The cmdty Yearbook 2019

cmdty by Barchart

www.barchart.com/solutions/cmdty

For general information on our other products and services or for technical support, please contact our Customer Support Department within the United States at (800) 238-5814 outside the United States at (312) 554-8122 or fax (312) 939-4135.

ISBN 978-0-910418-07-2

Printed in the United States of America

10 9 8 7 6 5 4 3 2 1

Barchart.com
209 W. Jackson Blvd, 2nd Floor
Chicago, Illinois 60606
Phone: 800.238.5814 or 312.554.8122
Fax: 312.939.4135
Website: www.barchart.com/solutions/cmdty
Email: info@cmdtydata.com

Table of Contents

cmdtyView®

advanced charting, tools, and data from a modern web-based platform

Charting

View any instrument - cash, crush, futures, indexes - in seasonal or interactive charts

Futures Trading

Access your trading account from any device with connectivity to 50+ brokers

Forward Curves

Prebuilt curves or customize for your needs. Create, edit, chart, and go

Local Cash Bids

Find the best price in your area or identify basis trends with our data and tools

Grain Indexes

Our indexes ensure that the price you're buying or selling is the fair market price

Newswires

Actionable news, market analysis, and proprietary content delivered in real-time

DataCenter

Give your business, app, or analytics an advantage with global commodities data that's been relied on for over fifty years.

cmdty leverages direct exchange connectivity to deliver institutional quality market data and information. Our coverage includes futures and options from 50 global exchanges - as well as spot pricing on hundreds of cash commodities, rates, and indexes. Many of our historical data sets go back to the 1950s or earlier.

Who uses DataCenter?

Hedge Funds — Software Providers — Brokers — Investment Advisors — Data Analysts

Available Packages	Content	History	Markets
Futures	Futures	1959 to date	320+
	Cash	1900 to date	450+
	COT	1986 to date	60+
Options on Futures	Options	2016 to date	90+
	Volatility	2016 to date	90+

cmdtydata.com
cmdty@barchart.com
312.566.9235

Barchart OnDemand
Market Data APIs

Our flexible cloud-based APIs make getting powerful data into your applications, workflows and products simple.

Power your business with Barchart OnDemand

Construct dynamic apps and tools

Integrate market data into your website

Simplify your current data strategy

Power charts with real-time or historical data

Get to market faster with built-in scale

Scale Your Business

Data is served through AWS ensuring reliability, redundancy, and built-in security that scales dynamically as your business grows

Always Compatible

Barchart OnDemand works with any operating system or programming language allowing you to start building in minutes

Reliable Performance

We embrace the cloud but also maintain physical data centers allowing us to cater to low latency requirements and provide a true physical back-up

Data Coverage

- Exchange Price Data
- Index Price Data
- Commodities
- Technical Data

- OTC & Cash Markets
- Economic Data
- News
- Weather

- Equities
- ETFs & Mutual Funds
- Forex
- Corporate Actions

Barchart Solutions
solutions@barchart.com
312.566.9235

Commodity Indexes

The Thomson Reuters Equal Weight Commodity Index (ticker symbol CCI) rallied to a new 4-year high in mid-2018 but then faded during the remainder of the year and closed the year down -7.1% yr/yr. The CCI index since 2017 has been consolidating near the bottom of the 2011/16 sell-off. The index in 2018 closed just mildly above the 10-year low posted in January 2016, where the index was down by -41% from its record high and retraced 66.7% of the 2001-11 bull market, which was the largest commodity rally in post-war history.

Bearish factors for commodity prices in 2018 included (1) the +4.4% rally in the dollar index seen in 2018, (2) the weaker global economy seen in 2018 due largely to trade tensions, (3) the Fed's one percentage point hike in interest rates in 2018, and (4) ample supply conditions in most commodity markets. Bullish factors for commodity prices included (1) a dovish turn in global monetary policies in late 2018 and early 2019, and (2) generally strong U.S. GDP growth in 2018 that helped support the world economy and commodity demand.

Five of the six CCI index sub-sectors closed lower in 2018 and only one closed higher. The ranked returns in 2018 were as follows: Grains +5.8%, Softs -5.1%, Livestock -6.8%, Metals -8.8%, Industrials -14.2%, and Energy -17.7%.

Energy

The CCI Energy sub-sector, which is composed of Crude Oil, Heating Oil, and Natural Gas, accounts for 18% of the overall index. The Energy sub-sector in 2018 closed sharply lower by -17.7%. On a nearest-futures basis, crude oil in 2018 closed down -24.8%, gasoline closed down -26.4%, heating oil closed down -19.0%, and natural gas closed down -0.4%. Crude oil prices and petroleum products fell sharply late in 2018 after Saudi Arabia boosted its production late in the year to offset production losses seen in Iran and Venezuela caused by U.S. sanctions.

Grains

The CCI Grains and Oilseeds sub-sector, which is composed of Corn, Soybeans, and Wheat, accounts for 18%

of the overall index. The Grains and Oilseeds sub-sector closed +5.8% higher in 2018, breaking the string of five consecutive yearly loses. On a nearest-futures basis, corn in 2018 rose +6.9%, soybeans fell -7.3%, and wheat rose +17.9%.

Industrials

The CCI Industrials sub-sector, which is composed of Copper and Cotton, accounts for 12% of the overall index. The Industrials sub-sector showed a -14.2% decline in 2018 following strong gains seen in the two previous years. Cotton in 2018 closed down -8.2%, reversing part of 2017's gain of +11.3%. Copper in 2018 fell sharply by -20.3%, reversing part of the +31.7% gain seen in 2017.

Livestock

The CCI Livestock sub-sector, which is composed of Live Cattle and Lean Hogs, accounts for 12% of the overall index. The Livestock sub-sector closed -6.8% lower in 2018, more than reversing 2017's gain of +5.9%. On a nearest-futures basis, live cattle futures in 2018 closed slightly higher by +1.5%, adding to the small gain of +3.4% seen in 2017. Lean hog futures in 2018 closed down -15.0%, more than reversing the +8.5% gain seen in 2017.

Precious Metals

The CCI Precious Metals sub-sector, which is composed of Gold, Platinum, and Silver, accounts for 17% of the overall index. The Precious Metals sub-sector closed down -8.8% in 2018, more than reversing the +8.2% gain seen in 2017. In 2018, gold fell by -2.1%, silver fell by -9.2%, and platinum fell by -14.8%.

Softs

The CCI Softs sub-sector, which is composed of Cocoa, Coffee, Orange Juice, and Sugar #11, accounts for 23% of the overall index. The Softs sub-sector in 2018 closed down -5.1%, adding to the sharp loss of -18.1% seen in 2017. In 2018, coffee closed down -19.3%, cocoa closed up +27.7%, sugar closed down -20.6%, and orange juice closed down -8.0%.

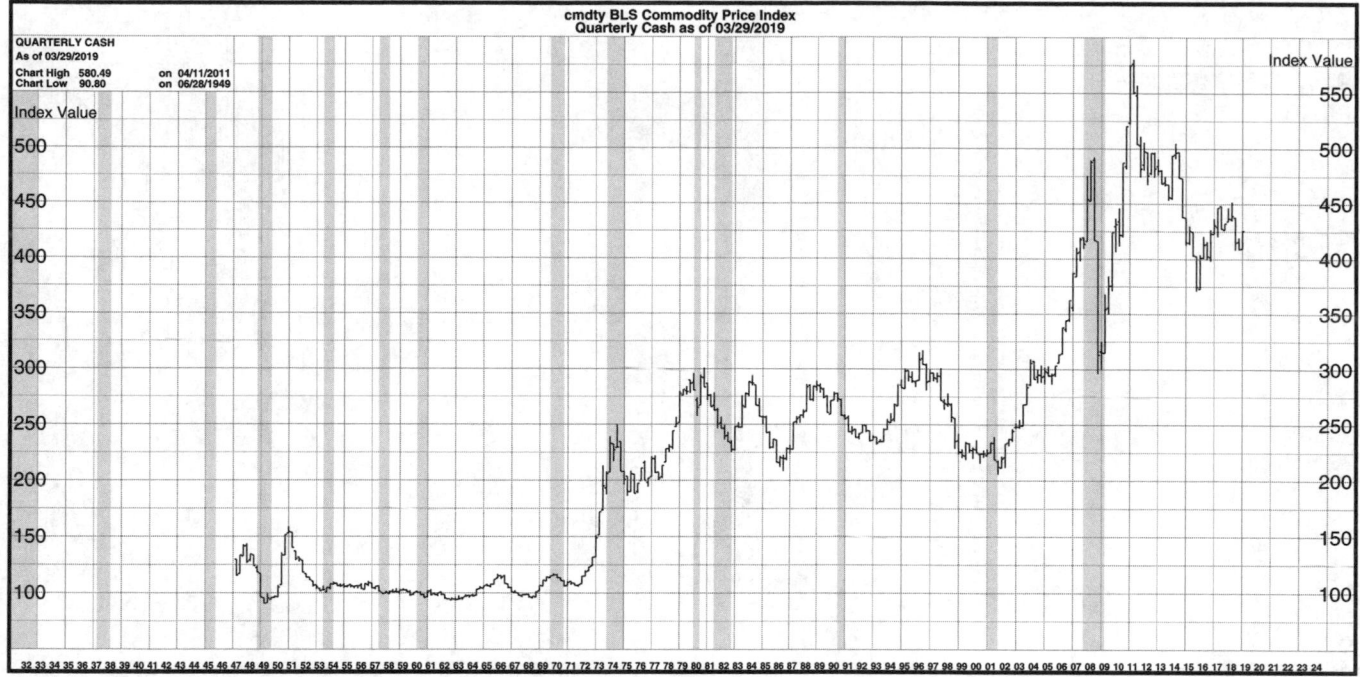

cmdty BLS Commodity Price Index
Quarterly Cash as of 03/29/2019

Unweighted Index of 23 Commodities: Hides, tallow, copper scrap, lead scrap, steel scrap, zinc, tin, burlap, cotton, print cloth, wool tops, rosin, rubber, hogs, steers, lard, butter, soybean oil, cocoa, corn, Kansas City wheat, Minneapolis wheat, and sugar.   Shaded areas indicate US recessions.

cmdty BLS Commodity Price Index
Weekly Cash as of 03/29/2019

Unweighted Index of 23 Commodities.   Shaded areas indicate US recessions.

cmdty BLS Commodity Price Index   (1967=100)

Year	Jan.	Feb.	Mar.	Apr.	May	June	July	Aug.	Sept.	Oct.	Nov.	Dec.	Average
2009	320.03	312.26	305.91	326.11	347.44	359.84	358.67	374.28	378.72	381.73	403.44	416.74	357.10
2010	428.27	417.21	433.51	441.48	431.40	420.89	425.03	449.12	473.29	489.05	491.25	507.30	450.65
2011	538.09	562.60	566.40	575.61	559.14	557.32	553.30	543.59	527.83	506.85	496.08	480.93	538.98
2012	488.60	498.90	501.77	490.93	480.92	474.62	480.69	488.41	493.34	486.07	477.98	484.25	487.21
2013	485.62	481.97	481.13	477.55	474.67	474.05	469.75	471.23	470.60	462.25	458.57	459.56	472.25
2014	457.25	465.09	487.18	497.58	500.90	495.60	491.20	484.78	479.78	465.82	455.62	445.75	477.21
2015	429.10	420.06	416.96	415.41	425.99	424.32	416.08	408.18	405.50	397.38	385.58	379.17	410.31
2016	377.44	385.09	396.03	410.34	413.55	416.74	411.76	409.65	402.79	401.09	411.91	424.17	405.05
2017	431.01	433.68	433.15	423.76	431.69	440.28	444.10	439.00	430.79	428.83	430.05	430.49	433.07
2018	438.94	441.96	442.40	441.42	444.86	445.13	434.09	417.91	412.39	416.93	415.79	413.91	430.48

Average.   *Source: cmdty by Barchart*

CMDTY INDEXES

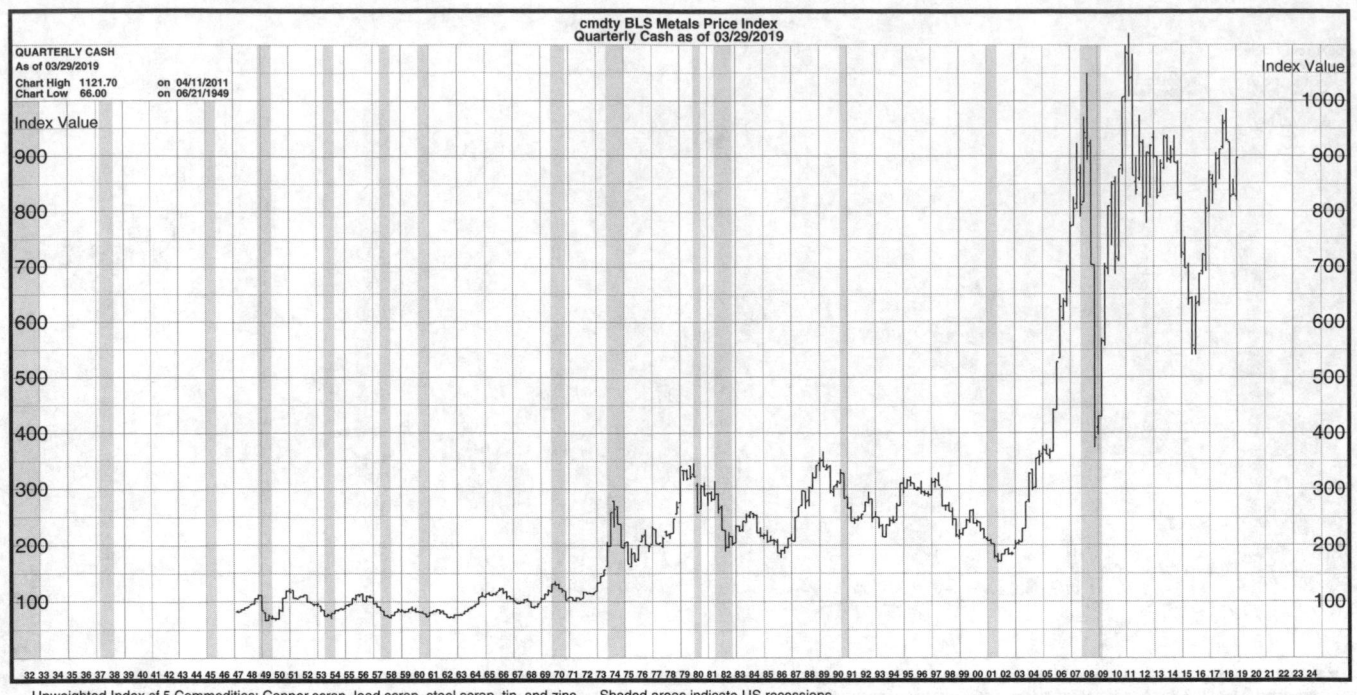

cmdty BLS Metals Price Index
Quarterly Cash as of 03/29/2019

QUARTERLY CASH
As of 03/29/2019

Chart High 1121.70 on 04/11/2011
Chart Low 66.00 on 06/21/1949

Unweighted Index of 5 Commodities: Copper scrap, lead scrap, steel scrap, tin, and zinc.   Shaded areas indicate US recessions.

cmdty BLS Metals Price Index
Weekly Cash as of 03/29/2019

WEEKLY CASH
As of 03/29/2019

Chart High 1121.70 on 04/11/2011
Chart Low 372.80 on 12/03/2008

Unweighted Index of 5 Commodities.   Shaded areas indicate US recessions.

cmdty BLS Metal Price Index   (1967=100)

Year	Jan.	Feb.	Mar.	Apr.	May	June	July	Aug.	Sept.	Oct.	Nov.	Dec.	Average
2009	409.17	416.80	421.44	455.21	410.21	552.61	591.59	651.17	688.67	704.55	716.43	767.81	565.47
2010	830.98	773.24	833.04	850.73	765.47	717.04	728.15	804.22	853.40	896.08	905.01	971.85	827.43
2011	1,029.49	1,085.28	1,066.15	1,096.80	1,033.85	1,023.86	1,063.60	994.80	942.14	874.77	868.19	849.37	994.03
2012	903.04	949.99	931.85	908.47	878.62	843.33	800.76	828.46	883.07	862.76	859.31	910.40	880.01
2013	929.61	930.76	908.99	870.31	850.59	841.39	838.54	875.10	881.56	883.73	891.08	919.04	885.06
2014	925.99	920.45	900.88	905.67	908.51	897.46	921.84	922.59	903.65	876.01	856.97	836.99	898.08
2015	808.63	753.27	725.64	726.61	741.70	717.50	693.73	662.74	649.72	619.91	560.90	546.74	683.92
2016	549.39	582.24	628.81	662.38	675.30	676.25	698.07	709.14	710.14	705.02	762.46	807.03	680.52
2017	834.55	840.10	854.85	833.46	828.55	825.47	849.85	882.09	891.55	884.15	871.25	885.11	856.75
2018	938.18	960.91	957.84	970.72	955.27	954.43	896.38	848.71	816.40	837.13	842.37	840.64	901.58

Average.   *Source: cmdty by Barchart*

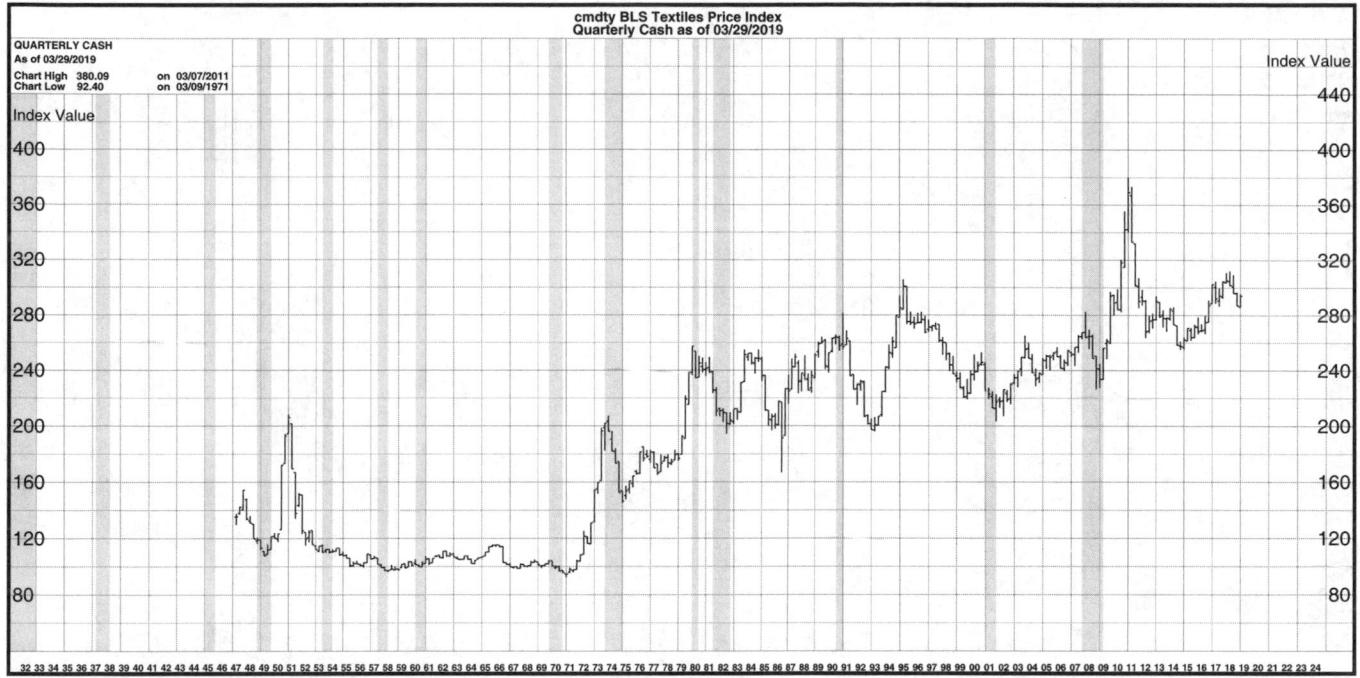

cmdty BLS Textiles Price Index
Quarterly Cash as of 03/29/2019

QUARTERLY CASH
As of 03/29/2019

Chart High 380.09   on 03/07/2011
Chart Low   92.40   on 03/09/1971

Unweighted Index of 4 Commodities: Burlap, cotton, print cloth, and wool tops.   Shaded areas indicate US recessions.

cmdty BLS Textiles Price Index
Weekly Cash as of 03/29/2019

WEEKLY CASH
As of 03/29/2019

Chart High 380.09   on 03/07/2011
Chart Low   226.60   on 11/12/2008

Unweighted Index of 4 Commodities.   Shaded areas indicate US recessions.

cmdty BLS Textiles Price Index   (1967=100)

Year	Jan.	Feb.	Mar.	Apr.	May	June	July	Aug.	Sept.	Oct.	Nov.	Dec.	Average
2009	241.13	237.01	229.83	240.05	252.00	253.03	258.94	253.52	257.42	265.67	280.85	293.96	255.28
2010	290.62	287.34	291.16	294.69	292.22	290.03	284.28	295.19	310.18	329.04	341.31	344.99	304.25
2011	347.26	365.82	372.19	365.44	352.18	344.70	319.66	310.92	310.19	303.37	299.19	289.50	331.70
2012	294.47	293.94	289.55	288.47	276.62	269.11	268.88	274.55	277.06	276.65	272.43	276.20	279.83
2013	279.44	283.14	289.79	286.96	286.20	283.33	278.59	278.23	275.03	274.73	269.70	275.78	280.08
2014	278.29	278.84	283.25	283.66	283.35	277.98	268.12	262.53	262.02	259.07	257.53	258.34	271.08
2015	257.16	260.85	261.80	265.21	265.95	267.24	267.42	267.46	263.78	266.74	268.72	271.68	265.33
2016	275.67	273.67	268.32	271.13	270.18	270.66	274.89	272.29	271.23	279.05	286.95	287.39	275.12
2017	292.60	296.28	299.77	300.52	299.68	293.69	290.06	292.93	295.83	293.56	295.50	301.02	295.95
2018	308.00	305.82	307.44	304.71	305.47	306.44	305.15	303.14	299.06	295.34	291.57	291.47	301.97

Average.   *Source: cmdty by Barchart*

CMDTY INDEXES

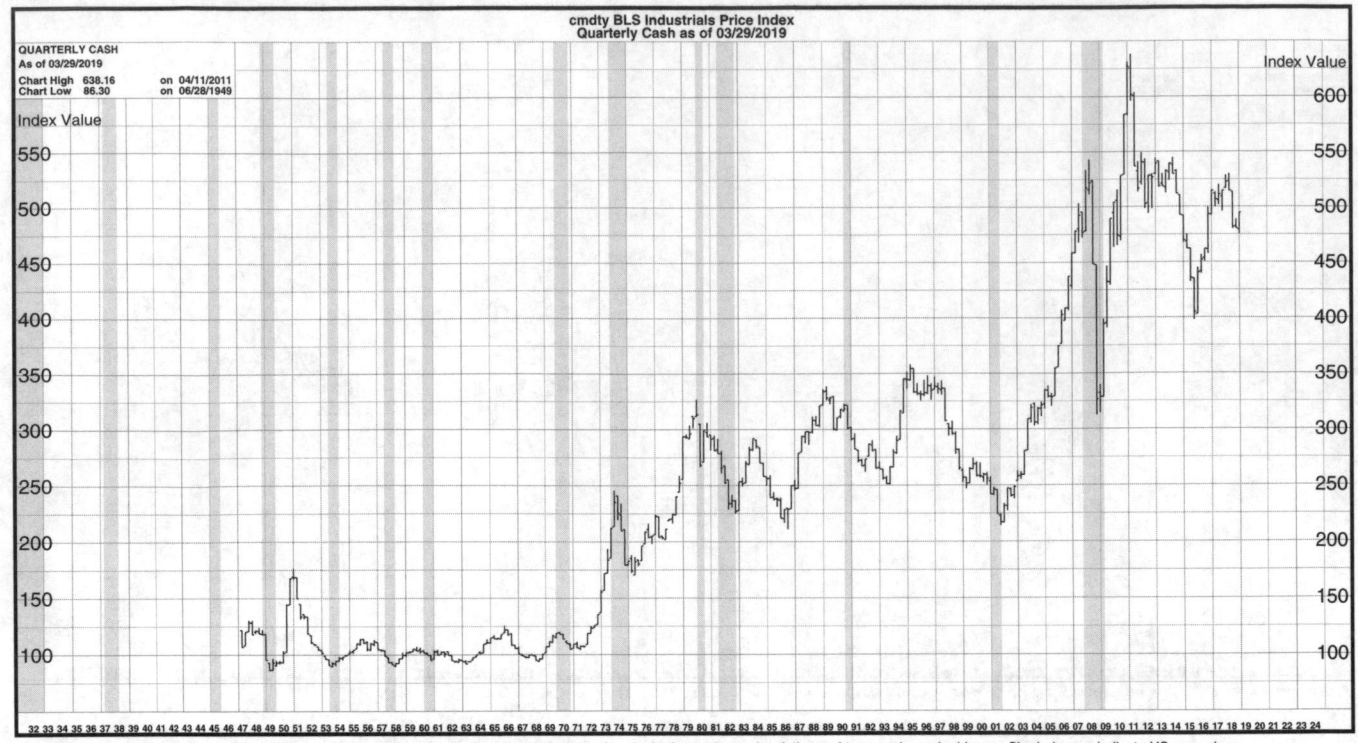

cmdty BLS Industrials Price Index
Quarterly Cash as of 03/29/2019

QUARTERLY CASH
As of 03/29/2019
Chart High 638.16 on 04/11/2011
Chart Low 86.30 on 06/28/1949

Unweighted Index of 13 Commodities: Hides, tallow, copper scrap, lead scrap, steel scrap, zinc, tin, burlap, cotton, print cloth, wool tops, rosin, and rubber.   Shaded areas indicate US recessions.

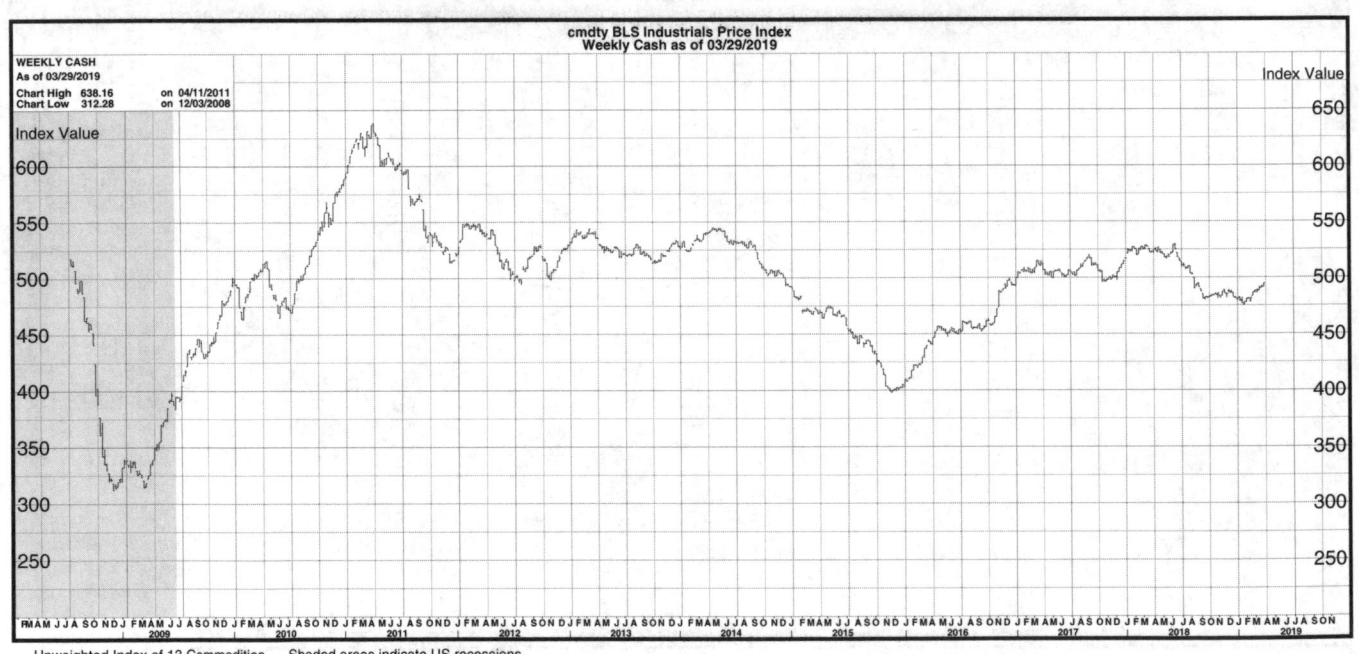

cmdty BLS Industrials Price Index
Weekly Cash as of 03/29/2019

WEEKLY CASH
As of 03/29/2019
Chart High 638.16 on 04/11/2011
Chart Low 312.28 on 12/03/2008

Unweighted Index of 13 Commodities.   Shaded areas indicate US recessions.

cmdty BLS Industrials Price Index   (1967=100)

Year	Jan.	Feb.	Mar.	Apr.	May	June	July	Aug.	Sept.	Oct.	Nov.	Dec.	Average
2009	335.09	331.50	321.35	343.49	370.17	391.18	403.99	431.59	439.72	435.97	455.27	480.02	394.95
2010	492.93	476.13	499.63	510.22	489.56	476.07	474.97	498.86	518.04	539.43	555.01	574.70	508.80
2011	595.51	619.22	621.89	628.72	606.29	602.99	596.81	573.01	559.74	536.77	528.95	519.49	582.45
2012	531.91	546.88	544.73	538.46	526.82	510.28	500.22	510.14	524.29	515.30	506.62	523.72	523.28
2013	534.06	538.69	539.87	532.46	524.75	523.74	520.86	525.30	521.20	514.92	519.98	529.58	527.12
2014	528.48	527.92	535.44	541.50	542.77	534.33	532.02	529.81	520.65	506.18	504.60	497.80	525.13
2015	485.52	474.22	470.13	467.83	471.58	466.96	451.80	443.96	439.86	424.27	403.04	401.58	450.06
2016	409.74	421.84	436.56	450.36	452.52	451.96	457.45	456.93	456.68	460.60	484.07	494.37	452.76
2017	503.07	506.20	510.83	505.47	504.70	502.57	504.42	511.92	513.67	502.70	499.14	506.88	505.96
2018	522.93	524.51	525.49	524.02	519.13	522.01	509.95	496.98	483.37	483.58	484.68	485.14	506.82

Average.   *Source: cmdty by Barchart*

cmdty BLS Foodstuffs Price Index
Quarterly Cash as of 03/29/2019

QUARTERLY CASH
As of 03/29/2019
Chart High 513.59 on 04/05/2011
Chart Low 89.20 on 12/22/1959

Unweighted Index of 10 Commodities: Hogs, steers, lard, butter, soybean oil, cocoa, corn, Kansas City wheat, Minneapolis wheat, and sugar.   Shaded areas indicate US recessions.

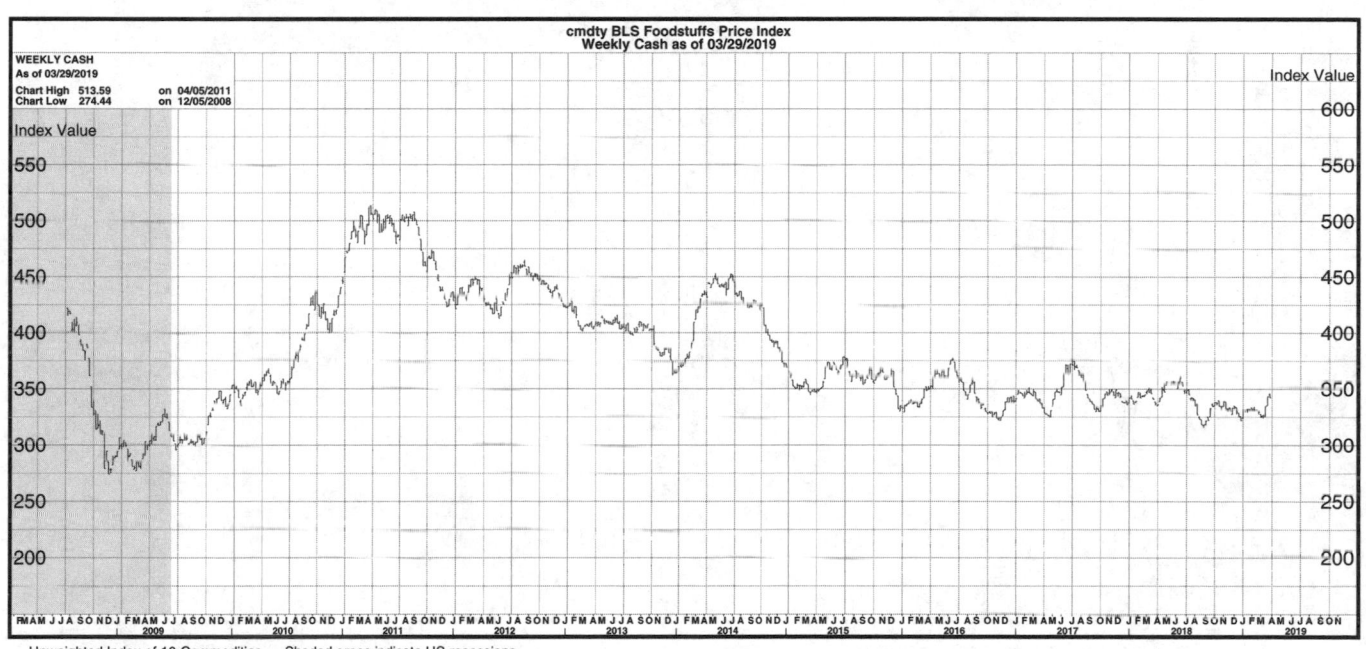

cmdty BLS Foodstuffs Price Index
Weekly Cash as of 03/29/2019

WEEKLY CASH
As of 03/29/2019
Chart High 513.59 on 04/05/2011
Chart Low 274.44 on 12/05/2008

Unweighted Index of 10 Commodities.   Shaded areas indicate US recessions.

cmdty BLS Foodstuffs Price Index   (1967=100)

Year	Jan.	Feb.	Mar.	Apr.	May	June	July	Aug.	Sept.	Oct.	Nov.	Dec.	Average
2009	299.83	286.21	284.71	302.35	316.81	318.81	301.83	304.44	305.01	314.86	338.56	339.54	309.41
2010	349.28	344.48	352.89	357.94	359.11	352.01	361.74	385.62	415.09	424.20	411.58	423.33	378.11
2011	464.45	489.47	494.49	506.33	497.04	497.00	495.67	503.38	484.57	466.21	451.87	429.91	481.70
2012	431.88	436.61	445.29	429.26	421.32	427.19	453.49	458.33	451.49	446.42	439.14	432.15	439.38
2013	422.99	410.14	407.07	407.78	410.33	410.17	404.33	402.51	405.75	395.29	382.14	374.23	402.73
2014	370.69	387.03	424.76	440.01	445.70	444.24	437.38	426.08	426.02	412.87	392.84	379.75	415.61
2015	358.69	352.29	350.34	349.61	367.54	369.24	369.14	361.25	360.32	361.29	361.42	348.87	359.17
2016	334.98	337.31	343.78	358.46	362.83	370.40	353.47	349.64	335.73	328.19	326.03	339.73	345.05
2017	344.49	346.60	341.09	328.23	344.21	363.46	369.20	351.43	333.86	340.67	346.50	339.79	345.79
2018	340.59	344.84	344.76	344.32	355.67	353.36	343.73	325.14	327.65	336.27	332.96	328.82	339.84

Average.   *Source: cmdty by Barchart*

CMDTY INDEXES

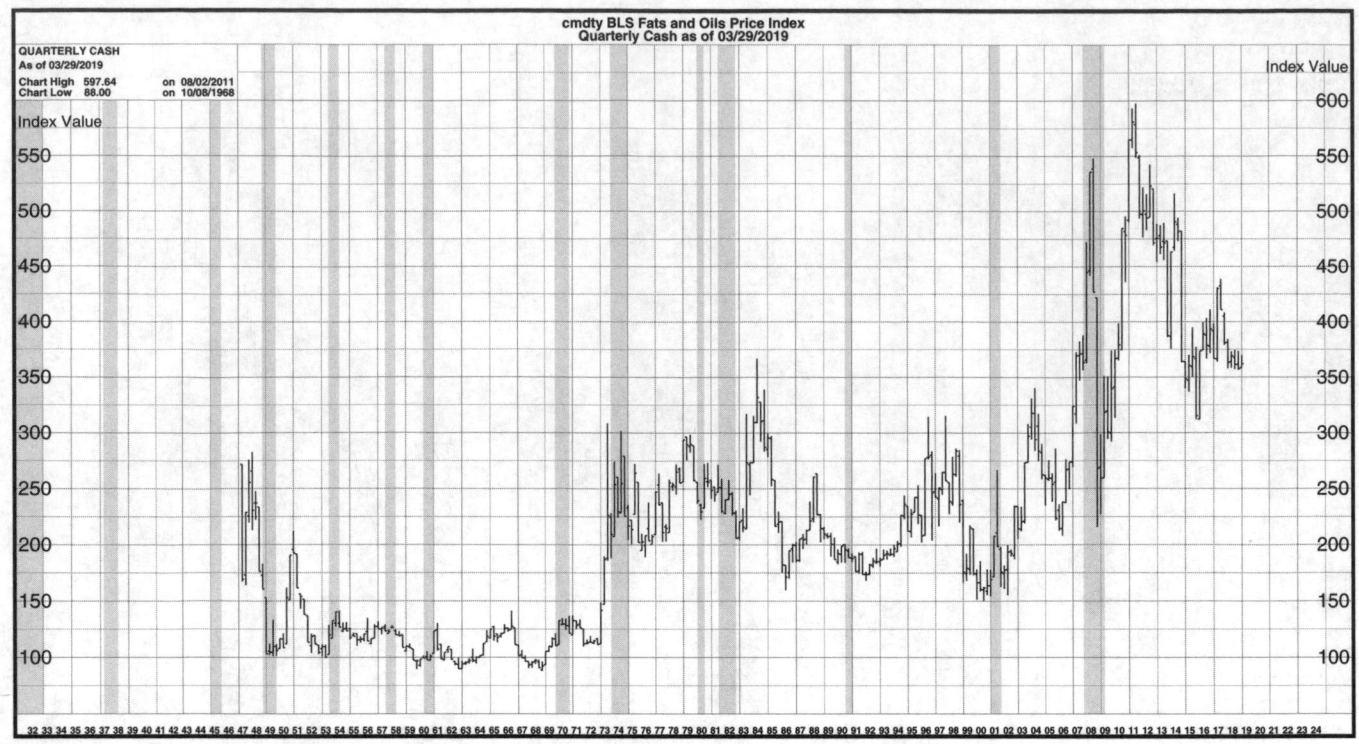

cmdty BLS Fats and Oils Price Index
Quarterly Cash as of 03/29/2019

QUARTERLY CASH
As of 03/29/2019
Chart High 597.64 on 08/02/2011
Chart Low 88.00 on 10/08/1968

Unweighted Index of 4 Commodities: Butter, cottonseed oil, lard, and tallow.   Shaded areas indicate US recessions.

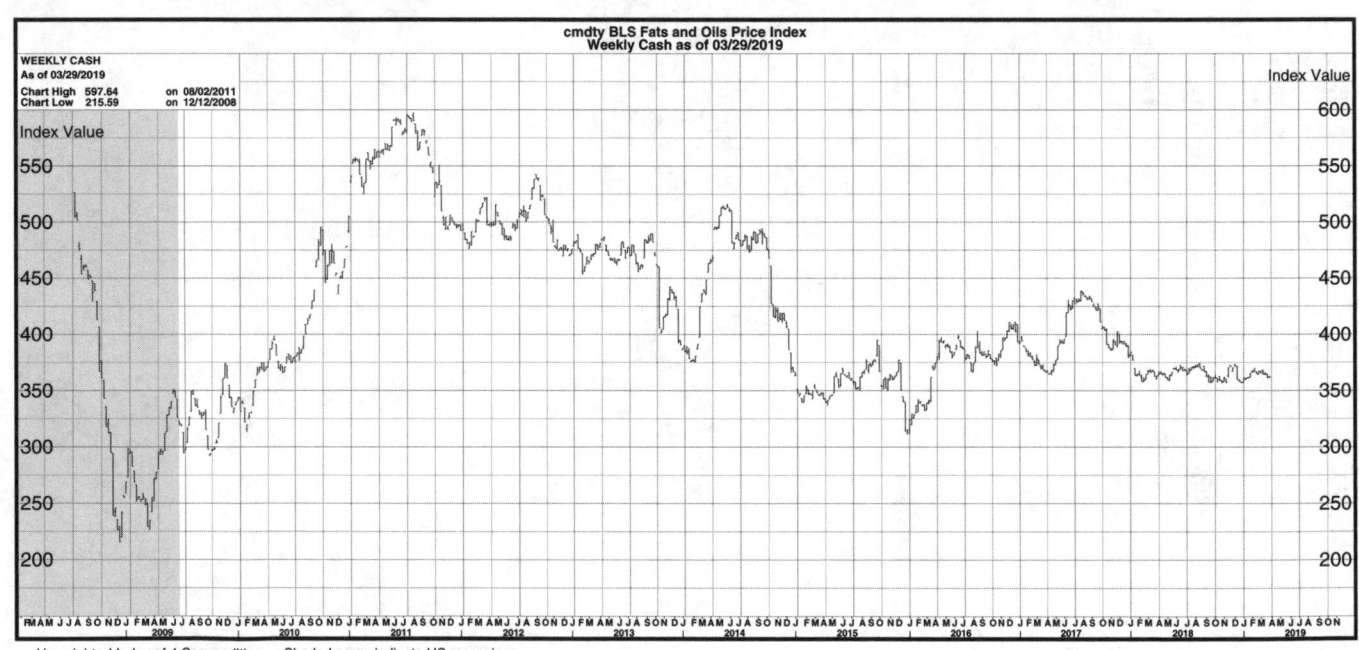

cmdty BLS Fats and Oils Price Index
Weekly Cash as of 03/29/2019

WEEKLY CASH
As of 03/29/2019
Chart High 597.64 on 08/02/2011
Chart Low 215.59 on 12/12/2008

Unweighted Index of 4 Commodities.   Shaded areas indicate US recessions.

cmdty BLS Fats and Oils Price Index   (1967=100)

Year	Jan.	Feb.	Mar.	Apr.	May	June	July	Aug.	Sept.	Oct.	Nov.	Dec.	Average
2009	283.42	254.79	243.41	285.09	321.74	335.76	308.54	340.28	324.64	298.33	343.85	344.85	307.06
2010	337.27	329.26	366.69	378.35	381.68	374.59	379.27	399.57	444.83	471.40	463.11	458.65	398.72
2011	536.41	542.91	553.67	561.25	569.84	588.10	587.94	578.55	567.28	536.83	502.49	499.60	552.07
2012	488.60	489.04	512.32	501.11	495.37	490.44	506.48	516.93	532.05	501.87	478.36	474.48	498.92
2013	478.78	463.85	472.83	480.48	466.32	473.86	473.76	463.55	484.31	435.85	427.75	414.70	461.34
2014	383.34	388.71	444.35	482.96	511.46	492.95	483.40	482.99	488.24	444.49	416.67	383.76	450.28
2015	345.69	348.02	348.93	342.31	357.64	363.99	355.78	368.38	378.59	356.58	362.48	345.06	356.12
2016	325.81	337.32	352.31	387.99	386.67	491.94	378.62	384.16	381.65	376.69	394.32	405.54	383.59
2017	390.86	379.46	372.45	367.41	387.20	417.41	431.12	432.99	422.43	398.69	392.43	390.23	398.56
2018	372.28	362.23	365.82	365.04	364.99	368.91	368.71	370.93	360.64	360.00	365.24	363.08	365.66

Average.   *Source: cmdty by Barchart*

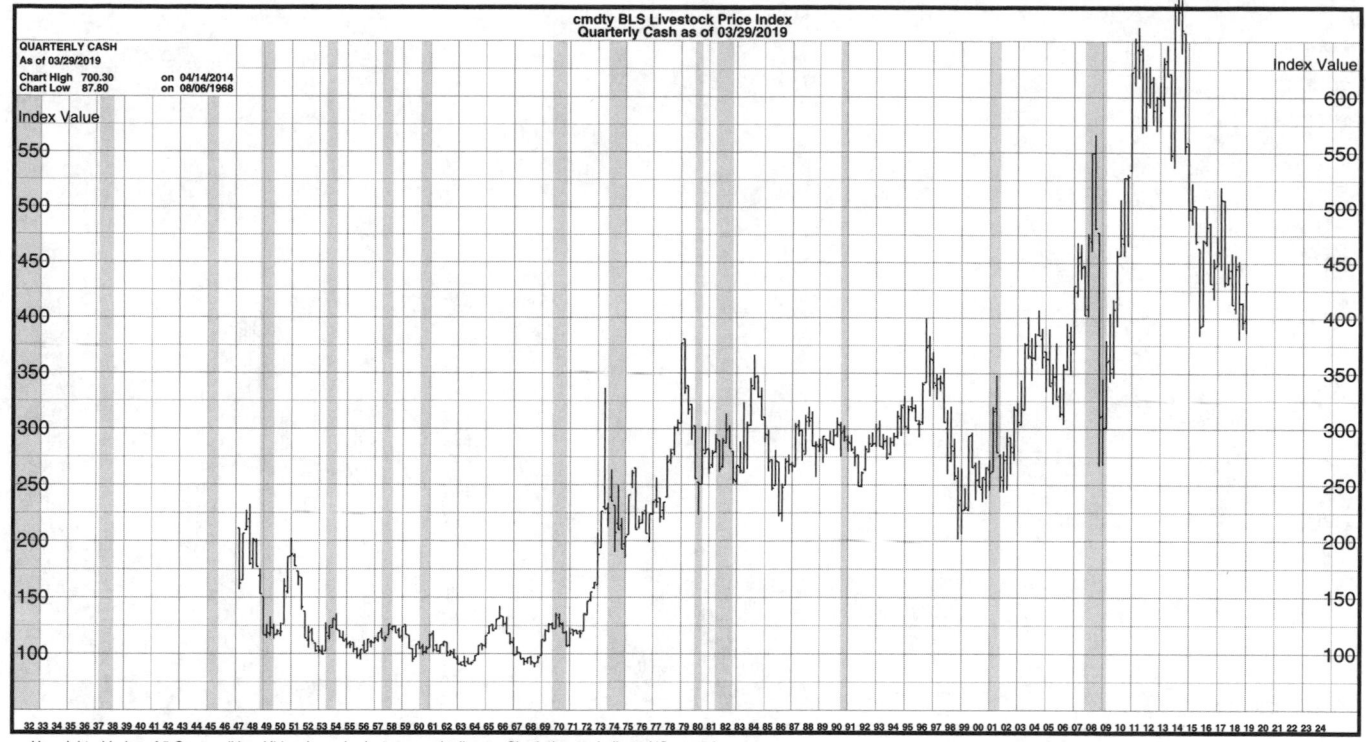

Unweighted Index of 5 Commodities: Hides, hogs, lard, steers, and tallow.   Shaded areas indicate US recessions.

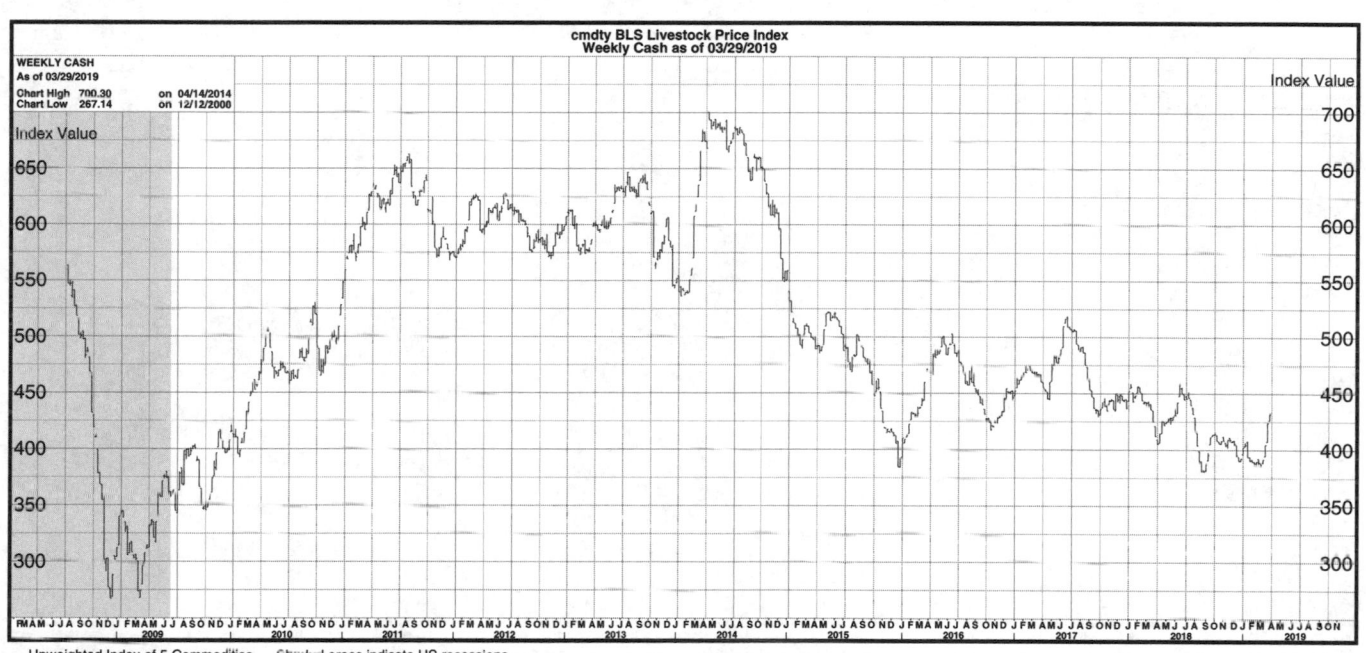

Unweighted Index of 5 Commodities.   Shaded areas indicate US recessions.

cmdty BLS Livestock Price Index   (1967=100)

Year	Jan.	Feb.	Mar.	Apr.	May	June	July	Aug.	Sept.	Oct.	Nov.	Dec.	Average
2009	333.60	310.58	288.18	321.58	347.01	368.85	362.91	393.37	389.53	350.90	386.75	403.06	354.69
2010	411.55	408.71	450.01	478.92	488.46	470.53	465.13	475.55	498.82	495.89	485.02	505.23	469.49
2011	561.16	577.76	601.55	629.36	618.46	635.68	646.41	644.21	626.64	618.26	580.65	580.02	610.01
2012	575.19	598.32	620.12	600.69	612.10	619.49	613.35	601.44	582.23	585.33	577.18	594.91	598.36
2013	606.27	584.54	580.26	598.17	601.26	626.31	634.54	630.72	637.72	591.03	583.70	571.43	603.83
2014	543.02	557.63	645.13	685.62	689.00	676.46	683.71	661.15	656.18	639.12	613.66	573.26	635.33
2015	523.85	500.96	503.91	491.27	517.22	513.03	484.28	490.90	477.86	452.68	419.99	404.96	481.74
2016	410.40	432.01	453.40	479.17	491.47	491.94	473.49	461.17	443.34	423.46	428.92	449.89	453.22
2017	459.17	470.78	466.97	452.02	478.49	506.82	500.73	478.13	439.94	438.59	442.67	443.87	464.85
2018	450.12	447.67	433.39	415.52	427.78	447.09	441.73	396.16	401.17	409.82	406.81	396.83	422.84

Average.   *Source: cmdty by Barchart*

CMDTY INDEXES

S&P Goldman Sachs Commodity Index
Quarterly Cash as of 03/29/2019

QUARTERLY CASH
As of 03/29/2019
Chart High 893.86 on 07/03/2008
Chart Low 98.92 on 05/26/1970

Standard & Poor's GSCI is a registered trademark of Standard & Poor's Financial Services LLC ("S&P"), a subsidiary of The McGraw-Hill Companies, Inc.
Currently the S&P GSCI includes 24 commodity nearby futures contracts.   Shaded areas indicate US recessions.

S&P Goldman Sachs Commodity Index
Weekly Cash as of 03/29/2019

WEEKLY CASH
As of 03/29/2019
Chart High 893.86 on 07/03/2008
Chart Low 268.40 on 01/20/2016

Standard & Poor's GSCI is a registered trademark of Standard & Poor's Financial Services LLC ("S&P"), a subsidiary of The McGraw-Hill Companies, Inc.
Currently the S&P GSCI includes 24 commodity nearby futures contracts.   Shaded areas indicate US recessions.

S&P GSCI Index   (12/31/1969=100)

Year	Jan.	Feb.	Mar.	Apr.	May	June	July	Aug.	Sept.	Oct.	Nov.	Dec.	Average
2009	346.03	327.48	350.86	367.12	410.82	458.22	429.21	466.68	453.77	492.51	509.71	505.07	426.46
2010	520.05	503.83	523.07	543.90	499.87	497.00	503.57	517.41	526.98	561.66	579.86	614.79	532.67
2011	634.64	661.44	707.87	744.48	695.62	679.91	689.47	651.63	638.94	625.65	653.51	642.72	668.82
2012	661.12	685.83	701.92	681.61	637.66	579.93	627.42	661.68	670.25	654.57	639.84	640.09	653.49
2013	658.10	669.41	648.20	624.14	627.04	622.56	639.34	645.98	645.31	633.40	614.88	631.12	638.29
2014	617.20	640.25	645.88	653.19	652.42	657.64	636.14	609.55	588.76	548.78	521.86	449.57	601.77
2015	388.27	412.87	403.39	423.64	443.38	436.70	402.75	360.85	362.48	364.45	345.91	315.98	388.39
2016	289.97	293.46	324.99	337.79	361.37	377.36	354.83	353.51	353.18	372.96	359.92	391.89	347.60
2017	396.61	402.05	385.28	390.60	381.04	364.63	374.75	380.46	394.88	401.99	425.01	425.39	393.56
2018	452.52	444.49	446.07	463.57	484.33	472.75	465.94	459.42	470.55	479.81	428.86	396.52	455.40

Average.   *Source: CME Group; Chicago Mercantile Exchange*

Bloomberg and Bloomberg Indices are trademarks or service marks of Bloomberg Finance L.P.   12/31/1990=100   Shaded areas indicate US recessions.

Bloomberg and Bloomberg Indices are trademarks or service marks of Bloomberg Finance L.P.   12/31/1990=100   Shaded areas indicate US recessions.

Bloomberg Commodity Index   (12/31/1990=100)

Year	Jan.	Feb.	Mar.	Apr.	May	June	July	Aug.	Sept.	Oct.	Nov.	Dec.	Average
2009	114.17	107.49	107.93	111.21	119.75	125.98	119.71	128.50	125.34	132.15	134.35	135.93	121.88
2010	137.76	131.70	132.79	134.85	127.45	125.94	127.89	132.81	137.28	144.46	148.49	156.14	136.46
2011	160.80	163.41	165.87	171.91	163.23	161.47	162.81	159.01	154.26	145.52	146.73	141.41	158.04
2012	143.34	146.45	144.63	139.84	134.79	129.46	141.40	143.91	147.64	146.02	142.06	140.45	141.67
2013	140.01	139.55	137.44	132.99	132.04	129.38	127.65	128.32	128.98	127.48	123.20	126.25	131.11
2014	125.24	130.97	134.71	136.56	135.81	134.75	130.44	126.39	121.57	117.97	116.95	109.39	126.73
2015	102.09	102.74	99.64	100.95	103.32	100.92	96.70	89.46	88.43	88.72	83.31	78.74	94.58
2016	75.41	75.36	79.16	81.15	84.40	88.25	85.82	84.51	84.08	85.97	83.99	87.30	82.95
2017	87.80	88.15	85.30	84.99	83.53	81.21	83.04	83.40	85.03	85.16	86.78	85.14	84.96
2018	89.02	88.02	87.59	88.72	90.37	88.31	84.53	83.90	83.50	85.94	83.10	80.58	86.13

Average.   Bloomberg and Bloomberg Indices are trademarks or service marks of Bloomberg Finance L.P.   Formerly the Dow Jones-UBS Commodity Index.   *Source: CME Group; Chicago Board of Trade*

COMMODITY PRICES FADE IN 2018 ON WEAKER GLOBAL ECONOMY

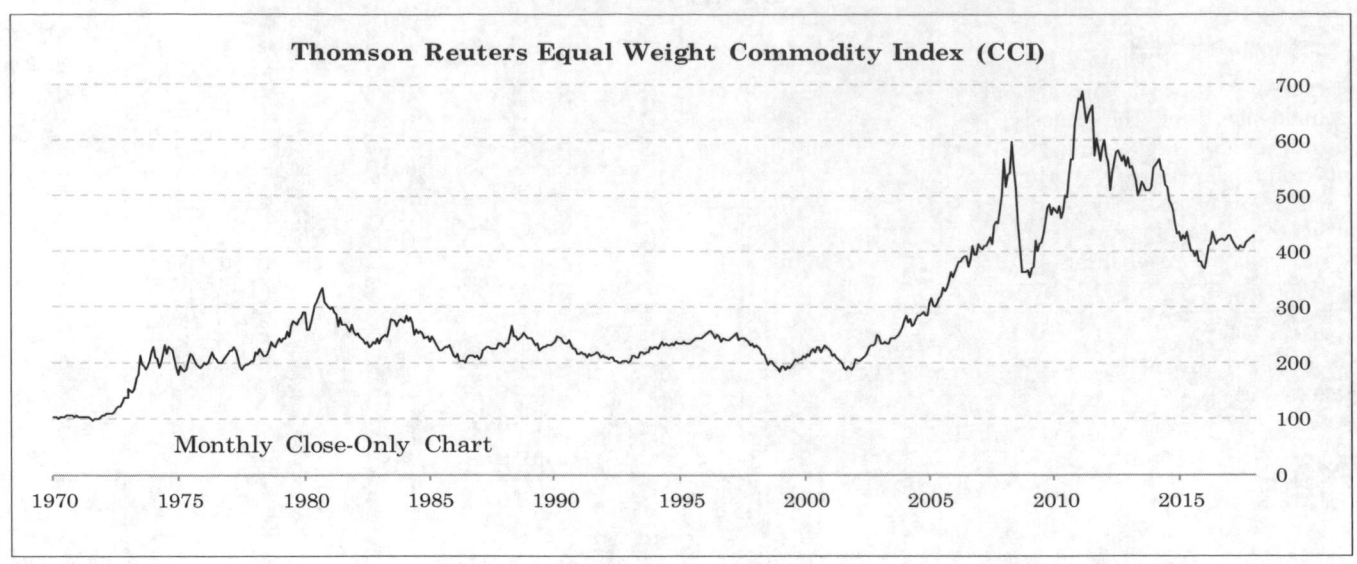

The Thomson Reuters Equal Weight Commodity Index (CCI) in 2018 showed some strength early in the year and rallied to a 4-year high, but then faded and closed the year down -7.1% yr/yr. For the last two years, the CCI index has been consolidating in a narrow range near the bottom of the 2011/16 sell-off, not far above the 10-year low posted in January 2016.

Looking back at recent history, the CCI index from 2001 through 2011 posted an extraordinary rally totaling +278%. That decade-long rally was by far the largest commodity bull market in post-war history, exceeding even the rallies seen in the 1970s. The 1971/74 and 1977/80 commodity bull markets were separated by two years of consolidation in 1975/76. Even if those two rallies were to be counted as one large bull market, that bull market of 250% is less than the 2001/2011 bull market of 278%.

The 2001/2011 commodity bull market was driven mainly by strong commodity demand from fast-growing emerging countries such as China, India, Brazil, and others. The fact that the rally was driven by demand, as opposed to a temporary supply disruption, accounted for its size and longevity.

Along with strong demand, the weak dollar was an important driver of the commodity bull market from 2001 through 2008. During that time frame, the dollar plunged and provided a powerfully bullish factor for commodity prices. As the value of the dollar falls, the price of hard assets tends to rise to account for the lower value of the currency in which the hard assets are priced. From 2008 through mid-2014, however, the dollar had less impact on commodity prices because the dollar was in a sideways consolidation mode.

The commodity bull market received a new head of steam in 2009/11 in the aftermath of the 2008/09 global financial crisis. Commodity prices were driven higher during 2009/11 by (1) extra liquidity from the Federal Reserve's extraordinarily easy monetary policy, and (2) safe-haven buying of commodities as protection in case the Federal Reserve's extraordinarily easy monetary policy might eventually cause hyperinflation and a plunge in the dollar.

However, commodity prices topped out in early 2011 and then plunged by -49% to the 9-year low in January 2016. Commodity prices during that period were driven lower by weak physical demand for commodities due to poor global economic growth. In addition, many investors were forced to give up on any imminent arrival of hyperinflation stemming from the Fed's extraordinarily easy monetary policy. Instead, the U.S. and global economies during that period continued to feel the deflationary pressures that stemmed from the 2007/08 global financial crisis and the Great Recession.

Ranked Commodity Bull Markets - Thomson-Reuters Equal Weight Commodity Index (CCI) (1960-2019[1])							
	-------- Low --------		-------- High --------		Percent Rally	Rally Duration Months	Avg CPI (yr-yr%)
2001-11	Oct-01	182.83	Apr-11	691.09	278.0%	114	2.4%
1971-74	Oct-71	96.40	Feb-74	237.80	146.7%	28	4.9%
1977-80	Aug-77	184.70	Nov-80	337.60	82.8%	39	10.2%
1986-88	Jul-86	196.16	Jun-88	272.19	38.8%	23	3.2%
1992-96	Aug-92	198.17	Apr-96	263.79	33.1%	44	2.8%

[1] Data as of February 2019.

The 2011/16 slump in commodity prices was also caused by an economic slowdown in China. It is no coincidence that the massive commodity bull market began in 2003 at the same time that the Chinese economy started to show double-digit growth. China's building and investment boom produced huge demand for various types of commodities. However, commodity prices started falling after 2011 because Chinese GDP growth slid from +9.5% in 2011 to +7.7% in 2012 and then steadily fell further to a 28-year low of +6.6% by 2018.

Commodity prices in 2015 and early 2016 were also pressured by the end of the Fed's quantitative easing (QE) programs in Oct 2014 as well as the Fed's first interest rate hike in December 2015. The end of the Fed's QE programs and rising interest rates meant that there was less liquidity fuel for the commodities markets and a reduced risk of eventual hyperinflation.

However, commodity prices in early 2016 were able to rally moderately and then remained steady during 2017 and 2018. Commodity prices in 2017 were supported by a 10% sell-off in the dollar index and by the generally strong global economy. However, commodity prices later in 2018 were then undercut by weakening global economic growth due to trade tensions, a +4.4% rally in the dollar index during 2018, and an overall 1 percentage point interest rate hike by the Federal Reserve.

The nearby chart shows how the majority of commodities saw price declines in 2018, led by energy and metals prices. Metal prices were undercut by the strong dollar and the slower global economy. Meanwhile, petroleum prices fell sharply late in 2018 as Saudi Arabia boosted its oil production and OPEC+ temporarily lost its production discipline.

Other commodity markets in 2018 showed a mixed price performance depending on supply/demand factors in each particular market. In the agriculture markets, supplies were generally plentiful with weather-specific moves in some markets.

Looking ahead to 2019, the outlook is mixed for commodity prices. Commodity prices should see support

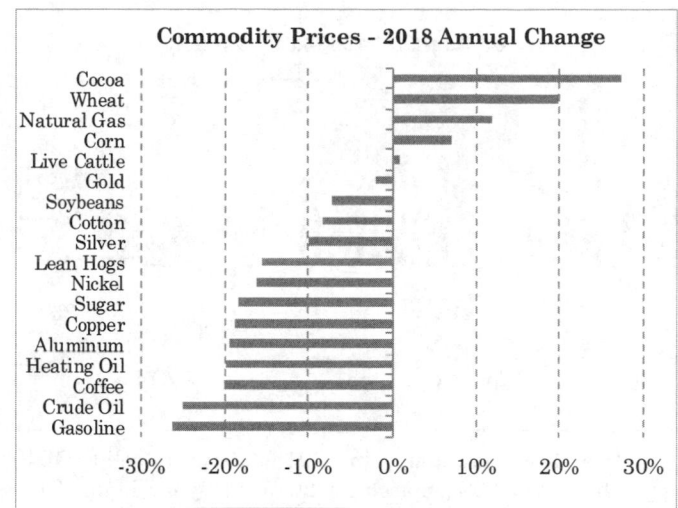

from continued growth in the global economy and from the dovish turn in global monetary policies in late 2018 and early 2019. Commodity prices are likely to be held back in 2019, however, by ample commodity supplies and the Federal Reserve's continued balance sheet reduction program, which is permanently draining reserves from the U.S. banking system and tightening liquidity.

Commodity prices in 2019 will likely depend mainly on the prospects for the Chinese economy. China's economy is decelerating due to trade tensions, high debt, and a hangover from decades of extremely rapid growth. The question is whether government efforts to revive growth will be successful or whether Chinese economic growth will continue to slide, thus undercutting commodity demand.

Over the long run, commodity prices will see support from firm demand from population growth and world development. The UN forecasts that the global population will grow by about 50% to 11.2 billion people by 2100. Meanwhile, the need in the developing world continues to be enormous for food, shelter and infrastructure, which are all sectors that utilize raw commodities. Some 80% of the world's population lives on less than $10 per day and many of these people will be slowly integrated into the global economy.

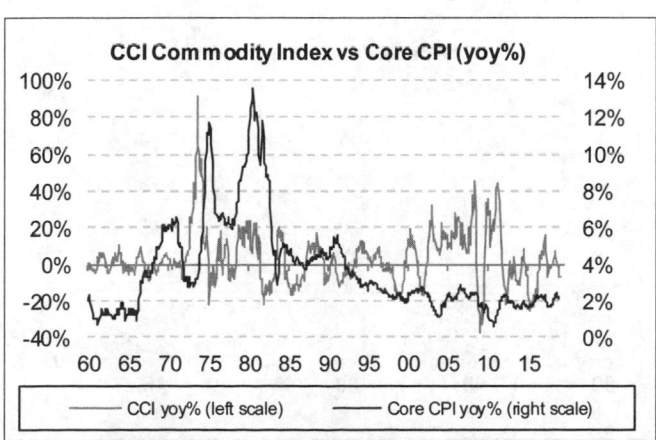

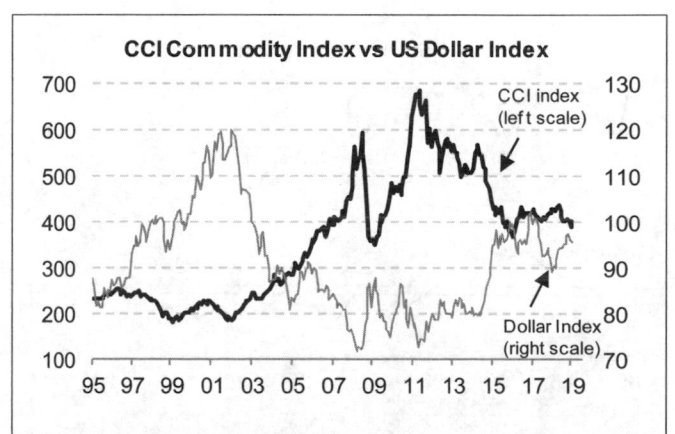

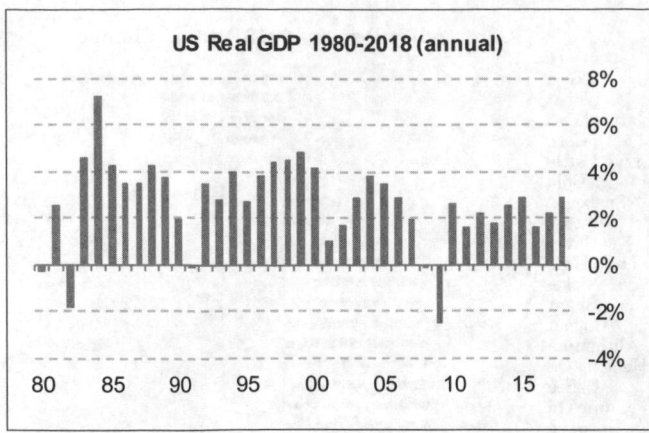

US Real GDP 1980-2018 (annual)

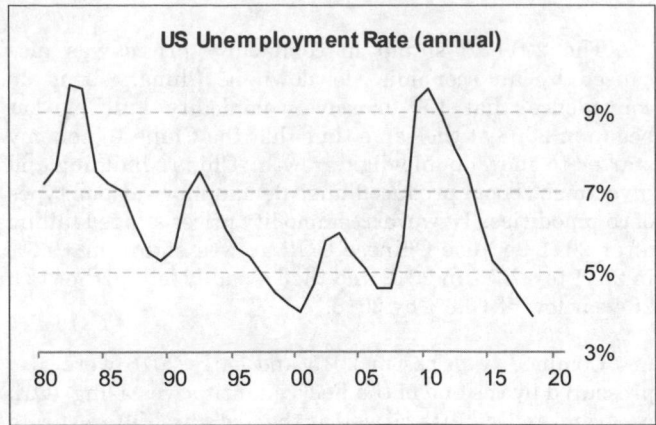

US Unemployment Rate (annual)

The U.S. economy in 2018 showed solid GDP growth near +2.9%, matching 2015's 13-year high. The U.S. economy in 2018 gained support mainly from the massive tax cuts that took effect on January 1, 2018. For individuals, the new tax law cut the top tax bracket for individuals to 37% from 39.6% and cut the tax rates for most other brackets. For corporations, the top corporate tax rate was cut sharply to 21% from 35% and the effective tax rate was also cut for pass-through business entities such LLCs and SubChapter S corporations.

The tax bill gave the U.S. economy a strong boost as both consumers and corporations had more cash to spend. Personal income in 2018 was strong at +4% and personal spending rose by +5%. Consumer confidence in 2018 was supported by (1) increased household cash flow from the 2018 tax cuts, (2) the strong labor market and rising wages, (3) rising household wealth with the continued rise in home prices and the generally strong stock market, and (4) low gasoline prices.

Negative factors for consumer confidence in 2018 included (1) Washington political uncertainty with the investigation into Russian interference in the 2016 U.S. election by Special Counsel Robert Mueller, (2) trade tensions as the Trump administration raised tariffs in an attempt to force trade deals, and (3) a sharp downside correction in stocks in Q4-2018.

The corporate tax cut supported business investment during 2018. Business investment contributed a quarterly average of 0.9 percentage points of growth to GDP during

2018, matching the 2017 level and remaining strong relative to weak business investment in 2015-16.

The U.S. manufacturing sector in 2018 grew by +3.2% yr/yr, which was substantially better than in previous years. However, the U.S. manufacturing sector was held back by trade tensions as the Trump administration slapped tariffs on steel and aluminum imports and on $250 billion of Chinese goods, which drew retaliatory tariffs on a variety of U.S. exports and disrupted global supply chains.

The ISM manufacturing index, which measures confidence in the manufacturing sector, rose to a 14-year high of 60.8 in August 2018 on the tax cuts and the generally strong U.S. and global economy. However, the index then slid to 54.3 by December due to trade tensions, slower global economic growth, and the Q4-2018 global stock market correction. Business confidence was strong in the service sectors of the U.S. economy with the ISM non-manufacturing index rising to a 13-year high of 60.8 in September 2018 but then tailing off to 58.0 by December.

The U.S. labor market in 2018 continued to strengthen with the unemployment rate falling to a 5-decade low of 3.7% in September 2018 before rebounding mildly higher to 3.9% by year-end. The unemployment rate fell even below the levels seen before the Great Recession in 2007-09, providing another illustration of how the U.S. economy finally returned to health. The December 2018 unemployment rate of 3.9% was substantially below the Fed's estimate of a longer-run natural unemployment rate of 4.4%, illustrating that wages should be on the rise with

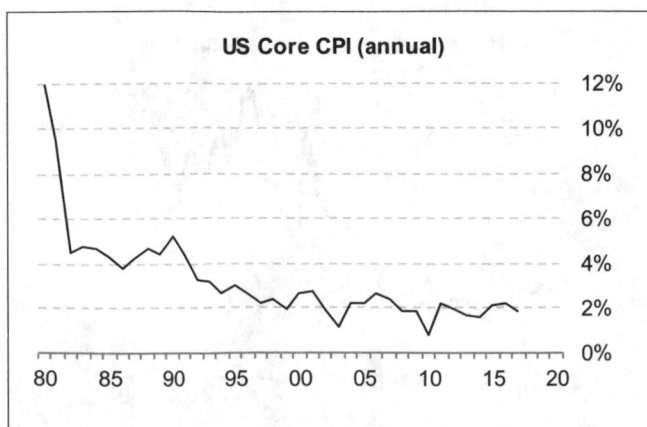

US Core CPI (annual)

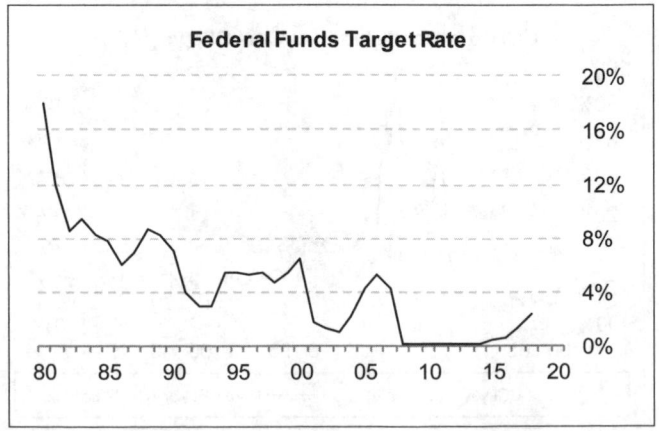

Federal Funds Target Rate

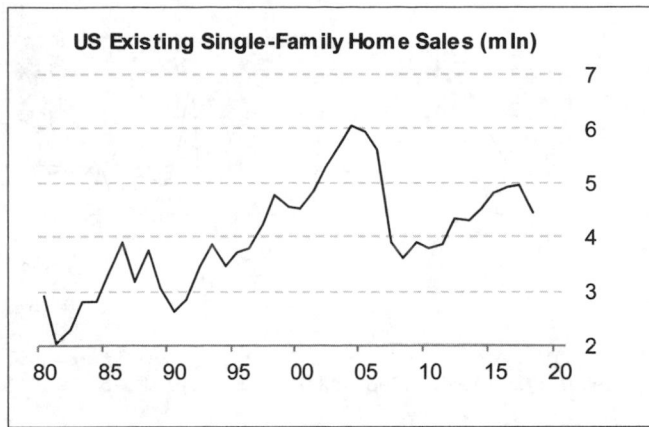

US Existing Single-Family Home Sales (mln)

US Existing Home Median Price ($'000)

the tight labor market. Indeed, hourly earnings growth at the end of 2018 reached a 10-year high of +3.3% yr/yr.

Non-farm payroll job growth in 2018 showed a strong monthly average of +223,000, stronger than the pace of +179,000 in 2017 and +193,000 in 2016. The U.S. economy since the Great Recession has created 20.6 million new jobs, bringing the total number of jobs in the U.S. in 2018 to a new record high of 151 million jobs.

The U.S. housing market continued to support the overall U.S. economy in 2018 but weakened somewhat during the year as the 30-year mortgage rate rose to an 8-year high of 4.94% in November 2018. However, the mortgage rate then dropped sharply to 4.35% by early 2019 as the Fed dropped its bias toward higher rates. U.S. existing home sales during 2018 faded to 5.00 million units/month by year-end from the 12-year high of 5.64 million units in November 2017. U.S. housing starts in 2018 nevertheless remained strong near an 11-year high.

As 2019 began, the prospects for the U.S. economy were generally favorable due to the Fed's halt to its rate-hike policy and continued support from the 2018 tax cuts. However, U.S. GDP growth is expected to edge lower to +2.4% in 2019 and +1.9% in 2020 as the effects of the tax cut fade and U.S. GDP growth falls back to the Federal Reserve's estimate of the long-term potential growth near +1.9%. Threats to U.S. economic growth in 2019 include the slowing Chinese and Eurozone economies and

continued trade tensions.

The 10-year T-note yield rose sharply starting in late 2017 as Congress moved toward passing a massive tax cut bill, which took effect on January 1, 2018. The tax cut caused the 10-year T-note yield to rise sharply during 2018 to a 7-year high of 3.26% by October 2018 because the tax cut boosted the economy and inflation and caused the Federal Reserve to maintain a hawkish policy. The Fed during 2018 raised interest rates four times by a total of 1 percentage point. The federal funds rate target reached an 11-year high of 3.25-3.50% by December 2018. The 10-year T-note yield then fell sharply in late 2018 as the stock market went into a steep correction and the global economy slowed due to trade tensions.

The S&P 500 index during 2018 extended the 2016-2017 rally to post a new record high in September 2018. The stock market was boosted mainly by a +24% yr/yr surge in earnings growth sparked by the massive corporate tax cut implemented on January 1, 2018. Stocks were also supported by the generally strong global economy seen during 2018 and by historically low interest rates.

However, the stock market went into a steep downward correction in Q4-2018 as the global economy stumbled on trade tensions and as the Fed's series of interest rates took their toll. The stock market was then able to partially recover in early 2019 after the Fed halted its rate-hike regime and moved to a neutral policy.

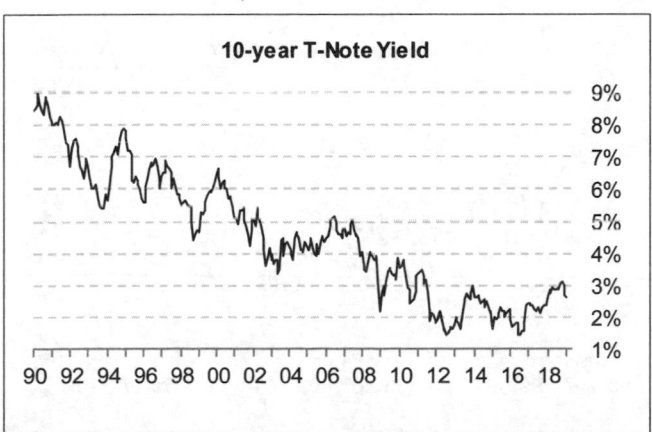

10-year T-Note Yield

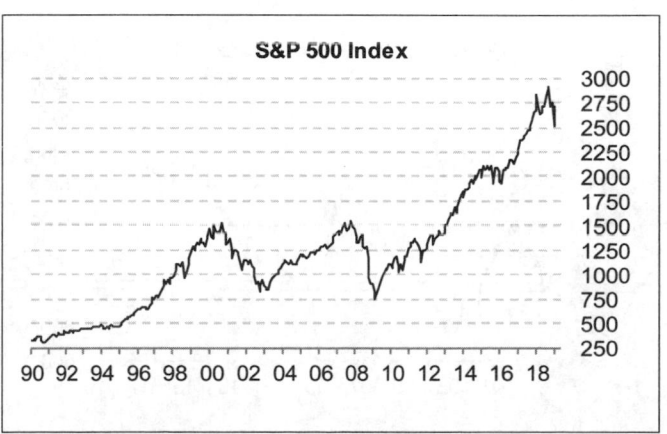

S&P 500 Index

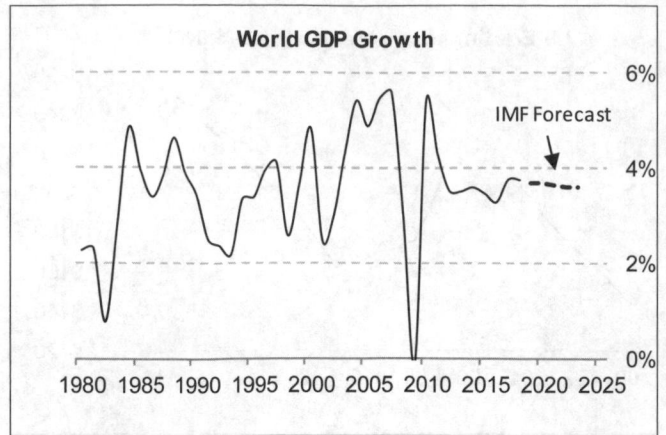

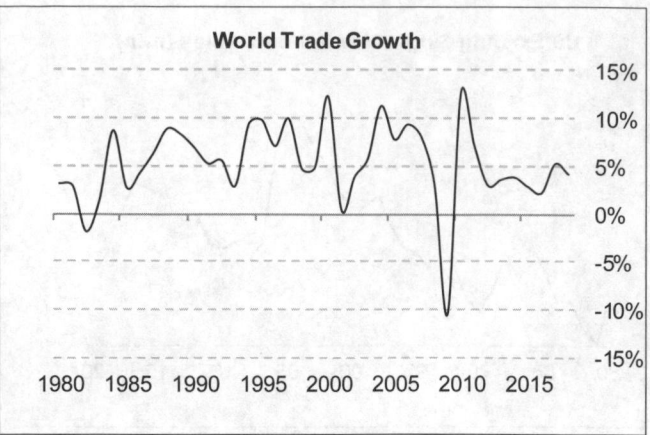

The world economy in 2018 remained relatively strong at +3.7%, unchanged from 2017 and better than the 9-year low of +3.2% seen in 2016.

The global economy in 2018 benefited from strong growth in the U.S. where the economy received a substantial boost from the massive 2018 tax cut. However, the prospects for the global economy sagged in the latter half of the year as the Chinese and Eurozone economies were hurt by trade tensions. The UK and Eurozone economies were also undercut by Brexit uncertainties.

In early 2018, President Trump imposed tariffs on imported solar panels, washing machines, steel, and aluminum. The U.S. tariffs caused a series of retaliatory tariffs against U.S. exports. The Trump administration in 2018 also imposed tariffs on $250 billion worth of Chinese goods, which caused China to impose retaliatory tariffs on $110 billion of U.S. goods. All those tariffs remained in effect as of February 2019.

U.S. GDP growth in 2018 improved to +2.9% from +2.2% in 2017 due to a strong boost from the massive personal and corporate tax cuts that took effect on January 1, 2018. Looking ahead, the consensus is for U.S. GDP growth to ease as the tax-cut stimulus fades, falling to +2.4% in 2019 and +1.9% in 2020.

The Eurozone economy in 2018 fell to +1.8% from +2.4% in 2017 on trade tensions, Brexit risks, and a

technical recession in Italy in the second half of the year. UK GDP was weak and fell to +1.4% in 2018 from +1.8% in 2017 as the UK Parliament dragged its feet on Brexit and caused a slump in business investment.

China's GDP growth in 2018 eased to a 28-year low of +6.6% on (1) the U.S.-Chinese trade war, (2) debt overhang, (3) excess capacity in many industries, and (4) the continued effects of the government's deleveraging efforts in 2017. Japan's GDP in 2018 fell to +0.8% from 2017's strong pace of +1.9% on trade tensions and carry-over weakness from China.

Looking ahead, the market consensus is for world GDP growth to ease to +3.4% in 2019, +3.3% in 2020, and +3.0% in 2021.

The global economy is expected to ease as trade tensions continue to disrupt exports and global supply chains and as China's economy slows to the growth rates more normally seen in large, developed countries. Trade tensions will likely continue to plague the global economy in 2019. The Chinese economy also continues to see threats from the massive levels of household and corporate debt, which could spark a debt crisis.

On the more positive side, the global economy in 2019 should see support from more dovish central bank policies. There could also be a resolution of the U.S.-Chinese trade war, which would give the global economy a boost.

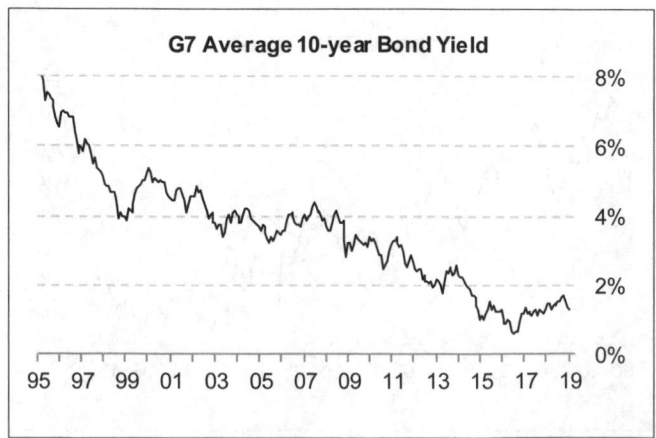

CRUDE OIL PRICES KEY ON OPEC+ PRODUCTION CUTS

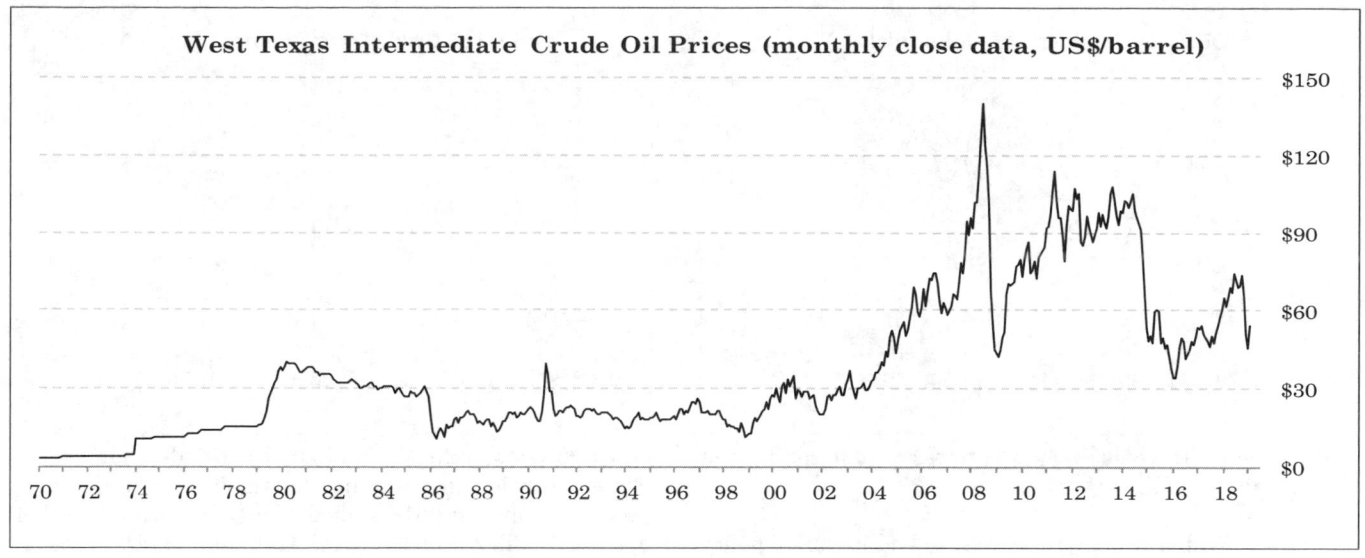

West Texas Intermediate Crude Oil Prices (monthly close data, US$/barrel)

The world crude oil market continues to be plagued by production over-capacity caused in large part by the sharp increase in U.S. shale oil production in recent years. This over-capacity has caused crude oil prices since 2014 to trade on a generally weak basis despite various oil supply disruptions.

U.S. shale oil production started to ramp up in 2012 when new technologies became available for extracting oil from pockets in shale rock formations. In fact, U.S. oil production in the space of just five years surged by +75% to a 44-year high of 9.6 million barrels per day (bpd) in June 2015. U.S. oil production temporarily dipped by 12% from mid-2015 through early-2016 due to the collapse in oil prices from Saudi Arabia's market-share-preservation policy However, U.S. oil production then recovered sharply with a +9% rise in 2017 and a +23% surge in 2018 to a record high of 12.1 million bpd by early 2019.

Saudi Arabia initially tried to halt rising U.S. oil production in 2014 by announcing a policy of maintaining its production level and market share at any cost, allowing oil prices to drop sharply in an attempt to permanently price high-cost producers out of the market. Saudi Arabia has some of the lowest production costs in the world, meaning that Saudi Arabia in theory would be the last

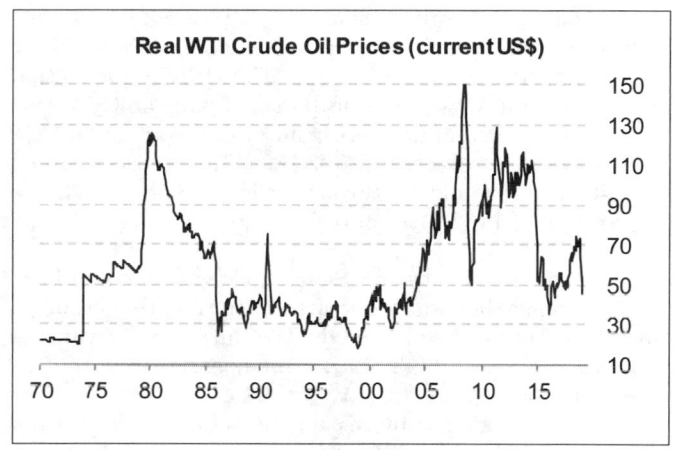

Real WTI Crude Oil Prices (current US$)

producer standing after a price war.

However, Saudi Arabia could not sustain its price war because Nymex West Texas Intermediate (WTI) crude oil futures prices during 2014/15 plunged by an extraordinary -76% from the 3-year high of $107.68 posted in mid-2014 to the 14-year low of $26.05 posted in February 2016. That plunge in oil prices devastated Saudi Arabia's government finances and caused its budget deficit to soar to 15% of GDP. Saudi Arabia was forced to cut government spending

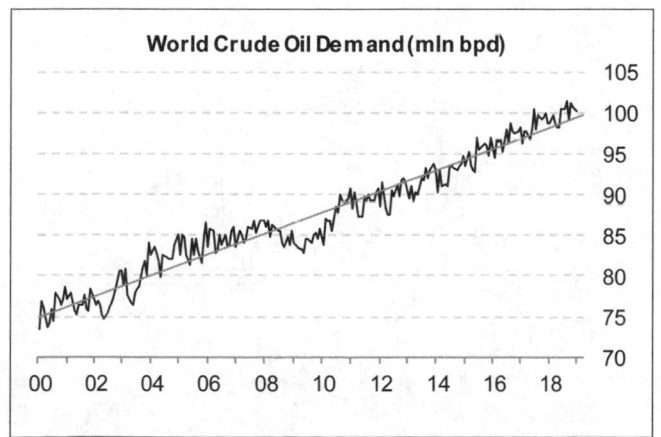

World Crude Oil Demand (mln bpd)

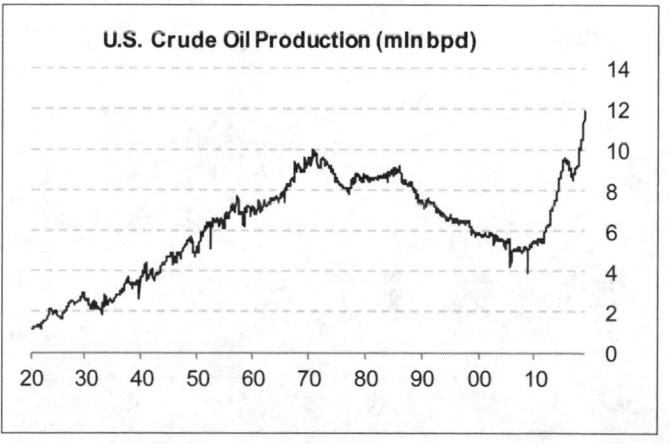

U.S. Crude Oil Production (mln bpd)

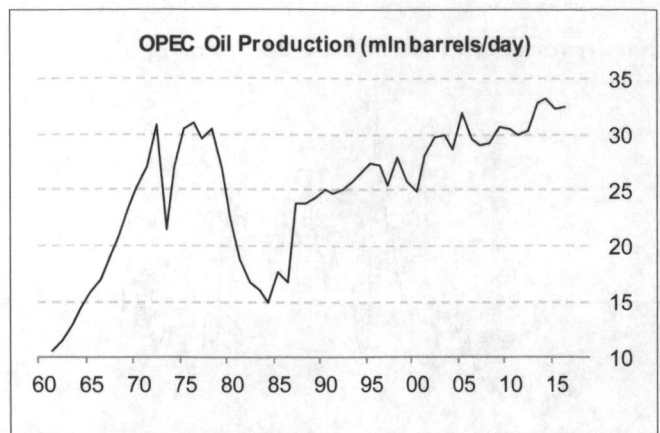

OPEC Oil Production (mln barrels/day)

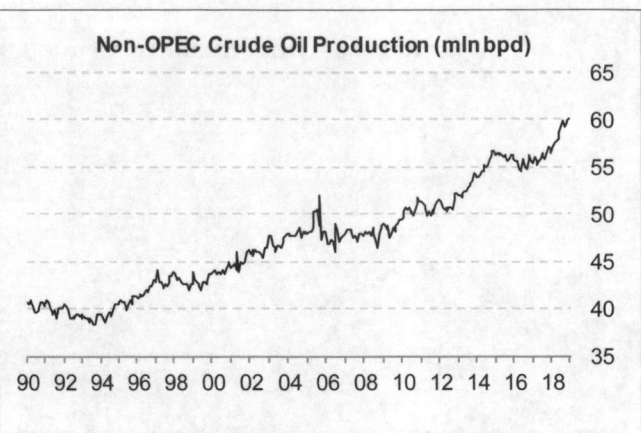

Non-OPEC Crude Oil Production (mln bpd)

and subsidies, thus risking social unrest and perhaps even the monarchy itself.

Saudi Arabia was finally forced to end its failed policy and OPEC in November 2016 reached an agreement to cut production by 1.2 million bpd. Non-OPEC countries such as Russia joined the agreement to bring the overall OPEC+ production cut to 1.8 million bpd. The OPEC+ production cut agreement was successful in bringing down excess global inventories and boosting oil prices, leading OPEC+ to extend the agreement into 2018. WTI oil prices rallied steadily from mid-2017 through mid-2018 and posted a 4-year high of $76.90 per barrel in October 2018.

The abject failure of Saudi Arabia's market-share preservation policy was illustrated by the fact that crude oil inventories in the developed OECD countries soared during 2015-16 to a record high of 3.1 billion barrels in July 2016 (see chart below). However, the OPEC+ production cut agreement was successful in causing oil inventories to drop sharply by -10% to 2.8 billion barrels by early 2018. That allowed OPEC+ to meet its goal of cutting inventories to the 5-year moving average, although inventories remained well above the pre-2014 levels.

The success of the OPEC+ production cut agreement started to fade in mid-2018 as higher oil prices prompted U.S. oil production to soar by +23% in 2018. In addition, the U.S. in May 2018 announced that it would withdraw from the Iran nuclear agreement and would reinstate sanctions on Iran in November 2018. In anticipation of a sharp drop in Iranian oil exports in late 2018, Saudi Arabia

and OPEC+ starting in mid-2018 boosted production to offset the anticipated drop in Iranian oil exports. OPEC oil production in mid-2018 spiked higher by about 1 million bpd to 33 million bpd as Saudi Arabian production rose to a record high of 11 million bpd.

The sharp rise in Saudi oil production during mid-2018 caused a renewed global oil surplus and caused OECD oil inventories to start rising again. Oil inventories in the U.S. also started rising in mid-2018 due to strong U.S. production. The result was that West Texas Intermediate crude oil futures prices (nearest-futures) plunged by -45% from October's 4-year high of $76.90 per barrel to a 1-1/2 year low in late-December 2018 of $42.36.

The plunge in oil prices in late 2018 forced OPEC+ to adopt a new production cut agreement totaling 1.2 million bpd for the first six months of 2019. As part of that agreement, Saudi Arabia slashed its production by a total of 800,000 bpd and Russia cut its production as well. In addition, Iran's oil production and exports plunged after the U.S. sanctions were reinstated in November 2018. Also, Venezuela's oil production extended its plunge after the U.S. imposed sanctions on the Maduro regime in late 2018. The tighter supply situation in early 2019 allowed oil prices to recover to the $58 per barrel area.

Looking ahead, the question is whether OPEC+ will be able to maintain its production cut discipline. If not, then oil prices are likely to see renewed weakness as U.S. oil production continues its relentless rise.

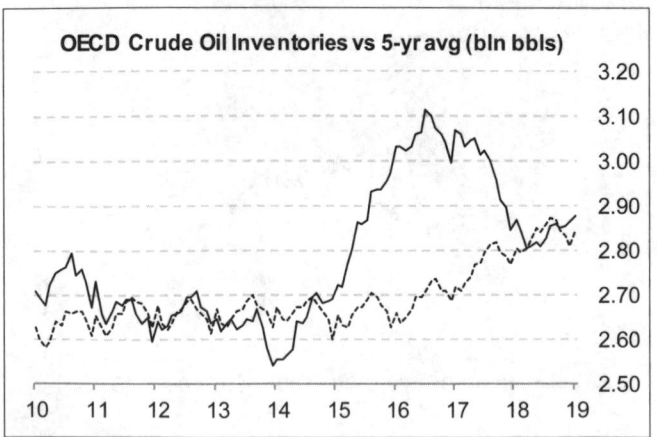

OECD Crude Oil Inventories vs 5-yr avg (bln bbls)

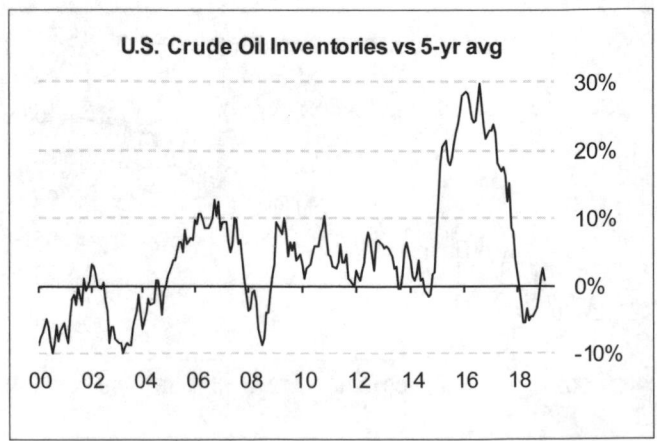

U.S. Crude Oil Inventories vs 5-yr avg

The dollar index in early 2018 fell to a 4-year low but then recovered modestly during the remainder of the year to post a 1-1/2 year high by late-2018. The 2018 rally in the dollar index retraced about 60% of the sharp sell-off seen in 2017 but fell short of challenging the 14-year high posted in early 2017.

The dollar index during 2018 saw support from the massive tax-cut bill that Congress passed in December 2017. The fiscal stimulus from the tax cut produced strong GDP growth in 2018 of +2.9%, well above the U.S. economy's long-term potential growth rate of +1.9%.

Strong U.S. GDP growth in turn caused the Federal Reserve to step up the pace of its interest rates hikes, which supported the dollar with improved interest rate differentials against U.S. trading partners. The Fed during 2018 raised its federal funds target rate four times for a total hike of one percentage point.

The Fed also tightened monetary policy during 2018 by reducing its balance sheet, providing further support for the dollar. The Fed in its balance sheet drawdown program let maturing securities roll off from its portfolio without replacing those securities, thus reducing the size of its balance sheet and permanently draining reserves from the banking system. The balance sheet drawdown program started at a maximum of $10 billion per month in Q4-2017 and accelerated to the maximum of $50 billion per month by Q4-2018.

The Fed during 2018 reduced the size of its balance sheet by a total of $370 billion (-8%) to $4.1 trillion. Despite that decline, the Fed's balance sheet level at the end of 2018 was still $3.2 trillion above the pre-crisis level, illustrating that a massive quantity of excess reserves continued to slosh around in the U.S. banking system.

The dollar was also supported during 2018 by corporate repatriation of capital from overseas. The 2018 tax bill imposed a tax on the $2.6 trillion of dollars that U.S. corporations earned and held overseas to avoid paying U.S. taxes. The new tax caused some corporations to bring their cash back to the U.S., which was bullish for the dollar since some of that overseas cash was held in foreign currencies that had to be converted into dollars.

The dollar also received support in 2018 as the sharp U.S. corporate tax cut encouraged foreign corporations to expand their operations in the U.S., thus leading to capital inflows. The 2018 tax law slashed the top U.S. corporate tax rate to 21% from 35% and made the U.S. a much more competitive tax domicile.

The dollar's rally in 2018 was held back by several bearish factors. The main bearish factor was that the market in late 2018 downgraded its expectations for Fed interest rate hikes in 2019 and beyond. By the end of 2018, the market was not expecting any more rate hikes by the Fed in 2019 and 2020. The FOMC at its meeting in January 2019 confirmed that it would at least temporarily

US Export Growth (yoy%)

00 01 02 03 04 05 06 07 08 09 10 11 12 13 14 15 16 17 18 19

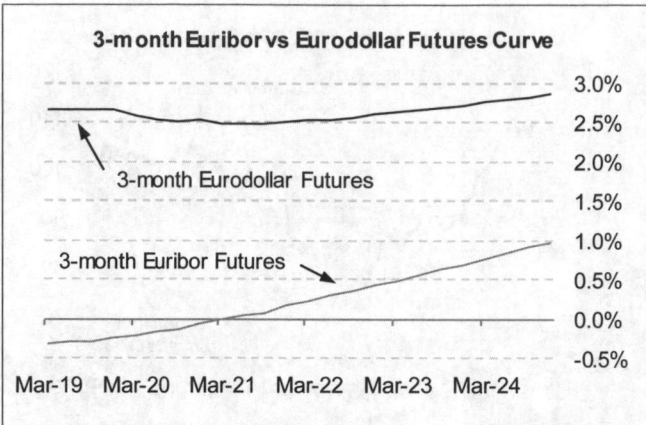

3-month Euribor vs Eurodollar Futures Curve

3-month Eurodollar Futures

3-month Euribor Futures

Mar-19 Mar-20 Mar-21 Mar-22 Mar-23 Mar-24

halt its rate-hike regime.

The Fed by late 2018 was forced to halt its rate-hike regime as the global economy slowed due in part to trade tensions. The Chinese economy progressively slowed during 2018 after the Trump administration in early 2018 slapped tariffs on $250 billion of Chinese goods and China retaliated with tariffs on $110 billion of U.S. goods. The Trump administration also slapped tariffs on imported steel and aluminum, which drew retaliatory tariffs on U.S. products sent overseas.

The dollar was also undercut during 2018 by political uncertainty as the investigation by Special Counsel Robert Mueller indicted some key Trump campaign and administration officials and a number of Russian nationals.

The large U.S. current account deficit continued to be a long-term underlying bearish factor for the dollar in 2018. The U.S. current account deficit, which is the broadest measure of U.S. trade, was reported at -$125 billion in Q3-2018. The deficit means that a net $1.4 billion worth of dollars are flowing out of the U.S. each calendar day to pay for goods and services.

Meanwhile, the euro was weak during 2018, falling from a 4-year high in 2018 to a 1-1/2 year low by late 2018. The euro was undercut by falling Eurozone GDP in the second half of 2018 where Italy saw a technical recession and Germany saw negative growth in Q3 and barely eked out a gain in Q4.

The weak Eurozone economy, combined with below-target inflation, caused the European Central Bank to remain in a dovish mode during 2018. The ECB ended its quantitative easing program at the end of 2018 but promised not to raise interest rates until at least summer 2019. Indeed, the markets believe that the ECB will not raise interest rates until 2020, thus depressing the euro's interest rate differentials and keeping downward pressure on the euro. The 10-year German government bund yield ended 2018 at 0.40%, far below the comparable U.S. 10-year Treasury yield level of 2.80%.

The yen also remained under pressure during 2018. While the Federal Reserve raised interest rates during 2018, the Bank of Japan was forced to keep Japanese interest rates near zero and continue its large quantitative easing program. The BOJ during 2018 maintained its policy of targeting the 10-year Japanese government bond (JGB) yield rate near zero.

In the big picture, the dollar is trading in the upper third of its 2011/2016 rally. The dollar in 2019 should continue to benefit from relative strength in the U.S. economy and much higher interest rates in the U.S. than in Europe and Japan. However, there are few catalysts for a new dollar rally since the U.S. economy is slowing and Fed policy is on hold. Meanwhile, the euro and yen have upside potential once their economies get onto stable ground and the ECB and BOJ start raising interest rates.

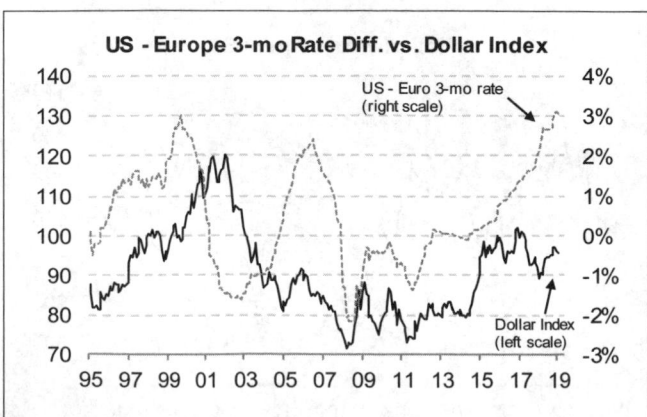

US - Europe 3-mo Rate Diff. vs. Dollar Index

US - Euro 3-mo rate (right scale)

Dollar Index (left scale)

95 97 99 01 03 05 07 09 11 13 15 17 19

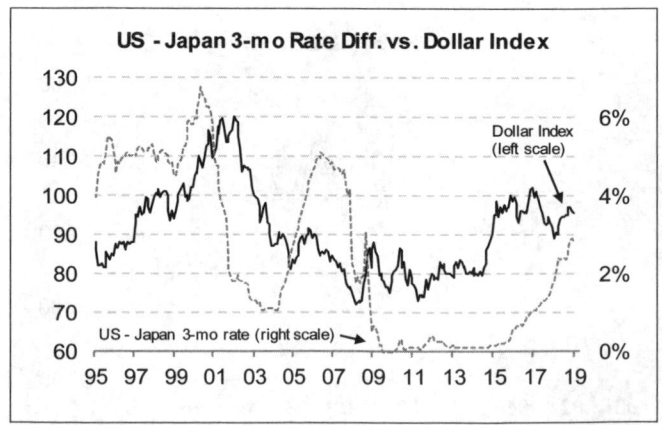

US - Japan 3-mo Rate Diff. vs. Dollar Index

Dollar Index (left scale)

US - Japan 3-mo rate (right scale)

95 97 99 01 03 05 07 09 11 13 15 17 19

FEDERAL RESERVE HITS PAUSE BUTTON AS GLOBAL ECONOMY SLOWS

The Federal Reserve at its January 2019 meeting surprised the markets by shifting to a neutral monetary policy and dropping its guidance for a further slow rise in interest rates. The Fed in January thereby halted its rate-hike regime with its federal funds rate target at 2.25%/2.50%.

Previously, the FOMC during 2015-18 raised its funds rate target a total of nine times in increments of 25 basis points from the 0.00%/0.25% level that prevailed after the 2007/09 global financial crisis to the 2.25%/2.50% level in December 2018.

Back in 2007, the Fed was forced to adopt the most stimulative monetary policy in American history in reaction to the Great Recession in 2007/09 and the global financial crisis. The Fed started cutting its federal funds rate target in October 2007 from 5.25% when the housing crisis started. By early 2009 the Fed had cut its federal funds rate target range to 0.00%/0.25%, which was the range that then prevailed until late 2015.

After the financial crisis erupted into global proportions in September 2008 with the bankruptcy of Lehman Brothers, the Fed also began its so-called "quantitative easing" (QE) operations whereby it bought securities to permanently inject reserves into the banking system and thus boost liquidity.

The Fed began its first quantitative easing move (QE1) in March 2008, which involved the purchase of a total of $1.425 trillion of securities by the time it ended in March 2010. When the economy continued to struggle in the first half of 2010, the Fed launched its QE2 program of buying another $600 billion worth of Treasury securities from November 2010 through June 2011.

The U.S. economy in the first half of 2011 and 2012 then faltered again due to a confluence of negative events including high gasoline prices, the Japanese earthquake/tsunami in March 2011, the U.S. debt ceiling debacle in early summer 2011, and the European sovereign debt crisis that began in 2011. As a result, the Fed in September 2012 began its QE3 program, which lasted until October 2014 and totaled $1.7 trillion.

By the time the Fed's QE3 program ended in October 2014, the Fed's QE programs totaled $3.7 trillion and the Fed's balance sheet had quintupled to $4.5 trillion from the pre-crisis level of $900 billion.

The purpose of the Fed's QE programs was to (1) keep banks fully supplied with excess reserves to reduce the chance of any liquidity squeeze and to provide plenty of reserves as a base for expanded lending, (2) keep long-term Treasury yields relatively low in order to hold down private rates such as corporate bond yields and mortgage rates, and (3) provide a boost to asset prices and the stock market in order to increase household confidence and wealth.

The Fed in December 2015 finally took its first step towards normalizing monetary policy by raising its federal funds rate target range by +25 basis points (bp) to 0.25%/0.50%. However, the U.S. economy was weak in the first half of 2016 and the Fed was forced to wait for a year before implementing its second +25 bp rate hike to a new range of 0.50%/0.75% in December 2016.

By 2017, the U.S. economy finally started showing signs of a solid expansion, thus allowing the Fed to accelerate the pace of its rate hikes. The Fed in 2017 accelerated its tightening process with three rate hikes totaling +75 bp to 1.25%/1.50% by the end of 2017.

The Fed in October 2017 also started to allow its balance sheet to decline by letting maturing securities roll off its balance sheet without replacement. The Fed allowed its balance sheet to decline by a maximum of $10 billion per month in Q4-2017. The Fed then increased that maximum by $10 billion per quarter until a maximum drawdown amount of $50 billion per month was reached in Q4-2018.

Upon starting its balance sheet drawdown program, the Fed said the program would be on autopilot and would be like "watching paint dry." Indeed, the balance sheet drawdown program in its first year was uneventful and drew little attention.

However, when the global stock markets took a nosedive in Q4-2018, some market participants started pointing fingers at the Fed's balance sheet drawdown program as one of the causes. The thinking was that if the QE programs and the Fed's rising balance sheet were

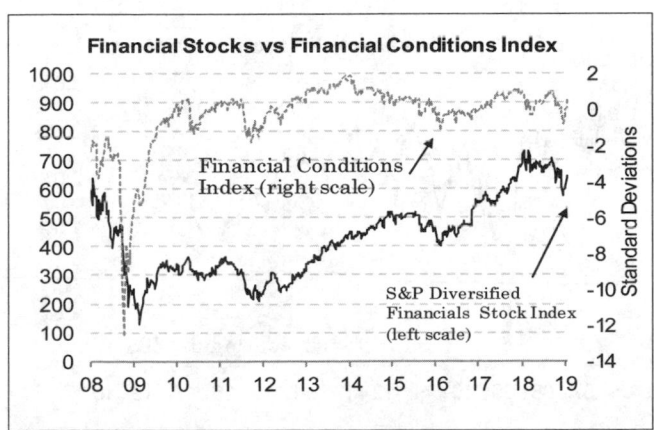

Financial Stocks vs Financial Conditions Index

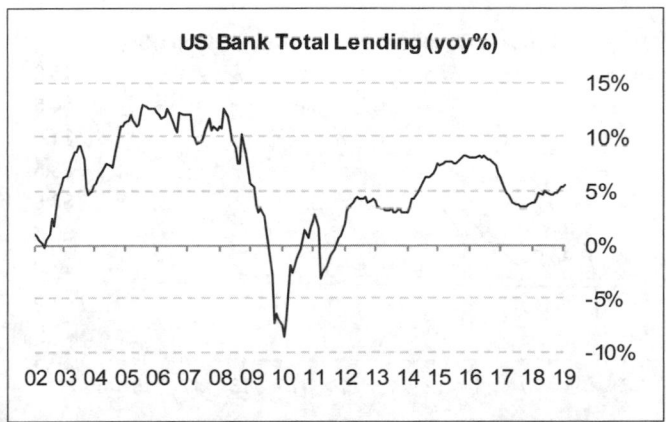

US Bank Total Lending (yoy%)

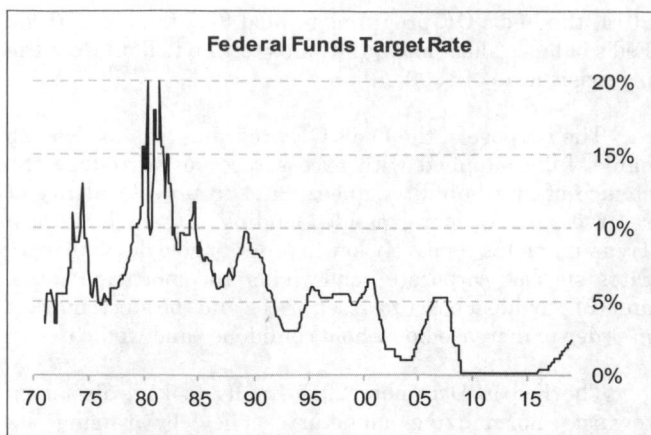

Federal Funds Target Rate

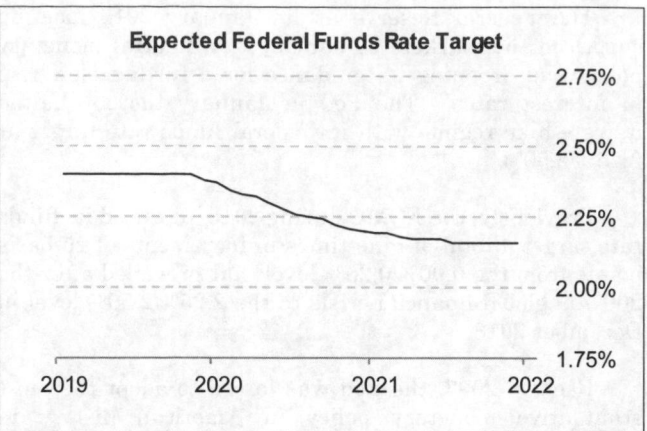

Expected Federal Funds Rate Target

bullish for both the economy and the stock market during 2009-2014, then the converse must also be true, i.e., that Fed's drawdown of its balance sheet (called "quantitative tightening" or QT) must be negative for both the U.S. economy and the stock market in 2018 as the Fed drained excess liquidity from the banking system.

In reaction to the market criticism about the balance sheet reduction program, Fed officials in early 2019 said that they could slow the program if necessary and said that program might end by late 2019. The Fed has not yet announced exactly when its drawdown program will end or what the ultimate target will be for its balance sheet level. However, Fed officials did say that they plan to continue using a floor-type system for running monetary policy, which indicates that the Fed will stop its program with a relatively high balance sheet level.

The Fed's interest rate pause in early 2019 occurred with the funds rate target at 2.25%/2.50%, which is still about 50 bp below the Fed's view of a long-run neutral funds rate of 2.75% The Fed would undoubtedly still like to push the funds rate up by another 50 bp to the 2.75%/3.00% range so that the funds rate is close to neutral and does not over-stimulate the economy or cause an inflation spike.

In addition, the funds rate level of 2.40% seen in early 2019 was only 40 bp above the Fed's 2.0% inflation target. A real federal funds rate level of 0.40% is well below the long-term average of 1.60% and indicates that U.S. monetary policy is still very simulative. If the Fed were

to raise the funds rate by another 50 bp to 2.90%, then the new real funds rate of 0.90% would be closer to a long-run equilibrium level.

While the Fed would probably prefer to raise interest rates by another 50 bp, the Fed will have to wait for that move until the coast becomes clear for the global macroeconomic outlook. The U.S. and global economies in early 2019 faced considerable uncertainty with the U.S. economy slowing as the 2018 tax-cut stimulus started wearing off. The Eurozone economy was seeing weakness and the Chinese economy was slowing due to trade tensions and high debt levels. The Fed will be under pressure to avoid further interest rate hikes at least until U.S./Chinese trade tensions are resolved and the Chinese economy stabilizes.

The good news is that the Fed has so far been able to raise interest rates by 225 bp without causing a recession. The Fed's rate-hike pause in early 2019 may be sufficient to allow the U.S. economy to maintain its firm underpinnings and avoid a recession over the next few years. If so, then the Fed will have done a remarkable job in getting its monetary policy back to something resembling normality. Still, there is a risk that the lagging effects of the Fed's overall 225 bp rate hike and the ongoing balance sheet reduction program might tip the U.S. economy into recession. If so, that recession would likely be shallow since the Fed could quickly start to cut interest rates again and stop its balance sheet reduction program.

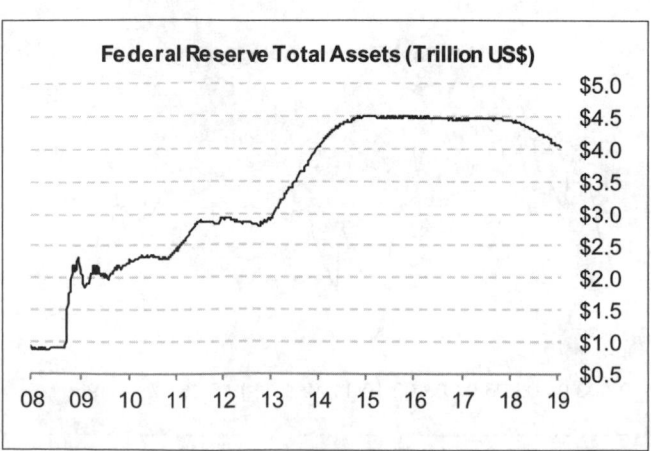

Federal Reserve Total Assets (Trillion US$)

U.S. 10-year Breakeven Inflation Expectations

10-yr T-note minus TIPS

SLOWING CHINESE ECONOMIC GROWTH SPARKS GLOBAL CONCERNS

The Chinese economy during 2018 decelerated and sparked major concerns for global investors. China's economy has a large effect on the overall global economy since China's economy accounts for about 19% of world GDP and accounts for an even larger 35% share of world GDP growth. Without growth in China, the world economy would likely dip towards a recession.

Chinese real GDP growth in 2018 extended its 7-year slide and fell to a 28-year low of +6.6%, the slowest pace since 1990. The market is expecting Chinese GDP to continue to slow in coming years to +6.2% in 2019, +6.0% in 2020, and +5.8% in 2021.

China's growth is slowing partly because the economy is maturing and is falling back to the more normal growth rate around +2% seen in developed countries. China is coming down from several decades of extraordinarily fast growth that was driven by urbanization, investment, and exports on a massive scale. China is now being forced to downshift to longer-term equilibrium with an economy that is more dependent on a middle class and consumer spending rather than on investment and exports.

China's biggest problem at present is a massive debt load by households and corporations. China's government responded to the 2007/09 global financial crisis with a big expansion of monetary stimulus and bank lending, as well as deficit government spending. The result has been that China's total debt, including government, household, and corporate debt, has soared to 271% of GDP from only 150% in 2008.

China's government debt has doubled to about 50% of GDP from 25% before the 2007/09 global financial crisis, but remains at a manageable level that is lower than the debt loads of other major nations. China's debt problem is actually not so much from government debt as it is from explosion of household and corporate debt to 220% of GDP from just 125% before the global financial crisis.

China's banking system is on shaky ground as the economy slows and as households and corporations have less cash to service their debt loads. Indeed, Chinese onshore corporate debt defaults during 2018 quadrupled from 2017 to a record $18 billion. Moreover, China has a serious problem with its shadow banking system that is highly leveraged and dependent on a variety of high-risk financial instruments and strategies.

China's GDP growth in 2018 was hurt in particular by the trade war with the U.S., which caused a significant drop in demand for Chinese products overseas and a disruption of global supply chains. The Trump administration launched the trade war in an attempt to force China to reduce its trade surplus with the U.S. and address structural issues such as alleged intellectual property theft, forced technology transfers, and subsidies to state-owned companies.

The Trump administration in early 2018 imposed a 25% tariff on $50 billion of Chinese products and a 10% tariff on $200 billion of additional Chinese products. Those tariffs covered about half of all U.S. imports from China. In retaliation, China slapped tariffs on $110 billion of U.S. products, accounting for nearly all of China's imports from the U.S. including nearly all U.S. farm products.

The U.S. and China as of February 2018 had yet to resolve their trade differences with President Trump threatening to further ratchet up tariffs on Chinese products.

The Chinese government in 2018 responded to the slowing economy with a variety of targeted stimulus moves. The Chinese central bank did not cut its benchmark interest rates because it did not want to weaken the yuan, which would have risked capital flight and fresh criticism by the Trump administration. However, the Chinese central bank did cut the bank reserve requirement to free up reserves and give banks room to boost their lending to households and corporations. The Chinese economy was also helped by the sharp drop in the Chinese 10-year government bond yield during 2018 to a 2-year low of 3.10% by early 2019.

China's stock market sold off sharply by +25% during 2018 to a 4-year low due to the U.S.-Chinese trade war and the slower Chinese economy. However, Chinese stocks showed a modest recovery in early 2019 on hopes for a resolution of the U.S.-Chinese trade war and on the halt by the U.S. Federal Reserve of its interest-rate-hike regime.

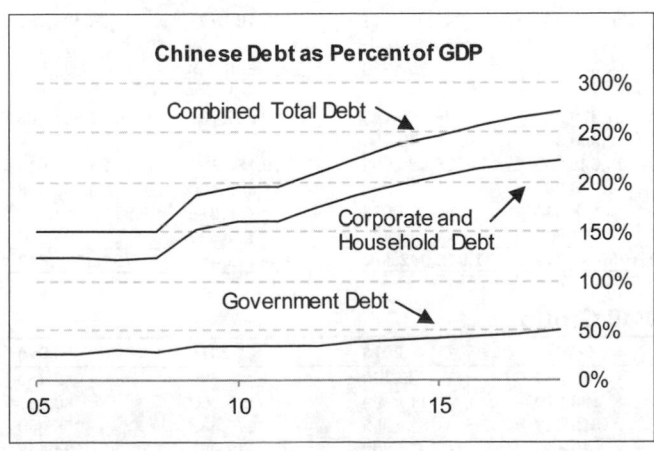

Chinese Debt as Percent of GDP

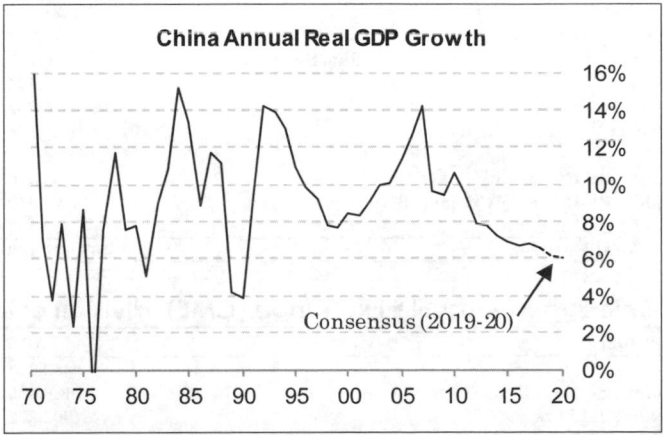

China Annual Real GDP Growth

Volume - U.S.

U.S. Futures Volume Highlights
2018 in Comparison with 2017

2018 Rank	EXCHANGE	2018 Contracts	%	2017 Contracts	%	2017 Rank
1	Chicago Mercantile Exchange (CME Group)	1,670,413,684	46.67%	1,353,316,208	42.04%	1
2	Chicago Board of Trade (CME Group)	1,467,662,478	41.00%	1,166,882,749	36.25%	2
3	New York Mercantile Exchange (CME Group)	572,332,919	15.99%	571,361,340	17.75%	3
4	ICE Futures U.S.	304,291,576	8.50%	306,687,921	9.53%	4
5	Commodity Exchange (CME Group)	139,202,852	3.89%	124,381,290	3.86%	5
6	CBOE Futures Exchange	75,555,327	2.11%	73,991,390	2.30%	6
7	NASDAQ NFX	13,581,864	0.38%	42,101,306	1.31%	7
8	OneChicago	7,066,292	0.20%	14,929,997	0.46%	8
9	Minneapolis Grain Exchange	2,275,557	0.06%	2,677,661	0.08%	9
10	ERIS Exchange	451,520	0.01%	435,881	0.01%	10
	Total Futures	**4,252,834,069**	**100.00%**	**3,656,765,743**	**100.00%**	

CBOE Futures Exchange (CFE)

FUTURE	2018	2017	2016	2015	2014
CBOE Bitcoin	1,219,083	56,092			
CBOE Russell 2000 Volatility Index (RVX)	1,930	6,060	5,795	5,677	5,340
CBOE S&P 500 Twelve-Month Variance (IIK)	12,212	70,343	1,290	5,011	2,308
CBOE Volatility Index (VX)	74,318,415	73,858,885	60,170,725	51,656,362	50,531,366
CBOE High Yield Corporate Bond	3,656				
CBOE Investment Grade Corporate Bond	18				
CBOE/CBOT 10 Year US Treasury Note Volatility	13	10		153	14
Total Futures	**75,555,327**	**73,991,390**	**60,177,810**	**51,675,531**	**50,615,305**

Chicago Board of Trade (CBT), division of the CME Group

FUTURE	2018	2017	2016	2015	2014
Chicago Soft Red Winter Wheat	36,805,171	33,717,805	31,059,726	31,100,598	25,853,004
Corn	97,387,154	89,876,782	85,625,219	83,094,271	69,437,304
EU Wheat	179,745	120,874	77,631		
Fertilizer	13,680	5,700			
Fertilizer Products	27,360	21,700	22,842	27,175	16,925
KC Hard Red Winter Wheat	15,341,514	12,623,018	9,690,816	7,359,946	5,868,505
Mini Corn	118,883	115,646	143,840	132,596	172,411
Mini Soybeans	273,669	204,819	296,336	229,208	316,771
Mini Wheat	88,021	67,718	74,698	82,987	101,124
Oats	172,939	169,252	225,230	194,575	200,531
Rough Rice	231,294	271,183	305,045	316,315	225,694
Soybeans	58,538,591	54,504,169	61,730,753	54,095,051	49,169,361
Soybean Meal	31,838,908	25,996,399	25,953,938	24,315,276	20,637,382
Soybean Oil	31,265,884	30,232,316	29,429,298	28,897,275	23,769,391
Ethanol	112,438	149,546	172,664	187,661	243,072
Mini-sized $5 Dow Jones Industrial Index	60,324,164	32,866,342	42,555,855	40,601,073	39,053,744
S&P 500 Index	500				
10-Year Treasury Note	457,719,304	375,338,442	350,762,158	328,341,066	340,485,319
10-Year Eris Swap	26,274				
10-Year USD Deliverable Interest Rate Swap	516,443	601,992	631,279	756,375	784,215
2-Year Treasury Note	135,499,156	97,249,457	81,874,197	83,040,660	71,814,288
2-Year Eris Swap	26,272				
30-Year Treasury Bond	92,661,809	73,337,240	70,203,290	71,901,544	93,189,109
30-Year Eris Swap	300				
30-Year USD Deliverable Interest Rate Swap	983	10,759	21,236	35,760	62,513
3-Year Eris Swap	1,628				
4-Year Eris Swap	3,016				
5 Year Treasury Note	287,221,081	226,441,088	201,904,771	190,707,727	196,429,135
5-Year Eris Swap	29,381				
5-Year USD Deliverable Interest Rate Swap	350,138	566,751	792,880	696,148	779,579
7-Year Eris Swap	3,404				
Federal Funds	65,336,892	47,978,260	33,299,445	20,247,761	7,894,868
Ultra 10-Year Treasury Note	47,350,198	29,309,367	16,979,453		
Ultra T-Bond	46,632,747	33,625,955	28,430,003	29,133,162	25,427,616
DJ UBS Commodity Index	950,480	1,093,237	417,312	369,468	255,563
DJ UBS Roll Select Commodity Index	20,570	8,640	5,036	8,018	4,072
DJ US Real Estate	592,487	374,968	241,475	177,627	121,166
Total Futures	**1,467,662,478**	**1,166,882,749**	**1,072,942,112**	**996,142,086**	**972,566,847**

Chicago Mercantile Exchange (CME), division of the CME Group

FUTURE	2018	2017	2016	2015	2014
Butter	52,623	40,323	39,170	30,896	2,480
Cash Settled Cheese	136,455	128,370	117,899	123,000	80,507
Class III Milk	302,252	319,828	321,959	275,539	358,659
Class IV Milk	10,864	10,447	14,302	12,071	24,447

Chicago Mercantile Exchange (CME), division of the CME Group (continued)

FUTURE	2018	2017	2016	2015	2014
Dry Whey	16,852	20,786	16,042	21,482	17,790
Feeder Cattle	3,528,965	3,541,833	2,537,955	2,493,051	2,116,262
Lean Hogs	13,551,711	11,242,021	9,195,000	9,575,882	10,656,944
Live Cattle	16,440,125	16,165,210	13,122,784	13,440,934	13,599,292
Malaysian Palm Oil Calendar Swap	51,474	105,112	117,440	54,412	43,020
Nonfat Dry Milk	59,405	60,375	55,375	50,714	28,461
USD Crude Palm Oil	8,680	6,434	3,140	200	
Australian Dollar	28,062,547	24,054,242	25,303,506	23,382,408	22,728,891
Australian Dollar / Canadian Dollar	60	838	69	234	1,022
Australian Dollar / Japanese Yen	50,269	33,516	52,139	49,242	70,201
Australian Dollar / New Zealand Dollar	1,026	1,160	733	605	2,200
Bitcoin	923,294	9,503			
Brazilian Real	1,624,599	1,147,242	1,004,902	703,676	648,815
British Pound	32,439,027	31,167,897	29,126,002	24,144,659	24,837,008
British Pound / Japanese Yen	37,470	40,981	22,624	15,468	51,224
British Pound / Swiss Franc	3,982	1,103	479	1,629	4,891
Canadian Dollar	21,019,365	19,222,524	18,697,306	17,301,876	15,096,546
Canadian Dollar / Japanese Yen	1,489	1,490	15	261	1,214
Chilean Peso	24,127	34,751	10	73	
Chinese Renimibi / Euro	117,420	19,826	21,091	13,267	
Chinese Renimibi / US Dollar	65	345	3,803	5,239	10,799
Czech Koruna	75				41
Czech Koruna (European)	8				
E-micro AUD/USD	1,313,037	1,012,132	1,218,358	652,469	519,173
E-micro EUR/USD	4,323,117	2,987,367	3,371,953	4,325,807	1,969,393
E-micro GBP/USD	545,675	681,701	1,038,606	488,050	362,251
E-micro INR/USD	62,787	31,089	29,960	2,576	
E-mini Euro FX	1,224,546	1,142,522	949,208	1,481,391	915,094
E-mini Japanese Yen	163,359	318,114	393,096	212,810	176,328
Euro FX	68,785,137	56,455,834	49,455,909	65,356,062	52,208,275
Euro / Australian Dollar	33,121	40,887	21,928	24,807	16,076
Euro / British Pound	1,064,898	1,029,005	956,015	772,968	742,968
Euro / Canadian Dollar	45,151	57,521	33,735	31,904	40,530
Euro / Japanese Yen	1,044,615	877,007	542,332	555,285	559,039
Euro / Norwegian Krone	4,440	3,149	11	769	1,198
Euro / Swedish Krona	10,058	10,456	3,527	5,059	8,972
Euro / Swiss Franc	377,760	464,544	477,722	411,198	459,297
Hungarian Forint	729			2	624
Hungarian Forint (European)	98				
Indian Rupee	1,089,152	472,388	160,255	130,396	50,949
Israeli Shekel	2,610	1,468		22	5,983
Japanese Yen	36,979,311	41,623,449	36,588,788	36,180,466	38,319,796
Korean Won	6,846	786	207	815	2,301
Mexican Peso	17,081,210	13,082,141	14,074,359	10,951,568	10,484,059
Micro CAD/USD	206,791	244,321	245,995	158,108	177,522
Micro CHF/USD	18,276	11,952	21,814	28,110	48,379
Micro JPY/USD	356,863	450,068	396,958	150,355	164,072
New Zealand Dollar	7,552,938	6,352,688	5,938,492	5,040,002	4,108,009
Norwegian Krone/US Dollar	64,580	25,688	23,898	14,381	14,647
Euro / Polish Zloty	232	444	19,906	6,483	36,075
Polish Zloty	1,212	4,046	23,053	8,434	24,500
Russian Ruble	769,150	700,678	481,686	399,570	972,959
South African Rand	593,301	671,568	242,283	216,350	122,259
Swedish Krona	61,886	35,201	26,231	15,398	12,163
Swiss Franc	7,262,353	6,978,111	5,968,783	5,634,413	9,638,920
Swiss Franc/Japanese Yen	199	32			16
Turkish Lira	38,992	27,812	420	126	20,215
US Dollar/South African Rand	15	1	46	580	1,476
CNX Nifty Index	54,444	142,778	117,092	18,485	
E-mini FTSE 100 Index	54,932	33,509	20,867	4,525	
E-mini NASDAQ 100 Index	124,195,504	69,559,095	65,750,522	67,310,282	75,483,720
E-mini Russell 1000 Growth Index	133,122	60,347	3,415	1,782	
E-mini Russell 1000 Index	183,158	68,918	5,213	2,913	
E-mini Russell 1000 Value Index	200,920	111,903	10,640	1,729	
E-mini Russell 2000 Index	37,825,110	11,255,598			
E-mini S&P 500 Index	445,199,191	365,601,616	472,678,663	429,803,221	425,020,210
E-mini S&P Consumer Discretionary Sector	237,902	95,698	150,939	134,064	36,813
E-mini S&P Consumer Staples Sector	336,374	216,011	315,638	154,403	67,346
E-mini S&P Energy Sector	459,339	200,581	141,747	94,819	93,174
E-mini S&P Financial Sector	661,070	392,947	174,419	63,667	40,078
E-mini S&P Healthcare Sector	304,283	184,740	146,804	144,470	56,750
E-mini S&P Industrial Sector	275,804	109,172	133,452	43,235	37,218
E-mini S&P Materials Sector	168,358	108,529	85,743	41,622	29,985
E-mini S&P MidCap 400 Index	4,951,100	4,332,040	5,405,757	5,381,033	5,285,715
E-mini S&P Real Estate Select Sector	116,335	73,426	14,213		

VOLUME - U.S.

Chicago Mercantile Exchange (CME), division of the CME Group (continued)

FUTURE	2018	2017	2016	2015	2014
E-mini S&P SmallCap 600 Index	1			1	57
E-mini S&P Technology Sector	490,180	137,930	81,412	60,448	41,290
E-mini S&P Utilities Sector	518,335	347,959	298,401	138,316	88,427
Ibovespa Index	13,032	8,560	8,878	5,090	4,431
NASDAQ Biotech	8,528	3,805	2,312	1,724	600
Nikkei 225 ($)	3,823,525	3,375,130	4,288,493	4,236,624	4,815,946
Nikkei 225 (Yen)	11,012,114	10,851,751	14,805,432	13,352,541	12,184,838
S&P 500 Index	1,654,823	1,509,263	2,245,436	3,024,624	3,387,740
S&P Citigroup Growth	93	285	290	401	803
S&P Citigroup Value	188,031	227,150	133,679	6,105	1,609
Topix (Yen)	13,365				
Eurodollar (3-month)	765,208,581	639,847,185	654,947,336	586,913,126	664,433,493
One Month Eurodollar	32,337	66,122	19,687	63,422	19,870
Secured Overnight Financing Rate (SOFR)	1,096,606				
Sterling Overnight Index Average (SONIA)	298,611				
CDD Seasonal Weather Strips	600	1,100	1,575	1,404	100
CDD Weather	2,150	26,250	3,375	5,992	7,407
CSI Housing Index	113	136	146	93	133
Euro HDD Seasonal Strip Weather	24,000	400	200	100	6,250
HDD Seasonal Weather Strips	50		350	952	800
HDD Weather	14,405	9,239	6,204	8,427	7,039
Random Lumber	216,586	205,099	174,982	201,352	160,497
Goldman Sachs Commodity Index	378,542	403,424	359,987	354,566	274,161
S&P GSCI Enhanced Excess Return Swap	41,362	134,259	116,459	104,576	80,586
GSCI Excess Return Index	472,094	437,683	344,822	254,115	201,879
Total Futures	**1,670,413,684**	**1,353,316,208**	**1,445,488,379**	**1,336,988,253**	**1,404,178,272**

Commodity Exchange (COMEX), division of the CME Group

FUTURE	2018	2017	2016	2015	2014
Alumina FOB Australia (Platts) (ALA)	5,755	6,685	60		
Aluminium European Premium Duty-Paid (Metal	17,730	10,865	10,453		
Aluminium European Premium Metal Bulletin (25mt-	20,068	29,963	13,573	4,651	
Aluminum A380 Alloy (S&P Global Platts) (A38)	112	30	167		
Aluminum Japan Premium (Platts) (MJP)	13,155	17,399	9,103		
Aluminum MW U.S. Transaction Premium Platts	98,922	85,683	68,872	37,447	5,431
Copper (HG)	32,710,103	27,051,503	21,524,547	16,986,055	14,591,200
Copper Financial Futures (HGS)	17,294	8,988	3,881	6,538	12,819
Copper Premium Grade A CIF Shanghai (Metal	205	329			
E-mini Copper Futures (QC)	5,195	8,269	6,675	9,171	11,304
Zinc Futures (ZNC)	14,057	141	230	386	
E-Micro Gold Futures (MGC)	1,801,078	1,141,590	976,950	407,643	276,815
Gold (GC)	80,301,590	72,802,171	57,564,840	41,847,338	40,518,804
Gold Kilo (GCK)	136	3,665	56,157	51,336	
miNY Gold Futures (QO)	96,481	92,442	130,190	66,758	51,504
miNY Silver Futures (QI)	13,401	9,704	14,985	9,823	12,160
1,000-oz. Silver Futures (SIL)	100,519	71,118	101,937	89,934	143,368
Silver (SI)	23,987,051	23,034,989	18,218,740	13,454,406	13,696,961
Total Futures	**139,202,852**	**124,381,290**	**98,709,628**	**72,975,530**	**69,326,368**

ERIS Exchange

FUTURE	2018	2017	2016	2015	2014
10-Year Standards	92,461	154,248	124,389	286,612	164,539
15-Year Standards	7,700				
2-Year Standards	135,271	24,404	27,655	37,500	44,965
20-Year Standards	314				
3-Year Standards	38,049	32,275	9,775		
30-Year Standards	3,072	5,809	4,225	2,769	2,196
4-Year Standards	13,029	6,045	7,456		
5-Year Standards	119,331	195,465	292,482	289,268	162,162
7-Year Standards	28,441	17,635	8,106	25,761	34,953
Flexes	13,852				
Total Futures	**451,520**	**435,881**	**474,094**	**660,462**	**489,305**

Minneapolis Grain Exchange (MGE)

FUTURE	2018	2017	2016	2015	2014
Hard Red Spring Wheat	2,275,557	2,677,449	2,162,166	2,288,655	2,153,083
Total Futures	**2,275,557**	**2,677,661**	**2,162,509**	**2,288,685**	**2,153,373**

ICE Futures U.S. (ICE)

FUTURE	2018	2017	2016	2015	2014
Canola[3]	4,828,030	5,391,355	6,244,156	5,559,469	5,553,922
Cocoa	12,035,589	11,061,606	9,862,218	7,913,036	6,315,792
Coffee 'C'	13,387,705	9,434,122	9,856,314	8,108,135	7,052,230
Cotton #2	8,876,095	7,907,507	7,703,046	6,725,842	5,787,883
Orange Juice, Frozen Concentrate	356,854	363,499	413,904	398,567	398,529
Sugar #11	37,011,007	30,961,148	33,115,334	34,394,482	29,396,597
Sugar #16	75,141	70,679	78,410	71,502	86,261
U.S. Wheat	50	115	83	128	271
U.S. Corn	40	73	119	443	294
U.S. Soybeans	2	41	220	179	108
U.S. Soybean Meal	72	94	74	20	8
U.S. Soybean Oil	51	34	26	20	123
Australian Dollar / Canadian Dollar	467	1,486	8,790	8,346	3,505
Australian Dollar / Japanese Yen	1,805	4,791	9,023	7,016	7,211
Australian Dollar / New Zealand Dollar	13,682	21,795	45,174	22,609	11,411
Australian Dollar / US Dollar (KAU)	13,337	17,705	14,044	10,312	4,172
British Pound / Australian Dollar	458	1,795	9,210	6,176	4,532
British Pound / Canadian Dollar	953	1,227	6,232	7,870	5,549
British Pound / Japanese Yen	8,889	14,255	18,168	42,001	33,124
British Pound / New Zealand Dollar	272	1,747	4,314	2,806	3,643
British Pound / Norwegian Krone	23,600	20,036	14,881	7,583	5,508
British Pound / South Africa Rand	279	959	1,115	714	1,020
British Pound / Swedish Krona	815	863	1,093	645	980
British Pound / Swiss Franc	9,969	8,680	9,651	19,869	22,049
Canadian Dollar / Japanese Yen	2,262	3,500	5,508	6,931	5,729
Canadian Dollar / US Dollar (KSV)	6,651	13,445	21,408	14,943	9,222
Colombian Peso / US Dollar	866	1,950			
Euro / Australian Dollar (KRA)	11,883	10,862	23,675	27,783	31,842
Euro / British Pound (KGB)	2,608	10,714	24,116	32,683	31,059
Euro / Canadian Dollar (KEP)	1,796	5,191	11,088	12,131	7,045
Euro/Czech Koruna	241				
Euro / Norwegian Krone (KOL)	15,449	53,267	30,993	13,683	48,624
Euro / South African Rand	6,712	18,002	641	693	1,624
Euro / Swedish Krona (KRK)	37,618	32,974	41,644	51,925	27,738
Euro / Swiss Franc (KRZ)	364	752	10,436	12,895	16,786
Euro / US Dollar (KEO)	69,149	47,062	141,885	230,182	221,758
Euro / Czech Koruna	4,591	4,371	4,302	25,929	18,904
Euro / Hungarian Forint	124,288	144,639	84,482	50,989	34,564
Israeli Shekel / US Dollar	7,818	7,278	15,272	7,845	
Japanese Yen / US Dollar (KSN)	5,944	10,779	24,463	18,606	15,742
Mexican Peso / US Dollar	954	3,162	322	1,400	160
New Zealand Dollar / US Dollar (KZX)	40	217	9,291	4,143	3,327
New Zealand Dollar / Japanese Yen	17,638	13,956	12,985	14,479	22,499
Norwegian Krone / Japanese Yen	370	508	658	571	878
Norwegian Krone / Swedish Koruna	74,309	78,548	77,292	19,931	31,714
Polish Zloty / Euro	44,555	66,392	24,868	26,182	
Polish Zloty / US Dollar	28,662	24,331	1,727	6,024	
Small British Pound / US Dollar	9,691	12,801	36,327	19,807	15,852
Swedish Krona / Japanese Yen	306	456	292	471	770
Swiss Franc / Japanese Yen (KZY)	6,256	8,479	8,097	10,955	11,225
Swiss Franc / US Dollar (KMF)	78	712	5,303	8,194	2,714
Turkish Lira / Euro	7,829	13,777	23,319	11,655	
Turkish Lira / US Dollar	48,204	53,285	43,974	25,963	
US Dollar Index	6,448,251	7,518,615	7,407,987	12,106,494	7,112,150
US Dollar / Czech Koruna (Half Size)	33,432	20,051	30,894	18,306	10,043
US Dollar / Hungarian Forint (Half Size)	20,412	36,922	16,744	24,160	12,587
US Dollar / Norwegian Krone (Half Size)	43,970	21,746	21,288	19,344	39,626
US Dollar / South African Rand	11,216	41,403	45,660	112,509	124,300
US Dollar / Swedish Krona (Half Size)	35,589	34,964	48,668	37,791	34,290
Global Oil Products	3,185,340				
North American Natural Gas	156,488,955	154,481,611	161,812,492	161,164,603	180,868,570
North American Power	12,689,753	17,143,215	26,957,208	28,326,978	27,169,421
FANG+ Index	361,012	13,846			
Mini MSCI ACWI Index	212	100			
MSCI ACWI NTR	303,832	376,085	383,969	139,820	143,859
Mini MSCI Canada Index	5	183	39	152	64
Mini MSCI EAFE Index	9,232,112	6,803,099	5,774,453	4,302,898	2,963,517
Mini MSCI Emerging Markets Asia NTR	35,866,309	523,135	129,558		2,398
Mini MSCI Emerging Markets	398,263	24,121,251	22,534,452	14,135,268	9,245,982
Mini MSCI Emerging Markets Latin America Index	11,560	7,764	11,137	10,749	3,152
Mini MSCI Europe Index	69	24,314	178,209	441,714	416,392
Mini MSCI USA Value Index	250				
Mini MSCI World Index	3,189	2,620	11,928	18,640	11,756
Mini Pan Euro Index	7,485	50,879	35,159	57,306	141,076
Russell 1000 Growth Index Mini	2,282	77,040	133,883	106,399	150,113

VOLUME - U.S.

ICE Futures U.S. (ICE) (continued)

FUTURE	2018	2017	2016	2015	2014
Russell 1000 Mini Index	9,006	150,297	201,101	269,188	372,183
Russell 1000 Value Index Mini	3,342	163,953	198,820	139,083	182,675
Russell 2000 Mini Index	1,540,931	28,732,125	29,192,489	28,367,406	34,606,377
Eris CDX HY Credit Index Future 5Y	6,378	7,342	10,232	905	
Eris CDX IG Credit Index Future 5Y	6,597	20,084	26,984	2,786	
100 oz. Gold	207	274	310	376	388
5,000 oz. Silver	272	730	380	209	118
Gold (Daily)	207,429	138,168			
Mini Gold	71,505	145,413	302,714	280,497	495,869
Mini Silver	58,058	79,482	138,169	129,850	188,863
Silver (Daily)	62,059	13,186			
Total Futures	**304,291,576**	**306,687,921**	**323,749,015**	**314,207,769**	**319,641,261**

New York Mercantile Exchange (NYMEX), division of the CME Group

FUTURE	2018	2017	2016	2015	2014
Cocoa (CJ)	5	92	2,607	1,816	317
Cotton Futures (TT)	22	20	578	585	737
No. 11 Sugar Futures (YO)	58	42	418	1,570	760
1% Fuel Oil Cargoes CIF MED (Platts) Futures (1W)	154	20	1,279	264	246
1% Fuel Oil Cargoes CIF NWE (Platts) Futures (1X)	120		54	206	238
1% Fuel Oil Cargoes FOB MED (Platts) BALMO	8	50	8	62	47
1% Fuel Oil Cargoes FOB NWE (Platts) Crack Spread	171		32	306	1,945
1% Fuel Oil Cargoes FOB NWE (Platts) vs. 3.5% Fuel	2,553	3,086	4,029	4,656	7,151
1.0% Fuel Oil Cargoes FOB NWE (Platts) Crack	30			31	15
3.5% Fuel Oil Barges FOB Rdam (Platts) Crack Spread	18,153	20,260	29,875	20,213	9,164
3.5% Fuel Oil Barges FOB Rdam (Platts) Crack Spread	808	1,836	3,172	3,082	3,042
3.5% Fuel Oil Barges FOB Rdam (Platts) Crack Spread	38,610	41,030	51,192	44,483	49,990
3.5% Fuel Oil Cargoes FOB MED (Platts) vs. 3.5% Fuel	860	4,466	9,548	10,806	7,869
3.5% Fuel Oil CIF MED (Platts) BALMO Futures (8D)	95	175	397	153	100
3.5% Fuel Oil CIF MED (Platts) Futures (7D)	622	1,035	3,291	896	1,094
3.5% Fuel Oil Rdam vs. 3.5% FOB MED Spread	217	859	1,840	1,245	1,619
Argus Gasoline Eurobob Oxy Barges NWE Crack	222	127	97	456	130
Argus LLS vs. WTI (Argus) Trade Month Futures (E5)	256,755	190,327	144,567	98,118	64,272
Argus Propane (Saudi Aramco) Futures (9N)	32,923	12,890	10,114	7,128	10,193
Argus Propane Far East Index BALMO Swap (22)	2,117	1,165	592	401	290
Argus Propane Far East Index Futures (7E)	68,590	32,339	18,219	5,791	3,031
Argus Propane Far East Index vs European Propane	5,018	3,497	2,007	356	310
Argus Propane Far East Index vs Japan C&F Naphtha	51				
Argus Sour Crude Index vs WTI Diff Spread Calendar	2,055		675	300	150
Brent CFD: Dated Brent (Platts) vs. Brent Second	300			950	6,075
Brent Crude Oil BALMO Futures (J9)	285	578	2,293	4,854	3,378
Brent Crude Oil Futures (BB)	20,864	43,043	3,094	73,795	73,495
Brent Last Day Financial (BZ)	21,825,780	21,839,889	23,713,109	26,251,078	18,493,384
Brent Crude Oil vs. Dubai Crude Oil (Platts) Futures	106,858	119,797	33,163	12,540	4,467
Brent Financial Futures (CY)	39,825	34,990	22,091	59,242	89,889
Canadian C5+ Condensate Index (Net Energy) (CC5)	555	690			
Chicago CBOB Gasoline (Platts) vs. RBOB Gasoline	1,075		2,090	345	238
Chicago Ethanol (Platts) (CU)	1,133,415	1,342,798	1,322,192	1,001,090	1,151,356
Chicago ULSD (Platts) vs. NY Harbor ULSD (5C)	5,838	2,208	2,888	4,402	5,166
CIG Rockies Natural Gas (Platts Gas Daily/Platts	0	720	1,054		
CIG Rockies Natural Gas (Platts IFERC) Basis	221	1,456	82,139	47,921	11,071
Clearbrook Bakken Sweet Crude Oil Index (Net	2,360	2,790	2,305		
Coal (API 5) fob Newcastle (Argus/McCloskey) Futures	570	1,720	3,078	4,120	4,275
Coal (API2) CIF ARA (ARGUS-McCloskey) (MTF)	274,172	501,130	1,793,838	2,131,742	1,559,529
Coal (API4) FOB Richards Bay (ARGUS-McCloskey)	33,286	55,540	191,566	283,926	393,262
Coal (ICI 4) Indonesian Coal Index (Argus/Coalindo)	1,760				
Columbia Gas TCO (Platts IFERC) Basis Futures (TC)	856	8,949	34,344	39,379	166,413
Columbia Gulf, Mainline Natural Gas (Platts IFERC)	214	999	22,041	25,715	48,877
Conway Natural Gasoline (OPIS) Futures (8L)	2,831	2,984	1,691	1,032	589
Conway Normal Butane (OPIS) BALMO Futures	80	52	30		50
Conway Normal Butane (OPIS) Futures (8M)	2,831	8,299	2,760	1,964	1,135
Conway Propane (OPIS) BALMO Futures (CPB)	3,608	3,532	1,482	506	628
Conway Propane (OPIS) Futures (8K)	186,616	109,794	88,313	55,695	45,438
CPC Blend CIF Med Cargoes (Platts) vs Dated Brent	2,956	700			
Crude Oil Financial Futures (WS)	15,639	75,600	94,928	201,068	117,285
CSX Coal (Platts OTC Broker Index) Futures (QX)	245	4,870	14,967	35,651	55,289
Daily European Naphtha CIF NWE (Platts) Futures	640	1,514	1,112	2,687	474
Dated Brent (Platts) Financial Futures (UB)	5,300	2,540	26,638	39,030	29,055
Dated Brent (Platts) to Frontline Brent Futures (FY)	3,360	14,450	21,815	31,885	15,270
Diesel 10ppm Barges FOB Rdam (Platts) vs. Low	5		225	10	28
Dominion, South Point Natural Gas (Platts IFERC)	126	53,117	230,295	85,651	63,229
Dubai Crude Oil (Platts) BALMO Futures (BI)	125	50	275	2,525	252
Dubai Crude Oil (Platts) Financial Futures (DC)	111,582	83,846	30,297	43,926	22,191
Dutch TTF Natural Gas (USD per MMBTU) (ICIS	885	1,181			

New York Mercantile Exchange (NYMEX), division of the CME Group (continued)

FUTURE	2018	2017	2016	2015	2014
Dutch TTF Natural Gas Calendar Month (TTF)	20,664				
East-West Fuel Oil Spread (Platts) Futures (EW)	187	1,255	398	10,226	6,521
East-West Gasoline Spread (Platts-Argus) Futures	58,413	32,545	22,001	18	152
East-West Naphtha: Japan C&F vs. Cargoes CIF	8,461	8,279	2,321	1,038	579
EIA Flat Tax On-Highway Diesel Futures (A5)	3,373	7,945	11,593	9,618	8,943
EIA Flat Tax U.S. Retail Gasoline Futures (JE)	111	420	439	565	20
Electricity Off-Peak (4P)	55,380			11,680	
E-mini Crude Oil (QM)	4,692,563	3,001,906	3,380,972	3,149,495	1,898,735
E-mini Natural Gas Futures (QG)	433,039	311,945	338,981	330,199	397,582
E-mini NY Harbor ULSD (QH)	47	35	105	98	119
E-mini RBOB Gasoline Futures (QU)	47	51	51	57	51
Enable Natural Gas (Platts IFERC) Basis Futures	36	999	13,180	22,747	11,549
ERCOT Houston 345 kV Hub 5 MW Off-Peak (I2)	19,600				
ERCOT Houston 345 kV Hub 5 MW Peak (I1)	1,950	3,880			
ERCOT North 345 kV Hub 5 MW Off-Peak Futures	19,600	191,440	4,280	28,797	145,365
ERCOT North 345 kV Hub 5 MW Peak Futures (I5)	5,050	6,810	235	3,051	9,719
Ethanol T2 FOB Rdam Including Duty (Platts)	40,167	45,681	33,306	29,375	21,891
Ethanol T2 FOB Rotterdam Including Duty (Platts)	5				
European 1% Fuel Oil Barges FOB Rdam (Platts)	3	39	142	166	260
European 1% Fuel Oil Cargoes FOB MED vs.	150	420	1,171	703	1,524
European 1% Fuel Oil Cargoes FOB NWE (Platts)	33	18	241	131	287
European 1% Fuel Oil Cargoes FOB NWE (Platts)	570	765	1,550	1,920	1,970
European 3.5% Fuel Oil Barges FOB Rdam (Platts)	5,732	5,048	4,754	6,365	4,604
European 3.5% Fuel Oil Barges FOB Rdam (Platts)	78,702	85,392	91,573	98,474	97,311
European 3.5% Fuel Oil Cargoes FOB MED (Platts)	185	323	597	169	246
European 3.5% Fuel Oil Cargoes FOB MED (Platts)	1,001	1,744	4,552	1,410	1,758
European Diesel 10 ppm Barges FOB Rdam (Platts)	370	430	796	1,064	1,556
European Jet Kerosene Cargoes CIF NWE (Platts)	39	105	38	499	119
European Low Sulphur Gasoil (100mt) Bullet Futures	7,105	31,421	1,574,187	770,779	6,040
European Low Sulphur Gasoil Brent Crack Spread	39,294	77,557	64,857	38,850	28,118
European Low Sulphur Gasoil Financial Futures (GX)	66	244	352	263	472
European Naphtha (Platts) BALMO Futures (KZ)	3,087	3,923	2,257	986	2,792
European Naphtha (Platts) Crack Spread Futures	106,790	80,745	69,363	77,928	108,341
European Naphtha Cargoes CIF NWE (Platts)	39,775	31,941	18,916	14,968	21,344
European Propane CIF ARA (Argus) BALMO Swap	1,745	1,281	817	615	785
European Propane CIF ARA (Argus) Futures (PS)	21,260	15,311	15,813	4,938	4,437
European Propane CIF ARA (Argus) vs. Naphtha	10,741	6,468	3,179	580	1,061
FOB Australia Premium Hard Coking Coal (TSI)	20	240			
Freight Route Liquid Petroleum Gas (Baltic) BALMO	5				
Freight Route Liquid Petroleum Gas (Baltic) Future	2,533	1,797	2,557	764	
Freight Route TC14 (Baltic) Futures (FRC)	600				40
Freight Route TC2 (Baltic) Futures (TM)	1,052	220		13	250
Freight Route TC5 (Platts) Futures (TH)	1,665	75	15	30	25
Freight Route TC6 (Baltic) Futures (TC6)	240				
Freight Route TD20 (Baltic) (T2D)	4,983				
Freight Route TD3 (Baltic) Futures (TL)	20,671	390			5
Freight Route TD3C (Platts) (TD3)	30				
Freight Route TD8 (Baltic) (TD8)	150				
Gasoil 0.1 Barges FOB Rdam (Platts) Futures (VL)	1,506	170	30	40	90
Gasoil 0.1 Barges FOB Rdam (Platts) vs. Low Sulphur	10	354	120	180	893
Gasoil 0.1 Cargoes CIF MED (Platts) vs. Low Sulphur	10	50	195	241	341
Gasoline Eurobob Non-Oxy NWE Barges (Argus) vs	5				
Gasoline Euro-bob Oxy NWE Barges (Argus) BALMO	3,083	2,657	3,632	3,148	5,551
Gasoline Euro-bob Oxy NWE Barges (Argus) Crack	1,235	1,207	2,052	2,181	6,943
Gasoline Euro-bob Oxy NWE Barges (Argus) Crack	206,227	223,046	176,701	205,698	277,461
Gasoline Euro-bob Oxy NWE Barges (Argus) Futures	86,232	72,390	82,333	80,515	80,573
German Power Baseload Calendar Month (DEB)	5,441				
Group Three Sub-Octane Gasoline (Platts) (A9)	425				
Group Three Sub-octane Gasoline (Platts) vs. RBOB	25,837	13,644	16,815	18,787	17,903
Group Three ULSD (Platts) Futures (A7)	250	125	300	200	474
Group Three ULSD (Platts) vs. NY Harbor ULSD	42,527	53,220	32,645	46,007	59,295
Guernsey Light Sweet Crude Oil Index (Net Energy)	105	200	230		
Gulf Coast 3.0% Fuel Oil (Platts) BALMO Futures	14,048	16,992	9,656	12,429	15,735
Gulf Coast CBOB Gasoline A2 (Platts) vs. RBOB	35,880	3,130	1,509	3,843	951
Gulf Coast Jet (Platts) Up-Down BALMO Futures	71,272	80,836	57,075	38,460	30,742
Gulf Coast Jet (Platts) Up-Down Futures (ME)	403,914	480,097	388,487	269,633	266,693
Gulf Coast Jet Fuel (Platts) Futures (GE)	1,606	1,270	1,923	3,668	3,689
Gulf Coast No. 2 (Platts) Up-Down Financial Futures	3,133	3,759	3,412	4,034	2,175
Gulf Coast No. 6 Fuel Oil (Platts) Crack Spread	40	555	379	100	240
Gulf Coast No. 6 Fuel Oil (Platts) Crack Spread	18,242	19,411	15,814	17,530	43,558
Gulf Coast No.6 Fuel Oil 3.0% (Platts) Brent Crack	14,947	11,328	15,304	11,990	11,378
Gulf Coast No. 6 Fuel Oil 3.0% (Platts) Futures (MF)	608,490	629,301	681,964	811,531	602,488
Gulf Coast No. 6 Fuel Oil 3.0% (Platts) vs. European	1,005	739	1,130	1,158	1,750
Gulf Coast No. 6 Fuel Oil 3.0% (Platts) vs. European	130,251	73,204	88,311	134,083	139,985
Gulf Coast ULSD (Platts) Crack Spread Futures (GY)	1,655	3,870	6,981	3,960	17,023

New York Mercantile Exchange (NYMEX), division of the CME Group (continued)

FUTURE	2018	2017	2016	2015	2014
Gulf Coast ULSD (Platts) Futures (LY)	3,950	5,953	10,572	8,713	13,066
Gulf Coast ULSD (Platts) Up-Down BALMO Futures	67,675	62,513	75,583	45,366	19,937
Gulf Coast ULSD (Platts) Up-Down Futures (LT)	383,467	551,389	619,919	499,641	371,429
Gulf Coast Unl 87 Gasoline M2 (Platts) Crack Spread	1,740	1,310	2,975	700	
Gulf Coast Unl 87 Gasoline M2 (Platts) vs. RBOB	14,760	13,553	4,760	50	300
Gulf Coast Unl 87 Gasoline M2 (Platts) vs. RBOB	187,871	181,036	109,698	6,306	5,770
Gulf Coast Unl 87 Gasoline M2 (Platts) (GCM)	163	59	388		
Henry Hub Natural Gas (NG)	114,256,078	108,391,797	97,480,591	81,772,492	74,206,602
Henry Hub Natural Gas (Platts Gas Daily/Platts	32,088	50,542	181,858	111,082	137,728
Henry Hub Natural Gas (Platts IFERC) Basis	32,088	52,732	200,555	147,869	146,260
Henry Hub Natural Gas Last Day Financial (NN)	1,955,712	2,275,687	5,002,282	5,330,807	6,332,365
Henry Hub Penultimate NP (NP)	422,431	973,379	1,330,312	2,200,047	4,476,844
In Delivery Month European Union Allowance (EUA)	1,248	2,850	37,241	104,603	122,156
ISO New England Mass Hub 5 MW Peak Calendar-	12,711	17,275	45,635	20,388	17,633
ISO New England Mass Hub Day-Ahead Off-Peak	136,440	235,140	519,369	319,140	365,739
Japan C&F Naphtha (Platts) BALMO Futures (E6)	637	1,418	486	505	845
Japan C&F Naphtha (Platts) Brent Crack Spread	1,890	7,398	4,944	3,237	1,488
Japan C&F Naphtha (Platts) Futures (JA)	23,044	18,408	15,520	11,776	14,376
Jet Aviation Fuel Cargoes FOB MED (Platts) Futures	39	102	20	90	31
Jet Aviation Fuel Cargoes FOB MED (Platts) vs. Low	5	36	172	279	280
Jet Cargoes CIF NWE (Platts) vs. Low Sulphur Gasoil	677	1,318	890	1,275	1,533
Light Sweet Oil (Net Energy) Monthly Index (LSW)	335	4,410			
LLS (Argus) Financial Futures (XA)	607				
LLS (Argus) vs. WTI Financial Futures (WJ)	60,624	64,990	71,223	110,156	115,106
LNG Japan/Korea Marker (Platts) Futures (JKM)	16,299	1,320			
LOOP Crude Oil Storage Futures (LPS)	53,385	46,199	57,915	30,548	
LOOP Gulf Coast Sour Crude Oil (MB)	2,319	18,177	19,795		
Los Angeles CARB Diesel (OPIS) vs. NY Harbor	3,287	2,220	7,904	7,675	11,206
Los Angeles CARBOB Gasoline (OPIS) (MH)	10				
Los Angeles CARBOB Gasoline (OPIS) vs. RBOB	5,670	3,225	5,950	5,941	7,200
Los Angeles Jet (OPIS) vs. NY Harbor ULSD (JS)	21,774	20,120	22,112	10,820	6,950
Low Sulphur Gasoil Crack Spread (1000mt) Financial	84	120	139	674	602
Low Sulphur Gasoil Mini Financial Futures (QA)	2,947	1,613	2,779	3,321	6,113
Mars (Argus) vs. WTI Financial Futures (YX)	22,295	36,539	54,086	74,060	49,005
Mars (Argus) vs. WTI Trade Month Futures (YV)	233,266	260,006	140,278	17,008	670
Methanol T2 FOB Rotterdam (ICIS) (MT2)	700				
Micro European 3.5% Fuel Oil Barges FOB Rdam	1,812				
Micro Singapore Fuel Oil 380CST (Platts) (MAF)	4,748				
Mini 1% Fuel Oil Cargoes FOB MED (Platts) Futures	100	247	1,126	907	1,156
Mini 3.5% Fuel Oil Barges FOB Rdam (Platts) Crack	4		30		
Mini 3.5% Fuel Oil Cargoes FOB MED (Platts)	260	534	1,996	1,939	851
Mini Argus Propane (Saudi Aramco) Futures (MAS)	2,251	405	1,010	355	642
Mini Argus Propane Far East Index Futures (MAE)	2,780	570	455	290	60
Mini Brent Financial Futures (MBC)	127		1,424	1,114	
Mini Dated Brent (Platts) Financial Futures (MDB)	224	426	2,513	390	
Mini Dubai Crude Oil (Platts) Futures (DBL)	99	2,036	850	32,612	1,400
Mini European 1% Fuel Oil Barges FOB Rdam	9	164	1,328	1,997	964
Mini European 1% Fuel Oil Cargoes FOB NWE	23	70	316	213	515
Mini European 1% Fuel Oil Cargoes FOB NWE	144	163	1,605	1,074	3,285
Mini European 3.5% Fuel Oil Barges FOB Rdam	249	4,137	11,781	6,094	3,195
Mini European 3.5% Fuel Oil Barges FOB Rdam	15,797	26,473	48,318	52,314	41,207
Mini European Diesel 10 ppm Barges FOB Rdam	173	910	1,301	957	1,716
Mini European Jet Kero Cargoes CIF NWE (Platts)	1,460	1,540	895	780	600
Mini European Naphtha (Platts) BALMO Futures	4,846	6,653	7,596	7,763	9,504
Mini European Naphtha CIF NWE (Platts) Futures	48,644	45,730	47,818	50,904	60,494
Mini European Propane CIF ARA (Argus) (MPS)	1,462	180			
Mini Gasoil 0.1 Barges FOB Rdam (Platts) vs. Low	220	150	40	434	253
Mini Gasoil 0.1 Cargoes CIF NWE (Platts) vs. Low	268	316	100	86	150
Mini Gasoline Euro-bob Oxy NWE Barges (Argus)	3,902	5,378	5,429	3,490	7,144
Mini Gasoline Euro-bob Oxy NWE Barges (Argus)	39,908	94,727	120,511	100,465	112,317
Mini Japan C&F Naphtha (Platts) BALMO Futures	714	242	502	862	870
Mini Japan C&F Naphtha (Platts) Futures (MJN)	22,700	20,833	16,148	19,125	21,227
Mini Middle East Naphtha FOB Arab Gulf (Platts)	60	50			
Mini RBOB Gasoline vs. Gasoline Euro-bob Oxy NWE	3,741	5,846	3,891	4,803	6,555
Mini RBOB Gasoline vs. Gasoline Euro-bob Oxy NWE	20,908	26,045	21,690	8,766	5,468
Mini Singapore Fuel Oil 180 cst (Platts) BALMO	286	709	2,397	1,345	1,893
Mini Singapore Fuel Oil 180 cst (Platts) Futures (0F)	6,014	11,717	15,080	11,368	14,538
Mini Singapore Fuel Oil 380 cst (Platts) BALMO	615	1,559	3,116	1,460	1,898
Mini Singapore Fuel Oil 380 cst (Platts) Futures	55,855	57,540	46,049	30,302	24,945
Mini Singapore Gasoil (Platts) Futures (MSG)	5,132	3,293	651	6,868	7,896
Mini Singapore Gasoil 500 PPM (Platts) (MGO)	221	130			
Mini ULSD 10ppm Cargoes CIF MED (Platts) vs. Low	80	295	353	578	618
Mini ULSD 10ppm Cargoes CIF NWE (Platts) vs.	923	1,126	1,689	1,903	1,052
Mini-Argus Butane (Saudi Aramco) (MAA)	50				
MISO Indiana Hub (formerly Cinergy Hub) 5 Month	1,505	25,625	68,221	20,718	20,915

New York Mercantile Exchange (NYMEX), division of the CME Group (continued)

FUTURE	2018	2017	2016	2015	2014
MISO Indiana Hub (formerly Cinergy Hub) Day-	13,630	19,513	22,142	10,579	22,269
Mont Belvieu Ethane (OPIS) BALMO Futures (8C)	1,900	3,205	1,920	2,765	1,605
Mont Belvieu Ethane (OPIS) Futures (C0)	189,923	256,776	590,762	92,745	55,129
Mont Belvieu Ethylene (PCW) BALMO Futures	321	550	84	245	809
Mont Belvieu Ethylene (PCW) Financial Futures	10,161	11,686	16,658	13,609	18,081
Mont Belvieu Iso-Butane (OPIS) Futures (8I)	6,893	7,021	3,257	5,223	3,027
Mont Belvieu LDH Iso-Butane (OPIS) Futures (MBL)	40	266	325	746	1,490
Mont Belvieu LDH Propane (OPIS) BALMO Futures	29,975	19,536	12,068	7,879	8,767
Mont Belvieu LDH Propane (OPIS) Futures (B0)	1,462,178	1,122,133	1,345,538	616,592	424,193
Mont Belvieu LDH Propane (OPIS) vs European CIF	23				2
Mont Belvieu Natural Gasoline (OPIS) BALMO	4,191	3,667	1,981	4,160	4,107
Mont Belvieu Natural Gasoline (OPIS) Futures (7Q)	97,757	85,506	91,566	64,931	86,123
Mont Belvieu Normal Butane (OPIS) BALMO	12,905	8,436	7,211	5,424	6,661
Mont Belvieu Normal Butane (OPIS) Futures (D0)	427,121	346,469	345,287	209,582	175,113
Mont Belvieu Normal Butane LDH (OPIS) Futures	20,582	19,968	21,979	15,956	14,978
Mont Belvieu Spot Ethylene In-Well Futures (MBE)	9,160	12,370	32,365	22,730	28,116
Naphtha Cargoes CIF NWE (Platts) Crack Spread	182	139	221	56	25
Naphtha Cargoes CIF NWE (Platts) Crack Spread	21,394	12,897	6,826	2,396	1,357
Natural Gas (Henry Hub) Last-day Financial (HH)	4,579,077	3,539,546	2,958,345	2,897,566	2,330,546
Natural Gas (Henry Hub) Penultimate Financial (HP)	1,438,019	1,669,023	1,574,185	1,067,919	678,445
New York Harbor 1.0% Fuel Oil (Platts) BALMO	50	25	151	531	1,001
New York Harbor Residual Fuel (Platts) Crack	50			100	450
New York Harbor Residual Fuel 1.0% (Platts) Futures	12,678	28,543	39,080	62,080	73,140
NGPL Mid-Con Natural Gas (Platts IFERC) Basis	4,748	4,674	30,002	50,587	7,234
NGPL TexOk Natural Gas (Platts IFERC) Basis	50,116	9,214	33,872	84,276	54,615
Northwest Europe Fuel Oil High-Low Sulfur Spread	125	75	60	305	186
NY 1% Fuel Oil (Platts) vs. Gulf Coast 3% Fuel Oil	50	109	1,008	200	830
NY 1% Fuel Oil (Platts) vs. Gulf Coast 3% Fuel Oil	15,373	25,857	29,944	27,649	52,582
NY 3.0% Fuel Oil (Platts) Futures (H1)	1,905	3,410	2,450	5,245	2,385
NY 3.0% Fuel Oil (Platts) vs. Gulf Coast No. 6 Fuel	7,275	7,878	11,945	8,150	3,678
NY Buckeye Jet Fuel (Platts) vs. NY Harbor ULSD	35,110	44,806	63,859	16,905	
NY Buckeye Jet Fuel (Platts) vs. NY Harbor ULSD	8,000	3,938			
NY Ethanol (Platts) Futures (EZ)	12,583	10,820	17,875	12,070	15,517
NY Harbor ULSD (HO)	46,277,883	43,596,206	39,389,349	36,947,020	33,946,420
NY Harbor ULSD BALMO Futures (1G)	243	1,057	479	1,814	525
NY Harbor ULSD Brent Crack Spread Futures (HOB)	9,206	35,033	38,059	38,784	14,554
NY Harbor ULSD Bullet Futures (BH)	120	340	5,578	2,146	670
NY Harbor ULSD Crack Spread Futures (HK)	8,636	14,244	22,662	31,218	45,901
NY Harbor ULSD Financial Futures (MP)	29,460	24,739	29,320	53,763	77,983
NY Harbor ULSD vs. Low Sulphur Gasoil (1,000bbl)	3,445	4,273	6,586	4,042	6,810
NY ULSD (Argus) vs. NY Harbor ULSD (7Y)	213	8,245	9,621	33,130	28,259
NYISO Lower Hudson Valley Capacity Calendar-	766	453	318		
NYISO NYC In-City Capacity Calendar-Month	795	2,306	1,977	3,723	1,134
NYISO Rest of the State Capacity Calendar-Month	395	2,899	2,473	5,170	1,917
NYISO Zone A Day-Ahead Off-Peak Calendar-Month	44,264	32,760	258,085	433,136	269,628
NYISO Zone A Day-Ahead Peak Calendar-Month 5	1,890	7,235	6,560	19,321	15,610
NYISO Zone G Day-Ahead Off-Peak Calendar-Month	626,384	789,929	444,481	256,288	123,931
NYISO Zone G Day-Ahead Peak Calendar-Month 5	21,159	60,668	40,288	35,469	12,130
OneOk, Oklahoma Natural Gas (Platts IFERC) Basis	2,704	1,788	1,411	2,991	2,476
Ontario Peak Calendar-Day Futures (OPD)	10	510	490	355	439
Panhandle Natural Gas (Platts IFERC) Basis Futures	275	3,060	97,142	131,807	43,650
Petro European Naphtha Crack Spread BALMO	3,414	3,619	2,378	3,738	3,676
PGP Polymer Grade Propylene (PCW) Financial	5,560	6,264	5,129	10,575	6,493
PJM AEP Dayton Hub 5MW Peak Calendar-Month	15,198	22,831	106,259	111,974	115,264
PJM AEP Dayton Hub Real-Time Off-Peak Calendar-	72,197	288,349	1,531,162	1,661,753	1,989,829
PJM Northern Illinois Hub 5 MW Peak Calendar-	7,220	79,300	94,649	69,427	27,630
PJM Northern Illinois Hub Day-Ahead LMP Peak	64	39,492	48,608	23,715	14,777
PJM Northern Illinois Hub Day-Ahead Off-Peak	770	689,738	1,186,752	506,843	236,798
PJM Northern Illinois Hub Real-Time Off-Peak	5,925	1,719,650	2,631,867	1,879,247	617,032
PJM PEPCO Zone 5MW Peak Cal Mth Day Ahead	2,960			650	
PJM PSEG Zone Off-Peak Calendar-Month Day-	78,780		163,800	1,960	
PJM PSEG Zone Peak Calendar-Month Day-Ahead	4,235		5,100	110	
PJM Western Hub Day-Ahead Off-Peak Calendar-	101,810	54,300	1,129,110	807,716	1,241,519
PJM Western Hub Day-Ahead Peak Calendar-Month	5,525	8,620	62,333	42,139	70,693
PJM Western Hub Peak Calendar-Month Real-Time	63,850	223,316	657,190	251,063	220,143
PJM Western Hub Real-Time Off-Peak Calendar-	392,520	2,208,775	6,738,450	3,630,757	3,609,397
Powder River Basin Coal (Platts OTC Broker Index)	25	2,520	9,342	26,220	35,735
Premium Unleaded Gasoline 10 ppm Barges FOB	83	7	7	84	38
Premium Unleaded Gasoline 10 ppm Barges FOB	366	37	274	340	358
Premium Unleaded Gasoline 10 ppm FOB MED	443	162	382	698	1,277
Premium Unleaded Gasoline 10 ppm FOB MED	3,158	914	2,889	3,391	4,876
Propane Non-LDH Mont Belvieu (OPIS) BALMO	7,013	5,252	5,997	2,513	480
Propane Non-LDH Mont Belvieu (OPIS) Futures (1R)	150,843	87,065	138,706	90,810	21,925
RBOB Gasoline BALMO Futures (1D)	11,687	12,245	11,080	13,121	9,281
RBOB Gasoline Brent Crack Spread Futures (RBB)	57,935	86,718	128,539	125,379	102,467

New York Mercantile Exchange (NYMEX), division of the CME Group (continued)

FUTURE	2018	2017	2016	2015	2014
RBOB Gasoline Bullet Futures (RT)	14,386	28,456	19,381	18,062	9,369
RBOB Gasoline Crack Spread Futures (RM)	9,658	11,362	18,804	12,795	17,019
RBOB Gasoline Financial Futures (RL)	65,352	83,819	80,700	85,040	100,107
RBOB Gasoline Physical (RB)	49,613,909	49,910,909	45,428,663	40,302,099	34,421,866
RBOB Gasoline vs. Euro-bob Oxy NWE Barges	32,982	28,899	20,434	13,510	13,702
RBOB Gasoline vs. Euro-bob Oxy NWE Barges	300			90	50
RBOB Gasoline vs. NY Harbor ULSD (RH)	1,975	17,720	21,905	12,265	6,025
Rockies Natural Gas (Platts IFERC) Fixed Price	59	334		991	3,608
San Juan Natural Gas (Platts IFERC) Basis Futures	58	2,254	76,144	29,833	2,632
San Juan Natural Gas (Platts IFERC) Fixed Price	360				336
Singapore Fuel Oil 180 cst (Platts) 6.35 Brent Crack	790	264	64	760	1,868
Singapore Fuel Oil 180 cst (Platts) 6.35 Dubai (Platts)	539	2,480	230	318	295
Singapore Fuel Oil 180 cst (Platts) BALMO Futures	499	772	590	458	854
Singapore Fuel Oil 180 cst (Platts) Futures (UA)	8,683	12,108	14,209	22,208	51,466
Singapore Fuel Oil 180 cst (Platts) vs. 380 cst (Platts)	100	120	70	10	20
Singapore Fuel Oil 180 cst (Platts) vs. 380 cst (Platts)	6,261	7,038	7,686	5,708	5,046
Singapore Fuel Oil 380 cst (Platts) BALMO Futures	2,454	2,693	1,933	1,271	909
Singapore Fuel Oil 380 cst (Platts) Futures (SE)	95,826	116,554	101,072	63,496	37,549
Singapore Fuel Oil 380 cst (Platts) vs. European 3.5%	125	178	165	15	5
Singapore Fuel Oil 380 cst (Platts) vs. European 3.5%	21,636	29,725	24,696	16,421	9,225
Singapore Fuel Oil 380cst (Platts) Brent Crack Spread	371	15	64		
Singapore Gasoil (Platts) BALMO Futures (VU)	1,339	3,223	4,063	1,316	8,976
Singapore Gasoil (Platts) Dubai (Platts) Crack Spread	250				
Singapore Gasoil (Platts) Futures (SG)	49,344	90,723	81,687	28,055	89,154
Singapore Gasoil (Platts) vs. Low Sulphur Gasoil	130,138	70,787	44,904	6,000	41,284
Singapore Gasoil 10 ppm (Platts) vs. Singapore Gasoil	4,300	1,123	180	250	1,165
Singapore Gasoil 500 PPM (Platts) (GHS)	9	60			
Singapore Gasoil 500 ppm (Platts) Dubai (Platts)	50				
Singapore Gasoil 500 PPM (Platts) vs Low Sulphur	325	168			
Singapore Jet Kerosene (Platts) BALMO Futures (BX)	215	536	156	550	270
Singapore Jet Kerosene (Platts) Futures (KS)	13,450	12,979	8,346	16,364	51,766
Singapore Jet Kerosene (Platts) vs. Gasoil (Platts)	400	50	50	50	50
Singapore Jet Kerosene (Platts) vs. Gasoil (Platts)	35,345	18,735	14,485	3,640	18,226
Singapore Mogas 92 Unleaded (Platts) BALMO	6,067	2,076	5,953	3,618	7,124
Singapore Mogas 92 Unleaded (Platts) Brent Crack	20,126	13,999	19,445	20,131	29,903
Singapore Mogas 92 Unleaded (Platts) Dubai (Platts)	100	525		50	
Singapore Mogas 92 Unleaded (Platts) Futures (1N)	162,080	85,721	120,268	80,419	179,698
Singapore Mogas 95 Unleaded (Platts) Futures (V0)	980	150	390	2,876	2,700
Singapore Mogas 95 Unleaded (Platts) vs. Singapore	553	40	340	600	300
Singapore Mogas 97 Unleaded (Platts) Futures (X0)	116		150	698	294
Singapore Naphtha (Platts) Futures (SP)	200			1,175	1,675
Sumas Natural Gas (Platts IFERC) Basis Futures	91	6,238	18,059	14,347	2,767
UK NBP Natural Gas (USD per MMBTU) (ICIS	26,818	5,326			
UK NBP Natural Gas Calendar Month (UKG)	49,382				
ULSD 10ppm Cargoes CIF NWE (Platts) vs. Low	21	727	948	1,460	1,170
ULSD 10ppm CIF MED (Platts) vs. Low Sulphur	14	81	198	1,119	627
Urals Med (Platts) vs Dated Brent (Platts) CFD (UMD)	4,800	600			
Urals North (Platts) vs Dated Brent (Platts) CFD	7,554	1,878			
Ventura Natural Gas (Platts IFERC) Basis Futures	100	132	9,216	5,722	7,759
Waha Natural Gas (Platts IFERC) Basis Futures (NW)	3,451	6,787	44,649	40,876	27,932
Western Canadian Select Oil (Net Energy) Monthly	73,558	88,576			
WTI BALMO Swap (42)	3,436	6,419	1,195	12,032	9,736
WTI Financial Futures (CS)	399,374	448,037	387,932	404,806	400,686
WTI Houston (Argus) vs. WTI Trade Month (HTT)	555,118	245,508	30,135		
WTI Houston Crude Oil (HCL)	24,641				
WTI Light Sweet Crude Oil (CL)	306,613,007	310,052,767	276,768,438	202,202,392	145,147,334
WTI Midland (Argus) vs. WTI Financial Futures (FF)	91,302	72,712	55,703	60,936	63,435
WTI Midland (Argus) vs. WTI Trade Month Futures	430,553	192,022	45,727	7,543	
WTI-Brent Bullet Futures (BY)	6,650	1,154	500		7,650
WTI-Brent Financial Futures (BK)	346,950	251,432	137,258	277,619	267,854
WTS (Argus) vs. WTI Trade Month Futures (FH)	6,345	9,936	12,370	19,453	12,470
Iron Ore 62% Fe, CFR China (TSI) Futures (TIO)	44,127	90,283	199,434	136,158	24,988
U.S. Midwest Busheling Ferrous Scrap (AMM)	20,175	1,465	972	558	34
U.S. Midwest Domestic Hot-Rolled Coil Steel (CRU)	119,569	63,229	53,884	58,817	48,230
UxC Uranium U3O8 Futures (UX)	7,162	6,393	7,583	4,548	3,453
Palladium Futures (PA)	1,433,712	1,402,740	1,435,863	1,344,426	1,573,972
Platinum (PL)	5,463,799	4,852,160	3,994,072	3,641,144	3,235,941
Total Futures	**572,332,919**	**571,361,340**	**536,490,550**	**432,608,496**	**350,416,385**

ONECHICAGO

FUTURE	2018	2017	2016	2015	2014
Exchange Traded Funds Futures	1,132,605	2,702,139	2,695,620	2,918,444	2,898,979
Single Stock Futures	5,933,687	12,227,858	9,695,835	8,795,571	8,008,998
Total Futures	**7,066,292**	**14,929,997**	**12,391,455**	**11,714,015**	**10,907,977**

Total Futures Volume

	2018	2017	2016	2015	2014
Total Futures	4,252,834,069	3,656,765,743	3,579,398,052	3,219,261,004	3,180,295,093
Precent Change	16.30%	2.16%	11.19%	1.23%	0.16%

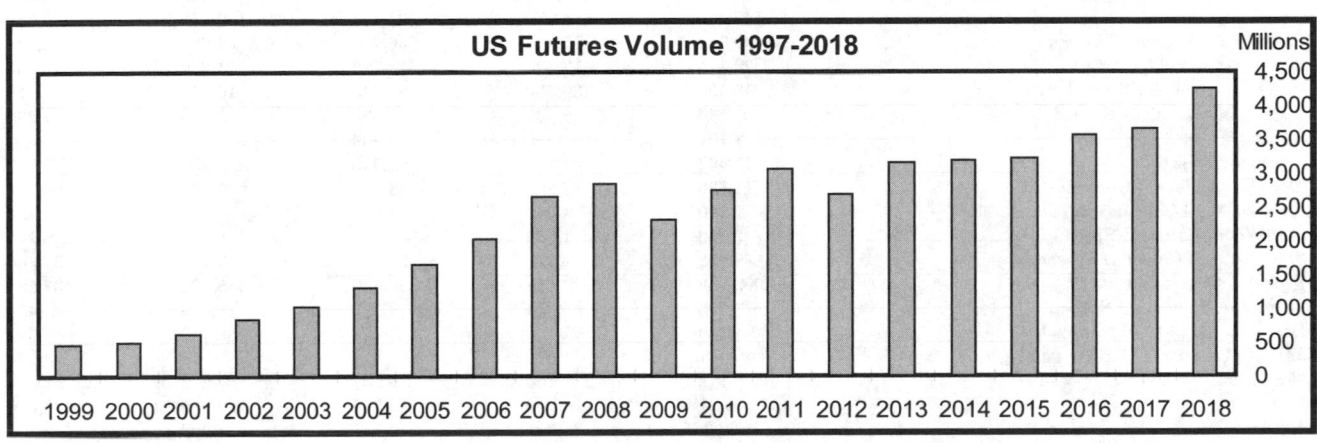

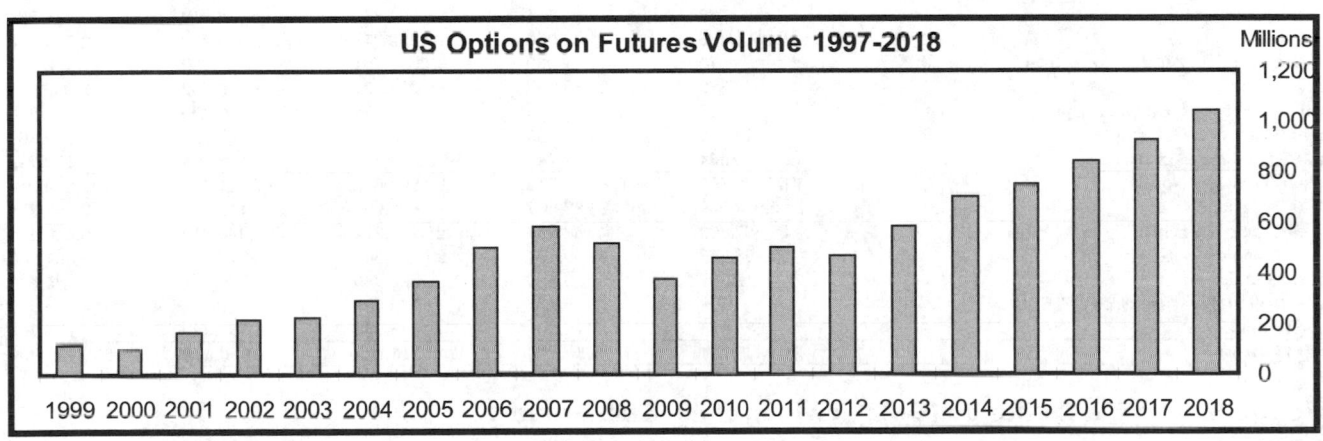

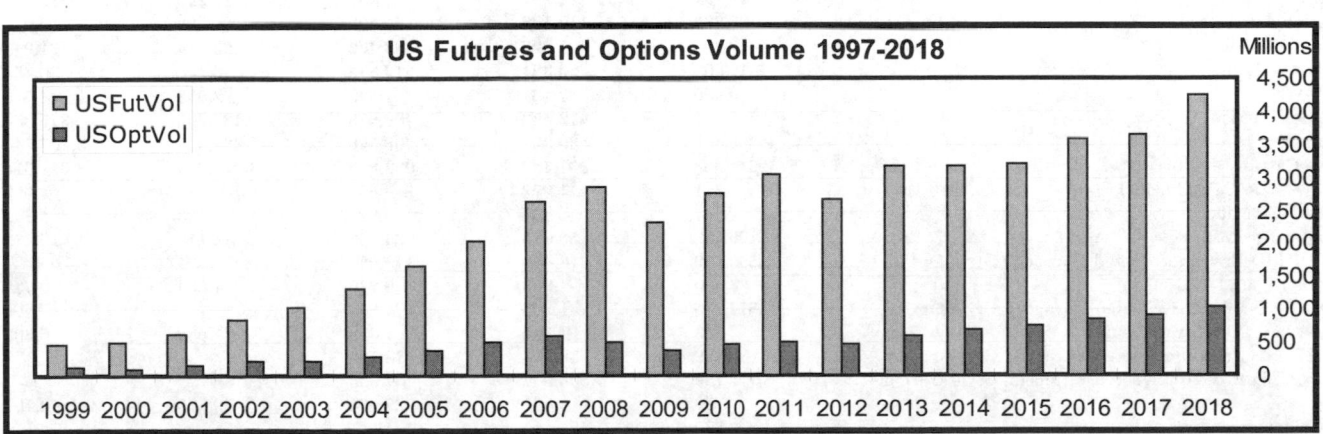

Options Traded on U.S. Futures Exchanges Volume Highlights
2018 in Comparison with 2017

2018 Rank	EXCHANGE	2018 Contracts	%	2017 Contracts	%	2017 Rank
1	Chicago Mercantile Exchange (CME Group)	589,217,258	69.58%	538,252,025	71.76%	1
2	Chicago Board of Trade (CME Group)	310,928,251	36.72%	241,151,596	32.15%	2
3	New York Mercantile Exchange (CME Group)	80,137,450	9.46%	81,933,810	10.92%	3
4	ICE Futures U.S.	41,294,620	4.88%	53,362,810	7.11%	4
5	Commodity Exchange (CME Group)	14,510,468	1.71%	11,630,993	1.55%	5
6	NASDAQ NFX	8,430,791	1.00%	7,006,803	0.93%	6
7	Minneapolis Grain Exchange	59,727	0.01%	121,704	0.02%	7
	Total Options	**1,044,578,565**	**100.00%**	**933,459,741**	**100.00%**	

Chicago Board of Trade (CBT), division of the CME Group

OPTION	2018	2017	2016	2015	2014
Chicago Soft Red Winter Wheat	9,403,524	7,513,694	6,977,412	7,435,420	6,141,089
Chicago SRW Wheat-Corn Intercommodity Spread	5,780	9,846	17,752	20,400	15,310
Corn	25,542,064	23,884,970	22,794,484	24,150,182	21,246,732
Corn Nearby + 2 Calendar Spread	40,753	15,940	36,758	52,620	89,104
Dec-Dec Corn Calendar Spread	20,775	12,136	18,778	4,240	2,787
Dec-July Corn Calendar Spread	19,499	39,888	26,543	10,070	1,010
Dec-July Wheat Calendar Spread	1,744	2,133	590	35	1,230
EU Wheat	7,107	486	409		
Intercommodity Spread	11,463	701	4,046	959	
July-Dec Corn Calendar Spread	11,696	17,802	36,834	36,161	89,967
July-Dec Soy Meal Calendar Spread	1,200	640	1,020	45	255
July-Dec Wheat Calendar Spread	2,620	1,614	33,619	15,671	6,116
July-Nov Soybean Calendar Spread	59,472	71,412	66,019	37,235	57,566
KC Hard Red Winter Wheat	1,009,253	530,134	346,680	465,301	437,286
Mar-July Wheat Calendar Spread	1,950	2,214	3,193	12,076	435
Nov-Dec Soybean Calendar Spread	130				690
Nov-July Soybean Calendar Spread	1	1,696		68	991
Nov-Nov Soybean Calendar Spread	118	164	2,982	272	
Oats	6,801	14,062	18,576	20,935	25,010
Rough Rice	18,279	24,741	19,775	23,200	16,261
September-December Soybean Meal CSO	1,170			1,060	
Soybeans	19,031,062	16,980,581	20,109,648	18,663,389	17,916,675
Soybean Crush	185	741	4,825	2,712	2,984
Soybean Meal	3,185,498	2,160,060	2,269,279	2,909,760	2,588,548
Soybean Nearby +2 Calendar Spread	10	1,060	1,701	280	8,463
Soybean Oil	1,425,379	2,050,228	2,298,191	2,159,102	1,739,640
Soymeal Nearby +2 Calendar Spread	8,415		3,785	300	210
Wheat Nearby +2 Calendar Spread	14,178	17,903	55,023	135,291	63,961
Mini $5 Dow Jones Industrial Index	125,334	74,244	127,484	138,575	150,742
10-Year Treasury Note	167,962,668	128,546,313	98,504,626	97,821,923	100,663,916
2-Year Treasury Note	5,973,549	2,292,507	1,683,900	2,412,018	2,487,998
30-Year Treasury Bond	35,397,862	27,156,898	21,244,372	21,046,810	16,405,485
5-Year Treasury Note	41,498,642	29,659,494	23,880,566	22,776,553	28,561,850
Federal Funds	19,257	16,880	94,739	339,751	25,533
Ultra 10-Year Treasury Note	128	8,487	42,788		
Ultra T-Bond	120,685	40,304	86,253	105,390	156,763
Total Options	**310,928,251**	**241,151,596**	**200,815,588**	**200,806,945**	**198,920,909**

Chicago Mercantile Exchange (CME), division of the CME Group

OPTION	2018	2017	2016	2015	2014
Cash Butter	49,184	22,987	15,851	12,220	12,020
Cash Settled Cheese	125,892	119,578	91,630	80,024	39,074
Class III Milk	428,200	421,226	383,472	265,414	361,945
Class IV Milk	15,501	20,321	13,873	8,446	20,734
Dry Whey	6,990	7,481	1,325	2,973	4,523
Feeder Cattle	338,741	412,553	409,638	437,202	375,384
Lean Hogs	2,769,669	2,536,927	2,208,546	2,837,639	3,107,748
Live Cattle	2,641,563	2,901,400	4,032,890	3,974,324	4,041,314
Live Cattle Calendar ISO	341	1,972	851	81	572
Mini BFP Milk	484	834	924	533	1,349
Nonfat Dry Milk	60,568	53,069	34,398	46,112	16,339
AUD/USD Premium Quoted European Style Option –	1,580,352	1,312,480	170,930		
British Pound (European)	280	4,609	9,270	7,684	9,717
CAD/USD Premium Quoted European Style Option –	1,872,860	1,741,208	174,857		
Canadian Dollar (European)	63	146	1,818	1,588	6,303
CHF/USD Premium Quoted European Style Option –	30,519	38,775	13,121		
EUR/USD Premium Quoted European Style Option –	8,711,729	7,803,347	737,055		
Euro FX European	59	509	28,664	59,879	90,707
Euro/Japanese Yen	2,870				
GBP/USD Premium Quoted European Style Option – 2	3,244,177	2,703,047	220,889		

Chicago Mercantile Exchange (CME), division of the CME Group (continued)

OPTION	2018	2017	2016	2015	2014
JPY/USD Premium Quoted European Style Option – 2	3,131,431	3,113,816	395,282		
Mexican Peso	24,211	37,948	50,933	17,624	9,809
New Zealand Dollar	1,050			13	753
E-Mini NASDAQ 100 Index	2,878,414	2,873,368	2,568,059	1,535,576	3,154,154
E-mini Russell 2000 Index (Weekly)	230,982	110,395			
E-mini Russell 2000 Index	388,874	69,951			
E-Mini S&P 500 Index	73,364,734	51,055,524	58,887,823	77,768,004	74,080,842
EOM E-Mini S&P 500 Index	31,194,081	24,790,850	20,898,070	13,277,837	11,522,506
EOM S&P 500 Index	2,170,861	2,347,874	2,069,567	1,280,558	1,023,767
EOW1 E-mini S&P 500 Index	14,069,450	12,669,333	11,710,684	11,552,239	10,419,487
EOW1 S&P 500 Index	1,016,605	1,092,049	706,582	381,560	530,588
EOW2 E-mini S&P 500 Index	15,832,156	12,649,778	12,992,775	12,558,487	10,554,604
EOW2 S&P 500 Index	2,014,974	2,097,086	1,539,741	952,275	933,010
EOW3 E-mini S&P 500 Index	43,285,692	39,320,303	27,113,276		
EOW3 S&P 500 Index	3,081,428	4,294,574	3,156,223		
EOW4 E-mini S&P 500 Index	13,910,378	11,434,439	12,923,810	11,744,931	9,137,555
S&P 500 Index	3,974,098	3,893,439	5,674,293	9,099,788	8,647,971
Eurodollar (3-month)	173,585,526	153,425,834	168,254,035	112,278,366	49,471,203
Eurodollar Mid-Curve	183,150,164	190,004,215	140,529,194	131,374,348	167,167,523
CDD Seasonal Strip Weather	700	2,800	29,250	67,000	34,480
Euro HDD Seasonal Strip Weather	500	2,500	2,500	7,500	34,800
HDD Seasonal Weather Strip	9,000	16,000	20,200	17,100	23,960
HDD Weather	350	1,250	2,000	2,800	6,125
Random Lumber	21,557	16,219	12,522	13,305	13,891
Total Options	**589,217,258**	**538,252,025**	**494,429,721**	**412,622,695**	**371,826,055**

Commodity Exchange (COMEX), division of the CME Group

OPTION	2018	2017	2016	2015	2014
Copper Options (HX)	351,780	107,490	38,472	27,111	21,022
Copper Weekly Options Wk 2 (H2E)	154				
Copper Weekly Options Wk 3 (H3E)	119				
Copper Weekly Options Wk 4 (H4E)	177				
Copper Weekly Options Wk 5 (H5E)	12				
Copper Weekly Wk 1 (H1E)	178				
Gold (OG)	11,751,255	9,892,533	9,916,049	7,534,527	8,415,139
Gold Weekly Options Wk 1 (OG1)	137,349	49,292	14,995	6,117	8,922
Gold Weekly Options Wk 2 (OG2)	129,124	49,145	20,626	7,513	4,224
Gold Weekly Options Wk 3 (OG3)	144,799	48,868	12,249	5,632	5,279
Gold Weekly Options Wk 4 (OG4)	88,255	27,923	8,208	3,235	3,771
Gold Weekly Options Wk 5 (OG5)	32,861	14,976	3,625	1,305	580
Silver Options (SO)	1,847,187	1,438,930	1,375,636	1,224,664	1,853,652
Silver Weekly Options Wk 1 (SO1)	5,789	686	559	428	1,538
Silver Weekly Options Wk 2 (SO2)	5,708	262	610	190	1,508
Silver Weekly Options Wk 3 (SO3)	8,489	629	797	194	1,298
Silver Weekly Options Wk 4 (SO4)	4,486	206	472	141	1,174
Silver Weekly Options Wk 5 (SO5)	2,746	53	258	203	381
Total Options	**14,510,468**	**11,630,993**	**11,392,565**	**8,811,260**	**10,318,488**

ICE Futures U.S. (ICE)

OPTION	2018	2017	2016	2015	2014
Canola	102,448	154,229	177,660	151,319	106,438
Canola 1 Month CSO	1,595	295	8,630	8,300	15,265
Cocoa	1,432,751	1,360,371	1,881,082	1,351,396	993,275
Coffee 'C'	3,073,591	2,365,261	2,230,914	1,817,282	2,726,981
Coffee 'C' 1-month	92,950	42,934	53,187	24,455	4,821
Coffee 'C' 2-month	14,730	8,300	5,475	3,660	
Cotton #2	2,402,085	1,824,315	2,074,521	1,740,642	1,780,315
Cotton #2 1-month	200	550	2,110	1,200	4,443
Cotton #2 2-month	9,313	9,180		5,425	287
Orange Juice Frozen Concentrate	60,625	86,104	71,379	62,187	87,559
Sugar #11	5,708,889	4,763,196	7,279,040	6,159,101	4,917,608
Sugar #11 1-month	33,069	16,510	38,178	36,793	46,678
US Dollar Index	5,708	10,210	22,893	16,099	23,399
Global Oil Products	329,163				
North American Natural Gas and Power	28,027,203	42,656,346	39,140,813	45,537,970	39,484,277
Mini MSCI Emerging Markets	300	600			
Total Options	**41,294,620**	**53,362,810**	**53,045,272**	**56,945,604**	**50,268,200**

VOLUME - U.S.

Minneapolis Grain Exchange (MGE)

OPTION	2018	2017	2016	2015	2014
Hard Red Spring Wheat - open outcry and electronic	59,727	121,684	22,429	26,200	24,127
Total Options	59,727	121,704	22,589	26,501	24,367

NASDAQ NFX

OPTION	2018	2017	2016	2015	2014
Brent Crude Oil Financial (BCQ)	124,989	58,856	26,120		
Henry Hub Natural Gas Penultimate Financial (10,000	8,004,597	6,757,704	5,018,242		
PJM Western Hub Real□Time Peak Calendar Year	92,618	12,750			
PJM Western Hub Real-Time Peak Financial (50MW)	30,723	61,988	14,679		
WTI Crude Oil Penultimate Financial (TOQ)	128,949	115,505	78,717		
CS5TC Capesize 5 T/C Average Financial (C5Q)	30,420				
PM4TC Panamax 4 T/C Average Financial (P4Q)	17,385				
SM6TC Supramax 6 T/C Average Financial (S6Q)	1,110				
Total Options	8,430,791	7,006,803	5,137,758		

New York Mercantile Exchange (NYMEX), division of the CME Group

OPTION	2018	2017	2016	2015	2014
Brent Crude Oil 1 Month Spread Option (AA)	3,000				200
Brent Crude Oil Futures-Style Margin Option (BZO)	1,967,269	540,735	259,439	720	
Brent Crude Oil Last Day Financial Calendar Spread	423,088				
Brent Crude Oil Last Day Financial Calendar Spread	2,000	2,000			
Brent Crude Oil Last Day Financial Calendar Spread	1,000				
Brent Financial Average Price Options (BA)	16,462	5,347	15,237	153,151	413,914
Brent Last Day Financial (European) Options (BE)	469,058	38,281	43,890	52,621	117,326
Brent Last Day Financial Options (OS)	1,290	3,912	12,234	55,192	228,871
Chicago Ethanol (Platts) Average Price Options (CVR)	70,070	73,329	85,662	72,994	100,845
Chicago Ethanol (Platts) Calendar Spread Option -	275	75	125		
Chicago Ethanol (Platts) Calendar Spread Option -	150	325	325		
Coal (API 2) cif ARA (Argus/McCloskey) Calendar	6,640	10,233	54,378	66,223	4,455
Coal (API 2) cif ARA (Argus/McCloskey) Options	290	1,600	9,505	8,995	26,945
Coal (API 2) cif ARA (Argus/McCloskey) Quarterly	3,655	825	103,884	100,652	3,765
Coal (API 4) fob Richards Bay (Argus/McCloskey)	25		100	1,400	1,240
Coal (API 4) fob Richards Bay (Argus/McCloskey)	2,145	275	2,485	1,875	6,540
Coal (API 4) fob Richards Bay (Argus/McCloskey)	60	30	1,540	600	430
Crude Oil (LO)	44,521,982	42,901,045	45,879,991	39,627,070	31,107,783
Crude Oil Calendar Strip Options (6F)	170				60
Crude Oil Short-Term D15 (C15)	500				
Crude Oil Weekly Options Wk 1 (LO1)	188,943	164,240	82,795	50,765	39,235
Crude Oil Weekly Options Wk 2 (LO2)	179,572	158,374	48,765	40,298	42,977
Crude Oil Weekly Options Wk 3 (LO3)	160,965	103,804	35,405	24,850	27,747
Crude Oil Weekly Options Wk 4 (LO4)	202,068	191,368	56,458	30,301	43,192
Crude Oil Weekly Options Wk 5 (LO5)	71,635	61,548	28,646	15,318	11,322
Dubai Crude Oil (Platts) Average Price Options (AH)	8,000		2,290	21,600	900
EIA Flat Tax On-Highway Diesel Average Price	792	72			
Gulf Coast Jet Fuel (Platts) Average Price Options	3,898	2,168	3,668	3,934	18,390
Light Sweet Crude Oil (WTI) Daily Physical Options	21,350	31,435	38,425	17,900	23,850
Light Sweet Crude Oil (WTI) Financial 1 Month	893,940	771,245	1,851,715	1,845,556	1,451,107
Light Sweet Crude Oil European Financial Option	149,026	258,029	344,468	487,003	220,375
LLS (Argus) vs. WTI Crude Oil Average Price Option	100	6,900	11,730	4,080	
Mont Belvieu Ethane (OPIS) Average Price Options	1,350	3,095	6,755	1,840	10,040
Mont Belvieu LDH Propane (OPIS) Average Price	6,662	8,572	11,486	13,341	22,579
Mont Belvieu Normal Butane (OPIS) Average Price	3,300	1,200	1,560		1,075
Natural Gas (American) (ON)	2,383,119	2,586,748	3,444,463	3,029,693	3,369,085
Natural Gas (European) (LN)	22,852,904	28,303,431	23,520,044	19,594,491	20,936,070
Natural Gas (Henry Hub) Daily Options (KD)	202,634	517,490	375,887	271,330	254,700
Natural Gas (Henry Hub) Last-day Financial 1 Month	570,809	487,016	168,709	271,714	883,039
Natural Gas (Henry Hub) Last-day Financial 2 Month	1,430	14,950	4,505	4,950	2,100
Natural Gas (Henry Hub) Last-day Financial 3 Month	44,246	159,825	228,182	65,445	67,783
Natural Gas (Henry Hub) Last-day Financial 5 Month	2,550	4,050	1,200	2,700	650
Natural Gas (Henry Hub) Last-day Financial 6 Month	102,850	70,320	11,275	46,900	41,678
Natural Gas (Henry Hub) Last-day Financial Options	52,503	47,791	28,902	23,660	65,737
Natural Gas Calendar Strip Options (6J)	37,282	14,670	28,068	13,020	14,066
Natural Gas Short-Term Options D01 (U01)	550	3,716	5,025	1,855	475
Natural Gas Short-Term Options D02 (U02)	2,798	4,258	4,800	6,013	2,175
Natural Gas Short-Term Options D03 (U03)	2,279	2,273	3,170	3,100	1,750
Natural Gas Short-Term Options D04 (U04)	1,975	2,613	5,000	2,330	1,200
Natural Gas Short-Term Options D05 (U05)	1,630	11,208	3,550	2,200	1,225
Natural Gas Short-Term Options D06 (U06)	1,500	9,148	2,905	2,325	2,850
Natural Gas Short-Term Options D07 (U07)	1,851	3,675	5,100	2,920	825
Natural Gas Short-Term Options D08 (U08)	1,477	5,637	3,522	1,975	1,550
Natural Gas Short-Term Options D09 (U09)	1,634	5,214	5,617	5,431	750
Natural Gas Short-Term Options D10 (U10)	1,250	6,029	4,595	3,750	1,900
Natural Gas Short-Term Options D11 (U11)	1,236	7,575	3,205	3,510	2,350

New York Mercantile Exchange (NYMEX), division of the CME Group (continued)

OPTION	2018	2017	2016	2015	2014
Natural Gas Short-Term Options D12 (U12)	1,900	4,740	4,450	2,065	1,100
Natural Gas Short-Term Options D13 (U13)	500	5,119	4,361	2,535	2,125
Natural Gas Short-Term Options D14 (U14)	863	3,980	5,225	1,675	1,100
Natural Gas Short-Term Options D15 (U15)	797	5,415	3,755	2,750	2,280
Natural Gas Short-Term Options D16 (U16)	700	7,010	4,175	3,025	675
Natural Gas Short-Term Options D17 (U17)	2,296	5,147	1,405	1,985	1,925
Natural Gas Short-Term Options D18 (U18)	1,622	2,565	3,055	1,100	1,175
Natural Gas Short-Term Options D19 (U19)	348	5,345	1,845	3,170	625
Natural Gas Short-Term Options D20 (U20)	1,425	4,330	1,680	1,730	405
Natural Gas Short-Term Options D21 (U21)	613	3,642	2,325	2,350	950
Natural Gas Short-Term Options D22 (U22)	1,271	3,527	4,205	1,560	3,150
Natural Gas Short-Term Options D23 (U23)	898	1,672	2,280	2,465	900
Natural Gas Short-Term Options D24 (U24)	879	3,225	2,080	2,105	625
Natural Gas Short-Term Options D25 (U25)	152	940	505	1,000	100
Natural Gas Short-Term Options D26 (U26)	600	292	1,580	1,075	425
Natural Gas Short-Term Options D27 (U27)	525	2,020	1,050	1,225	175
Natural Gas Short-Term Options D28 (U28)	100	3,255	3,925	450	350
Natural Gas Short-Term Options D29 (U29)	510	906	3,475	1,600	550
Natural Gas Short-Term Options D30 (U30)	100	4,745	2,100	4,075	250
Natural Gas Short-Term Options D31 (U31)	477	6,250	1,125	380	500
Natural Gas Winter Strip (6I)	2,700				
NY Harbor ULSD Average Price Option (AT)	35,782	36,891	67,799	165,910	287,936
NY Harbor ULSD Calendar Spread Option - 1 Month	2,600	1,700	5,900	3,500	21,960
NY Harbor ULSD European Financial Option (LB)	2,767	2,813	4,789	6,205	8,800
NY Harbor ULSD Option (OH)	386,859	395,078	606,514	606,659	785,306
PJM WES HUB PEAK CAL MTH (6OA)	860	4,100	1,220	200	
PJM Western Hub Real-Time Peak Calendar-Month 5	880		10,300		
PJM Western Hub Real-Time Peak Calendar-Month	7,488	14,257	11,935		
RBOB Gasoline 1 Month Calendar Spread Options	700	6,758	11,850		2,575
RBOB Gasoline Average Price Options (RA)	1,350	2,865	6,744	21,649	98,941
RBOB Gasoline Crack Spread (RX)	2				
RBOB Gasoline European Financial Option (RF)	125	1,335	60	5,440	12,090
RBOB Gasoline Physical Options (OB)	144,932	293,296	390,579	347,789	401,970
Rockies Natural Gas (Platts IFERC) "Pipe" Option	3,556	4,030	6,540	6,429	15,444
San Juan Natural Gas (Platts IFERC) "Pipe" Option	2,149	3,240	9,108	5,092	3,330
Western Canadian Select Oil (Net Energy) Monthly	390	11,770			
WTI Average Price Options (AO)	534,847	640,113	409,273	722,701	889,225
WTI Crude Oil 1 Month Calendar Spread (WA)	2,410,650	2,084,297	3,005,974	2,359,207	2,061,821
WTI-Brent Crude Oil Spread Options (BV)	856,315	564,527	279,675	268,360	554,571
Iron Ore 62% Fe, CFR China (TSI) Average Price	1,480	44,199	72,160	73,556	13,482
U.S. Midwest Domestic Hot-Rolled Coil Steel (CRU)	300	1,530			
Palladium Options (PAO)	29,533	66,745	42,072	42,981	137,511
Platinum Option (PO)	45,372	36,869	53,221	58,275	144,370
Total Options	**80,137,450**	**81,933,810**	**81,933,753**	**70,821,204**	**65,217,660**

Total Options Volume

	2018	2017	2016	2015	2014
Total Options	1,044,578,565	933,459,741	846,777,246	750,034,209	696,575,679
Percent Change	11.90%	10.24%	12.90%	7.67%	18.57%

Options Traded on U.S. Securities Exchanges Volume Highlights
2018 in Comparison with 2017

2018 Rank	EXCHANGE	2018 Contracts	%	2017 Contracts	%	2017 Rank
1	Chicago Board Options Exchange	1,283,269,272	31.51%	1,132,457,708	27.29%	1
2	NASDAQ PHLX	724,170,578	17.78%	641,637,538	15.46%	2
3	NYSE-ARCA	460,113,644	11.30%	302,568,725	7.29%	6
4	NASDAQ Options Market	428,650,957	10.53%	340,852,645	8.21%	4
5	BATS Exchange	422,706,669	10.38%	409,693,613	9.87%	3
6	International Securities Exchange	402,504,406	9.88%	334,888,824	8.07%	5
7	NYSE Amex Options (formerly American Stock	389,866,979	9.57%	293,548,459	7.07%	7
8	MIAX Pearl	220,609,083	5.42%	41,070,094	0.99%	13
9	International Securities Exchange Gemini	205,043,832	5.04%	191,019,945	4.60%	9
10	Miami International Securities Exchange	200,711,418	4.93%	191,153,873	4.61%	8
11	C2 Exchange	150,923,570	3.71%	141,207,528	3.40%	10
12	EDGX Options Exchange	118,429,304	2.91%	52,844,958	1.27%	12
13	Boston Options Exchange	106,794,504	2.62%	86,904,384	2.09%	11
14	NASDAQ Boston	17,424,846	0.43%	23,967,125	0.58%	14
15	North American Derivative Exchange	12,323,287	0.30%	10,416,392	0.25%	15
16	International Securities Exchange Mercury	5,982,457	0.15%	5,731,749	0.14%	16
	Total Options	**5,149,524,806**	**100.00%**	**4,199,963,560**	**100.00%**	

Volume - Worldwide

ASX, Australia

	2018	2017	2016	2015	2014
S&P/ASX Index	7,212	25,610	8,054	12,968	238,602
All Futures on Individual Equities	2,837,126	2,921,155	4,718,169	5,862,951	6,703,662
Total Futures	**2,844,338**	**2,946,765**	**4,726,223**	**5,875,919**	**6,942,264**
S&P / ASX Index	12,720,573	10,728,593	12,138,930	11,462,192	9,797,586
All Options on Individual Equities	72,126,000	86,902,467	85,174,090	89,218,026	108,984,616
Total Options	**84,846,573**	**97,631,060**	**97,313,020**	**100,680,218**	**118,782,202**

ASX 24, Australia

(formerly Sydney Futures Exchange)	2018	2017	2016	2015	2014
Australian Sorghum	20			432	4,412
Eastern Australia Feed Barley	3,413	2,510	6,490	4,546	15,773
Eastern Australia Wheat	84,217	76,374	28,931	100	
ASX Electricity Base Load $300 CAP Quarterly NSW	12,743	8,639	9,415	7,618	11,289
ASX Electricity Base Load $300 CAP Quarterly QLD	11,507	10,109	10,146	8,667	9,634
ASX Electricity Base Load $300 CAP Quarterly SA (GS)	2,697	762	962	1,722	2,159
ASX Electricity Base Load $300 CAP Quarterly VIC	10,776	6,887	9,763	7,535	10,342
ASX Electricity Base Load $300 Cap Strip Future (RN)	1,055	572	415	261	
ASX Electricity Base Load $300 Cap Strip Future (RQ)	832	787	323	215	
ASX Electricity Base Load $300 Cap Strip Future (RS)	130	11	55	5	
ASX Electricity Base Load $300 Cap Strip Future (RV)	618	147	350	165	
ASX Electricity Base Load Monthly Futures NSW (EN)	861	91	140	40	
ASX Electricity Base Load Monthly Futures QLD (EQ)	195	191	364	358	816
ASX Electricity Base Load Monthly SA ES	350		210		
ASX Electricity Base Load Quarterly NSW	36,040	29,615	34,554	40,785	56,033
ASX Electricity Base Load Quarterly QLD	42,101	40,575	41,378	44,392	46,800
ASX Electricity Base Load Quarterly SA	3,734	2,376	3,523	3,440	4,039
ASX Electricity Base Load Quarterly VIC	50,149	46,038	52,513	37,928	44,972
ASX Electricity Base Load Strip NSW	3,757	3,210	3,167	3,999	175
ASX Electricity Base Load Strip QLD	3,960	3,355	3,280	4,137	211
ASX Electricity Base Load Strip SA	342	133	191	157	18
ASX Electricity Base Load Strip VIC	4,973	4,754	5,904	3,041	206
ASX Electricity Peak Load Quarterly NSW	1,962	1,984	2,116	4,396	5,268
ASX Electricity Peak Load Quarterly QLD	2,423	1,436	1,353	979	1,188
ASX Electricity Peak Load Quarterly SA	40	85	36	134	110
ASX Electricity Peak Load Quarterly VIC	1,658	2,049	2,417	2,181	2,251
ASX Electricity Peak Load Strip Futures NSW (DN)	163	80	79	100	
ASX Electricity Peak Load Strip Futures QLD (DQ)	264	122	27	85	
ASX Electricity Peak Load Strip Futures SA DS	1		5		
ASX Electricity Peak Load Strip Futures VIC (DV)	95	196	60	38	
ASX NZ Electricity Base Load Calendar Month (ED)	56,747	53,691	26,871	5,271	1,657
ASX NZ Electricity Base Load Calendar Month (EH)	56,248	49,445	28,440	4,971	1,522
ASX NZ Electricity Base Load Quarterly (EA)	56,651	46,280	32,854	8,643	3,770
ASX NZ Electricity Base Load Quarterly (EE)	51,933	50,577	35,990	8,065	3,444
ASX NZ Base Load Calendar Month Electricity	10				
ASX NZ Electricity Base Load Strip OTAHUHU	210	30			
ASX NZ Electricity Peak Load Quarterly (EC)	1,580	1,130	1,890	282	52
ASX NZ Electricity Peak Load Quarterly (EG)	440	110	270	29	10
ASX VIC Monthly Base Load Electricity	271	364	298		70
VIC Gas	593	10	15		
VIC Gas Strip	70				
Mini-ASX SPI 200	3,008	6,949	29,059	9,752	
S&P/ASX 200 A-REIT Index	162,623	103,992	97,935	155,392	8,711
S&P/ASX 200 Financials-x-A-REIT Index	8	603	1,539	1,514	969
SPI 200	15,498,686	12,461,177	12,196,602	11,039,188	10,011,422
10 Year Treasury Bonds	51,250,531	43,578,795	40,121,694	31,786,345	27,186,944
20 Year Bonds	322,917	403,859	567,077	191,600	
3 Year Treasury Bonds	55,198,297	55,928,705	51,827,874	49,308,108	48,517,655
30 Day Interbank Cash Rate	1,604,936	1,980,701	3,762,252	4,325,909	2,347,004
Bank Bills 90 Day	32,850,509	30,326,252	29,899,739	28,492,027	26,392,134
New Zealand 90 Day Bank Bill	1,956,974	1,478,877	1,705,915	1,769,899	1,108,271
NZ White Pack 1st Yr Bank Bill Strip	110				
Red Pack 2nd yr IR Strip Futures	2,009				
White Pack 1st yr IR Strip Futures	1,174				50
Total Futures	**159,357,611**	**146,719,362**	**140,640,990**	**127,415,168**	**115,954,870**
ASX Electricity Base Load Quarterly NSW	3,924	2,564	2,536	5,206	2,393
ASX Electricity Base Load Quarterly QLD	3,265	2,855	3,796	4,710	5,775
ASX Electricity Base Load Quarterly SA	52	192	81	316	87
ASX Electricity Base Load Quarterly VIC	6,340	4,050	4,580	4,258	2,593
ASX Electricity Base Load Strip NSW	1,455	2,256	2,164	3,635	75
ASX Electricity Base Load Strip QLD	5,688	4,564	4,429	4,645	325
ASX Electricity Base Load Strip SA	75	15	75	135	
ASX Electricity Base Load Strip VIC	3,950	3,358	3,248	3,968	210
ASX NZ Electricity Base Load Quarterly (EA)	12,550	7,030	720	291	
ASX NZ Electricity Base Load Quarterly (EE)	7,350	3,860	240	150	
SPI 200	129,638	159,222	293,385	331,089	553,388

ASX 24, Australia (continued)

(formerly Sydney Futures Exchange)	2018	2017	2016	2015	2014
10 Year Treasury Bonds	30,540	13,856	14,950	4,235	41,899
Overnight 10 Year Treasury Bonds	3,550	4,900	125		
3 Year Treasury Bond	109,357	84,856	337,775	273,988	370,759
3 Year Bonds Intra-Day	349,454	416,542	581,801	732,605	1,245,326
Overnight 3 Year Treasury Bond	288,212	441,623	524,071	649,101	1,299,967
Total Options	**955,400**	**1,152,218**	**1,779,806**	**2,021,789**	**3,530,098**

Bolsa de Mercadorias & Futuros (BM&F), Brazil

	2018	2017	2016	2015	2014
Arabica Coffee	106,901	102,474	125,904	124,297	188,789
Arabica Coffee Rollover	7,279	14,188	9,852	11,154	13,942
Corn Cash Settled	980,296	792,259	741,933	685,723	968,841
Cross Listing Mini-Sized Soybean CME	95,443	69,177	84,272	43,789	57,465
Hydrous Ethanol	39,064	21,476	25,524	36,424	44,602
Live Cattle	285,685	502,727	429,292	545,842	813,312
Australian Dollar	121,237	62,966	48,949	51,707	86,940
Canadian Dollar	129,140	46,408	21,659	18,531	41,038
Chilean Peso	8,495	11,356	18,196	8,381	24,004
Euro	430,075	393,680	426,920	610,614	334,525
Mexican Peso	67,522	42,697	34,173	25,945	30,813
Mini Euro	192	208		11	464
Mini US Dollar	266,982,975	146,458,100	92,119,754	38,287,575	6,983,457
Mini US Dollar Rollover	111,815				
New Zealand Dollar	6,195	10,153	3,613	4,715	6,708
Pound Sterling	56,948	30,563	29,487	34,188	65,337
South African Rand	36,978	18,120	6,816	15,082	26,121
Swiss Franc	24,612	10,868	14,117	5,772	12,471
Turkish Lira	20,321	22,230	12,640	9,170	25,269
US Dollar	91,695,866	74,087,470	71,281,293	77,490,315	82,365,540
US Dollar forward points	4,556,775	5,010,115	4,966,735	5,021,955	4,929,440
US Dollar Rollover	8,076,875	14,939,854	16,838,265	22,384,437	25,029,948
Yen	93,619	62,017	33,087	54,561	85,125
West Texas Intermediate (WTI)	34,001	60,781	18,841	7,519	3,738
Bovespa Mini Index	706,224,217	290,827,570	150,763,004	89,671,637	69,989,607
Bovespa Rollover	2,559,215	5,079,920	4,509,610	6,251,834	4,968,870
Bovespa Stock Index Futures	23,827,497	18,945,370	19,212,830	16,924,855	20,496,231
E-mini S&P 500	229,142	136,135	164,886	260,013	343,009
E-mini S&P 500 Rollover	41,657	35,954	23,745	42,292	37,046
IBrX-50	29,547	16,146	19,623	92,637	117,869
Mini Ibovespa Rollover	79,274				
Forward Exchange Rate	33,742	102,823	31,911	17,521	86,381
ID x IPCA Spread Futures	3,174,330	2,104,405	332,245	1,805	
ID x US Dollar Spread Futures	1,471,403	1,738,831	3,201,458	3,175,476	1,073,054
DI x US Dollar Swap with reset	2,739,421	10,030	180,600	523,543	193,063
ID x US Dollar FRA	41,123,360	61,401,079	58,612,981	66,957,541	53,344,699
Interbank Deposits futures SELIC	423,000	20,000	376,265	2,432,536	2,310,699
Interest Rate Swap	120,585	152,501	102,014	222,770	1,324,955
Interest Rate x Exchange Rate	290,057	155,750	388,062	3,517,095	308,742
Interest Rate x Price Index	89,469	28,876	769,807	353,513	782,445
One Day Inter-Bank Deposit	371,801,536	354,386,047	302,518,177	309,308,981	286,125,664
US T-Note	81,195	41,098	16,189	9,848	45,039
Gold Spot (250g)	8,685	8,430	7,253	9,873	12,754
Odd-lot gold spot (0.225g)	34,821	43,560	29,399	19,385	
Odd-lot gold spot (10g.)	16,785	18,855	18,349	13,839	
Total Futures	**1,528,367,247**	**978,038,985**	**728,583,549**	**645,291,749**	**563,743,123**
Arabica Coffee	1,453	1,983	729	2,694	2,536
Corn Cash Settled	417,450	291,191	216,628	154,471	122,434
Live Cattle on Futures	214,768	350,240	158,381	214,298	204,757
Flexible US Dollar	57,378	126,079	724,841	371,643	166,743
US Dollar	8,826,246	8,684,500	7,578,200	7,154,790	8,419,449
US Dollar Volatility	100	1,945	27,280	142,420	235,510
Hydrous Ethanol	220				300
E-mini S&P 500	13,099				
Exchange Traded Funds	17,921,657	31,666,541	4,225,345	4,809,002	2,352,231
Flexible BOVA11 Index	35,233	72,103	8,003	1,600	2,080
Flexible Bovespa Stock Index	278,113	402,362	219,462	120,600	103,579
Ibovespa Index	848,522	1,091,642	1,416,900	1,063,917	1,626,643
All Options on Individual Equities	913,153,184	681,905,062	692,006,945	659,993,736	786,115,608
Flexible Spot Interest Rate Index	880,737	1,612,327	678,291	206,937	269,799
IDI Index	102,904,073	98,481,487	50,194,640	31,762,121	48,454,406
One Day Inter-Bank Deposit	152,490	6,596,925	1,264,615	6,191,959	
Gold Spot (250g)	1,208	35,548	1,580	7,996	
Total Options	**1,045,705,931**	**831,319,970**	**758,722,239**	**713,301,108**	**856,736,082**

Athens Derivatives Exchange S.A. (ADEX), Greece

	2018	2017	2016	2015	2014
FTSE/Athex Large Cap	640,572	629,413	895,527	2,134,904	3,572,231
All Futures on Individual Equities	13,212,566	18,698,023	14,496,353	12,410,089	6,969,083
Total Futures	**13,853,138**	**19,327,436**	**15,391,880**	**14,544,993**	**10,541,314**
FTSE/Athex Large Cap	81,295	95,203	66,983	94,728	227,510
All Options on Individual Equities	11,679	24,572	11,853	13,384	30,164
Total Options	**92,974**	**119,775**	**78,836**	**108,112**	**257,674**

Bolsa de Valores de Colombia (BCV), Colombia

	2018	2017	2016	2015	2014
Mini US Dollar	123,606	115,348	143,230	90,697	61,570
US Dollar	600,378	292,448	456,633	467,478	299,721
COLCAP Index	9,907	1,734	474	933	1,005
All Futures on Individual Equities	136,291	419,785	602,897	291,360	347,522
10-year Treasury Bond	62,651	144,516	74,754	71,017	1,918
2-year Treasury Bond	35,888	44,602	62,199	84,693	6,775
5-year Treasury Bond	86,972	78,328	33,602	35,909	9,163
IBR	9,104	19,267	29,775	6,072	59
Total Futures	**1,064,797**	**1,116,028**	**1,403,564**	**1,048,199**	**941,620**
US Dollar	5				
Total Options	**5**				

Borsa Istanbul, Turkey

(formerly TurkDEX)	2018	2017	2016	2015	2014
Cotton	109				
Wheat	726	15	4		
CNH/TRY	12,793	640			
EUR/USD Cross Currency	1,655,729	1,822,681	1,471,151	888,551	400,627
GBP/USD	42				
RUB/TRY	370	126			
TRY/EUR	4,250,947	2,003,497	2,432,494	2,336,850	434,442
TRY/USD	91,295,379	64,523,385	36,496,794	32,986,013	12,929,674
Base Load Electricity	25,805	33,428	246,169	23,647	26
BIST 30 Index	55,181,858	43,851,583	45,495,203	46,057,541	43,020,419
BIST Bank Index	528				
BIST Industrials Index	172				
FBIST ETF Futures	4,317	5,643	5,666	6,067	
All Futures on Individual Equities	54,692,782	15,949,196	7,081,902	2,739,426	194,377
Gold	19,363,020	5,033,306	3,551,717	989,478	929,006
USD/Ounce Gold	2,644,588	2,067,576	1,227,497	415,146	585,995
Total Futures	**229,129,165**	**135,291,078**	**98,008,597**	**86,442,719**	**58,494,568**
TRY/USD	4,522,535	7,711,002	6,080,600	1,323,524	25,494
BIST 30 Index	148,171	218,207	290,827	266,425	94,484
All Options on Individual Equities	2,593,550	2,902,061	2,873,483	847,500	88,919
Total Options	**7,264,256**	**10,831,270**	**9,244,910**	**2,437,449**	**208,897**

Borsa Italiana, Italy

	2018	2017	2016	2015	2014
Electricity	1,475	1,172	2,891	2,811	7,544
Mini S&P/MIB Index	3,837,339	3,039,553	4,789,081	4,920,082	4,204,244
S&P/MIB Index	8,405,118	7,201,735	10,603,083	9,563,659	8,493,311
All Futures on Individual Equities	3,114,540	2,668,343	3,708,532	3,772,920	605,592
Single Stock Dividend Futures	17,810	76,346	41,392	39,447	133,853
Total Futures	**15,376,282**	**12,987,323**	**19,145,698**	**18,299,887**	**13,445,424**
S&P/MIB Index	3,798,540	2,645,143	5,786,699	4,655,965	4,015,974
All Options on Individual Equities	17,061,970	18,518,552	24,091,505	21,416,914	21,585,798
Total Options	**20,860,510**	**21,163,695**	**29,878,204**	**26,072,879**	**25,601,772**

Bombay Stock Exchange, India

	2018	2017	2016	2015	2014
EUR/INR	995,115	1,232,645	1,655,492	778,180	328,954
EUR/USD	332,801				
GBP/INR	686,087	1,271,200	962,629	311,114	338,174
GBP/USD	138,891				
JPY/INR	187,853	353,801	715,899	247,796	599,336
US Dollar/Indian Rupee	453,709,423	262,138,344	319,413,292	258,083,484	171,642,176
USD/JPY	5,004				
S&P Sensex Index (BSX)	393	44,102	63,932	498,367	1,271,330
All Futures on Individual Equities	295	3,801	3,672	139,683	579,391
91-day Government of India (GOI) Treasury Bill	7,212,166	9,338,072	6,179,322	5,063,460	1,076,089
Total Futures	**463,268,028**	**274,381,965**	**328,994,243**	**265,122,143**	**175,921,040**
US Dollar/Indian Rupee	559,489,717	334,052,119	207,386,529	170,311,114	32,110,966
All Options on Individual Equities	2	6	126,898	7,071,245	2,012,537
Total Options	**559,489,719**	**334,052,239**	**214,064,265**	**349,772,380**	**554,252,129**

Budapest Stock Exchange (BSE), Hungary

	2018	2017	2016	2015	2014
Feed Corn	2	470	1,471	1,949	1,920
AUD/CAD	3,000			400	
AUD/CHF	1,000		200		
AUD/JPY	4,000				200
AUD/USD	10,500	1,800	3,700	7,600	6,650
CAD/CHF	1,000				
CAD/HUF	3,500	5,700	300	8,265	1,220
CAD/JPY	1,000	600			200
CHF/HUF	155,950	122,000	146,305	186,845	100,267
CHF/JPY	7,600		6,400	200	
CZK/HUF	240	50			
EUR/AUD	8,600	1,200		2,600	1,000
EUR/CAD	18,600	3,200	800	1,700	1,900
EUR/CHF	36,850	13,650	23,310	64,650	90,790
EUR/CZK	800	1,500		3,150	
EUR/GBP	24,350	25,365	66,245	19,200	7,850
EUR/HUF	2,952,475	2,134,171	2,832,411	3,462,873	3,174,892
EUR/NOK	14,900	11,150	24,450	17,300	6,750
EUR/PLN	1,900	28,900	2,900	3,000	3,700
EUR/RUB	1,050	700			10,180
EUR/SEK	4,500		2,600	300	1,100
EURO/JPY	47,550	58,150	1,000	33,150	41,100
EURO/TRY	90,576	72,915	102,307	130,945	164,470
EURO/USD	666,248	563,986	1,083,078	1,191,892	786,835
GBP/AUD	1,600			2,600	4,600
GBP/CAD	2,300			1,300	3,200
GBP/CHF	1,800		200	200	450
GBP/HUF	224,697	268,249	408,284	276,873	256,972
GBP/JPY	6,600		2,400	1,000	1,800
GBP/SEK	800				
GBP/USD	50,900	110,900	119,565	11,500	37,060
NOK/HUF	4,300		400		600
PLN/HUF	900	260	1,990	2,265	485
TRY/HUF	7,195	18,450	26,650	37,050	36,410
USD/CAD	4,703	13,873	46,670	11,030	14,390
USD/CHF	2,850	800	27,400	13,200	40,450
USD/HUF	1,539,878	2,819,431	2,276,697	2,341,642	1,281,715
USD/JPY	50,194	154,830	115,106	106,650	114,680
USD/NOK	20,000	8,750	4,400	5,600	1,800
USD/PLN	13,450	4,180	600	800	1,400
USD/RUB	000	1,500	7,100	100	100
USD/SEK	5,500	8,900	3,300	5,900	4,000
USD/TRY	42,210	21,910	32,000	41,700	22,150
All Futures on Individual Equities	596,858	522,503	426,601	498,889	567,669
Total Futures	**6,633,826**	**7,000,145**	**7,797,885**	**9,069,453**	**7,533,757**
EUR/HUF	64,850	1,900	2,550	27,200	
EUR/USD	500		600	200	2,400
EURO/TRY	3,000	4,600	6,400	2,200	17,250
GBP/USD	200				
USD/HUF	1,600	14,500	1,000	2,600	
Total Options	**70,150**	**21,100**	**10,550**	**35,204**	**29,300**

Dalian Commodity Exchange (DCE), China

	2018	2017	2016	2015	2014
Corn	66,812,732	127,323,949	122,362,964	42,090,235	9,329,939
Corn Starch	22,613,108	50,433,910	67,445,264	27,053,680	71,958
Egg	19,918,457	37,262,376	22,474,739	14,718,738	35,188,187
No. 1 Soybeans	22,111,727	26,324,058	32,570,158	18,810,903	27,197,413
No. 2 Soybeans	24,476,720	42,551	1,834	4,936	6,952
RBD Palm Olein	44,344,644	68,046,475	139,157,899	111,515,010	79,996,388
Soybean Meal	238,162,413	162,877,864	388,949,970	289,496,780	204,988,746
Soybean Oil	54,135,551	57,158,378	94,761,814	92,504,264	64,082,631
Coke	69,071,834	40,121,040	50,461,050	15,662,329	63,688,294
Hard Coking Coal	46,465,289	42,194,764	41,077,427	15,706,560	57,605,436
Iron Ore	236,491,632	328,743,737	342,265,309	259,572,085	96,359,128
Block Board	689	1,286	8,157	182,704	17,760,375
Ethylene Glycol	2,323,861				
Fibre Board	29,630	1,056	710	68,271	15,354,378
Linear Low Density Polyethylene (LLDPE)	36,735,543	61,420,753	100,931,133	119,856,998	71,754,393
Polypropylene	49,349,161	56,691,866	123,768,347	107,513,311	24,781,150
Polyvinyl Chloride (PVC)	36,362,787	39,000,407	11,242,993	1,566,571	1,471,673
Total Futures	**969,405,778**	**1,097,644,470**	**1,537,479,768**	**1,116,323,375**	**769,637,041**
Soybean Meal	12,521,591	3,635,682			
Total Options	**12,521,591**	**3,635,682**			

VOLUME - WORLDWIDE

Dubai Gold & Commodities Exchange

	2018	2017	2016	2015	2014
Australian Dollar	12,133	19,179	8,628	9,435	4,446
Canadian Dollar	17,367	23,427	4,054	5,212	3,588
Chinese Yuan	24,128	5,433	13,039	322	
Euro	376,991	275,723	122,150	112,945	72,908
Indian Rupee	12,509,330	10,216,672	11,670,100	10,567,072	9,428,978
Japanese yen	35,832	50,549	21,496	6,895	12,214
Mini Indian Rupee	1,861,404	1,120,475	1,060,546	1,154,820	1,401,306
Rupee Quanto	3,705,241	2,647,629	5,042,013	1,658,972	
Sterling Pound	142,024	169,056	137,457	51,544	29,102
Swiss Franc	11,144	9,940	1,879	2,460	1,586
USD/RUB	53	624	40	108	42
USD/ZAR	5,431	5,857	8,189	24,909	3
Brenrt Crude Oil	21,377	4,211	39		
WTI	66,847	66,426	103,486	43,309	24,317
WTI Mini	30,512	41,131	63,467	9,853	
S&P Sensex Index	75,226	140,615	174,984	182,873	204,732
Indian Single Stock Futures	2,674,548	1,353,725	76,618		
Copper	14,362	17,818	7,632	22,053	34,031
Gold	230,568	310,195	447,599	347,531	481,250
Gold Quanto	215,202	190,713	281,241	109,036	
Shanghai Gold	35,321	34,518			
Silver	7,385	20,982	37,770	29,643	63,448
Spot Gold	536	14,513	4,981	115	
Total Futures	**22,072,962**	**16,777,992**	**19,327,252**	**14,372,851**	**11,774,345**
Indian Rupee	187,174	661,666	342,534	132,465	14,718
Total Options	**187,174**	**661,666**	**342,534**	**132,465**	**14,718**

Dubai Mercantile Exchange (DME)

	2018	2017	2016	2015	2014
Brent vs. Dubai (Platts) Crude Oil	59,195	14,609	300		
Dubai Crude Oil (Platts)	52,249	80,207			
Oman Crude Oil	1,125,731	1,480,511	1,949,004	1,709,888	2,119,936
Total Futures	**1,237,175**	**1,575,427**	**1,949,658**	**1,709,888**	**2,119,936**

EUREX, Frankfurt, Germany

	2018	2017	2016	2015	2014
Bloomberg Agriculture Subindex (FCAG)	10	63		129	
AUD/USD (FCAU)	337				
AUD/USD Rolling Spot (RSAU)	321				
EUR/CHF (FCEF)	523				
EUR/CHF Rolling Spot (RSEF)	330				
EUR/GBP (FCEP)	749				
EUR/GBP Rolling Spot (RSEP)	648				
EUR/JPY (FCEY)	112				
EUR/JPY Rolling Spot (RSEY)	223				
EUR/USD Futures	3,808		4	47	6
EUR/USD Rolling Spot (RSEU)	4,770				
GBP/CHF Rolling Spot (RSPF)	20				
GBP/USD Futures	1,244			10	11
GBP/USD Rolling Spot (RSPU)	965				
NZD/USD (FCNU)	30				
NZD/USD Rolling Spot (RSNU)	10				
USD/CHF (FCUF)	60				11
USD/CHF Rolling Spot (RSUF)	20				
USD/JPY (FCUY)	9				
USD/JPY Rolling Spot (RSUY)	554				
ATX	169,647	237,373	349,325	330,033	270,120
ATX five	4,863	8,739	12,430	17,384	38,068
CECE EUR	14,182	15,703	20,853	12,594	6,179
Dax	26,563,806	21,547,762	27,261,861	29,991,539	29,718,354
DivDAX	23,096	19,163	11,883	12,215	13,700
Euro Stoxx	436,621	321,687	169,001	270,114	250,923
Euro Stoxx 50 ex Financials Index	51,884	43,821	31,301	37,213	6,436
Euro Stoxx 50 Index	318,635,725	282,107,311	374,452,071	341,824,375	293,837,558
Euro Stoxx 50 Index (USD) (FESQ)	71	74,669	47,222		
Euro Stoxx 50 Index Dividend	6,976,107	4,172,068	5,651,691	4,922,323	4,548,195
Euro Stoxx 50 Index Market-on-Close (FES1)	5,248	122			
Euro Stoxx 50 Index Total Return Futures (TESX) *	1,705,583	543,845	680		
Euro Stoxx 50 Variance Index	36,696	5,722			
Euro Stoxx Automobiles & Parts	119,174	78,994	108,800	65,743	47,282
Euro Stoxx Banks	73,510,289	55,560,883	42,645,554	24,155,819	19,744,140
Euro Stoxx Banks Index Dividend	226,855	33,135	7,759	11,899	7,900
Euro Stoxx Basic Resources	60,182	52,451	52,230	27,018	23,870

EUREX, Frankfurt, Germany (continued)

	2018	2017	2016	2015	2014
Euro Stoxx Chemicals	26,897	11,037	11,993	17,876	13,803
Euro Stoxx Construction & Materials	18,010	12,694	38,523	26,411	37,712
Euro Stoxx Financial Services	2,536	2,732	21,628	5,367	8,356
Euro Stoxx Food and Beverage	31,047	19,006	42,334	26,051	43,727
Euro Stoxx Healthcare	20,253	17,919	30,016	15,894	18,065
Euro Stoxx Industrial Goods & Services	12,950	16,730	25,320	18,156	31,224
Euro Stoxx Insurance	265,011	263,284	315,050	281,044	158,282
Euro Stoxx Large	13,469	7,859	9,557	7,955	10,020
Euro Stoxx Media	10,867	9,585	55,656	14,320	11,567
Euro Stoxx Mid	368,376	392,283	84,762	23,644	5,482
Euro Stoxx Oil & Gas	236,040	302,392	436,417	412,583	254,357
Euro Stoxx Personal & Household Goods	9,271	11,248	43,646	11,106	28,487
Euro Stoxx Real Estate	90,951	57,069	87,141	38,583	8,539
Euro Stoxx Retail	14,151	9,575	27,410	8,524	9,073
Euro Stoxx Select Dividend 30 Index	655,339	451,157	378,281	246,961	140,887
Euro Stoxx Select Dividend 30 Index Dividend	5,900	6,090	14,715	16,658	650
Euro Stoxx Small	272,896	188,880	254,510	108,962	75,857
Euro Stoxx Technology	22,597	25,055	57,178	19,157	37,800
Euro Stoxx Telecommunications	246,035	143,842	184,634	170,303	285,158
Euro Stoxx Travel & Leisure	10,134	4,745	53,180	22,710	16,800
Euro Stoxx Utilities	311,713	375,938	464,788	371,290	466,050
iShares Euro Stoxx 50 UCITS ETF (EUNF)	20	21			
iStoxx Europe Carry Factor Index (FXFC)	66,335	15,303			
iStoxx Europe Low Risk Factor Index (FXFR)	105,141	16,101			
iStoxx Europe Momentum Factor Index (FXFM)	86,725	41,770			
iStoxx Europe Quality Factor Index (FXFQ)	119,425	19,436			
iStoxx Europe Size Factor Index (FXFS)	49,059	20,546			
iStoxx Europe Value Factor Index (FXFV)	137,218	65,649			
MDAX	201,375	172,975	249,155	342,212	309,115
Eurex Daily Futures on Mini KOSPI 200 Futures (FMK2)	73,112	69,905	1,701		
Mini-DAX Futures	10,489,283	6,166,085	6,162,026	608,835	
Mini-Futures auf VSTOXX	15,538,785	13,423,085	10,085,067	7,225,150	6,960,491
MSCI AC ASEAN (FMSE)	105				
MSCI AC Asia ex Japan (FMXJ)	11,316	6,850			
MSCI AC Asia Pacific ex Japan	23,328	29,929	43,875	11,974	3,694
MSCI ACWI	29,686	1,912	8,256	10,290	
MSCI ACWI (EUR / NTR) (FMAE)	607				
MSCI ACWI ex USA (USD / NTR) (FMXU)	125				
MSCI Australia (FMAU)	298,239	242,242	38,367	30	
MSCI Canada (USD / GTR) (FMGC)	198,449	229,149	28,725		
MSCI Canada (USD / NTR) (FMCA)	165	17			
MSCI Chile	53,505	43,576	4,910	3,866	166
MSCI China Free	514,489	786,979	201,279	7,235	148
MSCI Colombia	11,463	9,292	2,080	1,299	80
MSCI Czech Rep (FMCZ)	991	1,698			
MSCI EAFE (USD, Price) (FMFP)	69,422	16,195			
MSCI EAFE NTR (USD) (FMFA)	101,739	31,506			
MSCI Egypt	1,731	986	169	55	219
MSCI EM Asia ex KR (USD / NTR) (FMXK)	1,629				
MSCI EM EMEA ex Turkey (FMXT)	985				
MSCI EM Growth (FMMG)	10				
MSCI EM LatAm ex Brazil (FMXB)	685				
MSCI Emerging Markets	710,041	613,520	64,859	9,020	7,790
MSCI Emerging Markets Asia	2,115,231	1,424,180	537,034	4,684	364
MSCI Emerging Markets EMEA	604,205	447,480	65,195	2,576	14
MSCI Emerging Markets Latin America	467,385	346,083	59,382	2,588	91
MSCI EMU (GTR, EUR) (FMGM)	2,656	6,414			
MSCI EMU (NTR, EUR) (FMMU)	223,704	86,676	10,688		
MSCI Europe	2,411,484	1,593,727	1,727,702	450,068	232,605
MSCI Europe (EUR / GTR) (FMGE)	547	91			
MSCI Europe (FMEF)	193,156	80,736	8,029	2,642	
MSCI Europe (FMEN)	50,474	28,987	37,526	19,055	
MSCI Europe (FMEP)	34,840	43,347	125,363	35,416	
MSCI Europe (NTR, USD) (FMED)	357,321	475,192	47,069		
MSCI Europe (USD / GTR) (FMGU)	5,640	3,772			
MSCI Europe Growth (FMEG)	23,651	17,578	2,420		
MSCI Europe Value (FMEV)	17,831	18,840	6,288		
MSCI France (EUR / GTR) (FMGF)	147	57,950			
MSCI France (EUR, NTR) (FMFR)	223	40			
MSCI Hong Kong	102,126	73,262	15,372	134	
MSCI Hungary (FMHU)	724	203		105	
MSCI India (FMIN)	11,914	33,094	15,285	139	
MSCI Indonesia	184,735	179,255	33,378	1,003	
MSCI Japan (GTR, USD) (FMJG)	2,756	313			
MSCI Japan Index	628,502	929,911	91,140	908	440

EUREX, Frankfurt, Germany (continued)

	2018	2017	2016	2015	2014
MSCI Kokusai (FMKN)	182	30	272	216	
MSCI Malaysia	137,679	122,203	16,883	2,012	345
MSCI Mexico	210,517	194,750	11,912	324	502
MSCI New Zealand (FMNZ)	1,738	1,290	339	125	
MSCI North America (USD / GTR) (FMGA)	5,163	46			
MSCI North America (USD / NTR) (FMNA)	338,659	223,766	941		
MSCI Pacific (NTR, USD) (FMAP)	6,679	11,479			
MSCI Pacific (NTR, USD) (FMPA)	78,295	146,649	17,429		
MSCI Pacific ex Japan (FMPX)	35,762	35,395	4,580	181	
MSCI Peru (FMPE)	12,703	1,899			
MSCI Philippines	56,698	47,103	7,922	954	88
MSCI Poland	23,434	17,550	4,062	751	284
MSCI Qatar	12,829	17,451	5,467	2,317	495
MSCI Russia	148,040	75,415	11,717	6,886	7,468
MSCI Russia Index	12,913	12,955	8,085	49,505	105,274
MSCI Singapore (FMSI)	12,466	10,792			
MSCI South Africa	164,337	107,033	11,593	305	121
MSCI Taiwan (FMTW)	1,121	3,187			
MSCI Thailand	183,868	196,266	59,576	229	368
MSCI UAE	6,724	7,533	1,584	604	129
MSCI UK	3,440	2,209	2,104	7,733	
MSCI UK (USD / NTR) (FMDK)	126,848	106,427	1,410		
MSCI USA (FMUS)	85,717	42,606	7,912	202	
MSCI USA (GTR, USD) (FMGS)	52,016	85			
MSCI USA Equal Weighted (NTR, USD) (FMUE)	2,780	5,463	652		
MSCI USA Momentum (NTR, USD) (FMUM)	7,619	14,683	10,966		
MSCI USA Quality (NTR, USD) (FMUQ)	7,550	9,490	6,016		
MSCI USA Value Weighted (NTR, USD) (FMUV)	24,985	39,378	10,197		
MSCI World (EUR / GTR) (FMWE)	857	1,609			
MSCI World (FMWN)	1,762,619	945,318	1,155,683	437,739	28,737
MSCI World (FMWO)	1,454,761	705,112	291,414	256,555	142,743
MSCI World (FMWP)	84,538	31,734	1,241	700	
MSCI World (USD / GTR) (FMWG)	110	101			
MSCI World Growth (FMOG)	8,260				
MSCI World Midcap (FMWM)	18,169	17,638	13,042	11,369	2,574
MSCI World Value (FMOV)	9,026				
OMX-Helsinki 25	127,858	78,477	142,486	169,775	103,876
RDX USD Index	634,628	771,787	1,045,762	759,353	917,116
SMI Index Dividend	1,049	1,095	1,795	1,795	2,096
Stoxx Europe 50 Index	875,239	732,831	776,440	901,275	686,507
Stoxx Europe 600	16,668,181	11,324,758	11,707,122	6,520,341	3,273,465
Stoxx Europe 600 Automobiles & Parts	840,193	681,659	475,406	477,859	492,680
Stoxx Europe 600 Banks	4,422,463	3,445,360	3,583,783	1,894,102	1,850,759
Stoxx Europe 600 Basic Resources	1,742,841	1,443,957	1,333,904	916,390	959,180
Stoxx Europe 600 Chemicals	70,748	94,424	82,140	57,366	61,840
Stoxx Europe 600 Construction & Materials	109,575	104,813	167,898	121,177	76,409
Stoxx Europe 600 Financial Services	119,564	105,130	68,535	65,563	29,359
Stoxx Europe 600 Food & Beverage	273,901	194,096	266,973	268,077	197,695
Stoxx Europe 600 Healthcare	400,083	384,617	445,425	265,689	252,262
Stoxx Europe 600 Industrial Goods & Services	326,405	302,349	381,840	199,465	235,237
Stoxx Europe 600 Insurance	420,464	591,707	665,868	601,403	359,704
Stoxx Europe 600 Media	209,846	112,557	97,764	98,076	105,441
Stoxx Europe 600 Oil & Gas	2,329,873	1,841,403	1,954,186	1,169,216	664,417
Stoxx Europe 600 Personal & Household Goods	69,954	106,706	88,258	99,603	58,716
Stoxx Europe 600 Real Estate	294,858	170,454	162,256	117,008	20,904
Stoxx Europe 600 Retail	198,033	102,170	72,615	78,718	55,441
Stoxx Europe 600 Technology	286,387	256,900	158,332	123,685	103,823
Stoxx Europe 600 Telecom	995,784	650,678	477,998	314,938	418,363
Stoxx Europe 600 Travel & Leisure	131,592	103,229	108,297	96,038	65,674
Stoxx Europe 600 Utilities	693,582	844,596	508,135	473,537	341,489
Stoxx Europe Large 200	91,542	78,041	103,773	122,014	105,646
Stoxx Europe Mid 200	146,037	176,942	263,100	260,514	298,166
Stoxx Europe Small 200	694,573	527,862	682,410	623,605	460,064
STOXX Global Select Dividend 100 Index	4,080	6,061	11,856	480	
Swiss Leader Index (SLI)	21,542	19,334	32,134	66,577	24,205
Swiss Market Index (SMI)	13,548,464	11,084,756	12,745,219	11,605,853	9,141,697
Swiss Market Index Mid-Cap (SMIM)	156,082	122,353	155,951	142,076	214,386
Tecdax	124,522	96,535	98,207	115,937	109,249
All Futures on Individual Equities	176,533,099	101,528,094	101,258,985	122,978,432	123,997,353
Single Stock Dividend	6,578,908	4,080,465	2,448,326	2,441,557	3,145,117
3 Month Euribor	70,761	74,505	169,335	376,042	160,355
Euro Stoxx 50 Corporate Bond (PI) (FCBI)	155	60			
Euro-BOBL	138,001,817	135,394,434	130,704,593	118,963,514	113,554,369
Euro-BONO	173,450	209,596	146,360	40,273	
Euro-BTP	30,283,789	28,950,808	28,339,932	25,543,794	17,356,789

EUREX, Frankfurt, Germany (continued)

	2018	2017	2016	2015	2014
Euro-BUND	202,027,816	195,580,025	186,714,728	177,107,346	179,136,822
Euro-BUXL	16,009,717	14,350,348	11,840,847	9,314,084	6,428,189
Euro-OAT	37,970,925	35,941,066	29,041,392	21,562,432	17,372,490
Euro-SCHATZ	108,326,655	86,000,890	73,660,249	70,279,064	71,376,790
Mid Term Euro-OAT	4	468	7,849	50,932	138,687
Short Term Euro-BTP	18,116,789	12,186,532	6,766,913	5,584,445	3,706,784
Swiss Government Bond (CONF)	91,981	106,716	102,360	104,041	115,674
Three-Month SARON (FSO3)	948				
Bloomberg Commodity Index	13,565	62,488	67,166	32,188	16,960
Bloomberg Energy Sub-Index	12,252				
Bloomberg Energy Subindex (XLEN)	3,253	27,489	10,806	469	2,513
Bloomberg ex-Agriculture & Livestock Index	3,020				
Bloomberg ex-Agriculture & Livestock XL Futures	8,881	8,544	9,350	5,587	6,032
Bloomberg Industrial Metals Sub-Index	80	57	257	177	741
Bloomberg Petroleum Sub-Index	10,292	7,949	7,518	16,562	14,646
Bloomberg Precious Metals Sub-Index	10	10	95		2,292
Bloomberg Softs Sub-Index	50	1,286	1,100	4,647	
Total Futures	**1,253,900,917**	**1,049,331,509**	**1,085,268,363**	**996,460,293**	**916,533,113**
ATX	1,265	1,115	7,400	28,249	7,418
CECE EUR	890	5,800	7,550	750	
CS ETF (CH) on SMI	59			1	
DAX	25,824,668	22,215,330	27,974,560	42,130,864	39,792,092
DAX 1st Friday Weekly	1,007,234	652,280	653,731	707,439	981,896
DAX 2nd Friday Weekly	857,549	623,562	671,853	672,894	788,852
DAX 4th Friday Weekly	904,474	694,396	782,122	978,252	1,027,793
DAX 5th Friday Weekly	321,539	248,808	321,664	295,736	371,679
db x-trackers MSCI Emerg. Markets TRN	15	381	522	632	
db x-trackers MSCI World TRN (DBXW)	5	4			
ETFS Gold (OPHA)	80,000	6,300			
Euro STOXX 50 Index	273,634,066	263,152,091	286,250,081	299,881,600	241,254,907
Euro STOXX 50 Index - 1st Friday	6,915,517	5,010,118	4,020,370	4,313,199	4,595,091
Euro STOXX 50 Index - 2nd Friday	5,363,211	3,815,340	4,237,875	3,204,106	3,136,464
Euro STOXX 50 Index - 4th Friday	7,252,612	6,317,176	4,771,520	5,282,926	4,839,024
Euro STOXX 50 Index - 5th Friday	2,321,001	2,462,702	2,190,098	1,777,432	1,731,467
Euro Stoxx 50 Index Dividend	2,372,411	1,063,310	1,332,581	1,515,550	1,968,591
Euro Stoxx 50 Index Options (OESX-MEEx) (OMSX)	585,205				
Euro Stoxx Automobiles & Parts	10,804	5,343	4,052	7,967	6,218
Euro Stoxx Banks	46,613,902	33,944,306	27,694,785	10,901,633	12,131,518
Euro Stoxx Banks 1st Friday	33,631	4,368	36,197	15,852	63,627
Euro Stoxx Banks 2nd Friday	14,534	6,810	5,397	14,000	43,342
Euro Stoxx Banks 4th Friday	31,560	36,323	48,468	31,793	7,104
Euro Stoxx Banks 5th Friday	9,135	12,295	19,767	4,079	32,720
Euro Stoxx Basic Resources	5,850	4,142	1,343	1,586	1,459
Euro Stoxx Chemicals	2,772	294	1,883	5,186	2,541
Euro Stoxx Construction & Materials	673	40	190	989	1,282
Euro Stoxx Food and Beverage	2,661	886	106	1,520	
Euro Stoxx Healthcare	590	634	1,870	4,161	2,975
Euro Stoxx Industrial Goods & Services	961	782	859	1,738	1,002
Euro Stoxx Insurance	52,230	35,279	68,583	24,945	5,472
Euro Stoxx Mid	0	1,400			
Euro Stoxx Oil & Gas	17,165	19,566	28,630	35,945	41,640
Euro Stoxx Personal & Household Goods	3,009	4,457	2,086	2,718	
Euro Stoxx Real Estate (OESL)	57,316	6,564			
Euro Stoxx Select Dividend 30 Index	189,924	121,100	47,480	9,300	1,001
Euro Stoxx Technology	6,877	3,146	13,310	5,588	
Euro Stoxx Telecom	87,635	4,634	3,331	9,723	23,668
Euro Stoxx Utilities	313,507	50,289	106,422	180,626	53,424
iShares DAX® UCITS ETF (DE)	7,500	18,589	31,466	24,612	
iShares EURO STOXX50® UCITS ETF	8,959	218,302	254,172	16,002	
iShares Euro Stoxx Banks 30-15 UCITS ETF (DE)	2,632	4,030			
iShares J.P. Morgan USD Emerging Market Bond UCITS	200				
iShares Physical Gold (IGLN)	1,311,740				
iShares Stoxx Europe 600 UCITS ETF (DE) (EXSA)	164	13			
iShares USD Corporate Bond ETF (OQDE)	220				
iShares USD High Yield Corporate Bond ETF (OHYU)	41,141				
Kospi 200	38,604,669	26,091,710	21,328,717	24,423,032	22,497,002
MDAX	1,869	2,498	11,100	11,292	19,352
MSCI AC Asia Pacific ex Japan (OMAS)	510				
MSCI EAFE (USD, Price) (OMFP)	128,079	47,333			
MSCI EM (OMEF)	30,393	11,362	91,779	24,999	
MSCI EM (OMEN)	105	16,406	36,032	34,459	4,551
MSCI Emerging Markets	222,786	224,960	186,950	83,844	75,816
MSCI Emerging Markets Asia (OMEA)	507,710	170,671	7,458	4,155	
MSCI World	290,718	335,599	185,360	52,530	25,730
MSCI World (OMWN)	16,326			6,075	

VOLUME - WORLDWIDE

EUREX, Frankfurt, Germany (continued)

	2018	2017	2016	2015	2014
MSCI World (OMWP)	199,062	16,307	15,100		
RDX USD Index	692,322	576,094	614,261	567,629	996,854
Stoxx Europe 50 Index	12,407	15,394	32,578	314	2,198
Stoxx Europe 600	196,912	629,772	97,847	154,649	13,500
Stoxx Europe 600 Automobiles & Parts	219,805	97,483	124,581	240,192	217,780
Stoxx Europe 600 Banks	271,058	205,981	636,435	316,735	305,576
Stoxx Europe 600 Basic Resources	235,487	220,448	334,456	346,945	594,603
Stoxx Europe 600 Financial Services	30	191	1,159	5,578	1,787
Stoxx Europe 600 Food & Beverage	4,100	9,505	26,220	12,585	14,558
Stoxx Europe 600 Healthcare	20,708	24,727	35,847	19,597	26,713
Stoxx Europe 600 Industrial Goods & Services	102,256	52,666	53,080	9,640	22,915
Stoxx Europe 600 Insurance	33,707	20,032	10,805	31,792	18,357
Stoxx Europe 600 Media	2,871	93	1,248	2,109	2,584
Stoxx Europe 600 Oil & Gas	262,267	334,032	436,129	309,696	159,504
Stoxx Europe 600 Personal & Household Goods	1,630	4,322	13,539	11,139	2,475
Stoxx Europe 600 Real Estate	23,500	11,750		600	
Stoxx Europe 600 Technology	6		99	1	8,750
Stoxx Europe 600 Telecom	229,264	65,796	50,763	27,099	112,944
Stoxx Europe 600 Travel & Leisure	369	148	35,825	26,175	6,227
Stoxx Europe 600 Utilities	28,813	45,908	28,059	15,172	25,185
Stoxx Europe Small 200 Index	2,000	7,105	619	963	
Stoxx Global Select Dividend 100 Index	14,880	17,716	33,110		
Swiss Leader Index (SLI)	103	2,919	12,631	14,655	6,532
Swiss Market Index (SMI)	4,345,091	3,929,715	3,950,989	3,801,588	3,566,161
Swiss Market Index (SMI) - 1st Friday	4,703	5,532	3,757		
Swiss Market Index (SMI) - 2nd Friday	8,403	4,002	2,015		
Swiss Market Index (SMI) - 4th Friday	7,905	7,819	2,489		
Swiss Market Index (SMI) - 5th Friday	1,669	1,942	1,687		
Swiss Market Index Mid-Cap (SMIM)	8,715	4,195	12,039	32,013	11,688
TecDAX	196	401	12,689	16,207	5,359
VSTOXX (OVS2)	8,583,691	2,008,927			
All Options on Austrian Equities	378,184	572,046	488,809	513,706	398,383
All Options on Belgian Equities	1,030,297	714,267	624,172	565,356	682,907
All Options on Dutch Equities	11,550,630	13,142,352	12,238,251	10,141,752	9,966,922
All Options on Finnish Equities	6,851,910	6,952,407	9,985,076	11,001,476	14,285,048
All Options on French Equities	24,312,363	22,017,290	21,643,909	21,544,339	20,060,331
All Options on German Equities	84,935,707	72,642,208	80,812,584	89,548,522	82,968,214
All Options on Great Britain	112,727	93,377	231,828	260,699	294,190
All Options on Ireland	10,275	43,370	10,702	14,954	6,925
All Options on Italian Equities	5,209,627	5,321,227	6,963,201	5,316,686	3,548,003
All Options on Russian Equities	1,059,310	263,758	500,913	187,557	125,092
All Options on Spanish Equities	5,305,355	5,799,277	7,976,521	6,280,385	6,065,820
All Options on Swedish Equities	11,202	12,680	12,054	5,263	1,021
All Options on Swiss Equities	48,123,718	41,610,620	45,029,440	41,045,258	38,002,420
All Options on US Equities	626				
3-Month Euribor	610	2,317	5,215	278,361	337,164
Bund Weekly - Week1 (OGB1)	107,490	90,376	82,582	272,071	
Bund Weekly - Week2 (OGB2)	67,033	70,284	119,226	214,920	
Bund Weekly - Week3 (OGB3)	35,948	42,217	93,612	124,112	
Bund Weekly - Week4 (OGB4)	22,882	10,127	23,564	35,159	
Bund Weekly - Week5 (OGB5)	22,360	29,157	44,313	62,748	
Euro-Bobl	12,012,901	12,918,246	9,580,664	14,979,787	8,242,904
Euro-BTP (OBTP)	1,717,815	85,678			
Euro-Bund	43,572,017	42,673,925	34,904,716	45,385,172	33,679,659
Euro-OAT	380,416	98,873	20		26,804
Euro-Schatz	19,444,653	17,319,057	14,428,689	18,277,115	9,050,906
Total Options	**697,862,164**	**626,566,801**	**641,553,408**	**676,188,190**	**574,008,711**

Euronext Derivatives Market

	2018	2017	2016	2015	2014
Corn	410,980	370,081	522,273	670,938	565,519
Milling Wheat	10,675,119	8,997,886	9,006,649	9,073,162	8,444,694
Rapeseed	2,348,117	2,790,491	2,567,941	2,143,032	1,775,676
Rapeseed Meal	1,428	9,739	15,725	19,171	155
AEX Dividend Index	300	300	2		
AEX Mini	13,511	13,381	65,529	48,127	59,961
AEX Stock Index (FTI)	8,980,034	8,741,565	9,919,048	10,657,589	9,458,794
Bel 20 Index (BXF)	981	2,578	3,396	15,429	31,924
CAC 40	30,279,622	32,457,671	33,784,414	35,646,788	36,653,426
CAC 40 Dividend Index	347,000	411,963	175,085	88,106	207,561
CAC 40 Mini	25,235	5,891	15,669	14,973	23,082
CAC 40 Total Return	1,110				
FTSE EPRA Euro Zone	304		1,589	998	32
FTSE EPRA Europe	106,285	108,322	102,981	154,732	87,836

Euronext Derivatives Market (continued)

	2018	2017	2016	2015	2014
Morningstar Eurozone 50 Index	38				
PSI 20 Index	130,941	170,838	197,332	271,991	263,883
All Futures on Individual Equities	1,092,497	378,951	257,004	87,490	21,652
Stock Dividend Futures	12,419	10,958	13,569	7,048	
Total Futures	**54,425,921**	**54,472,765**	**56,651,270**	**58,905,484**	**57,598,004**
Corn	39,446	34,238	71,369	92,099	82,086
Milling Wheat	973,588	734,663	1,222,123	1,961,639	1,846,385
Rapeseed	135,029	226,086	349,886	331,888	176,618
AEX Daily	2,918,897	1,959,405	1,386,412	1,611,387	2,107,194
AEX Mini	19,107	16,524	14,624	42,749	94,018
AEX-Index (AEX)	9,681,101	7,147,796	5,708,911	7,333,284	8,483,732
AEX Weekly	2,606,585	1,818,891	1,411,476	1,659,125	2,066,600
CAC 40 (€10)	3,811,892	3,713,089	2,282,839	3,348,106	4,427,108
CAC 40 (WEEKLY)	9,319	17,744	60,664		
ISHARES CORE FTSE 100 UCITS ETF (DIST)	93	137	15		
ISHARES EURO STOXX 50 UCITS ETF (DIST)	9,427	11,230	6,699	1,456	
ISHARES EURO STOXX 50 UCITS ETF (DIST)	120	1,864	9		
ISHARES MSCI EMERGING MARKETS UCITS ETF	12,334	3,692	370	800	
ISHARES MSCI EMERGING MARKETS UCITS ETF	4	35			
ISHARES MSCI EUROPE UCITS ETF (DIST)	1,673	1,563	492	1,046	
ISHARES MSCI JAPAN EUR HEDGED UCITS ETF	580	770	172	48	
ISHARES MSCI WORLD UCITS ETF (DIST)	1,524	4,202	552	865	
ISHARES MSCI WORLD UCITS ETF (DIST) (WEEKLY)	20	23			
ISHARES S&P 500 UCITS ETF (DIST)	4,684	5,387	2,067	1,699	
PSI 20 Index	30	3,656	1,000		
All Options on Individual Equities	74,602,767	70,084,311	57,015,075	60,094,108	66,791,184
Total Options	**94,828,220**	**85,804,162**	**69,590,712**	**76,610,199**	**86,460,872**

Hong Kong Futures Exchange (HKFE), Hong Kong

	2018	2017	2016	2015	2014
RMB Currency - AUD/CNH	1,304	409	88		
RMB Currency - CNH/USD	12,214	11,939	4,867		
RMB Currency - EUR/CNH	8,956	1,750	952		
RMB Currency - JPY/CNH	2,291	485	390		
RMB Currency - USD/CNH	1,755,130	732,569	538,594	262,433	205,049
CES China 120 Index	765	1,511	642	27,427	40,283
CES Gaming Top 10 Index	235				
Hang Seng Index	57,668,346	31,486,965	32,313,994	21,239,775	17,067,247
Hang Seng IT Hardware Index Futures	144	2			
Hang Seng Mainland Banks Index Futures	22,516	8,067	285		
Hang Seng Mainland Healthcare Index	62	2			
Hang Seng Mainland Oil & Gas Index Futures	20,973	2,637	6		
Hang Seng Mainland Properties Index Futures	28,456	4,744	5		
Hang Seng Software & Services Index Futures ^	103				
HSCEI Dividend Point Index	413,292	472,147	589,188	205,269	240,572
HSCEI Gross Total Return Index	2				
HSCEI Net Total Return Index	2				
H Shares Index	37,451,281	28,852,655	33,031,130	33,379,310	21,984,297
HSI Dividend Point Index	12,822	18,243	16,886	9,573	15,658
HSI Gross Total Return Index	14				
HSI Net Total Return Index	13				
HSI Volatility Index	1	68	87	464	475
Mini Hang Seng Index	24,664,381	11,487,207	12,477,552	10,046,556	6,959,838
Mini H-Shares Index	5,551,632	3,661,193	4,870,262	7,506,543	3,429,393
MSCI AC Asia ex Japan NTR Index	5,545				
All Futures on Individual Equities	863,027	121,532	225,978	729,013	427,609
One-Month Hibor	167	20		6	
Three-Month Hibor	592	568	52	90	35
Iron Ore (Monthly)	9,517	18,194			
London Aluminium Mini Futures	635	937	1,829	11,554	1,644
London Copper Mini Futures	124	731	3,354	27,388	4,318
London Nickel Mini Futures	323	325	11,550	155	
London Zinc Mini Futures	651	483	12,394	16,654	2,828
Gold (CNH)	25,006	110,763			
Gold (USD)	326,700	55,372			
Total Futures	**128,847,222**	**77,060,327**	**84,100,129**	**73,462,212**	**50,379,246**
RMB Currency - USD/CNH	30,067	10,473			
Flexible Hang Seng Index	762		560	5,300	36,621
Flexible H-shares Index	6,500	10,000	16,616	39,848	
Hang Seng Index	12,716,495	10,129,325	9,353,749	7,515,466	7,518,710
H-shares Index	24,258,084	19,777,920	19,475,726	15,304,245	8,998,897
Mini Hang Seng Index	2,461,296	1,640,881	1,424,379	1,033,813	961,354
Mini H-Shares Index	583,549	377,243	197,399		
All Options on Individual Equities	127,279,101	105,839,179	73,582,114	92,463,479	74,543,861
Total Options	**167,335,854**	**137,785,021**	**104,050,543**	**116,362,151**	**92,059,793**

ICE Futures Europe (ICE), United Kingdom

	2018	2017	2016	2015	2014
Cocoa	7,732,270	7,817,955	8,378,774	6,430,848	5,671,277
Robusta Coffee - 10 Tonne	4,268,610	4,458,111	4,378,442	3,982,365	3,707,464
UK Feed Wheat	113,009	91,701	108,264	123,284	152,373
White Sugar	3,442,923	2,874,270	2,654,375	2,340,302	2,023,273
Belgian Power Futures	26,486	17,312	21,574	24,305	18,360
Belgian ZTP Natural Gas	270				
ICE Brent	235,001,152	241,544,633	210,561,053	183,853,174	160,425,461
CER Futures	20,109	11,089	30,029	79,766	200,254
Dutch Power	141,732	167,323	156,556	131,783	194,805
Dutch TTF Gas	9,317,729	7,541,880	6,909,038	4,853,206	2,320,254
EUA Futures	7,776,993	4,891,577	5,137,885	5,195,957	7,008,526
EUA Phase 3 Daily	664,929	327,280	234,444	207,070	194,987
EUA UK Auction	202,106	211,920	160,516	149,916	132,440
EUAA Futures	1,684	26	651	5,732	1,630
EUAA UK Auction	1,720	1,451	1,842	5,041	5,415
French Power Futures	60				
gC Newcastle Coal	82,672,960	259,626	374,545	356,946	228,878
German Natural Gas Futures	185,488	4,387	1,555	1,215	2,234
German Power Futures	3,046	288	42		
ICE Gas Oil	21,677	74,686,410	66,158,348	63,239,874	52,800,084
ICE Global Oil Products	33,749,182	38,857,776	34,102,096	30,761,725	21,509,940
ICE Heating Oil	7,284,007	5,512,333	4,935,310	4,244,432	4,502,749
Italian Power Futures	1,891				
ICE Natural Gas	7,315	11,683,665	11,178,265	11,772,115	10,600,335
ICE NYH (RBOB) Gasoline (Monthly)	9,357,935	5,115,433	5,395,099	5,807,503	5,006,982
ICE Richards Bay Coal	5,192,657	56,312	84,875	64,850	85,481
ICE Rotterdam Coal	50,637	992,492	1,217,874	742,948	523,591
ICE UK Electricity Futures Peak (1MWh)	1,011,767	19,850	40,285	15,225	2,015
Italian PSV Natural Gas Futures	2,044	15,200	3,415	245	
ICE WTI Crude	56,802,221	54,967,258	47,289,665	39,802,954	31,600,959
FTSE 100 Declared Dividend	3,050	510	2,800	5,752	3,100
FTSE 100 Dividend Index	515,653	372,215	347,063	368,186	659,120
FTSE 100 Index	36,915,549	33,318,372	37,954,717	33,170,416	33,522,718
FTSE 250 £2	432,451	470,451	507,061	288,889	233,513
MSCI AC Asia Pacific Ex Japan Futures	2,450	1,432	6,701	42,442	
MSCI All Countries Asia Ex Japan Index Futures	199,615	166,770	275,561	221,987	
MSCI AWI NTR Index Future	102,873	381,114			
MSCI Brazil Index Future	232,864	225,688	41,406	17,369	
MSCI EM Asia Index Future	9		15	9,908	
MSCI EM Lat Am Index Future	48	96	5,175	14,474	
MSCI Emerging Markets (EM) Index Future	956,714	1,065,757	861,893	560,936	
MSCI Emerging Markets Net TR EUR Index Future	171,639	112,342	153,487	83,436	
MSCI Europe Consumer Disc NTR EUR Index Future	14,655	5,477	6,779	7,235	
MSCI Europe Consumer Stap NTR EUR Index Futures	7,474	1,280	3,032	850	
MSCI Europe Energy NTR EUR Index Future	9,122				
MSCI Europe Ex UK Index Futures	15,634	1,067	1,856	3,647	
MSCI Europe Financials NTR EUR Index Future	25,698	3,266	5,373	6,150	
MSCI Europe Health Care NTR EUR Index Future	9,393				
MSCI Europe Index Future	284,640	405,755	472,209	232,439	
MSCI Europe Industrials NTR EUR Index	7,992				
MSCI Europe IT NTR EUR Index Future	22,003				
MSCI Europe Materials NTR EUR Index	5,915	3,341	4,516	2,810	
MSCI Europe Net Total Return EUR Index Future	79,001	413,564	224,338	316,660	
MSCI Europe Tele Services NTR EUR Index Future	21,291				
MSCI Europe Utilities NTR EUR Index Future	14,186				
MSCI India Index Futures	248,842	424,783	221,953	74,657	
MSCI Japan Index Futures	15,729	6,685	1,508	254	6,465,262
MSCI Pacific ex Japan Index Futures	456,611	384,381	344,457	221,468	6,465,262
MSCI Switzerland Net Total Return CHF - Standard	5,840	4,878	13,544		
MSCI USA Index Futures	2,200	55,963	39,238	31,547	230
MSCI World Consumer Disc NTR USD Index Futures	1,564	13,081	13,199	18,744	
MSCI World Consumer Stap NTR USD Index Futures	54,103	66,184	17,554	7,089	13,217
MSCI World Energy Net TR USD Index Futures	78,133	34,748	6,442	9,261	
MSCI World Financials Net TR USD Index Futures	81,985	118,897	32,115	21,369	
MSCI World Health Care Net TR USD Index Futures	21,799	18,925	11,420	7,389	63,503,591
MSCI World Index Future	944,505	1,331,516	768,871	645,825	2,727,003
MSCI World Industrials Net TR USD Index Futures	8,256	15,066	11,105	979	2,571,293
MSCI World IT Net TR USD Index Futures	2,911	36,917	7,667	12,835	3,114,820
MSCI World Materials Net TR USD Index Futures	18,215	27,002	14,575	1,654	2,100,786
MSCI World Min Volatility NTR USD Index	10,195	17,333	5,211	1,136	29,299
MSCI World Net Total Return EUR Index Future	11,815	61,890	71,562	351,876	64,101
MSCI World Real Estate NTR Index Future	61,052	99,117	12,113		
MSCI World Telecom Net TR USD Index Futures	93,109	59,754	30,658	6,562	
MSCI World Utilities Net TR USD Index Futures	134,505	71,583	29,311	6,324	
Russell UK MID 150 NTR Index	199,255	322,438	134,747	21,667	2,246

ICE Futures Europe (ICE), United Kingdom (continued)

	2018	2017	2016	2015	2014
All Futures on Individual Equities	102,738,810	82,062,578	41,588,169	61,752,480	97,858,715
1 Month Secured Overnight Financing Rate	50,787				
3 Month Euribor	226,441,372	197,286,277	134,881,365	110,151,762	127,427,642
3 Month Euroswiss	7,397,204	6,496,257	5,760,114	6,740,041	7,800,896
3 Month Secured Overnight Financing Rate	51,783				
3-Month Short Sterling	216,984,337	198,845,679	153,940,833	146,337,942	149,357,479
ERIS Standard EUR 2 Year 0.00% Interest Rate Future	11,119	12,094	8,529	15	
ERIS Standard EUR 3 Year 0.00% Interest Rate Future	1,548	260	2,406		
ERIS Standard EUR 3 Year 0.25% Interest Rate Future	1,231	1,992			
ERIS Standard EUR 5 Year 0.00% Interest Rate	652	1,985			
ERIS Standard EUR 5 Year 0.25% Interest Rate	3,119	4,170			
ERIS Standard EUR 5 Year 0.50% Interest Rate Future	6,333		5,047	150	
ERIS Standard GBP 10 Year 1.75% Interest Rate Future	11,002	5,292	6,951		
ERIS Standard GBP 10 Year 4.00% Interest Rate	6,106				
ERIS Standard GBP 2 Year 1.00% Interest Rate Future	2,426	400	1,800	22	
ERIS Standard GBP 3 Year 0.75% Interest Rate	3,878	5,689			
ERIS Standard GBP 3 Year 1.25% Interest Rate Future	1,389			60	
ERIS Standard GBP 5 Year 1.50% Interest Rate Future	2,240			40	
Euribor 3 Year 0.00% Interest Rate Future	3,165	6,993	3,028		
GBP Libor 2 Year 1.25% Interest Rate Future	2,177		2,362		
GCF Repo US Treasury Index	52,037	221,976	160,679	273,792	
Long Gilt	64,887,815	51,162,865	53,144,942	47,917,051	44,582,727
Medium Gilt	5,337	17,710	25,651	39,632	29,207
Short Gilt	9,141	21,024	44,788	85,977	109,645
Swapnote € - 10 Yr	13,759	10,844	18,386	99,151	131,654
Swapnote € - 2 Yr	287,410	209,775	334,860	263,741	424,292
Swapnote € - 5 Yr	172,105	167,587	238,512	213,436	324,589
Three Month Euro (EONIA)	712,939	803			
Total Futures	**1,127,416,373**	**1,038,826,477**	**842,507,861**	**775,161,967**	**775,279,517**
Cocoa	1,193,032	1,456,382	2,692,602	1,883,865	1,733,250
Robusta Coffee 10 Tonne	805,450	930,305	835,963	633,806	742,481
UK Feed Wheat	1,025	957	2,613	1,583	3,673
White Sugar	5,314	7,943	11,556	5,650	2,942
Dutch TTF Gas	24,943,223	704,130	527,890	339,080	105,240
EUA	1,121,285	728,794	522,161	433,897	702,117
gC Newcastle Coal	2,515,690	68,934	93,258	105,550	38,505
German Power Options	123,535				
ICE Brent Crude Oil	18,410	18,282,452	16,152,414	13,594,212	13,285,768
ICE Gasoil	400	193,863	254,617	279,438	607,747
ICE Global Oil Products	2,309,684	1,693,696	1,252,118	1,668,712	3,473,601
ICE Natural Gas	567,805	1,506,030	1,604,115	2,032,675	1,336,920
ICE Richards Bay Coal	150	1,050	3,500	4,800	21,075
ICE Rotterdam Coal	290,365	331,229	792,480	559,574	459,801
ICE WTI Crude	5,074,934	3,957,901	4,642,881	4,942,451	3,998,924
FTSE 100 Euro FLEX Index	44,536	39,382	55,291	21,418	704,914
FTSE 100 (ESX)	12,856,406	12,378,557	15,846,915	16,804,267	19,928,232
FTSE 250 Index FLEX	10,763	6,948	14,371	6,010	9,180
All Options on Individual Equities	14,955,206	15,555,053	22,437,120	25,911,090	26,367,076
3 Month Euribor	13,698,090	10,512,677	10,485,675	15,984,090	20,455,410
3 Month Euribor 1 Year Mid Curve	9,517,322	6,973,347	6,285,825	6,234,485	8,565,948
3 Month Euribor 2 Year Mid Curve	8,220,483	7,078,526	4,542,141	7,157,550	7,263,456
3 Month Euribor 3 Year Mid Curve	3,923,186	4,895,059	2,118,763	2,492,075	3,309,290
3 Month Sterling	29,350,989	23,621,519	27,132,950	15,542,252	21,352,762
3 Month Sterling 2 Year Mid Curve	7,305,315	8,191,545	3,985,856	3,135,867	7,540,691
3 Month Sterling 3 Year Mid Curve	243,829	215,950	213,738	177,470	542,504
3 Month Sterling Mid Curve	9,429,538	8,763,610	8,843,680	6,627,443	15,161,256
Long Gilt	148,038	22,020			
Total Options	**148,674,003**	**128,121,359**	**131,350,493**	**126,603,647**	**157,739,517**

ICE Futures Singapore (ICE), Singapore

	2018	2017	2016	2015	2014
Malaysian Ringgit/US Dollar Futures	117,676	2,376	2		
Mini Onshore Renminbi Futures	57	10	3		
Mini US Dollar Index Futures	288,321	7,282	70		
Mini Brent Crude Futures (100 BBL)	1,807,071	1,767,406	1,694,092	134,575	
Mini Low Sulphur Gasoil Futures (10mt)	9,663	7,615	115,536	32,471	
Mini Low Sulphur Gasoil Futures (10mt)	334,813	503,621	187,530		
FANG+ Index	8,421				
Total Futures	**2,566,022**	**2,288,311**	**2,003,921**	**168,085**	

Indonesia Commodity & Derivatives Exchange, Indonesia

	2018	2017	2016	2015	2014
Olein	6,544	302	427	383	588
Palm Oil	36,949	49,194	383,024	439,635	603,168
Tin	15,062	15,594	12,614	13,496	11,373
Gold (GR)	100,481	138,506	157,745	117,276	66,707
Gold (ID)	12,486	30,280	3,971	1,451	949
Gold (UD)	150	117	197	295	
Total Futures	**171,672**	**234,030**	**558,409**	**575,896**	**691,238**

Japan Exchange, Japan

	2018	2017	2016	2015	2014
CNX Nifty Index	1,142	706	536	3,950	1,130
FTSE China Index 50	4				
JPX-Nikkei Index 400 Futures	8,152,838	7,669,469	7,370,575	10,474,332	1,606,338
Mini-TOPIX Futures	4,480,852	3,624,850	2,955,098	4,314,181	4,743,111
Nikkei 225	26,193,823	23,054,495	26,765,460	27,678,234	25,917,773
Nikkei 225 Dividend Index	2,926	6,682	19,305	6,272	7,840
Nikkei 225 Mini	273,327,463	219,518,050	233,940,373	247,159,359	199,121,967
Nikkei VI Futures	10,020	17,006	78,088	218,280	206,536
OSE DJIA	234,893	71,194	63,800	74,958	70,190
TAIEX Index	338,669	306,302	204		
TOPIX	224	1	22,560,705	22,303,956	20,877,250
TOPIX Banks Index	26,224,277	24,392,610	33,001	22,604	28,700
TOPIX Core30	401,396	172,701	5,440	4,772	3,827
TSE Mothers Index	3,302	2,830	54,171		
10 Year Japan Government Bond	687,027	254,100	7,383,298	8,677,576	8,791,553
Mini 10 Year Japan Government Bond	10,304,257	8,190,265	5,742	40,562	21,171
SL-JGB 20 Year Japan Government Bond	3,434	1,602	843	2,978	5,041
REIT Index Futures	152	303	253,607	175,450	132,531
Total Futures	**350,366,699**	**287,283,166**	**301,490,246**	**321,157,464**	**263,257,676**
Nikkei 225	35,502,311	32,594,768	33,763,728	37,806,896	43,958,283
Nikkei 225 Weekly	601,555	493,801	256,350	188,422	
TOPIX Index	179,262	259,384	145,716	329,529	320,313
All Options on Individual Equities (Combined)	869,163	915,787	922,341	834,886	1,062,389
10 Year Japan Government Bond	783,545	861,714	958,472	1,142,738	1,133,723
Total Options	**37,935,836**	**35,125,454**	**36,047,087**	**40,302,471**	**46,474,708**

Korea Futures Exchange (KFE), Korea

	2018	2017	2016	2015	2014
Euro	660,860	750,072	771,273	970,127	759,008
Japanese yen	683,645	566,382	521,657	374,364	370,112
US Dollar	74,821,050	60,882,377	64,308,611	52,508,299	48,663,722
Yuan	4,541	5,150	4,963	1,735	
KOSDAQ 150 Futures	13,353,982	2,984,151	1,204,706	47,775	
KOSPI 200	64,338,721	48,617,581	33,925,669	39,515,553	38,056,972
Mini KOSPI 200 Futures	20,906,086	14,738,747	8,992,497	2,276,951	
All Futures on Individual Equities	501,723,576	280,064,162	172,120,372	165,104,827	96,365,483
10 Year Treasury Bond	15,136,390	12,156,888	14,493,794	11,794,685	9,970,610
3 Year Treasury Bond	22,989,204	22,130,599	26,046,011	25,997,164	21,519,203
Total Futures	**714,618,055**	**442,896,109**	**322,389,553**	**298,626,183**	**215,715,833**
KOSPI 200	657,832,873	540,103,609	337,007,133	488,009,055	462,010,885
Mini KOSPI 200	17,063,243	14,661,725	22,029,182	7,580,506	
All Options on Individual Equities	18,743,585	17,674,231	11,564,672	719,582	28,962
Total Options	**693,639,701**	**572,439,565**	**370,600,987**	**496,309,143**	**462,049,295**

Malaysia Derivatives Exchange, Malaysia

	2018	2017	2016	2015	2014
Crude Palm Oil (FCPO)	10,471,357	11,919,425	10,415,755	10,984,549	10,088,131
RBD Palm Olein (FPOL)	507,394			60	656
KLSE Composite Index (FKLI)	2,497,513	2,034,237	2,750,951	3,023,971	2,094,807
Mini FTSE Bursa Malaysia Mid 70 Index (FM70)	173,132				
Gold	619	2,500	8,997	39,974	111,844
Total Futures	**13,650,015**	**13,956,213**	**13,175,743**	**14,053,525**	**12,308,588**
Crude Palm Oil (OCPO)	66,066	38,866	40,120	2,300	714
KLSE Composite Index (OKLI)	10,486	20,285	10,171	4,702	4,188
Total Options	**76,552**	**59,151**	**50,291**	**7,002**	**4,902**

London Metal Exchange (LME), United Kingdom

	2018	2017	2016	2015	2014
Aluminium	65,574,126	51,429,383	53,073,441	59,880,649	65,439,689
Aluminium Alloy	57,478	61,723	128,006	217,503	275,957
Cobalt	12,932	14,261	7,894	8,668	12,162
Copper - Grade A	38,599,069	33,885,113	36,947,881	38,557,831	38,811,609
North American Special Aluminum Alloy (NASAAC)	257,996	348,578	358,797	540,645	770,651
Primary Nickel	24,011,101	21,080,612	19,947,714	19,959,729	18,079,099
Special High Grade Zinc	33,430,054	29,642,124	26,942,407	28,751,185	30,323,897
Standard Lead	13,437,086	10,920,001	10,571,590	12,522,608	12,872,940
Steel Rebar	54,297	64,430	8,637		
Steel Scrap	484,843	307,532	49,099		
Tin	1,272,723	1,215,432	1,353,350	1,463,139	2,111,938
Gold	732,188	639,546			
Silver	148,566	95,625			
Total Futures	**178,072,459**	**149,704,368**	**149,388,960**	**161,902,341**	**168,712,316**
Aluminium Alloy	120				
Copper - Grade A	1,675,489	1,767,797	1,762,967	2,485,153	2,003,739
Copper Grade A TAPOs	50,056	30,736	28,806	5,625	19,689
High Grade Primary Aluminum	3,083,333	3,307,496	2,915,725	2,608,985	3,271,338
Lead TAPOs	2,399	4,934	320	1,552	852
Nickel TAPOs	7,950	1,776	9,942	13,643	43,712
North American Special Aluminum Alloy (NASAAC)	10	700	6,170	3,210	7,640
Primary Aluminium TAPOs	162,831	50,894	93,580	51,416	108,818
Primary Nickel	606,017	912,003	732,523	726,373	1,240,163
Special High Grade Zinc	906,392	1,360,303	1,159,365	1,284,521	1,453,349
Special High Grade Zinc TAPOs	6,427	2,955	22,032	1,333	61,845
Standard Lead	209,498	197,451	364,451	447,282	220,491
Tin	570	130	6,660	6,250	7,010
Total Options	**6,711,092**	**7,637,225**	**7,102,541**	**7,637,843**	**8,439,396**

MEFF Renta Variable (RV), Spain

	2018	2017	2016	2015	2014
Ibex 35	6,342,478	6,268,290	6,836,500	7,384,896	6,930,104
Ibex 35 Dividend Impact	70,725	43,372	58,044	32,499	23,939
Ibex 35 Sectoral	2,745	7,753	1,619		
Mini Ibex 35	1,490,232	1,618,857	2,498,973	3,181,287	3,034,973
All Futures on Individual Equities	10,703,192	11,671,215	9,467,294	10,054,830	13,119,374
Single Stock Dividend Futures Plus	200	880	760	1,152	
Stock Dividend	471,614	346,555	367,785	291,688	236,151
Total Futures	**19,081,186**	**19,956,922**	**19,231,335**	**20,954,364**	**23,349,888**
IBEX 35 Plus Index	4,183,154	4,303,701	3,222,390	5,444,156	7,319,962
All Options on Individual Equities	20,237,873	20,316,354	22,900,619	21,420,685	25,635,035
Total Options	**24,421,027**	**24,620,055**	**26,123,009**	**26,864,841**	**32,954,997**

Mercado a Termino de Buenos Aires (MATBA), Argentina

	2018	2017	2016	2015	2014
Corn	67,605	49,367	42,852	35,335	31,988
Corn Mini	53,827	4,980			
Sorghum	7	27		40	190
Soybean	192,993	151,427	164,779	153,351	128,156
Soybean 30 ton	825	6	11	10	
Soybean Index	138				
Soybean Mini	213,239	11,758			
Sunflower	2	8	1	10	68
Wheat	61,569	18,034	16,381	14,699	18,749
Wheat Mini	34,665	5,285			
Total Futures	**624,960**	**241,358**	**229,827**	**215,363**	**201,701**
Corn	7	6,025	4,662	4,297	5,131
Corn Mini	1				
Corn	13,575	33,010	39,741	24,566	26,348
Soybean Mini	42				
Sunflower	57,575	6			
Wheat	17,200	2,231	1,446	1,080	3,095
Total Options	**88,400**	**41,272**	**45,849**	**29,955**	**35,058**

Metropolitan Stock Exchange, India

	2018	2017	2016	2015	2014
EUR/Indian Rupee	100,465	92,975	582,240	2,154,619	4,509,383
EUR/US Dollar	200				
GBP/Indian Rupee	118,633	161,143	661,589	1,699,872	5,121,278
GBP/US Dollar	2				
JPY/Indian Rupee	3,826	65,848	333,927	570,706	2,157,102
US Dollar/Indian Rupee	10,060,783	19,488,001	45,178,861	53,568,902	112,458,175
Total Futures	**10,283,909**	**19,807,967**	**46,756,617**	**57,994,099**	**124,245,938**

VOLUME - WORLDWIDE

Mexican Derivatives Exchange (MEXDER), Mexico

	2018	2017	2016	2015	2014
Mexican Peso/Euro	78	296	5,638	74,685	69,394
Mexican Peso/US Dollar	6,265,233	8,576,423	8,627,126	7,949,772	19,855,606
IPC Stock Index	915,347	864,563	988,673	1,095,845	976,682
Mini IPC Stock Index	20,197	160,197	513,903	431,151	93,179
All Futures on Individual Equities	15,200	277,720	8,750	19,252	38,550
DC24 Bond	444,486	544,737	1,319,848	1,127,072	434,712
JN22 Bond	1,000				
JN27 Bond	39,100				
MR26 Bond	45,600	50,050	1,200		
MY31 Bond	1,100		2,800	42,400	85,007
NV42 Bond	1,500	45,876	155,012	32,850	
NV47 Bond	1,600				
TIIE 28	91,010	25,938	545,100	5,693,368	7,030,428
Total Futures	**7,841,451**	**10,613,400**	**12,528,580**	**16,548,629**	**29,230,798**
Mexican Peso/US Dollar	126,508	94,134	32,904	74,995	27,756
Exchange Traded Funds	1	247	293	13,602	39,559
IPC Stock Index	10,789	22,685	56,413	92,938	53,822
All Options on Individual Equities	352,759	300,820	322,308	257,524	524,309
Total Options	**490,057**	**417,886**	**411,918**	**439,059**	**683,174**

Montreal Exchange (ME), Canada

	2018	2017	2016	2015	2014
ETFs	10,300				
S&P/TSX 60 Index Mini Futures (SXM)	79,938	97,432	19,930	45,867	98,767
S&P/TSX 60 Index Standard Futures (SXF)	7,623,603	6,144,651	6,090,257	5,474,698	4,405,739
S&P/TSX Capped Energy Index (SXY)	65	51	66	189	
Banking Index (SXB)	25				
S&P/TSX Capped Utilities Index (SXU)	926		1,034	1,629	
S&P/TSX Composite Index Banks (Industry Group)	5,699	1,679	2,754	3,950	
S&P/TSX Composite Index Mini (SCF)	51	164	143	115	597
Share Futures	1,051,667	1,145,427	608		
10 Year Government of Canada Bond (CGB)	28,769,478	23,946,703	20,968,281	17,913,516	14,956,206
Bankers Acceptance 3 Months (BAX)	29,018,180	28,962,355	26,316,537	21,746,698	24,640,229
5 Year Canadian Gov't Bond (CGF)	406,782	358,078	116,799	176,269	301,026
Total Futures	**66,966,714**	**60,656,540**	**53,516,409**	**45,368,417**	**44,420,141**
US Dollar (USX)	128	9,008	19,006	2,491	2,170
ETFs	14,482,523	11,417,417	11,724,768	8,719,474	4,064,224
S&P Canada 60 Index (SXO) (incl. LEAPS)	198,698	193,038	671,462	541,759	428,590
All Options on Individual Equities	29,405,993	23,178,799	25,302,965	21,456,144	20,674,540
10 Year Government of Canada Bond Futures (OGB)	43,447	11,650	4,553	3,677	5,130
3 Month Bankers Acceptance Futures (OBX)	1,095,579	801,051	683,247	580,007	392,661
Total Options	**45,226,368**	**35,610,963**	**38,406,005**	**31,303,754**	**25,567,315**

Moscow Interbank Currency Exchange (MICEX), Russia

	2018	2017	2016	2015	2014
Sugar (cash settled - SA)	1,075	283	1,141	821	66
AUD/USD	539,229	461,766	614,498	486,061	569,862
CNY/RUB	405	825	2,837	28,158	
EUR/RUB	23,895,450	23,140,836	23,579,817	17,410,092	20,982,195
EUR/USD	58,384,706	40,782,844	34,882,762	59,826,374	26,179,646
GBP/USD	1,214,176	2,035,835	1,900,109	685,154	1,892,645
USD/CAD	176,629	266,011	467,540	128,779	
USD/CHF	77,234	92,989	95,846	289,536	304,197
USD/INR	7				
USD/JPY	1,423,892	3,303,245	3,652,237	777,702	763,907
USD/RUB	496,225,103	590,260,376	860,140,157	903,374,140	656,476,373
USD/TRY	5,289	2,380	66,637	30,331	
USD/UAH	7	87	499	7,806	28,290
Brent Oil	441,379,480	451,643,376	435,468,923	111,415,185	7,084,451
Light Sweet Crude Oil	584,178				
MICEX Index	6,980,201	5,180,920	4,652,963	3,995,588	1,728,304
MICEX Index (mini)	13,503,373	12,939,134	25,448,910	6,992,354	
RTS Index	118,174,805	134,467,991	204,593,580	184,124,166	243,320,038
RTS Standard Index	35	289	109	76	82
Russian Market Volatility	4,906	41,370	34,792	22,532	1,070
US 500 Index	336,425				
All Futures on Individual Equities	235,942,818	201,803,970	253,211,955	307,107,435	343,151,338
10 Year Federal Bond issued by Russian Federation	89,245	368,746	600,683	445,441	2,458,939
15 Year Federal Bond issued by Russian Federation	47,784	548,376	647,605	988,591	3,496,494
2-year Russian Federation Government Bond Futures	16,351	145,552	348,263	530,919	1,039,762
4-year Russian Federation Government Bond Futures	20,059	166,373	626,123	417,033	1,439,202
6-year Russian Federation Government Bond Futures	12,514	207,377	365,174	228,409	626,275
Ruble Overnight Index Average (RUONIA)	107,804	23,462	2,470	124	16

Moscow Interbank Currency Exchange (MICEX), Russia (continued)

	2018	2017	2016	2015	2014
Copper	449	939	31,718	1,160	3,125
Zinc	6				
Gold	14,526,824	23,562,649	22,656,213	10,784,533	11,519,763
Palladium	54,499	115,908	63,397	3,578	262
Platinum	240,011	180,024	191,923	128,311	97,461
Refined Silver	13,838,317	9,155,351	3,823,058	777,933	1,273,493
Total Options	**1,427,803,286**	**1,500,899,284**	**1,878,174,500**	**1,611,019,838**	**1,324,551,013**
EUR/RUB	207,263	248,956	464,423	61,665	103,972
EUR/USD	13,819	7,785	22,551	22,394	99,915
GBP/USD	802	2,760			
USD/JPY	292	6,664			
USD/RUB	32,220,569	36,555,667	30,184,048	22,379,627	43,240,578
Brent Crude Oil	7,660,935	6,652,353	4,513,050	126,593	47,493
Light Sweet Crude Oil	69,067				
MICEX Index (mini)	9,842	50,445	2,293,439	1,095,588	
MICEX Index	704	935	10,185	173,230	64,512
RTS Index	31,112,682	38,010,457	28,281,676	18,650,221	40,884,039
All Options on Individual Equities	1,230,677	2,154,952	6,146,989	5,866,674	4,059,807
Gold	26,099	26,579	35,276	36,367	153,854
Platinum	34	1	25	262	6,228
Refined Silver	19,186	16,127	16,643	7,572	10,785
Total Options	**72,571,971**	**83,733,681**	**71,970,718**	**48,421,746**	**88,671,183**

Nasdaq Exchanges Nordic Markets

	2018	2017	2016	2015	2014
OMX (Index)	42,008,960	38,820,112	42,405,041	39,853,871	32,935,776
All Futures on Individual Equities	2,794,528	3,431,710	3,550,905	4,426,022	2,523,612
10 Year Swedish Government Bond Future (SGB10H)	752,054	879,493	809,944	52,451	
2 Year Nordea Hypotek Bond Future (NDH2YH)	53,476	23,657	72,335	12,736	
2 Year Spintab Bond Future (SWH2YH)	87,581	86,203	168,943	21,339	
2 Year Stadshypotek Bond Future (STH2YH)	189,666	212,128	208,338	23,600	
2 Year Swedish Government Bond Future (SGB2YH)	922,069	826,965	597,913	40,224	
5 Year Nordea Hypotek Bond Future (NDH5YH)	84,571	104,924	128,571	10,396	
5 Year Spintab Bond Future (SWH5YH)	145,909	108,313	102,037	7,381	
5 Year Stadshypotek Bond Future (STH5YH)	419,471	374,548	357,908	24,840	
5 Year Swedish Government Bond Future (SGB5YH)	1,125,232	1,133,559	938,531	89,456	
Danish Mortgage Bond Futures (20MBF)	8,100	3,250	3,450	1,350	
Danish Mortgage Bond Futures (3MBF)	18,850	17,100	9,600	6,650	
Danish Mortgage Bond Futures (3YMBF)	13,400	9,920	15,500	8,205	
NIBOR-FRA	240,000	628,000	792,000	412,500	500,020
Policy Rate (RIBA)	2,074,019	2,691,300	1,718,140	3,233,280	2,728,500
STIBOR-FRA	9,226,260	7,689,266	5,467,864	8,444,508	9,544,148
Total Futures	**60,164,146**	**57,435,006**	**57,846,969**	**60,928,212**	**53,265,679**
OMX Index Options	6,499,806	6,108,213	8,260,077	9,911,654	9,276,282
All Options on Individual Equities	19,691,435	22,592,140	24,950,383	29,078,684	29,058,264
STIBOR-FRA	917,500	285,000	20,000	50,000	
Total Options	**27,108,741**	**28,985,353**	**33,230,460**	**39,078,838**	**38,533,796**

National Stock Exchange of India

	2018	2017	2016	2015	2014
EUR/Indian Rupee	23,507,247	17,924,752	14,993,193	18,041,680	12,482,953
EUR/US Dollar	5,725,331				
GBP/Indian Rupee	24,384,480	20,380,086	19,809,931	12,977,847	11,654,280
GBP/US Dollar	3,701,986				
JPY/Indian Rupee	9,331,971	7,472,207	10,465,101	5,556,373	4,856,701
US Dollar/Indian Rupee	537,847,778	312,477,915	351,162,981	358,801,689	294,069,368
US Dollar/JPY	220,697				
Bank Nifty Index	27,055,983	19,362,201	26,097,774	36,040,824	30,415,661
CNX IT Index	109,503	80,572	58,977	130,845	174,048
CNX Nifty Index	41,545,725	34,779,564	48,552,800	128,656,346	74,236,766
CNX PSE	2	34		76	67
FTSE 100	12	19	56	305	2,545
Nifty Midcap 50 Index	103,057	7,736	22	5,788	7,195
All Futures on Individual Equities	252,190,234	201,923,887	172,712,809	257,370,023	211,004,887
Total Futures	**925,724,006**	**614,511,019**	**644,017,804**	**817,753,199**	**639,121,739**
EUR/Indian Rupee	347,340				
EUR/US Dollar	3,331				
GBP/Indian Rupee	148,172				
GBP/US Dollar	418				
JPY/Indian Rupee	57,975				
US Dollar/Indian Rupee	484,853,286	371,600,526	351,632,420	216,130,236	98,750,882
US Dollar/JPY	5				
Bank Nifty Index	1,587,426,222	800,401,601	319,723,806	127,694,954	84,347,528

National Stock Exchange of India (continued)

	2018	2017	2016	2015	2014
CNX IT Index	35	66	136	1,365	190
CNX Nifty CPSE Index	20	7,224	18		
CNX Nifty Index	622,118,790	562,315,794	715,273,610	1,765,858,934	972,738,636
Nifty Midcap 50 Index	3,201				
All Options on Individual Equities	169,407,341	116,497,267	88,815,026	104,454,088	85,404,647
Total Options	**2,864,366,136**	**1,850,822,486**	**1,475,445,016**	**2,214,139,585**	**1,241,241,993**

Oslo Stock Exchange (OSE), Norway

	2018	2017	2016	2015	2014
OBX Index	2,723,548	2,810,099	3,426,747	2,916,233	3,408,114
Tailor Made Forwards/Futures	2,916,204	3,431,915	2,586,041	3,904,840	4,203,109
Single Stock Forwards/Futures	702,393	1,032,993	1,430,965	2,658,791	3,123,593
Total Futures	**6,342,145**	**7,275,007**	**7,443,753**	**9,479,864**	**10,734,816**
OBX Index	919,367	781,785	753,393	666,906	977,244
Tailor Made	2,270	835		1,000	12,560
All Options on Individual Equities	2,168,336	2,737,475	3,243,158	3,570,932	4,313,393
Total Options	**3,089,973**	**3,520,095**	**3,996,551**	**4,238,838**	**5,303,197**

Rosario Futures Exchange (ROFEX), Argentina

	2018	2017	2016	2015	2014
Chicago Corn	66,104	71,980	49,041	86,693	43,981
Chicago Soybean	134,520	241,780	192,082	140,560	80,624
Novillo Index (Cattle)	1,746	2,041			
Rosafe Soybean Index (ISR)	94,531	35,790	22,052	14,693	20,484
Soybean	37,283	38,804	42,852	56,079	76,161
Ternero Index (Cattle)	440	40			
U.S. Dollar	189,223,855	148,562,920	112,242,365	73,243,271	64,700,492
Oil Crude	240,875	247,371	178,855	33,244	34,168
Merval Stock Index	847,085	619,866	137,898	5,500	
ROFEX 20 Index	1,359,226				
Central Bank Bills (LEBACs)	16,648	10,588			
Goverment Bonds - BONAR 2024	26,079	33,696	30,224	17,798	3,922
Goverment Bonds - DICA	763	300	20,429	304	
Gold	73,094	65,933	51,650	19,446	17,117
Total Futures	**192,122,249**	**149,951,619**	**113,035,086**	**73,676,659**	**65,136,830**
Chicago Corn	59,515	20,488	19,856	15,921	15,145
Chicago Soybeans	68,236	68,245	256,547	20,907	27,743
Rosafe Soybean Index (ISR)	8,854	11,217	8,606	6,844	5,614
US Dollar (DLR)	45,348	72,365	32,639	142,305	2,540
Oil Crude	1,687	2,130			
Merval Srock Index	16,074	9,877	300		
ROFEX 20 Index	8,892				
Gold	9,363	426	14,512	8,280	
Total Options	**217,969**	**186,632**	**332,765**	**194,257**	**51,102**

SGX ASIACLEAR, Singapore

	2018	2017	2016	2015	2014
Coking Coal	117,895	144,701	8,450	5,210	4,210
Electricity (Monthly)	2,424	207			
Electricity Futures	7,043	2,537	1,889	933	
Energy Futures	4,709	8,035	12,119	38,430	31,715
LNG Gas	2,060	440	15		
Petrochemicals Futures	9,927	8,720	3,050		
Thermal Coal	48,700			3,820	850
Iron Ore 62%	10,473,351	12,804,720	11,787,611	6,039,555	2,049,821
Iron Ore 65%	19,070				
Iron Ore Lump Premium Futures	202,905	133,575	33,740	23,480	
Forward Freight Agreement	702,220	445,943	412,631	182,399	4,166
Total Futures	**11,590,304**	**13,548,878**	**12,260,112**	**6,299,405**	**2,730,965**
Coking Coal	4,900	4,400			
OTC Iron Ore	2,441,426	2,958,407	3,147,236	1,294,444	33,890
OTC Iron Ore Swap	700	7,201	76,314	266,722	188,977
OTC Forward Freight Agreements on Futures	141,490	47,075	135,904	45,975	
Total Options	**2,588,516**	**3,017,083**	**3,359,454**	**1,622,066**	**231,622**

Shanghai Metal Exchange, China

	2018	2017	2016	2015	2014
Rubber	61,845,475	89,341,052	97,371,256	83,067,547	88,631,586
Woodpulp	8,975,314				
Bitumen	69,802,079	97,440,530	186,814,247	32,397,823	650,169
Fuel Oil	39,268,835	1,432	2,922	3,875	1,469
Aluminum	46,618,361	65,423,439	44,391,785	22,900,691	13,926,276
Copper	51,247,050	54,100,135	72,394,915	88,318,558	70,510,306
Hot Rolled Coil	86,816,386	103,131,555	43,281,751	2,012,366	1,255,424
Lead	10,203,832	12,509,166	4,561,200	1,310,106	1,457,822
Nickel	114,818,738	74,154,526	100,249,941	63,590,118	
Steel Rebar	530,976,610	702,019,499	934,148,409	541,035,860	408,078,103
Tin	2,741,587	2,083,571	3,168,348	515,789	
Wire Rod	157,334	98	61	327	665
Zinc	92,348,782	91,449,266	73,065,922	45,237,435	40,429,347
Gold	16,123,891	19,478,090	34,759,523	25,317,200	23,865,406
Silver	42,250,568	53,111,169	86,501,561	144,786,451	193,487,650
Total Futures	**1,174,194,842**	**1,364,243,528**	**1,680,711,841**	**1,050,494,146**	**842,294,223**
Copper	1,193,828				
Total Options	**1,193,828**				

Singapore Exchange (SGX), Singapore

	2018	2017	2016	2015	2014
SICOM RSS3 Rubber	62,285	68,422	64,034	61,233	35,490
SICOM TSR20 Rubber	1,749,307	1,407,000	1,349,662	593,620	454,300
AUD/JPY	19	10	135	305	8,342
AUD/USD	3	14	838	192	3,781
CNY/USD	3,481	5,985	6,729	3,976	1,370
EUR/CNH	7,220	2,862	450	60	
INR/USD	12,814,105	7,955,136	5,666,369	3,832,462	597,738
KRW/USD	139,698	64,011	32,698	30,120	4,742
MYR/USD	1,245	401			
SGD/CNH	310	78	65	50	
THB/USD	13				9
TWD/USD	970	25	5	5	
USD/CNH	5,338,643	1,902,105	514,057	247,065	29,824
USD/JPY (Standard)	3	4,151	1,162	321	2,022
USD/SGD	63,997	61,757	62,895	88,221	30,221
CNX Nifty Banks Index Futures	219,604	726,690	120,166		
CNX Nifty Index	21,378,076	21,186,591	21,273,910	21,434,975	18,356,984
FTSE China A50 Index	88,028,881	67,407,030	70,107,740	95,845,784	41,346,887
Mini Nikkei 225	620,795	244,305	3,642	8,168	5,709
MSCI Australia NTR Index	149,502				
MSCI China Index Futures	12,644	39,165	39,536		
MSCI China NTR Index	368,978	2,391			
MSCI Emerging Markets Asia NTR Index	610,842	16,448			
MSCI Emerging Markets Index	3,070	46			
MSCI Emerging Markets NTR Index	411				
MSCI India Index	1,870	120,964	192,813	491,130	2,488
MSCI India NTR Index	675,490	77,785			
MSCI Indonesia Index	317,921	249,296	289,231	285,954	251,331
MSCI Indonesia NTR Index	72,515	6,142			
MSCI Japan Index	616,224				
MSCI Japan NTR (JPY) Index	1,156,350				
MSCI Japan NTR Index	610,839				
MSCI Malaysia Index	230	506	5,422	1,601	
MSCI Malaysia NTR Index	34,366				
MSCI Philippines NTR Index	8,345				
MSCI PSE Philippines	117	406	1,141	259	85
MSCI Singapore Index Futures	10,232,425	10,012,785	7,664,389	4,207,914	3,167,077
MSCI Singapore NTR Index	2,136	40			
MSCI Taiwan Index	20,952,086	19,314,868	18,146,726	16,719,529	17,216,807
MSCI Taiwan NTR Index	697,469	31,521			
MSCI Thailand Index	651	332	993	3,936	4,298
MSCI Thailand NTR Index	37,894				
Nikkei 225	23,813,108	21,724,646	24,335,028	25,542,958	27,179,349
Nikkei Stock Average Dividend Point Index	56,270	90,946	102,048	93,792	115,374
Straits Times Index	322	1,093	734	295	148
USD Nikkei 225	175	1,016	3,318	3,674	394
All Futures on Individual Equities	390,005				
Mini Japanese Government Bond	521,185	548,951	607,675	703,059	702,718
Total Futures	**191,671,095**	**153,276,051**	**150,595,133**	**170,200,843**	**109,517,621**
USD_CNH FX	75	284	20		
MSCI Singapore Index	426,551	293,407	940	11,295	350
Nikkei 225 Index	51,955	19,543	5,967,910	5,474,250	7,744,469
SGX S&P CNX Nifty Index	11,059,024	8,218,454	189,795	246,677	144,204
Total Options	**11,537,605**	**8,532,938**	**6,207,384**	**5,750,550**	**7,918,130**

VOLUME - WORLDWIDE

Taiwan Futures Exchange, Taiwan

	2018	2017	2016	2015	2014
AUD/USD FX (XAF)	49,032				
EUR/USD FX (XEF)	77,987	94,290	33,214		
GBP/USD FX (XBF)	75,468				
USD/CHN FX (RHF)	66,743	67,793	99,204	106,938	
USD/CNT FX (RTF)	283,451	269,020	523,716	1,046,265	
USD/JPY FX (XJF)	71,851	102,815	36,309		
Brent Crude Oil (BRF)	27,118				
CNX Nifty 50 Futures (I5F)	72,218	56,727	12,280		
DJIA Index (UDF)	1,466,111	403,078			
ETF Futures	1,520,673	1,224,271	1,748,371	2,129,871	183,440
GreTai Securities Weighted Stock Index (GTF)	7,881	8,117	3,320	2,613	4,655
Mini Taiex Futures (MTX)	37,268,930	21,552,246	23,864,953	21,021,527	13,286,373
S&P 500 (SPF)	125,444	38,658			
Taiex (TX)	46,946,307	34,014,500	34,534,902	33,059,533	24,759,873
Taiwan 50 Futures (T5F)	12,052	4,112	233	261	134
Taiwan Stock Exch NonFin/NonElec SubIndx (XIF)	96,311	78,376	110,869	138,726	139,097
Taiwan Stock Exchange Electronic Sector Index Futures	992,544	792,372	889,791	1,221,577	1,227,119
Taiwan Stock Exchange Finance Sector Index Futures	539,434	673,890	862,330	1,060,748	1,086,554
TOPIX Futures (TJF)	88,285	176,841	316,578	17,393	
All Futures on Individual Equities	22,812,494	18,763,068	9,954,514	12,189,434	9,325,030
Gold Futures (GDF)	20,396	12,933	10,131	2	1
NT Dollar Gold (TGF)	110,513	75,442	101,744	58,014	45,069
Total Futures	**112,731,243**	**78,408,549**	**73,102,459**	**72,052,902**	**50,057,345**
USD/CNH FX (RHO)	16,193	15,128	9,822		
USD/CNT FX (RTO)	118,833	123,562	140,488		
ETF Options (ETC)	153,669	165,967	330,369	8,626	
Taiex (TXO)	194,438,947	186,410,859	167,342,279	191,513,144	151,620,546
Taiwan Stock Exchange Electronic Sector Index Options	229,985	180,453	155,433	297,571	238,646
Taiwan Stock Exchange Finance Sector Index Options	139,980	145,482	234,487	379,912	330,969
All Options on Individual Equities	209,341	215,425	289,101	169,589	110,454
NTD-denominated Gold (TGO)	45,385	40,075	73,749	73,579	52,022
Total Options	**195,352,333**	**187,297,120**	**168,576,097**	**192,442,758**	**152,353,748**

Tel-Aviv Stock Exchange (TASE), Israel

	2018	2017	2016	2015	2014
TA-25 Index	3,659	12,457	18,644	17,398	52,945
Total Futures	**3,659**	**12,457**	**22,104**	**30,033**	**57,496**
Shekel-Dollar Rate	13,771,524	13,120,123	12,708,033	15,674,801	12,685,813
Shekel-Euro Rate Options	588,438	394,679	428,333	1,002,216	1,120,409
TA-Banks Index	70,240	107,668	123,258	133,909	130,167
TA-100 index	125,492	97,451	80,109	41,939	
TA-25 Index	32,902,984	32,183,095	37,745,708	47,646,434	48,264,048
All Options on Individual Equities	644,761	725,658	990,111	1,525,235	1,794,563
Total Options	**48,103,439**	**46,628,674**	**52,075,552**	**66,024,534**	**63,995,000**

Tokyo Commodity Exchange (TOCOM), Japan

	2018	2017	2016	2015	2014
Corn	170,754	266,411	385,035	469,557	423,597
Red Beans	11,154	14,313	19,594	21,355	20,823
Rubber	1,681,524	2,136,254	2,366,213	2,411,306	2,440,391
Rubber (TSR20)	126,785				
Soybeans	4,772	45,190	123,439	159,602	147,071
Chukyo Gasoline	11,300	12,281	10,159	15,070	22,214
Chukyo Kerosene	5,285	7,779	5,744	8,150	9,705
Crude Oil	4,537,185	5,286,870	5,963,788	3,651,528	840,192
Gas Oil (Barge Delivered)	4,025	4,845			
Gas Oil (Lorry Delivered)	4,029	4,842			
Gasoline	730,665	647,470	992,868	1,685,518	1,869,868
Gasoline (Barge Delivered)	3,999	4,945			
Gasoline (Lorry Delivered)	4,008	5,062			
Kerosene	186,753	228,833	237,165	418,314	689,541
Kerosene (Barge Delivered)	3,958	4,897			
Kerosene (Lorry Delivered)	4,032	4,852			
Gold	8,090,879	6,397,872	8,541,329	7,927,825	8,744,990
Gold (Daily Futures)	2,834,674	3,545,698	3,830,446	2,075,048	
Gold Mini	787,036	752,050	1,224,290	1,269,045	1,414,905
Gold Physical Transaction	281	304	130		
Palladium	37,731	32,745	31,621	62,574	76,823
Platinum	2,811,442	2,755,776	2,890,485	3,853,480	4,593,224
Platinum (Rolling Spot)	1,384,105	1,818,007			
Platinum Mini	141,473	157,623	233,847	307,921	418,695
Silver	19,918	22,426	61,136	62,575	85,963
Total Futures	**23,597,767**	**24,157,345**	**26,917,289**	**24,399,068**	**21,856,063**

Thailand Futures Exchange, Thailand

	2018	2017	2016	2015	2014
Rubber	34,482	10,613	250		
US Dollar	685,847	346,890	204,470	271,754	309,926
SET50	42,544,040	26,321,073	32,192,984	26,764,395	14,403,574
All Futures on Individual Equities	55,332,444	47,480,762	33,826,624	19,708,113	19,624,561
10 Baht Gold	4,102,613	3,500,669	2,721,773	1,328,932	1,303,151
50 Baht Gold	165,400	191,116	182,177	132,604	238,544
Gold (100 Grams)	106,443	57,770			
Gold Online	88,411				
Total Futures	**103,059,680**	**77,908,893**	**69,147,354**	**48,231,768**	**35,912,295**
SET 50	1,362,520	1,081,681	428,810	307,131	108,855
Total Options	**1,362,520**	**1,081,681**	**428,810**	**307,131**	**108,855**

Tokyo International Financial Futures Exchange (TIFFE), Japan

	2018	2017	2016	2015	2014
Australian Dollar/Japanese Yen	2,872,116	2,013,196	5,330,221	4,572,137	5,478,496
Australian Dollar/Japanese Yen (Large)	2,744	5,682	59,938	2,828	
Australian Dollar/US Dollar	224,403	355,991	486,770	563,014	500,322
British Pound/Australian Dollar	90,171	110,176	202,394	148,347	150,456
British Pound/Japanese Yen	2,477,581	2,135,877	5,023,899	2,291,868	2,522,602
British Pound/Japanese Yen (Large)	2,550	8,301	19,839	829	
British Pound/Swiss Franc	23,341	29,228	33,290	22,186	25,563
British Pound/US Dollar	470,655	658,807	1,078,624	212,126	193,658
Canadian Dollar/Japanese Yen	188,629	244,116	351,540	273,991	271,873
Euro/Australian Dollar	131,382	114,358	305,297	255,196	297,823
Euro/British Pound	71,368	75,466	241,636	73,122	46,566
Euro/Japanese Yen	1,787,220	1,700,235	2,365,744	3,348,524	2,968,883
Euro/Japanese Yen (Large)	9,190	6,335	18,816	1,721	
Euro/Swiss Franc	21,565	45,366	28,369	58,628	19,213
Euro/US Dollar	1,017,450	1,213,754	2,244,455	3,056,292	752,951
Euro/US Dollar (Large)	39,347	3,527	5,103	1,541	
Hong Kong Dollar/Japanese Yen	26,778	47,349	93,112	36,030	33,123
Mexican Peso/Japanese Yen	1,726,944	136,401			
New Zealand Dollar/Japanese Yen	1,081,621	1,057,673	2,026,071	2,467,301	1,878,175
New Zealand Dollar/US Dollar	92,851	142,729	213,060	249,845	205,664
Norway Krone/Japanese Yen	36,510	77,431	46,274	86,261	51,076
Polish Zloty/Japanese Yen	139,930	261,339	292,385	346,273	794,226
South African Rand/Japanese Yen	4,475,626	4,156,809	3,859,663	4,031,856	3,746,597
Sweden Krona/Japanese Yen	22,858	58,552	18,396	36,832	29,463
Swiss Franc/Japanese Yen	200,746	163,086	285,508	353,886	140,575
Turkish Lira /Japanese Yen	6,109,747	3,529,833	3,679,657	3,074,957	
US Dollar/Japanese Yen	8,363,218	10,478,227	14,992,697	12,919,505	12,550,958
US Dollar/Canadian Dollar	44,536	86,180	138,148	108,986	58,245
US Dollar/Japanese Yen (Large)	118,431	32,827	56,820	4,135	
US Dollar/Swiss Franc	40,733	46,742	95,729	88,915	30,212
DAX Margin	79,616	155,430	92,311	291,958	204,069
DJIA Margin	1,055,650	1,874,728	601,241		
FTSE 100 Margin	97,404	185,022	89,560	166,485	173,047
Nikkei 225 Margin	4,266,773	5,722,311	5,203,500	7,840,578	5,065,037
3 Month Euroyen	1,423,666	1,545,861	2,506,430	2,000,289	2,708,318
Total Futures	**38,833,350**	**38,478,945**	**52,086,497**	**48,986,442**	**40,900,423**

LSE Derivatives Market, London

(Formerly Turquoise Derivatives, EDX)	2018	2017	2016	2015	2014
BIST 30 Index	40	84			
OBX Index	1,526,904	1,350,031	1,450,377	1,193,117	1,100,864
IOB DR Futures on Individual Equities	826,154	738,970	186,258	111,916	923,860
3 Month Euribor	1,395,988	927,158	123,564		
3 Month SONIA	556,728				
3 Month Sterling	1,361,762	807,333	112,348		
Bobl	2,202	7,060	3,644		
Bund	4,882	8,403	3,908		
Long Gilt	2	866	774		
Schatz	492	19,871	8,284		
Total Futures	**5,675,154**	**4,033,786**	**2,305,245**	**1,510,566**	**2,080,134**
OBX Index	301,286	263,986	300,307	274,064	351,897
IOB DR Options on Individual Equities	3,129,672	2,920,238	942,459	1,237,534	7,646,176
Norwegian Options on Individual Equities	762,590	1,169,118	1,481,934	1,483,813	1,366,368
Total Options	**4,193,548**	**4,353,595**	**2,735,897**	**2,995,911**	**9,365,361**

VOLUME - WORLDWIDE

Warsaw Stock Exchange, Poland

	2018	2017	2016	2015	2014
CHFPLN	51,837	50,816	76,536	170,108	64,268
EURPLN	237,052	112,502	234,512	254,653	174,644
GBPPLN	28,666	34,916	3,392		
USDPLN	1,726,908	878,169	944,883	1,742,842	2,016,605
WIG20 Index	4,448,485	4,507,035	4,681,125	4,443,040	6,038,355
WIG40 Index	81,417	75,908	112,556	120,650	120,803
All Futures on Individual Equities	1,296,270	1,651,089	1,537,581	1,033,300	580,185
1 Month WIBOR	8	5	204	43	276
3 Month WIBOR	17	820	2,809	1,675	2,699
6 Month WIBOR	3	3			1,208
Long Term Bond	42	4,862	3,971	222	809
Total Futures	**7,870,705**	**7,318,662**	**7,597,905**	**7,766,891**	**9,001,819**
WIG20 Index	292,949	304,494	377,232	438,206	479,020
Total Options	**292,949**	**304,494**	**377,232**	**438,206**	**479,020**

Zhengzhou Commodity Exchange (ZCE), China

	2018	2017	2016	2015	2014
Apple (AP)	99,956,445	793,933			
Common Wheat (PM)	301	82	173	1,175	1,203
Cotton No. 1 (CF)	58,533,251	26,068,232	80,530,129	22,613,311	31,782,665
Cotton Yarn (CY)	1,533,644	124,156			
Early Rice (RI)	38,199	1,037	2,000	3,571	332,910
Japonica Rice (JR)	12,608	261	342	99	10,005
Late Rice (LR)	537,759	202	334	1,063	52,116
Rapeseed (RS)	1,354	1,908	18,879	45,703	17,219
Rapeseed Meal (RM)	104,361,264	79,736,545	246,267,758	261,487,209	303,515,966
Rapeseed Oil (OI)	35,083,678	25,994,757	27,312,246	7,780,455	13,897,650
Strong Gluten Wheat (WH)	107,031	377,494	500,078	460,729	1,025,946
White Sugar (SR)	64,004,805	61,073,198	117,293,884	187,323,456	97,726,662
Thermal Coal (ZC)	48,874,599	30,708,183	50,299,868	980,710	
Ferrosilicon	21,563,209	16,278,210	659,485	39,406	767,619
Silicon Manganese	18,856,010	24,921,207	1,364,525	50,439	361,462
Flat Glass (FG)	25,143,634	41,091,381	67,648,313	41,548,298	78,725,549
Methanol (MA)	163,897,244	137,007,280	136,739,016	314,357,813	14,048,540
PTA (TA)	170,871,552	140,399,689	172,659,870	231,578,021	117,865,244
Total Futures	**813,376,587**	**584,577,755**	**901,297,047**	**1,070,335,606**	**676,343,283**
White Sugar (SR)	4,593,395	1,492,393			
Total Options	**4,593,395**	**1,492,393**			

Total Worldwide Volume

	2018	2017	2016	2015	2014
Total Futures	**12,898,485,328**	**11,185,997,625**	**12,311,059,489**	**11,256,808,142**	**8,960,128,044**
Percent Change	4.77%	-0.63%	37.40%	24.49%	-20.40%
Total Options	**6,937,074,526**	**5,222,802,081**	**4,409,177,613**	**5,422,420,397**	**4,726,786,633**
Percent Change	57.33%	-3.68%	-6.72%	14.72%	-12.83%
Total Futures and Options	**19,835,559,854**	**16,408,799,706**	**16,720,237,102**	**16,679,228,539**	**13,686,914,677**
Percent Change	18.63%	-1.62%	22.16%	21.13%	-17.94%

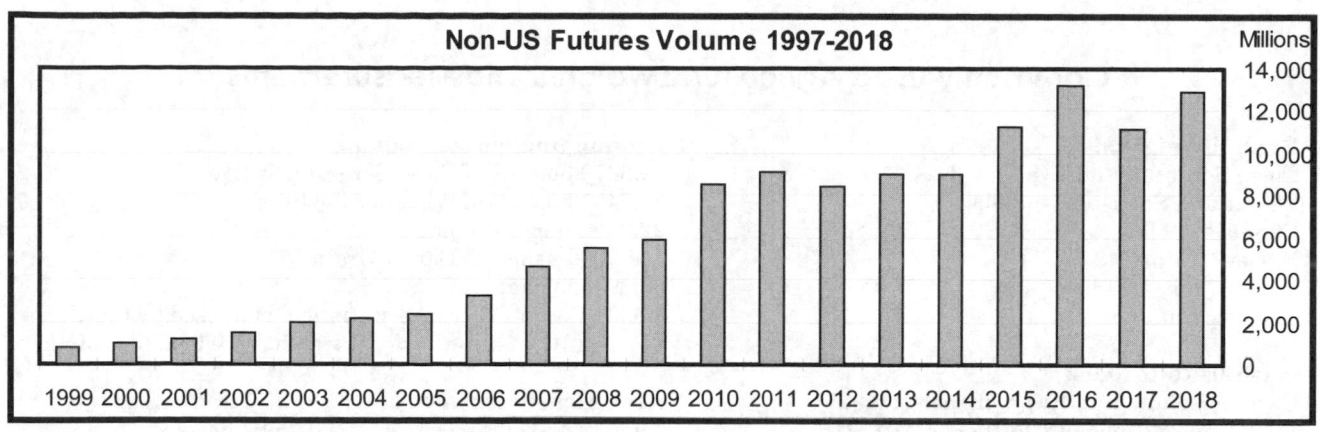

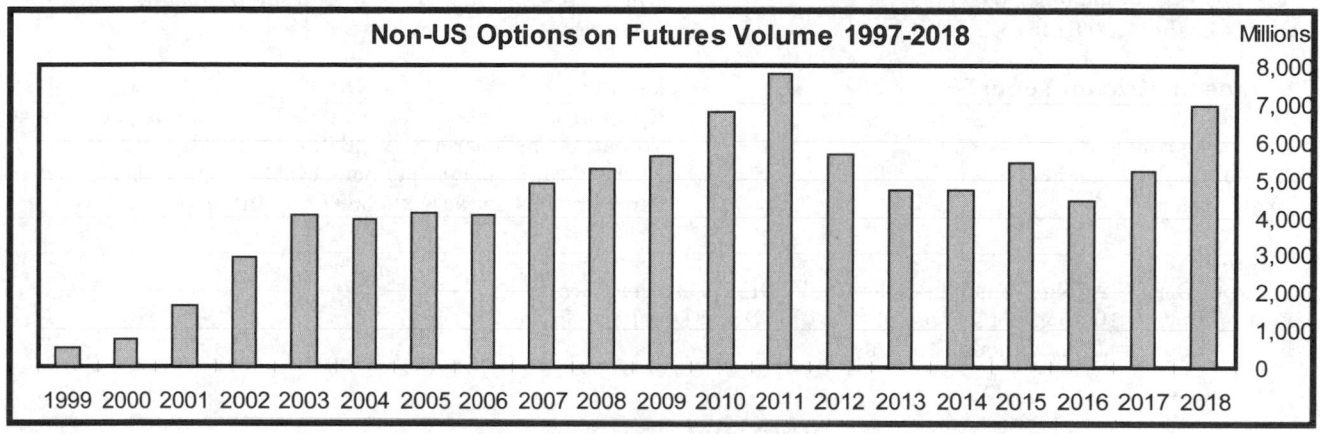

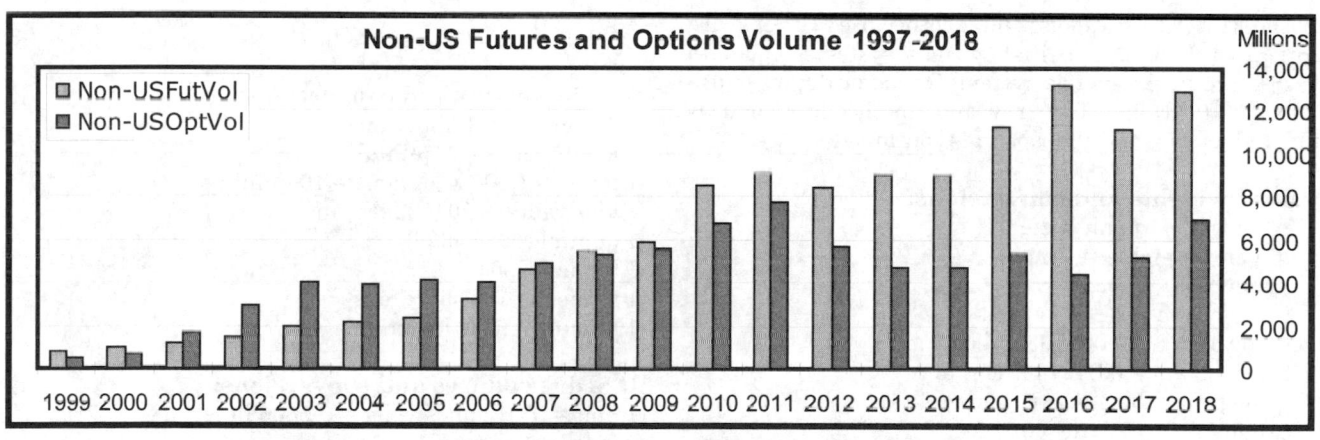

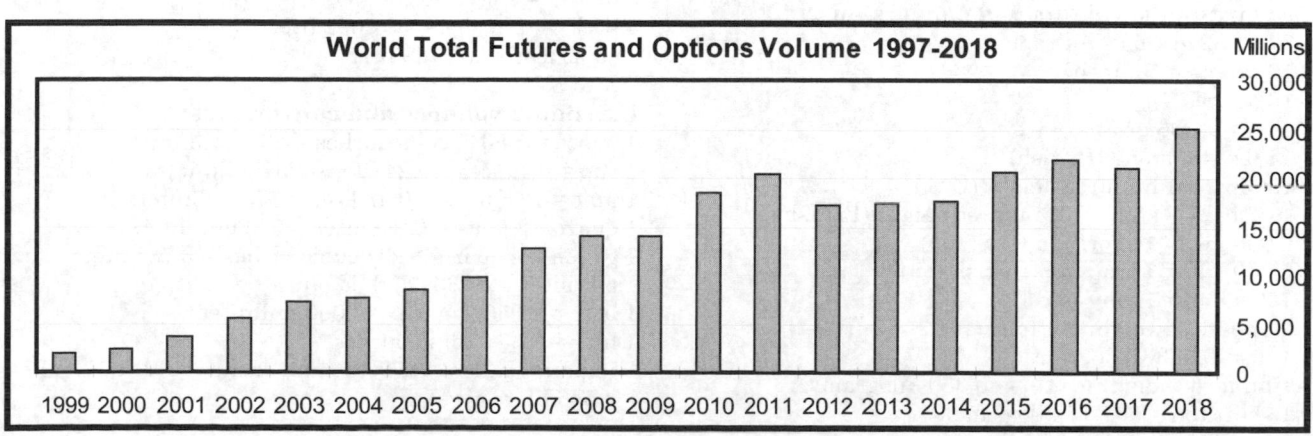

Conversion Factors

Commonly Used Agricultural Weights and Measurements

Bushel Weights:
Corn, Sorghum and Rye = 56 lbs.
Wheat and Soybeans = 60 lbs.
Canola = 50 lbs.
Barley Grain = 48 lbs.
Barley Malt = 34 lbs.
Oats = 32 lbs.

Bushels to tonnes:
Corn, Sorghum and Rye = bushels x 0.0254
Wheat and Soybeans = bushels x 0.027216
Barley Grain = bushels x 0.021772
Oats = bushels x 0.014515

1 tonne (metric ton) equals:
2204.622 lbs.
1,000 kilograms
22.046 hundredweight
10 quintals

Ethanol
1 bushel Corn = 2.75 gallons Ethanol = 18 lbs Dried Distillers Grain
1 tonne Corn = 101.0 gallons Ethanol = 661 lbs Dried Distillers Grain
1 tonne Sugar = 149.3 gallons Ethanol

1 tonne (metric ton) equals:
39.3679 bushels of Corn, Sorghum or Rye
36.7437 bushels of Wheat or Soybeans
22.046 hundredweight
45.9296 bushels of Barley Grain
68.8944 bushels of Oats
4.5929 Cotton bales (the statistical bale used by the USDA and ICAC contains a net weight of 480 pounds of lint)

Area Measurements:
1 acre = 43,560 square feet = 0.040694 hectare
1 hectare = 2.4710 acres = 10,000 square meters
640 acres = 1 square mile = 259 hectares

Yields:
Rye, Corn: bushels per acre x 0.6277 = quintals per hectare
Wheat: bushels per acre x 0.6725 = quintals per hectare
Barley Grain: bushels per acre x 0.538 = quintals per hectare
Oats: bushels per acre x 0.3587 = quintals per hectare

Commonly Used Weights

The troy, avoirdupois and apothecaries' grains are identical in U.S. and British weight systems, equal to 0.0648 gram in the metric system. One avoirdupois ounce equals 437.5 grains. The troy and apothecaries' ounces equal 480 grains, and their pounds contain 12 ounces.

Troy weights and conversions:
24 grains = 1 pennyweigh
20 pennyweights = 1 ounce
12 ounces = 1 pound
1 troy ounce = 31.103 grams
1 troy ounce = 0.0311033 kilogram
1 troy pound = 0.37224 kilogram
1 kilogram = 32.1507 troy ounces
1 tonne = 32,151 troy ounces

Avoirdupois weights and conversions:
27 11/32 grains = 1 dram
16 drams = 1 ounce
16 ounces = 1 lb.
1 lb. = 7,000 grains
14 lbs. = 1 stone (British)
100 lbs. = 1 hundredweight (U.S.)
112 lbs. = 8 stone = 1 hundredweight (British)
2,000 lbs. = 1 short ton (U.S. ton)
2,240 lbs. = 1 long ton (British ton)
160 stone = 1 long ton
20 hundredweight = 1 ton
1 lb. = 0.4536 kilogram
1 hundredweight (cwt.) = 45.359 kilograms
1 short ton = 907.18 kilograms
1 long ton = 1,016.05 kilograms

Metric weights and conversions:
1,000 grams = 1 kilogram
100 kilograms = 1 quintal
1 tonne = 1,000 kilograms = 10 quintals
1 kilogram = 2.204622 lbs.
1 quintal = 220.462 lbs.
1 tonne = 2204.6 lbs.
1 tonne = 1.102 short tons
1 tonne = 0.9842 long ton

U.S. dry volumes and conversions:
1 pint = 33.6 cubic inches = 0.5506 liter
2 pints = 1 quart = 1.1012 liters
8 quarts = 1 peck = 8.8098 liters
4 pecks = 1 bushel = 35.2391 liters
1 cubic foot = 28.3169 liters

U.S. liquid volumes and conversions:
1 ounce = 1.8047 cubic inches = 29.6 milliliters
1 cup = 8 ounces = 0.24 liter = 237 milliliters
1 pint = 16 ounces = 0.48 liter = 473 milliliters
1 quart = 2 pints = 0.946 liter = 946 milliliters
1 gallon = 4 quarts = 231 cubic inches = 3.785 liters
1 milliliter = 0.033815 fluid ounce
1 liter = 1.0567 quarts = 1,000 milliliters
1 liter = 33.815 fluid ounces
1 imperial gallon = 277.42 cubic inches = 1.2 U.S. gallons = 4.546 liters

Energy Conversion Factors

U.S. Crude OIl (average gravity)
1 U.S. barrel = 42 U.S. gallons
1 short ton = 6.65 barrels
1 tonne = 7.33 barrels

Barrels per tonne for various origins

Abu Dhabi	7.624
Algeria	7.661
Angola	7.206
Australia	7.775
Bahrain	7.335
Brunei	7.334
Canada	7.428
Dubai	7.295
Ecuador	7.580
Gabon	7.245
Indonesia	7.348
Iran	7.370
Iraq	7.453
Kuwait	7.261
Libya	7.615
Mexico	7.104
Neutral Zone	6.825
Nigeria	7.410
Norway	7.444
Oman	7.390
Qatar	7.573
Romania	7.453
Saudi Arabia	7.338
Trinidad	6.989
Tunisia	7.709
United Arab Emirates	7.522
United Kingdom	7.279
United States	7.418
Former Soviet Union	7.350
Venezuela	7.005
Zaire	7.206

Barrels per tonne of refined products:

aviation gasoline	8.90
motor gasoline	8.50
kerosene	7.75
jet fuel	8.00
distillate, including diesel	7.46

(continued above)

residual fuel oil	6.45
lubricating oil	7.00
grease	6.30
white spirits	8.50
paraffin oil	7.14
paraffin wax	7.87
petrolatum	7.87
asphalt and road oil	6.06
petroleum coke	5.50
bitumen	6.06
LPG	11.6

Approximate heat content of refined products:
(Million Btu per barrel, 1 British thermal unit is the amount of heat required to raise the temperature of 1 pound of water 1 degree F.)

Petroleum Product	Heat Content
asphalt	6.636
aviation gasoline	5.048
butane	4.326
distillate fuel oil	5.825
ethane	3.082
isobutane	3.974
jet fuel, kerosene	5.670
jet fuel, naptha	5.355
kerosene	5.670
lubricants	6.065
motor gasoline	5.253
natural gasoline	4.620
pentanes plus	4.620

Petrochemical feedstocks:

naptha less than 401*F	5.248
other oils equal to or greater than 401*F	5.825
still gas	6.000
petroleum coke	6.024
plant condensate	5.418
propane	3.836
residual fuel oil	6.287
special napthas	5.248
unfinished oils	5.825
unfractionated steam	5.418
waxes	5.537

Source: U.S. Department of Energy

Natural Gas Conversions

Although there are approximately 1,031 Btu in a cubic foot of gas, for most applications, the following conversions are sufficient:

Cubic Feet			MMBtu		
1,000	(one thousand cubic feet)	=	1 Mcf	=	1
1,000,000	(one million cubic feet)	=	1 MMcf	=	1,000
10,000,000	(ten million cubic feet)	=	10 MMcf	=	10,000
1,000,000,000	(one billion cubic feet)	=	1 Bcf	=	1,000,000
1,000,000,000,000	(one trillion cubic feet)	=	1 Tcf	=	1,000,000,000

Acknowledgments

The editors wish to thank the following for source material:

Agricultural Marketing Service (AMS)

Agricultural Research Service (ARS)

American Bureau of Metal Statistics, Inc. (ABMS)

American Iron and Steel Institute (AISI)

American Metal Market (AMM)

Bureau of the Census

Bureau of Economic Analysis (BEA)

Bureau of Labor Statistics (BLS)

Chicago Board of Trade (CBT)

Chicago Mercantile Exchange (CME / IMM / IOM)

Commodity Credit Corporation (CCC)

Commodity Futures Trading Commision (CFTC)

The Conference Board

Economic Research Service (ERS)

Edison Electric Institute (EEI)

Farm Service Agency (FSA)

Federal Reserve Bank of St. Louis

Food and Agriculture Organization of the United Nations (FAO)

Foreign Agricultural Service (FAS)

Futures Industry Association (FIA)

ICE Futures U.S, Canada, Europe (ICE)

International Cotton Advisory Committee (ICAC)

International Cocoa Organization (ICCO)

Johnson Matthey

Kansas City Board of Trade (KCBT)

Leather Industries of America

Minneapolis Grain Exchange (MGEX)

National Agricultural Statistics Service (NASS)

New York Mercantile Exchange (NYMEX)

Oil World

The Organisation for Economic Co-Operation and Development (OECD)

The Silver Institute

The Society of the Plastics Industry, Inc. (SPI)

United Nations (UN)

United States Department of Agriculture (USDA)

Wall Street Journal (WSJ)

Aluminum

Aluminum (atomic symbol Al) is a silvery, lightweight metal that is the most abundant metallic element in the earth's crust. Aluminum was first isolated in 1825 by a Danish chemist, Hans Christian Oersted, using a chemical process involving a potassium amalgam. A German chemist, Friedrich Woehler, improved Oersted's process by using metallic potassium in 1827. He was the first to show aluminum's lightness. In France, Henri Sainte-Claire Deville isolated the metal by reducing aluminum chloride with sodium and established a large-scale experimental plant in 1854. He displayed pure aluminum at the Paris Exposition of 1855. In 1886, Charles Martin Hall in the U.S. and Paul L.T. Heroult in France simultaneously discovered the first practical method for producing aluminum through electrolytic reduction, which is still the primary method of aluminum production today.

By volume, aluminum weighs less than a third as much as steel. This high strength-to-weight ratio makes aluminum a good choice for construction of aircraft, railroad cars, and automobiles. Aluminum is used in cooking utensils and the pistons of internal-combustion engines because of its high heat conductivity. Aluminum foil, siding, and storm windows make excellent insulators. Because it absorbs relatively few neutrons, aluminum is used in low-temperature nuclear reactors. Aluminum is also useful in boat hulls and various marine devices due to its resistance to corrosion in salt water.

Futures and options on Primary Aluminum and Aluminum Alloy are traded on the London Metal Exchange (LME). Aluminum futures are traded on the Multi Commodity Exchange of India, and the Shanghai Futures Exchange (SHFE). The London Metals Exchange aluminum futures contracts are priced in terms of dollars were metric tons.

Supply – World production of aluminum in 2018 rose by +1.0% yr/yr to a new record high of 60.0 million metric tons. The world's largest producers of aluminum are China with 55.0% of world production in 2018, Russia with 6.2%, Canada with 4.8%, Australia with 2.7%, and the U.S. with 1.5%. U.S. production of primary aluminum in 2018 rose 20.1% yr/yr to 890 thousand metric tons.

Demand – U.S. consumption of aluminum in 2018 fell -13.6% yr/yr to 4.900 million metric tons, up from the 3-decade low of 3.320 million metric tons in 2009.

Trade – U.S. exports in 2017 fell -0.4% yr/yr to 2.800 million metric tons, below the 2012 record high of 3.480 million metric tons. U.S. imports of aluminum in 2017 rose +16.8% yr/yr to 7.030 million metric tons which is a new record high. The U.S. was a net importer in 2017 and relied on imports for 59% of its consumption.

World Production of Primary Aluminum   In Thousands of Metric Tons

Year	Australia	Brazil	Canada	China	France	Germany	Norway	Russia	Spain	United Kingdom	United States	Vene-zuela	World Total
2009	1,943	1,536	3,030	12,900	345	292	1,139	3,815	360	253	1,727	561	37,200
2010	1,928	1,536	2,963	16,200	356	402	1,543	3,947	340	186	1,726	335	41,800
2011	1,945	1,440	2,988	20,000	334	432	1,389	3,993	365	213	1,986	380	46,800
2012	1,860	1,436	2,781	23,500	349	410	1,145	4,024	230	60	2,070	208	49,300
2013	1,777	1,304	2,967	26,500	346	492	1,155	3,601	235	44	1,946	186	52,200
2014	1,703	962	2,858	28,300	360	531	1,250	3,300	350	42	1,710	138	54,200
2015	1,646	772	2,880	31,400	420	541	1,225	3,530	350	47	1,587	119	58,100
2016	1,634	793	3,209	31,873	425	575	1,220	3,561	350	48	818	140	58,900
2017[1]	1,450	801	3,210	32,300			1,230	3,580			741		59,400
2018[2]	1,600	660	2,900	33,000			1,300	3,700			890		60,000

[1] Preliminary.   [2] Estimate.   Source: U.S. Geological Survey (USGS)

Production of Primary Aluminum (Domestic and Foreign Ores) in the U.S.   In Thousands of Metric Tons

Year	Jan.	Feb.	Mar.	Apr.	May	June	July	Aug.	Sept.	Oct.	Nov.	Dec.	U.S. Total
2009	193	149	154	145	147	132	135	133	129	137	133	140	1,727
2010	142	130	146	142	148	141	146	146	143	148	144	148	1,726
2011	152	140	162	162	170	167	171	172	169	175	171	177	1,986
2012	178	167	179	174	179	173	177	171	164	170	166	171	2,070
2013	171	155	172	167	171	165	168	163	157	154	149	154	1,946
2014	153	139	153	143	147	140	143	143	136	137	134	141	1,710
2015	142	130	143	138	142	133	134	135	128	128	121	113	1,587
2016	106	96	77	63	64	62	64	62	61	62	61	63	841
2017	62	56	63	60	64	61	63	63	60	63	61	64	741
2018[1]	66	61	71	71	73	63	68	76	76	84	88	95	892

[1] Preliminary.   Source: U.S. Geological Survey (USGS)

ALUMINUM

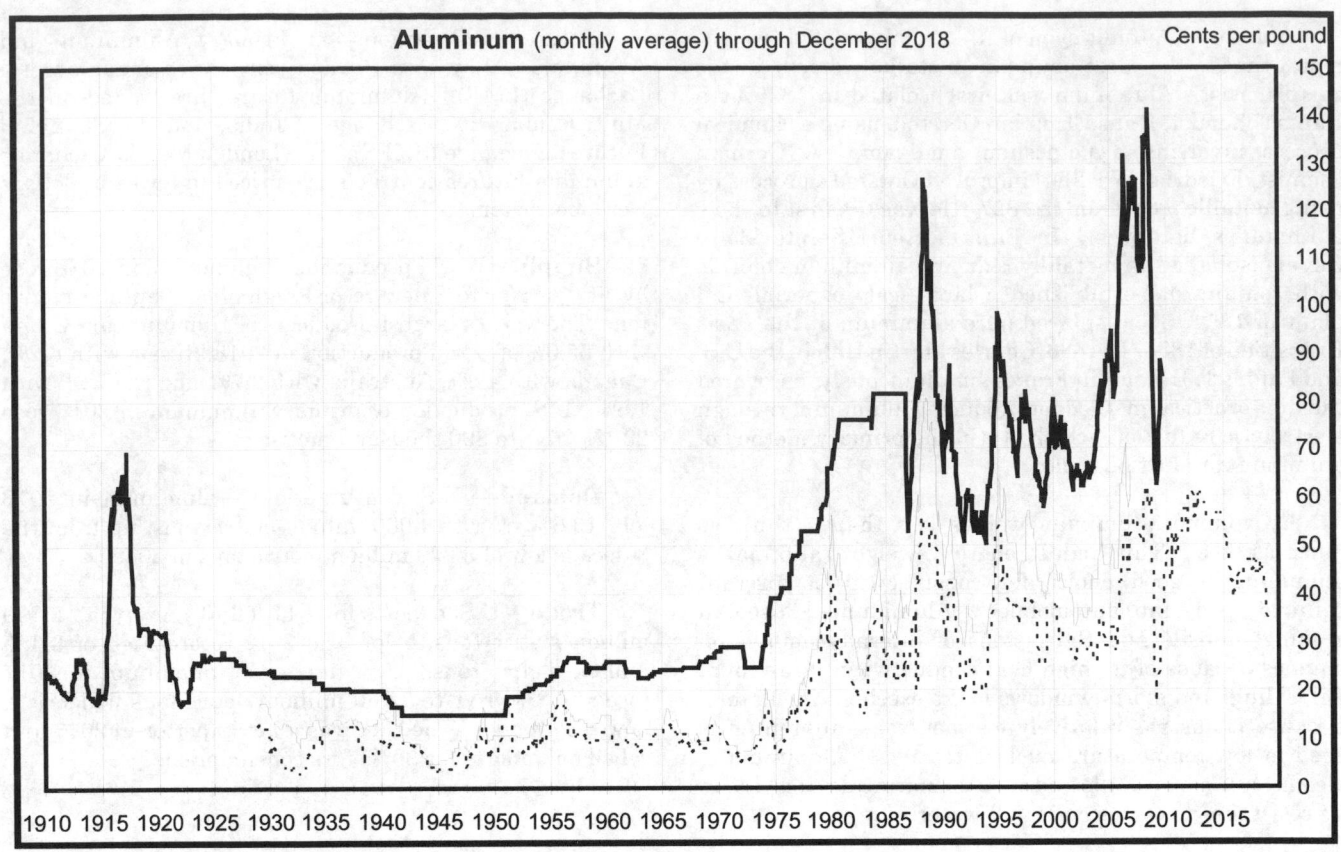

Aluminum (monthly average) through December 2018 — Cents per pound

Salient Statistics of Aluminum in the United States   In Thousands of Metric Tons

Year	Net Import Reliance as a % of Apparent Consump	Production Primary	Production Secondary	Primary Shipments	Recovery from Scrap Old	Recovery from Scrap New	Apparent Consumption	Plate, Sheet, Foil	Rolled Structural Shapes[3]	Extruded Shapes[4]	All	Permanent Mold	Die	Sand	All	Total All Net Shipments
2009	10	1,727	2,820	6,810	1,260	1,570	3,320	4,050	632	1,070	5,752	377	691	160	1,230	6,982
2010	14	1,726	2,790	7,720	1,250	1,540	3,460	4,450	703	1,530	6,683	475	949	147	1,580	8,263
2011	3	1,986	3,110	8,520	1,440	1,670	3,570	4,000	537	1,700	6,237	494	1,010	178	1,690	7,927
2012	11	2,070	3,380	9,670	1,630	1,760	3,950	4,770	915	2,130	7,815	589	1,110	127	1,860	9,675
2013	21	1,946	3,410	9,920	1,630	1,790	4,520	4,830	914	1,950	7,694	604	1,240	132	2,000	9,694
2014	33	1,710	3,230	9,960	1,690	1,870	5,070	5,020	887	2,100	8,007	563	1,330	214	2,120	10,127
2015	41	1,587	3,010	10,400	1,560	2,000	5,300	5,220	859	2,220	8,299	526	1,470	295	2,300	10,599
2016	53	818	2,820	10,600	1,570	2,010	5,090	5,400	890	2,250	8,540	550	1,500	300	2,360	10,900
2017	59	741			1,590	2,050	5,670									
2018[1]	50	890			1,600	2,100	4,900									

[1] Preliminary.   [2] To domestic industry.   [3] Also rod, bar & wire.   [4] Also rod, bar, tube, blooms & tubing.   [5] Consists of total shipments less shipments to other mills for further fabrication.   *Source: U.S. Geological Survey (USGS)*

Supply and Distribution of Aluminum in the United States   In Thousands of Metric Tons

Year	Apparent Consumption	Production Primary	Production From Old Scrap	Imports	Exports	Inventories December 31 Private	Inventories December 31 Government[3]	Year	Apparent Consumption	Production Primary	Production From Old Scrap	Imports	Exports	Inventories December 31 Private	Inventories December 31 Government[3]
2007	5,170	2,554	1,660	4,020	2,840	1,400	----	2013	4,520	1,946	1,630	4,725	3,390	1,130	----
2008	3,940	2,658	1,500	3,710	3,280	1,220	----	2014	5,070	1,710	1,690	4,849	3,240	1,280	----
2009	3,320	1,727	1,260	3,680	2,710	937	----	2015	5,300	1,587	1,560	5,081	3,010	1,350	----
2010	3,460	1,726	1,250	3,610	3,040	1,010	----	2016	5,090	818	1,570	6,019	2,810	1,400	----
2011	3,570	1,986	1,440	3,710	3,420	1,060	----	2017[1]	5,670	741	1,590	7,030	2,800	1,360	----
2012	3,950	2,070	1,630	4,349	3,480	1,140	----	2018[2]	4,900	890	1,600				----

[1] Preliminary.   [2] Estimate.   [3] National Defense Stockpile.   *Source: U.S. Geological Survey (USGS)*

Aluminum Products Distribution of End-Use Shipments in the United States   In Thousands of Metric Tons

Year	Containers & Packaging	Building & Construction	Trans-portation	Electrical	Consumer Durables	Machinery & Equipment	Other Markets	Total to Domestic Users	Exports	U.S. Total
2007	2,230	1,410	3,580	762	664	736	359	9,730	1,450	11,200
2008	2,240	1,180	2,830	700	607	688	334	8,570	1,490	10,100
2009	2,150	964	1,910	593	458	475	254	6,810	1,280	8,090
2010	2,200	1,030	2,390	668	547	564	318	7,720	1,460	9,180
2011	2,160	1,110	2,820	798	631	682	322	8,520	1,700	10,200
2012	2,110	1,180	3,220	861	672	696	343	9,080	1,690	10,800
2013	2,090	1,310	3,430	867	700	726	332	9,450	1,720	11,200
2014	2,090	1,390	3,810	807	748	768	343	9,960	1,620	11,600
2015	2,130	1,420	4,180	798	741	767	327	10,400	1,320	11,700
2016[1]	2,100	1,500	4,300	800	750	770	330	10,600	1,000	11,600

[1] Preliminary.   Source: U.S. Geological Survey (USGS)

Salient Statistics of Recycling Aluminum in the United States

Year	Percent Recycled	New Scrap[1]	Old Scrap[2]	Recycled Metal[3]	Apparent Supply	New Scrap[1]	Old Scrap[2]	Recycled Metal[3]	Apparent Supply
		In Metric Tons				Value in Thousands of Dollars			
2007	2,450,000	1,660,000	4,120,000	7,320,000	56.0	6,610,000	4,480,000	11,100,000	19,700,000
2008	2,130,000	1,500,000	3,630,000	6,070,000	60.0	5,660,000	3,970,000	9,640,000	16,100,000
2009	1,570,000	1,260,000	2,820,000	4,890,000	58.0	2,740,000	2,200,000	4,940,000	8,550,000
2010	1,540,000	1,250,000	2,790,000	5,000,000	56.0	3,550,000	2,880,000	6,430,000	11,500,000
2011	1,670,000	1,440,000	3,110,000	5,210,000	60.0	4,280,000	3,690,000	7,970,000	13,300,000
2012	1,750,000	1,620,000	3,380,000	5,880,000	57.0	3,900,000	3,620,000	7,510,000	13,100,000
2013	1,790,000	1,630,000	3,410,000	6,310,000	54.0	3,710,000	3,380,000	7,090,000	13,100,000
2014	1,870,000	1,690,000	3,570,000	6,940,000	51.0	4,310,000	3,900,000	8,210,000	16,000,000
2015	2,000,000	1,560,000	3,560,000	7,310,000	49.0	3,900,000	3,030,000	6,920,000	14,200,000
2016	2,010,000	1,580,000	3,580,000	7,100,000	50.0	3,560,000	2,790,000	6,350,000	12,600,000

[1] Scrap that results from the manufacturing process.   [2] Scrap that results from consumer products.   [3] Metal recovered from new plus old scrap.
Source: U.S. Geological Survey (USGS)

Producer Prices for Aluminum Used Beverage Can Scrap   In Cents Per Pound

Year	Jan.	Feb.	Mar.	Apr.	May	June	July	Aug.	Sept.	Oct.	Nov.	Dec.	Average
2009	43.70	41.42	41.91	44.00	46.80	50.64	54.27	61.62	58.00	61.43	64.42	71.16	53.28
2010	73.95	68.05	75.48	78.77	69.10	65.77	67.43	72.45	74.76	82.57	79.38	82.26	74.16
2011	86.78	89.11	90.98	96.08	94.72	94.05	90.95	86.54	83.69	78.07	75.25	73.18	86.62
2012	77.30	79.83	79.87	75.67	74.27	69.76	70.81	70.35	77.82	75.72	74.83	80.09	75.49
2013	79.03	79.19	75.69	76.25	75.18	73.08	71.02	72.27	68.95	69.74	68.16	68.76	73.11
2014	73.24	76.75	77.52	82.43	79.62	80.41	83.80	85.33	85.93	85.92	91.17	88.64	82.56
2015	83.85	81.13	75.14	71.00	61.70	56.09	57.86	58.00	60.24	59.30	56.84	59.89	65.09
2016	60.63	61.60	59.87	60.71	59.90	60.36	61.30	61.52	60.02	63.00	67.15	67.81	61.99
2017	70.30	72.37	73.35	71.55	68.27	67.23	67.05	70.98	73.12	74.09	72.88	69.95	70.93
2018	75.57	75.66	75.59	81.81	84.41	85.29	77.40	73.37	65.87	63.50	59.35	58.12	73.00

Source: American Metal Market (AMM)

Average Price of Cast Aluminum Scrap (Crank Cases) in Chicago[1]   In Cents Per Pound

Year	Jan.	Feb.	Mar.	Apr.	May	June	July	Aug.	Sept.	Oct.	Nov.	Dec.	Average
2009	17.50	17.50	22.27	22.50	22.50	22.50	24.55	27.50	37.50	37.50	37.50	42.24	27.63
2010	45.39	47.50	48.80	55.23	51.50	43.41	42.50	47.27	47.50	51.31	52.50	47.50	48.37
2011	48.75	52.50	52.50	52.50	52.50	52.50	56.00	57.50	56.93	54.50	54.70	52.45	53.61
2012	55.05	59.60	61.50	60.93	59.23	55.93	55.50	55.50	58.55	59.50	57.00	58.67	58.08
2013	60.50	60.45	59.50	59.00	58.50	58.35	55.50	56.00	55.90	55.54	55.55	54.50	57.44
2014	54.50	53.50	53.50	55.00	56.50	56.50	56.50	56.55	57.40	56.50	56.50	55.45	55.70
2015	53.40	52.50	51.32	50.50	51.00	46.50	46.41	43.88	42.45	41.41	38.97	38.64	46.42
2016	39.97	40.50	41.50	41.50	43.45	43.05	44.05	43.46	41.93	43.50	44.50	44.50	42.66
2017	45.60	45.97	46.93	47.00	45.95	44.95	44.50	44.65	46.50	46.50	45.95	44.00	45.71
2018	45.40	46.03	44.50	44.02	45.05	44.98	41.93	39.93	37.45	36.50	34.50	34.00	41.19

[1] Dealer buying prices.   Source: American Metal Market (AMM)

ALUMINUM

Aluminum Exports of Crude Metal and Alloys from the United States   In Thousands of Metric Tons

Year	Jan.	Feb.	Mar.	Apr.	May	June	July	Aug.	Sept.	Oct.	Nov.	Dec.	U.S. Total
2009	15.9	15.9	12.7	14.8	24.7	24.9	24.6	24.7	24.4	28.0	26.4	25.1	262.1
2010	20.2	22.0	22.4	16.8	20.5	25.6	22.8	24.5	35.2	24.4	26.0	23.5	283.9
2011	25.5	24.2	30.2	34.6	26.1	23.1	25.7	23.2	23.2	24.3	29.5	24.4	314.0
2012	30.8	29.5	32.0	29.9	31.0	30.6	31.6	32.2	24.3	24.3	33.0	24.5	353.7
2013	27.5	29.4	31.1	32.9	30.0	29.8	26.5	33.7	31.0	32.3	32.3	25.9	362.4
2014	31.1	25.6	30.5	30.7	33.0	31.0	28.7	31.5	30.0	33.7	26.9	28.2	360.9
2015	26.5	26.0	25.2	25.0	26.9	29.5	26.7	27.2	25.2	26.1	22.9	22.8	310.0
2016	25.7	24.5	25.3	22.1	22.7	18.7	19.4	20.1	23.6	21.7	21.2	17.1	262.1
2017	24.9	20.5	23.7	22.3	22.4	24.5	22.8	27.7	21.0	23.9	22.5	18.9	275.1
2018[1]	25.6	28.4	23.6	25.5	25.3	22.8	24.9	27.5	23.0	25.5	22.2	18.1	292.4

[1] Preliminary.   *Source: U.S. Geological Survey (USGS)*

Aluminum General Imports of Crude Metal and Alloys into the United States   In Thousands of Metric Tons

Year	Jan.	Feb.	Mar.	Apr.	May	June	July	Aug.	Sept.	Oct.	Nov.	Dec.	U.S. Total
2009	270.0	204.0	333.0	233.0	292.0	200.0	299.0	216.0	212.0	207.0	211.0	217.0	2,894.0
2010	238.0	209.0	230.0	257.0	233.0	232.0	223.0	207.0	224.0	203.0	209.0	179.0	2,644.0
2011	211.0	212.0	232.0	220.0	285.0	263.0	220.0	241.0	263.0	243.0	192.0	245.0	2,827.0
2012	281.0	284.0	248.0	231.0	293.0	240.0	233.0	234.0	214.0	204.0	196.0	244.0	2,902.0
2013	248.0	220.0	283.0	457.0	314.0	267.0	273.0	271.0	242.0	219.0	299.0	220.0	3,313.0
2014	253.0	221.0	439.0	291.0	290.0	294.0	237.0	270.0	253.0	271.0	213.0	270.0	3,302.0
2015	273.0	245.0	312.0	322.0	299.0	301.0	301.0	251.0	283.0	270.0	267.0	259.0	3,383.0
2016	362.0	270.0	385.0	350.0	336.0	401.0	346.0	345.0	349.0	316.0	392.0	381.0	4,233.0
2017	459.0	394.0	476.0	434.0	411.0	410.0	411.0	379.0	338.0	358.0	358.0	400.0	4,828.0
2018[1]	333.0	374.0	555.0	381.0	349.0	297.0	332.0	292.0	313.0	306.0	294.0	306.0	4,132.0

[1] Preliminary.   *Source: U.S. Geological Survey (USGS)*

Average Price of Aluminum (Cash) in London   In U.S. Dollars per Metric Ton

Year	Jan.	Feb.	Mar.	Apr.	May	June	July	Aug.	Sept.	Oct.	Nov.	Dec.	Average
2009	1,419.3	1,335.1	1,337.8	1,427.5	1,466.0	1,580.9	1,665.9	1,927.0	1,833.7	1,876.8	1,955.0	2,182.6	1,667.3
2010	2,230.7	2,052.7	2,208.0	2,319.5	2,043.2	1,926.5	1,988.7	2,115.6	2,163.9	2,347.1	2,328.6	2,353.3	2,173.1
2011	2,441.8	2,509.0	2,556.1	2,662.8	2,595.6	2,553.7	2,525.5	2,381.0	2,293.5	2,180.7	2,080.0	2,024.4	2,400.3
2012	2,151.4	2,207.9	2,184.2	2,048.5	2,002.6	1,885.5	1,876.3	1,842.1	2,064.1	1,974.4	1,948.9	2,086.8	2,022.7
2013	2,036.5	2,053.6	1,911.3	1,861.1	1,832.6	1,814.6	1,769.6	1,816.3	1,761.3	1,814.6	1,748.0	1,739.8	1,846.6
2014	1,727.4	1,695.2	1,705.4	1,810.7	1,751.1	1,839.0	1,948.3	2,030.5	1,990.4	1,946.2	2,055.6	1,909.5	1,867.4
2015	1,814.7	1,817.8	1,773.9	1,819.2	1,804.0	1,687.7	1,639.5	1,548.1	1,589.6	1,516.5	1,467.9	1,497.2	1,664.7
2016	1,481.1	1,531.3	1,531.0	1,571.2	1,550.6	1,593.5	1,629.1	1,639.3	1,592.4	1,665.9	1,737.1	1,727.7	1,604.2
2017	1,791.2	1,860.8	1,901.5	1,921.2	1,913.0	1,885.3	1,903.0	2,030.3	2,096.5	2,131.5	2,097.4	2,080.5	1,967.7
2018	2,209.7	2,182.4	2,070.8	2,254.7	2,299.7	2,237.6	2,082.2	2,051.5	2,026.5	2,029.9	1,938.5	1,920.4	2,108.7

Contract Size = 25 Metric Tons   *Source: London Metal Exchange (LME)*

Average Price of Aluminum (3-Month) in London   In U.S. Dollars per Metric Ton

Year	Jan.	Feb.	Mar.	Apr.	May	June	July	Aug.	Sept.	Oct.	Nov.	Dec.	Average
2009	1,456.4	1,373.5	1,373.2	1,465.6	1,502.0	1,608.4	1,698.9	1,957.6	1,868.8	1,911.6	1,988.3	2,211.6	1,701.3
2010	2,264.3	2,088.4	2,239.8	2,354.3	2,072.1	1,957.8	2,008.7	2,119.0	2,201.0	2,375.0	2,351.0	2,371.0	2,200.2
2011	2,458.4	2,539.2	2,586.4	2,689.4	2,591.9	2,584.3	2,554.8	2,414.2	2,327.7	2,207.7	2,098.4	2,034.6	2,423.9
2012	2,182.2	2,248.6	2,225.5	2,088.3	2,042.5	1,923.7	1,907.3	1,875.4	2,077.0	2,001.1	1,966.6	2,098.1	2,053.0
2013	2,073.3	2,094.8	1,950.5	1,893.3	1,864.5	1,854.9	1,814.3	1,863.4	1,808.0	1,860.5	1,793.5	1,784.6	1,888.0
2014	1,771.7	1,738.5	1,748.5	1,848.0	1,792.4	1,873.3	1,968.9	2,040.1	2,022.0	1,962.2	2,043.7	1,927.5	1,894.7
2015	1,827.3	1,835.0	1,781.7	1,809.7	1,836.8	1,726.6	1,680.2	1,576.4	1,605.3	1,541.0	1,482.0	1,497.9	1,683.3
2016	1,481.5	1,525.0	1,537.7	1,581.1	1,564.5	1,602.1	1,641.0	1,651.6	1,606.4	1,671.3	1,735.3	1,720.4	1,609.8
2017	1,786.8	1,870.7	1,912.3	1,933.4	1,917.1	1,892.1	1,921.1	2,036.7	2,122.6	2,150.6	2,114.8	2,096.7	1,979.6
2018	2,217.8	2,171.0	2,088.9	2,251.8	2,298.7	2,233.9	2,065.6	2,074.9	2,058.1	2,040.8	1,950.8	1,922.8	2,114.6

Contract Size = 25 Metric Tons   *Source: London Metal Exchange (LME)*

4

Antimony

Antimony (atomic symbol Sb) is a lustrous, extremely brittle and hard crystalline semi-metal that is silvery white in its most common allotropic form. Antimony is a poor conductor of heat and electricity. In nature, antimony has a strong affinity for sulfur and for such metals as lead, silver, and copper. Antimony is primarily a byproduct of the mining, smelting and refining of lead, silver, and copper ores. There is no longer any mine production of antimony in the U.S.

The most common use of antimony is in antimony trioxide, a chemical that is used as a flame retardant in textiles, plastics, adhesives and building materials. Antimony trioxide is also used in battery components, ceramics, bearings, chemicals, glass, and ammunition.

Prices – Antimony prices in 2018 fell -0.3% yr/yr to 377.34 cents per pound and remained well below the 2011 record high of 671.10 cents per pound. However, antimony prices are far above the over 3-decade low price of 66.05 cents per pound posted in 1999.

Supply – World mine production of antimony in 2018 rose +2.2% yr/yr to 140,000 metric tons, remaining below the 2008 & 2011 record high of 185,000 metric tons. China accounted for 71.4% of world antimony production in 2017. After China, the only significant producers were Russia and Tajikistan each with 10.0%, U.S. secondary production of antimony in 2017 fell -2.1% yr/yr to 3,700 metric tons.

Demand – U.S. industrial consumption of antimony in 2016 rose +9.7% yr/yr to 9,070 metric tons. Regarding consumption on antimony in the U.S. in 2016, 39% was used for metal product, 31% was used for flame-retardants, and 30.5% was used for non-metal products.

Trade –The total U.S. gross weight of imports of antimony ore in 2016 fell -61.4% yr/yr to 119 metric tons. The antimony content of the 2017 imported ore fell -16.0% yr/yr to 100 metric tons. The gross weight of U.S. imports of antimony oxide in 2017 fell -89.7% yr/yr to 2,400 metric tons. U.S. exports of antimony oxide in 2017 rose +12.8% yr/yr to 2,200 metric tons.

World Mine Production of Antimony (Content of Ore) In Metric Tons

Year	Australia	Bolivia	Canada	China	Kyrgyzstan	Russia	South Africa	Tajikistan	Turkey	World Total
2014	3,639	4,186	5	123,000	481	8,000	815	8,058	3,070	157,000
2015	3,712	3,843	1	111,000	500	8,000	400	8,000	1,950	143,000
2016	3,573	2,669	----	107,525	573	8,000	1,200	14,000	1,950	144,000
2017[1]	3,120	2,700	----	98,000	----	14,400	1,200	14,000	2,000	137,000
2018[2]	3,100	2,700		100,000		14,000		14,000	2,000	140,000

[1] Preliminary.   [2] Estimate.   [3] Less than 1/2 unit.   Source: U.S. Geological Survey (USGS)

Salient Statistics of Antimony in the United States   In Metric Tons

Year	Avg. Price Cents/lb. C.i.f. U.S. Ports	Primary[2] Mine	Primary[2] Smelter	Secondary (Alloys)[2]	Ore Gross Weight	Ore Antimony Content	Oxide (Gross Weight)	Exports (Oxide)	Metallic	Oxide	Sulfide	Other	Total
2015	326.51	----	W	3,850	473	308	22,500	3,200	198	751	----	340	1,290
2016	334.79	----	W	3,780	----	119	23,300	1,950	314	717	----	57	1,090
2017[1]	398.00	----	W	3,700	----	100	2,400	2,200				----	1,360
2018[2]	390.00	----	W		----							----	1,400

Column group headers: Production[3] (Primary[2], Secondary); Imports for Consumption (Ore: Gross Weight, Antimony Content; Oxide: Gross Weight); Industry Stocks, December 31[3]

[1] Preliminary.   [2] Estimate.   [3] Antimony content.   [4] Including primary antimony residues & slag.   W = Withheld proprietary data.
Source: U.S. Geological Survey (USGS)

Industrial Consumption of Primary Antimony in the United States   In Metric Tons (Antimony Content)

Year	Ammunition	Antimonial Lead[3]	Sheet & Pipe[4]	Bearing Metal & Bearings	Solder	Products	Flame Retardants Plastics	Flame Retardants Total	Ceramics & Glass	Pigments	Plastics	Total	Grand Total
2013	W	W	W	21	54	2,630	2,350	2,780	W	1,050	W	3,630	9,040
2014	W	W	W	18	46	2,440	2,440	2,820	W	877	W	3,260	8,520
2015	W	W	W	20	19	2,450	2,200	2,860	W	808	W	2,960	8,270
2016[1]	W	W	W	9	15	3,510	2,290	2,790	W	765	W	2,770	9,070

Column group headers: Metal Products; Non-Metal Products

[1] Preliminary.   [2] Estimated coverage based on 77% of the industry.   W = Withheld proprietary data.   Source: U.S. Geological Survey (USGS)

Average Price of Antimony[1] in the United States   In Cents Per Pound

Year	Jan.	Feb.	Mar.	Apr.	May	June	July	Aug.	Sept.	Oct.	Nov.	Dec.	Average
2015	368.32	354.52	378.08	397.36	400.64	374.53	334.38	313.63	288.95	278.34	252.23	232.62	331.13
2016	242.57	245.61	240.88	265.03	291.54	292.83	312.49	325.01	348.96	345.92	338.39	335.61	298.74
2017	343.19	358.05	393.84	406.65	408.04	397.31	364.01	379.44	384.42	370.76	366.18	370.33	378.52
2018	373.63	388.62	394.60	382.37	373.58	373.25	362.83	375.06	388.05	382.06	371.23	362.88	377.34

[1] Prices are for antimony metal (99.65%) merchants, minimum 18-ton containers, c.i.f. U.S. Ports.   Source: American Metal Market (AMM)

Apples

The apple tree is the common name of trees from the rose family, Rosaceae, and the fruit that comes from them. The apple tree is a deciduous plant and grows mainly in the temperate areas of the world. The apple tree is believed to have originated in the Caspian and Black Sea area. Apples were the favorite fruit of the ancient Greeks and Romans. The early settlers brought apple seeds with them and introduced them to America. John Champman, also known as Johnny Appleseed, was responsible for extensive planting of apple trees in the Midwestern United States.

Prices – The average monthly price of apples received by growers in the U.S. in 2018 fell by -12.7% yr/yr to 35.20 cents per pound.

Supply – World apple production in the 2018/19 marketing year fell -7.5% yr/yr to 68.645 million metric tons. The world's largest apple producers in 2018/19 were China (with 45.2% of world production), the European Union (20.4%), the U.S. (7.4%), and Turkey (4.4%). U.S. apple production in 2018/19 fell -0.6% to 5.048 million metric tons and remained far above the 2-decade low of 3.798 million metric tons posted in 2002-03.

Demand – The utilization breakdown of the 2017 apple crop showed that 67.6% of apples were for fresh consumption, 11.9% for juice and cider, 10.2% for canning, 3.2% for dried apples and 1.0% for frozen apples. U.S. per capita apple consumption in 2017 was 18.5 pounds.

World Production of Apples[3], Fresh (Dessert & Cooking)   In Thousands of Metric Tons

Year	Argen-tina	Brazil	Chile	China	European Union	India	Japan	Russia	South Africa	Turkey	Ukraine	United States	World Total
2011-12	860	1,341	1,360	33,670	12,338	2,203	794	1,124	813	2,700	1,127	4,231	68,804
2012-13	860	1,232	1,420	35,810	12,207	1,915	742	1,264	908	2,900	1,211	4,049	70,411
2013-14	630	1,379	1,310	36,300	11,865	2,498	816	1,417	793	2,930	1,085	4,690	71,621
2014-15	650	1,265	1,210	37,350	13,636	2,498	812	1,409	920	2,289	1,180	5,067	74,091
2015-16	600	1,049	1,335	38,900	12,453	2,520	765	1,311	924	2,740	1,099	4,521	74,459
2016-17	560	1,049	1,310	40,393	12,723	2,258	765	1,509	902	2,900	1,099	4,957	76,677
2017-18[1]	520	1,049	1,300	41,390	10,014	1,920	765	1,360	814	2,750	1,099	5,018	74,230
2018-19[2]	530	1,049	1,250	31,000	14,009	2,300	765	1,503	850	3,000	1,099	5,048	68,645

[1] Preliminary.   [2] Estimate.   Source: Foreign Agricultural Service, U.S. Department of Agriculture (FAS-USDA)

Salient Statistics of Apples[2] in the United States

	Production		Growers Prices		Utilization of Quantities Sold							Avg. Fram Price Cents/ lb.	Foreign Trade[4] Domestic				Fresh Per Capita Con-sump-tion
								Processed[5]								Imports Fresh	
Year	Total	Utilized	Fresh Cents/ lb.	Pro-cessing $/ton	Fresh	Canned	Dried	Frozen	Juice & Cider	Other[3]			Farm Value Million $	Exports Fresh	Dried[5] & Dried[5]		Lbs.
					Millions of Pounds								Million $	Metric Tons			
2010	9,282	9,205	32.6	187.0	6,249	1,088	176	206	1,266	74	25.1	2,313.6	748.1	22.1	225.7	16.2
2011	9,440	9,329	39.4	226.0	6,313	1,124	184	191	1,208	71	30.3	2,823.4	817.9	26.8	184.5	15.3
2012	8,992	8,927	45.3	281.0	6,595	749	223	67	1,112	53	37.1	3,315.0	856.8	28.5	219.3	15.4
2013	10,432	10,340	40.5	197.0	6,895	1,264	161	239	1,520	72	30.3	3,132.9	908.8	22.3	243.1	16.0
2014	11,814	11,171	32.7	178.0	7,882	1,135	171	251	1,480	60	25.7	2,870.7	848.7	23.7	243.9	17.3
2015	10,046	9,966	44.1	201.0	6,896	1,110	179	188	1,329	187	33.6	3,350.1	1,057.9	26.1	209.5	18.6
2016	11,378	10,928	40.5	215.0	7,680	1,215	339	138	1,286	136	31.7	3,460.0	747.3	28.0	233.6	17.4
2017[1]	11,406	11,062	40.6	248.0	7,714	1,166	370	119	1,354	176	32.1	3,549.7	868.2		171.2	18.5

[1] Preliminary.   [2] Commercial crop.   [3] Mostly crushed for vinegar, jam, etc.   [4] Year beginning July.   [5] Fresh weight basis.
Source: Economic Research Service, U.S. Department of Agriculture (ERS-USDA)

Price of Apples Received by Growers (for Fresh Use) in the United States   In Cents Per Pound

Year	Jan.	Feb.	Mar.	Apr.	May	June	July	Aug.	Sept.	Oct.	Nov.	Dec.	Average
2011	30.0	28.0	28.2	26.6	25.6	26.3	35.8	45.8	42.1	43.1	34.4	30.2	33.0
2012	32.0	30.6	33.2	30.0	30.0	38.4	41.9	49.3	58.7	52.2	51.9	45.4	41.1
2013	43.8	41.6	39.5	NQ	NQ	NQ	NQ	NQ	NQ	NQ	NQ	NQ	41.6
2014	NQ	NQ	NQ	39.2	37.2	34.4	33.2	38.8	46.9	40.2	35.8	31.8	37.5
2015	31.6	29.2	27.8	25.9	24.3	20.7	19.0	30.3	44.3	41.6	40.1	44.7	31.6
2016	44.7	44.7	45.9	45.1	39.1	38.0	40.6	46.1	53.0	45.2	39.9	39.6	43.5
2017	39.7	36.9	35.8	35.3	36.0	36.3	37.0	42.6	59.1	45.9	39.9	39.7	40.4
2018[1]	37.5	35.2	33.7	32.6	29.7	28.9	31.1	29.7	46.7	41.6	40.4	41.4	35.7

[1] Preliminary.   NQ = No quote.   Source: Economic Research Service, U.S. Department of Agriculture (ERS-USDA)

Arsenic

Arsenic (atomic symbol As) is a silver-gray, extremely poisonous, semi-metallic element. Arsenic, which is odorless and flavorless, has been known since ancient times, but it wasn't until the Middle Ages that its poisonous characteristics first became known. Metallic arsenic was first produced in the 17th century by heating arsenic with potash and soap. Arsenic is rarely found in nature in its elemental form and is generally recovered as a by-product of ore processing. Recently, small doses of arsenic have been found to put some forms of cancer into remission. It can also help thin blood. Homoeopathists have successfully used undetectable amounts of arsenic to cure stomach cramps.

The U.S. does not produce any arsenic and instead imports all its consumption needs for arsenic metals and compounds. More than 95 percent of the arsenic consumed in the U.S. is in compound form, mostly as arsenic trioxide, which in turn is converted into arsenic acid. Production of chromated copper arsenate, a wood preservative, accounts for about 90% of the domestic consumption of arsenic trioxide. Three companies in the U.S. manufacture chromate copper arsenate. Another company used arsenic acid to produce an arsenical herbicide. Arsenic metal is used to produce nonferrous alloys, primarily for lead-acid batteries.

One area where there is increased consumption of arsenic is in the semiconductor industry. Very high-purity arsenic is used in the production of gallium arsenide. High-speed and high-frequency integrated circuits that use gallium arsenide have better signal reception and lower power consumption. An estimated 30 metric tons per year of high-purity arsenic is used in the production of semiconductor materials.

In the early 2000's, as much as 88% of U.S. arsenic production was used for wood preservative treatments, so the demand for arsenic was closely tied to new home construction, home renovation, and deck construction. However, the total demand for arsenic in 2004 dropped by 69% from 2003, and due to arsenic's toxicity and tighter environmental regulation; only 65% of that much smaller amount was used for wood preservative treatments. Since then the specific percentage used for wood preservative treatments is no longer available.

Supply – World production of white arsenic (arsenic trioxide) in 2018 rose +1.2% yr/yr to 35,000 metric tons. The world's largest producer is China with 68.6% of world production, followed by Morocco with 17.1%, Namibia with 5.4%, Russia with 4.3%, and Belgium with 2.9%. China's production of arsenic was at its high around 2002 at about 40,000 metric tons per year but that has since dropped to about 25,000 in the last fifteen years or so. The U.S. supply of arsenic in 2018 fell -20.1% yr/yr to 5,530 metric tons.

Demand – U.S. demand for arsenic in 2018 fell 20.5% to 5,500 metric tons. Data on the use for arsenic is no longer available but in 2004 about 65% was for wood preservatives, 10% was for non-ferrous alloys and electric usage, 10% was for glass, and 3% was for other uses.

Trade – U.S. imports of trioxide arsenic in 2016 fell by -10.4% yr/yr to 7,000 metric tons, above the 2010 record low of 5,920 metric tons. U.S. exports of trioxide arsenic in 2018 fell -91.4% yr/yr to 60.0 metric tons, well below the record high of 3,270 metric tons in 2005.

World Production of White Arsenic (Arsenic Trioxide)   In Metric Tons

Year	Belgium	Bolivia	Chile	China	Japan	Mexico	Morocco	Peru	Morocco	Peru	Portugal	Russia	World Total
2011	1,000	99	11,000	25,000	45	----	8,154	1,750	----	1,500	37,600	1,500	60,900
2012	1,000	104	10,000	26,000	45	----	8,820	1,590	----	1,500	39,100	1,500	53,900
2013	1,000	120	10,000	25,000	45	----	8,968	1,520	----	1,500	38,200	1,500	50,500
2014	1,000	52	10,000	25,000	45	----	6,860	1,980	----	1,500	36,400	1,500	47,000
2015	1,000	50	----	25,000	45	----	6,900	1,960	----	1,500	36,500	1,500	52,400
2016	1,000	40	----	25,000	45	----	7,600	1,900	----	1,500	37,000	1,500	45,800
2017[1]	1,000	40	----	24,000	45	----	6,000	1,900	----	1,500	34,600	1,500	46,700
2018[3]	1,000	40	----	24,000	45	----	6,000	1,900	----	1,500	35,000	1,500	45,000

[1] Preliminary. [2] Estimate. [3] Output of Tsumeb Corp. Ltd. only. [4] Includes low-grade dusts that were exported to the U.S. for further refining.
Source: U.S. Geological Survey (USGS)

Salient Statistics of Arsenic in the United States   (In Metric Tons -- Arsenic Content)

	-------- Supply --------			--- Distribution ---		------ Estimated Demand Pattern ------						- Average Price -			
	---- Imports ----		Industry		Industry	Agricultural		Wood	Non-Ferrous			Trioxide	Metal		
Year	Metal	Compounds	Stocks Jan. 1	Total	Apparent Demand	Stocks Dec. 31	Chemicals	Glass	Preservatives	Alloys & Electric	Other	Total	Mexican Cents/Pound	Chinese	Imports Trioxide[3]	Exports
2011	628	4,990	----	5,618	5,620	----	----	----	----	----	----	5,620	----	74	6,570	705
2012	883	5,720	----	6,603	6,620	----	----	----	----	----	----	6,620	----	75	7,550	444
2013	514	6,290	----	6,804	6,810	----	----	----	----	----	----	6,810	----	72	8,310	1,630
2014	688	5,260	----	5,948	5,940	----	----	----	----	----	----	5,940	----	75	6,940	2,970
2015	514	5,920	----	6,434	6,430	----	----	----	----	----	----	6,430	----	84	7,810	1,670
2016	793	5,320	----	6,113	6,120	----	----	----	----	----	----	6,120	----	88	7,000	1,760
2017[1]	942	5,980	----	6,922	6,920	----	----	----	----	----	----	6,920	----			698
2018[2]	630	4,900	----	5,530	5,500	----	----	----	----	----	----	5,500	----			60

[1] Preliminary. [2] Estimate. [3] For Consumption.   *Source: U.S. Geological Survey (USGS)*

Barley

Barley is the common name for the genus of cereal grass and is native to Asia and Ethiopia. Barley is an ancient crop and was grown by the Egyptians, Greek, Romans and Chinese. Barley is now the world's fourth largest grain crop, after wheat, rice, and corn. Barley is planted in the spring in most of Europe, Canada and the United States. The U.S. barley crop year begins June 1. It is planted in the autumn in parts of California, Arizona and along the Mediterranean Sea. Barley is hardy and drought resistant and can be grown on marginal cropland. Salt-resistant strains are being developed for use in coastal regions. Barley grain, along with hay, straw, and several by-products are used for animal feed. Barley is used for malt beverages and in cooking. Barley, like other cereals, contains a large proportion of carbohydrate (67%) and protein (12.8%).

Barley futures are traded on the ASX 24 exchange and the National Commodity & Derivatives Exchange (NCDEX).

Prices – The monthly average price for all barley received by U.S. farmers in the 2018/19 marketing year rose by +1.4% yr/yr to $4.53 per bushel.

Supply – World barley production in the 2018/19 marketing year is forecasted to fall by -2.3% yr/yr to 140.724 million metric tons. The world's largest barley crop of 179.038 million metric tons occurred in 1990-91. The world's largest barley producers in 2018/19 are expected to be the European Union with 40.5% of world production, Russia with 11.7%, Canada with 6.0%, Ukraine with 5.4%, Turkey with 5.3%, and Australia with 5.2%.

U.S. barley production in the 2018/19 marketing year is expected to rise by +7.9% yr/yr to 153.082 million bushels but that is still only a quarter of the record U.S. barley crop of 608.532 million bushels seen in 1986-87. U.S. farmers are expected to harvest +1.2% yr/yr more acres in 2018/19 at 1.978 million acres. Barley yield in 2018/19 is expected to rise +6.6% yr/yr to 77.4 bushels per acre, which is not far down from the record high yield of 77.9 in 2016/17. Ending stocks for the 2017/18 marketing year fell -11.2% to 94.4 million bushels.

Demand – U.S. total barley disappearance in 2018/19 is expected to fall -21.4% yr/yr to 179.0 million bushels. About 97% of barley is used for food and alcoholic beverages, less than 3% for seed, and less than 1% for animal feed.

Trade – World exports of barley in 2018/19 are expected to fall -2.8% yr/yr to 27.364 million metric tons. The largest world exporters of barley in 2018/19 are expected to be Australia with 19.7% of the world exports, European Union with 19.0%, Russia with 17.2%, and Ukraine with 16.4%. The largest importers of barley in 2018/19 are expected to be China with 9.2 million metric tons (34% of total world imports) and Saudi Arabia with 8.0 million metric tons (24% of total world imports).

World Production of Barley   In Thousands of Metric Tons

Year	Argentina	Australia	Canada	Ethiopia	European Union	Iran	Kazakhstan	Morocco	Russia	Turkey	Ukraine	United States	World Total
2009-10	1,356	7,865	9,528	1,750	62,393	3,446	2,519	3,786	17,881	6,500	11,833	4,934	151,020
2010-11	2,950	7,995	7,627	1,703	53,691	3,290	1,313	2,566	8,350	5,900	8,484	3,924	122,710
2011-12	4,500	8,221	7,892	1,592	51,883	2,530	2,593	2,318	16,938	7,000	9,098	3,370	133,021
2012-13	5,000	7,472	8,012	1,782	54,875	2,770	1,500	1,201	13,952	5,500	6,935	4,768	129,217
2013-14	4,750	9,174	10,282	1,908	59,674	3,000	2,539	2,723	15,389	7,300	7,561	4,719	144,577
2014-15	2,900	8,646	7,117	1,953	60,609	3,200	2,412	1,638	20,026	4,000	9,450	3,953	141,984
2015-16	4,940	8,993	8,257	2,047	62,095	3,200	2,675	3,400	17,083	7,400	8,751	4,750	149,775
2016-17	3,300	13,506	8,839	2,025	59,866	3,000	3,231	620	17,547	4,750	9,874	4,353	147,055
2017-18[1]	3,740	8,900	7,891	2,100	58,837	3,100	3,305	2,000	20,183	6,400	8,695	3,090	144,013
2018-19[2]	4,000	7,300	8,400	2,170	56,950	3,100	4,200	2,910	16,500	7,400	7,600	3,333	140,724

[1] Preliminary.   [2] Estimate.   *Source: Foreign Agricultural Service, U.S. Department of Agriculture (FAS-USDA)*

World Exports of Barley   In Thousands of Metric Tons

Year	Argentina	Australia	Canada	Ethiopia	European Union	Iran	Kazakhstan	Morocco	Russia	Turkey	Ukraine	United States	World Total
2009-10	482	3,915	1,309	1,123	51	358	2,657	21	781	6,232	123	----	17,140
2010-11	1,614	4,664	1,207	4,873	11	233	267	11	23	2,794	165	----	15,916
2011-12	3,616	5,377	1,299	3,008	46	704	3,544	9	103	2,463	193	----	20,394
2012-13	3,581	4,484	1,432	4,966	267	164	2,237	17	----	2,134	193	107	19,630
2013-14	2,891	6,217	1,561	5,741	441	416	2,709	28	6	2,476	311	34	22,856
2014-15	1,552	5,219	1,517	9,547	431	483	5,336	21	9	4,456	311	43	29,016
2015-16	3,077	5,745	1,195	10,834	81	804	4,241	54	----	4,412	235	42	30,818
2016-17	2,556	9,190	1,546	5,667	1	682	2,951	26	14	5,354	95	114	28,323
2017-18[1]	2,600	5,725	2,021	5,899	1	1,400	5,873	50	20	4,300	111	5	28,145
2018-19[2]	2,800	5,400	2,200	5,200	50	2,000	4,700	80	100	4,500	109	150	27,364

[1] Preliminary.   [2] Estimate.   *Source: Foreign Agricultural Service, U.S. Department of Agriculture (FAS-USDA)*

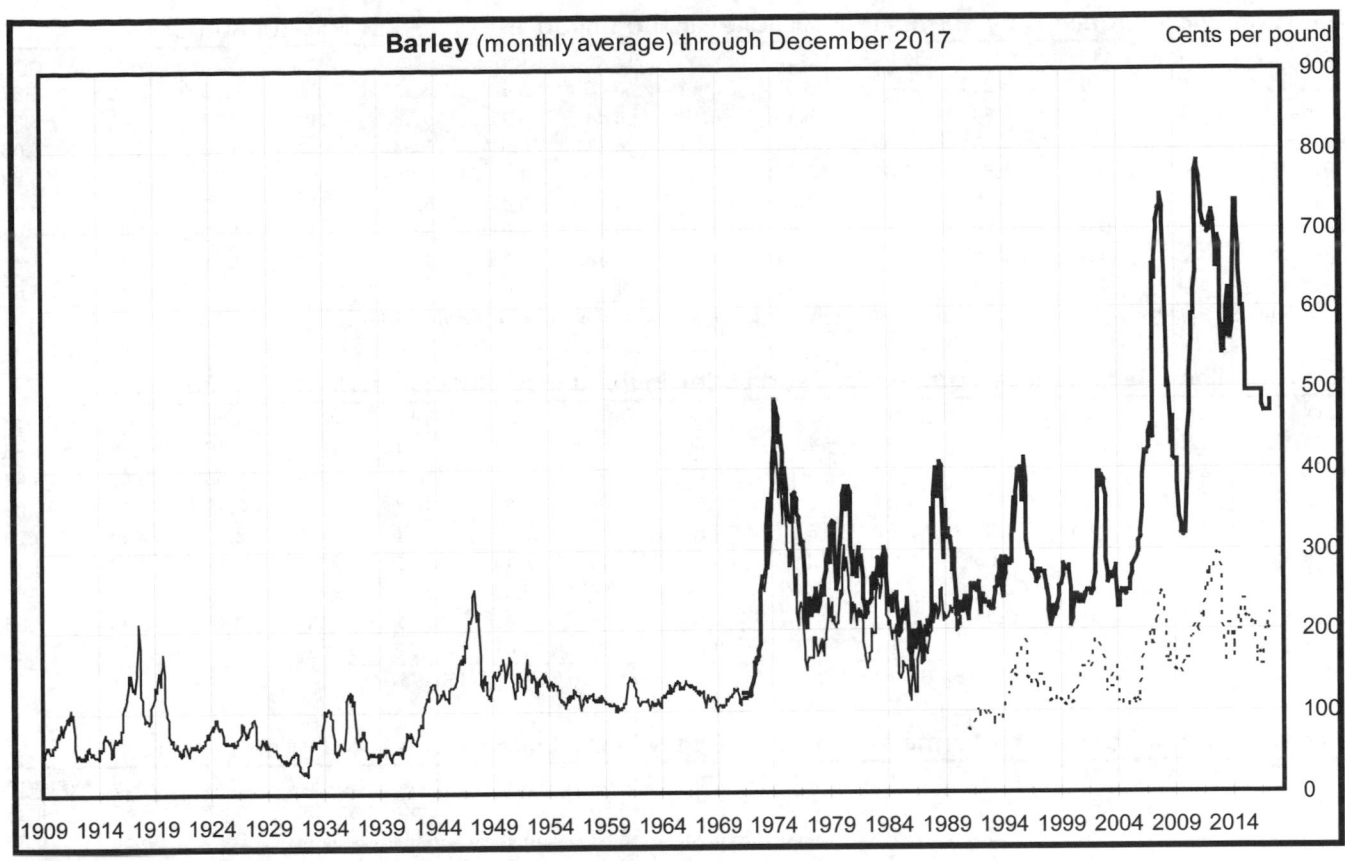

Barley (monthly average) through December 2017 — Cents per pound

Barley Acreage and Prices in the United States

Crop Year Beginning June 1	Acreage 1,000 Acres Planted	Acreage 1,000 Acres Harvested for Grain	Yield Per Harvested Acre -- Bushels --	Seasonal Prices — Received by Farmers[3] All	Seasonal Prices Feed[4]	Seasonal Prices Malting[4] Dollars per Bushel	Portland No. 2 Western	Government Price Support Operations National Average Loan Rate	Target Price	Put Under Support (mil. Bu.)	Percent of Production
2011-12	2,559	2,239	69.1	5.37	4.88	5.46	----	1.95	2.63	2.8	1.8
2012-13	3,660	3,274	66.9	6.36	5.62	6.50	----	1.95	2.63	3.1	1.4
2013-14	3,528	3,040	71.3	6.06	4.22	6.49	----	1.95	2.63	4.2	1.9
2014-15	3,031	2,497	72.7	5.22	3.20	5.77	----	1.95	4.95	3.9	2.1
2015-16	3,623	3,158	69.1	5.46	3.11	5.78	----	1.95	4.95	8.3	3.9
2016-17	3,059	2,565	77.9	4.97	2.73	5.26	----	1.95	4.95	9.3	4.9
2017-18[1]	2,486	1,962	73.0	4.47	3.00	4.67	----				
2018-19[2]	2,543	1,978	77.4	4.56	3.25	4.74	----				

[1] Preliminary.   [2] Estimate.   [3] Excludes support payments.   *Source: Economic Research Service, U.S. Department of Agriculture (ERS-USDA)*

Salient Statistics of Barley in the United States   In Millions of Bushels

Crop Year Beginning June 1	Supply Beginning Stocks	Supply Production	Supply Imports	Supply Total Supply	Disappearance / Domestic Use Food & Alcohol Beverage	Seed	Feed & Residual	Total	Exports	Total Disappearance	Ending Stocks Gov't Owned	Ending Stocks Privately Owned	Ending Stocks Total Stocks
2011-12	89.4	155.8	16.3	260.4	149.0	6.0	36.6	191.6	8.8	200.4	----	60.0	60.0
2012-13	60.0	219.0	23.3	302.3	141.0	5.8	66.2	213.0	8.9	221.9	----	80.4	80.4
2013-14	80.4	216.7	18.7	315.9	148.3	5.1	65.9	219.4	14.3	233.6	----	82.3	82.3
2014-15	82.3	181.5	23.6	287.4	154.3	5.9	34.4	194.5	14.3	208.8	----	78.6	78.6
2015-16	78.6	218.2	18.6	315.3	153.1	5.2	44.2	202.4	10.8	213.2	----	102.1	102.1
2016-17	102.1	199.9	9.6	311.7	158.2	4.2	38.5	200.9	4.4	205.3	----	106.4	106.4
2017-18[1]	106.4	143.3	9.1	257.4	153.0	4.3	0.6	157.8	5.1	162.9	----	94.5	94.5
2018-19[2]	94.5	153.1	10.0	257.6	150.5	4.5	15.0	170.0	5.0	175.0	----	87.6	

[1] Preliminary.   [2] Estimate.   [3] Uncommitted inventory.   [4] Includes quantity under loan & farmer-owned reserve.   [5] Included in Food & Alcohol.
Source: Economic Research Service, U.S. Department of Agriculture (ERS-USDA)

BARLEY

Average Price Received by Farmers for All Barley in the United States   In Dollars Per Bushel

Year	June	July	Aug.	Sept.	Oct.	Nov.	Dec.	Jan.	Feb.	Mar.	Apr.	May	Average
2011-12	4.65	5.07	5.27	5.45	5.51	5.44	5.46	5.44	5.41	5.34	5.69	5.72	5.37
2012-13	5.52	6.25	6.54	6.42	6.49	6.49	6.44	6.41	6.48	6.49	6.30	6.45	6.36
2013-14	6.35	6.38	6.15	5.88	5.94	6.20	6.11	6.04	5.94	5.94	5.90	5.94	6.06
2014-15	6.01	5.62	5.60	5.31	5.24	5.09	5.16	4.86	5.22	4.87	4.94	4.75	5.22
2015-16	5.04	5.19	5.59	5.49	5.54	5.55	5.88	5.47	5.51	5.43	5.29	5.59	5.46
2016-17	5.39	5.00	4.89	4.54	4.85	4.97	5.12	4.91	5.08	4.97	4.87	5.05	4.97
2017-18	4.47	4.54	4.52	4.32	4.44	4.60	4.38	4.45	4.58	4.46	4.44	4.45	4.47
2018-19[1]	4.61	4.52	4.53	4.49	4.27	4.78	4.68	4.60					4.56

[1] Preliminary.   Source: National Agricultural Statistical Service, U.S. Department of Agriculture (NASS-USDA)

Average Price Received by Farmers for Feed Barley in the United States   In Dollars Per Bushel

Year	June	July	Aug.	Sept.	Oct.	Nov.	Dec.	Jan.	Feb.	Mar.	Apr.	May	Average
2011-12	4.74	5.04	4.91	5.07	4.76	4.85	4.88	4.81	4.74	4.76	5.10	4.89	4.88
2012-13	5.46	5.53	5.61	5.58	5.72	5.67	5.53	5.60	5.91	5.61	5.55	5.68	5.62
2013-14	5.75	5.17	4.42	4.25	4.10	3.63	3.65	4.21	3.77	3.81	3.77	4.15	4.22
2014-15	4.32	3.85	3.31	2.97	3.13	2.84	2.99	2.99	2.94	3.08	3.05	2.90	3.20
2015-16	3.55	2.97	3.00	3.24	2.97	3.03	3.11	3.14	3.07	2.79	2.82	3.67	3.11
2016-17	3.38	3.18	2.75	2.39	2.52	2.49	2.87	2.61	2.75	2.50	2.64	2.69	2.73
2017-18	3.47	3.04	2.97	2.62	3.07	2.80	2.85	3.01	2.84	2.90	3.08	3.33	3.00
2018-19[1]	3.77	3.41	3.11	3.15	2.97	3.28	3.30	3.01					3.25

[1] Preliminary.   Source: National Agricultural Statistical Service, U.S. Department of Agriculture (NASS-USDA)

Average Price Received by Farmers for Malting Barley in the United States   In Dollars Per Bushel

Year	June	July	Aug.	Sept.	Oct.	Nov.	Dec.	Jan.	Feb.	Mar.	Apr.	May	Average
2011-12	4.60	5.09	5.31	5.57	5.69	5.57	5.55	5.54	5.50	5.43	5.87	5.84	5.46
2012-13	5.54	6.43	6.68	6.70	6.65	6.65	6.57	6.49	6.56	6.64	6.48	6.55	6.50
2013-14	6.68	6.56	6.56	6.44	6.49	6.61	6.52	6.52	6.43	6.30	6.45	6.37	6.49
2014-15	6.30	5.90	6.11	5.91	5.76	5.69	5.63	5.47	5.67	5.39	5.75	5.62	5.77
2015-16	5.68	5.73	5.91	5.74	5.78	5.80	5.99	5.68	5.70	5.64	5.71	6.03	5.78
2016-17	5.70	5.33	5.31	5.13	5.17	5.21	5.32	5.19	5.20	5.13	5.13	5.27	5.26
2017-18	4.66	4.78	4.70	4.64	4.64	4.81	4.51	4.60	4.77	4.60	4.73	4.58	4.67
2018-19[1]	4.88	4.79	4.68	4.75	4.47	4.87	4.81	4.69					4.74

[1] Preliminary.   Source: National Agricultural Statistical Service, U.S. Department of Agriculture (NASS-USDA)

Stocks of Barley in the United States   In Thousands of Bushels

Year	On Farms Mar. 1	On Farms June 1	On Farms Sept. 1	On Farms Dec. 1	Off Farms Mar. 1	Off Farms June 1	Off Farms Sept. 1	Off Farms Dec. 1	Total Stocks Mar. 1	Total Stocks June 1	Total Stocks Sept. 1	Total Stocks Dec. 1
2011	57,700	26,040	93,050	55,320	80,424	63,311	82,007	83,621	138,124	89,351	175,057	138,941
2012	26,480	9,670	111,550	72,580	67,248	50,317	85,226	85,473	93,728	59,987	196,776	158,053
2013	35,180	15,840	105,620	81,340	81,897	64,557	90,470	88,063	117,077	80,397	196,090	169,403
2014	43,830	19,110	97,820	74,510	77,734	63,145	81,997	81,625	121,564	82,255	179,817	156,135
2015	41,990	20,940	135,840	96,670	76,247	57,639	83,132	83,738	118,237	78,579	218,972	180,408
2016	57,910	27,740	130,600	99,100	79,832	74,370	99,737	93,408	137,742	102,110	230,337	192,508
2017	56,490	27,050	90,400	74,340	88,211	79,314	89,283	84,528	144,701	106,364	179,683	158,868
2018[1]	48,540	26,420	91,350	71,960	81,491	68,061	83,456	80,761	130,031	94,481	174,806	152,721

[1] Preliminary.   Source: National Agricultural Statistics Service, U.S. Department of Agriculture (NASS-USDA)

Production of Barley in the United States, by State   In Thousands of Bushels

Year	Arizona	California	Colorado	Idaho	Minnesota	Montana	North Dakota	Oregon	Pennsylvania	Virginia	Washington	Wyoming	U.S. Total
2011	8,000	4,725	7,938	46,500	3,060	31,000	16,450	2,400	3,575	6,160	8,510	6,111	155,780
2012	4,935	4,400	6,710	54,000	6,270	40,290	60,600	3,816	3,604	2,870	12,425	6,141	218,990
2013	8,142	3,150	7,714	57,660	5,175	43,160	46,080	3,500	4,080	3,608	14,040	6,052	216,745
2014	4,000	1,825	6,696	51,700	3,120	44,660	35,845	1,900	3,550	2,212	6,300	7,276	181,542
2015	1,920	1,595	8,190	56,260	9,240	44,720	67,200	1,924	2,600	1,200	5,040	8,170	218,187
2016	2,048	4,500	9,675	62,060	5,214	46,800	42,880	2,144	2,850	804	7,161	7,872	199,914
2017	2,227	1,450	8,976	48,450	5,168	28,815	26,000	2,356	3,150	803	4,505	6,426	143,258
2018[1]	900	1,794	7,540	53,530	5,092	33,600	28,490	1,378	2,079	630	4,891	5,000	153,082

[1] Preliminary.   Source: National Agricultural Statistics Service, U.S. Department of Agriculture (NASS-USDA)

Weekly Outstanding Export Sales and Cumulative Exports of U.S. Barley — In Thousands of Metric Tons

Marketing Year 2017/2018 Week Ending	Weekly Exports	Accumulated Exports	Net Sales	Outstanding Sales	Marketing Year 2018/2019 Week Ending	Weekly Exports	Accumulated Exports	Net Sales	Outstanding Sales
Jun 01, 2017			647	28,427	Jun 07, 2018	1,555	1,555		47,014
Jun 08, 2017	58	58	49	28,418	Jun 14, 2018	112	1,667	375	47,277
Jun 15, 2017	692	750	769	28,495	Jun 21, 2018	581	2,248		46,696
Jun 22, 2017	1,651	2,401		26,844	Jun 28, 2018	1,395	3,643		45,301
Jun 29, 2017	998	3,399	635	26,481	Jul 05, 2018	1,955	5,598	-5	43,341
Jul 06, 2017	506	3,905	290	26,265	Jul 12, 2018	1,324	6,922		42,017
Jul 13, 2017	235	4,140	5,542	31,572	Jul 19, 2018	1,582	8,504		40,435
Jul 20, 2017	135	4,275	75	31,512	Jul 26, 2018	1,388	9,892		39,047
Jul 27, 2017	1,142	5,417	500	30,870	Aug 02, 2018	1,350	11,242	200	37,897
Aug 03, 2017	539	5,956		30,331	Aug 09, 2018		11,242		37,897
Aug 10, 2017	451	6,407	-1	29,879	Aug 16, 2018	166	11,408	2,354	40,085
Aug 17, 2017	905	7,312		28,974	Aug 23, 2018	357	11,765	500	40,228
Aug 24, 2017	232	7,544		28,742	Aug 30, 2018	582	12,347	438	40,084
Aug 31, 2017	700	8,244		28,042	Sep 06, 2018	385	12,732	1,000	40,699
Sep 07, 2017	21	8,265		28,021	Sep 13, 2018	132	12,864		40,567
Sep 14, 2017	651	8,916		27,370	Sep 20, 2018	936	13,800	2,050	41,681
Sep 21, 2017	699	9,615	650	27,321	Sep 27, 2018	2,050	15,850	184	39,815
Sep 28, 2017	389	10,004	435	27,367	Oct 04, 2018	552	16,402		39,263
Oct 05, 2017	790	10,794	90	26,667	Oct 11, 2018	332	16,734		38,931
Oct 12, 2017	673	11,467		25,994	Oct 18, 2018	935	17,669	250	38,246
Oct 19, 2017	647	12,114		25,347	Oct 25, 2018	648	18,317	-96	37,502
Oct 26, 2017		12,114	75	25,422	Nov 01, 2018	732	19,049	-91	36,679
Nov 02, 2017	2,040	14,154	1	23,383	Nov 08, 2018	330	19,379	1	36,350
Nov 09, 2017		14,154	500	23,883	Nov 15, 2018	1,900	21,279	249	34,699
Nov 16, 2017	632	14,786	-7	23,244	Nov 22, 2018	550	21,829	991	35,140
Nov 23, 2017	1,163	15,949		22,081	Nov 29, 2018	772	22,601		34,368
Nov 30, 2017	378	16,327		21,703	Dec 06, 2018	97	22,698		34,271
Dec 07, 2017	916	17,243		20,787	Dec 13, 2018	2,888	25,586	5	31,388
Dec 14, 2017	866	18,109	-1,581	18,340	Dec 20, 2018	726	26,312	608	31,270
Dec 21, 2017	441	18,550		17,899	Dec 27, 2018	472	26,784	700	31,498
Dec 28, 2017	1,417	19,967		16,482	Jan 03, 2019	629	27,413		30,869
Jan 04, 2018	1,268	21,235		15,214	Jan 10, 2019		27,413		30,869
Jan 11, 2018		21,235	1,400	16,614	Jan 17, 2019		27,413		30,869
Jan 18, 2018	732	21,967	-4	15,878	Jan 24, 2019		27,413		30,869
Jan 25, 2018	554	22,521		15,324	Jan 31, 2019		27,413		30,869
Feb 01, 2018		22,521		15,324	Feb 07, 2019		27,413		30,869
Feb 08, 2018	628	23,149		14,696	Feb 14, 2019	3,032	30,445	-72	27,765
Feb 15, 2018	1,123	24,272		13,573	Feb 21, 2019	246	30,691		27,519
Feb 22, 2018	578	24,850		12,995	Feb 28, 2019	1,607	32,298	930	26,842
Mar 01, 2018	270	25,120	15,000	27,725	Mar 07, 2019	226	32,524	1,125	27,741
Mar 08, 2018	1,271	26,391		26,454	Mar 14, 2019	218	32,742	-890	26,633
Mar 15, 2018	522	26,913	1,600	27,532	Mar 21, 2019				
Mar 22, 2018	135	27,048	-14,927	12,470	Mar 28, 2019				
Mar 29, 2018	621	27,669	-1	11,848	Apr 04, 2019				
Apr 05, 2018	1,201	28,870	500	11,147	Apr 11, 2019				
Apr 12, 2018	247	29,117		10,900	Apr 18, 2019				
Apr 19, 2018	30	29,147		10,870	Apr 25, 2019				
Apr 26, 2018	444	29,591		10,426	May 02, 2019				
May 03, 2018	90	29,681		10,336	May 09, 2019				
May 10, 2018	454	30,135	-6,967	2,915	May 16, 2019				
May 17, 2018	948	31,083		1,967	May 23, 2019				
May 24, 2018	213	31,296	-569	1,185	May 30, 2019				
May 31, 2018		31,296		1,185	May 31, 2018				

Source: Foreign Agricultural Service, U.S. Department of Agriculture (FAS-USDA)

Bauxite

Bauxite is a naturally occurring, heterogeneous material comprised of one or more aluminum hydroxide minerals plus various mixtures of silica, iron oxide, titanium, alumina-silicates, and other impurities in trace amounts. Bauxite is an important ore of aluminum and forms by the rapid weathering of granite rocks in warm, humid climates. It is easily purified and can be converted directly into either alum or metallic aluminum. It is a soft mineral with hardness varying from 1 to 3, and specific gravity from 2 to 2.55. Bauxite is dull in appearance and may vary in color from white to brown. It usually occurs in aggregates in pea-sized lumps.

Bauxite is the only raw material used in the production of alumina on a commercial scale in the United States. Bauxite is classified according to the intended commercial application, such as abrasive, cement, chemical, metallurgical, and refractory. Of all the bauxite mined, about 95 percent is converted to alumina for the production of aluminum metal with some smaller amounts going to nonmetal uses as various forms of specialty alumina. Small amounts are used in non-metallurgical bauxite applications. Bauxite is also used to produce aluminum chemicals and is used in the steel industry.

Supply – World production of bauxite in 2018 fell -2.9% yr/yr to 300.000 million metric tons. The world's largest producer of bauxite is Australia with 25.0% of the world's production, followed by China with 23.3%, Guinea with 16.7%, Brazil with 9.0%, India with 8.0%, and Jamaica with 3.3%. Chinese production of bauxite has almost tripled in the past 15 years. India's bauxite production has also risen rapidly and is about double the amount seen 15 years ago.

Demand – U.S. consumption of bauxite in 2018 rose by +11.1% yr/yr to 3.900 million metric tons, well below the record high of 15.962 million metric tons seen in 1980. Back in 2014 the alumina industry took about 97% of bauxite production, 9.530 million metric tons. According to 2004 data (the latest data available) the refractory industry usually takes about 1.4% of the U.S. bauxite supply, the abrasive industry takes about 0.2%, and the chemical industry takes the rest.

Trade – The U.S. relies on imports for almost 100% of its consumption needs. Domestic ore, which provides less than 1 percent of the U.S. requirement for bauxite, is mined by one company from surface mines in the states of Alabama and Georgia. U.S. imports of bauxite in 2016 fell -53.2% yr/yr to 5.010 million metric tons, well below the record high of 14.976 million metric tons seen in 1974. U.S. exports of bauxite in 2016 rose +48.4% yr/yr to 5.000 million metric tons.

World Production of Bauxite   In Thousands of Metric Tons

Year	Australia	Brazil	China	Greece	Guinea	Guyana[3]	Hungary	India	Jamaica[3]	Russia[3]	Sierra Leone	Suriname	World Total
2009	65,231	26,074	40,000	1,935	13,600	1,485	267	16,000	7,817	5,775	757	3,388	209,000
2010	68,414	32,028	44,000	1,902	15,900	1,083	307	14,124	8,540	5,690	1,089	3,104	236,000
2011	69,976	33,625	45,000	2,324	15,696	1,818	155	13,000	10,189	5,943	1,300	3,236	254,000
2012	76,281	34,988	47,000	1,816	16,041	2,210	144	13,463	9,339	5,700	776	2,873	255,000
2013	81,119	33,896	50,400	1,844	16,887	1,649	94	20,664	9,435	6,028	616	2,706	295,000
2014	78,632	36,308	59,200	1,873	17,257	1,602	14	22,636	9,677	6,293	1,161	2,708	258,000
2015	80,910	37,057	65,000	1,832	16,303	1,500	8	27,757	9,629	5,900	1,334	1,600	299,000
2016	82,000	34,400	60,800	1,800	31,500	1,700	10	23,886	8,540	5,431	1,369	----	270,000
2017[1]	87,900	38,500	70,000	1,800	46,200	1,500	----	22,900	8,250	5,520	----	----	309,000
2018[2]	75,000	27,000	70,000		50,000			24,000	10,000	5,500		----	300,000

[1] Preliminary.   [2] Estimate.   [3] Dry Bauxite equivalent of ore processed.   *Source: U.S. Geological Survey (USGS)*

Salient Statistics of Bauxite in the United States   In Thousands of Metric Tons

Year	Net Import Reliance as a % of Apparent Consump	Average Price F.O.B. Mine $ per Ton	Consumption by Industry Total	Alumina	Abrasive	Chemical	Refractoty	Dry Equivalent Imports[4]	Exports[3]	Consumption	Stocks, December 31 Producers & Consumers	Gov't Owned	Total
2009	100	30	5,490	5,330	W	W	W	6,970	9	4,960	W	----	W
2010	100	29	8,180	8,050	W	W	W	8,120	21	8,180	W	----	W
2011	100	39	8,820	8,670	----	----	----	9,540	22	8,820	W	----	W
2012	>75	36	9,560	9,330	----	----	----	10,300	11	9,560	W	----	W
2013	>75	----	10,200	9,810	----	----	----	9,830	4	10,200	W	----	W
2014	>75	----	9,840	9,600	----	----	----	10,800	3	9,840	W	----	W
2015	>75	----	9,660	9,340	----	----	----	10,700	3	9,660	W	----	W
2016	>75	----	5,360	4,650	----	----	----	5,010	5	4,940	W	----	W
2017[1]	>75	----	3,510		----	----	----				W	----	W
2018[2]	>75	----	3,900		----	----	----				W	----	W

[1] Preliminary.   [2] Estimate.   [3] Including concentrates.   [4] For consumption.   W = Withheld.   *Source: U.S. Geological Survey (USGS)*

Bismuth

Bismuth (symbol Bi) is a rare metallic element with a pinkish tinge. Bismuth has been known since ancient times, but it was confused with lead, tin, and zinc until the middle of the 18th century. Among the elements in the earth's crust, bismuth is ranked about 73rd in natural abundance. This makes bismuth about as rare as silver. Most industrial bismuth is obtained as a by-product of ore extraction.

Bismuth is useful for castings because of the unusual way that it expands after solidifying. Some of bismuth's alloys have unusually low melting points. Bismuth is one of the most difficult of all substances to magnetize. It tends to turn at right angles to a magnetic field. Because of this property, it is used in instruments for measuring the strength of magnetic fields.

Bismuth finds a wide variety of uses such as pharmaceutical compounds, ceramic glazes, crystal ware, and chemicals and pigments. Bismuth is found in household pharmaceuticals and is used to treat stomach ulcers. Bismuth is opaque to X-rays and can be used in fluoroscopy. Bismuth has also found new use as a nontoxic substitute for lead in various applications such as brass plumbing fixtures, crystal ware, lubricating greases, pigments, and solders. There has been environmental interest in the use of bismuth as a replacement for lead used in shot for waterfowl hunting and in fishing sinkers. Another use has been for galvanizing to improve drainage characteristics of galvanizing alloys. Zinc-bismuth alloys have the same drainage properties as zinc-lead without being as hazardous.

Prices – The average price of bismuth (99.99% pure) in the U.S. in 2018 fell -6.3% yr/yr to $4.62 per pound, well below the 2007 record high of $13.32 per pound. Up until 2007, bismuth prices were lower in the range of $3.00 to $4.00 per pound.

Supply – World mine production of bismuth in 2016 fell -1.0% yr/yr to 10,200 metric tons, down from the 2015 record high of 10,300 metric tons. The world's largest producer in 2016 was China with 72.5% of world production, followed by Mexico with 6.9%. Regarding production of the refined metal in 2017 (latest data), China had 78.6% of production, Mexico had 3.9%, Japan had 3.1%, and Kazakhstan had 1.0%. The U.S. does not have any significant domestic refinery production of bismuth.

Demand – U.S. consumption of bismuth in 2018 fell by -10.1% yr/yr to 680 metric tons, still well below the record high of 2,630 metric tons in 2007. In 2016 the consumed uses of bismuth were 72.7% for chemicals and 11.1% for fusible alloys.

Trade – U.S. imports of bismuth in 2018 fell -0.7% yr/yr to 2,800 metric tons, well below the 2007 record high of 3,070 metric tons. In 2014 17.7% of U.S. imports came from Belgium and 3.0% from Peru. U.S. exports of bismuth and alloys in 2018 rose +48.0% yr/yr to 580 metric tons, but still well below the 2010 record high of 1,040 metric tons.

World Production of Bismuth   In Metric Tons (Mine Output=Metal Content)

	Mine Output, Metal Content						Refined Metal						
Year	Canada	China	Japan	Mexico	Peru	World Total	Belgium	China	Japan	Kazak-hastan[3]	Mexico	Peru	World Total
2010	91	6,500	----	952	----	7,700	----	14,000	454	150	952	----	16,000
2011	92	7,000	----	935	----	8,100	----	15,000	460	150	935	----	17,000
2012	121	6,000	----	800	----	7,100	----	14,000	470	150	940	----	16,000
2013	35	7,500	----	824	----	8,400	----	15,500	480	150	824	----	17,000
2014	3	7,600	----	948	----	8,600	----	15,300	480	150	948	----	17,000
2015[1]	3	7,500	----	700	----	10,300							
2016[2]	3	7,400	----	700	----	10,200							

[1] Preliminary.   [2] Estimate.   *Source U.S. Geological Survey (USGS)*

Salient Statistics of Bismuth in the United States   In Metric Tons

	Bismuth Consumed, By Uses							Imports from				
	Metal-lurgical Additives	Other Alloys & Uses	Fusible Alloys	Chem-icals[3]	Total Consumption	Consumer Stocks Dec. 31	Exports of Metal & Alloys	Metallic Bismuth from				Dealer Price $ Per Pound
Year								Belgium	Mexico	Preu	Total	
2011	----	15,000	460	150	935	----	17,000	674.0	0.4	0.5	1,620	8.76
2012	----	14,000	470	150	940	----	16,000	713.0	0.1	----	1,750	11.47
2013	----	15,500	480	150	824	----	17,000	505.0	----	----	1,700	10.10
2014	----	15,300	582	150	948	----	17,000	389.0	----	144.0	1,710	8.71
2015	----	14,800	773	150	606	----	17,000	303.0	----	71.6	2,270	11.14
2016[1]	----	14,000	428	140	539	----	17,100				1,950	6.43
2017[2]	----	11,000	430	140	540	----	14,000				2,200	4.50

[1] Preliminary.   [2] Estimate.   [3] Includes pharmaceuticals.   *Source: U.S. Geological Survey (USGS)*

Average Price of Bismuth (99.99%) in the United States   In Dollars Per Pound

Year	Jan.	Feb.	Mar.	Apr.	May	June	July	Aug.	Sept.	Oct.	Nov.	Dec.	Average
2015	10.06	8.42	7.65	7.09	6.90	6.68	6.08	5.33	5.18	5.11	4.72	4.43	6.47
2016	4.41	4.40	4.46	4.46	4.54	4.48	4.28	4.36	4.60	4.72	4.64	4.63	4.50
2017	4.72	4.63	4.70	4.84	4.93	4.87	4.85	4.87	5.17	5.20	5.20	5.25	4.94
2018	5.22	5.21	5.28	5.22	5.04	4.68	4.55	4.35	4.27	4.17	3.80	3.69	4.62

Source: American Metal Market (AMM)

Broilers

Broiler chickens are raised for meat rather than for eggs. The broiler industry was started in the late 1950's when chickens were selectively bred for meat production. Broiler chickens are housed in massive flocks mainly between 20,000 and 50,000 birds, with some flocks reaching over 100,000 birds. Broiler chicken farmers usually rear five or six batches of chickens per year.

After just six or seven weeks, broiler chickens are slaughtered (a chicken's natural lifespan is around seven years). Chickens marketed as pouissons, or spring chickens, are slaughtered after four weeks. A few are kept longer than seven weeks to be sold as the larger roasting chickens.

Prices – The average monthly price received by farmers for broilers (live weight) rose in 2018 by +5.1 yr/yr to 57.4 cents per pound. The average monthly price for wholesale broilers (ready-to-cook) in 2018 rose +5.3% to 98.51 cents per pound, but still below the 2014 record high of 104.88 cents per pound.

Supply – Total production of broilers in 2018 rose +2.4% yr/yr to 43.370 billion pounds. The number of broilers raised for commercial production in 2018 was up +2.5% yr/yr to 9.136 billion birds, for a new record high. The average live-weight per bird rose +0.9% to 6.26 pounds, which was a new record high and was about 70% heavier than the average bird weight of 3.62 pounds seen in 1970, attesting to the increased efficiency of the industry.

Demand – U.S. per capita consumption of broilers in 2018 rose by +1.8% to 92.4 pounds (ready-to-cook) per person per year, a new record high. U.S. consumption of chicken has nearly doubled in the past two decades, up from 47.0 pounds in 1980, as consumers have increased their consumption of chicken because of the focus on low-carb diets and because chicken is a leaner and healthier meat than either beef or pork.

Broiler Supply and Prices in the United States

Years and Quarters	Number (Million)	Average Weight (Pounds)	Liveweight Pounds (Mil. Lbs.)	Certified RTC³ Weight (Mil. Lbs.)	Total Production RTC³ (Mil. Lbs.)	Per Capita Consumption RTC³ Basis (Mil. Lbs.)	Farm	Georgia Dock⁴
		------ Federally Inspected Slaughter ------					------ Prices ------ Cents per Pound	
2013	8,504	5.92	50,357	37,826	37,830	81.8	60.25	103.26
2014	8,522	6.01	50,842	38,550	38,565	83.3	63.92	109.71
2015	8,688	6.12	53,165	40,046	40,048	89.0	52.92	113.83
2016	8,768	6.16	54,037	40,692	40,696	89.7	50.38	111.93
2017	8,916	6.20	55,313	41,661	41,662	90.8	54.58	----
2018¹	8,983	6.25	56,177	42,322	42,649	92.4	56.92	----
I	2,209	6.24	13,789	10,385	10,385	22.6	55.00	----
II	2,270	6.25	14,180	10,685	10,685	23.3	70.00	----
III	2,270	6.25	14,180	10,685	10,929	23.5	54.00	----
IV	2,235	6.28	14,027	10,567	10,650	23.0	48.67	----

¹ Preliminary. ² Estimate. ³ Total production equals federal inspected slaughter plus other slaughter minus cut-up & further processing condemnation. ⁴ Ready-to-cook basis. *Source: Economic Research Service, U.S. Department of Agriculture (ERS-USDA)*

Salient Statistics of Broilers in the United States

Year	Number (Mil. Lbs.)	Liveweight (Mil. Lbs.)	Liveweight Per Bird (Mil. Lbs.)	Average Price (cents Lb.)	Value of Production (Mil. $)	Federally Inspected	Other Chickens	Total January 1	Exports	Broiler Feed Ratio (pounds)	Total (Mil. Lbs.)	Per Capita⁴ (Pounds)
	Commercial Production		Average			Production		Storage Stocks			Consumption	
2012	8,429	49,350	5.85	51.4	24,828	37,035	396	37,431	590	7,274	3.1	29,413	80.39
2013	8,504	50,357	5.92	60.3	30,762	37,826		37,826	651	7,345	3.7	30,166	81.90
2014	8,545	51,379	6.01	63.9	32,728	38,550		38,550	669	7,301	5.0	30,957	83.30
2015	8,689	53,376	6.14	52.9	28,716	40,046		40,046	680	6,319	5.0	33,279	88.90
2016	8,768	54,037	6.16	50.4	25,936	40,692		40,692	832	6,740	4.7	34,211	90.90
2017¹	8,916	55,313	6.20	54.6	30,230	41,661		41,661			5.4		
2018²	9,031	56,511	6.26	56.9		42,577		42,577					

Preliminary. ² Estimate. ³ Ready-to-cook. ⁴ Retail weight basis. Source: Economic Research Service, U.S. Department of Agriculture (ERS-USDA)

Average Wholesale Broiler² Prices RTC (Ready-to-Cook)   In Cents Per Pound

Year	Jan.	Feb.	Mar.	Apr.	May	June	July	Aug.	Sept.	Oct.	Nov.	Dec.	Average
2012	81.76	86.59	93.23	85.01	87.26	85.41	82.62	82.89	82.68	84.05	95.42	97.81	87.06
2013	101.48	101.80	107.27	107.10	110.40	108.28	99.04	91.12	91.51	90.02	93.72	94.60	99.70
2014	96.45	92.45	106.26	110.11	117.59	113.40	107.16	99.69	107.05	106.68	103.68	98.07	104.88
2015	99.62	92.56	98.88	104.79	106.71	101.17	91.01	82.61	77.40	74.09	75.37	82.05	90.52
2016	87.90	81.52	84.46	88.41	93.72	96.93	88.62	79.71	76.68	70.73	79.28	84.04	84.33
2017	85.58	85.07	94.49	96.91	108.97	109.02	103.80	92.47	88.38	84.84	86.06	87.33	93.58
2018¹	94.00	91.08	101.97	108.73	117.59	118.92	110.60	87.33	83.13	83.56	86.75		98.51

¹ Preliminary. ² 12-city composite wholesale price. *Source: Economic Research Service, U.S. Department of Agriculture (ERS-USDA)*

Butter

Butter is a dairy product produced by churning the fat from milk, usually cow's milk, until it solidifies. In some parts of the world, butter is also made from the milk of goats, sheep, and even horses. Butter has been in use since at least 2,000 BC. Today butter is used principally as a food item, but in ancient times it was used more as an ointment, medicine, or illuminating oil. Butter was first churned in skin pouches thrown back and forth over the backs of trotting horses.

It takes about 10 quarts of milk to produce 1 pound of butter. The manufacture of butter is the third largest use of milk in the U.S. California is generally the largest producing state, followed closely by Wisconsin, with Washington as a distant third. Commercially finished butter is comprised of milk fat (80% to 85%), water (12% to 16%), and salt (about 2%). Although the price of butter is highly correlated with the price of milk, it also has its own supply and demand dynamics.

The consumption of butter has dropped in recent decades because pure butter has a high level of animal fat and cholesterol that have been linked to obesity and heart disease. The primary substitute for butter is margarine, which is produced from vegetable oil rather than milk fat. U.S. per capita consumption of margarine has risen from 2.6 pounds in 1930 to recent levels near 8.3 pounds, much higher than U.S. butter consumption.

Butter Futures and options are traded at the CME Group. The CME's butter futures contract calls for the delivery of 20,000 pounds of butter and is priced in cents per pound. Butter futures are traded on New Zealand Futures Exchange (NZFE)

Prices – The average monthly price of butter at the CME in 2018 fell -3.2% yr/yr to $2.2543/pound, down from last year's record high of $2.3278/pound.

Supply – World production of butter in 2019 is forecasted to rise 3.0% yr/yr to 10.810 million metric tons, a new record high. The world's largest producers of butter for 2019 are forecasted to be India with 54.1% of the world production, the European Union with 22.3%, the United States with 8.0%, New Zealand with 4.9%, and Russia with 2.5%. Production of creamery butter by U.S. factories in 2018 rose +1.8% yr/yr to 1.881 billion pounds, a new record high.

Demand – Total commercial use of creamery butter in the U.S. rose +3.5% yr/yr to 1.921 million pounds in 2018. That is about one-third more that the commercial use of butter back in the 1950's. Cold storage stocks of creamery butter in the U.S. on January 1, 2018 rose +1.7% yr/yr to 168,787 million pounds.

Trade – World imports of butter in 2019 are expected to fall -4.7% yr/yr to 264,000 metric tons. U.S. imports of butter in 2019 are expected to remain unchanged at 46,000 metric tons. World exports of butter in 2019 are expected to rise +0.5% yr/yr to 885,000 metric tons. U.S exports in 2019 are expected to fall -113.5% yr/yr to 45,000 metric tons, which is still be well below the 1993 record high of 145,000 metric tons.

Supply and Distribution of Butter in the United States   In Millions of Pounds

| | Supply | | | | Distribution | | | | | | 93 Score | |
| | | Cold Storage | | | | Domestic Disappearance | | Department of Agriculture | | | AA Wholesale Price | |
Year	Pro-duction	Stocks[3] Jan. 1	Imports	Total Supply	Total	Per Capita (Pounds)	Exports	Stocks[4] Jan. 1	Stocks[4] Dec 31	Removed by USDA Programs	Total Use	$ per Pound
2010	1,564.0	133,022	22.046	1,717	1,506	4.9	130	----	----	----	1,636	1.7280
2011	1,809.8	81,695	26.455	1,918	1,669	5.4	143	----	----	----	1,812	1.9618
2012	1,859.5	106,856	37.478	2,002	1,746	5.5	104	----	----	----	1,850	1.5943
2013	1,862.5	153,027	26.455	2,041	1,724	5.5	205	----	----	----	1,929	1.5451
2014	1,855.3	112,467	48.501	2,017	1,750	5.5	163				1,914	2.1361
2015	1,849.5	104,728	83.775	2,037	1,832	5.6	51	----	----	----	1,883	2.0670
2016	1,839.4	155,082	110.230	2,103	1,878	5.7	60	----	----	----	1,938	2.0777
2017[1]	1,847.5	166,043	99.207	2,112	1,889		62	----	----	----	1,951	
2018[2]	1,884.1	168,787	105.821	2,141	1,925		62	----	----	----	1,986	

[1] Preliminary.   [2] Estimates   [3] Includes butter-equivalent.   [4] Includes butteroil.   [5] Includes stocks held by USDA.
Source: Economic Research Service, U.S. Department of Agriculture (ERS-USDA)

Quarterly Commercial Disappearance of Creamery Butter In the United States   In Millions of Pounds

Year	First Quarter	Second Quarter	Third Quarter	Fourth Quarter	Total	Year	First Quarter	Second Quarter	Third Quarter	Fourth Quarter	Total
2007	337.8	284.3	349.2	459.2	1,430.5	2013	412.3	372.2	434.2	517.8	1,736.5
2008	350.1	321.4	369.0	477.0	1,517.5	2014	380.9	433.5	433.6	508.5	1,756.4
2009	371.0	352.3	343.2	457.9	1,524.6	2015	417.3	403.2	468.4	509.5	1,798.4
2010	362.6	353.0	365.1	443.5	1,524.1	2016	447.6	406.3	457.7	546.4	1,857.9
2011	387.0	372.0	426.3	494.5	1,679.7	2017	412.9	428.8	463.5	550.5	1,855.8
2012	402.5	403.6	435.6	491.3	1,733.0	2018[1]	429.0	421.6	467.7	640.1	1,958.5

[1] Preliminary.   *Source: Economic Research Service, U.S. Department of Agriculture (ERS-USDA)*

BUTTER

World Production of Butter[3] In Thousands of Metric Tons

Year	Argentina	Australia	Brazil	Canada	European Union	India	Japan	Mexico	New Zealand	Russia	Ukraine	United States	World Total
2012	58	119	81	98	2,100	4,525	69	174	527	216	88	843	9,011
2013	60	117	83	95	2,100	4,745	68	195	535	219	93	845	9,254
2014	52	125	85	88	2,250	4,887	61	207	580	252	115	842	9,651
2015	50	120	83	91	2,335	5,035	65	216	594	260	103	839	9,904
2016	47	110	82	93	2,345	5,200	66	217	570	246	103	834	10,031
2017	46	103	83	109	2,340	5,400	60	223	525	270	109	838	10,226
2018[1]	50	100	85	123	2,375	5,600	60	226	530	263	106	860	10,494
2019[2]	53	100	86	125	2,410	5,850	61	229	530	275	103	870	10,810

[1] Preliminary.　[2] Forecast.　[3] Factory (including creameries and dairies) & farm.　NA = Not available.
Source: Foreign Agricultural Service, U.S. Department of Agriculture (FAS-USDA)

Production of Creamery Butter in Factories in the United States In Thousands of Pounds

Year	Jan.	Feb.	Mar.	Apr.	May	June	July	Aug.	Sept.	Oct.	Nov.	Dec.	Total
2011	167,058	150,070	165,358	158,670	155,873	141,293	135,460	133,748	137,907	145,667	152,781	165,866	1,809,751
2012	181,563	170,575	176,287	169,896	164,133	137,046	133,581	129,531	136,299	144,544	142,938	173,144	1,859,537
2013	188,037	173,335	181,421	166,658	163,785	140,124	132,746	134,370	132,232	145,886	142,192	161,730	1,862,516
2014	184,030	166,097	166,626	167,730	166,285	140,391	137,788	129,092	131,802	151,201	144,518	169,755	1,855,315
2015	173,634	155,976	167,816	165,457	169,409	143,692	135,525	128,072	133,652	148,414	152,323	175,549	1,849,519
2016	170,746	168,272	174,916	171,210	166,178	147,705	135,169	123,523	135,283	139,858	143,086	163,453	1,839,399
2017	178,060	161,013	177,021	161,956	163,397	139,200	135,625	131,152	134,552	144,671	149,721	171,105	1,847,473
2018[1]	182,088	170,116	182,046	175,297	168,109	142,540	134,561	133,982	134,800	143,480	146,143	170,960	1,884,122

[1] Preliminary.　*Source: Economic Research Service, U.S. Department of Agriculture (ERS-USDA)*

Cold Storage Holdings of Creamery Butter in the United States, on First of Month In Millions of Pounds

Year	Jan.	Feb.	Mar.	Apr.	May	June	July	Aug.	Sept.	Oct.	Nov.	Dec.
2011	81,695	118,784	138,672	144,244	141,728	170,095	190,310	187,796	165,698	150,979	130,684	93,523
2012	106,856	170,348	205,172	208,253	254,184	261,586	243,235	234,352	201,135	195,819	145,098	127,282
2013	153,027	207,075	238,342	254,991	309,719	321,954	318,893	295,751	263,928	233,031	181,799	121,627
2014	112,467	143,890	171,773	191,755	186,914	209,430	199,248	180,834	172,789	152,361	147,956	107,566
2015	104,728	148,885	179,003	184,373	232,372	265,198	256,000	254,347	212,189	187,528	178,834	132,740
2016	155,082	192,101	235,559	243,134	295,771	324,942	328,149	332,848	318,774	269,125	228,158	161,203
2017	166,043	221,556	269,857	272,500	292,284	313,593	310,158	307,359	280,194	255,839	217,918	159,258
2018[1]	168,787	226,694	265,756	273,955	307,325	338,492	336,625	318,327	290,855	283,195	230,735	153,730

[1] Preliminary.　*Source: Agricultural Statistics Board, U.S. Department of Agriculture (ASB-USDA)*

Average Price of Butter at Chicago Mercantile Exchange In Cents Per Pound

Year	Jan.	Feb.	Mar.	Apr.	May	June	July	Aug.	Sept.	Oct.	Nov.	Dec.	Average
2011	2.0345	2.0622	2.0863	1.9970	2.0724	2.1077	2.0443	2.0882	1.8724	1.8295	1.7356	1.6119	1.9618
2012	1.5831	1.4273	1.4895	1.4136	1.3531	1.4774	1.5831	1.7687	1.8803	1.9086	1.7910	1.5590	1.6029
2013	1.4933	1.5713	1.6421	1.7197	1.5997	1.5105	1.4751	1.4013	1.5233	1.5267	1.6126	1.5963	1.5560
2014	1.7756	1.8047	1.9145	1.9357	2.1713	2.2630	2.4624	2.5913	2.9740	2.3184	1.9968	1.7633	2.1643
2015	1.5714	1.7293	1.7166	1.7937	1.9309	1.9065	1.9056	2.1542	2.6690	2.4757	2.8779	2.3318	2.0886
2016	2.1214	2.0840	1.9605	2.0563	2.0554	2.2640	2.2731	2.1776	1.9950	1.8239	1.9899	2.1763	2.0815
2017	2.2393	2.1534	2.1392	2.0992	2.2684	2.5688	2.6195	2.6473	2.4370	2.3293	2.2244	2.2078	2.3278
2018	2.1587	2.1211	2.2011	2.3145	2.3751	2.3270	2.2361	2.3009	2.2545	2.2600	2.2480	2.2071	2.2503

Source: Economic Research Service, U.S. Department of Agriculture (ERS-USDA)

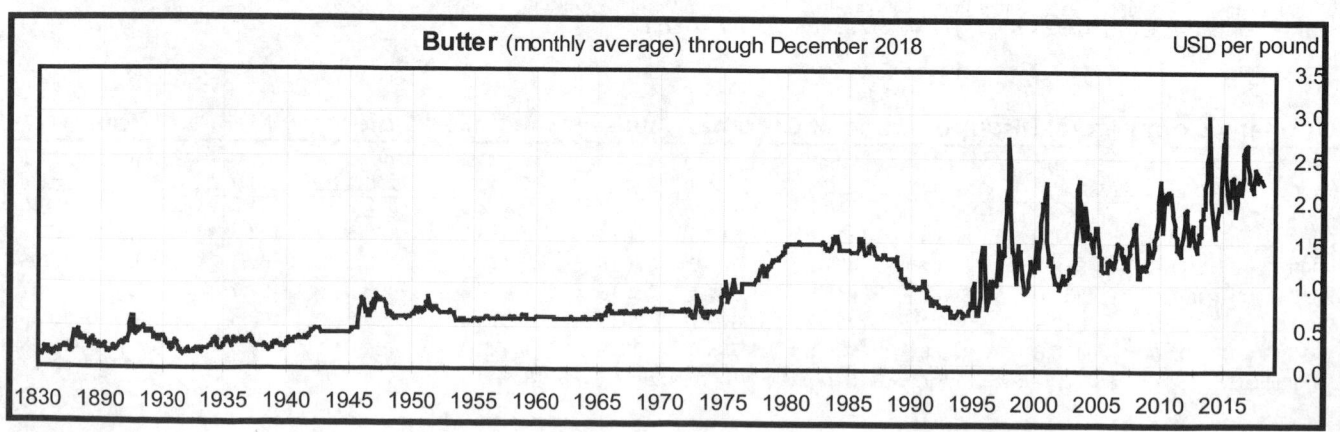

Butter (monthly average) through December 2018　USD per pound

Cadmium

Cadmium (atomic symbol Cd) is a soft, bluish-white, metallic element that can easily be shaped and cut with a knife. Cadmium melts at 321 degrees Celsius and boils at 765 degrees Celsius. Cadmium burns brightly in air when heated, forming the oxide CdO. In 1871, the German chemist Friedrich Stromeyer discovered cadmium in incrustations in zinc furnaces.

Rare greenockite is the only mineral bearing cadmium. Cadmium occurs most often in small quantities associated with zinc ores, such as sphalerite. Electrolysis or fractional distillation is used to separate the cadmium and zinc. About 80% of world cadmium output is a by-product from zinc refining. The remaining 20% comes from secondary sources and recycling of cadmium products. Cadmium recycling is practical only from nickel-cadmium batteries and from some alloys and dust from electric-arc furnaces.

Cadmium is used primarily for metal plating and coating operations in transportation equipment, machinery, baking enamels, photography, and television phosphors. It is also used in solar modules, pigments and lasers, and in nickel-cadmium and solar batteries.

Prices –Cadmium prices rallied sharply during 2005-07 and posted a record high of $334.28 per pound in 2007. In 2018, the average cadmium price rose by +64.8% yr/yr to $130.94 per pound.

Supply – World cadmium production in 2018 rose by 2.4% yr/yr to 25,000 metric tons, a new record high. The largest producer was China with 31.5% of total world production followed by South Korea with 21.57%, Japan with 8.1%, and Canada with 6.9%. U.S. production in 2010 fell by -0.6% yr/yr to 637 metric tons, which was just above the 2009 record low of 633 metric tons.

Demand – U.S. cadmium consumption in 2010 (latest available data) rose by +139.7% yr/yr to 477 metric tons. Of the total apparent consumption, generally about 75% is used for batteries, 12% for pigments, 8% for coatings and plating, 4% for nonferrous alloys, and 1% for other uses.

Trade – The U.S. has been a net exporter of cadmium since 2004. In 2018 the U.S. imports fell -32.4% yr/yr to 200 metric tons. U.S. exports of cadmium in 2018 fell -48.6% yr/yr to 220 metric tons, well below the 2-decade high of 661 metric tons in 2009.

World Refinery Production of Cadmium   In Metric Tons

Year	Australia	Canada	China	Germany	India	Japan	Kazakh stan	Korea, South	Mexico	Nether- lands	Russia	United States[3]	World Total
2011	390	1,240	6,672	400	470	1,755	1,280	3,005	1,485	570	1,500	W	21,300
2012	380	1,286	7,265	400	396	1,855	1,166	3,904	1,482	560	1,500	W	22,500
2013	380	1,313	7,496	400	285	1,826	1,319	3,904	1,451	610	1,200	W	22,600
2014	350	1,187	8,201	400	107	1,829	1,633	4,090	1,409	640	1,200	W	23,700
2015	380	1,159	8,200	400	200	1,959	1,459	3,600	1,283	640	1,200	W	22,800
2016	400	2,305	8,200	400	21	1,988	1,500	3,600	1,188	630	1,300	W	23,900
2017[1]		1,800	8,200			2,140	1,500	5,600	1,160	600	1,200	W	25,400
2018[2]		1,800	8,200			2,100	1,500	5,600	1,200	900	1,200	W	26,000

[1] Preliminary.   [2] Estimate.   [3] Primary and secondary metal.   *Source: U.S. Geological Survey (USGS)*

Salient Statistics of Cadmium in the United States   In Metric Tons of Contained Cadmium

Year	Net import Reliance As a % of Apparent Consumption	Production (Metal)	Producer Shipments	Cadmium Sulfide Production	Production Other Compounds	Imports of Cadmium Metal[3]	Exports[4]	Apparent Consumption	Industry Stocks Dec. 31[5]	New York Dealer Price $ Per Lb.
2012	E	W	W	----	----	192	631	W	W	.92
2013	<25	W	W	----	----	388	417	W	W	.87
2014	E	W	W	----	----	139	270	W	W	.88
2015	E	W	W	----	----	326	596	W	W	.67
2016	<25	W	W	----	----	292	540	W	W	.61
2017[1]	<25	W	W	----	----	296	428	W	W	.79
2018[2]	<25	W	W	----	----	200	220	W	W	1.32

[1] Preliminary.   [2] Estimate.   [3] For consumption.   [4] Cadmium metal, alloys, dross, flue dust.   [5] Metallic, Compounds, Distributors.   [6] Sticks & Balls in 1 to 5 short ton lots of metal (99.95%).   E = Net exporter.   *Source: U.S. Geological Survey (USGS)*

Average Price of Cadmium (99.95%) in the United States   In Dollars Per Pound

Year	Jan.	Feb.	Mar.	Apr.	May	June	July	Aug.	Sept.	Oct.	Nov.	Dec.	Average
2014	82.98	82.50	80.71	80.00	80.00	80.00	80.00	81.90	85.00	85.00	83.06	80.00	81.76
2015	79.90	73.82	64.61	54.91	50.25	44.66	41.97	39.16	35.50	36.11	39.33	42.83	50.25
2016	46.79	52.36	58.74	68.79	73.00	71.64	64.29	54.30	50.77	54.05	63.89	67.50	60.51
2017	67.50	70.75	74.20	77.90	78.35	74.32	70.69	70.50	71.64	90.86	104.55	102.14	79.45
2018	101.00	121.85	152.50	155.43	143.46	130.83	129.66	127.50	127.50	127.50	127.50	126.50	130.94

Source: American Metal Market (AMM)

Canola (Rapeseed)

Canola is a genetic variation of rapeseed that was developed by Canadian plant breeders specifically for its nutritional qualities and its low level of saturated fat. The term Canola is a contraction of "Canadian oil." The history of canola oil begins with the rapeseed plant, a member of the mustard family. The rape plant is grown both as feed for livestock and birdfeed. For 4,000 years, the oil from the rapeseed was used in China and India for cooking and as lamp oil. During World War II, rapeseed oil was used as a marine and industrial lubricant. After the war, the market for rapeseed oil plummeted. Rapeseed growers needed other uses for their crop, and that stimulated the research that led to the development of canola. In 1974, Canadian plant breeders from the University of Manitoba produced canola by genetically altering rapeseed. Each canola plant produces yellow flowers, which then produce pods. The tiny round seeds within each pod are crushed to produce canola oil. Each canola seed contains approximately 40% oil. Canola oil is the world's third largest source of vegetable oil accounting for 13% of world vegetable oils, following soybean oil at 32%, and palm oil at 28%. The rest of the seed is processed into canola meal, which is used as high protein livestock feed.

The climate in Canada is especially suitable for canola plant growth. Today, over 13 million acres of Canadian soil are dedicated to canola production. Canola oil is Canada's leading vegetable oil. Due to strong demand from the U.S. for canola oil, approximately 70% of Canada's canola oil is exported to the U.S. Canola oil is used as a salad oil, cooking oil, and for margarine as well as in the manufacture of inks, biodegradable greases, pharmaceuticals, fuel, soap, and cosmetics.

Canola futures and options are traded at the ICE U.S. Exchange. The futures contract calls for the delivery of 20 metric tons of canola and 5 contracts are together called a "1 board lot." The futures contract is priced in Canadian dollars per metric ton.

Prices – ICE U.S. canola prices on the nearest-futures chart (Barchart.com symbol code RS) in 2018 moved higher early but then moved lower to close down by -8.0% at CD\$473.00 per metric ton. The average monthly wholesale price of canola oil in the Midwest in 2018 fell -1.6% yr/yr to 38.02 cents per pound. The average monthly wholesale price of canola meal (delivery Pacific Northwest) in the 2018/19 crop year fell -4.1% to \$279.23 per short ton.

Supply – World canola production in the 2018/19 marketing year is forecasted to fall -5.1% yr/yr to 70.217 million metric tons, down from last year's record high. The world's largest canola producers are expected to be Canada with 30.0% of world production in 2018/19, European Union with 27.0%, China with 18.3%, and India with 8.5%. U.S. production of canola in 2018/19 is expected to rise +15.6% yr/yr to 1.646 million metric tons. Regarding canola products, world production of canola oil in 2018/19 is expected to fall by -0.5% to 27.707 million metric tons. U.S. production of canola oil in 2018/19 is expected to rise by +10.2% to 829,000 metric tons, a new record high. World production of canola meal in 2018/19 is expected to be unchanged at 39.058 million metric tons, a record high.

Demand – World crush demand for canola in 2018/19 is expected to fall -5.1% yr/yr to 67.670 million metric tons. World consumption of canola oil in 2018/19 is expected to fall by -2.9% yr/yr to 27.825 million metric tons, down from last year's record high. World consumption of canola meal in 2018/19 is expected to fall -0.6% to 39.996 million metric tons.

Trade – World canola exports in 2018/19 are expected to rise by +4.3% to 17.052 million metric tons, a new record high. World canola oil exports are expected to rise by +4.5% to 4.826 million metric tons, a new record high, and world canola meal exports to fall -2.8% yr/yr to 6.162 million metric tons. World canola imports in 2018/19 are expected to rise by +4.3% to 17.052 million metric tons, world canola oil imports are expected to rise +5.9% to 4.765 million metric tons, and world canola meal imports are expected to rise 0.1% to 6.125 million metric tons. Regarding U.S. canola trade, U.S. canola imports in 2018/19 are expected to fall -11.9% to 570.000 metric tons and U.S. exports to rise 20.1% to 193.000 metric tons.

World Production of Canola (Rapeseed) In Thousands of Metric Tons

Year	Australia	Bangla-desh	Belarus	Canada	China	European Union	India	Kazakh-stan	Pakistan	Russia	Ukraine	United States	World Total
2009-10	1,907	223	611	12,898	13,536	21,633	6,030	107	162	605	1,873	665	60,789
2010-11	2,359	246	374	12,789	12,788	20,782	7,100	109	192	608	1,470	1,112	60,523
2011-12	3,427	262	379	14,608	13,137	19,240	6,030	148	179	956	1,437	694	61,228
2012-13	4,142	294	705	13,869	13,401	19,560	6,851	117	220	945	1,300	1,087	63,305
2013-14	3,832	230	676	18,551	13,523	21,306	6,650	242	190	1,259	2,352	1,004	70,590
2014-15	3,540	230	730	16,410	13,914	24,587	5,080	241	220	1,324	2,200	1,141	70,429
2015-16	2,775	230	382	18,377	13,859	21,997	5,920	138	215	1,001	1,744	1,306	68,740
2016-17[1]	4,313	230	260	19,599	13,128	20,538	6,620	170	200	997	1,250	1,409	69,436
2017-18[2]	3,670	230	603	21,328	13,274	22,145	6,450	279	225	1,497	2,217	1,424	74,028
2018-19[3]	2,300	230	550	21,100	12,850	19,600	6,000	275	225	2,000	2,700	1,646	70,217

[1] Preliminary. [2] Estimate. [3] Forecast. *Source: Economic Research Service, U.S. Department of Agriculture (ERS-USDA); The Oil World*

CANOLA - ICE-US
Weekly Nearest Futures as of 03/29/2019

WEEKLY NEAREST FUTURES
As of 03/29/2019

Chart High 691.10 on 07/10/2012
Chart Low 360.00 on 05/12/2010

Nearby Futures through Last Trading Day.

Volume of Trading of Canola Futures in Winnipeg   In 20 Metric Ton Units

Year	Jan.	Feb.	Mar.	Apr.	May	June	July	Aug.	Sept.	Oct.	Nov.	Dec.	Total
2009	265,415	345,108	267,276	358,030	286,069	326,924	161,569	188,651	268,629	340,368	211,160	332,594	3,351,793
2010	239,347	349,512	283,156	415,932	232,711	534,781	200,250	277,736	351,663	500,943	284,703	447,694	4,118,428
2011	345,505	483,744	342,887	417,453	326,805	436,050	268,144	331,289	490,065	443,909	361,250	406,052	4,653,153
2012	375,738	588,006	536,713	535,291	367,014	399,329	299,775	279,962	332,661	487,242	279,767	388,733	4,870,261
2013	413,545	558,269	295,056	489,741	355,341	347,609	276,608	381,094	523,431	654,471	479,983	716,539	5,491,687
2014	536,669	570,465	454,015	552,959	369,170	424,087	331,748	298,308	486,457	615,158	346,000	568,886	5,553,922
2015	489,637	486,854	400,209	447,467	327,911	644,971	335,432	365,804	447,279	624,741	403,539	585,625	5,559,469
2016	408,059	641,600	441,094	619,493	518,643	644,052	358,823	385,481	407,031	702,156	490,671	627,053	6,244,156
2017	397,507	549,415	508,671	521,424	344,251	530,093	331,900	298,854	390,755	625,937	381,367	511,181	5,391,355
2018	349,016	530,467	351,802	541,694	324,795	561,388	269,381	251,140	260,732	537,386	333,575	516,654	4,828,030

Contract size = 20 tonnes.   Source: ICE Futures Canada (ICE)

Average Open Interest of Canola Futures in Winnipeg   In 20 Metric Ton Units

Year	Jan.	Feb.	Mar.	Apr.	May	June	July	Aug.	Sept.	Oct.	Nov.	Dec.
2009	88,487	100,072	97,016	104,423	111,922	109,921	94,574	104,426	95,168	99,968	93,108	99,736
2010	112,406	125,895	122,112	133,172	134,768	159,949	154,881	150,209	155,712	181,660	199,487	193,948
2011	204,715	207,186	188,138	176,678	166,554	166,105	150,624	166,066	188,592	166,852	160,276	140,345
2012	151,192	181,837	200,941	228,092	242,231	224,287	220,919	224,646	233,085	198,147	157,664	147,883
2013	155,134	189,913	178,763	164,200	143,013	129,283	118,115	145,257	186,811	177,248	200,975	226,220
2014	230,796	224,847	230,852	219,844	168,705	165,651	147,462	165,501	173,282	159,986	142,371	139,732
2015	170,492	217,729	205,075	168,204	151,739	189,500	180,410	173,734	172,828	186,334	174,098	187,855
2016	187,904	177,999	171,820	162,225	173,204	172,984	155,301	173,698	195,884	190,086	208,329	210,792
2017	181,938	181,007	185,572	185,411	178,603	159,381	117,599	128,345	180,168	173,585	192,341	171,325
2018	171,262	180,496	184,370	210,695	207,565	200,361	172,198	173,769	178,603	147,365	168,872	175,750

Contract size = 20 tonnes.   Source: ICE Futures Canada (ICE)

World Supply and Distribution of Canola and Products — In Thousands of Metric Tons

Year	Canola Production	Imports	Exports	Crush	Ending Stocks	Canola Meal Production	Imports	Exports	Consumption	Ending Stocks	Canola oil Production	Imports	Exports	Consumption	Ending Stocks
2011-12	61,228	13,244	12,988	60,455	6,829	34,924	5,557	5,560	34,878	1,103	24,719	4,076	3,980	23,794	3,302
2012-13	63,305	12,831	12,572	62,093	5,503	35,969	5,613	5,698	36,007	980	25,386	3,933	3,952	23,729	4,940
2013-14	70,590	15,549	15,099	66,236	7,725	38,319	6,501	6,351	38,525	924	27,018	3,817	3,828	25,682	6,265
2014-15	70,429	14,318	15,105	67,095	7,257	38,715	5,991	6,067	38,585	978	27,411	3,949	4,065	27,044	6,516
2015-16	68,740	14,146	14,347	66,717	6,161	38,606	5,704	5,689	38,504	1,095	27,340	4,132	4,166	28,178	5,644
2016-17	69,436	15,528	15,800	67,352	4,989	38,765	5,886	6,031	38,685	1,030	27,537	4,391	4,522	28,898	4,152
2017-18[1]	74,028	15,151	16,355	67,825	6,728	39,044	6,121	6,340	39,244	611	27,860	4,499	4,620	28,652	3,239
2018-19[2]	70,217	16,731	17,052	67,670	5,972	39,058	6,125	6,162	38,996	636	27,707	4,765	4,826	27,825	3,060

[1] Preliminary. [2] Estimate. [3] Forecast. *Source: Economic Research Service, U.S. Department of Agriculture (ERS-USDA); The Oil World*

Salient Statistics of Canola and Canola Oil in the United States — In Thousands of Metric Tons

Year	Canola Supply Stocks June 1	Production	Imports	Total Supply	Disappearance Exports	Crush	Total[3]	Canola Oil Supply Stocks Oct. 1	Production	Imports	Total Supply	Disappearance Exports	Domestic	Total
2011-12	102	694	622	1,418	153	1,168	1,418	136	499	1,492	2,127	301	1,741	2,127
2012-13	70	1,087	394	1,551	177	1,266	1,551	85	578	1,252	1,915	216	1,635	1,915
2013-14	81	1,004	927	2,012	159	1,689	2,012	64	710	1,536	2,310	119	2,066	2,310
2014-15	129	1,141	777	2,047	160	1,740	2,047	125	704	1,675	2,504	110	2,273	2,504
2015-16	110	1,306	359	1,775	176	1,542	1,775	121	722	1,797	2,640	111	2,414	2,640
2016-17	161	1,409	697	2,267	119	2,003	2,267	115	798	2,000	2,913	123	2,656	2,913
2017-18[1]	108	1,424	647	2,179	153	1,766	2,179	134	752	1,852	2,738	105	2,545	2,738
2018-19[2]	88	1,646	570	2,304	193	1,972	2,304	88	829	2,030	2,947	110	2,710	2,947

[1] Preliminary. [2] Forecast. [3] Includes planting seed and residual. *Source: Economic Research Service, U.S. Department of Agriculture (ERS-USDA)*

Wholesale Price of Canola Oil in Midwest — In Cents Per Pound

Year	Jan.	Feb.	Mar.	Apr.	May	June	July	Aug.	Sept.	Oct.	Nov.	Dec.	Average
2011	59.50	60.13	60.25	62.05	60.19	59.56	60.70	60.00	58.45	56.81	56.13	55.40	59.10
2012	55.06	56.94	59.10	60.94	55.88	54.10	57.44	58.75	59.75	57.50	58.20	57.13	57.57
2013	57.19	59.38	58.95	60.44	60.45	57.50	53.25	48.05	46.00	44.88	45.05	42.63	52.81
2014	39.75	42.56	45.75	47.63	47.50	46.00	43.63	40.10	38.94	39.45	38.94	39.25	42.46
2015	38.80	38.94	35.69	37.19	38.55	40.19	38.30	35.13	33.31	34.20	33.63	36.50	36.70
2016	34.06	34.63	35.55	36.80	35.06	35.10	33.55	36.94	37.25	38.94	39.25	40.20	36.44
2017	38.69	37.25	37.30	36.13	37.06	37.85	39.75	41.19	41.15	39.06	39.69	38.65	38.65
2018[1]	38.31	37.44	37.10	37.31	38.25	37.75	38.69	38.75	38.19	38.94	37.45	36.75	37.91

[1] Preliminary. *Source: Economic Research Service, U.S. Department of Agriculture (ERS-USDA)*

Average Price of Canola in Vancouver — In Canadian Dollars Per Metric Ton

Year	Jan.	Feb.	Mar.	Apr.	May	June	July	Aug.	Sept.	Oct.	Nov.	Dec.	Average
2011	567.16	577.71	558.19	569.44	555.48	574.44	563.30	547.52	528.64	509.52	513.06	502.88	547.28
2012	512.75	539.92	591.55	626.52	624.60	629.57	657.26	632.65	644.75	627.09	594.75	601.67	606.92
2013	613.04	636.36	635.99	641.70	643.47	626.04	571.91	513.54	473.76	457.25	461.44	418.96	557.79
2014	386.37	380.71	412.23	435.66	459.42	453.37	446.33	430.27	397.71	404.23	423.82	419.92	420.84
2015	432.04	437.63	444.39	443.37	448.45	488.36	514.22	475.87	457.49	460.78	454.54	460.90	459.84
2016	466.39	454.66	450.95	482.41	508.73	502.94	461.72	437.87	426.82	457.28	484.44	488.93	468.60
2017	484.48	493.42	489.15	497.87	516.16	508.58	521.58	482.09	468.24	481.75	496.16	484.15	493.64
2018	475.97	488.09	504.44	516.61	520.50	511.14	491.80	475.69	465.45	Disc.	----	----	494.41

Source: ICE Futures Canada (ICE)

Average Wholesale Price of Canola Meal, 36% Pacific Northwest — In Dollars Per Short Ton

Year	Oct.	Nov.	Dec.	Jan.	Feb.	Mar.	Apr.	May	June	July	Aug.	Sept.	Average
2011-12	238.70	235.20	NA	253.98	257.63	277.83	313.38	333.69	335.26	378.86	388.13	370.79	307.59
2012-13	354.49	334.46	349.55	347.22	359.23	356.74	340.42	362.51	376.19	374.89	340.44	354.55	354.22
2013-14	334.95	342.86	373.60	365.48	384.21	383.68	398.39	407.14	387.65	317.81	303.74	316.94	359.70
2014-15	301.75	356.31	349.31	311.56	296.21	279.54	261.35	274.60	305.85	328.03	285.83	264.01	301.20
2015-16	257.69	248.98	240.64	231.76	224.34	228.87	247.53	329.01	345.14	306.03	255.35	231.00	262.20
2016-17	225.05	234.78	243.30	267.41	276.90	276.33	270.66	279.64	281.66	307.73	289.45	262.33	267.94
2017-18	257.73	255.74	266.53	270.20	315.95	334.58	332.16	336.93	302.75	279.84	274.55	266.86	291.15
2018-19[1]	279.40	279.16	291.42	----	----								283.33

[1] Preliminary. *Source: Economic Research Service, U.S. Department of Agriculture (ERS-USDA)*

Cattle and Calves

The beef cycle begins with the cow-calf operation, which breeds the new calves. Most ranchers breed their herds of cows in summer, thus producing the new crop of calves in spring (the gestation period is about nine months). This allows the calves to be born during the milder weather of spring and provides the calves with ample forage through the summer and early autumn. The calves are weaned from the mother after 6-8 months and most are then moved into the "stocker" operation. The calves usually spend 6-10 months in the stocker operation, growing to near full-sized by foraging for summer grass or winter wheat. When the cattle reach 600-800 pounds, they are typically sent to a feedlot and become "feeder cattle." In the feedlot, the cattle are fed a special food mix to encourage rapid weight gain. The mix includes grain (corn, milo, or wheat), a protein supplement (soybean, cottonseed, or linseed meal), and roughage (alfalfa, silage, prairie hay, or an agricultural by-product such as sugar beet pulp). The animal is considered "finished" when it reaches full weight and is ready for slaughter, typically at around 1,200 pounds, which produces a dressed carcass of around 745 pounds. After reaching full weight, the cattle are sold for slaughter to a meat packing plant. Futures and options on live cattle and feeder cattle are traded at the CME Group. Both the live and feeder cattle futures contracts trade in terms of cents per pound.

Prices – CME live cattle futures prices (Barchart.com electronic symbol LE) pushed higher in early 2018 and posted the high for the year in February at $1.30525 a pound. Robust foreign demand for U.S. beef was positive for prices in early 2018 as U.S. 2017 beef exports rose +12% yr/yr to 2.862 bln lbs and the USDA projected U.S. 2018 beef exports would rise +5.7% yr/yr to a record high 3.025 bln lbs. Cattle prices then tumbled to a 2-year low of $1.1010 a pound in April on demand concerns and abundant supplies. The Trump administration's imposition of tariffs attracted retaliatory tariffs on a range of U.S. farm exports. China announced a 25% tariff on U.S. beef exports to China. Cattle prices were also undercut by supply concerns after the USDA projected that U.S. 2018 beef production would rise +5.8% yr/yr to a record 27.752 bln lbs. Also, the September Cattle on Feed report showed cattle on feed as of September 1 rose +5.9% yr/yr to a record for a September at 11.125 mln head as the number of cattle on feed climbed for twenty straight months. In addition, the August Cold Storage report showed U.S. beef supplies in cold storage rose to a record high for the month of August of 503.449 mln lbs. Cattle prices then crept higher into year-end as foreign demand for U.S. beef remained firm despite trade frictions. U.S. 2018 beef exports Jan-Oct were up +12% yr/yr at 2.627 bln lbs. Cattle prices finished 2018 slightly higher by +1.5% yr at $1.2480 a pound.

Supply – The world's number of cattle as of January 1, 2019, rose +0.5% to 1.007 billion head. As of January 1, 2018, the number of cattle on farms in India (the world's largest herd) rose +0.5% to 306.500 million head and on Brazilian farms (the world's second largest herd) rose by +2.5% to 238.150 million head. As of January 1, 2019, the number of cattle and calves on U.S. farms rose by +0.6% yr/yr to 95.000 million head. The USDA reported that U.S. commercial production of beef in 2017 rose 4.3% yr/yr to 27.590 billion pounds.

Demand – The federally-inspected slaughter of cattle in the U.S., a measure of cattle consumption, rose by +3.0% yr/yr to 32.654 million head in 2018, up from the 5-decade low of 28.296 million head in 2015.

Trade – U.S. imports of live cattle in 2018 fell -.05% yr/yr to 1.796 million head. U.S. exports of live cattle in 2017 rose +180.1% yr/yr to 194.600 head, up sharply from last year's 69,500. U.S. imports of beef in 2018 rose +1.0% to 3.025 billion pounds. U.S. exports of beef in 2018 rose +9.2% yr/yr to 3.124 billion pounds, a new record high.

World Cattle and Buffalo Numbers as of January 1   In Thousands of Head

Year	Argentina	Australia	Brazil	Canada	China	European Union	India	Mexico	New Zealand	Russia	United States	Uraguay	World Total
2010	49,057	27,906	185,159	12,670	107,265	89,829	304,500	22,192	9,917	20,677	94,081	11,828	1,008,954
2011	48,156	27,550	190,925	12,155	106,264	87,831	302,500	21,456	9,864	19,970	92,887	11,241	1,002,413
2012	49,597	28,506	197,550	12,230	103,605	87,054	300,000	20,090	10,021	20,134	91,160	11,232	1,001,706
2013	51,095	28,418	203,273	12,240	103,434	87,106	299,606	18,521	10,180	19,930	90,095	11,384	1,005,225
2014	51,545	29,291	207,959	12,050	103,000	87,619	300,600	17,760	10,183	19,564	88,526	11,903	1,008,403
2015	51,545	29,102	213,035	11,640	100,450	88,406	301,100	17,120	10,368	19,152	89,143	12,053	979,636
2016	52,565	27,413	219,180	11,610	100,275	89,152	302,600	16,615	10,033	18,879	91,918	12,016	988,487
2017	53,515	24,971	226,045	11,535	99,173	89,152	303,600	16,490	10,152	18,638	93,705	11,864	995,357
2018[1]	53,715	25,500	232,350	11,575	96,850	88,439	305,000	16,584	10,146	18,564	94,399	11,744	1,001,829
2019[2]	54,215	25,200	238,150	11,520	94,700	87,290	306,500	16,815	10,200	18,500	95,000	11,500	1,007,263

[1] Preliminary.   [2] Forecast.   *Source: Foreign Agricultural Service, U.S. Department of Agriculture (FAS-USDA)*

CATTLE AND CALVES

Cattle Supply and Distribution in the United States   In Thousands of Head

Year	Cattle & Calves on Farms Jan. 1	Imports	Calves Born	Total Supply	Federally Inspected	Other[3]	All Commercial	Farm	Total Slaughter	Deaths on Farms	Exports	Total Disappearance
					Livestock Slaughter - Cattle and Calves	*Commercial*						
2009	94,521	2,002	35,939	132,462	33,696	587	34,283	185	34,468	4,064	58	38,590
2010	94,081	2,284	35,740	132,105	34,566	561	35,128	197	35,325	4,001	91	39,417
2011	92,887	2,107	35,357	130,352	34,394	546	34,939	169	35,108	4,017	194	39,319
2012	91,160	2,283	34,469	127,912	33,185	538	33,723	149	33,872	3,881	191	37,944
2013	90,095	2,033	33,730	125,858	32,698	526	33,224	130	33,355	3,870	161	37,385
2014	88,526	2,358	33,522	124,406	30,242	494	30,734	124	30,857	3,850	108	34,815
2015	89,143	1,985	34,087	125,214	28,742	462	29,204	116	29,320	3,880	73	33,273
2016	91,918	1,708	35,093	128,719	30,602	472	31,066	123	31,189	3,875	69	35,133
2017[1]	93,705	1,806	35,758	131,269	32,208		32,702	116	32,817		195	
2018[2]	94,298	1,860	36,403	132,561	33,090							

[1] Preliminary.   [2] Estimate.   [3] Wholesale and retail.   Source: Economic Research Service, U.S. Department of Agriculture (ERS-USDA)

Beef Supply and Utilization in the United States

Years and Quarters	Beginning Stocks	Commercial	Total	Imports	Total Supply	Exports	Ending Stocks	Total Disappearance	Carcass Weight	Retail Weight Total
		Production							*Per Capita Disappearance*	
2015	----	23,698	23,698	3,371	27,069	2,267	----	----	----	54.0
I	----	5,665	5,665	878	6,543	523	----	----	----	13.1
II	----	5,856	5,856	990	6,846	607	----	----	----	13.6
III	----	6,068	6,068	890	6,958	542	----	----	----	13.9
IV	----	6,109	6,109	613	6,722	595	----	----	----	13.3
2016	----	25,221	25,221	3,012	28,233	2,557	----	----	----	55.6
I	----	5,938	5,938	792	6,730	535	----	----	----	13.6
II	----	6,187	6,187	831	7,018	621	----	----	----	13.9
III	----	6,472	6,472	751	7,223	660	----	----	----	14.1
IV	----	6,625	6,625	638	7,263	740	----	----	----	14.0
2017	----	26,187	26,187	2,993	29,180	2,860	----	----	----	56.9
I	----	6,303	6,303	700	7,003	653	----	----	----	14.0
II	----	6,407	6,407	812	7,219	680	----	----	----	14.2
III	----	6,736	6,736	814	7,550	746	----	----	----	14.4
IV	----	6,742	6,742	668	7,410	781	----	----	----	14.3
2018[1]	----	26,868	26,868	2,998	29,866	3,156	----	----	----	57.0
I	----	6,465	6,465	722	7,187	730	----	----	----	13.9
II	----	6,724	6,724	805	7,529	799	----	----	----	14.4
III	----	6,820	6,820	807	7,627	826	----	----	----	14.3
IV	----	6,859	6,859	664	7,523	801	----	----	----	14.3
2019[2]	----	27,300	27,300	3,010	30,310	3,255	----	----	----	57.3
I	----	6,390	6,390	720	7,110	770	----	----	----	13.6
II	----	6,810	6,810	810	7,620	805	----	----	----	14.5
III	----	7,070	7,070	800	7,870	840	----	----	----	14.7
IV	----	7,030	7,030	680	7,710	840	----	----	----	14.5

[1] Preliminary.   [2] Forecast.   Source: Economic Research Service, U.S. Department of Agriculture (ERS-USDA)

United States Cattle on Feed in 13 States   In Thousands of Head

Year	Number on Feed[3]	Placed on Feed	Marketings	Other Disappearance	Year	Number on Feed[3]	Placed on Feed	Marketings	Other Disappearance
2015	10,626	20,432	19,660	823	2017[1]	10,605	23,513	21,899	730
I	10,626	5,149	4,772	206	I	10,605	5,792	5,313	165
II	10,797	4,748	5,097	212	II	10,919	5,737	5,643	192
III	10,236	5,120	4,955	173	III	10,821	5,693	5,546	155
IV	10,228	5,415	4,836	232	IV	10,813	6,291	5,397	218
2016	10,575	21,604	20,873	701	2018[2]	11,489	23,297	22,310	786
I	10,575	5,381	4,927	176	I	11,489	5,806	5,373	193
II	10,853	5,078	5,364	211	II	11,729	5,617	5,865	194
III	10,356	5,346	5,313	133	III	11,287	5,863	5,575	175
IV	10,256	5,799	5,269	181	IV	11,400	6,011	5,497	224

[1] Preliminary.   [2] Estimate.   [3] Beginning of period.   Source: Economic Research Service, U.S. Department of Agriculture (ERS-USDA)

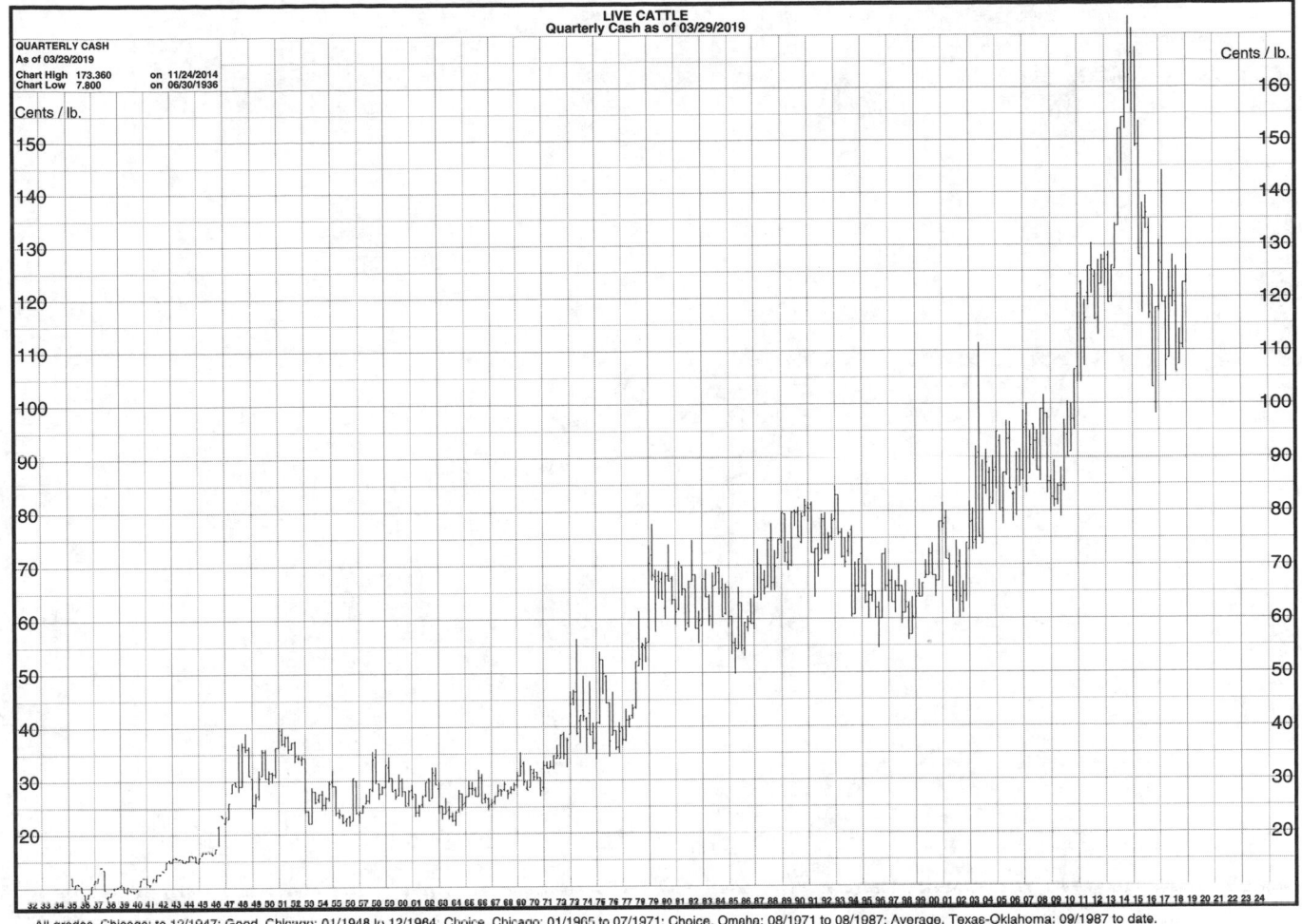

LIVE CATTLE
Quarterly Cash as of 03/29/2019

QUARTERLY CASH
As of 03/29/2019

Chart High 173.360 on 11/24/2014
Chart Low 7.800 on 06/30/1936

All grades, Chicago: to 12/1947; Good, Chicago: 01/1948 to 12/1964, Choice, Chicago: 01/1965 to 07/1971; Choice, Omaha: 08/1971 to 08/1987; Average, Texas-Oklahoma: 09/1987 to date.

United States Cattle on Feed, 1000+ Capacity Feedlots, on First of Month   In Thousands of Head

Year	Jan.	Feb.	Mar.	Apr.	May	June	July	Aug.	Sept.	Oct.	Nov.	Dec.
2009	11,234	11,288	11,228	11,162	10,822	10,407	9,752	9,637	9,900	10,474	11,134	11,277
2010	10,983	10,959	10,849	10,742	10,428	10,495	10,071	9,880	10,181	10,788	11,497	11,620
2011	11,513	11,571	11,386	11,257	11,175	10,902	10,433	10,579	10,700	11,282	11,889	12,055
2012	11,861	11,811	11,677	11,482	11,110	11,077	10,710	10,656	10,647	10,989	11,254	11,348
2013	11,172	11,070	10,845	10,924	10,760	10,767	10,375	10,025	9,876	10,110	10,585	10,724
2014	10,523	10,678	10,716	10,792	10,554	10,497	10,043	9,752	9,719	9,985	10,571	10,816
2015	10,626	10,713	10,688	10,797	10,640	10,571	10,236	10,002	9,986	10,228	10,809	10,800
2016	10,575	10,709	10,770	10,853	10,783	10,804	10,356	10,165	10,135	10,256	10,665	10,652
2017	10,605	10,782	10,772	10,919	10,998	11,096	10,821	10,604	10,504	10,813	11,332	11,516
2018[1]	11,489	11,630	11,715	11,729	11,558	11,553	11,287	11,093	11,125	11,400	11,692	11,739

[1] Preliminary.   Source: Economic Research Service, U.S. Department of Agriculture (ERS-USDA)

United States Cattle Placed on Feed, 1000+ Capacity Feedlots   In Thousands of Head

Year	Jan.	Feb.	Mar.	Apr.	May	June	July	Aug.	Sept.	Oct.	Nov.	Dec.	Total
2009	1,858	1,678	1,808	1,600	1,638	1,391	1,863	2,119	2,388	2,474	1,844	1,526	22,187
2010	1,822	1,674	1,856	1,634	2,030	1,628	1,758	2,271	2,463	2,505	1,959	1,789	23,389
2011	1,889	1,667	1,914	1,785	1,810	1,695	2,135	2,246	2,469	2,492	2,037	1,673	23,812
2012	1,847	1,714	1,792	1,521	2,084	1,664	1,922	2,007	2,004	2,180	1,943	1,576	22,254
2013	1,869	1,438	1,884	1,720	2,055	1,551	1,684	1,772	1,988	2,378	1,867	1,654	21,860
2014	2,014	1,658	1,801	1,623	1,909	1,468	1,559	1,725	2,014	2,368	1,794	1,537	21,470
2015	1,789	1,551	1,809	1,548	1,719	1,481	1,547	1,632	1,941	2,286	1,602	1,527	20,432
2016	1,779	1,710	1,892	1,664	1,889	1,525	1,572	1,879	1,895	2,171	1,843	1,785	21,604
2017	1,981	1,694	2,117	1,848	2,119	1,770	1,615	1,928	2,150	2,393	2,099	1,799	23,513
2018[1]	2,068	1,817	1,921	1,695	2,124	1,798	1,742	2,070	2,051	2,248	1,996	1,767	23,297

[1] Preliminary.   Source: Economic Research Service, U.S. Department of Agriculture (ERS-USDA)

CATTLE AND CALVES

CATTLE, LIVE - CME
Weekly Selected Futures as of 03/29/2019

WEEKLY SELECTED FUTURES
As of 03/29/2019
Chart High 171.975 on 10/31/2014
Chart Low 78.700 on 12/10/2009

Nearby Futures through Last Trading Day.

United States Cattle Marketings, 1000+ Capacity Feedlots[2] In Thousands of Head

Year	Jan.	Feb.	Mar.	Apr.	May	June	July	Aug.	Sept.	Oct.	Nov.	Dec.	Total
2009	1,737	1,682	1,824	1,871	1,952	1,989	1,935	1,800	1,767	1,755	1,635	1,745	21,692
2010	1,776	1,716	1,903	1,857	1,865	1,997	1,901	1,923	1,802	1,734	1,774	1,830	22,078
2011	1,774	1,791	1,990	1,807	2,002	2,092	1,918	2,053	1,813	1,787	1,774	1,776	22,577
2012	1,816	1,755	1,918	1,815	2,017	1,965	1,913	1,955	1,598	1,837	1,761	1,678	22,028
2013	1,892	1,603	1,724	1,815	1,948	1,880	1,970	1,871	1,692	1,827	1,660	1,736	21,618
2014	1,788	1,549	1,660	1,778	1,865	1,847	1,787	1,692	1,683	1,685	1,475	1,655	20,464
2015	1,625	1,516	1,631	1,639	1,711	1,747	1,725	1,588	1,642	1,630	1,532	1,674	19,660
2016	1,589	1,591	1,747	1,658	1,794	1,912	1,713	1,868	1,732	1,705	1,787	1,777	20,873
2017	1,751	1,648	1,914	1,703	1,951	1,989	1,784	1,979	1,783	1,801	1,844	1,752	20,873
2018[1]	1,858	1,675	1,840	1,803	2,056	2,006	1,873	1,983	1,719	1,887	1,869	1,741	22,310

[1] Preliminary. *Source: Economic Research Service, U.S. Department of Agriculture (ERS-USDA)*

Quarterly Trade of Live Cattle in the United States In Head

	Imports					Exports				
Year	First Quarter	Second Quarter	Third Quarter	Fourth Quarter	Total	First Quarter	Second Quarter	Third Quarter	Fourth Quarter	Total
2009	612,188	423,742	342,988	622,956	2,001,874	6,903	18,153	16,354	16,613	58,023
2010	598,853	596,339	406,926	681,767	2,283,885	15,526	20,853	17,552	37,159	91,090
2011	580,696	488,356	376,602	661,649	2,107,303	35,446	41,142	45,749	71,571	193,908
2012	672,076	650,094	326,509	634,109	2,282,788	41,379	45,837	36,427	67,241	190,884
2013	595,623	474,806	309,404	653,290	2,033,123	30,707	50,454	38,259	41,258	160,678
2014	599,440	562,937	415,409	780,581	2,358,367	27,541	25,988	25,813	28,342	107,684
2015	564,315	534,024	413,354	472,875	1,984,568	12,576	23,575	15,664	20,744	72,559
2016	490,504	459,089	288,205	470,251	1,708,049	13,498	11,733	10,219	34,035	69,485
2017	517,913	439,901	317,584	530,501	1,805,899	31,987	32,447	34,867	95,332	194,633
2018[1]	467,307	497,270	364,205	564,143	1,859,866	37,834	47,737	62,942	105,666	238,862

[1] Preliminary. *Source: Economic Research Service, U.S. Department of Agriculture (ERS-USDA)*

FEEDER CATTLE
Quarterly Cash as of 03/29/2019

QUARTERLY CASH
As of 03/29/2019
Chart High 244.990 on 12/03/2014
Chart Low 24.750 on 01/31/1975

Oklahoma City: to date.

Average Slaughter Steer Price, Choice 2-4, Nebraska Direct (1100-1300 Lb.)   In Dollars Per 100 Pounds

Year	Jan.	Feb.	Mar.	Apr.	May	June	July	Aug.	Sept.	Oct.	Nov.	Dec.	Average
2012	123.73	125.74	127.16	122.26	122.07	119.27	114.95	119.50	125.14	125.61	125.75	125.65	123.07
2013	124.33	125.47	126.83	128.08	120.48	121.70	120.41	123.78	124.23	130.09	132.23	131.18	126.10
2014	143.33	146.45	151.93	149.01	146.19	149.55	158.57	158.35	159.86	164.91	170.04	163.09	155.11
2015	165.13	160.29	163.42	162.98	160.76	151.13	149.17	149.06	136.28	132.88	126.90	125.00	148.58
2016	133.15	133.85	137.83	129.52	129.90	122.95	117.10	116.91	106.22	101.76	106.23	115.24	120.70
2017	119.92	121.83	126.91	131.18	138.42	130.10	118.08	113.01	107.73	113.40	122.49	119.73	121.90
2018[1]	124.35	127.93	124.97	121.11	116.14	110.10	112.39	109.98	110.69	111.53	115.28	120.34	117.07

[1] Preliminary.   Source: Economic Research Service, U.S. Department of Agriculture (ERS-USDA)

Average Price of Feeder Steers in Oklahoma City   In Dollars Per 100 Pounds

Year	Jan.	Feb.	Mar.	Apr.	May	June	July	Aug.	Sept.	Oct.	Nov.	Dec.	Average
2012	150.15	155.24	155.34	150.24	149.53	152.85	140.49	138.43	142.56	144.22	144.25	147.32	147.55
2013	147.99	142.75	136.98	136.75	133.75	135.78	144.26	152.68	156.92	161.92	165.05	166.20	148.41
2014	170.98	170.61	174.43	178.55	185.49	201.90	216.19	221.28	228.15	239.59	240.37	233.67	205.10
2015	224.57	210.18	212.80	218.29	219.14	226.34	219.98	215.14	200.97	188.55	181.41	159.43	206.40
2016	162.19	158.82	160.13	154.07	146.07	144.74	142.23	146.88	136.34	124.66	126.85	131.41	144.53
2017	132.65	127.78	129.29	136.04	144.23	150.36	149.39	146.20	149.54	155.21	157.93	152.81	144.29
2018	149.61	147.91	141.90	136.73	136.14	140.75	147.25	150.14	153.97	156.14	149.97	146.09	146.38

Source: Economic Research Service, U.S. Department of Agriculture (ERS-USDA)

Federally Inspected Slaughter of Cattle in the United States   In Thousands of Head

Year	Jan.	Feb.	Mar.	Apr.	May	June	July	Aug.	Sept.	Oct.	Nov.	Dec.	Total
2012	2,666	2,515	2,713	2,528	2,836	2,826	2,755	2,952	2,497	2,897	2,740	2,500	32,425
2013	2,785	2,315	2,545	2,689	2,823	2,693	2,856	2,778	2,568	2,851	2,527	2,518	31,947
2014	2,634	2,204	2,413	2,556	2,597	2,568	2,562	2,463	2,490	2,591	2,210	2,398	29,684
2015	2,377	2,135	2,342	2,346	2,345	2,430	2,459	2,288	2,435	2,469	2,259	2,414	28,296
2016	2,320	2,252	2,493	2,373	2,479	2,670	2,443	2,711	2,578	2,592	2,632	2,572	30,115
2017	2,533	2,330	2,726	2,425	2,713	2,821	2,577	2,903	2,655	2,753	2,726	2,543	31,704
2018[1]	2,714	2,378	2,661	2,599	2,868	2,842	2,729	2,937	2,577	2,908	2,762	2,544	32,518

[1] Preliminary.   Source: National Agricultural Statistics Service, U.S. Department of Agriculture (NASS-USDA)

CATTLE AND CALVES

CATTLE, FEEDER - CME
Weekly Nearest Futures as of 03/29/2019

WEEKLY NEAREST FUTURES
As of 03/29/2019
Chart High 245.200 on 10/09/2014
Chart Low 87.600 on 02/23/2009

Nearby Futures through Last Trading Day using Selected contract months: February, April, June, August, October and December.

Volume of Trading of Live Cattle Futures Chicago   In Thousands of Contracts

Year	Jan.	Feb.	Mar.	Apr.	May	June	July	Aug.	Sept.	Oct.	Nov.	Dec.	Total
2009	819.5	616.8	789.3	641.3	721.5	617.8	855.4	657.9	854.6	739.7	844.3	638.9	8,797.0
2010	901.0	782.9	1,167.2	863.2	1,204.5	785.8	923.8	868.3	1,158.8	827.1	1,066.3	783.9	11,332.7
2011	1,181.8	910.9	1,531.6	928.4	1,293.3	1,097.4	1,148.8	1,034.4	1,325.4	1,067.2	1,136.1	877.4	13,532.6
2012	1,179.7	1,078.3	1,516.9	1,180.1	1,399.6	1,022.4	1,293.1	1,097.1	1,185.9	977.2	1,090.4	964.8	13,985.4
2013	1,484.1	1,069.5	1,249.3	977.9	1,189.7	831.3	1,020.8	884.5	972.5	1,040.2	986.9	756.2	12,463.0
2014	1,381.4	970.0	1,270.2	847.7	1,139.3	1,126.6	1,503.5	1,023.5	1,303.4	1,061.5	962.5	1,009.6	13,599.3
2015	1,282.2	918.7	1,163.5	959.6	1,139.1	955.3	1,166.5	901.6	1,344.2	1,222.5	1,213.9	1,173.9	13,440.9
2016	1,127.6	956.2	1,187.4	1,010.7	1,234.8	852.5	1,070.5	990.9	1,335.8	1,028.2	1,257.5	1,070.7	13,122.8
2017	1,300.9	958.4	1,552.2	1,260.5	2,164.7	1,201.2	1,487.1	1,155.8	1,364.4	1,228.1	1,501.6	990.4	16,165.2
2018	1,493.4	1,078.6	1,621.7	1,294.7	1,680.4	1,170.3	1,476.9	1,205.5	1,433.2	1,397.4	1,466.9	1,121.1	16,440.1

Contract size = 40,000 lbs.   *Source: CME Group; Chicago Mercantile Exchange (CME)*

Average Open Interest of Live Cattle Futures in Chicago   In Contracts

Year	Jan.	Feb.	Mar.	Apr.	May	June	July	Aug.	Sept.	Oct.	Nov.	Dec.
2009	207,768	203,912	207,221	206,462	204,424	211,978	222,562	233,578	251,083	260,285	266,293	262,738
2010	276,265	294,225	343,951	362,939	362,895	327,910	323,477	339,349	344,298	317,349	321,039	332,858
2011	344,671	358,852	366,250	380,138	346,614	326,592	322,313	309,147	324,714	336,225	325,195	315,700
2012	333,921	350,623	358,333	351,179	337,579	318,041	305,336	290,534	294,356	289,303	327,964	331,211
2013	329,529	330,784	335,436	325,462	315,201	290,113	275,925	289,980	295,826	314,058	333,154	323,189
2014	354,327	371,310	369,611	352,639	345,372	352,223	343,096	313,046	315,722	313,134	317,289	286,556
2015	261,167	243,091	259,858	273,309	296,935	287,815	241,553	236,485	258,984	258,122	271,979	256,669
2016	274,078	272,513	291,131	282,634	271,110	247,299	248,641	247,108	262,608	268,144	278,901	294,562
2017	333,745	332,286	360,860	404,610	421,183	403,152	372,623	320,894	327,393	334,666	380,212	341,419
2018	353,135	370,641	362,617	348,766	356,141	329,947	317,434	301,001	314,505	335,731	342,814	347,681

Contract size = 40,000 lbs.   *Source: CME Group; Chicago Mercantile Exchange (CME)*

Beef Steer-Corn Price Ratio[1] in the United States

Year	Jan.	Feb.	Mar.	Apr.	May	June	July	Aug.	Sept.	Oct.	Nov.	Dec.	Average
2009	19.7	21.7	21.8	22.9	22.1	21.2	23.7	25.6	26.3	23.4	23.4	23.3	22.9
2010	23.9	25.5	27.0	29.6	28.6	27.8	27.5	26.9	24.4	22.9	22.2	21.6	25.7
2011	22.3	19.6	21.3	19.2	18.2	17.2	18.2	16.6	18.3	21.3	21.6	21.5	19.6
2012	21.4	20.9	20.8	20.2	19.7	19.5	16.4	15.7	18.1	18.7	18.3	18.6	19.0
2013	18.7	17.8	17.8	18.2	18.2	17.8	17.8	19.6	23.0	27.6	30.2	29.9	21.4
2014	31.7	33.3	33.2	31.8	31.2	32.9	38.7	43.8	45.3	45.7	46.9	43.8	38.2
2015	43.5	42.5	42.5	43.7	44.2	43.5	39.5	40.5	38.0	35.1	36.5	33.7	40.3
2016	36.1	37.4	38.5	37.4	35.1	33.2	33.3	36.8	33.9	31.0	32.7	34.0	35.0
2017	35.0	35.2	36.4	37.9	40.0	38.8	34.7	35.2	32.7	34.0	38.4	37.2	36.3
2018[1]	37.4	37.6	36.2	34.1	33.2	31.6	32.3	33.3	32.4	32.8	33.7	33.6	34.0

[1] Bushels of corn equal in value to 100 pounds of steers and heifers.   [2] Preliminary.   *Source: Economic Research Service, U.S. Department of Agriculture*

Average Price Received by Farmers for Beef Cattle in the United States   In Dollars Per 100 Pounds

Year	Jan.	Feb.	Mar.	Apr.	May	June	July	Aug.	Sept.	Oct.	Nov.	Dec.	Average
2009	80.10	78.90	79.10	83.80	83.20	80.10	80.90	80.40	80.50	79.20	79.60	78.50	80.36
2010	82.10	85.70	90.40	95.60	94.70	90.40	91.70	93.50	94.10	93.10	94.00	98.10	91.95
2011	107.00	108.00	115.00	119.00	112.00	107.00	111.00	111.00	112.00	117.00	120.00	120.00	113.25
2012	125.00	127.00	128.00	124.00	122.00	121.00	114.00	117.00	121.00	123.00	123.00	124.00	122.42
2013	126.00	123.00	125.00	125.00	126.00	122.00	120.00	121.00	122.00	127.00	130.00	130.00	124.75
2014	138.00	144.00	148.00	148.00	146.00	147.00	156.00	158.00	157.00	161.00	167.00	164.00	152.83
2015	164.00	159.00	160.00	162.00	160.00	155.00	149.00	148.00	139.00	128.00	129.00	122.00	147.92
2016	130.00	132.00	135.00	131.00	128.00	125.00	119.00	117.00	108.00	101.00	104.00	111.00	120.08
2017	117.00	119.00	125.00	128.00	136.00	132.00	120.00	114.00	105.00	109.00	119.00	118.00	120.17
2018[1]	120.00	125.00	125.00	119.00	120.00	112.00	110.00	110.00	108.00	110.00	113.00	117.00	115.75

[1] Preliminary.   *Source: National Agricultural Statistics Service, U.S. Department of Agriculture (NASS-USDA)*

Average Price Received by Farmers for Calves in the United States   In Dollars Per 100 Pounds

Year	Jan.	Feb.	Mar.	Apr.	May	June	July	Aug.	Sept.	Oct.	Nov.	Dec.	Average
2009	106.00	104.00	106.00	100.00	111.00	109.00	108.00	108.00	105.00	103.00	104.00	105.00	106.50
2010	109.00	113.00	117.00	124.00	124.00	122.00	122.00	123.00	118.00	121.00	125.00	130.00	120.67
2011	136.00	139.00	148.00	147.00	137.00	133.00	138.00	134.00	132.00	145.00	153.00	157.00	141.58
2012	169.00	184.00	184.00	178.00	176.00	166.00	144.00	155.00	162.00	164.00	161.00	163.00	167.17
2013	168.00	170.00	163.00	159.00	157.00	152.00	162.00	178.00	200.00	190.00	192.00	197.00	174.00
2014	208.00	209.00	216.00	222.00	229.00	249.00	257.00	271.00	279.00	307.00	305.00	303.00	254.58
2015	288.00	277.00	290.00	288.00	288.00	292.00	275.00	273.00	241.00	234.00	217.00	193.00	263.00
2016	196.00	201.00	199.00	183.00	173.00	168.00	145.00	158.00	142.00	134.00	144.00	148.00	165.92
2017	152.00	151.00	159.00	164.00	171.00	164.00	157.00	163.00	173.00	177.00	177.00	174.00	165.17
2018[1]	174.00	180.00	175.00	170.00	165.00	158.00	153.00	160.00	169.00	174.00	169.00	166.00	167.75

[1] Preliminary.   *Source: National Agricultural Statistics Board, U.S. Department of Agriculture (NASS-USDA)*

Federally Inspected Slaughter of Calves and Vealers in the United States   In Thousands of Head

Year	Jan.	Feb.	Mar.	Apr.	May	June	July	Aug.	Sept.	Oct.	Nov.	Dec.	Total
2009	83.6	73.0	78.8	67.1	64.2	76.0	78.9	75.6	79.9	82.2	80.0	91.1	930.4
2010	81.6	72.9	78.8	67.4	59.1	67.3	74.1	74.8	70.0	70.0	71.7	76.6	864.3
2011	70.8	67.9	71.8	57.9	60.0	71.5	72.4	78.9	72.5	71.5	71.9	71.8	838.9
2012	66.6	59.3	58.5	55.4	58.2	55.0	66.5	71.6	63.2	71.6	69.4	64.5	759.8
2013	69.9	58.7	61.6	57.7	57.6	56.7	69.1	63.5	62.0	68.5	59.7	65.8	750.8
2014	62.0	51.5	52.9	48.0	45.9	44.6	47.8	43.0	41.8	42.6	35.2	42.2	557.5
2015	39.3	36.1	39.2	34.7	32.7	34.5	36.0	33.9	36.8	39.6	38.2	44.5	445.5
2016	41.2	37.8	41.3	34.2	34.9	37.0	37.1	40.3	41.8	47.6	46.6	48.1	487.9
2017	45.9	39.6	44.3	38.4	38.5	39.6	38.3	45.4	42.9	43.2	41.7	45.6	503.4
2018[1]	48.4	40.4	43.0	42.1	45.7	44.6	47.0	51.6	47.8	52.9	54.9	53.0	571.4

[1] Preliminary.   *Source: Crop Reporting Board, U.S. Department of Agriculture (CRB-USDA)*

Cement

Cement is made in a wide variety of compositions and is used in many different ways. The best-known cement is *Portland cement*, which is bound with sand and gravel to create concrete. Concrete is used to unite the surfaces of various materials and to coat surfaces to protect them from various chemicals. Portland cement is almost universally used for structural concrete. It is manufactured from lime-bearing materials, usually limestone, together with clays, blast-furnace slag containing alumina and silica or shale. The combination is usually approximately 60 percent lime, 19 percent silica, 8 percent alumina, 5 percent iron, 5 percent magnesia, and 3 percent sulfur trioxide. To slow the hardening process, gypsum is often added. In 1924, the name "Portland cement" was coined by Joseph Aspdin, a British cement maker, because of the resemblance between concrete made from his cement and Portland stone. The United States did not start producing Portland cement in any great quantity until the 20th century. Hydraulic cements are those that set and harden in water. Clinker cement is an intermediate product in cement manufacture. The production and consumption of cement is directly related to the level of activity in the construction industry.

Prices – The average value (F.O.B. mill) of Portland cement in 2018 rose by +4.5% yr/yr to $126.50 per ton, posting a new record high.

Supply – World production of hydraulic cement in 2018 rose by +1.2% to 4.100 billion metric tons, just below the 2014 record high of 4.190 billion. The world's largest hydraulic cement producers were China with 57.8% of world production in 2018, India with 7.1%, U.S. with 2.2%, and Turkey with 2.0%.

U.S. production of cement in 2018 rose +2.0% yr/yr to 87.800 million metric tons, but still below the 2005 record high of 99.319 million metric tons. U.S. shipments of cement from mills in the U.S. in 2018 rose +2.7% to 100.000 million metric tons but remained below the 2005 record high of 128.000 million metric tons.

Demand – U.S. consumption of cement in 2018 rose +4.7% to 102.000 million metric tons but was still far below the 2005 record high of 128.260 million metric tons.

Trade – The U.S. relied on imports for 14% of its cement consumption in 2018. The two main suppliers of cement to the U.S. were Canada and Mexico. U.S. exports of cement in 2018 fell -3.4% yr/yr to 1.000 million metric tons.

World Production of Hydraulic Cement   In Thousands of Short Tons

Year	Brazil	China	France	Germany	India	Italy	Japan	Korea, South	Russia	Spain	Turkey	United States	World Total
2011	64,093	2,099,000	19,270	32,779	240,000	33,120	51,291	48,249	56,200	22,178	63,405	68,639	3,630,000
2012	69,323	2,210,000	17,810	32,432	270,000	26,240	54,737	46,862	61,700	15,939	63,879	74,934	3,820,000
2013	69,975	2,411,000	18,018	31,308	280,000	23,100	57,962	47,291	66,503	13,736	71,337	77,415	4,070,000
2014	71,254	2,492,000	16,400	32,099	280,000	21,400	57,913	47,048	69,139	14,587	71,329	83,124	4,190,000
2015	65,283	2,359,000	15,600	31,160	300,000	22,000	54,827	52,044	62,104	15,000	71,419	84,940	4,100,000
2016	57,000	2,400,000			280,000		53,300	57,000	56,000		75,400	85,000	4,100,000
2017[1]	53,000	2,320,000			290,000		55,200	56,500	54,700		80,600	86,600	4,050,000
2018[2]	52,000	2,370,000			290,000		55,500	56,000	55,000		84,000	88,500	4,100,000

[1] Preliminary.   [2] Estimate.   *Source: U.S. Geological Survey (USGS)*

Salient Statistics of Cement in the United States

Year	Net Import Reliance as a % of Apparent Consump	Production Portland	Other[3]	Total --- 1,000 Metric tons ----	Capacity Used at Portland Mills %	Shipments --- From Mills Total (Mil. MT)	Value[4] (Mil. $)	Average Value (F.O.B. Mill) $ per MT	Stocks at Mills Dec. 31	Exports	Apparent Consumption	Imports for Consumption[5] by Country Canada	Japan	Mexico	Spain	Total
2011	7	66,136	1,759	67,895	54.1	72,100	6,440	89.50	6,270	1,414	72,200	3,416	1	354	[6]	6,418
2012	7	72,222	1,929	74,151	59.9	78,300	7,020	89.50	6,900	1,749	77,900	3,709	1	300	38	6,893
2013	7	74,689	2,115	76,804	62.6	83,187	7,760	95.00	6,570	1,670	81,800	3,615	2	308	[6]	7,095
2014	8	80,315	2,285	82,600	67.1	90,204	8,930	100.50	6,140	1,404	89,145	3,739	1	354	[6]	8,304
2015	11	82,093	2,312	84,405	68.5	93,338	9,800	106.50	7,230	1,288	92,403	4,497	2	338	270	11,318
2016[1]	13			84,695		95,373		111.00	7,420	1,283	94,964					
2017[2]	13			86,100		97,359		121.00	7,400	1,035	97,400					
2018[2]	14			87,800		100,000		126.50	8,050	1,000	102,000					

[1] Preliminary.   [2] Estimate.   [3] Masonry, natural & pozzolan (slag-line).   [4] Value received F.O.B. mill, excluding cost of containers.   [5] Hydraulic & clinker cement for consumption.   [6] Less than 1/2 unit.   *Source: U.S. Geological Survey (USGS)*

Shipments of Finished Portland Cement from Mills in the United States   In Thousands of Metric Tons

Year	Jan.	Feb.	Mar.	Apr.	May	June	July	Aug.	Sept.	Oct.	Nov.	Dec.	Total
2012	4,256.6	4,375.9	5,565.9	6,172.8	6,858.9	6,984.9	6,709.5	7,455.3	6,340.6	7,371.7	6,094.6	4,341.5	72,528.2
2013	4,413.4	4,290.4	5,344.9	6,098.7	7,022.2	6,954.2	7,422.6	7,856.7	7,287.9	7,965.3	6,025.7	4,708.3	75,390.3
2014	4,405.2	4,336.7	5,644.2	6,786.1	7,503.4	7,598.1	8,240.1	7,970.4	8,187.0	8,742.4	5,905.7	5,685.6	81,018.8
2015	4,874.8	4,288.7	5,697.8	6,890.4	6,920.1	7,977.7	8,318.2	8,169.8	9,035.5	8,311.3	6,512.3	5,930.7	82,927.4
2016	4,725.8	5,376.4	6,723.3	6,763.5	7,136.6	8,268.5	7,237.9	8,272.8	7,741.7	7,958.6	7,008.8	5,414.3	82,628.2
2017	4,869.2	5,398.2	6,687.5	6,673.6	7,738.1	8,236.3	7,507.0	8,497.2	7,606.4	8,222.6	7,253.1	5,515.0	84,204.1
2018[1]	5,161.1	5,082.8	6,603.5	7,233.3	8,253.8	8,140.2	8,028.7	8,885.2	7,295.0	8,532.0			87,858.8

[1] Preliminary.   *Source: U.S. Geological Survey (USGS)*

Cheese

Since prehistoric times, humans have been making and eating cheese. Dating back as far as 6,000 BC, archaeologists have discovered that cheese had been made from cow and goat milk and stored in tall jars. The Romans turned cheese making into a culinary art, mixing sheep and goat milk and adding herbs and spices for flavoring. By 300 AD, cheese was being exported regularly to countries along the Mediterranean coast.

Cheese is made from the milk of cows and other mammals such as sheep, goats, buffalo, reindeer, camels, yaks, and mares. More than 400 varieties of cheese exist. There are three basic steps common to all cheese making. First, proteins in milk are transformed into curds, or solid lumps. Second, the curds are separated from the milky liquid (or whey) and shaped or pressed into molds. Finally, the shaped curds are ripened according to a variety of aging and curing techniques. Cheeses are usually grouped according to their moisture content into fresh, soft, semi-soft, hard, and very hard. Many classifications overlap due to texture changes with aging.

Cheese is a multi-billion-dollar a year industry in the U.S. Cheddar cheese is the most common natural cheese produced in the U.S., accounting for 35% of U.S. production. Cheeses originating in America include Colby, cream cheese, and Monterey Jack. Varieties other than American cheeses, mostly Italian, now have had a combined level of production that easily exceeds American cheeses.

Cheese futures are traded at the CME Group. The CME's cheese futures contract calls for the delivery of 20,000 pounds of cheese and is priced in U.S. Dollars per pound.

Prices – Average monthly cheese prices at the CME Group in 2018 fell -3.1% yr/yr to $1.5614 per pound, far below the 2014 record high of $2.1094 cents per pound.

Supply – World production of cheese in 2019 is expected to rise +1.2% yr/yr to 20.779 million metric tons, which would be a new record high. The European Union is expected to be the world's largest producer of cheese with 49.3% of the total world production in 2019. The U.S. production was the next largest with 28.8% of the total. U.S. production of cheese in 2017 rose +3.9% to 12.659 billion pounds, which was a new record high.

World Production of Cheese   In Thousands of Metric Tons

Year	Argentina	Australia	Brazil	Canada	European Union	Japan	Korea, South	Mexico	New Zealand	Russia	Ukraine	United States	World Total
2010	540	343	648	383	8,959	48	27	275	268	776	269	4,737	17,486
2011	572	337	679	378	8,981	45	25	275	300	753	254	4,806	17,598
2012	564	352	700	386	9,287	47	23	293	328	790	245	4,938	18,154
2013	549	318	722	388	9,368	49	22	316	311	713	247	5,036	18,223
2014	562	328	736	396	9,560	46	24	343	325	760	203	5,222	18,733
2015	566	343	754	419	9,740	46	23	363	355	861	190	5,367	19,270
2016	552	344	745	445	9,810	47	25	375	360	865	186	5,525	19,556
2017	514	348	771	497	10,050	46	35	396	378	951	190	5,742	20,180
2018[1]	555	360	755	510	10,160	45	43	410	380	975	192	5,878	20,538
2019[2]	585	355	770	515	10,235	46	45	422	384	965	195	5,992	20,779

[1] Preliminary.   [2] Forecast.   NA = Not available.   Source: Foreign Agricultural Service, U.S. Department of Agriculture (FAS-USDA)

Production of Cheese in the United States   In Millions of Pounds

	-------- American --------			Swiss, Including			Lim-burger	Crean & Neufchatel	Italian	Blue	All Other	Total of All	----- Cottage Cheese -----		
Year	Whole Milk	Part Skim	Total	Block	Munster	Brick	burger	Cheese	Varieties	Mond	Varieties	Cheese[2]	Lowfat	Curd[3]	Cream-ed[4]
2008	4,109	----	4,109	294.0	117.2	6.9	.6	763.6	4,120.8	[5]	307.5	9,913	389.2	428.1	325.0
2009	4,203	----	4,203	322.3	115.5	9.4	[5]	766.9	4,180.6	[5]	270.0	10,074	389.0	432.3	342.4
2010	4,289	----	4,289	336.5	117.6	6.7	[5]	744.9	4,415.7	[5]	136.7	10,443	389.0	432.9	331.2
2011	4,227	----	4,227	329.1	146.6	11.4	[5]	714.6	4,585.3	[5]	147.5	10,595	381.5	423.7	322.1
2012	4,355	----	4,355	320.6	152.5	12.5	[5]	807.7	4,632.8	[5]	146.6	10,886	386.1	423.9	323.2
2013	4,420	----	4,420	294.5	163.2	9.3	[5]	842.3	4,735.5	[5]	151.9	11,102	370.3	389.4	307.4
2014	4,588	----	4,588	297.8	163.7	2.9	[5]	851.7	4,950.2	[5]	154.2	11,512	364.6	381.1	303.1
2015	4,694	----	4,694	312.0	177.5	3.4	[5]	876.3	5,081.8	[5]		11,831	363.0	400.6	317.5
2016	4,756	----	4,756	312.0	181.3	2.8	[5]	909.0	5,292.6	[5]		12,158	367.8	406.4	329.4
2017[1]	5,008	----	5,008	314.2			[5]	942.4	5,381.9	[5]		12,478	344.1	389.8	327.0

[1] Preliminary.   [2] Excludes full-skim cheddar and cottage cheese.   [3] Includes cottage, pot, and baker's cheese with a butterfat content of less than 4%.
[4] Includes cheese with a butterfat content of 4 to 19 %.   [5] Included in All Other Varieties.   NA = Not available.
Source: Economic Research Service, U.S. Department of Agriculture ERS-USDA)

CHEESE

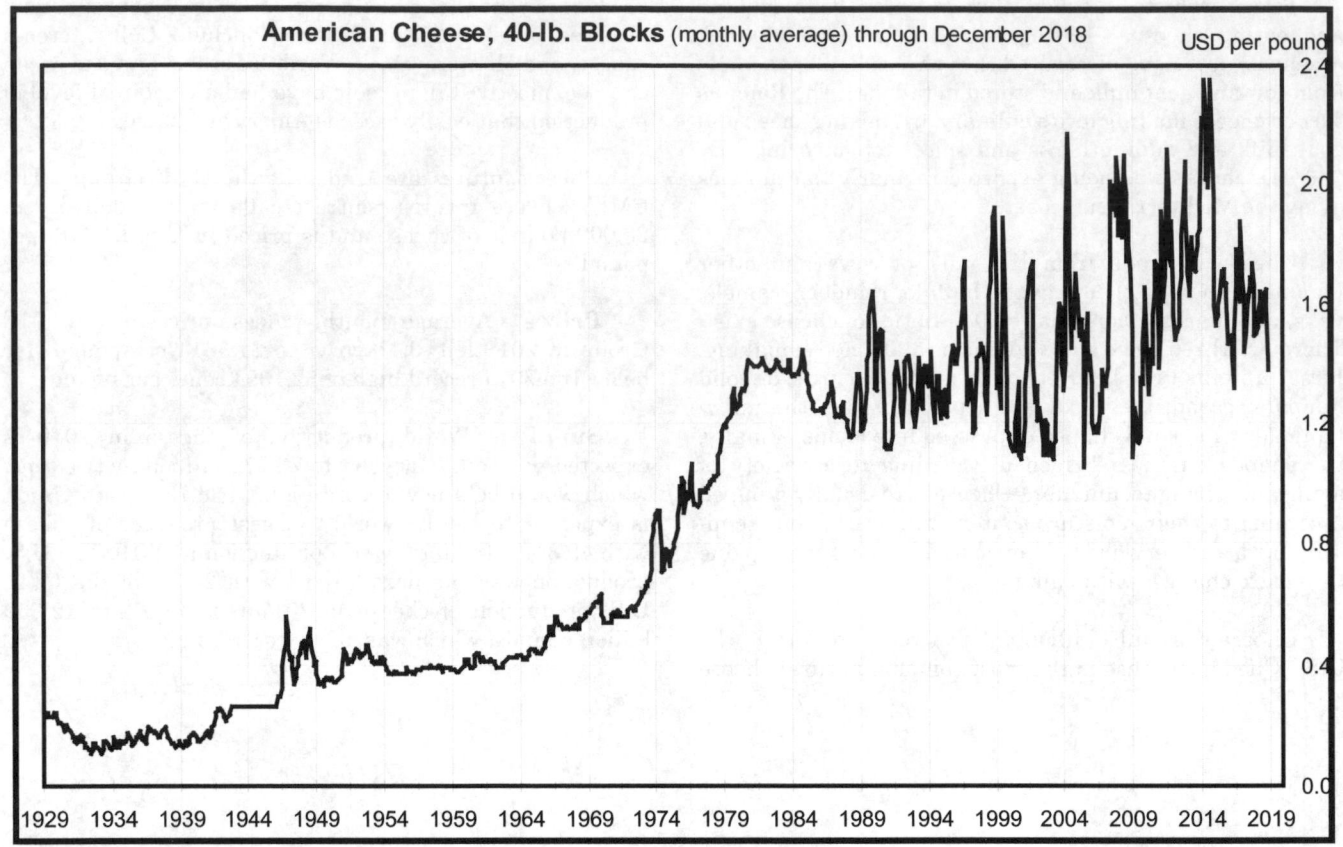

American Cheese, 40-lb. Blocks (monthly average) through December 2018   USD per pound

Average Price of Cheese, 40-lb. Blocks, Chicago Mercantile Exchange   In U.S. Dollars Per Pound

Year	Jan.	Feb.	Mar.	Apr.	May	June	July	Aug.	Sept.	Oct.	Nov.	Dec.	Average
2009	1.0833	1.2171	1.2455	1.2045	1.1394	1.1353	1.1516	1.3474	1.3294	1.4709	1.5788	1.6503	1.2961
2010	1.4536	1.4526	1.2976	1.4182	1.4420	1.3961	1.5549	1.6367	1.7374	1.7246	1.4619	1.3807	1.4964
2011	1.5140	1.9064	1.8125	1.6036	1.6858	2.0995	2.1150	1.9725	1.7561	1.7231	1.8716	1.6170	1.8064
2012	1.5546	1.4793	1.5193	1.5039	1.5234	1.6313	1.6855	1.8262	1.9245	2.0757	1.9073	1.7448	1.6980
2013	1.6965	1.6420	1.6240	1.8225	1.8052	1.7140	1.7072	1.7493	1.7956	1.8236	1.8478	1.9431	1.7642
2014	2.2227	2.1945	2.3554	2.2439	2.0155	2.0237	1.9870	2.1820	2.3499	2.1932	1.9513	1.5938	2.1094
2015	1.5218	1.5382	1.5549	1.5890	1.6308	1.7052	1.6659	1.7111	1.6605	1.6674	1.6176	1.4616	1.6103
2016	1.4757	1.4744	1.4877	1.4194	1.3174	1.5005	1.6613	1.7826	1.6224	1.6035	1.8775	1.7335	1.5797
2017	1.6866	1.6199	1.4342	1.4976	1.6264	1.6022	1.6586	1.6852	1.6370	1.7305	1.6590	1.4900	1.6106
2018[1]	1.4938	1.5157	1.5614	1.6062	1.6397	1.5617	1.5364	1.6341	1.6438	1.5874	1.3951	1.3764	1.5460

[1] Preliminary.   *Source: Economic Research Service, U.S. Department of Agriculture (ERS-USDA)*

Average Price of American Cheese, Barrels, Chicago Mercantile Exchange   In U.S. Dollars Per Pound

Year	Jan.	Feb.	Mar.	Apr.	May	June	July	Aug.	Sept.	Oct.	Nov.	Dec.	Average
2009	1.0832	1.1993	1.2738	1.1506	1.0763	1.0884	1.1349	1.3271	1.3035	1.4499	1.4825	1.4520	1.2518
2010	1.4684	1.4182	1.2782	1.3854	1.4195	1.3647	1.5161	1.6006	1.7114	1.7120	1.4520	1.3751	1.4751
2011	1.4876	1.8680	4.8049	1.5756	1.6902	2.0483	2.1124	1.9571	1.7010	1.7192	1.8963	1.5839	2.0370
2012	1.5358	1.4823	1.5152	1.4524	1.4701	1.5871	1.6826	1.7889	1.8780	2.0240	1.8388	1.6634	1.6599
2013	1.6388	1.5880	1.5920	1.7124	1.7251	1.7184	1.6919	1.7425	1.7688	1.7714	1.7833	1.8651	1.7165
2014	2.1727	2.1757	2.2790	2.1842	1.9985	1.9856	1.9970	2.1961	2.3663	2.0782	1.9326	1.5305	2.0747
2015	1.4995	1.4849	1.5290	1.6135	1.6250	1.6690	1.6313	1.6689	1.5840	1.6072	1.5305	1.4638	1.5756
2016	1.4842	1.4573	1.4530	1.4231	1.3529	1.5301	1.7363	1.8110	1.5415	1.5295	1.7424	1.6132	1.5562
2017	1.5573	1.6230	1.4072	1.4307	1.4806	1.3972	1.4396	1.5993	1.5691	1.6970	1.6656	1.5426	1.5341
2018[1]	1.3345	1.4096	1.5071	1.4721	1.5870	1.4145	1.3707	1.5835	1.4503	1.3152	1.3100	1.2829	1.4198

[1] Preliminary.   *Source: Economic Research Service, U.S. Department of Agriculture (ERS-USDA)*

Production of Cheese[2] in the United States   In Millions of Pounds

Year	Jan.	Feb.	Mar.	Apr.	May	June	July	Aug.	Sept.	Oct.	Nov.	Dec.	Total
2009	826.9	768.0	870.5	847.6	856.1	838.1	842.8	850.7	842.5	862.8	839.5	863.9	10,109.3
2010	842.5	779.0	895.3	864.6	881.0	883.3	878.0	871.2	873.2	882.2	884.5	908.5	10,443.3
2011	883.5	804.6	912.2	883.3	912.3	889.0	854.9	861.9	867.9	899.1	895.6	930.6	10,595.0
2012	911.8	860.6	955.6	898.5	918.2	901.2	882.6	891.2	870.6	930.4	914.3	951.2	10,886.2
2013	931.7	848.7	954.3	929.8	943.9	912.1	893.9	931.7	899.2	954.8	922.5	979.3	11,101.7
2014	962.4	859.4	976.0	967.3	977.2	951.0	965.0	935.6	943.0	987.8	965.2	1,022.1	11,512.1
2015	994.1	896.7	1,013.0	977.3	988.2	976.1	1,002.0	979.0	965.5	1,018.0	986.4	1,035.1	11,831.4
2016	1,025.7	947.5	1,028.6	1,003.2	1,010.7	998.4	1,020.8	1,006.8	991.4	1,052.2	1,029.2	1,067.0	12,181.5
2017	1,064.2	957.7	1,071.8	1,057.8	1,076.2	1,045.9	1,051.7	1,046.0	1,024.8	1,086.9	1,070.7	1,105.5	12,659.1
2018[1]	1,096.5	986.0	1,108.4	1,073.4	1,084.6	1,062.5	1,082.8	1,078.4	1,054.5	1,129.9	1,081.0	1,093.0	12,931.0

[1] Preliminary.   [2] Excludes cottage cheese.   *Source: National Agricultural Statistics Service, U.S. Department of Agriculture (NASS-USDA)*

Production of American Cheese[2] in the United States   In Thousands of Pounds

Year	Jan.	Feb.	Mar.	Apr.	May	June	July	Aug.	Sept.	Oct.	Nov.	Dec.	Total
2009	357,200	323,370	364,359	354,781	368,021	356,869	354,695	347,088	342,921	349,403	331,593	352,199	4,202,499
2010	350,806	322,263	365,376	361,362	372,538	371,189	368,900	351,807	353,196	357,850	346,555	367,499	4,289,341
2011	356,983	327,255	363,518	355,848	369,073	362,050	349,031	337,523	337,549	351,654	348,331	367,855	4,226,670
2012	366,533	343,759	378,063	363,348	367,591	360,364	356,169	353,167	347,486	370,139	364,541	384,092	4,355,252
2013	377,258	347,262	384,770	376,891	387,590	362,977	345,707	381,125	347,449	371,125	356,220	381,474	4,419,848
2014	388,420	345,464	387,071	385,322	399,239	374,373	385,175	376,203	369,843	393,414	383,500	399,999	4,588,023
2015	402,222	357,376	395,823	396,691	407,667	390,447	397,235	394,943	379,550	392,592	380,004	399,921	4,694,471
2016	402,377	368,000	402,001	398,750	403,040	392,166	401,815	393,459	379,456	403,397	400,983	423,444	4,768,888
2017	434,627	390,314	429,558	434,657	443,083	419,260	414,495	414,280	403,544	430,485	413,714	443,974	5,071,991
2018[1]	433,670	397,364	443,491	443,257	443,503	429,895	440,653	426,427	417,313	438,187	422,011	425,245	5,161,016

[1] Preliminary.   [2] Includes Cheddar, Colby, Monterey, and Jack.   *Source: National Agricultural Statistics Service, U.S. Department of Agriculture*

Production of Cheddar Cheese in the United States   In Thousands of Pounds

Year	Jan.	Feb.	Mar.	Apr.	May	June	July	Aug.	Sept.	Oct.	Nov.	Dec.	Total
2009	278,181	244,440	279,290	272,091	287,422	276,646	269,533	264,743	259,004	263,443	248,076	263,062	3,207,137
2010	268,758	245,100	283,712	272,412	287,658	286,238	275,646	261,425	257,172	265,485	256,551	274,834	3,234,991
2011	270,755	239,469	262,728	260,547	279,567	266,254	256,667	243,255	247,264	247,636	251,795	270,413	3,096,350
2012	271,840	252,207	274,434	263,771	268,475	260,253	258,484	250,658	242,852	262,610	259,112	278,747	3,143,443
2013	280,944	251,977	284,123	279,144	281,307	259,631	246,804	269,747	241,687	268,497	252,211	273,767	3,189,839
2014	283,595	254,140	283,494	290,713	293,923	274,257	274,163	265,918	262,230	277,835	266,025	290,745	3,317,038
2015	296,767	262,602	287,042	287,350	296,447	287,956	286,435	279,379	271,551	278,915	265,947	292,720	3,393,111
2016	297,480	258,530	286,426	300,166	293,238	280,220	284,607	281,932	271,561	284,058	286,571	309,709	3,434,498
2017	327,328	291,508	323,442	329,671	327,456	302,090	298,285	298,306	291,755	307,833	296,598	327,062	3,721,334
2018[1]	318,254	293,255	321,144	318,849	319,684	313,351	326,370	303,563	290,846	307,510	301,795	306,902	3,721,523

[1] Preliminary.   *Source: National Agricultural Statistics Service, U.S. Department of Agriculture (NASS-USDA)*

Production of Mozzarella Cheese in the United States   In Thousands of Pounds

Year	Jan.	Feb.	Mar.	Apr.	May	June	July	Aug.	Sept.	Oct.	Nov.	Dec.	Total
2009	267,299	246,429	280,012	270,604	271,395	268,901	273,782	272,632	270,262	278,106	279,105	288,779	3,267,306
2010	282,976	258,367	299,356	287,350	293,088	289,727	290,158	290,489	290,266	291,195	298,573	307,896	3,479,441
2011	307,978	273,554	310,367	300,077	308,898	298,100	287,392	286,670	286,434	296,943	296,616	321,399	3,574,428
2012	311,892	291,441	318,710	302,550	306,314	299,675	291,932	286,230	286,444	297,141	297,676	324,843	3,614,848
2013	311,837	278,522	323,187	302,643	307,092	307,964	307,910	296,420	301,973	318,997	307,484	335,960	3,699,989
2014	333,319	300,506	335,385	332,466	331,181	328,829	327,914	311,973	319,861	326,866	326,093	350,532	3,924,925
2015	341,183	305,421	344,459	330,958	333,451	331,196	338,554	316,045	316,408	332,824	335,210	363,227	3,988,936
2016	353,001	323,713	358,081	340,584	345,063	339,993	350,089	328,118	334,808	346,013	338,728	359,555	4,117,746
2017	352,768	314,602	361,368	347,399	350,530	349,363	352,014	335,867	332,180	347,688	351,511	365,309	4,160,599
2018[1]	366,988	327,413	371,264	353,725	357,591	353,869	367,215	358,177	358,006	373,332	363,893	378,867	4,330,340

[1] Preliminary.   *Source: National Agricultural Statistics Service, U.S. Department of Agriculture (NASS-USDA)*

CHEESE

Cold Storage of All Varieties of Cheese in the United States, on First of Month In Thousands of Pounds

Year	Jan.	Feb.	Mar.	Apr.	May	June	July	Aug.	Sept.	Oct.	Nov.	Dec.
2009	851,960	882,376	892,541	915,189	938,914	970,320	987,399	1,000,171	997,620	983,941	969,185	961,745
2010	966,758	981,608	995,915	1,004,763	1,018,614	1,026,807	1,037,819	1,070,127	1,058,957	1,060,596	1,057,815	1,026,117
2011	1,047,926	1,052,397	1,035,332	1,029,494	1,040,145	1,049,185	1,051,424	1,084,946	1,065,363	1,046,014	1,017,627	977,765
2012	991,616	1,020,057	1,026,405	1,045,473	1,072,146	1,069,086	1,094,965	1,092,617	1,049,484	1,040,006	995,363	985,871
2013	1,023,102	1,032,196	1,068,756	1,105,725	1,121,293	1,150,039	1,149,377	1,146,131	1,100,351	1,070,697	1,019,716	996,609
2014	1,009,381	1,015,053	1,010,132	1,018,290	1,037,586	1,065,540	1,055,442	1,054,892	1,041,408	1,013,782	995,666	1,017,192
2015	1,017,936	1,048,243	1,067,060	1,068,645	1,085,909	1,111,854	1,142,241	1,161,796	1,167,393	1,152,446	1,146,191	1,148,060
2016	1,146,086	1,178,194	1,182,308	1,191,394	1,209,222	1,249,382	1,250,328	1,275,546	1,241,119	1,235,452	1,222,315	1,182,646
2017	1,198,334	1,192,166	1,226,457	1,262,244	1,303,328	1,308,929	1,316,698	1,369,506	1,333,551	1,308,072	1,267,950	1,258,630
2018[1]	1,280,484	1,278,637	1,317,731	1,324,662	1,345,289	1,385,513	1,388,638	1,412,958	1,358,526	1,377,710	1,370,107	1,352,815

Quantities are given in "net weight."   [1] Preliminary.   *Source: National Agricultural Statistics Service, U.S. Department of Agriculture (NASS-USDA)*

Cold Storage of Natural American Cheese in the United States, on First of Month In Thousands of Pounds

Year	Jan.	Feb.	Mar.	Apr.	May	June	July	Aug.	Sept.	Oct.	Nov.	Dec.
2009	538,105	533,402	541,739	548,568	577,391	586,053	602,049	605,022	598,710	596,191	579,808	583,056
2010	584,981	588,186	599,152	602,077	609,588	614,935	627,053	639,525	633,573	636,946	639,035	625,348
2011	630,789	637,935	621,023	611,200	622,121	622,672	619,147	648,834	647,268	639,175	619,376	583,993
2012	610,998	642,204	634,614	651,005	663,532	652,052	662,387	670,734	649,397	641,685	610,931	611,687
2013	635,590	643,184	661,019	684,653	698,655	714,637	710,604	701,964	668,361	661,046	626,161	613,965
2014	618,265	630,820	628,679	639,067	648,900	656,446	655,239	660,438	648,784	631,279	623,336	635,776
2015	627,769	636,019	645,670	634,270	644,113	669,464	685,745	698,029	709,029	698,875	696,781	699,794
2016	701,073	716,370	716,357	725,837	734,121	757,530	756,950	769,705	742,497	742,804	736,017	713,231
2017	726,403	722,449	744,640	772,702	804,645	816,266	810,234	831,538	800,994	780,466	740,404	733,378
2018[1]	746,846	741,772	762,770	766,624	780,270	804,570	800,379	823,322	786,416	803,812	811,399	803,352

Quantities are given in "net weight."   [1] Preliminary.   *Source: National Agricultural Statistics Service, U.S. Department of Agriculture (NASS-USDA)*

Cold Storage of Other Natural American Cheese in the United States, on First of Month In Thousands of Lbs.

Year	Jan.	Feb.	Mar.	Apr.	May	June	July	Aug.	Sept.	Oct.	Nov.	Dec.
2009	291,266	325,826	327,480	343,386	338,668	362,165	362,283	371,879	375,496	364,640	365,840	354,435
2010	356,986	367,234	369,384	375,736	382,266	384,533	383,788	402,900	397,005	395,982	390,175	371,892
2011	385,645	378,142	379,698	385,737	386,597	392,811	397,914	401,944	384,518	375,535	366,010	354,919
2012	352,981	351,944	364,742	365,596	379,769	387,458	402,201	391,272	371,295	369,388	354,411	343,278
2013	355,765	358,611	377,607	390,483	394,135	406,351	407,426	411,452	399,984	379,676	365,632	356,542
2014	366,428	358,812	354,511	351,798	360,370	378,556	372,231	369,861	365,539	356,819	346,730	356,997
2015	368,885	389,813	397,035	409,802	417,810	420,966	435,655	442,176	436,161	431,534	428,006	425,601
2016	420,426	437,724	441,248	440,928	450,509	466,885	468,886	480,139	472,603	466,593	461,870	444,666
2017	447,731	445,787	454,818	463,489	471,721	466,421	480,969	510,959	505,726	502,198	503,269	500,319
2018[1]	507,271	508,132	527,077	528,958	535,826	549,537	556,947	557,447	541,149	543,050	528,826	520,491

Quantities are given in "net weight."   [1] Preliminary.   *Source: National Agricultural Statistics Service, U.S. Department of Agriculture (NASS-USDA)*

Cold Storage of Swiss Cheese in the United States, on First of Month In Thousands of Pounds

Year	Jan.	Feb.	Mar.	Apr.	May	June	July	Aug.	Sept.	Oct.	Nov.	Dec.
2009	22,589	23,148	23,322	23,235	22,855	22,102	23,067	23,270	23,414	23,110	23,537	24,254
2010	24,791	26,188	27,379	26,950	26,760	27,339	26,978	27,702	28,379	27,668	28,605	28,877
2011	31,492	36,320	34,611	32,557	31,427	33,702	34,363	34,168	33,577	31,304	32,241	30,073
2012	27,637	25,909	27,049	28,872	28,845	29,576	30,377	30,611	28,792	28,933	30,021	30,906
2013	31,747	30,401	30,130	30,589	28,503	29,051	31,347	32,715	32,006	29,975	27,923	26,102
2014	24,688	25,421	26,942	27,425	28,316	30,538	27,972	24,593	27,085	25,684	25,600	24,419
2015	21,282	22,411	23,587	24,573	23,986	21,424	20,841	21,591	22,203	22,037	21,404	22,665
2016	24,587	24,100	24,703	24,629	24,592	24,967	24,492	25,702	26,019	26,055	24,428	24,749
2017	24,200	23,930	26,999	26,053	26,962	26,242	25,495	27,009	26,831	25,408	24,277	24,933
2018[1]	26,367	28,733	27,885	27,884	29,193	31,406	31,312	32,189	30,961	30,848	29,882	28,972

Quantities are given in "net weight."   [1] Preliminary.   *Source: National Agricultural Statistics Service, U.S. Department of Agriculture (NASS-USDA)*

Chromium

Chromium (atomic symbol Cr) is a steel-gray, hard, and brittle, metallic element that can take on a high polish. Chromium and its compounds are toxic. Discovered in 1797 by Louis Vauquelin, chromium is named after the Greek word for color, *khroma*. Vauquelin also discovered that an emerald's green color is due to the presence of chromium. Many precious stones owe their color to the presence of chromium compounds.

Chromium is primarily found in chromite ore. The primary use of chromium is to form alloys with iron, nickel, or cobalt. Chromium improves hardness and resistance to corrosion and oxidation in iron, steel, and nonferrous alloys. It is a critical alloying ingredient in the production of stainless steel, making up 10% or more of the final composition. More than half of the chromium consumed is used in metallic products, and about one-third is used in refractories. Chromium is also used as a lustrous decorative plating agent, in pigments, leather processing, plating of metals, and catalysts.

Supply – World mine production of chromium in 2018 rose +0.8% yr/yr to 36.000 billion metric tons, a record high. The world's largest producers of chromium in 2018 were South Africa with 44.4% of world production, Turkey with 18.1%, Kazakhstan with 12.8%, and India with 9.7%. South Africa's production in 2018 fell -3.0% yr/yr to 16.000 million metric tons which is down from last year's record high of 16.500. Turkey has emerged as a major producer with 6.500 million metric tons, more than triple its levels in the late-1990s. India has emerged as a major producer of chromium in the past three decades. Kazakhstan's production in 2018 was up +0.4% yr/yr to 4.600 million metric tons, but down from the 2016 record high of 5.543 million. India's 2018 production level of 3.500 million metric tons was more than ten times the level of 360,000 metric tons seen 30 years earlier.

Trade – The U.S. relied on imports for 71% of its chromium consumption in 2018. That is well below the record high of 91% posted back in the 1970s. U.S. chromium imports in 2017 rose +110.9% yr/yr to 734,000 metric tons. U.S. exports of chromium in 2015 (latest available data) rose +387.8% yr/yr to 13,310 metric tons.

World Mine Production of Chromite   In Thousands of Metric Tons (Gross Weight)

Year	Albania	Brazil	Cuba	Finland	India	Iran	Kazakhstan	Madagascar	Philippines	South Africa	Turkey	Zimbabwe	World Total[1]
2009	284	365	----	247	4,073	269	3,544	133	14	7,561	1,574	194	19,700
2010	328	520	----	598	3,426	394	3,760	135	15	11,340	1,904	510	25,200
2011	161	494	----	693	4,326	418	5,059	67	25	10,824	2,282	599	26,900
2012	380	425	----	425	3,255	412	5,233	112	37	11,317	3,295	408	26,900
2013	521	430	----	982	2,633	344	5,255	88	35	13,690	4,141	355	30,000
2014	652	556	----	1,035	2,374	359	5,411	97	47	14,038	4,100	408	30,500
2015	680	500	----	946	2,660	320	5,383	198	16	15,656	3,500	208	31,200
2016	660	500	----	1,070	3,200	300	5,543	200	29	14,705	2,800	275	30,400
2017[1]			----		3,500		4,580			16,500	6,500		35,700
2018[2]			----		3,500		4,600			16,000	6,500		36,000

[1] Preliminary.   [2] Estimate.   *Source: U.S. Geological Survey (USGS)*

Salient Statistics of Chromite in the United States   In Thousands of Metric Tons (Gross Weight)

Year	Net Import Reliance as a % of Apparent Consumpn	Production of Ferro-chromium	Exports	Imports for Consumption	Reexports	Consumption by -- Primary Consumer Group -- Total	Metallurgical & Chemical	Refractory	Government[5] Stocks, Dec. 31 Metallurgical & Chemical	Refractory	Total Stocks	$/Metric Ton South Africa[3]	Turkish[4]
2009	12	W	17	181	----	W	W	W	----	----	----	NA	NA
2010	63	W	28	367	----	W	W	W	----	----	----	NA	NA
2011	67	W	25	399	----	W	W	W	----	----	----	NA	NA
2012	73	W	27	416	----	W	W	W	----	----	----	NA	NA
2013	69	W	23	355	----	W	W	W	----	----	----	NA	NA
2014	75	W	21	441	----	W	W	W	----	----	----	NA	NA
2015	67	W	9	329	----	W	W	W	----	----	----	NA	NA
2016	66	W	3	348	----	W	W	W	----	----	----	NA	NA
2017[1]	71	W	13	735	----	W	W	W	----	----	----	NA	NA
2018[2]	71	W			----	W	W	W	----	----	----	NA	NA

[1] Preliminary.   [2] Estimate.   [3] Cr_2O_3, 44% (Transvaal).   [4] 48% Cr_2O_3.   [5] Data through 1999 are for Consumer.   W = Withheld.
Source: U.S. Geological Survey (USGS)

Coal

Coal is a sedimentary rock composed primarily of carbon, hydrogen, and oxygen. Coal is a fossil fuel formed from ancient plants buried deep in the Earth's crust over 300 million years ago. Historians believe coal was first used commercially in China for smelting copper and for casting coins around 1,000 BC. Almost 92% of all coal consumed in the U.S. is burned by electric power plants, and coal accounts for about 55% of total electricity output. Coal is also used in the manufacture of steel. The steel industry first converts coal into coke, then combines the coke with iron ore and limestone, and finally heats the mixture to produce iron. Other industries use coal to make fertilizers, solvents, medicine, pesticides, and synthetic fuels.

There are four types of mined coal: anthracite (used in high-grade steel production), bituminous (used for electricity generation and for making coke), sub-bituminous, and lignite (both used primarily for electricity generation).

Prices – Coal futures trade at the CME Group. The contract trades in units of 1,550 tons and is priced in terms of dollars and cents per ton.

Supply – U.S. production of bituminous coal in 2018 fell -2.6% yr/yr to 752.793 million tons, the lowest level since 1978.

Demand – U.S. consumption of coal in 2017 fell -1.9% to 716.856 million tons, the lowest level since 1983.

Trade – U.S. exports of coal in 2017 rose +60.9% yr/yr to 96.953 million tons. U.S. imports in 2017 fell -21.0% yr/yr to 7.777 million tons. The major exporting destinations for the U.S. are Europe and Asia.

World Production of Primary Coal   In Thousands of Short Tons

Year	Australia	China	Colombia	Germany	India	Indonesia	Kazakhstan	Poland	Russia	South Africa	Turkey	United States	World Total
2007	431,046	3,042,256	72,486	225,526	541,303	239,143	107,837	159,773	318,591	273,005	83,074	1,146,635	7,285,300
2008	432,383	3,200,453	81,065	214,351	544,931	274,217	109,119	157,993	336,163	278,472	87,526	1,171,809	7,531,162
2009	449,631	3,434,086	80,309	203,738	548,559	321,044	111,172	148,355	304,228	276,219	87,633	1,074,923	7,666,856
2010	467,823	3,779,212	82,021	202,286	578,216	358,251	122,278	146,257	329,258	280,403	80,908	1,084,368	8,152,994
2011	461,799	4,149,575	94,625	208,846	590,753	445,904	128,364	152,680	325,887	276,853	82,885	1,095,628	8,698,397
2012	492,786	4,348,754	98,207	217,144	680,568	496,691	132,858	158,197	363,058	285,031	77,458	1,016,458	9,035,517
2013	521,124	4,380,935	94,247	210,493	671,435	522,904	131,808	156,875	385,818	282,780	72,877	984,842	9,054,981
2014	555,812	4,270,260	97,640	205,597	713,454	504,965	125,647	150,374	393,765	288,695	75,094	1,000,049	8,979,787
2015[1]	556,120	4,129,851	94,300	203,612	747,074	508,789	118,299	149,147	409,701	278,003	67,025	896,941	8,735,276
2016[2]	554,764	3,759,543	99,772	193,593	761,662	502,653	113,620	143,996	423,095	277,952	80,473	728,364	8,199,981

[1] Preliminary.   [2] Estimate.   NA = Not available.   *Source: United Nations*

Production of Bituminous & Lignite Coal in the United States   In Thousands of Short Tons

Year	Alabama	Colorado	Illinois	Indiana	Kentucky	Montana	Ohio	Pennsylvania	Texas	West Virginia	Virginia	Wyoming	U.S. Total
2008	20,611	32,028	32,918	35,893	120,323	44,786	26,251	65,414	39,017	24,712	157,778	467,644	1,171,809
2009	18,796	28,267	33,748	35,655	107,338	39,486	27,501	57,979	35,093	21,019	137,127	431,107	1,074,923
2010	19,915	25,163	33,241	34,950	104,960	44,732	26,707	58,593	40,982	22,385	135,220	442,522	1,084,368
2011	19,071	26,890	37,770	37,426	108,766	42,008	28,166	59,182	45,904	22,523	134,662	438,673	1,095,628
2012	19,321	28,566	48,486	36,720	90,862	36,694	26,328	54,719	44,178	18,965	120,425	401,442	1,016,458
2013	18,620	24,236	52,147	39,102	80,380	42,231	25,113	54,009	42,851	16,619	112,786	387,924	984,842
2014	16,363	24,007	57,969	39,267	77,335	44,562	22,252	60,910	43,654	15,059	112,187	395,665	1,000,049
2015	13,191	18,879	56,101	34,295	61,425	41,864	17,041	50,031	35,918	13,914	95,633	375,773	896,941
2016[1]	9,643	12,634	43,422	28,767	42,868	32,336	12,564	45,720	39,001	12,910	79,757	297,218	728,364
2017[2]	12,613	15,047	48,128	31,418	42,608	35,232	9,336	49,065	36,338	13,205	92,733	316,454	774,118

[1] Preliminary.   [2] Estimate.   *Source: Energy Information Administration, U.S. Department of Energy (EIA-DOE)*

Production[2] of Bituminous Coal in the United States   In Thousands of Short Tons

Year	Jan.	Feb.	Mar.	Apr.	May	June	July	Aug.	Sept.	Oct.	Nov.	Dec.	Total
2009	97,022	89,688	96,062	89,072	85,236	88,708	90,847	90,308	88,185	88,002	85,564	86,229	1,074,923
2010	85,711	83,087	96,904	90,960	85,401	88,621	90,795	93,350	93,360	91,831	91,558	92,791	1,084,368
2011	91,355	85,575	96,548	88,563	86,850	88,878	85,498	95,495	94,013	94,643	94,109	94,101	1,095,628
2012	95,102	85,914	85,849	77,514	81,717	81,816	86,321	90,816	81,818	85,239	84,147	80,205	1,016,458
2013	82,529	77,414	84,381	78,724	83,075	80,841	84,344	90,013	82,707	80,435	80,408	77,827	982,699
2014	82,835	75,177	86,794	82,835	83,645	78,929	84,275	87,167	83,410	85,286	81,587	86,163	998,102
2015	86,548	72,210	81,430	74,704	69,942	66,484	76,618	82,777	77,868	75,705	68,613	63,036	895,936
2016	60,413	57,181	55,186	48,089	52,983	59,356	61,667	68,118	64,947	68,578	67,006	63,176	726,700
2017	68,236	64,221	64,167	58,598	61,950	66,053	62,834	70,434	62,759	66,201	64,184	63,061	772,697
2018[1]	61,796	60,098	65,318	57,876	61,032	61,392	62,791	69,131	62,263	65,354	62,264	63,000	752,315

[1] Preliminary.   [2] Includes small amount of lignite.   *Source: Energy Information Administration, U.S. Department of Energy (EIA-DOE)*

Production[2] of Pennsylvania Anthracite Coal   In Thousands of Short Tons

Year	Jan.	Feb.	Mar.	Apr.	May	June	July	Aug.	Sept.	Oct.	Nov.	Dec.	Total
2009	150	141	153	153	139	154	172	168	171	176	168	177	1,921
2010	129	128	156	158	140	151	161	169	168	131	140	143	1,776
2011	163	156	176	177	180	186	185	218	205	191	199	198	2,235
2012	198	185	193	205	213	206	210	224	195	186	179	174	2,368
2013	183	172	187	186	196	191	174	186	171	168	168	163	2,143
2014	157	143	165	147	148	140	174	180	172	176	168	177	1,947
2015	170	142	160	182	171	162	204	220	207	192	174	160	2,145
2016	156	147	142	128	141	157	117	129	123	147	144	135	1,665
2017	178	168	168	156	165	176	133	149	133	167	162	159	1,912
2018[1]	141	137	149	156	164	165	155	170	153				1,390

[1] Preliminary.   [2] Represents production in Pennsylvania only.   *Source: Energy Information Administration, U.S. Department of Energy (EIA-DOE)*

Salient Statistics of Coal in the United States   In Thousands of Short Tons

Year	Production	Imports	Consumption	Exports Brazil	Exports Canada	Exports Europe	Exports Asia	Exports Total	Total Ending Stocks[2]	Losses & Unaccounted For[3]
2008	1,171,809	34,208	1,120,548	6,380	22,979	40,306	5,269	81,519	205,112	5,740
2009	1,074,923	22,639	997,478	7,416	10,599	30,073	6,483	59,097	244,780	14,985
2010	1,084,368	19,353	1,048,514	7,925	11,400	38,208	17,896	81,716	231,740	182
2011	1,095,628	13,088	1,002,948	8,680	6,845	53,942	27,533	107,259	231,951	11,506
2012	1,016,458	9,159	889,185	7,954	7,211	66,399	32,512	125,746	238,853	14,980
2013	984,842	8,906	924,442	8,610	7,110	60,755	27,245	117,659	200,335	1,451
2014	1,000,049	11,350	917,731	8,032	6,724	52,469	19,450	97,257	197,727	11,101
2015	896,941	11,318	798,115	6,339	5,958	37,894	17,544	73,958	238,431	5,452
2016	728,364	9,850	731,071	6,939	5,011	27,381	15,714	60,271	192,990	2,452
2017[1]	774,609	7,777	716,856	7,563	5,286	39,561	32,841	96,953	163,539	4,562

[1] Preliminary.   [2] Producer & distributor and consumer stocks, excludes stocks held by retail dealers for consumption by the residential and commercial sector.   [3] Equals production plus imports minus the change in producer & distributor and consumer stocks minus consumption minus exports.
Source: Energy Information Administraion, U.S. Department of Energy (EIA-DOE)

Consumption and Stocks of Coal in the United States   In Thousands of Short Tons

Year	Consumption Electric Utilities Anthracite	Bituminous	Lignite	Total	Industrial Coke Plants	Other Industrial[2]	Residential and Commercial	Total	Stocks, Dec. 31 Consumer Electric Utilities	Coke Plants	Other Industrials	Producers and Distributors
2008	----	----	----	1,040,580	22,070	54,393	3,506	1,120,548	161,589	2,331	6,007	34,688
2009	----	----	----	933,627	15,326	45,314	3,210	997,478	189,467	1,957	5,109	47,718
2010	----	----	----	975,052	21,092	49,289	3,081	1,048,514	174,917	1,925	4,525	49,820
2011	----	----	----	932,484	21,434	46,238	2,793	1,002,948	172,387	2,610	4,455	51,897
2012	----	----	----	823,551	20,751	42,838	2,045	889,185	185,116	2,522	4,475	46,157
2013	----	----	----	857,962	21,171	43,055	1,951	924,442	147,884	2,200	4,097	45,652
2014	----	----	----	851,602	21,297	42,946	1,887	917,731	151,548	2,640	4,196	38,894
2015	----	----	----	738,444	19,708	38,459	1,503	798,115	195,548	2,236	4,382	35,871
2016	----	----	----	678,554	16,485	34,849	1,183	731,071	162,009	1,675	3,637	25,309
2017[1]	----	----	----	664,749	17,538	33,613	1,061	716,961	137,155	1,718	3,249	21,108

[1] Preliminary.   [2] Including transportation.   [3] Excludes stocks held at retail dealers for consumption by the residential and commercial sector.
Source: Energy Information Administration, U.S. Department of Energy (EIA-DOE)

Average Prices of Coal in the United States   In Dollars Per Short Ton

Year	End-Use Sector Electric Utilities	Coke Plants	Other Industrial[2]	Imports[3]	Exports Steam	Metal-lurgical	Total Average[3]	Year	End-Use Sector Electric Utilities	Coke Plants	Other Industrial[2]	Imports[3]	Exports Steam	Metal-lurgical	Total Average[3]
2008	NA	118.09	63.44	59.83	57.35	134.62	97.68	2013	----	156.99	69.32	83.35	69.23	115.50	95.06
2009	----	143.01	64.87	63.91	73.63	117.73	101.44	2014	----	----	----	80.96	67.05	99.49	87.08
2010	----	153.59	64.38	71.77	65.54	145.44	120.41	2015	----	----	----	71.61	56.44	89.31	76.89
2011	----	184.44	70.62	103.32	80.42	185.99	148.86	2016	----	----	----	65.72	48.58	71.13	73.66
2012	----	190.55	70.33	96.78	76.16	152.23	118.43	2017[1]	----	----	----	78.15	58.02	140.09	106.33

[1] Preliminary.   [2] Manufacturing plants only.   [3] Based on the free alongside ship (F.A.S.) value.
Source: Energy Information Administration, U.S. Department of Energy (EIA-DOE)

COAL

Trends in Bituminous Coal, Lignite and Pennsylvania Anthracite in the United States   In Thousands of Short Tons

	Bituminous Coal and Lignite				Labor Productivity			Pennsylvania Anthracite				Labor Productivity	All Mines Labor Productivity
	Production				Under-Ground	Surface	Average						
Year	Under-Ground	Surface	Total	Miners[1] Employd	Under-Ground	Surface	Average	Under-Ground	Surface	Total	Miners[1] Employed	Short Tons Miner/Hr.	Short Tons Miner/Hr.
					—— Short Tons Per Miner Per Hour—								
2008	357,079	814,729	1,171,809	86,859	3.15	9.82	5.96	227	2,455	2,682	929	.91	5.96
2009	332,062	742,862	1,074,923	87,592	2.99	9.22	5.61	176	1,555	1,731	941	.95	5.61
2010	337,155	747,214	1,084,368	86,057	2.89	9.47	5.55	139	1,566	1,705	928	.98	5.55
2011	345,606	750,022	1,095,628	91,482	2.72	8.97	5.19	166	1,965	2,131	952	1.11	5.19
2012	342,387	674,072	1,016,458	89,838	2.84	8.97	5.19	120	2,215	2,335	1,146	1.02	5.19
2013	341,685	643,157	984,842	80,396	3.07	9.69	5.53	95	1,965	2,060	1,095	1.01	5.53
2014	354,704	645,345	1,000,049	74,931	3.35	10.42	5.95	93	1,740	1,833	956	.98	5.96
2015	306,821	590,119	896,941	65,971	3.45	10.95	6.28	86	1,867	1,953	1,005	.94	6.28
2016	252,106	476,258	728,364	51,795	3.83	10.73	6.61	91	1,409	1,500	952	.83	6.61
2017	273,129	501,480	774,609	53,051	3.77	10.92	6.55	79	1,788	1,867	914	1.07	6.55

[1] Excludes miners employed at mines producing less than 10,000 tons.
Source: Energy Information Administration, U.S. Department of Energy (EIA-DOE)

Average Mine Prices of Coal in the United States   In Dollars Per Short Ton

| | Average Mine Prices by Method | | | Average Mine Prices by Rank | | | | Bituminous & Lignite FOB Mines[2] | Anthracite FOB Mines[2] | All Coal CIF[3] Electric Utility Plants |
Year	Under-ground	Surface	Total	Lignite	Sub-bituminous	Bituminous	Anthracite[1]			
2008	51.35	22.35	31.25	16.50	12.31	51.40	60.76	51.40	60.76	41.32
2009	55.77	23.24	33.24	17.26	13.35	55.44	57.10	55.44	57.10	44.47
2010	60.73	24.13	35.61	18.76	14.11	60.88	59.61	60.88	59.61	44.27
2011	70.47	27.00	41.01	18.77	14.07	68.50	75.70	68.50	75.70	46.29
2012	66.56	26.43	39.95	19.60	15.34	66.04	80.21	66.04	80.21	45.77
2013	60.98	24.50	37.24	19.96	14.86	60.61	87.82	60.61	87.82	45.03
2014	56.97	22.83	34.83	19.44	14.72	55.99	90.98	55.99	90.98	45.66
2015	52.20	21.47	31.83	22.36	14.63	51.57	97.91	51.57	97.91	42.58
2016	49.02	20.47	30.57	48.40	14.83	19.99	97.61	19.99	97.61	40.39
2017	56.99	20.95	33.72	55.60	14.29	19.51	93.17	19.51	93.17	33.72

[1] Produced in Pennsylvania.   [2] FOB = free on board.   [3] CIF = cost, insurance and freight.   W = Withheld data.
Source: Energy Information Adminstration, U.S. Department of Energy (EIA-DOE)

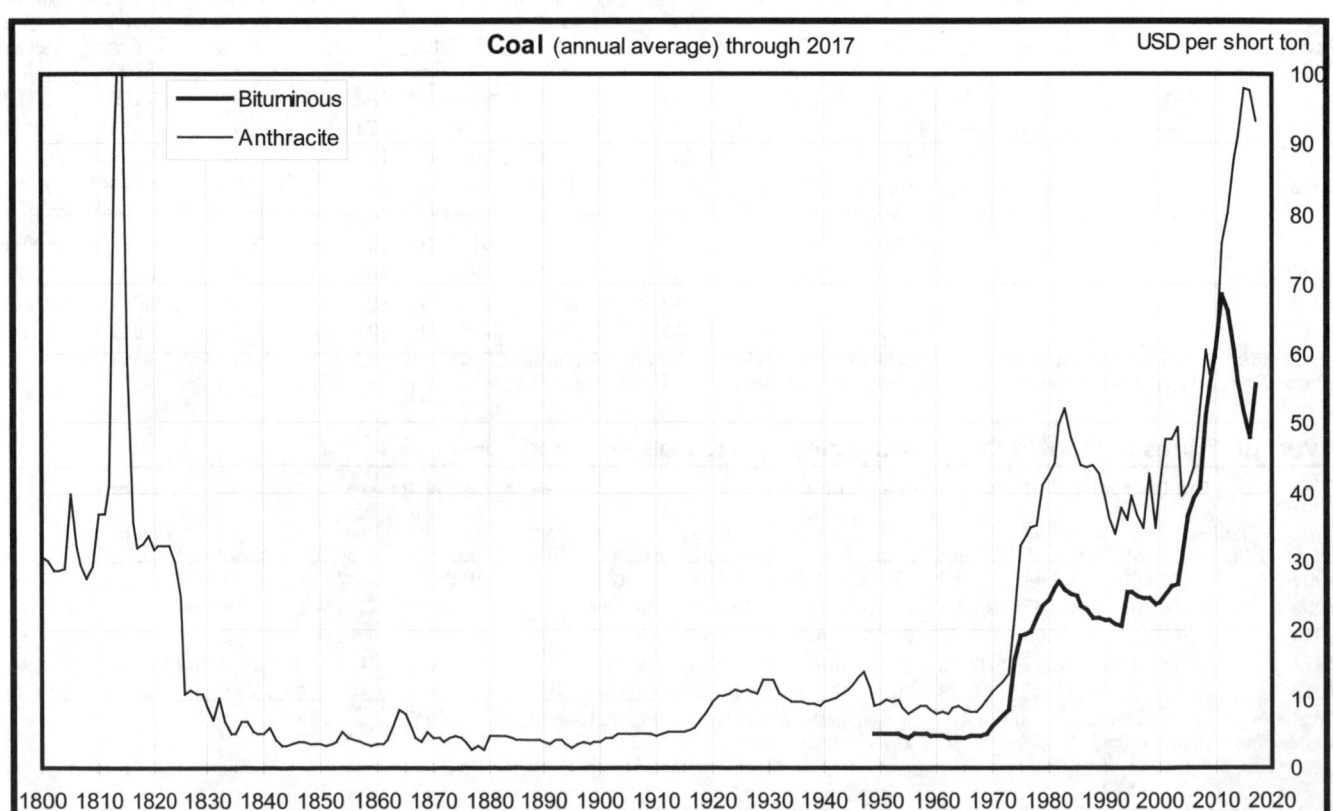

Coal (annual average) through 2017   USD per short ton
— Bituminous
— Anthracite

Cobalt

Cobalt (atomic symbol Co) is a lustrous, silvery-white, magnetic, metallic element used chiefly for making alloys. Cobalt was known in ancient times and used by the Persians in 2250 BC to color glass. The name *cobalt* comes from the German word *kobalt* or *kobold*, meaning evil spirit. Miners gave cobalt its name because it was poisonous and troublesome since it polluted and degraded other mined elements, like nickel. In the 1730s, George Brandt first isolated metallic cobalt and was able to show that cobalt was the source of the blue color in glasses. In 1780, it was recognized as an element. Cobalt is generally not found in nature as a free metal and is instead found in ores. Cobalt is generally produced as a by-product of nickel and copper mining.

Cobalt is used in a variety of applications: high temperature steel alloys; fasteners in gas turbine engines; magnets and magnetic recording media; drying agents for paints and pigments; and steel-belted radial tires. Cobalt-60, an important radioactive tracer and cancer-treatment agent, is an artificially produced radioactive isotope of cobalt.

Prices – The price of cobalt in 2018 rose by +40.95% yr/yr to $38.00 per pound, but still a little below the 2008 record high of $39.01 per pound, and more than 6 times the 20-year low of $6.91 per pound in 2002.

Supply – World production of cobalt in 2018 rose by +16.7% yr/yr to 140,000 metric tons, a new record high. The world's largest cobalt mine producers in 2018 were the Congo with 64.3% of world production, China with 6.0%, Russia with 4.2%, Cuba with 3.5%, and Australia with 3.4%.

The U.S. does not specifically mine or refine cobalt although some cobalt is produced as a by-product of other mining operations. Imports, stock releases, and secondary materials comprise the U.S. cobalt supply. Secondary production includes extraction from super-alloy scrap, cemented carbide scrap, and spent catalysts. In the U.S. there are two domestic producers of extra-fine cobalt powder. One company produces the powder from imported primary metal and the other from recycled materials. There are only about seven companies that produce cobalt compounds. U.S. secondary production of cobalt in 2018 rose +1.8% yr/yr to 2,800 metric tons, still below the record high of 3,080 metric tons seen in 1998.

Demand – U.S. consumption of cobalt in 2017 fell -19.2% yr/yr to 7,200 metric tons, well below the 2005 record high of 11,800 metric tons. In 2015, the largest use of cobalt by far was for super-alloys with 38.4% of consumption. Other smaller-scaled applications for cobalt include cutting and wear-resistant materials at 8.1% and magnetic alloys at 3.3%. Demand for some other uses is not available as proprietary information.

Trade – U.S. imports of cobalt in 2018 rose +0.8% to 12,000 metric tons, down from the 2016 record high of 12,800. In 2017, the U.S. relied on imports for 61% of its cobalt consumption, which is down from the 99% level seen in the early 1970s.

World Mine Production of Cobalt   In Metric Tons (Cobalt Content)

Year	Australia	Botswana	Brazil	Canada	China	Congo[3] (Kinshasa)	Cuba	Indonesia	Morocco	New Caledonia	Russia	Zambia	World Total
2009	4,345	342	2,075	3,919	6,000	40,000	4,600	1,200	2,610	2,000	6,100	4,900	80,200
2010	3,852	272	3,139	4,636	6,980	60,000	4,800	1,600	3,110	2,850	6,200	8,648	110,000
2011	3,848	149	3,623	6,836	6,800	59,000	5,100	1,600	2,160	3,100	6,100	7,702	111,000
2012	5,870	195	2,900	3,698	2,200	52,000	4,700	1,700	2,000	2,670	6,300	5,435	96,800
2013	6,410	248	3,500	4,005	2,600	56,000	4,000	1,700	2,000	3,190	6,300	5,919	106,000
2014	5,978	196	3,828	3,907	2,800	62,000	3,700	1,300	2,150	4,040	6,300	4,600	115,000
2015	6,000	316	3,800	4,339	3,000	66,000	4,300	1,300	2,250	3,690	6,200	4,000	121,000
2016	5,500	281	300	4,245	3,100	64,000	5,100	1,200	2,400	3,390	5,500	3,000	113,000
2017[1]	5,030			3,870	3,100	73,000	5,000		2,200	2,800	5,900	2,900	120,000
2018[2]	4,700			3,800	3,100	90,000	4,900		2,300		5,900		140,000

[1] Preliminary.   [2] Estimate.   [3] Formerly Zaire.   *Source: U.S. Geological Survey (USGS)*

Salient Statistics of Cobalt in the United States   In Metric Tons (Cobalt Content)

Year	Net Import Reliance As a % of Apparent Consump	Cobalt Secondary Production	Processor and Consumer Stocks Dec. 31	Imports for Consumption	Ground Coal Frit	Stainless & Heat Resisting	Catalysts	Super-alloys	Tool Steel	Magnetic Alloys	Pigments	Drier in Paints, etc.	Cutting & Wear-Resistant Material	Welding Materials	Total Apparent Uses	Price $ Per Pound[4]
2009	76	1,790	780	7,680	W	W	W	3,570	W	287	W	W	503	331	7,470	17.86
2010	81	2,000	880	11,100	W	W	W	3,740	W	357	W	W	696	364	8,030	20.85
2011	76	2,210	1,040	10,600	W	W	W	4,650	W	313	W	W	773	438	9,230	17.99
2012	77	2,160	980	11,100	W	W	W	4,190	W	285	W	W	774	414	9,540	14.07
2013	75	2,160	1,070	10,400	W	W	W	3,770	W	303	W	W	705	397	8,660	12.89
2014	75	2,200	1,410	11,300	----	----	----	3,930	----	328	----	----	783	573	8,710	14.48
2015	73	2,750	1,320	11,400	----	----	----	3,960	----	----	----	----	726	----	10,300	13.44
2016	76	2,750	1,220	12,800	----	----	----	4,080	----	----	----	----	672	----	11,500	12.01
2017[1]	69	2,750	1,270	11,900											8,910	26.97
2018[2]	61	2,800	1,200	12,000											7,200	38.00

[1] Preliminary.   [2] Estimate.   [3] Or related usage.   [4] Annual spot for cathodes.   W = Withheld.   *Source: U.S. Geological Survey (USGS)*

Cocoa

Cocoa is the common name for a powder derived from the fruit seeds of the cacao tree. The Spanish called cocoa "the food of the gods" when they found it in South America 500 years ago. Today, it remains a valued commodity. Dating back to the time of the Aztecs, cocoa was mainly used as a beverage. The processing of the cacao seeds, also known as cocoa beans, begins when the harvested fruit is fermented or cured into a pulpy state for three to nine days. The cocoa beans are then dried in the sun and cleaned in special machines before they are roasted to bring out the chocolate flavor. After roasting, they are put into a crushing machine and ground into cocoa powder. Cocoa has a high food value because it contains as much as 20 percent protein, 40 percent carbohydrate, and 40 percent fat. It is also mildly stimulating because of the presence of theobromine, an alkaloid that is closely related to caffeine. Roughly two-thirds of cocoa bean production is used to make chocolate and one-third to make cocoa powder.

Four major West African cocoa producers, the Ivory Coast, Ghana, Nigeria and Cameroon, together account for about two-thirds of world cocoa production. Outside of West Africa, the major producers of cocoa are Indonesia, Brazil, Malaysia, Ecuador, and the Dominican Republic. Cocoa producers like Ghana and Indonesia have been making efforts to increase cocoa production while producers like Malaysia have been switching to other crops. Ghana has had an ongoing problem with black pod disease and with smuggling of the crop into neighboring Ivory Coast. Brazil was once one of the largest producers of cocoa but has had problems with witches' broom disease. In West Africa, the main crop harvest starts in the September-October period and can be extended into the January-March period. Cocoa trees reach maturity in 5-6 years but can live to be 50 years old or more. During a growing season, the cocoa tree will produce thousands of flowers but only a few will develop into cocoa pods.

Cocoa futures and options are traded at the ICE Futures U.S. and ICE Futures Europe exchanges. The futures contracts call for the delivery of 10 metric tons of cocoa and the contract is priced in US dollars per metric ton.

Prices – ICE cocoa futures prices (Barchart.com symbol CC) posted the low for 2018 in January at $1,836 per metric ton on tepid demand after North American Q4 cocoa grindings unexpectedly fell -1.3% yr/yr, weaker than expectations of a +2.5% yr/yr increase and after Asia Q4 cocoa grindings rose +4.2% yr/yr, below expectations of +8% yr/yr. Cocoa prices then rallied sharply into mid-year and posted a 2-1/4 year high of $2,914 per metric ton in May 2018 as production fell and demand picked up. The International Cocoa Organization (ICCO) forecasted that global 2017/18 cocoa production would fall -2.3% yr/yr to 4.64 MMT and that the 2017/18 global surplus would shrink to +22,000 MT from a +296,000 MT surplus in 2016/17. Global cocoa demand climbed as European Q1 cocoa grindings rose +5.5% yr/yr to a record for the quarter at 358,432 MT and Asian Q1 cocoa grindings rose +7.2% to a record for the quarter at 190,244 MT (data since 2001). Cocoa prices fell back into October as favorable weather in West Africa improved the outlook for the cocoa crops of the Ivory Coast and Ghana, the world's two largest cocoa producers. Also, Barry Callebaut, the world's largest cocoa processor, forecasted a balanced global cocoa market into 2019. Cocoa prices climbed into year-end on signs of tighter supplies after ICE-monitored cocoa inventories fell to a 2-year low in December. Cocoa prices finished 2018 sharply higher by +28% yr/yr at $2,416 per metric ton.

Supply – The world production of cocoa beans in the 2017/18 crop year rose by +11.5% yr/yr to 5.201 million metric tons. The world's largest cocoa producer by far is the Ivory Coast with 39.1% of total world production in 2017/18 with 2.034 million metric tons. After the Ivory Coast the major producers are Ghana with 17.0% of total world production in 2017/18, Indonesia with 12.7%, Nigeria with 6.3%, Cameroon with 5.7%, Brazil with 4.5%, and Ecuador with 4.0%. Closing stocks of cocoa in the 2017/18 crop year rose +1/3% yr/yr to 1.748 metric tons.

Demand – World seasonal grindings of cocoa in 2017/18 rose +3.9% yr/yr to 4.570 million metric tons, a new record high. The European Union is by far the largest global consumer of cocoa, consuming about 34.4 of the global crop.

Trade – U.S. imports of cocoa and cocoa products in 2018 (annualized through November) fell -5.1% yr/yr to 1.382 million metric tons, down from the 2017 record high of 1.456.

World Supply and Demand Cocoa — In Thousands of Metric Tons

Crop Year Beginning Oct. 1	Stocks Oct. 1	Net World Production[4]	Total Availability	Seasona Grindings	Closing Stocks	Stock Change	Stock/Consumption Ratio %
2008-09	1,538	3,592	5,130	3,537	1,557	19	44.0
2009-10	1,557	3,634	5,191	3,737	1,418	-139	37.9
2010-11	1,418	4,309	5,727	3,938	1,746	328	44.3
2011-12	1,746	4,095	5,841	3,972	1,828	82	46.0
2012-13	1,828	3,943	5,771	4,180	1,552	-276	37.1
2013-14	1,552	4,370	5,922	4,335	1,543	-9	35.6
2014-15	1,543	4,252	5,795	4,152	1,600	57	38.5
2015-16[1]	1,600	3,997	5,597	4,127	1,430	-170	34.6
2016-17[2]	1,430	4,740	6,170	4,397	1,726	296	39.3
2017-18[3]	1,726	4,638	6,364	4,570	1,748	22	38.2

[1] Preliminary. [2] Estimate. [3] Forecast. [4] Obtained by adjusting the gross world crop for a one percent loss in weight.
Source: International Cocoa Organization (ICO

World Production of Cocoa Beans   In Metric Tons

Crop Year Beginning Oct. 1	Brazil	Cameroon	Colombia	Côte d'Ivoire	Dominican Republic	Ecuador	Ghana	Indonesia	Malaysia	Mexico	Nigeria	Papau New Guinea	World Total
2008-09	202,030	229,203	44,740	1,382,441	45,291	94,300	680,781	803,593	27,955	50,000	367,020	51,500	4,266,013
2009-10	218,487	235,500	44,740	1,223,153	54,994	120,581	710,638	809,583	18,152	60,000	363,510	59,400	4,211,424
2010-11	235,389	264,077	39,534	1,301,347	58,334	132,099	632,037	844,626	15,654	50,114	399,200	39,400	4,329,437
2011-12	248,524	240,000	37,202	1,511,255	54,279	224,163	700,020	712,200	4,605	42,175	391,000	47,600	4,614,870
2012-13	253,211	268,941	41,670	1,485,882	72,225	133,323	879,348	740,500	3,645	38,825	383,000	38,700	4,613,415
2013-14	256,186	275,000	46,739	1,448,992	68,021	128,446	835,466	720,900	2,809	33,284	367,000	41,200	4,484,827
2014-15	273,793	269,228	47,732	1,613,241	69,913	156,216	858,720	728,400	2,665	26,969	329,870	44,402	4,710,254
2015-16[1]	278,299	274,559	54,798	1,796,000	75,500	180,192	858,720	593,331	1,729	28,007	302,066	45,235	4,791,742
2016-17[2]	213,843	289,312	56,785	1,634,000	81,246	177,551	858,720	656,817	1,757	26,863	298,029	44,491	4,659,027
2017-18[3]	235,809	295,028	56,808	2,034,000	86,599	205,955	883,652	659,776	1,029	27,287	328,263	44,504	5,201,108

[1] Preliminary.   [2] Estimate.   [3] Forecast.   *Source: Food and Agricultural Organization of the United Nations (FAO)*

World Consumption of Cocoa[4]   In Thousands of Metric Tons

Crop Year Beginning Oct. 1	Canada	Côte d'Ivoire	Brazil	European Union	Ghana	Indonesia	Japan	Malaysia	Singapore	Turkey	United States	Russia	World Total
2008-09	55	419	216	1,357	133	120	41	278	80	57	361	54	3,537
2009-10	59	411	226	1,409	212	130	42	298	83	68	382	52	3,737
2010-11	62	361	239	1,492	230	190	40	305	83	70	401	61	3,938
2011-12	60	431	243	1,383	212	270	40	297	83	75	387	63	3,972
2012-13	64	471	241	1,443	225	290	40	293	77	75	429	71	4,180
2013-14	67	519	240	1,461	234	340	44	259	79	88	446	62	4,335
2014-15	62	558	224	1,432	234	335	45	195	81	86	400	46	4,152
2015-16[1]	62	492	225	1,483	202	382	47	194	81	84	398	49	4,127
2016-17[2]	62	577	227	1,502	250	455	49	216	82	101	390	52	4,397
2017-18[3]	62	580	230	1,571	280	490	52	233	88	105	385	57	4,570

[1] Preliminary.   [2] Estimate.   [3] Forecast.   [4] Figures represent the "grindings" of cocoa beans in each country.
Source: International Cocoa Organization (ICO)

Imports of Cocoa Butter in Selected Countries   In Metric Tons

Year	Australia	Austria	Belgium	Canada	France	Germany	Italy	Japan	Netherlands	Sweden	Switzerland	United Kingdom	United States
2009	13,110	3,856	70,155	20,759	64,495	84,939	21,735	22,038	72,609	3,699	24,820	42,921	84,498
2010	15,024	4,929	65,336	20,885	57,639	88,713	22,439	19,365	70,529	6,416	26,462	50,639	102,878
2011	15,081	5,155	75,003	22,463	61,948	89,511	21,988	19,475	91,297	6,010	26,813	43,440	92,572
2012	15,971	5,090	75,402	24,090	71,043	92,370	25,999	26,566	72,416	6,219	26,430	51,541	72,085
2013	17,900	5,425	75,585	25,929	65,205	109,853	30,310	24,260	92,547	6,192	28,795	50,789	80,676
2014	16,074	4,912	79,049	26,250	68,073	124,839	28,364	27,351	82,319	6,400	28,767	47,171	97,774
2015	17,527	4,119	81,283	24,950	62,998	106,110	28,406	21,305	62,409	6,284	27,548	59,164	95,125
2016	16,293	4,970	93,024	26,218	64,443	130,642	28,150	22,362	77,969	6,247	27,545	53,109	82,678
2017	17,798	5,557	95,598	25,385	78,733	145,287	28,914	23,553	86,544	6,519	29,483	53,778	111,696
2018[1]	16,176	5,416	106,980	21,324	71,464	137,196	33,836	27,324	68,004	5,940	26,292	58,020	119,256

[1] Preliminary.   *Sources: Food and Agricultural Organization of the United Nations (FAO)*

Imports of Cocoa Liquor and Cocoa Powder in Selected Countries   In Metric Tons

	Cocoa Liquor						Cocoa Powder						
Year	France	Germany	Japan	Netherlands	United Kingdom	United States	Belgium	France	Germany	Italy	Japan	Netherlands	United States
2009	59,017	64,206	7,515	44,915	6,635	19,367	19,058	42,022	49,689	26,708	15,613	35,034	163,874
2010	59,205	94,860	6,006	60,067	10,073	29,709	20,820	53,861	54,056	26,161	18,765	45,047	172,904
2011	84,704	79,039	9,358	82,633	12,108	22,996	18,324	58,723	54,215	27,717	17,361	53,899	162,723
2012	83,905	82,605	9,351	74,125	14,907	20,461	16,226	53,499	52,762	25,370	17,201	45,494	161,081
2013	96,205	81,726	8,487	98,497	9,934	18,379	19,336	65,479	59,576	26,630	15,897	49,255	150,266
2014	94,219	77,645	9,829	112,010	9,238	22,302	18,833	59,356	69,838	28,444	17,705	56,878	154,294
2015	69,450	74,768	11,884	76,553	10,348	14,764	47,539	56,542	69,652	33,407	19,771	28,048	137,590
2016	73,167	78,359	12,215	79,963	16,134	32,559	46,881	46,516	69,627	33,500	19,768	30,216	180,582
2017	96,669	63,007	14,719	115,370	13,957	30,067	29,992	41,469	68,300	35,693	21,258	71,285	182,884
2018[1]	82,884	51,800	16,004	120,612	14,704	41,036	27,512	42,628	75,428	40,508	19,556	81,836	149,012

[1] Preliminary.   *Source: Food and Agricultural Organization of the United Nations (FAO)*

COCOA

Imports of Cocoa and Products in the United States   In Metric Tons

Year	Jan.	Feb.	Mar.	Apr.	May	June	July	Aug.	Sept.	Oct.	Nov.	Dec.	Total
2009	113,518	97,987	87,642	95,112	82,460	98,606	80,011	87,970	103,220	103,319	94,175	125,717	1,169,736
2010	153,823	99,689	133,915	85,380	94,230	78,143	79,620	84,394	109,595	88,503	100,412	114,736	1,222,436
2011	132,295	144,126	88,224	89,816	91,987	138,011	125,210	121,553	93,780	97,723	90,074	100,511	1,313,310
2012	147,347	152,455	115,034	99,232	82,919	90,586	91,538	95,556	83,121	91,707	88,361	99,904	1,237,761
2013	118,129	125,897	119,255	106,917	136,359	88,132	112,058	94,986	93,586	91,863	90,006	126,702	1,303,889
2014	105,743	141,186	165,373	133,870	95,607	94,784	104,583	98,192	91,016	93,453	80,532	91,672	1,296,010
2015	109,669	121,573	132,182	138,943	115,781	124,700	107,942	88,465	101,383	105,487	87,698	105,521	1,339,343
2016	123,193	144,838	122,403	125,085	99,749	95,351	97,444	109,180	100,657	114,504	105,660	129,828	1,367,892
2017	143,196	143,358	175,485	162,652	129,538	111,460	108,712	100,961	90,012	95,449	95,478	99,473	1,455,775
2018[1]	149,657	134,349	134,869	129,987	111,950	93,772	104,645	111,269	92,118	105,331	99,051	108,658	1,375,657

[1] Preliminary.   Source: Foreign Agricultural Service, U.S. Department of Agriculture (FAS-USDA)

Visible Stocks of Cocoa in Port of Hampton Road Warehouses[1], at End of Month   In Thousands of Bags

Year	Jan.	Feb.	Mar.	Apr.	May	June	July	Aug.	Sept.	Oct.	Nov.	Dec.
2009	14.9	14.9	14.9	14.9	14.9	14.9	13.7	13.7	13.7	13.7	13.7	13.7
2010	13.3	12.3	12.3	12.3	12.3	12.3	12.3	12.3	12.3	12.3	12.3	12.3
2011	10.4	12.3	12.3	12.3	12.3	12.3	12.3	12.3	11.6	11.6	11.6	11.6
2012	11.6	11.6	11.6	11.6	11.6	11.6	11.6	11.6	11.6	11.3	11.3	11.3
2013	11.3	11.3	11.3	9.6	9.6	9.6	10.5	10.5	5.1	9.6	9.5	9.6
2014	9.6	9.6	9.6	9.6	9.6	9.6	9.6	9.6	9.6	9.6	9.6	9.6
2015	9.6	9.6	9.6	9.6	9.6	7.2	7.2	7.2	7.2	7.2	7.2	7.2
2016	7.2	7.2	7.2	7.2	7.2	7.2	7.2	7.2	7.2	7.2	7.2	7.2
2017	7.2	6.5	6.5	6.5	6.5	6.5	6.5	6.5	6.5	6.5	2.7	2.7
2018	2.4	2.4	2.0	2.0	1.9	1.9	1.4	1.4	0	0	0	0

[1] Licensed warehouses approved by ICE.   Source: ICE Futures U.S. (ICE)

Visible Stocks of Cocoa in Philadelphia (Del. River) Warehouses[1], at End of Month   In Thousands of Bags

Year	Jan.	Feb.	Mar.	Apr.	May	June	July	Aug.	Sept.	Oct.	Nov.	Dec.
2009	2,062.7	2,339.1	2,292.6	2,530.2	2,456.1	2,405.8	2,137.2	2,059.1	1,938.5	1,931.4	2,105.8	2,196.4
2010	2,699.9	3,217.3	3,442.6	3,400.3	3,317.0	3,128.8	2,935.7	2,602.8	2,491.2	2,159.6	1,985.2	2,197.6
2011	2,551.7	2,900.4	2,856.1	2,633.1	2,546.0	2,971.6	3,388.2	3,089.4	3,055.1	2,758.3	2,559.1	2,856.1
2012	3,210.7	3,538.5	4,156.0	4,123.5	3,985.5	3,815.8	3,792.4	3,655.2	3,442.7	3,204.1	2,895.2	2,956.3
2013	3,070.3	3,690.7	3,924.4	3,884.4	4,110.6	4,035.9	3,945.1	3,897.9	3,583.0	3,170.0	2,921.9	3,050.1
2014	3,215.1	3,687.7	4,395.1	4,862.6	4,647.1	4,354.2	4,167.4	3,909.4	3,569.5	3,168.6	2,816.0	2,494.7
2015	2,640.6	2,953.7	3,044.0	3,700.4	3,780.4	4,166.1	4,013.1	3,788.7	3,568.2	3,286.3	3,146.1	2,956.1
2016	3,186.6	3,464.0	3,960.3	3,809.4	3,690.7	3,441.0	3,155.1	2,908.5	2,606.9	2,546.0	2,479.5	2,493.6
2017	2,961.9	3,695.8	4,460.4	5,117.8	5,394.3	5,245.8	4,992.7	4,669.1	4,318.8	3,834.3	3,462.8	3,147.5
2018	3,746.2	4,259.6	4,501.8	5,054.0	4,870.3	4,579.7	4,386.0	4,215.1	3,955.9	3,633.1	3,269.1	3,236.1

[1] Licensed warehouses approved by ICE.   Source: ICE Futures U.S. (ICE)

Visible Stocks of Cocoa in New York Warehouses[1], at End of Month   In Thousands of Bags

Year	Jan.	Feb.	Mar.	Apr.	May	June	July	Aug.	Sept.	Oct.	Nov.	Dec.
2009	291.7	413.2	423.9	472.0	501.5	557.3	672.2	664.2	653.9	726.0	714.6	722.3
2010	831.4	1,005.7	1,099.3	1,042.0	954.2	825.2	730.7	662.7	618.4	572.3	524.9	487.3
2011	499.4	604.9	701.2	711.1	639.3	661.5	719.8	734.1	807.6	884.8	875.5	857.6
2012	845.1	881.2	1,031.7	1,016.7	962.8	944.4	862.3	928.4	877.0	829.7	752.3	716.5
2013	679.9	619.6	621.1	708.3	779.6	779.6	717.2	660.4	589.3	529.2	451.3	475.6
2014	391.0	386.7	364.5	482.6	619.3	566.5	505.4	435.9	419.3	380.9	317.1	308.3
2015	276.6	266.0	245.3	260.4	286.9	366.0	342.2	314.5	284.7	277.7	278.0	287.8
2016	283.3	353.2	412.3	388.1	317.4	302.9	299.7	311.3	312.4	289.8	250.2	274.9
2017	336.9	318.2	344.6	388.7	424.8	399.4	367.4	331.1	291.6	252.7	244.0	232.2
2018	271.1	281.8	288.4	315.4	278.3	264.7	265.4	240.5	224.6	206.8	197.7	230.7

[1] Licensed warehouses approved by ICE.   Source: ICE Futures U.S. (ICE)

COCOA
Quarterly Cash as of 03/29/2019

QUARTERLY CASH
As of 03/29/2019

Chart High 5732.0 on 09/14/1977
Chart Low   92.0 on 07/31/1939

USD/metric ton

Exchange Standard: to 10/1946; ACCRA: 11/1946 to 09/1980; Ivory Coast: 10/1980 to date.

Average Cash Price of Cocoa, Ivory Coast in New York   In Dollars Per Metric Ton

Year	Jan.	Feb.	Mar.	Apr.	May	June	July	Aug.	Sept.	Oct.	Nov.	Dec.	Average
2009	2,985	2,977	2,781	2,830	2,699	2,892	3,047	3,186	3,427	3,634	3,596	3,782	3,153
2010	3,851	3,611	3,452	3,580	3,535	3,539	3,602	3,455	3,269	3,314	3,279	3,354	3,487
2011	3,507	3,937	3,992	3,697	3,565	3,360	3,422	3,312	3,199	2,949	2,831	2,396	3,347
2012	2,448	2,621	2,647	2,553	2,605	2,506	2,595	2,759	2,956	2,787	2,745	2,724	2,662
2013	2,519	2,455	2,428	2,492	2,566	2,494	2,521	2,672	2,819	2,988	2,998	3,099	2,671
2014	3,068	3,281	3,325	3,340	3,287	3,476	3,494	3,591	3,523	3,455	3,176	3,191	3,351
2015	3,170	3,181	3,181	3,129	3,331	3,493	3,590	3,424	3,546	3,434	3,630	3,632	3,395
2016	3,297	3,124	3,327	3,333	3,412	3,439	3,482	3,434	3,288	3,070	2,800	2,620	3,219
2017	2,493	2,379	2,381	2,214	2,200	2,235	2,195	2,256	2,231	2,354	2,411	2,190	2,295
2018	2,148	2,362	2,701	2,974	2,952	2,800	2,748	2,573	2,626	2,511	2,569	2,530	2,625

Source: Economic Research Service, U.S. Department of Agriculture (ERS-USDA)

Total Visible Stocks of Cocoa in Warehouses[1], at End of Month   In Thousands of Bags

Year	Jan.	Feb.	Mar.	Apr.	May	June	July	Aug.	Sept.	Oct.	Nov.	Dec.
2009	2,557.4	2,996.2	2,956.5	3,266.2	3,179.4	3,166.2	3,000.9	2,909.0	2,751.1	2,783.3	2,932.8	3,027.8
2010	3,639.8	4,330.1	4,727.3	4,636.9	4,477.2	4,170.8	3,901.1	3,492.1	3,318.1	2,884.6	2,645.7	2,801.8
2011	3,158.1	3,611.9	3,757.3	3,520.8	3,324.1	3,729.7	4,185.3	3,892.5	3,928.4	3,704.4	3,491.6	3,767.1
2012	4,108.5	4,627.0	5,393.6	5,343.0	5,149.2	4,947.6	4,834.9	4,758.7	4,483.8	4,161.4	3,753.2	3,763.1
2013	3,814.6	4,416.3	4,653.7	4,690.9	4,987.5	4,966.3	4,745.1	4,632.7	4,232.5	3,754.5	3,436.3	3,574.1
2014	3,648.9	4,117.1	4,800.1	5,384.4	5,305.6	4,960.0	4,711.8	4,384.1	4,027.5	3,588.3	3,171.9	2,824.9
2015	2,939.1	3,241.1	3,310.7	3,978.6	4,085.2	4,546.7	4,369.9	4,117.8	3,867.5	3,578.7	3,438.3	3,255.3
2016	3,481.4	3,828.6	4,384.0	4,209.0	4,019.5	3,755.4	3,465.7	3,230.7	2,930.3	2,846.7	2,740.7	2,779.4
2017	3,309.3	4,023.4	4,814.4	5,515.9	5,828.5	5,654.6	5,369.5	5,009.6	4,617.9	4,096.9	3,714.4	3,386.7
2018	4,025.4	4,549.1	4,793.7	5,372.4	5,151.2	4,847.1	4,653.5	4,457.3	4,180.9	3,840.3	3,467.2	3,467.2

[1] Licensed warehouses approved by ICE.   *Source: ICE Futures U.S. (ICE)*

COCOA

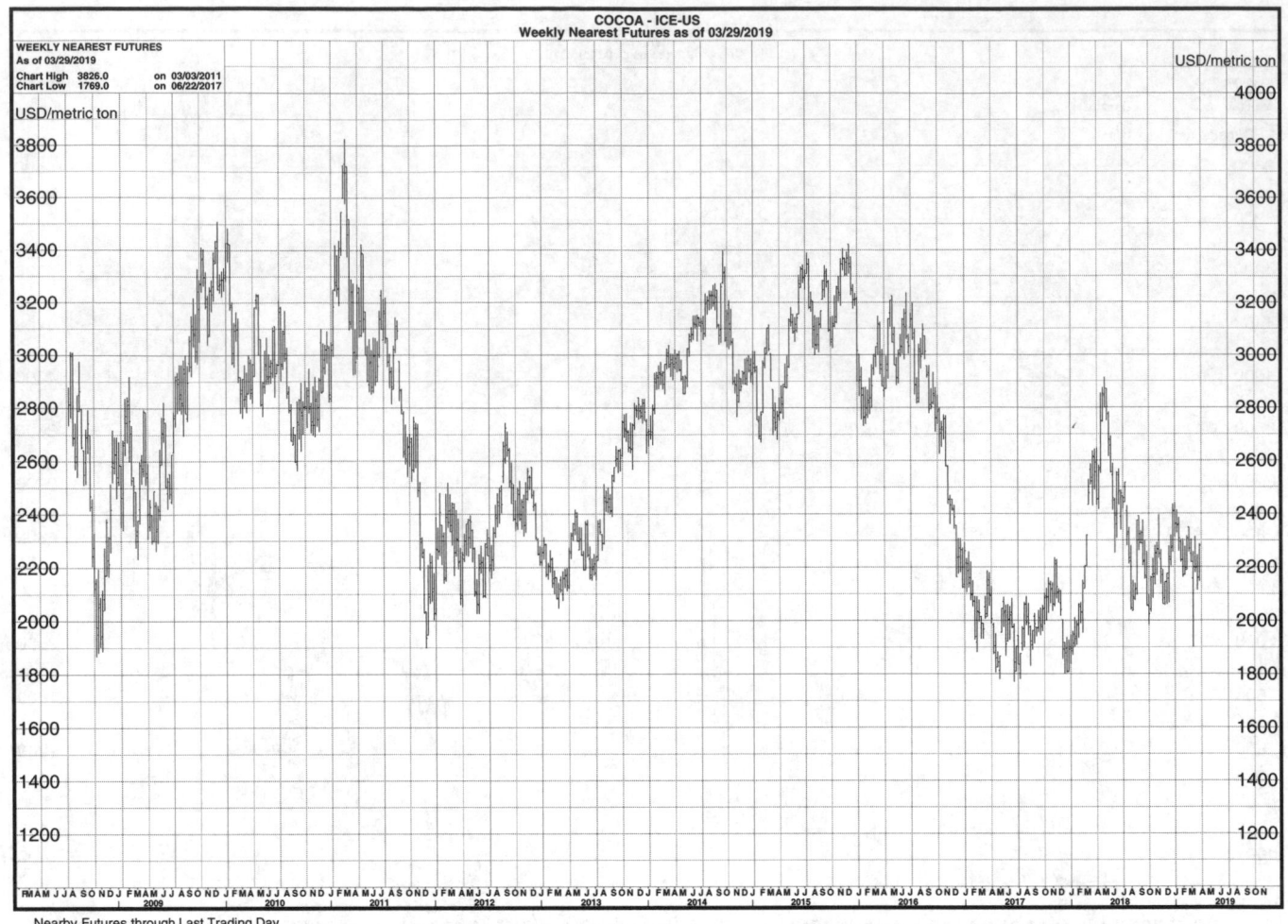

COCOA - ICE-US
Weekly Nearest Futures as of 03/29/2019

WEEKLY NEAREST FUTURES
As of 03/29/2019

Chart High 3826.0 on 03/03/2011
Chart Low 1769.0 on 06/22/2017

Nearby Futures through Last Trading Day.

Volume of Trading of Cocoa Futures in New York   In Contracts

Year	Jan.	Feb.	Mar.	Apr.	May	June	July	Aug.	Sept.	Oct.	Nov.	Dec.	Total
2009	265,308	282,200	242,110	279,621	214,640	303,030	216,046	292,552	188,138	289,133	338,296	175,892	3,086,966
2010	255,025	361,068	282,222	372,997	290,545	366,645	253,289	425,322	247,749	284,483	404,682	253,652	3,797,679
2011	395,349	401,740	390,590	423,879	357,282	454,217	328,156	571,410	335,481	388,486	554,320	347,142	4,948,052
2012	395,832	586,013	474,613	605,217	459,683	620,166	457,510	627,854	346,794	467,949	651,655	306,527	5,999,813
2013	505,589	598,270	425,547	752,332	541,022	792,100	504,933	646,114	379,515	484,417	621,749	332,158	6,583,746
2014	571,906	588,461	453,219	593,071	454,372	625,401	551,959	541,132	478,549	617,492	508,452	331,778	6,315,792
2015	586,564	679,362	694,091	739,813	520,024	710,582	531,381	801,763	602,091	770,424	775,633	501,308	7,913,036
2016	940,394	950,705	667,648	927,406	857,735	778,284	712,599	987,963	730,541	856,408	829,030	623,505	9,862,218
2017	797,471	929,400	906,294	974,013	927,022	1,095,512	790,389	1,116,901	660,699	1,066,289	1,049,735	747,881	11,061,606
2018	973,387	1,122,890	1,135,854	1,266,511	972,472	1,176,038	884,333	1,090,296	707,925	1,021,630	1,077,251	607,002	12,035,589

Source: ICE Futures U.S. (ICE)

Average Open Interest of Cocoa Futures in New York   In Contracts

Year	Jan.	Feb.	Mar.	Apr.	May	June	July	Aug.	Sept.	Oct.	Nov.	Dec.
2009	119,496	118,145	114,051	111,859	117,027	114,792	112,079	112,935	121,226	133,635	129,171	129,296
2010	137,675	127,994	129,562	128,298	130,258	119,074	124,335	119,070	127,315	138,385	136,708	137,345
2011	148,426	158,965	163,700	159,411	157,851	162,945	172,670	166,766	176,524	191,211	168,734	167,339
2012	171,138	165,555	170,143	178,362	183,549	174,848	186,439	190,328	202,142	202,142	189,765	193,643
2013	197,848	192,704	200,696	199,773	220,741	196,543	176,618	183,556	201,739	219,812	212,717	213,685
2014	210,130	216,867	215,297	206,091	204,253	216,264	214,879	213,149	208,448	199,236	177,425	186,443
2015	200,884	193,672	211,199	199,675	208,637	215,736	219,497	182,777	200,200	216,932	232,054	234,884
2016	227,549	234,056	238,732	234,122	242,073	198,093	215,818	206,006	210,888	251,984	244,643	254,911
2017	275,443	265,621	285,852	284,418	296,408	257,541	273,750	244,093	258,013	253,440	241,566	251,261
2018	275,944	263,249	296,500	289,878	304,760	266,004	247,961	240,819	242,329	264,377	241,641	235,570

Source: ICE Futures U.S. (ICE)

Coconut Oil and Copra

Coconut oil and copra come from the fruit of the coconut palm tree, which originated in Southeast Asia. Coconut oil has been used for thousands of years as cooking oil, and is still a staple in the diets of many people living in tropical areas. Until shortages of imported oil developed during WWII, Americans also used coconut oil for cooking.

Copra is the meaty inner lining of the coconut. It is an oil-rich pulp with a light, slightly sweet, nutty flavor. Copra is used mainly as a source of coconut oil and is also used shredded for baking. High-quality copra contains about 65% to 72% oil, and oil made from the copra is called crude coconut oil. Crude coconut oil is processed from copra by expeller press and solvent extraction. It is not considered fit for human consumption until it has been refined, which consists of neutralizing, bleaching and deodorizing it at high heat with a vacuum. The remaining oil cake obtained as a by-product is used for livestock feed.

Premium grade coconut oil, also called virgin coconut oil, is oil made from the first pressing without the addition of any chemicals. Premium grade coconut oil is more expensive than refined or crude oil because the producers use only selected raw materials and there is a lower production yield due to only one pressing.

Coconut oil accounts for approximately 20% of all vegetable oils used worldwide. Coconut oil is used in margarines, vegetable shortening, salad oils, confections, and in sports drinks to boost energy and enhance athletic performance. It is also used in the manufacture of soaps, detergents, shampoos, cosmetics, candles, glycerin and synthetic rubber. Coconut oil is very healthy, unless it is hydrogenated, and is easily digested.

Supply – World production of copra in 2018 was up +15.0% at 4.579 million metric tons but remained below the record high of 5.662 million metric tons posted in 2001. The world's largest producers of copra in 2018 were the Philippines with 36.7% of world production, Indonesia with 29.5%, India with 11.8%, and Mexico with 4.7%. World production of coconut oil in the 2017/18 marketing year rose +10.3% yr/yr to 2.734 million metric tons.

Demand – Virtually all of world production of copra goes for crushing into coconut meal and oil (over 99%). World consumption of coconut oil in 2017/18 rose by +7.8% yr/yr to 2.643 million metric tons, but still below the 2009-10 record high of 3.574 million metric tons.

Trade – Copra is generally crushed in the country of origin, meaning that less than 4% of copra itself is exported; the rest is exported in the form of coconut oil. World exports of coconut oil in 2017/18 rose by +8.1% yr/yr to 1.810 million metric tons, but still below the 2009-10 record high of 2.406 million metric tons.

World Production of Copra   In Thousands of Metric Tons

Year	India	Indonesia	Ivory Coast	Malaysia	Mexico	Mozam-bique	Papua New Guinea	Philip-pines	Sri Lanka	Thailand	Vanuatu	Vietnam	World Total
2009	680	1,520	46	54	228	48	100	2,040	89	69	31	55	5,284
2010	690	1,440	46	63	211	48	102	2,680	85	48	32	57	5,816
2011	680	1,400	46	51	209	48	115	1,700	87	44	32	57	4,791
2012	670	1,550	46	58	216	49	85	2,030	90	48	32	57	5,247
2013	640	1,470	29	79	207	50	80	2,300	90	49	25	57	5,392
2014	670	1,530	27	62	203	52	72	1,740	80	49	25	57	4,881
2015	620	1,540	28	64	203	54	95	1,680	83	49	18	57	4,806
2016[1]	580	1,290	26	58	208	50	97	1,280	95	46	28	55	4,128
2017[2]	420	1,160	28	67	231	52	114	1,370	90	46	27	56	3,981
2018[3]	540	1,350	30	68	215	52	100	1,680	94	48	21	57	4,579

[1] Preliminary.   [2] Estimate.   [3] Forecast.   *Source: The Oil World*

World Supply and Distribution of Coconut Oil   In Thousands of Metric Tons

	Production							Consumption						Ending Stocks		
Year	India	Indo-nesia	Malay-sia	Philip-pines	World Total	World Exports	World Imports	European Union	India	Indo-nesia	Philip-pines	United States	World Total	Philip-pines	United States	World Total
2008-09	396	851	44	1,239	3,099	1,766	1,795	632	411	181	441	419	3,087	145	83	442
2009-10	400	890	45	1,732	3,621	2,406	2,374	794	404	179	445	587	3,574	55	84	457
2010-11	398	847	50	1,240	3,090	1,948	1,973	730	409	153	336	474	3,237	70	62	336
2011-12	393	914	47	1,208	3,114	1,908	1,907	594	402	143	375	487	3,067	110	77	381
2012-13	380	850	51	1,654	3,471	2,078	2,086	716	381	193	564	521	3,423	80	80	436
2013-14	391	933	51	1,153	3,050	1,866	1,859	646	392	176	364	518	3,119	68	65	359
2014-15	377	937	51	1,093	2,970	1,964	1,953	537	389	161	233	531	2,896	69	61	423
2015-16[1]	346	805	45	888	2,594	1,641	1,653	536	341	166	198	469	2,685	74	66	344
2016-17[2]	270	691	45	953	2,479	1,674	1,637	476	262	184	119	439	2,453	58	52	333
2017-18[3]	300	790	46	1,067	2,734	1,810	1,817	522	292	197	132	470	2,643	78	72	431

[1] Preliminary.   [2] Estimate.   [3] Forecast.   *Source: The Oil World*

COCONUT OIL AND COPRA

Supply and Distribution of Coconut Oil in the United States   In Millions of Pounds

Year	Rotterdam Copra Tonne $ U.S.	Rotterdam Coconut Oil, CIF $ U.S.	Imports For Con-sumption	Stocks Oct. 1	Total Supply	Exports	Disapearance Total Domestic	Disapearance Edible Products	Disapearance Inedible Products	Production of Coconut Oil (Refined) Total	Production Oct.-Dec.	Production Jan.-Mar.	Production April-June	Production July-Sept.
2008-09	487	735	961	181	1,143	37	1,293	364	394	586.6	147.6	131.1	122.8	185.2
2009-10	613	921	1,338	183	1,521	41	1,836	441	W	833.0	190.1	214.9	211.2	216.8
2010-11	1,188	1,772	1,080	186	1,266	85	1,045	467	W	808.8	202.2	NA	NA	NA
2011-12	829	1,244	1,165	169	1,334	60	1,073	NA	NA	NA	NA	NA	NA	NA
2012-13	570	858	1,214	176	1,390	56	1,149	NA	NA	NA	NA	NA	NA	NA
2013-14	854	1,278	1,173	143	1,316	64	1,142	----	----	----	----	----	----	----
2014-15	749	1,128	1,261	134	1,395	99	1,171	----	----	----	----	----	----	----
2015-16	907	1,360	1,157	146	1,302	111	1,034	----	----	----	----	----	----	----
2016-17[1]	1,076	1,620	1,036	115	1,151	98	969	----	----	----	----	----	----	----
2017-18[2]	895	1,343	1,168	159	1,327	88	1,036	----	----	----	----	----	----	----

[1] Preliminary.   [2] Forecast.   *Source: Bureau of Census, U.S. Department of Commerce*

Average Price of Coconut Oil (Crude) Tank Cars in New York   In Cents Per Pound

Year	Jan.	Feb.	Mar.	Apr.	May	June	July	Aug.	Sept.	Oct.	Nov.	Dec.	Average
2008	58.02	62.33	70.98	67.38	67.38	71.73	70.33	59.62	55.82	47.73	37.46	35.51	58.69
2009	35.25	33.14	30.07	31.58	37.84	37.34	32.78	35.00	35.75	35.75	35.75	35.53	34.65
2010	36.20	35.75	37.88	41.99	43.60	44.00	46.49	54.31	55.94	63.65	69.00	79.50	50.69
2011	87.00	92.50	85.00	91.80	95.50	96.50	87.00	81.75	74.40	57.75	57.00	61.00	80.60
2012	68.25	68.00	64.90	63.63	59.25	54.00	52.75	50.30	47.75	43.75	41.40	38.88	54.40
2013	39.38	41.25	39.30	38.00	38.20	40.75	41.50	41.50	46.00	45.00	59.30	61.00	44.26
2014	59.70	63.00	65.38	62.75	65.70	65.31	62.88	56.60	55.31	53.75	55.69	56.50	60.21
2015	56.30	54.94	52.94	49.50	52.25	53.19	52.30	51.56	50.75	51.05	50.31	52.20	52.27
2016	53.69	54.44	67.75	76.90	68.38	69.35	70.85	72.06	74.30	70.00	73.50	78.20	69.12
2017[1]	83.63	90.00	73.90	82.81	84.00	83.60	81.00	85.88	86.63	68.50	72.25	72.10	80.36

[1] Preliminary.   *Source: Economic Research Service, U.S. Department of Agriculture (ERS-USDA)*

Consumption of Coconut Oil in End Products (Edible and Inedible) in the United States   In Millions of Pounds

Year	Jan.	Feb.	Mar.	Apr.	May	June	July	Aug.	Sept.	Oct.	Nov.	Dec.	Total
2002	55.4	41.3	50.8	59.3	53.9	46.4	50.7	51.8	45.9	54.3	56.1	49.4	615.4
2003	51.2	49.3	56.8	50.6	52.3	46.7	48.9	49.6	50.3	47.8	41.8	38.5	583.7
2004	50.0	51.7	58.5	54.6	48.5	55.6	52.9	55.1	48.9	48.2	64.3	51.7	640.0
2005	46.7	52.0	47.9	48.8	51.4	55.5	47.2	58.1	49.2	52.8	53.4	58.1	621.1
2006	70.4	62.7	50.4	47.5	50.7	51.6	43.1	51.6	43.8	49.6	44.4	40.8	606.4
2007	49.8	48.5	47.0	51.2	53.7	60.3	60.3	74.2	67.5	71.8	71.3	62.7	718.3
2008	63.6	72.1	64.8	74.4	69.7	70.4	65.8	67.6	65.8	63.0	63.6	53.6	794.5
2009	67.9	62.8	60.2	66.9	66.9	27.6	36.5	28.1	29.4	32.8	32.1	30.6	541.8
2010	41.0	36.6	45.3	34.9	39.8	38.6	37.2	40.4	32.1	41.4	39.9	70.8	498.0
2011[1]	34.6	37.0	40.6	38.0	39.0	37.0	26.7	NA	NA	NA	NA	NA	433.5

[1] Preliminary.   *Source: Bureau of Census, U.S. Department of Commerce*

Stocks of Coconut Oil (Crude and Refined) in the United States, on First of Month   In Millions of Pounds

Year	Jan.	Feb.	Mar.	Apr.	May	June	July	Aug.	Sept.	Oct.	Nov.	Dec.
2002	245.9	238.8	249.6	251.3	233.5	231.6	303.3	301.6	245.8	226.5	273.8	264.1
2003	195.2	194.0	214.3	224.9	223.7	187.8	162.2	202.9	195.6	218.9	184.6	186.1
2004	167.2	160.3	192.6	181.7	131.4	108.7	90.6	132.8	149.2	131.3	147.7	182.5
2005	225.9	163.7	188.4	191.0	170.6	187.7	263.5	250.4	253.7	242.1	252.3	273.3
2006	268.3	236.9	224.5	227.3	260.2	229.1	213.8	214.4	204.7	224.5	179.2	180.2
2007	214.4	228.5	261.5	223.1	191.8	157.9	171.2	154.4	127.7	128.4	142.5	212.6
2008	205.6	192.9	180.9	191.9	223.9	203.9	187.8	181.5	180.4	182.2	163.3	174.6
2009	164.1	183.7	215.6	167.2	143.9	138.0	134.8	133.2	102.3	182.3	159.0	154.7
2010	220.2	204.5	172.1	144.6	119.3	120.3	172.2	179.3	197.1	185.8	166.7	167.2
2011[1]	181.5	150.2	162.7	154.6	150.0	157.6	158.4	190.9	NA	NA	NA	NA

[1] Preliminary.   *Source: Bureau of Census, U.S. Department of Commerce*

Coffee

Coffee is one of the world's most important cash commodities. Coffee is the common name for any type of tree in the genus madder family. It is actually a tropical evergreen shrub that has the potential to grow 100 feet tall. The coffee tree grows in tropical regions between the Tropics of Cancer and Capricorn in areas with abundant rainfall, year-round warm temperatures averaging about 70 degrees Fahrenheit, and no frost. In the U.S., the only areas that produce any significant amount of coffee are Puerto Rico and Hawaii. The coffee plant will produce its first full crop of beans at about 5 years old and then be productive for about 15 years. The average coffee tree produces enough beans to make about 1 to 1 ½ pounds of roasted coffee per year. It takes approximately 4,000 handpicked green coffee beans to make a pound of coffee. Wine was the first drink made from the coffee tree using the coffee cherries, honey, and water. In the 17th century, the first coffee house, also known as a "penny university" because of the price per cup, opened in London. The London Stock Exchange grew from one of these first coffee houses.

Coffee is generally classified into two types of beans: arabica and robusta. The most widely produced coffee is arabica, which makes up about 70 percent of total production. It grows mostly at high altitudes of 600 to 2,000 meters, with Brazil and Colombia being the largest producers. Arabic coffee is traded at the ICE Futures U.S. exchange. The stronger of the two types is robusta. It is grown at lower altitudes with the largest producers being Indonesia, West Africa, Brazil, and Vietnam. Robusta coffee is traded on the ICE Futures Europe exchange.

Ninety percent of the world coffee trade is in green (unroasted) coffee beans. Seasonal factors have a significant influence on the price of coffee. There is no extreme peak in world production at any one time of the year, although coffee consumption declines by 12 percent or more below the year's average in the warm summer months. Therefore, coffee imports and roasts both tend to decline in spring and summer and pick up again in fall and winter.

Very low prices for coffee can create serious long-term problems for coffee producers. When prices fall below the costs of production, there is little or no economic incentive to produce coffee and coffee trees may be neglected or completely abandoned. When prices are low, producers cannot afford to hire the labor needed to maintain the trees and pick the crop at harvest. The result is that trees yield less due to reduced use of fertilizer and fewer employed coffee workers. One effect is a decline in the quality of the coffee that is produced. Higher quality Arabica coffee is often produced at higher altitudes, which entails higher costs. It is this coffee that is often abandoned. Although the pressure on producers can be severe, the market eventually comes back into balance as supply declines in response to low prices.

Coffee prices are subject to upward spikes in June, July and August due to possible freeze scares in Brazil during the winter months in the Southern Hemisphere. The Brazilian coffee crop is harvested starting in May and extending for several weeks into what are the winter months in Brazil. A major freeze in Brazil occurs roughly every five years on average.

Coffee futures and options are traded at the ICE Futures U.S. and ICE Futures Europe exchanges, and the B3 Exchange (formerly BM&F/BOVESPA). Coffee futures are traded on the JSE Securities Exchange (JSE).

Prices – ICE Arabica coffee futures prices (Barchart. com symbol KC) posted the high for 2018 in January at 131.35 cents per pound on signs of smaller supplies after CeCafe reported Brazil 2017 green coffee exports fell -10% to 27.3 mln bags, a 5-year low, and after the International Coffee Organization (ICO) reported that global coffee exports for the first two months of the 2017/18 crop year (Oct-Nov) were down -11% yr/yr at 17.62 mln bags. Coffee prices then ratcheted lower into September and posted a 13-year low of 92.00 cents per pound on the prospects for robust global production and abundant supplies. Conab projected that Brazil's 2018 coffee production would climb +37% yr/yr to a record 61.7 mln bags since the crop was in the higher-yielding half of its biennial cycle. In addition, the USDA forecasted that global 2018/19 coffee production would climb +7.1% yr/yr to a record 171.166 mln bags and that global 2018/19 coffee ending stocks would increase by +11.6% to a 3-year high of 32.812 mln bags. A plunge in the Brazilian real to a 3-1/4 low against the dollar in September further exacerbated the downside in coffee prices since the weak real provided incentive to Brazil's coffee producers to boost more-profitable exports that are priced in dollars. ICO reported that global 2017/18 coffee exports rose +2% yr/yr to 121.9 mln bags and that ICE-monitored coffee inventories climbed to a 4-1/2 year high of 2.463 mln bags in December. Prices recovered into year-end but still finished 2018 down -19.3% yr/yr at 101.85 cents per pound.

Supply – World coffee production of green coffee in the 2018/19 marketing year (July-June) is forecasted to rise +9.8% yr/yr to 174.493 million bags (1 bag equals 60 kilograms or 132.3 pounds), to a new record high. Coffee ending stocks in the 2018/19 marketing year are forecasted to rise +23.7% yr/yr to 37.056 million bags. Brazil is forecasted to be the world's largest coffee producer by far with 63.4 million bags of production in 2018/19, which is 38.0% of total world production. Other key producers include Vietnam with 17.0% of the world's production Columbia with 8.0%, and Indonesia with 6.0%. Brazil's coffee production in 2018/19 is forecasted to rise +24.6% yr/yr to 63.400 million bags. Vietnam has become a major coffee producer in recent years, expected to boost its production to a record 30.400 million bags in 2018/19, up from less than a million bags in 1990.

Demand – U.S. coffee consumption in 2018 fell -2.8% yr/yr to 27.138 million bags, down from last year's record high of 27.921.

Trade – World coffee exports in 2018/19 are forecasted to rise +4.2% yr/yr to 136.737 million bags, a new record high. The world's largest exporters of coffee in 2018/19 are forecasted to be Brazil with 25.8% of world exports, Vietnam with 20.6%, and Columbia with 9.7%. U.S. coffee imports in 2017 rose +1.5% yr/yr to 27.921 million bags, a new record high. The key countries from which the U.S. imported coffee in 2017 were Brazil with 22.3% of U.S. imports, Columbia with 20.8%, Mexico with 4.7%, and Guatemala with 4.6%.

COFFEE

World Supply and Distribution of Coffee for Producing Countries   In Thousands of 60 Kilogram Bags

Year	Beginning Stocks	Production	Imports	Total Supply	Total Exports	Bean Exports	Rst/Grn Exports	Soluble Exports	Domestic Use	Ending Stocks
2009-10	39,593	129,774	91,776	273,455	106,334	92,306	2,193	11,835	138,276	28,845
2010-11	28,845	141,409	96,401	279,597	116,462	100,403	2,278	13,781	134,495	28,640
2011-12	28,640	144,837	98,113	284,935	117,661	101,144	2,411	14,106	141,526	25,748
2012-13	25,748	158,018	102,077	300,351	122,847	104,993	2,730	15,124	142,139	35,365
2013-14	35,365	160,054	102,615	312,430	128,877	110,004	3,220	15,653	142,389	41,164
2014-15	41,164	153,816	102,517	312,384	123,643	103,734	3,523	16,386	145,637	43,104
2015-16	43,104	152,939	107,068	320,516	133,389	112,971	3,417	17,001	152,728	34,393
2016-17[1]	34,393	161,814	107,270	322,761	133,662	113,921	3,737	16,004	154,294	34,790
2017-18[2]	34,790	158,882	108,325	318,887	131,190	111,259	3,780	16,151	160,274	29,966
2018-19[3]	29,966	174,493	113,360	332,202	136,737	117,035	3,622	16,080	163,589	37,056

[1] Preliminary.   [2] Estimate.   [3] Forecast.   132.276 Lbs. Per Bag   Source: Foreign Agricultural Service, U.S. Department of Agriculture (FAS-USDA)

World Production of Green Coffee   In Thousands of 60 Kilogram Bags

Crop Year	Brazil	Colombia	Costa Rica	Cote d'Ivoire	El Salvador	Ethiopia	Guatemala	India	Indonesia	Mexico	Uganda	Vietnam	World Total
2009-10	44,800	8,100	1,475	2,350	1,300	6,000	4,010	4,825	10,500	4,150	2,870	18,500	129,774
2010-11	54,500	8,525	1,575	1,600	1,860	6,125	3,960	5,035	9,325	4,000	3,212	19,415	141,409
2011-12	49,200	7,655	1,775	1,600	1,200	6,320	4,410	5,230	7,970	4,300	3,075	26,000	144,837
2012-13	57,600	9,927	1,675	1,750	1,250	6,500	4,010	5,303	11,900	4,650	3,600	26,500	158,018
2013-14	57,200	12,075	1,450	1,675	550	6,345	3,515	5,075	11,900	3,950	3,850	29,833	160,054
2014-15	54,300	13,300	1,400	1,400	700	6,475	3,185	5,440	10,470	3,180	3,550	27,400	153,816
2015-16	49,400	14,000	1,625	1,600	560	6,510	3,295	5,800	12,100	2,300	3,650	28,930	152,939
2016-17[1]	56,100	14,600	1,300	1,090	600	6,943	3,570	5,200	10,600	3,300	5,200	26,700	161,814
2017-18[2]	50,900	13,825	1,500	1,250	650	7,055	3,780	5,266	10,400	4,075	4,350	29,300	158,882
2018-19[3]	63,400	14,300	1,350	1,400	650	7,100	3,890	5,200	10,900	4,500	4,800	30,400	174,493

[1] Preliminary.   [2] Estimate.   [3] Forecast.   132.276 Lbs. Per Bag   Source: Foreign Agricultural Service, U.S. Department of Agriculture (FAS-USDA)

World Exportable[4] Production of Green Coffee   In Thousands of 60 Kilogram Bags

Crop Year	Brazil	Colombia	Cote d'Ivoire	Ethiopia	Guatemala	Honduras	India	Indonesia	Mexico	Peru	Uganda	Vietnam	World Total
2009-10	29,780	7,435	2,045	3,250	3,890	3,200	4,265	8,750	2,480	3,150	2,670	18,670	106,334
2010-11	35,010	8,385	985	3,235	3,725	3,900	5,515	9,730	2,560	3,880	3,150	18,640	116,462
2011-12	29,843	7,360	1,620	3,140	3,840	5,290	5,223	7,145	3,365	5,140	3,000	24,495	117,661
2012-13	30,660	8,855	1,680	3,500	3,770	4,480	4,858	10,325	3,616	4,100	3,575	24,643	122,847
2013-14	34,146	11,040	1,570	3,285	3,175	3,940	5,013	10,380	2,725	4,100	3,600	28,289	128,877
2014-15	36,573	12,420	1,350	3,500	3,070	4,760	4,894	8,720	2,560	2,750	3,400	21,530	123,643
2015-16	35,543	12,390	1,540	3,405	3,044	5,000	5,693	9,896	2,340	3,300	3,500	29,500	133,389
2016-17[1]	33,081	13,755	990	3,853	3,330	7,290	6,158	8,174	2,865	4,025	4,600	27,550	133,662
2017-18[2]	30,450	12,715	1,300	3,950	3,555	7,200	6,224	8,010	3,160	4,185	4,500	27,900	131,190
2018-19[3]	35,330	13,300	1,300	3,980	3,605	7,300	5,425	8,140	3,220	4,200	4,600	28,200	136,737

[1] Preliminary.   [2] Estimate.   [3] Forecast.   [4] Marketing year begins in October in some countries and April or July in others. Exportable production represents total harvested production minus estimated domestic consumption.   132.276 Lbs. Per Bag
Source: Foreign Agricultural Service, U.S. Department of Agriculture (FAS-USDA)

Coffee Imports in the United States   In Thousands of 60 Kilogram Bags

Year	Brazil	Colombia	Costa Rica	Republic	Ecuador	El Salvador	Ethiopia	Guatemala	Indonesia	Mexico	Peru	Venezuela	World Total
2009	5,642	3,425	750	56	65	463	202	1,739	1,318	1,642	854	7	22,465
2010	6,302	3,017	715	6	56	366	306	1,311	1,352	1,371	882	7	23,165
2011	6,971	3,552	707	26	73	657	283	1,576	990	1,639	1,051	0	24,912
2012	5,582	3,009	749	77	45	397	207	1,787	1,328	1,989	863	0	24,841
2013	6,090	4,241	762	34	54	427	268	1,696	1,344	1,923	869	4	25,683
2014	7,326	4,611	671	23	71	205	293	1,390	1,117	1,393	873		26,221
2015	7,817	5,376	586	4	54	287	366	1,190	1,218	1,230	776		26,415
2016	6,704	5,253	648	4	52	217	292	1,011	1,212	1,030	1,112		27,500
2017	6,217	5,767	492	9	41	273	439	1,282	1,247	1,305	1,065		27,917
2018[1]	6,347	5,709	603	7	4	248	425	1,379	969	1,365	1,052	71	27,225

[1] Preliminary.   132.276 Lbs. Per Bag   Source: Bureau of Census, U.S. Department of Commerce

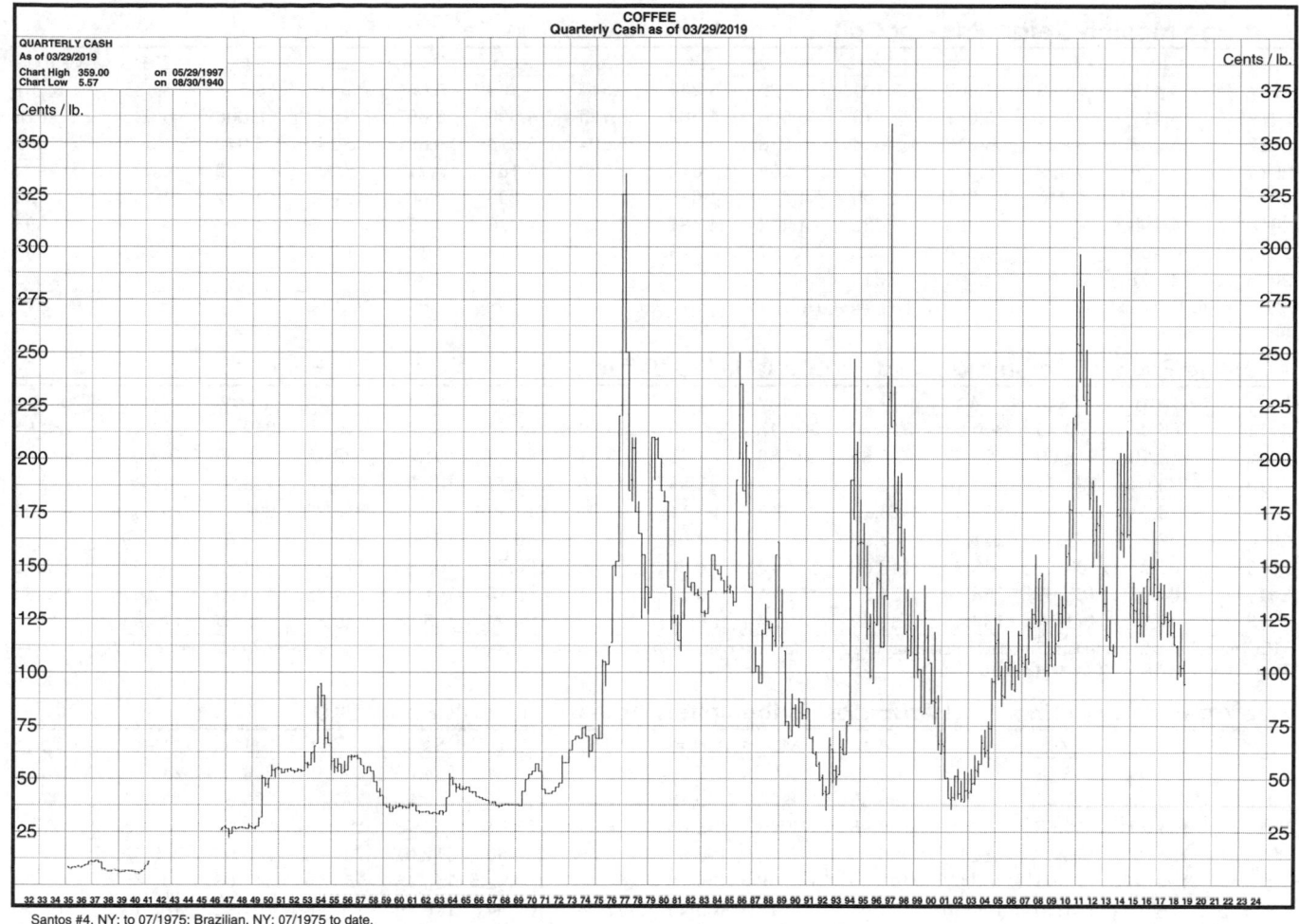

COFFEE
Quarterly Cash as of 03/29/2019

QUARTERLY CASH
As of 03/29/2019

Chart High   359.00   on 05/29/1997
Chart Low   5.57   on 08/30/1940

Cents / lb.

Cents / lb.

Santos #4, NY: to 07/1975; Brazilian, NY: 07/1975 to date.

Monthly Coffee Imports in the United States   In Thousands of 60 Kilogram Bags (132.276 Lbs. Per Bag)

Year	Jan.	Feb.	Mar.	Apr.	May	June	July	Aug.	Sept.	Oct.	Nov.	Dec.	Total
2009	1,872	1,680	1,998	1,978	2,042	2,197	2,357	1,895	1,661	1,605	1,389	1,793	22,465
2010	1,705	1,696	1,989	1,989	2,036	1,988	1,870	2,095	1,863	1,826	2,054	2,053	23,165
2011	2,058	1,913	2,389	2,187	2,105	2,092	2,050	1,830	1,871	2,013	2,138	2,267	24,912
2012	2,376	1,891	2,186	1,945	2,172	2,081	2,269	2,246	2,055	1,803	1,893	1,923	24,841
2013	2,200	1,933	2,090	2,154	2,629	2,283	2,459	2,184	1,875	1,933	1,828	2,115	25,683
2014	1,919	1,895	2,407	2,489	2,545	2,468	2,356	2,357	2,174	2,019	1,640	1,943	26,219
2015	1,780	1,708	2,430	2,255	2,489	2,407	2,338	2,265	2,269	2,120	2,154	2,194	26,410
2016	2,135	2,166	2,293	2,305	2,551	2,408	2,316	2,333	2,382	2,014	2,419	2,179	27,503
2017	2,349	2,362	2,681	2,280	2,476	2,532	2,350	2,437	2,109	2,119	1,992	2,235	27,921
2018[1]	2,090	2,220	2,420	2,382	2,542	2,225	2,274	2,186	2,013	2,260	2,266	2,349	27,225

[1] Preliminary.   Source: Bureau of the Census, U.S. Department of Commerce

Average Price of Brazilian[1] Coffee in New York   In Cents Per Pound

Year	Jan.	Feb.	Mar.	Apr.	May	June	July	Aug.	Sept.	Oct.	Nov.	Dec.	Average
2009	101.43	100.45	97.48	101.46	113.13	109.81	104.55	114.01	114.12	122.84	126.21	131.23	111.39
2010	128.11	121.61	125.28	124.94	121.66	136.18	146.74	152.91	162.02	163.86	179.16	186.05	145.71
2011	209.26	237.43	257.24	271.39	266.02	247.19	242.66	251.78	251.70	230.62	233.13	225.59	243.67
2012	222.41	211.95	188.15	177.20	170.39	151.55	171.69	158.75	162.59	155.77	146.35	138.80	171.30
2013	139.36	133.37	129.74	130.11	129.82	116.91	114.89	111.97	106.33	103.58	98.82	100.48	117.95
2014	107.49	142.75	174.89	182.89	170.89	154.02	154.00	171.99	168.11	181.58	169.10	157.87	161.30
2015	151.21	143.32	127.81	129.02	123.49	124.97	119.77	121.21	113.14	118.43	122.95	123.73	126.59
2016	121.21	122.24	130.38	128.10	129.05	138.38	144.76	141.41	149.80	153.15	157.72	137.14	137.78
2017	145.70	137.68	134.07	130.39	125.40	122.39	127.26	128.24	124.46	120.01	117.26	114.00	127.24
2018	115.60	114.19	112.99	112.56	113.34	110.44	107.20	102.41	98.17	111.21	109.59	100.61	109.03

[1] And other Arabicas.   Source: Foreign Agricultural Service, U.S. Department of Agriculture (FAS-USDA)

COFFEE

Average Monthly Retail[1] Price of Coffee in the United States   In Cents Per Pound

Year	Jan.	Feb.	Mar.	Apr.	May	June	July	Aug.	Sept.	Oct.	Nov.	Dec.	Average
2011	4.417	4.218	4.642	5.101	5.129	5.234	5.547	5.766	5.651	5.511	5.636	5.437	5.191
2012	5.497	5.382	5.558	5.513	5.596	5.582	5.723	5.693	5.693	5.888	6.066	5.921	5.676
2013	5.902	5.742	6.014	5.674	5.678	5.588	5.394	5.214	5.091	5.149	5.040	4.948	5.453
2014	5.025	5.002	5.005	5.204	5.153	4.670	5.099	5.167	5.215	5.032	4.713	4.590	4.990
2015	4.738	4.910	4.827	4.990	4.715	4.686	4.790	4.808	4.669	4.609	4.412	4.486	4.720
2016	4.498	4.447	4.405	4.428	4.443	4.481	4.428	4.316	4.372	4.309	4.306	4.281	4.393
2017	4.468	4.583	4.650	4.622	4.597	4.545	4.335	4.373	4.323	4.327	4.324	4.285	4.453
2018	4.291	4.267	4.343	4.313	4.294	----	----	----	4.306	----	----	----	4.302

[1] Roasted in 13.1 to 20 ounce cans.   *Source: Foreign Agricultural Service, U.S. Department of Agriculture (FAS-USDA)*

Average Price of Colombian Mild Arabicas[1] in the United States   In Cents Per Pound

Year	Jan.	Feb.	Mar.	Apr.	May	June	July	Aug.	Sept.	Oct.	Nov.	Dec.	Average
2011	280.05	289.49	300.93	314.26	301.48	290.19	286.46	288.43	283.51	256.86	259.74	254.41	283.82
2012	258.70	248.09	224.69	215.85	207.66	184.45	203.31	189.27	191.54	182.73	172.55	167.67	203.88
2013	170.64	164.74	163.46	164.52	161.14	148.56	147.70	142.47	135.93	130.14	123.92	125.82	148.25
2014	133.51	173.96	213.63	223.79	213.45	196.14	194.91	210.42	202.77	219.27	203.71	191.53	198.09
2015	182.32	171.68	151.94	157.06	150.19	152.02	144.52	146.96	135.55	143.10	138.63	139.89	151.16
2016	135.21	137.17	145.20	143.66	144.49	156.86	164.46	160.78	168.85	172.28	177.85	156.64	155.29
2017	164.96	163.67	158.40	154.97	151.41	146.12	152.51	155.15	151.47	144.26	144.09	141.62	152.39
2018	143.77	141.50	139.45	139.29	140.26	138.55	133.92	129.99	125.74	140.83	139.27	127.86	136.70

[1] ICO monthly and composite indicator prices on the New York Market, 1979 ICA Agreement basis.   *Source: Foreign Agricultural Service, U.S. Department of Agriculture (FAS-USDA)*

Average Price of Other Mild Arabicas[1] in the United States   In Cents Per Pound

Year	Jan.	Feb.	Mar.	Apr.	May	June	July	Aug.	Sept.	Oct.	Nov.	Dec.	Average
2011	262.94	288.08	294.48	303.59	293.06	277.78	269.18	273.54	274.38	248.49	249.50	243.40	273.20
2012	239.43	225.49	201.85	193.35	186.35	169.79	190.77	175.97	179.60	172.37	160.64	154.65	187.52
2013	158.27	153.00	152.96	152.96	151.43	138.86	138.44	135.63	132.78	128.83	122.75	127.05	141.08
2014	135.03	176.28	216.06	226.99	215.24	198.91	198.59	214.50	212.01	227.06	212.93	200.59	202.85
2015	190.90	179.94	160.02	164.00	158.48	159.76	154.45	156.92	146.15	153.25	147.98	148.66	160.04
2016	145.03	147.70	157.50	154.22	155.19	165.45	171.76	167.54	176.30	178.96	184.12	161.78	163.80
2017	168.61	166.35	160.15	155.40	150.00	143.22	149.66	149.88	146.56	140.71	140.90	137.42	150.74
2018	138.81	136.28	135.03	134.34	135.61	134.03	130.60	125.21	121.18	137.34	137.11	127.10	132.72

[1] ICO monthly and composite indicator prices on the New York Market, 1979 ICA Agreement basis.   *Source: Foreign Agricultural Service, U.S. Department of Agriculture (FAS-USDA)*

Average Price of Robustas 1976[1] in the United States   In Cents Per Pound

Year	Jan.	Feb.	Mar.	Apr.	May	June	July	Aug.	Sept.	Oct.	Nov.	Dec.	Average
2011	106.03	114.62	122.46	121.55	126.30	122.15	116.58	119.00	113.47	107.34	108.18	114.23	115.99
2012	109.40	111.25	113.60	111.71	116.01	113.34	113.37	113.01	110.87	109.89	102.94	102.26	110.64
2013	105.79	109.70	112.47	107.58	105.76	97.05	102.41	100.73	93.48	90.01	85.67	95.30	100.50
2014	92.93	101.14	111.90	110.68	108.35	104.63	107.23	105.07	105.57	109.39	106.81	103.51	105.60
2015	102.33	103.74	98.07	92.06	87.56	90.25	87.12	85.78	81.50	82.78	81.74	79.28	89.35
2016	74.71	74.04	75.60	80.18	83.93	85.94	90.82	91.79	96.88	103.65	103.72	101.85	88.59
2017	108.32	106.49	106.73	103.58	98.36	101.95	104.94	104.52	99.18	98.39	91.33	87.59	100.95
2018	88.65	89.24	88.18	88.31	88.74	86.07	84.42	80.74	76.70	85.32	83.52	77.57	84.79

[1] ICO monthly and composite indicator prices on the New York Market, 1979 ICA Agreement basis.   *Source: Foreign Agricultural Service, U.S. Department of Agriculture (FAS-USDA)*

Average Price of Composite 1979[1] in the United States   In Cents Per Pound

Year	Jan.	Feb.	Mar.	Apr.	May	June	July	Aug.	Sept.	Oct.	Nov.	Dec.	Average
2011	197.35	216.03	224.33	231.24	227.97	215.58	210.36	212.19	213.04	193.90	193.66	189.02	210.39
2012	188.90	182.29	167.77	160.46	157.68	145.31	159.07	148.50	151.28	147.12	136.35	131.31	156.34
2013	135.38	131.51	131.38	129.55	126.96	117.58	118.93	116.45	111.82	107.03	100.99	106.56	119.51
2014	110.75	137.81	165.03	170.58	163.94	151.92	152.50	163.08	161.79	172.88	162.17	150.66	155.26
2015	148.24	141.10	127.04	129.02	123.49	124.97	119.77	121.21	113.14	118.43	122.95	114.63	125.33
2016	110.89	111.75	117.83	117.93	119.91	127.05	132.98	131.00	138.22	142.68	145.82	131.70	127.31
2017	139.07	145.50	139.67	136.09	131.21	123.71	129.19	131.93	129.67	124.55	124.28	121.47	131.36
2018	123.67	120.83	119.80	118.76	119.57	115.10	110.54	104.46	99.87	115.59	113.27	102.10	113.63

[1] ICO monthly and composite indicator prices on the New York Market, 1979 ICA Agreement basis.   *Source: Foreign Agricultural Service, U.S. Department of Agriculture (FAS-USDA)*

COFFEE 'C' - ICE-US
Weekly Nearest Futures as of 03/29/2019

WEEKLY NEAREST FUTURES
As of 03/29/2019
Chart High 306.25 on 05/03/2011
Chart Low 92.00 on 09/18/2018

Nearby Futures through Last Trading Day.

Volume of Trading of Coffee "C" Futures in New York   In Contracts

Year	Jan.	Feb.	Mar.	Apr.	May	June	July	Aug.	Sept.	Oct.	Nov.	Dec.	Total
2009	309,386	406,786	328,940	404,635	305,326	435,239	244,504	388,567	244,371	332,043	535,063	300,489	4,235,349
2010	336,188	544,197	388,468	586,602	372,641	791,873	384,464	601,583	336,930	370,233	519,808	255,209	5,488,196
2011	390,345	471,890	408,416	516,121	388,052	555,238	332,701	577,095	391,134	420,084	483,740	239,722	5,174,538
2012	401,399	578,415	541,098	628,814	494,615	642,772	466,738	581,141	406,023	503,577	603,866	277,026	6,125,484
2013	555,032	758,665	468,082	904,549	609,068	742,238	590,940	703,755	347,915	423,480	700,471	319,834	7,124,029
2014	567,574	1,140,881	596,963	736,494	458,676	596,745	404,407	619,641	394,962	583,259	610,793	341,845	7,052,230
2015	586,593	795,022	615,139	786,626	596,214	847,139	540,970	964,634	490,262	633,066	864,055	388,415	8,108,135
2016	665,155	983,217	863,904	1,009,149	777,352	1,181,746	553,988	908,304	600,690	695,422	1,092,826	524,561	9,856,314
2017	621,047	824,746	618,426	1,018,525	642,116	1,079,212	637,351	983,180	599,210	701,745	1,135,521	573,043	9,434,122
2018	931,694	1,202,836	818,537	1,357,172	937,402	1,313,761	939,824	1,698,417	734,886	1,493,016	1,342,642	617,518	13,387,705

Contract size = 37,500 lbs   Source: ICE Futures U.S. (ICE)

Average Open Interest of Coffee "C" Futures in New York   In Contracts

Year	Jan.	Feb.	Mar.	Apr.	May	June	July	Aug.	Sept.	Oct.	Nov.	Dec.
2009	129,577	130,101	135,143	134,290	134,827	127,263	107,711	100,880	97,935	114,065	118,016	123,699
2010	129,749	126,850	124,238	133,961	136,711	151,959	169,669	156,086	143,454	139,801	138,738	134,477
2011	139,619	133,869	123,270	120,639	113,874	109,539	108,411	108,089	114,318	119,559	107,527	102,687
2012	113,404	131,880	149,533	151,527	148,352	147,775	137,737	137,322	141,421	147,434	141,940	141,395
2013	151,087	161,116	170,696	168,341	164,440	167,032	153,493	151,666	154,791	160,797	159,934	146,729
2014	146,800	162,005	169,201	160,266	162,103	163,163	161,218	156,931	154,752	168,847	156,410	155,382
2015	166,609	172,443	195,176	190,207	190,814	183,516	186,782	178,827	187,577	188,355	188,664	169,129
2016	193,283	190,752	194,420	190,067	190,161	182,825	182,322	175,300	180,542	194,806	205,128	187,602
2017	184,650	177,790	184,499	200,509	210,358	220,709	222,738	197,922	197,826	225,779	216,415	211,636
2018	232,027	234,405	257,968	267,133	256,291	272,561	306,898	319,784	326,360	303,193	252,010	262,406

Contract size = 37,500 lbs.   Source: ICE Futures U.S. (ICE)

Coke

Coke is the hard and porous residue left after certain types of bituminous coals are heated to high temperatures (up to 2,000 degrees Fahrenheit) for about 17 hours. It is blackish-gray and has a metallic luster. The residue is mostly carbon. Coke is used as a reducing agent in the smelting of pig iron and the production of steel. Petroleum coke is made from the heavy tar-like residue of the petroleum refining process. It is used primarily to generate electricity.

Supply – Production of petroleum coke in the U.S. in 2018 (annualized through November) fell -0.5% yr/yr to 327.460 million barrels and remains below the U.S. production record of 369.305 million barrels posted back in 1957. U.S. stocks of coke at coke plants (Dec 31) in 2017 fell -3.6% yr/yr to 558,000 tons.

Trade – U.S. coke exports in 2017 rose +20.9% yr/yr to 1.209 million tons, and 63.8% of that went to Canada. U.S. coke imports in 2017 rose +74.4% yr/yr to 58.480 thousand tons. About 38% of the imports were from Poland and 32% from Columbia.

Salient Statistics of Coke in the United States   In Thousands of Short Tons

Year	Total Production	Coke Total	Breeze Total	Consumption[2]	Producer and Distributor Stocks: Dec. 31	Exports	Imports
2011	16,531	15,420	1,110	15,825	745	970	1,418
2012	16,139	15,172	967	15,472	606	974	1,135
2013	16,226	15,320	906	14,351	872	840	138
2014	NA	15,154	NA	14,359	797	946	77
2015	14,470	13,755	715	13,128	707	857	140
2016	12,416	11,855	561	11,212	579	1,000	229
2017[1]	13,554	12,948	606	11,818	558	1,209	58

[1] Preliminary.   [2] Equal to production plus imports minus the change in producer and distributor stocks minus exports.
W = Withheld.   *Source: Energy Information Administration, U.S. Department of Energy (EIA-DOE)*

Production of Petroleum Coke in the United States   In Thousands of Barrels

Year	Jan.	Feb.	Mar.	Apr.	May	June	July	Aug.	Sept.	Oct.	Nov.	Dec.	Total
2012	25,427	23,451	24,656	24,774	26,408	25,602	26,785	26,670	25,385	26,477	26,303	28,543	310,481
2013	26,197	22,792	25,535	25,051	26,308	27,314	28,718	28,243	26,440	26,890	26,215	28,168	317,871
2014	26,979	23,225	26,073	26,851	26,716	26,020	29,087	28,017	26,498	26,383	26,383	28,485	320,717
2015	27,131	23,655	26,744	25,434	26,722	26,531	28,090	27,341	25,749	25,858	27,078	28,384	318,717
2016	27,669	25,498	27,657	26,846	27,638	27,488	29,710	29,120	27,782	26,504	27,713	29,251	332,876
2017	28,715	24,498	26,747	27,709	29,018	28,113	29,113	28,358	24,187	26,703	27,286	28,556	329,003
2018[1]	27,460	24,563	27,740	27,003	28,074	27,423	28,199	29,609	26,529	26,862	26,718		327,469

[1] Preliminary.   *Source: Energy Information Administration, U.S. Department of Energy (EIA-DOE)*

Coke and Breeze Production at Coke Plants in the United States   In Thousands of Short Tons

Year	Middle Atlantic	East North Central	East South Central	Other	U.S. Total	Coke Total	Breeze Total
2011	W	8,907	W	7,624	16,531	15,420	1,110
2012	W	9,355	W	6,784	16,139	15,172	967
2013	W	8,864	W	7,362	16,226	15,320	906
2014	NA	NA	NA	NA	NA	15,154	NA
2015	4,722	7,562	1,270	916	14,470	13,755	715
2016	3,560	6,645	1,231	980	12,416	11,855	561
2017[1]	4,066	7,181	1,238	1,069	13,554	12,948	606

[1] Preliminary.   W = Withheld.   *Source: Energy Information Administration, U.S. Department of Energy (EIA-DOE)*

Coal Carbonized and Coke and Breeze Stocks at Coke Plants in the United States   In Thousands of Short Tons

	Coal Carbonized at Coke Plants — By Census Division					Stocks at Coke Plants, Dec. 31 — By Census Division						
Year	Middle Atlantic	East North Central	East South Central	Other	Total	Middle Atlantic	East North Central	East South Central	Other	Total	Coke Total	Breeze Total
2011	W	11,673	W	9,761	21,434	W	571	W	236	807	745	62
2012	W	12,125	W	8,626	20,751	W	513	W	194	707	606	101
2013	W	11,948	W	9,526	21,474	W	739	W	344	1,083	872	211
2014	NA	NA	NA	NA	NA	NA	NA	NA	NA	NA	NA	NA
2015	6,219	10,584	1,204	1,701	19,708	797	1,172	197	70	2,236	----	----
2016	4,694	8,947	1,253	1,591	16,485	304	1,024	203	144	1,675	----	----
2017[1]	5,347	9,295	1,308	1,588	17,538	355	1,042	145	176	1,718	----	----

[1] Preliminary.   W = Withheld.   *Source: Energy Information Administration, U.S. Department of Energy (EIA-DOE)*

Copper

The word *copper* comes from name of the Mediterranean island Cyprus that was a primary source of the metal. Dating back more than 10,000 years, copper is the oldest metal used by humans. From the Pyramid of Cheops in Egypt, archeologists recovered a portion of a water plumbing system whose copper tubing was found in serviceable condition after more than 5,000 years.

Copper is one of the most widely used industrial metals because it is an excellent conductor of electricity, has strong corrosion-resistance properties, and is very ductile. It is also used to produce the alloys of brass (a copper-zinc alloy) and bronze (a copper-tin alloy), both of which are far harder and stronger than pure copper. Electrical uses of copper account for about 75% of total copper usage, and building construction is the single largest market (the average U.S. home contains 400 pounds of copper). Copper is biostatic, meaning that bacteria will not grow on its surface, and it is therefore used in air-conditioning systems, food processing surfaces, and doorknobs to prevent the spread of disease.

Copper futures and options are traded on the London Metal Exchange (LME) and the CME Group. Copper futures are traded on the Shanghai Futures Exchange. The CME copper futures contract calls for the delivery of 25,000 pounds of Grade 1 electrolyte copper and is priced in terms of cents per pound.

Prices – CME copper futures prices (Barchart.com symbol HG) moved sideways to higher the first half of 2018 and posted a 5-year high of $3.3155 per pound in June. Strength in the U.S. economy and record highs in the stock market bolstered the outlook for strong copper demand in 2018. Also, copper prices soared on concern that workers

at Chile's Escondida mine, the world's largest, would strike over wage demands. However, copper prices retreated into August to a 1-1/2 year low of $2.5520 per pound as concerns emerged that trade tensions between the U.S. and China would hurt Chinese copper demand. Copper prices then moved sideways in the bottom half of the year's range as a slump in global equity markets and a slowdown in China's economy limited the upside in copper. The S&P 500 fell to a 1-1/2 year low in December and China's Q4 GDP slid to 6.4% yr/yr, the weakest pace since 2009. Copper prices finished 2018 down -20% yr/yr at $2.6280 per pound.

Supply – World production of copper in 2018 rose +5.0% yr/yr to 21.000 million metric tons, a new record high. The largest producer of copper was Chile with 27.6% of the world's production, followed by Peru with 11.4%, China with 7.6%, the U.S. with 5.7%, and Australia with 4.5%. U.S. production of refined copper in 2018 rose +5.8% yr/yr to 1.100 million short tons, far below the record U.S. production level of 2.140 million short tons seen in 1998.

Demand – U.S. consumption of copper in 2015 rose +2.8% yr/yr to 1.810 million metric tons. The primary users of copper in the U.S. in 2015 by class of consumer are wire rod mills with 72.9% of usage, brass mills with 23.3% of usage, and nominal use of 2% or less by each of foundries, ingot makers, and chemical plants.

Trade – U.S. exports of refined copper in 2018 rose +80.0% yr/yr to 169,464 metric tons, a new record high. U.S. imports of copper in 2018 rose +0.7% yr/yr to 818,400 metric tons, below the record high of 1.070 million metric tons in 2006.

World Mine Production of Copper (Content of Ore)   In Thousands of Metric Tons

Year	Australia	Canada[3]	Chile	China	Indonesia	Mexico	Peru	Poland	Russia	South Africa	United States[3]	Zambia	World Total[2]
2009	854.0	485.6	5,394.4	1065	998.5	241.0	1,276.2	439.0	666	107.6	1,181	698.0	15,980
2010	870.4	523.0	5,418.9	1195	878.4	270.0	1,247.1	425.4	703	102.6	1,109	672.0	16,140
2011	957.9	569.8	5,262.8	1310	534.9	444.0	1,235.3	426.7	713	96.6	1,113	663.0	16,100
2012	914.0	579.5	5,433.9	1590	394.0	500.0	1,298.7	427.1	720	81.0	1,167	695.0	16,900
2013	1,001.0	631.9	5,776.0	1720	504.0	480.0	1,375.6	429.3	722	76.5	1,249	760.0	18,250
2014	970.0	673.0	5,749.6	1780	374.4	515.0	1,379.6	421.7	742	87.6	1,357	708.0	18,410
2015	971.0	697.0	5,764.0	1710	574.5	594.0	1,700.8	426.2	732	77.4	1,383	712.0	19,130
2016	948.0	708.0	5,500.0	1900	727.0	752.0	2,350.0		710		1,430	763.0	20,100
2017[1]	860.0	620.0	5,500.0	1710	622.0	742.0	2,450.0		705		1,260	740.0	20,000
2018[2]	950.0		5,800.0	1600	780.0	760.0	2,400.0		710		1,200	870.0	21,000

[1] Preliminary.   [2] Estimate.   [3] Recoverable.   *Source: U.S. Geological Survey (USGS)*

Commodity Exchange Warehouse Stocks of Copper, on First of Month   In Short Tons

Year	Jan. 1	Feb. 1	Mar. 1	Apr. 1	May 1	June 1	July 1	Aug. 1	Sept. 1	Oct. 1	Nov. 1	Dec. 1
2009	32,145	40,240	45,329	46,476	54,129	56,814	59,795	54,068	53,461	55,027	55,027	70,675
2010	94,489	94,489	94,489	102,012	101,151	101,928	101,925	100,438	95,346	84,883	74,285	70,831
2011	64,951	73,220	82,935	84,725	82,468	80,732	80,716	82,753	85,773	88,511	89,917	87,737
2012	90,055	89,703	91,159	86,523	75,051	59,070	53,335	48,129	49,757	50,336	56,551	63,632
2013	70,712	74,111	75,025	76,241	85,562	79,838	71,733	64,565	36,518	31,099	26,347	19,076
2014	13,033	19,224	13,589	19,967	18,292	16,378	19,653	23,912	27,984	34,162	29,759	28,137
2015	26,157	21,289	18,034	26,864	23,316	22,518	30,120	37,283	36,860	40,153	53,517	72,749
2016	69,753	65,615	67,502	71,991	65,495	61,044	62,445	65,416	67,282	70,575	71,961	78,310
2017	88,902	102,072	125,849	144,120	155,295	157,922	163,072	171,314	181,926	196,210	206,099	209,143
2018	210,972	221,036	230,376	233,927	248,744	231,364	223,981	200,039	189,050	172,440	157,434	135,536

Source: CME Group; Commodity Exchange (COMEX)

COPPER

Salient Statistics of Copper in the United States   In Thousands of Metric Tons

Year	New Copper Produced - From Domestic Ores - Mines	Smelters	Refineries	From Foreign Ores	Total New	Secondary Recovery	Imports[5] Unmanufactured	Refined	Exports Ore, Concentrate[6]	Refined[7]	COMEX	Primary Producers (Refined)	Blister & Material in Solution	Apparent Consumption Refined Copper (Reported)	Primary & Old Copper[8]
2009	1,180	597	588	48	1,110	138	788	664	151	81	90	434	16	1,650	1,580
2010	1,110	601	606	21	1,060	143	760	605	137	78	59	384	21	1,760	1,760
2011	1,110	538	545	----	992	153	----	670	252	40	80	409	13	1,760	1,730
2012	1,170	485	491	----	962	164	----	630	301	169	64	236	12	1,760	1,760
2013	1,250	516	518	----	993	166	----	734	348	111	15	259	13	1,830	1,760
2014	1,360	522	535	----	1,050	173	----	620	410	127	24	190	10	1,760	1,780
2015	1,380	527	503	----	1,090	166	----	687	392	86	63	209	14	1,810	1,820
2016	1,430			----	1,180	149	----	708	331	134		223		1,800	1,880
2017[1]	1,260			----	1,040	146	----	813	237	94		265		1,800	1,870
2018[2]	1,200			----	1,100	150	----	820	230	170		280		1,800	1,850

[1] Preliminary.   [2] Estimate.   [3] Also from matte, etc., refinery reports.   [4] From old scrap only.   [5] For consumption.   [6] Blister (copper content).   [7] Ingots, bars, etc.   [8] Old scrap only.   W = Withheld.   *Source: U.S. Geological Survey (USGS)*

Consumption of Refined Copper[3] in the United States   In Thousands of Metric Tons

Year	Cathodes	Wire Bars	By-Products Ingots and Ingot Bars	Cakes & Slabs	Billets	Other[4]	By Class of Consumer Wire Rod Mills	Brass Mills	Chemical Plants	Ingot Makers	Foundries	Miscellaneous[5]	Total Consumption
2006	1,910.0	W	30.8	37.1	W	135.0	1,570.0	490.0	1.0	4.5	21.4	24.1	2,110.0
2007	1,930.0	W	28.8	42.7	W	135.0	1,610.0	476.0	1.0	4.5	19.4	25.7	2,140.0
2008	1,820.0	W	28.6	45.0	W	130.0	1,490.0	479.0	0.3	4.5	20.4	24.7	2,020.0
2009	1,450.0	W	27.4	43.6	W	125.0	1,140.0	454.0	0.4	4.5	19.1	30.1	1,650.0
2010	1,570.0	W	22.5	44.1	W	127.0	1,250.0	459.0	0.4	4.5	18.2	34.6	1,760.0
2011	1,580.0	W	2.5	43.8	W	136.0	1,270.0	430.0	1.5	5.0	17.7	37.5	1,760.0
2012	1,610.0	W	2.3	42.8	W	102.0	1,280.0	424.0	0.3	4.5	19.9	34.3	1,760.0
2013	1,680.0	W	2.1	43.5	W	103.0	1,310.0	457.0	0.2	4.5	18.5	36.2	1,830.0
2014[1]	1,620.0	----	2.9	43.7	----	92.5	1,270.0	424.0	0.2	W	27.9	26.1	1,760.0
2015[2]	1,670.0	----	3.0	42.3	----	99.4	1,320.0	422.0	6.6	----	32.8	26.0	1,810.0

[1] Preliminary.   [2] Estimate.   [3] Primary & secondary.   [4] Includes Wirebars and Billets.   [5] Includes iron and steel plants, primary smelters producing alloys other than copper, consumers of copper powder and copper shot, and other manufacturers.   W = Withheld.
Source: U.S. Geological Survey (USGS)

Salient Statistics of Recycling Copper in the United States

Year	New Scrap[1] (Metric Tons)	Old Scrap[2]	Recycled Metal[3]	Apparent Supply	Percent Recycled	New Scrap[1] (Value in Thousands of Dollars)	Old Scrap[2]	Recycled Metal[3]	Apparent Supply
2007	772,000	162,000	933,000	3,050,000	30.6	5,580,000	1,170,000	6,750,000	22,000,000
2008	700,000	159,000	859,000	2,700,000	31.8	4,930,000	1,120,000	6,050,000	18,900,000
2009	639,000	138,000	777,000	2,220,000	35.0	3,400,000	734,000	4,130,000	11,800,000
2010	642,000	143,000	785,000	2,400,000	32.7	4,930,000	1,100,000	6,030,000	18,400,000
2011	649,000	153,000	802,000	2,380,000	33.7	5,810,000	1,370,000	7,180,000	21,300,000
2012	642,000	164,000	807,000	2,400,000	34.0	5,200,000	1,330,000	6,530,000	19,400,000
2013	630,000	166,000	797,000	2,390,000	33.0	4,720,000	1,250,000	5,970,000	17,900,000
2014	672,000	173,000	845,000	2,450,000	35.0	4,710,000	1,210,000	5,930,000	17,200,000
2015	640,000	166,000	806,000	2,460,000	33.0	3,610,000	940,000	4,550,000	13,900,000
2016	690,000	150,000	839,000	2,570,000	33.0	3,420,000	740,000	4,160,000	12,700,000

[1] Scrap that results from the manufacturing process.   [2] Scrap that results from consumer products.   [3] Metal recovered from new plus old scrap.
Source: U.S. Geological Survey (USGS)

Copper Refined from Scrap in the United States   In Metric Tons

Year	Jan.	Feb.	Mar.	Apr.	May	June	July	Aug.	Sept.	Oct.	Nov.	Dec.	Total
2009	5,390	4,810	4,390	4,420	4,030	4,200	4,090	2,900	2,980	2,960	3,040	3,210	46,400
2010	2,920	3,170	2,830	3,290	2,960	3,280	3,180	3,450	3,330	3,240	3,200	2,850	37,700
2011	3,830	2,970	3,240	2,970	3,240	3,060	3,030	3,200	3,010	3,110	3,010	2,630	37,300
2012	3,060	3,350	2,960	2,950	2,940	3,030	2,810	2,770	3,070	4,510	4,010	3,870	39,500
2013	3,870	3,660	4,550	4,770	4,910	4,910	4,680	3,800	3,780	3,990	3,970	4,450	46,900
2014	3,860	3,870	3,750	3,960	3,810	3,900	3,930	3,430	4,210	3,900	3,800	3,600	46,000
2015	4,030	3,810	4,150	4,180	4,360	3,310	3,570	3,890	4,200	5,010	4,250	4,050	48,800
2016	4,250	7,190	4,900	3,200	3,180	3,260	3,280	3,300	3,810	3,410	3,220	3,330	46,330
2017	3,240	4,090	3,240	3,230	3,380	3,280	3,220	3,340	3,310	3,280	3,240	3,250	40,100
2018[1]	3,220	3,260	3,220	3,260	3,330	3,400	3,390	3,220	3,810	4,180	3,370		41,084

[1] Preliminary.   *Source: U.S. Geological Survey (USGS)*

Imports of Refined Copper into the United States   In Metric Tons

Year	Jan.	Feb.	Mar.	Apr.	May	June	July	Aug.	Sept.	Oct.	Nov.	Dec.	Total
2009	76,400	67,700	80,000	53,900	52,600	35,700	54,200	36,400	56,000	39,900	55,200	55,500	664,000
2010	60,300	61,300	46,200	46,700	46,700	61,600	66,000	37,700	35,300	45,600	34,400	63,300	605,000
2011	57,400	50,500	66,200	73,100	65,500	45,500	69,500	32,300	64,300	46,700	50,300	48,900	670,000
2012	37,800	51,100	47,100	51,600	52,400	57,200	53,400	49,500	46,200	52,700	64,700	86,800	630,000
2013	86,800	64,600	88,200	55,600	83,600	69,200	70,000	50,200	42,800	40,300	33,900	48,500	734,000
2014	42,900	36,200	45,100	56,200	54,100	53,000	62,900	46,700	59,900	58,600	46,000	58,500	620,000
2015	70,900	50,300	68,700	60,500	56,100	64,500	78,500	47,400	47,800	51,700	44,200	45,400	686,000
2016	57,700	57,700	52,000	53,600	51,800	55,100	61,100	60,200	55,200	64,500	67,100	72,000	708,000
2017	72,600	59,600	84,800	51,900	63,500	66,100	72,500	55,200	86,800	76,500	65,200	58,400	813,100
2018[1]	88,300	77,000	72,900	61,800	64,600	66,200	59,500	59,700	67,300	64,700	51,000		799,636

[1] Preliminary.   Source: U.S. Geological Survey (USGS)

Exports of Refined Copper from the United States   In Metric Tons

Year	Jan.	Feb.	Mar.	Apr.	May	June	July	Aug.	Sept.	Oct.	Nov.	Dec.	Total
2009	893	1,650	3,770	6,510	21,400	19,200	8,870	6,280	3,980	2,110	3,030	3,160	80,800
2010	6,200	13,900	13,600	10,400	4,670	4,520	4,200	5,250	6,980	1,540	1,220	5,690	78,300
2011	1,640	5,010	3,130	2,120	3,500	1,930	1,850	5,140	2,140	2,350	6,870	4,690	40,400
2012	9,610	18,300	26,000	37,900	33,000	10,200	4,940	5,700	4,280	3,160	3,320	3,540	159,000
2013	3,540	5,300	5,110	5,380	5,740	4,890	8,270	17,100	14,900	10,300	15,200	17,700	113,000
2014	9,420	9,000	8,630	5,470	7,670	6,270	10,200	8,360	11,000	11,100	17,300	22,900	127,000
2015	5,860	8,490	10,100	6,620	7,190	9,400	5,870	6,430	4,490	6,110	8,690	7,270	86,500
2016	6,390	16,800	24,800	9,650	22,000	5,600	6,510	6,420	6,630	7,750	13,100	8,040	133,690
2017	12,300	9,100	9,760	12,200	9,230	6,140	7,140	6,680	7,190	5,210	4,400	4,810	94,160
2018[1]	9,550	7,270	12,100	13,700	13,800	11,200	11,300	15,700	15,600	31,000	36,200		193,549

[1] Preliminary.   Source: U.S. Geological Survey (USGS)

Production of Refined Copper in the United States   In Short Tons

Year	Jan.	Feb.	Mar.	Apr.	May	June	July	Aug.	Sept.	Oct.	Nov.	Dec.	Total
2009	105,000	96,700	95,900	93,700	91,800	90,300	94,400	97,600	94,300	101,000	98,000	101,000	1,160,000
2010	96,200	91,300	95,200	89,500	85,400	89,300	95,600	94,400	94,200	90,100	84,100	89,200	1,090,000
2011	86,800	76,300	84,900	79,700	82,900	86,400	79,200	79,700	93,600	89,600	95,100	96,500	1,030,000
2012	88,500	82,400	78,400	74,400	78,200	68,300	82,600	87,900	82,400	94,100	92,900	91,300	1,000,000
2013	89,300	76,200	85,700	88,500	83,000	80,300	83,800	85,300	81,100	94,800	92,800	99,200	1,040,000
2014	96,600	87,300	88,400	95,500	99,600	98,400	103,000	101,000	91,600	80,900	70,000	82,300	1,090,000
2015	83,700	85,500	93,900	90,700	86,700	91,000	94,400	93,000	97,600	104,000	107,000	113,000	1,140,000
2016	110,000	99,200	110,000	100,000	103,000	97,500	100,000	101,000	103,000	105,000	98,500	94,100	1,221,300
2017	101,000	93,900	105,000	91,000	84,800	83,000	90,600	99,400	95,700	82,400	70,900	81,200	1,078,900
2018[1]	92,800	92,300	98,000	85,200	90,900	88,000	95,300	97,100	87,000	93,400	96,400		1,108,800

Recoverable Copper Content.   [1] Preliminary.   Source: U.S. Geological Survey (USGS)

Mine Production of Recoverable Copper in the United States   In Thousands of Metric Tons

Year	Recoverable Copper			Contained Copper		
	Arizona	Others[2]	Total	Electrowon	Concentrates[3]	Total
2009	711.4	470.3	1,181.8	476.4	727.6	1,203.9
2010	703.2	406.0	1,109.2	428.3	700.9	1,128.9
2011	751.3	361.0	1,112.5	448.9	689.7	1,138.4
2012	763.3	404.1	1,167.9	471.0	724.0	1,196.4
2013	795.0	453.0	1,250.0	475.0	804.0	1,280.0
2014	893.0	464.0	1,360.0	514.0	871.0	1,380.0
2015	985.0	419.0	1,410.0	588.0	851.0	1,440.0
2016	968.5	461.2	1,431.0	614.5	848.9	1,464.0
2017	867.7	391.1	1,257.5	557.5	729.6	1,287.0
2018[1]	797.8	418.3	1,216.5	530.4	712.0	1,241.8

[1] Preliminary.   [2] Includes production from Alaska, Idaho, Missouri, Montana, Nevada, New Mexico, and Utah.   [3] Includes copper content of precipitates and other metal concentrates.   Source: U.S. Geological Survey (USGS)

COPPER

Production of Recoverable Copper in Arizona   In Thousands of Short Tons

Year	Jan.	Feb.	Mar.	Apr.	May	June	July	Aug.	Sept.	Oct.	Nov.	Dec.	Total
2009	65.8	57.3	57.8	53.7	58.7	59.0	62.7	58.2	56.5	60.7	59.0	62.0	711.4
2010	62.6	53.1	56.6	56.6	61.5	58.6	59.1	56.2	57.7	60.0	57.6	63.6	703.2
2011	57.3	53.0	60.8	59.3	66.5	63.9	61.9	65.0	64.4	66.5	67.1	65.6	751.3
2012	62.8	64.5	65.7	64.6	65.2	56.7	60.7	66.2	60.9	64.0	67.5	64.5	763.3
2013	65.7	57.7	66.5	64.1	70.7	64.6	68.2	65.1	66.6	68.5	65.9	71.3	795.0
2014	69.7	66.6	75.1	70.3	68.6	73.1	75.8	76.2	73.3	82.3	72.1	85.6	893.0
2015	78.4	70.5	80.5	75.9	76.5	77.2	81.3	84.1	83.9	89.3	85.7	90.3	985.0
2016	84.5	79.4	81.6	81.2	83.5	79.8	80.2	86.4	80.1	81.0	74.2	76.6	968.5
2017	71.0	64.2	77.5	72.5	75.1	71.9	73.5	71.2	75.0	66.9	72.8	76.1	867.7
2018[1]	68.8	61.5	68.2	65.4	69.3	70.6	66.8	69.1	63.0	64.3	64.3		797.8

[1] Preliminary.   *Source: U.S. Geological Survey (USGS)*

Copper Stocks in the United States at Yearend   In Metric Tons

	Crude	Refineries[3]	Wire-rod Mills[3]	Brass Mills[3]	Other[4]	Comex	LME[5]	Total
Year	Copper[2]							Refined
2008	19.8	15.7	22.6	8.3	5.8	31.3	106.0	190.0
2009	15.5	23.7	25.3	7.6	3.2	90.0	283.0	433.0
2010	21.1	10.3	19.7	6.4	4.3	58.6	284.0	384.0
2011	13.0	8.4	24.0	6.9	4.4	79.8	286.0	409.0
2012	12.3	12.9	28.1	6.5	4.3	64.1	120.0	236.0
2013	12.7	15.0	32.6	6.7	4.2	15.0	185.0	258.0
2014	9.9	9.5	42.0	6.4	4.4	24.2	102.0	189.0
2015	13.9	12.0	36.2	7.6	7.6	63.3	83.8	210.0
2016	14.4	4.2	26.7	7.4	5.7	80.1	98.9	223.0
2017[1]	12.6	5.8	27.8	7.9	5.5	192.0	27.1	265.0

[1] Preliminary.   [2] Copper content of blister and anode.   [3] Stocks of refined copper as reported; no estimates are made for nonrespondents.   [4] Monthly estimates based on reported and 2011 annual data, comprising stocks at ingot makers, chemical plants, foundries, and miscellaneous manufacturers.
[5] London Metal Exchange Ltd., U.S. warehouses.   *Source: U.S. Geological Survey (USGS)*

Stocks of Crude Copper[2] in the United States, at End of Month   In Thousands of Metric Tons

Year	Jan.	Feb.	Mar.	Apr.	May	June	July	Aug.	Sept.	Oct.	Nov.	Dec.
2009	24.7	16.0	21.3	25.2	22.5	23.8	26.1	32.5	27.1	28.9	28.2	15.5
2010	25.8	25.2	25.5	24.4	23.8	18.1	23.7	22.4	19.9	17.6	23.4	21.1
2011	25.2	24.8	24.7	24.9	27.2	20.1	20.1	13.0	14.3	18.5	14.5	13.0
2012	10.9	14.2	16.5	19.2	15.0	12.6	12.3	12.5	16.7	19.7	18.6	12.3
2013	8.6	20.1	17.9	21.8	28.7	11.5	12.8	10.7	11.2	14.2	15.3	12.7
2014	13.4	13.8	18.4	15.1	22.2	14.7	10.3	15.9	15.7	11.3	9.7	9.9
2015	14.2	11.3	11.3	11.3	16.6	15.4	13.2	14.3	21.2	17.9	13.5	13.9
2016	13.7	14.5	13.6	12.4	16.1	19.5	13.5	12.5	12.6	14.7	13.8	14.4
2017	11.7	13.2	13.5	26.1	11.0	11.0	11.0	7.4	12.1	13.6	16.7	12.6
2018[1]	15.0	14.6	9.0	9.9	8.1	14.3	9.7	9.0	9.1	8.9		

[1] Preliminary.   [2] Copper content of blister and anode.   *Source: U.S. Geological Survey (USGS)*

Total Stocks of Refined Copper in the United States, at End of Month   In Thousands of Metric Tons

Year	Jan.	Feb.	Mar.	Apr.	May	June	July	Aug.	Sept.	Oct.	Nov.	Dec.
2009	258.0	289.0	337.0	337.0	312.0	284.0	293.0	298.0	323.0	339.0	379.0	433.0
2010	467.0	487.0	467.0	455.0	434.0	431.0	422.0	407.0	381.0	364.0	356.0	384.0
2011	282.0	383.0	372.0	366.0	365.0	359.0	368.0	370.0	377.0	383.0	387.0	409.0
2012	393.0	358.0	309.0	268.0	235.0	210.0	199.0	192.0	187.0	194.0	203.0	236.0
2013	261.0	275.0	308.0	325.0	318.0	314.0	306.0	292.0	273.0	260.0	250.0	258.0
2014	246.0	239.0	258.0	246.0	222.0	201.0	198.0	202.0	215.0	210.0	193.0	189.0
2015	182.0	186.0	195.0	197.0	178.0	171.0	166.0	185.0	187.0	190.0	198.0	210.0
2016	220.0	215.0	187.0	172.0	163.0	134.0	149.0	152.0	177.0	192.0	210.0	223.0
2017	241.0	242.0	248.0	243.0	218.0	219.0	222.0	246.0	256.0	268.0	266.0	265.0
2018[1]	286.0	283.0	297.0	315.0	323.0	344.0	357.0	347.0	316.0	283.0		

[1] Preliminary.   *Source: U.S. Geological Survey (USGS)*

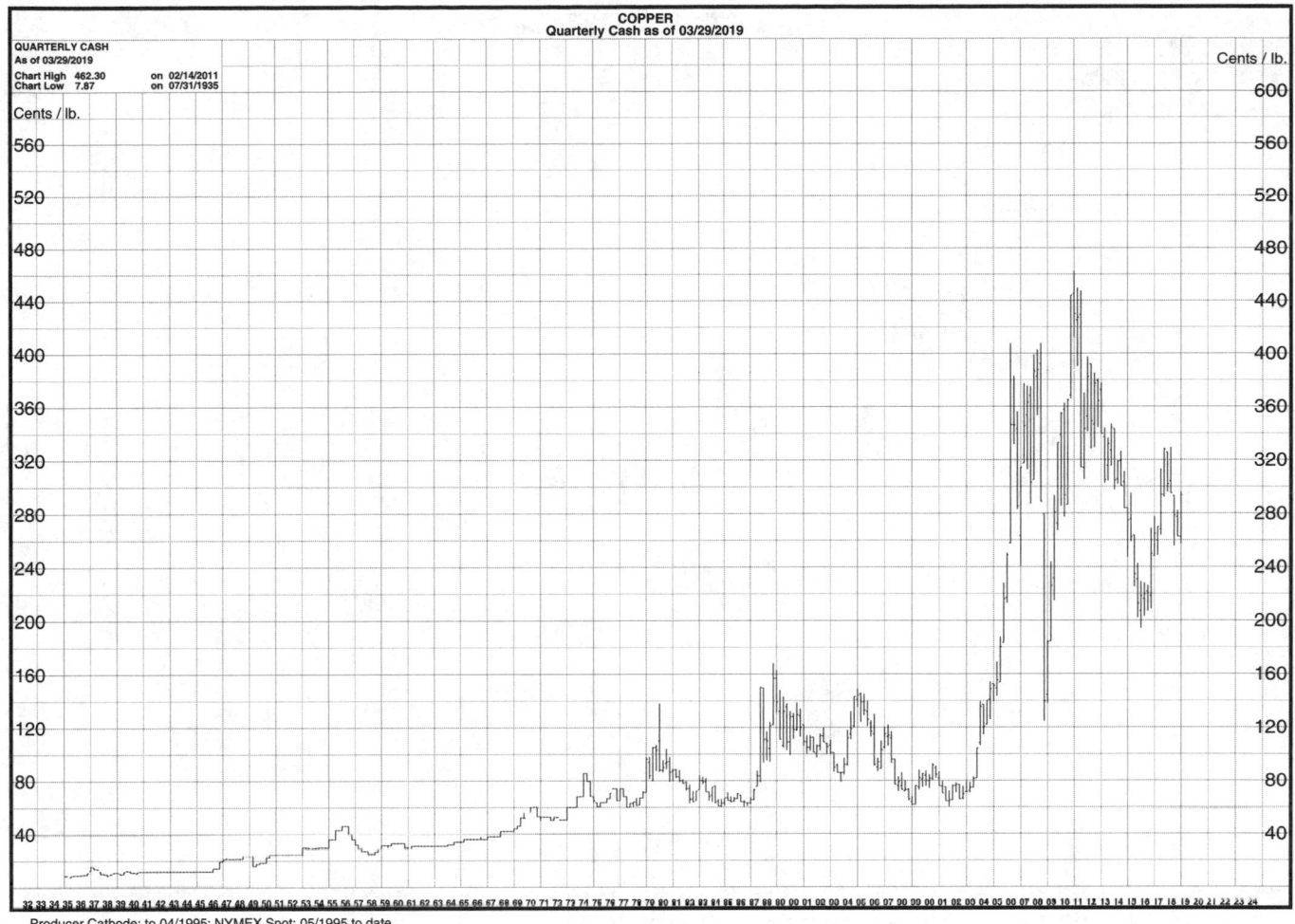

COPPER
Quarterly Cash as of 03/29/2019

QUARTERLY CASH
As of 03/29/2019

Chart High 462.30 on 02/14/2011
Chart Low 7.87 on 07/31/1935

Cents / lb.

Producer Cathode: to 04/1995; NYMEX Spot: 05/1995 to date.

Producers' Price of Electrolytic (Wirebar) Copper, Delivered to U.S. Destinations   In Cents Per Pound

Year	Jan.	Feb.	Mar.	Apr.	May	June	July	Aug.	Sept.	Oct.	Nov.	Dec.	Average
2009	153.55	155.38	176.45	209.36	215.36	233.23	243.36	285.81	285.91	292.24	307.45	320.57	239.89
2010	337.71	315.88	343.54	356.46	315.33	299.00	312.18	337.50	357.31	382.81	390.16	419.69	347.30
2011	439.85	454.13	436.70	435.63	410.49	415.91	445.11	412.86	378.78	339.15	349.89	348.73	405.60
2012	371.87	389.59	389.13	377.51	362.32	340.76	349.95	348.05	378.12	374.24	356.44	368.84	367.24
2013	372.47	371.83	351.31	332.72	337.45	325.95	321.50	335.18	334.13	334.93	328.07	339.43	340.41
2014	342.10	334.93	315.05	313.99	320.45	317.04	329.34	322.01	315.28	309.62	308.64	296.46	318.74
2015	271.73	268.95	277.04	281.50	295.59	273.57	254.27	239.79	243.31	243.04	222.34	214.01	257.10
2016	206.43	213.16	228.88	224.08	217.34	216.02	226.98	220.02	219.50	219.55	251.14	262.05	225.43
2017	267.08	274.55	269.56	264.04	260.33	265.44	278.13	301.13	303.66	314.81	314.38	315.32	285.70
2018	324.91	322.49	312.22	314.51	312.31	318.18	286.26	276.64	276.71	283.18	282.25	279.59	299.10

Source: American Metal Market (AMM)

Dealers' Buying Price of No. 2 Heavy Copper Scrap in Chicago   In Cents Per Pound

Year	Jan.	Feb.	Mar.	Apr.	May	June	July	Aug.	Sept.	Oct.	Nov.	Dec.	Average
2009	80.00	92.24	104.32	124.40	134.00	155.23	166.59	182.02	192.50	194.40	203.55	224.61	154.49
2010	245.13	220.92	258.37	275.68	244.50	214.32	214.64	255.68	260.36	273.93	277.50	268.29	250.78
2011	285.00	292.50	299.13	295.00	290.72	295.23	315.00	311.41	293.69	241.55	261.50	256.97	286.48
2012	262.50	287.75	292.50	283.93	280.00	259.64	262.50	262.50	275.39	282.50	270.25	281.39	275.07
2013	287.74	292.24	287.02	272.50	263.18	269.00	255.23	260.55	265.00	274.63	272.76	277.76	273.13
2014	287.02	277.50	266.55	262.73	270.36	269.07	270.64	268.26	262.64	257.24	255.50	240.31	265.65
2015	220.60	205.08	215.50	218.86	232.50	219.77	212.86	195.79	195.12	193.91	184.97	165.64	205.05
2016	160.61	158.50	168.02	169.50	170.26	166.27	173.15	172.20	169.21	170.40	182.00	198.45	171.55
2017	194.80	202.97	199.67	195.50	193.23	191.95	195.50	205.93	213.85	218.95	222.00	220.00	204.53
2018	229.79	231.50	227.50	223.02	222.59	228.17	212.93	201.80	192.45	201.50	199.00	201.50	214.31

Source: American Metal Market (AMM)

COPPER

COPPER, HIGH GRADE - COMEX
Weekly Selected Futures as of 03/29/2019

WEEKLY SELECTED FUTURES
As of 03/29/2019
Chart High 464.95 on 02/15/2011
Chart Low 137.30 on 01/23/2009

Nearby Futures through Last Trading Day using selected contract months: March, May, July, September and December.

Volume of Trading of Copper Futures in Chicago   In Thousands of Contracts

Year	Jan.	Feb.	Mar.	Apr.	May	June	July	Aug.	Sept.	Oct.	Nov.	Dec.	Total
2009	343.5	446.0	361.0	592.9	373.6	661.9	499.5	746.2	511.2	599.7	809.3	454.0	6,399.0
2010	645.5	996.3	772.6	1,049.0	894.7	1,051.1	724.9	980.5	604.4	822.3	1,132.3	631.8	10,305.7
2011	777.6	1,079.7	931.9	1,079.4	915.2	1,170.7	765.9	1,312.5	1,142.5	1,268.8	1,234.6	812.7	12,491.5
2012	1,131.5	1,572.7	1,222.8	1,768.1	1,491.4	1,790.3	1,163.1	1,478.0	1,084.8	1,137.7	1,469.8	848.6	16,158.8
2013	1,163.8	1,547.7	1,199.1	2,262.6	1,646.6	1,760.9	1,307.1	1,696.7	913.6	1,265.4	1,443.0	920.9	17,127.4
2014	1,049.9	1,236.2	1,401.8	1,422.9	933.0	1,434.3	1,081.3	1,276.8	1,089.7	1,269.0	1,459.4	927.7	14,582.2
2015	1,376.3	1,513.4	1,327.0	1,570.8	1,078.6	1,638.6	1,410.3	1,753.1	1,197.7	1,227.4	1,843.6	1,049.2	16,986.1
2016	1,324.0	1,754.8	1,611.4	2,018.8	1,522.9	2,148.7	1,510.2	1,876.0	1,294.0	1,498.6	3,531.3	1,433.8	21,524.5
2017	1,697.3	2,348.1	1,823.1	2,266.8	1,867.4	2,297.6	1,740.5	2,945.0	2,309.5	2,410.7	2,992.4	2,353.2	27,051.5
2018	2,761.2	3,000.6	2,510.6	3,091.0	2,562.9	3,619.8	2,833.2	3,402.4	2,349.7	2,625.9	2,546.7	1,406.1	32,710.1

Source: CME Group; Commodity Exchange (COMEX)

Average Open Interest of Copper Futures in Chicago   In Contracts

Year	Jan.	Feb.	Mar.	Apr.	May	June	July	Aug.	Sept.	Oct.	Nov.	Dec.
2009	82,402	85,831	90,636	103,517	106,511	111,555	111,849	118,935	117,782	127,204	146,612	149,621
2010	147,311	126,659	131,619	151,712	132,069	134,323	132,119	140,543	142,628	160,288	156,869	162,683
2011	162,325	157,918	138,261	134,959	122,036	128,861	148,876	130,312	120,015	126,973	124,770	115,634
2012	134,294	159,589	152,255	154,073	147,975	149,350	138,220	148,201	147,632	153,484	148,322	148,754
2013	160,188	174,428	166,007	179,530	162,279	180,744	165,350	160,513	149,129	150,400	162,528	160,424
2014	160,638	155,280	153,880	153,104	148,544	148,751	171,388	153,255	146,669	170,902	167,274	155,661
2015	175,389	178,359	165,403	163,159	173,340	174,453	165,716	180,019	153,941	160,277	181,603	175,301
2016	192,827	185,631	174,735	192,037	197,457	211,980	174,617	187,041	193,526	198,811	230,065	233,247
2017	253,784	288,886	266,753	273,442	249,694	258,588	280,781	328,948	300,294	297,370	283,754	254,501
2018	287,421	266,506	275,877	253,876	256,236	273,982	294,730	270,229	234,947	241,389	235,321	214,508

Source: CME Group; Commodity Exchange (COMEX)

Corn

Corn is a member of the grass family of plants and is a native grain of the American continents. Fossils of corn pollen that are over 80,000 years old have been found in lake sediment under Mexico City. Archaeological discoveries show that cultivated corn existed in the southwestern U.S. for at least 3,000 years, indicating that the indigenous people of the region cultivated corn as a food crop long before the Europeans reached the New World. Corn is a hardy plant that grows in many different areas of the world. It can grow at altitudes as low as sea level and as high as 12,000 feet in the South American Andes Mountains. Corn can also grow in tropical climates that receive up to 400 inches of rainfall per year, or in areas that receive only 12 inches of rainfall per year. Corn is used primarily as livestock feed in the United States and the rest of the world. Other uses for corn are alcohol additives for gasoline, adhesives, corn oil for cooking and margarine, sweeteners, and as food for humans. Corn is the largest crop in the U.S., both in terms of the value of the crop and of the acres planted.

The largest futures market for corn is at the CME Group. Corn futures also trade at the Bolsa de Mercadorias & Futuros (BM&F) in Brazil, the Budapest Commodity Exchange, the Marche a Terme International de France (MATIF), the Mercado a Termino de Buenos Aires in Argentina, the Kanmon Commodity Exchange (KCE) in Korea, and the Tokyo Grain Exchange (TGE). The CME futures contract calls for the delivery of 5000 bushels of No. 2 yellow corn at par contract price, No. 1 yellow at 1-1/2 cents per bushel over the contract price, or No. 3 yellow at 1-1/2 cents per bushel below the contract price.

Prices – CME corn futures prices (Barchart.com electronic symbol code ZC) trended higher the first half of 2018 and posted a 2-1/2 year high of $4.1225 a bushel in May. The plunge in the dollar index to a 4-year low in February 2018 bolstered U.S. corn export prospects and prompted the USDA to raise its U.S. corn export estimates and to cut its global corn ending stocks estimates. The USDA in May 2018 projected that U.S. 2018/19 corn exports would climb to a record 2.475 billion bushels and that global 2018/19 corn ending stocks would tumble -19.6% yr/yr to a 6-year low of 159.35 MMT. Also, near-record U.S. ethanol production cut into U.S. corn ending stocks as the USDA projected a 2018/19 U.S. stocks-to-use ratio at a 5-year low of 12.0% and a world stocks-to-use ratio at a 45-year low of 14.4%. In addition, the USDA projected that 2018/19 U.S. corn planted acreage would fall to a 3-year low of 89.1 million acres. In June, however, corn prices plunged and fell to a 1-1/2 year low in July of $3.2975 a bushel. An increase in trade tensions undercut corn prices after China added tariffs on U.S. agricultural products in retaliation for U.S. tariffs. Also, near-perfect weather in the Midwest benefitted yields that led to a bumper U.S. corn crop as the weekly USDA Crop Progress report showed that 75% of the U.S. corn crop on July 8 was in good-to-excellent condition, the best condition for that time of year since 2004. The USDA projected the U.S. 2018/19 corn crop at 14.778 billion bushels, the second biggest crop ever, and projected the global 2018/19 corn crop at 1068.31 MMT, also the second largest corn crop

ever. Corn prices then recovered from their worst levels and ratcheted higher into year-end on improved trade prospects after the announcement of the U.S.-Mexico-Canada trade deal. Also, in December, President Trump and Chinese President Xi Jinping announced a 90-day suspension of any new tariffs as they worked toward a trade deal. The USDA forecast that China would import 5 MMT of U.S. corn in the 2018/19 marketing year, the most in 4 years, after China's 2018 corn production fell to 257.3 MMT, the lowest since 2014. Corn prices finished 2018 up +6.9% yr/yr at $3.7500 a bushel.

Supply – World production of corn in the 2018/19 marketing year is forecasted to rise +2.2% yr/yr to 1.100 billion metric tons, but still below the 2016-17 record high of 1.122 billion. The world's largest corn producers are forecasted to be the U.S. with 33.8% of world production, China with 23.3%, and Brazil with 8.6%. Production in both China and Brazil has more than tripled since 1980. Production in the U.S. over that same time frame has about doubled. The world area harvested with corn in 2018/19 are forecasted to rise +1.1% yr/yr to 322.5 million hectares, down from the 2016/17 three-decade high of 329.7 million hectares. World ending stocks of corn and coarse grains in 2018/19 are forecasted to fall -17.9% yr/yr to 181.6 million metric tons.

U.S. corn production for the 2018/19 marketing year (Sep-Aug) is forecasted to rise rise +0.2% yr/yr to 14.626 billion bushels. U.S. farmers are forecasted to harvest 81.767 million acres of corn for grain usage in 2018/19, which is down -1.1% yr/y. The U.S. corn yield in 2018/19 is forecasted to rise +1.3% yr/yr to 178.9 bushels per acre, which is a new record high. U.S. 2018/19 ending stocks are forecasted to fall -16.8% yr/yr to 1.781 billion bushels. The largest corn producing states in the U.S. in 2018 were Iowa with 17.3% of U.S. production, Illinois with 15.6%, Nebraska with 12.3%, Minnesota with 9.4%, and Indiana with 6.9%. The value of the U.S. corn crop in 2017/18 was $48.485 billion.

Demand – World consumption of corn and rough grains in the 2018/19 crop year is expected to rise +1.5% yr/yr to 1.376 billion metric tons, down from the 2014/15 record high of 1.277. The U.S. forecasted distribution table for corn shows that in 2017/18 the largest category of usage, aside from animal feed, is for ethanol production (alcohol fuel) with 5.475 billion bushels, which is 79.1% of total non-feed usage. That was up +0.7% yr/yr. Corn usage for ethanol is more than nine times the usage in 2000. After ethanol, the largest non-feed usage categories are for high fructose corn syrup (HFCS) with 6.6% of U.S. usage, glucose and dextrose sugars with 5.3%, corn starch with 3.4%, cereal and other corn products with 3.0%, and alcoholic beverages with 2.2%.

Trade – U.S. exports of corn in 2017/18 rose +14.4% yr/yr to 63.505 million tons. The largest destination countries for U.S. corn exports are Mexico with 24.4% of total exports, Japan with 21.7, South Korea with 9.5%, and Taiwan with 4.3%.

CORN

World Production of Corn or Maize   In Thousands of Metric Tons

Crop Year Beginning Oct. 1	Argentina	Brazil	Canada	China	European Union	India	Indonesia	Mexico	Russia	South Africa	Ukraine	United States	World Total
2009-10	25,000	56,100	9,796	173,259	59,540	16,719	6,900	20,374	3,963	13,420	10,486	331,921	833,942
2010-11	25,200	57,400	12,043	190,752	58,618	21,726	6,800	21,058	3,075	10,924	11,919	315,618	849,420
2011-12	21,000	73,000	11,359	211,316	68,316	21,759	8,850	18,726	6,962	12,759	22,838	312,789	909,315
2012-13	27,000	81,500	13,060	229,559	59,142	22,258	8,500	21,591	8,213	12,365	20,922	273,192	898,047
2013-14	26,000	80,000	14,191	248,453	64,931	24,259	9,100	22,880	11,635	14,925	30,900	351,272	1,025,895
2014-15	29,750	85,000	11,606	249,764	75,734	24,170	9,000	25,480	11,325	10,629	28,450	361,091	1,056,779
2015-16	29,500	67,000	13,680	264,992	58,748	22,570	10,500	25,971	13,168	8,214	23,333	345,506	1,013,222
2016-17[1]	41,000	98,500	13,889	263,613	61,884	25,900	10,900	27,575	15,305	17,551	27,969	384,778	1,122,411
2017-18[2]	32,000	82,000	14,095	259,071	62,104	28,720	11,400	27,450	13,229	13,525	24,115	370,960	1,076,180
2018-19[3]	42,500	94,500	13,900	256,000	60,400	26,000	11,900	26,000	11,250	12,000	35,000	371,517	1,099,912

[1] Preliminary.   [2] Estimate.   [3] Forecast.   Source: Foreign Agricultural Service, U.S. Department of Agriculture (FAS-USDA)

World Supply and Demand of Coarse Grains   In Millions of Metric Tons/Hectares

Crop Year Beginning Oct. 1	Area Harvested	Yield	Production	World Trade	Total Consumption	Ending Stocks	Stocks as % of Consumption[3]
2009-10	306.0	3.60	1,114.9	118.8	1,113.6	191.9	17.2
2010-11	305.4	3.60	1,098.3	115.8	1,131.3	159.0	14.1
2011-12	315.0	3.70	1,155.8	133.3	1,154.6	160.1	13.9
2012-13	316.6	3.60	1,135.0	132.4	1,132.5	162.6	14.4
2013-14	325.9	3.90	1,283.2	165.3	1,236.7	209.1	16.9
2014-15	327.2	4.00	1,311.8	173.9	1,276.9	244.0	19.1
2015-16	318.8	4.00	1,262.6	184.9	1,258.5	248.1	19.7
2016-17	329.7	4.20	1,369.8	181.5	1,355.6	262.2	19.3
2017-18[1]	319.1	4.10	1,315.2	188.8	1,356.3	221.1	16.3
2018-19[2]	322.5	4.10	1,336.8	195.0	1,376.3	181.6	13.2

[1] Preliminary.   [2] Estimate.   [3] Represents the ratio of marketing year ending stocks to total consumption.   Source: Foreign Agricultural Service, U.S. Department of Agriculture (FAS-USDA)

Acreage and Supply of Corn in the United States   In Millions of Bushels

Crop Year Beginning Sept. 1	Planted	Harvested For Grain	Harvested For Silage	Yield Per Harvested Acre Bushels	Carry-over, Sept. 1 On Farms	Carry-over, Sept. 1 Off Farms	Supply Beginning Stocks	Supply Production	Supply Imports	Supply Total Supply
	------- In Thousands of Acres ----------									
2009-10	86,382	79,490	5,605	164.7	607,500	1,065,811	1,673	13,110	8	14,774
2010-11	88,192	81,446	5,567	152.8	485,100	1,222,687	1,708	12,447	28	14,161
2011-12	91,936	83,989	5,935	147.2	314,950	812,695	1,128	12,360	29	13,471
2012-13	97,291	87,365	7,419	123.1	313,700	675,327	989	10,755	160	11,904
2013-14	95,365	87,451	6,281	158.1	275,000	546,185	821	13,829	36	14,686
2014-15	90,597	83,136	6,371	171.0	462,000	769,904	1,232	14,216	32	15,479
2015-16	88,019	80,753	6,237	168.4	593,000	1,138,164	1,731	13,602	68	15,401
2016-17	94,004	86,748	6,186	174.6	627,400	1,109,658	1,737	15,148	57	16,942
2017-18[1]	90,167	82,703	6,434	176.6	787,000	1,506,303	2,293	14,604	36	16,939
2018-19[2]	89,129	81,740	6,113	176.4	620,000	1,520,335	2,140	14,420	40	16,600

[1] Preliminary.   [2] Estimate.   Source: Economic Research Service, U.S. Department of Agriculture (ERS-USDA)

Production of Corn (For Grain) in the United States, by State   In Millions of Bushels

Year	Illinois	Indiana	Iowa	Kansas	Michigan	Minnesota	Missouri	Nebraska	Ohio	South Dakota	Texas	Wisconsin	US Total
2009	2,053.2	933.7	2,420.6	598.3	309.3	1,244.1	446.8	1,575.3	546.4	706.7	254.8	448.3	13,110.1
2010	1,946.8	898.0	2,153.3	581.3	315.0	1,292.1	369.0	1,469.1	533.0	569.7	301.6	502.2	12,446.9
2011	1,946.8	839.5	2,356.4	449.4	335.1	1,201.2	350.0	1,536.0	508.8	653.4	136.7	517.9	12,359.6
2012	1,286.3	597.0	1,876.9	375.3	314.2	1,374.5	247.5	1,292.2	438.0	535.3	200.0	396.0	10,755.1
2013	2,100.4	1,031.9	2,140.2	504.0	345.7	1,294.3	435.2	1,614.0	649.0	802.8	265.2	439.4	13,829.0
2014	2,350.0	1,084.8	2,367.4	566.2	355.8	1,177.8	628.7	1,602.1	610.7	787.4	294.5	485.2	14,215.5
2015	2,012.5	822.0	2,505.6	580.2	335.3	1,428.8	437.4	1,692.8	498.8	799.8	266.0	492.0	13,602.0
2016	2,255.7	946.3	2,740.5	698.6	320.3	1,544.0	570.5	1,699.9	524.7	825.9	323.9	573.2	15,148.0
2017	2,201.0	936.0	2,605.8	686.4	300.5	1,480.2	552.5	1,683.3	557.6	736.6	313.6	509.8	14,604.1
2018[1]	2,278.5	982.8	2,508.8	645.0	296.8	1,363.2	466.2	1,787.5	617.1	777.6	189.0	545.2	14,420.1

[1] Preliminary.   Source: National Agricultural Statistics Service, U.S. Department of Agriculture (NASS-USDA)

Quarterly Supply and Disappearance of Corn in the United States   In Millions of Bushels

Crop Year Beginning Sept. 1	Beginning Stocks	Pro-duction	Imports	Total Supply	Food & Alcohol	Seed	Feed & Residual	Total	Exports	Total Disap-pearance	Total Ending Stocks
2014-15	1,232	14,216	31.6	15,479	6,568	29.3	5,284	11,881	1,867	13,748	1,731.2
Sept.-Nov.	1,232	14,216	5.0	15,452	1,615	----	2,225	3,840	401	4,241	11,211.4
Dec.-Feb.	11,211	----	5.9	11,217	1,622	----	1,445	3,067	400	3,468	7,749.8
Mar.-May	7,750	----	10.0	7,760	1,646	27.7	1,094	2,767	540	3,307	4,453.0
June-Aug.	4,453	----	10.8	4,464	1,685	1.5	520	2,207	526	2,733	1,731.2
2015-16	1,731	13,602	67.6	15,401	6,617	30.6	5,118	11,765	1,899	13,664	1,737.1
Sept.-Nov.	1,731	13,602	12.9	15,346	1,631	----	2,178	3,810	301	4,111	11,235.2
Dec.-Feb.	11,235	----	17.7	11,253	1,652	----	1,438	3,089	341	3,431	7,822.2
Mar.-May	7,822	----	20.6	7,843	1,627	27.9	914	2,569	563	3,132	4,711.1
June-Aug.	4,711	----	16.4	4,727	1,707	2.6	587	2,297	694	2,990	1,737.1
2016-17	1,737	15,148	57.1	16,942	6,856	29.3	5,470	12,355	2,294	14,649	2,293.3
Sept.-Nov.	1,737	15,148	14.3	16,899	1,689	----	2,279	3,968	548	4,516	12,383.5
Dec.-Feb.	12,383	----	11.8	12,395	1,711	----	1,523	3,235	539	3,773	8,622.0
Mar.-May	8,622	----	17.3	8,639	1,714	27.3	982	2,723	687	3,410	5,229.1
June-Aug.	5,229	----	13.7	5,243	1,741	2.1	686	2,430	520	2,949	2,293.3
2017-18[1]	2,293	14,609	36.3	16,939	7,027	29.6	5,304	12,360	2,438	14,799	2,140.3
Sept.-Nov.	2,293	14,609	10.8	16,914	1,743	----	2,255	3,998	349	4,347	12,566.5
Dec.-Feb.	12,567	----	8.7	12,575	1,738	----	1,503	3,242	441	3,683	8,892.1
Mar.-May	8,892	----	7.6	8,900	1,753	28.2	943	2,724	871	3,595	5,304.8
June-Aug.	5,305	----	9.3	5,314	1,792	1.5	603	2,396	777	3,174	2,140.3
2018-19[2]	2,140	14,420	40.0	16,600	7,009	30.9	5,375	12,415	2,450	14,865	1,735.4
Sept.-Nov.	2,140	14,420	6.2	16,567	1,706	----	2,275	3,981	633	4,614	11,952.4

[1] Preliminary.   [2] Estimate.   *Source: Economic Research Service, U.S. Department of Agriculture (ERS-USDA)*

Corn Production Estimates and Cash Price in the United States

	Corn for Grain Production Estimates					St. Louis No. 2 Yellow	Omaha No. 2 Yellow	Gulf Ports No. 2 Yellow	Kansas City No. 2 White	Chicago No. 2 Yellow	Average Farm Price[2]	Value of Pro-duction (Mil. $)
Year	Aug. 1	Sept. 1	Oct. 1	Nov. 1	Final			Dollars Per Bushel				
2009-10	12,760,986	12,954,500	13,018,058	12,920,928	13,110,062	3.69	3.49	4.14	3.71	3.64	3.53	46,734
2010-11	13,365,225	13,159,700	12,663,949	12,539,646	12,446,865	6.50	6.29	7.04	6.55	6.38	5.51	64,643
2011-12	12,914,085	12,497,070	12,432,910	12,309,936	12,359,612	6.95	6.65	7.22	7.37	6.73	6.36	76,940
2012-13	10,778,589	10,727,364	10,705,729	10,725,191	10,755,111	6.94	7.20	7.58	7.52	7.17	6.88	74,155
2013-14	13,763,025	13,843,320	NA	13,988,720	13,828,964	4.91	4.35	5.16	4.63	4.47	4.48	61,928
2014-15	14,031,915	14,395,350	14,474,920	14,407,420	14,215,532	3.82	3.60	4.35	3.75	3.76	3.69	52,952
2015-16	13,686,063	13,584,945	13,554,923	13,653,507	13,601,964	3.80	3.49	4.18	3.75	3.75	3.61	49,339
2016-17	15,153,472	15,092,908	15,057,404	15,225,586	15,148,038	3.64	3.28	3.95	3.62	3.55	3.37	51,304
2017-18	14,152,966	14,184,466	14,280,112	14,577,502	14,604,067	3.63	3.46	4.07	3.71	3.55	3.40	48,466
2018-19[1]	14,586,485	14,826,690	14,777,826	14,625,974	14,420,101	3.71	3.47	4.15	3.81	3.57	3.46	

[1] Preliminary.   [2] Season-average price based on monthly prices weigthed by monthly marketings.
Source: Economic Research Service, U.S. Department of Agriculture (ERS-USDA)

Distribution of Corn in the United States   In Millions of Bushels

Crop Year Beginning Sept. 1	HFCS	Glucose & Dextrose	Starch	Fuel	Bev-rage[3]	Seed	Cereal & Other Products	Total	Livestock Feed[4]	Exports (Including Grain Equiv. of Products)	Domestic Disap-pearance	Total Utilization
2008-09	489	245	234	3,709	134	21.9	192	5,025	5,133	1,848.9	10,159	12,008
2009-10	512	257	250	4,591	134	22.3	194	5,961	5,101	1,979.0	11,062	13,041
2010-11	521	272	258	5,019	135	23.0	197	6,426	4,770	1,830.9	11,202	13,033
2011-12	513	297	254	5,000	137	24.5	203	6,428	4,512	1,539.2	10,943	12,482
2012-13	491	292	249	4,641	140	31.0	199	6,044	4,309	730.1	10,353	11,083
2013-14	478	307	251	5,124	141	29.7	200	6,531	5,002	1,920.8	11,533	13,454
2014-15	479	299	246	5,200	142	29.3	201	6,597	5,284	1,866.9	11,881	13,748
2015-16	472	337	239	5,224	143	30.6	203	6,648	5,114	1,901.0	11,763	13,664
2016-17[1]	460	360	235	5,435	146	29.7	204	6,870	5,425	2,295.0	12,295	14,590
2017-18[2]	460	370	235	5,475	149	29.5	207	6,925	5,475	1,850.0	12,400	14,250

[1] Preliminary.   [2] Estimate.   [3] Also includes nonfuel industrial alcohol.   [4] Feed and waste (residual, mostly feed).
Source: Economic Research Service, U.S. Department of Agriculture (ERS-USDA)

CORN

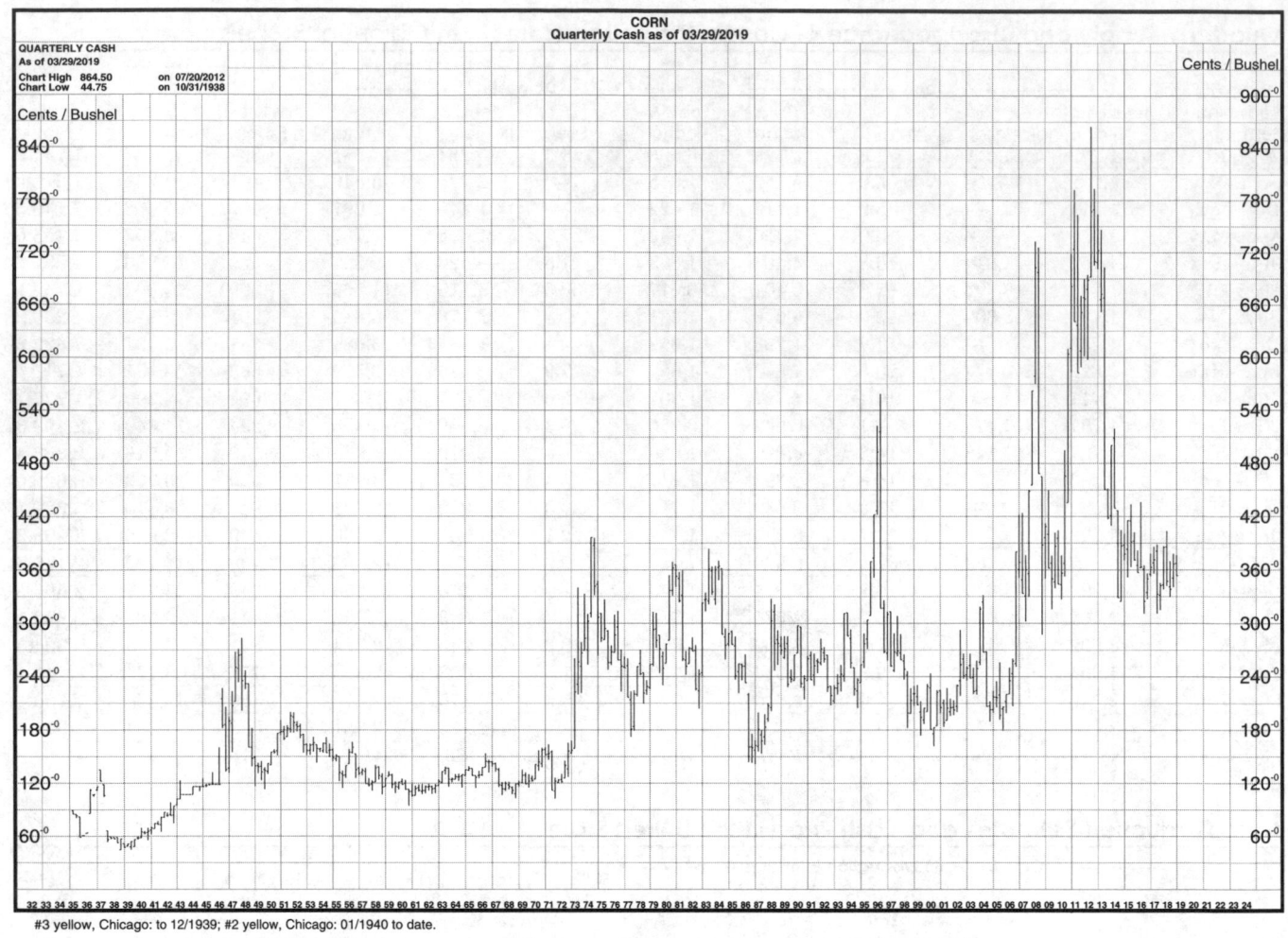

CORN
Quarterly Cash as of 03/29/2019

QUARTERLY CASH
As of 03/29/2019

Chart High 864.50 on 07/20/2012
Chart Low   44.75   on 10/31/1938

#3 yellow, Chicago: to 12/1939; #2 yellow, Chicago: 01/1940 to date.

Average Cash Price of Corn, No. 2 Yellow in Central Illinois   In Dollars Per Bushel

Year	Sept.	Oct.	Nov.	Dec.	Jan.	Feb.	Mar.	Apr.	May	June	July	Aug.	Average
2009-10	3.10	3.52	3.62	3.59	3.52	3.39	3.40	3.36	3.43	3.24	3.49	3.77	3.45
2010-11	4.51	5.19	5.33	5.65	6.10	6.69	6.59	7.33	7.08	7.17	6.96	7.30	6.33
2011-12	6.77	6.23	6.26	5.96	6.25	6.41	6.46	6.34	6.27	6.30	7.85	8.15	6.60
2012-13	7.70	7.48	7.39	7.23	7.17	7.15	7.33	6.57	6.83	6.94	6.61	5.98	7.03
2013-14	4.78	4.20	4.10	4.13	4.13	4.33	4.64	4.98	4.72	4.37	3.74	3.59	4.31
2014-15	3.16	3.09	3.45	3.75	3.67	3.65	3.66	3.59	3.49	3.52	3.85	3.51	3.53
2015-16	3.55	3.67	3.62	3.62	3.55	3.56	3.54	3.61	3.74	3.91	3.28	3.09	3.56
2016-17	3.09	3.27	3.28	3.34	3.45	3.51	3.40	3.41	3.47	3.49	3.51	3.27	3.37
2017-18	3.15	3.15	3.14	3.21	3.29	3.45	3.52	3.54	3.73	3.38	3.22	3.24	3.34
2018-19[1]	3.12	3.28	3.36	3.53	3.53	3.50							3.39

[1] Preliminary.   Source: Economic Research Service, U.S. Department of Agriculture (ERS-USDA)

Average Cash Price of Corn, No. 2 Yellow at Gulf Ports[2]   In Dollars Per Bushel

Year	Sept.	Oct.	Nov.	Dec.	Jan.	Feb.	Mar.	Apr.	May	June	July	Aug.	Average
2009-10	3.82	4.25	4.36	4.18	4.25	4.11	4.04	3.99	4.15	3.88	4.15	4.46	4.14
2010-11	5.23	5.99	6.05	6.36	6.73	7.44	7.38	8.11	7.82	7.89	7.64	7.88	7.04
2011-12	7.50	6.98	6.97	6.57	6.94	7.10	7.13	6.96	6.84	6.79	8.46	8.44	7.22
2012-13	8.15	8.16	8.18	7.85	7.70	7.70	7.85	7.11	7.50	7.58	7.10	6.07	7.58
2013-14	5.27	5.13	5.06	5.06	5.03	5.32	5.65	5.65	5.51	5.14	4.64	4.48	5.16
2014-15	4.14	4.15	4.54	4.55	4.44	4.41	4.43	4.38	4.23	4.24	4.56	4.14	4.35
2015-16	4.22	4.36	4.22	4.17	4.09	4.06	4.05	4.17	4.30	4.62	4.11	3.82	4.18
2016-17	3.78	3.88	3.83	3.88	4.07	4.14	4.04	3.98	4.03	4.01	4.00	3.77	3.95
2017-18	3.74	3.77	3.78	3.79	3.96	4.15	4.36	4.46	4.55	4.19	3.98	4.13	4.07
2018-19[1]	3.93	4.07	4.09	4.25	4.24	4.31							4.15

[1] Preliminary.   [2] Barge delivered to Louisiana Gulf.   Source: Economic Research Service, U.S. Department of Agriculture (ERS-USDA)

Weekly Outstanding Export Sales and Cumulative Exports of U.S. Corn   In Thousands of Metric Tons

Marketing Year 2017/2018 Week Ending	Weekly Exports	Accumu-lated Exports	Net Sales	Out-standing Sales	Marketing Year 2018/2019 Week Ending	Weekly Exports	Accumu-lated Exports	Net Sales	Out-standing Sales
Sep 07, 2017	714,557	714,557	1,046,709	9,788,435	Sep 06, 2018	727,204	727,204	3,700,402	14,444,245
Sep 14, 2017	703,696	1,418,253	526,867	9,611,606	Sep 13, 2018	1,077,716	1,804,920	1,383,724	14,750,253
Sep 21, 2017	727,477	2,145,730	320,242	9,204,371	Sep 20, 2018	1,358,773	3,163,693	1,712,785	15,104,265
Sep 28, 2017	896,945	3,042,675	744,994	9,052,420	Sep 27, 2018	1,408,067	4,571,760	1,430,999	15,127,197
Oct 05, 2017	655,443	3,698,118	1,579,002	9,975,979	Oct 04, 2018	1,605,212	6,176,972	1,006,676	14,528,661
Oct 12, 2017	339,252	4,037,370	1,254,868	10,891,595	Oct 11, 2018	1,100,435	7,277,407	382,534	13,810,760
Oct 19, 2017	604,356	4,641,726	1,288,332	11,575,571	Oct 18, 2018	1,213,221	8,490,628	349,531	12,947,070
Oct 26, 2017	598,247	5,239,973	811,417	11,788,741	Oct 25, 2018	755,036	9,245,664	394,441	12,586,475
Nov 02, 2017	489,835	5,729,808	2,364,487	13,663,393	Nov 01, 2018	1,355,355	10,601,019	701,477	11,932,597
Nov 09, 2017	417,468	6,147,276	949,521	14,195,446	Nov 08, 2018	1,112,973	11,713,992	892,529	11,712,153
Nov 16, 2017	695,754	6,843,030	1,080,865	14,580,557	Nov 15, 2018	834,853	12,548,845	877,424	11,754,724
Nov 23, 2017	651,220	7,494,250	599,157	14,528,494	Nov 22, 2018	1,053,231	13,602,076	1,266,460	11,967,953
Nov 30, 2017	592,319	8,086,569	876,394	14,812,569	Nov 29, 2018	1,166,285	14,768,361	1,177,470	11,979,138
Dec 07, 2017	690,824	8,777,393	866,918	14,988,663	Dec 06, 2018	952,132	15,720,493	903,164	11,930,170
Dec 14, 2017	701,915	9,479,308	1,558,325	15,845,073	Dec 13, 2018	975,577	16,696,070	1,974,392	12,928,985
Dec 21, 2017	521,046	10,000,354	1,245,458	16,569,485	Dec 20, 2018	899,618	17,595,688	1,699,449	13,728,816
Dec 28, 2017	657,645	10,657,999	101,198	16,013,038	Dec 27, 2018	1,005,951	18,601,639	503,117	13,225,982
Jan 04, 2018	889,270	11,547,269	437,200	15,560,968	Jan 03, 2019	664,975	19,266,614	459,822	13,020,829
Jan 11, 2018	618,590	12,165,859	1,847,220	16,789,598	Jan 10, 2019		19,266,614		13,020,829
Jan 18, 2018	598,965	12,764,824	1,445,876	17,636,509	Jan 17, 2019		19,266,614		13,020,829
Jan 25, 2018	1,046,104	13,810,928	1,850,584	18,440,989	Jan 24, 2019		19,266,614		13,020,829
Feb 01, 2018	961,200	14,772,128	1,769,595	19,249,384	Jan 31, 2019		19,266,614		13,020,829
Feb 08, 2018	864,485	15,636,613	1,974,467	20,359,366	Feb 07, 2019		19,266,614		13,020,829
Feb 15, 2018	852,058	16,488,671	1,555,410	21,062,718	Feb 14, 2019	5,489,592	24,756,206	6,028,535	13,559,772
Feb 22, 2018	1,240,289	17,728,960	1,717,544	21,539,973	Feb 21, 2019	769,089	25,525,295	1,239,914	14,030,597
Mar 01, 2018	1,076,777	18,805,737	1,857,557	22,320,753	Feb 28, 2019	744,006	26,269,301	969,742	14,256,333
Mar 08, 2018	1,406,330	20,212,067	2,505,077	23,419,500	Mar 07, 2019	785,767	27,055,068	371,981	13,842,547
Mar 15, 2018	1,375,343	21,587,410	1,470,242	23,514,399	Mar 14, 2019	764,246	27,819,314	855,944	13,934,245
Mar 22, 2018	1,376,064	22,963,474	1,353,108	23,491,443	Mar 21, 2019				
Mar 29, 2018	1,265,694	24,229,168	898,268	23,124,017	Mar 28, 2019				
Apr 05, 2018	1,912,070	26,141,043	839,914	22,051,861	Apr 04, 2019				
Apr 12, 2018	1,593,803	27,734,846	1,091,654	21,549,712	Apr 11, 2019				
Apr 19, 2018	1,635,379	29,370,225	631,441	20,545,774	Apr 18, 2019				
Apr 26, 2018	1,474,322	30,844,547	1,019,863	20,091,315	Apr 25, 2019				
May 03, 2018	1,784,742	32,629,289	695,568	19,002,141	May 02, 2019				
May 10, 2018	1,560,982	34,190,271	982,911	18,424,070	May 09, 2019				
May 17, 2018	1,469,334	35,659,605	854,304	17,809,040	May 16, 2019				
May 24, 2018	1,894,810	37,554,415	993,090	16,907,320	May 23, 2019				
May 31, 2018	1,448,476	39,002,891	838,616	16,297,460	May 30, 2019				
Jun 07, 2018	1,405,719	40,408,610	936,440	15,828,181	Jun 06, 2019				
Jun 14, 2018	1,762,860	42,171,470	165,917	14,231,238	Jun 13, 2019				
Jun 21, 2018	1,479,913	43,651,383	849,871	13,601,196	Jun 20, 2019				
Jun 28, 2018	1,514,791	45,166,174	440,696	12,527,101	Jun 27, 2019				
Jul 05, 2018	1,396,662	46,562,836	402,102	11,532,541	Jul 04, 2019				
Jul 12, 2018	1,293,041	47,855,877	640,997	10,880,497	Jul 11, 2019				
Jul 19, 2018	1,281,906	49,137,783	338,514	9,937,105	Jul 18, 2019				
Jul 26, 2018	1,624,574	50,762,357	292,022	8,604,553	Jul 25, 2019				
Aug 02, 2018	1,428,779	52,191,128	554,492	7,730,266	Aug 01, 2019				
Aug 09, 2018	1,152,128	53,343,256	271,115	6,849,253	Aug 08, 2019				
Aug 16, 2018	1,313,370	54,656,626	173,360	5,709,243	Aug 15, 2019				
Aug 23, 2018	1,344,383	56,001,009	175,448	4,540,308	Aug 22, 2019				
Aug 30, 2018	1,208,363	57,209,372	30,108	3,362,053	Aug 29, 2019				
Sep 06, 2018	264,317	57,473,689	-171,577	2,926,159					

Source: Foreign Agricultural Service, U.S. Department of Agriculture (FAS-USDA)

CORN

Average Price Received by Farmers for Corn in the United States   In Dollars Per Bushel

Year	Sept.	Oct.	Nov.	Dec.	Jan.	Feb.	Mar.	Apr.	May	June	July	Aug.	Average
2009-10	3.25	3.61	3.65	3.60	3.66	3.55	3.55	3.41	3.48	3.41	3.49	3.65	3.53
2010-11	4.08	4.32	4.55	4.82	4.94	5.65	5.53	6.36	6.32	6.38	6.33	6.88	5.51
2011-12	6.38	5.73	5.83	5.86	6.07	6.28	6.35	6.34	6.34	6.37	7.14	7.63	6.36
2012-13	6.89	6.78	7.01	6.87	6.96	7.04	7.13	6.97	6.97	6.97	6.79	6.21	6.88
2013-14	5.40	4.63	4.37	4.41	4.42	4.35	4.52	4.71	4.71	4.50	4.06	3.63	4.48
2014-15	3.49	3.57	3.60	3.79	3.82	3.79	3.81	3.75	3.64	3.59	3.80	3.68	3.69
2015-16	3.68	3.67	3.59	3.65	3.66	3.58	3.56	3.56	3.68	3.82	3.60	3.21	3.61
2016-17	3.22	3.29	3.24	3.32	3.40	3.44	3.49	3.43	3.45	3.43	3.49	3.27	3.37
2017-18	3.27	3.26	3.15	3.23	3.29	3.38	3.51	3.58	3.67	3.58	3.47	3.36	3.40
2018-19[1]	3.39	3.41	3.41	3.54	3.56								3.46

[1] Preliminary.   Source: Economic Research Service, U.S. Department of Agriculture (ERS-USDA)

Corn Price Support Data in the United States

Crop Year Beginning Sept. 1	National Average Loan Rate[3] --- Dollars Per Bushel -----	Target Price	Placed Under Loan	% of Production	Acquired by CCC	Owned by CCC Aug. 31	CCC Inventory ----- As of Dec. 31 ----- CCC Owned	Under CCC Loan	Quantity Pledged (Thousands of Bushels)	Face Amount (Thousands of Dollars)
					--------------------------- Millions of Bushels --------------------------					
2007-08	1.95	2.63	1,217	9.3	0	0	1	----	1,217,822	2,332,929
2008-09	1.95	2.63	1,074	8.9	0	0	0	----	1,078,175	2,025,300
2009-10	1.95	2.63	934	7.1	0	0	0	----	935,064	1,707,057
2010-11	1.95	2.63	801	6.4	0	0	0	----	801,131	1,455,091
2011-12	1.95	2.63	574	4.6	0	0	0	----	574,224	1,050,954
2012-13	1.95	2.63	368	3.4	0	0	0	----	367,998	675,046
2013-14	1.95	2.63	460	3.3	0	0	0	----	460,885	823,153
2014-15	1.95	3.70	574	4.0	0	0	0	----	7,822	16,432
2015-16[1]	1.95	3.70	746	5.5	0	0	0	----	44,185	110,902
2016-17[2]	1.95	3.70	880	5.8	0	0	0	----	59,619	116,982

[1] Preliminary.   [2] Estimate.   [3] Findley or announced loan rate.   NA = Not available.
Source: National Agricultural Statistics Service, U.S. Department of Agriculture (NASS-USDA)

U.S. Exports[1] of Corn (Including Seed), By Country of Destination   In Thousands of Metric Tons

Crop Year Beginning Oct. 1	Algeria	Canada	Egypt	Israel	Japan	Mexico	Korea, South	Russia	Saudi Arabia	Spain	Taiwan	Vene-zuela	Total
2008-09	95	1,810	2,445	138	15,491	5,735	7,710		440	3	3,713	1,145	47,658
2009-10	64	1,935	2,961	330	14,616	6,795	8,243		706	3	3,012	1,121	49,642
2010-11		962	2,939	679	13,762	6,059	7,476		574	330	2,731	852	45,109
2011-12		718	298	29	11,703	3,189	9,878		361	1	1,500	1,398	38,282
2012-13		451		0	6,511	296	4,861		345	9	514	1,079	18,176
2013-14	76	604	2,940	469	12,379	5,312	10,895		1,030	693	1,772	1,058	50,599
2014-15	239	1,444	1,127	26	11,832	3,645	11,220	1	1,184	66	1,830	806	46,758
2015-16	663	926	792	388	11,225	3,881	13,535		1,522	66	2,305	1,078	51,031
2016-17	91	650	258	107	12,539	4,762	14,312		2,029	205	2,663	384	55,492
2017-18[2]	48	1,724	1,587	757	13,784	6,051	15,506		1,577	1,167	2,738	440	63,505

[1] Excludes exports of corn by-products.   [2] Preliminary.   Source: Foreign Agricultural Service, U.S. Department of Agriculture (FAS-USDA)

Stocks of Corn (Shelled and Ear) in the United States   In Millions of Bushels

Year	On Farms Mar. 1	June 1	Sept. 1	Dec. 1	Off Farms Mar. 1	June 1	Sept. 1	Dec. 1	Total Stocks Mar. 1	June 1	Sept. 1	Dec. 1
2009	4,085,000	2,205,400	607,500	7,405,000	2,869,145	2,056,027	1,065,811	3,497,460	6,954,145	4,261,427	1,673,311	10,902,460
2010	4,548,000	2,131,400	485,100	6,302,000	3,145,787	2,178,671	1,222,687	3,754,769	7,693,787	4,310,071	1,707,787	10,056,769
2011	3,384,000	1,681,500	314,950	6,175,000	3,139,228	1,988,338	812,695	3,472,466	6,523,228	3,669,838	1,127,645	9,647,466
2012	3,192,000	1,482,000	313,700	4,586,000	2,831,356	1,666,204	675,327	3,446,732	6,023,356	3,148,204	989,027	8,032,732
2013	2,669,200	1,260,100	275,000	6,380,000	2,730,726	1,506,144	546,185	4,072,532	5,399,926	2,766,244	821,185	10,452,532
2014	3,860,500	1,863,200	462,000	7,087,000	3,147,623	1,988,516	769,904	4,124,380	7,008,123	3,851,716	1,231,904	11,211,380
2015	4,380,000	2,275,000	593,000	6,829,000	3,369,806	2,177,988	1,138,164	4,406,178	7,749,806	4,452,988	1,731,164	11,234,178
2016	4,335,000	2,471,400	627,400	7,611,000	3,487,233	2,239,679	1,109,658	4,774,776	7,822,233	4,711,079	1,737,058	12,385,776
2017	4,908,000	2,841,400	787,000	7,739,000	3,713,992	2,387,682	1,506,303	4,827,501	8,621,992	5,229,082	2,293,303	12,566,501
2018[1]	5,002,000	2,750,100	620,000	7,451,000	3,890,126	2,554,704	1,520,335	4,501,444	8,892,126	5,304,804	2,140,335	11,952,444

[1] Preliminary.   Source: National Agricultural Statistics Service, U.S. Department of Agriculture (NASS-USDA)

Nearby Futures through Last Trading Day using selected contract months: March, May, July, September and December.

Volume of Trading of Corn Futures in Chicago   In Thousands of Contracts

Year	Jan.	Feb.	Mar.	Apr.	May	June	July	Aug.	Sept.	Oct.	Nov.	Dec.	Total
2009	3,041.3	4,487.1	3,684.9	4,567.6	4,151.8	5,636.8	4,765.8	4,441.8	3,159.8	4,374.0	5,509.1	3,194.9	50,948.8
2010	4,025.9	5,217.5	3,935.4	6,466.0	4,240.6	6,207.8	4,863.8	6,899.6	7,033.7	7,501.1	9,169.7	4,280.4	69,841.4
2011	5,981.0	7,473.1	7,552.4	8,715.1	5,676.9	8,639.5	5,119.3	6,834.9	5,385.7	5,568.2	8,003.4	4,055.2	79,004.8
2012	6,194.8	7,388.6	6,538.5	7,418.0	6,162.5	8,027.0	6,825.3	6,003.0	4,164.7	4,701.6	6,406.8	3,353.5	73,184.3
2013	5,151.4	6,347.6	4,929.5	7,089.9	4,937.7	5,823.6	4,824.9	6,128.2	3,436.3	4,919.5	7,695.2	3,039.0	64,322.6
2014	5,790.8	7,614.4	5,772.2	6,996.2	4,613.5	6,677.8	4,938.4	5,781.3	3,784.4	5,875.4	7,439.7	4,153.1	69,437.3
2015	5,468.9	6,810.9	6,111.2	7,860.2	5,957.5	10,795.4	8,553.2	7,835.9	4,880.3	5,708.6	8,736.5	4,375.5	83,094.3
2016	5,878.1	7,858.5	6,061.1	11,510.4	6,909.2	11,322.0	6,258.8	7,704.5	4,498.0	5,321.4	8,319.7	3,983.4	85,625.2
2017	5,911.2	8,379.3	6,001.8	8,751.1	6,167.8	11,804.7	8,516.1	9,294.9	4,606.4	5,878.6	10,685.8	3,879.2	89,876.8
2018	6,474.5	10,818.8	8,754.6	10,249.8	8,164.3	11,485.8	6,613.3	8,637.0	5,584.7	6,586.2	9,690.5	4,327.7	97,387.2

Contract size = 5,000 bu.   *Source: CME Group; Chicago Board of Trade (CBT)*

Average Open Interest of Corn Futures in Chicago   In Thousands of Contracts

Year	Jan.	Feb.	Mar.	Apr.	May	June	July	Aug.	Sept.	Oct.	Nov.	Dec.
2009	806.7	801.1	767.8	823.3	860.6	971.7	894.1	862.6	850.1	923.9	1,002.9	969.2
2010	1,105.4	1,149.6	1,124.2	1,169.6	1,196.2	1,204.5	1,161.3	1,324.5	1,405.8	1,509.8	1,629.6	1,511.5
2011	1,595.6	1,697.7	1,598.8	1,617.6	1,439.8	1,406.3	1,196.7	1,244.3	1,214.8	1,220.0	1,268.5	1,156.4
2012	1,209.5	1,289.9	1,312.4	1,330.4	1,212.9	1,125.0	1,138.0	1,211.6	1,175.6	1,247.8	1,282.1	1,168.4
2013	1,187.9	1,275.3	1,264.8	1,270.8	1,160.8	1,196.6	1,135.7	1,166.2	1,114.6	1,252.2	1,335.0	1,193.8
2014	1,284.5	1,343.4	1,318.8	1,396.1	1,338.9	1,370.7	1,332.4	1,316.6	1,254.5	1,289.5	1,298.1	1,216.6
2015	1,291.3	1,332.4	1,296.8	1,360.9	1,370.6	1,428.7	1,350.7	1,346.0	1,253.1	1,309.6	1,365.9	1,291.4
2016	1,374.6	1,372.9	1,349.8	1,432.1	1,364.2	1,438.5	1,297.8	1,353.5	1,303.9	1,322.3	1,345.3	1,227.3
2017	1,306.7	1,431.1	1,403.8	1,443.3	1,364.3	1,406.1	1,377.3	1,412.7	1,378.6	1,496.8	1,641.6	1,522.8
2018	1,623.6	1,670.6	1,821.7	1,837.2	1,852.3	1,950.0	1,850.8	1,729.7	1,693.3	1,659.4	1,702.9	1,574.6

Contract size = 5,000 bu.   *Source: CME Group; Chicago Board of Trade (CBT)*

Corn Oil

Corn oil is a bland, odorless oil produced by refining the crude corn oil that is mechanically extracted from the germ of the plant seed. High-oil corn, the most common type of corn used to make corn oil, typically has an oil content of 7% or higher compared to about 4% for normal corn. Corn oil is widely used as cooking oil, for making margarine and mayonnaise, and for making inedible products such as soap, paints, inks, varnishes, and cosmetics. For humans, studies have shown that no vegetable oil is more effective than corn oil in lowering blood cholesterol levels.

Prices – The average monthly price of corn oil (wet mill price in Chicago) in the latest data available for the 2017-18 marketing year (Oct-Sep) fell into the range of 32.0-35.0 cents per pound, still well below the 2007-08 record high of 69.40 cents per pound. Seasonally, prices tend to be highest around March/April and lowest late in the calendar year.

Supply – U.S. corn oil production in the 2017/18 marketing year rose +3.47% yr/yr to 6.050 billion pounds, a new record high. Seasonally, production tends to peak around December and March and reaches a low in July. U.S. stocks in the 2017/18 marketing year (beginning Oct 1) fell -23.0% to 127 million pounds.

Demand – U.S. usage (domestic disappearance) in 2017/18 rose +10.7% to 5.342 billion pounds.

Exports – U.S. corn oil exports in 2017/18 fell -33.9% to 750 million pounds. U.S. corn oil imports in 2017/18 fell by -11.0% to 65.000 million pounds.

Supply and Disappearance of Corn Oil in the United States — In Millions of Pounds

| | Supply | | | | Disappearance | | | | | | |
Year	Stocks Oct. 1	Pro-duction	Imports	Total Supply	Baking and Frying Fats	Salad and Cooking Oil	Marg-arine	Total Edible Products	Domestic Disap-pearance	Exports	Total Disap-pearance
2008-09	205	2,418	43.5	2,667	W	1,722	W	1,591	1,568	814	2,382
2009-10	286	2,485	37.0	2,808	W	1,930	W	1,589	1,895	774	2,669
2010-11	139	3,650	47.6	3,836	W	2,375	W	1,691	2,805	792	3,596
2011-12	240	3,625	45.8	3,911	NA	NA	NA	NA	2,742	1,003	3,746
2012-13	165	3,685	60.0	3,910	----	----	----	----	2,726	1,019	3,745
2013-14	165	3,890	42.1	4,097	----	----	----	----	2,928	1,004	3,932
2014-15	165	4,740	38.8	4,944	----	----	----	----	3,870	909	4,779
2015-16[1]	165	5,300	82.8	5,548	----	----	----	----	4,289	1,094	5,383
2016-17[2]	165	5,850	73.0	6,088	----	----	----	----	4,826	1,135	5,961
2017-18[2]	127	6,050	65.0	6,242	----	----	----	----	5,342	750	6,092

[1] Preliminary. [2] Estimate. W = Withheld. Source: Economic Research Service, U.S. Department of Agriculture (ERS-USDA)

Production[2] of Crude Corn Oil in the United States — In Millions of Pounds

Year	Oct.	Nov.	Dec.	Jan.	Feb.	Mar.	Apr.	May	June	July	Aug.	Sept.	Total
2004-05	208.8	187.1	191.0	205.2	182.5	206.6	217.2	188.2	211.5	206.7	198.5	189.0	2,392
2005-06	207.5	199.9	200.3	209.2	184.8	217.6	191.7	218.7	206.7	215.3	222.0	209.0	2,483
2006-07	228.7	216.0	226.1	224.7	187.9	216.4	194.1	214.4	212.7	219.8	209.5	209.4	2,560
2007-08	213.5	213.0	214.0	205.4	193.7	222.5	190.7	220.9	193.7	214.9	217.3	207.3	2,507
2008-09	206.3	210.6	198.7	200.3	199.8	218.8	189.4	202.5	189.0	186.0	201.4	215.8	2,419
2009-10	212.9	205.2	203.2	197.9	188.1	212.4	214.7	205.4	214.7	216.8	213.6	200.1	2,485
2010-11[1]	205.1	211.2	198.9	220.9	199.4	218.1	203.1	215.0	216.3	205.7			2,512

[1] Preliminary. [2] Not seasonally adjusted. Source: Bureau of the Census, U.S. Department of Commerce

Average Corn Oil Price, Wet Mill in Chicago — In Cents Per Pound

Year	Oct.	Nov.	Dec.	Jan.	Feb.	Mar.	Apr.	May	June	July	Aug.	Sept.	Average
2009-10	37.59	38.12	40.02	40.34	37.54	38.37	38.50	38.50	38.93	39.29	41.48	42.85	39.29
2010-11	47.50	51.96	54.71	57.91	63.39	67.72	68.89	68.33	66.70	62.00	62.00	57.95	60.76
2011-12	54.24	53.98	53.36	54.00	56.30	59.31	60.75	58.05	52.90	54.76	57.26	58.21	56.09
2012-13	54.75	51.93	50.63	52.06	51.71	47.76	47.06	45.23	42.50	38.91	38.93	38.46	46.66
2013-14	37.85	38.79	38.31	38.79	41.07	43.19	41.94	41.02	40.01	39.02	38.00	35.17	39.43
2014-15	34.50	33.96	33.68	34.86	36.13	37.73	39.27	39.50	40.34	41.49	40.75	37.55	37.48
2015-16	36.60	36.43	38.25	39.93	40.29	41.05	42.12	40.33	39.94	38.86	39.06	38.11	39.25
2016-17	36.22	36.83	38.12	37.89	38.11	37.90	37.63	37.71	38.00	37.53	36.75	36.48	37.43
2017-18	34.96	34.46	33.96	30.68	29.72	29.66	29.50	29.65	29.54	28.76	26.80	26.46	30.35
2018-19[1]	27.18	26.37	26.46	26.21	25.65								26.37

[1] Preliminary. Source: Economic Research Service, U.S. Department of Agriculture (ERS-USDA)

Cotton

Cotton is a natural vegetable fiber that comes from small trees and shrubs of a genus belonging to the mallow family, one of which is the common American Upland cotton plant. Cotton has been used in India for at least the last 5,000 years and probably much longer, and was also used by the ancient Chinese, Egyptians, and North and South Americans. Cotton was one of the earliest crops grown by European settlers in the U.S.

Cotton requires a long growing season, plenty of sunshine and water during the growing season, and then dry weather for harvesting. In the United States, the Cotton Belt stretches from northern Florida to North Carolina and westward to California. In the U.S., planting time varies from the beginning of February in Southern Texas to the beginning of June in the northern sections of the Cotton Belt. The flower bud of the plant blossoms and develops into an oval boll that splits open at maturity. At maturity, cotton is most vulnerable to damage from wind and rain. Approximately 95% of the cotton in the U.S. is now harvested mechanically with spindle-type pickers or strippers and then sent off to cotton gins for processing. There it is dried, cleaned, separated, and packed into bales.

Cotton is used in a wide range of products from clothing to home furnishings to medical products. The value of cotton is determined according to the staple, grade, and character of each bale. Staple refers to short, medium, long, or extra-long fiber length, with medium staple accounting for about 70% of all U.S. cotton. Grade refers to the color, brightness, and amount of foreign matter and is established by the U.S. Department of Agriculture. Character refers to the fiber's diameter, strength, body, maturity (ratio of mature to immature fibers), uniformity, and smoothness. Cotton is the fifth leading cash crop in the U.S. and is one of the nation's principal agricultural exports. The weight of cotton is typically measured in terms of a "bale," which is deemed to equal 480 pounds.

Cotton futures and options are traded at the Intercontinental Exchange (ICE). Cotton futures are also traded on the Bolsa de Mercadorias & Futuros (BM&F). Cotton yarn futures are traded on the Central Japan Commodity Exchange (CCOM) and the Osaka Mercantile Exchange (OME). The New York Cotton Exchange's futures contract calls for the delivery of 50,000 pounds net weight (approximately 100 bales) of No. 2 cotton with a quality rating of Strict Low Middling and a staple length of 1-and-2/32 inch. Delivery points include Texas (Galveston and Houston), New Orleans, Memphis, and Greenville/Spartanburg in South Carolina.

Prices – ICE cotton futures prices (Barchart.com symbol CT) zigzagged higher in the first half of 2018 and posted a 5-year high of 96.50 cents per pound in June. Adverse weather around the globe in 2018 reduced forecasts for global cotton production. Cotton production in China, the world's second-largest producer, was negatively impacted by lower-than-normal temperatures and excessive rains, while cotton production in the U.S., the world's third biggest producer, took a hit from several hurricanes that made landfall in the southeastern U.S. In addition, cotton production in India, the world's biggest cotton producer, fell as the USDA's FAS forecasted India's 2018/19 cotton production at -1.7% yr/yr to 28.5 mln bales after India's monsoon rains were 9% below normal. The USDA projected that global 2018/19 cotton ending stocks would drop to a 7-year low of 74.45 million bales on increased usage as the USDA projected global 2018/19 cotton use would climb to a record high 127.76 mln bales. Cotton prices tumbled into year-end and posted a 1-year low of 71.87 cents per pound in December on increased U.S. cotton acreage and the U.S.-China trade war. The USDA estimated that U.S. 2018/19 cotton acreage would rise +11.3% yr/yr to a 7-year high of 14.04 million acres. The USDA also projected that U.S. 2018/19 cotton exports would fall -2.2% yr/yr to 15.5 mln bales and that U.S. cotton ending stocks would climb +16.3% yr/yr to an 11-year high of 5.0 million bales. Trade tensions prompted China to boost subsidies to its cotton farmers to boost domestic output and China 2018 cotton production rose +7.8% yr/yr to a 4-year high of 6.1 MMT. Cotton prices finished 2018 down -8.2% yr/yr at 72.20 cents a pound.

Supply – World cotton production in 2018/19 is forecasted to fall -4.0% yr/yr to 118.742 million bales (480 pounds per bale) remaining below the 2011/12 record high of 127.243 million bales The world's largest cotton producers were forecasted to be India with 23.2% of world production in 2018/19, China with 22.7%, the U.S. with 15.7%, Brazil with 9,3%, and Pakistan with 6.2%. World ending stocks in 2018/19 are forecasted to all -9.0% yr/yr to 73.190 million bales, farther down from the 2014/15 record high of 106.857.

The U.S. cotton crop in 2018/19 is forecasted to fall -11.2% yr/yr to 18.588 million bales, farther below the 2005-06 record high of 23.890 million bales. U.S. farmers are forecasted to harvest 10.374 million acres of cotton in 2018/19, down -6.5% yr/yr. The U.S. cotton yield in 2018/19 is forecasted to fall -5.0% yr/yr to 860 pound per acre, down from last year's record high of 905 pounds per acre. The leading U.S. producing states of cotton in 2018 were Texas with 37.8% of U.S. production, Georgia with 10.2%, Mississippi with 8.0%, Arkansas with 6.2%, California with 4.8%, Alabama with 4.7%, and Missouri with 4.6%.

Demand – World consumption of cotton in 2018/19 is forecasted to rise +1.9% yr/yr to 125.983 million bales, a new record high. However, consumption of cotton continues to move toward countries with low wages, where the raw cotton is utilized to produce textiles and other cotton products. The largest consumers of cotton in 2018/19 are expected to be China with 32.9% of the world total, India with 20.1%, and Pakistan with 8.4%. U.S. consumption of cotton cloth has fallen sharply by almost half in the past decade due to the movement of the textile industry out of the U.S. to low-wage foreign countries. U.S. consumption of cotton by mills in 2018/19 is expected to fall by -1.0% yr/yr to 3.493 million bales.

Trade – World exports of cotton in 2018/19 are expected to rise +1.8% yr/yr to 41.728 million bales, but that is still below the 2012/13 record high of 46.435 million bales. U.S. cotton exports in 2017/18 rose by +9.3% yr/yr to 16.736 million bales., The U.S. is still the world's largest cotton exporter by far and accounts for 35.9% of world cotton exports. The main destinations for U.S. exports in 2017/18 were China with 15.7% of total exports, Indonesia with 9.5%, Mexico with 5.7%, and South Korea with 3.6%. Major world cotton importers for 2018/19 are expected to be Bangladesh with 19.8% of total world imports, Vietnam with 18.5%, China with 17.1%, Indonesia with 8.9%, and Turkey with 7.1%.

COTTON

Supply and Distribution of All Cotton in the United States   In Thousands of 480-Pound Bales

Crop Year Beginning Aug. 1	Planted --- 1,000 Acres ---	Harvested	Yield Lbs./Acre	Beginning Stocks[3]	Production[4]	Imports	Total	Mill Use	Exports	Total	Unaccounted	Ending Stocks	Farm Price[5]	"A" Index Price[6]	Value of Production Million USD
2009-10	9,150	7,534	776	6,337	12,183	0	18,520	3,550	12,037	15,587	14	2,947	64.8	78.13	3,788.0
2010-11	10,974	10,699	812	2,947	18,102	9	21,058	3,900	14,376	18,276	-182	2,600	84.6	164.29	7,348.1
2011-12	14,735	9,461	790	2,600	15,573	19	18,192	3,300	11,714	15,014	172	3,350	93.5	----	6,986.0
2012-13	12,264	9,322	892	3,350	17,314	10	20,674	3,500	13,026	16,526	-348	3,800	75.7	----	6,291.8
2013-14	10,407	7,544	821	3,800	12,909	13	16,722	3,550	10,530	14,080	-292	2,350	82.5	----	5,191.5
2014-15	11,037	9,347	838	2,350	16,319	12	18,681	3,575	11,246	14,821	-210	3,650	65.7	----	5,147.2
2015-16	8,581	8,075	766	3,650	12,888	33	16,571	3,450	9,153	12,603	-168	3,800	64.5	----	3,989.0
2016-17	10,074	9,508	867	3,800	17,170	7	20,977	3,250	14,917	18,167	-60	2,750	69.7	----	5,813.8
2017-18[1]	12,718	11,100	905	2,750	20,923	3	23,676	3,225	15,847	19,072	-304	4,300	71.0	----	7,227.3
2018-19[2]	14,099	10,531	838	4,300	18,390	5	22,713	3,300	15,000	18,300	-113	4,300	74 - 80	----	

[1] Preliminary.   [2] Estimate.   [3] Excludes preseason ginnings (adjusted to 480-lb. bale net weight basis).   [4] Includes preseason ginnings.   [5] Marketing year average price.   [6] Average of 5 cheapest types of SLM 1 3/32" staple length cotton offered on the European market.
Source: Economic Research Service, U.S. Department of Agriculture (ERS-USDA)

World Production of All Cotton   In Thousands of 480-Pound Bales

Crop Year Beginning Aug. 1	Australia	Brazil	Burkina	China	Greece	India	Mexico	Pakistan	Turkey	Turkmenistan	United States	Uzbekistan	World Total
2009-10	1,775	5,480	695	32,000	940	24,200	475	9,240	1,750	1,470	12,183	3,900	103,084
2010-11	4,200	9,000	645	30,500	940	26,900	732	8,640	2,110	1,750	18,102	4,200	117,298
2011-12	5,500	8,620	795	34,000	1,330	28,700	1,180	10,600	3,440	1,525	15,573	4,000	127,243
2012-13	4,600	6,020	1,215	35,000	1,194	28,500	1,036	9,300	2,650	1,700	17,314	4,600	123,891
2013-14	4,100	7,960	1,250	32,750	1,369	31,000	933	9,500	2,300	1,550	12,909	4,100	120,356
2014-15	2,300	7,180	1,350	30,000	1,286	29,500	1,319	10,600	3,200	1,525	16,319	3,900	119,219
2015-16	2,850	5,920	1,100	22,000	1,010	25,900	943	7,000	2,650	1,450	12,888	3,800	96,156
2016-17	4,050	7,020	1,310	22,750	1,033	27,000	765	7,700	3,200	1,325	17,170	3,725	106,663
2017-18[1]	4,700	9,220	1,300	27,500	1,240	29,000	1,560	8,200	4,000	1,340	20,923	3,860	123,696
2018-19[2]	2,500	11,000	1,400	27,000	1,350	27,500	1,725	7,400	4,300	1,000	18,588	3,300	118,742

[1] Preliminary.   [2] Estimate.   *Source: Foreign Agricultural Service, U.S. Department of Agriculture (FAS-USDA)*

World Consumption of Cotton   In Thousands of 480-Pound Bales

Crop Year Beginning Aug. 1	Bangladesh	Brazil	China	India	Indonesia	Mexico	Pakistan	Thailand	Turkey	United States	Uzbekistan	Vietnam	World Total
2009-10	4,010	4,300	50,000	19,750	2,650	1,925	10,425	1,800	5,900	3,536	1,100	1,600	119,482
2010-11	4,210	4,250	46,000	20,550	2,650	1,725	9,925	1,725	5,600	4,082	1,250	1,625	115,611
2011-12	3,710	4,000	38,000	19,450	2,450	1,725	10,025	1,325	5,600	3,128	1,350	1,675	103,906
2012-13	4,710	4,100	36,000	21,050	3,050	1,825	10,775	1,525	6,050	3,848	1,450	2,250	107,900
2013-14	5,310	4,200	34,500	23,050	3,050	1,875	10,425	1,550	6,300	3,842	1,600	3,200	109,998
2014-15	5,810	3,400	34,500	24,500	3,250	1,875	10,625	1,500	6,400	3,785	1,750	4,100	112,499
2015-16	6,310	3,100	36,000	24,750	3,000	1,875	10,325	1,295	6,700	3,618	1,800	4,500	113,506
2016-17	6,810	3,200	38,500	24,350	3,300	1,775	10,325	1,225	6,550	3,310	2,000	5,400	116,380
2017-18[1]	7,510	3,400	41,000	24,700	3,500	1,925	10,825	1,175	7,350	3,529	2,500	6,600	123,638
2018-19[2]	8,010	3,500	41,500	25,300	3,600	1,975	10,625	1,175	7,000	3,493	2,700	7,500	125,983

[1] Preliminary.   [2] Estimate.   *Source: Foreign Agricultural Service, U.S. Department of Agriculture (FAS-USDA)*

World Ending Stocks of Cotton   In Thousands of 480-Pound Bales

Crop Year Beginning Aug. 1	Argentina	Australia	Bangladesh	Brazil	China	India	Mexico	Pakistan	Turkey	Turkmenistan	United States	Uzbekistan	World Total
2009-10	803	852	888	4,553	14,246	7,999	617	3,042	1,605	1,404	2,947	948	46,179
2010-11	966	2,762	992	8,006	10,603	9,549	595	2,520	1,319	2,004	2,600	1,248	49,263
2011-12	881	3,807	768	7,863	31,081	8,319	710	2,835	1,241	2,254	3,350	1,398	72,149
2012-13	789	2,399	1,166	5,541	50,361	9,195	646	2,710	1,315	2,554	3,800	1,548	89,335
2013-14	942	1,807	1,271	7,218	62,707	8,559	584	2,475	1,357	1,879	2,350	1,748	99,950
2014-15	727	1,818	1,331	7,112	66,420	10,586	693	2,890	1,596	1,279	3,650	1,298	106,857
2015-16	632	1,880	1,515	5,709	56,698	7,044	605	2,615	1,533	829	3,800	1,098	90,328
2016-17	472	2,193	1,630	6,929	45,919	7,880	445	2,315	1,528	654	2,750	1,073	80,404
2017-18[1]	520	2,940	1,855	8,657	38,019	8,675	655	2,830	1,877	644	4,300	1,533	80,446
2018-19[2]	710	1,805	2,080	10,432	30,369	8,075	705	2,355	1,677	494	4,400	1,333	73,190

[1] Preliminary.   [2] Estimate.   *Source: Foreign Agricultural Service, U.S. Department of Agriculture (FAS-USDA)*

World Exports of Cotton   In Thousands of 480-Pound Bales

Crop Year Beginning Aug. 1	Australia	Benin	Brazil	Burkina	Cote d'Ivoire	Greece	India	Malaysia	Mali	Turkmen-istan	United States	Uzbek-istan	World Total
2009-10	2,112	400	1,990	775	420	850	6,550	43	440	1,150	12,037	3,800	35,804
2010-11	2,500	300	2,000	675	300	750	5,000	80	450	725	14,376	2,650	34,900
2011-12	4,640	275	4,792	650	480	1,100	11,080	825	625	700	11,714	2,500	45,874
2012-13	6,168	350	4,307	1,200	620	1,092	7,761	700	800	800	13,026	3,000	46,435
2013-14	4,852	600	2,230	1,250	830	1,288	9,261	210	900	1,625	10,530	2,300	40,947
2014-15	2,404	750	3,910	1,300	860	1,165	4,199	81	850	1,500	11,246	2,600	35,878
2015-16	2,828	650	4,314	1,100	780	959	5,764	142	1,000	1,250	9,153	2,200	34,621
2016-17	3,727	800	2,789	1,150	625	1,017	4,550	111	1,100	850	14,917	1,750	37,902
2017-18[1]	3,918	1,000	4,174	1,250	620	1,076	5,182	152	1,300	700	15,847	900	40,994
2018-19[2]	3,600	1,175	5,800	1,350	800	1,200	4,400	300	1,300	475	15,000	800	41,728

[1] Preliminary.   [2] Estimate.   Source: Foreign Agricultural Service, U.S. Department of Agriculture (FAS-USDA)

World Imports of Cotton   In Thousands of 480-Pound Bales

Crop Year Beginning Aug. 1	Bangla-desh	China	India	Indonesia	Korea, South	Malaysia	Mexico	Pakistan	Taiwan	Thailand	Turkey	Vietnam	World Total
2009-10	4,000	10,903	480	2,700	1,010	271	1,393	1,574	1,016	1,806	4,394	1,695	36,928
2010-11	4,250	11,979	200	2,500	1,038	325	1,196	1,443	803	1,752	3,350	1,569	36,297
2011-12	3,400	24,533	600	2,500	1,170	1,125	1,000	900	863	1,263	2,382	1,625	45,423
2012-13	5,000	20,327	1,187	3,137	1,314	900	950	1,800	941	1,511	3,692	2,410	47,630
2013-14	5,300	14,122	675	2,989	1,286	350	1,040	1,200	857	1,546	4,246	3,200	41,204
2014-15	5,750	8,284	1,226	3,345	1,321	280	830	950	873	1,475	3,675	4,275	36,065
2015-16	6,375	4,406	1,072	2,941	1,175	443	975	3,300	707	1,275	4,218	4,600	35,442
2016-17	6,800	5,032	2,736	3,391	1,025	392	1,000	2,450	644	1,226	3,679	5,500	37,695
2017-18[1]	7,600	5,725	1,677	3,498	904	739	925	3,300	632	1,149	4,024	6,900	40,978
2018-19[2]	8,100	7,000	1,600	3,650	800	675	900	2,900	600	1,175	2,900	7,600	41,713

[1] Preliminary.   [2] Estimate.   Source: Foreign Agricultural Service, U.S. Department of Agriculture (FAS-USDA)

Average Spot Cotton, 1-3/32", Price (SLM) at Designated U.S. Markets[2]   In Cents Per Pound (Net Weight)

Year	Aug	Sept	Oct	Nov	Dec	Jan	Feb	Mar	Apr	May	June	July	Average
2009-10	57.77	59.82	64.58	69.23	72.59	70.45	72.47	79.02	79.81	78.99	79.37	80.30	72.03
2010-11	87.38	95.48	112.06	130.62	139.68	148.24	181.61	199.76	185.94	155.89	148.73	117.00	141.87
2011-12	106.41	105.50	100.97	97.13	89.53	94.10	89.52	87.76	88.07	77.26	72.12	70.91	89.94
2012-13	74.76	74.19	72.87	72.06	75.42	77.99	81.37	87.28	85.39	84.29	86.63	86.07	79.86
2013-14	87.80	85.65	83.66	78.84	83.15	85.69	87.45	90.94	89.71	87.41	82.74	73.89	84.74
2014-15	68.94	68.70	67.32	63.40	63.13	62.12	66.02	64.89	67.33	67.30	67.09	66.60	66.07
2015-16	66.09	63.93	65.06	65.17	66.47	64.76	62.05	59.91	63.51	64.42	66.74	73.12	65.10
2016-17	72.48	71.58	71.93	73.41	73.31	75.24	75.92	77.10	76.91	78.55	72.72	69.05	74.02
2017-18	70.52	71.93	69.47	71.10	76.32	80.83	78.44	82.77	82.52	85.57	88.85	87.33	78.80
2018-19[1]	84.10	80.10	77.12	77.06	76.07	72.23	70.61						76.76

[1] Preliminary.   Source: Agricultural Marketing Service, U.S. Department of Agriculture (AMS-USDA)

Average Producer Price Index of Gray Cotton Broadwovens   Index 1982 = 100

Year	Jan.	Feb.	Mar.	Apr.	May	June	July	Aug.	Sept.	Oct.	Nov.	Dec.	Average
2009	111.0	111.0	111.0	107.2	107.2	107.2	107.2	107.5	107.5	107.5	108.9	108.9	108.5
2010	109.8	113.7	113.7	113.7	114.9	116.6	119.0	118.8	118.8	118.8	119.1	119.1	116.3
2011	144.8	145.4	147.0	153.5	154.3	154.3	162.1	162.0	161.3	148.5	148.5	141.1	151.9
2012	139.1	139.2	139.2	135.0	135.0	135.2	126.1	126.1	126.1	124.7	123.6	122.7	131.0
2013	122.6	122.3	123.3	126.9	126.4	126.4	126.4	126.4	126.4	127.7	127.7	127.7	125.9
2014	124.5	124.5	121.8	124.7	124.7	124.7	124.8	124.8	124.8	123.3	123.3	123.3	124.1
2015	118.2	121.2	121.2	121.5	121.5	121.5	123.7	123.7	123.7	123.5	123.5	123.5	122.2
2016	122.6	122.6	122.6	121.9	121.9	121.9	122.6	122.6	122.6	123.6	123.6	123.6	122.7
2017	125.2	125.3	125.3	129.2	129.2	129.2	128.5	128.5	128.5	126.4	126.4	126.4	127.3
2018[1]	127.3	127.3	127.3	133.1	133.1	133.1	133.1	----	----	----	----	----	130.6

[1] Preliminary.   Source: Bureau of Labor Statistics (0337-01), U.S. Department of Commerce

COTTON

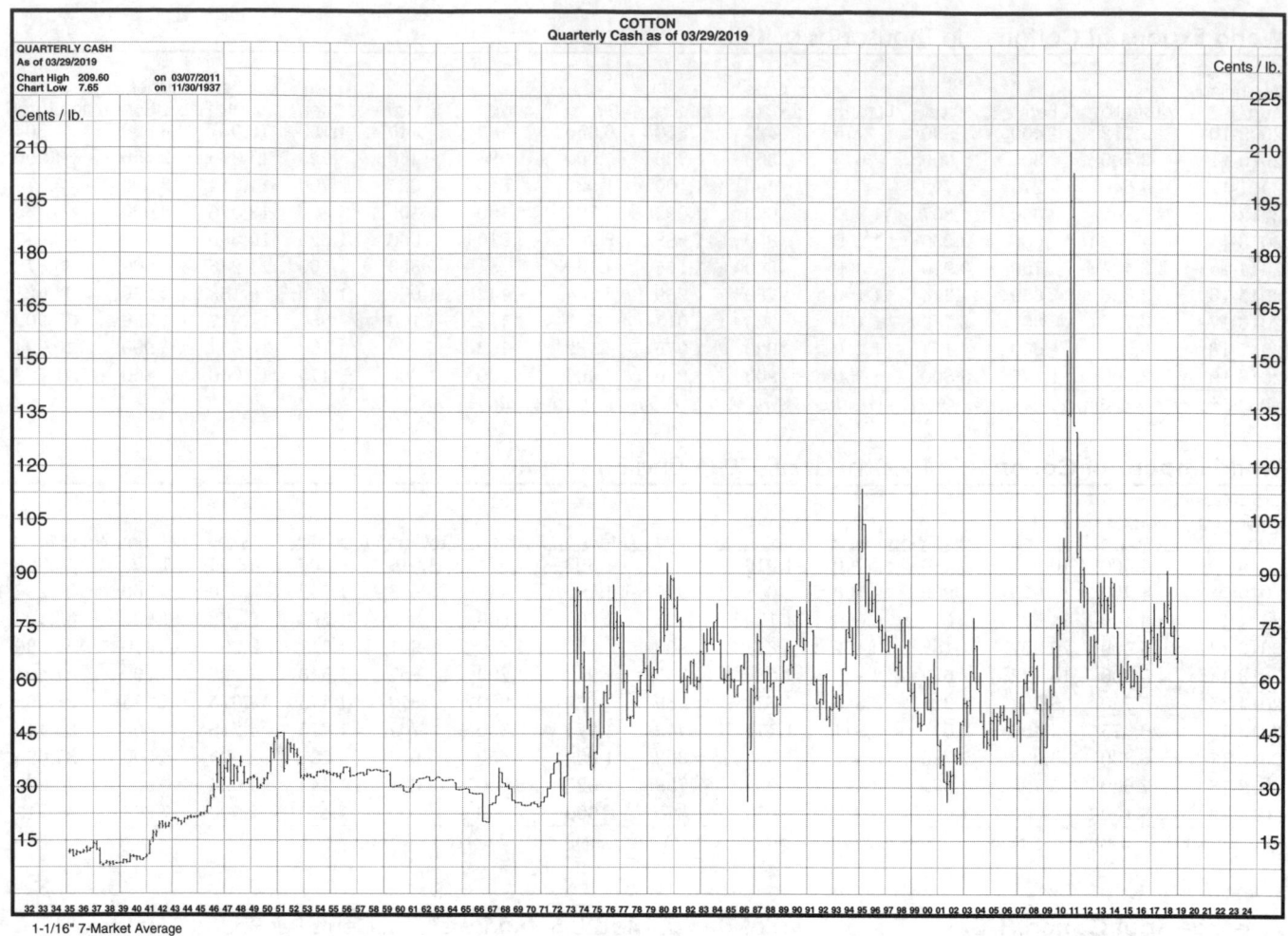

QUARTERLY CASH
As of 03/29/2019

Chart High 209.60 on 03/07/2011
Chart Low   7.65   on 11/30/1937

Cents / lb.

1-1/16" 7-Market Average

Average Price of SLM 1-1/16", Cotton/5 at Designated U.S. Markets   In Cents Per Pound (Net Weight)

Year	Aug.	Sept.	Oct.	Nov.	Dec.	Jan.	Feb.	Mar.	Apr.	May	June	July	Average
2009-10	53.77	55.78	60.44	64.90	68.11	65.93	68.08	74.54	75.46	74.70	75.19	76.16	67.76
2010-11	81.16	91.53	108.26	126.62	135.46	144.79	177.65	195.79	181.98	151.93	144.77	113.03	137.75
2011-12	102.89	102.06	97.63	93.59	85.99	89.83	85.17	83.14	83.37	72.51	67.35	66.14	85.81
2012-13	69.97	69.38	68.03	67.34	70.61	73.33	76.87	82.80	80.94	79.84	82.18	81.62	75.24
2013-14	83.36	81.25	77.37	74.43	78.75	81.43	83.21	86.70	85.48	83.20	78.54	69.63	80.28
2014-15	64.99	64.83	63.51	59.64	59.38	58.19	61.74	60.65	63.08	63.06	62.86	62.36	62.02
2015-16	61.85	59.70	60.83	60.99	62.32	60.69	58.06	55.96	59.65	60.36	62.78	69.25	61.04
2016-17	68.57	67.65	68.04	69.42	69.69	71.81	73.02	74.33	74.13	75.75	69.85	66.24	70.71
2017-18	67.71	69.12	66.67	68.09	73.13	77.58	75.24	79.57	79.34	82.40	85.54	83.95	75.70
2018-19[1]	80.75	76.72	73.90	73.72	72.66	68.72							74.41

[1] Preliminary.   [2] Grade 41, leaf 4, staple 34, mike 35-36 and 43-49 , strength 23.5-26.4.   Source: Agricultural Marketing Service, U.S. Department of Agriculture (AMS-USDA)

Average Price[1] Received by Farmers for Upland Cotton in the United States   In Cents Per Pound

Year	Aug.	Sept.	Oct.	Nov.	Dec.	Jan.	Feb.	Mar.	Apr.	May	June	July	Average
2009-10	47.7	55.0	58.5	59.5	63.4	60.8	65.0	65.0	66.7	66.6	68.5	68.5	62.1
2010-11	77.2	74.7	77.3	81.5	81.2	82.1	92.9	84.4	86.7	83.2	83.3	82.5	82.3
2011-12	94.0	93.5	92.2	92.6	88.9	90.1	92.3	90.0	90.4	84.4	77.1	76.6	88.5
2012-13	71.4	70.7	69.8	69.2	71.8	72.9	76.9	77.5	78.4	78.3	79.3	80.9	74.8
2013-14	76.9	74.6	77.8	75.9	77.2	77.5	80.2	81.7	82.7	81.7	83.9	84.7	79.6
2014-15	70.5	68.9	64.5	62.7	60.8	59.1	57.8	61.3	62.6	65.9	66.8	69.3	64.2
2015-16	58.0	60.3	57.9	60.0	61.3	60.3	59.8	58.2	58.7	63.2	67.0	74.5	61.6
2016-17	67.1	67.0	66.0	67.2	67.9	67.0	68.8	69.2	69.3	69.9	70.4	73.0	68.6
2017-18	64.7	64.1	66.5	67.3	68.6	68.9	67.7	67.7	66.7	68.8	73.5	74.1	68.2
2018-19[2]	69.7	71.0	72.3	73.0	72.7	65.3							70.7

[1] Weighted average by sales.   [2] Preliminary.   Source: Agricultural Marketing Service, U.S. Department of Agriculture (AMS-USDA)

Purchases Reported by Exchanges in Designated U.S. Spot Markets[1]   In Running Bales

Crop Year Beginning Aug. 1	Aug.	Sept.	Oct.	Nov.	Dec.	Jan.	Feb.	Mar.	Apr.	May	June	July	Market Total
2009-10	34,279	54,457	57,362	179,007	199,006	75,580	175,053	69,900	34,523	9,790	13,412	1,732	904,101
2010-11	1,431	5,498	69,122	126,009	153,780	130,932	59,520	27,102	10,609	27,288	33,804	7,581	652,676
2011-12	9,762	31,213	95,360	122,388	131,642	227,089	115,427	119,698	25,990	20,764	20,687	36,712	956,732
2012-13	38,533	55,227	81,437	408,050	417,927	382,992	112,442	62,556	65,991	27,923	25,573	12,135	1,690,786
2013-14	20,398	26,066	52,042	198,579	433,317	345,007	141,663	57,669	24,792	24,878	7,569	6,815	1,338,795
2014-15	21,486	35,934	141,203	200,756	593,113	425,345	404,710	121,097	117,746	26,509	19,259	20,128	2,127,286
2015-16	18,634	24,429	56,127	220,807	424,830	297,380	196,419	128,004	61,364	28,446	16,622	56,367	1,529,429
2016-17	9,555	26,482	54,441	251,092	253,534	549,344	214,644	159,483	38,442	8,097	2,411	3,121	1,570,646
2017-18	16,659	20,322	57,282	341,259	429,829	427,512	255,750	152,678	156,773	152,630	35,949	13,783	2,060,426
2018-19	11,511	5,796	18,533	79,339	122,132	226,334							926,238

[1] Seven markets.   *Source: Agricultural Marketing Service, U.S. Department of Agriculture (AMS-USDA)*

Production of All Cotton in the United States   In Thousands of 480-Pound Bales

Year	Alabama	Arizona	Arkansas	California	Georgia	Louisiana	Mississippi	Missouri	North Carolina	South Carolina	Ten- nessee	Texas	U.S. Total
2009	345	447	852	601	1,860	349	415	502	763	207	492	4,651	12,188
2010	480	614	1,176	844	2,250	437	848	685	951	376	681	7,871	18,104
2011	685	820	1,277	1,341	2,465	511	1,200	741	1,026	519	813	3,540	15,573
2012	745	612	1,297	1,261	2,910	478	993	731	1,225	593	743	5,015	17,314
2013	590	483	720	943	2,320	326	719	496	766	360	414	4,185	12,909
2014	653	520	787	714	2,570	404	1,078	570	995	528	494	6,203	16,319
2015	554	308	471	526	2,255	189	672	400	527	155	305	5,748	12,888
2016	706	395	840	747	2,180	268	1,081	566	343	250	575	8,133	17,170
2017[1]	808	515	1,074	865	2,225	404	1,351	750	741	471	732	9,296	20,923
2018[2]	860	469	1,150	902	1,950	410	1,430	835	700	440	780	6,935	18,390

[1] Preliminary.   [2] Forecast.   *Source: Agricultural Statistics Board, U.S. Department of Agriculture (ASB-USDA)*

Cotton Production and Yield Estimates in the United States

Year	Forecasts of Production (1,000 Bales of 480 Lbs.[1])						Actual Crop	Forecasts of Yield (Lbs. Per Harvested Acre)						Actual Yield
	Aug.1	Sept.1	Oct. 1	Nov. 1	Dec. 1	Jan. 1		Aug.1	Sept.1	Oct. 1	Nov. 1	Dec. 1	Jan. 1	
2009	13,207	13,438	12,998	12,496	12,592	----	12,183	816	816	807	776	782	----	776
2010	18,634	18,841	18,873	18,418	18,268	----	18,102	837	839	841	821	814	----	812
2011	16,554	16,556	16,608	16,300	15,827	----	15,573	822	807	809	794	771	----	790
2012	17,651	17,109	17,287	17,447	17,257	----	17,314	784	786	795	802	793	----	892
2013	13,053	12,899	NA	13,105	13,069	----	12,909	813	796	NA	808	806	----	821
2014	17,502	16,538	16,255	16,397	15,923	----	16,319	820	803	790	797	773	----	838
2015	13,082	13,428	13,338	13,281	13,031	----	12,888	795	789	784	782	768	----	766
2016	15,879	16,142	16,034	16,162	16,524	----	17,170	800	802	797	803	821	----	867
2017	20,545	21,758	21,115	21,377	21,440	----	20,923	892	908	889	900	902	----	905
2018	19,235	19,682	19,763	18,408	18,588	----	18,588	911	895	901	852	860	----	860

[1] Net weight bales.   *Source: Agricultural Statistics Board, U.S. Department of Agriculture (ASB-USDA)*

Supply and Distribution of Upland Cotton in the United States   In Thousands of 480-Pound Bales

Crop Year Beginning Aug. 1	Area			Supply				Disappearance				Farm Price[5] Cents/ Lb.
	Planted	Harvested	Yield	Beginning Stocks[3]	Pro- duction	Imports	Total Supply	Mill Use	Exports	Total	Ending Stocks	
	1,000 Acres		Lbs./Acre									
2009-10	9,008	7,391	766	6,032	11,783		17,815	3,529	11,343	14,872	2,929	62.1
2010-11	10,770	10,497	805	2,929	17,598	2	20,529	3,874	13,881	17,755	2,572	82.3
2011-12	14,428	9,156	772	2,572	14,722	13	17,307	3,278	11,120	14,398	3,081	88.5
2012-13	12,026	9,085	874	3,081	16,534	6	19,621	3,478	12,182	15,660	3,613	74.8
2013-14	10,206	7,345	802	3,613	12,275	6	15,894	3,527	9,850	13,377	2,225	79.6
2014-15	10,845	9,157	826	2,225	15,753	9	17,987	3,550	10,836	14,386	3,391	64.2
2015-16	8,422	7,903	756	3,391	12,455	30	15,876	3,425	8,619	12,044	3,664	61.6
2016-17	9,878	9,320	855	3,664	16,601	5	20,270	3,221	14,303	17,524	2,686	68.6
2017-18[1]	12,465	10,850	895	2,686	20,223	1	22,910	3,198	15,211	18,409	4,197	68.2
2018-19[2]	13,850	10,283	821	4,197	17,637	5	21,839	3,270	14,350	17,620	4,106	70.7

[1] Preliminary.   [2] Estimate.   [3] Excludes preseason ginnings (adjusted to 480-lb. bale net weight basis).   [4] Includes preseason ginnings.
[5] Marketing year average price.   *Source: Economic Research Service, U.S. Department of Agriculture (ERS-USDA)*

COTTON

COTTON #2 - ICE-US
Weekly Selected Futures as of 03/29/2019

WEEKLY SELECTED FUTURES
As of 03/29/2019

Chart High 227.00 on 03/07/2011
Chart Low 40.01 on 03/09/2009

Nearby Futures through Last Trading Day using selected contract months: March, May, July, October and December.

Volume of Trading of Cotton #2 Futures in New York   In Contracts

Year	Jan.	Feb.	Mar.	Apr.	May	June	July	Aug.	Sept.	Oct.	Nov.	Dec.	Total
2009	276,977	326,853	272,091	373,379	274,983	372,124	187,347	177,989	228,815	347,989	509,375	227,073	3,574,995
2010	321,331	570,117	344,389	567,774	365,998	550,206	327,296	331,579	440,411	600,977	887,594	425,234	5,732,906
2011	457,454	719,075	590,294	602,903	325,606	536,555	293,608	290,265	307,617	350,452	598,711	215,914	5,288,454
2012	471,729	605,161	499,276	660,539	564,011	826,818	308,028	339,672	349,649	584,358	632,610	288,501	6,130,352
2013	599,171	738,954	474,475	725,015	494,848	729,167	282,565	464,074	273,354	487,233	588,624	297,544	6,155,024
2014	544,180	602,542	446,810	568,063	399,736	611,785	362,461	338,548	460,119	477,742	625,593	350,304	5,787,883
2015	474,061	764,365	532,511	774,667	504,552	748,679	391,137	541,234	378,522	492,136	718,549	405,429	6,725,842
2016	556,311	939,909	544,144	920,712	567,195	802,595	582,169	538,811	437,283	528,534	876,713	408,670	7,703,046
2017	621,642	919,593	648,217	805,263	728,004	731,750	367,996	499,490	527,357	539,450	954,722	564,023	7,907,507
2018	908,692	1,040,986	697,571	967,537	865,014	966,955	395,024	544,209	451,364	641,924	889,009	507,810	8,876,095

Contract size = 50,000 lbs.   *Source: ICE Futures U.S. (ICE)*

Average Open Interest of Cotton #2 Futures in New York   In Contracts

Year	Jan.	Feb.	Mar.	Apr.	May	June	July	Aug.	Sept.	Oct.	Nov.	Dec.
2009	130,049	120,331	128,054	128,973	134,079	120,861	122,153	127,019	136,585	165,683	180,594	182,489
2010	178,305	166,475	185,608	190,458	184,193	171,459	160,118	201,962	231,513	235,834	217,587	201,510
2011	204,871	198,798	176,675	180,626	150,430	148,695	138,168	144,300	150,834	155,592	149,292	146,219
2012	156,940	180,632	183,618	186,859	188,255	185,629	171,383	180,207	183,282	199,026	179,969	165,382
2013	185,106	201,378	205,753	188,311	181,012	173,729	162,260	191,013	178,447	203,972	172,006	164,247
2014	180,149	171,213	178,245	178,514	190,808	169,165	152,321	167,437	181,359	190,436	181,192	175,349
2015	197,949	192,586	182,898	180,941	191,700	175,835	177,911	185,267	180,786	192,945	184,447	188,025
2016	188,149	196,230	211,958	203,691	191,903	197,043	216,925	236,332	238,644	251,736	250,363	248,786
2017	263,192	275,644	277,202	252,849	254,360	219,791	213,858	221,829	238,371	230,544	232,469	262,608
2018	301,515	271,212	272,354	270,033	290,493	289,963	257,708	260,562	253,033	259,661	241,659	217,465

Contract size = 50,000 lbs.   *Source: ICE Futures U.S. (ICE)*

Average Spot Prices of U.S. Cotton,[2] Base Quality (SLM) at Designated Markets   In Cents Per Pound

Crop Year Beginning Aug. 1	Dallas (EastTex.-Okl.)	Fresno (San Joaquin Valley)	Greenville (South-east)	Greenwood (South Delta)	Lubbock (West Texas)	Memphis (North Delta)	Phoenix Desert (Southwest)	Average
2009-10	66.57	67.20	70.13	69.30	66.38	69.30	65.40	67.76
2010-11	139.31	137.94	135.69	139.73	135.14	138.94	139.06	137.88
2011-12	86.95	85.73	83.30	87.75	83.31	86.74	86.91	85.81
2012-13	73.79	74.74	77.50	76.56	73.68	76.56	73.89	75.24
2013-14	79.27	78.88	82.74	81.85	79.14	81.85	78.23	80.28
2014-15	60.75	62.32	63.55	62.64	60.71	62.64	61.57	62.02
2015-16	59.29	60.88	63.32	62.44	59.16	62.44	59.73	61.04
2016-17	70.25	69.62	72.91	71.81	70.06	71.81	68.51	70.71
2017-18	66.90	68.63	71.13	69.63	66.67	69.63	67.38	68.57
2018-19[1]	67.14	67.42	69.92	68.42	66.05	68.42	66.17	67.65

[1] Preliminary   [2] Prices are for mixed lots, net weight, uncompressed in warehouse.
Source: Agricultural Marketing Service, U.S. Department of Agriculture (AMS-USDA)

Cotton Ginnings[1] in the United States To: In Thousands of Running Bales

Crop Year	Aug. 1	Sept. 1	Sept. 15	Oct. 1	Oct. 15	Nov. 1	Nov. 15	Dec. 1	Dec. 15	Jan. 1	Jan. 15	Feb. 1	Mar. 1	Total Crop
2009-10	5	110	175	234	552	2,189	4,957	7,873	9,728	10,812	11,383	11,706	----	11,832
2010-11	W	287	747	2,284	4,716	7,947	10,576	13,170	15,126	16,442	17,138	17,518	----	17,643
2011-12	203	822	1,095	1,734	3,467	6,440	9,214	11,668	13,064	13,949	14,458	14,805	----	15,153
2012-13	60	473	756	1,552	2,943	6,307	9,394	12,263	14,194	15,327	16,029	16,547	----	16,834
2013-14	W	132	274	486	1,101	3,038	5,723	8,260	10,459	11,402	12,053	12,391	----	12,521
2014-15	1	367	696	1,154	2,108	4,807	7,530	10,246	12,601	14,214	15,030	15,538	----	15,876
2015-16	----	105	293	635	1,448	3,704	5,738	7,955	9,830	11,092	11,737	12,251	12,517	12,529
2016-17	35	438	701	1,167	2,313	5,016	7,584	10,296	12,261	13,858	14,840	15,881	16,559	16,710
2017-18	107	571	789	1,249	2,298	4,915	7,878	11,287	13,963	16,153	17,430	18,654	19,557	20,441
2018-19[2]	20	489	745	1,287	2,422	4,877	7,078	10,265	12,261	NA	NA	16,663	17,471	

[1] Excluding linters.   [2] Preliminary.   W = Withheld.   *Source: National Agricultural Statistics Service, U.S. Department of Agriculture (NASS-USDA)*

Exports of All Cotton[2] from the United States   In Thousands of Running Bales

Year	Aug.	Sept.	Oct.	Nov.	Dec.	Jan.	Feb.	Mar.	Apr.	May	June	July	Total
2009-10	885	809	664	570	778	942	1,174	1,447	1,175	1,354	1,344	1,373	12,515
2010-11	1,023	467	449	1,141	1,688	2,057	1,839	2,085	1,561	1,163	706	533	14,714
2011-12	302	303	422	776	930	1,284	1,583	1,672	1,322	1,241	942	785	11,561
2012-13	743	743	494	731	1,098	1,549	1,796	1,730	1,445	1,394	913	694	13,330
2013-14	767	533	414	606	975	1,417	1,345	1,347	1,087	873	607	446	10,418
2014-15	499	380	354	572	1,024	1,126	1,430	1,596	1,418	1,369	945	769	11,482
2015-16	560	404	370	396	643	776	918	1,083	1,083	1,077	1,042	909	9,261
2016-17	966	799	569	828	1,291	1,580	1,734	1,936	1,634	1,592	1,209	1,175	15,313
2017-18	933	577	447	727	1,399	1,647	1,980	2,329	2,198	1,989	1,428	1,088	16,741
2018-19[1]	815	715	609	681	976								9,109

[1] Preliminary.   *Source: Foreign Agricultural Service, U.S. Department of Agriculture (FAS-USDA)*

U.S. Exports of American Cotton to Countries of Destination   In Thousands of 480 Pound Bales

Crop Year Beginning Aug. 1	Canada	China	Hong Kong	Indo-nesia	Italy	Japan	Korea, South	Mexico	Philip-pines	Taiwan	Thailand	United Kingdom	Total
2008-09	19	3,770	184	1,057	23	158	302	1,320	52	436	615	----	13,179
2009-10	9	3,886	69	660	21	150	353	1,490	51	424	605	----	12,515
2010-11	10	4,863	47	889	53	186	513	1,245	37	357	712	1	14,714
2011-12	3	6,279	45	329	15	97	329	956	16	271	275	0	11,561
2012-13	2	5,615	105	533	8	120	355	979	31	419	353	0	13,330
2013-14	2	2,646	13	701	9	115	461	1,009	39	299	457	0	10,418
2014-15	2	2,709	16	978	22	114	670	950	42	349	466	7	11,460
2015-16	1	842	0	690	9	124	476	994	34	330	379	0	9,259
2016-17[1]	1	2,311	1	1,476	9	121	598	1,007	65	422	577	1	15,315
2017-18[2]	1	2,623	2	1,593	14	122	607	949	57	465	668	1	16,736

[1] Preliminary.   [2] Estimate.   *Source: Foreign Agricultural Service, U.S. Department of Agriculture (FAS-USDA)*

Cotton[1] Government Loan Program in the United States

Crop Year Beginning Aug. 1	Support Price	Target Price	Put Under Support	% of Pro- duction	Acquired	Owned July 31	Crop Year Beginning Aug. 1	Support Price	Target Price	Put Under Support	% of Pro- duction	Acquired	Owned July 31
	--- Cents Per Lb. ---		Ths Bales		----- Ths. Bales -----			--- Cents Per Lb. ---		Ths Bales		----- Ths. Bales -----	
2007-08	52.00	72.4	14,636	79.7	169	0	2012-13	52.00	71.3	8,330	50.4	0	0
2008-09	52.00	71.3	10,005	80.7	4	0	2013-14	52.00	71.3	3,981	32.4	0	0
2009-10	52.00	71.3	8,278	70.2	0	0	2014-15	52.00	NA	7,625	48.4	0	0
2010-11	52.00	71.3	11,403	64.8	0	0	2015-16	52.00	NA	6,758	54.3	0	0
2011-12	52.00	71.3	7,268	49.3	1	0	2016-17[1]	52.00	NA	9,373	56.4	0	0

[1] Upland.   [2] Preliminary.   NA = Not applicable.   *Source: Economic Research Service, U.S. Department of Agriculture (ERS-USDA)*

Weekly Outstanding Export Sales and Cumulative Exports of U.S. Cotton   In Running Bales

Marketing Year 2017/2018 Week Ending	Weekly Exports	Accumu- lated Exports	Net Sales	Out- standing Sales	Marketing Year 2018/2019 Week Ending	Weekly Exports	Accumu- lated Exports	Net Sales	Out- standing Sales
Aug 03, 2017	113,953	113,953	821,144	5,829,015	Aug 02, 2018	43,138	43,138	1,704,287	8,201,988
Aug 10, 2017	200,354	314,307	186,686	5,815,347	Aug 09, 2018	240,271	283,409	77,718	8,039,435
Aug 17, 2017	221,848	536,155	277,643	5,871,142	Aug 16, 2018	157,374	440,783	188,021	8,070,082
Aug 24, 2017	156,318	692,473	230,696	5,945,520	Aug 23, 2018	172,615	613,398	150,635	8,048,102
Aug 31, 2017	164,259	856,732	116,109	5,897,370	Aug 30, 2018	177,327	790,725	92,162	7,962,937
Sep 07, 2017	108,523	965,255	65,216	5,854,063	Sep 06, 2018	135,731	926,456	81,719	7,908,925
Sep 14, 2017	175,725	1,140,980	219,850	5,898,188	Sep 13, 2018	148,892	1,075,348	97,773	7,857,806
Sep 21, 2017	131,894	1,272,874	194,198	5,960,492	Sep 20, 2018	138,859	1,214,207	70,290	7,789,237
Sep 28, 2017	114,942	1,387,816	161,013	6,006,563	Sep 27, 2018	179,733	1,393,940	21,845	7,631,349
Oct 05, 2017	118,009	1,505,825	154,423	6,042,977	Oct 04, 2018	208,416	1,602,356	97,997	7,520,930
Oct 12, 2017	86,125	1,591,950	253,182	6,210,034	Oct 11, 2018	135,325	1,737,681	32,656	7,418,261
Oct 19, 2017	94,659	1,686,609	289,094	6,404,469	Oct 18, 2018	139,155	1,876,836	40,589	7,319,695
Oct 26, 2017	86,838	1,773,447	209,504	6,527,135	Oct 25, 2018	109,778	1,986,614	-49,004	7,160,913
Nov 02, 2017	124,292	1,897,739	205,297	6,608,140	Nov 01, 2018	150,982	2,137,596	91,007	7,100,938
Nov 09, 2017	94,207	1,991,946	506,668	7,020,601	Nov 08, 2018	112,973	2,250,569	67,593	7,055,558
Nov 16, 2017	85,560	2,077,506	357,026	7,292,067	Nov 15, 2018	150,827	2,401,396	210,464	7,115,195
Nov 23, 2017	112,207	2,189,713	276,491	7,456,351	Nov 22, 2018	126,148	2,527,544	176,787	7,165,834
Nov 30, 2017	246,763	2,436,476	186,579	7,396,167	Nov 29, 2018	158,554	2,686,098	94,866	7,102,146
Dec 07, 2017	166,568	2,603,044	259,661	7,489,260	Dec 06, 2018	154,547	2,840,645	47,099	6,994,698
Dec 14, 2017	148,200	2,751,244	326,520	7,667,580	Dec 13, 2018	154,246	2,994,891	142,349	6,982,801
Dec 21, 2017	276,729	3,027,973	163,680	7,554,531	Dec 20, 2018	207,113	3,202,004	373,100	7,148,788
Dec 28, 2017	208,468	3,236,441	193,942	7,540,005	Dec 27, 2018	189,798	3,391,802	228,202	7,187,192
Jan 04, 2018	281,647	3,518,088	274,533	7,532,891	Jan 03, 2019	181,091	3,572,893	299,767	7,305,868
Jan 11, 2018	289,866	3,807,954	275,060	7,518,085	Jan 10, 2019		3,572,893		7,305,868
Jan 18, 2018	232,547	4,040,501	67,684	7,353,222	Jan 17, 2019		3,572,893		7,305,868
Jan 25, 2018	305,086	4,345,587	303,345	7,351,481	Jan 24, 2019		3,572,893		7,305,868
Feb 01, 2018	432,463	4,778,050	402,411	7,321,429	Jan 31, 2019		3,572,893		7,305,868
Feb 08, 2018	324,692	5,102,742	364,771	7,361,508	Feb 07, 2019		3,572,893		7,305,868
Feb 15, 2018	333,531	5,436,273	399,123	7,427,100	Feb 14, 2019	1,431,483	5,004,376	977,144	6,851,529
Feb 22, 2018	278,682	5,714,955	294,078	7,442,496	Feb 21, 2019	345,654	5,350,030	85,544	6,591,419
Mar 01, 2018	524,187	6,239,142	383,926	7,302,235	Feb 28, 2019	358,976	5,709,006	114,028	6,346,471
Mar 08, 2018	414,403	6,653,545	321,416	7,209,248	Mar 07, 2019	287,001	5,996,007	166,125	6,225,595
Mar 15, 2018	425,093	7,078,638	338,370	7,122,525	Mar 14, 2019	350,146	6,346,153	124,985	6,000,434
Mar 22, 2018	438,357	7,516,995	304,271	6,988,439	Mar 21, 2019				
Mar 29, 2018	452,415	7,969,410	367,567	6,903,591	Mar 28, 2019				
Apr 05, 2018	499,560	8,468,970	179,354	6,583,385	Apr 04, 2019				
Apr 12, 2018	361,952	8,830,922	290,248	6,511,681	Apr 11, 2019				
Apr 19, 2018	421,431	9,252,353	311,973	6,402,223	Apr 18, 2019				
Apr 26, 2018	432,550	9,684,903	189,870	6,159,543	Apr 25, 2019				
May 03, 2018	510,541	10,195,444	193,065	5,842,067	May 02, 2019				
May 10, 2018	420,535	10,615,979	151,070	5,572,602	May 09, 2019				
May 17, 2018	402,955	11,018,934	50,664	5,220,311	May 16, 2019				
May 24, 2018	373,286	11,392,220	16,667	4,863,692	May 23, 2019				
May 31, 2018	576,413	11,968,633	6,792	4,294,071	May 30, 2019				
Jun 07, 2018	459,935	12,428,568	34,819	3,868,955	Jun 06, 2019				
Jun 14, 2018	312,768	12,741,336	-112,393	3,443,794	Jun 13, 2019				
Jun 21, 2018	367,762	13,109,098	-18,884	3,057,148	Jun 20, 2019				
Jun 28, 2018	411,615	13,520,713	17,990	2,663,523	Jun 27, 2019				
Jul 05, 2018	257,409	13,778,122	121,603	2,527,717	Jul 04, 2019				
Jul 12, 2018	227,320	14,005,442	12,935	2,313,332	Jul 11, 2019				
Jul 19, 2018	293,277	14,298,719	2,313	2,022,368	Jul 18, 2019				
Jul 26, 2018	259,093	14,557,812	19,649	1,782,924	Jul 25, 2019				
Aug 02, 2018	272,800	14,830,612	17,526	1,527,650					

Source: Foreign Agricultural Service, U.S. Department of Agriculture (FAS-USDA)

Cottonseed and Products

Cottonseed is crushed to produce both oil and meal. Cottonseed oil is typically used for cooking oil and cottonseed meal is fed to livestock. Before the cottonseed is crushed for oil and meal, it is de-linted of its linters. Linters are used for padding in furniture, absorbent cotton swabs, and for the manufacture of many cellulose products. The sediment left by cottonseed oil refining, called foots, provides fatty acids for industrial products. The value of cottonseeds represents a substantial 18% of a cotton producer's income.

Prices – The average monthly price of cottonseed oil in 2018 fell by -20.7% yr/yr to 30.56 cents per pound, farther below the 2008 record high of 68.09 cents per pound. The average monthly price of cottonseed meal in 2018 rose by +27.1% yr/yr to $266.295 per short ton, but still below the 2014 record high of $368.98 per short ton.

Supply – World production of cottonseed in the 2018/19 marketing year is forecasted to fall -3.8% to 43.392

million metric tons, farther below the 2011-12 record high of 48.007. The world's largest cottonseed producers in 2018/19 are expected to be the European Union with 26.9% of world production, Burma with 24.4%, the U.S. with 12.2%, and Pakistan with 7.4%. U.S. production of cottonseed in the 2018/19 marketing year is expected to fall by -8.8% yr/yr to 5.858 million tons. U.S. production of cottonseed oil in 2018/19 is expected to fall by -0.2% to 560 million pounds, far below the 20-year high of 957 million pounds posted in 2004-05.

Demand – U.S. cottonseed crushed (consumed) in the U.S. in the 2018/19 marketing year is expected to fall -2.9% to 1.800 million tons, which was still far below the levels of over 4 million tons seen in the 1970s.

Trade – U.S. exports of cottonseed in 2018/19 are expected to fall -11.1% to 425 million tons. U.S. imports in 2018/19 are expected to remain at zero.

World Production of Cottonseed   In Thousands of Metric Ton

Crop Year Beginning Oct. 1	Argentina	Australia	Brazil	China	Egypt	Greece	India	Mexico	Pakistan	Turkey	United States	Former USSR	World Total
2010-11	1,299	3,229	179	383	11,953	383	11,420	108	134	3,762	690	5,530	44,182
2011-12	1,676	3,019	220	387	13,325	551	12,185	147	243	4,616	1,050	4,872	47,873
2012-13	1,377	2,019	335	389	13,720	484	12,100	163	246	4,000	870	5,140	46,348
2013-14	1,205	2,671	345	368	12,835	479	13,161	133	241	4,100	740	3,813	45,235
2014-15	664	2,349	373	370	11,757	510	12,525	94	294	4,616	1,050	4,649	44,357
2015-16	881	1,937	304	295	8,600	409	10,996	79	276	3,032	870	3,668	35,759
2016-17	1,250	2,298	362	285	8,800	418	11,463	112	351	3,336	1,050	4,871	39,083
2017-18[1]	1,500	3,019	359	310	10,800	493	12,312	117	382	3,552	1,300	5,826	45,128
2018-19[2]	751	3,601	387	295	10,600	530	11,675	127	396	3,222	1,404	5,314	43,392

[1] Preliminary.   [2] Estimate.   *Source: The Oil World*

Salient Statistics of Cottonseed in the United States   In Thousands of Short Tons

Crop Year Beginning Aug. 1	Stocks	Pro- duction	Imports	Total Supply	Crush	Exports	Other	Total	Farm Price USD/Ton	Value of Pro- duction Mil. USD	Oil (Million Pounds)	Meal (1,000 Short Tons)
				In Thousands of Short Tons								
2010-11	342	6,098	0	6,440	2,563	275	2,984	5,822	161.0	989	835	1,163
2011-12	618	5,370	72	6,059	2,400	133	3,096	5,629	260.0	1,413	755	1,090
2012-13	430	5,666	182	6,278	2,500	191	3,094	5,786	252.0	1,456	800	1,125
2013-14	492	4,203	198	4,893	2,000	219	2,250	4,468	246.0	1,054	630	900
2014-15	425	5,125	60	5,610	1,900	228	3,045	5,173	194.0	1,016	610	855
2015-16	437	4,043	16	4,496	1,500	136	2,469	4,105	227.0	933	465	705
2016-17	391	5,369	51	5,811	1,769	342	3,300	5,411	195.0	1,056	542	805
2017-18[1]	400	6,422	0	6,822	1,854	478	4,040	6,372	139.0	949	561	845
2018-19[2]	450	5,794	0	6,244	1,900	425	3,599	5,924	115-155		590	855

[1] Preliminary.   [2] Estimate.   *Source: Economic Research Service, U.S. Department of Agriculture (ERS-USDA)*

Average Wholesale Price of Cottonseed Meal (41% Solvent)[2] in Memphis   In Dollars Per Short Ton

Year	Jan.	Feb.	Mar.	Apr.	May	June	July	Aug.	Sept.	Oct.	Nov.	Dec.	Average
2010	286.25	253.75	213.00	175.00	171.25	176.00	183.75	198.00	200.00	225.31	235.00	240.63	213.16
2011	245.63	258.75	256.50	240.00	275.50	307.50	313.13	342.50	345.63	255.63	240.50	220.63	275.16
2012	213.00	190.00	225.00	240.63	270.00	294.38	350.50	407.50	393.75	343.00	376.88	345.00	304.14
2013	327.50	279.38	301.88	314.50	311.88	329.38	344.50	330.00	374.38	355.00	345.00	401.88	334.60
2014	378.34	388.75	401.25	405.50	416.88	412.50	359.50	310.00	360.63	346.88	313.13	334.38	368.98
2015	313.75	302.50	310.50	288.13	274.38	281.00	299.38	295.63	293.50	292.50	291.88	267.50	292.55
2016	248.75	238.13	216.50	207.50	242.50	284.00	280.00	280.00	285.00	241.88	221.00	217.50	246.90
2017	223.50	221.88	210.63	195.00	179.50	179.38	200.84	198.50	213.75	229.00	228.75	232.50	209.44
2018[1]	259.00	303.13	323.13	263.13	262.50	257.50	253.13	260.00	258.75	249.00	240.00	243.75	264.42

[1] Preliminary.   *Source: Economic Research Service, U.S. Department of Agriculture (ERS-USDA)*

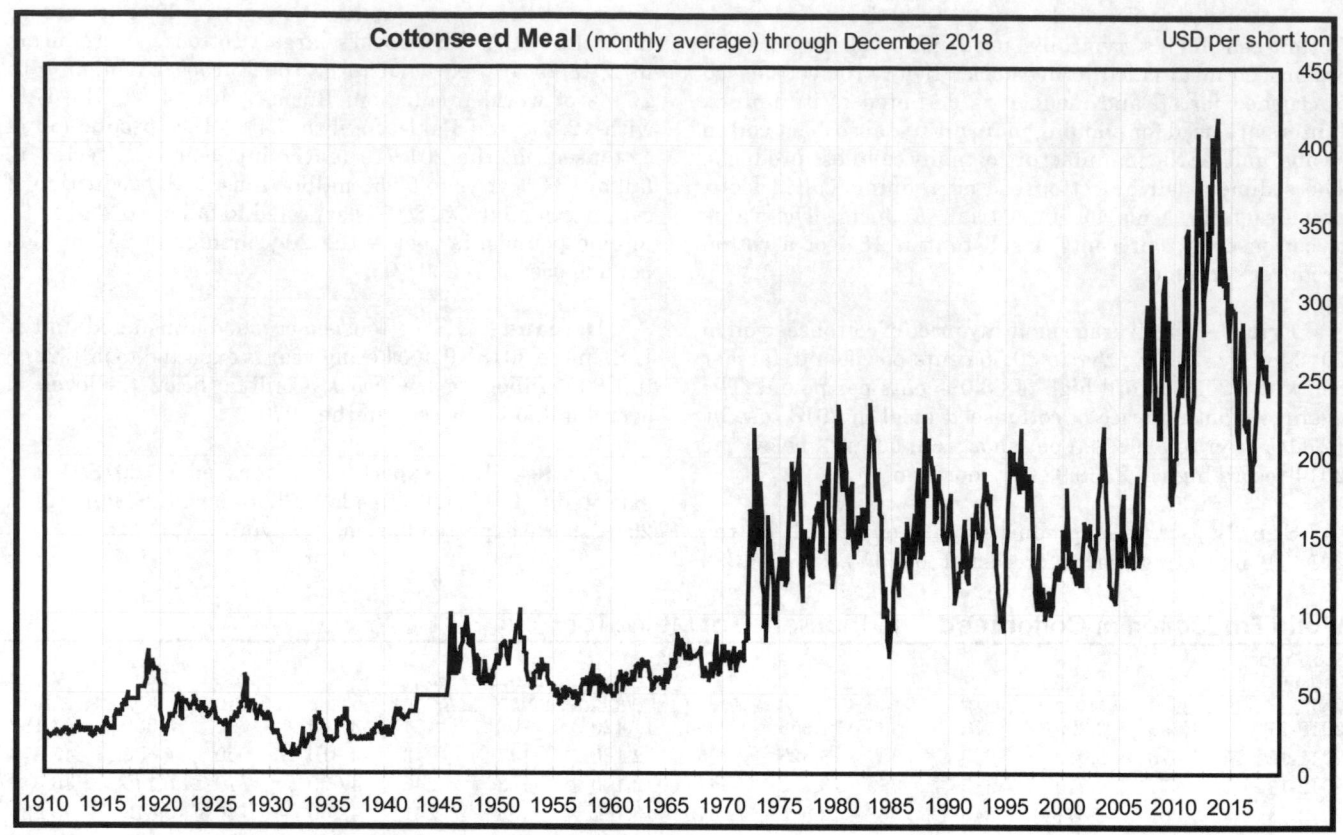

Cottonseed Meal (monthly average) through December 2018 — USD per short ton

Supply and Distribution of Cottonseed Oil in the United States   In Millions of Pounds

Crop Year Beginning Oct. 1	Supply				Disappearance			Per Capita Consumption of Salad & Cooking Oils --- In Lbs. ---	Utilization Food Uses			Prices	
	Stocks	Pro-duction	Imports	Total Supply	Domestic	Exports	Total		Short-ening	Salad & Cooking Oils	Total	U.S.[3] (Crude) --- $/Metric Ton ---	Rott[4] (Cif)
2009-10	121	617	0	738	551	94	646	51	W	509	509	888	895
2010-11	93	835	0	928	599	164	763	54	123	521	644	1,201	1,258
2011-12	165	755	10.0	930	572	259	830	NA	NA	NA	NA	1,173	1,188
2012-13	100	800	20.0	920	599	221	820	----	----	----	----	1,071	1,121
2013-14	100	630	32.0	762	514	148	662	----	----	----	----	1,337	
2014-15	90	610	17.0	717	541	119	659	----	----	----	----	1,008	
2015-16	58	465	7.0	530	433	55	488	----	----	----	----	1,011	
2016-17	42	542	0	583	435	104	539	----	----	----	----	902	
2017-18[1]	44	561	0	605	461	112	573	----	----	----	----	703	
2018-19[2]	32	590	1.0	623	476	115	591	----	----	----	----	706	

[1] Preliminary.   [2] Estimate.   [3] Valley Points FOB; Tank Cars.   [4] Rotterdam; US, PBSY, fob gulf.   W = Withheld.
Source: Economic Research Service, U.S. Department of Agriculture (ERS-USDA)

Exports of Cottonseed Oil (Crude and Refined) from the United States   In Thousands of Pounds

Year	Jan.	Feb.	Mar.	Apr.	May	June	July	Aug.	Sept.	Oct.	Nov.	Dec.	Total
2009	14,423	20,981	15,258	19,313	12,296	14,087	12,070	10,915	11,370	8,506	14,923	8,455	162,597
2010	6,767	9,348	7,075	6,728	6,189	4,234	3,539	5,523	12,740	19,988	16,878	7,038	106,046
2011	8,142	11,103	19,150	17,085	15,053	9,531	11,479	14,273	13,515	25,841	31,753	18,691	195,617
2012	18,551	12,596	31,375	19,626	20,622	24,030	17,908	21,019	16,715	21,956	17,805	15,878	238,080
2013	19,609	20,389	16,582	21,550	21,218	19,340	15,042	15,886	15,406	15,674	13,338	11,094	205,128
2014	13,667	19,061	18,084	20,029	8,709	7,165	2,999	5,895	12,687	12,384	11,780	14,205	146,664
2015	19,843	8,117	10,559	11,852	6,246	6,162	4,005	8,573	4,379	8,700	4,634	6,080	99,149
2016	5,390	1,338	3,211	5,406	4,703	3,031	2,271	5,894	4,168	6,622	15,929	10,107	68,070
2017	10,899	8,438	9,269	8,538	6,577	5,865	5,385	11,003	5,265	7,084	8,038	6,769	93,130
2018[1]	16,387	9,282	10,793	6,797	7,626	6,980	18,567	8,421	4,152	13,262	13,725	4,527	120,518

[1] Preliminary.   *Source: Economic Research Service, U.S. Department of Agriculture (ERS-USDA)*

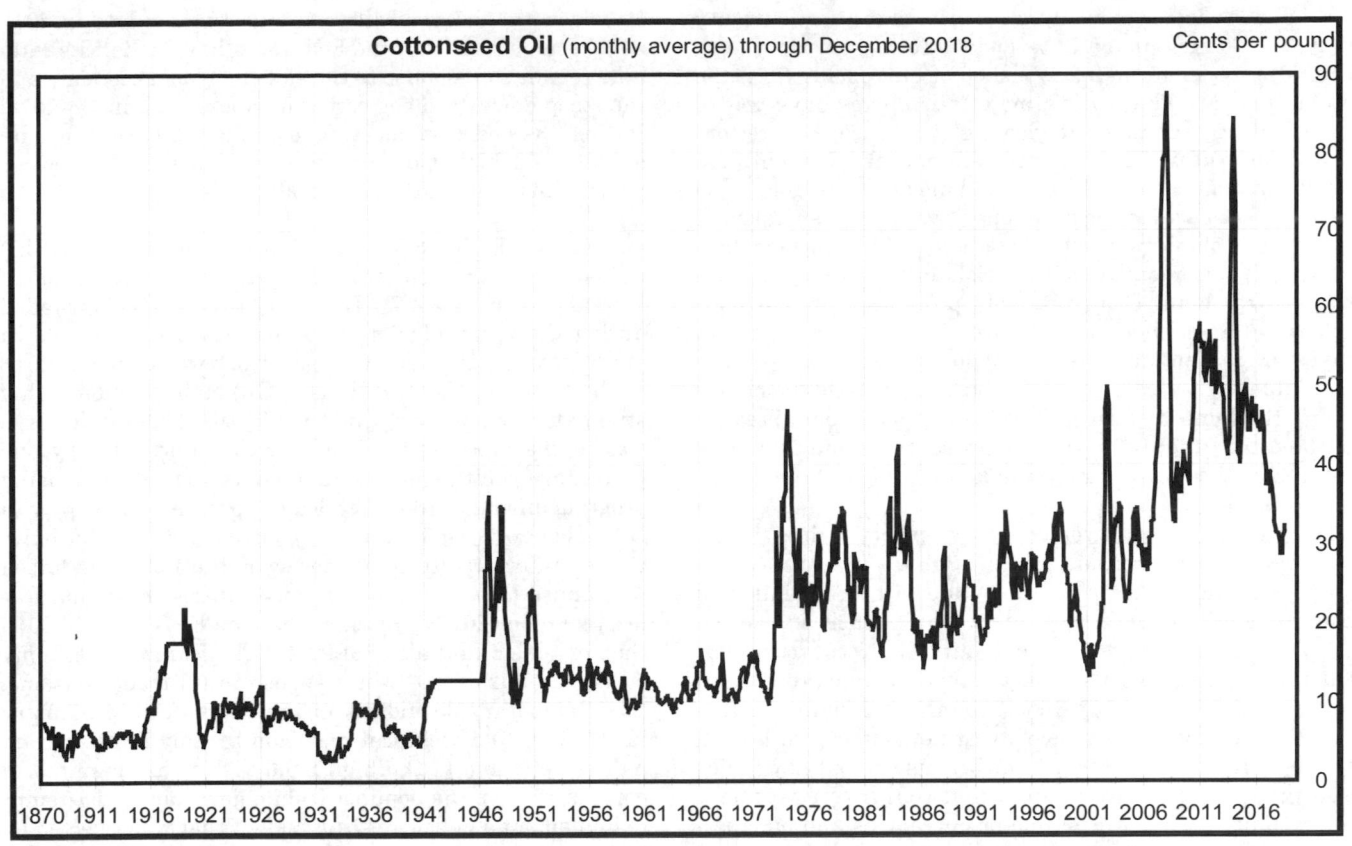

Cottonseed Oil (monthly average) through December 2018 — Cents per pound

Average Price of Crude Cottonseed Oil, PBSY, Greenwood, MS.[1] in Tank Cars   In Cents Per Pound

Year	Jan.	Feb.	Mar.	Apr.	May	June	July	Aug.	Sept.	Oct.	Nov.	Dec.	Average
2009	35.70	33.19	32.63	37.38	39.90	38.75	36.55	39.13	36.44	37.90	40.69	41.40	37.47
2010	39.00	39.13	39.88	38.75	37.38	40.00	42.45	43.69	43.00	47.20	50.75	54.00	42.94
2011	55.92	56.75	55.50	57.70	56.06	55.25	54.75	54.75	55.35	51.56	50.50	51.10	54.60
2012	52.19	54.56	55.95	56.88	52.00	50.05	53.75	54.65	55.50	51.31	49.05	50.06	53.00
2013	50.94	51.56	50.20	49.94	49.75	48.25	46.19	43.10	42.81	41.19	42.05	43.19	46.60
2014	47.10	57.81	69.94	75.00	84.25	83.31	73.15	61.25	49.63	41.45	40.75	40.31	60.33
2015	44.95	48.81	46.06	48.19	48.90	49.94	49.15	46.25	44.13	44.25	45.19	48.35	47.01
2016	47.31	46.06	46.20	47.35	46.06	45.55	44.75	45.25	44.15	44.88	45.81	46.40	45.81
2017	44.56	41.50	39.45	37.56	38.63	38.60	38.88	36.38	38.45	37.06	37.00	34.25	38.63
2018[1]	32.75	31.44	31.35	31.19	31.25	29.90	28.75	28.60	28.88	30.56	31.45	32.06	30.68

[1] Preliminary.   *Source: Economic Research Service, U.S. Department of Agriculture (ERS-USDA)*

Exports of Cottonseed Oil to Important Countries from the United States   In Metric Tons

Year	Canada	Dominican Republic	Egypt	Guate-mala	Japan	Mexico	Nether-lands	El Salvador	Korea, South	Turkey	Venez-uela	Total
2009	36,995.6		----	----	2,569.4	8,667.6	18,061.2	89.6	187.8	----	----	73,753.5
2010	17,573.3		----	----	1,415.9	925.9	25,962.2	----	----	----	----	48,101.9
2011	39,847.8	.8	----	----	----	920.0	45,845.7	----	----	2.8	----	88,730.9
2012	30,697.9	.9	----	----	510.0	----	73,891.0	226.8	----	25.9	----	107,992.2
2013	22,335.7	----	----	----	222.5	35.1	63,532.9	1,169.8	----	321.9	----	93,045.6
2014	11,934.5	----	----	----	2,118.0	----	36,433.4	925.6	----	315.9	----	66,688.9
2015	12,316.0	----	----	134.2	913.4	529.0	24,767.3	466.8	----	67.5	----	44,990.0
2016	3,473.7	----	----	311.2	473.6	512.3	19,599.3	.8	----	.6	----	30,837.0
2017	5,141.1	----	----	206.7	591.0	----	22,013.1	2.3	----	29.1	----	41,770.0
2018[1]	6,230.3	----	3,149.7	----	1,100.6	42.7	17,088.9	----	----	20.3	----	54,666.8

[1] Preliminary.   *Source: Foreign Agricultural Service, U.S. Department of Agriculture (FAS-USDA)*

Currencies

A "currency" rate involves the price of the base currency (e.g., the dollar) quoted in terms of another currency (e.g., the yen), or in terms of a basket of currencies (e.g., the dollar index). The world's major currencies have traded in a floating exchange rate regime ever since the Bretton-Woods international payments system broke down in 1971 when President Nixon broke the dollar's peg to gold. The two key factors affecting a currency's value are central bank monetary policy and the trade balance. An easy monetary policy (low interest rates) is bearish for a currency because the central bank is aggressively pumping new currency reserves into the marketplace and because foreign investors are not attracted to the low interest rate returns available in the country. By contrast, a tight monetary policy (high interest rates) is bullish for a currency because of the tight supply of new currency reserves and attractive interest rate returns for foreign investors.

The other key factor driving currency values is the nation's current account balance. A current account surplus is bullish for a currency due to the net inflow of the currency, while a current account deficit is bearish for a currency due to the net outflow of the currency. Currency values are also affected by economic growth and investment opportunities in the country. A country with a strong economy and lucrative investment opportunities will typically have a strong currency because global companies and investors want to buy into that country's investment opportunities. Futures on major currencies and on cross-currency rates are traded primarily at the CME Group.

Dollar – The dollar index (Barchart.com symbol DXY00) fell to a 4-year low in early 2018 but then rallied through the remainder of the year and closed 2018 up +4.4% yr/yr. The dollar's rally in 2018 was limited and the dollar index was unable to fully recover the 2017 sell-off and indeed remained well below the 16-year high posted in early 2017. The dollar index was supported in 2018 by the strong U.S. economy and by the four interest rate hikes by the Federal Reserve. The U.S. economy in 2018 showed strong GDP growth of +2.9% due to the stimulus from the massive personal and corporate tax cuts that took effect on January 1, 2018. Meanwhile, the Fed during 2018 raised its federal funds rate target by a total of one percentage point to a new range of 2.25%/2.50% by December 2018. That sharp one percentage rate hike, compared with no rate hikes by Europe or Japan, produced a big improvement in the dollar's interest rate differentials, which was a major supportive factor for the dollar index. The Fed also tightened monetary policy during 2018 by reducing the size of its balance sheet, thus tightening liquidity.

However, the dollar's rally ran out of steam late in 2018 as it became clear that the Fed would have to halt its rate-hike regime in response to the slowing global economy and the steep downward correction in stocks seen in Q4-2018. Indeed, the Fed at its meeting in January 2019 dropped its guidance for higher interest rates and moved to a neutral policy, thus undercutting the dollar index.

Euro – EUR/USD (Barchart.com symbol ^EURUSD) posted a 4-year high in early 2018 on an extension of the rally seen in 2017. However, EUR/USD then faded during the remainder of 2018 and closed the year down -4.5% yr/yr. EUR/USD was generally weak during 2018 as the European Central Bank (ECB) maintained a highly stimulative monetary policy while the Federal Reserve was in the process of raising U.S. interest rates by one percentage point. The ECB tapered its quantitative easing program during 2018 and ended the program altogether in December 2018, which was a supportive factor for the euro. On the interest rate front, however, the ECB was forced to promise that it would not raise interest rates until at least summer 2019, a promise that the ECB in early 2019 then extended to the end of 2019. The Eurozone economy weakened during 2018 in response to (1) trade tensions, (2) a temporary downdraft in the German auto industry in Q3, and (3) a technical recession in Italy in the second half of 2018 due to the high bond yields that resulted in early 2018 from the populist Italian government's attempt to implement a deficit-busting budget that was rejected by the European Commission.

Yen – USD/JPY (Barchart.com symbol ^USDJPY) fell to a 2-year low in early 2018 but then recovered to close the year down -2.6% yr/yr, meaning that the yen closed the year up +2.6% against the dollar. The yen showed weakness in 2018 from April through September since the Bank of Japan maintained its extraordinarily easy monetary policy all during 2018 while the Federal Reserve raised interest rates. The Bank of Japan during 2018 continued the policy it adopted in September 2016 of yield-curve control (YCC) where it targeted the 10-year Japanese government bond (JGB) yield near zero and its short-term policy rate at -0.1%. The yen therefore suffered from very poor interest rate differentials against the dollar all year. However, the BOJ did engage in some stealth tapering of its bond-buying program since not as much bond buying was necessary to keep the 10-year JGB yield near its target of zero, which was a supportive factor for the yen. The yen was also supported late in 2018 by some flight-to-quality buying as the global stock markets took a steep dive in late 2018.

BRITISH POUND - CME
Weekly Selected Futures as of 03/29/2019

WEEKLY SELECTED FUTURES
As of 03/29/2019

Chart High 1.7184 on 07/15/2014
Chart Low   1.2001 on 01/17/2017

Nearby Futures through Last Trading Day.

U.S. Dollars per British Pound

Year	Jan.	Feb.	Mar.	Apr.	May	June	July	Aug.	Sept.	Oct.	Nov.	Dec.	Average
2009	1.4484	1.4417	1.4197	1.4727	1.5460	1.6379	1.6387	1.6532	1.6312	1.6196	1.6610	1.6230	1.5661
2010	1.6160	1.5621	1.5059	1.5337	1.4658	1.4758	1.5302	1.5652	1.5575	1.5858	1.5953	1.5599	1.5461
2011	1.5789	1.6137	1.6158	1.6385	1.6338	1.6219	1.6150	1.6359	1.5776	1.5773	1.5799	1.5587	1.6039
2012	1.5522	1.5806	1.5829	1.6009	1.5909	1.5556	1.5598	1.5718	1.6113	1.6073	1.5964	1.6144	1.5854
2013	1.5961	1.5468	1.5083	1.5309	1.5287	1.5498	1.5184	1.5505	1.5875	1.6089	1.6112	1.6383	1.5646
2014	1.6468	1.6566	1.6617	1.6747	1.6841	1.6916	1.7075	1.6700	1.6303	1.6077	1.5773	1.5631	1.6476
2015	1.5139	1.5334	1.4969	1.4960	1.5454	1.5586	1.5558	1.5581	1.5334	1.5335	1.5193	1.4984	1.5286
2016	1.4387	1.4309	1.4256	1.4315	1.4523	1.4210	1.3145	1.3103	1.3148	1.2336	1.2441	1.2471	1.3554
2017	1.2351	1.2487	1.2348	1.2643	1.2923	1.2812	1.2999	1.2956	1.3317	1.3202	1.3232	1.3405	1.2890
2018	1.3828	1.3962	1.3976	1.4070	1.3462	1.3285	1.3169	1.2879	1.3057	1.3011	1.2896	1.2663	1.3355

Average. Source: FOREX

Volume of Trading of British Pound Futures in Chicago   In Thousands of Contracts

Year	Jan.	Feb.	Mar.	Apr.	May	June	July	Aug.	Sept.	Oct.	Nov.	Dec.	Total
2009	1,446.3	1,457.1	1,721.8	1,509.2	1,736.4	2,609.0	2,127.0	2,126.5	2,644.3	2,864.8	2,389.1	2,222.4	24,853.8
2010	2,258.4	2,538.3	3,253.0	2,367.8	3,139.4	2,906.1	2,170.7	2,349.4	2,541.7	2,305.1	2,299.2	2,091.1	30,220.2
2011	2,520.0	2,519.3	2,933.2	2,170.3	2,578.2	2,683.0	2,159.4	2,348.8	2,732.7	2,313.8	2,015.5	2,054.4	29,028.8
2012	1,688.5	2,010.0	2,445.6	2,058.2	2,510.7	2,495.4	2,189.7	2,168.2	2,372.3	2,133.3	1,941.9	2,152.6	26,166.3
2013	2,460.2	2,647.5	2,948.2	2,172.0	2,678.5	3,067.9	2,504.8	2,298.1	2,348.2	2,002.0	1,936.9	2,173.5	29,237.8
2014	2,123.0	2,139.8	2,315.4	1,415.6	1,592.2	2,547.6	1,728.8	1,781.2	3,181.2	2,283.2	1,740.6	1,988.2	24,837.0
2015	2,024.6	1,677.7	2,854.7	1,918.6	2,234.4	2,374.3	1,744.8	2,048.9	2,139.5	1,635.5	1,506.4	1,985.3	24,144.7
2016	1,919.1	2,025.0	2,574.4	1,967.0	1,953.3	4,034.0	2,337.1	1,855.1	2,559.9	2,714.9	2,678.6	2,507.8	29,126.0
2017	2,491.4	1,975.1	3,110.3	2,009.6	2,313.0	3,147.8	1,991.9	2,124.7	3,406.7	2,570.9	2,940.8	3,085.7	31,167.9
2018	2,930.4	2,739.3	3,020.1	2,256.6	2,838.9	3,023.7	2,501.4	2,318.6	2,974.4	2,407.6	2,873.0	2,555.1	32,439.0

Contract size = 62,500 GBP.   Source: CME Group; Chicago Mercantile Exchange (CME)

Average Open Interest of British Pound Futures in Chicago   In Contracts

Year	Jan.	Feb.	Mar.	Apr.	May	June	July	Aug.	Sept.	Oct.	Nov.	Dec.
2009	81,141	84,191	88,354	82,933	91,683	92,365	90,994	98,358	88,658	104,344	96,882	83,847
2010	86,016	116,480	136,357	122,843	145,514	136,099	126,486	138,872	97,056	89,011	95,465	80,042
2011	92,434	118,770	118,434	114,166	111,901	103,047	106,501	100,953	142,668	174,087	162,814	206,391
2012	198,201	190,107	167,722	159,541	191,394	150,584	115,951	115,580	166,427	165,761	156,794	188,125
2013	165,256	184,350	248,526	201,357	202,681	172,212	145,625	145,596	167,475	181,110	186,634	226,964
2014	207,609	232,142	231,703	226,479	236,374	262,034	246,579	231,599	184,224	135,955	160,534	165,669
2015	178,585	173,893	187,709	180,094	179,361	174,693	167,418	168,889	163,232	155,414	169,080	191,263
2016	252,441	261,454	274,786	240,358	242,020	225,029	231,642	245,379	247,713	259,915	250,809	229,322
2017	223,750	212,997	257,227	252,578	258,691	226,183	199,970	215,422	220,244	182,430	180,126	203,247
2018	220,399	202,010	190,552	186,782	193,666	210,213	186,764	243,357	252,436	216,670	227,938	229,210

Contract size = 62,500 GBP.   Source: CME Group; Chicago Mercantile Exchange (CME)

CURRENCIES

CANADIAN DOLLAR - CME
Weekly Selected Futures as of 03/29/2019

WEEKLY SELECTED FUTURES
As of 03/29/2019
Chart High 1.06170 on 07/26/2011
Chart Low .68090 on 01/20/2016

Nearby Futures through Last Trading Day.

Canadian Dollars per U.S. Dollar

Year	Jan.	Feb.	Mar.	Apr.	May	June	July	Aug.	Sept.	Oct.	Nov.	Dec.	Average
2009	1.2244	1.2449	1.2638	1.2244	1.1502	1.1274	1.1225	1.0878	1.0812	1.0547	1.0587	1.0558	1.1413
2010	1.0435	1.0561	1.0233	1.0052	1.0415	1.0397	1.0433	1.0408	1.0335	1.0180	1.0128	1.0081	1.0305
2011	0.9939	0.9875	0.9767	0.9574	0.9682	0.9771	0.9558	0.9814	1.0023	1.0201	1.0253	1.0238	0.9891
2012	1.0132	0.9970	0.9934	0.9929	1.0106	1.0275	1.0137	0.9930	0.9788	0.9872	0.9969	0.9899	0.9995
2013	0.9919	1.0094	1.0240	1.0185	1.0206	1.0315	1.0404	1.0404	1.0354	1.0367	1.0488	1.0637	1.0301
2014	1.0947	1.1054	1.1106	1.0992	1.0890	1.0825	1.0734	1.0922	1.1007	1.1214	1.1332	1.1542	1.1047
2015	1.2128	1.2500	1.2610	1.2338	1.2183	1.2354	1.2851	1.3144	1.3270	1.3071	1.3275	1.3710	1.2786
2016	1.4229	1.3790	1.3212	1.2814	1.2949	1.2890	1.3037	1.3000	1.3091	1.3247	1.3446	1.3351	1.3255
2017	1.3206	1.3110	1.3382	1.3435	1.3597	1.3293	1.2698	1.2608	1.2295	1.2599	1.2766	1.2767	1.2980
2018	1.2432	1.2586	1.2930	1.2729	1.2867	1.3129	1.3133	1.3036	1.3033	1.3014	1.3205	1.3447	1.2962

Average.   Source: FOREX

Volume of Trading of Canadian Dollar Futures in Chicago   In Thousands of Contracts

Year	Jan.	Feb.	Mar.	Apr.	May	June	July	Aug.	Sept.	Oct.	Nov.	Dec.	Total
2009	625.5	685.7	1,040.2	964.4	1,222.0	1,691.7	1,318.6	1,319.2	1,644.8	1,626.3	1,569.5	1,773.2	15,481.2
2010	1,391.4	1,623.9	1,989.7	1,742.0	2,329.7	2,120.7	1,774.7	1,839.7	1,905.7	1,841.7	1,889.4	1,635.3	22,083.8
2011	1,477.5	1,505.0	2,143.4	1,403.3	1,943.9	2,213.2	1,557.3	2,545.8	2,479.4	2,000.8	1,624.9	1,522.3	22,416.7
2012	1,441.3	1,790.3	2,203.3	1,812.6	2,260.5	2,546.9	1,947.1	1,871.8	2,213.3	1,713.8	1,467.8	1,530.9	22,799.4
2013	1,472.2	1,439.5	1,815.4	1,502.0	1,770.9	1,891.0	1,434.3	1,327.6	1,256.7	1,077.0	986.0	1,455.2	17,427.8
2014	1,495.5	1,064.6	1,572.7	903.8	917.2	1,253.6	1,064.6	1,057.9	1,612.2	1,569.7	1,191.6	1,393.1	15,096.5
2015	1,371.7	1,298.8	1,881.8	1,394.8	1,170.1	1,595.7	1,447.1	1,477.1	1,710.6	1,283.7	1,040.4	1,630.2	17,301.9
2016	1,794.8	1,487.2	1,748.1	1,481.8	1,476.4	1,665.3	1,240.5	1,408.3	1,860.5	1,507.1	1,614.2	1,413.1	18,697.3
2017	1,405.8	1,093.9	1,726.1	1,277.3	1,559.2	2,136.4	1,641.9	1,517.9	2,143.3	1,559.1	1,420.4	1,741.3	19,222.5
2018	1,721.5	1,622.3	2,110.0	1,530.7	1,964.4	2,133.5	1,410.3	1,639.3	1,688.7	1,667.5	1,544.8	1,986.5	21,019.4

Contract size = 100,000 CAD.   Source: CME Group; Chicago Mercantile Exchange (CME)

Average Open Interest of Canadian Dollar Futures in Chicago   In Contracts

Year	Jan.	Feb.	Mar.	Apr.	May	June	July	Aug.	Sept.	Oct.	Nov.	Dec.
2009	59,962	70,940	70,863	63,119	83,214	88,873	87,203	98,521	91,989	97,587	89,022	94,758
2010	106,475	92,349	143,969	148,414	125,802	102,117	87,121	100,655	101,319	113,964	116,126	110,800
2011	123,984	139,328	141,949	141,548	124,951	108,081	118,209	111,898	102,180	118,239	127,296	143,821
2012	119,930	126,823	147,325	128,867	141,093	120,545	101,536	134,628	225,238	185,312	168,662	167,449
2013	142,358	161,037	216,418	167,325	145,528	128,346	126,955	115,698	127,754	114,266	121,783	158,005
2014	159,815	152,844	144,262	119,310	123,899	117,918	125,230	111,259	91,900	100,526	106,812	106,069
2015	108,171	115,078	124,649	120,477	120,938	101,560	143,112	167,447	148,706	121,352	137,170	164,083
2016	165,688	157,798	129,610	111,929	124,671	127,872	117,139	122,876	115,488	105,483	122,002	102,506
2017	98,335	125,839	131,989	145,292	209,032	184,268	169,578	192,761	210,929	173,057	147,137	136,029
2018	158,422	156,598	142,004	125,633	132,447	160,264	154,993	145,448	136,094	119,192	130,139	163,042

Contract size = 100,000 CAD.   Source: CME Group; Chicago Mercantile Exchange (CME)

EURO FX - CME
Weekly Selected Futures as of 03/29/2019

WEEKLY SELECTED FUTURES
As of 03/29/2019

Chart High 1.5144 on 11/25/2009
Chart Low 1.0368 on 12/15/2016

Nearby Futures through Last Trading Day.

Euro per U.S. Dollar

Year	Jan.	Feb.	Mar.	Apr.	May	June	July	Aug.	Sept.	Oct.	Nov.	Dec.	Average
2009	1.3253	1.2805	1.3074	1.3207	1.3675	1.4014	1.4087	1.4267	1.4565	1.4817	1.4926	1.4577	1.3939
2010	1.4270	1.3681	1.3574	1.3427	1.2536	1.2212	1.2803	1.2899	1.3092	1.3899	1.3640	1.3227	1.3272
2011	1.3374	1.3661	1.4018	1.4472	1.4324	1.4400	1.4289	1.4339	1.3754	1.3727	1.3551	1.3148	1.3921
2012	1.2910	1.3238	1.3213	1.3164	1.2788	1.2546	1.2293	1.2403	1.2873	1.2969	1.2837	1.3124	1.2863
2013	1.3306	1.3340	1.2956	1.3025	1.2978	1.3202	1.3090	1.3320	1.3362	1.3638	1.3496	1.3704	1.3285
2014	1.3616	1.3669	1.3827	1.3811	1.3733	1.3600	1.3538	1.3315	1.2895	1.2680	1.2474	1.2307	1.3289
2015	1.1605	1.1352	1.0830	1.0817	1.1157	1.1237	1.0997	1.1144	1.1236	1.1218	1.0728	1.0896	1.1101
2016	1.0868	1.1106	1.1143	1.1339	1.1298	1.1241	1.1065	1.1205	1.1214	1.1023	1.0786	1.0538	1.1069
2017	1.0630	1.0640	1.0688	1.0718	1.1057	1.1238	1.1531	1.1820	1.1906	1.1757	1.1745	1.1835	1.1297
2018	1.2202	1.2345	1.2339	1.2274	1.1814	1.1675	1.1686	1.1548	1.1661	1.1483	1.1363	1.1377	1.1814

Average.   Source: FOREX

Volume of Trading of Euro FX Futures in Chicago   In Thousands of Contracts

Year	Jan.	Feb.	Mar.	Apr.	May	June	July	Aug.	Sept.	Oct.	Nov.	Dec.	Total
2009	3,574.5	3,903.4	4,564.5	3,155.7	3,758.9	5,261.4	4,675.6	4,220.4	5,123.9	5,429.9	5,419.9	5,305.7	54,393.6
2010	5,407.6	6,439.6	7,562.4	7,157.1	9,578.8	7,913.1	6,006.4	6,418.2	7,294.2	7,476.0	8,241.8	6,737.2	86,232.4
2011	7,402.8	6,451.9	7,437.7	5,453.1	7,657.0	7,504.8	6,906.8	8,061.0	8,376.7	7,008.3	6,638.4	5,338.4	84,236.8
2012	5,611.6	5,984.0	6,055.0	4,864.4	6,510.0	7,165.7	5,311.9	5,059.1	5,927.6	5,197.0	5,281.1	4,440.5	67,407.7
2013	5,675.6	6,088.9	6,391.7	5,480.1	6,055.8	5,970.9	5,093.7	4,390.9	4,120.9	3,988.5	4,047.7	3,981.0	61,285.6
2014	4,422.1	3,733.1	4,781.4	3,046.6	3,338.3	4,261.9	3,048.4	3,507.4	6,106.3	5,900.3	4,564.9	5,497.7	52,208.3
2015	5,560.3	3,639.7	7,724.4	5,745.4	5,549.4	6,980.8	4,666.0	5,245.6	5,468.3	4,455.2	4,243.0	6,077.9	65,356.1
2016	4,077.1	4,559.6	5,453.9	3,688.1	3,192.6	4,996.0	2,734.2	2,994.6	4,677.7	3,357.0	4,596.8	5,128.3	49,455.9
2017	4,328.4	3,667.0	5,810.9	3,353.5	4,129.2	5,345.8	4,449.8	4,681.0	5,929.7	4,704.7	4,593.7	5,462.1	56,455.8
2018	6,129.6	4,985.2	6,336.2	4,410.2	7,312.1	7,459.5	4,527.2	6,009.6	6,216.1	5,419.0	4,626.7	5,353.7	68,785.1

Contract size = 125,000 EUR.   Source: CME Group; Chicago Mercantile Exchange (CME)

Average Open Interest of Euro FX Futures in Chicago   In Contracts

Year	Jan.	Feb.	Mar.	Apr.	May	June	July	Aug.	Sept.	Oct.	Nov.	Dec.
2009	127,134	156,321	141,863	110,261	124,438	130,793	129,062	133,469	156,493	168,629	169,331	155,488
2010	169,083	199,832	211,780	216,500	285,206	251,763	226,656	242,448	198,817	203,635	198,138	172,703
2011	190,755	202,950	225,190	244,014	257,695	222,331	184,688	178,500	231,100	228,018	251,778	297,070
2012	301,627	288,301	275,581	277,812	349,794	369,192	321,319	318,368	276,124	220,770	225,676	217,375
2013	214,230	236,476	211,778	220,576	242,334	232,139	217,712	237,132	250,358	270,275	239,030	258,190
2014	251,507	285,722	289,786	266,980	270,902	302,019	322,167	390,128	429,750	434,763	467,267	427,194
2015	430,963	443,172	477,046	453,055	436,488	388,813	358,550	366,585	340,638	357,347	432,251	432,591
2016	402,675	425,594	367,707	340,746	352,037	344,370	380,293	367,126	350,287	403,624	430,112	425,424
2017	413,834	410,809	414,949	414,920	429,990	435,606	439,731	464,075	459,095	444,328	467,275	505,655
2018	587,907	576,878	540,887	501,746	521,277	539,601	491,694	522,487	503,058	486,553	526,379	541,129

Contract size = 125,000 EUR.   Source: CME Group; Chicago Mercantile Exchange (CME)

CURRENCIES

Nearby Futures through Last Trading Day.

Japanese Yen per U.S. Dollar

Year	Jan.	Feb.	Mar.	Apr.	May	June	July	Aug.	Sept.	Oct.	Nov.	Dec.	Average
2009	90.33	92.86	97.74	98.94	96.49	96.67	94.46	94.90	91.40	90.32	89.12	89.99	93.60
2010	91.13	90.17	90.71	93.49	91.88	90.81	87.56	85.38	84.38	81.79	82.58	83.23	87.76
2011	82.61	82.57	81.65	83.18	81.14	80.47	79.29	77.05	76.88	76.68	77.54	77.83	79.74
2012	76.93	78.60	82.54	81.28	79.69	79.36	78.98	78.68	78.16	79.00	81.04	83.86	79.84
2013	89.19	93.11	94.88	97.75	100.97	97.30	99.64	97.80	99.18	97.85	100.12	103.55	97.61
2014	103.80	102.12	102.34	102.51	101.83	102.07	101.75	102.97	107.37	108.03	116.37	119.42	105.88
2015	118.27	118.75	120.36	119.52	120.85	123.67	123.31	123.04	120.08	120.15	122.63	121.63	121.02
2016	118.20	114.63	112.94	109.58	109.00	105.46	104.08	101.31	101.84	103.85	108.63	116.12	108.80
2017	114.94	112.98	112.90	110.05	112.23	110.96	112.37	109.85	110.81	112.93	112.82	112.92	112.14
2018	110.89	107.87	106.09	107.62	109.69	110.13	111.48	111.04	112.04	112.77	113.35	112.25	110.43

Average.   Source: FOREX

Volume of Trading of Japanese Yen Futures in Chicago   In Thousands of Contracts

Year	Jan.	Feb.	Mar.	Apr.	May	June	July	Aug.	Sept.	Oct.	Nov.	Dec.	Total
2009	1,644.2	1,802.9	1,796.0	1,469.3	1,600.9	1,932.6	2,061.8	1,924.0	2,260.9	2,157.6	1,916.7	2,182.7	22,749.6
2010	2,321.3	2,382.1	2,664.8	2,397.2	3,481.7	3,094.9	2,712.4	2,591.6	3,065.3	2,171.1	2,484.6	2,495.8	31,862.8
2011	2,542.6	2,572.2	3,764.0	2,438.4	2,297.9	2,563.3	2,023.5	2,701.8	2,393.6	2,135.9	1,425.0	1,510.9	28,369.1
2012	1,445.7	1,772.5	2,609.4	1,752.1	1,820.9	2,037.7	1,397.4	1,721.5	2,223.2	1,912.0	2,189.4	2,638.8	23,520.6
2013	3,831.3	4,175.7	3,820.2	4,510.5	4,431.7	5,387.8	2,849.1	2,885.5	3,045.1	2,564.9	2,379.8	2,880.5	42,762.3
2014	3,335.1	2,865.2	3,324.4	2,335.1	2,285.1	2,615.9	2,143.3	2,335.6	3,904.6	4,728.3	3,791.3	4,655.9	38,319.8
2015	4,041.9	2,593.2	3,160.9	2,462.5	2,548.1	3,539.0	2,236.0	3,410.2	3,926.7	2,985.0	2,201.2	3,075.8	36,180.5
2016	3,637.8	3,997.1	3,022.3	2,736.8	2,141.9	3,547.6	2,632.9	2,225.8	3,262.3	2,343.2	3,889.4	3,151.8	36,588.8
2017	3,844.0	2,739.9	4,044.3	2,989.3	3,355.7	3,767.5	2,819.8	3,398.4	4,610.2	3,425.4	3,496.3	3,132.6	41,623.4
2018	3,479.6	3,457.9	3,574.2	2,600.7	3,248.2	3,097.7	2,775.9	2,522.3	2,585.9	3,624.0	2,707.5	3,305.4	36,979.3

Contract size = 12,500,000 JPY.   Source: CME Group; Chicago Mercantile Exchange (CME)

Average Open Interest of Japanese Yen Futures in Chicago   In Contracts

Year	Jan.	Feb.	Mar.	Apr.	May	June	July	Aug.	Sept.	Oct.	Nov.	Dec.
2009	112,194	108,893	90,828	79,142	86,624	81,378	95,456	80,087	119,014	118,478	123,821	110,809
2010	116,578	121,216	117,096	131,315	143,384	111,812	129,460	135,623	130,539	142,646	133,612	111,840
2011	112,265	119,793	118,104	123,251	102,290	101,702	121,491	128,615	135,195	151,744	147,224	168,945
2012	162,827	160,215	161,521	145,491	143,219	151,494	127,493	147,320	152,104	136,446	176,769	226,165
2013	203,930	217,961	246,456	211,493	222,136	199,960	182,942	168,128	184,355	160,423	204,490	251,937
2014	217,565	201,386	190,296	174,544	163,960	170,679	163,460	202,088	234,084	205,740	233,431	252,694
2015	218,141	204,791	206,382	190,770	217,291	275,725	249,546	259,312	213,125	181,162	237,763	217,541
2016	243,541	246,520	196,787	171,510	161,320	155,959	156,403	163,674	156,868	157,987	177,739	247,079
2017	206,164	203,979	208,760	199,364	209,490	199,979	238,520	221,773	210,652	262,262	270,180	240,954
2018	242,152	261,583	232,642	151,792	163,587	159,871	195,077	189,113	204,846	225,418	222,065	225,312

Contract size = 12,500,000 JPY.   Source: CME Group; Chicago Mercantile Exchange (CME)

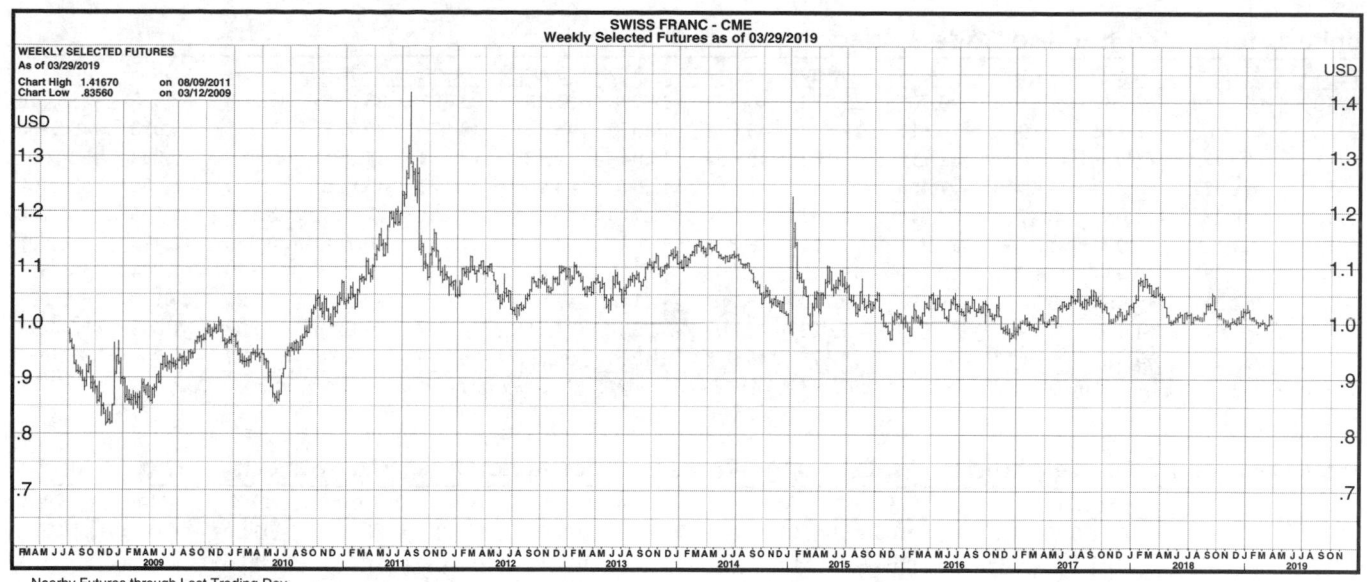

SWISS FRANC - CME
Weekly Selected Futures as of 03/29/2019

WEEKLY SELECTED FUTURES
As of 03/29/2019

Chart High 1.41670 on 08/09/2011
Chart Low .83560 on 03/12/2009

Nearby Futures through Last Trading Day.

Swiss Francs per U.S. Dollar

Year	Jan.	Feb.	Mar.	Apr.	May	June	July	Aug.	Sept.	Oct.	Nov.	Dec.	Average
2009	1.1280	1.1635	1.1540	1.1472	1.1057	1.0810	1.0784	1.0677	1.0399	1.0218	1.0117	1.0304	1.0858
2010	1.0341	1.0719	1.0660	1.0682	1.1325	1.1263	1.0531	1.0392	1.0012	0.9688	0.9852	0.9671	1.0428
2011	0.9567	0.9495	0.9187	0.8964	0.8733	0.8404	0.8221	0.7810	0.8734	0.8963	0.9086	0.9335	0.8875
2012	0.9377	0.9119	0.9129	0.9131	0.9397	0.9574	0.9771	0.9685	0.9394	0.9327	0.9388	0.9212	0.9375
2013	0.9243	0.9215	0.9465	0.9368	0.9564	0.9330	0.9446	0.9255	0.9232	0.9032	0.9126	0.8937	0.9268
2014	0.9039	0.8934	0.8805	0.8830	0.8888	0.8955	0.8977	0.9100	0.9367	0.9526	0.9641	0.9769	0.9152
2015	0.9412	0.9361	0.9796	0.9602	0.9325	0.9309	0.9544	0.9685	0.9723	0.9697	1.0099	0.9938	0.9624
2016	1.0070	0.9916	0.9809	0.9642	0.9792	0.9691	0.9820	0.9716	0.9737	0.9872	0.9969	1.0201	0.9853
2017	1.0079	1.0017	1.0022	1.0007	0.9863	0.9678	0.9602	0.9653	0.9626	0.9820	0.9913	0.9869	0.9846
2018	0.9605	0.9346	0.9478	0.9686	0.9972	0.9901	0.9945	0.9879	0.9682	0.9940	1.0009	0.9922	0.9780

Average.   Source: FOREX

Volume of Trading of Swiss Franc Futures in Chicago   In Thousands of Contracts

Year	Jan.	Feb.	Mar.	Apr.	May	June	July	Aug.	Sept.	Oct.	Nov.	Dec.	Total
2009	677.7	624.5	813.9	641.5	731.2	1,094.1	844.8	727.0	1,015.2	1,098.5	1,206.6	1,143.5	10,618.6
2010	1,046.8	954.5	1,218.2	1,105.8	1,299.4	1,066.8	813.5	806.1	997.7	847.7	940.4	914.3	12,011.2
2011	848.8	1,025.6	1,266.4	827.0	928.5	1,074.6	936.2	1,098.0	643.1	539.6	489.5	561.4	10,238.7
2012	552.9	773.9	1,034.3	865.2	1,140.5	1,163.6	870.0	855.3	827.8	623.8	599.5	604.6	9,911.3
2013	767.5	643.9	860.4	696.4	1,085.0	938.7	805.1	677.3	688.4	711.0	632.6	705.7	9,061.8
2014	714.1	552.0	819.7	535.8	607.3	792.8	721.4	758.5	1,121.3	1,026.6	834.4	1,154.9	9,638.9
2015	752.0	244.8	537.2	472.1	421.0	513.2	379.8	433.0	433.6	381.7	458.4	607.8	5,634.4
2016	406.6	559.6	531.2	399.3	393.9	650.6	328.1	418.4	596.9	454.4	604.0	625.8	5,968.8
2017	474.3	372.0	598.5	391.8	645.0	638.1	603.4	687.9	772.9	551.5	527.2	715.5	6,978.1
2018	712.9	521.6	651.2	504.3	626.3	699.4	502.7	633.4	709.1	564.5	483.6	653.0	7,262.1

Contract size = 125,000 CHF.   Source: CME Group; Chicago Mercantile Exchange (CME)

Average Open Interest of Swiss Franc Futures in Chicago   In Contracts

Year	Jan.	Feb.	Mar.	Apr.	May	June	July	Aug.	Sept.	Oct.	Nov.	Dec.
2009	26,083	32,701	33,518	28,613	34,585	40,027	35,918	39,324	49,537	51,736	52,912	41,890
2010	36,523	41,531	36,834	38,093	49,842	48,989	52,203	55,870	58,484	53,703	45,087	44,460
2011	42,658	46,656	62,300	65,373	70,315	61,349	50,716	20,516	33,972	25,587	29,848	44,100
2012	40,696	48,122	50,263	40,932	59,311	68,970	60,351	56,214	47,686	36,825	43,328	47,914
2013	42,982	44,119	58,519	49,385	59,413	47,741	36,890	38,631	39,298	51,347	45,586	53,657
2014	42,329	48,122	56,682	47,081	49,564	42,368	38,273	52,798	61,701	58,348	60,929	63,108
2015	54,230	35,769	42,525	32,785	32,615	26,518	26,717	40,075	40,143	37,866	64,828	62,677
2016	50,939	51,074	43,286	40,453	46,929	48,028	42,074	42,193	43,527	58,626	57,887	63,292
2017	48,235	47,924	48,104	45,251	49,672	45,409	40,566	40,367	41,027	56,027	80,732	88,812
2018	72,099	71,614	56,365	60,123	100,513	102,678	91,755	89,149	66,738	65,735	78,129	79,614

Contract size = 125,000 CHF.   Source: CME Group; Chicago Mercantile Exchange (CME)

CURRENCIES

United States Merchandise Trade Balance[2] In Millions of Dollars

Year	Jan.	Feb.	Mar.	Apr.	May	June	July	Aug.	Sept.	Oct.	Nov.	Dec.	Total
2009	-37,842	-27,767	-29,162	-29,705	-25,372	-26,367	-32,790	-31,267	-34,491	-33,826	-37,203	-37,983	-383,775
2010	-37,302	-41,116	-39,848	-40,817	-41,347	-46,644	-40,670	-45,011	-43,876	-39,737	-37,842	-41,015	-495,225
2011	-47,352	-44,068	-43,621	-42,173	-47,163	-49,505	-45,943	-44,984	-43,744	-44,974	-46,888	-49,283	-549,698
2012	-51,077	-43,675	-50,088	-47,406	-45,786	-43,536	-43,570	-44,280	-40,127	-43,032	-46,700	-38,132	-537,409
2013	-41,288	-42,039	-35,741	-38,714	-42,687	-35,764	-37,710	-38,253	-41,461	-37,615	-35,158	-34,705	-461,135
2014	-39,113	-41,093	-41,656	-44,271	-40,941	-39,878	-39,909	-37,906	-41,768	-40,762	-39,856	-42,429	-489,582
2015	-41,037	-35,934	-48,737	-40,519	-38,746	-42,208	-40,705	-44,463	-42,363	-41,769	-40,439	-41,605	-498,525
2016	-42,217	-45,695	-37,350	-38,192	-40,170	-43,737	-41,136	-41,635	-39,000	-42,644	-46,127	-44,100	-502,003
2017	-46,879	-44,171	-43,909	-46,074	-45,823	-44,803	-44,221	-44,163	-44,407	-46,986	-48,952	-51,889	-552,277
2018[1]	-53,158	-55,787	-47,517	-46,521	-43,578	-46,978	-51,240	-54,509	-55,379	-56,304	-50,297	-59,769	-621,037

[1] Preliminary. [2] Not seasonally adjusted. Source: Bureau of Economic Analysis, U.S. Department of Commerce (BEA)

Index of Real Trade-Weighted Dollar Exchange Rates for Total Agriculture[3] (U.S. Markets) (2000 = 100)

Year	Jan.	Feb.	Mar.	Apr.	May	June	July	Aug.	Sept.	Oct.	Nov.	Dec.
2009	108.0	111.0	112.5	109.2	106.3	106.2	105.5	104.3	103.6	102.0	101.5	101.3
2010	101.0	101.7	100.7	100.0	102.2	102.5	101.3	100.3	99.4	96.8	96.7	97.2
2011	96.3	95.9	95.6	94.7	94.8	94.8	93.8	94.6	96.6	97.2	97.2	97.5
2012	97.0	95.5	96.5	96.7	97.9	99.0	97.9	97.3	96.5	96.0	96.2	95.7
2013	96.1	97.3	98.1	97.7	98.2	99.2	99.6	99.5	99.5	98.2	98.6	99.0
2014	100.2	100.4	100.5	99.8	99.5	99.7	99.5	99.9	101.0	101.9	103.1	104.7
2015	106.2	107.7	109.5	108.7	108.6	110.0	111.7	113.8	114.3	112.9	113.8	114.7
2016	117.0	115.9	113.7	112.1	113.4	113.8	114.0	113.1	113.9	114.6	117.9	120.1
2017[1]	120.2	118.3	117.8	116.9	117.0	115.6	113.9	112.9	112.3	114.0	114.2	113.6
2018[2]	111.8	111.2	111.7	111.8	114.7	116.5	116.7	117.1	117.3	117.1	116.9	116.9

[1] Preliminary. [2] Forecast. [3] Real indexes adjust nominal exchange rates for differences in rates of inflation, to avoid the distortion caused by high-inflation countries. A higher value means the dollar has appreciated. Federal Reserve Board Index of trade-weighted value of the U.S. dollar against 10 major currencies. Weights are based on relative importance in world financial markets.
Source: Bureau of Economic Analysis, U.S. Department of Commerce (BEA)

Index of Real Trade-Weighted Dollar Exchange Rates for Total Agriculture[3] (U.S. Competitors) (2000 = 100)

Year	Jan.	Feb.	Mar.	Apr.	May	June	July	Aug.	Sept.	Oct.	Nov.	Dec.
2009	107.8	111.3	110.9	108.0	104.5	102.7	102.0	100.4	98.9	96.9	96.1	97.0
2010	97.9	100.3	99.7	99.5	103.9	105.4	102.3	101.1	99.7	95.7	96.3	97.8
2011	97.1	95.9	94.7	92.5	93.1	92.8	92.7	93.0	96.6	97.2	97.6	99.1
2012	99.8	97.3	98.0	98.5	101.1	102.9	102.9	102.2	100.4	99.6	100.0	98.4
2013	97.7	97.9	99.5	98.9	99.6	100.5	101.3	101.2	101.0	98.9	100.0	99.8
2014	101.3	101.6	100.7	100.2	100.5	101.2	101.0	102.0	104.4	105.9	106.8	108.1
2015	111.8	114.0	118.0	117.6	116.0	116.9	119.0	120.1	121.5	120.5	122.8	122.9
2016	125.7	123.8	121.9	119.4	120.0	120.3	120.6	119.4	120.1	121.0	123.4	125.2
2017[1]	124.7	123.3	122.9	122.2	120.8	119.7	117.6	116.0	115.4	116.7	117.0	115.9
2018[2]	113.8	113.4	113.9	114.5	119.2	121.2	121.7	122.7	121.9	121.2	120.4	120.0

[1] Preliminary. [2] Forecast. [3] Real indexes adjust nominal exchange rates for differences in rates of inflation, to avoid the distortion caused by high-inflation countries. A higher value means the dollar has appreciated. Federal Reserve Board Index of trade-weighted value of the U.S. dollar against 10 major currencies. Weights are based on relative importance in world financial markets.
Source: Bureau of Economic Analysis, U.S. Department of Commerce (BEA)

Merchandise Trade and Current Account Balances[3] In Billions of Dollars

| | Merchanise Trade Balance | | | | | Current Account Balance | | | | |
Year	Canada	Germany	Japan	Switzerland	United Kingdom	Canada	Germany	Japan	Switzerland	United Kingdom
2009	-20.3	169.8	29.2	41.6	-44.2	-40.7	195.3	146.5	40.7	-84.4
2010	-30.9	174.8	83.2	62.2	-54.3	-58.2	185.7	221.3	86.1	-83.0
2011	-21.6	180.7	-34.1	58.9	-29.6	-49.7	226.3	128.1	54.5	-51.5
2012	-35.9	217.1	-95.8	70.0	-40.6	-65.7	250.5	62.5	71.3	-101.3
2013	-30.3	226.5	-119.0	83.4	-45.9	-59.4	254.7	46.3	79.7	-142.3
2014	-17.6	271.4	-120.9	83.5	-48.7	-43.1	292.9	36.6	60.2	-149.3
2015	-38.6	269.5	-18.4	79.5	-41.2	-56.1	302.5	136.4	75.6	-142.1
2016	-37.2	271.2	49.1	77.6	-41.8	-49.4	296.2	189.2	66.1	-139.7
2017[1]	-37.8	281.5	45.1	73.8	-29.1	-48.9	297.1	196.6	64.4	-98.6
2018[2]	-42.2	279.0	10.3	82.2	-21.3	-52.8	311.0	163.6	78.6	-94.4

[1] Estimate. [2] Projection. [3] Not seasonally adjusted. Source: Organization for Economic Cooperation and Development (OECD)

EURO / SWISS FRANC
Weekly Cash as of 03/29/2019

WEEKLY CASH
As of 03/29/2019
Chart High 1.6377 on 05/19/2008
Chart Low .8597 on 01/15/2015

EURO / BRITISH POUND
Weekly Cash as of 03/29/2019

WEEKLY CASH
As of 03/29/2019
Chart High .98020 on 12/29/2008
Chart Low .69371 on 07/17/2015

BRITISH POUND / JAPANESE YEN
Weekly Cash as of 03/29/2019

WEEKLY CASH
As of 03/29/2019
Chart High 215.870 on 07/24/2008
Chart Low 116.868 on 09/22/2011

EURO / JAPANESE YEN
Weekly Cash as of 03/29/2019

WEEKLY CASH
As of 03/29/2019
Chart High 169.96 on 07/23/2008
Chart Low 94.12 on 07/24/2012

Forex.

Diamonds

The diamond, which is the mineral form of carbon, is the hardest, strongest natural material known on earth. The name *diamond* is derived from *adamas*, the ancient Greek term meaning "invincible." Diamonds form deep within the Earth's crust and are typically billions of years old. Diamonds have also have been found in and near meteorites and their craters. Diamonds are considered precious gemstones but lower grade diamonds are used for industrial applications such as drilling, cutting, grinding and polishing.

Supply – World production of natural gem diamonds in 2018 fell by -1.2% yr/yr to 87.000 million carats, well below the 2008 record high of 114.000 million carats (one carat equals 1/5 gram or 200 milligrams). The world's largest producers of natural gem diamonds are Russia with 29.8% of world production in 2014, Botswana with 24.0%, Angola with 11.0%, and South Africa with 8.3%. World production of natural industrial diamonds in 2014 fell -11.9% yr/yr to 52.800 million carats. The main producers of natural industrial diamonds in 2018 were Russia with 26.4% of world production and Botswana with 18.4%. World production of synthetic diamonds in 2011 remained at 4.380 million carats. The main producer of synthetic diamonds in 2011 was China with 91.3% of world production.

Trade – The U.S. in 2018 imported 850,000 carats of natural diamonds and relied on imports for 89% of its consumption.

World Production of Natural Gem Diamonds   In Thousands of Carats

Year	Angola	Australia	Botswana	Brazil, unspec-ified	Central African Republic	China, unspec-ified	Congo (Kinshasa)	Ghana, unspec-ified	Namibia	Russia	Sierra Leone	South Africa	World Total
2013	7,740	235	16,200	49	65	1	3,140	169	1,689	21,200	487	6,520	70,100
2014	7,910	186	17,300	57	----	----	3,130	242	1,918	21,500	496	5,950	72,000
2015	8,120	271	14,500	32	----	----	3,200	174	2,053	23,500	400	5,780	70,900
2016	8,120	279	14,400	184	9	5	4,640	142	1,718	22,600	439	6,650	73,200
2017[1]	8,500	343	16,000	255		230	3,780		1,950	23,800	231	7,750	88,100
2018[2]	8,500	340	16,000	250		230	3,700		1,900	23,000	230	7,700	87,000

[1] Preliminary.   [2] Estimate.   [3] Less than 1/2 unit.   *Source: U.S. Geological Survey (USGS)*

World Production of Natural Industrial Diamonds[4]   In Thousands of Carats

Year	Angola	Australia	Botswana	Brazil	Central African Republic	China	Congo (Kinshasa)	Ghana	Russia	Sierra Leone	South Africa	Vene-zuela	World Total
2013	860	11,500	6,960	----	16	----	12,500	----	1,670	122	1,630	----	44,800
2014	879	9,100	7,400	----	----	----	12,500	----	16,900	124	1,490	----	52,800
2015	902	13,300	6,230	----	----	----	12,800	----	18,400	100	1,440	----	56,500
2016	902	13,700	6,150	----	2	----	18,600	----	17,700	110	1,660	----	60,900
2017[1]		17,000	7,000	----		----	15,000	----	19,000		2,000	----	63,000
2018[2]		17,000	7,000	----		----	15,000	----	19,000		2,000	----	63,000

[1] Preliminary.   [2] Estimate.   [3] Formerly Zaire.   *Source: U.S. Geological Survey (USGS)*

U.S. Exports of Industrial Diamonds   In Thousands of Carats

Year	Belgium	France	Hong Kong	India	Israel	Mexico	Singa-pore	Switzer-land	Thailand	United Arab Emirates	United Kingdom	Other	World Total
2011	269.0	1.2	2,320.0	768.0	293.0	604.0	6.1	190.0	168.0	131.0	492.0	12.5	5,450.0
2012	393.0	0.9	2,390.0	525.0	576.0	473.0	3.6	9.3	116.0	45.1	8.7	10.7	4,800.0
2013	90.9	10.8	2,140.0	489.0	346.0	420.0	1.9	10.8	154.0	49.1	19.7	13.2	4,060.0
2014	55.6	3.3	1,980.0	381.0	78.5	416.0	3.9	2.2	153.0	88.7	26.3	5.6	3,470.0
2015[1]	187.0	67.1	1,660.0	672.0	243.0	316.0	6.8	12.3	146.0	391.0	6.7	6.2	4,020.0
2016[2]	564.0	9.4	1,170.0	669.0	184.0	331.0	5.1	44.2	148.0	408.0	49.7	6.3	3,790.0

[1] Preliminary.   [2] Estimate.   *Source: U.S. Geological Survey (USGS)*

Salient Statistics of Industrial Diamonds in the United States   In Millions of Carats

	Bort, Grit & Powder & Dust Natural and Synthetic							Stones (Natural)					Net Import Reliance % of Con-sumption
	--- Production ---							Secon-dary Pro-duction					
Year	Manu-factured Diamond	Secon-dary	Imports for Con-sumption	Exports & Reexports	In Manu-factured Products	Gov't Sales	Apparent Con-sumption	Price Value of Imports $/Carat	Imports for Con-sumption	Exports & Reexports	Gov't Sales	Apparent Con-sumption	Price Value of Imports $/Carat
2013	----	38.1	728.0	149.0	----	----	663.0	.11	----	1.9	----	----	----	15.50	87
2014	----	43.7	682.0	163.0	----	----	616.0	.11	----	2.2	----	----	----	14.40	84
2015	----	63.5	275.0	140.0	----	----	238.0	.20	----	1.3	----	----	----	17.50	57
2016	----	66.1	216.0	134.0	----	----	190.0	.23	----	1.4	----	----	----	13.60	43
2017[1]	----	11.0	399.0	161.0	----	----	290.0	.16	----	1.2	----	----	----	12.90	82
2018[2]	----	12.0	580.0	140.0	----	----	495.0	.12	----	.9	----	----	----	8.10	89

[1] Preliminary.   [2] Estimate.   [3] Less than 1/2 unit.   *Source: U.S. Geological Survey (USGS)*

Eggs

Eggs are a low-priced protein source and are consumed worldwide. Each commercial chicken lays between 265-280 eggs per year. In the United States, the grade and size of eggs are regulated under the federal Egg Products Inspection Act (1970). The grades of eggs are AA, A, and B, and must have sound, whole shells and must be clean. The difference among the grades of eggs is internal and mostly reflects the freshness of the egg. Table eggs vary in color and can be determined by the color of the chicken's earlobe. For example, chickens with white earlobes lay white eggs and chickens with reddish-brown earlobes lay brown eggs. In the U.S., egg size is determined by the weight of a dozen eggs, not individual eggs, and range from Peewee to Jumbo. Store-bought eggs in the shell stay fresh for 3 to 5 weeks in a home refrigerator, according to the USDA.

Eggs are primarily used as a source of food, although eggs are also widely used for medical purposes. Fertile eggs, as a source of purified proteins, are used to produce many vaccines. Flu vaccines are produced by growing single strains of the flu virus in eggs, which are then extracted to make the vaccine. Eggs are also used in biotechnology to create new drugs. The hen's genetic make-up can be altered so the whites of the eggs are rich in tailored proteins that form the basis of medicines to fight cancer and other diseases. The U.S. biotech company Viragen and the Roslin Institute in Edinburgh have produced eggs with 100 mg or more of the easily-extracted proteins used in new drugs to treat various illnesses including ovarian and breast cancers.

Prices – The average monthly price of all eggs received by farmers in the U.S. in 2018 rose by +33.6% yr/yr to 115.4 cents per dozen, but still down from the 2015 record high of 164.6 cents.

Supply – World egg production in 2017 rose +2.4% at 1.417 billion eggs. The world's largest egg producers were China with 37.9% of world production, the U.S. with 7.5%, Mexico with 3.9%, Brazil with 3.6% and Japan with 3.1%. U.S. egg production in 2018 rose +1.5% to 107.267 billion eggs, which is a new record high. The average number of hens and pullets on U.S. farms in 2017 rose by +2.7% yr/yr to 375,845 million, a new record high.

Demand – U.S. consumption of eggs in 2017 rose +0.7% yr/yr to 7.275 billion dozen eggs, a new record high. U.S. consumption of eggs is up sharply by about 30% from ten years earlier, reflecting the increased popularity of eggs in American diets. U.S. per capita egg consumption in 2019 is forecasted to fall -1.0% yr/yr to 276.7 eggs per year per person. Per capita egg consumption was at a high of 277.2 eggs in 1970, fell sharply in the 1990s to a low of 174.9 in 1995, and then began rebounding in 1997 to current levels of about 275 eggs per year.

Trade – U.S. imports of eggs in 2017 fell -41.2% yr/yr to 60.000 million dozen eggs. U.S. exports of eggs in 2017 rose +7.1% yr/yr to 295.000 million dozen eggs down from the 2014 record high of 393.844 million dozen.

World Production of Eggs   In Millions of Eggs

Year	Brazil	China	France	Germany	Italy	Japan	Mexico	Russia	Spain	Ukraine	United Kingdom	United States	World Total
2009	38,438	472,671	14,601	10,754	14,509	41,750	47,206	39,188	13,166	15,303	10,319	90,737	1,183,251
2010	38,961	476,403	15,094	10,191	13,157	41,900	47,623	40,392	12,896	16,865	11,274	91,811	1,205,346
2011	40,731	484,633	14,088	12,035	13,482	41,377	49,170	40,778	12,995	18,428	11,201	92,450	1,228,760
2012	41,676	493,184	14,155	12,246	13,661	41,780	46,361	41,548	11,409	18,919	10,806	94,364	1,256,024
2013	43,431	495,741	15,766	12,593	12,679	42,033	50,317	40,779	11,787	19,419	11,517	97,555	1,285,109
2014	44,811	459,063	15,935	12,685	12,749	41,699	51,344	41,313	12,498	19,391	11,653	100,879	1,273,636
2015	45,219	516,844	16,319	11,807	13,093	42,015	53,051	42,093	12,780	16,615	11,966	97,208	1,342,430
2016[1]	45,635	537,354	16,029	11,979	13,300	42,704	54,404	43,087	13,183	14,799	12,370	102,112	1,383,121
2017[2]	50,943	536,818	15,917	12,087	13,220	43,353	55,418	44,351	13,503	15,351	12,885	106,689	1,416,675

[1] Preliminary.   [2] Forecast.   [3] Selected countries.   Source: Food and Agricultural Organization of the United Nations (FAO)

Salient Statistics of Eggs in the United States

	--- Hens & Pullets ---		Rate of Lay	----- Eggs -----					----- Consumption -----			
		Average	Per Layer		Price		Total					Per
	On Farm	Number During	During	Total	in cents Per	Value of Pro-	Egg Pro-			Used for		Capita
Year	Dec. 1[3]	Year	Year[4]	Produced	Dozen	duction[5]	duction	Imports[6]	Exports[6]	Hatching	Total	Eggs[6]
	----- Thousands -----		(Number)	----- Millions -----		Million USD	-------------------- Million Dozen --------------------					Number
2010	341,551	340,335	269	91,472	86.5	6,553	7,656	21.8	258.4	982.2	6,436	247.9
2011	338,472	338,475	271	91,915	97.7	7,356	7,755	20.9	276.5	950.1	6,501	250.0
2012	346,965	341,052	274	93,533	100.1	7,929	7,930	18.5	301.7	941.4	6,666	254.6
2013	356,923	354,844	275	96,698	108.8	8,679	8,186	16.9	371.8	964.8	6,827	258.0
2014	370,637	364,707	277	101,186	125.8	10,258	8,404	34.7	393.8	980.6	7,106	267.5
2015	346,343	352,411	276	97,208	164.6	13,608	8,101	123.3	313.6	995.6	6,781	256.3
2016	377,371	365,997	279	102,112	76.6	6,514	8,496	102.1	275.4	1,007.3	7,222	271.6
2017[1]	382,266	375,845	281	105,693	86.3	7,551	8,550	60.0	295.0	1,040.0	7,275	276.3
2018[2]	391,802			107,924	115.5							278.8

[1] Preliminary.   [2] Forecast.   [3] All layers of laying age.   [4] Number of eggs produced during the year divided by the average number of all layers of laying age on hand during the year.   [5] Value of sales plus value of eggs consumed in households of producers. 6/ Shell-egg equivalent of eggs and egg products.
Source: National Agricultural Statistics Service, U.S. Department of Agriculture (NASS-USDA)

EGGS

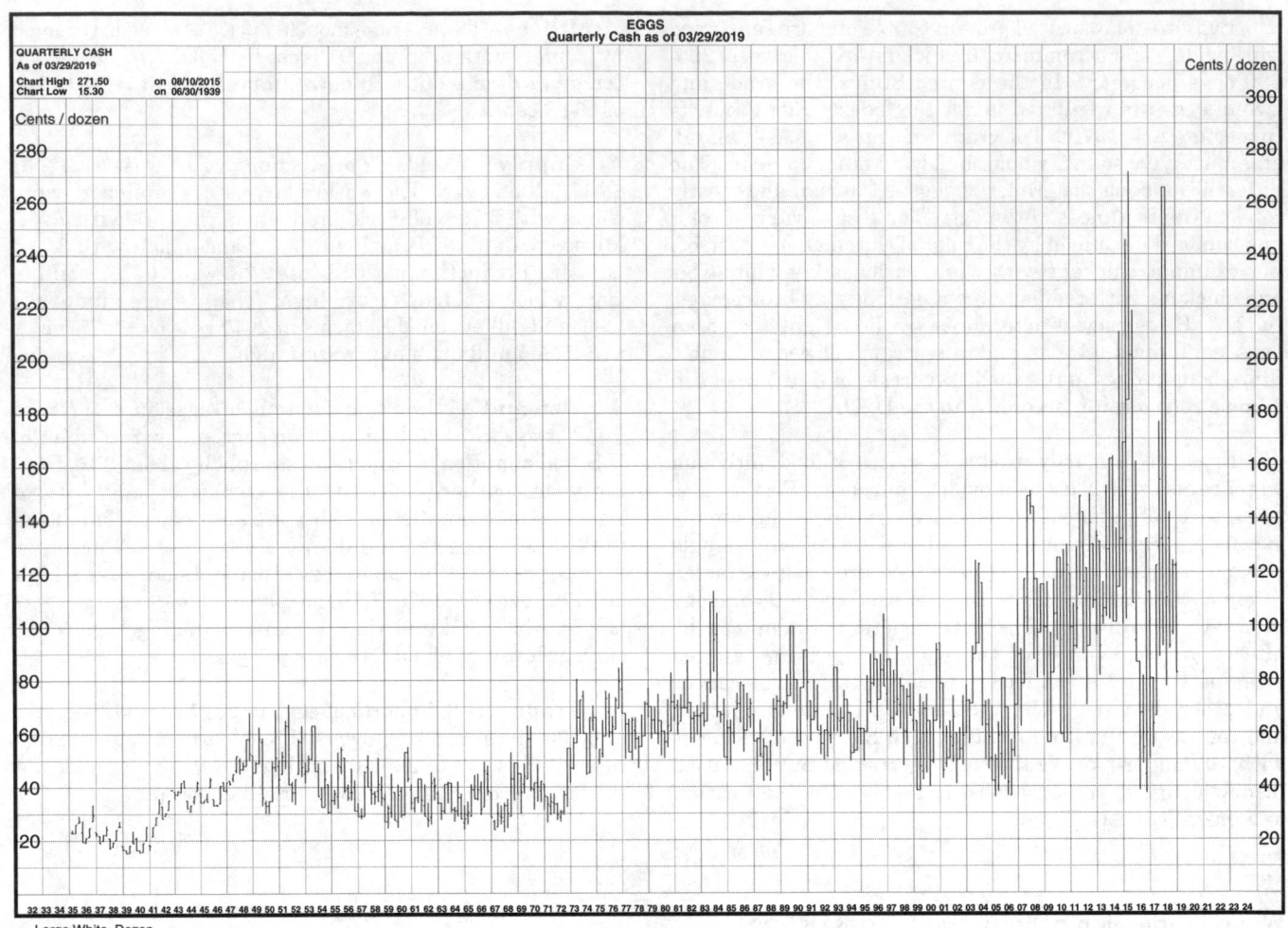

QUARTERLY CASH
As of 03/29/2019
Chart High 271.50   on 08/10/2015
Chart Low   15.30   on 06/30/1939

Cents / dozen

Cents / dozen

Large White, Dozen

Average Price Received by Farmers for All Eggs in the United States   In Cents Per Dozen

Year	Jan.	Feb.	Mar.	Apr.	May	June	July	Aug.	Sept.	Oct.	Nov.	Dec.	Average
2009	103.0	80.9	81.6	92.0	61.7	59.4	70.8	75.8	74.4	80.0	101.0	105.0	82.1
2010	103.0	91.7	116.0	79.4	63.3	61.9	70.9	78.9	68.4	83.6	113.0	108.0	86.5
2011	85.0	95.4	84.9	105.0	82.2	88.6	88.0	115.0	102.0	102.0	102.0	122.0	97.7
2012	87.9	88.5	99.5	86.5	82.8	90.7	96.9	113.0	122.0	102.0	118.0	113.0	100.1
2013	106.0	99.3	115.0	88.5	117.0	93.0	104.0	108.0	103.0	104.0	132.0	136.0	108.8
2014	112.0	140.0	124.0	127.0	117.0	109.0	124.0	108.0	105.0	114.0	152.0	177.0	125.8
2015	125.0	129.0	154.0	108.0	173.0	200.0	190.0	239.0	190.0	143.0	200.0	124.0	164.6
2016	118.0	108.0	96.7	67.6	54.7	53.7	64.8	65.1	60.1	51.0	58.8	121.0	76.6
2017	79.5	62.3	78.3	63.3	61.9	63.5	82.3	74.9	109.0	90.1	138.0	133.0	86.3
2018[1]	115.0	126.0	201.0	120.0	85.7	103.0	110.0	109.0	93.6	91.8	114.0	117.0	115.5

[1] Preliminary.   Source: Economic Research Service, U.S. Department of Agriculture (ERS-USDA)

Average Wholesale Price of Shell Eggs (Large) Delivered, Chicago   In Cents Per Dozen

Year	Jan.	Feb.	Mar.	Apr.	May	June	July	Aug.	Sept.	Oct.	Nov.	Dec.	Average
2009	113.40	92.29	85.64	99.26	64.55	72.41	73.55	85.69	80.17	86.14	110.75	114.41	89.86
2010	111.50	107.55	116.80	84.81	64.15	69.68	73.74	88.73	83.17	76.88	124.79	124.73	93.88
2011	100.20	99.08	86.37	106.05	87.31	86.95	92.70	114.07	105.93	111.79	112.50	130.07	102.75
2012	106.25	91.47	98.59	96.10	76.55	92.50	105.45	131.33	119.50	114.28	123.93	123.90	106.65
2013	112.93	112.92	114.30	97.86	105.45	89.75	104.77	106.82	106.50	106.41	133.60	150.21	111.79
2014	113.10	135.97	133.93	145.98	116.21	115.83	122.16	116.02	111.93	117.11	143.18	194.45	130.49
2015	111.10	133.50	149.18	113.10	136.20	223.82	206.55	260.40	217.02	161.95	192.55	157.14	171.88
2016	106.71	131.80	93.05	62.93	55.45	46.18	69.70	57.24	64.74	44.07	58.07	94.31	73.69
2017	78.47	65.84	63.76	68.39	55.77	60.32	74.45	80.85	104.85	110.00	130.74	169.80	88.60
2018[1]	116.40	150.24	205.07	177.93	90.95	88.93	129.55	105.22	93.45	99.54	115.26	120.80	124.45

[1] Preliminary.   Source: National Agricultural Statistics Service, U.S. Department of Agriculture (NASS-USDA)

Total Egg Production in the United States   In Millions of Eggs

Year	Jan.	Feb.	Mar.	Apr.	May	June	July	Aug.	Sept.	Oct.	Nov.	Dec.	Total
2009	7,678	6,903	7,737	7,472	7,607	7,360	7,590	7,593	7,376	7,696	7,569	7,853	90,434
2010	7,724	6,935	7,839	7,578	7,716	7,484	7,719	7,765	7,514	7,698	7,573	7,927	91,472
2011	7,833	7,013	7,840	7,617	7,773	7,503	7,732	7,719	7,503	7,783	7,612	7,987	91,915
2012	7,892	7,283	7,916	7,653	7,850	7,582	7,798	7,869	7,625	7,965	7,874	8,226	93,533
2013	8,125	7,321	8,195	7,929	8,139	7,857	8,082	8,178	7,969	8,267	8,098	8,538	96,698
2014	8,490	7,636	8,522	8,298	8,523	8,242	8,597	8,591	8,289	8,632	8,521	8,845	101,186
2015	8,656	7,730	8,688	8,352	8,141	7,577	7,850	7,878	7,647	7,970	7,875	8,261	97,208
2016	8,308	7,948	8,622	8,333	8,643	8,349	8,672	8,751	8,507	8,851	8,707	9,100	102,112
2017	9,053	8,124	9,007	8,687	8,918	8,636	8,953	8,922	8,578	8,920	8,791	9,104	105,693
2018[1]	8,985	8,145	9,099	8,806	9,123	8,832	9,100	9,166	8,914	9,251	9,069	9,436	107,924

[1] Preliminary.   Source: National Agricultural Statistics Service, U.S. Department of Agriculture (NASS-USDA)

Per Capita Disappearance of Eggs[4] in the United States   In Number of Eggs

Year	First Quarter	Second Quarter	Third Quarter	Fourth Quarter	Total	Year	First Quarter	Second Quarter	Third Quarter	Fourth Quarter	Total
2008	61.8	61.3	62.0	63.8	248.3	2014	65.6	66.2	67.2	68.5	267.5
2009	62.0	61.5	61.4	62.9	248.2	2015	65.7	62.9	61.9	65.7	256.3
2010	61.5	61.4	62.2	62.8	247.9	2016	67.4	66.3	67.3	70.6	271.6
2011	61.3	61.5	62.8	64.3	250.0	2017[1]	68.5	68.6	69.3	69.9	276.3
2012	63.3	62.3	63.3	65.6	254.6	2018[2]	68.2	68.9	70.3	71.4	278.8
2013	64.2	63.3	64.5	66.0	258.0	2019[3]	69.4	69.6	70.4	72.4	281.8

[1] Preliminary.   [2] Estimate.   [3] Forecast.   Source: Economic Research Service, U.S. Department of Agriculture (ERS-USDA)

Egg-Feed Ratio[1] in the United States

Year	Jan.	Feb.	Mar.	Apr.	May	June	July	Aug.	Sept.	Oct.	Nov.	Dec.	Average
2009	9.0	7.0	7.2	8.4	4.3	3.8	5.6	6.5	6.8	7.3	10.0	10.3	7.2
2010	10.1	8.9	12.2	7.0	5.1	5.0	6.0	6.9	4.6	6.5	9.5	8.1	7.5
2011	5.8	6.0	5.1	6.4	4.5	4.9	4.9	6.7	6.3	6.8	6.8	8.7	6.1
2012	5.1	5.0	5.7	4.5	5.0	4.8	4.8	5.6	7.0	5.6	6.6	6.3	5.5
2013	5.6	5.0	6.1	4.2	6.3	4.4	5.3	6.1	6.4	7.3	10.4	10.7	6.5
2014	8.0	10.9	8.9	8.9	7.9	7.3	9.6	8.6	9.0	10.5	15.1	17.7	10.2
2015	11.4	12.2	15.3	9.6	18.2	21.8	19.5	26.5	20.7	14.7	22.9	12.2	17.1
2016	11.4	10.2	8.8	4.6	2.7	2.5	4.0	4.4	3.9	2.6	3.7	12.1	5.9
2017	6.7	4.3	6.4	4.4	4.2	4.5	6.9	6.1	10.0	8.3	15.3	14.4	7.7
2018[1]	11.6	12.9	22.2	11.4	6.9	9.3	10.6	11.0	8.7	8.5	11.8	11.8	11.4

[1] Pounds of laying feed equivalent in value to one dozen eggs.   [2] Preliminary.   Source: Economic Research Service, U.S. Department of Agriculture (ERS-USDA)

Hens and Pullets of Laying Age (Layers) in the United States, on First of Month   In Thousands

Year	Jan.	Feb.	Mar.	Apr.	May	June	July	Aug.	Sept.	Oct.	Nov.	Dec.
2009	341,373	341,388	340,716	341,067	339,239	334,953	333,064	332,371	332,808	334,917	336,671	339,526
2010	341,411	339,747	341,191	342,969	339,635	339,018	340,442	339,384	340,749	336,691	337,300	341,551
2011	344,255	340,247	339,296	342,237	339,520	336,232	336,559	334,997	335,794	334,826	336,909	338,472
2012	340,522	339,826	340,926	343,073	341,885	341,486	338,416	337,525	339,302	341,076	345,269	346,965
2013	344,920	344,916	347,025	348,468	344,363	345,740	343,944	349,862	351,870	349,950	352,971	356,923
2014	363,828	362,628	363,000	364,610	364,840	363,604	363,572	365,799	365,748	366,306	366,329	370,637
2015	368,380	364,996	365,857	366,022	357,858	332,788	332,422	334,040	334,912	338,273	340,554	346,343
2016	356,109	359,429	366,253	366,749	366,217	365,830	364,432	364,935	368,128	370,254	371,438	377,371
2017	377,198	376,955	375,688	376,790	374,671	372,584	372,241	372,995	374,769	376,694	379,323	382,266
2018[1]	382,305	382,169	385,963	387,033	386,443	386,172	385,592	384,282	385,775	385,860	389,150	391,802

[1] Preliminary.   Source: National Agricultural Statistics Service, U.S. Department of Agriculture (NASS-USDA)

EGGS

Eggs Laid Per Hundred Layers in the United States   In Number of Eggs

Year	Jan.	Feb.	Mar.	Apr.	May	June	July	Aug.	Sept.	Oct.	Nov.	Dec.	Average
2009	2,249	2,024	2,269	2,197	2,256	2,203	2,281	2,283	2,209	2,292	2,239	2,303	2,234
2010	2,267	2,036	2,291	2,220	2,273	2,203	2,271	2,283	2,218	2,284	2,231	2,311	2,241
2011	2,289	2,064	2,301	2,234	2,300	2,230	2,303	2,301	2,238	2,317	2,254	2,351	2,265
2012	2,320	2,140	2,315	2,234	2,297	2,229	2,307	2,325	2,241	2,321	2,275	2,347	2,279
2013	2,327	2,090	2,326	2,259	2,329	2,249	2,315	2,331	2,271	2,352	2,281	2,354	2,290
2014	2,337	2,105	2,342	2,275	2,340	2,267	2,357	2,349	2,265	2,356	2,312	2,388	2,308
2015	2,349	2,103	2,360	2,292	2,339	2,258	2,334	2,332	2,247	2,319	2,261	2,335	2,294
2016	2,322	2,190	2,352	2,274	2,361	2,287	2,378	2,387	2,304	2,386	2,328	2,411	2,332
2017	2,400	2,159	2,394	2,312	2,387	2,319	2,403	2,386	2,283	2,360	2,308	2,381	2,341
2018[1]	2,350	2,121	2,354	2,277	2,361	2,289	2,364	2,380	2,310	2,387	2,322	2,404	2,327

[1] Preliminary.   Source: National Agricultural Statistics Service, U.S. Department of Agriculture (NASS-USDA)

Egg-Type Chicks Hatched by Commercial Hatcheries in the United States   In Thousands

Year	Jan.	Feb.	Mar.	Apr.	May	June	July	Aug.	Sept.	Oct.	Nov.	Dec.	Total
2009	37,826	36,809	41,752	42,808	40,772	41,980	36,227	38,078	40,310	37,392	34,525	39,502	467,981
2010	39,815	38,854	44,189	47,132	44,039	41,474	38,831	37,172	39,761	41,965	38,794	38,367	490,393
2011	40,587	37,412	43,600	42,956	42,946	38,918	36,948	41,428	39,803	37,616	37,503	38,889	478,606
2012	41,290	40,523	43,101	43,202	44,564	38,829	35,968	42,269	38,319	37,901	36,492	40,985	483,443
2013	43,831	42,236	43,584	46,031	50,154	42,252	39,936	38,794	42,166	42,506	41,845	41,144	514,479
2014	44,345	41,269	44,801	46,384	49,684	44,271	42,489	39,731	43,671	44,665	36,544	42,991	520,845
2015	43,868	43,774	50,187	50,193	48,315	47,212	42,790	47,131	49,391	50,194	45,848	46,679	565,582
2016	47,775	54,289	57,055	51,266	57,306	57,562	41,609	43,258	44,892	43,344	41,648	45,731	585,735
2017	45,367	48,127	55,919	52,762	53,506	49,722	41,862	45,861	42,725	51,495	48,344	46,080	581,770
2018[1]	52,313	50,148	58,147	58,986	60,063	53,486	50,752	53,207	49,610	54,960	46,844	46,779	635,295

[1] Preliminary.   Source: National Agricultural Statistics Service, U.S. Department of Agriculture (NASS-USDA)

Cold Storage Holdings of Frozen Eggs in the United States, on First of Month   In Thousands of Pounds[2]

Year	Jan.	Feb.	Mar.	Apr.	May	June	July	Aug.	Sept.	Oct.	Nov.	Dec.
2009	22,638	22,558	22,065	20,343	18,241	21,714	21,655	22,578	22,558	21,590	22,912	21,158
2010	23,644	24,340	24,106	21,623	22,388	22,419	25,010	24,684	24,688	26,054	25,552	22,910
2011	25,357	26,788	28,143	27,287	27,681	29,025	33,813	33,924	31,009	31,889	33,895	32,967
2012	36,491	37,415	36,326	33,669	32,528	34,498	40,191	38,654	35,856	31,375	28,971	27,251
2013	27,376	29,659	28,620	27,138	29,339	28,856	30,591	26,118	30,144	33,577	33,832	29,754
2014	30,350	34,687	34,631	29,044	27,430	28,300	30,142	31,453	29,820	31,126	31,960	30,349
2015	30,718	34,670	35,648	31,978	31,260	28,216	26,890	27,408	30,572	32,324	37,486	36,013
2016	40,896	42,158	37,400	31,741	33,670	35,961	37,960	37,209	31,725	33,084	34,344	36,490
2017	35,652	36,913	41,071	41,911	41,176	39,033	41,712	40,193	35,166	33,934	32,928	27,911
2018[1]	30,162	31,041	32,308	28,175	27,763	30,236	30,705	29,808	31,990	28,935	30,267	29,621

[1] Preliminary.   [2] Converted on basis 39.5 pounds frozen eggs equals 1 case.   Source: National Agricultural Statistics Service, U.S. Department of Agriculture (NASS-USDA)

Electric Power Production by Electric Utilities in the United States   In Millions of Kilowatt Hours

Year	Jan.	Feb.	Mar.	Apr.	May	June	July	Aug.	Sept.	Oct.	Nov.	Dec.	Total
2009	216,218	179,859	184,963	174,130	189,695	213,482	221,545	222,452	193,720	184,019	179,276	213,417	2,372,776
2010	222,362	195,895	188,491	172,441	199,835	228,551	243,756	240,185	203,521	178,917	179,858	217,820	2,471,632
2011	220,900	188,700	195,148	183,567	196,994	225,535	253,142	242,540	199,144	181,359	176,515	197,306	2,460,850
2012	196,498	176,554	175,331	169,095	194,593	210,514	242,595	229,579	191,871	178,825	178,834	194,884	2,339,173
2013	207,123	180,975	189,129	173,761	190,354	213,033	232,867	229,557	198,719	182,713	181,991	207,837	2,388,059
2014	222,165	191,345	193,194	170,329	191,866	212,311	227,343	225,392	194,390	176,990	180,869	196,279	2,382,473
2015	208,073	194,871	184,609	165,379	184,165	208,270	229,212	223,696	196,273	172,561	165,247	182,965	2,315,323
2016	203,384	179,182	171,452	162,936	179,569	213,557	234,890	232,277	195,105	171,134	164,301	197,136	2,304,923
2017	199,391	164,437	179,245	164,153	183,781	205,299	233,807	220,364	185,458	174,251	168,569	195,521	2,274,276
2018[1]	214,312	170,605	173,577	164,625	189,778	211,327	235,146	230,053	197,602	177,218	176,642		2,335,511

[1] Preliminary.   Source: Energy Information Administration, U.S. Department of Energy (EIA-DOE)

Electric Power

The modern electric utility industry began in the 1800s. In 1807, Humphry Davy constructed a practical battery and demonstrated both incandescent and arc light. In 1831, Michael Faraday built the first electric generator proving that rotary mechanical power could be converted into electric power. In 1879, Thomas Edison perfected a practical incandescent light bulb. The electric utility industry evolved from gas and electric carbon-arc commercial and street lighting systems. In 1882, in New York City, Thomas Edison's Pearl Street electricity generating station established the industry by displaying the four key elements of a modern electric utility system: reliable central generation, efficient distribution, successful end use, and a competitive price.

Electricity is measured in units called watts and watt-hours. Electricity must be used when it is generated and cannot be stored to any significant degree. That means the power utilities must match the level of electricity generation to the level of demand in order to avoid wasteful over-production. The power industry has been deregulated to some degree in the past decade and now major utility companies sell power back and forth across major national grids in order to meet supply and demand needs. The rapid changes in the supply-demand situation mean that the cost of electricity can be very volatile.

Electricity futures trade at the CME Group. The futures contract is a financially settled contract, which is priced based on electricity prices in the PJM western hub at 111 delivery points, mainly on the utility transmission systems of Pennsylvania Electric Co. and the Potomac Electric Co. The contract is priced in dollars and cents per megawatt hours.

Supply – U.S. electricity production in 2018 (annualized through November) fell -2.7% yr/yr to 2.336 trillion kilowatt-hours. That was still well below the record high of 3.212 trillion kilowatt-hours in 1998 and indicated that recent electricity production has been reduced mainly because of more efficient production and distribution systems, and to some extent by conservation of electricity by both business and residential consumers. U.S. electricity generation in 2018 required the use of 11.012 billion cubic feet of natural gas (up +15.8% yr/yr), 633 million tons of coal (down -4.7% yr/yr), and 44 million barrels of fuel oil (up +13.3% yr/yr).

In terms of kilowatt-hours, natural gas is the most widely used source of electricity production in the U.S. accounting for 30.9% of electricity production in 2017 (latest data available), followed by coal (30.9%), nuclear (20.8%), hydro (7.7%), and fuel oil (0.5%). Alternative sources of fuel for electricity generation that are gaining favor include geothermal, biomass, solar, wind, etc. but so far, they only account for 9.1% of total electricity production in the U.S.

Demand – Residential use of electricity accounts for the largest single category of electricity demand with usage of 1.379 trillion kilowatt hours in 2017 accounting for 37.0% of overall usage. Business users in total use more electricity than residential users, but business users are broken into the categories of commercial with 36.3% of usage and industrial with 26.4% of usage.

World Net Generation of Electricity   In Billions of Kilowatt Hours

Year	Brazil	Canada	China	France	Germany	India	Japan	Korea, South	Russia	Spain	United Kingdom	United States	World Total
2007	437.2	612.9	3,108.0	538.4	597.8	775.9	1,100.0	402.4	958.4	286.8	367.6	4,157.4	18,923.9
2008	454.7	614.7	3,297.5	544.2	599.3	803.7	1,028.5	419.0	982.5	295.9	360.6	4,120.5	19,212.4
2009	458.7	595.1	3,527.3	507.7	557.3	866.0	1,001.4	425.9	937.8	278.6	349.0	3,951.8	19,145.9
2010	506.7	584.0	3,984.0	540.1	591.7	916.2	1,067.1	468.3	980.9	284.2	355.2	4,127.4	20,416.8
2011	522.9	613.6	4,461.7	535.6	574.8	1,005.6	1,059.0	490.2	996.8	277.6	342.2	4,103.8	21,126.9
2012	542.5	613.4	4,735.5	536.1	591.4	1,053.4	989.1	500.1	1,012.3	279.2	338.6	4,053.7	21,561.5
2013	559.0	638.3	5,170.7	543.2	601.0	1,116.9	1,014.7	506.1	1,001.8	268.9	334.1	4,074.1	22,233.6
2014	577.0	638.5	5,387.9	535.3	590.8	1,213.7	993.9	513.3	1,005.7	263.0	316.0	4,104.8	22,673.3
2015[1]	568.6	649.0	5,562.5	542.2	610.2	1,287.4	984.3	516.5	1,008.4	264.4	318.0	4,091.7	23,105.5
2016[2]	567.9	649.6	5,882.9	529.1	612.8	1,386.4	989.3	526.0	1,031.3	258.6	318.2	4,095.5	23,765.8

[1] Preliminary.   [2] Estimate.   NA = Not avaliable.   *Source: Energy Information Administration, U.S. Department of Energy (EIA-DOE)*

World Consumption of Electricity   In Billions of Kilowatt Hours

Year	Brazil	Canada	China	France	Germany	India	Italy	Japan	Korea, South	Russia	United Kingdom	United States	World Total
2007	404.2	535.4	2,891.5	450.0	551.9	593.3	315.7	1,049.0	387.0	840.7	345.0	3,890.2	17,212.5
2008	419.8	529.8	3,070.9	462.8	549.1	628.8	315.5	977.2	402.9	855.6	343.6	3,866.2	17,471.9
2009	418.5	508.6	3,290.1	446.8	520.1	679.1	298.0	950.9	409.1	816.1	323.7	3,723.7	17,417.1
2010	455.6	510.1	3,713.7	474.0	552.8	727.3	307.0	1,020.0	450.2	858.5	331.0	3,886.8	18,643.3
2011	471.3	523.5	4,178.9	443.0	546.2	802.3	311.0	1,012.2	472.7	874.8	320.5	3,882.6	19,324.1
2012	488.4	516.5	4,435.1	454.5	546.3	845.8	305.3	945.9	482.8	889.1	322.2	3,832.3	19,712.9
2013	504.3	532.9	4,845.4	456.7	544.3	898.3	296.5	967.2	487.8	881.1	322.0	3,868.3	20,340.0
2014	517.6	535.1	5,066.5	434.3	532.7	974.2	290.9	950.6	495.0	891.1	309.1	3,903.3	20,760.7
2015[1]	510.0	524.3	5,251.2	442.8	536.3	1,046.6	296.2	943.7	498.5	890.1	310.4	3,900.2	21,191.7
2016[2]	509.1	522.2	5,563.9	450.8	536.5	1,136.5	293.5	943.7	507.6	909.6	309.2	3,902.3	21,801.2

[1] Preliminary.   [2] Estimate.   NA = Not avaliable.   *Source: Energy Information Administration, U.S. Department of Energy (EIA-DOE)*

ELECTRIC POWER

World Installed Capacity of Electricity   In Billions of Kilowatt Hours

Year	Brazil	Canada	China	France	Germany	India	Italy	Japan	Russia	Spain	United Kingdom	United States	World Total
2007	97.9	125.3	718.5	116.5	136.5	169.1	93.6	278.2	223.2	88.8	83.5	994.9	4,505.4
2008	101.6	126.5	794.2	117.7	143.4	177.1	98.7	280.9	222.8	93.7	84.9	1,010.2	4,677.8
2009	105.0	131.6	878.8	119.1	152.0	189.6	101.6	283.6	224.1	96.7	86.7	1,025.4	4,883.4
2010	113.7	132.3	969.7	124.1	162.9	207.8	106.6	286.2	229.3	102.1	92.9	1,039.1	5,126.1
2011	117.1	132.9	1,066.3	125.3	168.0	237.3	118.8	288.8	232.8	102.9	93.1	1,051.3	5,358.9
2012	121.4	130.7	1,151.5	128.4	178.4	261.6	124.6	294.8	234.8	105.3	95.3	1,063.0	5,602.9
2013	128.1	133.3	1,265.1	128.0	185.3	283.9	124.5	302.4	238.9	106.1	93.0	1,060.1	5,829.7
2014	134.8	136.8	1,377.0	127.8	197.5	313.3	121.7	272.9	259.5	106.2	96.1	1,068.4	6,084.4
2015[1]	141.7	147.6	1,516.2	129.9	203.4	345.6	117.0	283.0	257.3	106.6	96.7	1,064.1	6,360.5
2016[2]	150.8	143.5	1,653.2	130.8	208.5	367.8	114.2	295.9	244.9	105.9	97.1	1,074.3	6,628.0

[1] Preliminary.   [2] Estimate.   NA = Not avaliable.   *Source: Energy Information Administration, U.S. Department of Energy (EIA-DOE)*

Electricity in the United States   In Billions of Kilowatt Hours

	Net Generation				Trade			T&D Losses[6] and Unaccounted for[7]	End Use		
Year	Electric Power Sector[2]	Commercial Sector[3]	Industrial Sector[4]	Total	Imports[5]	Exports[5]	Net Imports[5]		Retail Sales[8]	Direct Use[9]	Total
2009	3,809.8	8.2	132.3	3,950.3	52.2	18.1	34.1	260.6	3,596.9	126.9	3,723.8
2010	3,972.4	8.6	144.1	4,125.1	45.1	19.1	26.0	264.6	3,754.5	131.9	3,886.4
2011	3,948.2	10.1	141.9	4,100.1	52.3	15.0	37.3	254.8	3,749.8	132.8	3,882.6
2012	3,890.4	11.3	146.1	4,047.8	59.3	12.0	47.3	262.7	3,694.7	137.7	3,832.3
2013	3,903.7	12.2	150.0	4,066.0	70.4	11.4	59.0	256.6	3,724.9	143.5	3,868.3
2014	3,937.0	12.5	144.1	4,093.6	66.5	13.3	53.2	243.5	3,764.7	138.6	3,903.3
2015	3,919.3	12.6	145.7	4,077.6	75.8	9.1	66.7	244.1	3,759.0	141.2	3,900.2
2016	3,918.1	12.7	145.9	4,076.7	72.7	6.2	66.5	240.9	3,762.5	139.8	3,902.3
2017	3,877.4	13.1	143.8	4,034.3	65.7	9.4	56.3	225.6	3,723.8	141.1	3,864.9
2018[1]	4,032.7	13.3	145.7	4,191.6	59.5	13.8	45.7	282.9	3,811.4	143.1	3,954.4

[1] Preliminary.   [2] Electricity-only and combined-heat-and-power (CHP) plants within the NAICS 22 category whose primary business is to sell electricity, or electricity and heat, to the public.   [3] Commercial combined-heat-and-power (CHP) and commercial electricity-only plants.   [4] Industrial combined-heat-and-power (CHP) and industrial electricity-only plants.   [5] Electricity transmitted across U.S. borders. Net imports equal imports minus exports.   [6] Transmission and distribution losses.   [7] Data collection frame differences and nonsampling error.   [8] Electricity retail sales to ultimate customers by electric utilities and other energy service providers.   [9] Use of electricity that is 1) self-generated, 2) produced by either the same entity that consumes the power or an affiliate, and 3) used in direct support of a service or industrial process located within the same facility or group of facilities that house the generating equipment. Direct use is exclusive of station use.   *Source: U.S. Geological Survey (USGS)*

Electricity Net Generation in the United States by Sector   In Millions of Kilowatt Hours

	Fossil Fuels					Renewable Energy						
Year	Coal[2]	Petroleum[3]	Natural Gas[4]	Other Gases[5]	Nuclear electric power	Hydro-electric Pumped Storage[6]	Conventional Hydro-electric Power	Biomass: Wood[7]	Biomass: Waste[8]	Geo-thermal	Solar/ PV[9]	Wind	Total
2009	1,755,904	38,937	920,979	10,632	798,855	-4,627	273,445	36,050	18,443	15,009	891	73,886	3,950,331
2010	1,847,290	37,061	987,697	11,313	806,968	-5,501	260,203	37,172	18,917	15,219	1,212	94,652	4,125,060
2011	1,733,430	30,182	1,013,689	11,566	790,204	-6,421	319,355	37,449	19,222	15,316	1,818	120,177	4,100,141
2012	1,514,043	23,190	1,225,894	11,898	769,331	-4,950	276,240	37,799	19,823	15,562	4,327	140,822	4,047,765
2013	1,581,115	27,164	1,124,836	12,853	789,016	-4,681	268,565	40,028	20,830	15,775	9,036	167,840	4,065,964
2014	1,581,710	30,232	1,126,609	12,022	797,166	-6,174	259,367	42,340	21,650	15,877	17,691	181,655	4,093,606
2015	1,352,398	28,249	1,333,482	13,117	797,178	-5,091	249,080	41,929	21,703	15,918	24,893	190,719	4,077,601
2016	1,239,149	24,205	1,378,307	12,807	805,694	-6,686	267,812	40,947	21,813	15,826	36,054	226,993	4,076,827
2017	1,205,835	21,390	1,296,415	12,469	804,950	-6,495	300,333	41,152	21,610	15,927	53,286	254,303	4,034,268
2018[1]	1,144,690	24,865	1,486,905	12,220	802,277	-5,872	292,338	41,621	21,305	16,624	69,225	272,838	4,191,637

[1] Preliminary.   [2] Anthracite, bituminous coal, subbituminous coal, lignite, waste coal, and coal synfuel.   [3] Distillate fuel oil, residual fuel oil, petroleum coke, jet fuel, kerosene, other petroleum, waste oil, and propane.   [4] Natural gas, plus a small amount of supplemental gaseous fuels.   [5] Blast furnace gas, and other manufactured and waste gases derived from fossil fuels.   [6] Pumped storage facility production minus energy used for pumping.   [7] Wood and wood-derived fuels.   [8] Municipal solid waste from biogenic sources, landfill gas, sludge waste, agricultural byproducts, and other biomass.   [9] Solar thermal and photovoltaic (PV) energy.   *Source: U.S. Geological Survey (USGS)*

Total Electricity Net Generation in the United States   In Billions of Kilowatt Hours

Year	Jan.	Feb.	Mar.	Apr.	May	June	July	Aug.	Sept.	Oct.	Nov.	Dec.	Total
2009	355.0	300.9	310.6	289.5	311.3	347.7	372.5	381.2	327.4	307.0	296.6	350.5	3,950.3
2010	361.0	319.7	312.2	287.8	327.9	375.8	409.7	408.9	346.0	307.9	306.0	362.1	4,125.1
2011	362.9	313.1	318.7	302.4	323.6	367.7	418.7	406.5	337.9	308.7	304.1	335.7	4,100.1
2012	339.5	309.4	309.1	295.2	336.5	360.8	414.6	395.7	334.6	311.7	306.0	334.6	4,047.8
2013	349.0	309.7	325.4	299.3	322.2	356.8	394.8	385.3	340.9	314.9	314.5	353.0	4,066.0
2014	377.3	324.3	331.8	297.6	324.7	357.8	385.8	384.3	339.9	314.5	317.5	338.0	4,093.6
2015	360.5	334.5	324.2	294.1	322.1	362.4	400.4	392.1	350.1	312.1	300.7	324.4	4,077.6
2016	352.7	313.7	304.4	292.9	316.8	367.8	411.9	409.7	351.5	312.9	297.1	345.3	4,076.7
2017	343.2	289.7	317.9	294.3	322.5	357.9	404.4	384.3	335.9	320.4	310.3	353.5	4,034.3
2018[1]	374.3	306.1	321.0	301.7	339.7	372.4	412.5	408.0	356.7	325.6	322.4	337.3	4,177.8

[1] Preliminary.   Source: Energy Information Administration, U.S. Department of Energy (EIA-DOE)

Imports[2] of Electricity in the United States   In Billions of Kilowatt Hours

Year	Jan.	Feb.	Mar.	Apr.	May	June	July	Aug.	Sept.	Oct.	Nov.	Dec.	Total
2009	4.3	3.9	2.9	3.3	4.1	4.7	5.5	5.8	4.5	4.7	3.8	4.6	52.2
2010	5.3	4.4	4.4	3.9	3.1	4.1	4.3	3.6	2.9	2.5	2.7	4.0	45.1
2011	4.3	3.7	4.0	3.8	4.9	4.5	6.0	5.6	4.0	3.7	3.5	4.3	52.3
2012	4.1	3.6	4.2	5.0	5.5	5.4	6.7	6.3	4.9	4.4	4.7	4.4	59.3
2013	5.8	5.3	5.8	5.0	5.9	6.0	6.7	6.9	5.6	5.6	6.0	5.9	70.4
2014	5.5	4.4	5.6	4.8	5.4	5.5	6.3	6.7	6.0	5.4	5.6	5.4	66.5
2015	6.0	5.6	6.6	6.5	6.6	6.7	6.9	7.2	6.6	5.3	5.8	5.9	75.8
2016	6.5	5.4	5.8	4.7	5.6	6.7	7.7	7.3	5.3	5.8	6.4	5.4	72.7
2017	7.0	5.7	6.0	5.6	5.1	6.0	5.9	6.5	5.2	4.0	3.9	4.8	65.7
2018[1]	5.2	4.8	5.6	4.5	5.2	5.5	5.4	6.1	4.3	3.7	3.8	4.1	58.3

[1] Preliminary.   [2] Electricity transmitted across U.S. borders. Net imports equal imports minus exports.   Source: Energy Information Administration, U.S. Department of Energy (EIA-DOE)

Exports[2] of Electricity in the United States   In Billions of Kilowatt Hours

Year	Jan.	Feb.	Mar.	Apr.	May	June	July	Aug.	Sept.	Oct.	Nov.	Dec.	Total
2009	2.3	1.5	1.7	1.5	1.4	1.6	1.4	1.4	1.4	1.4	1.3	1.4	18.1
2010	1.2	1.0	1.3	1.3	1.7	1.6	1.5	1.8	2.4	2.1	1.9	1.4	19.1
2011	1.6	1.5	1.5	1.6	1.3	1.3	1.3	1.0	1.0	0.9	1.1	0.9	15.0
2012	0.9	0.9	1.2	1.3	1.2	1.2	1.0	0.9	0.9	0.7	0.8	1.1	12.0
2013	1.0	0.8	0.9	1.2	1.0	0.8	1.0	0.9	0.7	1.0	0.9	1.1	11.4
2014	1.3	1.3	1.9	1.3	0.8	1.0	1.0	0.9	0.8	1.0	0.9	1.1	13.3
2015	0.8	1.4	0.9	0.6	0.6	0.6	0.6	0.7	0.7	0.7	0.7	0.8	9.1
2016	0.4	0.6	0.7	0.5	0.4	0.6	0.6	0.6	0.6	0.4	0.4	0.6	6.2
2017	0.5	0.7	1.0	1.1	0.8	0.8	0.7	0.8	0.7	0.7	0.8	0.7	9.4
2018[1]	1.1	1.3	1.2	1.6	1.1	1.2	0.9	1.1	1.1	0.9	1.3	0.9	13.8

[1] Preliminary.   [2] Electricity transmitted across U.S. borders. Net imports equal imports minus exports.   Source: Energy Information Administration, U.S. Department of Energy (EIA-DOE)

Total End Use of Electricity in the United States   In Billions of Kilowatt Hours

Year	Jan.	Feb.	Mar.	Apr.	May	June	July	Aug.	Sept.	Oct.	Nov.	Dec.	Total
2009	331.7	296.5	294.0	275.3	285.0	315.5	349.5	356.9	322.1	298.1	278.4	320.8	3,723.8
2010	342.9	308.6	303.4	277.1	294.3	341.9	380.7	384.0	338.9	298.4	285.4	330.7	3,886.4
2011	345.3	306.9	302.4	285.6	298.7	339.9	382.8	385.0	337.5	298.6	286.1	313.6	3,882.6
2012	322.6	298.0	294.7	281.3	308.3	336.6	383.5	377.2	329.5	301.9	289.5	309.2	3,832.3
2013	333.0	302.6	309.2	288.9	301.0	332.2	371.7	366.3	335.2	306.0	293.2	329.1	3,868.3
2014	353.3	319.6	313.8	286.7	302.6	334.2	363.9	364.3	338.5	307.9	296.7	321.8	3,903.3
2015	341.9	317.5	316.5	286.1	299.3	338.3	375.9	374.7	345.0	307.6	287.6	309.8	3,900.2
2016	332.8	307.9	297.4	280.4	296.1	341.6	384.7	393.9	348.4	308.0	288.6	322.4	3,902.3
2017	330.3	286.7	303.1	284.0	303.4	340.6	380.4	372.9	333.0	310.9	294.8	324.8	3,864.9
2018[1]	352.9	299.1	303.8	285.2	309.7	345.2	382.3	390.6	343.7	315.8	297.6	319.6	3,945.5

[1] Preliminary.   Source: Energy Information Administration, U.S. Department of Energy (EIA-DOE)

Ethanol

World Production of Fuel Ethanol   In Thousands of Barrels per Day

Year	Australia	Brazil	Canada	China	Colombia	France	Germany	India	Jamaica	Spain	Thailand	United States	World Total
2007	22.4	6,230.2	224.2	464.5	75.3	148.9	108.9	72.1	78.5	112.1	48.0	6,521.0	14,815.0
2008	40.0	7,463.5	240.2	544.5	70.5	256.3	160.2	80.1	102.5	96.1	91.3	9,308.8	19,459.6
2009	56.0	6,610.0	362.4	680.6	47.4	247.3	200.4	27.6	----	126.9	115.6	10,937.8	20,660.0
2010	75.9	7,112.2	378.7	684.2	54.9	268.9	212.7	13.8	----	137.7	124.5	13,297.9	23,681.2
2011	88.0	5,803.4	445.6	708.2	63.5	272.0	199.3	100.7	----	127.5	134.1	13,929.1	23,296.6
2012	95.5	6,036.6	471.1	786.6	77.9	251.5	213.5	84.2	----	105.2	130.0	13,218.0	23,864.6
2013	84.2	6,978.0	465.0	809.8	81.7	259.6	229.4	105.4	----	123.2	262.2	13,292.7	25,342.0
2014	71.6	7,128.7	472.6	814.5	84.0	262.1	241.8	96.6	----	120.8	292.0	14,312.8	26,628.5
2015[1]	68.8	7,669.3	477.1	849.5	119.8	264.0	248.1	189.1	----	129.1	324.0	14,807.2	27,824.4
2016[2]	68.8	7,374.4	486.8	868.4	122.6	249.4	247.3	306.4	26.1	102.6	352.2	15,413.2	

[1] Preliminary.   [2] Estimate.   *Source: Renewable Fuels Association*

Salient Statistics of Ethanol in the United States

Year	Ethanol Plants	Ethanol Production Capacity (mgy)	Plants Under Con-struction	Capacity Under Construction (mgy)	Farmer Owned Plants	Farmer Owned Capacity (mgy)	Percent of Total Capacity Farmer	Farmer Owned UC Plants	Farmers Owned UC Capacity	Percent of Total UC Capacity	States with Ethanol Plants
2009	170	12,475.4	24	2,066.0	NA	NA	NA	NA	NA	NA	26
2010	189	13,028.4	15	1,432.0	----	----	----	----	----	----	26
2011	204	14,071.4	10	560.0	----	----	----	----	----	----	29
2012	209	14,906.9	2	140.0	----	----	----	----	----	----	29
2013	211	14,837.4	2	50.0	----	----	----	----	----	----	28
2014	210	14,879.5	7	167.0	----	----	----	----	----	----	28
2015	213	15,077.0	3	100.0	----	----	----	----	----	----	29
2016	214	15,594.0	3	162.0	----	----	----	----	----	----	28
2017[1]	213	15,998.0	3	91.0	----	----	----	----	----	----	28
2018[2]	211	16,241.0	7	465.0	----	----	----	----	----	----	28

[1] Preliminary.   [2] Estimate.   *Source: Renewable Fuels Association*

Production of Fuel Ethanol in the United States   In Thousands of Barrels

Year	Jan.	Feb.	Mar.	Apr.	May	June	July	Aug.	Sept.	Oct.	Nov.	Dec.	Total
2009	19,561	18,255	20,121	19,374	21,024	21,125	22,887	23,136	22,218	23,467	24,122	25,134	260,424
2010	25,625	23,802	26,486	25,384	26,244	25,632	26,584	26,964	26,221	27,471	27,747	28,457	316,617
2011	28,467	25,300	28,178	26,538	27,720	27,224	27,541	27,976	26,588	28,013	28,383	29,718	331,646
2012	29,038	26,647	27,548	26,346	27,616	26,513	25,236	26,092	24,376	24,976	24,744	25,582	314,714
2013	24,778	22,494	25,620	25,601	27,197	26,722	26,923	26,279	25,564	27,995	27,915	29,405	316,493
2014	28,194	25,269	28,120	27,733	28,888	28,629	29,413	28,665	27,807	28,644	28,588	30,831	340,781
2015	29,770	26,814	29,485	27,910	29,666	29,684	30,249	29,762	28,571	29,886	29,675	31,081	352,553
2016	30,452	28,810	30,957	28,208	30,346	30,443	31,469	31,856	30,048	31,006	30,706	32,680	366,981
2017	32,887	29,307	32,393	29,639	31,863	30,794	31,384	32,672	30,701	32,212	32,631	32,952	379,435
2018[1]	32,428	29,519	32,216	30,532	32,215	31,924	33,496	33,773	30,667	32,380	31,514	31,736	382,400

[1] Preliminary.   *Source: Energy Information Administration, U.S. Department of Energy (EIA-DOE)*

Stocks of Fuel Ethanol in the United States   In Thousands of Barrels

Year	Jan.	Feb.	Mar.	Apr.	May	June	July	Aug.	Sept.	Oct.	Nov.	Dec.
2009	14,514	15,834	16,411	15,322	14,173	13,974	14,223	14,671	15,283	14,933	15,578	16,594
2010	18,251	19,297	20,222	20,042	19,851	18,565	17,809	17,380	17,437	17,278	18,150	17,941
2011	20,826	21,016	21,593	21,065	20,609	19,217	18,788	18,123	18,465	18,038	18,308	18,238
2012	21,475	22,393	22,583	22,050	21,635	21,239	20,224	19,180	19,921	18,626	19,992	20,350
2013	19,894	19,009	18,410	17,370	16,804	16,428	17,072	16,945	15,986	15,750	15,569	16,424
2014	17,153	16,865	17,310	17,610	18,330	18,785	18,696	18,218	18,724	17,341	17,035	18,739
2015	20,647	21,057	20,878	20,854	20,154	20,128	19,701	19,390	18,944	18,984	20,099	21,596
2016	23,347	23,171	22,730	21,336	20,962	21,284	21,381	21,198	20,713	20,113	19,463	19,758
2017	22,679	23,195	23,981	23,671	22,855	21,770	21,167	21,186	21,507	21,663	23,203	23,043
2018[1]	24,229	24,335	22,883	23,256	22,636	21,880	22,802	22,833	24,422	23,675	23,679	23,338

[1] Preliminary.   *Source: Energy Information Administration, U.S. Department of Energy (EIA-DOE)*

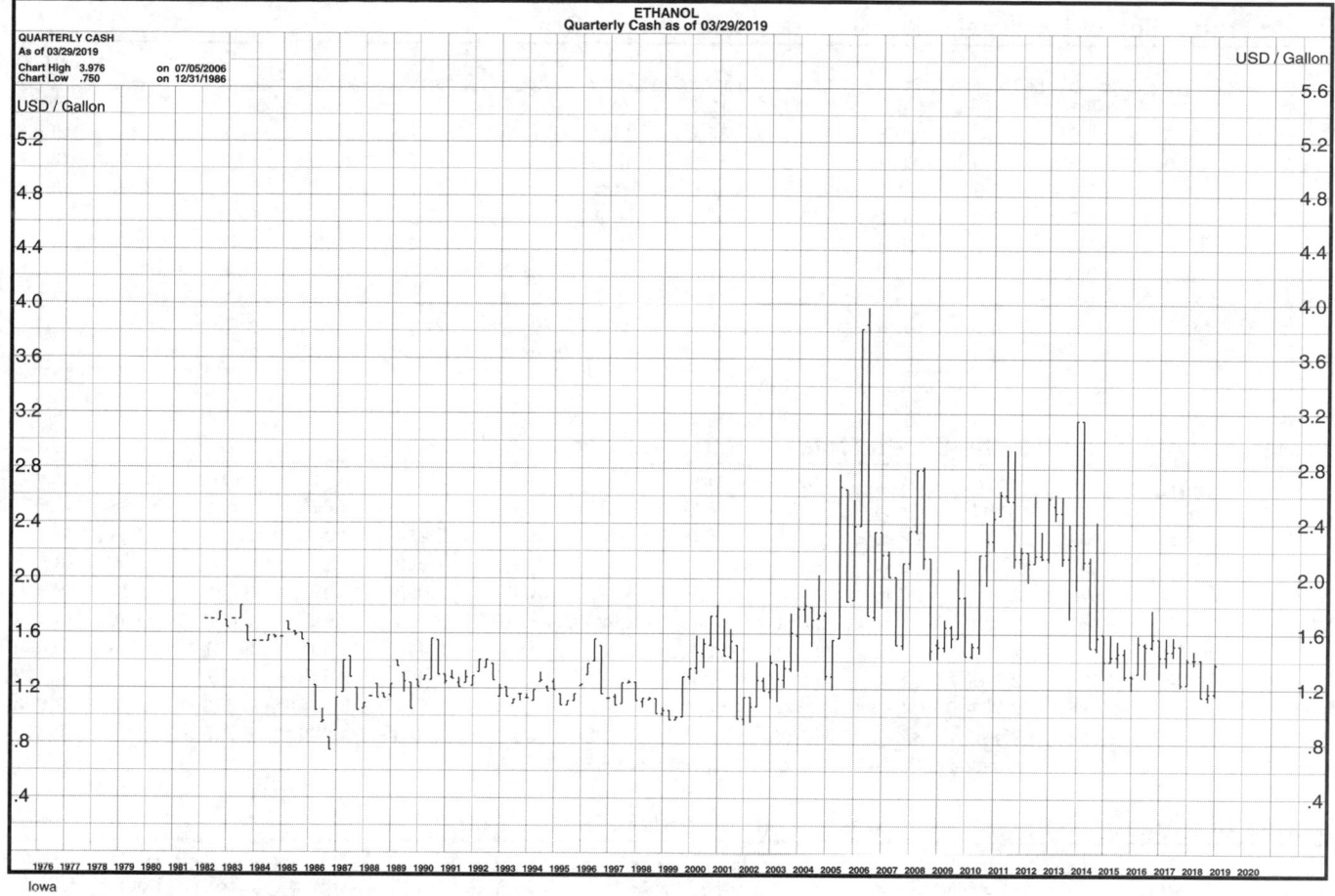

ETHANOL
Quarterly Cash as of 03/29/2019

QUARTERLY CASH
As of 03/29/2019

Chart High 3.976   on 07/05/2006
Chart Low   .750   on 12/31/1986

USD / Gallon

Iowa

Average Price of Ethanol in the United States[1]   In Dollars Per Gallon

Year	Jan.	Feb.	Mar.	Apr.	May	June	July	Aug.	Sept.	Oct.	Nov.	Dec. Average
2011	2.268	2.292	2.435	2.504	2.546	2.600	2.718	2.830	2.745	2.596	2.825	2.324 2.562
2012	2.128	2.089	2.177	2.152	2.107	2.002	2.399	2.532	2.397	2.296	2.301	2.265 2.237
2013	2.197	2.331	2.473	2.478	2.553	2.571	2.430	2.287	2.346	2.096	1.942	2.314 2.335
2014	2.073	1.946	2.478	2.800	2.237	2.225	2.100	2.096	1.827	1.561	2.019	1.995 2.113
2015	1.382	1.313	1.386	1.479	1.568	1.440	1.493	1.418	1.408	1.472	1.425	1.347 1.428
2016	1.235	1.304	1.273	1.417	1.466	1.562	1.480	1.333	1.430	1.519	1.545	1.649 1.434
2017	1.400	1.381	1.378	1.541	1.446	1.505	1.472	1.487	1.510	1.407	1.357	1.267 1.429
2018	1.270	1.338	1.408	1.430	1.397	1.403	1.406	1.341	1.223	1.196	1.230	1.156 1.317

[1] Northeast and Northwest Iowa.   Source: Agricultural Marketing Service, U.S. Department of Agriculture (AMS-USDA)

Volume of Trading of Ethanol Futures in Chicago   In Contracts

Year	Jan.	Feb.	Mar.	Apr.	May	June	July	Aug.	Sept.	Oct.	Nov.	Dec.	Total
2013	29,052	31,990	37,290	40,033	30,116	30,695	27,053	22,140	16,027	13,413	11,025	9,884	298,718
2014	18,334	20,874	20,547	24,319	20,168	24,842	18,015	17,399	20,134	22,580	19,087	16,773	243,072
2015	24,040	13,103	17,508	20,055	20,013	17,466	17,981	11,506	10,947	10,938	11,211	12,893	187,661
2016	14,151	11,923	15,335	13,085	13,549	20,010	14,181	12,121	13,043	11,682	16,030	17,554	172,664
2017	18,902	15,630	18,607	16,246	17,896	9,817	6,524	9,114	6,012	10,185	9,943	10,670	149,546
2018	10,502	9,213	8,683	9,238	9,476	9,346	6,682	8,319	8,239	9,346	12,343	11,051	112,438

Contract size = 29,000 US gallons.   Source: CME Group; Chicago Board of Trade (CBT)

Average Open Interest of Ethanol Futures in Chicago   In Contracts

Year	Jan.	Feb.	Mar.	Apr.	May	June	July	Aug.	Sept.	Oct.	Nov.	Dec.
2013	9,090	9,812	11,152	10,792	10,018	9,985	9,137	7,796	6,382	4,724	3,798	3,278
2014	3,944	5,403	5,556	6,826	7,137	6,617	6,381	6,252	6,519	6,796	5,810	5,548
2015	6,518	6,892	7,296	6,781	7,978	7,336	6,511	5,381	4,905	5,167	5,098	4,253
2016	4,270	4,361	4,130	4,449	5,193	5,170	4,828	4,361	4,477	5,054	5,571	5,352
2017	5,783	4,991	4,743	4,849	3,660	2,551	2,062	1,742	1,501	1,674	2,011	2,332
2018	2,812	2,162	1,970	1,982	1,916	1,957	1,899	2,069	2,177	2,367	2,598	2,796

Contract size = 29,000 US gallons.   Source: CME Group; Chicago Board of Trade (CBT)

ETHANOL

World Production of Biodiesel   In Thousands of Barrels per Day

Year	Argentina	Austria	Belgium	Brazil	China	France	Germany	Indo-nesia	Italy	Spain	Thailand	United States	World Total
2007	3.7	5.1	----	5.8	6.1	19.1	58.9	4.7	4.0	3.6	1.8	32.0	180.7
2008	14.6	4.9	----	19.3	9.2	35.2	49.9	10.9	13.1	4.4	7.3	44.1	265.3
2009	23.0	5.2	2.6	27.7	10.2	41.8	48.3	5.7	15.7	14.6	10.5	33.7	307.5
2010	38.7	5.4	6.9	41.1	9.8	40.0	61.2	12.8	15.7	16.9	11.4	22.4	364.4
2011	51.7	4.7	6.2	46.1	12.7	36.6	60.9	31.0	11.6	13.6	10.9	63.1	449.0
2012	52.2	4.1	6.2	46.8	15.7	43.7	55.6	37.9	5.6	9.9	15.7	64.5	482.5
2013	39.4	3.5	6.1	50.3	18.6	43.1	59.7	48.3	9.0	14.5	18.6	88.7	537.2
2014	51.3	5.2	9.0	59.0	19.5	47.0	68.1	51.7	11.4	24.0	20.2	83.4	597.7
2015[1]	35.9	6.8	5.0	67.8	9.4	48.6	61.9	20.3	11.4	22.0	21.5	82.4	547.9
2016[2]	48.3	5.7	4.7	65.5	8.6	45.1	62.4	63.0	11.0	26.8	21.4	102.0	

[1] Preliminary.   [2] Estimate.   *Source: Renewable Fuels Association*

Production of Biodiesel in the United States   In Thousands of Barrels (mbbl)

Year	Jan.	Feb.	Mar.	Apr.	May	June	July	Aug.	Sept.	Oct.	Nov.	Dec.	Average
2010	633	696	804	814	760	644	657	653	723	676	528	588	8,177
2011	842	961	1,419	1,692	1,838	1,938	2,183	2,273	2,284	2,508	2,494	2,604	23,035
2012	1,751	1,887	2,251	2,237	2,428	2,223	2,127	2,176	1,949	1,792	1,363	1,406	23,588
2013	1,640	1,672	2,412	2,548	2,645	2,699	3,072	3,086	3,025	3,272	3,080	3,217	32,368
2014	1,727	1,801	2,361	2,223	2,531	2,645	2,926	2,987	2,754	2,928	2,610	2,958	30,452
2015	1,727	1,851	2,326	2,568	2,784	2,901	2,883	2,933	2,479	2,535	2,521	2,573	30,080
2016	2,490	2,504	2,861	2,856	3,222	3,205	3,331	3,385	3,206	3,433	3,408	3,425	37,327
2017	2,208	2,238	2,761	3,020	3,242	3,344	3,560	3,559	3,507	3,515	3,523	3,515	37,993
2018[1]	2,945	2,996	3,493	3,344	3,538	3,718	3,892	4,028	3,850	4,039	3,783	3,991	43,616

[1] Preliminary.   *Source: Energy Information Administration, U.S. Department of Energy (EIA-DOE)*

Stocks of Biodiesel in the United States   In Thousands of Barrels (Mbbl)

Year	Jan.	Feb.	Mar.	Apr.	May	June	July	Aug.	Sept.	Oct.	Nov.	Dec.
2012	2,503	2,888	2,886	2,773	2,710	2,348	2,262	2,011	2,049	2,176	1,862	1,984
2013	2,002	2,026	2,390	2,507	2,460	2,485	2,683	2,549	2,509	2,483	3,360	3,810
2014	3,708	3,726	3,604	3,402	3,135	2,798	3,089	2,786	2,293	2,641	3,084	3,131
2015	4,032	4,245	4,244	4,071	3,599	3,063	3,404	3,333	3,021	3,070	3,600	3,943
2016	4,222	4,133	4,167	4,358	4,091	4,726	4,443	4,265	4,227	4,690	5,314	6,398
2017	6,397	6,475	6,189	5,706	4,909	5,052	5,405	5,356	4,849	4,485	4,233	4,268
2018[1]	4,557	4,924	4,916	4,681	4,257	3,845	3,583	3,412	3,360	3,647	4,056	4,684

[1] Preliminary.   *Source: Energy Information Administration, U.S. Department of Energy (EIA-DOE)*

Imports of Biodiesel in the United States   In Thousands of Barrels (mbbl)

Year	Jan.	Feb.	Mar.	Apr.	May	June	July	Aug.	Sept.	Oct.	Nov.	Dec.	Average
2011	50	39	55	54	49	50	64	67	67	85	69	241	890
2012	48	72	25	32	75	132	166	55	108	60	9	71	853
2013	38	88	439	372	410	698	358	385	781	1,177	1,641	1,765	8,152
2014	222	161	240	135	133	235	493	571	352	507	989	540	4,578
2015	372	526	340	330	336	673	1,157	961	1,062	863	701	1,078	8,399
2016	248	287	565	969	1,117	1,630	1,681	1,873	1,835	1,822	2,184	2,668	16,879
2017	241	549	650	681	948	1,736	1,670	1,582	205	386	222	504	9,374
2018[1]	246	146	457	308	325	296	157	281	277	468	416	536	3,913

[1] Preliminary.   *Source: Energy Information Administration, U.S. Department of Energy (EIA-DOE)*

Exports of Biodiesel in the United States   In Thousands of Barrels (mbbl)

Year	Jan.	Feb.	Mar.	Apr.	May	June	July	Aug.	Sept.	Oct.	Nov.	Dec.	Average
2011	224	91	204	229	198	120	147	74	199	136	135	40	1,799
2012	258	125	189	230	320	392	426	403	295	209	65	143	3,056
2013	16	37	176	371	563	587	429	687	511	415	408	476	4,675
2014	134	141	91	261	208	263	320	264	136	40	65	51	1,974
2015	22	23	191	240	255	260	255	275	200	161	76	133	2,091
2016	42	49	234	246	335	220	250	235	150	114	143	80	2,098
2017	42	59	136	283	239	226	453	387	100	217	49	35	2,228
2018[1]	102	103	255	217	382	275	259	263	190	188	156	61	2,453

[1] Preliminary.   *Source: Energy Information Administration, U.S. Department of Energy (EIA-DOE)*

Fertilizer

Fertilizer is a natural or synthetic chemical substance, or mixture, that enriches soil to promote plant growth. The three primary nutrients that fertilizers provide are nitrogen, potassium, and phosphorus. In ancient times, and still today, many commonly used fertilizers contain one or more of the three primary ingredients: manure (containing nitrogen), bones (containing small amounts of nitrogen and large quantities of phosphorus), and potash (containing potassium).

At least fourteen different nutrients have been found essential for crops. These include three organic nutrients (carbon, hydrogen, and oxygen, which are taken directly from air and water), three primary chemical nutrients (nitrogen, phosphorus, and potassium), and three secondary chemical nutrients (magnesium, calcium, and sulfur). The others are micronutrients or trace elements and include iron, manganese, copper, zinc, boron, and molybdenum.

Prices – The average price of ammonia (Gulf Coast delivery), a key source of ingredients for fertilizers, fell by -10.1% yr/yr in 2017 to $240 per metric ton, far below the 2008 record high of $590 per metric ton. The average price of potash in the U.S. in 2016 rose by +36.8% yr/yr to $360.00 per metric ton, below the 2009 record high of $800.00 per metric ton.

Supply – World production of ammonia (as contained in nitrogen) in 2018 fell -1.4% to 140.000 million metric tons, below the 2015 record high of 147.000. The world's largest producers of nitrogen in 2018 were China with 31.4% of world production, Russia with 10.0%, the U.S. with 8.9%, and India with 7.9%. U.S. nitrogen production in 2018 rose +7.8% to 12.500 million metric tons. World production of phosphate rock, basic slag and guano in 2018 rose +0.4% yr/yr to 270.000 million metric tons. The world's largest producers of phosphate rock in 2018 were China with 51.9% of world production, Morocco with 12.2%, the U.S. with 10.0%, and Russia with 4.8%. U.S. production in 2018 fell -3.2% yr/yr to 27.000 million metric tons.

World production of marketable potash in 2018 rose +1.4% yr/yr to 42.000 million metric tons. The world's largest producers of potash in 2018 were Canada with 28.6% of world production, Russia with 17.9%, Belarus with 16.9%, and China with 13.1%. U.S. production of potash in 2017 rose +4.2% to 500,000 metric tons.

Demand – U.S. consumption of phosphate rock in 2018 fell -6.3% to 27.000 million metric tons. U.S. consumption of potash in 2018 rose by +1.6% yr/yr to 6.3 million metric tons. U.S. consumption of nitrogen in 2016 fell -0.8% to 11.900 million metric tons.

Trade – U.S. imports of nitrogen in 2018 fell -15.9% yr/yr to 2.600 million metric tons and the U.S. relied on imports for 14% of its consumption. U.S. imports of phosphate rock in 2018 rose +18.0% yr/yr to 3.000 million metric tons. U.S. imports of potash in 2018 rose +0.5% to 5.900 million metric tons, higher than the 4-decade low of 2.220 million metric tons posted in 2009. Imports accounted for 92% of U.S. consumption.

World Production of Ammonia   In Thousands of Metric Tons of Contained Nitrogen

Year	Canada	China	France	Germany	India	Indo-nesia	Japan	Mexico	Nether-lands	Poland	Russia	United States	Total
2010	3,620	40,870	3,517	2,677	10,600	4,800	968	824	1,800	1,700	10,902	8,290	132,000
2011	3,946	43,250	3,500	2,821	10,500	5,000	995	709	1,800	1,918	11,418	9,350	138,000
2012	3,942	45,520	2,644	2,823	10,650	5,100	867	772	2,200	2,026	11,401	8,730	139,000
2013	3,942	48,326	2,640	2,757	10,840	5,000	828	1,136	2,300	2,119	11,879	9,170	144,000
2014	3,807	45,642	2,600	2,540	10,780	5,000	787	1,089	2,200	2,200	12,030	9,330	141,000
2015	4,140	49,706	2,600	2,500	10,800	5,000	790	1,100	2,300	2,200	12,485	9,590	147,000
2016	4,140	46,000	2,600	2,500	10,800	5,000	790	1,100	2,300	2,200	12,500	10,150	144,000
2017[1]	3,750	43,600	1,010	2,500	10,800	5,000		1,100	2,300	2,340	14,000	11,600	142,000
2018[2]	3,800	44,000	1,000	2,500	11,000	6,000			2,300	2,300	14,000	12,500	140,000

[1] Preliminary.   [2] Estimate.   *Source: U.S. Geological Survey (USGS)*

Salient Statistics of Nitrogen[3] (Ammonia) in the United States   In Thousands of Metric Tons

Year	Net Import Reliance As a % of Apparent Consumption	Production[3] (Fixed) Fertilizer	Non-fertilizer	Total	Imprts[4] (Fixed)	Exports	Nitrogen[5] Compounds Pro-duced	Con-sumption	Stocks, Dec. 31 Am-monia	Fixed Nitrogen Com-pounds	Ammonia Con-sumption (Apparent)	Urea FOB Gulf[6] Coast	Urea FOB Corn Belt	Ammonium Nitrate: FOB Corn Belt	Ammonia FOB Gulf Coast
2010	40	7,130	1,160	8,290	5,540	36	8,597	11,200	165	328	13,800	370-380	415-440	640-685	396
2011	37	8,170	1,180	9,350	5,600	26	8,759	11,600	178	178	14,900	360-375	410-450	670-710	531
2012	37	7,600	1,140	8,730	5,170	31	8,579	12,300	180	180	13,900	393-410	440-480	760-820	579
2013	34	8,070	1,100	9,170	4,960	196	8,759	11,900	240	240	13,900	325-342	370-380	510-550	541
2014	30	8,210	1,120	9,330	4,150	111	8,391	11,400	280	280	13,300	322-333	360-385	570-640	531
2015	30	8,440	1,150	9,590	4,320	93	8,266	12,000	420	420	13,700	225-230	265-295	445-470	481
2016	26	8,930	1,220	10,200	3,840	183	8,918	11,900	400	400	13,800	232-242	255-275	290-405	267
2017[1]	18			11,600	3,090	612			320	410	14,100				240
2018[2]	14			12,500	2,600	430			400		14,600				

[1] Preliminary.   [2] Estimate.   [3] Anhydrous ammonia, synthetic.   [4] For consumption.   [5] Major downstream nitrogen compounds.   [6] Granular.
Source: U.S. Geological Survey (USGS)

FERTILIZER

World Production of Phosphate Rock, Basic Slag & Guano   In Thousands of Metric Tons (Gross Weight)

Year	Brazil	China	Egypt	Israel	Jordan	Morocco	Russia	Senegal	Syria	Togo	Tunisia	United States	World Total
2009	6,084	60,200	6,227	2,697	5,282	18,307	9,500	949	2,128	726	7,409	26,400	161,000
2010	6,192	68,000	3,435	3,135	6,529	26,603	11,000	1,079	3,167	695	8,149	25,800	184,000
2011	6,738	81,000	4,746	3,105	7,594	28,052	10,300	1,411	3,541	866	2,479	28,100	200,000
2012	6,740	95,300	6,236	3,514	6,383	27,060	10,300	1,381	1,534	1,159	2,762	30,100	216,000
2013	6,715	111,700	5,922	3,578	5,399	26,400	11,000	800	1,000	1,214	3,283	31,200	232,000
2014	6,513	120,000	5,400	3,357	7,144	27,390	11,000	900	1,230	1,086	3,784	25,300	237,000
2015	6,100	120,000	5,500	3,538	8,335	29,000	11,600	1,240	750	1,100	2,800	27,400	241,000
2016	5,200	135,000	5,000	3,950	7,990	26,900	12,400	2,200		850	3,660	27,100	255,000
2017[1]	5,200	144,000	4,400	3,850	8,690	30,000	13,300	1,390		825	4,420	27,900	269,000
2018[2]	5,400	140,000	4,600	3,900	8,800	33,000	13,000	1,500		850	3,300	27,000	270,000

[1] Preliminary.   [2] Estimate.   *Source: U.S. Geological Survey (USGS)*

Salient Statistics of Phosphate Rock in the United States   In Thousands of Metric Tons

Year	Mine Production	Marketable Production	Value Million Dollars	Imports for Consumption	Exports	Apparent Consumption	Producer Stocks, Dec. 31	Avg. Price FOB Mine $/Metric Ton	Avg. Price of Florida & N. Carolina - $/Met. Ton - FOB Mine (-60% to +74%) - Domestic	Export	Average
2009	107,000	26,400	3,360	2,000	----	27,500	8,120	127.19	----	----	NA
2010	106,000	25,800	1,980	2,400	----	30,500	5,620	76.69	----	----	----
2011	129,000	28,100	2,720	3,750	----	32,000	4,580	96.64	----	----	----
2012	150,000	30,100	3,080	3,570	----	30,900	6,700	102.54	----	----	----
2013	139,000	31,200	2,850	3,170	----	31,900	9,000	91.11	----	----	----
2014	112,000	25,300	1,990	2,380	----	29,100	5,880	78.59	----	----	----
2015	127,000	27,400	1,980	1,960	----	28,100	6,730	72.41	----	----	----
2016		27,100		1,590	----	28,200	7,450	76.90	----	----	----
2017[1]		27,900		2,520	----	28,800	8,440	73.67	----	----	----
2018[2]		27,000		3,000	----	27,000	11,000	68.00	----	----	----

[1] Preliminary.   [2] Estimate.   *Source: U.S. Geological Survey (USGS)*

World Production of Marketable Potash   In Thousands of Metric Tons (K_2O Equivalent)

Year	Belarus	Brazil	Canada	Chile	China	Germany	Israel	Jordan	Russia	Spain	United Kingdom	United States	World Total
2009	2,485	453	4,297	691	3,200	1,825	1,900	683	3,727	400	411	715	20,800
2010	5,223	418	9,700	929	3,600	3,024	1,650	1,166	6,283	514	427	930	33,900
2011	5,306	395	10,686	832	3,800	3,215	1,610	1,355	6,498	521	470	1,000	35,800
2012	4,840	347	8,976	1,018	3,770	3,149	1,830	1,094	5,563	632	549	900	32,800
2013	4,243	311	10,196	1,153	5,300	3,075	1,824	1,046	6,100	711	549	960	35,600
2014	6,306	311	10,818	1,130	6,110	3,127	1,842	1,255	7,439	685	610	850	40,800
2015	6,468	293	11,420	1,200	6,200	3,100	1,260	1,413	6,993	690	610	740	40,700
2016	6,180	301	10,800	1,200	6,200	2,800	2,050	1,200	6,480	670	450	500	39,300
2017[1]	7,100	290	12,200	1,100	5,510	2,700	2,000	1,390	7,300	610	250	480	41,400
2018[2]	7,100	300	12,000	1,000	5,500	2,900	2,000	1,400	7,500	560	190	500	42,000

[1] Preliminary.   [2] Estimate.   *Source: U.S. Geological Survey (USGS)*

Salient Statistics of Potash in the United States   In Thousands of Metric Tons (K_2O Equivalent)

Year	Net Import Reliance As a % of Apparent Consump	Production	Sales by Producers	Value Million Dollars	Imports for Consumption	Exports	Apparent Consumption	Producer Stocks Dec. 31	Avg Value of Product	Avg Value of K_2O Equiv	Avg. Price[3] (Metric Ton)
2009	73	720	630	500.0	2,220	303	2,500	----	330.00	800.00	800.00
2010	83	930	1,000	660.0	4,760	297	5,500	----	275.00	630.00	605.00
2011	83	1,000	990	740.0	4,980	175	5,800	----	320.00	745.00	730.00
2012	82	900	980	750.0	4,240	200	5,000	----	340.00	765.00	650.00
2013	82	960	880	630.0	4,650	255	5,300	----	315.00	715.00	590.00
2014	85	850	930	680.0	4,970	100	5,800	----	345.00	735.00	555.00
2015	87	740	620	550.0	5,000	106	5,500	----	360.00	810.00	570.00
2016	90	510	600	410.0	4,550	96	5,000	----	305.00	765.00	360.00
2017[1]	92	480	490		5,870	128	6,200	----		790.00	
2018[2]	92	500	550		5,900	110	6,300				

[1] Preliminary.   [2] Estimate.   [3] Unit of K_2O, standard 60% muriate F.O.B. mine.   *Source: U.S. Geological Survey (USGS)*

Fish

Fish are the primary source of protein for a large portion of the world's population. The worldwide yearly harvest of all sea fish (including aquaculture) is between 85 and 130 million metric tons. There are approximately 20,000 species of fish, of which 9,000 are regularly caught. Only 22 fish species are harvested in large amounts. Ground-fish, which are fish that live near or on the ocean floor, account for about 10% of the world's fishery harvest, and include cod, haddock, pollock, flounder, halibut and sole. Large pelagic fish such as tuna, swordfish, marlin, and mahi-mahi, account for about 5% of world harvest. The fish eaten most often in the United States is canned tuna.

Rising global demand for fish has increased the pressure to harvest more fish to the point where all 17 of the world's major fishing areas have either reached or exceeded their limits. Atlantic stocks of cod, haddock and blue-fin tuna are all seriously depleted, while in the Pacific, anchovies, salmon and halibut are all over-fished. Aquaculture, or fish farming, reduces pressure on wild stocks and now accounts for nearly 20% of world harvest.

Supply – The U.S. grand total of fishery products in 2016 rose by +0.4% to 21.508 billion pounds, which is a new record high. The U.S. total domestic catch in 2016 fell -1.5% to 9.572 billion pounds, and that comprised 44.5% of total U.S. supply. Of the U.S. total domestic catch in 2016, 66.8% of the catch was finfish for human consumption, 21.8% of the catch was a variety of fish for industrial use, and 11.4% was shellfish for human consumption. The principal species of U.S. fishery landings in 2016 were Pollock with 3.381 billion pounds, Menhaden with 1.728 billion pounds, Flounder with 565.4 million pounds, Pacific Salmon with 561.0 million pounds, and Sea Herring with 191.6 million pounds.

About 30% of the fish harvested in the world are processed directly into fishmeal and fish oil. Fishmeal is used primarily in animal feed. Fish oil is used in both animal feed and human food products. World fishmeal production in the 2017/18 marketing year fell by -2.1% to 4.874 million metric tons. Peru, the European Union and Thailand are the world's largest producers of fish meal. World production of fish oil in the 2017/18 marketing year rose +4.8% to 973.2 thousand metric tons. Peru, Chile and the U.S. are the world's largest producers of fish oil.

Trade – U.S. imports of fishery products in 2016 rose +1.90% yr/yr to 11.936 billion pounds, nearing the 2014 record high of 11.945, comprising 55.5% of total U.S. supply.

		-- For Human Food --		For	**Domestic Catch**		**-- For Human Food --**		For	**Imports**		**-- For Human Food --**		For
Year	Grand Total	Finfish	Shellfish[3]	Industrial Use[4]	Total	Percent of Grand Total	Finfish	Shellfish[3]	Industrial Use[4]	Total	Percent of Grand Total	Finfish	Shellfish[3]	Industrial Use[4]
2011	21,106	13,644	5,088	2,374	9,858	46.7	6,540	1,369	1,949	11,248	53.3	7,104	3,719	425
2012	20,757	13,159	4,907	2,692	9,634	46.4	6,163	1,314	2,157	11,123	53.6	6,996	3,592	535
2013	20,988	13,787	4,786	2,416	9,870	47.0	6,777	1,266	1,827	11,118	53.0	7,009	3,520	589
2014	21,431	14,060	5,054	2,317	9,486	44.3	6,588	1,240	1,658	11,945	55.7	7,473	3,814	659
2015	21,426	13,862	4,986	2,579	9,718	45.4	6,621	1,129	1,968	11,709	54.6	7,241	3,857	611
2016	21,542	13,746	5,034	2,762	9,572	44.4	6,393	1,092	2,088	11,970	55.6	7,353	3,942	675
2017[1]	22,266	14,421	5,384	2,461	9,916	44.5	7,121	1,107	1,688	12,350	55.5	7,301	4,276	773

[1] Preliminary. [2] Live weight, except percent. [3] For univalue and bivalues mollusks (conchs, clams, oysters, scallops, etc.) the weight of meats, excluding the shell is reported. [4] Fish meal and sea herring. *Source: Fisheries Statistics Division, U.S. Department of Commerce*

Fisheries -- Landings of Principal Species in the United States   In Millions of Pounds

Year	Cod, Atlantic	Flounder	Halibut	Herring, Sea	Man-haden	Pollock	Salmon, Pacific	Tuna	Whiting	Clams (Meats)	Crabs	Lobsters American	Oysters (Meats)	Scallops (Meats)	Shrimp
2011	18	707	43	276	1,875	2,827	780	50	17	86	369	126	29	59	313
2012	11	703	34	270	1,771	2,887	636	60	16	91	367	150	33	57	303
2013	5	717	30	298	1,467	3,014	1,069	56	14	91	332	149	35	41	283
2014	5	714	23	309	1,256	3,156	720	59	16	91	295	148	34	34	295
2015	3	555	25	247	1,618	3,269	1,066	57	14	86	326	146	28	36	327
2016	3	565	25	192	1,728	3,361	561	56	14	89	317	159	33	41	271
2017[1]	2	545	26	180	1,413	3,396	1,008	55	12	85	275	133	32	52	283

[1] Preliminary. *Source: National Marine Fisheries Service, U.S. Department of Commerce*

U.S. Fisheries: Quantity & Value of Domestic Catch & Consumption & World Fish Oil Production

Year	Fresh & Frozen	Canned	Cured	For Meal, Oil, etc.	Total	For Human Food	For Industrial Products	Ex-vessel Value[3] (Million $)	Average Price (Cents /Lb.)	Per Capita Consumption (Pounds)	World[2] Fish Oil Production (1,000 Tons)
2011	7,817	371	52	1,618	9,858	7,909	1,949	5,289	----	15.0	1,079
2012	7,541	299	82	1,712	9,634	7,477	2,157	5,103	----	14.4	933
2013	8,009	365	45	1,451	9,870	8,043	1,827	5,466	----	14.5	941
2014	7,916	196	63	1,311	9,486	7,828	1,658	5,448	----	14.6	917
2015	7,622	364	65	1,667	9,718	7,750	1,968	5,203	----	15.5	903
2016	7,509	186	57	1,820	9,572	7,484	2,088	5,312	----	14.9	861
2017[1]	8,091	289	136	1,400	9,916	8,228	1,688	5,421	----	16.0	883

[1] Preliminary. [2] Crop years on a marketing year basis. [3] At the Dock Prices. *Source: Fisheries Statistics Division, U.S. Department of Commerce*

FISH

Imports of Seafood Products into the United States   In Thousands of Pounds

Year	Trout, fresh and frozen	Atlantic salmon, fresh	Pacific salmon, fresh[2]	Atlantic salmon, frozen	Pacific salmon, frozen[2]	Atlantic salmon, fillets	Salmon, canned and pre-pared[3]	Tilapia[4]	Shrimp, frozen	Shrimp, fresh and prepared[5]	Oysters[6]	Mussels[6]	Clams[6]	Scallops[6]
2011	11,082	192,231	19,704	5,694	85,406	201,601	25,167	433,162	948,460	323,579	26,779	63,813	44,832	56,804
2012	19,616	222,313	9,770	4,828	65,491	276,703	27,539	503,644	922,877	253,456	18,566	75,384	45,518	34,021
2013	18,713	190,427	12,153	5,604	71,480	317,981	37,106	504,698	865,142	248,812	19,830	70,916	48,705	60,429
2014	19,312	172,283	11,070	6,853	76,248	360,274	32,381	508,484	989,966	265,538	21,356	74,665	50,989	60,041
2015	26,708	236,674	10,051	6,112	78,790	371,476	32,387	496,083	996,935	292,139	24,498	71,002	52,969	48,365
2016	31,366	239,288	14,670	8,223	89,165	371,643	30,619	434,606	1,039,918	290,126	25,096	78,855	54,918	50,178
2017	27,929	262,434	9,658	6,367	96,676	390,821	33,591	402,899	1,139,623	325,786	25,775	78,107	51,859	40,077
2018[1]	34,711	273,299	9,070	6,172	105,785	439,428	35,107	416,012	1,182,612	353,853	29,578	67,385	56,243	45,498

[1] Preliminary.   [2] Includes salmon with no specific species noted.   [3] Includes smoked and cured salmon.   [4] Frozen whole fish plus fresh and frozen fillets.   [5] Canned, breaded or otherwise prepared.   [6] Fresh or prepared.   *Source: Bureau of the Census, U.S. Department of Commerce*

Exports of Seafood Products From the United States   In Thousands of Pounds

Year	Trout, fresh and frozen	Atlantic salmon, fresh	Pacific salmon, fresh[2]	Atlantic salmon, frozen	Pacific salmon, frozen[2]	Salmon, canned and prepared[3]	Shrimp, frozen	Shrimp, fresh and prepared[4]	Oysters[5]	Mussels[5]	Clams[5]	Scallops[5]
2011	503	7,537	20,881	667	337,058	137,878	9,980	16,449	10,376	1,141	13,526	32,136
2012	1,779	17,234	20,934	380	222,933	92,838	14,951	9,260	7,781	931	14,056	28,756
2013	2,148	15,574	24,129	223	359,834	101,469	14,760	7,897	7,624	1,043	18,114	21,206
2014	2,232	11,868	17,704	295	310,551	94,793	15,251	12,972	8,229	1,275	17,483	20,064
2015	1,317	9,590	23,825	335	413,075	87,624	25,699	11,931	8,370	1,217	18,491	16,824
2016	2,188	23,094	33,543	1,342	272,351	82,959	11,441	13,367	7,765	1,262	19,494	18,236
2017	3,836	12,655	26,168	1,516	427,477	64,451	8,020	9,535	7,539	1,944	16,612	16,437
2018[1]	3,422	18,173	14,633	648	280,101	56,270	8,344	12,030	7,468	1,311	15,369	14,125

[1] Preliminary.   [2] Includes salmon with no specific species noted.   [3] Includes smoked and cured salmon.   [4] Canned, breaded, or prepared.   [5] Fresh or prepared.   *Source: Bureau of the Census, U.S. Department of Commerce*

World Production of Fish Meal   In Thousands of Metric Tons

Year	Chile	Denmark	European Union	Iceland	Japan	Norway	Peru	Russia	South Africa	Spain	Thailand	United States	World Total
2010-11	564.1	176.2	394.0	96.6	185.7	113.0	1,286.0	82.8	90.0	30.4	503.0	277.4	5,052.1
2011-12	464.5	90.0	307.2	130.3	189.8	86.0	1,413.8	76.9	96.2	30.0	489.0	278.6	5,046.2
2012-13	336.6	140.4	368.2	123.0	207.0	101.0	775.0	81.9	28.4	30.5	462.5	236.7	4,334.2
2013-14	395.9	161.8	392.3	82.0	201.0	132.7	1,070.9	75.3	74.8	30.1	460.0	227.0	4,744.5
2014-15	338.8	192.0	427.1	152.0	198.0	174.1	671.2	87.8	72.2	30.4	430.0	279.1	4,460.5
2015-16[1]	236.9	175.0	417.4	90.0	194.8	139.0	558.7	93.4	85.1	30.0	400.0	252.5	4,250.7
2016-17[2]	313.2	222.1	469.4	117.0	192.0	142.7	1,087.0	98.8	80.3	31.0	366.0	245.3	4,976.6
2017-18[3]	350.0	205.0	459.1	123.3	194.0	152.0	930.0	95.0	71.0	32.0	385.0	220.0	4,874.4

[1] Preliminary.   [2] Estimate.   [3] Forecast.   *Source: The Oil World*

World Production of Fish Oil   In Thousands of Metric Tons

Year	Canada	Chile	China	Denmark	Iceland	Japan	Norway	Peru	Africa	Russia	United States	World Total	Fish Oil CIF[4] $ Per Tonne
2010-11	5.7	131.6	16.7	61.8	53.1	55.7	49.3	237.9	5.0	4.2	69.1	963.4	1,502
2011-12	6.0	117.5	17.8	35.2	59.9	56.2	36.0	307.4	5.8	5.7	56.5	1,053.7	1,718
2012-13	6.2	91.1	18.7	46.8	50.5	58.4	36.0	137.6	2.2	7.3	78.1	892.9	2,190
2013-14	6.0	137.9	20.0	50.1	44.3	60.0	53.2	174.4	4.8	8.6	60.8	969.4	1,791
2014-15	6.1	110.3	24.0	50.1	48.2	62.6	58.8	85.7	7.3	8.6	64.8	867.4	1,909
2015-16[1]	6.1	87.9	40.0	53.7	29.2	61.3	53.0	77.0	7.6	21.0	80.7	839.5	1,713
2016-17[2]	6.0	111.9	32.0	55.7	35.6	61.0	50.4	165.7	7.3	7.5	49.6	928.2	1,445
2017-18[3]	6.0	123.0	31.0	58.9	39.5	63.0	53.0	152.4	6.0	13.1	69.3	973.2	1,903

[1] Preliminary.   [2] Estimate.   [3] Forecast.   [4] Any origin, N.W. Europe.   *Source: The Oil World*

Average Price of Fish Meal, 60% protein, Domestic, East Coast   In U.S. Dollars Per Ton

Year	Oct.	Nov.	Dec.	Jan.	Feb.	Mar.	Apr.	May	June	July	Aug.	Sept.	Average
2012-13	1,265.00	1,415.00	1,427.50	1,441.50	1,511.88	1,525.00	1,525.00	1,525.00	1,500.00	1,477.50	1,465.63	1,395.63	1,456.22
2013-14	1,347.00	1,335.00	1,322.50	1,328.75	1,334.38	1,333.75	1,345.00	1,345.00	1,400.00	1,479.00	1,505.00	1,512.50	1,382.32
2014-15	1,546.25	1,718.13	1,821.88	1,861.25	1,825.00	1,791.50	1,740.63	1,518.13	1,412.50	1,380.00	1,329.00	1,312.50	1,604.73
2015-16	1,353.75	1,431.25	1,437.50	1,437.50	1,437.50	1,432.50	1,398.88	1,335.00	1,377.50	1,392.50	1,381.00	1,368.75	1,398.64
2016-17	1,359.38	1,362.50	1,362.50	1,362.50	1,362.50	1,343.75	1,300.00	1,290.00	1,300.00	1,302.50	1,310.00	1,312.50	1,330.68
2017-18[1]	1,327.50	1,355.00	1,394.17	1,480.50	1,500.00	1,500.00	1,500.00	1,500.00	----	----	----	----	1,444.65
2018-19[1]	----	----	----	----									

[1] Preliminary.   *Source: Economic Research Service, U.S. Department of Agriculture (ERS-USDA)*

Catfish Sales of Foodsize Fish in the United States   In Thousands of Fish

Year	Alabama	Arkansas	California	Mississippi	North Carolina	Texas	Other[2]	U.S. Total
2008	82,600	51,100	2,220	143,000	4,040	11,100	2,530	304,010
2009	66,600	31,200	2,550	146,000	3,120	10,500	1,680	266,310
2010	73,700	26,000	2,110	143,000	3,250	10,300	1,020	263,420
2011	62,300	14,800	1,360	107,000	2,970	10,400	1,240	201,880
2012	64,700	11,300	1,260	117,000	2,940	7,700	1,160	206,630
2013	62,400	15,500	1,510	106,000	2,750	10,200	2,400	201,810
2014	63,400	9,980	1,340	97,900	1,990	7,050	2,940	184,600
2015	63,000	9,560	1,050	110,000	2,120	7,880	1,900	195,510
2016	62,300	10,300	1,150	105,000	1,930	8,020	1,880	190,580
2017[1]	66,300	11,100	910	112,000	1,380	6,740	1,400	199,830

[1] Preliminary.   [2] Other States include State estimates not shown and States suppressed due to disclosure.
Source: National Agricultural Statistics Service, U.S. Department of Agriculture (NASS-USDA)

Catfish Sales of Foodsize Fish in the United States   In Thousands of Pounds (Live Weight)

Year	Alabama	Arkansas	California	Mississippi	North Carolina	Texas	Other[2]	U.S. Total
2008	131,600	83,700	3,150	252,370	8,050	16,900	3,750	514,920
2009	128,900	58,100	3,400	249,000	6,150	16,100	2,800	475,950
2010	137,700	49,400	3,100	257,400	5,850	16,000	2,000	478,850
2011	119,200	25,500	2,850	173,900	5,200	16,900	2,200	348,000
2012	122,600	20,000	2,150	174,800	5,200	12,700	1,960	340,166
2013	109,300	25,300	2,800	175,300	4,000	15,800	3,500	337,130
2014	105,300	17,200	2,550	161,500	3,400	14,300	3,248	307,498
2015	107,500	14,500	2,200	171,700	3,250	15,600	2,694	317,444
2016	109,000	16,300	1,640	172,000	3,500	15,400	2,334	320,174
2017[1]	112,900	16,800	1,580	180,500	2,600	14,000	2,048	330,428

[1] Preliminary.   [2] Other States include State estimates not shown and States suppressed due to disclosure.
Source: National Agricultural Statistics Service, U.S. Department of Agriculture (NASS-USDA)

Trout Sales of Fish 12" or longer (Foodsize) in the United States   In Thousands of Fish

Year	California	Colorado	Georgia	Idaho	Michigan	North Carolina	Pennsylvania	Virginia	Washington	West Virginia	Wisconsin	Other[2]	U.S. Total
2008	2,290	W	174	27,600	300	3,820	1,340	640	1,040	305	480	2,200	40,401
2009	1,400	440	140	29,800	300	3,400	1,240	600	400	630	480	1,850	40,822
2010	1,310	370	130	28,500	260	2,980	1,210	500	420	490	520	1,860	38,700
2011	1,260	260	150	27,600	220	3,450	1,710	490	210	370	470	1,950	38,215
2012	1,120	220	W	30,900	230	3,180	1,030	460	W	420	470	3,580	41,700
2013	W	250	145	30,100	145	3,310	870	430	W	440	480	4,380	41,170
2014	1,310	210	W	36,100	105	3,310	880	480	W	420	410	4,150	48,285
2015	1,350	310	W	32,700	W	3,220	910	590	W	550	440	4,460	45,350
2016	W	380	W	33,000	W	3,960	980	460	W	630	W	6,035	46,305
2017[1]	W	340	W	27,300	W	3,500	970	500	W	590	W	5,965	40,265

[1] Preliminary.   [2] Other States include State estimates not shown and States suppressed due to disclosure.   W = Withheld.
Source: National Agricultural Statistics Service, U.S. Department of Agriculture (NASS-USDA)

Trout Sales of Fish 12" or longer (Foodsize) in the United States   In Thousands of Pounds (Live Weight)

Year	California	Colorado	Georgia	Idaho	Michigan	North Carolina	Pennsylvania	Virginia	Washington	West Virginia	Wisconsin	Other[2]	U.S. Total
2008	2,950	W	206	35,400	296	3,550	1,460	634	3,700	450	446	3,096	52,410
2009	1,660	420	174	35,600	340	3,750	1,320	600	1,220	812	459	2,210	48,714
2010	1,620	360	165	32,800	283	3,600	1,270	540	1,250	426	482	2,317	45,285
2011	1,580	410	167	33,000	214	3,350	1,570	552	620	506	450	2,300	44,786
2012	1,370	393	W	36,600	251	3,250	1,100	525	W	515	465	10,960	55,529
2013	W	441	163	35,700	167	3,700	1,050	498	W	551	447	13,178	56,666
2014	1,550	404	W	42,200	119	4,050	1,030	489	W	518	403	9,121	60,733
2015	1,600	405	W	39,100	W	3,700	1,050	567	W	464	414	9,767	57,947
2016	W	441	W	39,700	W	4,400	1,090	427	W	569	W	11,598	59,087
2017[1]	W	333	W	33,300	W	4,150	1,070	524	W	515	W	12,168	53,286

[1] Preliminary.   [2] Other States include State estimates not shown and States suppressed due to disclosure.   W = Withheld.
Source: National Agricultural Statistics Service, U.S. Department of Agriculture (NASS-USDA)

Flaxseed and Linseed Oil

Flaxseed, also called linseed, is an ancient crop that was cultivated by the Babylonians around 3,000 BC. Flaxseed is used for fiber in textiles and to produce oil. Flaxseeds contain approximately 35% oil, of which 60% is omega-3 fatty acid. Flaxseed or linseed oil is obtained through either the expeller extraction or solvent extraction method. Manufacturers filter the processed oil to remove some impurities and then sell it as unrefined. Unrefined oil retains its full flavor, aroma, color, and naturally occurring nutrients. Flaxseed oil is used for cooking and as a dietary supplement as well as for animal feed. Industrial linseed oil is not for internal consumption due to possible poisonous additives and is used for making putty, sealants, linoleum, wood preservation, varnishes, and oil paints.

Prices – The average monthly price received by U.S. farmers for flaxseed in the 2018/19 marketing year (through January 2019) rose by +3.7% yr/yr to $9.84 per bushel, but still below the record high of $14.10 per bushel posted in the 2012/13 marketing year.

Supply – World production of flaxseed in the 2017/18 marketing year fell by -7.1% yr/yr to 2.551 million metric tons, only slightly below the 10-year high of 2.864 million metric tons in 2005-06. The world's largest producer of

flaxseed in 2017/18 was Russia at 44.8% of total world production, Canada with 21.8%, China with 12.2%, and India with 5.5%. U.S. production of flaxseed in 2017 fell -55.6% to 3,842 million bushels, but still up from the 2011 record low of 2.791 million bushels. North Dakota is by far the largest producing state for flaxseed and accounted for 89.4% of flaxseed production in 2017, followed by Montana 8.9% and South Dakota with 1.7% of production.

World production of linseed oil in 2017/18 fell by -5.1% yr/yr to 732,200 metric tons. The world's largest producers of linseed oil were China with 29.2% of world production in 2017/18, Belgium with 16.6%, the U.S. with 10.9%, and Germany with 7.2%. U.S. production of linseed oil in 2017/18 fell by -14.1% yr/yr to 176.000 million pounds.

Demand – U.S. distribution of flaxseed in 2017/18 fell by -17.2% yr/yr to 10.337 million bushels. The breakdown of use was 87.1% for crushing into meal and oil, 5.3% for exports, 5.2% for residual, 2,4% for seed.

Trade – U.S. exports of flaxseed in 2017/18 fell by -53.8% yr/yr to 550,000 thousand bushels. U.S. imports of flaxseed in 2017/18 rose +65.8% yr/yr to 5.125 million bushels.

World Production of Flaxseed   In Thousands of Metric Tons

Crop Year	Argen-tina	Australia	Bang-ladesh	Canada	China	Egypt	France	Hungary	India	Romania	United States	Former USSR	World Total
2008-09	19	8	8	861	475	12	15	1	150	----	145	145	2,098
2009-10	52	8	7	930	318	8	21	1	154	1	189	206	2,163
2010-11	32	7	7	419	353	12	36	----	147	2	230	326	1,806
2011-12	21	7	7	399	359	5	31	1	152	3	147	571	2,136
2012-13	17	7	6	489	391	5	26	----	149	4	147	571	2,053
2013-14	20	6	6	731	399	2	16	1	140	4	85	618	2,255
2014-15	17	6	9	840	350	5	23	1	155	3	162	688	2,457
2015-16[1]	20	6	5	943	330	5	48	1	125	4	256	873	2,835
2016-17[2]	17	6	5	591	320	5	42	1	160	3	221	1,140	2,747
2017-18[3]	14	6	5	555	310	5	42	2	140	3	98	1,143	2,551

[1] Preliminary.   [2] Estimate.   [3] Forecast.   *Source: The Oil World*

Supply and Distribution of Flaxseed in the United States   In Thousands of Bushels

Crop Year Beginning June 1	Planted	Harvested	Yield Per Acre (Bushels)	Beginning Stocks	Pro-duction	Imports	Total Supply	Seed	Crush	Exports	Residual	Total
	---- 1,000 Acres ----											
2009-10	317	314	23.6	2,552	7,423	6,283	16,258	341	12,000	1,752	608	14,701
2010-11	421	418	21.7	1,557	9,056	6,040	16,653	144	11,635	2,130	573	14,483
2011-12	178	173	16.1	2,170	2,791	8,286	13,247	279	10,500	654	694	12,127
2012-13	349	336	17.3	1,120	5,798	6,928	13,846	147	11,000	1,020	755	12,922
2013-14	181	172	19.5	924	3,356	6,759	11,039	252	8,700	599	725	10,276
2014-15	311	302	21.1	763	6,368	7,464	14,595	375	11,850	528	1,034	13,787
2015-16	463	456	22.1	808	10,095	4,481	15,339	303	10,700	825	598	12,425
2016-17[1]	374	366	23.7	2,914	8,656	3,091	14,661	245	10,500	1,190	556	12,491
2017-18[2]	303	272	14.1	2,170	3,842	5,125	11,137	247	9,000	550	540	10,337
2018-19[3]	168	160										

[1] Preliminary.   [2] Estimate.   [3] Forecast.   NA = not avaliable.   *Source: Economic Research Service, U.S. Department of Agriculture (ERS-USDA)*

Supply and Distribution of Linseed Meal in the United States   In Millions of Pounds

Crop Year Beginning June 1	Supply				Disappearance			Ending Stocks	Average Price at Minneapolis (34% Protein) Cents/Lb.
	Stocks June 1	Production	Imports	Total Supply	Domestic Disappear-ance	Exports	Total Disappear-ance		
2008-09	5	147	10	162	130	28	157	5	227.66
2009-10	5	216	3	224	210	10	219	5	217.24
2010-11	5	209	7	221	208	7	216	5	223.23
2011-12	5	189	8	202	194	3	197	5	238.35
2012-13	5	198	6	209	199	5	204	5	320.13
2013-14	5	157	1	163	153	6	158	5	359.42
2014-15	5	213	3	221	212	4	216	5	263.90
2015-16	5	193	7	205	196	4	200	5	234.78
2016-17[1]	5	189	6	200	190	5	195	5	313.17
2017-18[2]	5	162	5	172	163	4	167	5	220-250

[1] Preliminary.   [2] Forecast.   Source: Economic Research Service, U.S. Department of Agriculture (ERS-USDA)

Supply and Distribution of Linseed Oil in the United States   In Millions of Pounds

Crop Year Beginning June 1	Supply			Disappearance			Average Price at Minneapolis Cents/Lb.
	Stocks June 1	Production	Total Supply	Exports	Domestic Disappearance	Total Disappearance	
2008-09	26	159	191	66	52	118	86.5
2009-10	73	234	312	103	172	275	67.5
2010-11	37	227	270	101	131	232	NA
2011-12	38	205	248	89	124	213	NA
2012-13	35	215	255	94	126	220	NA
2013-14	35	170	210	58	117	175	NA
2014-15	35	231	270	52	183	235	NA
2015-16	35	209	248	17	196	213	NA
2016-17[1]	35	205	244	15	194	209	NA
2017-18[2]	35	176	216	18	163	181	NA

[1] Preliminary.   [2] Forecast.   Source: Economic Research Service, U.S. Department of Agriculture (ERS-USDA)

World Production and Price of Linseed Oil   In Thousands of Metric Tons

Year	Argen-tina	Bang-ladesh	Belgium	China	Egypt	Germany	India	Japan	United Kingdom	United States	Former USSR	World Total	Rotterdam Ex-TankUSD $/Tonne
2008-09	2.1	2.3	77.4	121.3	6.4	37.7	47.9	2.8	3.2	84.8	14.2	524.3	975
2009-10	1.7	2.1	96.9	159.2	5.2	34.5	45.2	2.0	2.6	115.7	21.9	587.7	1,114
2010-11	1.9	2.0	107.2	120.4	4.3	40.9	41.4	1.6	5.9	103.1	25.1	538.9	1,451
2011-12	1.1	2.3	108.8	144.5	4.3	49.5	41.1	1.6	5.6	100.2	24.3	609.5	1,267
2012-13	1.6	2.0	107.2	152.0	2.9	44.8	38.6	2.0	4.9	94.3	21.4	592.5	1,217
2013-14	----	----	112.0	186.6	2.9	48.7	35.3	1.5	6.7	81.6	21.8	640.9	1,191
2014-15	----	----	123.2	210.7	3.5	49.4	38.6	2.6	6.1	108.7	27.9	679.2	1,162
2015-16	----	----	131.8	207.7	4.5	49.4	34.3	----	6.9	97.8	38.9	715.9	825
2016-17[1]	----	----	125.4	207.7	4.5	52.6	40.9	----	8.5	90.4	53.6	771.6	828
2017-18[2]	----	----	121.6	213.7	7.1	52.6	37.6	----	8.5	79.8	58.4	732.2	830

[1] Preliminary.   [2] Forecast.   Source: The Oil World

Production of Flaxseed in the United States, by States   In Thousands of Bushels

Year	Minnesota	Montana	North Dakota	South Dakota	U.S. Total
2008	69	72	5,491	84	5,716
2009	63	160	7,032	168	7,423
2010	56	255	8,536	209	9,056
2011	45	208	2,426	112	2,791
2012	45	156	5,478	119	5,798
2013	76	240	2,920	120	3,356
2014	48	425	5,805	90	6,368
2015	42	450	9,315	288	10,095
2016	----	616	7,896	144	8,656
2017[1]	----	342	3,435	65	3,842

[1] Preliminary.   Source: National Agricultural Statistics Service, U.S. Department of Agriculture (NASS-USDA)

FLAXSEED AND LINSEED OIL

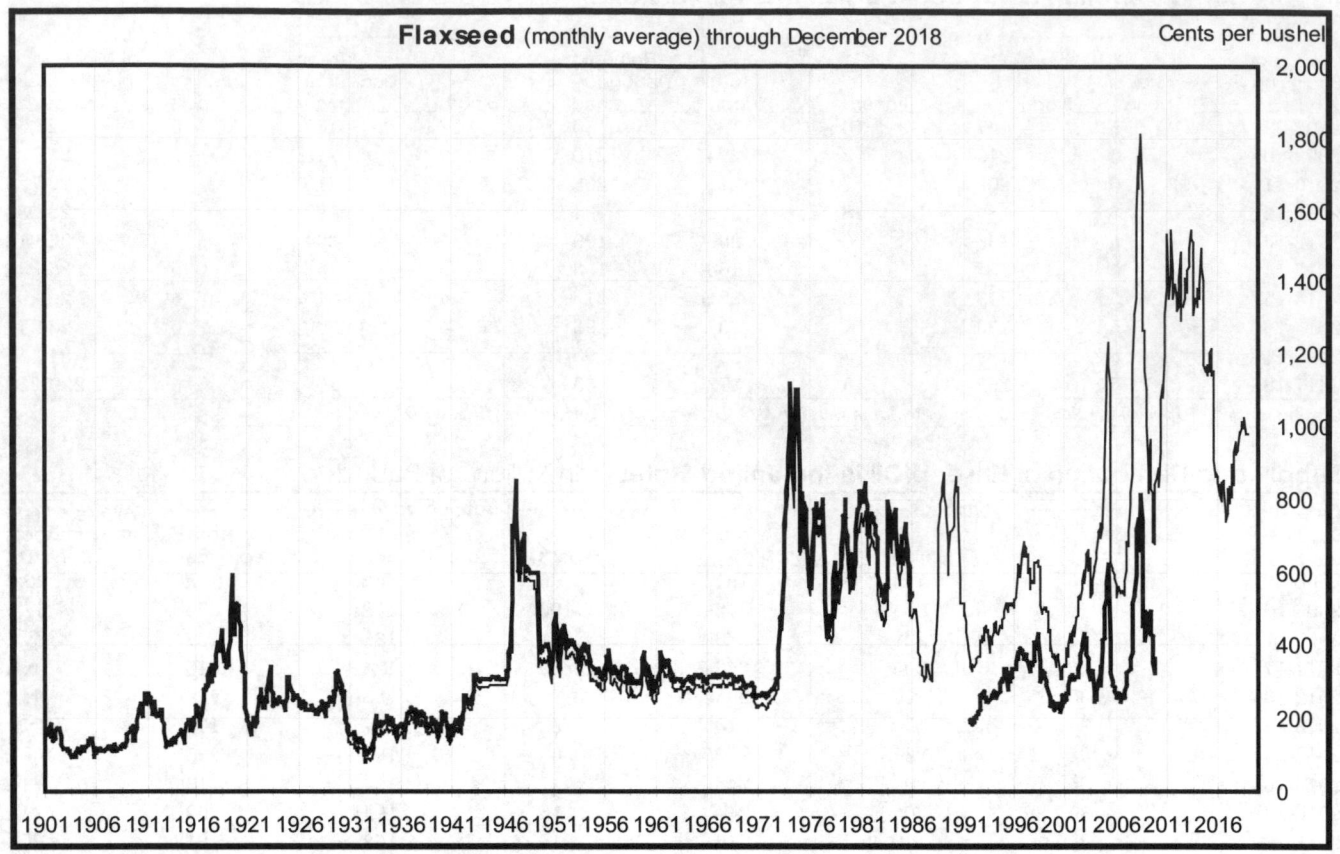

Flaxseed (monthly average) through December 2018   Cents per bushel

Average Price Received by Farmers for Flaxseed in the United States   In Dollars Per Bushel

Year	July	Aug.	Sept.	Oct.	Nov.	Dec.	Jan.	Feb.	Mar.	Apr.	May	June	Average
2009-10	8.28	8.14	6.79	6.78	8.12	8.40	8.53	8.57	8.82	8.53	8.34	9.26	8.21
2010-11	10.70	11.10	10.80	11.90	12.60	13.10	13.80	15.30	13.70	13.50	14.20	15.40	13.01
2011-12	15.40	14.30	13.50	13.90	13.90	13.50	13.70	13.20	13.30	14.10	14.80	12.90	13.88
2012-13	13.30	13.30	13.30	13.50	14.10	13.80	13.70	14.30	14.40	14.90	15.40	15.20	14.10
2013-14	15.10	14.90	13.10	13.50	13.40	13.40	13.30	13.80	13.50	13.90	14.90	14.40	13.93
2014-15	14.00	13.30	11.70	11.50	11.60	11.40	11.70	11.50	11.50	12.00	12.10	11.40	11.98
2015-16	11.50	10.00	9.07	8.57	8.71	8.62	8.46	8.10	8.37	8.10	7.93	8.44	8.82
2016-17	8.48	8.25	7.61	7.37	7.36	7.59	8.26	7.86	8.34	8.03	8.96	8.52	8.05
2017-18	8.40	9.30	9.55	9.23	9.21	9.36	9.40	9.81	9.76	9.92	10.10	9.98	9.50
2018-19[1]	9.96	10.20	9.79	9.79	9.76	9.66	9.75						9.84

[1] Preliminary.   *Source: National Agricultural Statistics Service, U.S. Department of Agriculture (NASS-USDA)*

Average Price of Linseed Meal (34% protein) at Minneapolis   In Dollars Per Ton

Year	July	Aug.	Sept.	Oct.	Nov.	Dec.	Jan.	Feb.	Mar.	Apr.	May	June	Average
2009-10	226.90	217.00	195.20	185.00	220.00	256.50	228.75	222.50	201.50	200.83	202.75	189.50	212.20
2010-11	199.38	204.00	200.00	208.75	237.50	234.38	255.00	256.25	236.50	225.63	231.88	254.38	228.64
2011-12	260.63	247.50	239.38	243.75	239.00	221.25	209.00	193.75	216.25	256.25	279.00	287.50	241.11
2012-13	343.00	358.75	340.63	334.00	297.50	335.83	296.00	303.75	303.75	309.00	331.88	340.00	324.51
2013-14	382.50	317.50	400.00	363.75	316.25	328.75	330.00	377.50	413.75	388.00	355.00	323.75	358.06
2014-15	295.00	252.50	302.50	214.38	283.75	287.50	250.00	230.63	230.50	239.38	256.88	258.00	258.42
2015-16	284.38	287.50	256.00	215.00	209.80	200.00	195.00	197.50	195.00	218.13	301.50	375.63	244.62
2016-17	364.38	335.00	316.25	305.63	296.00	290.00	297.00	299.38	297.50	291.25	290.00	282.63	305.42
2017-18	250.63	253.00	236.88	214.00	205.00	209.17	215.50	233.13	237.50	238.13	267.50	271.25	235.97
2018-19[1]	278.00	265.63	235.00	196.50	209.38	225.83	219.00	225.00					231.79

[1] Preliminary.   *Source: Economic Research Service, U.S. Department of Agriculture (ERS-USDA)*

Fruits

A fruit is any seed-bearing structure produced from a flowering plant. A widely used classification system divides fruit into fleshy or dry types. Fleshy fruits are juicy and include peaches, mangos, apples, and blueberries. Dry fruits include tree nuts such as almonds, walnuts, and pecans. Some foods that are commonly called vegetables, such as tomatoes, squash, peppers and eggplant, are technically fruits because they develop from the ovary of a flower.

Worldwide, over 430 million tons of fruit are produced each year and are grown everywhere except the Arctic and the Antarctic. The tropics, because of their abundant moisture and warm temperatures, produce the most diverse and abundant fruits. Mexico and Chile produce more than half of all the fresh and frozen fruit imported into the U.S. In the U.S., the top three fruits produced are oranges, grapes, and apples. Virtually all U.S. production of almonds, pistachios, and walnuts occurs in California, which leads the U.S. in tree nut production.

Prices – Overall fruit prices were fairly strong in 2016 with the fresh fruit Consumer Price Index (CPI) rising +2.2% to 359.8 and the processed fruit CPI index rising +0.4% to 158.2. Individual fruit prices, however, were mixed in 2016 (latest data): Red Delicious apples (+6.2% to $1.442 per pound), bananas (-1.6% to 57.7 cents per pound), Anjou pears (+33.7% to $1.674 per pound), Thompson seedless grapes (+6.4% to $2.758 per pound), lemons (+2.8% to $2.037 per pound), grapefruit (-11.1% to $0.97 per pound), and navel oranges (-4.5% to $1.246 cents per pound).

Supply – U.S. commercial production of selected fruits in 2016 rose + 0.6% to 28.9584 million short tons. By weight, grapes accounted for 28.4% of that U.S. fruit production figure, followed by oranges at 22.6%, and apples at 20.9%. The value of U.S. fruit production in 2016 rose +1.4% yr/yr to $28,808 billion.

Demand – U.S. per capita fresh fruit consumption in 2016 rose +3.1% to 116.05 pounds per year, a new record high. The highest per capita consumption categories for non-citrus fruits in 2016 were bananas (27.55 pounds) and apples (18.55 pounds). Per capital consumption of citrus fruits were oranges (9.17 pounds), tangerines & tangelos (5.28 pounds), lemons (4.15 pounds), Limes (3.46 pounds) and grapefruit (1.97 pounds). The utilization breakdown for 2016 shows that total U.S. non-citrus fruit was used for fresh fruit (43.0%), wine (25.1%), dried fruit (9.8%), juice (8.3%), canned fruit (6.6%), and frozen fruit (4.8%). The value of utilized non-citrus fruit production in 2016 was virtually unchanged at $16.608 billion.

Commercial Production for Selected Fruits in the United States   In Thousands of Short Tons

Year	Apples	Cherries[2]	Cran-berries	Grapes	Grape-fruit	Lemons	Nect-arines	Oranges	Peach-es	Pears	Pine-apple[3]	Prunes & Plums	Straw-berries	Tang-elos	Tang-erines	Total All Fruits
2011	4,720	450	386	7,409	1,264	920	225	8,905	1,071	966	----	617	1,451	52	657	29,555
2012	4,496	467	402	7,531	1,153	850	189	8,982	968	851	----	564	1,526	52	644	28,832
2013	5,216	479	448	8,632	1,204	912	162	8,268	904	877	----	364	1,524	45	682	30,071
2014	5,907	516	420	7,884	1,047	824	205	6,768	853	832	----	452	1,512	40	732	28,342
2015	5,023	462	428	7,621	910	904	176	6,353	847	817	----	441	1,533	30	863	26,791
2016	5,689	515	481	7,697	803	904	168	6,088	796	739	----	292	1,578	18	935	27,015
2017[1]	5,703	567	419	7,363	698	882	158	5,088	697	738	----	467	1,598		1,029	25,722

[1] Preliminary.   [2] Sweet and tart.   [3] Utilized production.   Source: Economic Research Service, U.S. Department of Agriculture (ERS-USDA)

Utilized Production for Selected Fruits in the United States   In Thousands of Short Tons

| | ------- Utilized Production ------- | | | | ------- Value of Production ------- | | | |
Year	Citrus[2]	Noncitrus	Tree nuts[3]	Total	Citrus[2]	Noncitrus	Tree nuts[3]	Total
	In Thousands of Short Tons				In Thousands of Dollars			
2011	11,798	18,111	2,584	32,493	3,240,896	13,886,156	7,007,694	24,134,746
2012	11,681	17,635	2,636	31,952	3,712,817	15,611,441	8,337,036	27,661,294
2013	11,111	19,433	2,659	33,203	3,169,544	16,220,440	10,462,270	29,852,254
2014	9,411	19,151	2,567	31,129	3,704,444	16,410,049	11,816,331	31,930,824
2015	9,060	18,334	2,552	29,946	3,353,750	16,602,493	8,461,676	28,417,919
2016	8,748	18,690	3,132	30,570	3,435,675	17,865,364	8,690,836	29,991,875
2017[1]	7,697	18,455	3,025	29,177	3,532,125	18,589,066	9,024,205	31,145,396

[1] Preliminary.   [2] Year harvest was completed.   [3] Tree nuts on an in-shell equivalent.
Source: Economic Research Service, U.S. Department of Agriculture (ERS-USDA)

Annual Average Retail Prices for Selected Fruits in the United States   In Dollars Per Pound

Year	Red Delicious Apples	Bananas	Anjou Pears	Thompson Seedless Grapes	Lemons	Grapefruit	Oranges Navel	Oranges Valencias
2011	1.350	.610	1.409	2.386	1.581	.976	1.096	1.009
2012	1.377	.602	1.253	2.488	1.565	1.078	1.053	----
2013	1.386	.600	----	2.494	1.582	1.048	1.151	1.032
2014	1.354	.588	----	2.639	1.968	1.109	1.319	----
2015	1.358	.586	----	2.591	1.981	1.091	1.304	----
2016	1.442	.573	1.674	2.758	2.037	.970	1.246	----
2017[1]	1.294	.563	1.603	2.641	2.007	1.279	1.341	----

[1] Estimate.   Source: Economic Research Service, U.S. Department of Agriculture (ERS-USDA)

FRUITS

Utilization of Noncitrus Fruit Production, and Value in the United States   1,000 Short Tons (Fresh Equivalent)

Year	Utilized Production	Fresh	Canned	Dried	Juice	Frozen	Wine	Other Processed	Value of Utilized Production $1,000
2008	17,558	7,203	1,406	2,413	1,228	682	3,944	289	11,547,473
2009	18,021	7,514	1,394	2,148	1,235	742	4,373	269	12,232,459
2010	17,835	7,414	1,386	2,318	1,103	706	4,271	298	12,751,568
2011	18,111	7,666	1,301	2,399	1,153	737	4,155	316	13,886,156
2012	17,635	7,443	1,100	2,091	1,213	707	4,707	374	15,611,441
2013	19,433	7,718	1,373	2,321	1,630	827	5,068	497	16,220,440
2014	19,151	8,267	1,208	2,194	1,617	857	4,526	483	16,410,049
2015	18,334	7,702	1,253	2,323	1,391	881	4,255	530	16,602,493
2016	18,690	8,042	1,224	1,858	1,519	890	4,668	479	17,865,364
2017[1]	18,455	8,107	1,188	1,755	1,477	731	4,665	532	18,589,066

[1] Preliminary.   Source: Economic Research Service, U.S. Department of Agriculture (ERS-USDA)

Average Price Indexes for Fruits in the United States

Year	Index of all Fruit & Nut Prices Received by Growers (1990-92=100)	Producer Price Index — Fresh Fruit (1982 = 100)	Dried Fruit	Canned Fruits and Juices	Frozen Fruits and Juices	Consumer Price Index — Fresh Fruit (1982-84 = 100)	Processed Fruit
2008	89.0	122.9	----	179.0	146.7	345.4	135.6
2009	84.0	110.4	----	186.9	150.5	324.4	142.8
2010	87.0	123.8	----	187.3	148.7	322.3	141.0
2011	100.0	117.7	----	195.4	160.0	333.1	146.0
2012	112.4	119.0	----	203.8	168.9	336.6	150.4
2013	119.0	121.2	----	206.4	170.3	343.2	154.5
2014	136.3	124.5	----	208.7	172.7	359.7	154.0
2015	138.2	124.2	----	217.1	176.8	352.0	157.5
2016	138.5	138.7	----	223.2	177.0	359.8	158.2
2017[1]	126.3	147.9	----	229.4	180.4	361.4	156.4

[1] Estimate.   NA = Not availavle.   Source: Economic Research Service, U.S. Department of Agriculture (ERS-USDA)

Fresh Fruit: Per Capita Consumption[1] in the United States   In Pounds

Year	Oranges	Tangerines & Tangelos	Lemons	Limes	Grapefruit	U.S. Total	Apples	Apricots	Avocados	Bananas	Blueberries	Cherries	Cranberries
2008	9.93	3.08	1.97	2.48	3.16	20.62	15.88	.13	3.83	25.04	.80	1.00	.10
2009	9.06	3.16	3.12	2.55	2.80	20.69	16.20	.14	4.25	22.01	.96	1.56	.09
2010	9.68	3.78	2.79	2.57	2.76	21.58	15.29	.12	4.00	25.61	1.12	1.31	.06
2011	9.96	4.14	3.46	2.50	2.71	22.79	15.45	.12	5.10	25.54	1.29	1.30	.06
2012	10.47	4.17	3.94	2.57	2.37	23.51	16.02	.10	5.61	26.89	1.33	1.50	.07
2013	10.38	4.49	3.48	2.96	2.64	23.95	17.33	.11	6.11	27.97	1.38	.99	.08
2014	9.37	5.00	3.42	3.07	2.40	23.26	18.60	.12	6.97	27.83	1.51	1.17	.07
2015	8.67	5.22	3.59	3.01	2.23	22.72	17.35	.08	7.18	27.90	1.61	1.15	.12
2016	9.17	5.28	4.14	3.47	1.97	24.03	18.91	.13	6.87	27.40	1.77	1.17	.12
2017[1]	8.01	5.85	4.25	3.74	1.91	23.77	17.69	.09	7.47	28.54	1.74	1.47	.09

Cutrus Fruit / Noncitrus Fruit

[1] All data on calendar-year basis except for citrus fruits; apples, August; grapes and pears, July; grapefruit, September; lemons, August of prior year; all other citrus, November.   [2] Preliminary.   Source: Economic Research Service, U.S. Department of Agriculture (ERS-USDA)

Fresh Fruit: Per Capita Consumption[1] in the United States   In Pounds

Noncitrus Fruit Continued

Year	Grapes	Kiwifruit	Mangos	Peaches	Pears	Pineapples	Papaya	Prunes	Strawberries	Total Noncitrus	Total Fruit
2008	8.26	.46	2.10	5.08	3.11	5.07	.98	.92	6.45	79.23	99.84
2009	7.66	.50	2.02	4.41	3.19	5.09	1.20	.73	7.17	77.17	97.85
2010	7.93	.50	2.24	4.73	2.90	5.70	1.17	.78	7.23	80.87	102.46
2011	7.35	.58	2.53	4.47	3.21	5.72	1.05	.87	7.36	82.31	105.09
2012	7.57	.54	2.49	3.86	2.76	6.42	.97	.62	7.97	85.06	108.57
2013	7.75	.46	2.87	3.01	2.84	6.74	1.12	.51	8.00	87.64	111.58
2014	7.66	.55	2.52	3.26	2.85	7.19	1.14	.58	7.95	90.48	113.73
2015	7.86	.63	2.60	3.02	2.66	6.98	1.32	.64	7.71	89.64	112.36
2016	8.07	.58	2.96	2.85	2.75	7.27	1.43	.82	8.05	91.98	116.02
2017[1]	8.20	.60	3.21	2.73	2.69	7.74	1.36	.82	8.33	93.67	117.44

[1] All data on calendar-year basis except for citrus fruits; apples, August; grapes and pears, July; grapefruit, September; lemons, August of prior year; all other citrus, November.   [2] Preliminary.   Source: Economic Research Service, U.S. Department of Agriculture (ERS-USDA)

Average Price Received by Growers for Grapefruit in the United States   In Dollars Per Box

Year	Jan.	Feb.	Mar.	Apr.	May	June	July	Aug.	Sept.	Oct.	Nov.	Dec.	Average
2009	4.19	3.74	3.61	2.99	6.21	8.23	7.15	6.15	6.55	16.41	10.78	8.82	7.07
2010	8.86	7.10	5.93	4.19	4.05	5.40	1.30	0.50	4.70	7.62	12.06	8.06	5.81
2011	6.94	6.31	5.69	5.27	7.55	9.50	8.20	7.10	9.50	8.67	7.90	7.18	7.48
2012	6.83	6.79	6.91	10.20	9.62	15.43	13.23	10.33	10.13	12.49	7.68	6.87	9.71
2013	7.19	5.71	4.29	4.33	8.26	8.76	6.66	6.36	8.76	7.96	8.54	7.51	7.03
2014	7.30	5.78	5.60	5.34	7.89	7.69	7.19	8.05	13.40	12.33	9.82	8.92	8.28
2015	7.03	4.83	5.34	5.33	5.47	12.21	9.33	5.63	7.79	13.21	13.36	11.43	8.41
2016	10.70	9.13	8.86	12.77	14.81	13.82	15.26	14.08	W	19.08	13.14	12.14	13.07
2017	11.25	11.57	11.95	13.62	16.44	15.18	14.10	W	14.66	20.91	19.88	16.13	15.06
2018[1]	15.88	13.12	11.78	12.55	16.25	14.41	13.98	9.57	14.82	20.36	18.84	16.31	14.82

On-tree equivalent.   [1]Preliminary.   *Source: National Agricultural Statistics Service, U.S. Department of Agriculture (NASS-USDA)*

Average Price Received by Growers for Lemons in the United States   In Dollars Per Box

Year	Jan.	Feb.	Mar.	Apr.	May	June	July	Aug.	Sept.	Oct.	Nov.	Dec.	Average
2009	5.90	2.62	1.80	4.26	5.68	11.34	12.21	20.79	17.60	15.59	14.60	11.81	10.35
2010	9.88	8.48	8.68	10.06	9.13	11.24	12.59	16.60	19.72	19.92	18.51	9.51	12.86
2011	8.84	3.91	5.70	8.54	10.26	12.32	16.16	21.99	17.98	12.87	14.10	14.29	12.25
2012	12.97	11.38	12.51	15.55	17.19	16.10	17.29	11.89	14.94	16.38	13.96	11.60	14.31
2013	10.65	7.28	7.08	9.18	14.77	16.35	18.98	28.45	27.85	32.77	26.65	23.52	18.63
2014	21.17	21.69	21.31	22.39	24.54	29.91	40.05	33.68	37.40	38.47	29.54	21.15	28.44
2015	18.53	13.44	16.14	21.65	31.76	38.51	37.34	29.40	31.71	36.54	30.18	24.42	27.47
2016	23.05	22.04	24.29	25.09	31.67	29.95	26.47	29.54	31.84	31.49	27.88	23.13	27.20
2017	23.44	25.12	24.65	27.10	31.30	40.90	41.85	29.79	29.58	25.49	28.32	30.84	29.87
2018[1]	30.17	23.28	21.57	18.20	21.36	29.14	40.34	53.01	53.26	40.97	32.73	25.44	32.46

On-tree equivalent.   [1]Preliminary.   *Source: National Agricultural Statistics Service, U.S. Department of Agriculture (NASS-USDA)*

Average Price Received by Growers for Grapes In the United States   In Dollars Per Box

Year	Jan.	Feb.	Mar.	Apr.	May	June	July	Aug.	Sept.	Oct.	Nov.	Dec.	Average
2009	NQ	NQ	NQ	NQ	1,380	1,120	610	310	470	630	630	1,220	796
2010	NQ	NQ	NQ	NQ	NQ	650	460	430	420	430	500	750	520
2011	NQ	NQ	NQ	NQ	NQ	1,080	1,480	960	820	790	980	1,040	1,021
2012	NQ	NQ	NQ	NQ	NQ	1,410	1,030	980	1,130	1,540	1,770	1,780	1,377
2013	NQ	NQ	NQ	NQ	NQ	NQ	NQ	NQ	NQ	NQ	NQ	NQ	NQ
2014	NQ	NQ	NQ	NQ	NQ	1,870	1,550	1,360	1,350	1,530	1,660	1,680	1,571
2015	NQ	NQ	NQ	NQ	2,330	1,690	1,340	1,470	1,490	1,590	1,810	2,070	1,724
2016	NQ	NQ	NQ	NQ	NQ	NQ	1,480	1,330	1,360	1,460	1,520	2,310	1,577
2017	NQ	NQ	NQ	NQ	NQ	NQ	1,590	1,500	1,500	1,460	1,540	1,660	1,542
2018[1]	NQ	NQ	NQ	NQ	NQ	2,550	1,600	1,310	1,210	1,080	1,030	1,140	1,417

Fresh.   [1]Preliminary.   NQ = No quote.   *Source: National Agricultural Statistics Service, U.S. Department of Agriculture (NASS-USDA)*

Average Price Received by Growers for Peaches in the United States   In Dollars Per Box

Year	Jan.	Feb.	Mar.	Apr.	May	June	July	Aug.	Sept.	Oct.	Nov.	Dec.	Average
2009	NQ	NQ	NQ	NQ	846	794	644	676	655	NQ	NQ	NQ	723
2010	NQ	NQ	NQ	NQ	1,080	587	573	568	506	NQ	NQ	NQ	663
2011	NQ	NQ	NQ	NQ	1,290	705	666	704	564	NQ	NQ	NQ	786
2012	NQ	NQ	NQ	NQ	1,100	836	780	737	689	NQ	NQ	NQ	828
2013	NQ	NQ	NQ	NQ	NQ	NQ	NQ	NQ	NQ	NQ	NQ	NQ	NQ
2014	NQ	NQ	NQ	NQ	NQ	1,270	1,180	1,070	954	NQ	NQ	NQ	1,119
2015	NQ	NQ	NQ	NQ	1,480	1,110	937	1,030	835	NQ	NQ	NQ	1,078
2016	NQ	NQ	NQ	NQ	1,220	993	1,230	1,320	1,080	NQ	NQ	NQ	1,169
2017	NQ	NQ	NQ	NQ	NQ	1,530	1,710	1,400	1,310	NQ	NQ	NQ	1,488
2018[1]	NQ	NQ	NQ	NQ	NQ	1,130	1,140	1,110	918	NQ	NQ	NQ	1,075

Fresh.   [1]Preliminary.   NQ = No quote.   *Source: National Agricultural Statistics Service, U.S. Department of Agriculture (NASS-USDA)*

FRUITS

Average Price Received by Growers for Pears in the United States — In Dollars Per Box

Year	Jan.	Feb.	Mar.	Apr.	May	June	July	Aug.	Sept.	Oct.	Nov.	Dec.	Average
2009	539	473	452	462	518	642	537	424	383	481	449	398	480
2010	381	368	350	426	533	640	598	496	485	622	548	587	503
2011	639	636	625	599	571	565	561	576	490	533	512	474	565
2012	428	386	301	286	353	594	673	583	601	692	686	713	525
2013	774	778	753	NQ	NQ	NQ	NQ	NQ	NQ	NQ	NQ	NQ	768
2014	NQ	NQ	NQ	592	686	893	695	531	631	696	692	702	680
2015	725	729	652	610	619	633	635	706	690	747	778	813	695
2016	844	785	749	793	914	1,050	810	810	816	829	787	756	829
2017	782	806	722	668	694	734	631	764	829	848	832	888	767
2018[1]	879	856	777	677	680	798	788	688	660	663	616	614	725

Fresh.   [1]Preliminary.   NA = Not available.   *Source: National Agricultural Statistics Service, U.S. Department of Agriculture (NASS-USDA)*

Average Price Received by Growers for Strawberries in the United States — In Dollars Per Box

Year	Jan.	Feb.	Mar.	Apr.	May	June	July	Aug.	Sept.	Oct.	Nov.	Dec.	Average
2009	116.00	128.00	91.10	78.90	76.10	62.80	74.80	73.50	75.00	108.00	87.60	210.00	98.48
2010	218.00	179.00	116.00	75.70	78.90	67.70	62.00	81.70	73.30	87.60	139.00	285.00	121.99
2011	217.00	126.00	99.20	93.50	80.80	72.70	89.20	78.80	87.60	66.90	84.40	153.00	104.09
2012	137.00	113.00	103.00	94.40	82.70	74.40	74.00	85.00	87.60	90.10	139.00	222.00	108.52
2013	109.00	123.00	117.00	NA	NA	NA	NA	NA	NA	NA	NA	NA	116.33
2014	NA	NA	NA	87.60	96.10	91.80	89.30	92.70	133.00	112.00	152.00	209.00	118.17
2015	135.00	101.00	63.60	76.80	72.60	61.50	60.20	86.70	71.30	100.00	190.00	193.00	100.98
2016	195.00	167.00	81.00	84.30	68.60	60.50	59.40	69.40	50.90	71.00	167.00	154.00	102.34
2017	147.00	128.00	94.90	66.60	53.20	59.20	74.10	84.70	109.00	98.00	164.00	182.00	105.06
2018[1]	169.00	125.00	118.00	105.00	55.30	52.70	66.60	50.50	84.00	67.30	99.00	W	90.22

Fresh.   [1]Preliminary.   NA = Not available..   *Source: National Agricultural Statistics Service, U.S. Department of Agriculture (NASS-USDA)*

Cold Storage Stocks of Frozen Apples in the United States, on First of Month — In Thousands of Pounds

Year	Jan.	Feb.	Mar.	Apr.	May	June	July	Aug.	Sept.	Oct.	Nov.	Dec.
2009	69,090	76,213	82,134	87,781	89,443	80,700	75,916	65,915	53,452	46,569	52,235	62,256
2010	71,643	80,614	87,070	90,246	85,975	80,162	76,030	71,496	63,194	55,183	68,354	81,069
2011	89,093	91,277	85,564	74,199	74,565	67,990	58,857	55,216	45,730	46,911	53,790	61,286
2012	73,898	76,390	73,470	70,943	66,459	60,688	59,358	57,905	55,178	51,344	51,748	54,843
2013	56,202	51,297	48,411	46,119	42,047	39,547	34,354	34,202	31,733	32,414	37,339	50,486
2014	49,831	56,312	60,384	61,220	60,693	58,666	56,046	55,517	52,050	49,676	53,072	52,828
2015	55,400	55,350	53,314	52,079	50,761	49,547	46,985	42,987	36,586	31,854	35,761	38,917
2016	37,596	38,707	37,994	37,761	39,147	38,682	39,040	36,171	32,361	29,104	28,198	32,407
2017	34,929	37,963	36,919	38,679	44,495	40,049	37,418	34,995	34,475	29,471	26,836	29,408
2018[1]	32,007	34,420	35,915	36,968	35,087	32,441	33,715	30,609	24,822	22,366	21,603	23,791

[1] Preliminary.   *Source: Economic Research Service, U.S. Department of Agriculture (ERS-USDA)*

Cold Storage Stocks of Frozen Apricots in the United States, on First of Month — In Thousands of Pounds

Year	Jan.	Feb.	Mar.	Apr.	May	June	July	Aug.	Sept.	Oct.	Nov.	Dec.
2009	5,471	4,850	4,768	3,829	3,563	3,103	12,685	8,468	7,582	6,930	5,857	5,662
2010	4,845	3,905	2,724	2,803	2,340	1,837	7,288	10,191	8,659	8,244	6,329	5,576
2011	4,833	3,519	3,517	2,944	2,034	2,192	6,003	12,132	8,630	6,564	4,982	4,643
2012	4,863	3,593	3,460	3,003	2,591	1,990	9,440	11,011	9,636	8,737	6,318	4,053
2013	4,018	3,395	2,340	1,907	1,452	1,668	11,874	7,871	7,204	6,276	4,639	4,501
2014	3,895	3,532	3,406	3,380	2,384	1,974	12,488	9,847	7,852	7,533	6,471	6,191
2015	5,941	5,246	4,720	4,162	4,051	3,390	11,760	11,058	10,059	7,931	6,128	5,640
2016	4,921	4,319	3,804	3,434	2,968	3,301	11,086	16,226	13,454	11,690	9,998	8,958
2017	8,456	6,506	4,103	3,163	2,848	2,279	11,696	11,048	8,512	7,335	6,098	5,506
2018[1]	4,873	4,295	3,616	2,974	2,275	1,664	8,301	9,538	8,843	8,148	7,549	6,640

[1] Preliminary.   *Source: Economic Research Service, U.S. Department of Agriculture (ERS-USDA)*

Cold Storage Stocks of Frozen Blackberries[2] in the United States, on First of Month — In Thousands of Pounds

Year	Jan.	Feb.	Mar.	Apr.	May	June	July	Aug.	Sept.	Oct.	Nov.	Dec.
2009	26,148	22,370	20,797	17,505	15,256	13,742	11,081	39,708	40,099	37,329	34,855	32,393
2010	27,630	25,010	23,056	21,793	19,425	16,174	12,879	26,312	31,930	32,384	28,823	26,794
2011	23,857	18,649	14,941	14,603	13,864	13,113	11,946	20,833	36,913	38,718	37,111	33,876
2012	31,909	26,925	24,149	21,359	19,248	18,076	15,138	40,692	40,867	39,689	37,508	36,152
2013	35,272	33,021	25,975	24,247	21,792	17,887	18,727	40,606	39,237	37,880	33,468	32,048
2014	30,066	28,823	27,183	22,994	21,110	21,107	22,053	42,581	40,339	37,494	34,756	32,368
2015	30,925	28,843	25,499	23,071	20,892	19,931	25,158	34,001	35,240	33,078	30,553	28,366
2016	26,594	24,457	23,752	23,008	20,296	19,131	36,373	43,885	43,330	38,711	36,110	33,134
2017	31,753	29,540	26,983	24,151	23,147	20,956	22,085	36,913	34,707	31,603	28,024	26,682
2018[1]	24,449	21,402	18,205	16,089	14,699	12,534	14,481	38,977	33,607	32,294	29,964	26,923

[1] Preliminary. [2] Includes IQF, Pails and Tubs, Barrels (400lbs net), and Concentrate. *Source: Economic Research Service, U.S. Department of Agriculture (ERS-USDA)*

Cold Storage Stocks of Frozen Blueberries in the United States, on First of Month — In Thousands of Pounds

Year	Jan.	Feb.	Mar.	Apr.	May	June	July	Aug.	Sept.	Oct.	Nov.	Dec.
2009	153,445	141,089	130,964	115,615	100,820	87,790	81,404	106,327	189,893	189,628	173,849	154,647
2010	141,883	123,579	109,095	93,342	75,482	61,331	57,332	100,100	163,387	155,105	140,707	129,877
2011	116,485	104,091	93,103	80,016	65,583	50,865	57,467	76,551	167,015	174,805	160,156	147,757
2012	136,966	124,003	114,066	96,723	85,700	73,717	82,218	148,315	238,510	234,207	215,588	196,702
2013	171,296	165,932	152,187	137,358	119,814	100,876	103,559	166,382	260,094	251,279	235,007	217,393
2014	201,834	172,718	150,626	130,825	117,065	98,716	102,012	171,661	269,537	265,303	240,830	229,225
2015	208,324	187,523	166,469	152,745	133,836	119,276	132,732	236,349	273,614	280,085	259,198	245,754
2016	224,696	211,459	191,351	164,927	154,142	145,414	157,928	260,675	315,436	332,379	308,554	294,135
2017	268,895	241,947	223,211	195,417	184,367	157,140	147,915	197,723	276,632	266,423	256,727	230,843
2018[1]	222,060	192,354	162,564	134,469	116,387	96,891	99,912	175,185	244,902	247,396	228,308	200,002

[1] Preliminary. *Source: Economic Research Service, U.S. Department of Agriculture (ERS-USDA)*

Cold Storage Stocks of Frozen Cherries[2] in the United States, on First of Month — In Thousands of Pounds

Year	Jan.	Feb.	Mar.	Apr.	May	June	July	Aug.	Sept.	Oct.	Nov.	Dec.
2009	101,892	96,533	90,052	79,608	69,139	59,714	53,206	128,571	193,312	185,263	179,608	167,716
2010	156,136	145,923	136,313	124,138	113,941	103,008	96,431	161,826	150,298	136,233	128,236	118,223
2011	110,166	97,223	87,153	71,167	62,380	50,776	40,803	96,444	124,646	108,842	98,395	90,339
2012	83,622	73,371	65,185	54,211	44,684	32,532	26,924	59,120	51,815	50,514	49,966	56,135
2013	51,161	44,651	38,315	33,746	26,644	19,127	14,227	114,938	150,224	139,064	128,171	114,676
2014	112,101	99,639	91,631	82,926	71,746	58,869	50,181	103,362	178,542	164,429	153,521	144,280
2015	134,908	129,319	120,870	105,707	98,519	85,866	79,028	146,251	158,170	159,154	141,734	132,880
2016	123,378	113,844	102,584	91,204	81,431	72,293	63,925	173,739	196,001	184,839	174,878	156,973
2017	142,913	131,911	121,549	111,923	102,192	93,736	83,809	155,363	166,554	158,660	154,858	142,281
2018[1]	134,946	125,530	115,381	108,226	98,931	88,879	74,151	167,724	184,463	169,664	156,442	145,503

[1] Preliminary. [2] Tart (ripe tart pitted). *Source: Economic Research Service, U.S. Department of Agriculture (ERS-USDA)*

Cold Storage Stocks of Frozen Peaches in the United States, on First of Month — In Thousands of Pounds

Year	Jan.	Feb.	Mar.	Apr.	May	June	July	Aug.	Sept.	Oct.	Nov.	Dec.
2009	76,356	69,001	59,525	45,757	40,755	34,667	29,049	32,155	48,217	59,280	56,959	57,070
2010	52,278	48,051	48,298	44,625	41,204	40,744	31,570	30,403	52,904	64,624	63,093	60,595
2011	56,317	52,137	46,376	39,799	35,267	31,398	27,005	28,034	56,462	77,798	73,554	73,053
2012	66,344	60,950	60,096	48,374	44,074	39,734	35,430	36,517	59,775	70,173	67,100	55,085
2013	50,717	45,535	40,062	33,489	28,880	22,290	19,137	36,193	59,642	72,610	73,147	65,548
2014	61,092	53,367	47,862	39,621	32,936	25,714	19,497	34,001	54,810	63,033	57,543	52,384
2015	47,465	44,353	38,646	35,803	30,722	27,566	26,877	41,488	63,360	78,572	75,817	75,253
2016	74,308	68,463	62,266	54,489	52,746	49,601	48,346	62,290	83,003	93,794	91,530	88,731
2017	81,881	74,285	69,924	64,477	58,878	53,696	53,066	62,003	83,564	87,901	85,238	84,813
2018[1]	76,686	68,986	60,036	54,898	46,755	40,717	35,517	37,621	47,952	69,189	69,578	65,013

[1] Preliminary. *Source: Economic Research Service, U.S. Department of Agriculture (ERS-USDA)*

FRUITS

Cold Storage Stocks of Frozen Raspberries[2] in the United States, on First of Month   In Thousands of Pounds

Year	Jan.	Feb.	Mar.	Apr.	May	June	July	Aug.	Sept.	Oct.	Nov.	Dec.
2009	34,083	29,155	25,817	24,155	20,797	18,742	15,963	75,263	65,422	59,133	52,459	48,339
2010	41,572	38,012	30,972	28,317	25,137	20,192	19,296	67,816	63,950	59,331	53,098	46,875
2011	42,151	37,949	33,062	28,151	27,424	23,199	21,531	66,893	73,113	71,489	65,330	62,067
2012	56,868	51,127	45,651	38,328	34,302	31,284	26,663	77,169	73,056	68,773	61,981	56,825
2013	53,505	44,526	39,815	32,916	31,666	26,920	25,369	72,447	82,984	79,479	72,788	65,095
2014	62,102	52,730	45,071	38,418	33,673	31,353	30,226	87,492	81,541	74,858	67,095	62,337
2015	57,298	52,133	47,260	42,776	37,243	32,411	40,185	76,637	70,585	69,798	63,343	61,126
2016	57,362	50,125	46,477	41,902	40,581	38,234	65,383	101,557	93,436	86,090	81,042	76,043
2017	68,388	61,275	54,772	48,895	44,148	39,664	33,818	83,871	93,184	87,305	80,655	79,382
2018[1]	75,614	67,234	64,955	57,902	56,206	50,897	48,562	113,881	111,557	103,198	95,489	86,933

[1] Preliminary .   [2] Red: Includes IQF, Pails and Tubs, Barrels (400 lbs net), and Concentrate.   *Source: Economic Research Service, U.S. Department of Agriculture (ERS-USDA)*

Cold Storage Stocks of Frozen Strawberries[2] in the United States, on First of Month   In Thousands of Pounds

Year	Jan.	Feb.	Mar.	Apr.	May	June	July	Aug.	Sept.	Oct.	Nov.	Dec.
2009	235,241	198,713	182,112	151,904	212,641	281,133	390,580	423,878	412,766	389,377	364,611	342,063
2010	322,452	289,623	269,111	236,089	273,591	274,438	358,348	421,410	385,612	355,255	322,577	297,494
2011	263,147	233,644	203,393	177,108	180,773	244,433	333,190	384,184	367,425	350,563	348,285	323,160
2012	291,697	259,308	224,105	199,485	206,876	305,961	399,764	424,417	414,358	399,632	381,561	343,201
2013	302,987	265,250	240,083	218,149	334,359	397,352	421,128	463,698	428,160	392,032	345,152	320,036
2014	279,977	240,382	215,168	211,064	233,147	257,783	357,526	362,127	330,666	294,969	270,553	236,828
2015	206,841	175,520	163,599	186,817	199,290	238,106	341,295	360,045	328,775	314,350	278,860	253,146
2016	235,852	208,274	190,132	203,784	225,525	264,440	390,681	396,716	377,156	376,035	367,939	331,389
2017	304,827	289,622	274,147	255,978	266,206	312,244	357,628	411,241	402,915	363,542	333,050	309,351
2018[1]	281,076	253,019	216,083	195,941	187,043	249,528	377,233	373,131	350,742	328,176	286,222	253,170

[1] Preliminary.   [2] Includes IQF and Poly, Pails and Tubs, Barrels and Drums, and Juice Stock.   *Source: Economic Research Service, U.S. Department of Agriculture (ERS-USDA)*

Cold Storage Stocks of Other Frozen Fruit in the United States, on First of Month   In Thousands of Pounds

Year	Jan.	Feb.	Mar.	Apr.	May	June	July	Aug.	Sept.	Oct.	Nov.	Dec.
2009	509,807	467,363	414,907	360,587	343,101	311,835	286,675	246,058	215,985	198,200	551,910	530,591
2010	486,760	449,112	399,408	355,773	318,497	289,097	246,690	209,745	174,476	225,587	502,560	473,224
2011	439,996	404,540	367,245	345,131	294,806	254,167	217,588	189,747	150,499	160,415	452,421	452,416
2012	423,367	388,229	360,867	331,923	294,833	256,890	220,723	194,871	170,723	224,022	525,515	510,323
2013	493,200	444,506	417,678	382,611	355,428	316,247	284,810	277,685	238,619	224,171	470,098	589,226
2014	575,025	528,790	475,527	440,532	389,071	341,283	305,249	286,727	264,490	293,231	542,534	576,843
2015	535,775	482,436	434,463	385,477	348,811	321,532	297,358	309,251	309,356	377,612	659,912	665,020
2016	587,967	603,399	557,741	521,065	525,633	489,438	473,450	483,812	464,629	514,081	853,189	872,413
2017	808,397	764,821	738,926	665,196	604,047	543,809	491,595	502,270	493,106	515,569	700,422	709,259
2018[1]	666,624	595,561	554,544	487,759	462,211	399,596	404,649	395,232	361,493	398,684	741,610	710,686

[1] Preliminary.   *Source: Economic Research Service, U.S. Department of Agriculture (ERS-USDA)*

Cold Storage Stocks of Total Frozen Fruit in the United States, on First of Month   In Millions of Pounds

Year	Jan.	Feb.	Mar.	Apr.	May	June	July	Aug.	Sept.	Oct.	Nov.	Dec.
2009	1,245.6	1,134.2	1,038.1	911.0	916.8	910.6	973.2	1,154.3	1,257.8	1,200.7	1,501.1	1,428.2
2010	1,328.6	1,226.0	1,125.9	1,014.5	971.8	902.7	921.1	1,124.3	1,118.5	1,113.1	1,335.7	1,259.8
2011	1,165.1	1,060.7	950.9	847.7	770.1	750.6	785.5	953.4	1,058.5	1,063.6	1,317.2	1,269.3
2012	1,189.3	1,082.2	989.1	881.4	813.3	835.1	889.5	1,077.5	1,145.4	1,178.0	1,425.6	1,342.3
2013	1,246.6	1,123.5	1,030.1	934.9	985.0	962.6	954.1	1,251.3	1,335.0	1,270.0	1,431.1	1,489.0
2014	1,405.6	1,261.1	1,140.4	1,052.0	981.1	912.1	972.2	1,176.0	1,317.9	1,286.1	1,461.4	1,426.8
2015	1,315.4	1,191.8	1,084.2	1,016.4	949.2	921.6	1,028.1	1,294.3	1,322.6	1,385.6	1,580.9	1,535.4
2016	1,398.6	1,349.4	1,240.4	1,165.4	1,163.7	1,141.0	1,309.2	1,611.2	1,658.5	1,707.9	1,993.9	1,934.0
2017	1,788.9	1,673.4	1,585.8	1,439.9	1,360.5	1,291.0	1,262.8	1,530.3	1,633.1	1,585.8	1,707.8	1,650.3
2018[1]	1,547.8	1,390.3	1,256.2	1,118.8	1,041.1	992.9	1,117.5	1,379.8	1,419.1	1,425.1	1,677.2	1,557.1

[1] Preliminary.   *Source: Economic Research Service, U.S. Department of Agriculture (ERS-USDA)*

Gas

Natural gas is a fossil fuel that is colorless, shapeless, and odorless in its pure form. It is a mixture of hydrocarbon gases formed primarily of methane, but it can also include ethane, propane, butane, and pentane. Natural gas is combustible, clean burning, and gives off a great deal of energy. Around 500 BC, the Chinese discovered that the energy in natural gas could be harnessed. They passed it through crude bamboo-shoot pipes and then burned it to boil sea water to create potable fresh water. Around 1785, Britain became the first country to commercially use natural gas produced from coal for streetlights and indoor lights. In 1821, William Hart dug the first well specifically intended to obtain natural gas and he is generally regarded as the "father of natural gas" in America. There is a vast amount of natural gas estimated to still be in the ground in the U.S. Natural gas as a source of energy is significantly less expensive than electricity per Btu.

Natural gas futures and options are traded at the CME Group. The CME natural gas futures contract calls for the delivery of natural gas representing 10,000 million British thermal units (mmBtu) at the Henry Hub in Louisiana, which is the nexus of 16 intra-state and inter-state pipelines. The contract is priced in terms of U.S. Dollars per mmBtu. CME also has basic swap futures contracts available for 30 different natural gas pricing locations versus the benchmark Henry Hub location. Natural gas futures are also traded at ICE Futures Europe.

Prices – CME natural gas futures (Barchart.com symbol code NG) on the nearest-futures chart started 2018 at $2.995 per mmBtu, moved lower most of the year to finally close the year down -6.0% at $2.814 per mmBtu.

Supply – U.S. recovery of natural gas in 2017 rose +1.6% to a record high of 33.170 billion cubic feet. The top U.S. producing states for natural gas in 2017 were Texas with 23.7% of U.S. production, Pennsylvania with 19.0%, Oklahoma with 8.7%, Louisiana with 7.4%, Colorado with 5.9%, Wyoming with 5.4%, and New Mexico with 4.4%. In 2017 the world's largest natural gas producers were the U.S. with 2,680,036 Terajoules and Russia with 1,999,581 Terajoules of production.

Demand – U.S. total delivered consumption of natural gas in 2017 fell -1.6% yr/yr to 24,794 billion cubic feet, of which about 37.3% was delivered to electrical utility plants, 31.9% to industrial establishments, 17.8% to residences, and 12.8% to commercial establishments.

Trade – U.S. imports of natural gas (consumed) in 2017 rose +1.2% yr/yr to 3,042 billion cubic feet, down from the 2007 record high of 4,608 billion cubic feet. U.S. exports of natural gas in 2017 rose +35.6% yr/yr to 3,168 billion cubic feet for a new record high.

World Dry Natural Gas Production   In Billion Cubic Feet

Year	Algeria	Canada	China	Indonesia	Iran	Nether-lands	Norway	Qatar	Russia	Saudi Arabia	United States	Uzbek-istan	World Total
2006	3,079	6,548	2,067	2,199	3,836	2,732	3,094	1,790	21,736	2,594	18,504	2,216	101,621
2007	2,996	6,416	2,446	2,422	3,952	2,687	3,168	2,232	21,595	2,628	19,266	2,302	104,141
2008	3,055	6,046	2,685	2,472	4,107	2,957	3,503	2,719	21,515	2,841	20,159	2,387	107,858
2009	2,876	5,634	2,975	2,557	4,986	2,786	3,664	3,154	18,890	2,770	20,624	2,169	105,418
2010	2,988	5,390	3,334	2,917	5,161	3,131	3,756	4,121	20,915	2,969	21,316	2,123	112,438
2011	2,923	5,218	3,629	2,693	5,361	2,851	3,576	5,130	22,202	3,127	22,902	2,226	116,690
2012	3,053	5,070	3,666	2,619	5,640	2,843	4,052	5,546	21,764	3,439	24,033	2,222	119,302
2013	2,813	5,129	3,986	2,606	5,696	3,053	3,841	5,800	22,139	3,462	24,334	2,106	120,879
2014[1]	2,942	5,349	4,360	2,594	6,162	2,482	3,843	5,650	21,225	3,547	25,890	2,180	122,305
2015[2]	2,933	5,295	4,487	2,571	6,526	1,935	4,139	5,794	21,141	3,614	27,059	1,967	124,090

[1] Preliminary.   [2] Estimate.   Source: Energy Information Administration, U.S. Department of Energy (EIA-DOE)

Marketed Production of Natural Gas in the United States, by States   In Million Cubic Feet

Year	Alaska	Arkansas	California	Colorado	Kansas	Louisiana	New Mexico	Oklahoma	Pennsyl-vania	Texas	Wyoming	Total
2008	398,442	446,457	296,469	1,389,399	374,310	1,377,969	1,446,204	1,886,710	198,295	6,960,693	2,274,850	21,112,053
2009	397,077	679,952	276,575	1,499,070	354,440	1,548,607	1,383,004	1,901,556	273,869	6,818,973	2,335,328	21,647,936
2010	374,226	926,639	286,841	1,578,379	324,720	2,210,099	1,292,185	1,827,328	572,902	6,715,294	2,305,525	22,381,873
2011	356,225	1,072,212	250,177	1,637,576	309,124	3,029,206	1,237,303	1,888,870	1,310,592	7,112,863	2,159,422	24,036,352
2012	351,259	1,146,168	246,822	1,709,376	296,299	2,955,437	1,215,773	2,023,461	2,256,696	7,475,495	2,022,275	25,283,278
2013	338,182	1,139,654	252,310	1,604,860	292,467	2,360,202	1,171,640	1,993,754	3,259,042	7,633,618	1,858,207	25,562,232
2014	345,310	1,122,733	238,988	1,643,487	286,480	1,960,813	1,229,519	2,331,086	4,257,693	7,985,019	1,794,413	27,497,754
2015	343,625	1,010,382	236,648	1,688,733	284,184	1,805,197	1,245,145	2,499,599	4,812,983	7,890,459	1,808,519	28,772,044
2016	338,095	823,223	205,024	1,701,735	243,459	1,743,259	1,251,013	2,468,312	5,313,258	7,203,012	1,664,604	28,479,288
2017[1]	344,385	700,861	201,954	1,691,700	220,259	2,119,509	1,272,297	2,513,304	5,461,259	6,831,318	1,554,455	28,806,552

[1] Preliminary.   Source: Energy Information Administration, U.S. Department of Energy (EIA-DOE)

GAS

World Production of Natural Gas Plant Liquids   Thousand Barrels per Day

Year	Algeria	Canada	Mexico	Saudi Arabia	Russia	United States	Persian Gulf[2]	OAPEC[3]	OPEC-12[4]	OPEC-11[4]	World
2006	270	685	338	472	1,860	1,739	2,722	2,554	3,292	3,270	8,178
2007	260	726	328	486	1,940	1,783	2,813	2,582	3,407	3,383	8,394
2008	250	677	318	500	2,080	1,784	2,985	2,592	3,550	3,540	8,514
2009	325	640	326	539	1,980	1,910	2,922	2,744	3,562	3,552	8,641
2010	340	597	332	574	1,920	2,074	2,935	2,972	3,592	3,582	8,901
2011	322	591	334	611	1,920	2,216	3,102	2,958	3,637	3,627	9,130
2012	342	611	318	647	1,920	2,408	3,152	3,164	3,786	3,776	9,502
2013	300	639	320	684	1,920	2,606	3,141		3,685	3,673	9,636
2014[1]	300	665	320	720	1,800	2,964	3,117		3,644	3,629	10,013

Average.   [1] Preliminary.   [2] Bahrain, Iran, Iraq, Kuwait, Qatar, Saudi Arabia, and the United Arab Emirates.   [3] Organization of Arab Petroleum Exporting Countriess: Algeria, Iraq, Kuwait, Libya, Qatar, Saudi Arabia, and the United Arab Emirates.   [4] OPEC-12: Organization of the Petroleum Exporting Countries: Algeria, Angola, Indonesia, Iran, Iraq, Kuwait, Libya, Nigeria, Qatar, Saudi Arabia, the United Arab Emirates, and Venezuela. OPEC-11 does not include Angola.   *Source: Energy Information Administration, U.S. Department of Energy (EIA-DOE)*

Recoverable Reserves and Deliveries of Natural Gas in the United States   In Billions of Cubic Feet

Year	Gross With-drawals	Recoverable Reserves of Natural Gas Dec. 31[2]	Residential	Commercial	Electric Utility Plants[3]	Industrial	Total	Lease & Plant Fuel	Used as Pipline Fuel	Heating Value BTU per Cubic Foot
2010	26,816	304,625	4,782	3,103	7,387	6,826	22,127	1,286	674	1,023
2011	28,479	334,067	4,714	3,155	7,574	6,994	22,467	1,323	688	1,022
2012	29,542	308,036	4,150	2,895	9,111	7,226	23,411	1,396	731	1,024
2013	29,523	338,264	4,897	3,295	8,191	7,425	23,839	1,483	833	1,027
2014	31,405	368,704	5,087	3,466	8,146	7,646	24,381	1,512	700	1,032
2015	32,915	307,730	4,613	3,202	9,613	7,522	24,989	1,576	678	1,037
2016	32,592	322,234	4,347	3,110	9,985	7,729	25,212	1,545	687	1,037
2017	33,357	438,460	4,412	3,164	9,250	7,949	24,824	1,564	722	1,036
2018[1]	36,991		4,980	3,485	10,626	8,268	27,402	1,753	797	1,036

[1] Preliminary.   [2] Estimated proved recoverable reserves of dry natural gas.   [3] Figures include gas other than natural (impossible to segregate); therefore, shown separately from other consumption.   *Source: Energy Information Administration, U.S. Department of Energy (EIA-DOE)*

Salient Statistics of Natural Gas in the United States

	Supply						Disposition				Average Price Delivered to Customers						
Year	Mar-keted Pro-duction	Extrac-tion Loss	Dry Pro-duction	Storage With-drawals	Imports (Con-sumed)	Total Supply	Con-sump-tion	Exports	Added to Storage	Total Dis-position	Well-head Price	Imports	Exports	Resi-dential	Com-mercial	Indus-trial	Electric Utilities
	In Billions of Cubic Feet										Dollars Per Thousand Cubic Feet						
2009	21,648	1,024	20,624	2,966	3,751	28,365	22,910	1,072	3,315	27,297	3.67	4.19	4.47	12.14	10.06	5.33	4.93
2010	22,382	1,066	21,316	3,274	3,741	29,397	24,087	1,137	3,291	28,515	4.48	4.52	5.02	11.39	9.47	5.49	5.27
2011	24,036	1,134	22,902	3,074	3,469	30,579	24,477	1,506	3,422	29,405	3.95	4.24	4.64	11.03	8.91	5.13	4.89
2012	25,283	1,250	24,033	2,818	3,138	31,239	25,538	1,619	2,854	30,011	2.66	2.88	3.25	10.65	8.10	3.88	3.54
2013	25,562	1,357	24,206	3,702	2,883	32,147	26,155	1,572	3,156	30,883	----	3.83	4.08	10.32	8.08	4.64	4.49
2014	27,498	1,608	25,890	3,586	2,695	33,779	26,593	1,514	3,839	31,946	----	5.30	5.51	10.97	8.90	5.62	5.19
2015	28,772	1,707	27,065	3,100	2,718	34,590	27,244	1,784	3,638	32,666	----	2.99	3.07	10.38	7.91	3.93	3.38
2016[1]	28,400	1,808	26,592	3,325	3,006	34,731	27,444	2,335	2,977	32,756	----	2.24	2.79	10.05	7.28	3.52	2.99
2017[2]	29,197	1,906	27,291	3,559	3,042	35,798	27,126	3,168	3,308	33,601	----	2.72	3.54	10.98	7.89	4.14	3.52

[1] Preliminary.   [2] Estimate.   *Source: Energy Information Administration, U.S. Department of Energy (EIA-DOE)*

Average Price of Natural Gas at Henry Hub   In Dollars Per MMBtu

Year	Jan.	Feb.	Mar.	Apr.	May	June	July	Aug.	Sept.	Oct.	Nov.	Dec.	Average
2009	5.24	4.52	3.96	3.50	3.83	3.80	3.38	3.14	2.99	4.01	3.66	5.35	3.95
2010	5.83	5.32	4.29	4.03	4.14	4.80	4.63	4.32	3.89	3.43	3.71	4.25	4.39
2011	4.49	4.09	3.97	4.24	4.31	4.54	4.42	4.06	3.90	3.57	3.24	3.17	4.00
2012	2.67	2.51	2.17	1.95	2.43	2.46	2.95	2.84	2.85	3.32	3.54	3.34	2.75
2013	3.33	3.33	3.81	4.17	4.04	3.83	3.62	3.43	3.62	3.68	3.64	4.24	3.73
2014	4.71	6.00	4.90	4.66	4.58	4.59	4.05	3.91	3.92	3.78	4.12	3.48	4.39
2015	3.00	2.88	2.83	2.61	2.85	2.78	2.84	2.77	2.66	2.34	2.09	1.94	2.63
2016	2.29	1.98	1.73	1.92	1.93	2.59	2.82	2.82	3.00	2.98	2.54	3.59	2.52
2017	3.28	2.86	2.88	3.11	3.15	2.98	2.98	2.90	2.98	2.88	3.01	2.82	2.99
2018	3.91	2.67	2.69	2.80	2.80	2.96	2.83	2.96	3.00	3.26	4.12	3.97	3.16

Source: Energy Information Administration, U.S. Department of Energy (EIA-DOE)

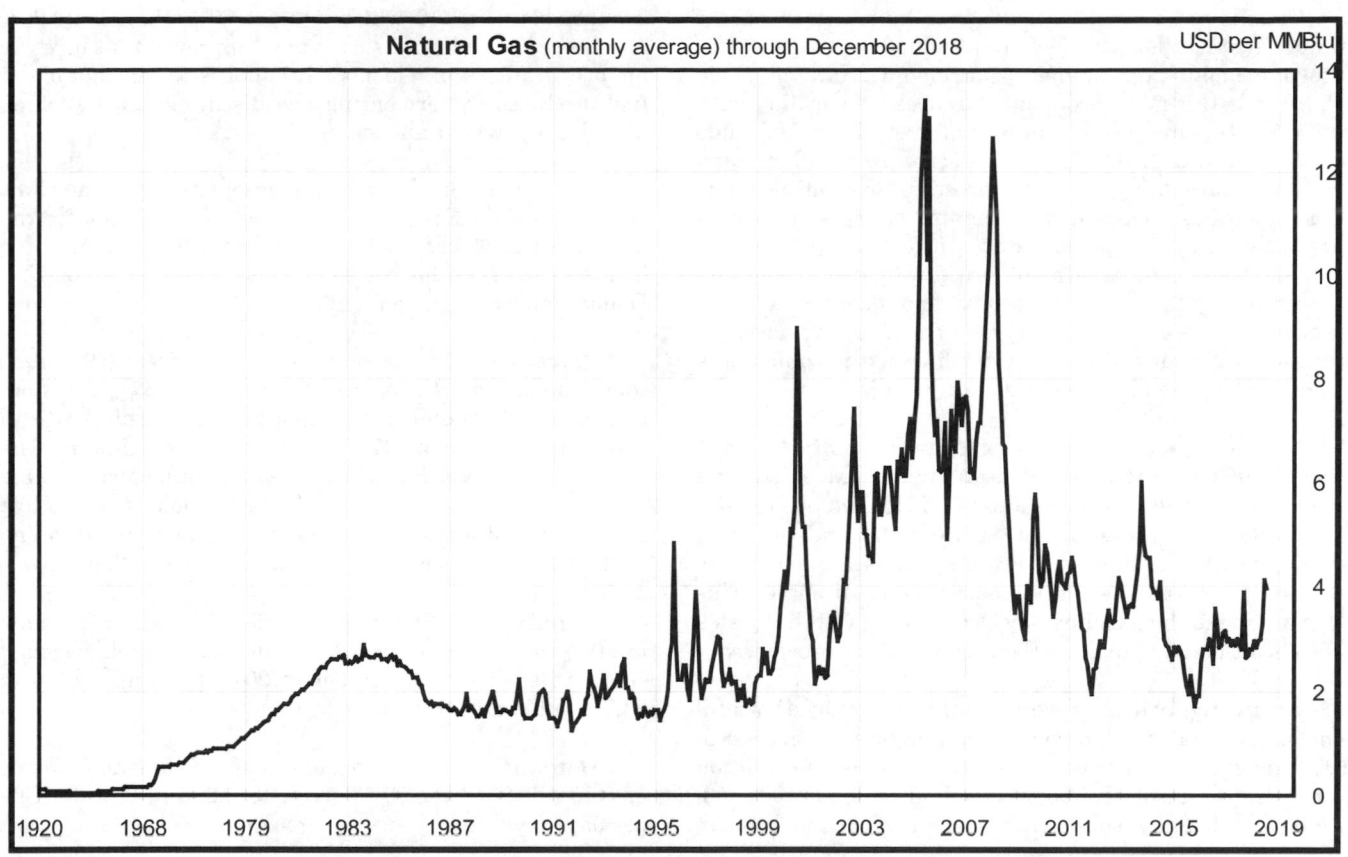

Natural Gas (monthly average) through December 2018 — USD per MMBtu

Volume of Trading of Natural Gas Futures in New York   In Thousands of Contracts

Year	Jan.	Feb.	Mar.	Apr.	May	June	July	Aug.	Sept.	Oct.	Nov.	Dec.	Total
2009	2,343.7	2,780.6	2,989.9	2,493.1	3,479.0	4,486.6	3,979.4	4,445.9	5,597.7	5,594.7	4,413.7	5,347.2	47,951.4
2010	4,501.7	4,557.7	4,690.9	5,740.4	4,729.9	5,911.9	5,267.7	5,791.0	5,428.1	5,920.0	5,780.8	6,002.9	64,323.1
2011	6,468.6	6,123.2	7,284.0	6,432.0	6,015.2	6,760.5	6,317.9	6,904.9	6,363.8	7,199.9	6,117.1	5,878.9	76,864.9
2012	9,328.0	8,723.2	6,798.8	7,488.9	8,660.3	8,639.0	7,412.7	8,579.0	7,272.7	9,259.2	6,262.3	6,375.6	94,799.5
2013	7,329.4	6,910.3	8,343.9	9,484.9	6,796.2	6,271.5	5,626.2	6,944.2	5,741.2	6,991.3	5,618.2	8,225.0	84,282.5
2014	8,872.0	8,301.5	4,804.4	5,114.8	5,031.3	5,425.1	5,022.7	5,374.9	5,623.7	6,087.8	7,980.1	6,568.4	74,206.6
2015	7,617.0	7,014.7	6,255.0	6,141.5	6,663.2	7,705.9	6,403.9	6,458.0	5,714.9	7,578.3	6,236.2	7,984.0	81,772.5
2016	6,472.9	7,003.9	7,649.5	8,350.1	7,090.1	8,875.2	6,769.1	8,506.9	7,646.7	10,240.1	9,073.3	9,802.9	97,480.6
2017	8,858.0	8,035.1	9,138.2	7,911.2	9,389.8	9,195.0	7,515.3	8,159.4	8,498.8	10,583.3	10,006.5	10,500.6	108,391.8
2018	14,188.6	8,454.1	7,287.5	8,409.2	8,241.5	8,010.4	7,091.6	8,462.0	9,776.6	12,263.9	14,219.3	7,851.3	114,256.1

Contract size = 10,000 MMBtu.   *Source: CME Group; New York Mercantile Exchange (NYMEX)*

Average Open Interest of Natural Gas Futures in New York   In Thousands of Contracts

Year	Jan.	Feb.	Mar.	Apr.	May	June	July	Aug.	Sept.	Oct.	Nov.	Dec.
2009	693.3	709.0	652.4	649.9	678.4	709.2	737.5	731.6	713.8	710.0	713.6	719.6
2010	762.0	786.4	839.2	855.4	860.8	817.7	783.9	819.2	812.4	800.8	783.7	774.4
2011	820.8	917.0	922.1	948.1	956.5	980.4	977.0	990.3	952.1	969.6	977.2	981.2
2012	1,122.7	1,241.6	1,226.2	1,271.3	1,221.7	1,177.7	1,120.4	1,089.0	1,106.9	1,184.3	1,166.7	1,157.0
2013	1,172.0	1,196.1	1,315.3	1,539.1	1,511.7	1,434.8	1,389.5	1,356.6	1,306.4	1,263.8	1,271.2	1,302.4
2014	1,278.0	1,246.6	1,160.8	1,104.7	1,021.9	1,032.9	1,017.1	962.3	970.3	914.8	952.5	939.1
2015	991.0	1,004.6	979.6	1,016.3	1,015.3	1,038.6	1,001.3	957.0	918.7	977.8	1,011.8	1,007.1
2016	912.6	995.9	1,076.7	1,117.9	1,081.1	1,061.2	1,014.6	1,057.1	1,059.3	1,142.7	1,169.7	1,220.4
2017	1,195.9	1,247.4	1,364.8	1,432.0	1,537.9	1,421.3	1,337.6	1,324.8	1,317.7	1,374.0	1,377.5	1,505.8
2018	1,426.6	1,365.8	1,392.4	1,463.5	1,484.9	1,512.8	1,507.3	1,583.4	1,642.3	1,621.5	1,409.2	1,258.8

Contract size = 10,000 MMBtu.   *Source: CME Group; New York Mercantile Exchange (NYMEX)*

Gasoline

Gasoline is a complex mixture of hundreds of lighter liquid hydrocarbons and is used chiefly as a fuel for internal-combustion engines. Petroleum crude, or crude oil, is still the most economical source of gasoline with refineries turning more than half of every barrel of crude oil into gasoline. The three basic steps to all refining operations are the separation process (separating crude oil into various chemical components), conversion process (breaking the chemicals down into molecules called hydrocarbons), and treatment process (transforming and combining hydrocarbon molecules and other additives). Another process, called *hydro treating*, removes a significant amount of sulfur from finished gasoline as is currently required by the state of California.

Octane is a measure of a gasoline's ability to resist pinging or knocking noise from an engine. Most gasoline stations offer three octane grades of unleaded fuel—regular at 87 (R+M)/2, mid-grade at 89 (R+M)/2, and premium at 93 (R+M)/2. Additional refining steps are needed to increase the octane, which increases the retail price. This does not make the gasoline any cleaner or better, but yields a different blend of hydrocarbons that burn more slowly.

In an attempt to improve air quality and reduce harmful emissions from internal combustion engines, Congress in 1990 amended the Clean Air Act to mandate the addition of ethanol to gasoline. Some 2 billion gallons of ethanol are now added to gasoline each year in the U.S. The most common blend is E10, which contains 10% ethanol and 90% gasoline. Auto manufacturers have approved that mixture for use in all U.S. vehicles. Ethanol is an alcohol-based fuel produced by fermenting and distilling crops such as corn, barley, wheat and sugar.

RBOB gasoline futures and options trade at the CME Group. The CME's gasoline futures contract calls for the delivery of 1,000 barrels (42,000 gallons) of RBOB gasoline in the New York harbor and is priced in terms of U.S. Dollars and cents per gallon.

Price – CME gasoline futures prices (Barchart. com symbol code RB) opened 2018 at $1.8937 per gallon, rallied until September and then moved sharply lower to close the year down -27.3% at $1.3376 per gallon. The average monthly retail price of regular unleaded gasoline in 2018 rose +13.6% yr/yr to $2.74 per gallon. The average monthly retail price of unleaded premium motor gasoline in the U.S. in 2018 rose +12.3% to $3.17 per gallon.

Supply – U.S. production of finished motor gasoline in 2018 rose +1.0% yr/yr to10.054 million barrels per day. Gasoline stocks in November of 2018 were up +2.8% to 24.267 million barrels.

Demand – U.S. consumption of finished motor gasoline in 2018 fell -0.3% yr/yr to 9.298 million barrels per day, down from last year's record.

World Production of Motor Gasoline   In Thousands of Barrels Per Day

Year	Brazil	Canada	China	France	Germany	India	Italy	Japan	Mexico	Russia	United Kingdom	United States	World Total
2007	331.0	750.4	1,394.8	224.8	492.9	233.0	288.2	929.2	735.4	672.0	410.6	9,285.7	21,669.0
2008	327.0	742.7	1,524.0	206.9	482.6	257.0	264.9	900.5	764.0	738.0	385.7	8,989.2	21,434.5
2009	329.0	756.8	1,586.5	199.2	467.1	308.0	254.1	925.2	766.0	731.0	367.3	8,996.5	21,890.8
2010	393.0	782.9	1,806.5	184.9	454.1	319.0	239.4	940.1	775.4	779.0	349.6	8,992.7	22,315.8
2011	467.0	789.3	2,011.6	174.3	453.8	338.0	244.1	918.0	773.0	789.0	333.7	8,752.8	22,344.1
2012	530.0	791.3	2,157.8	164.8	426.8	368.0	216.3	957.2	774.8	819.0	319.7	8,682.2	22,745.4
2013	547.0	814.5	2,463.2	160.3	426.5	400.0	201.5	947.7	761.1	834.0	306.2	8,843.0	23,466.0
2014	576.0	803.8	2,614.8	161.9	428.9	445.8	204.8	922.3	750.9	853.1	300.3	8,920.8	23,895.8
2015[1]		810.9		164.2	421.9		183.9	893.4	766.9		294.3	9,178.4	
2016[2]		847.5		169.3	420.9		181.2	896.8	795.9		289.8		

[1] Preliminary.   [2] Estimate.   *Source: Energy Information Administration, U.S. Department of Energy (EIA-DOE)*

World Imports of Motor Gasoline   In Thousands of Barrels Per Day

Year	Australia	Canada	Indonesia	Iran	Malaysia	Mexico	Netherlands	Nigeria	Saudi Arabia	Singapore	United Kingdom	United States	World Total
2004	59.6	65.0	99.7	142.6	54.7	161.7	181.3	136.9	----	161.6	50.2	496.4	2,891.4
2005	57.5	81.7	125.2	156.0	66.3	214.2	212.2	128.1	41.1	166.6	55.1	602.7	3,242.9
2006	56.1	98.8	128.9	172.9	76.3	245.5	242.4	126.4	79.2	172.4	87.8	475.2	3,212.4
2007	46.8	75.3	145.3	119.8	73.3	284.7	170.7	135.4	75.2	200.0	75.6	412.6	3,040.0
2008	70.7	94.2	94.8	130.0	78.1	307.1	225.2	107.4	108.0	230.3	53.7	301.6	3,030.0
2009	77.1	89.1	199.3	132.5	74.0	307.6	234.1	140.0	102.9	20.2	77.8	223.4	2,943.9
2010	47.3	79.9	219.0	93.9	97.1	354.4	217.2	162.7	86.2	324.9	85.3	134.3	3,366.9
2011	57.2	90.4	268.8	31.1	104.6	386.8	240.5	142.0	51.9	323.3	88.0	104.8	3,508.0
2012[1]	57.3	62.2	307.9	9.6	134.9	374.9	276.2	137.3	92.2	305.7	111.5	44.1	3,628.2
2013[2]	63.6	54.7				319.4	225.1				108.7	45.0	

[1] Preliminary.   [2] Estimate.   *Source: Energy Information Administration, U.S. Department of Energy (EIA-DOE)*

World Exports of Motor Gasoline   In Thousands of Barrels Per Day

Year	Canada	France	Germany	India	Italy	Nether-lands	Russia	Singa-pore	United Kingdom	United States	Vene-zuela	Virgin Islands	World Total
2004	156.2	161.7	121.5	67.5	127.6	340.4	98.3	240.4	169.3	124.3	178.0	158.9	3,358.6
2005	161.4	179.1	132.1	53.1	161.3	376.4	138.4	332.0	152.5	135.5	172.0	159.3	3,655.9
2006	138.8	160.0	128.6	86.4	161.3	400.4	147.4	330.2	161.5	141.8	132.0	131.6	3,669.6
2007	147.4	147.0	125.4	105.3	208.7	297.6	140.4	376.5	169.7	127.0	115.1	140.1	3,562.2
2008	129.3	182.6	132.2	126.8	196.6	357.1	104.3	428.7	162.6	171.7	117.0	131.9	3,635.9
2009	136.5	148.4	125.5	228.1	166.8	376.0	105.2	216.8	177.2	195.4	127.5	115.8	3,564.1
2010	149.7	133.2	112.1	318.9	192.7	382.9	69.2	525.4	208.4	295.8	9.5	107.9	3,887.4
2011	130.7	118.5	109.6	329.1	187.2	348.7	90.3	535.7	214.3	478.8	27.9	102.3	4,052.4
2012[1]	138.4	107.9	114.9	336.8	201.8	448.9	74.9	530.9	196.5	408.9	8.7	18.0	4,020.3
2013[2]	143.2	85.8	115.4		180.4	409.3			238.5	373.0			

[1] Preliminary.   [2] Estimate.   Source: Energy Information Administration, U.S. Department of Energy (EIA-DOE)

Production of Finished Motor Gasoline in the United States   In Thousand Barrels per Day

Year	Jan.	Feb.	Mar.	Apr.	May	June	July	Aug.	Sept.	Oct.	Nov.	Dec.	Average
2009	8,445	8,408	8,646	8,724	8,793	9,068	8,952	8,856	8,829	8,770	8,905	9,006	8,784
2010	8,348	8,510	8,913	9,062	9,113	9,211	9,500	9,426	9,143	9,049	9,134	9,252	9,055
2011	8,714	8,866	8,908	8,978	9,157	9,289	9,166	9,264	9,140	8,932	9,141	9,128	9,057
2012	8,385	8,606	8,705	8,720	8,950	9,157	9,073	9,237	8,888	9,176	9,156	9,051	8,925
2013	8,718	8,926	8,971	9,042	9,299	9,472	9,374	9,340	9,190	9,484	9,476	9,495	9,232
2014	8,849	9,111	9,368	9,652	9,834	9,809	9,983	9,741	9,404	9,552	9,607	9,898	9,567
2015	9,260	9,504	9,524	9,720	9,771	9,846	9,989	9,998	9,878	9,935	9,799	9,806	9,752
2016	9,378	9,834	9,932	9,876	10,058	10,280	10,224	10,293	10,020	10,059	9,969	10,013	9,995
2017	9,281	9,507	9,802	9,855	10,126	10,270	10,164	10,176	9,778	10,129	10,220	10,104	9,951
2018[1]	9,519	9,800	10,052	9,964	10,130	10,326	10,166	10,243	9,926	10,299	10,240	10,020	10,057

[1] Preliminary.   Source: Energy Information Administration, U.S. Department of Energy (EIA-DOE)

Disposition of Finished Motor Gasoline, Total Product Supplied in the United States   In Thousand Barrels per Day

Year	Jan.	Feb.	Mar.	Apr.	May	June	July	Aug.	Sept.	Oct.	Nov.	Dec.	Average
2009	8,623	8,836	8,903	9,029	9,084	9,180	9,260	9,295	8,911	8,986	8,906	8,931	8,995
2010	8,520	8,579	8,793	9,108	9,162	9,311	9,301	9,255	9,112	9,016	8,816	8,911	8,990
2011	8,370	8,604	8,799	8,796	8,817	9,067	9,031	8,925	8,744	8,649	8,537	8,683	8,752
2012	8,190	8,598	8,582	8,741	8,979	8,996	8,810	9,154	8,561	8,701	8,483	8,389	8,682
2013	8,331	8,395	8,641	8,855	9,033	9,078	9,146	9,124	8,946	8,944	8,923	8,670	8,841
2014	8,273	8,647	8,697	8,955	9,023	9,039	9,249	9,311	8,822	9,148	8,921	8,941	8,919
2015	8,639	8,829	9,057	9,189	9,262	9,417	9,470	9,460	9,289	9,245	9,112	9,148	9,176
2016	8,653	9,221	9,373	9,176	9,417	9,608	9,578	9,687	9,484	9,093	9,233	9,283	9,317
2017	8,507	9,008	9,325	9,295	9,550	9,772	9,595	9,752	9,378	9,357	9,110	9,247	9,325
2018[1]	8,742	8,817	9,446	9,187	9,550	9,798	9,640	9,748	9,118	9,273	9,247	9,219	9,315

[1] Preliminary.   Source: Energy Information Administration, U.S. Department of Energy (EIA-DOE)

Stocks of Finished Gasoline[2] on Hand in the United States, at End of Month   In Thousands of Barrels

Year	Jan.	Feb.	Mar.	Apr.	May	June	July	Aug.	Sept.	Oct.	Nov.	Dec.
2009	95,266	86,907	85,864	86,034	83,542	88,643	86,143	86,729	84,658	79,383	83,016	84,927
2010	87,152	83,618	81,941	78,134	75,189	71,787	71,882	72,412	70,207	65,103	65,537	63,257
2011	69,617	67,835	61,206	54,636	56,353	55,521	53,335	54,546	56,308	55,052	57,573	60,631
2012	61,550	58,671	54,112	50,538	49,986	51,896	51,952	48,294	47,788	49,668	52,626	55,211
2013	55,228	53,143	47,327	45,108	46,376	48,634	49,726	47,655	39,780	37,595	37,548	38,976
2014	39,790	37,687	34,274	30,710	31,057	28,854	28,320	27,514	28,773	27,432	29,532	30,615
2015	29,923	30,558	26,891	25,898	26,580	25,678	24,418	26,048	29,028	27,638	27,805	28,453
2016	26,800	27,218	26,468	25,039	23,708	24,874	24,773	25,641	25,088	25,892	26,525	28,610
2017	28,496	25,727	21,728	21,828	21,983	22,480	23,157	24,584	21,765	23,154	23,595	24,641
2018[1]	25,230	24,986	23,129	22,808	23,873	24,709	24,295	23,299	24,801	24,914	24,267	25,732

[1] Preliminary.   [2] Includes oxygenated and other finished.   Source: Energy Information Administration, U.S. Department of Energy (EIA-DOE)

GASOLINE

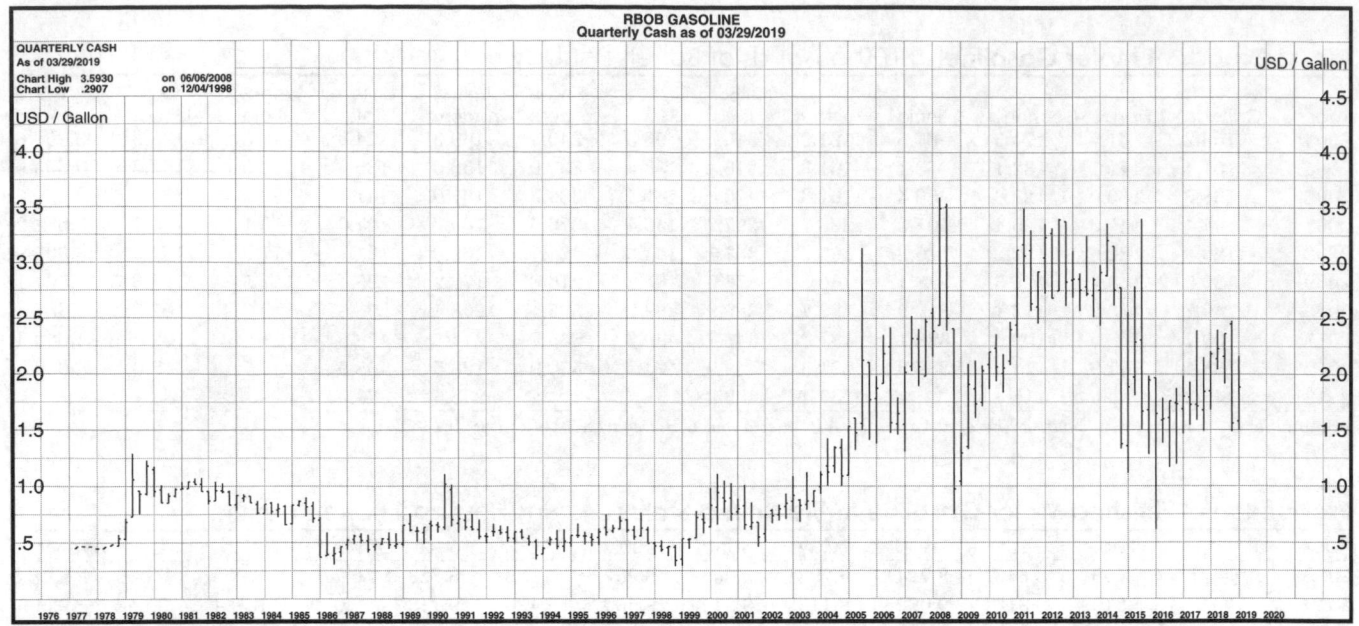

Unleaded: to 12/2006; RBOB: 01/1997 to date.

Average Spot Price of Unleaded Gasoline in New York   In Dollars Per Gallon

Year	Jan.	Feb.	Mar.	Apr.	May	June	July	Aug.	Sept.	Oct.	Nov.	Dec.	Average
2009	1.1460	1.2160	1.2880	1.3790	1.6890	1.9060	1.7500	1.9300	1.7790	1.9240	1.9830	1.9190	1.6650
2010	2.0400	1.9630	2.1400	2.2270	2.0190	2.0140	1.9950	1.9430	1.9690	2.1640	2.2440	2.3890	2.0950
2011	2.4480	2.5580	2.8380	3.1780	3.0240	2.8350	3.0210	2.8350	2.7680	2.7720	2.6290	2.6340	2.7970
2012	2.8220	3.0440	3.1670	3.2060	2.8770	2.6020	2.7470	3.0220	3.2700	2.9750	2.8170	2.7270	2.9390
2013	2.8520	3.0530	2.9140	2.7060	2.7420	2.7400	2.9240	2.9330	2.7970	2.6850	2.6730	2.7360	2.8110
2014	2.6720	2.7950	2.7530	2.8960	2.8620	2.8960	2.8020	2.7050	2.7210	2.3980	2.1650	1.6830	2.6100
2015	1.3640	1.6070	1.6440	1.7930	1.9380	2.0050	1.8600	1.6200	1.4600	1.3970	1.3770	1.2760	1.6120
2016	1.1210	1.0580	1.2010	1.4480	1.5660	1.5060	1.3540	1.3790	1.4380	1.5220	1.4620	1.6340	1.3908
2017	1.6200	1.5470	1.4920	1.6110	1.5400	1.4450	1.5620	1.6880	1.8670	1.7150	1.8300	1.7570	1.6395
2018	1.8990	1.8170	1.8340	1.9950	2.1290	2.0300	2.0740	2.0770	2.0930	2.0280	1.6250	1.4490	1.9208

Source: Energy Information Administration, U.S. Department of Energy (EIA-DOE)

Average Refiner Price of Finished Motor Gasoline to End Users[2] in the United States   In Dollars Per Gallon

Year	Jan.	Feb.	Mar.	Apr.	May	June	July	Aug.	Sept.	Oct.	Nov.	Dec.	Average
2009	1.358	1.468	1.503	1.601	1.856	2.187	2.067	2.157	2.086	2.104	2.173	2.144	1.888
2010	2.240	2.173	2.301	2.370	2.353	2.251	2.247	2.250	2.219	2.319	2.378	2.514	2.301
2011	2.615	2.712	3.072	3.340	3.419	3.184	3.172	3.134	3.090	2.980	2.922	2.808	3.050
2012	2.914	3.087	3.389	3.405	3.289	3.061	2.981	3.248	3.357	3.261	2.994	2.828	3.154
2013	2.850	3.221	3.233	3.102	3.188	3.184	3.146	3.097	3.059	2.893	2.759	2.759	3.041
2014	2.816	2.913	3.104	3.214	3.245	3.265	3.128	3.016	2.936	2.670	2.406	2.013	2.894
2015	1.673	1.858	2.054	2.058	2.322	2.374	2.338	2.218	1.920	1.849	1.711	1.604	1.998
2016	1.505	1.332	1.552	1.725	1.869	1.961	1.804	1.754	1.788	1.819	1.759	1.849	1.726
2017	1.900	1.862	1.904	1.997	1.963	1.906	1.871	1.952	2.154	2.042	2.122	2.034	1.976
2018[1]	2.108	2.127	2.160	2.315	2.494	2.469	2.442	2.421	2.428	2.441	2.205	1.973	2.299

[1] Preliminary.   [2] Excludes aviation and taxes.   *Source: Energy Information Administration, U.S. Department of Energy (EIA-DOE)*

Average Retail Price of All-Types[2] Motor Gasoline[3] in the United States   In Dollars Per Gallon

Year	Jan.	Feb.	Mar.	Apr.	May	June	July	Aug.	Sept.	Oct.	Nov.	Dec.	Average
2009	1.838	1.979	2.000	2.107	2.314	2.681	2.594	2.677	2.626	2.613	2.709	2.671	2.401
2010	2.779	2.709	2.829	2.906	2.915	2.783	2.783	2.795	2.754	2.843	2.899	3.031	2.836
2011	3.139	3.215	3.594	3.863	3.982	3.753	3.703	3.680	3.664	3.521	3.475	3.329	3.577
2012	3.447	3.622	3.918	3.976	3.839	3.602	3.502	3.759	3.908	3.839	3.542	3.386	3.695
2013	3.407	3.748	3.792	3.647	3.682	3.693	3.687	3.658	3.616	3.434	3.310	3.333	3.584
2014	3.378	3.422	3.590	3.717	3.745	3.750	3.690	3.540	3.463	3.241	2.945	2.618	3.425
2015	2.170	2.308	2.544	2.545	2.832	2.889	2.893	2.745	2.463	2.357	2.249	2.125	2.510
2016	2.034	1.833	2.021	2.196	2.324	2.422	2.287	2.218	2.269	2.304	2.246	2.289	2.204
2017	2.409	2.360	2.386	2.479	2.448	2.400	2.344	2.436	2.688	2.545	2.608	2.521	2.469
2018[1]	2.596	2.632	2.631	2.795	2.963	2.970	2.930	2.919	2.930	2.945	2.733	2.479	2.794

[1] Preliminary.   [2] Also includes types of motor oil not shown separately.   [3] Including taxes   *Source: Energy Information Administration, U.S. Department of Energy (EIA-DOE)*

BLENDSTOCK GASOLINE (RBOB) - NYMEX
Weekly Nearest Futures as of 03/29/2019

WEEKLY NEAREST FUTURES
As of 03/29/2019
Chart High 3.4800 on 04/29/2011
Chart Low   .8975   on 02/09/2016

Nearby Futures through Last Trading Day.

Volume of Trading of Gasoline, RBOB[1] Futures in New York   In Thousands of Contracts

Year	Jan.	Feb.	Mar.	Apr.	May	June	July	Aug.	Sept.	Oct.	Nov.	Dec.	Total
2009	1,597.7	1,592.3	1,594.4	1,612.9	1,841.8	2,060.8	1,748.6	1,773.9	1,600.3	2,082.5	1,908.8	1,746.5	21,160.5
2010	1,979.2	1,978.8	2,318.0	2,829.9	2,537.8	2,186.6	1,946.1	2,402.3	2,325.4	2,614.0	2,529.1	2,251.3	27,898.7
2011	2,315.2	2,274.1	2,342.8	2,592.4	3,390.6	2,720.4	2,078.4	2,874.5	2,745.1	2,791.8	2,780.3	2,223.6	31,129.3
2012	2,899.2	2,844.2	3,480.0	3,789.4	3,257.2	3,107.9	2,844.9	3,043.1	3,015.4	3,298.3	2,674.1	2,350.2	36,603.8
2013	2,981.2	3,000.0	3,079.8	3,578.7	3,090.8	2,566.9	3,105.3	2,810.5	2,516.6	2,664.8	2,777.1	2,298.6	34,470.3
2014	2,470.9	2,417.0	2,562.7	3,316.9	3,240.6	2,679.3	3,001.7	2,894.1	3,173.3	3,170.5	2,713.5	2,781.4	34,421.9
2015	3,070.7	3,387.9	3,396.1	3,449.5	3,113.9	3,869.0	3,621.4	3,736.9	2,961.2	3,158.0	3,171.9	3,365.6	40,302.1
2016	3,362.4	3,841.7	3,723.6	3,546.6	3,874.1	4,362.3	3,427.0	4,134.4	4,677.2	3,413.1	3,844.7	3,221.5	45,428.7
2017	3,748.5	4,433.7	4,380.3	3,721.6	4,343.5	4,454.4	4,065.8	5,803.7	4,139.1	3,734.5	3,717.3	3,368.5	49,910.9
2018	4,290.5	3,815.0	3,992.9	4,067.4	4,569.1	4,175.0	3,959.4	4,858.9	3,901.0	4,626.3	3,953.8	3,404.7	49,613.9

[1] Data thru September 2005 are Unleaded, October 2005 thru December 2006 are Unleaded and RBOB.
Contract size = 42,000 US gallons.   *Source: CME Group; New York Mercantile Exchange (NYMEX)*

Average Open Interest of Gasoline, RBOB[1] Futures in New York   In Contracts

Year	Jan.	Feb.	Mar.	Apr.	May	June	July	Aug.	Sept.	Oct.	Nov.	Dec.
2009	192,691	187,748	199,423	204,956	220,450	215,256	200,537	217,625	205,517	219,883	256,151	238,789
2010	262,247	258,312	304,437	320,529	275,659	245,923	239,242	246,901	241,014	270,830	282,949	273,638
2011	280,084	274,277	275,857	293,452	280,369	251,349	245,309	250,244	268,974	273,495	280,706	275,994
2012	312,848	345,884	374,449	348,606	306,453	293,802	258,931	273,299	290,070	279,312	276,945	282,942
2013	312,415	328,903	318,974	301,346	283,215	277,107	270,359	271,797	264,119	232,420	240,735	246,590
2014	252,519	274,087	283,756	310,549	332,460	314,754	307,808	274,978	283,206	310,119	334,015	349,589
2015	366,741	362,191	372,013	383,705	383,960	372,487	367,208	378,562	371,326	345,971	360,109	365,200
2016	379,473	406,615	420,305	392,100	405,314	401,323	389,932	406,922	395,691	408,750	380,734	390,804
2017	425,330	421,979	398,661	406,054	403,723	402,039	392,477	408,427	415,138	403,480	429,908	400,346
2018	437,285	434,342	424,422	450,029	479,806	461,515	441,321	459,928	438,527	406,263	406,427	406,667

[1] Data thru September 2005 are Unleaded, October 2005 thru December 2006 are Unleaded and RBOB.
Contract size = 42,000 US gallons.   *Source: CME Group; New York Mercantile Exchange (NYMEX)*

GASOLINE

Average Retail Price of Unleaded Premium Motor Gasoline[2] in the United States   In Dollars per Gallon

Year	Jan.	Feb.	Mar.	Apr.	May	June	July	Aug.	Sept.	Oct.	Nov.	Dec.	Average
2009	2.036	2.182	2.197	2.309	2.511	2.883	2.806	2.887	2.845	2.826	2.917	2.882	2.607
2010	2.987	2.922	3.035	3.113	3.124	3.000	2.997	3.015	2.968	3.055	3.109	3.234	3.047
2011	3.345	3.424	3.807	4.074	4.192	3.972	3.915	3.893	3.887	3.745	3.700	3.553	3.792
2012	3.663	3.840	4.138	4.194	4.062	3.825	3.726	3.991	4.140	4.079	3.782	3.626	3.922
2013	3.646	3.990	4.038	3.901	3.936	3.957	3.951	3.919	3.881	3.702	3.585	3.604	3.843
2014	3.651	3.694	3.858	3.986	4.020	4.027	3.976	3.835	3.758	3.547	3.262	2.940	3.713
2015	2.497	2.621	2.867	2.868	3.166	3.218	3.252	3.120	2.860	2.749	2.640	2.532	2.866
2016	2.455	2.248	2.411	2.585	2.710	2.807	2.702	2.629	2.682	2.719	2.675	2.698	2.610
2017	2.815	2.793	2.827	2.909	2.894	2.859	2.800	2.883	3.120	2.996	3.056	2.985	2.911
2018[1]	3.042	3.091	3.101	3.258	3.423	3.440	3.399	3.384	3.400	3.431	3.251	3.015	3.270

[1] Preliminary.   [2] Including taxes.   *Source: Energy Information Administration, U.S. Department of Energy (EIA-DOE)*

Average Retail Price of Unleaded Regular Motor Gasoline[2] in the United States   In Dollars per Gallon

Year	Jan.	Feb.	Mar.	Apr.	May	June	July	Aug.	Sept.	Oct.	Nov.	Dec.	Average
2009	1.787	1.928	1.949	2.056	2.265	2.631	2.543	2.627	2.574	2.561	2.660	2.621	2.350
2010	2.731	2.659	2.780	2.858	2.869	2.736	2.736	2.745	2.704	2.795	2.852	2.985	2.788
2011	3.091	3.167	3.546	3.816	3.933	3.702	3.654	3.630	3.612	3.468	3.423	3.278	3.527
2012	3.399	3.572	3.868	3.927	3.792	3.552	3.451	3.707	3.856	3.786	3.488	3.331	3.644
2013	3.351	3.693	3.735	3.590	3.623	3.633	3.628	3.600	3.556	3.375	3.251	3.277	3.526
2014	3.320	3.364	3.532	3.659	3.691	3.695	3.633	3.481	3.403	3.182	2.887	2.560	3.367
2015	2.110	2.249	2.483	2.485	2.775	2.832	2.832	2.679	2.394	2.289	2.185	2.060	2.448
2016	1.967	1.767	1.958	2.134	2.264	2.363	2.225	2.155	2.208	2.243	2.187	2.230	2.142
2017	2.351	2.299	2.323	2.418	2.386	2.337	2.281	2.374	2.630	2.484	2.548	2.459	2.408
2018[1]	2.539	2.575	2.572	2.737	2.907	2.914	2.873	2.862	2.873	2.887	2.671	2.414	2.735

[1] Preliminary.   [2] Including taxes.   *Source: Energy Information Administration, U.S. Department of Energy (EIA-DOE)*

Average Retail Price of All-Types[2] Motor Gasoline[3] in the United States   In Dollars per Gallon

Year	Jan.	Feb.	Mar.	Apr.	May	June	July	Aug.	Sept.	Oct.	Nov.	Dec.	Average
2009	1.838	1.979	2.000	2.107	2.314	2.681	2.594	2.677	2.626	2.613	2.709	2.671	2.401
2010	2.779	2.709	2.829	2.906	2.915	2.783	2.783	2.795	2.754	2.843	2.899	3.031	2.836
2011	3.139	3.215	3.594	3.863	3.982	3.753	3.703	3.680	3.664	3.521	3.475	3.329	3.577
2012	3.447	3.622	3.918	3.976	3.839	3.602	3.502	3.759	3.908	3.839	3.542	3.386	3.695
2013	3.407	3.748	3.792	3.647	3.682	3.693	3.687	3.658	3.616	3.434	3.310	3.333	3.584
2014	3.378	3.422	3.590	3.717	3.745	3.750	3.690	3.540	3.463	3.241	2.945	2.618	3.425
2015	2.170	2.308	2.544	2.545	2.832	2.889	2.893	2.745	2.463	2.357	2.249	2.125	2.510
2016	2.034	1.833	2.021	2.196	2.324	2.422	2.287	2.218	2.269	2.304	2.246	2.289	2.204
2017	2.409	2.360	2.386	2.479	2.448	2.400	2.344	2.436	2.688	2.545	2.608	2.521	2.469
2018[1]	2.596	2.632	2.631	2.795	2.963	2.970	2.930	2.919	2.930	2.945	2.733	2.479	2.794

[1] Preliminary.   [2] Also includes types of motor oil not shown separately.   [3] Including taxes.   *Source: Energy Information Administration, U.S. Department of Energy (EIA-DOE)*

Average Refiner Price of Finished Aviation Gasoline to End Users[2] in the United States   In Dollars per Gallon

Year	Jan.	Feb.	Mar.	Apr.	May	June	July	Aug.	Sept.	Oct.	Nov.	Dec.	Average
2009	1.857	1.974	1.977	2.150	2.423	2.707	2.607	2.764	2.684	2.693	2.845	2.799	2.442
2010	2.914	2.855	3.103	3.201	3.129	2.981	3.028	2.967	2.893	3.000	3.095	3.218	3.028
2011	3.323	3.374	3.767	4.132	4.091	3.913	4.027	3.920	3.915	3.697	3.620	W	3.803
2012	3.732	W	4.133	4.313	W	W	W	4.091	4.262	4.064	3.561	3.599	3.971
2013	W	4.060	4.022	3.860	3.900	4.191	4.224	4.298	3.982	3.653	3.673	3.678	3.932
2014	W	4.142	W	W	W	W	W	W	W	W	W	W	3.986
2015	W	W	W	W	W	W	W	W	W	W	W	W	W
2016	W	W	W	W	W	W	W	W	W	W	W	W	W
2017	W	W	W	W	W	W	W	W	W	W	W	W	W
2018[1]	W	W	W	W	W	W	W	W	W	W	W	W	W

[1] Preliminary.   [2] Excluding taxes.   NA = Not available.   W = Withheld proprietary data.   *Source: Energy Information Administration, U.S. Department Energy (EIA-DOE)*

Gold

Gold is a dense, bright yellow metallic element with a high luster. Gold is an inactive substance and is unaffected by air, heat, moisture, and most solvents. Gold has been coveted for centuries for its unique blend of rarity, beauty, and near indestructibility. The Egyptians mined gold before 2,000 BC. The first known, pure gold coin was made on the orders of King Croesus of Lydia in the sixth century BC.

Gold is found in nature in quartz veins and secondary alluvial deposits as a free metal. Gold is produced from mines on every continent apart from Antarctica, where mining is forbidden. Because it is virtually indestructible, much of the gold that has ever been mined still exists above ground in one form or another. The largest producer of gold in the U.S. by far is the state of Nevada, with Alaska and California running a distant second and third.

Gold is a vital industrial commodity. Pure gold is one of the most malleable and ductile of all the metals. It is a good conductor of heat and electricity. The prime industrial use of gold is in electronics. Another important sector is dental gold where it has been used for almost 3,000 years. Other applications for gold include decorative gold leaf, reflective glass, and jewelry.

In 1792, the United States first assigned a formal monetary role for gold when Congress put the nation's currency on a bimetallic standard, backing it with gold and silver. Under the gold standard, the U.S. government was willing to exchange its paper currency for a set amount of gold, meaning the paper currency was backed by a physical asset with real value. However, President Nixon in 1971 severed the convertibility between the U.S. dollar and gold, which led to the breakdown of the Bretton Woods international payments system. Since then, the prices of gold and of paper currencies have floated freely. U.S. and other central banks now hold physical gold reserves primarily as a store of wealth.

Gold futures and options are traded at the CME Group. Gold futures are traded on the Bolsa de Mercadorias and Futuros (BM&F) and on the Tokyo Commodity Exchange (TOCOM), the Chicago Board of Trade (CBOT) and the Korea Futures Exchange (KOFEX). The Nymex gold futures contract calls for the delivery of 100 troy ounces of gold (0.995 fineness), and the contract trades in terms of dollars and cents per troy ounce.

Prices – CME gold futures prices (Barchart.com symbol GC) rallied early in 2018 to a 2-1/2 year high of $1,365 an ounce due to a slumping dollar. The dollar index plunged to a 4-year low in February on concern that the Trump administration's tax cut bill would widen the U.S. budget deficit and expand the U.S. current account deficit. Gold prices remained firm into April when they matched their 2-1/2 year nearest-futures high as geopolitical risks in the Middle East spurred fund buying as long gold positions in ETFs climbed to a 5-1/2 year high in May. Also, U.S. March core CPI rose to +2.1% yr/yr, above the Fed's 2.0% target and the largest year-on-year gain in 13 months, which boosted demand for gold as an inflation hedge. However, gold prices sold off into August to a 2-year low of $1,161 an ounce after the dollar index climbed to a 1-1/2 year high as U.S. economic strength underpinned the dollar and the prospects for additional Fed tightening. Gold prices recovered into year-end after a slide in global equity markets boosted safe-haven demand for gold. Gold prices finished 2018 slightly lower by -2.1% yr/yr at $1,281 an ounce.

Supply – World mine production of gold in 2018 rose +0.9% yr/yr at 3.260 million kilograms, which is a new record high (1 kilogram = 32.1507 troy ounces) The world's largest producers of gold in 2018 were China with 12.3% of world production, followed by Australia with 9.5%, Russia with 9.0%, the U.S with 6.4%, Peru with 4.4% and South Africa with 3.7%.

Gold mine production has been moving lower in many major gold-producing countries such as South Africa and the U.S. For example, South Africa's production of 120,000 kilograms in 2018 was less than one-quarter the production levels of more than 600,000 kilograms seen in the 1980s and early 1990s. U.S. gold mine production in 2018 fell -11.4% yr/yr to 210,000 kilograms. On the other hand, Canada's gold production in 2018 rose +12.8% yr/yr to a record high of 185,000 kilograms.

U.S. refinery production of gold from domestic and foreign ore sources in 2018 rose +5.7% yr/yr to 200,000 kilograms. U.S. refinery production of gold from secondary scrap sources in 2018 fell -1.0% yr/yr to 95,000 kilograms.

Demand – U.S. consumption of gold in 2018 fell -0.7% yr/yr to 145,000 kilograms. The most recent data available from the early 1990s showed that 71% of that gold demand came from jewelry and the arts, 22% from industrial uses, and 7% from dental uses.

Trade – U.S. exports of gold (excluding coinage) in 2018 rose +4.1% yr/yr to 480,000 kilograms, well below the 2012 record high of 699,000 kilograms. U.S. imports of gold for consumption in 2018 fell -13.7% yr/yr to 220,000 kilograms.

World Mine Production of Gold   In Kilograms (1 Kilogram = 32.1507 Troy Ounces)

Year	Australia	Brazil	Canada	China	Ghana	Indonesia	Papua New Guinea	Peru	Russia	South Africa	United States	Uzebek- istan	World Total
2010	261,000	62,047	102,693	345,000	76,332	106,316	62,900	164,084	189,000	188,702	231,000	90,000	2,590,000
2011	260,000	65,209	102,624	362,000	82,598	77,722	62,200	166,187	199,642	180,293	234,000	91,000	2,680,000
2012	250,000	66,773	107,486	403,000	86,972	69,291	59,100	161,544	217,800	155,286	235,000	93,000	2,750,000
2013	267,000	79,573	133,636	428,000	89,224	59,804	54,092	156,264	231,700	160,016	230,000	98,000	2,930,000
2014	273,963	81,038	152,460	451,000	90,754	69,349	57,939	140,090	249,100	151,622	210,000	100,000	3,030,000
2015	279,000	83,280	162,504	450,000	80,325	92,339	60,046	147,110	251,210	144,504	214,000	102,000	3,090,000
2016	290,000	85,000	165,034	453,000	79,199	80,000	62,293	153,029	253,150	144,500	222,000	102,000	3,120,000
2017[1]	301,000	80,000	164,000	426,000	128,000	75,000	64,000	151,000	270,000	137,000	237,000	104,000	3,230,000
2018[2]	310,000	81,000	185,000	400,000	130,000	85,000	65,000	145,000	295,000	120,000	210,000	105,000	3,260,000

[1] Preliminary.   [2] Estimate.   *Source: U.S. Geological Survey (USGS)*

GOLD

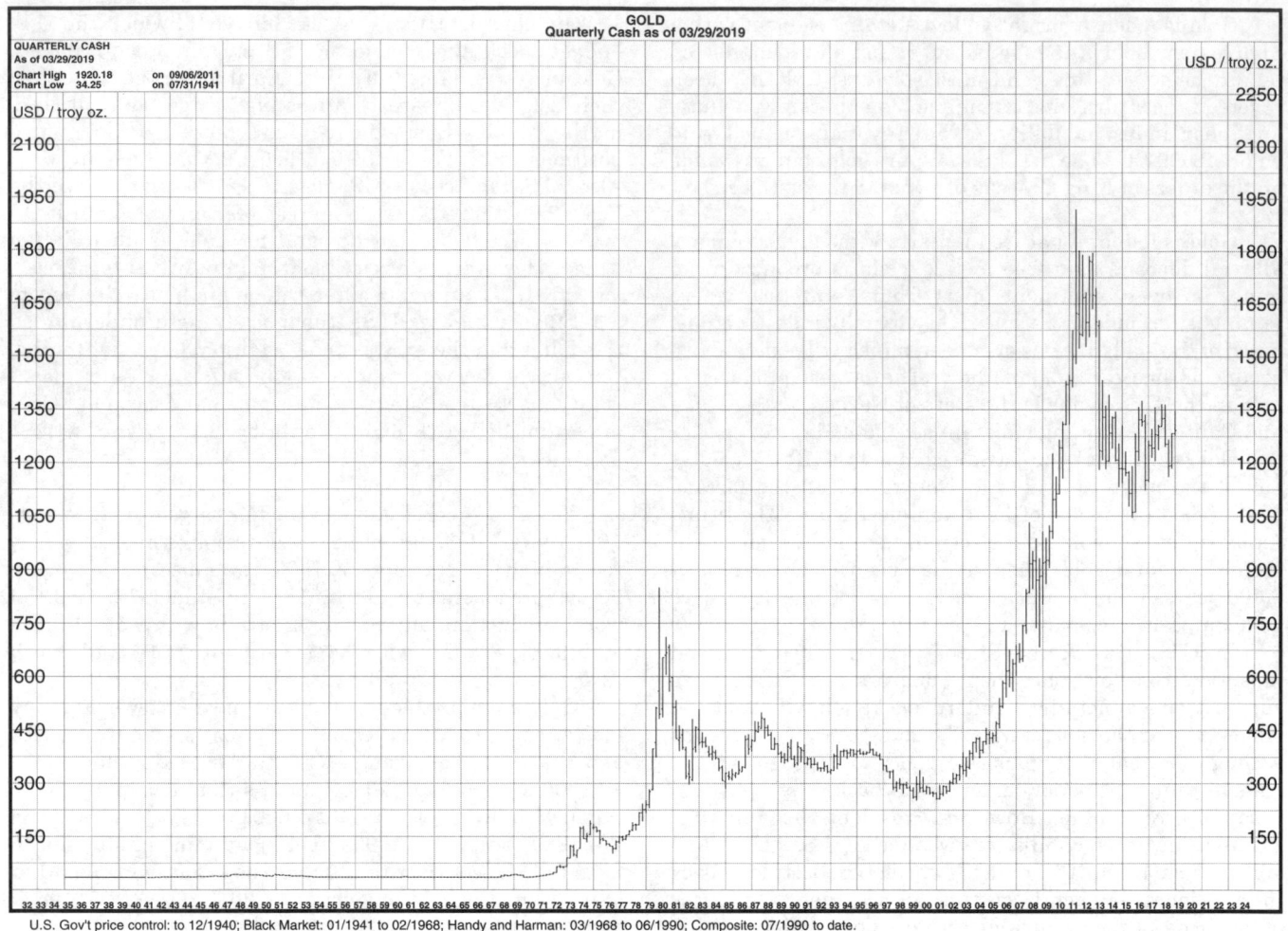

U.S. Gov't price control: to 12/1940; Black Market: 01/1941 to 02/1968; Handy and Harman: 03/1968 to 06/1990; Composite: 07/1990 to date.

Salient Statistics of Gold in the United States   In Kilograms (1 Kilogram = 32.1507 Troy Ounces)

			- Refinery Production -				-------- Stocks, Dec. 31 ---------			----------- Consumption -----------				
Year	Mine Pro- duction	Value Million $	Domestic & Foreign Ores	Secondary (Old Scrap)	Exports, Excluding Coinage	Imports for Con- sumption	Treasury Depart- ment[3]	Futures Exchange	Industry	Official World Reserves[4]	Dental	Indus- trial[5]	Jewelry & Arts	Total
2008	233,000	6,550.0	168,000	181,000	567,000	231,000	8,140,000	265,000	W	28,700	----	----	----	176,000
2009	223,000	7,000.0	170,000	189,000	381,000	320,000	8,140,000	305,000	9,200	30,400	----	----	----	173,000
2010	231,000	9,130.0	175,000	198,000	383,000	616,000	8,140,000	361,000	6,810	30,700	----	----	----	180,000
2011	234,000	11,800.0	220,000	263,000	664,000	550,000	8,140,000	353,000	6,470	31,100	----	----	----	168,000
2012	235,000	12,600.0	218,000	215,000	699,000	326,000	8,140,000	344,000	4,070	31,700	----	----	----	147,000
2013	230,000	10,400.0	223,000	210,000	686,000	315,000	8,140,000	243,000	5,940	31,900	----	----	----	160,000
2014	210,000	8,570.0	253,000	135,000	492,000	308,000	8,140,000	325,000	7,540	31,400	----	----	----	152,000
2015	214,000	8,000.0	248,000	124,000	478,000	265,000	8,140,000	198,000	7,330	32,800	----	----	----	164,000
2016[1]	222,000		248,000	123,000	393,000	374,000	8,140,000				----	----	----	165,000
2017[2]	229,800		250,000	120,000	480,000	240,000	8,140,000				----	----	----	

[1] Preliminary.   [2] Estimate.   [3] Includes gold in Exchange Stabilization Fund.   [4] Held by market economy country central banks and governments and international monetary orgainzations.   [5] Including space and defense.   NA = Not available.   *Source: U.S. Geological Survey (USGS)*

Monthly Average Gold Price (Handy & Harman) in New York   Dollars Per Troy Ounce

Year	Jan.	Feb.	Mar.	Apr.	May	June	July	Aug.	Sept.	Oct.	Nov.	Dec. Average
2009	859.98	943.20	924.27	890.50	927.34	945.67	934.31	949.34	996.76	1,043.16	1,122.03	1,212.50	979.09
2010	1,116.74	1,095.26	1,114.36	1,147.70	1,204.50	1,232.92	1,192.25	1,217.11	1,272.02	1,342.02	1,370.46	1,389.70	1,224.59
2011	1,359.39	1,371.13	1,424.01	1,478.55	1,511.63	1,528.66	1,576.70	1,757.21	1,765.99	1,665.36	1,743.83	1,645.50	1,569.00
2012	1,656.88	1,743.10	1,673.77	1,649.72	1,588.34	1,598.98	1,592.98	1,627.97	1,747.24	1,748.69	1,719.98	1,684.18	1,669.32
2013	1,670.17	1,628.47	1,592.85	1,490.22	1,415.91	1,342.36	1,288.31	1,349.30	1,346.63	1,316.19	1,276.94	1,220.65	1,411.50
2014	1,244.53	1,300.60	1,336.08	1,298.45	1,288.74	1,279.10	1,310.59	1,295.13	1,236.14	1,222.49	1,175.33	1,200.62	1,265.65
2015	1,250.75	1,227.08	1,178.63	1,198.93	1,198.63	1,181.50	1,128.31	1,117.93	1,124.88	1,159.25	1,086.44	1,068.25	1,160.05
2016	1,097.81	1,199.50	1,245.14	1,242.26	1,260.95	1,276.40	1,336.66	1,340.17	1,326.01	1,266.57	1,238.35	1,150.13	1,248.33
2017	1,192.10	1,234.20	1,231.09	1,266.88	1,246.04	1,260.26	1,236.84	1,283.04	1,314.07	1,279.51	1,281.90	1,264.44	1,257.53
2018	1,331.30	1,330.73	1,324.66	1,334.76	1,303.45	1,281.57	1,237.71	1,201.71	1,198.39	1,215.37	1,220.65	1,250.94	1,269.27

Source: U.S. Geological Survey (USGS)

GOLD - COMEX
Weekly Selected Futures as of 03/29/2019

WEEKLY SELECTED FUTURES
As of 03/29/2019

Chart High 1920.80 on 09/06/2011
Chart Low 801.50 on 01/15/2009

Nearby Futures through Last Trading Day using selected contract months: February, April, June, August, October and December.

Volume of Trading of Gold Futures in Chicago   In Thousands of Contracts

Year	Jan.	Feb.	Mar.	Apr.	May	June	July	Aug.	Sept.	Oct.	Nov.	Dec.	Total
2009	3,073.0	2,444.2	3,385.0	1,808.4	2,766.7	2,305.0	2,846.2	1,815.6	2,831.4	3,216.7	4,564.3	4,083.1	35,139.5
2010	4,574.3	3,616.1	4,385.6	2,932.3	4,824.1	3,024.7	4,097.3	2,184.9	2,732.1	3,858.8	5,530.4	2,969.7	44,730.3
2011	4,724.6	2,740.4	4,512.3	3,145.2	4,955.3	3,078.9	4,278.2	6,406.6	5,300.5	3,026.4	4,105.3	2,901.9	49,175.6
2012	4,146.5	3,506.7	4,860.6	2,834.8	4,913.7	3,479.4	3,732.7	2,793.5	3,460.8	3,147.0	4,380.3	2,637.3	43,893.3
2013	4,221.1	3,632.3	3,906.6	5,218.8	5,312.3	3,744.7	4,647.2	3,466.7	3,331.9	3,458.2	3,577.1	2,777.7	47,294.6
2014	3,754.8	2,607.5	4,200.3	2,692.9	3,631.1	2,508.1	3,848.3	2,381.8	3,205.8	3,703.7	4,676.7	3,307.7	40,518.8
2015	4,507.9	2,558.8	4,403.4	3,057.0	3,721.5	2,856.0	4,554.8	3,431.6	2,917.1	3,070.1	4,034.0	2,735.2	41,847.3
2016	4,102.0	4,369.5	5,720.2	3,902.5	5,880.1	4,936.3	5,798.5	4,387.9	4,022.6	3,815.0	7,108.7	3,521.6	57,564.8
2017	5,978.9	4,392.4	6,119.4	4,612.2	6,367.4	4,906.6	5,957.0	6,808.8	7,184.1	6,665.5	8,623.3	5,186.6	72,802.2
2018	9,161.9	6,078.6	8,036.1	6,655.1	8,676.6	5,739.0	7,231.2	6,274.2	5,495.6	6,470.2	6,351.2	4,132.0	80,301.6

Contract size = 100 oz.   *Source: CME Group; Commodity Exchange (COMEX)*

Average Open Interest of Gold Futures in Chicago   In Contracts

Year	Jan.	Feb.	Mar.	Apr.	May	June	July	Aug.	Sept.	Oct.	Nov.	Dec.
2009	331,891	359,420	376,201	341,491	366,468	382,960	380,301	383,826	454,286	493,909	522,556	504,102
2010	512,723	469,214	489,600	521,976	574,107	579,416	561,781	541,408	595,118	619,536	626,630	589,823
2011	556,448	479,014	507,118	522,520	513,744	504,841	522,091	517,064	494,932	438,488	453,477	424,014
2012	426,896	445,515	434,210	402,740	423,294	417,783	424,790	400,896	471,946	469,628	461,382	430,717
2013	442,707	435,425	437,300	416,489	431,460	383,314	424,302	388,278	380,768	382,216	395,583	383,980
2014	397,700	381,045	404,828	369,755	395,313	385,660	400,977	365,066	381,961	400,455	433,102	372,432
2015	415,408	399,097	415,894	397,632	411,656	417,416	451,224	430,894	416,389	448,795	425,138	398,843
2016	403,929	421,355	491,060	496,873	561,027	553,721	616,676	571,588	576,954	508,303	484,383	401,266
2017	444,716	423,037	436,599	458,759	447,814	462,182	468,238	490,304	562,694	524,694	530,233	460,378
2018	563,606	528,812	525,719	505,825	496,142	461,716	499,723	471,934	468,159	472,864	490,986	416,930

Contract size = 100 oz.   *Source: CME Group; Commodity Exchange (COMEX)*

GOLD

Commodity Exchange Warehouse Stocks of Gold, on First of Month   In Thousands of Troy Ounces

Year	Jan. 1	Feb. 1	Mar. 1	Apr. 1	May 1	June 1	July 1	Aug. 1	Sept. 1	Oct. 1	Nov. 1	Dec. 1
2009	8,548.5	8,556.8	8,635.9	8,508.6	8,322.6	8,725.8	8,893.4	9,144.6	9,173.0	9,316.2	9,316.2	9,508.9
2010	9,679.4	9,679.4	9,679.4	10,022.9	10,184.3	10,736.8	10,923.5	11,112.1	10,816.9	10,896.7	11,311.9	11,488.4
2011	11,694.3	11,401.9	11,075.3	11,033.0	11,140.8	11,310.3	11,439.7	11,431.5	11,559.8	11,246.8	11,236.9	11,301.8
2012	11,469.4	11,434.6	11,405.2	11,350.5	10,895.2	10,978.4	10,831.7	10,806.6	10,844.5	11,009.3	11,243.3	11,151.0
2013	11,058.7	11,009.3	10,289.3	9,279.4	8,129.2	8,054.9	7,534.5	6,991.4	7,013.2	6,862.8	7,153.7	7,247.9
2014	7,828.1	7,081.3	7,177.1	7,740.8	7,935.6	8,262.7	8,298.5	8,684.3	9,927.3	9,127.3	8,056.0	7,928.7
2015	7,932.1	7,983.9	8,321.5	8,010.7	7,718.4	7,871.5	8,043.6	7,572.3	7,221.1	6,852.5	6,700.8	6,377.6
2016	6,352.5	6,427.0	6,785.0	6,851.2	7,250.3	8,452.7	9,286.6	10,718.8	10,932.9	10,702.4	10,600.9	10,002.9
2017	9,158.9	8,986.3	8,942.2	8,956.9	8,931.0	8,750.3	8,616.7	8,660.6	8,693.6	8,761.4	8,707.2	8,914.8
2018	9,142.7	9,257.9	9,132.9	9,060.6	9,049.6	9,017.2	8,564.6	8,641.4	8,388.7	8,330.7	8,066.5	8,020.7

Source: CME Group; Commodity Exchange (COMEX)

Central Gold Bank Reserves   In Millions of Troy Ounces

Year	Belgium	Canada	France	Ger-many	Italy	Japan	Nether-lands	Switzer-land	United Kingdom	United States	World Total
2009	7.3	0.1	78.3	109.5	78.8	24.6	19.7	33.4	10.0	261.5	980.9
2010	7.3	0.1	78.3	109.3	78.8	24.6	19.7	33.4	10.0	261.5	990.4
2011	7.3	0.1	78.3	109.2	78.8	24.6	19.7	33.4	10.0	261.5	1,002.2
2012	7.3	0.1	78.3	109.0	78.8	24.6	19.7	33.4	10.0	261.5	1,017.5
2013	7.3	0.1	78.3	108.9	78.8	24.6	19.7	33.4	10.0	261.5	1,023.0
2014	7.3	0.1	78.3	108.8	78.8	24.6	19.7	33.4	10.0	261.5	1,028.7
2015	7.3	0.1	78.3	108.7	78.8	24.6	19.7	33.4	10.0	261.5	1,051.5
2016	7.3	----	78.3	108.6	78.8	24.6	19.7	33.4	10.0	261.5	1,069.3
2017	7.3	----	78.3	108.5	78.8	24.6	19.7	33.4	10.0	261.5	1,081.9
2018[1]	7.3	----	78.3	108.3	78.8	24.6	19.7	33.4	10.0	261.5	1,084.8

[1] Preliminary.   [2] International Monetary Fund.   Source: American Metal Market (AMM)

Mine Production of Recoverable Gold in the United States   In Kilograms

Year	Alaska	California	Nevada	Washington	Other States[2]	Total
2009	W	W	161,000	W	62,500	223,000
2010	28,100	W	166,000	W	36,900	231,000
2011	25,800	W	172,000	W	36,100	234,000
2012	27,700	W	175,000	W	31,400	235,000
2013	32,200	W	170,000	W	27,800	230,000
2014	31,400	W	151,000	W	27,800	210,000
2015	28,000	W	162,000	W	24,200	214,000
2016	27,600	W	165,000	W	30,000	222,000
2017	26,200	W	173,000	W	37,400	237,000
2018[1]	20,640	W	159,300	W	31,250	211,300

[1] Preliminary.   W = Withheld proprietary data, included in "Other States."   [2] Includes Arizona, California, Colorado, Idaho, Montana, New Mexico, South Dakota, Utah, and Washington.   Source: U.S. Geological Survey (USGS)

U.S. Exports of Gold, Total   In Kilograms

Year	Australia	Canada	China	Germany	Hong Kong	India	Mexico	South Africa	Switzer-land	Thailand	United Arab Emirates	United Kingdom	Total
2007	2,470	9,210	10	664	1,170	17,000	5,890	----	266,000	1,330	20,000	191,000	519,000
2008	12,300	11,800	219	305	4,280	18,800	4,660	5,270	296,000	8,510	20,700	181,000	568,000
2009	26,700	3,110	51	832	844	21,000	3,120	----	103,000	----	147	220,000	381,000
2010	14,200	8,750	558	1,390	18,400	30,900	2,270	9,510	113,000	5,000	3,080	170,000	383,000
2011	18,200	1,460	5,150	1,440	111,000	15,500	5,160	11,900	105,000	21,200	10,300	161,000	474,000
2012	5,140	18,400	1,200	2,230	133,000	66,900	7,040	8,260	280,000	9,280	64,200	137,000	692,000
2013	5,200	18,900	14,400	941	217,000	32,500	947	19,600	284,000	27,000	34,300	29,000	691,000
2014	6,430	3,300	12,600	232	147,000	27,300	434	----	173,000	13,800	20,300	80,000	500,000
2015	336	2,650	5,730	694	120,000	60,500	2,910	----	167,000	6,490	17,900	96,200	478,000
2016	952	5,390	4,500	1,430	69,900	41,400	1,880	----	150,000	2,030	17,000	94,900	393,000

Source: U.S. Geological Survey (USGS)

Grain Sorghum

Grain sorghums include milo, kafir, durra, feterita, and kaoliang. Grain sorghums are tolerant of drought by going into dormancy during dry and hot conditions and then resuming growth as conditions improve. Grain sorghums are a staple food in China, India, and Africa but in the U.S. they are mainly used as livestock feed. The two key U.S. producing states are Texas and Kansas, each with about one-third of total U.S. production. U.S. sorghum production has become more popular with the breeding of dwarf grain sorghum hybrids which are only about 3 feet tall (versus up to 10 feet tall for wild sorghum) and are easier to harvest with a combine. The U.S. sorghum crop year begins September 1.

Prices – The monthly average price for sorghum grain received by U.S. farmers in the 2018/19 marketing year (Sep-Aug) fell by -5.6% yr/yr to $5.51 per hundred pounds (annualized through November 2018). The value of U.S. grain sorghum production in the 2017/18 marketing year fell -13.1% to $1.175 billion.

Supply – World production of sorghum in the 2018/19 marketing year is expected to rise +1.9% to 58.914 million metric tons, below the 10-year high of 66.653 million metric tons posted in 2007-08. U.S. grain sorghum production in 2018/19 is expected to be virtually unchanged yr/yr at 363.668 million bushels. Sorghum acreage harvested in 2018/19 is forecasted to rise 1.0% to 5.093 million acres, only slightly above the 2006/07 figure of 4.937 acres which was the smallest sorghum acreage since the late 1930s. The harvested yield in 2018/19 is expected to fall -1.0% to 71.4 bushels per acre.

Demand – World utilization (consumption) of grain sorghum in the 2018/19 marketing year is expected to rise 2.0% to 59.440 million metric tons. The biggest consumers will be Nigeria utilizing 11.3% of the world supply and the U.S. utilizing 11.1%.

Trade – World exports of sorghum in the 2018/19 marketing year is expected to fall -30.2% to 4.897 million metric tons, below the 2014-15 record high of 12.162 million metric tons. U.S. exports in 2018/19 are expected to fall -51.3% yr/yr to 2.540 million metric tons, accounting for 52.0% of total world exports. The other major exporters are Australia with 1.4 million metric tons and Argentina with 500,000 metric tons of exports expected in 2018/19. World imports of sorghum in 2018/19 is expected to fall -24.7% yr/yr to 5.174 million metric tons. Major world importers are China with the European Union a distant second.

World Production of Grain Sorghum   In Thousands of Metric Tons

Crop Year	Argentina	Australia	Brazil	Burkina	China	Ethiopia	India	Mexico	Niger	Nigeria	Sudan	United States	World Total
2009-10	1,900	1,205	1,675	1,600	1,900	3,200	6,600	9,700	950	5,200	4,500	5,866	57,327
2010-11	1,900	1,405	2,075	1,950	2,200	3,700	6,800	9,400	1,250	7,050	3,000	5,277	60,254
2011-12	1,900	1,105	2,175	1,550	2,200	3,700	6,000	8,100	950	5,650	4,500	3,916	56,128
2012-13	2,300	1,080	2,300	1,850	3,200	3,700	5,150	8,100	1,200	5,794	2,650	4,796	56,811
2013-14	2,700	905	2,000	1,900	6,800	3,900	5,200	8,300	1,300	5,258	4,600	4,130	59,816
2014-15	2,800	505	2,000	1,700	12,900	4,100	5,100	6,600	1,450	6,833	6,000	2,459	66,092
2015-16	2,900	905	1,150	1,465	11,000	4,700	4,600	6,300	2,000	6,905	3,100	6,130	64,157
2016-17[1]	2,900	675	1,700	1,640	8,300	4,700	4,500	5,300	2,000	6,850	6,450	6,282	63,497
2017-18[2]	2,700	950	2,100	1,400	7,800	4,200	4,700	4,700	1,850	6,250	4,100	4,047	58,273
2018-19[3]	2,700	800	1,900	1,700	5,500	4,100	4,600	5,000	1,800	6,700	4,250	6,604	59,440

[1] Preliminary.   [2] Estimate.   [3] Forecast.   *Source: Foreign Agricultural Service, U.S. Department of Agriculture (FAS-USDA)*

Salient Statistics of Grain Sorghum in the United States

Crop Year Beginning Sept. 1	Acreage Planted[4] for All Purposes	Acreage Harvested	Production (1,000 Bushels)	Yield Per Harvested Acre (Bushels)	Price in Cents Per Bushel	Value of Production (Million $)	For Silage Acreage Harvested (1,000 Acres)	For Silage Production (1,000 Tons)	For Silage Yield Per Harvested Acre (Tons)	On Farms Dec. 1	Off Farms Dec. 1	On Farms June 1	Off Farms June 1
	-- 1,000 Acres --										1,000 Bushels		
2013-14	8,076	6,585	392,331	59.6	428	1,716.9	380	5,420	14.3	32,950	198,441	4,500	87,924
2014-15	7,138	6,401	432,575	67.6	403	1,721.3	315	4,123	13.1	30,500	192,094	2,960	31,329
2015-16	8,459	7,851	596,751	76.0	331	2,064.6	306	4,475	14.6	51,500	21,035	9,700	80,654
2016-17[1]	6,690	6,163	480,261	77.9	279	1,352.4	298	4,171	14.0	43,000	265,149	8,620	76,088
2017-18[2]	5,626	5,044	361,871	71.7	322	1,175.1	284	3,772	13.4	33,800	193,692	5,220	60,113
2018-19[3]	5,690	5,061	364,986	72.1	310-350		264	3,326	12.6	36,800	209,528		

[1] Preliminary.   [2] Estimate.   [3] Forecast.   *Source: Foreign Agricultural Service, U.S. Department of Agriculture (FAS-USDA)*

Production of All Sorghum for Grain in the United States, by States   In Thousands of Bushels

Year	Arkansas	Colorado	Illinois	Kansas	Louisiana	Mississippi	Missouri	Nebraska	New Mexico	Oklahoma	South Dakota	Texas	Total
2013	12,750	5,760	1,880	168,150	12,091	5,828	4,920	9,715	2,312	14,850	22,000	128,800	392,331
2014	16,005	8,400	2,226	199,800	8,928	8,400	7,373	13,120	2,520	17,360	9,450	137,250	432,575
2015	43,120	22,000	3,196	281,600	6,290	9,085	13,160	23,040	4,230	21,320	18,260	149,450	596,751
2016	3,212	20,750	1,488	268,450	4,692	979	5,130	17,850	3,485	20,350	15,800	115,500	480,261
2017	546	18,720	1,245	200,900	1,183	288	2,461	11,570	1,680	15,635	11,560	94,500	361,871
2018[1]	770	17,225	1,776	233,200	504	270	2,100	15,980	1,786	12,000	16,000	62,100	364,986

[1] Preliminary.   *Source: National Agricultural Statistics Service, U.S. Department of Agriculture (NASS-USDA)*

Quarterly Supply and Disappearance of Grain Sorghum in the United States   In Millions of Bushels

Crop Year Beginning Sept. 1	Beginning Stocks	Pro-duction	Imports[3]	Total Supply	Food & Alcohol	Seed	Feed & Residual	Total	Exports[3]	Total Disap-pearance	Gov't Owned[4]	Privately Owned[5]	Total Stocks
2015-16	18.4	596.8	4.6	619.7	136.1	.8	104.3	241.3	341.8	583.1	----	----	36.6
Sept.-Nov.	18.4	596.8	3.6	618.8	22.1	0	159.6	181.8	114.4	296.2	----	----	322.5
Dec.-Feb.	322.5	----	1.0	323.5	41.8	0	-6.1	35.6	86.3	121.9	----	----	201.6
Mar.-May	201.6	----	.0	201.6	43.0	.3	-5.5	37.8	73.5	111.2	----	----	90.4
June-Aug.	90.4	----	.0	90.4	29.3	.5	-43.6	-13.9	67.6	53.7	----	----	36.6
2016-17	36.6	480.3	1.7	518.6	113.9	.7	132.7	247.4	237.8	485.2	----	----	33.5
Sept.-Nov.	36.6	480.3	.0	516.9	21.6	0	144.4	166.0	41.8	207.8	----	----	309.1
Dec.-Feb.	309.1	----	.0	309.1	33.1	0	6.0	39.0	89.3	128.3	----	----	180.7
Mar.-May	180.7	----	.0	180.7	34.3	.3	2.4	37.0	59.0	96.0	----	----	84.7
June-Aug.	84.7	----	1.7	86.4	24.9	.4	-20.0	5.3	47.7	53.0	----	----	33.5
2017-18[1]	33.5	361.9	2.0	397.3	59.4	.7	97.3	157.3	205.1	362.5	----	----	34.9
Sept.-Nov.	33.5	361.9	1.9	397.2	13.9	0	110.1	124.0	45.7	169.7	----	----	227.5
Dec.-Feb.	227.5	----	.1	227.5	10.2	0	5.7	16.0	71.3	87.3	----	----	140.3
Mar.-May	140.3	----	.0	140.3	15.1	.4	-14.1	1.4	73.6	74.9	----	----	65.3
June-Aug.	65.3	----	.0	65.4	20.1	.3	-4.4	16.0	14.5	30.5	----	----	34.9
2018-19[2]	34.9	365.0		399.8	109.2	.8	125.0	235.0	100.0	335.0	----	----	64.8
Sept.-Nov.	34.9	365.0		399.8	25.6	0	111.6	137.1	16.4	153.5	----	----	246.3

[1] Preliminary.   [2] Estimate.   [3] Uncommitted inventory.   [4] Includes quantity under loan and farmer-owned reserve.   *Source: Economic Research Service, U.S. Department of Agriculture (ERS-USDA)*

Average Price of Sorghum Grain, No. 2, Yellow in Kansas City   In Dollars Per Hundred Pounds (Cwt.)

Year	Sept.	Oct.	Nov.	Dec.	Jan.	Feb.	Mar.	Apr.	May	June	July	Aug.	Average
2011-12	11.79	10.90	11.30	10.91	11.27	11.36	11.14	10.61	10.04	9.90	12.96	13.46	11.30
2012-13	12.74	12.65	12.88	12.74	12.74	12.59	12.63	11.38	11.82	11.97	11.00	8.61	11.98
2013-14	8.15	7.57	7.40	7.52	7.62	8.08	8.64	8.89	8.74	7.98	6.79	6.05	7.79
2014-15	5.31	5.67	6.71	7.25	6.93	6.85	8.16	7.92	6.79	7.23	7.76	6.65	6.94
2015-16	6.09	6.31	6.22	6.53	....	....	5.91	5.92	6.00	6.34	5.05	4.90	5.93
2016-17	4.94	5.18	5.09	5.28	5.48	5.67	5.50	5.61	5.94	5.88	5.66	5.32	5.46
2017-18	5.39	5.49	5.51	5.85	6.12	5.81	6.13	6.17	6.22	6.07	5.62	5.73	5.84
2018-19[1]	5.41	5.50	5.64	5.98	5.92	5.97							5.73

[1] Preliminary.   *Source: Economic Research Service, U.S. Department of Agriculture (ERS-USDA)*

Exports of Grain Sorghum, by Country of Destination from the United States   In Metric Tons

Year	Canada	Ecuador	Eritrea (Ethiopia)	Israel	Japan	Jordan	Mexico	South Africa	Spain	Sudan	Turkey	World Total
2011-12	2,979	----	----	----	127,396	----	1,153,494	20,000	295	108,480	----	1,529,460
2012-13	3,347	----	----	----	220,070	----	1,336,805	38,720	35,500	178,240	813	2,099,421
2013-14	5,368	----	----	----	254,692	----	135,236	27,963	18,910	155,813	----	5,664,432
2014-15	6,053	----	----	----	86,137	----	12,515	10,000	----	179,450	----	9,243,031
2015-16	5,505	----	----	----	71,133	----	640,676	99,264	8,540	188,490	----	7,887,407
2016-17[1]	4,937	----	----	----	169,619	----	530,086	68,936	----	121,825	----	5,932,296
2017-18[2]	5,257	----	30,047	----	329,511	----	72,470	42,266	143,821	135,904	----	4,927,917

[1] Preliminary.   [2] Estimate.   *Source: Economic Research Service, U.S. Department of Agriculture (ERS-USDA)*

Grain Sorghum Price Support Program and Market Prices in the United States

Year	Price Support Quantity	% of Pro-duction	Aquired by CCC	Owned by CCC at Year End	Basic Loan Rate	Target Price	Findley Loan Rate	Effective Base[3] (Million Acres)	Partici-pation Rate[4] % of Base	Kansas City	Texas High Plains	Los Angeles	Gulf Ports
	---- Million Cwt. ----				---- Dollars Per Bushel ----					---- No. 2 Yellow ($ Per Cwt.) ----			
2010-11	.5	.3	0	0	3.48	4.70	1.95	----	----	11.04	10.61	----	11.92
2011-12	.2	.2	0	0	3.48	4.70	1.95	----	----	11.30	10.92	----	12.33
2012-13	.2	.1	0	0	3.48	4.70	1.95	----	----	11.98	----	----	12.66
2013-14	.3	.1	0	0	3.48	4.70	1.95	----	----	7.79	----	----	9.53
2014-15	.4	.2	0	0	3.48	7.05	1.95	----	----	6.94	----	----	9.10
2015-16[1]	1.4	.4	0	0	3.48	7.05	1.95	----	----	5.93	----	----	8.07
2016-17[2]	1.9	.7	0	0	3.48	7.05		----	----	5.46	----	----	7.56

[1] Preliminary.   [2] Estimate.   [3] National effective crop acreage base as determined by ASCS.   [4] Percentage of effective base acres enrolled in acreage reduction programs.   5/ Beginning with the 1996-7 marketing year, target prices are no longer applicable.   *Source: Economic Research Service, U.S. Department of Agriculture (ERS-USDA)*

Hay

Hay is a catchall term for forage plants, typically grasses such as timothy and Sudan-grass, and legumes such as alfalfa and clover. Alfalfa and alfalfa mixtures account for nearly half of all hay production. Hay is generally used to make cured feed for livestock. Curing, which is the proper drying of hay, is necessary to prevent spoilage. Hay, when properly cured, contains about 20% moisture. If hay is dried excessively, however, there is a loss of protein, which makes it less effective as livestock feed. Hay is harvested in virtually all of the lower 48 states.

Prices – The average monthly price of hay received by U.S. farmers in the first eight months of the 2018/19 marketing year (May through April) rose by +13.3% yr/yr

to $161.86 per ton, but still below the record high of $189.67 per ton seen in 2012-13. The farm production value of hay produced in 2017/18 rose +3.9% to $16,155 million.

Supply – U.S. hay production in 2018/19 is expected to rise +2.2% yr/yr to 134.384 million tons. U.S. farmers are expected to harvest 55.068 million acres of hay in 2018/19, up by 2.4%. The yield in 2018/19 is expected to remain at 2.44 tons per acre, below the 2004/05 record high of 2.55. U.S. carryover (May 1) in 2018/19 is expected to fall -35.8% to 15.869 million tons. The largest hay producing states in the U.S. for 2017 were Texas with 7.9% of U.S. hay production; Nebraska with 4.7%; Missouri, California, and Oklahoma with 4.6%; South Dakota with 3.6%; and North Dakota with 2.7%.

Salient Statistics of All Hay in the United States

Crop Year Beginning May 1	Acres Harvested (1,000 Acres)	Yield Per Acre (Tons)	Pro- duction	Carry- over May 1	Disap- pearance	Supply pearance Per Animal Unit	Disap- pearance	Animal Units Fed[3] (Millions)	Farm Price ($ Per Ton)	Farm Pro- duction Value Million $	Alfalfa (Certified)	Timothy	Red Clover	Sudan- grass
			Millions of Tons			In Tons					Dollars Per Cwt.			
2013-14	57,897	2.33	135.0	14.2	130.0	2.23	1.95	66.8	177.9	19,815	456.00	193.00	226.00	103.00
2014-15	57,062	2.45	139.9	19.2	134.6	2.36	2.00	67.0	171.1	19,099	469.00	198.00	231.00	105.00
2015-16	54,447	2.47	134.5	24.5	133.9	2.29	1.93	69.0	145.3	16,549				
2016-17	53,185	2.52	134.1	25.1	135.5	2.26	1.91	71.0	129.8	15,552				
2017-18[1]	52,777	2.43	128.2	24.4		2.19	1.97		143.0	16,155				
2018-19[2]	52,839	2.34	123.6	15.3		2.10								

[1] Preliminary.   [2] Estimate.   [3] Roughage-consuming animal units fed annually.   NA = Not available.
Source: Economic Research Service, U.S. Department of Agriculture (ERS-USDA)

Production of All Hay in the United States, by States   In Thousands of Tons

Year	California	Idaho	Iowa	Minne- sota	Missouri	New York	North Dakota	Ohio	Okla- homa	South Dakota	Texas	Wisconsin	Total
2013	7,646	4,976	3,377	3,895	7,921	4,935	5,090	2,495	4,981	5,905	8,880	3,760	135,002
2014	7,513	4,881	3,675	4,486	7,100	6,028	5,460	2,710	6,121	6,665	11,746	4,866	139,923
2015	6,891	4,860	3,939	3,979	6,398	6,360	4,975	2,532	5,914	6,580	9,720	4,073	134,502
2016	6,790	5,126	3,210	4,440	6,066	5,717	4,285	2,471	5,611	5,425	11,714	3,926	134,082
2017	6,388	5,128	3,268	3,797	5,985	5,955	3,423	2,371	5,638	4,603	9,548	3,522	128,207
2018[1]	5,682	5,019	2,998	3,077	5,408	6,985	4,419	2,356	5,121	5,788	8,374	2,953	123,600

[1] Preliminary.   *Source: Agricultural Statistics Board, U.S. Department of Agriculture (ASB-USDA)*

Hay Production and Farm Stocks in the United States   In Thousands of Short Tons

Year	Alfalfa & Mixtures	All Others	All Hay	Corn for Silage[1]	Sorghum Silage[1]	Farm Stocks May 1	Farm Stocks Dec. 1
2013	57,217	77,785	135,002	118,296	5,420	14,156	89,304
2014	61,451	78,472	139,923	128,048	4,123	19,176	92,052
2015	58,974	75,528	134,502	127,311	4,475	24,517	94,993
2016	58,601	75,481	134,082	126,020	4,171	25,140	95,837
2017	55,812	72,395	128,207	127,434	3,772	24,400	84,422
2018[2]	52,634	70,966	123,600	121,361	3,326	15,348	79,055

[1] Not included in all tame hay.   [2] Preliminary.   *Source: Agricultural Statistics Board, U.S. Department of Agriculture (ASB-USDA)*

Mid-Month Price Received by Farmers for All Hay (Baled) in the United States   In Dollars Per Ton

Year	May	June	July	Aug.	Sept.	Oct.	Nov.	Dec.	Jan.	Feb.	Mar.	Apr.	Average
2013-14	203.0	199.0	190.0	177.0	174.0	174.0	168.0	163.0	162.0	167.0	170.0	188.0	177.9
2014-15	202.0	197.0	185.0	181.0	172.0	171.0	162.0	156.0	149.0	153.0	157.0	168.0	171.1
2015-16	175.0	162.0	152.0	143.0	142.0	143.0	138.0	139.0	134.0	135.0	136.0	144.0	145.3
2016-17	140.0	134.0	128.0	130.0	128.0	129.0	126.0	123.0	122.0	124.0	131.0	143.0	129.8
2017-18	147.0	145.0	141.0	137.0	137.0	141.0	138.0	137.0	140.0	143.0	148.0	162.0	143.0
2018-19[1]	167.0	160.0	159.0	161.0	163.0	162.0	161.0	164.0	166.0				162.6

[1] Preliminary.   [2] Marketing year average.   *Source: Economic Research Service, U.S. Department of Agriculture (ERS-USDA)*

Heating Oil

Heating oil is a heavy fuel oil that is derived from crude oil. Heating oil is also known as No. 2 fuel oil and accounts for about 25% of the yield from a barrel of crude oil. That is the second largest "cut" after gasoline. The price to consumers of home heating oil is generally comprised of 42% for crude oil, 12% for refining costs, and 46% for marketing and distribution costs (Source: EIA's Petroleum Marketing Monthly, 2001). Generally, a $1 increase in the price of crude oil translates into a 2.5-cent per gallon rise in heating oil. Because of this, heating oil prices are highly correlated with crude oil prices, although heating oil prices are also subject to swift supply and demand shifts due to weather changes or refinery shutdowns.

The primary use for heating oil is for residential heating. In the U.S., approximately 8.1 million households use heating oil as their main heating fuel. Most of the demand for heating oil occurs from October through March. The Northeast region, which includes the New England and the Central Atlantic States, is most reliant on heating oil. This region consumes approximately 70% of U.S. heating oil. However, demand for heating oil has been dropping as households switch to a more convenient heating source like natural gas. In fact, demand for heating oil is down by about 10 billion gallons/year from its peak use in 1976 (Source: American Petroleum Institute).

Refineries produce approximately 85% of U.S. heating oil as part of the "distillate fuel oil" product family, which includes heating oil and diesel fuel. The remainder of U.S. heating oil is imported from Canada, the Virgin Islands, and Venezuela.

Recently, a team of Purdue University researchers developed a way to make home heating oil from a mixture of soybean oil and conventional fuel oil. The oil blend is made by replacing 20% of the fuel oil with soybean oil, potentially saving 1.3 billion gallons of fuel oil per year. This soybean heating oil can be used in conventional furnaces without altering existing equipment. The soybean heating oil is relatively easy to produce and creates no sulfur emissions.

The "crack-spread" is the processing margin earned when refiners buy crude oil and refine it into heating oil and gasoline. The crack-spread ratio commonly used in the industry is the 3-2-1, which involves buying 1 heating oil contract and 2 gasoline futures contracts, and then selling 3 crude oil contracts. As long as the crack spread is positive, it is profitable for refiners to buy crude oil and refine it into products. The NYMEX has a crack-spread calculator on their web site at www.NYMEX.com.

Heating oil futures and options are traded at the CME Group. The CME's heating oil futures contract calls for the delivery of 1,000 barrels of fungible No. 2 heating oil in the New York harbor. Futures are also traded on ICE Futures Europe and the Multi Commodity Exchange of Index (MCX).

Prices – CME heating oil futures prices (Barchart.com symbol code HO) on the nearest-futures chart in 2018 opened at $2.0681 per gallon, moved generally higher into October and then moved sharply lower in November to close the year down -18.8% at $1.6794 per gallon.

Supply – U.S. production of distillate fuel oil in 2018 rose +2.7% yr/yr to 5.158 million barrels per day, a new record high. Stocks of distillate fuel oil in November 2018 were down -4.8% yr/yr at 126.356 million barrels. U.S. production of residual fuel in 2018 fell by 0.4% yr/yr to an average of 425,736 barrels per day, which was less than half the production level of over 1 million barrels per day produced in the 1970s. U.S. stocks of residual fuel oil as of November 2018 were down -6.2% to 29.793 million barrels, down from the 2015 record of 42.189 million barrels.

Demand – U.S. usage of distillate fuel oil in 2018 rose +5.4% yr/yr to 4.143 million barrels per day, down from the 2007 high of 4.198 million barrels a day.

Trade – U.S. imports of distillate fuel oil in 2018 rose +17.4% to an average of 174,613 barrels per day, down from the 2006 record high of 365,000 barrels per day. U.S. exports of distillate fuel oil in 2013 rose by +12.8% yr/yr to 1.134 million barrels per day. U.S. imports of residual fuel oil in 2017 fell -8.1% yr/yr to 187,912 barrels per day, far less than that the levels of over 1 million barrels per day seen back in the 1970s.

World Production of Distillate Fuel Oil   In Thousands of Barrels Per Day

Year	Brazil	Canada	China	France	Germany	India	Italy	Japan	Korea, South	Russia	Saudi Arabia	United States	World Total
2007	756.0	558.5	2,560.2	981.1	956.6	974.0	657.6	991.8	419.0	508.0	532.3	4,195.9	24,349.7
2008	793.0	557.0	2,767.5	991.2	1,104.4	1,054.0	642.0	908.7	388.3	640.0	577.8	3,945.4	25,436.2
2009	758.0	516.7	2,777.0	985.1	1,062.7	1,182.0	617.1	820.8	385.9	570.0	605.0	3,631.1	24,930.4
2010	855.0	569.6	3,011.3	983.7	1,096.5	1,226.0	614.5	825.8	399.4	583.0	618.9	3,800.3	25,369.0
2011	927.0	601.8	3,195.3	962.2	1,049.0	1,298.0	608.9	807.6	393.3	641.0	651.0	3,898.9	25,986.1
2012	992.0	582.7	3,461.4	962.9	1,076.1	1,420.0	569.5	811.3	405.2	582.0	704.8	3,741.4	26,616.3
2013	996.0	592.3	3,503.2	970.8	1,125.3	1,385.0	550.6	796.4	423.7	596.0	729.6	3,827.5	26,851.6
2014	1,023.0	580.8	3,513.6	949.2	1,079.8	1,417.7	568.2	772.8	432.2	577.1	753.3	4,037.2	27,229.2
2015[1]		571.5		965.1	1,100.8		558.0	770.1	472.6			3,995.2	
2016[2]		541.1		953.5	1,114.9		548.9	774.8	501.0				

[1] Preliminary.   [2] Estimate.   Source: Energy Information Administration, U.S. Department of Energy (EIA-DOE)

HEATING OIL

World Imports of Distillate Fuel Oil   In Thousands of Barrels Per Day

Year	Australia	Belgium	France	Germany	Indonesia	Nether-lands	Singa-pore	Spain	Turkey	United Kingdom	United States	Vietnam	World Total
2004	63.0	164.7	322.3	265.8	130.1	203.0	112.5	230.1	77.8	81.8	325.5	111.6	4,268.5
2005	81.7	198.1	380.7	277.6	170.2	196.2	78.9	263.4	84.7	98.6	328.8	120.4	4,499.6
2006	105.7	166.1	317.3	332.0	176.1	278.0	125.2	264.9	130.9	158.3	364.7	110.8	4,906.3
2007	105.2	148.9	271.6	187.8	229.7	188.4	127.0	286.6	162.3	159.0	304.1	132.5	5,090.9
2008	147.8	156.4	292.1	317.2	211.6	250.9	178.6	246.3	169.8	152.6	212.9	132.6	5,466.6
2009	144.0	124.6	380.2	297.0	146.7	333.5	155.0	234.1	186.2	127.5	225.1	132.9	5,485.7
2010	141.7	111.8	414.0	318.9	259.0	385.2	393.5	220.7	197.9	193.0	228.4	100.5	6,318.7
2011	176.6	161.7	408.0	278.9	244.3	375.1	383.0	174.1	207.5	191.4	178.7	108.5	6,444.8
2012[1]	202.0	128.3	469.9	276.1	290.2	384.2	279.2	136.4	226.1	218.6	126.2	113.6	6,523.9
2013[2]	226.8	246.5	478.1	322.7		378.6		95.2	245.5	217.2	154.7		

[1] Preliminary.   [2] Estimate.   Source: Energy Information Administration, U.S. Department of Energy (EIA-DOE)

World Exports of Distillate Fuel Oil   In Thousands of Barrels Per Day

Year	Belgium	Germany	India	Italy	Japan	Korea, South	Kuwait	Nether-lands	Russia	Singa-pore	Taiwan	United States	World Total
2004	167.0	166.1	148.5	187.3	29.4	185.8	225.3	411.2	614.3	294.0	119.9	109.6	4,692.3
2005	182.3	204.4	173.0	179.8	64.1	234.3	221.2	430.4	649.2	300.0	149.2	138.4	5,038.9
2006	162.1	223.0	238.0	160.2	70.5	250.6	185.5	495.9	752.6	341.3	150.0	215.1	5,394.9
2007	177.9	250.6	292.4	183.5	137.2	281.9	194.0	420.4	751.9	359.3	176.5	267.7	5,268.0
2008	171.7	203.2	300.2	170.2	220.5	357.6	190.2	464.7	767.8	406.8	181.1	528.3	5,830.8
2009	140.2	181.8	377.3	168.2	215.7	343.6	152.8	562.3	812.9	346.3	206.6	587.4	6,153.4
2010	142.4	138.8	376.5	189.1	197.4	358.0	143.8	636.1	851.0	540.0	177.2	656.0	6,209.9
2011	156.2	132.2	430.5	153.6	160.0	436.8	143.8	631.1	807.8	553.7	157.5	854.1	6,404.8
2012[1]	160.7	128.9	459.1	178.8	120.2	481.8	153.0	608.5	840.9	469.8	191.7	1,007.2	6,781.3
2013[2]	226.4	135.0		142.8	167.6	446.6		604.1				1,133.9	

[1] Preliminary.   [2] Estimate.   Source: Energy Information Administration, U.S. Department of Energy (EIA-DOE)

Production of Distillate Fuel Oil in the United States   In Thousand Barrels per Day

Year	Jan.	Feb.	Mar.	Apr.	May	June	July	Aug.	Sept.	Oct.	Nov.	Dec.	Average
2009	4,283.5	4,231.3	3,938.7	4,131.8	4,092.9	4,047.5	3,928.9	3,964.8	4,098.8	3,983.6	4,018.5	3,877.2	4,049.8
2010	3,551.3	3,658.1	3,835.0	4,156.5	4,374.8	4,407.8	4,424.7	4,403.9	4,341.4	4,315.3	4,502.9	4,669.7	4,220.1
2011	4,303.3	4,033.2	4,326.0	4,188.8	4,283.3	4,470.8	4,656.4	4,667.7	4,576.5	4,538.7	4,902.4	4,918.8	4,488.8
2012	4,500.4	4,407.7	4,262.8	4,351.7	4,547.3	4,631.8	4,660.1	4,599.7	4,565.5	4,509.8	4,668.8	4,884.4	4,549.2
2013	4,479.8	4,280.5	4,283.8	4,416.4	4,767.1	4,791.5	4,933.8	4,930.0	4,888.4	4,814.8	5,049.7	5,121.6	4,729.8
2014	4,685.3	4,594.5	4,779.7	4,987.9	5,026.1	4,896.0	5,021.2	5,042.5	4,939.8	4,662.0	5,011.6	5,322.9	4,914.1
2015	4,835.2	4,752.4	4,893.7	4,991.4	4,982.8	5,031.8	5,101.2	5,106.6	5,060.8	4,816.5	5,169.0	5,042.1	4,982.0
2016	4,530.3	4,667.8	4,848.3	4,658.8	4,760.4	4,953.6	4,933.4	4,939.2	4,888.1	4,614.1	5,066.0	5,147.6	4,834.0
2017	4,785.5	4,656.6	4,792.5	5,018.9	5,215.5	5,283.8	5,161.9	5,044.1	4,559.7	4,972.0	5,362.1	5,407.9	5,021.7
2018[1]	5,009.9	4,583.6	4,824.8	5,119.0	5,213.4	5,405.6	5,256.4	5,368.7	5,229.6	5,035.6	5,350.1	5,575.6	5,164.4

[1] Preliminary.   Source: Energy Information Administration; U.S. Department of Energy (EIA-DOE)

Stocks of Distillate Fuel in the United States, on First of Month   In Thousands of Barrels

Year	Jan.	Feb.	Mar.	Apr.	May	June	July	Aug.	Sept.	Oct.	Nov.	Dec.
2009	143,730	148,105	145,301	150,058	156,706	162,723	165,940	168,649	172,731	171,164	171,125	165,964
2010	163,527	155,333	146,817	144,802	150,041	157,944	166,628	170,334	166,735	161,510	161,991	164,306
2011	163,086	154,077	149,239	142,919	144,847	143,870	154,455	155,064	153,399	142,327	143,857	149,212
2012	147,210	139,289	133,697	124,665	121,445	119,890	126,454	127,309	127,384	118,653	117,993	134,809
2013	131,268	121,963	118,737	118,791	122,132	122,463	126,020	129,060	129,326	118,035	121,118	127,543
2014	114,534	112,897	115,337	116,827	121,757	121,674	125,559	128,132	131,289	120,093	126,085	136,065
2015	131,992	123,137	128,294	129,022	134,028	139,437	142,144	152,145	148,846	143,317	156,666	160,741
2016	160,583	162,696	160,620	154,692	154,389	149,239	155,969	159,534	160,378	153,884	160,173	165,456
2017	168,937	162,241	151,080	154,640	153,793	151,608	151,068	147,820	137,461	129,885	132,700	145,574
2018[1]	141,129	138,578	130,391	120,591	115,199	120,379	127,081	132,037	137,060	124,183	126,356	140,006

[1] Preliminary.   Source: Energy Information Administration; U.S. Department of Energy (EIA-DOE)

Imports of Distillate Fuel Oil in the United States   In Thousand of Barrels per Day

Year	Jan.	Feb.	Mar.	Apr.	May	June	July	Aug.	Sept.	Oct.	Nov.	Dec.	Average
2009	368	327	269	166	206	245	191	166	205	177	164	224	225
2010	462	293	179	220	189	237	170	246	189	163	178	219	229
2011	337	206	190	191	170	127	157	148	179	128	138	175	179
2012	157	142	137	98	113	87	117	112	86	88	188	190	126
2013	213	174	146	238	168	121	107	123	132	128	145	164	155
2014	283	337	324	181	198	121	129	143	126	120	136	245	195
2015	349	388	324	243	191	132	143	140	103	101	150	155	202
2016	172	231	150	177	123	88	123	164	150	75	145	167	147
2017	204	199	108	116	124	102	111	112	112	134	180	282	149
2018[1]	290	284	157	91	122	90	144	175	172	161	227	183	175

[1] Preliminary.   Source: Energy Information Administration, U.S. Department of Energy (EIA-DOE)

Disposition of Distillate Fuel Oil, Total Product Supplied in the United States   In Thousand of Barrels per Day

Year	Jan.	Feb.	Mar.	Apr.	May	June	July	Aug.	Sept.	Oct.	Nov.	Dec.	Average
2009	4,078.6	3,863.6	3,743.6	3,455.0	3,436.3	3,513.0	3,394.6	3,426.2	3,560.3	3,654.1	3,595.8	3,861.5	3,631.9
2010	3,700.5	3,854.5	3,834.6	3,758.6	3,638.6	3,742.7	3,544.0	3,829.5	3,886.2	3,772.9	3,873.3	4,175.5	3,800.9
2011	3,958.0	3,913.5	4,045.1	3,754.5	3,699.4	3,947.4	3,563.7	4,008.9	3,936.0	4,003.4	4,109.4	3,853.2	3,899.4
2012	3,860.9	3,922.9	3,714.8	3,718.9	3,756.3	3,732.5	3,556.6	3,743.0	3,674.3	3,852.4	3,847.6	3,528.8	3,742.4
2013	4,061.8	3,984.4	3,769.1	3,854.4	3,749.0	3,662.9	3,621.0	3,693.2	3,724.6	4,038.8	3,893.2	3,886.8	3,828.3
2014	4,340.0	4,160.3	4,066.2	3,989.8	3,951.6	3,901.6	3,866.5	3,874.8	3,933.4	4,266.3	3,917.2	4,178.2	4,037.1
2015	4,185.7	4,559.2	4,078.1	4,027.4	3,777.5	3,896.8	3,901.2	3,914.7	4,063.0	4,014.1	3,740.2	3,831.1	3,999.1
2016	3,850.3	3,996.1	3,947.0	3,798.9	3,732.0	3,852.7	3,597.4	3,880.4	3,912.0	3,986.3	3,938.4	4,043.1	3,877.9
2017	3,735.6	3,934.8	4,126.6	3,762.8	3,955.0	3,963.6	3,641.8	4,003.5	3,921.2	4,011.2	4,157.4	3,975.3	3,932.4
2018[1]	4,393.9	3,961.9	4,168.6	4,153.7	4,273.5	3,954.1	3,958.1	4,173.0	4,006.6	4,378.4	4,261.2	4,031.0	4,142.8

[1] Preliminary.   Source: Energy Information Administration, U.S. Department of Energy (EIA-DOE)

World Production of Residual Fuel Oil   In Thousands of Barrels Per Day

Year	Brazil	China	India	Iran	Italy	Japan	Korea, South	Mexico	Russia	Saudi Arabia	United States	Vene-zuela	World Total
2007	206.0	895.6	396.0	293.2	225.4	539.6	397.1	298.3	303.0	350.6	722.9	49.8	10,748.2
2008	213.0	738.9	241.0	328.2	212.7	546.7	331.7	265.1	264.0	363.7	622.2	100.5	10,323.9
2009	160.0	684.5	295.0	359.9	180.1	411.4	320.5	246.0	324.0	275.5	511.1	105.0	10,102.6
2010	184.0	878.4	179.0	318.6	144.0	395.6	321.3	224.0	303.0	272.0	535.1	117.0	9,855.0
2011	161.0	609.1	185.0	379.2	115.9	446.6	277.7	242.6	423.0	316.9	461.1	123.1	9,534.3
2012	167.0	583.7	184.0	420.3	107.2	565.4	268.8	244.9	407.0	330.9	368.8	115.0	9,373.6
2013	114.0	580.3	155.0	357.6	82.6	475.1	256.8	226.9	350.0	370.2	318.6	109.1	9,044.7
2014	139.3	552.9	148.4	335.3	72.7	413.3	218.8	164.7	243.5	438.3	257.2	71.3	8,846.6
2015[1]					77.7	368.1	237.3	144.6			259.3		
2016[2]					64.4	340.2	277.0	133.0					

[1] Preliminary.   [2] Estimate.   Source: Energy Information Administration, U.S. Department of Energy (EIA-DOE)

Supply and Disposition of Residual Fuel Oil in the United States

	---------------- Supply ----------------		------------------------- Disposition -------------------------			Ending Stocks (Million	Average Sales to End Users[3]
Year	Total Production	Imports	Stock Change	Exports	Product Supplied	Barrels)	(USD per Gallon)
	----------------------------------- In Thousands of Barrels Per Day -----------------------------------						
2008	620	349	NA	NA	622	36	1.96
2009	598	331	NA	NA	511	37	1.34
2010	585	366	----	----	535	41	1.71
2011	537	328	----	----	461	34	2.40
2012	501	256	----	----	369	34	2.59
2013	467	225	----	----	319	38	2.48
2014	435	173	----	----	257	34	2.33
2015	417	192	----	----	259	42	1.29
2016	418	205	----	----	326	41	0.95
2017[1]	429	188	----	----	359	29	1.29

[1] Preliminary.   [2] Less than +500 barrels per day and greater than -500 barrels per day.   [3] Refiner price excluding taxes.
Source: Energy Information Administration, U.S. Department of Energy (EIA-DOE)

HEATING OIL

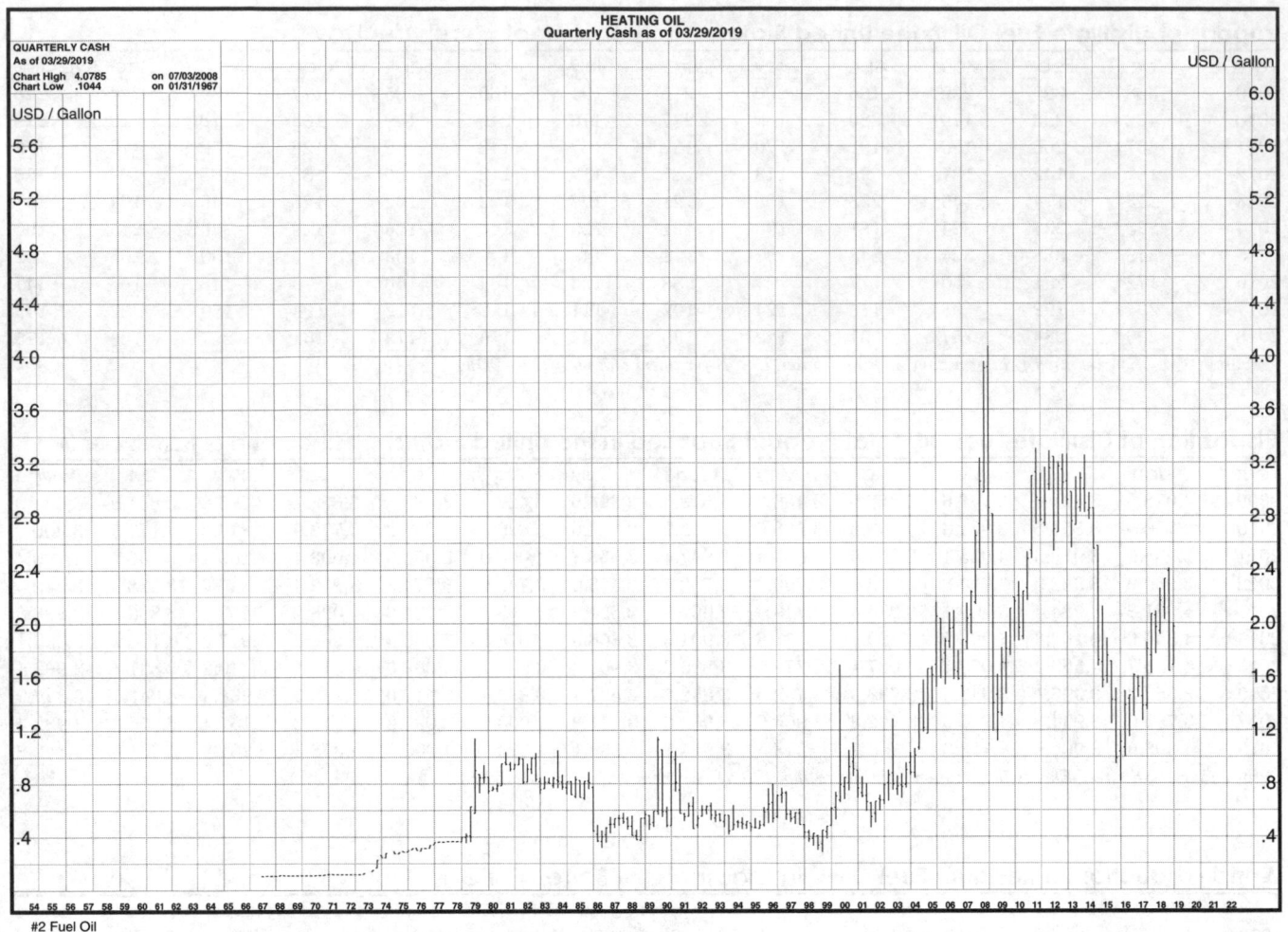

HEATING OIL
Quarterly Cash as of 03/29/2019

QUARTERLY CASH
As of 03/29/2019

Chart High 4.0785   on 07/03/2008
Chart Low   .1044   on 01/31/1967

USD / Gallon

USD / Gallon

#2 Fuel Oil

Production of Residual Fuel Oil in the United States   In Thousands of Barrels per Day

Year	Jan.	Feb.	Mar.	Apr.	May	June	July	Aug.	Sept.	Oct.	Nov.	Dec.	Average
2009	584.6	571.3	583.1	474.9	604.9	613.1	586.0	631.1	604.5	671.6	624.4	623.7	597.8
2010	633.1	631.8	581.3	597.5	615.0	558.9	575.8	553.6	588.3	528.4	563.7	595.2	585.2
2011	552.5	529.4	525.7	534.3	538.2	553.5	562.6	604.0	516.1	529.8	515.7	485.9	537.3
2012	499.8	547.8	577.3	524.9	508.6	538.2	486.0	495.1	507.7	480.5	457.5	387.7	500.9
2013	395.4	504.1	569.4	508.2	488.1	469.0	481.4	416.9	433.8	420.3	466.2	454.8	467.3
2014	476.3	427.5	460.8	420.4	454.3	454.7	402.1	438.7	409.8	415.6	462.0	401.2	435.3
2015	376.7	419.5	478.3	466.8	435.5	413.3	426.1	403.7	414.1	419.3	376.5	376.4	417.2
2016	395.0	403.4	399.9	435.0	427.0	389.4	400.6	419.8	436.0	454.8	450.1	400.9	417.7
2017	485.2	482.5	405.7	416.6	407.7	406.3	390.5	452.5	459.2	442.2	407.8	372.5	427.4
2018[1]	467.1	461.5	402.6	450.4	414.8	347.6	444.2	391.3	429.3	397.2	449.8	440.3	424.7

[1] Preliminary.   Source: Energy Information Administration, U.S. Department of Energy (EIA-DOE)

Average Price of Heating Oil #2   In Dollars Per Gallon

Year	Jan.	Feb.	Mar.	Apr.	May	June	July	Aug.	Sept.	Oct.	Nov.	Dec.	Average
2009	1.4643	1.2778	1.2830	1.3595	1.4787	1.7472	1.6318	1.8659	1.7305	1.9334	1.9848	1.9722	1.6441
2010	2.0523	1.9752	2.0847	2.2126	2.0378	2.0344	1.9775	2.0224	2.0948	2.2423	2.3174	2.4643	2.1263
2011	2.6035	2.7638	3.0339	3.1956	2.9514	2.9651	3.0692	2.9427	2.9199	2.9500	3.0524	2.8875	2.9446
2012	3.0452	3.1941	3.2146	3.1472	2.9123	2.6201	2.8200	3.0459	3.1295	3.1383	3.0107	2.9591	3.0198
2013	3.0720	3.1669	2.9468	2.7278	2.6882	2.7424	2.8863	2.9581	2.9613	2.9422	2.9228	3.0325	2.9206
2014	3.0633	3.0656	2.9124	2.8878	2.8603	2.8822	2.7758	2.7535	2.6332	2.4237	2.2493	1.8555	2.6969
2015	1.6163	1.8727	1.6315	1.7404	1.8317	1.7680	1.5505	1.3875	1.4311	1.4042	1.3198	1.0392	1.5494
2016	0.9396	0.9721	1.1289	1.1877	1.3527	1.4162	1.2850	1.3251	1.3521	1.4877	1.3872	1.5521	1.2822
2017	1.5474	1.5622	1.4925	1.5202	1.4521	1.3320	1.4248	1.5412	1.7915	1.7111	1.8216	1.8619	1.5882
2018	2.0315	1.8541	1.8698	2.0372	2.1880	2.1132	2.1067	2.1246	2.2260	2.3158	2.0360	1.7877	2.0576

Source: Energy Information Administration, U.S. Department of Energy (EIA-DOE)

ULSD NY HARBOR - NYMEX
Weekly Nearest Futures as of 03/29/2019

WEEKLY NEAREST FUTURES
As of 03/29/2019
Chart High 3.3700 on 01/31/2014
Chart Low .8487 on 01/21/2016

Nearby Futures through Last Trading Day.

Volume of Trading of Heating Oil #2 Futures in New York   In Thousands of Contracts

Year	Jan.	Feb.	Mar.	Apr.	May	June	July	Aug.	Sept.	Oct.	Nov.	Dec.	Total
2009	1,789.0	1,512.9	1,670.1	1,633.3	1,644.5	1,809.7	2,004.2	1,652.6	1,777.3	1,975.9	1,921.9	2,035.1	21,426.5
2010	2,096.3	1,872.5	2,230.6	2,459.2	2,493.3	2,305.2	1,963.7	2,409.5	2,548.9	2,230.9	2,165.8	2,194.1	26,970.1
2011	2,545.9	2,600.7	2,805.0	2,206.5	2,645.6	2,624.9	2,022.6	2,843.7	2,889.1	2,964.2	3,071.0	2,619.4	31,838.6
2012	3,149.6	3,203.3	2,953.3	2,693.2	2,913.9	3,172.8	2,875.1	3,071.6	2,812.8	3,887.9	2,913.4	2,440.8	36,087.7
2013	3,122.0	2,801.6	2,900.0	3,057.7	2,852.8	2,540.0	2,700.0	2,490.4	2,384.5	2,932.3	2,608.5	2,359.7	32,749.6
2014	3,400.6	2,893.3	2,533.8	2,209.6	2,253.3	2,483.3	2,857.3	2,719.9	2,875.9	3,409.5	3,126.2	3,183.6	33,946.4
2015	3,247.1	3,451.1	3,022.4	2,733.6	2,616.5	2,981.7	3,024.6	3,254.2	2,906.7	3,473.0	2,765.9	3,470.1	36,947.0
2016	3,341.1	3,201.8	2,861.8	3,286.1	3,452.2	3,431.1	3,052.5	3,455.0	3,288.4	3,183.1	3,518.7	3,317.7	39,389.3
2017	3,322.5	3,332.7	3,497.4	3,091.7	3,867.4	3,642.3	3,601.1	4,759.9	3,577.9	3,849.6	3,549.3	3,504.4	43,596.2
2018	4,542.6	3,826.2	3,715.8	4,066.3	4,334.6	3,738.0	3,326.2	3,566.0	3,440.1	3,966.1	4,516.8	3,239.0	46,277.9

Contract size = 42,000 US gallons.   Source: CME Group; New York Mercantile Exchange (NYMEX)

Average Open Interest of Heating Oil #2 Futures in New York   In Contracts

Year	Jan.	Feb.	Mar.	Apr.	May	June	July	Aug.	Sept.	Oct.	Nov.	Dec.
2009	237,894	252,753	261,552	259,008	260,646	283,068	294,270	308,022	311,296	312,653	322,505	309,113
2010	317,506	306,607	319,389	310,085	311,994	313,624	304,866	305,549	325,342	327,588	319,732	308,661
2011	306,262	312,145	305,872	310,288	310,053	316,026	306,360	307,607	323,485	303,460	291,931	274,679
2012	273,761	299,758	286,319	296,190	314,645	323,256	313,376	320,011	332,853	316,594	303,742	280,933
2013	297,517	316,763	297,280	304,306	307,574	291,583	287,422	290,885	284,372	280,863	298,480	292,422
2014	281,102	294,144	280,719	263,461	269,766	285,931	313,266	353,133	373,004	390,505	391,923	355,367
2015	375,870	384,974	375,278	361,933	360,017	362,447	388,442	425,342	399,488	382,414	367,273	348,763
2016	349,641	365,010	367,707	389,364	399,419	404,855	370,778	396,411	391,168	408,496	395,976	431,825
2017	422,678	424,439	413,555	428,260	418,050	405,141	411,503	404,442	444,276	442,998	445,430	443,590
2018	469,402	433,230	401,046	436,876	438,501	403,757	403,666	390,752	420,964	422,927	376,499	369,267

Contract size = 42,000 US gallons.   Source: CME Group; New York Mercantile Exchange (NYMEX)

Hides and Leather

Hides and leather have been used since ancient times for boots, clothing, shields, armor, tents, bottles, buckets, and cups. Leather is produced through the tanning of hides, pelts, and skins of animals. The remains of leather have been found in the Middle East dating back at least 7,000 years.

Today, most leather is made of cowhide but it is also made from the hides of lamb, deer, ostrich, snakes, crocodiles, and even stingray. Cattle hides are the most valuable byproduct of the meat packing industry. U.S. exports of cowhides bring more than $1 billion in foreign trade, and U.S. finished leather production is worth about $4 billion.

Prices – The average monthly price of wholesale cattle hides (packer heavy native steers FOB Chicago) in 2018 fell -12.5% yr/yr to 59.15 cents per pound, well below the 2014 record high of 110.19 cents per pound.

Supply – World production of cattle and buffalo hides in 2013 rose by +1.4% yr/yr to 9.078, down from 2009's record high of 9.135 million metric tons. The world's largest producers of cattle and buffalo hides in 2013 were the U.S. with 12.4% of world production, Brazil with 9.9%, and Argentina with 4.2%.

U.S. new supply of cattle hides from domestic slaughter in 2009 fell 3.0% yr/yr to 33.338 million hides, which is far below the record high of 43.582 million hides posted in 1976. U.S. production of leather footwear has been dropping sharply in recent years due to the movement of production offshore to lower cost producers. U.S. production of leather footwear in 2003 fell -46.0% yr/yr to 22.3 million pairs and was a mere 4% of the 562.3 million pairs produced in 1970.

Demand – World consumption of cowhides and skins in 2000, the last reporting year for the series, rose +1.4% to 4,774 metric tons, which was a record high for the data series, which goes back to 1984. The world's largest consumers of cowhides and skins in 2000 were the U.S. with 13.0% of world consumption, Italy (10.6%), Brazil (8.9%), Mexico, (6.0%), Argentina (6.0%), and South Korea (5.9%).

Trade – The total value of U.S. leather exports in 2004 was $1.344 billion. U.S. net exports of cattle hides in 2017 rose +5.7% to 17.107 million hides. The largest destinations for U.S. exports in 2017 were China (which took 61.7% of U.S. exports), South Korea (14.8%), Mexico (9.0%), Thailand (5.1%), and Taiwan (3.2%).

World Production of Cattle and Buffalo Hides   In Metric Tons

Year	Argentina	Australia	Brazil	Canada	Colombia	France	Germany	Italy	Mexico	Russia	United Kingdom	United States	World Total
2005	427,551	245,000	850,000	111,860	85,800	147,563	132,000	125,839	191,700	202,772	67,500	1,015,986	8,401,720
2006	402,565	233,000	886,000	103,875	85,467	142,813	135,000	124,139	196,500	183,154	74,000	1,076,440	8,585,029
2007	448,670	251,550	914,200	95,510	87,604	142,296	132,000	121,558	199,200	180,139	74,500	1,085,784	8,757,386
2008	439,809	239,000	873,500	96,098	93,500	143,148	135,000	115,315	201,900	182,363	73,700	1,104,271	8,801,379
2009	481,591	235,900	856,400	92,630	84,169	144,432	134,500	115,304	206,900	178,557	70,350	1,102,973	8,907,858
2010	356,481	230,000	855,000	93,640	79,721	144,562	134,500	115,450	212,900	177,054	75,900	1,130,384	8,915,811
2011	325,951	230,000	848,500	84,848	85,809	145,236	132,000	116,198	219,900	162,732	79,450	1,123,459	8,904,854
2012[1]	342,864	230,000	872,400	77,763	90,742	138,628	129,700	118,060	222,900	163,078	79,450	1,123,459	8,949,143
2013[2]	378,759	230,000	902,500	76,660	89,231	130,396	129,700	116,258	219,900	162,821	79,450	1,123,459	9,078,146
2014[2]	----	----	----	----	----	----	----	----	----	----	----	----	----

[1] Preliminary.   [2] Forecast.   Source: Food and Agricultural Organization of the United Nations (FAO-UN)

Imports of Bovine Hides and Skins in the United States   In Thousands of Hides

Year	Australia	Belgium-Luxembourg	Brazil	Canada	China	Colombia	Italy	Mexico	New Zealand	Pakistan	Thailand	Turkey	World Total
2009	0.0	21.8	13.4	975.0	197.1	19.4	34.2	97.2	76.3	5.9	5.9	----	1,475.2
2010	3.9	13.8	21.2	1,063.7	26.7	15.2	6.0	147.1	37.5	0.9	6.4	0.6	1,388.3
2011	0.3	10.0	4.7	931.9	16.5	6.2	18.9	196.3	16.6	24.7	6.9	48.5	1,305.7
2012	7.2	10.0	36.9	1,209.4	36.9	10.3	3.9	240.8	7.5	2.6	6.8	17.3	1,609.7
2013	2.6	11.4	15.2	1,007.6	80.6	0.9	12.2	432.9	4.4	2.5	5.3	22.0	1,623.0
2014	72.2	24.4	7.1	1,181.0	92.9	0.6	5.0	638.2	6.8	0.5	6.9	0.8	2,077.4
2015	97.2	43.8	1.0	1,218.8	5.2	33.7	5.9	375.8	1.0	0.1	8.8	0.8	2,193.2
2016	0.0	139.4	8.2	794.2	8.5	107.1	11.9	69.4	1.9	1.1	20.3	0.7	2,336.2
2017	5.2	203.7	18.5	625.1	0.2	27.1	10.3	16.6	4.1	0.8	5.7	0.0	1,449.8
2018[1]	3.4	196.5	19.6	653.8	4.9	13.7	10.6	9.2	16.5	1.2	4.7	0.0	1,404.6

[1] Preliminary.   Source: Foreign Agricultural Service, U.S. Department of Agriculture (FAS-USDA)

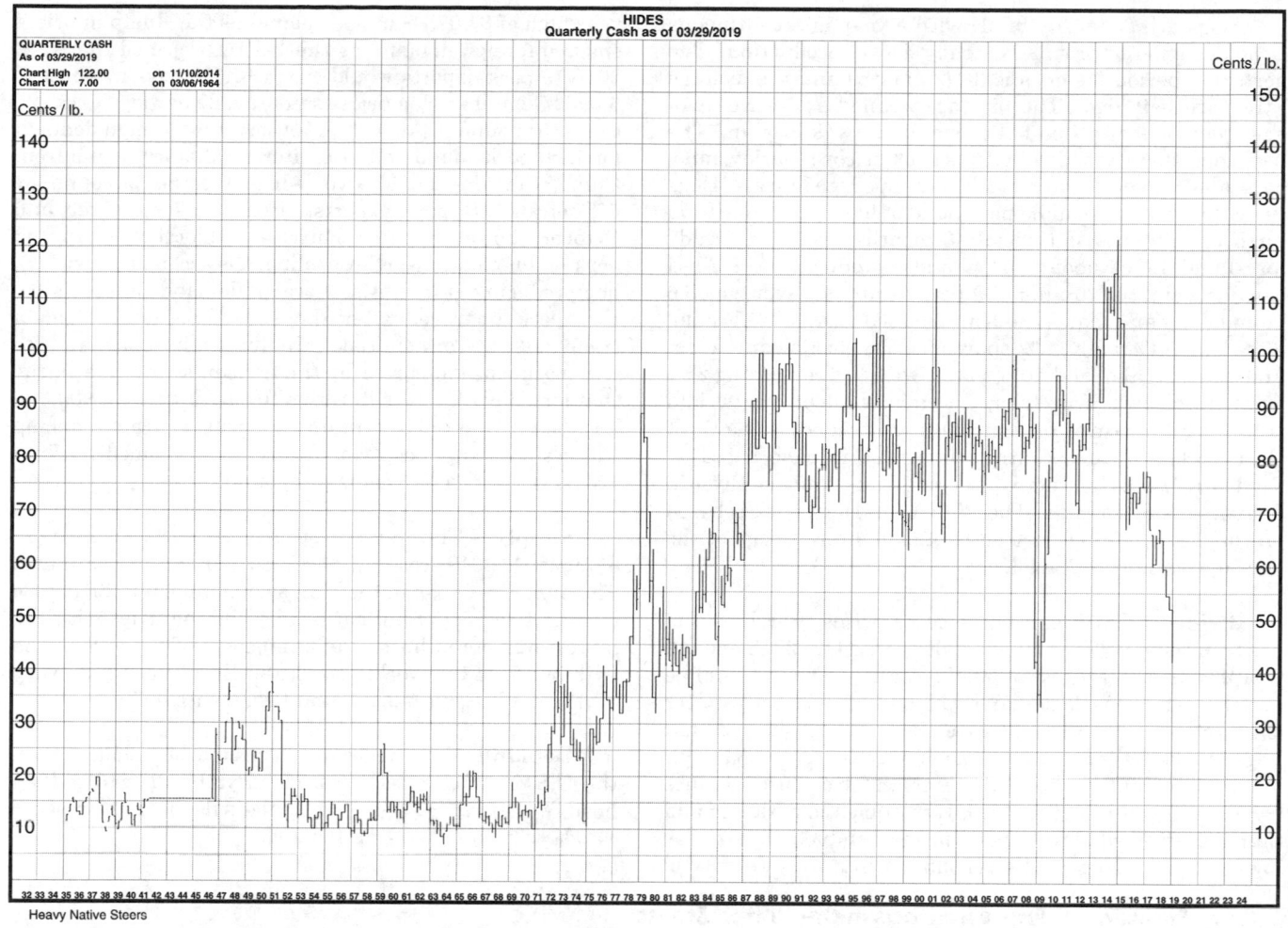

HIDES
Quarterly Cash as of 03/29/2019

QUARTERLY CASH
As of 03/29/2019
Chart High 122.00 on 11/10/2014
Chart Low 7.00 on 03/06/1964

Cents / lb.

Heavy Native Steers

Exports of Bovine Hides and Skins from the United States   In Thousands of Hides

Year	Canada	China	Hong Kong	Italy	Japan	Korea, South	Mexico	Nether lands	Taiwan	Thailand	Turkey	Vietnam	World Total
2009	345	7,851	1,160	407	189	2,379	1,510	124	1,249	574	97	374	16,661
2010	193	5,974	1,334	1,014	148	2,042	1,423	120	1,446	460	233	737	15,440
2011	179	8,245	1,141	1,703	347	3,002	1,062	84	1,194	382	241	895	18,814
2012	97	10,761	399	547	211	3,473	1,264	13	983	400	182	597	19,200
2013	62	9,319	348	228	97	2,426	1,075	15	865	173	53	257	15,173
2014	33	10,881	227	174	180	2,282	1,277	127	1,232	221	37	53	16,882
2015	57	9,835	36	172	153	2,307	1,275	163	620	281	65	147	15,260
2016	79	9,856	39	292	164	2,538	1,906	69	481	292	65	115	16,180
2017		10,540	29	192	152	2,540	1,541	33	557	881	101	51	17,095
2018[1]		8,884	12	182	177	2,483	1,670	64	374	1,496	114	30	16,058

[1] Preliminary.   Source: Foreign Agricultural Service, U.S. Department of Agriculture (FAS-USDA)

Wholesale Price of Hides (Packer Heavy Native Steers) F.O.B. Chicago   In Cents Per Pound

Year	Jan.	Feb.	Mar.	Apr.	May	June	July	Aug.	Sept.	Oct.	Nov.	Dec.	Average
2009	43.75	43.09	34.55	36.22	38.33	46.84	53.76	73.02	68.86	65.35	74.23	77.51	54.63
2010	79.31	78.31	83.78	91.83	93.38	93.69	92.86	91.36	88.90	90.68	90.44	90.90	88.79
2011	78.24	81.78	85.20	88.18	84.12	86.26	85.60	85.66	82.40	79.54	76.76	72.10	82.15
2012	72.19	78.90	83.55	84.32	85.95	83.71	84.10	85.89	83.66	86.48	88.52	91.10	84.03
2013	91.45	97.00	96.81	103.14	99.66	98.93	99.32	95.39	91.50	94.39	106.00	105.38	98.25
2014	104.76	107.00	110.62	112.00	108.90	108.14	108.59	112.00	114.43	114.37	114.29	107.16	110.19
2015	104.20	103.24	103.68	98.57	95.90	94.00	73.86	71.86	75.90	73.64	68.95	71.64	86.29
2016	72.37	70.85	73.18	72.93	71.86	72.77	73.80	73.70	73.81	75.43	77.33	75.45	73.62
2017	75.15	75.61	77.04	74.79	68.50	67.64	63.90	61.74	61.17	60.80	61.19	64.15	67.64
2018	66.17	66.24	65.89	63.86	61.36	59.98	57.52	55.63	54.92	54.17	52.10	52.00	59.15

Source: National Agricultural Statistics Service, U.S. Department of Agriculture (NASS-USDA)

Hogs

Hogs are generally bred twice a year in a continuous cycle designed to provide a steady flow of production. The gestation period for hogs is 3-1/2 months and the average litter size is 9 pigs. The pigs are weaned at 3-4 weeks of age. The pigs are then fed to maximize weight gain. The feed consists primarily of grains such as corn, barley, milo, oats, and wheat. Protein is added from oilseed meals. Hogs typically gain 3.1 pounds per pound of feed. The time from birth to slaughter is typically 6 months. Hogs are ready for slaughter at about 254 pounds, producing a dressed carcass weight of around 190 pounds and an average 88.6 pounds of lean meat. The lean meat consists of 21% ham, 20% loin, 14% belly, 3% spareribs, 7% Boston butt roast and blade steaks, and 10% picnic, with the remaining 25% going into jowl, lean trim, fat, miscellaneous cuts, and trimmings. Futures on lean hogs are traded at the CME Group. The futures contract is settled in cash based on the CME Lean Hog Index price, meaning that no physical delivery of hogs occurs. The CME Lean Hog Index is based on the 2-day average net price of slaughtered hogs at the average lean percentage level.

Prices – CME lean hog futures prices (Barchart.com electronic symbol HE) trended lower into Q2- 2018 and fell to a 2-year low in April of 50.475 cents per pound. Ample supplies amid slack demand weighed on hog prices after the U.S. Q1 Quarterly Hogs & Pigs report showed that hogs marketed for slaughter as of March 1 rose +3.3% yr/yr to 66.708 million hogs, the highest for a March 1 since the data began in 1964. Also, U.S. domestic pork demand plunged after wholesale pork prices tumbled to a 2-year low in April. Hog prices rebounded into July to a 1-1/2 year high of 84.075 cents per pound as the slump in prices spurred foreign demand as the USDA projected that U.S. 2018/19 pork exports would climb +2.1% yr/yr to a record 6.095 billion lbs. Hog prices sank to a 2-year low of 48.925 cents per pound in August on concern that foreign demand for U.S. pork would collapse after retaliatory tariffs from China, Canada and Mexico, which together account for 60% of all U.S. pork exports. Hog prices recovered into October, however, after Hurricane Florence disrupted pork production in North Carolina, the second largest U.S. hog-producing state. Also, foreign-demand prospects for U.S. pork improved after the new U.S.-Mexico-Canada trade deal was announced. Finally, Chinese demand for U.S. pork was supported by the African swine fever virus that forced pig farmers in China to cull more than 900,000 hogs in 2018 to try to contain the virus, sharply reducing China's pork supplies. Hog futures prices ended 2017 up +8.5% yr/yr at 71.775 cents per pound.

Supply – The number of hogs on world farms as of January 1, 2019, rose by +1.1% to 781.565 million head. The number of hogs in the U.S. as of January 1, 2019, rose by +3.1% to 75.750 million head. The countries with the largest number of hogs as of January 1, 2019, were China with 56.3% of the world's hogs, the European Union with 19.1%, the U.S. with 9.7%, and Brazil with 4.9%.

Demand – The federally-inspected hog slaughter in the U.S. in 2017 rose by +2.7% yr/yr to 120.516 million head, a new record high. U.S. hog sales in 2017 rose by +3.7% yr/yr to 171.422 million head.

Salient Statistics of Pigs and Hogs in the United States

	Pig Crop						Value of Hogs on Farms, Dec. 1		Hog Mar-ketings (1,000 Head)	Quantity Pro-duced (Live Wt.) (Mil. Lbs.)	Value of Pro-duction (Million$)	Hogs Slaughtered, Thousand Head --- Commercial				
	Spring[3]			Fall[4]												
	Sows Farrowed	Pig Crop	Pigs Per	Sows Farrowed	Pig Crop	Pigs Per	$ Per	Total				Federally		U.S.		U.S.
Year	--- 1,000 Head ---		Litter	--- 1,000 Head ---		Litter	Head	Million $				Inspected	Other	Total	Farm	Total
2009	6,029	57,564	9.55	5,874	56,978	9.70	83.0	5,417	150,107	31,359	12,590	112,613	1,006	113,619	114	113,732
2010	5,801	56,326	9.71	5,824	57,359	9.85	106.0	6,899	144,486	30,437	16,095	109,315	945	110,260	107	110,367
2011	5,760	57,118	9.92	5,857	58,720	10.03	----	----	145,665	31,066	20,176	109,956	904	110,860	96	110,956
2012	5,759	57,749	10.03	5,810	58,906	10.14	----	----	151,353	31,961	20,224	112,265	898	113,163	83	113,247
2013	5,595	57,020	10.19	5,670	58,115	10.25	----	----	154,923	32,620	21,666	111,248	829	112,077	84	112,161
2014	5,573	53,821	9.66	5,985	61,035	10.20	----	----	149,069	32,182	24,222	106,123	753	106,876	82	106,958
2015	5,749	59,219	10.30	5,946	62,191	10.46	----	----	159,945	35,886	18,877	114,616	811	115,427	87	115,514
2016	5,896	61,236	10.39	6,103	64,703	10.60	----	----	165,321	35,951	17,383	117,388	831	118,219	84	118,303
2017[1]	6,007	63,025	10.49	6,209	66,402	10.69	----	----	171,422	37,055	19,218	120,517	801	121,317	73	121,390
2018[2]	6,134	65,042	10.60	6,343	68,133	10.74	----	----								

[1] Preliminary. [2] Estimate. [3] December-May. [4] June-November. *Source: Economic Research Service, U.S. Department of Agriculture (ERS-USDA)*

World Hog Numbers in Specified Countries as of January 1   In Thousands of Head

Year	Australia	Belarus	Brazil	Canada	China	European Union	Japan	Korea, South	Mexico	Russia	Ukraine	United States	World Total
2010	2,302	3,782	35,122	12,465	469,960	152,780	10,000	8,721	8,979	17,236	7,577	64,687	793,611
2011	2,289	3,887	36,652	12,615	464,600	152,361	9,768	8,449	9,007	17,231	7,960	64,725	789,544
2012	2,285	3,989	38,336	12,770	468,627	149,809	9,735	8,171	9,276	17,258	7,373	66,259	793,888
2013	2,138	4,243	38,577	12,745	475,922	146,982	9,685	9,916	9,510	18,816	7,577	66,224	802,335
2014	2,098	3,267	38,844	12,835	474,113	146,172	9,537	9,912	9,775	19,081	7,922	64,775	798,331
2015	2,308	2,925	39,395	13,180	465,830	148,341	9,440	10,090	9,788	19,405	7,492	67,776	795,970
2016	2,272	3,205	39,422	13,630	451,130	148,716	9,313	10,187	10,043	21,345	7,240	68,919	785,422
2017	----	3,145	39,215	13,935	435,040	147,188	9,346	11,487	10,229	21,888	6,816	71,545	769,834
2018[1]	----	3,156	38,829	14,250	433,250	150,000	9,280	11,273	10,410	23,058	6,236	73,445	773,187
2019[2]	----	3,100	38,235	14,200	440,000	148,900	9,260	11,800	10,540	23,850	5,930	75,750	781,565

[1] Preliminary.   [2] Forecast.   *Source: Foreign Agricultural Service, U.S. Department of Agriculture (FAS-USDA)*

Hogs and Pigs on Farms in the United States on December 1   In Thousands of Head

Year	Georgia	Illinois	Indiana	Iowa	Kansas	Minne-sota	Missouri	Neb-raska	North Carolina	Ohio	South Dakota	Wis-consin	U.S. Total
2009	195	4,250	3,600	19,000	1,810	7,200	3,100	3,100	9,600	2,010	1,190	350	64,887
2010	160	4,400	3,650	19,100	1,820	7,700	2,900	3,150	9,000	2,040	1,290	340	64,925
2011	155	4,650	3,800	20,000	1,890	7,800	2,750	3,150	8,900	2,200	1,400	340	66,361
2012	155	4,600	3,800	20,600	1,900	7,650	2,750	3,000	9,000	2,050	1,200	320	66,374
2013	141	4,550	3,650	20,200	1,750	7,800	2,750	3,050	8,500	2,200	1,200	295	64,775
2014	155	4,700	3,700	21,300	1,840	8,100	2,850	3,200	8,800	2,230	1,270	310	67,776
2015	160	5,100	3,850	20,900	1,940	8,100	3,050	3,300	8,900	2,500	1,360	320	68,919
2016	65	5,100	4,100	22,200	1,910	8,500	3,100	3,400	9,300	2,700	1,450	335	71,545
2017	80	5,400	4,000	22,800	2,110	8,500	3,400	3,600	9,000	2,700	1,560	305	73,145
2018[1]	67	5,300	4,200	23,300	2,050	8,900	3,550	3,500	9,100	2,550	1,740	325	74,550

[1] Preliminary.   *Source: National Agricultural Statistics Service, U.S. Department of Agriculture (NASS-USDA)*

Cold Storage Holdings of Frozen Pork[2] in the United States, on First of Month   In Thousands of Pounds

Year	Jan.	Feb.	Mar.	Apr.	May	June	July	Aug.	Sept.	Oct.	Nov.	Dec.
2009	555,642	606,936	624,477	594,127	612,290	584,544	577,914	539,700	530,148	528,681	516,300	482,816
2010	471,125	492,287	515,911	513,066	483,710	446,049	412,983	391,193	388,292	424,322	481,653	467,950
2011	475,829	538,754	574,236	574,398	549,279	548,322	495,064	454,337	442,903	491,910	488,721	495,117
2012	484,497	585,307	622,673	610,318	659,726	636,017	592,880	549,621	585,796	630,446	603,502	558,688
2013	551,510	606,425	633,399	647,784	700,977	658,947	565,063	543,668	548,975	567,827	565,020	546,238
2014	554,328	618,746	654,712	575,539	583,891	575,818	537,447	533,259	543,666	550,622	533,076	492,752
2015	503,792	595,673	686,063	672,431	701,083	655,301	634,525	633,214	653,760	655,930	603,454	560,915
2016	545,696	625,246	628,948	613,803	637,320	616,124	586,479	598,592	608,955	642,303	599,010	518,813
2017	475,387	524,215	567,855	545,463	590,324	588,216	559,010	554,854	575,698	618,563	598,374	502,324
2018[1]	490,047	580,714	609,780	611,003	634,720	623,725	561,879	549,648	581,511	589,402	570,894	507,557

[1] Preliminary. [2] Excludes lard.   *Source: Economic Research Service, U.S. Department of Agriculture (ERS-USDA)*

Cold Storage Holdings of Frozen Pork Belly in the United States, on First of Month   In Thousands of Pounds

Year	Jan.	Feb.	Mar.	Apr	May	June	July	Aug.	Sept.	Oct.	Nov.	Dec.
2009	51,593	69,166	75,668	72,940	79,543	78,801	76,333	60,238	48,958	38,481	37,127	44,638
2010	56,764	53,584	55,552	58,762	49,656	44,201	35,369	21,380	7,202	4,817	23,248	37,696
2011	50,677	51,326	50,900	52,487	53,185	57,123	48,645	29,503	15,162	9,297	8,734	26,599
2012	41,469	53,685	61,577	66,031	74,927	65,648	49,034	27,962	14,210	15,668	18,720	23,837
2013	36,037	36,425	42,976	51,473	56,352	54,829	42,033	28,177	19,335	23,491	26,674	48,298
2014	80,367	87,171	87,675	79,721	83,579	85,888	83,936	64,644	45,562	34,311	29,006	35,894
2015	47,455	53,507	67,794	68,297	70,412	64,805	44,432	23,634	13,738	10,872	17,853	41,160
2016	53,392	60,698	61,433	65,028	72,592	77,683	62,921	50,733	32,053	25,084	20,386	18,526
2017	17,986	13,995	16,153	20,570	33,536	31,589	22,291	17,602	19,213	20,897	32,268	35,164
2018[1]	39,620	43,810	49,012	59,202	64,563	61,234	53,279	40,654	34,805	30,353	26,690	36,859

[1] Preliminary.   *Source: National Agricultural Statistics Service, U.S. Department of Agriculture (NASS-USDA)*

Hog-Corn Price Ratio[2] in the United States   In Bushels

Year	Jan.	Feb.	Mar.	Apr.	May	June	July	Aug.	Sept.	Oct.	Nov.	Dec.	Average
2009	9.8	11.3	11.4	11.4	11.3	10.8	12.0	11.2	11.6	10.5	11.0	12.5	11.2
2010	13.2	13.8	14.7	16.6	17.9	17.1	16.8	16.8	15.0	12.3	10.5	10.9	14.6
2011	11.3	10.9	11.4	10.7	10.9	10.9	11.3	11.0	10.5	12.0	11.0	10.8	11.1
2012	10.5	10.4	10.3	9.9	9.9	11.0	10.1	8.8	8.1	9.1	8.7	9.1	9.7
2013	9.2	9.2	8.3	8.9	9.8	10.7	11.2	11.9	13.1	14.8	14.6	13.9	11.3
2014	13.8	15.1	18.1	18.9	17.6	18.8	23.0	22.9	21.7	21.6	18.5	17.0	18.9
2015	15.0	13.3	13.2	13.1	16.2	16.7	15.4	16.0	14.8	15.1	12.8	11.7	14.4
2016	11.9	13.9	14.0	14.3	15.5	15.9	16.5	16.4	14.8	12.7	12.0	13.0	14.2
2017	14.1	15.8	15.2	14.1	15.5	18.1	19.3	18.8	15.0	14.5	15.9	15.0	15.9
2018[1]	16.0	16.2	14.2	12.7	14.0	16.5	16.9	13.2	12.7	14.8	13.5	12.3	14.4

[1] Preliminary.   [2] Bushels of corn equal in value to 100 pounds of hog, live weight.   *Source: Economic Research Service, U.S. Department of Agriculture (ERS-USDA)*

HOGS

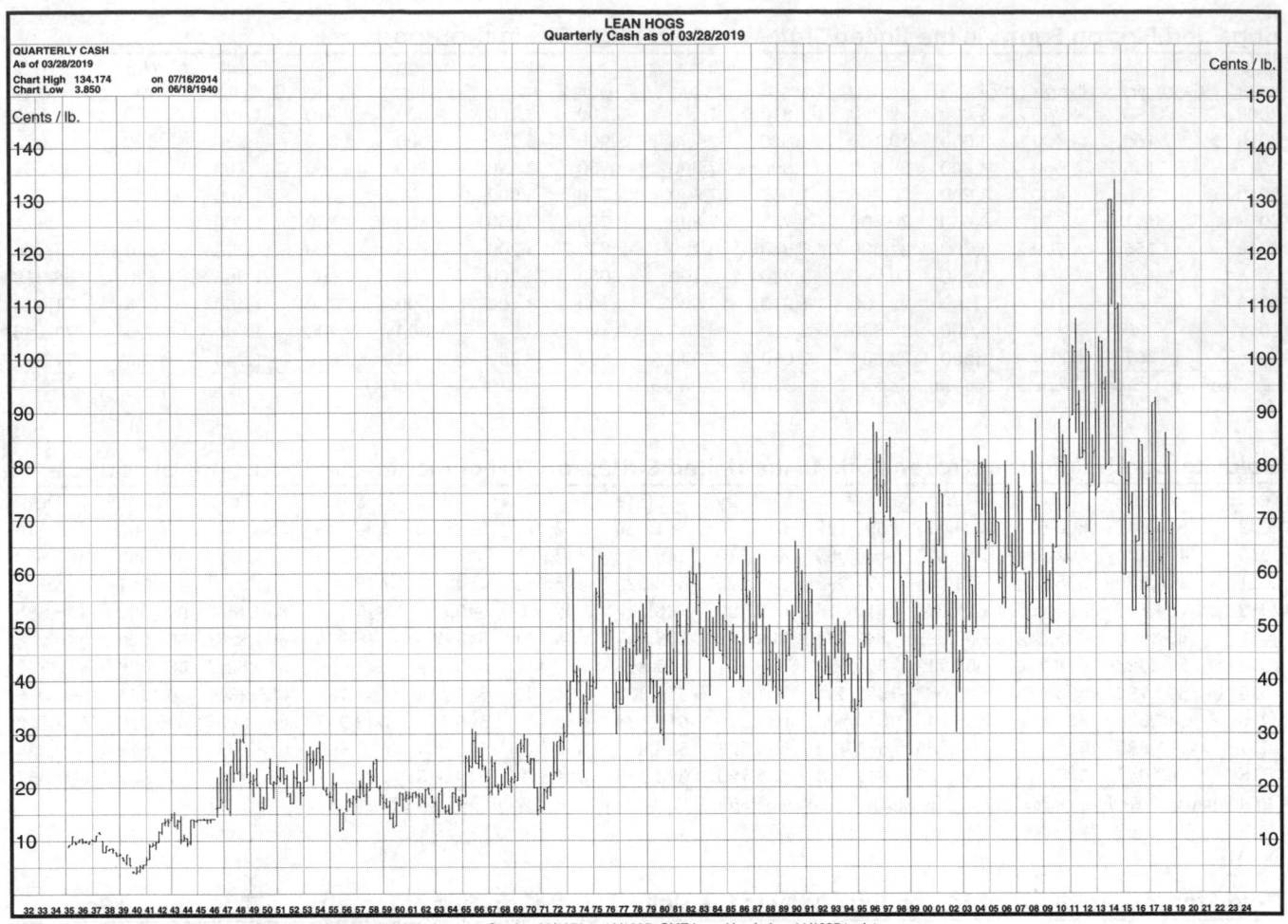

QUARTERLY CASH
As of 03/28/2019
Chart High 134.174 on 07/16/2014
Chart Low 3.850 on 06/18/1940

Cents / lb.

Cents / lb.

Top, Chicago: to 03/1968; Farrowing, Chicago: 04/1968 to 05/1970; Average, Omaha: 05/1970 to 10/1995; CME Lean Hog Index: 11/1995 to date.

Average Price of Hogs, National Base 51-52% lean   In Dollars Per Hundred Pounds (Cwt.)

Year	Jan.	Feb.	Mar.	Apr.	May	June	July	Aug.	Sept.	Oct.	Nov.	Dec.	Average
2009	41.43	42.43	42.47	42.83	43.18	42.21	42.74	36.56	37.41	37.65	40.12	45.82	41.24
2010	49.81	48.98	52.43	57.43	63.13	58.23	58.25	61.49	60.64	52.41	47.00	50.92	55.06
2011	55.56	61.62	62.63	68.10	68.41	69.88	71.65	76.09	65.45	68.44	63.40	62.14	66.11
2012	62.18	63.94	61.86	58.99	58.51	67.87	69.93	63.51	50.85	59.06	57.67	59.16	61.13
2013	61.22	61.59	54.28	57.71	66.03	72.65	72.88	71.03	67.84	64.95	60.21	58.16	64.05
2014	58.36	63.88	83.82	89.09	81.76	85.35	95.17	80.39	74.36	75.24	63.76	61.24	76.03
2015	54.05	45.75	45.61	45.13	57.23	57.25	56.21	55.91	51.64	52.68	42.01	39.30	50.23
2016	40.34	46.61	46.95	47.96	54.75	58.42	56.28	48.12	43.36	37.07	34.45	39.45	46.15
2017	45.60	53.02	50.56	44.04	50.46	60.61	65.15	57.99	43.64	43.75	46.46	44.23	50.46
2018[1]	50.40	51.49	45.46	39.88	46.86	56.99	55.38	37.88	38.43	47.54	42.19	38.58	45.92

[1] Preliminary.   Source: Economic Research Service, U.S. Department of Agriculture (ERS-USDA)

Average Price Received by Farmers for Hogs in the United States   In Cents Per Pound

Year	Jan.	Feb.	Mar.	Apr.	May	June	July	Aug.	Sept.	Oct.	Nov.	Dec.	Average
2009	42.8	43.8	43.9	44.0	44.6	43.3	43.3	37.3	37.7	37.8	40.3	45.0	42.0
2010	48.4	48.9	52.1	56.5	62.2	58.2	58.5	58.2	61.0	53.3	47.8	52.3	54.8
2011	55.8	61.4	62.9	67.8	68.6	69.7	71.7	75.8	67.1	68.7	64.4	63.5	66.5
2012	63.5	65.5	65.2	62.8	62.8	70.2	72.1	66.9	55.7	62.0	61.1	62.4	64.2
2013	63.8	64.5	59.2	61.8	68.6	74.4	75.8	74.2	70.7	68.5	63.6	61.5	67.2
2014	61.2	65.5	81.9	88.8	82.8	84.8	93.3	83.2	75.7	77.0	66.7	64.3	77.1
2015	57.4	50.4	50.3	49.0	58.9	59.9	58.7	59.0	54.5	55.5	45.9	42.8	53.5
2016	43.6	49.6	50.0	51.0	57.2	60.6	59.4	52.6	47.8	41.7	39.0	43.1	49.6
2017	48.1	54.4	53.0	48.4	53.6	62.1	67.3	61.5	48.9	47.3	50.0	48.6	53.6
2018[1]	52.5	54.6	50.0	45.3	51.5	59.1	58.6	44.3	43.2	50.3	46.2	43.4	49.9

[1] Preliminary.   Source: Economic Research Service, U.S. Department of Agriculture (ERS-USDA)

Quarterly Hogs and Pigs Report in the United States, 10 States   In Thousands of Head

Year[2]	Inventory[3]	Breeding[3]	Market[3]	Farrowings	Pig Crop	Year[2]	Inventory[3]	Breeding[3]	Market[3]	Farrowings	Pig Crop
2009	67,148	6,062	61,087	11,903	114,542	2014	64,775	5,757	59,018	11,558	114,856
I	67,148	6,062	61,087	3,011	28,552	I	64,775	5,757	59,018	2,763	26,326
II	65,819	5,992	59,828	3,018	29,012	II	61,494	5,851	55,643	2,810	27,495
III	66,809	5,968	60,842	2,959	28,718	III	61,568	5,855	55,713	2,991	30,402
IV	66,716	5,875	60,842	2,915	28,260	IV	65,979	5,920	60,059	2,994	30,633
2010	64,887	5,850	59,037	11,626	113,685	2015	67,776	5,939	61,838	11,695	121,411
I	64,887	5,850	59,037	2,872	27,596	I	67,776	5,939	61,838	2,895	29,627
II	63,568	5,760	57,808	2,929	28,730	II	67,399	5,982	61,418	2,854	29,593
III	64,650	5,788	58,862	2,944	28,871	III	67,165	5,926	61,240	3,017	31,343
IV	65,971	5,770	60,201	2,881	28,488	IV	69,185	5,986	63,200	2,929	30,848
2011	64,625	5,778	59,147	11,616	115,838	2016	68,919	6,002	62,917	11,998	125,939
I	64,625	5,778	59,147	2,843	27,866	I	68,919	6,002	62,917	2,927	30,139
II	63,684	5,788	57,896	2,917	29,252	II	68,124	5,980	62,144	2,968	31,097
III	65,320	5,803	59,517	2,927	29,355	III	69,281	5,979	63,302	3,057	32,331
IV	67,234	5,806	61,428	2,929	29,365	IV	71,786	6,016	65,770	3,046	32,372
2012	66,361	5,803	60,558	11,567	116,655	2017	71,545	6,110	65,435	12,217	129,429
I	66,361	5,803	60,558	2,813	28,037	I	71,545	6,110	65,435	2,990	31,187
II	64,787	5,820	58,967	2,945	29,712	II	70,916	6,098	64,818	3,018	31,839
III	66,609	5,862	60,747	2,921	29,587	III	71,210	6,109	65,101	3,106	33,075
IV	68,172	5,788	62,384	2,888	29,319	IV	73,309	6,117	67,192	3,103	33,328
2013	66,374	5,819	60,555	11,264	115,135	2018[1]	73,145	6,179	66,966	12,477	133,176
I	66,374	5,819	60,555	2,788	28,099	I	73,145	6,179	66,966	3,034	32,101
II	65,071	5,834	59,237	2,806	28,921	II	72,748	6,210	66,538	3,100	32,942
III	65,188	5,884	59,304	2,890	29,862	III	72,866	6,320	66,546	3,185	34,155
IV	66,906	5,816	61,090	2,780	28,253	IV	74,941	6,330	68,611	3,158	33,978

[1] Preliminary.   [2] Quarters are Dec. preceding year-Feb.(I), Mar.-May(II), June-Aug.(III) and Sept.-Nov.(IV).
[3] Beginning of period.   Source: National Agricultural Statistics Service, U.S. Department of Agriculture (NASS-USDA)

Federally Inspected Hog Slaughter in the United States   In Thousands of Head

Year	Jan.	Feb.	Mar.	Apr.	May	June	July	Aug.	Sept.	Oct.	Nov.	Dec.	Total
2009	9,846	8,840	9,574	9,353	8,379	9,101	9,062	9,250	9,848	10,230	9,385	9,742	112,613
2010	8,838	8,619	9,947	8,980	7,897	8,968	8,396	9,030	9,257	9,651	9,895	9,838	109,315
2011	9,036	8,440	9,795	8,559	8,470	8,866	8,089	9,440	9,603	9,822	9,968	9,868	109,956
2012	9,467	8,975	9,454	8,757	9,212	8,481	8,493	9,858	9,376	10,770	10,030	9,393	112,265
2013	9,885	8,526	9,252	9,292	9,147	8,132	9,003	9,474	8,952	10,341	9,579	9,665	111,248
2014	9,726	8,609	8,614	8,794	8,561	8,040	8,394	8,199	8,762	9,880	8,754	9,788	106,123
2015	9,698	9,018	9,818	9,612	8,686	9,364	9,332	9,272	9,652	10,173	9,700	10,292	114,616
2016	9,682	9,364	10,015	9,303	9,114	9,505	8,696	10,308	10,096	10,369	10,539	10,398	117,388
2017	10,059	9,310	10,611	9,282	9,886	9,809	8,953	10,583	10,213	10,922	10,487	10,400	120,517
2018[1]	10,653	9,578	10,661	9,939	10,163	9,553	9,532	11,081	9,583	11,571	10,982	10,403	123,696

[1] Preliminary.   Source: National Agricultural Statistics Service, U.S. Department of Agriculture (NASS-USDA)

Average Live Weight of all Hogs Slaughtered Under Federal Inspection   In Pounds Per Head

Year	Jan.	Feb.	Mar.	Apr.	May	June	July	Aug.	Sept.	Oct.	Nov.	Dec.	Average
2009	272	272	272	272	272	270	268	268	270	272	272	270	271
2010	272	271	272	273	273	271	269	267	271	276	278	278	273
2011	278	278	278	277	276	273	268	266	271	276	279	278	275
2012	279	278	279	279	277	274	269	269	271	274	276	276	275
2013	277	277	277	277	276	274	271	271	273	279	283	283	277
2014	284	283	285	287	287	285	284	283	283	286	287	287	285
2015	287	285	285	285	284	282	280	278	280	284	286	285	283
2016	286	284	284	285	283	281	278	276	280	282	283	283	282
2017	285	284	284	285	282	279	277	278	282	283	286	286	283
2018[1]	286	286	287	287	285	280	277	278	280	283	286	286	283

[1] Preliminary.   Source: National Agricultural Statistics Service, U.S. Department of Agriculture (NASS-USDA)

HOGS

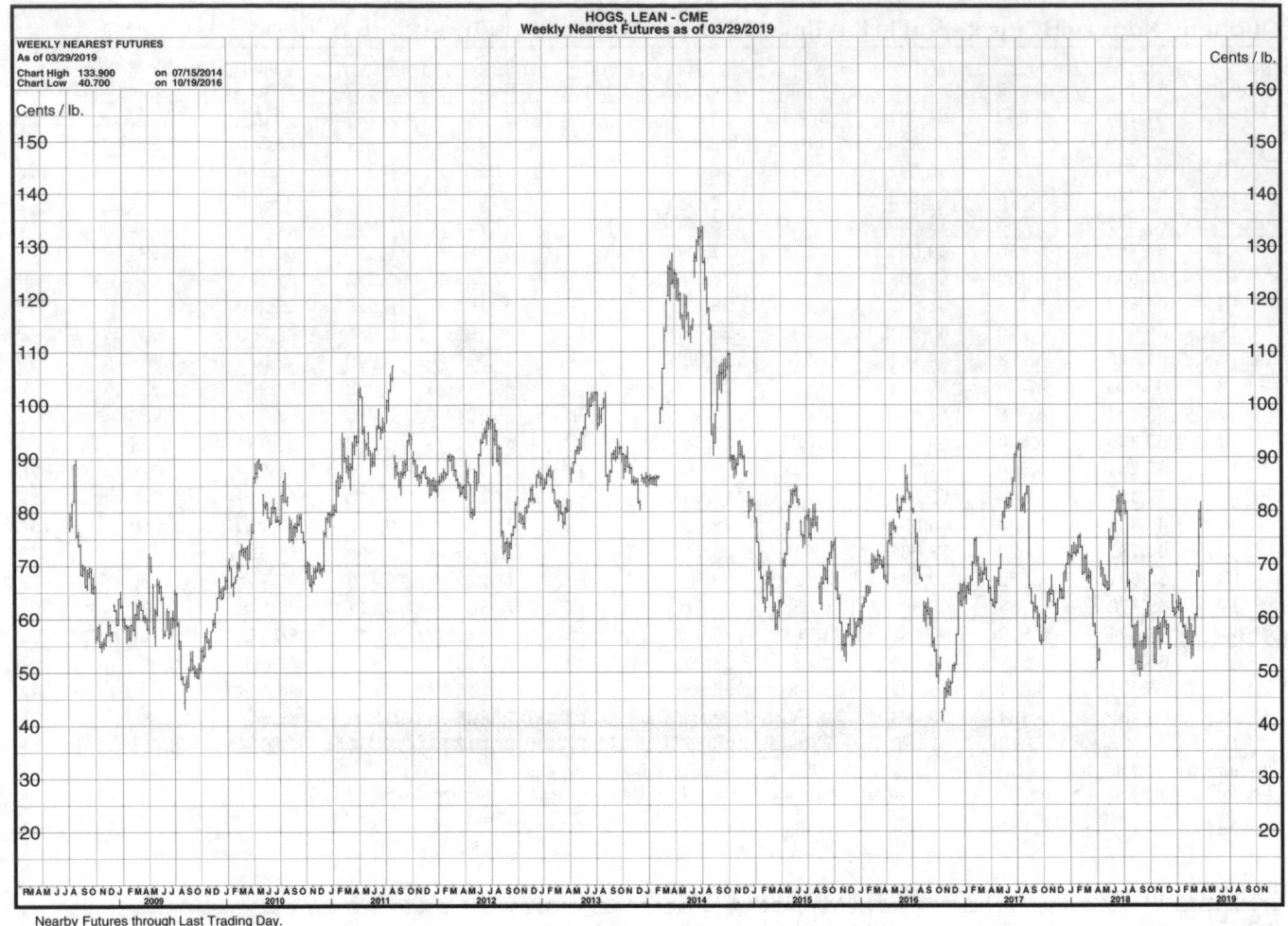

Nearby Futures through Last Trading Day.

Volume of Trading of Lean Hog Futures in Chicago   In Contracts

Year	Jan.	Feb.	Mar.	Apr.	May	June	July	Aug.	Sept.	Oct.	Nov.	Dec.	Total
2009	614,928	390,054	593,621	503,180	620,260	727,565	644,070	510,721	657,827	540,591	590,062	426,182	6,819,061
2010	672,191	464,868	706,267	567,410	740,462	803,035	763,584	627,870	808,561	683,542	753,457	485,288	8,076,535
2011	879,859	660,332	925,083	660,983	881,184	991,400	900,953	770,608	1,047,769	785,722	857,709	608,359	9,969,961
2012	908,368	715,081	1,093,713	882,705	1,312,891	1,189,274	1,082,496	819,332	979,379	869,169	949,221	660,263	11,461,892
2013	999,025	807,974	1,017,485	832,949	1,100,627	1,151,018	1,076,200	778,067	1,155,621	861,514	833,759	662,790	11,277,029
2014	940,059	880,082	1,402,273	760,629	892,977	937,458	1,046,618	818,841	1,000,387	674,141	707,984	595,495	10,656,944
2015	883,049	743,293	961,823	716,421	830,092	962,100	971,169	640,789	745,310	717,480	836,679	567,677	9,575,882
2016	665,222	645,429	797,006	589,363	726,478	937,796	826,532	645,478	849,779	762,690	915,391	833,836	9,195,000
2017	847,298	742,428	963,173	690,533	1,012,116	1,120,066	981,241	976,007	1,124,085	955,604	1,098,220	731,250	11,242,021
2018	992,415	936,449	1,149,911	962,589	1,236,082	1,312,538	1,250,892	1,308,397	1,241,177	1,140,731	1,267,228	753,302	13,551,711

Contract size = 40,000 lbs.   *Source: Chicago Mercantile Exchange (CME)*

Average Open Interest of Lean Hog Futures in Chicago   In Contracts

Year	Jan.	Feb.	Mar.	Apr.	May	June	July	Aug.	Sept.	Oct.	Nov.	Dec.
2009	137,693	122,594	126,377	134,363	143,493	135,606	131,683	130,844	143,952	152,820	164,819	174,739
2010	194,351	179,300	197,407	217,304	217,779	190,933	197,940	214,535	230,240	209,159	198,160	200,932
2011	218,818	243,878	226,344	233,168	222,193	221,633	242,921	253,224	247,476	273,568	257,632	246,758
2012	243,120	256,724	262,970	259,367	268,655	258,585	231,982	224,131	237,138	219,733	230,592	242,093
2013	244,228	226,691	235,834	229,097	247,125	279,932	297,930	306,652	326,192	302,314	282,782	263,509
2014	266,366	282,321	288,484	265,981	256,474	248,869	248,878	234,967	237,877	236,417	230,578	216,735
2015	208,643	192,716	208,128	216,998	219,669	221,626	210,767	196,682	196,033	198,965	204,049	173,053
2016	168,096	191,458	218,393	224,392	233,337	255,818	234,949	212,182	215,947	227,447	225,542	199,554
2017	210,582	227,286	214,122	207,945	223,068	251,117	272,856	258,984	256,269	253,357	260,573	239,469
2018	246,345	232,492	230,504	241,846	244,654	231,674	233,594	230,352	222,734	225,483	227,359	207,286

Contract size = 40,000 lbs.   *Source: Chicago Mercantile Exchange (CME)*

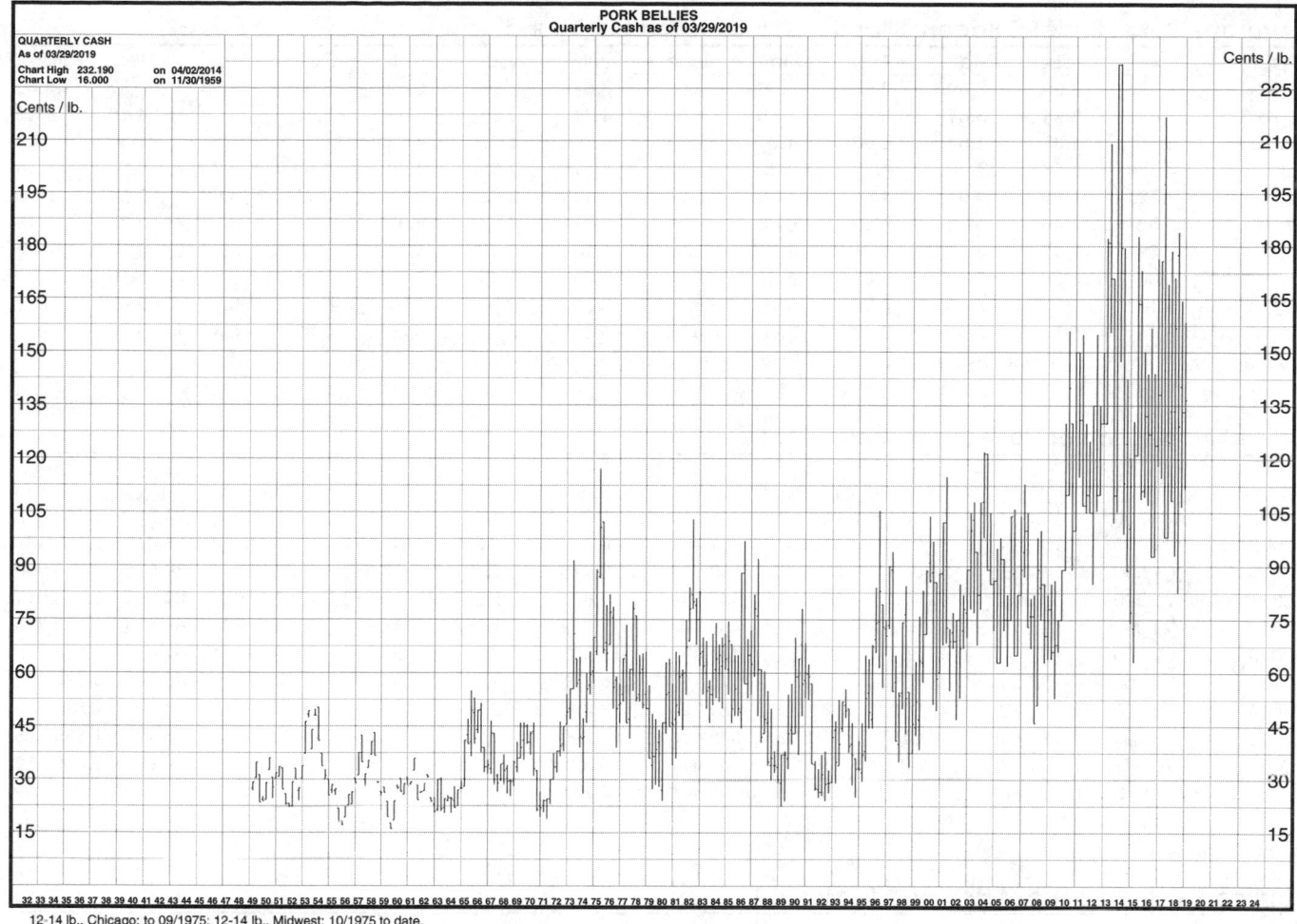

PORK BELLIES
Quarterly Cash as of 03/29/2019

QUARTERLY CASH
As of 03/29/2019
Chart High 232.190 on 04/02/2014
Chart Low 16.000 on 11/30/1959

12-14 lb., Chicago: to 09/1975; 12-14 lb., Midwest: 10/1975 to date.

Average Price of Pork Bellies (12-14 lbs.), Central, U.S.   In Cents Per Pound

Year	Jan.	Feb.	Mar.	Apr.	May	June	July	Aug.	Sept.	Oct.	Nov.	Dec.	Average
2009	69.88	71.00	65.25	77.50	57.00	50.00	80.36	42.25	45.83	47.33	60.50	64.00	60.91
2010	82.00	NA	NA	106.25	NA	NA	NA	122.50	88.00	76.67	NA	NA	95.08
2011	NA	NA	NA	144.17	NA	NA	121.00	135.09	NA	111.00	91.33	NA	120.52
2012	96.50	NA	90.00	80.00	NA	NA	NA	NA	NA	NA	NA	NA	88.83
2013	NA	NA	NA	151.44	161.60	175.55	163.12	177.24	149.62	134.99	128.41	127.35	152.15
2014	124.07	137.58	176.77	191.73	156.63	173.03	174.29	139.46	120.57	127.81	111.33	105.57	144.90
2015	122.30	102.97	81.14	75.33	82.51	108.15	NA	184.67	166.82	165.54	127.35	114.96	121.07
2016	128.18	NA	NA	134.91	119.13	130.09	146.67	115.14	96.21	127.29	120.69	121.10	123.94
2017	136.39	NA	158.66	136.79	139.18	176.76	216.28	170.18	116.74	107.75	135.04	142.64	148.76
2018[1]	137.69	157.64	133.63	111.96	110.14	157.22	NA	106.71	109.96	NA	181.14	131.26	133.73

[1] Preliminary.   *Source: Economic Research Service, U.S. Department of Agriculture (ERS-USDA)*

Average Price of Pork Loins (12-14 lbs.)[2], Central, U.S.   In Cents Per Pound

Year	Jan.	Feb.	Mar.	Apr.	May	June	July	Aug.	Sept.	Oct.	Nov.	Dec.	Average
2009	94.96	94.83	90.46	92.10	97.73	91.58	101.03	90.33	89.08	85.98	82.63	103.03	92.81
2010	110.94	104.08	108.14	122.64	137.62	114.17	118.47	132.73	120.09	110.36	104.06	108.22	115.96
2011	119.02	119.98	123.08	131.20	138.84	136.21	139.57	149.33	131.78	131.07	116.40	117.61	129.51
2012	116.21	118.22	123.09	119.81	128.27	149.14	127.43	119.00	108.86	117.45	105.20	105.56	119.85
2013	107.12	111.73	108.86	106.77	120.28	138.64	129.84	128.96	116.92	115.78	107.25	106.24	116.53
2014	115.27	128.19	165.28	147.55	135.39	153.75	167.79	150.01	153.69	152.92	117.50	115.82	141.93
2015	108.25	99.88	100.25	101.55	124.08	112.35	111.13	107.61	102.46	103.50	88.44	85.76	103.77
2016	100.14	93.52	90.52	89.61	111.77	112.56	104.71	98.27	110.10	89.52	76.73	85.90	96.95
2017	91.73	90.66	99.36	88.58	106.12	118.21	118.69	100.58	94.97	89.85	85.62	82.96	97.28
2018[1]	83.63	89.53	88.98	84.45	96.25	101.34	98.72	98.35	107.17	92.36	98.72	75.40	92.91

[1] Preliminary.   *Source: Economic Research Service, U.S. Department of Agriculture (ERS-USDA)*

HOGS

Average Retail Price of Bacon, Sliced   In U.S. Dollars Per Pound

Year	Jan.	Feb.	Mar.	Apr.	May	June	July	Aug.	Sept.	Oct.	Nov.	Dec.	Average
2009	3.73	3.62	3.59	3.58	3.66	3.62	3.64	3.59	3.59	3.60	3.50	3.57	3.61
2010	3.63	3.64	3.67	3.64	3.86	4.05	4.21	4.35	4.57	4.77	4.70	4.16	4.11
2011	4.25	4.37	4.54	4.66	4.77	4.84	4.76	4.77	4.82	4.59	4.64	4.55	4.63
2012	4.57	4.66	4.60	4.53	4.39	4.33	4.37	4.61	4.69	4.66	4.64	4.64	4.56
2013	4.72	4.83	4.91	4.89	5.09	5.33	5.49	5.62	5.68	5.71	5.62	5.54	5.29
2014	5.56	5.46	5.55	5.69	6.05	6.11	6.01	6.07	5.95	5.76	5.57	5.53	5.78
2015	5.59	5.47	5.37	5.21	4.94	5.06	5.18	5.41	5.73	5.90	5.85	5.73	5.45
2016	5.66	5.39	5.49	5.61	5.55	5.37	5.45	5.45	5.48	5.38	5.11	5.10	5.42
2017	5.18	5.33	5.75	5.78	5.70	5.67	5.82	6.24	6.37	6.07	5.71	5.63	5.77
2018[1]	5.65	5.53	5.53	5.42	5.45	5.25	5.42	5.58	5.50	5.37	5.39	5.50	5.47

[1] Preliminary.   Source: Economic Research Service, U.S. Department of Agriculture (ERS-USDA)

World Production of Honey   In Metric Tons

Year	Argentina	Australia	Brazil	Canada	China	Germany	Japan	Mexico	Russia	United States	World Total
2008	72,000	17,600	37,836	30,910	407,219	15,727	2,791	59,682	57,440	74,293	1,517,882
2009	62,000	15,663	39,030	33,510	407,367	16,460	2,656	56,071	53,598	66,413	1,505,462
2010	59,000	14,418	38,073	38,900	409,149	23,178	2,639	55,684	51,535	80,042	1,533,900
2011	72,000	10,000	41,793	38,020	446,089	25,831	2,684	57,783	60,010	67,294	1,615,914
2012	76,000	12,006	33,932	43,230	462,203	17,869	2,763	58,602	64,898	64,544	1,650,335
2013	67,500	13,864	35,365	36,420	461,431	18,953	2,766	56,907	68,446	67,812	1,722,109
2014	60,000	13,539	38,481	40,750	474,786	20,195	2,839	60,624	74,868	80,862	1,783,614
2015	52,600	13,212	37,859	39,630	484,726	23,398	2,865	61,881	67,736	71,008	1,824,828
2016	68,123	12,884	39,619	39,212	562,875	21,600	2,774	55,358	69,764	73,429	1,859,228
2017[1]	76,379	12,557	41,594	39,180	551,476	20,392	2,706	51,066	65,678	66,968	1,860,712

[1] Preliminary.   Source: Food and Agricultural Organization of the United Nations (FAO)

United States Imports of Honey   In Metric Tons

Year	Argentina	Brazil	Canada	India	Mexico	New Zealand	Taiwan	Thailand	Turkey	Ukraine	Uruguay	Vietnam	World Total
2008	10,043	13,598	17,305	13,648	1,411	650	3,983	956	54	84	227	19,378	104,984
2009	10,899	17,709	8,302	13,137	1,625	1,022	5,576	1,847	73	635	19	17,430	95,475
2010	17,414	10,036	11,053	18,462	3,325	1,048	1,755	1,699	37	440	852	20,738	113,930
2011	33,502	14,981	7,148	26,912	2,846	965	903	1,637	183	453	7,083	27,826	130,764
2012	42,482	11,303	15,971	21,454	6,179	966	1,324	258	1,073	1,302	10,877	20,700	141,016
2013	44,221	11,677	9,385	25,867	5,648	1,234	1,827	846	1,897	3,308	8,710	33,586	153,102
2014	36,888	19,249	5,612	20,290	7,254	1,625	2,523	3,458	2,581	8,876	5,362	47,107	165,777
2015	27,081	15,440	8,234	36,123	5,364	1,992	4,442	10,753	5,196	11,411	7,243	36,973	175,244
2016	34,708	19,062	13,487	29,364	4,557	1,858	1,662	4,238	1,852	11,086	1,767	38,514	166,477
2017[1]	35,378	24,031	15,786	45,170	4,783	----	1,649	4,490	2,396	19,362	4,025	36,288	203,069

[1] Preliminary.   Source: Foreign Agricultural Service, U.S. Department of Agriculture (FAS-USDA)

Production of Honey in the United States   In Thousands of Pounds

Year	California	Florida	Georgia	Idaho	Louisiana	Michigan	Minnesota	Montana	North Dakota	South Dakota	Texas	Wisconsin	U.S. Total
2009	11,715	11,560	2,665	4,738	3,811	3,960	7,930	10,220	34,650	17,820	5,607	3,780	146,416
2010	27,470	13,800	2,530	2,619	2,880	4,118	8,448	11,618	46,410	15,370	7,200	4,096	176,462
2011	17,760	10,980	2,795	3,132	2,772	4,736	6,360	13,340	32,660	16,500	4,524	3,591	148,357
2012	11,550	12,352	3,009	2,944	3,526	4,161	8,375	7,540	33,120	16,380	4,784	4,140	142,296
2013	10,890	13,420	3,350	2,656	4,900	4,675	7,540	14,946	33,120	14,840	6,254	3,540	149,499
2014	12,480	14,700	4,526	3,400	4,032	5,733	7,920	14,256	42,140	24,360	9,048	2,862	178,270
2015	8,250	11,880	2,760	2,848	4,356	5,220	8,296	12,118	36,260	19,140	8,316	3,484	156,544
2016	11,160	10,750	3,744	3,298	4,300	5,340	7,316	12,243	37,830	19,880	9,310	3,348	161,882
2017[1]	13,735	8,815	3,168	4,180	3,483	3,915	7,812	10,440	33,670	14,535	7,920	2,968	147,638
2018[1]	Report	delayed											

[1] Preliminary.   Source: National Agricultural Statistics Service, U.S. Department of Agriculture (NASS-USDA)

Honey

Honey is the thick, supersaturated sugar solution produced by bees to feed their larvae. It is composed of fructose, glucose and water in varying proportions and also contains several enzymes and oils. The color of honey varies due to the source of nectar and age of the honey. Light colored honeys are usually of higher quality than darker honeys. The average honeybee colony can produce more than 700 pounds of honey per year but only 10 percent is usually harvested by the beekeeper. The rest of the honey is consumed by the colony during the year. American per capita honey consumption is 1 pound per person per year. Honey is said to be humanity's oldest sweet, and beeswax the first plastic.

Honey is used in many ways, including direct human consumption, baking, and medicine. Honey has several healing properties. Its high sugar content nourishes injured tissues, thus enhancing faster healing time. Honey's phytochemicals create a form of hydrogen peroxide that cleans out the wound, and the thick consistency protects the wound from contact with air. Honey has also proven superior to antibiotic ointments for reducing rates of infection in people with burns.

Prices – U.S. average domestic honey prices in 2017 rose by +4.7% to 201.0 cents per pound, but still down from the 2014 record high of 207.1 cents per pound. The value of U.S. honey production in 2017 fell by -7.2% to $318 million, down from the 2014 record high of $388 million.

Supply – World production of honey in 2017 rose +0.1% to 1.861 million metric tons, a new record high. The major producers of honey in 2017 were China with 29.6% of the world's total, Argentina with 4.1%, U.S. with 3.6%, and Russia with 3%.

U.S. production of honey in 2017 fell -8.8% to 147.638 million pounds, remaining well below the 20-year high of 220.339 million pounds posted in 2000. Stocks fell by -25.9% to 30.577 million pounds in 2017 (latest data), which is far below 2000's 18-year high of 85.328 million pounds. Yield per colony in 2017 fell by -5.1% to 55.3 pounds per colony. The number of colonies in 2017 fell by -3.8% to 2,669.

Trade – U.S. imports of honey in 2017 rose by +22.0% to 447.688 million pounds, a new record high U.S. exports of honey in 2017 fell -11.0% to 9.900 million pounds.

Salient Statistics of Honey in the United States   In Millions of Pounds

Year	Number of Colonies (1,000)	Yield Per Colony (Pounds)	Stocks Jan. 1	Total U.S. Pro- duction	Imports for Con- sumption	Domestic Disap- pearance	Exports	Total Supply	Domestic Avg. Price All Honey (cents/lb.)	Value of Pro- duction ($1,000)	U.S. Pro- duction: Beeswax	Domestic Avg. Price: Beeswax (cents/lb.)
2009	2,498	58.6	37.516	146.416	210.427	----	9.656	394.4	147.3	215.671	----	----
2010	2,692	65.6	45.018	176.462	251.170	----	9.543	472.7	161.9	285.692	----	----
2011	2,491	59.6	36.761	148.357	288.283	----	11.889	473.4	176.5	261.850	----	----
2012	2,539	56.0	31.829	142.296	310.884	----	12.287	485.0	199.2	283.454	----	----
2013	2,640	56.6	38.160	149.499	337.529	----	11.952	525.2	214.1	320.077	----	----
2014	2,740	65.1	41.192	178.270	365.472	----	10.937	584.9	217.3	387.381	----	----
2015	2,660	58.9	42.203	156.544	386.341	----	11.258	585.1	208.3	326.081	----	----
2016	2,775	58.3	41.253	161.882	367.015	----	11.127	570.2	211.9	343.028	----	----
2017[1]	2,669	55.3	30.577	147.638	447.688	----	9.900	625.9	215.6	318.308	----	----
2018[1]	Report	delayed									----	----

[1] Preliminary.   Source: Economic Research Service, U.S. Department of Agriculture (ERS-USDA)

Average Price of Honey, by Color Class in the United States   In Cents Per Pound

	Co-op and Private					Retail					All				
Year	Water White, Extra White, White	Extra Light Amber	Light Amber, Amber, Dark Amber	All Other Honey, Area Special- ties	All Honey	Water White, Extra White, White	Extra Light Amber	Light Amber, Amber, Dark Amber	All Other Honey, Area Special- ties	All Honey	Water White, Extra White, White	Extra Light Amber	Light Amber, Amber, Dark Amber	All Other Honey, Area Special- ties	All Honey
2009	142.6	144.5	135.1	179.8	141.5	252.6	252.5	291.4	414.3	283.7	144.0	150.4	148.2	247.9	147.3
2010	157.5	151.1	148.9	172.1	154.1	297.1	266.3	330.5	471.4	311.6	159.8	157.6	167.0	208.1	161.9
2011	170.1	164.4	165.7	182.6	167.7	274.1	307.1	315.4	461.0	314.7	172.9	171.1	183.4	225.2	176.5
2012	192.3	195.4	183.0	213.4	191.3	323.9	303.5	352.4	519.5	348.0	194.2	200.2	205.8	281.6	199.2
2013	210.9	204.0	197.3	222.4	205.8	340.9	330.6	405.1	492.5	382.4	212.9	209.0	219.2	248.9	214.1
2014	204.6	209.6	208.8	255.4	207.1	328.5	392.2	417.1	535.2	405.4	206.2	218.3	234.2	318.2	217.3
2015	188.6	202.5	200.4	284.9	195.0	305.4	411.8	412.1	656.6	409.9	190.6	213.2	234.7	351.5	208.3
2016	189.1	190.8	194.8	245.7	192.0	463.8	433.7	452.9	781.6	474.5	195.5	200.8	233.0	385.2	211.9
2017[1]	199.9	202.7	198.4	285.9	201.0	380.1	458.8	484.8	624.1	477.7	201.6	213.5	232.2	373.8	215.6
2018[1]	Report	delayed													

[1] Preliminary.   Source: National Agricultural Statistics Service, U.S. Department of Agriculture (NASS-USDA)

Interest Rates - U.S.

U.S. interest rates can be characterized in two main ways, by credit quality and by maturity. Credit quality refers to the level of risk associated with a particular borrower. U.S. Treasury securities, for example, carry the lowest risk. Maturity refers to the time at which the security matures and must be repaid. Treasury securities carry a full spectrum of maturities, from short-term cash management bills, to T-bills (4-weeks, 3-months, 6-months), T-notes (2-year, 3-year, 5-year, 7-year, and 10-year), and 30-year T-bonds. The most active futures markets are the 10-year T-note futures, 30-year T-bond futures, and Eurodollar futures, all of which are traded at the CME Group.

Prices – CME 10-year T-note futures prices (Barchart. com electronic symbol ZN) were generally weak during 2018, closing the year down 2-3/64 points. The 10-year T-note yield in 2018 closed the year mildly higher by +28 basis points at 2.68%. 10-year T-note futures prices during 2018 extended the sharp sell-off that began in 2016, posting an 8-1/2 year nearest-futures low in late 2018. T-note prices were undercut in 2018 by the strong U.S. economy and the Fed's hawkish monetary policy. However, T-note prices were able to rebound higher in late 2018 due to (1) the sharp sell-off in the global stock markets in Q4-2018, (2) slower global economic growth, and (3) anticipation of the Fed's switch in early 2019 to a more dovish monetary policy.

The U.S. economy in 2018 was strong with GDP growth of +2.9% due to the big personal and corporate tax cuts that took effect on January 1, 2018. The strength of the economy boosted inflation and forced the Federal Reserve to maintain a hawkish monetary policy. On a quarterly basis, U.S. GDP growth in Q2-2018 reached its peak of a 4-year high of +4.2% (quarter-on-quarter annualized),

before easing to +3.4% in Q3 and +2.6% in Q4. U.S. GDP eased later in 2018 due to trade tensions, slower growth in China and the Eurozone, and the fading stimulus from the January 1 tax cuts.

Inflation expectations remained generally strong in 2018 and undercut T-note prices. The 10-year breakeven inflation expectations rate, which measures the difference between nominal and inflation-adjusted TIPS T-notes, rose to a 4-year high of 2.21% in May 2018 and then moved sideways through the summer. T-note expectations were boosted during the first three quarters of 2018 by the strong U.S. economy and by the sharp recovery rally in crude oil prices. Crude oil futures prices rallied to a 4-year high of $76.90 in early October 2018 due to the success of the OPEC+ production cut agreement in reducing global oil inventories. However, inflation expectations then fell sharply in late 2018 due to the slowing global economy and the plunge in oil prices seen during Q4-2018.

The Federal Reserve's hawkish policy during 2018 was a bearish factor for T-note prices. The Fed continued its string of interest rate hikes that began in 2015 with four more rate hikes in 2018 totaling one percentage point. By the end of 2018, the Fed had pushed its federal funds rate target range up to an 11-year high of 2.25%/2.50%. The Fed during 2018 also conducted a hawkish monetary policy by allowing its balance sheet to decline by a total of $370 billion (-8%) down to $4.1 trillion, thus draining excess liquidity from the banking system. However, the Fed at its January 2019 FOMC meeting surprised the markets by dropping its guidance for higher interest rates and switching to a neutral policy where the next policy move could either be a rate hike or a rate cut. Anticipation of that more dovish Fed policy allowed T-note prices to rebound higher in late 2018 and early 2019.

U.S. Producer Price Index[2] for All Commodities   1982 = 100

Year	Jan.	Feb.	Mar.	Apr.	May	June	July	Aug.	Sept.	Oct.	Nov.	Dec.	Average
2009	171.2	169.3	168.1	169.1	170.8	174.1	172.5	175.0	174.1	175.2	177.4	178.1	172.9
2010	181.9	181.0	183.3	184.4	184.8	183.5	184.1	184.9	184.9	186.6	187.7	189.7	184.7
2011	192.7	195.8	199.2	203.1	204.1	203.9	204.6	203.2	203.7	201.1	201.4	199.8	201.1
2012	200.7	201.6	204.2	203.7	201.9	199.8	200.1	202.7	204.4	203.5	201.8	201.5	202.2
2013	202.5	204.3	204.0	203.5	204.1	204.3	204.4	204.2	203.9	202.5	201.2	202.0	203.4
2014	203.8	205.7	207.0	208.3	208.0	208.3	208.0	207.0	206.4	203.4	200.9	197.0	205.3
2015	192.0	191.1	191.5	190.9	193.4	194.8	193.9	191.9	189.1	187.5	185.7	183.5	190.4
2016	182.6	181.3	182.1	183.2	185.3	187.6	187.7	186.6	186.9	186.7	186.3	188.2	185.4
2017	190.7	191.6	191.5	193.0	192.8	193.6	193.5	193.8	194.8	194.9	195.9	196.3	193.5
2018[1]	197.9	199.3	199.3	200.3	203.2	204.2	204.3	203.4	203.6	204.6	201.5	202.1	202.0

[1] Preliminary.   [2] Not seasonally adjusted.   *Source: Bureau of Labor Statistics, U.S. Department of Commerce (BLS)*

U.S. Consumer Price Index[2] for All Urban Consumers   1982-84 = 100

Year	Jan.	Feb.	Mar.	Apr.	May	June	July	Aug.	Sept.	Oct.	Nov.	Dec.	Average
2009	211.1	212.2	212.7	213.2	213.9	215.7	215.4	215.8	216.0	216.2	216.3	215.9	214.5
2010	216.7	216.7	217.6	218.0	218.2	218.0	218.0	218.3	218.4	218.7	218.8	219.2	218.1
2011	220.2	221.3	223.5	224.9	226.0	225.7	225.9	226.5	226.9	226.4	226.2	225.7	224.9
2012	226.7	227.7	229.4	230.1	229.8	229.5	229.1	230.4	231.4	231.3	230.2	229.6	229.6
2013	230.3	232.2	232.8	232.5	232.9	233.5	233.6	233.9	234.1	233.5	233.1	233.0	233.0
2014	233.9	234.8	236.3	237.1	237.9	238.3	238.3	237.9	238.0	237.4	236.2	234.8	236.7
2015	233.7	234.7	236.1	236.6	237.8	238.6	238.7	238.3	237.9	237.8	237.3	236.5	237.0
2016	236.9	237.1	238.1	239.3	240.2	241.0	240.6	240.8	241.4	241.7	241.4	241.4	240.0
2017	242.8	243.6	243.8	244.5	244.7	245.0	244.8	245.5	246.8	246.7	246.7	246.5	245.1
2018[1]	247.9	249.0	249.6	250.5	251.6	252.0	252.0	252.1	252.4	252.9	252.0	251.2	251.1

[1] Preliminary.   [2] Not seasonally adjusted.   *Source: Bureau of Labor Statistics, U.S. Department of Commerce (BLS)*

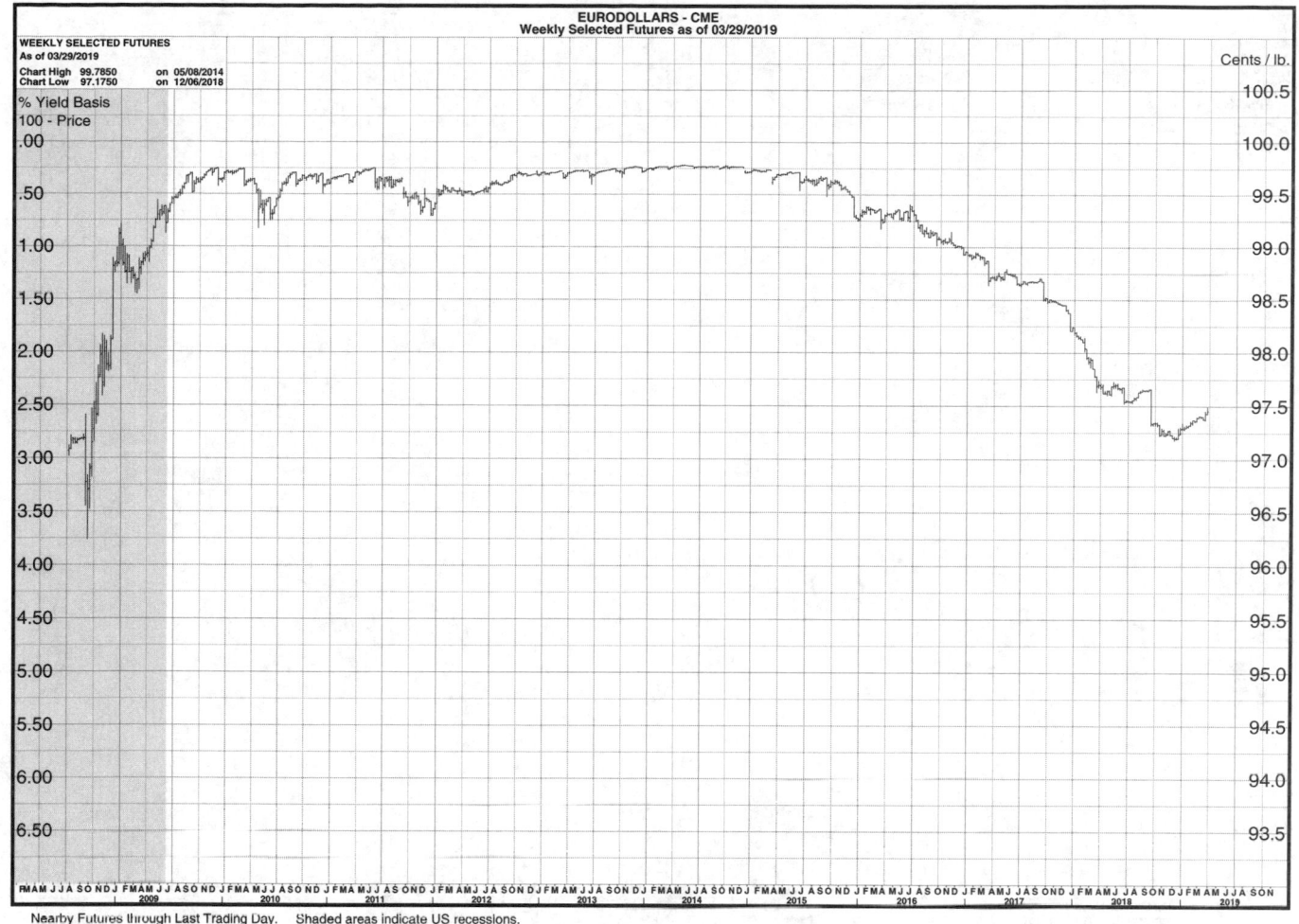

EURODOLLARS - CME
Weekly Selected Futures as of 03/29/2019

WEEKLY SELECTED FUTURES
As of 03/29/2019

Chart High 99.7850 on 05/08/2014
Chart Low 97.1750 on 12/06/2018

% Yield Basis
100 - Price

Nearby Futures through Last Trading Day.   Shaded areas indicate US recessions.

Volume of Trading of 3-month Eurodollar Futures in Chicago   In Thousands of Contracts

Year	Jan.	Feb.	Mar.	Apr.	May	June	July	Aug.	Sept.	Oct.	Nov.	Dec.	Total
2009	31,370.9	29,422.6	35,280.3	29,706.3	34,665.5	51,021.4	40,062.0	36,483.1	39,604.4	40,397.6	32,914.4	36,656.6	437,585
2010	36,569.3	37,746.7	47,459.2	52,132.3	57,806.8	36,986.7	32,120.3	34,582.2	38,196.5	34,205.0	55,512.9	47,637.1	510,955
2011	42,213.1	51,117.3	62,877.0	49,748.5	46,199.0	62,516.2	46,462.8	61,739.9	38,864.4	34,186.8	39,340.0	28,821.7	564,087
2012	41,620.4	38,145.0	46,496.1	32,895.5	40,756.4	38,105.8	28,199.5	34,119.2	37,238.4	35,652.7	26,998.6	26,210.8	426,438
2013	40,800.6	32,152.3	37,526.2	30,235.7	51,371.9	69,283.3	41,177.9	38,851.4	51,413.1	43,321.9	39,422.5	41,693.4	517,250
2014	54,761.3	38,750.1	57,945.4	46,118.3	54,063.9	55,196.8	57,448.5	47,862.5	67,835.8	86,823.2	34,561.1	63,066.5	664,433
2015	60,557.7	53,474.6	56,886.5	39,486.9	46,358.9	55,022.2	45,717.3	51,075.2	47,750.9	44,983.2	39,937.9	45,661.9	586,913
2016	60,730.2	58,698.8	53,857.5	41,209.6	46,085.8	56,564.7	49,539.9	49,707.1	49,586.2	42,365.9	84,793.1	61,808.7	654,947
2017	62,542.9	57,145.8	72,934.8	51,369.1	53,434.7	54,122.6	40,527.4	44,393.5	54,731.0	52,213.9	49,599.8	46,831.7	639,847
2018	69,710.4	90,635.0	87,329.3	54,086.4	68,834.0	53,227.4	38,782.1	43,758.4	55,084.0	72,841.9	58,947.3	71,972.4	765,209

Contract size = $1,000,000.   Source: CME Group; International Monetary Market (IOM), division of the Chicago Mercantile Exchange (CME)

Average Open Interest of 3-month Eurodollar Futures in Chicago   In Thousands of Contracts

Year	Jan.	Feb.	Mar.	Apr.	May	June	July	Aug.	Sept.	Oct.	Nov.	Dec.
2009	6,772.8	6,857.6	6,371.3	6,055.5	6,480.5	6,383.2	6,540.1	6,748.5	6,659.5	6,937.8	7,382.3	6,876.4
2010	6,957.6	7,607.2	7,643.6	7,850.9	7,728.4	7,297.3	7,652.9	7,876.1	7,528.6	7,953.2	8,245.8	7,433.0
2011	7,675.5	8,820.5	9,086.9	9,494.8	10,101.6	10,117.4	10,018.2	9,997.3	9,011.2	8,239.0	8,624.3	8,123.4
2012	7,787.5	8,387.6	8,508.1	8,593.1	8,776.6	8,213.4	7,889.8	7,858.5	8,210.5	8,269.0	8,508.1	8,292.0
2013	8,320.7	8,898.0	9,261.8	9,350.3	9,681.0	9,020.2	8,685.1	9,291.6	9,141.1	9,420.5	10,163.4	10,422.3
2014	10,142.7	10,022.8	10,453.9	10,875.2	11,635.9	11,593.8	12,101.1	12,734.0	13,139.9	11,819.9	11,685.4	10,902.1
2015	10,860.6	11,099.2	10,806.9	10,972.8	11,415.8	11,292.4	11,483.9	12,050.4	11,528.6	11,072.0	11,202.6	10,704.9
2016	10,869.1	10,865.4	10,132.9	10,143.2	10,621.0	10,281.7	10,434.1	10,977.1	11,138.0	11,410.5	12,131.6	12,064.2
2017	11,865.7	12,254.8	12,710.3	13,160.6	13,531.5	13,596.4	12,979.5	13,523.7	13,474.4	12,863.1	13,241.6	13,513.2
2018	14,034.4	15,871.7	17,114.1	16,815.8	16,141.1	14,660.5	14,124.0	14,084.0	14,114.7	14,373.2	14,151.3	13,543.0

Contract size = $1,000,000.   Source: CME Group; International Monetary Market (IOM), division of the Chicago Mercantile Exchange (CME)

INTEREST RATES - U.S.

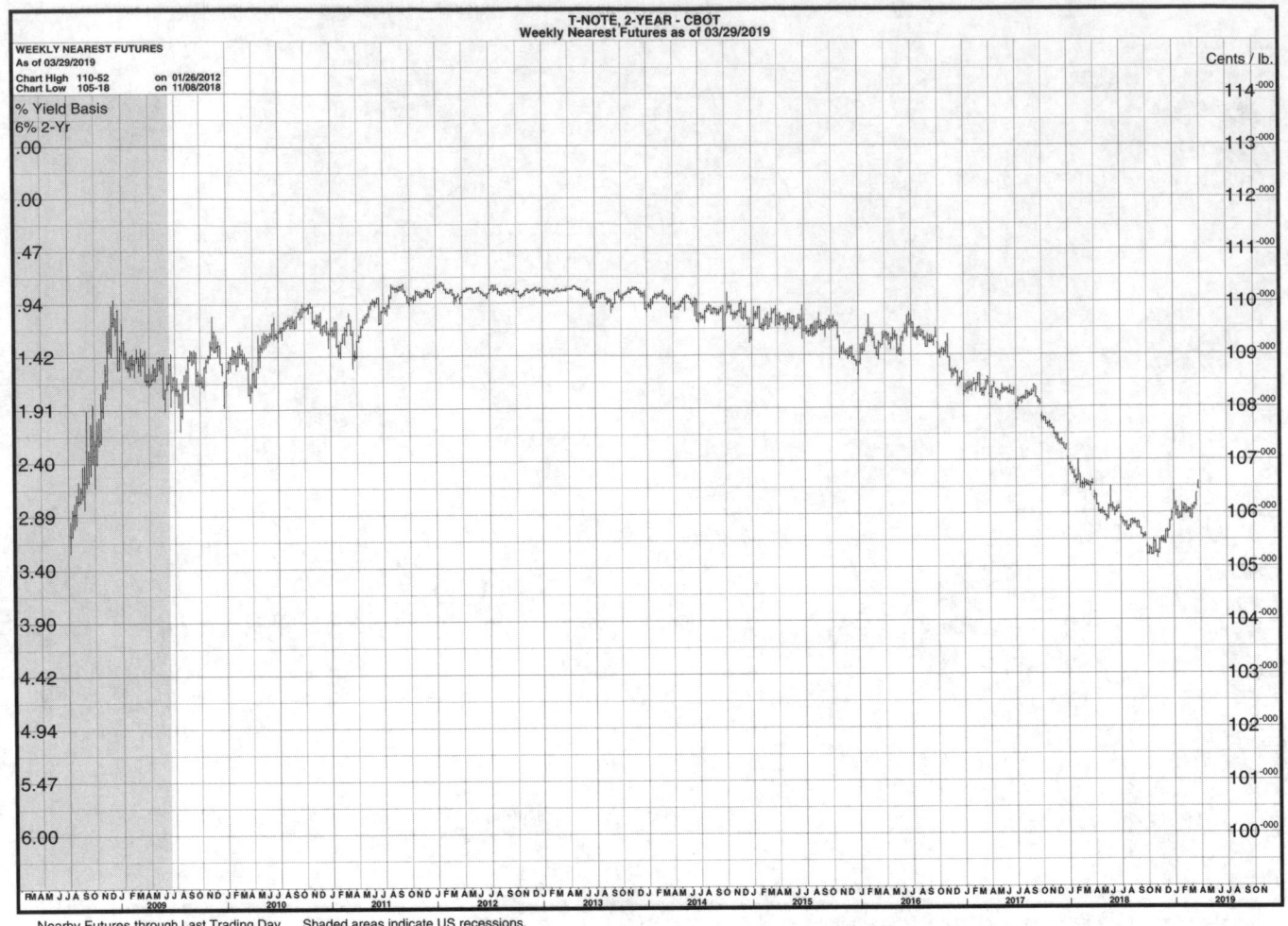

T-NOTE, 2-YEAR - CBOT
Weekly Nearest Futures as of 03/29/2019

WEEKLY NEAREST FUTURES
As of 03/29/2019

Chart High 110-52 on 01/26/2012
Chart Low 105-18 on 11/08/2018

% Yield Basis
6% 2-Yr

Nearby Futures through Last Trading Day.   Shaded areas indicate US recessions.

Volume of Trading of 2-Year U.S. Treasury Note Futures in Chicago   In Thousands of Contracts

Year	Jan.	Feb.	Mar.	Apr.	May	June	July	Aug.	Sept.	Oct.	Nov.	Dec.	Total
2009	2,117.4	3,797.2	2,486.1	2,219.7	4,409.0	3,818.7	3,094.7	5,931.9	3,915.7	5,012.4	7,205.5	4,150.6	48,158.9
2010	4,487.2	8,143.4	6,164.3	6,164.1	9,494.2	4,398.8	4,083.6	6,491.7	3,719.2	3,189.8	6,849.9	3,791.0	66,977.2
2011	4,172.3	9,276.8	7,161.9	5,363.7	8,520.4	6,814.1	5,166.5	9,198.7	3,990.7	3,743.3	6,105.9	2,664.6	72,178.8
2012	3,162.6	6,083.1	4,858.3	3,568.9	6,748.6	3,626.2	3,831.4	6,593.6	3,575.3	3,318.0	6,615.1	3,127.6	55,108.7
2013	4,249.9	7,408.8	3,786.5	3,169.7	8,812.1	4,703.0	3,008.5	6,380.5	4,134.8	3,133.0	5,982.2	3,046.9	57,815.9
2014	4,004.9	4,637.1	4,670.2	4,402.3	8,206.8	4,404.6	3,913.5	9,120.7	6,155.0	6,801.9	8,643.1	5,054.2	70,014.3
2015	5,113.2	11,269.7	6,108.6	4,349.9	10,776.5	6,555.7	4,983.7	10,933.2	5,556.6	4,681.9	7,946.4	4,765.3	83,040.7
2016	5,229.6	9,923.0	5,521.3	4,421.2	8,907.1	6,095.0	5,000.2	8,969.9	5,775.0	5,733.4	11,524.6	4,773.8	81,874.2
2017	5,753.0	10,850.4	6,893.6	5,031.7	11,816.4	6,878.7	4,794.3	11,174.2	6,379.3	6,749.4	14,716.4	6,212.1	97,249.5
2018	8,227.0	19,349.2	9,652.2	7,441.3	17,938.9	6,815.9	5,398.5	14,407.6	6,704.9	10,226.4	20,088.5	9,248.8	135,499.2

Contract size = $200,000.   *Source: CME Group; Chicago Board of Trade (CBT)*

Average Open Interest of 2-Year U.S. Treasury Note Futures in Chicago   In Thousands of Contracts

Year	Jan.	Feb.	Mar.	Apr.	May	June	July	Aug.	Sept.	Oct.	Nov.	Dec.
2009	505.7	495.1	473.4	487.5	514.2	535.3	627.8	741.6	772.4	935.2	1,052.2	911.8
2010	885.7	982.1	891.3	1,001.7	1,022.3	900.3	847.1	805.6	708.2	734.8	710.8	664.9
2011	711.7	900.2	892.0	1,031.0	1,066.2	1,030.5	1,012.9	976.2	772.3	714.5	748.0	698.8
2012	781.4	904.4	842.3	835.7	975.7	928.1	953.8	1,012.6	963.5	942.0	1,030.2	1,015.8
2013	998.1	1,046.5	989.2	916.5	945.3	816.8	791.7	864.5	863.5	925.2	978.2	866.6
2014	858.0	934.8	942.0	1,077.5	1,153.4	1,051.2	1,164.8	1,400.5	1,546.2	1,425.6	1,432.8	1,292.8
2015	1,269.4	1,462.5	1,346.2	1,378.7	1,363.1	1,183.6	1,274.7	1,356.3	1,143.8	1,117.1	1,091.9	989.4
2016	1,048.4	1,164.5	961.0	1,021.2	1,117.2	1,004.6	1,053.3	1,124.5	1,008.8	1,225.0	1,202.6	1,140.2
2017	1,215.9	1,444.9	1,412.6	1,378.3	1,392.5	1,350.8	1,354.0	1,488.8	1,527.0	1,667.8	1,837.2	1,765.6
2018	1,900.4	2,030.6	1,896.1	1,973.5	2,138.0	1,828.2	1,930.1	4,255.5	2,164.6	2,268.6	2,682.1	2,636.3

Contract size = $200,000.   *Source: CME Group; Chicago Board of Trade (CBT)*

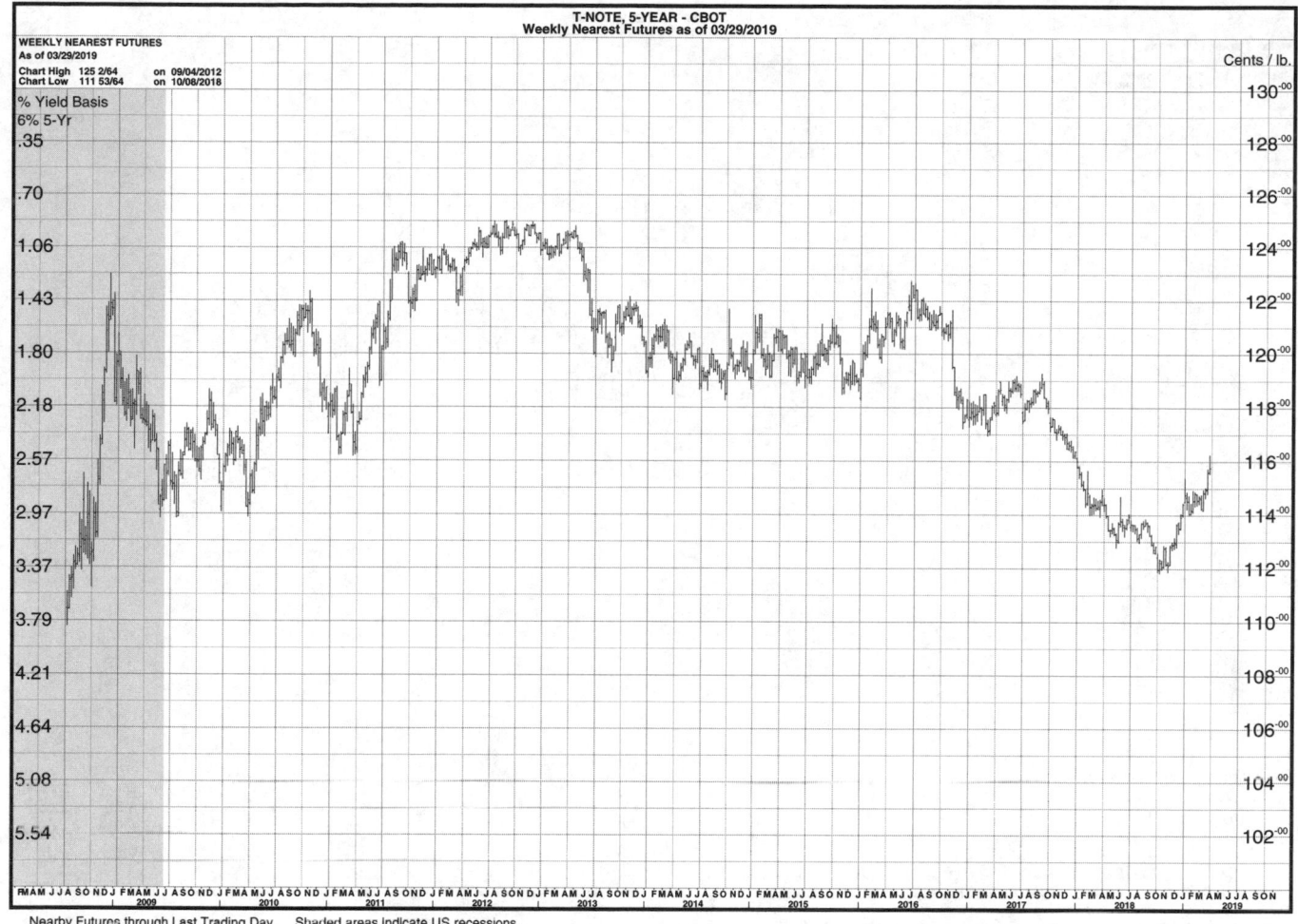

T-NOTE, 5-YEAR - CBOT
Weekly Nearest Futures as of 03/29/2019

WEEKLY NEAREST FUTURES
As of 03/29/2019
Chart High 125 2/64   on 09/04/2012
Chart Low   111 53/64 on 10/08/2018

Nearby Futures through Last Trading Day.   Shaded areas indicate US recessions.

Volume of Trading of 5-Year U.S. Treasury Note Futures in Chicago   In Thousands of Contracts

Year	Jan.	Feb.	Mar.	Apr.	May	June	July	Aug.	Sept.	Oct.	Nov.	Dec.	Total
2009	4,821.3	8,349.9	7,388.4	5,837.7	9,658.3	8,314.8	8,034.1	10,588.0	8,259.3	9,242.9	10,231.8	7,664.7	98,391
2010	7,434.9	11,815.6	10,096.3	9,631.3	16,093.0	10,212.4	9,662.0	13,062.2	9,627.7	9,404.1	14,828.5	10,282.0	132,150
2011	10,654.1	16,398.4	16,604.1	11,371.9	17,958.8	16,524.9	13,314.4	21,004.3	12,074.6	11,607.0	15,320.7	7,729.7	170,563
2012	9,260.0	14,543.1	12,251.9	8,980.8	14,647.3	10,565.4	7,291.7	13,493.4	10,510.3	9,281.0	13,968.6	8,549.0	133,342
2013	12,206.3	18,750.5	11,971.1	11,023.9	20,914.4	17,072.7	11,763.4	18,021.9	13,464.8	10,198.2	16,397.4	10,543.6	175,328
2014	13,081.6	18,022.0	16,060.6	14,088.2	20,473.5	13,605.3	14,182.4	20,546.3	16,596.0	20,858.3	15,933.0	12,982.0	196,429
2015	14,739.3	20,925.8	14,020.7	11,619.5	20,929.9	15,289.6	12,668.2	22,856.6	12,974.5	12,321.4	20,512.7	11,849.6	190,708
2016	13,618.7	24,294.8	13,229.2	11,144.4	22,079.7	15,245.5	11,120.9	23,442.5	12,453.2	11,484.3	30,046.2	13,745.4	201,905
2017	15,623.7	26,990.8	17,509.9	13,761.0	26,563.2	16,462.0	12,784.2	24,543.1	14,990.7	14,944.5	27,741.3	14,526.8	226,441
2018	18,302.4	35,388.6	19,974.6	16,208.0	36,454.5	14,379.4	14,187.0	30,353.9	15,664.4	25,561.2	36,989.9	20,757.0	284,221

Contract size = $100,000.   Source: CME Group; Chicago Board of Trade (CBT)

Average Open Interest of 5-Year U.S. Treasury Note Futures in Chicago   In Thousands of Contracts

Year	Jan.	Feb.	Mar.	Apr.	May	June	July	Aug.	Sept.	Oct.	Nov.	Dec.
2009	965.5	964.7	897.8	812.7	860.8	774.2	761.1	831.9	800.3	770.9	854.0	831.6
2010	805.1	939.1	942.4	937.2	1,045.8	932.2	940.4	1,095.6	925.0	1,012.8	1,136.6	1,010.9
2011	1,075.8	1,293.9	1,223.4	1,364.8	1,524.6	1,576.9	1,513.4	1,435.6	1,326.7	1,200.4	1,277.5	1,261.2
2012	1,398.3	1,444.8	1,390.1	1,306.6	1,384.1	1,144.6	1,145.8	1,236.3	1,330.2	1,399.5	1,461.6	1,506.2
2013	1,532.5	1,653.7	1,733.6	1,847.6	1,842.2	1,535.0	1,584.4	1,641.0	1,668.5	1,745.1	1,968.7	1,865.1
2014	1,939.7	2,002.5	1,959.1	2,036.7	2,126.3	2,070.6	2,130.6	2,190.1	2,130.5	1,992.7	1,993.5	1,844.4
2015	1,837.5	1,983.8	1,992.9	2,016.3	2,038.9	2,096.2	2,200.8	2,398.5	2,352.1	2,422.1	2,469.2	2,371.4
2016	2,497.2	2,734.3	2,476.6	2,477.3	2,575.0	2,632.8	2,676.0	2,866.4	2,799.2	2,756.9	2,961.3	2,924.3
2017	3,019.1	3,313.3	3,035.8	3,103.9	3,261.9	3,144.0	1,350.8	3,000.0	3,144.0	2,998.1	3,293.4	3,051.2
2018	3,236.9	3,538.2	3,376.7	3,519.0	3,813.1	3,742.6	3,892.1	4,255.5	4,380.4	4,536.9	4,922.3	4,702.5

Contract size = $100,000.   Source: CME Group; Chicago Board of Trade (CBT)

INTEREST RATES - U.S.

Nearby Futures through Last Trading Day.   Shaded areas indicate US recessions.

Volume of Trading of 10-year U.S. Treasury Note Futures in Chicago   In Thousands of Contracts

Year	Jan.	Feb.	Mar.	Apr.	May	June	July	Aug.	Sept.	Oct.	Nov.	Dec.	Total
2009	9,778.0	14,548.1	15,116.1	11,893.7	17,309.8	16,994.6	16,420.7	19,292.8	16,099.0	19,268.8	19,037.2	14,093.3	189,852
2010	16,865.3	23,588.6	19,582.2	22,070.6	35,156.5	24,198.2	22,294.5	30,744.0	26,070.6	22,947.9	29,360.3	20,840.2	293,719
2011	22,260.8	27,531.8	29,500.1	20,162.8	31,149.4	31,897.7	25,851.1	39,911.1	24,612.4	23,559.8	26,614.2	14,351.4	317,403
2012	19,336.4	26,546.0	24,188.9	20,706.8	32,255.6	24,036.4	16,688.1	25,178.8	18,527.4	18,740.5	23,319.0	15,473.1	264,997
2013	24,720.9	33,572.4	24,606.7	23,859.0	43,005.7	32,912.7	21,673.6	31,715.3	23,332.3	21,265.7	27,463.8	17,800.2	325,928
2014	23,218.1	29,772.2	27,675.3	25,202.1	34,569.3	24,098.5	23,402.1	34,087.3	28,122.5	39,126.2	28,205.8	23,005.8	340,485
2015	27,499.2	33,705.2	24,770.7	22,343.8	38,005.7	29,805.4	23,574.7	34,287.1	22,586.7	23,505.9	28,612.5	19,644.2	328,341
2016	27,310.1	41,327.8	24,480.8	22,290.2	32,571.1	28,364.5	23,198.0	34,699.7	24,140.8	22,878.3	46,296.5	23,204.4	350,762
2017	28,552.5	38,619.2	29,608.9	25,570.4	39,797.5	28,177.2	24,476.4	39,078.3	27,756.7	28,826.3	41,497.4	23,377.8	375,338
2018	32,939.1	51,555.5	33,837.1	27,450.9	53,075.1	31,980.5	25,504.3	44,233.8	27,721.0	48,099.0	49,321.5	32,001.5	457,719

Contract size = $100,000.   *Source: CME Group; Chicago Board of Trade (CBT)*

Average Open Interest of 10-year U.S. Treasury Note Futures in Chicago   In Thousands of Contracts

Year	Jan.	Feb.	Mar.	Apr.	May	June	July	Aug.	Sept.	Oct.	Nov.	Dec.
2009	1,034.9	1,027.6	1,007.0	1,010.0	1,132.3	1,070.9	1,056.2	1,139.7	1,120.2	1,239.1	1,327.5	1,203.9
2010	1,292.9	1,420.4	1,423.8	1,632.0	1,838.8	1,756.8	1,802.2	1,973.0	1,686.3	1,617.2	1,527.4	1,335.3
2011	1,360.1	1,521.3	1,563.5	1,643.4	1,854.0	1,834.0	1,843.5	1,937.7	1,627.4	1,504.3	1,505.7	1,460.6
2012	1,647.6	1,847.4	1,796.4	1,804.4	1,949.8	1,806.5	1,787.3	1,640.5	1,593.8	1,685.3	1,783.4	1,674.9
2013	1,815.9	2,089.8	2,125.6	2,230.3	2,331.8	2,132.2	2,199.4	2,308.6	2,031.6	2,079.2	2,341.3	2,261.2
2014	2,260.5	2,426.0	2,433.4	2,526.5	2,720.3	2,591.6	2,679.0	2,853.2	2,705.4	2,776.0	2,855.5	2,652.6
2015	2,684.1	2,610.3	2,690.8	2,822.7	2,884.8	2,730.7	2,751.9	2,941.1	2,729.8	2,776.5	2,680.6	2,594.4
2016	2,747.8	3,065.1	2,714.8	2,726.7	2,732.6	2,750.5	2,815.6	2,849.5	2,818.1	2,890.3	3,017.2	3,026.9
2017	3,130.7	3,343.9	3,139.4	3,137.3	3,365.2	3,179.9	3,162.4	3,384.4	3,277.1	3,132.4	3,399.8	3,271.5
2018	3,420.6	3,740.6	3,480.6	3,590.4	3,854.8	3,462.9	3,696.0	3,990.4	3,963.9	4,153.7	4,281.3	4,136.0

Contract size = $100,000.   *Source: CME Group; Chicago Board of Trade (CBT)*

T-BOND - CBOT
Weekly Nearest Futures as of 03/29/2019

WEEKLY NEAREST FUTURES
As of 03/29/2019
Chart High 177 22/64 on 07/11/2016
Chart Low 113 8/64 on 06/11/2009

% Yield Basis
6% 20-Yr

Cents / lb.

Nearby Futures through Last Trading Day.   Shaded areas indicate US recessions.

Volume of Trading of 30-year U.S. Treasury Bond Futures in Chicago   In Thousands of Contracts

Year	Jan.	Feb.	Mar.	Apr.	May	June	July	Aug.	Sept.	Oct.	Nov.	Dec.	Total
2009	3,805.9	6,062.7	4,525.5	3,224.8	6,465.1	5,192.0	4,995.2	7,238.3	4,297.6	5,133.4	6,978.4	4,313.9	62,233
2010	4,617.8	7,345.1	5,748.7	6,033.7	10,457.5	5,899.4	5,711.8	9,165.6	6,774.8	6,806.7	9,379.5	5,569.2	83,510
2011	6,272.2	8,551.9	7,823.2	5,528.4	9,231.3	8,358.3	6,471.5	11,892.5	7,487.1	6,694.3	9,057.7	4,969.9	92,339
2012	6,143.3	8,623.0	7,335.2	5,890.8	11,326.7	9,060.1	6,493.7	8,685.7	6,680.1	6,866.2	8,530.8	6,109.6	91,745
2013	7,892.2	10,758.6	7,691.9	8,269.7	13,337.5	9,601.6	5,788.0	8,792.7	6,759.6	6,193.9	7,712.2	5,165.3	97,963
2014	5,871.1	8,211.2	6,867.7	6,259.9	9,648.8	7,044.9	6,719.0	9,948.4	7,678.1	10,370.2	7,827.0	6,742.1	93,188
2015	7,956.2	8,611.4	5,183.2	4,747.5	6,832.7	5,708.3	5,453.9	7,438.7	4,884.1	4,927.9	5,625.7	4,531.9	71,902
2016	5,569.8	8,184.8	5,000.5	4,428.4	6,276.8	5,736.6	4,734.9	6,655.2	5,245.9	5,042.9	8,707.2	4,620.4	70,203
2017	5,165.8	7,149.6	5,818.2	4,614.0	7,713.7	6,144.7	4,672.2	7,620.6	5,442.3	5,668.0	8,212.6	5,115.4	73,337
2018	6,648.4	10,573.9	6,380.0	5,517.2	10,025.2	6,048.6	5,244.4	8,677.5	5,961.9	10,301.0	10,299.4	6,984.4	92,662

Contract size = $100,000.   Source: CME Group; Chicago Board of Trade (CBT)

Average Open Interest of 30-year U.S. Treasury Bond Futures in Chicago   In Contracts

Year	Jan.	Feb.	Mar.	Apr.	May	June	July	Aug.	Sept.	Oct.	Nov.	Dec.
2009	726,062	733,323	712,813	708,243	724,577	706,818	696,641	727,674	749,290	739,723	777,241	704,259
2010	656,438	676,778	648,845	663,991	740,180	663,330	682,310	738,206	669,950	683,476	654,901	563,632
2011	552,937	613,356	609,003	573,206	702,197	668,848	628,174	661,826	647,168	618,884	634,941	597,183
2012	612,937	615,616	583,579	576,419	661,058	664,479	636,745	610,065	570,346	564,706	623,227	586,502
2013	551,333	632,060	630,148	681,045	667,210	568,046	574,724	626,392	630,549	644,843	696,333	656,867
2014	666,663	716,926	712,174	722,390	780,781	738,607	758,214	870,115	860,417	870,759	850,561	889,272
2015	829,094	640,877	414,934	437,101	478,017	484,216	500,019	533,913	505,812	501,845	491,806	519,574
2016	517,291	562,305	510,970	525,831	528,077	570,427	575,832	583,950	562,062	562,046	574,628	586,673
2017	616,403	637,810	646,801	644,707	706,590	737,002	729,176	873,263	730,878	740,311	798,709	772,841
2018	790,518	834,751	806,285	798,849	878,533	804,968	826,864	878,497	859,024	917,822	964,126	966,317

Contract size = $100,000.   Source: CME Group; Chicago Board of Trade (CBT)

INTEREST RATES - U.S.

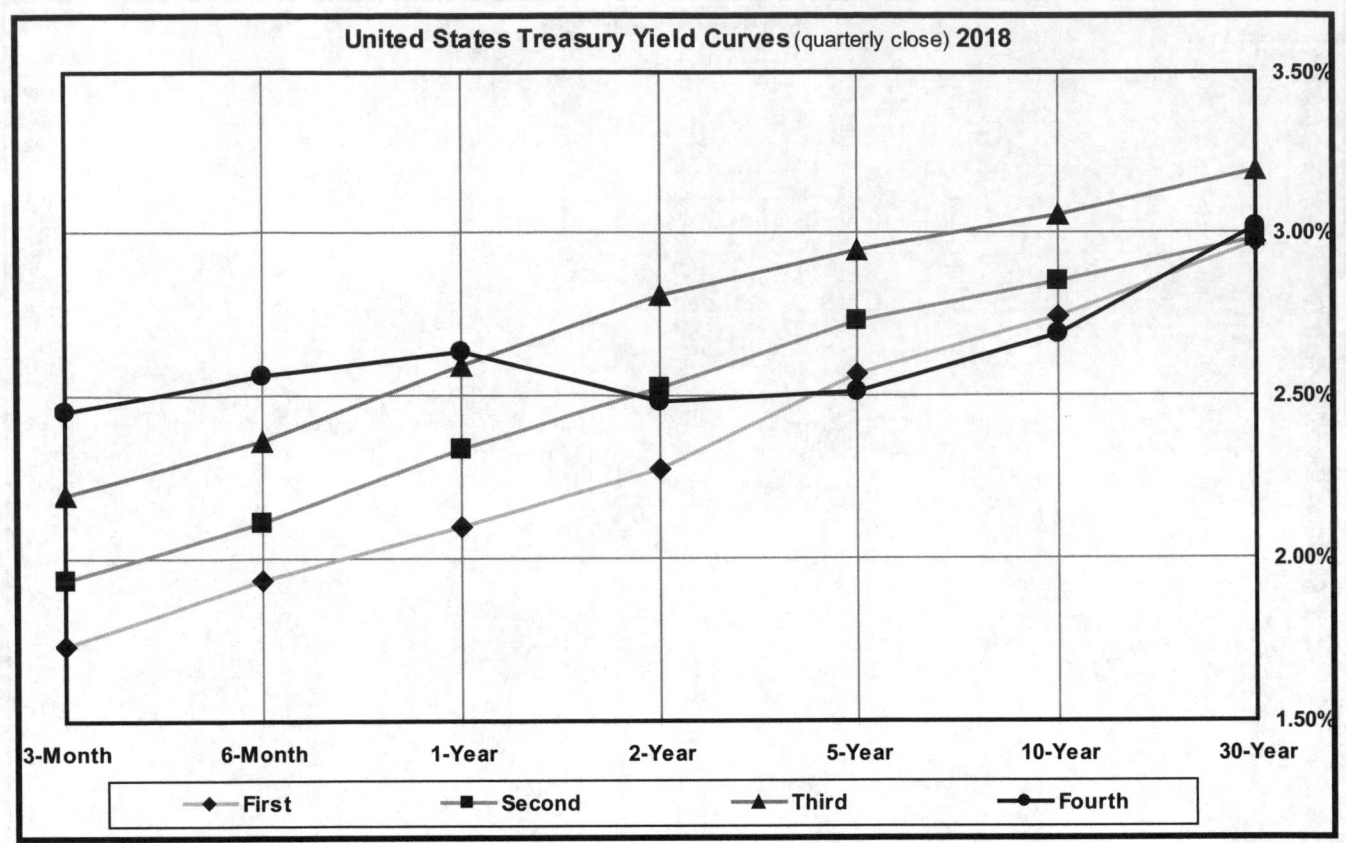

United States Treasury Yield Curves (quarterly close) **2018**

Legend: ◆ First ■ Second ▲ Third ● Fourth

U.S. Federal Funds Rate   In Percent

Year	Jan.	Feb.	Mar.	Apr.	May	June	July	Aug.	Sept.	Oct.	Nov.	Dec.	Average
2009	0.15	0.22	0.18	0.15	0.18	0.21	0.16	0.16	0.15	0.12	0.12	0.12	0.16
2010	0.11	0.13	0.16	0.20	0.20	0.18	0.18	0.19	0.19	0.19	0.19	0.18	0.18
2011	0.17	0.16	0.14	0.10	0.09	0.09	0.07	0.10	0.08	0.07	0.08	0.07	0.10
2012	0.08	0.10	0.13	0.14	0.16	0.16	0.16	0.13	0.14	0.16	0.16	0.16	0.14
2013	0.14	0.15	0.14	0.15	0.11	0.09	0.09	0.08	0.08	0.09	0.08	0.09	0.11
2014	0.07	0.07	0.08	0.09	0.09	0.10	0.09	0.09	0.09	0.09	0.09	0.12	0.09
2015	0.11	0.11	0.11	0.12	0.12	0.13	0.13	0.14	0.14	0.12	0.12	0.24	0.13
2016	0.34	0.38	0.36	0.37	0.37	0.38	0.39	0.40	0.40	0.40	0.41	0.54	0.40
2017	0.65	0.66	0.79	0.90	0.91	1.04	1.15	1.16	1.15	1.15	1.16	1.30	1.00
2018	1.41	1.42	1.51	1.69	1.70	1.82	1.91	1.91	1.95	2.19	2.20	2.27	1.83

Source: Bureau of Economic Analysis, U.S. Department of Commerce (BEA)

U.S. Municipal Bond Yield[1]   In Percent

Year	Jan.	Feb.	Mar.	Apr.	May	June	July	Aug.	Sept.	Oct.	Nov.	Dec.	Average
2007	4.23	4.22	4.15	4.26	4.31	4.60	4.56	4.64	4.51	4.39	4.46	4.42	4.40
2008	4.27	4.64	4.93	4.70	4.58	4.69	4.68	4.69	4.86	5.50	5.23	5.56	4.86
2009	5.07	4.90	4.99	4.78	4.56	4.81	4.72	4.60	4.24	4.20	4.37	4.21	4.62
2010	4.33	4.36	4.36	4.41	4.29	4.36	4.32	4.03	3.87	3.87	4.40	4.92	4.29
2011	5.28	5.15	4.92	4.99	4.59	4.51	4.52	4.02	4.01	4.13	4.05	3.95	4.51
2012	3.68	3.66	3.91	3.95	3.77	3.94	3.78	3.74	3.73	3.65	3.46	3.48	3.73
2013	3.60	3.72	3.96	3.92	3.72	4.27	4.56	4.82	4.79	4.56	4.60	4.73	4.27
2014	4.59	4.44	4.46	4.35	4.29	4.35	4.33	4.23	4.13	3.96	3.96	3.70	4.23
2015	3.40	3.58	3.59	3.51	3.76	3.82	3.79	3.74	3.78	3.67	3.68	3.57	3.66
2016	3.41	3.30	3.38	3.30	3.29	3.13	2.83	2.85	2.93	3.20	Discontinued		3.16

[1] 20-bond average.   *Source: Bureau of Economic Analysis, U.S. Department of Commerce (BEA)*

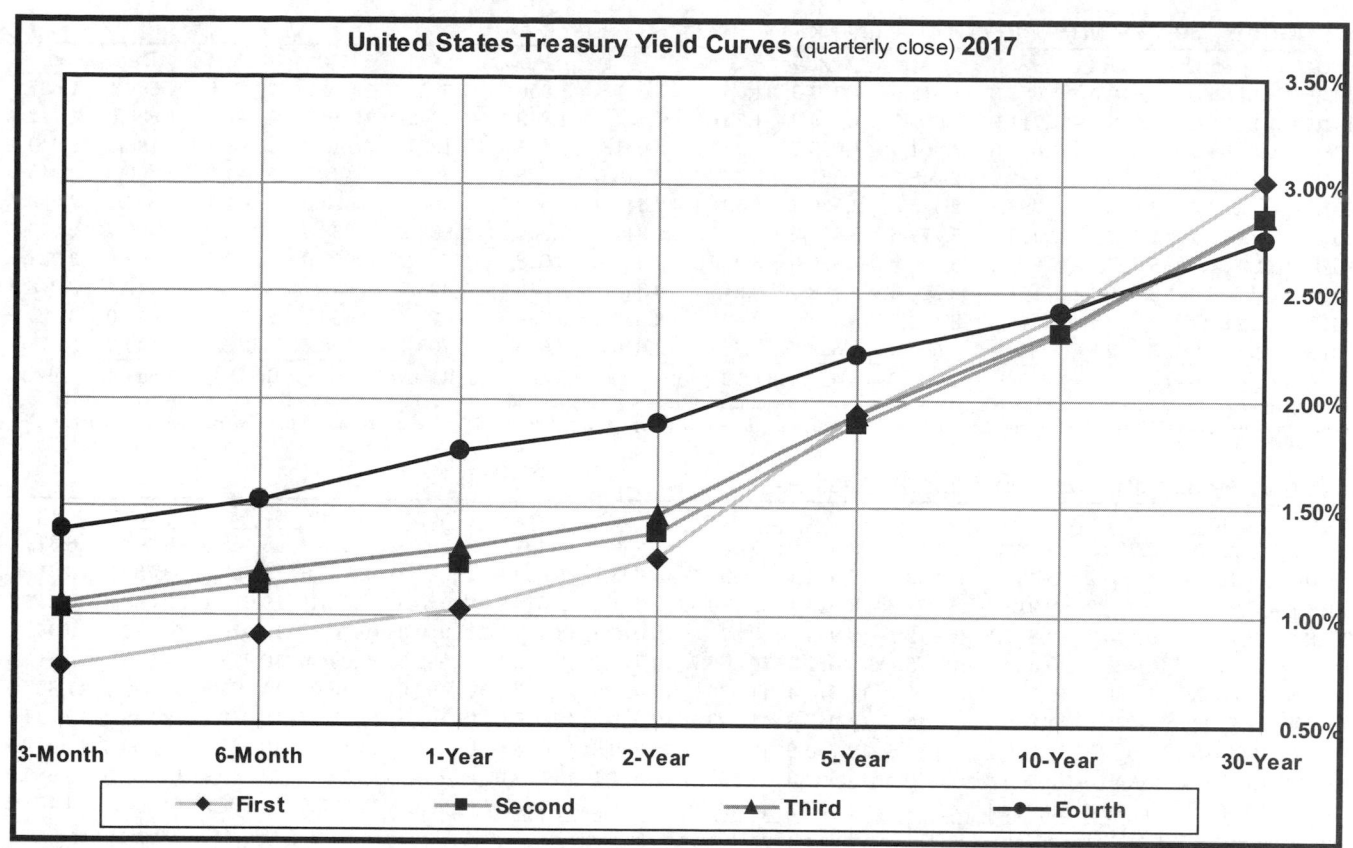

United States Treasury Yield Curves (quarterly close) **2017**

Legend: ◆ First ■ Second ▲ Third ● Fourth

U.S. Industrial Production Index[1]   1997 = 100

Year	Jan.	Feb.	Mar.	Apr.	May	June	July	Aug.	Sept.	Oct.	Nov.	Dec.	Average
2009	91.2	90.6	89.2	88.5	87.6	87.2	88.2	89.1	89.8	90.2	90.4	90.8	89.4
2010	91.7	92.0	92.6	93.0	94.3	94.4	94.8	95.1	95.4	95.1	95.1	96.0	94.1
2011	95.9	95.5	96.5	96.1	96.3	96.6	97.1	97.7	97.6	98.3	98.2	98.8	97.1
2012	99.4	99.6	99.2	99.9	100.1	100.0	100.3	99.9	99.9	100.1	100.6	100.9	100.0
2013	100.9	101.4	101.8	101.7	101.8	101.9	101.4	102.2	102.7	102.5	102.9	103.2	102.0
2014	102.7	103.6	104.6	104.7	105.1	105.4	105.6	105.5	105.8	105.8	106.7	106.5	105.2
2015	105.9	105.4	105.1	104.6	104.1	103.7	104.2	104.1	103.7	103.4	102.7	102.3	104.1
2016	103.0	102.3	101.5	101.7	101.6	101.9	102.1	102.1	101.9	102.1	101.8	102.8	102.1
2017	102.5	102.2	102.7	103.7	103.7	103.8	103.6	103.2	103.2	104.8	105.3	105.8	103.7
2018[1]	105.4	105.9	106.4	107.7	106.8	107.4	107.9	108.8	109.0	109.3	110.0	110.1	107.9

[1] Total Index of the Federal Reserve Index of Quantity Output, seasonally adjusted.   [2] Preliminary.   *Source: Bureau of Economic Analysis, U.S. Department of Commerce (BEA)*

U.S. Gross National Product, National Income, and Personal Income   In Billions of Constant Dollars[1]

	----------- Gross Domestic Product -----------					--------------- National Income ---------------					--------------- Personal Income ---------------				
Year	First Quarter	Second Quarter	Third Quarter	Fourth Quarter	Total	First Quarter	Second Quarter	Third Quarter	Fourth Quarter	Total	First Quarter	Second Quarter	Third Quarter	Fourth Quarter	Total
2009	14,395	14,353	14,420	14,628	14,449	12,007	11,996	12,122	12,374	12,125	12,039	12,099	12,057	12,134	12,082
2010	14,721	14,926	15,080	15,241	14,992	12,457	12,621	12,869	13,012	12,740	12,235	12,413	12,544	12,716	12,477
2011	15,286	15,496	15,592	15,796	15,543	13,091	13,256	13,455	13,607	13,352	13,078	13,195	13,347	13,398	13,255
2012	16,020	16,152	16,257	16,359	16,197	13,943	13,997	14,062	14,246	14,062	13,662	13,814	13,867	14,317	13,915
2013	16,570	16,638	16,849	17,083	16,785	14,276	14,382	14,479	14,642	14,445	13,904	14,017	14,135	14,238	14,074
2014	17,103	17,426	17,720	17,838	17,522	14,734	15,037	15,311	15,494	15,144	14,486	14,714	14,925	15,149	14,818
2015	17,970	18,221	18,331	18,354	18,219	15,553	15,720	15,785	15,901	15,740	15,301	15,516	15,626	15,769	15,553
2016	18,409	18,641	18,800	18,979	18,707	15,888	15,954	16,081	16,313	16,059	15,947	16,032	16,171	16,352	16,125
2017	19,163	19,359	19,588	19,832	19,485	16,525	16,661	16,823	17,015	16,756	16,604	16,721	16,895	17,103	16,831
2018[1]	20,041	20,412	20,658	20,891	20,501	17,266	17,424	17,659		17,450	17,319	17,467	17,657	17,882	17,581

[1] Seasonally adjusted at annual rates.   [2] Preliminary.   *Source: Bureau of Economic Analysis, U.S. Department of Commerce (BEA)*

INTEREST RATES - U.S.

U.S. Money Supply M1[2]   In Billions of Dollars

Year	Jan.	Feb.	Mar.	Apr.	May	June	July	Aug.	Sept.	Oct.	Nov.	Dec.	Average
2009	1,586.3	1,570.0	1,580.8	1,612.6	1,617.5	1,655.6	1,656.4	1,658.7	1,661.8	1,676.2	1,681.5	1,694.1	1,637.6
2010	1,674.6	1,699.7	1,711.9	1,699.6	1,710.6	1,731.7	1,724.4	1,749.3	1,766.5	1,780.9	1,826.2	1,835.8	1,742.6
2011	1,853.4	1,872.5	1,891.3	1,901.4	1,938.7	1,956.2	2,001.9	2,113.8	2,128.1	2,140.2	2,164.1	2,163.5	2,010.4
2012	2,201.8	2,209.9	2,229.0	2,248.8	2,257.2	2,277.3	2,318.5	2,348.9	2,390.1	2,422.5	2,421.2	2,460.6	2,315.5
2013	2,473.3	2,472.4	2,480.4	2,515.8	2,530.7	2,531.4	2,545.8	2,552.1	2,584.5	2,623.0	2,623.1	2,664.4	2,549.7
2014	2,696.4	2,726.4	2,754.8	2,778.6	2,795.2	2,829.5	2,841.6	2,802.9	2,862.2	2,868.8	2,884.9	2,940.7	2,815.2
2015	2,941.0	3,007.1	2,999.6	3,000.9	2,986.6	3,020.0	3,039.7	3,028.5	3,044.2	3,018.6	3,081.7	3,094.9	3,021.9
2016	3,099.0	3,130.4	3,151.1	3,200.3	3,238.7	3,245.7	3,247.9	3,315.1	3,326.5	3,335.7	3,354.1	3,342.4	3,248.9
2017	3,390.9	3,404.7	3,445.5	3,454.2	3,517.3	3,525.9	3,550.9	3,580.7	3,574.2	3,606.7	3,630.6	3,612.0	3,524.5
2018[1]	3,653.2	3,622.5	3,656.4	3,660.3	3,654.7	3,655.0	3,676.8	3,679.7	3,703.4	3,718.7	3,695.2	3,744.0	3,676.7

[1] Preliminary.   [2] M1 -- The sum of currency held outside the vaults of depository institutions, Federal Reserve Banks, and the U.S. Treasury; travelers checks; and demand and other checkable deposits issued by financial institutions (except demand deposits due to the Treasury and depository institutions), minus cash items in process of collection and Federal Reserve float. Seasonally adjusted.   *Source: Board of Governors of the Federal Reserve System*

U.S. Money Supply M2[2]   In Billions of Dollars

Year	Jan.	Feb.	Mar.	Apr.	May	June	July	Aug.	Sept.	Oct.	Nov.	Dec.	Average
2009	8,238.9	8,269.5	8,337.6	8,341.5	8,397.9	8,405.2	8,406.8	8,404.2	8,399.8	8,429.2	8,462.3	8,460.3	8,379.4
2010	8,445.6	8,495.2	8,492.3	8,522.6	8,577.4	8,596.5	8,606.1	8,656.4	8,687.4	8,736.6	8,757.2	8,789.1	8,613.5
2011	8,825.8	8,871.2	8,915.6	8,977.8	9,029.1	9,113.3	9,301.2	9,514.9	9,539.5	9,571.1	9,612.1	9,650.9	9,243.5
2012	9,730.2	9,773.0	9,817.7	9,872.1	9,903.7	9,973.5	10,046.6	10,117.7	10,200.0	10,261.3	10,319.8	10,445.6	10,038.4
2013	10,471.4	10,468.3	10,539.8	10,575.1	10,611.3	10,665.7	10,721.7	10,780.1	10,832.5	10,945.4	10,953.1	11,015.7	10,715.0
2014	11,066.2	11,148.7	11,190.3	11,246.7	11,314.4	11,366.6	11,427.8	11,457.1	11,492.0	11,552.4	11,591.5	11,670.1	11,377.0
2015	11,733.2	11,852.4	11,868.8	11,916.1	11,947.6	11,993.1	12,045.3	12,096.8	12,153.8	12,187.7	12,277.4	12,335.9	12,034.0
2016	12,461.3	12,533.5	12,595.2	12,684.8	12,750.9	12,819.4	12,880.6	12,968.0	13,031.3	13,105.2	13,178.4	13,209.6	12,851.5
2017	13,282.3	13,340.0	13,405.3	13,470.4	13,521.3	13,551.6	13,617.1	13,672.0	13,717.9	13,779.8	13,809.9	13,851.9	13,585.0
2018[1]	13,867.7	13,890.4	13,941.1	13,974.1	14,035.2	14,107.5	14,148.5	14,190.4	14,224.9	14,250.9	14,276.5	14,387.7	14,107.9

[1] Preliminary.   [2] M2 -- M1 plus savings deposits (including money market deposit accounts) and small-denomination (less than $100,000) time deposits issued by financial institutions; and shares in retail money market mutual funds (funds with initial investments of less than $50,000), net of retirement accounts. Seasonally adjusted.   *Source: Board of Governors of the Federal Reserve System*

U.S. Money Supply MZM[2]   In Billions of Dollars

Year	Jan.	Feb.	Mar.	Apr.	May	June	July	Aug.	Sept.	Oct.	Nov.	Dec.	Average
2009	9,326.4	9,399.7	9,501.5	9,533.4	9,623.0	9,636.1	9,643.9	9,614.9	9,590.5	9,578.2	9,578.1	9,540.8	9,547.2
2010	9,491.2	9,500.3	9,443.9	9,408.9	9,436.0	9,447.7	9,480.0	9,557.6	9,612.8	9,674.2	9,714.8	9,740.0	9,542.3
2011	9,745.1	9,784.2	9,866.3	9,972.1	10,058.2	10,133.9	10,300.5	10,437.0	10,491.0	10,531.3	10,574.4	10,625.4	10,210.0
2012	10,708.1	10,752.8	10,818.0	10,877.9	10,918.3	10,989.7	11,072.9	11,164.1	11,258.4	11,319.6	11,383.2	11,530.3	11,066.1
2013	11,591.2	11,599.4	11,659.7	11,714.3	11,753.8	11,824.9	11,893.9	11,952.8	12,037.8	12,145.5	12,159.9	12,210.3	11,878.6
2014	12,274.0	12,359.2	12,395.3	12,439.2	12,509.1	12,557.7	12,623.4	12,641.8	12,695.2	12,779.8	12,838.9	12,940.7	12,587.9
2015	13,012.5	13,131.5	13,166.6	13,212.8	13,259.4	13,325.0	13,414.1	13,493.7	13,542.7	13,611.1	13,707.2	13,745.8	13,385.2
2016	13,795.8	13,886.7	13,988.5	14,084.8	14,162.3	14,245.4	14,314.8	14,415.7	14,457.0	14,489.1	14,568.4	14,599.0	14,250.6
2017	14,643.3	14,699.4	14,757.5	14,828.4	14,894.3	14,915.7	14,966.2	15,050.3	15,117.9	15,185.7	15,201.7	15,267.7	14,960.7
2018[1]	15,285.4	15,306.1	15,359.4	15,395.4	15,439.3	15,514.8	15,542.1	15,561.8	15,589.6	15,589.9	15,604.3	15,699.0	15,490.6

[1] Preliminary.   [2] MZM (money, zero maturity): M2 minus small-denomination time deposits, plus institutional money market mutual funds (that is, those included in M3 but excluded from M2). The label MZM was coined by William Poole (1991); the aggregate itself was proposed earlier by Motley (1988). Seasonally adjusted.   *Source: Board of Governors of the Federal Reserve System*

U.S. Money Supply M3[2]   In Billions of Dollars

Year	Jan.	Feb.	Mar.	Apr.	May	June	July	Aug.	Sept.	Oct.	Nov.	Dec.	Average
1997	5,013.2	5,041.7	5,080.2	5,119.8	5,147.1	5,177.4	5,235.8	5,291.4	5,332.3	5,376.3	5,417.1	5,460.5	5,224.4
1998	5,508.8	5,541.3	5,611.5	5,647.3	5,686.9	5,728.4	5,750.0	5,815.0	5,882.0	5,953.7	6,010.1	6,051.9	5,765.6
1999	6,080.7	6,129.5	6,133.6	6,172.3	6,201.0	6,237.7	6,269.0	6,299.1	6,323.0	6,378.4	6,464.1	6,551.8	6,270.0
2000	6,605.5	6,642.2	6,704.0	6,767.3	6,776.9	6,823.6	6,875.2	6,945.0	7,003.5	7,027.0	7,038.3	7,117.6	6,860.5
2001	7,237.2	7,308.5	7,372.0	7,507.8	7,564.1	7,644.7	7,691.9	7,696.3	7,853.2	7,897.8	7,973.0	8,035.4	7,648.5
2002	8,063.9	8,109.3	8,117.3	8,142.6	8,175.1	8,190.8	8,244.2	8,298.1	8,331.5	8,368.9	8,498.8	8,568.0	8,259.0
2003	8,588.1	8,628.7	8,648.8	8,686.0	8,741.9	8,791.6	8,888.7	8,918.2	8,906.5	8,896.8	8,880.3	8,872.3	8,787.3
2004	8,930.2	9,000.3	9,080.7	9,149.6	9,243.8	9,275.7	9,282.7	9,314.4	9,351.8	9,359.4	9,395.1	9,433.0	9,234.7
2005	9,487.2	9,531.6	9,565.3	9,620.9	9,665.0	9,725.3	9,762.4	9,864.6	9,950.8	10,032.0	10,078.5	10,154.0	9,786.5
2006[1]	10,242.8	10,298.7	Discontinued										10,270.8

[1] Preliminary.   [2] M3 -- M2 plus large-denomination ($100,000 or more) time deposits; repurchase agreements issued by depository institutions; Eurodollar deposits, specifically, dollar-denominated deposits due to nonbank U.S. addresses held at foreign offices of U.S. banks worldwide and all banking offices in Canada and the United Kingdom; and institutional money market mutual funds (funds with initial investments of $50,000 or more). Seasonally adjusted.
Source: Board of Governors of the Federal Reserve System

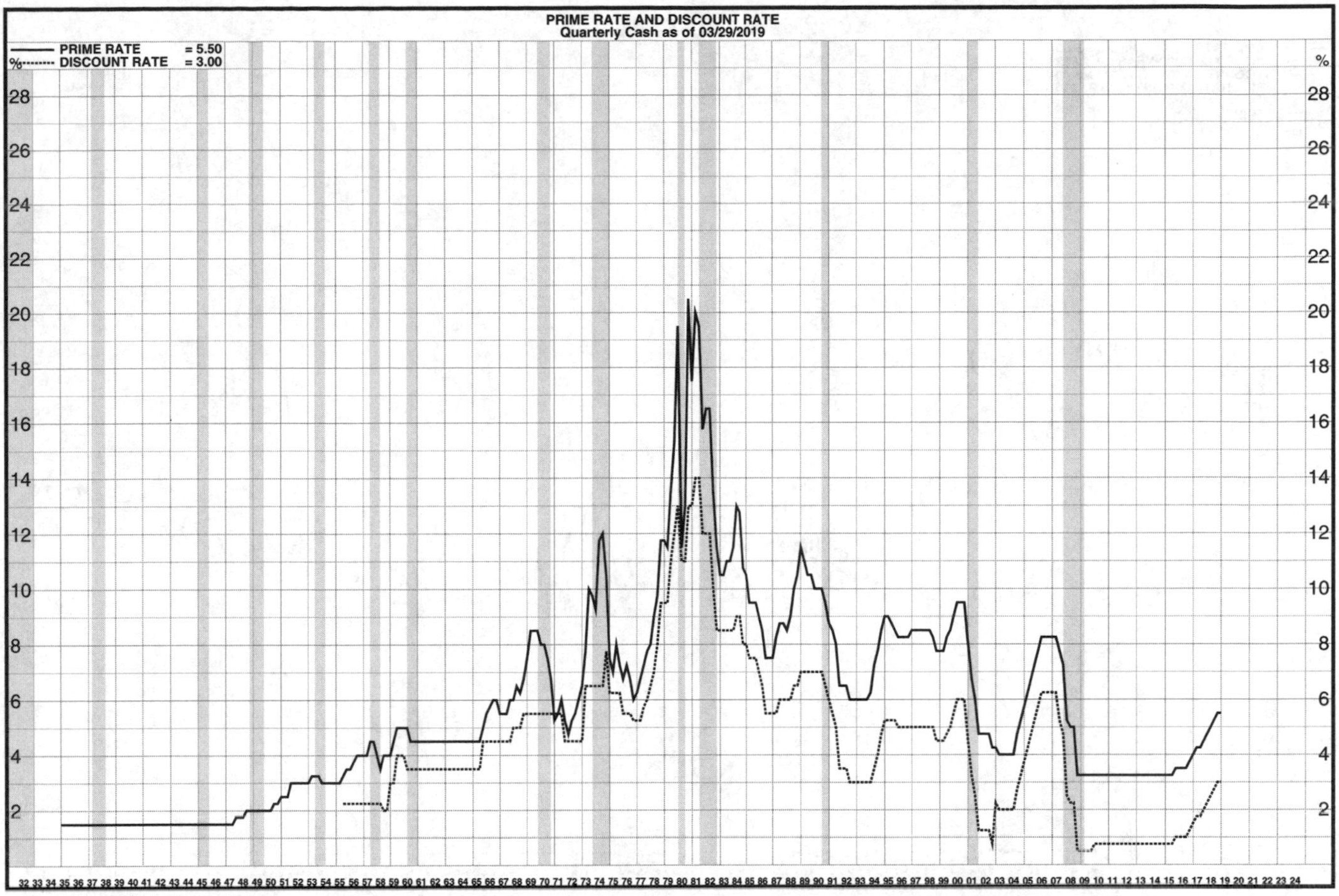

PRIME RATE AND DISCOUNT RATE
Quarterly Cash as of 03/29/2019

—— PRIME RATE	= 5.50
········ DISCOUNT RATE	= 3.00

Shaded areas indicate US recessions.

MUNICIPAL BONDS AND CORPORATE AAA BOND YIELDS
Quarterly Cash as of 03/29/2019

—— MUNICIPAL BOND YIELD	= 3.06
········ CORPORATE AAA BOND YIELD	= 3.44

Shaded areas indicate US recessions.

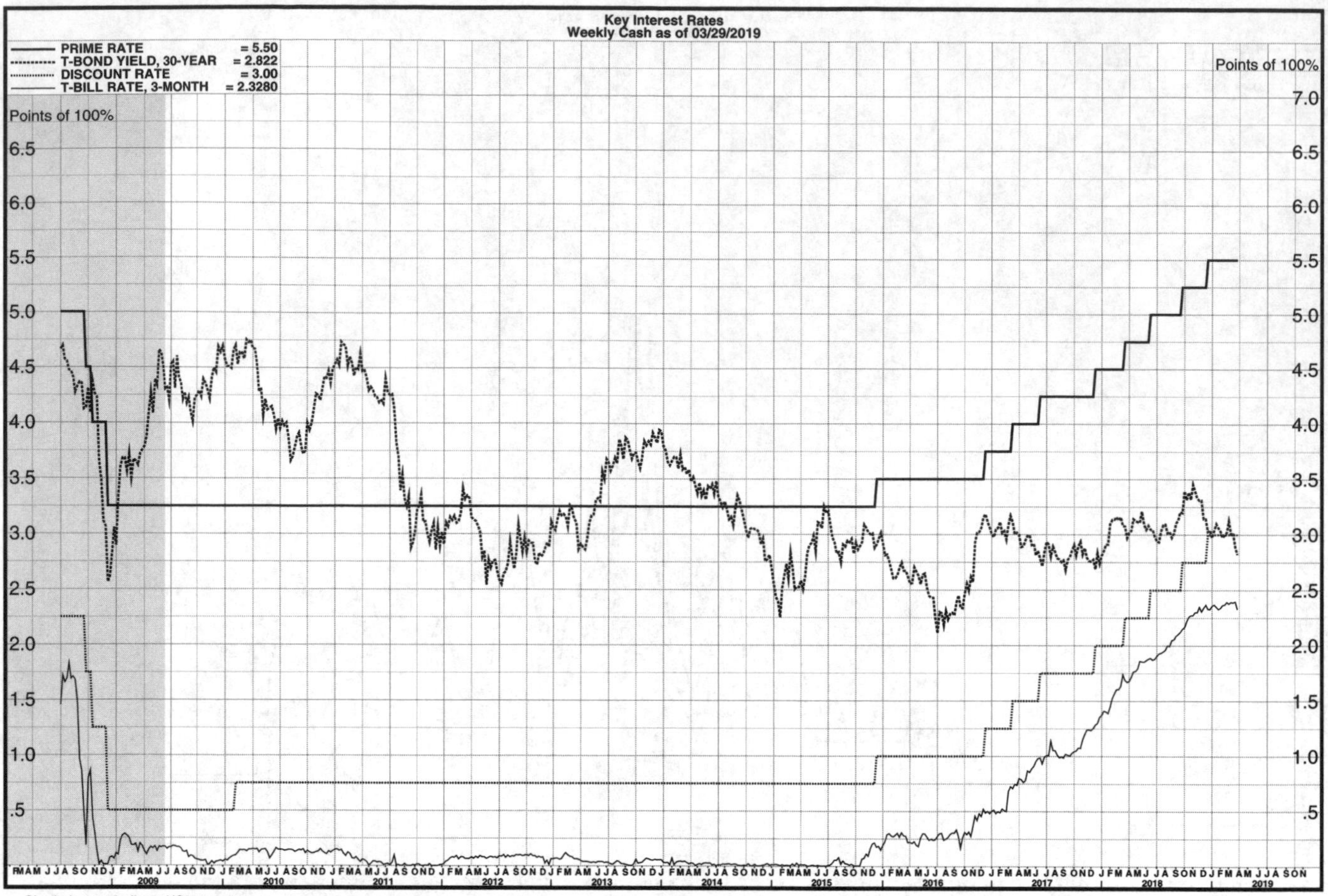

INTEREST RATES - U.S.

Key Interest Rates
Weekly Cash as of 03/29/2019

PRIME RATE = 5.50
T-BOND YIELD, 30-YEAR = 2.822
DISCOUNT RATE = 3.00
T-BILL RATE, 3-MONTH = 2.3280

Points of 100%

Points of 100%

Shaded areas indicate US recessions.

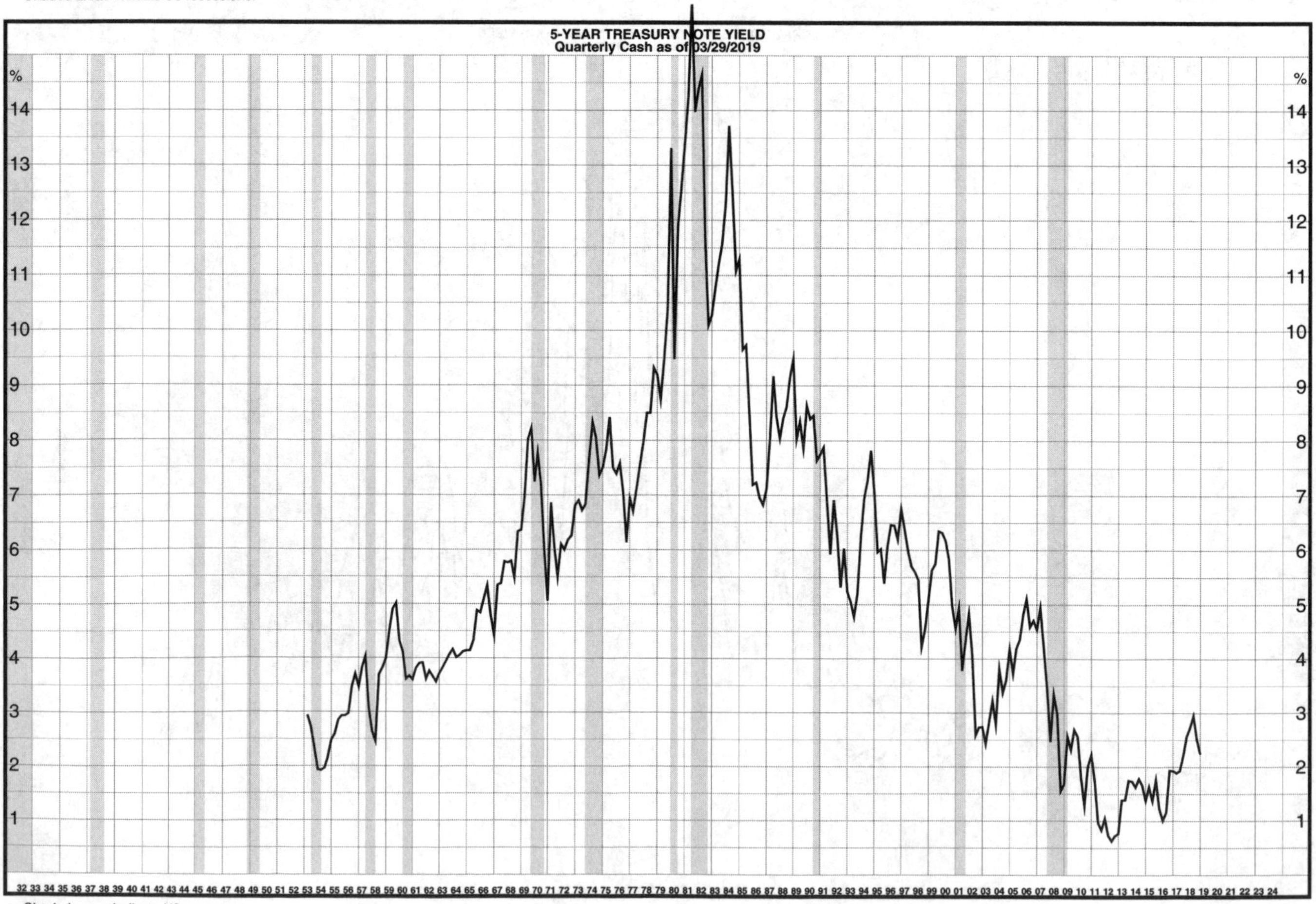

5-YEAR TREASURY NOTE YIELD
Quarterly Cash as of 03/29/2019

Shaded areas indicate US recessions.

150

Interest Rates - Worldwide

Interest rate futures contracts are widely traded throughout the world. The most popular futures contracts are generally 10-year government bonds and 3-month interest rate contracts. In Europe, futures on German interest rates are traded at the Eurex Exchange. Futures on UK interest rates are traded at the Liffe Exchange in London. Futures on Canadian interest rates are traded at the Montreal Exchange. Futures on Japanese interest rates are traded at the Singapore Exchange (SGX) and at the Tokyo Stock Exchange. A variety of other interest rate futures contracts are traded throughout the rest of the world (please see the front of this Yearbook for a complete list).

Euro-Zone – The Eurex German 10-year Euro Bund futures contract (Barchart.com symbol GG) traded mostly sideways during 2018, closing the year mildly higher by +1.86 points. The Eurex French 10-year OAT bond futures contract (Barchart.com symbol FN) also traded mostly sideways, closing the year down -4.38 points. The Eurex Italy Euro BTP 10-year bond futures contract (Barchart.com symbol II) fell sharply during spring 2018 but then stabilized and closed the year down -8.32 points.

European 10-year bond prices were generally stable in 2018 as the Eurozone economy showed tepid growth and as the European Central Bank (ECB) maintained its easy monetary policy. The Eurozone economy ended 2017 with a strong growth of +2.7% yr/yr in Q4-2017 and then remained relatively strong at +2.4% in Q1-2018 and +2.1% in Q2-2018, thus putting downward pressure on bond prices. However, the Eurozone economy then tailed off to +1.6% in Q3-2018 and +1.1% in Q4-2018 as the cumulative effects started stacking up from trade tensions and slower growth in China. In addition, German GDP growth turned negative in Q3-2018 and Italy's GDP growth was slightly negative in both Q3 and Q4.

Eurozone bond prices during 2018 saw support from weak inflation and a continued expansive monetary policy from the European Central Bank (ECB). The Eurozone core CPI remained weak in 2018 in the narrow range of 0.7%-1.2%, well below the ECB's target of just under 2%. The ECB kept its main refinancing rate at zero percent and its deposit rate at -0.40% during all of 2018. The ECB promised to keep its interest rates unchanged at least through summer 2019 and then in early 2019 extended that promise for unchanged rates until the end of 2019. The ECB's guidance for unchanged policy rates was a bullish factor for European bond prices.

The ECB reduced the size of its quantitative easing (QE) program during 2018 and ended its bond-buying program altogether in December 2018. Upon ending its QE program, the ECB promised to keep its balance sheet constant "for an extended period of time past the date when it starts raising the key ECB interest rates," which was supportive for European bond prices since it meant that the ECB would not be draining reserves from the banking system.

UK – The Liffe U.K. 10-year Gilt government bond futures contract (Barchart.com symbol G) fell to a 3-year low in early 2018 but then recovered and closed the year mildly higher by +2.08 points. Gilt prices were undercut in early 2018 as inflation remained high due to the plunge in sterling that followed the UK's vote in June 2016 to leave the EU (referred to as "Brexit"). The UK's CPI rose to a 6-year high of +3.1% y/y in November 2017 and remained high in early 2018, thus undercutting gilt prices and keeping pressure on the Bank of England (BOE) to raise interest rates. Indeed, the BOE in August 2018 did raise its base rate by +25 basis points to 0.75%, the highest level since 2009. However, the BOE was forced to back off its threats for another interest rate hike after the UK economy lost momentum later in 2018 and as Brexit negotiations became more troubled. UK GDP growth was relatively solid at +1.8% in 2016-17 but then tailed off to +1.4% in 2018. The BOE also backed off its threat for higher interest rates after UK inflation eased during 2018. The UK CPI eased to +2.1% by December 2018 and the core CPI eased to +1.9% y/y, thus roughly matching the BOE's inflation target. The UK interest rate outlook as of early 2019 depended mainly on whether the UK would be able to pull off a successful Brexit transition. The UK economy lost ground in late 2018 and early 2019 as some businesses gave up on a smooth Brexit transition and as business investment dropped.

Canada – The Montreal Exchange's Canadian 10-year government note futures contract (Barchart.com symbol CG) fell to a 4-year low in early 2018 but then recovered and closed the year mildly higher by +1.99 points. Canadian bond prices were undercut during 2018 by the Bank of Canada's (BOC) hawkish monetary policy. The BOC in 2018 raised its overnight lending rate three times by a total of 75 basis points to 1.75% by the end of 2018, bringing the overall rate hike since mid-2017 to a total of 1.25 percentage points. The BOC essentially followed the U.S. Federal Reserve in raising interest rates in an attempt to normalize monetary policy. The Canadian economy showed strong GDP growth of +3.0% in 2017 but then slid to +1.8% in 2018. Canadian GDP was particularly weak at +0.4% (quarter-on-quarter annualized) in Q4-2018 due to (1) trade tensions, (2) the slump in oil prices that hurt the Canadian oil industry, and (3) weaker global economic growth. The weaker Canadian economy in late 2018 allowed Canadian bond futures prices to rebound higher and close the year mildly higher.

Japan – The SGX Japan 10-year Japanese government bond (JGB) futures contract (Barchart.com symbol JX) traded sideways during most of 2018 but then rallied late in the year to post a new 2-year high and close the year mildly higher by +1.79 points. The Bank of Japan (BOJ) since September 2016 has pursued a yield-curve control policy where the central bank enforced a steeper yield curve with the 10-year JGB yield near zero, potentially allowing its 80-trillion-yen per year bond-purchase program to fluctuate in size to meet its yield target. The 10-year JGB yield has therefore been trading very close to the zero level. The BOJ on July 31, 2018 expanded the permissible range around the target to +/- 0.20% from 0.10%, potentially allowing the yield to trade as high as 0.20%. However, the BOJ also provided guidance that rates would remain very low for an "extended period," suggesting that the BOJ may not start raising rates until after the planned sales tax hike in Oct 2019 to 10% from 8% when the BOJ will see whether there will be a recession.

INTEREST RATES - WORLDWIDE

GILT, LONG - ICE-LIFF
Weekly Nearest Futures as of 03/29/2019

WEEKLY NEAREST FUTURES
As of 03/29/2019
Chart High 133.63   on 12/28/2011
Chart Low   106.00   on 01/02/2014

Points of 100%

% Yield Basis
6% 10-Yr

% Yield	Points
1.30	148
1.65	144
2.01	140
2.38	136
2.77	132
3.18	128
3.60	124
4.04	120
4.50	116
4.98	112
5.48	108
6.00	104
6.55	100
	96

2009 2010 2011 2012 2013 2014 2015 2016 2017 2018 2019

Nearby Futures through Last Trading Day.

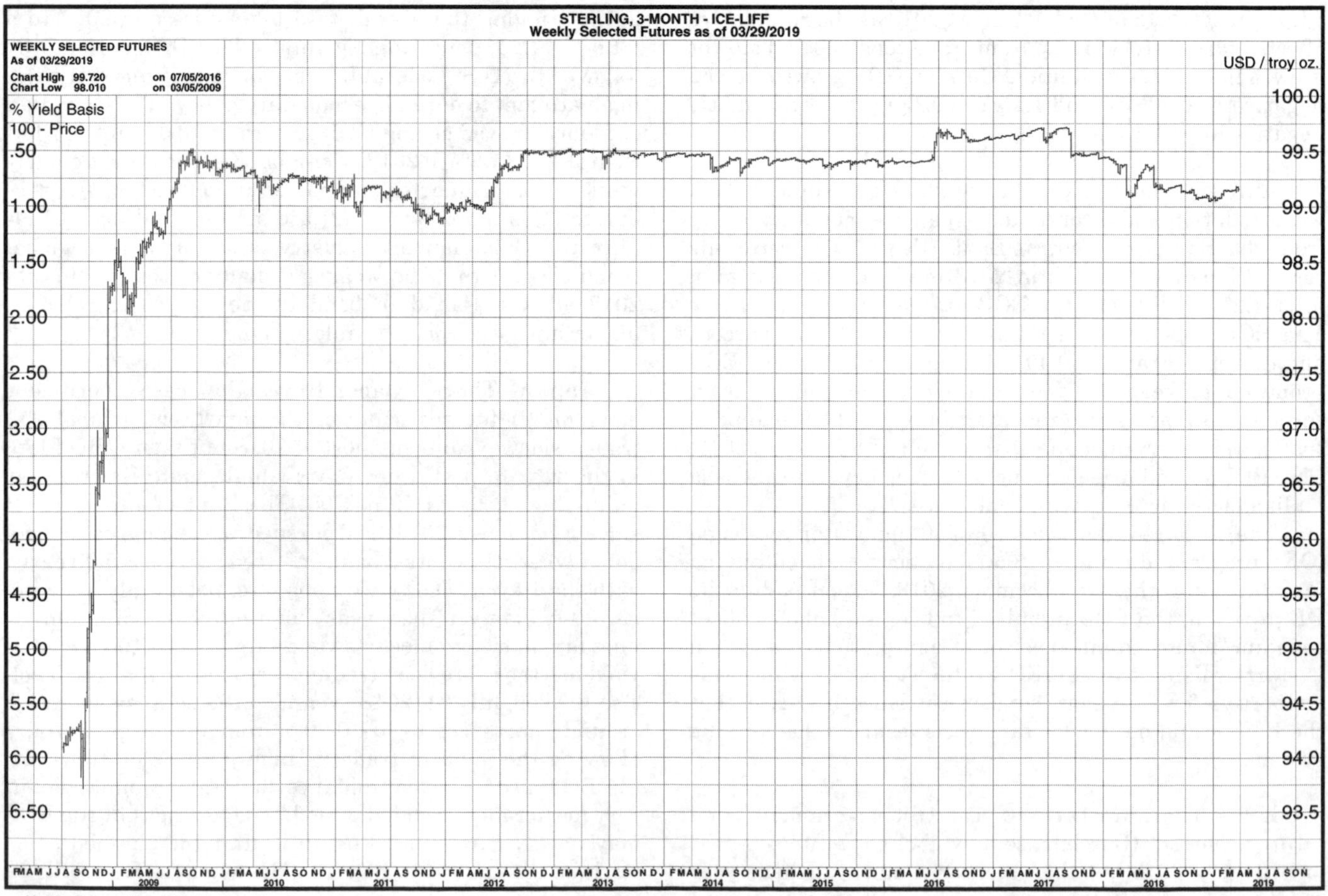

STERLING, 3-MONTH - ICE-LIFF
Weekly Selected Futures as of 03/29/2019

WEEKLY SELECTED FUTURES
As of 03/29/2019
Chart High 99.720   on 07/05/2016
Chart Low   98.010   on 03/05/2009

USD / troy oz.

% Yield Basis
100 - Price

% Yield	Price
.50	100.0
1.00	99.5
1.50	99.0
2.00	98.5
2.50	98.0
3.00	97.5
3.50	97.0
4.00	96.5
4.50	96.0
5.00	95.5
5.50	95.0
6.00	94.5
6.50	94.0
	93.5

2009 2010 2011 2012 2013 2014 2015 2016 2017 2018 2019

Nearby Futures through Last Trading Day.

152

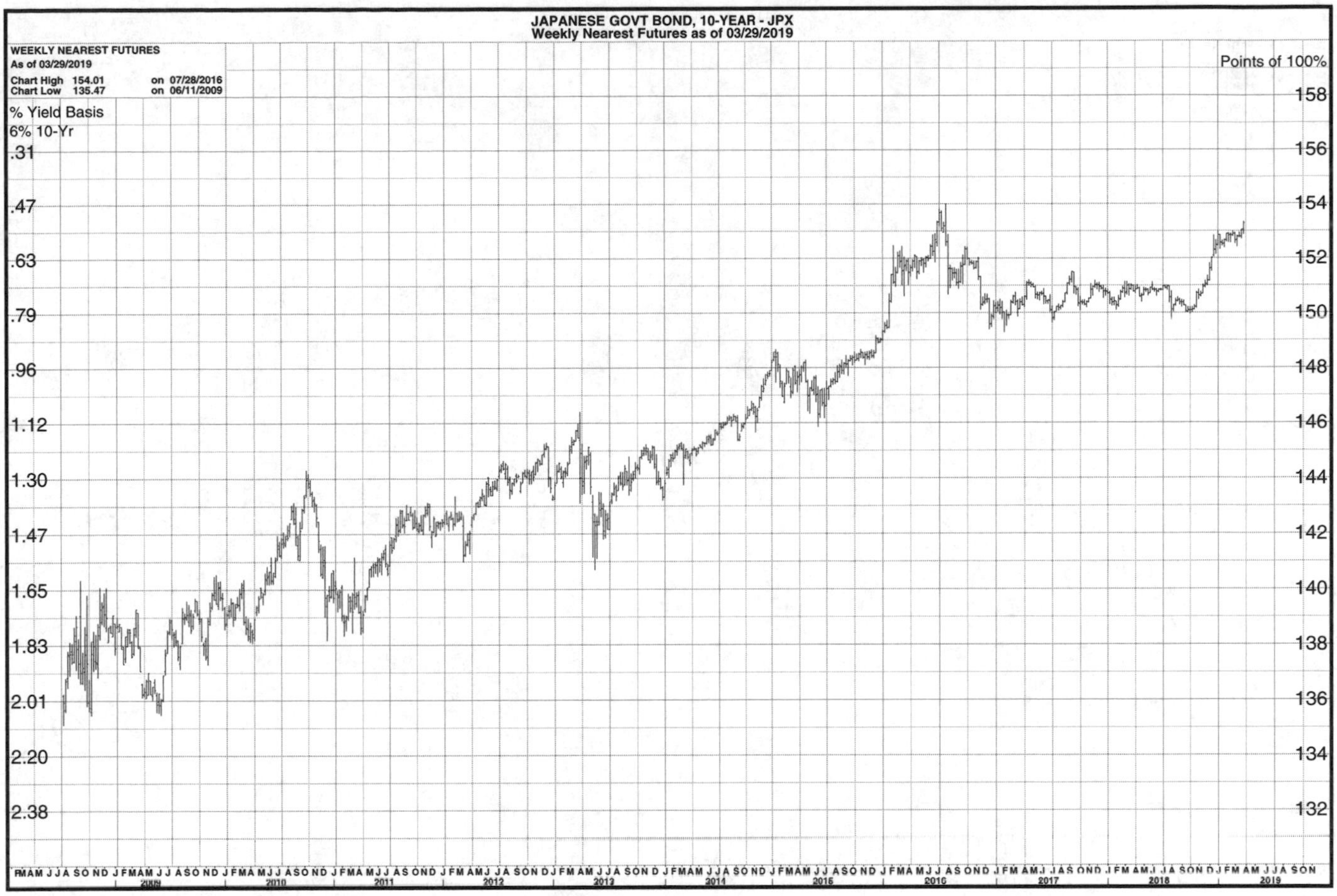

JAPANESE GOVT BOND, 10-YEAR - JPX
Weekly Nearest Futures as of 03/29/2019

WEEKLY NEAREST FUTURES
As of 03/29/2019

| Chart High | 154.01 | on 07/28/2016 |
| Chart Low | 135.47 | on 06/11/2009 |

Points of 100%

% Yield Basis
6% 10-Yr

Nearby Futures through Last Trading Day.

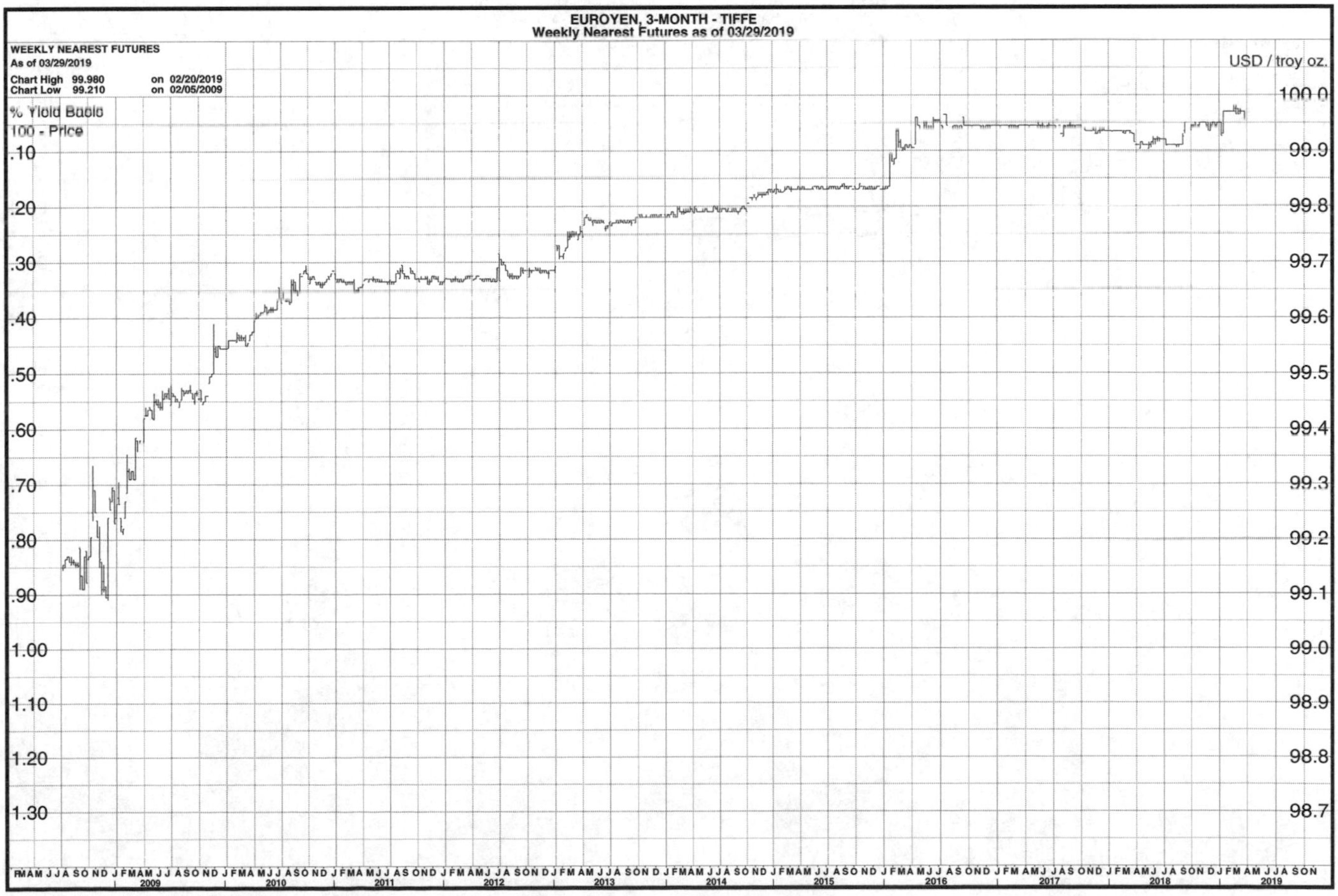

EUROYEN, 3-MONTH - TIFFE
Weekly Nearest Futures as of 03/29/2019

WEEKLY NEAREST FUTURES
As of 03/29/2019

| Chart High | 99.980 | on 02/20/2019 |
| Chart Low | 99.210 | on 02/05/2009 |

USD / troy oz.

% Yield Basis
100 - Price

Nearby Futures through Last Trading Day.

INTEREST RATES - WORLDWIDE

CANADIAN GOVT BOND, 10-YR - MNTRL
Weekly Nearest Futures as of 03/29/2019

WEEKLY NEAREST FUTURES
As of 03/29/2019
Chart High 149.390   on 07/08/2016
Chart Low   116.210   on 04/20/2010

% Yield Basis
6% 10-Yr

Points of 100%

Left axis	Right axis
.63	156
.96	152
1.30	148
1.65	144
2.01	140
2.38	136
2.77	132
3.18	128
3.60	124
4.04	120
4.50	116
4.98	112
5.48	108
	104

2009 2010 2011 2012 2013 2014 2015 2016 2017 2018 2019

Nearby Futures through Last Trading Day.

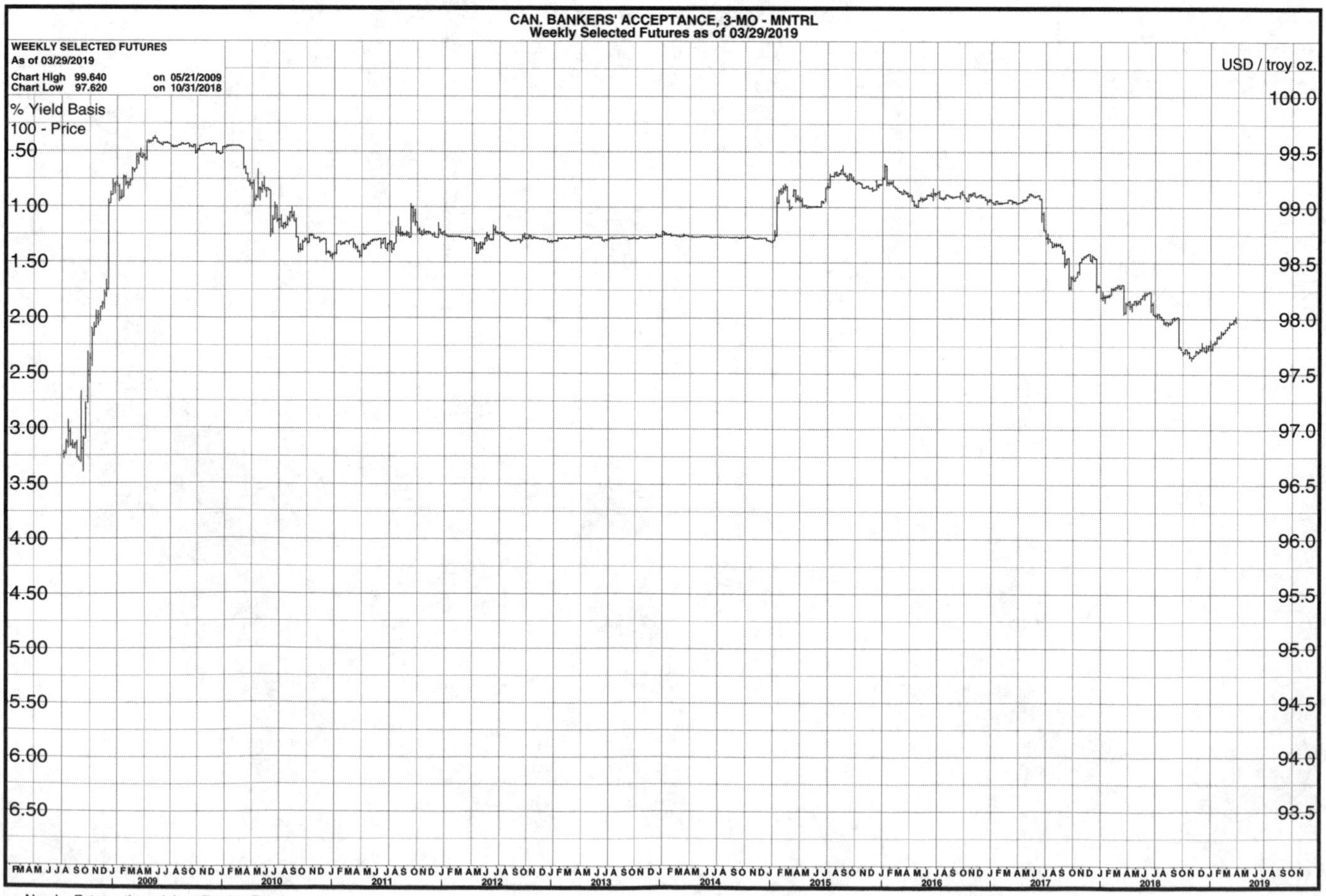

CAN. BANKERS' ACCEPTANCE, 3-MO - MNTRL
Weekly Selected Futures as of 03/29/2019

WEEKLY SELECTED FUTURES
As of 03/29/2019
Chart High 99.640   on 05/21/2009
Chart Low   97.620   on 10/31/2018

% Yield Basis
100 - Price

USD / troy oz.

Left axis	Right axis
.50	100.0
1.00	99.5
1.50	99.0
2.00	98.5
2.50	98.0
3.00	97.5
3.50	97.0
4.00	96.5
4.50	96.0
5.00	95.5
5.50	95.0
6.00	94.5
6.50	94.0
	93.5

2009 2010 2011 2012 2013 2014 2015 2016 2017 2018 2019

Nearby Futures through Last Trading Day.

154

Australia -- Economic Statistics   Percentage Change from Previous Period

Year	Real GDP	Nominal GDP	Real Private Consumption	Real Public Consumption	Grossed Fixed Investment	Real Total Domestic Demand	Real Exports of Goods & Services	Real Imports of Goods & Services	Consumer Prices[3]	Unemployment Rate
2011	2.7	7.7	3.5	3.9	7.1	5.0	-.4	10.6	3.3	5.1
2012	3.9	3.3	2.5	1.5	10.0	4.2	5.9	5.7	1.7	5.2
2013	2.2	3.5	1.9	1.9	-1.9	.4	5.8	-2.0	2.5	5.7
2014	2.5	2.9	2.5	.1	-2.3	.9	6.9	-1.4	2.5	6.1
2015	2.5	1.7	2.4	4.3	-3.4	1.3	6.3	1.7	1.5	6.1
2016	2.6	3.8	2.9	4.1	-2.2	1.9	6.8	.5	1.3	5.7
2017	2.2	5.8	2.7	3.7	3.4	3.0	3.7	7.8	1.9	5.6
2018[1]	3.1	4.6	2.5	4.4	3.4	3.1	4.6	5.6	2.0	5.4
2019[2]	2.9	4.1	2.1	3.2	4.0	2.7	4.1	6.1	2.2	5.3

[1] Estimate.   [2] Projection.   [3] National accounts implicit private consumption deflator.   *Source: Organization for Economic Co-operation and Development (OECD)*

Canada -- Economic Statistics   Percentage Change from Previous Period

Year	Real GDP	Nominal GDP	Real Private Consumption	Real Public Consumption	Grossed Fixed Investment	Real Total Domestic Demand	Real Exports of Goods & Services	Real Imports of Goods & Services	Consumer Prices[3]	Unemployment Rate
2011	3.1	6.5	2.3	1.3	4.6	2.2	4.8	5.6	2.9	7.5
2012	1.7	3.0	1.9	.7	4.9	2.1	2.6	3.6	1.5	7.3
2013	2.5	4.1	2.6	-.7	1.3	3.4	2.7	1.6	.9	7.1
2014	2.9	4.9	2.6	.5	2.4	1.8	5.9	2.3	1.9	6.9
2015	1.0	.2	2.2	1.6	-5.1	.1	3.5	.7	1.1	6.9
2016	1.4	2.0	2.3	2.2	-3.0	.8	1.0	-1.0	1.4	7.0
2017	3.0	5.4	3.4	2.3	2.8	3.8	1.1	3.6	1.5	6.4
2018[1]	2.1	4.1	2.3	2.4	3.8	2.6	2.6	4.2	1.9	6.1
2019[2]	2.2	4.2	2.3	1.4	2.5	2.1	3.4	3.2	2.0	5.9

[1] Estimate.   [2] Projection.   [3] National accounts implicit private consumption deflator.   *Source: Organization for Economic Co-operation and Development (OECD)*

France -- Economic Statistics   Percentage Change from Previous Period

Year	Real GDP[1]	Nominal GDP	Real Private Consumption	Real Public Consumption	Grossed Fixed Investment	Real Total Domestic Demand	Real Exports of Goods & Services	Real Imports of Goods & Services	Consumer Prices[3]	Unemployment Rate
2011	2.2	3.2	.6	1.1	2.2	2.2	6.6	6.2	2.3	9.1
2012	.4	1.6	-.4	1.6	.4	-.4	3.0	.4	2.2	9.8
2013	.6	1.4	.6	1.5	-.7	.7	2.1	2.5	1.0	10.3
2014	1.0	1.6	.8	1.3	.0	1.5	3.4	4.9	.6	10.3
2015	1.0	2.2	1.4	1.0	.9	1.5	4.4	5.7	.1	10.4
2016	1.1	1.3	1.9	1.4	2.7	1.6	1.5	3.1	.3	10.1
2017	2.3	3.0	1.2	1.4	4.7	2.2	4.7	4.1	1.1	9.4
2018[1]	1.6	2.6	1.0	.9	2.9	1.1	3.3	1.5	1.1	9.2
2019[2]	1.6	3.0	1.6	.8	2.4	1.5	3.6	3.2	1.3	8.8

[1] Estimate.   [2] Projection.   [3] National accounts implicit private consumption deflator.   *Source: Organization for Economic Co-operation and Development (OECD)*

Germany -- Economic Statistics   Percentage Change from Previous Period

Year	Real GDP	Nominal GDP	Real Private Consumption	Real Public Consumption	Grossed Fixed Investment	Real Total Domestic Demand	Real Exports of Goods & Services	Real Imports of Goods & Services	Consumer Prices[3]	Unemployment Rate
2011	3.7	4.8	1.3	.9	7.4	3.0	8.4	7.2	2.5	5.9
2012	.7	2.2	1.4	1.1	-.1	-.8	3.5	.4	2.1	5.4
2013	.6	2.6	.8	1.4	-1.2	1.0	1.9	3.1	1.6	5.2
2014	2.2	4.0	1.1	1.6	3.9	1.6	4.6	3.6	.8	5.0
2015	1.5	3.5	1.6	2.9	1.0	1.4	4.7	5.2	.1	4.6
2016	2.2	3.6	1.9	4.0	3.4	2.9	2.1	4.0	.4	4.2
2017	2.5	4.0	2.0	1.6	3.6	2.2	5.3	5.3	1.7	3.7
2018[1]	1.6	3.5	1.2	1.2	3.0	2.0	2.5	3.6	1.8	3.5
2019[2]	1.6	3.9	1.8	2.5	2.5	2.2	2.9	4.4	2.0	3.4

[1] Estimate.   [2] Projection.   [3] National accounts implicit private consumption deflator.   *Source: Organization for Economic Co-operation and Development (OECD)*

INTEREST RATES - WORLDWIDE

Italy -- Economic Statistics   Percentage Change from Previous Period

Year	Real GDP	Nominal GDP	Real Private Consumption	Real Public Consumption	Grossed Fixed Investment	Real Total Domestic Demand	Real Exports of Goods & Services	Real Imports of Goods & Services	Consumer Prices[3]	Unemployment Rate
2011	.7	2.2	.0	-1.8	-1.7	-.5	6.1	1.1	2.9	8.4
2012	-2.9	-1.5	-4.0	-1.4	-9.4	-5.7	2.0	-8.2	3.3	10.7
2013	-1.7	-.6	-2.4	-.3	-6.6	-2.7	.9	-2.3	1.2	12.1
2014	.2	1.1	.2	-.7	-2.2	.3	2.4	3.0	.2	12.6
2015	.8	1.8	1.9	-.6	1.9	1.4	4.2	6.6	.1	11.9
2016	1.0	1.8	1.4	.6	3.3	1.3	2.6	3.8	-.1	11.7
2017	1.6	2.2	1.4	.1	3.9	1.3	6.0	5.7	1.4	11.2
2018[1]	1.0	2.5	.8	.1	4.5	1.4	.2	1.6	1.2	10.5
2019[2]	.9	2.5	.7	.2	3.5	1.1	2.7	3.5	1.4	10.1

[1] Estimate.   [2] Projection.   [3] National accounts implicit private consumption deflator.   *Source: Organization for Economic Co-operation and Development (OECD)*

Japan -- Economic Statistics   Percentage Change from Previous Period

Year	Real GDP	Nominal GDP	Real Private Consumption	Real Public Consumption	Grossed Fixed Investment	Real Total Domestic Demand	Real Exports of Goods & Services	Real Imports of Goods & Services	Consumer Prices[3]	Unemployment Rate
2011	-.1	-1.8	-.4	1.9	1.7	.7	-.2	5.8	-.3	4.6
2012	1.5	.7	2.0	1.7	3.5	2.3	-.1	5.4	.0	4.4
2013	2.0	1.7	2.4	1.5	4.9	2.4	.8	3.3	.3	4.0
2014	.4	2.1	-.9	.5	3.1	.4	9.3	8.3	2.8	3.6
2015	1.4	3.5	.0	1.5	1.7	1.0	2.9	.8	.8	3.4
2016	1.0	1.2	.1	1.3	1.1	.4	1.7	-1.6	-.1	3.1
2017	1.7	1.5	1.0	.4	2.5	1.2	6.7	3.5	.4	2.8
2018[1]	.9	.7	.4	.5	1.7	.8	2.8	2.6	1.0	2.8
2019[2]	1.0	1.2	.9	.6	1.5	1.0	1.4	1.4	1.7	2.8

[1] Estimate.   [2] Projection.   [3] National accounts implicit private consumption deflator.   *Source: Organization for Economic Co-operation and Development (OECD)*

Switzerland -- Economic Statistics   Percentage Change from Previous Period

Year	Real GDP	Nominal GDP	Real Private Consumption	Real Public Consumption	Grossed Fixed Investment	Real Total Domestic Demand	Real Exports of Goods & Services	Real Imports of Goods & Services	Consumer Prices[3]	Unemployment Rate
2011	1.8	2.2	.8	1.7	4.3	3.9	5.2	9.3	.2	4.4
2012	1.0	.8	2.3	1.5	3.4	-1.4	1.1	-2.5	-.7	4.5
2013	1.9	1.9	2.6	2.3	.6	-.7	15.2	13.6	-.2	4.7
2014	2.5	1.8	1.3	2.2	2.9	2.7	-6.1	-7.7	.0	4.8
2015	1.3	.6	1.7	1.1	2.3	2.2	2.5	4.3	-1.1	4.8
2016	1.6	1.0	1.5	1.2	3.4	.3	6.7	5.9	-.4	4.9
2017	1.7	1.2	1.2	.9	3.3	1.5	-.1	-.7	.6	4.8
2018[1]	2.9	3.6	1.2	1.0	3.1	1.7	1.4	-.8	.6	4.5
2019[2]	1.6	2.7	1.5	1.0	2.9	2.6	1.9	3.8	.6	4.4

[1] Estimate.   [2] Projection.   [3] National accounts implicit private consumption deflator.   *Source: Organization for Economic Co-operation and Development (OECD)*

United Kingdom -- Economic Statistics   Percentage Change from Previous Period

Year	Real GDP	Nominal GDP	Real Private Consumption	Real Public Consumption	Grossed Fixed Investment	Real Total Domestic Demand	Real Exports of Goods & Services	Real Imports of Goods & Services	Consumer Prices[3]	Unemployment Rate
2011	1.6	3.6	-.6	.1	2.6	.1	6.4	.7	4.5	8.1
2012	1.4	3.0	1.5	1.2	2.1	1.9	1.4	3.0	2.8	8.0
2013	2.0	4.0	1.8	-.2	3.4	2.5	1.5	3.2	2.6	7.6
2014	2.9	4.7	2.0	2.2	7.2	3.4	2.3	3.8	1.5	6.2
2015	2.3	2.8	2.6	1.4	3.4	2.7	4.4	5.5	.1	5.4
2016	1.8	3.9	3.1	.8	2.3	2.5	1.0	3.3	.6	4.9
2017	1.7	3.8	1.8	-.1	3.3	1.2	5.7	3.2	2.7	4.4
2018[1]	1.3	3.2	1.5	.8	.0	1.0	1.2	.2	2.6	4.4
2019[2]	1.4	3.2	1.1	1.9	.8	1.1	1.1	.1	2.2	4.6

[1] Estimate.   [2] Projection.   [3] National accounts implicit private consumption deflator.   *Source: Organization for Economic Co-operation and Development (OECD)*

Iron and Steel

Iron (atomic symbol Fe) is a soft, malleable, and ductile metallic element. Next to aluminum, iron is the most abundant of all metals. Pure iron melts at about 1535 degrees Celsius and boils at 2750 degrees Celsius. Archaeologists in Egypt discovered the earliest iron implements dating back to about 3000 BC, and iron ornaments were used even earlier.

Steel is an alloy of iron and carbon, often with an admixture of other elements. The physical properties of various types of steel and steel alloys depend primarily on the amount of carbon present and how it is distributed in the iron. Steel is marketed in a variety of sizes and shapes, such as rods, pipes, railroad rails, tees, channels, and I-beams. Steel mills roll and form heated ingots into the required shapes. The working of steel improves the quality of the steel by refining its crystalline structure and making the metal tougher. There are five classifications of steel: carbon steels, alloy steels, high-strength low-alloy steels, stainless steel, and tool steels.

Prices – In 2018 the average wholesale price for No. 1 heavy-melting steel scrap in Chicago rose +22.8% yr/yr to $319.26 per metric ton.

Supply – World production of iron ore in 2017 rose +2.1% yr/yr to 2.400 billion metric tons, a new record high. The world's largest producers of iron ore are Australia with 36.7% of world production, Brazil with 18.3%, and China

with 14.2%. The U.S. accounted for only 1.9% of world iron ore production in 2017.

World production of raw steel (ingots and castings) in 2018 rose +6.5 % yr/yr to 1.800 billion metric tons. The largest producers were China with 49.4% of world production, Japan with 6.1%, and Russia with 3.9%. U.S. production of steel ingots in 2018 rose by +6.1% yr/yr to 87.0 million metric tons, up from the 2009 record low of 59.400 million metric tons.

U.S. production of pig iron (excluding ferro-alloys) in 2018 (annualized through October) rose +6.8% yr/yr to 23.928 million short tons.

Demand – U.S. consumption of ferrous scrap and pig iron in 2016 rose +0.8% yr/yr to 80.180 million metric tons, up from the 2015 record low of 79.530. The largest consumers of ferrous scrap and pig iron were the manufacturers steel ingots and castings with 87.8% of consumption. Iron foundries and miscellaneous users accounted for 8.3% of consumption and manufacturers of steel castings (scrap) accounted for 3.9% of consumption.

Trade – The U.S. imported 3.010 million metric tons of iron ore in 2016, down -33.8% yr/yr. The bulk of U.S. iron ore imports came from Brazil (58.5% with 1.760 million metric tons) and Canada (18.5% with 557,000 metric tons).

World Production of Raw Steel (Ingots and Castings)   In Thousands of Metric Tons

Year	Brazil	Canada	China	France	Germany	Italy	Japan	Korea, South	Russia	Ukraine	United Kindom	United States	World Total
2009	26,506	9,245	572,180	12,836	32,671	19,737	87,534	48,752	59,800	29,855	10,079	59,400	1,230,000
2010	32,928	13,003	637,230	15,416	43,830	25,751	109,599	58,914	66,800	33,559	9,709	80,500	1,430,000
2011	35,220	12,891	701,968	15,780	44,284	28,735	107,601	68,519	68,852	35,332	9,478	86,400	1,540,000
2012	34,524	13,507	723,880	15,609	42,661	27,257	107,232	69,073	70,392	33,511	9,579	88,700	1,560,000
2013	34,163	12,417	779,040	15,685	42,645	23,093	110,595	66,061	68,861	32,771	11,858	86,900	1,610,000
2014	33,912	12,730	822,300	16,143	42,943	23,714	110,666	71,542	70,548	27,373	12,120	88,200	1,670,000
2015	33,300	12,473	803,820	14,984	42,676	22,018	105,134	69,670	69,421	22,935	10,907	78,800	1,620,000
2016	31,275	12,646	808,366	14,413	42,080	23,373	104,775	68,576	70,808	24,128	7,635	78,500	1,630,000
2017[1]	34,000	14,000	832,000	16,000	43,000		105,000	71,000	70,000	21,000	8,000	82,000	1,690,000
2018[2]	35,000	15,000	890,000	17,000	44,000		110,000	75,000	71,000	22,000		87,000	1,800,000

[1] Preliminary.   [2] Estimate.   *Source: U.S. Geological Survey (USGS)*

Average Wholesale Prices of Iron and Steel in the United States

	No. 1 Heavy Melting Steel Scrap		Sheet Bars			Hot Rolled Strip	Carbon Steel Plates	Cold Rolled Strip	Galvanized Sheets	Rail Road Steel Scrap[2]	Used Steel Cans[3]
	Pittsburg	Chicago	Hot Rolled	Hot Rolled	Cold Finished						
Year	$ Per Gross Ton		Cents Per Pound							$ Per Gross Ton	
2002	101.06	89.92	16.46	----	23.26	----	----	----	22.00	NA	66.71
2003	128.32	113.82	14.80	----	25.15	----	----	----	20.08	----	116.21
2004	221.05	220.13	30.84	----	38.67	----	----	----	36.69	----	192.80
2005	199.10	196.75	27.83	----	44.96	----	----	----	33.77	----	172.00
2006	222.39	225.21	29.78	----	44.02	----	----	----	38.09	----	212.63
2007	250.98	262.80	26.89	----	45.26	----	----	----	38.25	----	244.65
2008	365.62	357.88	44.56	----	61.67	----	----	----	54.91	----	314.63
2009	204.21	206.14	24.60	----	42.10	----	----	----	34.23	----	121.84
2010	339.54	334.48	31.65	----	50.82	----	----	----	41.72	----	296.91
2011[1]	408.64	417.00	38.02	----	63.63	----	----	----	48.45	----	391.50

[1] Preliminary.   [2] Specialties scrap.   [3] Consumer buying prices.   NA = Not available.   *Source: American Metal Market (AMM)*

IRON AND STEEL

Salient Statistics of Steel in the United States   In Thousands of Short Tons

Year	Pig Iron Production	Producer Price Index for Steel Mill Products (1982=100)	Raw Steel Production — By Type of Furnace — Basic Oxygen	Open Hearth	Electric[2]	Raw Steel Production — Stainless	Carbon	Alloy	Total	Net Shipments Steel Mill Products	Total Steel Products — Exports	Imports
2009	19,000	165.2	21,274	----	39,793	1,786	60,847	2,888	65,477	56,400	8,420	14,700
2010	26,800	191.7	30,975	----	54,343	2,425	81,129	5,159	88,735	75,700	11,000	21,700
2011	30,200	216.2	34,943	----	57,430	2,282	87,192	5,754	95,239	83,300	12,200	25,900
2012	30,100	208.0	36,817	----	57,761	2,183	90,278	5,258	97,774	87,000	12,500	30,400
2013	30,300	195.0		----		2,238	88,956	4,530	95,790	86,600	11,500	29,200
2014	29,400	200.2		----		2,634	89,727	4,872	97,223	89,100	10,900	40,200
2015	25,400	177.1		----		2,590	81,129	3,230	86,861	78,500	9,050	35,200
2016	22,300	167.8		----		2,734	80,688	3,108	86,531	78,500	8,450	30,000
2017	22,400	187.4		----								
2018[1]	24,000	207.0		----								

[1] Preliminary.   [2] Includes crucible steels.   *Sources: American Iron & Steel Institute (AISI); U.S. Geological Survey (USGS)*

Production of Steel Ingots, Rate of Capability Utilization[1] in the United States   In Percent

Year	Jan.	Feb.	Mar.	Apr.	May	June	July	Aug.	Sept.	Oct.	Nov.	Dec.	Average
2009	42.6	45.5	42.9	40.8	42.8	46.9	52.4	57.7	62.1	62.3	61.4	60.9	51.5
2010	64.2	71.1	73.2	74.0	74.8	75.4	69.6	68.1	70.2	67.3	68.3	68.4	70.4
2011	73.2	75.4	75.0	74.2	72.7	76.2	75.0	75.7	76.1	71.9	73.0	75.2	74.5
2012	77.6	80.7	79.6	80.9	79.2	74.8	73.3	76.3	70.4	68.0	70.1	71.7	75.2
2013	76.5	78.3	76.2	76.7	76.5	76.1	77.3	77.6	78.3	76.5	76.2	74.0	76.7
2014	75.8	77.9	77.7	76.6	77.3	78.5	79.6	80.2	78.1	76.5	77.2	74.6	77.5
2015	76.4	72.1	67.7	69.8	72.1	74.4	73.2	72.2	70.5	68.1	62.7	62.1	70.1
2016	68.7	73.1	72.1	72.6	74.3	75.1	71.3	70.8	68.0	65.4	67.1	67.8	70.5
2017	73.3	75.9	73.6	73.6	73.7	74.9	74.3	75.8	73.4	73.2	73.3	71.9	73.9
2018[2]	73.6	77.9	78.3	76.0	77.1	77.4	78.4	79.4	79.6	80.2	81.2		78.1

[1] Based on tonnage capability to produce raw steel for a full order book.   [2] Preliminary.   *Sources: American Iron and Steel Institute (AISI); U.S. Geological Survey (USGS)*

World Production of Pig Iron (Excludes Ferro-Alloys)   In Thousands of Metric Tons

Year	Belgium	Brazil	China	France	Germany	India	Italy	Japan	Russia	Ukraine	United Kingdom	United States	World Total
2009	3,087	25,135	552,830	8,105	20,104	38,233	5,719	66,943	43,930	25,682	7,674	19,000	984,000
2010	4,688	30,878	597,330	10,137	28,560	39,560	8,549	82,283	48,000	27,361	7,235	26,800	1,110,000
2011	5,815	33,319	640,510	9,698	27,563	43,624	9,838	81,028	48,117	28,876	6,625	30,200	1,170,000
2012	4,073	26,900	663,500	9,532	26,493	47,987	9,424	81,405	50,459	28,484	7,183	32,100	1,190,000
2013	4,343	26,200	708,970	10,276	26,678	51,359	6,933	83,849	49,945	29,089	9,471	30,300	1,240,000
2014	4,388	27,016	713,740	10,866	27,379	55,166	6,371	83,872	51,460	24,801	9,705	29,400	1,260,000
2015	4,248	27,803	691,410	10,095	27,842	58,393	5,051	81,011	52,411	21,863	8,774	25,400	1,230,000
2016	4,868	26,031	700,740	9,722	27,264	62,994	6,048	80,170	51,829	23,613	6,218	22,288	1,240,000
2017[1]		28,000	711,000	11,000	28,000	66,000		78,000	52,000	20,000	6,000	22,000	1,170,000
2018[2]		29,000	723,000	12,000	29,000	69,000		82,000	53,000	21,000		24,000	1,200,000

[1] Preliminary.   [2] Estimate.   *Source: U.S. Geological Survey (USGS)*

Production of Pig Iron (Excludes Ferro-Alloys) in the United States   In Thousands of Short Tons

Year	Jan.	Feb.	Mar.	Apr.	May	June	July	Aug.	Sept.	Oct.	Nov.	Dec.	Total
2009	1,450	1,510	1,630	1,410	1,370	1,380	1,840	2,090	1,930	2,510	2,240	2,410	21,770
2010	2,350	2,530	2,870	2,030	2,830	2,800	2,450	2,490	2,600	2,150	2,470	2,340	29,910
2011	2,400	2,490	2,790	2,550	2,870	2,820	2,520	2,610	2,540	3,010	2,990	3,190	32,780
2012	3,080	3,050	3,430	2,920	3,320	2,970	2,930	2,860	2,440	2,260	2,820	2,900	34,980
2013	3,060	2,760	3,040	2,800	2,880	2,760	2,760	2,890	2,880	2,870	2,760	2,780	34,240
2014	2,430	2,450	2,820	2,580	2,710	2,760	2,930	2,920	2,740	2,690	2,740	2,860	32,630
2015	2,760	2,310	2,390	2,330	2,530	2,670	2,830	2,690	2,390	2,270	2,120	2,110	29,400
2016	2,200	2,260	2,380	2,150	1,910	2,280	2,220	1,860	1,770	1,610	1,660	1,810	24,110
2017	1,940	1,930	1,960	1,870	1,940	1,830	1,860	1,930	1,850	1,690	1,770	1,840	22,410
2018[1]	1,920	1,790	1,970	1,930	2,070	2,060	2,100	2,030	2,010	2,060			23,928

[1] Preliminary.   *Source: American Iron and Steel Institute*

Salient Statistics of Ferrous Scrap and Pig Iron in the United States   In Thousands of Metric Tons

| | Consumption: Ferrous Scrap & Pig Iron Charged To | | | | | | | | | | | | Stocks, Dec. 31 Ferrous Scrap & Pig Iron at Consumers | | |
| | Mfg. of Pig Iron & Steel Ingots & Castings | | | Iron Foundries & Misc. Users | | | Mfg. of Steel | All Uses | | | Imports of | Exports of | | | |
Year	Scrap	Pig Iron	Total	Scrap	Pig Iron	Total	Castings (Scrap)	Ferrous Scrap	Pig Iron	Grand Total	Scrap[2]	Scrap[3]			Total
2007	54,600	36,500	93,140	9,080	1,290	10,374	1,380	65,000	37,800	104,850	3,700	16,500	4,140	771	5,275
2008	56,600	33,500	92,050	7,760	844	8,608	2,070	66,400	34,400	102,760	3,600	21,500	4,340	885	5,660
2009	47,600	28,300	77,240	838	17	859	838	53,100	30,200	84,660	2,990	22,400	3,070	506	3,810
2010	53,100	34,100	88,690	5,180	1,910	7,093	1,810	60,100	36,000	97,590	3,780	20,500	3,330	418	3,909
2011	56,400	34,900	92,920	5,960	1,970	7,933	756	63,100	36,900	101,620	4,010	24,300	3,980	423	4,529
2012	55,800	35,400	94,780	6,710	1,980	8,693	639	63,100	37,400	104,080	3,720	21,400	4,170	405	4,722
2013	52,100	31,800	88,390	5,660	2,260	7,923	1,180	59,000	34,100	97,590	3,930	18,500	4,180	444	4,731
2014	51,900	25,900	82,590	5,560	2,100	7,663	1,190	58,600	28,100	91,490	4,220	15,300	4,330	469	5,016
2015	46,100	22,200	72,430	4,420	632	5,055	1,970	52,500	22,900	79,530	3,510	12,800	4,390	690	5,296
2016[1]	44,900	20,700	70,380	5,020	1,620	6,643	3,100	53,000	22,400	80,180	3,860	12,600	4,730	453	5,420

[1] Preliminary.   [2] Includes tinplate and terneplate.   [3] Excludes used rails for rerolling and other uses and ships, boats, and other vessels for scrapping.
Source: U.S. Geological Survey (USGS)

Consumption of Pig Iron in the United States, by Type of Furance or Equipment   In Thousands of Metric Tons

Year	Open Hearth	Electric	Cupola	Basic Oxygen Process	Air & Other Furnace	Direct Casting	Total
2007	----	3,980	401	33,400	8	36	37,800
2008	----	3,350	401	30,600	5	36	33,600
2009	----	4,140	148	25,900	----	36	30,200
2010	----	4,740	55	31,200	----	16	36,000
2011	----	5,410	76	31,300	12	36	36,900
2012	----	5,790	57	31,500	10	36	37,400
2013	----	4,150	345	29,600	----	----	34,100
2014	----	4,230	148	23,800	----	----	28,100
2015	----	2,350	152	20,300	----	----	22,900
2016[1]	----	3,620	155	18,600	----	----	22,400

[1] Preliminary.   W = Withheld.   *Source: U.S. Geological Survey (USGS)*

Volume of Trading of Hot Rolled Steel Futures in New York   In Contracts

Year	Jan.	Feb.	Mar.	Apr.	May	June	July	Aug.	Sept.	Oct.	Nov.	Dec.	Total
2009	25	740	350	350	900	132	4,645	310	3,250	360	17	2,410	13,489
2010	1,236	725	2,173	2,136	342	1,678	3,740	974	4,284	309	3,150	866	21,613
2011	1,727	1,036	1,549	684	2,128	1,320	4,588	3,197	3,098	5,021	5,205	2,185	31,738
2012	6,214	5,905	1,187	1,772	4,421	2,848	4,081	3,055	3,838	5,301	2,823	2,422	43,867
2013	4,567	6,619	6,814	6,972	3,415	3,700	2,874	2,572	1,728	8,033	3,869	2,630	53,793
2014	3,953	2,376	6,002	4,292	4,220	1,082	3,543	905	4,863	5,777	7,661	3,556	48,230
2015	3,096	2,344	4,705	6,489	4,084	3,083	6,478	6,156	7,222	6,559	5,405	3,196	58,817
2016	3,058	7,225	4,165	8,576	2,303	4,454	3,415	5,006	4,506	5,836	2,623	2,717	53,884
2017	5,501	2,870	2,897	1,182	7,188	4,905	6,639	7,316	7,495	7,107	4,598	5,531	63,229
2018	10,435	9,072	9,655	12,074	9,487	5,226	10,861	17,235	6,668	9,665	11,986	7,205	119,569

Contract size – 20 short tons.   *Source: CME Group; New York Mercantile Exchange (CME-NYMEX)*

Average Open Interest of Hot Rolled Steel Futures in New York   In Contracts

Year	Jan.	Feb.	Mar.	Apr.	May	June	July	Aug.	Sept.	Oct.	Nov.	Dec.
2009			498	781	1,338	1,432	3,770	5,773	6,549	9,137	8,445	9,051
2010	8,088	7,631	7,292	7,897	7,767	7,149	9,023	8,495	10,683	10,956	9,566	8,807
2011	7,951	7,919	8,287	8,459	8,827	9,592	10,330	11,253	9,604	9,774	11,324	10,568
2012	10,469	12,009	13,228	12,572	13,910	14,995	13,809	12,914	13,181	12,982	12,382	10,394
2013	9,679	10,033	12,210	14,098	14,810	14,668	14,328	14,565	14,114	13,517	13,613	11,741
2014	10,308	10,308	9,720	9,537	10,242	10,769	11,092	11,507	12,037	15,739	19,703	22,501
2015	21,609	20,954	18,637	18,859	19,351	19,356	20,474	20,783	21,273	22,758	23,472	24,299
2016	23,157	24,528	24,610	22,721	21,525	20,796	19,304	18,927	17,829	18,390	16,825	14,694
2017	13,068	12,862	13,145	12,646	12,815	13,952	13,369	14,007	14,493	14,065	13,384	13,600
2018	12,892	12,056	13,044	14,466	14,375	13,879	13,800	16,712	15,926	16,338	17,185	16,261

Contract size = 20 short tons.   *Source: CME Group; New York Mercantile Exchange (CME-NYMEX)*

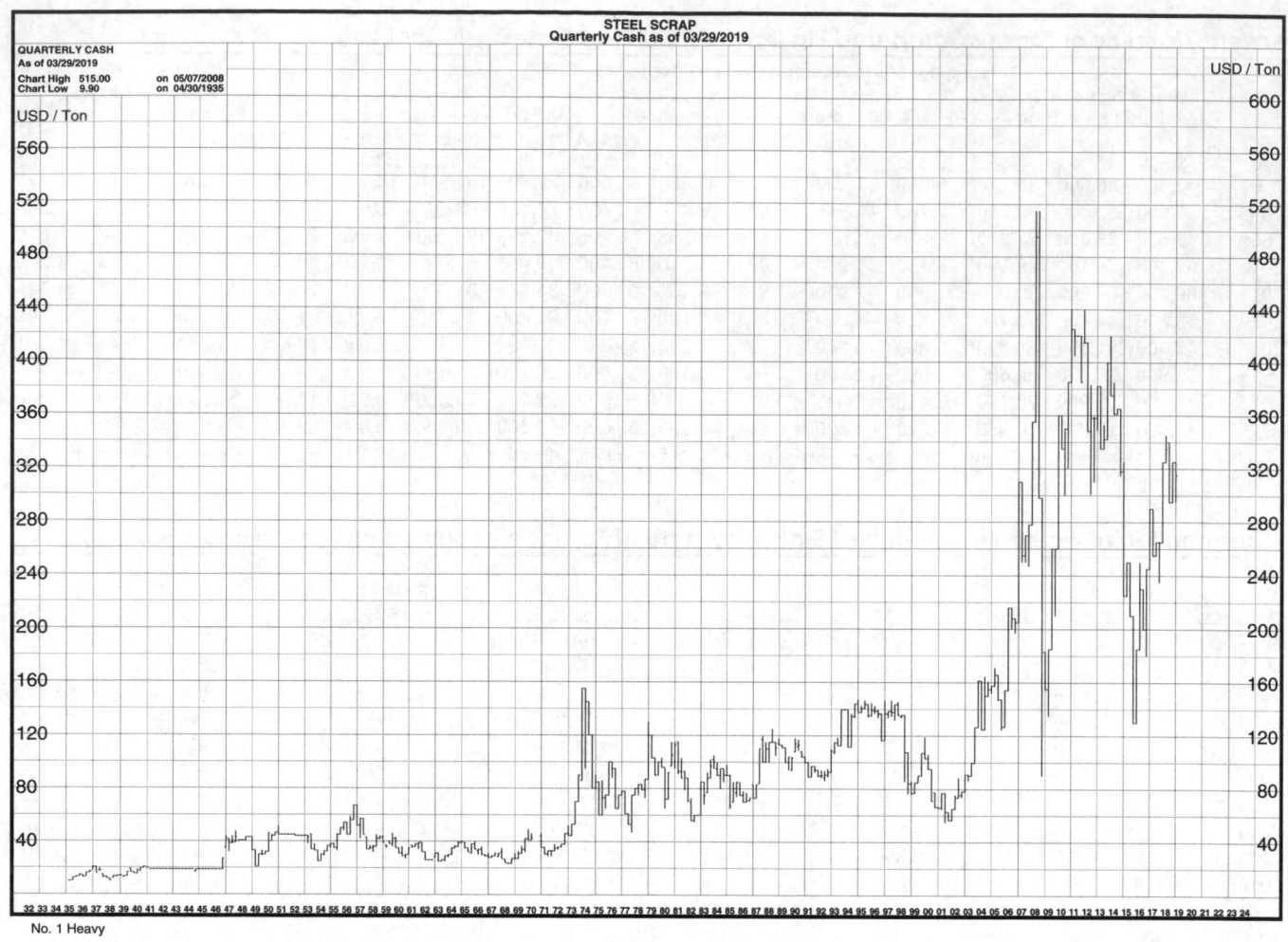

STEEL SCRAP
Quarterly Cash as of 03/29/2019

QUARTERLY CASH
As of 03/29/2019
Chart High 515.00 on 05/07/2008
Chart Low 9.90 on 04/30/1935

No. 1 Heavy

Wholesale Price of No. 1 Heavy Melting Steel Scrap in Chicago   In Dollars Per Metric Ton

Year	Jan.	Feb.	Mar.	Apr.	May	June	July	Aug.	Sept.	Oct.	Nov.	Dec.	Average
2009	183.00	176.68	157.73	150.00	179.25	185.00	230.00	244.29	257.86	244.76	216.32	251.05	206.33
2010	297.63	305.00	352.83	360.00	338.75	335.00	305.00	325.91	347.14	324.29	338.00	380.00	334.13
2011	429.00	427.37	425.00	425.00	407.86	419.32	420.00	420.00	420.00	411.43	388.75	408.68	416.87
2012	436.25	417.50	415.00	406.43	405.00	358.86	310.05	372.30	361.95	320.43	349.20	358.17	375.93
2013	358.00	350.89	375.71	363.86	342.82	336.20	351.36	351.18	343.35	344.61	370.26	395.16	356.95
2014	414.29	396.00	378.10	383.64	373.67	362.90	362.55	363.00	364.71	350.13	322.11	317.43	365.71
2015	323.60	250.00	225.91	225.00	229.00	246.36	242.27	222.86	211.43	171.36	136.32	130.00	217.84
2016	146.84	150.00	180.43	221.43	246.19	233.64	222.00	220.00	204.76	183.81	198.75	235.48	203.61
2017	274.75	261.58	283.91	266.00	260.00	255.91	255.00	263.26	265.00	240.45	235.00	259.00	259.99
2018	289.29	295.00	319.55	341.19	336.82	335.00	340.00	321.74	300.26	303.26	324.00	325.00	319.26

Source: American Metal Market (AMM)

World Production of Iron Ore[3]   In Thousands of Metric Tons (Gross Weight)

Year	Australia	Brazil	Canada	China	India	Maur-itania	Russia	South Africa	Sweden	Ukraine	United States	Venezula	World Total
2008	342,000	350,707	32,102	824,000	213,033	11,296	99,900	48,983	27,713	72,688	53,600	20,650	2,210,000
2009	394,000	298,528	31,704	880,000	217,155	10,524	92,000	55,313	20,389	66,476	26,700	13,801	2,230,000
2010	433,000	372,120	36,178	371,231	207,157	11,534	95,272	58,709	28,797	63,773	49,900	14,004	1,870,000
2011	488,000	398,131	35,705	442,179	168,582	11,400	103,607	58,057	26,100	65,807	56,200	17,037	2,030,000
2012	555,500	400,822	38,892	420,206	136,618	11,170	104,010	67,100	26,433	66,379	54,700	15,124	2,080,000
2013	682,700	386,270	42,063	417,287	152,433	13,038	102,156	71,645	27,900	67,020	52,800	16,800	2,230,000
2014	774,200	385,440	44,196	410,123	129,103	13,244	102,019	80,759	26,900	67,874	56,100	18,000	2,290,000
2015	816,689	396,531	45,954	374,838	155,898	11,296	100,985	73,000	24,500	66,815	46,100	11,394	2,290,000
2016[1]	858,000	430,000	47,000	348,000	185,000		101,000	66,000	27,000	63,000	42,000		2,350,000
2017[2]	880,000	440,000	47,000	340,000	190,000		100,000	68,000	27,000	63,000	46,000		2,400,000

[1] Preliminary.   [2] Estimate.   [3] Iron ore, iron ore concentrates and iron ore agglomerates.   *Source: U.S. Geological Survey (USGS)*

Salient Statistics of Iron Ore[3] in the United States   In Thousands of Metric Tons

Year	Net Import Reliance As a % of Apparent Consump	Production Total	Lake Superior	Other Regions	Ship-ments	Value Million $ (at Mine)	Average Value $ at Mine Per Ton	Stock, Dec. 31 Mines	Con-suming Plants	Lake Erie Docks	Imports	Exports	Con-sumption	Total
2009	E	26,700	NA	NA	27,600	2,560.0	92.76	5,060	----	----	3,870	3,920	31,000	376.0
2010	E	49,900	----	----	50,600	5,000.0	98.79	3,470	----	----	6,420	10,000	42,300	703.0
2011	E	54,700	----	----	55,600	5,850.0	99.45	3,260	----	----	5,300	11,100	49,100	841.0
2012	E	54,700	----	----	53,900	5,080.0	116.48	4,440	----	----	5,200	11,200	46,500	759.0
2013	E	52,800	----	----	53,400	4,610.0	87.42	2,350	----	----	3,200	11,000	47,100	426.0
2014	E	56,100	----	----	55,000	4,730.0	84.43	4,460	----	----	5,140	12,400	46,700	676.0
2015	E	46,100	----	----	43,500	3,750.0	81.19	7,860	----	----	4,550	8,030	39,300	455.0
2016	E	41,800	----	----	46,600	3,050.0	73.11	4,660	----	----	3,010	8,770	39,200	241.0
2017[1]	E	47,900	----	----	46,900		80.15	6,120	----	----	3,700	10,600	39,500	
2018[2]	E	49,000	----	----	49,000		82.00	7,600	----	----	3,400	13,000	38,000	

[1] Preliminary.   [2] Estimate.   [3] Usable iron ore exclusive of ore containing 5% or more manganese and includes byproduct ore.
NA = Not available.   *Source: U.S. Geological Survey (USGS)*

U.S. Imports (for Consumption) of Iron Ore[2]   In Thousands of Metric Tons

Year	Australia	Brazil	Canada	Chile	Mauritania	Peru	Sweden	Venezuela	Total
2007	----	3,210	5,520	279	----	140	141	58	9,400
2008	----	2,620	5,900	215	----	59	88	68	9,250
2009	----	188	3,140	203	----	34	31	21	3,870
2010	----	506	4,490	131	----	14	54	251	6,420
2011	----	562	3,910	165	----	14	81	279	5,270
2012	----	739	3,820	104	----	44	72	75	5,160
2013	----	630	2,090	152	----	12	49	----	3,250
2014	----	1,730	2,860	----	----	35	154	----	5,100
2015	----	2,050	2,040	1	----	22	85	25	4,550
2016[1]	----	1,760	557	1	----	66	351	28	3,010

[1] Preliminary.   [2] Including agglomerates.   [3] Less than 1/2 unit.   *Source: U.S. Geological Survey (USGS)*

Iron Ore Stocks in the United States, at End of Month   In Thousands of Metric Tons

Year	Jan.	Feb.	Mar.	Apr.	May	June	July	Aug.	Sept.	Oct.	Nov.	Dec.
2009	8,680	10,900	12,500	12,300	10,600	9,010	7,410	5,990	5,430	5,130	3,900	3,120
2010	3,760	6,080	7,040	6,070	5,400	4,160	3,730	3,240	3,150	3,410	3,320	2,860
2011	4,250	7,470	9,750	9,250	8,970	8,200	7,060	6,380	5,140	4,660	4,250	3,390
2012	3,200	6,750	8,910	7,730	6,410	5,340	3,850	2,980	2,660	2,970	3,020	2,200
2013	3,290	6,580	8,960	7,830	6,350	5,390	4,130	3,320	2,770	2,110	2,470	3,690
2014	6,530	9,240	12,400	13,600	12,500	11,300	9,770	8,190	7,320	6,600	6,290	5,430
2015	6,640	10,600	14,500	14,800	13,100	11,500	9,740	8,040	7,460	7,070	7,550	7,490
2016	8,940	11,800	13,600	12,100	11,000	10,200	9,470	8,300	7,630	7,170	6,500	6,050
2017	6,730	9,970	12,400	12,200	11,200	10,100	9,080	7,670	6,470	6,210	6,300	6,120
2018[1]	8,290	12,000	14,700	14,300	13,000	12,200	10,900	9,520	8,270	7,480		

[1] Preliminary.   *Source: U.S. Geological Survey (USGS)*

Lard

Lard is the layer of fat found along the back and underneath the skin of a hog. The hog's fat is purified by washing it with water, melting it under constant heat, and straining it several times. Lard is an important byproduct of the meatpacking industry. It is valued highly as cooking oil because there is very little smoke when it is heated. However, demand for lard in cooking is declining because of the trend toward healthier eating. Lard is also used for medicinal purposes such as ointments, plasters, liniments, and occasionally as a laxative for children. Lard production is directly proportional to commercial hog production, meaning the largest producers of hogs are the largest producers of lard.

Prices – The average monthly wholesale price of lard in 2018 fell by -7.7% to 32.55 cents per pound, far below the 2011 record high of 54.55 cents per pound.

Supply – World production of lard in the 2017/18 marketing year rose by +2.1% yr/yr to 8.908 million metric tons, which was a new record high. The world's largest lard producers were China with 42.1% of world production, the U.S with 7.7%, Russia with 6.7%, Germany with 6.3%, Brazil with 5.3%, Spain with 4.2%, and Poland with 2.9%. U.S. production of lard in 2015/16 rose +2.8% yr/yr to 1.450 billion pounds.

Demand – U.S. consumption of lard in 2011 rose +0.5% to 148.316 million pounds, down from 2008 record high of 490.602 million pounds. The current level of consumption is less than 10% of the consumption of 1.574 billion pounds in 1971.

Trade – U.S. exports of lard in 2016/17 fell by -9.5% to 38.0 million pounds and accounted for only 2.6% of U.S. production.

World Production of Lard   In Thousands of Metric Tons

Year	Brazil	Canada	China	France	Germany	Italy	Japan	Poland	Romania	Spain	United States	Ex-USSR	World Total
2009-10	411.4	122.7	3,402.7	136.5	554.9	210.4	52.6	220.4	71.9	287.2	576.7	423.4	7,893.7
2010-11	429.5	130.7	3,421.7	136.6	566.7	208.4	51.0	234.3	76.2	302.2	586.9	448.3	8,024.4
2011-12	443.0	132.8	3,546.2	133.2	561.5	208.4	51.4	222.7	75.4	309.3	599.7	466.2	8,185.7
2012-13	439.6	131.9	3,670.5	132.1	562.3	213.0	51.3	213.9	73.7	301.3	598.7	499.2	8,356.7
2013-14	443.5	131.3	3,745.1	132.1	558.0	186.3	51.0	231.5	74.3	310.7	594.3	514.7	8,455.5
2014-15	444.3	132.5	3,623.4	133.5	570.4	190.9	49.0	243.7	76.7	334.4	625.1	529.3	8,459.7
2015-16[1]	459.5	136.9	3,640.9	135.6	566.1	198.4	51.0	252.6	76.4	356.0	639.9	557.6	8,606.5
2016-17[2]	463.4	137.7	3,684.7	143.2	565.6	193.7	50.5	253.9	76.0	362.4	657.6	579.6	8,727.3
2017-18[3]	473.6	137.3	3,752.0	150.3	562.9	196.6	51.2	258.0	77.3	374.4	682.3	596.1	8,907.6

[1] Preliminary.   [2] Estimate.   [3] Forecast.   *Source: The Oil World*

Supply and Distribution of Lard in the United States   In Millions of Pounds

	Supply			Disappearance						
Year	Production	Stocks Oct. 1	Total Supply	Domestic	Baking or Frying Fats	Margarine[3]	Exports	Total Disap-pearance	Direct Use	Per Capita (Lbs.)
2008-09	1,316.8	13.9	1,330.7	800.9	W	W	81.4	882.3	310.3	1.0
2009-10	1,271.4	17.5	1,288.9	847.4	W	W	71.6	847.4	479.8	1.5
2010-11	1,293.9	25.6	1,319.5	870.8	W	W	76.7	870.8	NA	NA
2011-12	1,322.1	20.0	1,342.1	884.9	W	W	54.7	884.9	NA	NA
2012-13	1,319.9	20.0	1,339.9	881.2	W	W	61.5	881.2	NA	NA
2013-14	1,310.2	20.0	1,330.2	873.7	W	W	51.8	873.7	NA	NA
2014-15	1,378.1	20.0	1,398.1	927.7	W	W	46.6	927.7	NA	NA
2015-16[1]	1,410.7	8.6	1,419.3	943.5	W	W	42.1	943.5	NA	NA
2016-17[2]	1,449.7	8.0	1,457.7	972.7	W	W	38.0	972.7	NA	NA

[1] Preliminary.   [2] Forecast.   [3] Includes edible tallow.   W = Withheld.
Source: Economic Research Service, U.S. Department of Agriculture (ERS-USDA)

Consumption of Lard (Edible and Inedible) in the United States   In Millions of Pounds

Year	Jan.	Feb.	Mar.	Apr.	May	June	July	Aug.	Sept.	Oct.	Nov.	Dec.	Total
2002	26.4	26.1	21.8	26.7	24.8	21.2	22.9	26.4	23.6	26.4	28.1	28.7	303.2
2003	22.6	22.3	23.4	21.4	23.3	24.0	23.0	21.4	22.5	24.3	20.2	21.0	269.5
2004	22.9	25.8	25.9	23.9	23.5	22.0	19.1	19.7	21.3	22.4	21.9	19.9	268.1
2005	19.0	15.4	21.4	18.7	19.9	20.4	18.9	19.5	20.1	19.7	22.2	17.9	233.1
2006	15.7	16.4	20.6	21.4	20.2	16.7	14.9	17.7	17.8	18.9	22.3	20.9	223.4
2007	21.6	16.2	22.2	19.7	20.5	20.8	22.8	23.9	22.8	31.1	29.7	31.4	282.8
2008	34.8	32.2	44.6	50.7	50.8	44.4	47.8	39.7	44.0	37.5	31.7	32.2	490.6
2009	23.4	17.3	26.8	26.0	26.3	25.8	21.3	20.5	25.4	32.4	29.9	27.0	302.3
2010	22.2	W	38.8	W	30.4	30.8	30.4	32.4	30.1	31.1	30.4	28.8	366.6
2011[1]	22.2	26.3	36.0	W	28.8	29.6	31.4	W	W	W	W	W	348.7

[1] Preliminary.   *Source: Bureau of the Census, U.S. Department of Commerce*

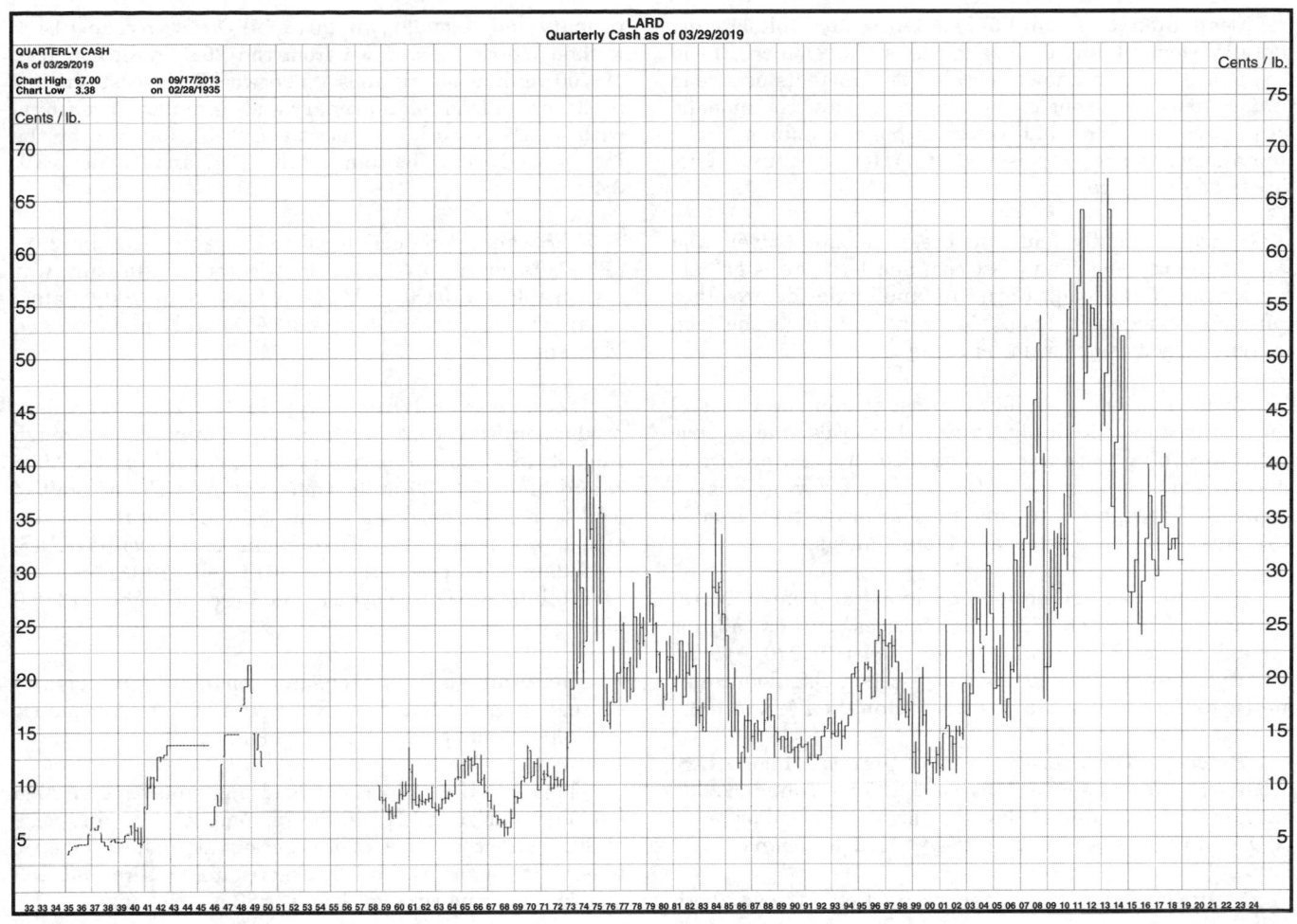

LARD
Quarterly Cash as of 03/29/2019

QUARTERLY CASH
As of 03/29/2019
Chart High 67.00   on 09/17/2013
Chart Low   3.38   on 02/28/1935

Cents / lb.

Average Wholesale Price of Lard--Loose, Tank Cars, in Chicago   In Cents Per Pound

Year	Jan.	Feb.	Mar.	Apr.	May	June	July	Aug.	Sept.	Oct.	Nov.	Dec.	Average
2009	25.36	20.31	19.49	23.36	29.00	30.06	27.63	32.20	29.73	25.75	30.07	28.75	26.81
2010	28.60	28.25	32.95	33.95	34.24	32.98	31.42	33.33	43.59	46.64	37.32	38.30	35.13
2011	48.50	49.60	52.00	51.50	54.31	56.75	63.00	58.96	61.33	61.10	48.86	48.71	54.55
2012	NA	52.55	54.60	52.59	54.82	54.83	53.00	NA	NA	51.60	57.00	NA	53.87
2013	52.45	45.56	NA	43.50	44.50	48.50	53.25	56.89	64.78	43.00	48.00	41.50	49.27
2014	33.00	38.00	40.67	53.00	NA	45.00	NA	46.50	50.67	48.00	42.81	35.91	43.36
2015	29.50	28.00	NA	26.64	28.00	NA	31.00	31.00	NA	34.23	35.50	28.80	30.30
2016	24.00	NA	29.00	33.00	NA	NA	NA	36.53	36.75	34.00	NA	31.00	32.04
2017	30.10	NA	NA	NA	NA	34.50	NA	NA	35.75	36.00	38.17	37.00	35.25
2018	32.08	32.20	NA	NA	NA	32.50	NA	32.38	32.93	33.00	34.33	31.00	32.55

Source: Economic Research Service, U.S. Department of Agriculture (ERS-USDA)

Cold Storage Holdings of all Lard[1] in the United States, on First of Month   In Millions of Pounds

Year	Jan.	Feb.	Mar.	Apr.	May	June	July	Aug.	Sept.	Oct.	Nov.	Dec.
2002	13.2	18.0	16.4	16.5	20.3	22.4	18.9	18.3	12.0	10.5	14.6	11.3
2003	10.5	14.0	19.6	18.7	16.5	13.5	11.9	9.7	8.4	9.3	10.1	12.4
2004	13.3	19.8	18.6	20.3	20.5	15.0	12.9	10.8	10.3	11.8	11.4	13.2
2005	13.7	14.6	20.6	19.0	17.8	12.3	12.0	12.3	12.5	13.0	12.2	14.7
2006	9.6	11.5	13.7	13.6	9.3	9.9	13.0	12.4	13.0	11.5	16.1	16.0
2007	16.4	14.9	13.3	18.5	10.9	14.6	11.3	12.8	11.0	9.2	14.6	18.8
2008	14.0	22.4	20.4	22.9	23.0	19.5	22.7	13.6	18.0	17.8	16.1	20.4
2009	12.1	13.6	15.4	16.2	14.5	18.8	17.3	21.6	20.5	26.7	18.5	15.4
2010	13.9	14.5	21.0	22.9	26.1	15.7	19.4	17.9	14.1	13.8	15.6	15.5
2011[2]	17.5	20.5	25.3	20.9	26.2	19.9	23.4	23.9	NA	NA	NA	NA

[1] Stocks in factories and warehouses (except that in hands of retailers).   [2] Preliminary.   *Source: Bureau of the Census, U.S. Department of Commerce*

Lead

Lead (atomic symbol Pb) is a dense, toxic, bluish-gray metallic element, and is the heaviest stable element. Lead was one of the first known metals. The ancients used lead in face powders, rouges, mascaras, paints, condiments, wine preservatives, and water supply plumbing. The Romans were slowly poisoned from lead because of its diverse daily usage.

Lead is usually found in ore with zinc, silver, and most often copper. The most common lead ore is galena, containing 86.6% lead. Cerussite and angleside are other common varieties of lead. More than half of the lead currently used comes from recycling.

Lead is used in building construction, bullets and shot, tank and pipe lining, storage batteries, and electric cable sheathing. Lead is used extensively as a protective shielding for radioactive material (e.g., X-ray apparatus) because of its high density and nuclear properties. Lead is also part of solder, pewter, and fusible alloys.

Lead futures and options trade at the London Metal Exchange (LME). The LME lead futures contract calls for the delivery of 25 metric tons of at least 99.970% purity lead ingots (pigs). The contract is priced in U.S. dollars per metric ton. Lead first started trading on the LME in 1903.

Prices – The average price of pig lead among U.S. producers reached a record high of $1.25 per pound in 2007 but has since remained below that level. Pig lead prices in 2018 ended the year down -2.9% at $1.12 per pound.

Supply – World smelter production of lead (both primary and secondary) in 2015 fell -1.9% yr/yr to 10.400 million metric tons, down from the 2013 record high of 10.700 million metric tons. The world's largest smelter producers of lead (both primary and secondary) are China with 42.3% of world production in 2015, followed by the U.S. with 10.1%, Germany with 3.6%, and Mexico with 3.4%.

U.S. mine production of recoverable lead in 2017 fell -7.4% yr/yr to 311,000 metric tons. Missouri was responsible for 94% of U.S. production in 2009 (latest data), with the remainder produced mainly by Idaho and Montana.

Lead recovered from scrap in the U.S. (secondary production) rose +0.2% yr/yr in 2018 (annualized through August) to 1.133 million metric tons, down from the 2008 record high of 1.220 million metric tons. The amount of lead recovered from scrap is almost three times the amount of lead produced in the U.S. from mines. The value of U.S. secondary lead production in 2015 fell -20.1% yr/yr to $2.110 billion, well below the 2008 record high of $3.040 billion.

Demand – U.S. lead consumption in 2018 (annualized through August) fell -5.3% yr/yr to 1.667 million metric tons, down from the 2017 record high.

Trade – U.S. imports of lead pigs and bars in 2015 fell -11.8% yr/yr to 521,000 metric tons. U.S. lead exports in 2015 were comprised of ore concentrate (349,000 metric tons), unwrought lead (55,900 metric tons), scrap (40,200 metric tons), and wrought lead (2,880 metric tons).

World Smelter (Primary and Secondary) Production of Lead   In Thousands of Metric Tons

Year	Australia[3]	Belgium[4]	Canada[3]	China[2]	France	Germany	Italy	Japan	Mexico[3]	Spain	United Kingdom[3]	United States	World Total
2007	229.0	236.7	2,790.0	405.1	257.8	210.0	276.3	255.0	212.0	128.0	263.0	1,303	8,320
2008	248.0	259.1	3,200.0	415.1	294.0	211.8	279.5	244.1	243.8	125.0	283.0	1,275	8,730
2009	229.0	258.9	3,710.0	390.6	332.0	149.0	192.4	326.9	239.4	138.0	279.0	1,213	8,850
2010	204.0	272.9	4,200.0	404.0	367.0	150.0	215.8	327.9	286.0	165.0	295.0	1,255	9,610
2011	213.0	282.6	4,600.0	429.0	419.0	149.5	218.0	416.9	317.7	177.0	269.0	1,248	10,300
2012	184.0	278.1	4,590.0	430.0	460.0	138.4	209.0	460.0	415.4	160.0	312.0	1,221	10,400
2013	201.0	288.3	4,780.0	400.0	471.0	180.0	210.0	427.7	400.0	157.0	292.0	1,264	10,700
2014[1]	226.0	282.0	4,740.0	379.0	477.0	210.0	240.0	639.0	364.0	166.0	267.0	1,020	10,600
2015[2]	223.0	273.0	4,400.0	378.0	501.0	208.0	232.0	641.0	356.0	172.0	308.0	1,050	10,400

[1] Preliminary.   [2] Estimate.   [3] Refinded & bullion.   [4] Includes scrap.   *Source: U.S. Geological Survey (USGS)*

Consumption of Lead in the United States, by Products   In Metric Tons

Year	Ammunition: Shot and Bullets	Bearing Metals	Brass and Bronze	Cable Covering	Calking Lead	Casting Metals	Pipes, Traps & Bends[2]	Sheet Lead	Solder	Storage Batteries: Total	Other Metal Products[3]	Other Oxides[4]	Total U.S. Consumption
2007	69,400	1,410	2,870	W	W	31,500	1,230	28,600	7,220	1,380,000	23,600	15,800	1,490,000
2008	67,400	1,250	2,460	W	W	20,100	1,190	26,400	6,610	1,290,000	7,670	10,700	1,570,000
2009	67,900	1,100	1,370	W	W	15,900	1,130	25,400	6,450	1,140,000	5,790	10,100	1,440,000
2010	65,700	1,230	1,410	W	W	16,400	990	23,400	6,420	1,280,000	8,800	9,760	1,290,000
2011	75,100	1,150	1,620	W	W	16,000	6,110	7,170	6,170	1,250,000	23,100	9,760	1,430,000
2012	73,900	1,090	1,120	W	W	16,700	6,240	7,390	6,280	1,190,000	18,500	9,740	1,410,000
2013	84,800	1,110	1,420	W	W	20,400	7,030	4,870	8,200	1,200,000	177	9,740	1,350,000
2014	85,300	1,150	2,990	W	W	19,100	6,900	6,090	7,380	1,320,000	33,000	9,740	1,390,000
2015[1]	79,300	1,080	2,080	W	W	14,300	7,460	12,200	6,500	1,350,000	33,200	11,500	1,540,000

[1] Preliminary.   [2] Including building.   [3] Including terne metal, type metal, and lead consumed in foil, collapsible tubes, annealing, plating, galvanizing and fishing weights.   [4] Includes paints, glass and ceramic products, and other pigments and chemicals.   W = Withheld.
Source: U.S. Geological Survey (USGS)

Salient Statistics of Lead in the United States   In Thousands of Metric Tons

Year	Net Import Reliance as a % of Apparent Consump	Production of Refined Lead From Domestic Ores[3]	Foreighn Ores[3]	Total Primary	Total Value of Refined Million $	Secondary Lead Recovered — As Soft Lead	In Anti-monial Lead	In Other Alloys	Total	Total Value of Secondary Million USD	Stocks, Dec. 31 — Primary	Con-sumer[4]	Average Price — Cents Per Pound — New York	London
2009	13	103	W	103	----	960	151	----	1,110	2,130	W	63.3	86.87	77.95
2010	13	115	W	115	----	968	174	----	1,140	2,740	W	64.8	108.91	97.42
2011	19	118	W	118	----	966	167	----	1,130	3,040	W	48.3	121.70	108.92
2012	26	111	W	111	----	863	236	----	1,110	2,790	W	71.7	114.16	93.53
2013	26	114	W	114	----	860	282	----	1,150	2,910	W	69.9	----	97.15
2014	35	----	W	----	----	786	224	8.8	1,020	2,640	W	66.4	----	95.04
2015	31	----	W	----	----	827	222	2.6	1,050	2,110	W	64.0	----	81.02
2016	33	----	W	----	----				986		W	101.0	----	84.80
2017[1]	36	----	W	----	----				1,130		W	----	----	105.10
2018[2]	29	----	W	----	----				1,300		W	----	----	104.00

[1] Preliminary.   [2] Estimate.   [3] And base bullion.   [4] Also at secondary smelters.   W = Withheld.   E = Net exporter.
Source: U.S. Geological Survey (USGS)

U.S. Foreign Trade of Lead   In Thousands of Metric Tons

Year	Exports — Ore Con-centrate	Un-wrought Lead[3]	Wrought Lead[4]	Scrap	Ash & Re-sidues[5]	Imports for Consumption — Ores, Flue Dust or Fume & Mattes	Base Bullion	Pigs & Bars	Re-claimed Scrap, Etc.	Value Million $	General Import From: Ore, Flue, Dust & Matte — Aus-tralia	Can-ada	Peru	Pigs & Bars — Can-ada	Mexico	Peru
2006	297.6	52.7	15.8	120.9	----	----	0.5	331.0	1.6	450.8	----	----	----	222.0	15.8	34.6
2007	300.0	51.8	4.6	129.0	----	----	2.0	263.0	2.4	591.4	----	----	----	208.0	35.6	16.5
2008	277.0	68.1	6.2	175.0	----	----	2.7	309.0	1.3	681.6	----	----	----	219.0	58.1	10.6
2009	287.0	77.6	4.3	140.0	----	----	0.8	251.0	1.3	418.8	----	----	----	205.0	41.1	1.0
2010	299.0	77.7	5.6	43.5	----	----	0.6	271.0	3.7	575.9	----	----	----	237.0	29.4	----
2011	223.0	40.1	7.0	31.1	----	----	0.4	313.0	2.4	718.4	----	----	----	250.0	56.0	0.1
2012	214.0	47.0	6.3	25.9	----	1.5	1.0	349.0	16.8	730.4	----	----	----	240.0	56.1	0.0
2013	215.0	41.6	6.6	34.9	----	0.0	1.9	500.0	15.6	1,060.4	----	----	----	257.0	111.0	39.6
2014[1]	356.0	55.3	5.0	36.4	----	----	1.1	593.0	11.4	1,243.8	----	----	----	264.0	120.0	49.7
2015[2]	349.0	55.9	2.9	46.2	----	----	0.3	521.0	7.5	992.2	----	----	----	249.0	111.0	----

[1] Preliminary.   [2] Estimate.   [3] And lead alloys.   [4] Blocks, pigs, etc.   [5] Less than 1/2 unit.   Source: U.S. Geological Survey (USGS)

Annual Mine Production of Recoverable Lead in the United States   In Metric Tons

Year	Idaho	Missouri	Montana	Total
2008	W	360,000	W	399,000
2009	W	370,000	W	395,000
2010	W	W	W	356,000
2011	W	W	W	334,000
2012	----	----	----	336,000
2013	----	----	----	331,000
2014	----	----	----	367,000
2015	----	----	----	360,000
2016[1]	----	----	----	336,000
2017[2]	----	----	----	311,000

[1] Preliminary.   [2] Estimate.   W = Withheld, included in Total.   Source: U.S. Geological Survey (USGS)

Mine Production of Recoverable Lead in the United States   In Metric Tons

Year	Jan.	Feb.	Mar.	Apr.	May	June	July	Aug.	Sept.	Oct.	Nov.	Dec.	Total
2009	33,800	30,500	32,800	34,700	33,600	33,700	29,900	35,700	35,600	36,900	28,500	32,800	395,000
2010	31,800	28,600	32,700	31,500	29,700	26,500	29,500	26,900	30,100	31,300	27,800	30,000	356,000
2011	30,400	25,100	29,500	32,500	27,400	27,200	29,300	24,400	29,200	25,200	28,100	30,700	334,000
2012	28,700	27,900	27,600	27,300	27,600	28,100	27,500	29,700	27,000	27,500	27,700	29,100	336,000
2013	27,000	25,717	26,000	28,600	28,900	28,000	28,500	28,700	29,600	27,200	25,700	28,600	331,000
2014	30,300	26,600	28,800	31,300	32,800	29,600	30,500	30,389	31,200	32,000	32,700	34,500	367,000
2015	28,200	30,100	35,700	32,100	31,300	28,900	31,200	31,500	26,100	27,100	27,200	27,400	360,000
2016	29,100	26,000	27,900	30,100	27,000	28,400	24,800	30,400	28,400	28,000	22,000	20,000	336,000
2017	25,400	25,500	31,300	27,900	24,400	25,300	23,100	25,400	21,000	24,900	27,500	21,900	311,000
2018[1]	21,700	17,400	20,700	22,200	23,000	23,400	24,000	W	W				261,257

[1] Preliminary.   W = Withheld to avoid disclosing company proprietary data.   Source: U.S. Geological Survey (USGS)

LEAD

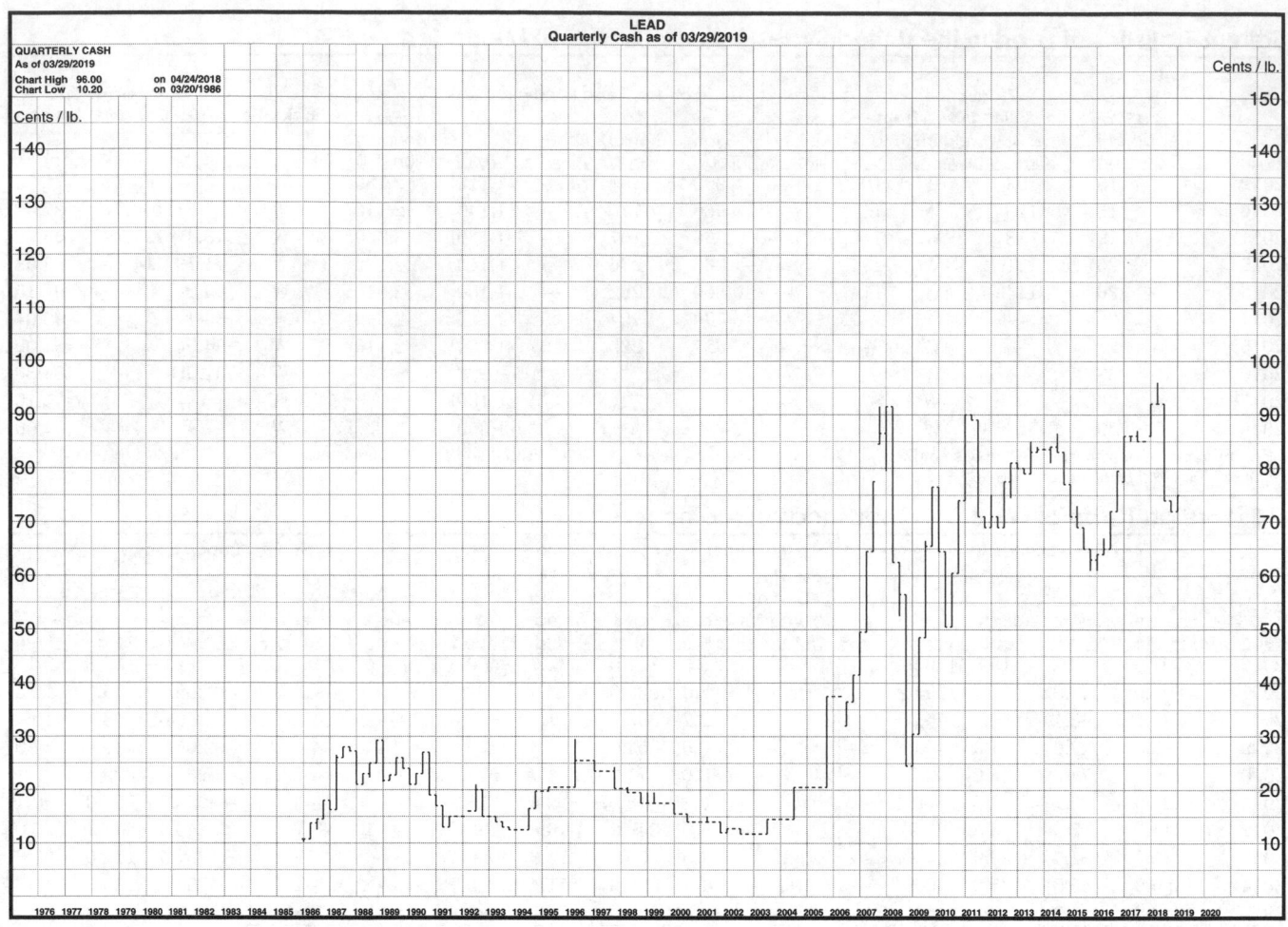

LEAD
Quarterly Cash as of 03/29/2019

QUARTERLY CASH
As of 03/29/2019
Chart High 96.00   on 04/24/2018
Chart Low   10.20   on 03/20/1986

Average Price of Pig Lead, U.S. Primary Producers (Common Corroding)[1]   In Cents Per Pound

Year	Jan.	Feb.	Mar.	Apr.	May	June	July	Aug.	Sept.	Oct.	Nov.	Dec.	Average
2009	57.27	55.74	61.81	67.86	70.02	80.87	81.05	91.57	104.06	105.75	109.61	110.96	83.05
2010	113.15	102.18	104.73	108.78	92.43	83.23	89.48	99.29	104.31	113.11	113.59	114.22	103.21
2011	123.37	122.83	124.67	130.68	117.43	121.38	129.14	116.63	111.36	95.84	97.61	100.19	115.93
2012	103.68	105.11	101.81	100.71	98.42	91.70	92.52	93.54	106.29	112.62	113.81	117.08	103.11
2013	120.19	121.68	112.79	106.17	105.82	109.38	106.18	111.56	107.53	108.72	107.97	109.40	110.62
2014	110.40	108.69	106.23	107.71	107.99	108.35	112.31	114.44	108.97	105.16	104.11	100.29	107.89
2015	95.45	94.25	93.41	102.60	103.12	94.25	92.01	93.72	91.66	88.54	84.72	89.21	93.58
2016	86.75	92.12	93.74	90.37	89.89	89.70	95.09	95.44	100.00	103.71	109.36	111.81	96.50
2017	111.53	114.71	112.58	110.76	106.56	106.67	112.97	116.68	117.90	123.74	121.73	123.64	114.96
2018	127.40	126.93	118.69	116.99	116.98	120.64	109.97	103.62	101.77	99.98	97.87	99.13	111.66

[1] New York Delivery.   Source: American Metal Market

Refiners Production[1] of Lead in the United States   In Metric Tons

Year	Jan.	Feb.	Mar.	Apr.	May	June	July	Aug.	Sept.	Oct.	Nov.	Dec.	Total
2001	NA	NA	NA	NA	NA	NA	NA	NA	NA	NA	NA	NA	290,000
2002	NA	NA	NA	NA	NA	NA	NA	NA	NA	NA	NA	NA	262,000
2003	NA	NA	NA	NA	NA	NA	NA	NA	NA	NA	NA	NA	245,000
2004	NA	NA	NA	NA	NA	NA	NA	NA	NA	NA	NA	NA	NA
2005	NA	NA	NA	NA	NA	NA	NA	NA	NA	NA	NA	NA	143,000
2006	NA	NA	NA	NA	NA	NA	NA	NA	NA	NA	NA	NA	143,000
2007	NA	NA	NA	NA	NA	NA	NA	NA	NA	NA	NA	NA	NA
2008	NA	NA	NA	NA	NA	NA	NA	NA	NA	NA	NA	NA	NA
2009	NA	NA	NA	NA	NA	NA	NA	NA	NA	NA	NA	NA	NA
2010[2]	NA	NA	NA	NA	NA	NA	NA	NA	NA	NA	NA	NA	NA

[1] Represents refined lead produced from domestic ores by primary smelters plus small amounts of secondary material passing through these smelters. Includes GSA metal purchased for remelt.   [2] Preliminary.   NA = Not available.   Source: U.S. Geological Survey (USGS)

Total Stocks of Lead[1] in the United States at Refiners, at End of Month   In Metric Tons

Year	Jan.	Feb.	Mar.	Apr.	May	June	July	Aug.	Sept.	Oct.	Nov.	Dec.
2009	70,600	70,100	77,900	68,100	70,200	65,600	56,300	53,800	54,500	55,200	59,100	61,700
2010	60,200	60,200	55,700	50,700	55,500	57,200	57,600	59,100	59,800	58,700	67,700	67,400
2011	67,100	53,000	53,200	61,100	62,600	61,500	62,800	60,500	58,800	56,300	53,500	54,800
2012	58,700	63,300	54,800	54,000	51,800	56,600	62,600	65,700	63,400	63,800	56,000	57,500
2013	69,900	76,200	83,100	94,300	98,000	93,400	83,600	81,400	77,400	69,300	65,100	69,400
2014	68,100	63,600	65,400	65,700	64,000	66,600	62,500	62,080	63,300	63,100	66,300	66,300
2015	64,900	63,800	63,600	64,100	62,700	62,400	60,800	66,900	69,500	68,600	67,900	64,500
2016	97,300	63,800	63,200	65,500	70,000	67,100	66,900	85,300	84,600	74,800	79,800	101,000
2017[1]	111,000	103,000	113,000	106,000	126,000	128,000	131,000	132,000	115,000	116,000	139,000	161,000
2018[1]	----	----	----	----	----	----	----	----	----			

[1] Preliminary.   [2] Secondary smelters and consumers.   *Source: U.S. Geological Survey (USGS)*

Total[2] Lead Consumption in the United States   In Metric Tons

Year	Jan.	Feb.	Mar.	Apr.	May	June	July	Aug.	Sept.	Oct.	Nov.	Dec.	Total
2009	123,000	119,000	116,000	124,000	116,000	117,000	116,000	115,000	118,000	122,000	121,000	117,000	1,424,000
2010	120,000	118,000	114,000	115,000	117,000	118,000	116,000	117,000	118,000	117,000	118,000	117,000	1,405,000
2011	131,000	118,000	118,000	133,000	132,000	133,000	132,000	133,000	132,000	132,000	132,000	131,000	1,557,000
2012	122,000	130,000	135,000	123,000	121,000	122,000	120,000	122,000	121,000	122,000	122,000	123,000	1,483,000
2013	146,000	123,000	118,000	117,000	117,000	117,000	116,000	118,000	117,000	119,000	115,000	134,000	1,750,000
2014	159,000	159,000	148,000	153,000	148,000	146,000	131,000	155,309	128,000	134,000	131,000	138,000	1,670,000
2015	132,000	121,000	135,000	151,000	130,000	135,000	128,000	125,000	121,000	145,000	134,000	129,000	1,590,000
2016	97,300	120,000	136,000	133,000	128,000	133,000	134,000	125,000	119,000	129,000	149,000	153,000	1,490,000
2017	146,000	157,000	167,000	156,000	171,000	125,000	147,000	128,000	147,000	130,000	129,000	120,000	1,760,000
2018[1]	129,000	154,000	161,000	139,000	129,000	144,000	127,000	128,000	144,000				1,673,333

[1] Preliminary.   [1] Represents total consumption of primary & secondary lead as metal, in chemicals, or in alloys.   *Source: U.S. Geological Survey (USGS)*

Lead Recovered from Scrap in the United States   In Metric Tons (Lead Content)

Year	Jan.	Feb.	Mar.	Apr.	May	June	July	Aug.	Sept.	Oct.	Nov.	Dec.	Total
2009	97,300	99,000	101,000	90,200	91,600	93,800	97,000	97,200	90,900	96,300	98,000	98,000	1,150,300
2010	96,200	95,200	92,100	86,300	89,800	92,900	94,200	98,000	95,600	101,000	100,000	96,300	1,137,600
2011	104,000	96,200	95,500	104,000	101,000	100,000	102,000	103,000	95,400	95,900	98,800	99,600	1,195,400
2012	102,000	101,000	97,800	98,000	99,400	102,000	100,000	98,000	97,300	100,000	100,000	99,200	1,194,700
2013	104,000	96,700	100,000	97,300	100,000	98,100	97,200	100,000	99,500	104,000	102,000	95,000	1,200,000
2014	92,700	91,100	97,300	96,300	94,500	94,500	96,900	93,796	94,800	94,400	88,600	94,800	1,130,000
2015	88,600	88,900	92,200	94,600	93,600	92,900	92,500	95,400	96,300	97,500	96,100	89,700	1,120,000
2016	94,300	90,800	92,300	93,500	91,900	86,500	83,900	92,600	86,700	106,000	102,000	102,000	1,000,000
2017	82,900	105,000	108,000	107,000	101,000	83,700	85,000	85,300	83,300	84,600	81,400	84,300	1,130,000
2018[1]	93,800	90,300	96,300	97,300	91,400	92,400	97,000	96,600	92,900				1,130,667

[1] Preliminary.   *Source: U.S. Geological Survey (USGS)*

Domestic Shipments[1] of Lead in the United States, by Refiners   In Thousands of Short Tons

Year	Jan.	Feb.	Mar.	Apr.	May	June	July	Aug.	Sept.	Oct.	Nov.	Dec.	Total
1989	29.3	28.5	32.2	35.7	45.1	36.4	32.8	41.5	40.0	44.2	40.2	31.1	437.1
1990	39.3	33.9	39.1	33.5	38.4	32.9	32.6	38.9	36.6	38.9	37.9	31.7	433.7
1991	35.4	33.8	34.3	39.8	33.9	26.0	31.8	37.9	35.1	35.7	28.7	26.7	399.2
1992	31.3	23.9	30.4	26.3	25.6	27.2	27.3	28.7	26.3	28.5	26.3	21.7	323.5
1993	24.6	23.6	32.5	30.0	31.3	35.1	28.9	34.0	35.5	35.5	31.7	33.5	376.2
1994	35.9	32.8	35.2	32.7	34.7	36.7	31.6	33.4	34.8	34.3	34.0	33.3	409.3
1995	36.5	30.3	35.1	31.1	33.7	31.9	28.6	40.3	34.9	40.9	33.2	29.8	406.4
1996	37.2	32.4	29.5	30.2	29.4	26.7	27.7	33.5	30.1	33.5	28.1	27.6	366.0
1997[2]	31.5	27.8	24.7	35.2	39.2	36.1	33.4	29.4	26.4	31.5	30.4	28.1	377.8
1998[2]	Data no longer available.												

[1] Includes GSA metal.   [2] Preliminary.   *Source: American Metal Market (AMM)*

Lumber and Plywood

Humans have utilized lumber for construction for thousands of years, but due to the heaviness of timber and the manual methods of harvesting, large-scale lumbering didn't occur until the mechanical advances of the Industrial Revolution. Lumber is produced from both hardwood and softwood. Hardwood lumber comes from deciduous trees that have broad leaves. Most hardwood lumber is used for miscellaneous industrial applications, primarily wood pallets, and includes oak, gum, maple, and ash. Hardwood species with beautiful colors and patterns are used for such high-grade products as furniture, flooring, paneling, and cabinets and include black walnut, black cherry, and red oak. Wood from cone-bearing trees is called softwood, regardless of its actual hardness. Most lumber from the U.S. is softwood. Softwoods, such as southern yellow pine, Douglas fir, ponderosa pine, and true firs, are primarily used as structural lumber such as 2x4s and 2x6s, poles, paper and cardboard.

Plywood consists of several thin layers of veneer bonded together with adhesives. The veneer sheets are layered so that the grain of one sheet is perpendicular to that of the next, which makes plywood exceptionally strong for its weight. Most plywood has from three to nine layers of wood. Plywood manufacturers use both hard and soft woods, although hardwoods serve primarily for appearance and are not as strong as those made from softwoods. Plywood is primarily used in construction, particularly for floors, roofs, walls, and doors. Homebuilding and remodeling account for two-thirds of U.S. lumber consumption. The price of lumber and plywood is highly correlated with the strength of the U.S. home-building market.

The forest and wood products industry is dominated by Weyerhaeuser Company (ticker symbol WY), which has about $20 billion in annual sales. Weyerhaeuser is a forest products conglomerate that engages not only in growing and harvesting timber, but also in the production and distribution of forest products, real estate development, and construction of single-family homes. Forest products include wood products, pulp and paper, and containerboard. The timberland segment of the business manages 7.2 million acres of company-owned land and 800,000 acres of leased commercial forestlands in North America. The company's Canadian division has renewable, long-term licenses on about 35 million acres of forestland in five Canadian provinces. In order to maximize its long-term yield from its acreage, Weyerhaeuser engages in a number of forest management activities such as extensive planting, suppression of non-merchantable species, thinning, fertilization, and operational pruning.

Lumber futures and options are traded at the CME Group. The CME Group's lumber futures contract calls for the delivery of 111,000 board feet (one 73-foot rail car) of random length 8 to 12-foot 2 x 4s, the type used in construction. The contract is priced in terms of dollars per thousand board feet.

Lumber futures and options are traded at the CME Group. The CME Group's lumber futures contract calls for the delivery of 111,000 board feet (one 73-foot rail car) of random length 8 to 12-foot 2 x 4s, the type used in construction. The contract is priced in terms of dollars per thousand board feet.

Prices – CME lumber futures prices (Barchart.com electronic symbol code LS) on the nearest-futures chart in 2018 moved higher until May when the price fell sharply but then recovered to close the year down -11.6% at $416.20 per thousand board feet. The price rise continued into early 2019.

Supply – The U.S. led the world in the production of industrial round wood and in 2017 production fell -0.4% yr/yr to 355.208 million cubic meters, followed by Russia up by +0.3% to 197.611 million cubic meters, and then Canada, up by +1.0% at 153.071 cubic meters.

The U.S. also led the world in the production of plywood in 2017 with 9.590 million cubic meters of production (+2.0% yr/yr), followed by Russia with 3.729 million cubic meters (-0.8% yr/yr), and then Japan with 3.063 million cubic meters (unchanged yr/yr).

Trade – World exports of plywood in 2017 rose by +2.5% yr/yr to 30.582 million cubic meters. The world's largest exporter of plywood is Russia with an 8.1% share of world plywood exports in 2017, followed by Finland with 3.4%, U.S. with 3.1%, Finland with 3.1%, Canada with 2.2%, and Baltic States with 1.4%. In 2017 U.S. exports were up by +34.2% yr/yr to 936,000 cubic meters.

World exports of industrial roundwood in 2017 fell by -3.3% yr/yr to 128.897 million cubic meters. Russia was the world's largest exporter of roundwood in 2017 with a 15.1% share of world exports, followed by the U.S. with an 10.5% share, Czech Republic with 6.5%, and Canada with a 6.3% share. Russian exports of industrial roundwood in 2017 fell by 3.1% yr/yr to 19.423 million cubic meters. U.S. exports of industrial roundwood in 2017 rose by +10.5% yr/yr to 13.483 million cubic meters.

World Production of Industrial Roundwood by Selected Countries   In Thousands of Cubic Meters

Year	Austria	Canada	Czech Republic	Finland	France	Germany	Poland	Romania	Russia	Spain	Sweden	Turkey	United States
2008	16,772	136,096	14,307	45,965	27,724	46,806	30,470	9,517	149,256	14,427	64,900	14,462	336,895
2009	12,144	113,306	13,769	36,701	29,081	38,987	30,475	8,587	146,310	11,900	59,200	14,252	292,091
2010	13,281	138,802	14,771	45,977	29,634	45,388	31,343	10,548	161,595	10,969	66,300	15,695	336,135
2011	13,631	146,735	13,467	45,526	28,387	45,358	32,200	10,344	175,625	11,528	66,000	16,423	354,704
2012	12,831	146,741	13,041	44,614	24,945	42,863	32,972	11,050	177,455	11,627	63,599	17,701	347,076
2013	12,433	147,751	13,149	49,331	24,451	42,052	33,795	10,091	180,378	12,124	63,700	16,762	354,937
2014	12,030	148,825	13,365	49,202	25,750	43,243	35,677	10,471	188,300	12,686	67,400	18,535	356,812
2015	12,570	151,358	13,827	51,446	25,043	45,119	35,878	10,235	190,507	12,905	67,300	20,008	354,678
2016[1]	12,173	154,694	15,362	54,327	25,314	42,780	37,106	9,953	198,194	13,325	67,900	20,389	356,586
2017[2]	12,738	153,071	15,398	55,330	25,324	43,562	40,384	10,651	197,611	13,340	68,470	19,462	355,208

[1] Preliminary.   [2] Estimate.   *Source: Food and Agriculture Organization of the United Nations (FAO)*

Imports of Industrial Roundwood by Selected Countries   In Thousands of Cubic Meters

Year	Austria	Belgium	Canada	Finland	France	Germany	Italy	Norway	Poland	Portugal	Spain	Sweden	United States
2008	7,550	3,669	4,608	13,371	2,358	5,758	3,478	1,808	1,868	521	2,860	6,781	1,430
2009	8,036	3,031	4,636	3,761	1,503	4,534	2,703	933	1,874	473	1,868	4,676	696
2010	8,041	4,193	4,745	6,256	1,690	7,656	3,198	1,288	2,289	855	1,839	6,276	816
2011	7,427	4,326	4,275	5,736	1,454	7,005	3,328	1,355	3,419	1,717	2,135	6,724	959
2012	7,319	4,338	4,495	5,457	1,368	6,567	2,802	940	2,469	1,644	1,727	6,855	1,167
2013	8,214	4,507	4,872	6,694	1,244	8,442	2,691	661	2,270	2,320	2,047	7,532	926
2014	7,239	4,472	4,262	6,257	1,512	8,417	2,913	447	2,633	2,600	1,750	8,127	909
2015	7,849	4,021	4,616	5,709	1,349	8,745	2,665	378	2,535	2,014	751	6,941	1,191
2016[1]	9,188	3,899	6,185	5,911	1,444	8,697	2,763	417	2,482	2,131	596	6,807	1,248
2017[2]	8,649	3,637	6,491	4,831	1,224	8,681	2,357	503	1,704	2,000	454	7,695	1,154

[1] Preliminary.   [2] Estimate.   *Source: Food and Agricultural Organization of the United Nations (FAO)*

Exports of Industrial Roundwood by Selected Countries   In Thousands of Cubic Meters

Year	Canada	Czech Republic	Estonia	France	Germany	Hungary	Latvia	Lithuania	Russia	Slovakia	Sweden	Switzerland	United States
2008	2,839	1,906	1,469	3,547	7,037	661	3,193	1,171	36,784	2,192	2,349	1,155	10,200
2009	2,723	2,596	1,080	5,047	3,857	684	2,503	673	21,700	2,538	1,177	575	9,619
2010	4,019	1,743	2,250	6,665	3,726	873	4,158	1,329	20,983	2,434	1,217	796	9,641
2011	5,706	3,487	2,610	6,380	3,658	881	4,401	1,844	20,429	2,533	846	926	13,755
2012	6,094	3,912	2,392	4,571	3,398	858	4,107	1,464	17,652	2,085	794	801	12,227
2013	7,023	4,292	2,747	4,740	3,316	975	3,737	1,809	19,045	2,662	756	740	14,700
2014	6,696	4,931	2,758	4,398	3,387	871	3,836	1,716	20,909	2,932	630	764	13,962
2015	6,060	4,530	2,431	4,311	3,747	680	3,002	1,406	19,437	2,358	570	641	11,561
2016[1]	8,172	5,863	2,527	4,000	3,947	683	2,676	1,467	20,046	2,157	573	559	12,047
2017[2]	8,083	8,381	2,527	4,085	3,963	683	2,195	1,467	19,423	1,955	778	570	13,483

[1] Preliminary.   [2] Estimate.   *Source: Food and Agricultural Organization of the United Nations (FAO)*

U.S. Housing Starts: Seasonally Adjusted Annual Rate   In Thousands

Year	Jan.	Feb.	Mar.	Apr.	May	June	July	Aug.	Sept.	Oct.	Nov.	Dec.	Average
2009	490	582	505	478	540	585	594	586	585	534	588	581	554
2010	614	604	636	687	583	536	546	599	594	543	545	539	586
2011	630	517	600	554	561	608	623	585	650	610	711	694	612
2012	723	704	695	753	708	757	740	754	847	915	833	976	784
2013	888	970	999	826	920	852	891	898	860	921	1,104	1,010	928
2014	902	948	973	1,038	987	928	1,085	984	999	1,094	994	1,081	1,001
2015	1,101	893	964	1,192	1,063	1,213	1,147	1,132	1,189	1,073	1,171	1,160	1,108
2016	1,123	1,209	1,128	1,164	1,119	1,190	1,223	1,164	1,062	1,328	1,149	1,268	1,177
2017	1,225	1,289	1,179	1,165	1,122	1,225	1,185	1,172	1,158	1,265	1,303	1,210	1,208
2018[1]	1,334	1,290	1,327	1,276	1,329	1,177	1,184	1,280	1,237	1,209	1,206	1,140	1,241

[1] Preliminary.   Total Privately owned.   *Source: Bureau of the Census, U.S. Department of Commerce*

LUMBER AND PLYWOOD

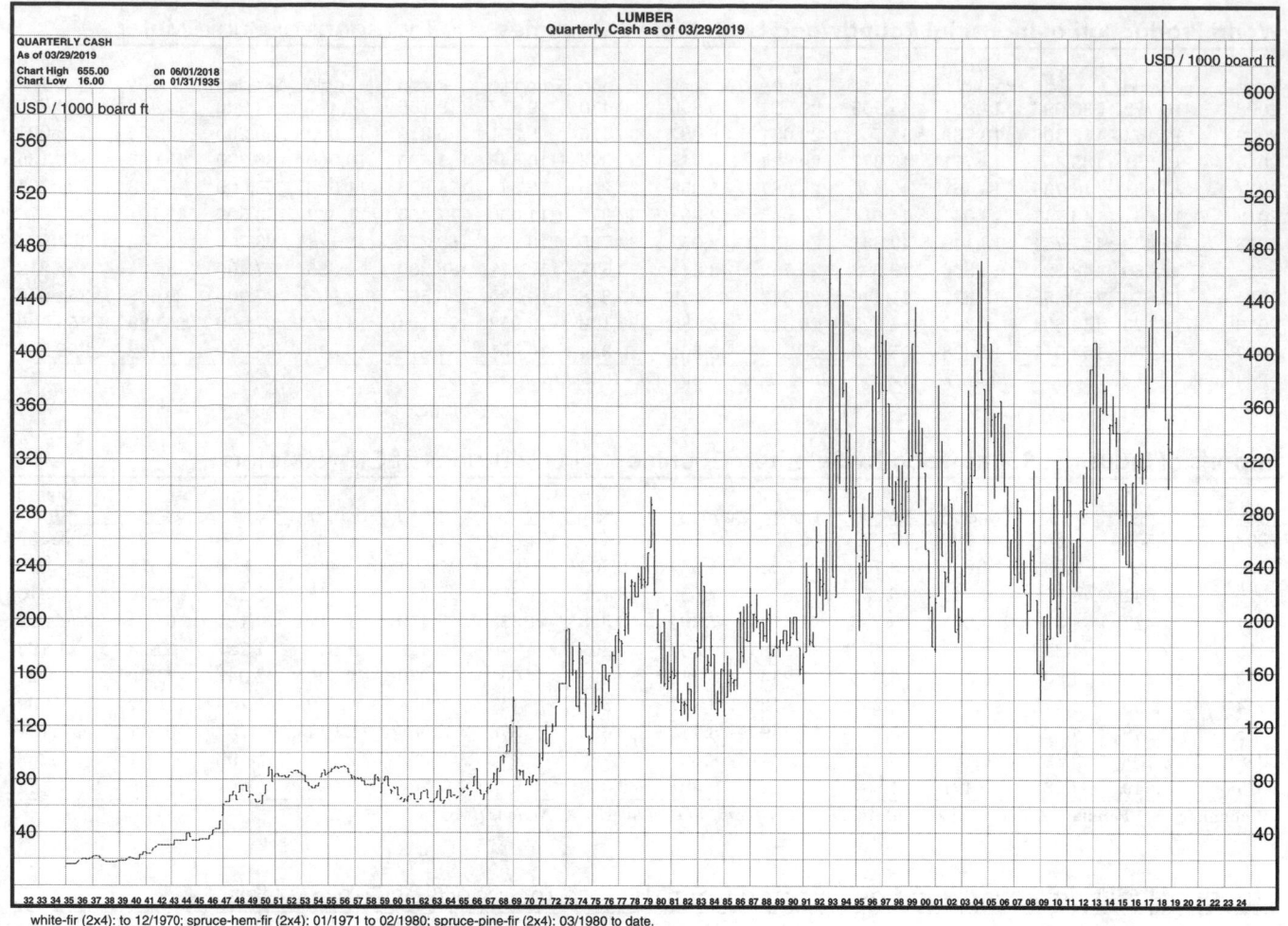

LUMBER
Quarterly Cash as of 03/29/2019

QUARTERLY CASH
As of 03/29/2019
Chart High 655.00 on 06/01/2018
Chart Low   16.00   on 01/31/1935

USD / 1000 board ft

white-fir (2x4): to 12/1970; spruce-hem-fir (2x4): 01/1971 to 02/1980; spruce-pine-fir (2x4): 03/1980 to date.

Average Price of Lumber in the United States   In Dollars per Thousand Board Feet

Year	Jan.	Feb.	Mar.	Apr.	May	June	July	Aug.	Sept.	Oct.	Nov.	Dec.	Average
2009	150.60	158.00	154.75	166.00	161.80	193.00	185.00	200.25	186.25	191.00	210.00	223.67	181.69
2010	238.50	287.00	281.50	312.00	272.50	207.50	203.40	219.75	231.75	245.80	275.33	283.80	254.90
2011	307.25	286.25	294.25	269.50	227.25	222.75	254.50	231.75	250.80	236.50	230.25	248.00	254.92
2012	253.50	262.67	280.75	281.25	305.50	300.00	294.25	310.20	292.33	298.00	339.50	370.00	299.00
2013	382.25	377.33	401.50	386.60	325.50	298.40	312.25	326.00	346.75	360.25	381.80	364.25	355.24
2014	373.20	364.00	362.75	339.00	342.00	323.75	351.50	361.00	355.25	347.00	333.75	337.75	349.25
2015	326.00	313.50	283.75	261.50	256.40	292.25	294.25	267.75	246.00	259.20	259.75	267.25	277.30
2016	258.75	251.50	292.00	298.60	317.50	319.50	323.40	326.00	313.60	318.75	306.25	319.60	303.79
2017	309.50	374.75	359.20	405.33	387.75	368.40	403.25	394.50	413.80	446.25	485.00	461.40	400.76
2018	492.50	523.25	524.20	551.75	621.33	617.80	564.25	468.20	413.75	316.33	338.00	320.25	479.30

Source: National Agricultural Statistics Service, U.S. Department of Agriculture (NASS-USDA)

Average Price of Plywood in the United States   In Dollars per Thousand Board Feet

Year	Jan.	Feb.	Mar.	Apr.	May	June	July	Aug.	Sept.	Oct.	Nov.	Dec.	Average
2009	151.00	163.00	150.75	148.00	140.80	153.75	174.00	186.00	176.50	158.00	171.25	186.33	163.28
2010	191.50	220.00	233.00	353.75	330.00	206.25	217.20	171.25	164.50	183.00	189.33	196.40	221.35
2011	210.75	196.75	189.25	178.25	167.25	180.25	171.25	192.25	188.60	190.75	185.00	192.00	186.86
2012	201.00	194.67	213.25	212.50	233.75	252.00	257.50	331.00	343.33	300.00	343.75	354.50	269.77
2013	401.50	412.67	430.00	410.00	354.33	279.25	256.25	254.40	244.75	263.00	244.00	227.75	314.83
2014	226.60	215.00	214.50	210.33	233.00	210.25	212.25	215.40	222.00	222.00	219.00	204.00	217.03
2015	200.80	194.25	183.50	177.50	194.00	207.25	194.00	200.50	218.33	239.20	257.00	233.50	208.32
2016	232.50	230.75	224.25	244.20	275.75	278.00	295.40	306.25	300.00	287.00	285.75	282.00	270.15
2017	278.50	291.25	307.00	327.00	329.75	330.40	378.00	412.00	432.20	454.25	396.25	304.00	353.38
2018	318.75	377.50	405.00	405.00	418.33	445.00	403.75	347.00	342.50	268.33	242.00	208.25	348.45

Source: National Agricultural Statistics Service, U.S. Department of Agriculture (NASS-USDA)

LUMBER - CME
Weekly Nearest Futures as of 03/29/2019

WEEKLY NEAREST FUTURES
As of 03/29/2019

Chart High 659.00 on 05/14/2018
Chart Low 137.90 on 01/29/2009

USD / 1000 board ft

Nearby Futures through Last Trading Day.

Volume of Trading of Random Lumber Futures in Chicago   In Contracts

Year	Jan.	Feb.	Mar.	Apr.	May	June	July	Aug.	Sept.	Oct.	Nov.	Dec.	Total
2009	18,478	29,930	22,193	25,349	24,351	34,027	24,340	29,548	22,271	33,768	21,817	31,155	317,227
2010	25,483	26,365	20,928	32,393	24,763	29,446	18,360	24,660	26,107	31,689	23,662	28,046	311,902
2011	22,691	25,642	25,141	32,161	20,134	30,740	18,440	32,615	28,562	26,650	22,589	33,968	319,333
2012	20,678	33,593	25,208	30,526	24,563	26,638	23,663	32,211	19,595	31,797	24,513	31,538	324,523
2013	26,219	29,842	18,671	26,472	23,349	19,914	18,572	18,118	19,271	17,021	11,100	15,073	243,622
2014	13,001	14,025	12,632	14,563	13,365	17,276	10,119	14,977	11,766	16,481	8,959	13,333	160,497
2015	13,744	16,696	14,710	21,116	16,757	19,374	14,253	20,509	15,592	21,061	11,475	16,065	201,352
2016	13,340	14,415	16,933	15,931	12,953	16,806	10,911	19,397	13,373	16,510	13,574	12,839	176,982
2017	11,400	20,115	14,942	21,705	16,706	15,346	14,333	15,684	16,030	21,713	18,739	18,386	205,099
2018	15,690	21,225	15,354	22,545	22,211	23,128	15,731	19,983	14,424	20,532	14,222	11,541	216,586

Contract size = 110,000 board feet.   *Source: CME Group; Chicago Mercantile Exchange (CME)*

Average Open Interest of Random Lumber Futures in Chicago   In Contracts

Year	Jan.	Feb.	Mar.	Apr.	May	June	July	Aug.	Sept.	Oct.	Nov.	Dec.
2009	7,912	7,937	6,852	7,732	7,815	9,039	7,910	8,873	9,248	9,593	10,174	9,557
2010	9,674	10,231	9,538	10,571	8,358	9,402	8,675	9,498	8,812	9,707	9,620	10,018
2011	11,235	10,223	9,471	9,813	10,090	10,408	9,233	10,170	9,465	10,314	9,663	10,768
2012	9,261	10,228	10,192	9,962	9,226	7,885	7,666	9,259	8,153	8,275	10,713	10,624
2013	9,354	8,222	8,609	7,345	5,872	6,726	5,816	5,539	5,699	4,816	4,672	4,086
2014	3,945	4,602	4,618	5,020	4,422	5,013	4,080	4,419	3,751	3,698	4,610	4,289
2015	4,831	5,256	6,336	6,860	6,379	4,660	4,389	6,151	6,104	5,553	3,974	4,158
2016	4,619	5,292	4,478	4,561	5,050	4,782	4,692	5,167	3,479	4,323	3,818	4,005
2017	3,786	4,992	5,353	6,044	5,180	4,378	4,158	4,510	5,489	6,494	6,800	6,278
2018	6,775	7,290	6,406	6,964	6,827	6,550	5,649	4,714	3,986	4,078	4,120	3,984

Contract size = 110,000 board feet.   *Source: CME Group; Chicago Mercantile Exchange (CME)*

LUMBER AND PLYWOOD

Production of Plywood by Selected Countries   In Thousands of Cubic Meters

Year	Austria	Canada	Finland	France	Germany	Italy	Japan	Poland	Romania	Russia	Spain	Sweden	United States
2008	133	633	2,149	402	581	1,459	530	3,583	635	192	131	1,486	3,059
2009	116	527	861	229	397	1,066	417	2,948	457	144	53	1,164	2,647
2010	155	544	1,750	219	544	1,288	485	3,255	495	152	68	1,264	2,551
2011	196	593	1,554	262	492	1,423	463	3,809	620	185	74	1,330	2,632
2012	209	533	1,621	270	374	1,336	420	3,645	476	173	86	1,285	3,113
2013	145	537	1,469	266	368	1,338	428	3,765	399	155	99	1,370	2,829
2014	160	554	1,587	266	429	1,369	453	3,597	468	163	184	1,399	2,872
2015	190	525	1,492	211	420	1,412	448	2,996	552	150	182	1,466	4,253
2016[1]	181	575	1,228	242	478	1,458	458	2,881	536	175	192	1,479	4,877
2017[2]	232	447	1,742	242	528	1,509	507	2,881	632	206	203	1,535	4,934

[1] Preliminary.   [2] Estimate.   Source: Food and Agricultural Organization of the United Nations (FAO)

Imports of Plywood by Selected Countries   In Thousands of Cubic Meters

Year	Austria	Belgium	Canada	Denmark	France	Germany	Italy	Japan	Nether-lands	Sweden	Switzer-land	United Kingdom	United States
2008	133	633	2,149	402	581	1,459	530	3,583	635	192	131	1,486	3,059
2009	116	527	861	229	397	1,066	417	2,948	457	144	53	1,164	2,647
2010	155	544	1,750	219	544	1,288	485	3,255	495	152	68	1,264	2,551
2011	196	593	1,554	262	492	1,423	463	3,809	620	185	74	1,330	2,632
2012	209	533	1,621	270	374	1,336	420	3,645	476	173	86	1,285	3,113
2013	145	537	1,469	266	368	1,338	428	3,765	399	155	99	1,370	2,829
2014	160	554	1,587	266	429	1,369	453	3,597	468	163	184	1,399	2,872
2015	190	525	1,492	211	420	1,412	448	2,996	552	150	182	1,466	4,253
2016[1]	181	575	1,228	242	478	1,458	458	2,881	536	175	192	1,479	4,877
2017[2]	232	447	1,742	242	528	1,509	507	2,881	632	206	203	1,535	4,934

[1] Preliminary.   [2] Estimate.   Source: Food and Agricultural Organization of the United Nations (FAO)

Exports of Plywood by Selected Countries   In Thousands of Cubic Meters

Year	Austria	Baltic States	Belgium	Canada	Finland	France	Germany	Italy	Nether-lands	Poland	Russia	Spain	United States
2008	278	197	470	583	1,083	275	342	184	51	133	1,326	213	506
2009	278	211	374	306	683	162	277	148	49	117	1,334	122	529
2010	304	289	440	301	833	163	337	218	50	133	1,512	141	871
2011	353	302	437	359	863	127	355	228	63	141	1,600	165	837
2012	334	310	368	287	855	143	298	201	89	169	1,717	152	914
2013	339	312	369	426	920	141	297	192	71	181	1,758	166	888
2014	346	302	403	482	998	145	310	210	75	203	1,969	189	828
2015	298	345	381	647	981	156	334	215	68	250	2,206	224	643
2016[1]	340	437	437	625	940	153	349	240	73	257	2,458	252	697
2017[2]	349	437	403	670	1,039	171	373	263	83	312	2,470	382	936

[1] Preliminary.   [2] Estimate.   Source: Food and Agricultural Organization of the United Nations (FAO)

Magnesium

Magnesium (atomic symbol Mg) is a silvery-white, light, and fairly tough, metallic element and is relatively stable. Magnesium is one of the alkaline earth metals. Magnesium is the eighth most abundant element in the earth's crust and the third most plentiful element found in seawater. Magnesium is ductile and malleable when heated, and with the exception of beryllium, is the lightest metal that remains stable under ordinary conditions. First isolated by the British chemist Sir Humphrey Davy in 1808, magnesium today is obtained mainly by electrolysis of fused magnesium chloride.

Magnesium compounds, primarily magnesium oxide, are used in the refractory material that line the furnaces used to produce iron and steel, nonferrous metals, glass, and cement. Magnesium oxide and other compounds are also used in the chemical, agricultural, and construction industries. Magnesium's principal use is as an alloying addition for aluminum. These aluminum-magnesium alloys are used primarily in beverage cans. Due to their lightness and considerable tensile strength, the alloys are also used in structural components in airplanes and automobiles.

Prices – The average price of magnesium in 2018 rose +6.5% yr/yr to $1.99 per pound, well below the 2008 record high of $3.38 per pound.

Supply – World primary production of magnesium in 2018 fell -7.6% yr/yr to 970,000 metric tons which is down from last year's record high. The current level of magnesium production is about four times what it was in the mid-1970s. Total U.S. consumption of primary magnesium in 2017 fell -14.9% yr/yr to 40,000 metric tons. The world's largest primary producer of magnesium in 2018 was China with 800,000 metric tons, which is 82.5% of the world's total production. Russia produced 65,000 metric tons and Israel produced 25,000 metric tons.

The U.S. production amount is not available because it is considered proprietary data but is probably less than about 50,000 metric tons. China increased production from 70,500 metric tons in 1998 to their new record high of 930,000 in 2017.

Demand -- Total U.S. consumption of magnesium for all structural products in 2016 rose +9.1% yr/yr to 11,349 metric tons. Of the structural product consumption category, 83.5% was for castings and the remaining 16.5% was for wrought products. U.S. consumption of magnesium for aluminum alloys fell -48.1% yr/yr to 11,100 metric tons. The consumption of magnesium for other uses rose +35.9% yr/yr to 57,900 metric tons.

Trade – U.S. exports of magnesium in 2018 fell -14.3% yr/yr to 12,000 metric tons, but still well above the 2005 record low of 9,650 metric tons. U.S. imports of magnesium in 2018 rose 16.7% yr/yr to 49,000 metric tons.

World Production of Magnesium (Primary)   In Metric Tons

Year	Brazil	Canada	China	Israel	Kazakhstan	Russia	Serbia	Ukraine	United States	Total
2013	16,000	----	770,000	27,399	13,000	66,000	----	10,300	W	910,000
2014	16,000	----	874,000	25,993	9,500	62,000	----	7,200	W	1,000,000
2015	15,000	----	859,000	19,307	8,100	60,000	----	7,700	W	979,000
2016	16,000	----	871,000	23,000	10,000	58,000	----	5,000	W	998,000
2017[1]	15,000	----	930,000	23,000	9,000	40,000	----	8,000	W	1,050,000
2018[2]	15,000	----	800,000	25,000	23,000	65,000	----	19,000	W	970,000

[1] Preliminary.   [2] Estimate.   W = Withheld.   Source: U.S. Geological Survey (USGS)

Salient Statistics of Magnesium in the United States   In Metric Tons

Year	Production Primary (Ingot)	Secondary New Scrap	Secondary Old Scrap	Total	Imports Exports[3]	Imports for Con-sumption	Stocks Dec. 31[4]	Price $ Per Pound[5]	Castings Structural Products	Wrought Structural Products	Total	Aluminum Alloys	Other Uses	Total
2013	W	54,200	25,000	79,300	16,100	45,900	W	2.13	10,829	2,240	13,069	24,400	44,100	68,500
2014	W	55,200	25,000	81,000	17,000	52,000	W	2.15	9,638	2,340	11,978	22,600	41,400	64,000
2015	W	65,600	22,900	88,000	15,000	49,000	W	2.15	9,361	1,040	10,401	21,400	42,600	64,000
2016	W	72,800	23,200	102,000	19,000	46,000	W	2.15	9,479	1,870	11,349	11,100	57,900	69,000
2017[1]	W			114,000	14,000	42,000	W	2.15						65,000
2018/[2]	W			100,000	12,000	49,000	W	2.15						70,000

[1] Preliminary.   [2] Estimate.   [3] Metal & alloys in crude form & scrap.   [4] Estimate of Industry Stocks, metal.   [5] Magnesium ingots (99.8%), f.o.b. Valasco, Texas.   [6] Distributive or sacrificial purposes.   W = Withheld proprietary data.   Source: U.S. Geological Survey (USGS)

Average Price of Magnesium   In Dollars Per Pound

Year	Jan.	Feb.	Mar.	Apr.	May	June	July	Aug.	Sept.	Oct.	Nov.	Dec.	Average
2014	2.08	2.06	2.05	2.05	2.05	2.03	2.02	2.02	2.02	2.02	2.02	2.02	2.04
2015	1.96	1.92	1.90	1.90	1.92	1.92	1.92	1.92	1.92	1.92	1.87	1.74	1.90
2016	1.74	1.74	1.75	1.75	1.85	1.79	1.77	1.80	1.84	1.90	1.94	1.95	1.82
2017	1.91	1.81	1.84	1.87	1.87	1.87	1.84	1.86	1.87	1.87	1.87	1.90	1.87
2018	1.94	1.99	2.00	1.98	1.99	1.99	1.99	1.99	1.99	1.99	1.99	1.99	1.99

Source: American Metal Market (AMM)

Manganese

Manganese (atomic symbol Mn) is a silvery-white, very brittle, metallic element used primarily in making alloys. Manganese was first distinguished as an element and isolated in 1774 by Johan Gottlieb Gahn. Manganese dissolves in acid and corrodes in moist air.

Manganese is found in the earth's crust in the form of ores such as rhodochrosite, franklinite, psilomelane, and manganite. Pyrolusite is the principal ore of manganese. Pure manganese is produced by igniting pyrolusite with aluminum powder or by electrolyzing manganese sulfate.

Manganese is used primarily in the steel industry for creating alloys, the most important ones being ferromanganese and spiegeleisen. In steel, manganese improves forging and rolling qualities, strength, toughness, stiffness, wear resistance, and hardness. Manganese is also used in plant fertilizers, animal feed, pigments, and dry cell batteries.

Prices – The average monthly price of ferromanganese (high carbon, FOB plant) in 2018 fell -2.3% yr/yr to $1,446.60 per gross ton, and still well below the 2008 record high of $2,953.84 per gross ton. The 2018 price, however, is still about three times the 25-year low price of $447.44 per gross ton posted as recently as 2001.

Supply – World production of manganese ore in 2015 fell -10.7% yr/yr to 51.800 million metric tons. The world's largest producers of manganese ore in 2015 were South Africa with 30.8% of world production, Russia with 25.1%, Australia with 14.5%, and Gabon with 7.0%. China's production in 2015 was down -33.8% yr/yr at 13.024 million metric tons.

Demand – U.S. consumption of manganese ore in 2018 rose +3.2% yr/yr to 390,000 metric tons. U.S. consumption of ferromanganese in 2018 rose +4.3% yr/yr to 360,000 metric tons, but still down from the 2012 record high of 382,000 metric tons. The 2018 figure is about 25% of the U.S. consumption back in the early 1970s.

Trade – The U.S. still relies on imports for 100% of its manganese consumption, as it has since 1985. U.S. imports of manganese ore for consumption in 2018 rose +44.8% yr/yr to 390,000 metric tons, up from 2009's 20-year low of 269,000 metric tons. U.S. imports of ferromanganese for consumption in 2018 rose +39.0% yr/yr to 460,000 metric tons. U.S. imports of silico-manganese in 2018 rose +19.7% yr/yr to 420,000 metric tons, well above 2009's 27-year low of 130,000 metric tons.

World Production of Manganese Ore   In Thousands of Metric Tons (Gross Weight)

Year	Australia[2] (37%-53%)	Brazil (37%)	China (20%-30%)	Gabon (45%-53%)	Ghana (32%-34%)	India (10%-54%)	Kazakh-stan (29%-30%)	Malaysia (32%-45%)	Mexico (27%-50%)	South Africa (30%-48%+)	Ukraine (30%-35%)	Other	World Total
2006	4,556	3,390	8,000	3,000	1,659	2,084	2,531	----	346	5,213	1,606	752	33,100
2007	5,289	1,570	10,000	3,300	1,854	2,016	1,003	57	423	5,996	1,720	1,270	34,500
2008	4,812	3,200	11,000	3,248	914	2,293	1,117	537	472	6,807	1,447	1,700	37,900
2009	4,451	2,575	12,000	1,992	882	2,347	982	469	330	4,579	932	1,660	33,800
2010	6,474	3,125	13,000	3,201	1,530	2,858	1,094	900	485	7,172	1,589	1,450	44,000
2011	6,963	2,738	14,000	4,070	1,689	2,015	1,096	598	468	8,652	972	1,410	45,700
2012	7,172	2,796	14,500	3,637	1,467	1,916	1,071	1,100	515	8,943	1,234	1,340	46,400
2013	7,447	2,883	17,547	3,997	1,812	3,112	1,121	1,125	580	10,958	1,525	1,670	54,600
2014	7,670	2,723	19,671	3,787	1,496	2,200	1,092	835	652	14,051	1,526	1,670	58,000
2015[1]	7,500	2,816	13,024	4,112	1,478	2,117	615	480	600	15,952	1,203	1,470	51,800

[1] Preliminary.   [2] Metallurgical Ore.   [3] Concentrate.   [4] Ranges of percentage of manganese.   *Source: U.S. Geological Survey (USGS)*

Salient Statistics of Manganese in the United States   In Thousands of Metric Tons (Gross Weight)

Year	Net Import Reliance As a % of Apparent Consump	Manganese Ore (35% or More Manganese) Imports for Consumption	Exports	Consumption	Stocks Dec. 31[3]	Ferromanganese Imports for Consumption	Exports	Consumption	Avg Price Mn. Metallurgical Ore $/Lg. Ton Unit[4]	Silicomanganese Exports	Imports
2009	100	269	15	422	115	153	24	242	7.95	18.8	130.0
2010	100	489	14	450	168	326	19	292	8.45	9.4	297.0
2011	100	552	1	532	250	348	5	303	6.67	8.5	348.0
2012	100	506	2	538	203	401	5	382	4.97	5.9	348.0
2013	100	558	1	523	217	335	2	368	4.61	6.0	329.0
2014	100	387	1	508	189	365	6	360	4.49	3.0	448.0
2015	100	441	1	451	187	292	5	344	3.53	1.0	301.0
2016	100	282	1	410	207	229	7	342	3.41	2.0	264.0
2017[1]	100	297	1	378	148	331	9	345	6.19	8.0	351.0
2018[2]	100	430	4	390	180	460	9	360	9.60	4.0	420.0

[1] Preliminary.   [2] Estimate.   [3] Including bonded warehouses; excludes Gov't stocks; also excludes small tonnages of dealers' stocks.
[4] 46-48% Mn, C.I.F. U.S. Ports.   *Source: U.S. Geological Survey (USGS)*

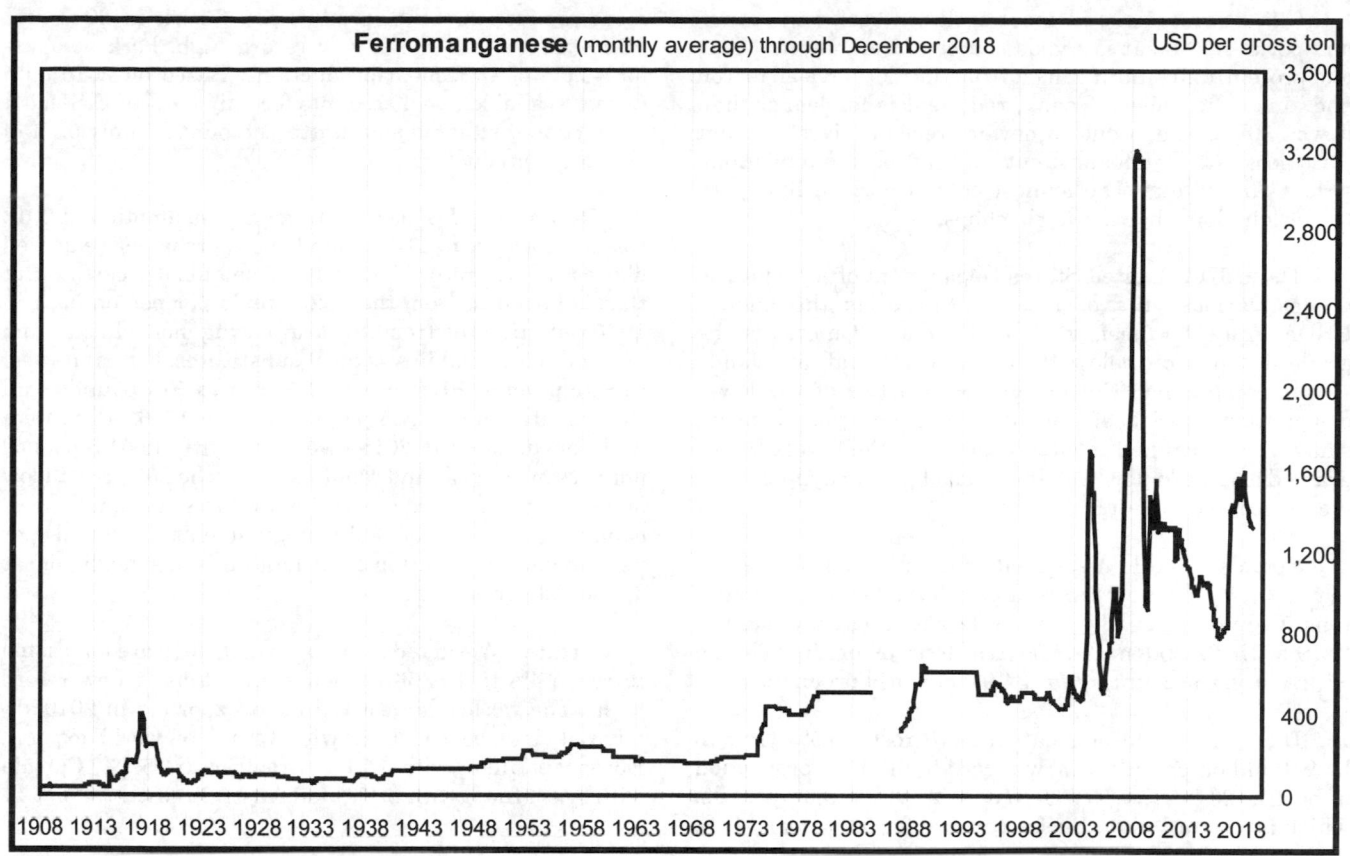

Ferromanganese (monthly average) through December 2018 — USD per gross ton

Imports[3] of Manganese Ore (20% or More Mn) in the United States — In Metric Tons (Mn Content)

Year	Australia	Brazil	Gabon	Mexico	Morocco	South Africa	Total	Customs Value ($1,000)
2008	51,900	34,400	181,000	----	----	14,600	289,000	154,000
2009	15,400	1,540	96,500	671	9	----	154,000	82,600
2010	65,200	3,440	125,000	1,050	791	40,100	255,000	133,000
2011	70,500	4,750	183,000	1,640	454	5,530	266,000	145,000
2012	15,000	3,970	152,000	2,200	2,670	46,400	226,000	101,000
2013	29,200	3,850	192,000	4,810	3,800	12,900	263,000	126,000
2014	17,500	1,690	149,400	3,440	910	17,280	192,000	88,300
2015	16,700	4,400	184,100	2,144	90	23,778	232,000	92,500
2016[1]	3,510	290	106,530	8,820	87	14,968	135,000	40,700
2017[2]	9,770	340	134,640	10,690	135	14,400	170,000	73,300

[1] Preliminary. [2] Estimate. [3] Imports for consumption. *Source: U.S. Geological Survey (USGS)*

Average Price of Ferromanganese[1] — In Dollars Per Gross Ton -- Carloads

Year	Jan.	Feb.	Mar.	Apr.	May	June	July	Aug.	Sept.	Oct.	Nov.	Dec.	Average
2009	2,225.00	1,300.00	1,300.00	1,038.10	950.00	928.18	955.45	1,071.43	1,344.52	1,481.67	1,431.84	1,365.26	1,282.62
2010	1,326.58	1,387.50	1,530.43	1,559.09	1,507.00	1,389.09	1,310.00	1,320.45	1,327.38	1,345.00	1,345.00	1,345.00	1,391.04
2011	1,336.25	1,320.00	1,320.00	1,327.62	1,321.43	1,315.00	1,315.00	1,327.39	1,330.00	1,330.00	1,330.00	1,303.95	1,323.05
2012	1,171.50	1,179.38	1,285.23	1,317.86	1,280.68	1,263.34	1,238.45	1,220.33	1,214.48	1,202.39	1,171.25	1,144.58	1,224.12
2013	1,140.00	1,128.16	1,128.81	1,121.14	1,076.94	1,071.25	1,037.50	1,037.50	1,031.88	1,000.00	1,000.00	1,000.00	1,064.43
2014	1,006.19	1,066.50	1,088.58	1,090.00	1,080.00	1,078.22	1,041.25	1,060.00	1,053.34	1,055.22	1,060.00	1,039.53	1,059.90
2015	1,042.00	1,036.06	1,029.09	944.66	939.75	929.77	876.82	875.00	841.67	836.36	825.00	797.73	914.49
2016	779.34	792.00	797.50	805.00	813.57	821.59	836.25	835.00	836.67	845.00	1,012.12	1,320.24	874.52
2017	1,410.00	1,438.42	1,430.87	1,406.50	1,418.64	1,470.68	1,509.00	1,547.39	1,568.50	1,552.84	1,540.00	1,473.12	1,480.50
2018	1,500.60	1,564.21	1,595.45	1,527.62	1,509.32	1,438.57	1,433.57	1,404.57	1,375.00	1,345.65	1,337.50	1,327.12	1,446.60

[1] Domestic standard, high carbon, FOB plant, carloads. *Source: American Metal Market (AMM)*

Meats

U.S. commercial red meat includes beef, veal, lamb, and pork. Red meat is a good source of iron, vitamin B12, and protein, and eliminating it from the diet can lead to iron and zinc deficiencies. Today, red meat is far leaner than it was 30 years ago due to newer breeds of livestock that carry less fat. The leanest cuts of beef include tenderloin, sirloin, and flank. The leanest cuts of pork include pork tenderloin, loin chops, and rib chops.

The USDA (United States Department of Agriculture) grades various cuts of meat. "Prime" is the highest USDA grade for beef, veal, and lamb. "Choice" is the grade designation below Prime for beef, veal, and lamb. "Commercial" and "Cutter" grades are two of the lower designations for beef, usually sold as ground meat, sausage, and canned meat. "Canner" is the lowest USDA grade designation for beef and is used primarily in canned meats not sold at retail.

Supply – World meat production in 2019 is forecasted to rise +1.3% to a new record high of 178.208 million metric tons. China will be the world's largest meat producer in 2019 with 62.200 million metric tons of production (up +1.2% yr/yr), accounting for 34.9% of world production.

U.S. production of meat in 2018 rose +5.5% yr/yr to 54.919 billion pounds, a new record high. U.S. production of beef in 2018 rose +5.9% yr/yr to 27.792 billion pounds, which is a record high. Beef accounted for 50.6% of all U.S.

meat production. U.S. production of pork in 2018 rose +5.1% yr/yr to 26.901, a new record high. Pork accounts for 49.0% of U.S. meat production. Based on 2015 data (latest available), veal accounts for only 0.4% of U.S. meat production, and lamb and mutton account for only 0.1% of U.S. meat production.

Demand – U.S. per-capita meat consumption in 2018 rose +3.7% yr/yr to 112.3 pounds per person per year, well above the 2014 record low of 101.7 pounds per person. But that is far down from the 192 pounds per person back in 1970 reflecting the trend towards eating more chicken and fish and the availability of meat substitutes. Per-capita beef consumption in 2018 rose +2.0% yr/yr to 56.7 pounds, half the record high of 127.5 pounds seen in 1976. Per capita pork consumption in 2018 rose +3.4% yr/yr to 51.8 pounds per person per year and remains above the 2011 record low of 45.7 pounds. Based on 2015 data (latest available), per-capita consumption of veal is negligible at 0.2 pounds per person and lamb/mutton consumption is also negligible at 1.0 pound per person.

Trade – World red meat exports in 2019 are forecasted to rise 1.4% to 19.366 million metric tons, a new record high. The world's largest red meat exporters in 2019 are forecasted to be the U.S. with 22.1% of world exports, European Union with 18.1%, Brazil with 15.2%, Canada with 9.7%. India with 8.4%, and Australia with 8.0%.

World Total Meat Production[4]   In Thousands of Metric Tons

Year	Argentina	Australia	Brazil	Canada	China[4]	European Union	India	Mexico	New Zealand	Russia	South Africa	United States	World Total
2010	2,899	2,468	12,310	3,059	57,243	30,728	3,125	2,779	690	3,416	1,078	22,220	162,096
2011	2,831	2,473	12,257	2,958	57,079	31,067	3,308	2,862	651	3,424	1,075	22,309	162,388
2012	2,951	2,504	12,637	2,904	60,050	30,234	3,491	2,911	673	3,555	1,058	22,399	166,242
2013	3,266	2,719	13,010	2,878	61,660	29,747	3,800	2,937	667	3,785	1,119	22,276	169,229
2014	3,142	2,957	13,123	2,905	63,600	29,983	4,100	2,962	705	3,885	1,207	21,443	171,312
2015	3,204	2,921	12,944	2,946	61,570	30,933	4,100	3,014	734	3,970	1,271	21,938	170,132
2016	3,172	2,511	12,984	3,044	59,990	31,746	4,200	3,090	693	4,205	1,333	22,827	170,617
2017	3,405	2,557	13,275	3,160	60,660	31,526	4,250	3,192	700	4,336	1,253	23,554	172,662
2018[1]	3,540	2,730	13,575	3,200	61,475	32,015	4,300	3,270	715	4,575	1,298	24,278	175,836
2019[2]	3,600	2,600	13,975	3,215	62,200	31,800	4,330	3,360	703	4,665	1,360	25,346	178,208

[1] Preliminary.   [2] Forecast.   [4] Predominately pork production.   *Source: Foreign Agricultural Service, U.S. Department of Agriculture (FAS-USDA)*

Production and Consumption of Red Meats in The United States

	Beef			Veal			Lamb & Mutton			Pork (Excluding Lard)			All Meats		
	Commercial Production	Consumption		Commercial Production	Consumption		Commercial Production	Consumption		Commercial Production	Consumption		Commercial Production	Consumption	
		Total	Per Capita		Total	Per Capita		Total	Per Capita		Total	Per Capita		Total	Per Capita
Year	- Million Pounds -		Lbs.	- Million Pounds -		Lbs.	- Million Pounds -		Lbs.	- Million Pounds -		Lbs.	- Million Pounds -		Lbs.
2010	26,304	26,390	59.6	145	150	0.4	168	317	0.9	22,437	19,077	47.8	49,183	45,935	108.6
2011	26,195	25,538	57.3	130	137	0.4	149	295	0.8	22,758	18,382	45.7	49,232	44,351	104.2
2012	25,913	25,755	57.3	118	123	0.3	156	299	0.8	23,253	18,607	45.9	49,439	44,784	104.4
2013	25,720	25,476	56.3	111	119	0.3	156	324	0.9	23,187	19,104	46.8	49,174	45,022	104.3
2014	24,250	24,687	54.2	94	97	0.3	156	340	0.9	22,843	19,071	45.8	47,345	44,195	101.7
2015	23,698	24,773	54.0	82	88	0.2	150	357	1.0	24,501	20,593	49.8	48,520	45,810	105.0
2016	25,288	25,673	55.6	----	----	----	----	----	----	24,956	20,891	50.1	50,480	47,018	106.9
2017[1]	26,250	26,492	56.9	----	----	----	----	----	----	25,598	21,035	50.1	52,078	48,000	108.2
2018[2]	26,931	26,759	57.0	----	----	----	----	----	----	26,329	21,496	50.8	53,499	48,760	109.2
2019[3]	27,363	27,105	57.3	----	----	----	----	----	----	27,444	22,323	52.3	55,045	49,931	110.9

[1] Preliminary.   [2] Estimate.   [3] Forecast.   *Source: Economic Research Service, U.S. Department of Agriculture (ERS-USDA)*

Total Red Meat Imports (Carcass Weight Equivalent) of Principal Countries   In Thousands of Metric Tons

Year	Brazil	Canada	Egypt	European Union	Hong Kong	Japan	Korea, South	Mexico	Philippines	Russia	Taiwan	United States	World Total
2010	36	416	260	467	501	1,919	748	983	292	1,974	188	1,432	12,577
2011	41	476	217	384	584	1,999	1,071	859	284	1,965	188	1,297	13,170
2012	63	530	250	369	655	1,996	872	921	273	2,097	148	1,371	13,600
2013	60	504	195	391	872	1,983	763	1,015	317	1,906	170	1,419	14,110
2014	84	486	270	386	993	2,071	872	1,024	364	1,448	201	1,796	14,250
2015	62	485	360	375	736	1,977	1,013	1,156	320	1,030	242	2,034	14,373
2016	68	458	340	380	882	2,080	1,128	1,209	358	871	231	1,861	15,692
2017	58	451	250	352	1,006	2,292	1,176	1,279	410	891	271	1,864	15,843
2018[1]	52	470	300	385	1,035	2,345	1,295	1,385	440	555	295	1,856	16,484
2019[2]	47	485	330	385	1,090	2,375	1,250	1,455	475	510	315	1,887	17,085

[1] Preliminary.   [2] Forecast.   Source: Foreign Agricultural Service, U.S. Department of Agriculture (FAS-USDA)

Total Red Meat Exports (Carcass Weight Equivalent) of Principal Countries   In Thousands of Metric Tons

Year	Argentina	Australia	Brazil	Canada	China	European Union	India	New Zealand	Russia	Ukraine	United States	Uruguay	World Total
2010	278	1,409	2,177	1,682	329	2,042	917	530	6	20	2,958	347	13,832
2011	214	1,451	1,924	1,623	299	2,595	1,268	503	7	35	3,620	320	15,067
2012	165	1,443	2,185	1,578	277	2,461	1,450	517	19	52	3,552	359	15,458
2013	187	1,629	2,434	1,578	274	2,471	1,881	529	11	41	3,436	340	16,269
2014	198	1,888	2,465	1,598	307	2,465	2,082	579	15	43	3,477	350	16,987
2015	187	1,890	2,332	1,636	255	2,695	1,806	639	17	81	3,300	372	16,823
2016	218	1,518	2,530	1,761	214	3,481	1,764	587	35	54	3,537	421	17,785
2017	296	1,528	2,642	1,801	225	3,229	1,849	594	49	66	3,853	436	18,264
2018[1]	504	1,679	2,785	1,850	190	3,400	1,665	604	57	53	4,152	440	19,095
2019[2]	579	1,555	2,935	1,880	165	3,500	1,625	589	65	50	4,285	415	19,366

[1] Preliminary.   [2] Forecast.   Source: Foreign Agricultural Service, U.S. Department of Agriculture (FAS-USDA)

Exports and Imports of Meats in the United States (Carcass Weight Equivalent)[3]

Year	Exports Beef and Veal	Exports Lamb and Mutton	Exports Pork[3]	Exports All Meat	Imports Beef and Veal	Imports Lamb and Mutton	Imports Pork[3]	Imports All Meat
2008	1,996	12	4,667	6,660	2,538	183	832	3,553
2009	1,935	16	4,126	6,045	2,626	171	834	3,631
2010	2,299	16	4,223	6,539	2,297	166	859	3,322
2011	2,785	----	5,196	7,981	2,057	162	803	3,022
2012	2,452	----	5,379	7,831	2,220	154	802	3,176
2013	2,589	----	4,988	7,577	2,250	173	880	3,303
2014	2,573	----	4,857	7,430	2,947	195	1,008	4,150
2015	2,265	----	5,009	7,274	3,371	213	1,116	4,700
2016[1]	2,550	----	5,233	7,783	3,016	195	1,092	4,303
2017[2]	2,725	----	5,670	8,395	2,745	----	1,045	3,790

[1] Preliminary.   [2] Estimate.   [3] Includes meat content of minor meats and of mixed products.
Source: Economic Research Service, U.S. Department of Agriculture (FAS-USDA)

Average Wholesale Prices of Meats in the United States   In Cent Per Pound

Year	Composite Retail Price of Beef, Choice, Grade 3	Composite Retail Price of Pork[3]	Wholesale Value[4] Beef	Wholesale Value[4] Pork	Net Farm Value[5] of Pork	Cow Beef Canner & Cutter, Central US	Boxed Beef Cut-out, Choice1-3, Central US 550-700 Lb.	Pork Carcass Cut-out, U.S., No. 2	Lamb Carcass, Choice-Prime, E. Coast 55-65 lbs.	Pork[6] Loins, Central US 14-18 lbs.	Skinned Ham, Central US 17-20 lbs.	Pork Bellies, Central US 12-14 lbs.
2009	425.81	291.97	217.18	111.19	71.56	NA	140.77	58.13	225.45	92.81	51.34	60.91
2010	438.40	311.36	241.08	141.16	95.68	----	156.91	81.25	263.02	115.96	76.41	95.08
2011	480.73	343.35	275.82	158.89	113.93	----	181.29	93.69	364.95	129.51	82.19	120.52
2012	498.59	346.67	290.59	147.10	104.88	----	190.68	84.65	329.48	119.85	73.04	88.83
2013	528.93	364.39	298.48	157.58	110.07	----	195.64	91.69	281.52	116.53	79.12	152.15
2014	597.03	401.88	364.71	187.66	131.80	----	238.94	110.10	339.65	141.93	107.00	144.90
2015	628.89	385.25	362.78	145.72	87.39	----	237.48	78.96	343.07	103.77	65.11	121.07
2016	596.38	374.67	316.78	150.12	80.05	----	207.00	78.36	332.90	96.95	66.73	123.94
2017[1]	590.86	378.42	321.47	155.37	87.41	----	209.74	84.02	339.16	97.28	64.63	148.76
2018[2]	592.33	374.45	328.55	140.14	79.16	----	214.06	76.09	----	92.91	56.80	133.73

[1] Preliminary.   [2] Estimate.   [3] Sold as retail cuts (ham, bacon, loin, etc.).   [4] Quantity equivalent to 1 pound of retail cuts.
[5] Portion of gross farm value minus farm by-product allowance.   Source: Economic Research Service, U.S. Department of Agriculture (ERS-USDA)

MEATS

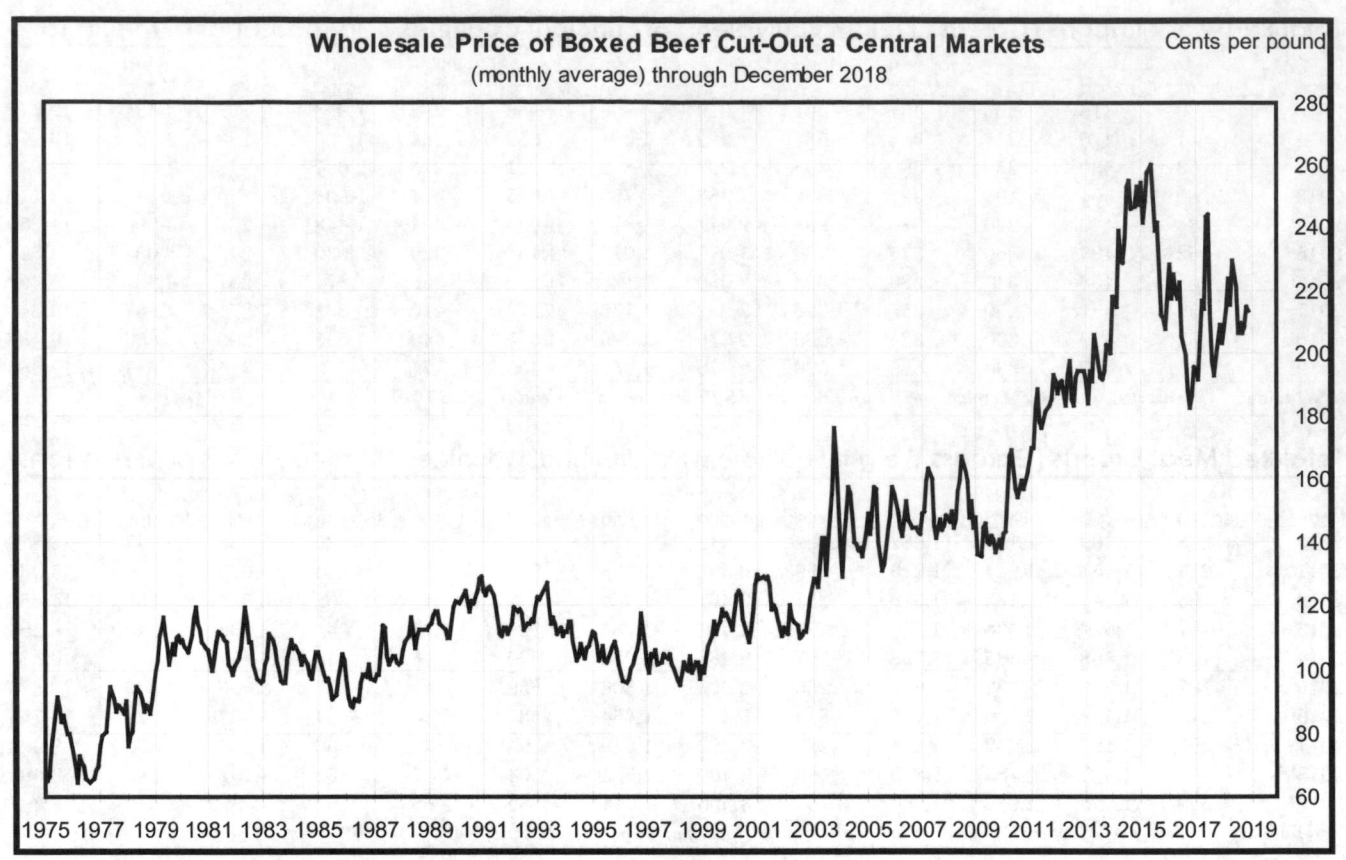

Wholesale Price of Boxed Beef Cut-Out a Central Markets (monthly average) through December 2018 — Cents per pound

Average Wholesale Price of Boxed Beef Cut-Out[2], Choice 1-3, at Central US   In Cents Per Pound

Year	Jan.	Feb.	Mar.	Apr.	May	June	July	Aug.	Sept.	Oct.	Nov.	Dec.	Average
2009	147.68	136.03	135.91	144.42	146.22	140.22	139.59	142.13	140.94	137.15	140.60	138.35	140.77
2010	142.87	143.22	155.73	167.37	168.80	156.54	154.53	156.67	159.20	156.58	159.25	162.20	156.91
2011	169.96	169.82	182.52	188.05	177.96	176.02	178.44	181.12	183.05	185.34	192.51	190.72	181.29
2012	186.77	190.46	190.54	183.43	192.84	197.24	185.25	186.82	192.09	194.19	194.22	194.25	190.68
2013	191.12	183.60	193.79	191.01	205.64	200.83	191.87	191.66	194.01	202.33	202.01	199.77	195.64
2014	218.00	214.43	239.03	229.14	228.96	236.60	252.87	254.83	246.14	246.80	253.18	247.35	238.94
2015	254.45	241.30	247.62	257.44	260.25	250.06	238.91	241.81	227.68	212.10	210.63	207.46	237.48
2016	227.76	217.46	224.61	218.88	216.91	222.59	204.88	199.30	187.77	182.29	186.27	195.23	207.00
2017	194.40	191.42	216.36	213.78	243.43	244.16	212.22	197.48	192.79	198.65	209.08	203.09	209.74
2018[1]	207.94	213.66	223.50	215.29	229.34	221.03	206.32	209.15	206.07	208.18	214.59	213.60	214.06

[1] Preliminary.   [2] 600-900 pounds.   *Source: Economic Research Service, U.S. Department of Agriculture (ERS-USDA)*

Production (Commercial) of All Red Meats in the United States   In Millions of Pounds (Carcass Weight)

Year	Jan.	Feb.	Mar.	Apr.	May	June	July	Aug.	Sept.	Oct.	Nov.	Dec.	Total
2009	4,170.2	3,827.0	4,141.8	4,085.1	3,919.5	4,162.0	4,124.5	4,077.0	4,262.7	4,391.2	3,963.8	4,148.7	49,274
2010	3,915.9	3,735.8	4,281.2	4,012.3	3,731.2	4,176.5	3,955.5	4,125.9	4,160.1	4,262.1	4,329.2	4,352.9	49,039
2011	4,041.1	3,809.9	4,346.8	3,867.8	3,914.8	4,218.8	3,792.2	4,303.5	4,192.1	4,270.6	4,258.9	4,215.2	49,232
2012	4,122.9	3,914.0	4,171.4	3,855.3	4,182.7	4,022.5	3,945.3	4,391.0	3,948.0	4,580.1	4,309.3	3,996.9	49,439
2013	4,348.4	3,673.2	3,994.3	4,091.6	4,151.4	3,859.7	4,158.0	4,203.2	3,937.9	4,509.5	4,119.5	4,136.0	49,183
2014	4,248.9	3,653.1	3,814.8	3,976.9	3,952.8	3,824.0	3,906.9	3,795.3	3,958.8	4,319.3	3,759.3	4,136.2	47,346
2015	4,087.0	3,731.8	4,064.3	4,015.5	3,805.3	4,017.4	4,038.5	3,901.4	4,140.2	4,313.4	4,033.2	4,274.0	48,422
2016	4,055.6	3,904.2	4,261.8	3,982.9	3,997.1	4,225.9	3,866.0	4,432.2	4,323.1	4,426.5	4,498.4	4,402.2	50,376
2017	4,291.4	3,937.9	4,535.1	3,968.1	4,276.0	4,350.8	3,988.9	4,630.5	4,403.8	4,635.3	4,553.2	4,402.4	51,973
2018[1]	4,587.0	4,059.0	4,520.9	4,276.6	4,501.2	4,327.1	4,235.9	4,766.3	4,188.5	4,899.7	4,680.9	4,367.6	53,411

[1] Preliminary.   *Source: Economic Research Service, U.S. Department of Agriculture (ERS-USDA)*

Production (Commercial) of Beef in the United States   In Millions of Pounds (Carcass Weight)

Year	Jan.	Feb.	Mar.	Apr.	May	June	July	Aug.	Sept.	Oct.	Nov.	Dec.	Total
2009	2,117.9	1,986.0	2,144.0	2,133.4	2,179.4	2,289.0	2,271.2	2,184.2	2,234.1	2,275.7	2,016.1	2,134.4	25,965
2010	2,081.8	1,955.2	2,211.2	2,139.2	2,087.2	2,320.0	2,229.6	2,286.6	2,252.2	2,234.9	2,235.5	2,270.9	26,304
2011	2,122.9	2,020.4	2,266.2	2,052.5	2,131.9	2,375.0	2,134.1	2,386.9	2,215.2	2,215.1	2,148.8	2,126.3	26,195
2012	2,113.1	2,008.9	2,159.5	1,990.6	2,231.9	2,250.7	2,201.4	2,368.6	2,015.5	2,344.8	2,207.5	2,020.1	25,913
2013	2,260.0	1,873.7	2,038.6	2,127.3	2,228.0	2,161.4	2,293.5	2,241.6	2,073.6	2,316.5	2,057.3	2,046.5	25,718
2014	2,141.1	1,788.9	1,938.4	2,042.8	2,071.6	2,068.7	2,085.9	2,024.4	2,067.4	2,171.5	1,850.6	2,000.7	24,252
2015	1,963.8	1,768.7	1,931.6	1,928.5	1,924.9	2,001.2	2,046.1	1,934.1	2,085.7	2,125.3	1,934.1	2,045.9	23,690
2016	1,953.5	1,885.0	2,096.0	1,964.0	2,029.5	2,193.0	2,024.4	2,264.4	2,179.2	2,210.1	2,239.3	2,173.3	25,212
2017	2,118.3	1,933.7	2,247.7	1,962.7	2,162.1	2,279.1	2,107.5	2,401.2	2,222.3	2,300.7	2,289.6	2,148.0	26,173
2018[1]	2,278.0	1,983.4	2,203.5	2,116.4	2,307.0	2,300.5	2,232.0	2,430.0	2,158.1	2,429.2	2,313.5	2,115.8	26,867

[1] Preliminary.   Source: Economic Research Service, U.S. Department of Agriculture (ERS-USDA)

Production (Commercial) of Pork in the United States   In Millions of Pounds (Carcass Weight)

Year	Jan.	Feb.	Mar.	Apr.	May	June	July	Aug.	Sept.	Oct.	Nov.	Dec.	Total
2009	2,027.0	1,817.3	1,969.7	1,925.0	1,716.8	1,847.7	1,828.5	1,868.9	2,002.1	2,089.0	1,921.7	1,985.3	22,999
2010	1,809.7	1,757.5	2,040.1	1,849.1	1,621.3	1,831.7	1,702.2	1,815.3	1,883.5	2,002.7	2,068.0	2,055.4	22,437
2011	1,896.2	1,768.1	2,054.4	1,790.7	1,759.7	1,820.0	1,637.1	1,892.1	1,954.4	2,033.2	2,086.7	2,065.6	22,758
2012	1,987.3	1,883.0	1,987.7	1,841.9	1,926.8	1,750.5	1,721.9	1,998.1	1,911.2	2,210.7	2,079.2	1,954.2	23,253
2013	2,065.5	1,779.0	1,932.7	1,941.8	1,900.0	1,677.1	1,840.8	1,938.7	1,844.1	2,169.9	2,041.3	2,066.5	23,197
2014	2,086.1	1,844.4	1,854.5	1,910.5	1,859.5	1,734.3	1,799.3	1,752.1	1,871.9	2,126.7	1,890.7	2,114.5	22,845
2015	2,104.7	1,945.2	2,111.5	2,066.8	1,861.9	1,995.8	1,972.6	1,949.1	2,035.5	2,168.9	2,080.2	2,207.1	24,499
2016	2,084.2	2,000.6	2,145.1	2,000.1	1,948.6	2,013.3	1,824.6	2,149.1	2,125.7	2,198.1	2,240.3	2,209.0	24,939
2017	2,154.5	1,987.4	2,267.3	1,988.1	2,095.8	2,053.0	1,864.7	2,210.1	2,164.2	2,316.3	2,244.8	2,235.0	25,581
2018[1]	2,289.9	2,058.0	2,297.1	2,141.7	2,174.4	2,008.5	1,985.7	2,316.4	2,013.0	2,450.2	2,347.9	2,232.1	26,315

[1] Preliminary.   Source: Economic Research Service, U.S. Department of Agriculture (ERS-USDA)

Cold Storage Holdings of All[2] Meats in the United States, on First of Month   In Millions of Pounds

Year	Jan.	Feb.	Mar.	Apr.	May	June	July	Aug.	Sept.	Oct.	Nov.	Dec.
2009	1,078.5	1,096.2	1,084.9	1,045.3	1,050.6	1,030.1	1,043.1	1,014.7	980.2	984.0	968.4	936.8
2010	924.9	938.4	941.9	921.8	876.3	837.8	816.1	808.6	803.4	844.7	918.6	925.3
2011	939.9	1,017.4	1,050.6	1,036.6	1,009.5	1,014.9	949.4	894.2	896.7	944.9	929.3	961.1
2012	961.5	1,092.6	1,118.7	1,139.8	1,201.0	1,157.7	1,087.6	1,039.1	1,047.7	1,082.8	1,060.9	1,023.4
2013	1,043.8	1,114.8	1,148.1	1,182.4	1,238.0	1,166.3	1,071.3	1,035.5	1,005.0	1,041.0	1,033.0	1,021.9
2014	1,022.2	1,077.0	1,093.6	1,012.3	1,015.9	981.4	930.1	939.1	934.0	970.8	956.5	930.3
2015	988.5	1,131.2	1,224.3	1,196.3	1,229.0	1,172.9	1,147.6	1,136.2	1,170.0	1,202.1	1,159.5	1,122.8
2016	1,105.9	1,213.4	1,182.7	1,142.9	1,151.1	1,129.1	1,099.2	1,118.1	1,130.5	1,205.1	1,173.3	1,079.2
2017	1,083.8	1,101.3	1,112.9	1,051.4	1,092.7	1,042.4	1,012.8	1,029.8	1,100.0	1,159.7	1,149.4	1,032.3
2018[1]	1,021.2	1,129.2	1,118.6	1,124.4	1,159.7	1,142.2	1,064.1	1,094.0	1,136.4	1,150.8	1,135.6	1,069.2

[1] Preliminary.   [2] Includes beef and veal, mutton and lamb, pork and products, rendered pork fat, and miscellaneous meats. Excludes lard.
Source: Economic Research Service, U.S. Department of Agriculture (ERS-USDA)

Cold Storage Holdings of Frozen Beef in the United States, on First of Month   In Millions of Pounds

Year	Jan.	Feb.	Mar.	Apr.	May	June	July	Aug.	Sept.	Oct.	Nov.	Dec.
2009	492.6	462.5	435.5	425.9	410.7	417.9	434.8	444.8	420.1	428.9	427.7	430.9
2010	430.3	426.3	404.5	384.6	369.5	362.8	374.2	388.8	387.4	396.8	414.6	435.2
2011	445.0	461.7	459.8	445.5	443.2	447.6	432.8	415.2	428.6	427.6	417.0	443.8
2012	457.2	485.1	470.8	503.2	517.9	497.9	468.7	461.1	432.8	424.9	430.3	441.8
2013	465.7	484.6	490.0	511.2	510.1	482.6	481.2	462.6	430.2	445.2	440.1	450.8
2014	439.4	429.3	409.5	405.8	402.3	377.6	358.2	367.9	346.6	378.2	380.9	400.8
2015	444.4	492.0	491.9	481.5	484.3	474.6	474.3	460.1	470.3	498.3	509.1	510.6
2016	512.5	534.1	506.4	481.8	467.8	461.7	464.5	469.7	476.6	519.0	533.1	531.0
2017	567.9	538.2	502.4	464.0	458.4	411.5	415.3	431.8	476.6	496.0	507.0	485.2
2018[1]	488.1	501.7	459.3	464.0	471.0	464.7	448.6	484.1	501.3	507.2	515.6	514.7

[1] Preliminary.   Source: Economic Research Service, U.S. Department of Agriculture (ERS-USDA)

Mercury

Mercury (atomic symbol Hg) was known to the ancient Hindus and Chinese, and was also found in Egyptian tombs dating back to 1500 BC. The ancient Greeks used mercury in ointments, and the Romans used it in cosmetics. Alchemists thought mercury turned into gold when it hardened.

Mercury, also called quicksilver, is a heavy, silvery, toxic, transitional metal. Mercury is the only common metal that is liquid at room temperatures. When subjected to a pressure of 7,640 atmospheres (7.7 million millibars), mercury becomes a solid. Mercury dissolves in nitric or concentrated sulfuric acid but is resistant to alkalis. It is a poor conductor of heat. Mercury has superconductivity when cooled to sufficiently low temperatures. It has a freezing point of about –39 degrees Celsius and a boiling point of about 357 degrees Celsius.

Mercury is found in its pure form or combined in small amounts with silvers, but is found most often in the ore cinnabar, a mineral consisting of mercuric sulfide. By heating the cinnabar ore in air until the mercuric sulfide breaks down, pure mercury metal is produced. Mercury forms alloys called amalgams with all common metals except iron and platinum. Most mercury is used for the manufacture of industrial chemicals and for electrical and electronic applications. Other uses for mercury include its use in gold recovery from ores, barometers, diffusion pumps, laboratory instruments, mercury-vapor lamps, pesticides, batteries, and catalysts. A decline in mercury production and usage since the 1970s reflects a trend for using mercury substitutes due to its toxicity.

Prices – The average monthly price of mercury in 2018 rose +113.3% yr/yr to $2,776.76 per flask (34.5 kilograms), but still below the record high of $3,438.59 posted in 2013.

Supply – World mine production of mercury in 2018 was down -11.3% yr/yr at 3,360 metric tons, down from the 2017 record high of 3,790. The record low of 1,150 metric tons was posted in 2006.

The world's largest miners of mercury are China with 89.3% of world production and Mexico with 6.0%. China has posted a new record high most years since 2009. China's record low of 190 metric tons was posted in 2001.

Demand – The breakdown of domestic consumption of mercury by particular categories is no longer available. However, in 1997 records showed that chlorine and caustic soda accounted for 46% of U.S. mercury consumption, followed by wiring devices and switches (17%), dental equipment (12%), electrical lighting (8%), and measuring control instruments (7%). Substitutes for mercury include lithium and composite ceramic materials.

Trade – U.S. foreign trade in mercury has been relatively small and U.S. imports of mercury in 2018 were down -50.0% yr/yr at 10 metric tons, far below the almost 3-decade high of 294 metric tons in 2010. By contrast the U.S.'s record high imports were in 1974 at 1,799 metric tons. U.S. imports were mostly from Chile and Peru. U.S. exports of mercury in 2012 fell by -22.6% yr/yr to 103 metric tons, but still above 2007's 13-year low of 84 metric tons.

World Mine Production of Mercury   In Metric Tons (1 tonne = 29.008216 flasks)

Year	Chile (byproduct)	China	Finland	Kyrgyzstan	Mexico (Exports)	Morocco	Peru (Exports)	Russia	Tajikistan	United States	World Total
2009	88	1,430	6	140	15	10	107	50	30	NA	1,960
2010	176	1,600	9	99	15	10	159	50	15	NA	2,180
2011	89	1,493	----	113	120	9	53	NA	30	NA	1,960
2012	49	1,350	----	75	235	8	17	NA	30	NA	1,830
2013	19	1,820	----	71	266	8	45	NA	32	NA	2,330
2014	10	2,260	----	48	301	8	40	NA	34	NA	2,770
2015	10	1,860	----	46	300	5	35	NA	30	NA	2,330
2016	10	2,000	----	50	300	5	40	NA	30	NA	2,480
2017[1]		3,380	----	20	197		40		100	NA	3,790
2018[2]		3,000	----	20	200		40		100		34,000

[1] Preliminary.   [2] Estimate.   NA = Not available   W = Withheld.   *Source: U.S. Geological Survey (USGS)*

Salient Statistics of Mercury in the United States   In Metric Tons

Year	Producing Mines	Secondary Production – Industrial	Secondary Production – Government[3]	NDS[4] Shipments	Consumer & Dealer Stocks, Dec. 31	Industrial Demand	Exports	Imports
2009	NA	NA	----	----	30	NA	753	206
2010	NA	NA	----	----	NA	NA	459	294
2011	NA	NA	----	----	NA	NA	133	110
2012	NA	NA	----	----	NA	NA	103	249
2013	NA	NA	----	----	NA	NA	(/5)	38
2014	NA	NA	----	----	NA	NA	----	49
2015	NA	NA	----	----	NA	NA	----	26
2016	NA	NA	----	----	NA	NA	----	24
2017[1]	NA	NA	----	----	NA	NA	----	20
2018[2]	NA	NA	----	----	NA	NA	----	10

[1] Preliminary.   [2] Estimate.   [3] Secondary mercury shipped from the Department of Energy.   [4] National Defense Stockpile.   [5] Less than 1/2 unit.   NA = Not available.   *Source: U.S. Geological Survey (USGS)*

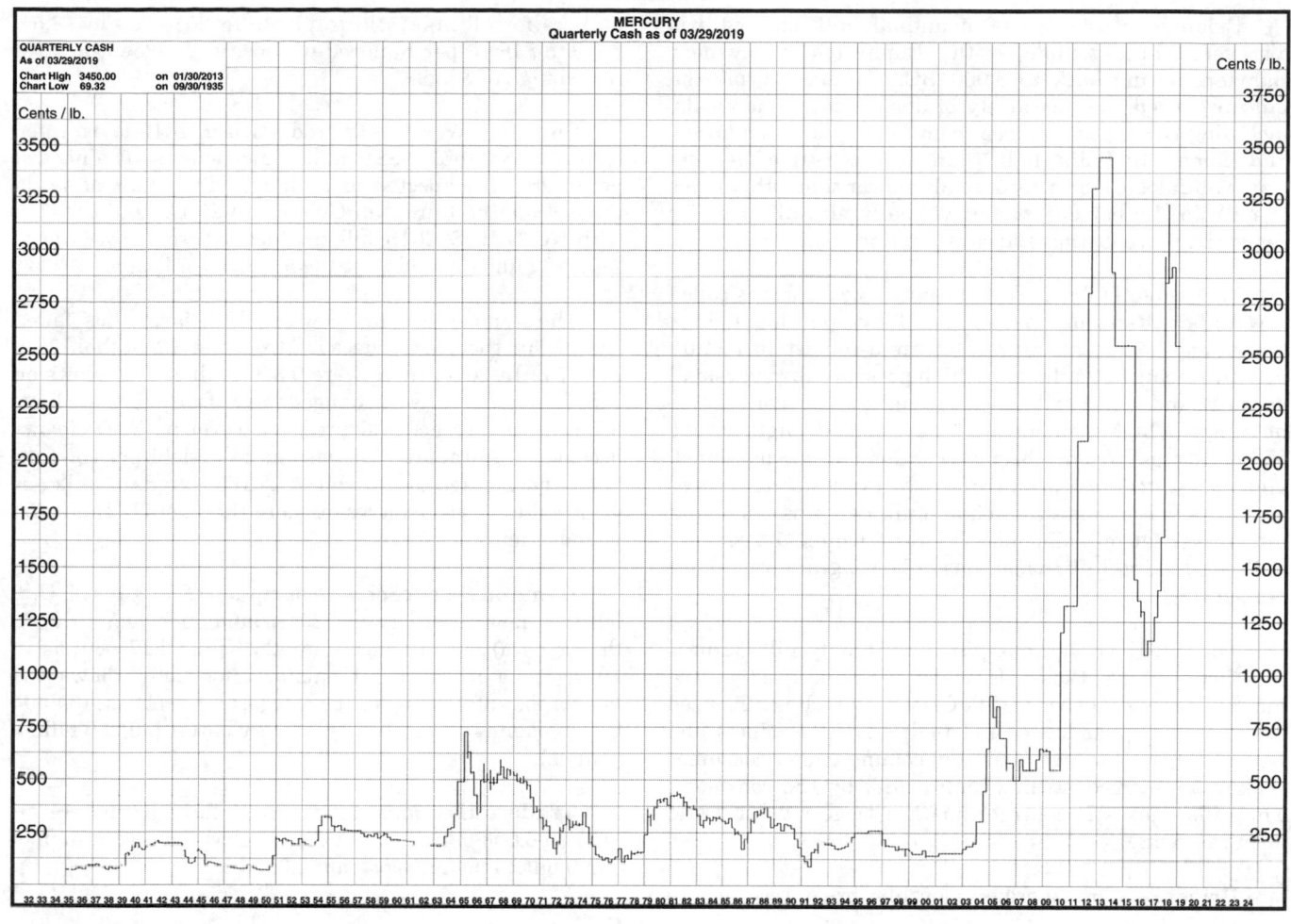

Average Price of Mercury in New York In Dollars Per Flask of 76 Pounds (34.5 Kilograms)

Year	Jan.	Feb.	Mar.	Apr.	May	June	July	Aug.	Sept.	Oct.	Nov.	Dec.	Average
2009	650.00	647.00	640.00	640.00	642.86	640.00	640.00	640.00	603.18	550.00	550.00	550.00	616.09
2010	550.00	550.00	550.00	550.00	828.57	1,129.55	1,213.64	1,293.18	1,325.00	1,325.00	1,325.00	1,325.00	997.08
2011	1,325.00	1,325.00	1,325.00	1,325.00	1,325.00	1,325.00	1,370.24	2,073.91	2,100.00	2,100.00	2,100.00	2,100.00	1,649.51
2012	2,100.00	2,100.00	2,100.00	2,100.00	2,547.83	2,800.00	2,800.00	2,800.00	3,100.00	3,300.00	3,300.00	3,300.00	2,695.65
2013	3,313.05	3,450.00	3,450.00	3,450.00	3,450.00	3,450.00	3,450.00	3,450.00	3,450.00	3,450.00	3,450.00	3,450.00	3,438.59
2014	3,269.57	3,175.00	2,991.67	2,850.00	2,563.64	2,550.00	2,550.00	2,550.00	2,550.00	2,550.00	2,550.00	2,550.00	2,724.99
2015	2,550.00	2,550.00	2,550.00	2,550.00	2,550.00	2,550.00	2,550.00	2,550.00	2,550.00	2,515.91	1,716.67	1,484.78	2,388.95
2016	1,450.00	1,450.00	1,406.52	1,350.00	1,350.00	1,304.55	1,155.24	1,110.00	1,095.68	1,095.00	1,107.27	1,162.50	1,253.06
2017	1,162.50	1,162.50	1,162.50	1,168.12	1,275.00	1,275.00	1,275.00	1,351.09	1,400.00	1,400.00	1,400.00	1,590.48	1,301.85
2018	1,971.74	2,603.00	2,901.82	3,030.95	2,875.00	2,875.00	2,915.91	2,925.00	2,925.00	2,925.00	2,822.73	2,550.00	2,776.76

Source: American Metal Market (AMM)

Mercury Consumed in the United States In Metric Tons

Year	Batteries[3]	Chlorine & Caustic Soda	Catalysts, Misc.	Dental Equip.	Electrical Lighting[3]	General Lab Use	Measuring Control Instrument	Paints	Wiring Devices & Switches[3]	Other Uses	Grand Total
1989	250	379	40	39	31	18	87	192	141	32	1,212
1990	106	247	29	44	33	32	108	14	70	38	720
1991	18	184	26	41	39	30	90	6	71	49	554
1992	13	209	20	42	55	28	80	----	82	92	621
1993	10	180	18	35	38	26	65	----	83	103	558
1994	6	135	25	24	27	24	53	----	79	110	483
1995	----	154	----	32	30	----	43	----	84	93	436
1996[1]	----	136	----	31	29	----	41	----	49	86	372
1997[2]	----	160	----	40	29	----	24	----	57	36	346
	Data No Longer Available										

[1] Preliminary. [2] Estimate. W = Withheld proprietary data. *Source: U.S. Geological Survey (USGS)*

Milk

Evidence of man's use of animal milk as food was discovered in a temple in the Euphrates Valley near Babylon, dating back to 3,000 BC. Humans drink the milk produced from a variety of domesticated mammals, including cows, goats, sheep, camels, reindeer, buffaloes, and llama. In India, half of all milk consumed is from water buffalo. Camels' milk spoils slower than other types of milk in the hot desert, but virtually all milk used for commercial production and consumption comes from cows.

Milk directly from a cow in its natural form is called raw milk. Raw milk is processed by spinning it in a centrifuge, homogenizing it to create a consistent texture (i.e., by forcing hot milk under high pressure through small nozzles), and then sterilizing it through pasteurization (i.e., heating to a high temperature for a specified length of time to destroy pathogenic bacteria). Condensed, powdered, and evaporated milk are produced by evaporating some or all of the water content. Whole milk contains 3.5% milk fat. Lower-fat milks include 2% low-fat milk, 1% low- fat milk, and skim milk, which has only 1/2 gram of milk fat per serving.

The CME Group has three different milk futures contracts: Milk Class III which is milk used in the manufacturing of cheese, Milk Class IV which is milk used in the production of butter and all dried milk products, and Nonfat Dry Milk which is used in commercial or consumer cooking or to reconstitute nonfat milk by the consumer. The Milk Class III contract has the largest volume and open interest.

Prices – The average monthly price received by farmers for all milk sold to plants in 2018 fell by -8.5% yr/yr to $16.15 per hundred pounds, well below the 2014 record high of $23.98.

Supply – World milk production in 2019 is expected to rise +1.8% to 616.881 million metric tons. The biggest producers are expected to be India with 28.2% of world production, the European Union with 26.1%, and the U.S. with 16.2%. U.S. 2018 milk production rose +1.0% yr/yr to 217.523 billion pounds, setting a new record high.

The number of dairy cows on U.S. farms has fallen sharply in the past 3 decades from the 12 million seen in 1970. In 2018, there were 9.389 million dairy cows on U.S. farms, virtually unchanged yr/yr. Dairy farmers have been able to increase milk production even with fewer cows because of a dramatic increase in milk yield per cow. In 2018, the average cow produced 23,168 pounds of milk per year, a +1.0% yr/yr increase, more than double the 9,751 pounds seen in 1970.

Demand – Per capita consumption of milk in the U.S. fell to a new record low of 204 pounds per year in 2008 (latest data), down sharply by -26% from 277 pounds in 1977. The utilization breakdown for 2002 shows the largest manufacturing usage categories are cheese (64.504 billion pounds of milk) and creamery butter (30.250 billion pounds).

Trade – U.S. imports of milk in 2017 fell by -14.7% yr/yr to 6.003 billion pounds, well below the record high of 7.500 billion pounds posted in 2005-06.

World Fluid Milk Production (Cow's Milk)   In Thousands of Metric Tons

Year	Argentina	Australia	Brazil	Canada	China	European Union	India	Mexico	New Zealand	Russia	Ukraine	United States	World Total
2011	11,470	9,551	22,449	8,400	32,379	142,920	123,000	11,213	18,965	31,646	11,085	89,020	528,363
2012	11,679	9,794	23,008	8,614	33,109	143,750	129,000	11,434	20,567	31,831	11,378	91,010	542,097
2013	11,519	9,309	24,259	8,443	31,458	144,850	134,500	11,451	20,200	30,529	11,488	91,277	545,950
2014	11,326	9,798	25,489	8,437	33,149	150,850	140,500	11,624	21,893	30,499	11,426	93,465	565,141
2015	11,552	10,091	25,650	8,773	33,298	154,550	147,000	11,900	21,587	30,548	10,864	94,618	577,462
2016	10,191	9,486	25,857	9,081	32,240	155,550	154,000	12,122	21,224	30,510	10,625	96,345	584,281
2017	10,090	9,462	26,766	9,675	31,886	158,000	160,000	12,288	21,510	30,934	10,520	97,734	595,994
2018[1]	10,837	9,440	25,662	9,940	31,250	159,450	167,000	12,449	22,155	31,450	10,300	98,792	605,803
2019[2]	11,380	9,300	26,210	10,115	31,100	160,860	174,000	12,549	22,200	31,875	10,120	100,063	616,881

[1] Preliminary.   [2] Forecast.   *Source: Foreign Agricultural Service, U.S. Department of Agriculture (FAS-USDA)*

Salient Statistics of Milk in the United States   In Millions of Pounds

Year	Number of Milk Cows on Farms[3] (Thousands)	Production Per Cow[4] (Pounds)	Production Total[4]	Beginning Stocks[5]	Imports	Total Supply	Exports[5]	Domestic Fed to Calves	Domestic Humans	Total Use	All Milk, Wholesale	Milk, Eligible for Fluid Market	Milk, Manufacturing Grade	Per Capita Consumption[6] (Fluid Milk in Lbs)
2011	9,194	21,346	196,245	10,086	3,504	209,835	9,059	867	188,559	198,485	20.14	----	----	
2012	9,232	21,696	200,324	10,226	4,110	214,660	8,499	858	193,258	202,615	18.48	----	----	
2013	9,215	21,413	201,218	11,403	3,772	216,393	12,065	877	192,137	205,079	20.04	----	----	
2014	9,257	22,259	206,046	10,344	4,372	220,762	12,159	872	196,308	209,340	23.98	----	----	
2015	9,314	22,396	208,633	10,487	5,759	224,879	8,500	879	202,260	211,639	17.11	----	----	
2016	9,328	22,775	212,436	12,335	7,034	231,805	8,417	898	211,412	220,727	16.30	----	----	
2017[1]	9,392	22,941	215,466	12,720	6,003	234,189	9,267	887	214,487	224,641	17.66	----	----	
2018[2]	9,399	23,149	217,575			217,575					16.18	----	----	

[1] Preliminary.   [2] Estimate.   [3] Average number on farms during year including dry cows, excluding heifers not yet fresh.   [4] Excludes milk sucked by calves.   [5] Government and commercial.   [6] Product pounds of commercial sales and on farm consumption.
Source: Economic Research Service, U.S. Department of Agriculture (ERS-USDA)

Milk-Feed Price Ratio[1] in the United States   In Pounds

Year	Jan.	Feb.	Mar.	Apr.	May	June	July	Aug.	Sept.	Oct.	Nov.	Dec.	Average
2009	1.60	1.51	1.56	1.59	1.48	1.45	1.57	1.80	2.00	2.11	2.26	2.42	1.78
2010	2.33	2.36	2.18	2.19	2.17	2.26	2.31	2.36	2.36	2.40	2.23	1.98	2.26
2011	1.96	2.01	2.12	1.81	1.73	1.87	1.91	1.83	1.84	1.82	1.89	1.81	1.88
2012	1.72	1.56	1.48	1.41	1.34	1.38	1.34	1.37	1.59	1.74	1.74	1.65	1.53
2013	1.57	1.52	1.48	1.54	1.53	1.52	1.53	1.68	1.88	2.10	2.27	2.30	1.74
2014	2.46	2.59	2.54	2.42	2.24	2.20	2.36	2.63	2.96	2.92	2.75	2.40	2.54
2015	2.11	2.05	2.01	1.95	1.97	2.07	2.01	2.10	2.23	2.30	2.45	2.29	2.13
2016	2.18	2.18	2.12	1.99	1.89	1.91	2.16	2.44	2.49	2.38	2.59	2.73	2.26
2017	2.71	2.62	2.40	2.22	2.20	2.31	2.27	2.51	2.46	2.47	2.54	2.38	2.42
2018[1]	2.18	2.03	1.97	1.90	1.90	1.98	1.92	2.03	2.10	2.20	2.18	2.04	2.04

[1] Pounds of 16% protein mixed dairy feed equal in value to one pound of whole milk.   [2] Preliminary.   *Source: Economic Research Service, U.S. Department of Agriculture (ERS-USDA)*

Milk Production[2] in the United States   In Millions of Pounds

Year	Jan.	Feb.	Mar.	Apr.	May	June	July	Aug.	Sept.	Oct.	Nov.	Dec.	Total
2009	16,135	14,754	16,485	16,148	16,805	15,935	16,018	15,737	15,038	15,420	15,070	15,775	189,320
2010	16,020	14,758	16,614	16,416	17,040	16,353	16,436	16,094	15,540	15,900	15,498	16,150	192,819
2011	16,393	15,077	16,989	16,652	17,278	16,518	16,479	16,422	15,783	16,278	15,820	16,556	196,245
2012	17,016	16,310	17,718	17,232	17,601	16,676	16,585	16,403	15,687	16,267	16,008	16,821	200,324
2013	17,109	15,759	17,677	17,249	17,813	16,935	16,788	16,789	15,831	16,475	16,003	16,790	201,218
2014	17,284	15,907	17,829	17,480	18,094	17,323	17,435	17,224	16,514	17,071	16,551	17,334	206,046
2015	17,685	16,166	18,085	17,788	18,428	17,504	17,665	17,403	16,617	17,130	16,689	17,473	208,633
2016	17,693	16,904	18,401	17,947	18,613	17,771	17,908	17,692	16,990	17,565	17,100	17,852	212,436
2017	18,128	16,694	18,740	18,332	18,952	18,060	18,268	18,049	17,156	17,769	17,260	18,058	215,466
2018[1]	18,437	16,973	18,989	18,412	19,131	18,288	18,329	18,245	17,395	17,873	17,348	18,155	217,575

[1] Preliminary.   [2] Excludes milk sucked by calves.   *Source: Economic Research Service, U.S. Department of Agriculture (ERS-USDA)*

Milk Cows[2] in the United States   In Thousands of Head

Year	Jan.	Feb.	Mar.	Apr.	May	June	July	Aug.	Sept.	Oct.	Nov.	Dec.	Total
2009	9,312	9,289	9,283	9,282	9,270	9,228	9,191	9,162	9,123	9,094	9,085	9,082	9,200
2010	9,089	9,092	9,099	9,108	9,119	9,129	9,135	9,123	9,121	9,123	9,125	9,141	9,117
2011	9,160	9,163	9,180	9,182	9,194	9,196	9,198	9,200	9,201	9,212	9,213	9,223	9,194
2012	9,242	9,257	9,271	9,273	9,263	9,241	9,222	9,217	9,195	9,189	9,201	9,218	9,232
2013	9,222	9,223	NA	NA	NA	NA	9,235	9,229	9,208	9,203	9,198	9,202	9,215
2014	9,212	9,212	9,223	9,240	9,252	9,267	9,268	9,268	9,274	9,277	9,284	9,299	9,257
2015	9,308	9,308	9,311	9,316	9,324	9,323	9,314	9,315	9,317	9,320	9,322	9,320	9,314
2016	9,304	9,311	9,321	9,321	9,322	9,326	9,329	9,334	9,331	9,335	9,344	9,354	9,328
2017	9,359	9,365	9,383	9,392	9,401	9,404	9,404	9,404	9,399	9,395	9,398	9,400	9,392
2018[1]	9,438	9,436	9,430	9,418	9,422	9,414	9,392	9,389	9,368	9,367	9,358	9,353	9,399

[1] Preliminary.   [2] Includes dry cows, excludes heifers not yet fresh.   *Source: Economic Research Service, U.S. Department of Agriculture (ERS-USDA)*

Milk Per Cow[2] in the United States   In Pounds

Year	Jan.	Feb.	Mar.	Apr.	May	June	July	Aug.	Sept.	Oct.	Nov.	Dec.	Total
2009	1,733	1,588	1,776	1,740	1,812	1,726	1,744	1,718	1,649	1,695	1,658	1,737	20,576
2010	1,763	1,623	1,826	1,802	1,869	1,791	1,799	1,764	1,704	1,743	1,698	1,767	21,149
2011	1,790	1,645	1,851	1,814	1,879	1,796	1,792	1,785	1,715	1,767	1,717	1,795	21,346
2012	1,841	1,762	1,911	1,858	1,900	1,805	1,798	1,780	1,706	1,770	1,740	1,825	21,696
2013	1,855	1,709	NA	NA	NA	NA	1,818	1,819	1,719	1,790	1,740	1,825	21,413
2014	1,876	1,727	1,933	1,892	1,956	1,869	1,881	1,858	1,781	1,840	1,783	1,864	22,259
2015	1,900	1,737	1,942	1,909	1,976	1,878	1,897	1,868	1,784	1,838	1,790	1,875	22,396
2016	1,902	1,815	1,974	1,925	1,997	1,906	1,920	1,895	1,821	1,882	1,830	1,908	22,775
2017	1,937	1,783	1,997	1,952	2,016	1,920	1,943	1,919	1,825	1,891	1,837	1,921	22,941
2018[1]	1,953	1,799	2,014	1,955	2,030	1,943	1,952	1,943	1,857	1,908	1,854	1,941	23,149

[1] Preliminary.   [2] Excludes milk sucked by calves.   *Source: Economic Research Service, U.S. Department of Agriculture (ERS-USDA)*

MILK

Average Price Received by Farmers for All Milk (Sold to Plants)   In Dollars Per Hundred Pounds (Cwt.)

Year	Jan.	Feb.	Mar.	Apr.	May	June	July	Aug.	Sept.	Oct.	Nov.	Dec.	Average
2009	13.30	11.60	11.80	11.90	11.60	11.30	11.30	12.10	13.00	14.30	15.40	16.50	12.84
2010	16.10	15.90	14.80	14.60	15.00	15.40	15.90	16.70	17.70	18.50	17.90	16.70	16.27
2011	16.70	19.10	20.40	19.60	19.60	21.10	21.80	22.10	21.10	20.00	20.50	19.70	20.14
2012	19.00	17.70	17.20	16.80	16.20	16.30	16.90	18.20	18.90	21.60	22.10	20.80	18.48
2013	19.90	19.50	19.10	19.50	19.70	19.50	19.10	19.60	20.10	20.90	21.60	22.00	20.04
2014	23.50	24.90	25.10	25.30	24.20	23.20	23.30	24.20	25.70	24.90	23.00	20.40	23.98
2015	17.60	16.80	16.60	16.50	16.80	17.00	16.70	16.70	17.50	17.70	18.20	17.20	17.11
2016	16.10	15.70	15.30	15.10	14.50	14.80	16.10	17.20	17.40	16.70	17.80	18.90	16.30
2017	18.90	18.50	17.30	16.50	16.70	17.30	17.20	18.10	17.90	18.10	18.20	17.20	17.66
2018[1]	16.10	15.30	15.60	15.80	16.20	16.30	15.40	15.90	16.70	17.40	17.00	16.40	16.18

[1] Preliminary.   *Source: Economic Research Service, U.S. Department of Agriculture (ERS-USDA)*

Production of Nonfat Dry Milk in the United States   In Thousands of Pounds

Year	Jan.	Feb.	Mar.	Apr.	May	June	July	Aug.	Sept.	Oct.	Nov.	Dec.	Total
2009	158,286	125,902	137,301	141,397	150,452	146,065	133,175	107,049	87,808	92,800	102,156	126,720	1,509,111
2010	129,679	118,999	138,305	152,945	154,757	136,990	131,704	119,562	109,286	114,595	116,653	139,043	1,562,518
2011	114,896	106,785	124,065	145,323	147,290	145,125	131,502	113,299	103,115	99,751	119,686	148,640	1,499,477
2012	152,085	171,394	189,227	190,728	193,362	168,394	140,169	106,014	84,498	95,064	115,854	157,660	1,764,449
2013	142,799	137,674	146,576	160,117	150,531	130,901	116,616	106,039	74,026	85,830	101,185	125,570	1,477,864
2014	138,661	141,187	167,853	160,342	162,139	148,648	166,602	116,134	112,467	134,973	151,402	164,224	1,764,632
2015	167,705	150,960	180,878	180,771	180,013	165,441	155,265	123,892	119,974	118,360	127,939	151,150	1,822,348
2016	137,463	142,978	172,003	170,796	165,837	146,643	150,787	117,550	125,486	140,051	128,105	154,935	1,752,634
2017	153,848	143,231	160,916	172,821	167,910	162,814	151,825	136,753	134,572	145,008	141,440	164,014	1,835,152
2018[1]	160,301	157,833	178,694	163,859	159,893	146,911	144,296	122,805	108,826	125,067	131,703	142,741	1,742,929

[1] Preliminary.   *Source: Economic Research Service, U.S. Department of Agriculture (ERS-USDA)*

Production of Dry Whey in the United States   In Thousands of Pounds

Year	Jan.	Feb.	Mar.	Apr.	May	June	July	Aug.	Sept.	Oct.	Nov.	Dec.	Total
2009	79,395	74,668	82,785	83,218	87,125	92,639	93,640	82,555	79,006	81,709	79,361	85,059	1,001,160
2010	85,766	78,206	92,496	87,728	89,255	86,045	87,529	81,519	77,718	77,888	79,506	89,327	1,012,983
2011	90,192	82,035	94,304	92,037	91,293	83,740	81,752	79,759	76,800	77,517	77,614	83,074	1,010,117
2012	95,588	89,274	88,348	84,014	86,760	83,819	79,807	77,543	74,810	77,195	72,559	89,181	998,898
2013	86,558	77,097	83,248	81,653	75,535	75,425	76,416	73,122	68,692	71,883	74,718	108,633	952,980
2014	70,011	65,603	71,504	71,629	82,480	79,309	73,475	71,192	69,537	68,684	70,994	75,283	869,701
2015	75,342	76,630	86,409	76,512	80,778	85,506	81,225	83,585	78,823	75,576	82,959	94,223	977,568
2016	83,459	74,891	82,762	82,075	81,836	80,002	82,354	76,505	75,864	83,966	72,893	78,534	955,141
2017	82,255	77,895	86,689	84,640	82,950	88,064	100,402	94,276	91,302	80,750	81,657	86,024	1,036,904
2018[1]	90,319	89,599	90,653	85,149	85,521	87,803	92,595	78,954	71,228	86,967	74,616	74,505	1,007,909

[1] Preliminary.   Excludes all modified dry whey products.   *Source: Economic Research Service, U.S. Department of Agriculture (ERS-USDA)*

Production of Whey Protein Concentrate in the United States   In Thousands of Pounds

Year	Jan.	Feb.	Mar.	Apr.	May	June	July	Aug.	Sept.	Oct.	Nov.	Dec.	Total
2009	35,177	32,340	35,259	32,971	34,705	34,572	35,221	35,284	34,810	35,830	34,061	34,785	415,015
2010	34,765	31,417	37,775	36,265	36,811	35,307	36,441	35,142	36,005	35,583	34,952	37,447	427,910
2011	34,871	32,701	36,809	34,668	36,669	36,292	34,683	35,248	35,571	37,323	36,818	39,285	430,938
2012	38,845	35,064	41,433	39,077	38,417	39,942	35,590	36,804	37,469	38,627	37,735	40,471	459,474
2013	39,262	36,941	41,742	40,396	43,391	41,501	40,265	39,461	39,386	45,542	43,194	46,567	497,648
2014	44,325	42,165	45,076	46,127	46,630	43,871	44,876	44,945	41,621	46,971	46,066	47,428	540,101
2015	44,061	38,365	42,234	42,375	43,812	39,307	41,736	39,380	37,474	41,302	40,137	42,766	492,949
2016	42,602	39,780	41,851	39,027	39,349	38,037	38,437	35,665	36,745	38,060	39,419	39,457	468,429
2017	40,329	36,110	42,354	42,062	41,612	40,297	41,192	38,339	38,720	40,796	40,551	41,914	484,276
2018[1]	43,461	39,391	44,932	40,926	41,870	39,862	39,798	41,767	42,020	42,890	40,188	40,851	497,956

[1] Preliminary.   *Source: Economic Research Service, U.S. Department of Agriculture (ERS-USDA)*

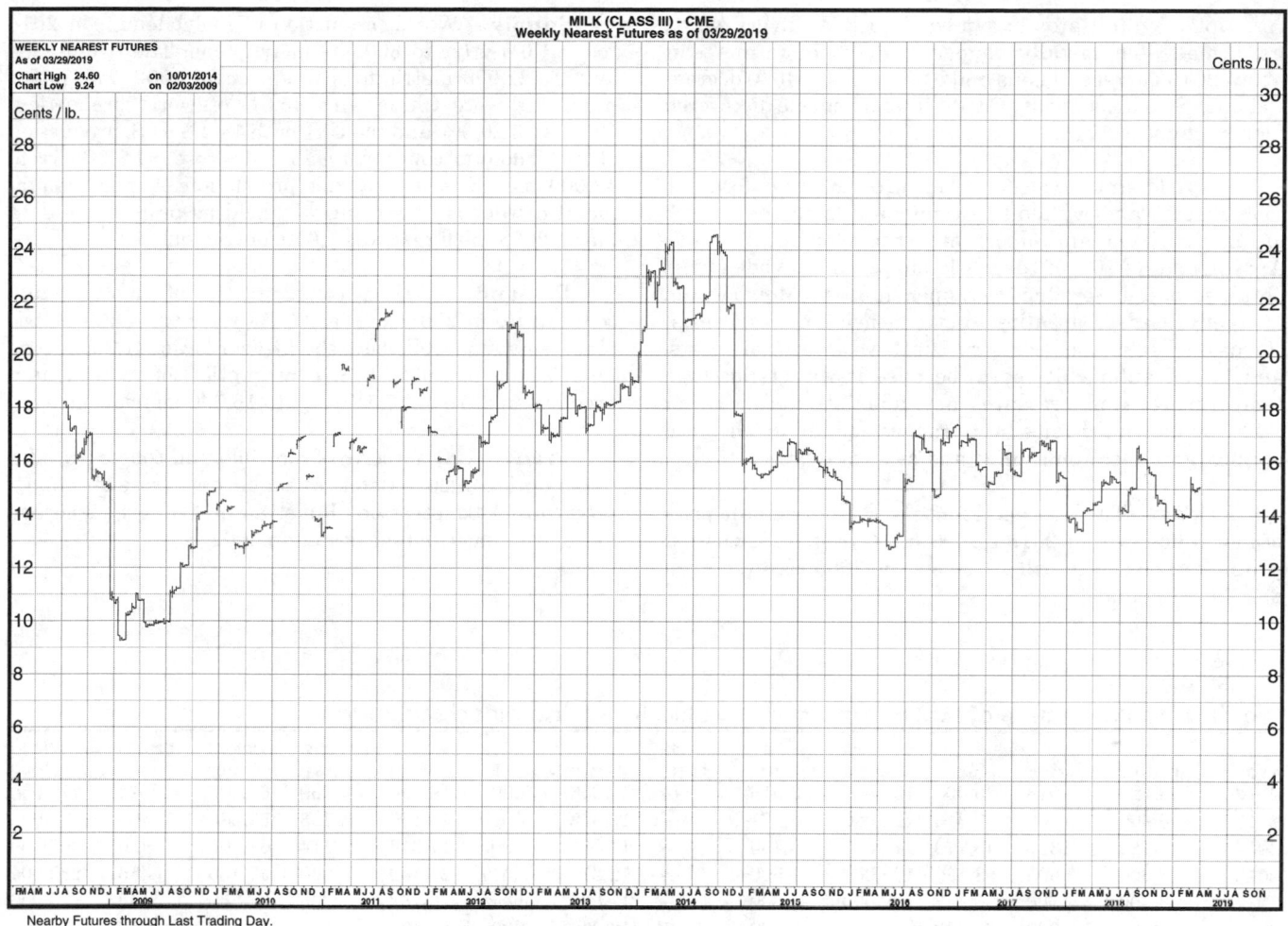

MILK (CLASS III) - CME
Weekly Nearest Futures as of 03/29/2019

WEEKLY NEAREST FUTURES
As of 03/29/2019

Chart High 24.60   on 10/01/2014
Chart Low   9.24   on 02/03/2009

Nearby Futures through Last Trading Day.

Volume of Trading of Class III Milk Futures in Chicago   In Contracts

Year	Jan.	Feb.	Mar.	Apr.	May	June	July	Aug.	Sept.	Oct.	Nov.	Dec.	Total
2009	29,313	21,085	22,708	19,126	21,625	26,902	26,248	21,781	20,214	25,391	17,874	28,369	280,636
2010	28,947	22,118	25,828	22,661	21,808	16,183	19,302	17,900	19,066	25,489	33,175	25,383	277,860
2011	48,169	40,246	37,892	16,713	24,145	30,885	27,495	37,989	29,503	25,880	25,522	24,175	368,614
2012	27,318	27,399	31,079	21,345	22,468	19,617	27,152	28,798	23,819	25,021	22,239	18,242	294,497
2013	22,182	20,654	25,964	29,668	24,403	22,482	23,762	28,680	19,519	24,806	21,210	30,611	293,941
2014	37,317	27,468	31,390	23,084	22,764	21,118	26,702	28,532	38,651	33,233	25,464	42,936	358,659
2015	30,448	29,457	23,844	22,999	21,087	21,649	23,920	16,422	19,958	18,049	22,488	25,218	275,539
2016	20,769	20,574	19,533	22,613	27,322	44,457	18,030	30,654	28,089	24,141	28,134	37,643	321,959
2017	27,439	28,001	33,774	20,263	30,371	25,574	25,564	31,494	22,438	22,205	27,303	25,402	319,828
2018	23,610	18,682	17,419	19,020	21,425	33,116	23,538	27,829	22,004	35,993	30,999	28,617	302,252

Contract size = 200,000 lbs.   *Source: CME Group; Chicago Mercantile Exchange (CME)*

Average Open Interest of Class III Milk Futures in Chicago   In Contracts

Year	Jan.	Feb.	Mar.	Apr.	May	June	July	Aug.	Sept.	Oct.	Nov.	Dec.
2009	37,081	36,447	33,843	30,337	28,648	28,695	27,551	25,535	24,131	23,388	23,538	24,950
2010	27,126	29,049	30,462	29,520	29,035	28,974	27,487	26,200	26,869	25,722	28,261	30,694
2011	33,741	38,813	38,723	34,509	33,021	35,150	35,730	36,553	33,284	31,322	33,127	33,472
2012	32,511	33,482	31,516	28,476	26,706	24,376	24,511	26,462	26,559	25,497	22,784	20,226
2013	19,320	20,206	21,408	23,180	22,062	21,456	21,802	23,267	23,463	22,153	22,480	24,287
2014	26,264	28,094	29,393	28,695	27,114	26,298	26,128	29,218	32,844	36,731	39,197	43,959
2015	46,134	44,918	42,292	37,710	34,509	31,725	28,890	28,792	26,554	25,839	27,821	29,784
2016	32,267	33,051	31,996	31,881	32,970	30,976	30,323	29,969	31,548	31,845	31,605	33,695
2017	31,058	31,194	34,015	34,006	31,200	28,498	28,226	25,863	25,933	23,510	24,940	25,949
2018	24,834	23,883	23,021	22,280	22,375	22,572	23,397	22,391	22,843	25,498	29,760	28,206

Contract size = 200,000 lbs.   *Source: CME Group; Chicago Mercantile Exchange (CME)*

Molybdenum

Molybdenum (atomic symbol Mo) is a silvery-white, hard, malleable, metallic element. Molybdenum melts at about 2610 degrees Celsius and boils at about 4640 degrees Celsius. Swedish chemist Carl Wilhelm Scheele discovered molybdenum in 1778.

Molybdenum occurs in nature in the form of molybdenite and wulfenite. Contributing to the growth of plants, it is an important trace element in soils. Approximately 70% of the world supply of molybdenum is obtained as a by-product of copper mining. Molybdenum is chiefly used as an alloy to strengthen steel and resist corrosion. It is used for structural work, aircraft parts, and forged automobile parts because it withstands high temperatures and pressures and adds strength. Other uses include lubricants, a refractory metal in chemical applications, electron tubing, and as a catalyst.

Prices – The average monthly U.S. merchant price of molybdic oxide in 2018 rose +45.6% yr/yr to $12.04 per pound, but that was still far below the 2005 record high of $32.70 per pound.

Supply – World production of molybdenum in 2018 rose +1.0% yr/yr to 300,000 metric tons. The two-decade low of 122,000 metric tons was seen in 2002. The major producers were China with 45.3% of world production, Chile with 20.3%, and the U.S. with 14.4%. U.S. production of molybdenum concentrate in 2018 rose +3.2% yr/yr to 42,000 metric tons. U.S. net production of molybdenum metal powder is now being withheld as proprietary data but in 2008 the figure was 1,640 metric tons.

Demand – U.S. consumption of molybdenum concentrate in 2008 rose by +1.4% yr/yr to 44,500 metric tons, remaining well above the 14-year low of 21,200 metric tons posted in 2002. U.S. consumption of molybdenum products in 2018 fell 7.5% yr/yr to 16,000 metric tons.

Trade – U.S. imports of molybdenum concentrate for consumption in 2016 (latest available data) rose by +15.5% yr/yr to 14,900 metric tons, but still well above the 2-decade low of 4,710 metric tons posted in 2002.

World Mine Production of Molybdenum   In Metric Tons (Contained Molybdenum)

Year	Armenia	Canada[3]	Chile	China	Iran	Kazak-hstan	Mexico	Mongolia	Peru	Russia	United States	Uzbek-isten	World Total
2012	6,526	8,936	35,090	120,000	3,516	----	11,366	1,904	16,790	4,939	60,400	522	272,000
2013	6,900	7,956	38,715	122,000	3,471	----	12,562	1,819	18,140	4,753	61,000	490	281,000
2014	7,162	9,358	48,770	129,000	3,494	----	14,370	1,999	17,018	3,114	68,200	450	306,000
2015	6,300	2,505	52,579	135,000	3,500	----	12,279	2,557	20,153	3,000	47,400	450	288,000
2016	6,300	2,708	55,647	129,000	3,500	----	11,896	2,444	25,757	3,000	36,200	450	278,000
2017[1]	5,800	5,290	62,500	130,000	3,500	----	14,000	1,800	28,100	3,100	40,700	450	297,000
2018[2]	5,000	5,100	61,000	130,000	3,500	----	15,000	1,800	28,000	3,100	42,000	450	300,000

[1] Preliminary. [2] Estimate. [3] Shipments. *Source: U.S. Geological Survey (USGS)*

Salient Statistics of Molybdenum in the United States   In Metric Tons (Contained Molybdenum)

| | Concentrate | | | | | | | Primary Products[4] | | | | | | |
| | | Shipments | | | | | | Net Production | | | Shipments | | |
Year	Production	Total (Including Exports)	Value Million $	For Exports	Consumption	Imports For Consumption	Stocks Dec. 31[3]	Grand Total	Molybolic Oxide[5]	Molybdenum Metal Powder	Avg Price Value $ / Kg.[6]	Domestic Destinations	To Oxide for Exports, Gross Weight	Consumption	Producer Stocks, Dec. 31
2012	60,400	60,200	----	----	W	12,000	W	----	----	----	28.09	W	1,590	19,400	W
2013	61,000	68,100	----	----	W	13,100	W	----	----	----	22.85	W	1,320	18,600	W
2014	68,200	71,900	----	----	W	15,800	W	----	----	----	25.84	W	1,740	19,500	W
2015	47,400	50,500	----	----	W	12,900	W	----	----	----	15.01	W	1,300	17,600	W
2016	36,200	38,600	----	----	W	14,900	W	----	----	----	14.40	W	853	15,800	W
2017[1]	40,700		----	----	W		W	----	----	----	18.06	W		17,300	W
2018[2]	42,000		----	----	W		W	----	----	----	27.00	W		16,000	W

[1] Preliminary. [2] Estimate. [3] At mines & at plants making molybdenum products. [4] Comprises ferromolybdenum, molybdic oxide, & molybdenum salts & metal. [5] Includes molybdic oxide briquets, molybdic acid, molybdenum trioxide, all other. [6] U.S. producer price per kilogram of molybdenum oxide contained in technical-grade molybdic oxide. W = Withheld proprietary data. E = Net exporter. *Source: U.S. Geological Survey (USGS)*

US Merchant Price of Molybdic Oxide   In Dollars Per Pound

Year	Jan.	Feb.	Mar.	Apr.	May	June	July	Aug.	Sept.	Oct.	Nov.	Dec.	Average
2012	13.87	14.56	14.38	14.21	14.09	13.53	12.79	11.69	11.68	10.87	10.76	11.06	12.79
2013	11.71	11.44	11.11	11.05	11.10	11.06	9.87	9.29	9.50	9.36	9.67	9.75	10.41
2014	9.92	10.26	10.29	11.60	14.05	14.72	13.55	13.25	12.84	10.59	9.78	9.59	11.70
2015	9.41	8.58	8.17	8.02	7.63	7.32	6.04	6.11	5.88	5.01	4.73	5.02	6.83
2016	5.32	5.45	5.45	5.55	6.87	7.95	6.91	7.11	7.13	6.88	6.82	6.71	6.51
2017	7.22	7.75	8.38	9.03	8.56	7.49	7.41	8.22	8.76	8.53	8.53	9.33	8.27
2018	11.42	12.33	12.96	12.48	11.95	11.43	11.28	12.15	12.16	12.06	12.01	12.22	12.04

Source: American Metal Market (AMM)

Nickel

Nickel (atomic symbol Ni) is a hard, malleable, ductile metal that has a silvery tinge that can take on a high polish. Nickel is somewhat ferromagnetic and is a fair conductor of heat and electricity. Nickel is primarily used in the production of stainless steel and other corrosion-resistant alloys. Nickel is used in coins to replace silver, in rechargeable batteries, and in electronic circuitry. Nickel plating techniques, like electro-less coating or single-slurry coating, are employed in such applications as turbine blades, helicopter rotors, extrusion dies, and rolled steel strip.

Nickel futures and options trade at the London Metal Exchange (LME). The nickel futures contract calls for the delivery of 6 metric tons of primary nickel with at least 99.80% purity in the form of full plate, cut cathodes, pellets or briquettes. The contract is priced in terms of U.S. dollars per metric ton.

Prices – Nickel prices posted a record high of $17.75 per pound in 2007 but have since remained well below that level. The average price of nickel in 2018 rose +26.9% yr/yr to $6.62 per pound.

Supply – World mine production of nickel in 2018 rose +6.5% yr/yr to 2.300 million metric tons, but still below the 2013 record high of 2.790 million metric tons. The current levels are almost triple the production seen in 1970. The world's largest mine producers of nickel in 2018 were Indonesia with 24.3% of the world production, Philippines with 14.8%, and Russia and New Caledonia with 9.1% each. U.S. secondary nickel production in 2015 fell -0.9% yr/yr to 90,050 metric tons, still below the 2006 decade-high of 103,630 metric tons.

Demand – U.S. consumption of nickel in 2018 rose + 3.1% yr/yr to 270,000 metric tons. In 2015, the primary U.S. nickel consumption use was for stainless and heat-resisting steels, which accounted for 58.8% of U.S. consumption. Other consumption uses in 2015 were super alloys at 11.4%, nickel alloys at 6.6%, electro-plating anodes at 3.6%, alloy steels at 2.2%, copper base alloys at 1.0%, and chemicals at 0.9%.

Trade – The U.S. relied on imports for 52% of its nickel consumption in 2017. U.S. imports of primary and secondary nickel in 2018 rose +6.3% yr/yr to 200,000 metric tons, still well above the 2009 record low of 117,600 metric tons. U.S. exports of primary and secondary nickel in 2018 rose +44.0% yr/yr to 90,000 metric tons.

World Mine Production of Nickel — In Metric Tons (Contained Nickel)

Year	Australia[3]	Botswana	Brazil	Canada	China	Dominican Republic	Greece	Indonesia	New Caledonia	Philippines	Russia	South Africa	Total
2012	244,000	17,948	139,531	211,701	103,860	25,590	21,980	648,400	131,693	455,000	296,650	45,945	2,570,000
2013	234,000	22,848	104,829	227,743	107,160	15,825	19,100	834,200	164,406	466,000	281,000	51,208	2,790,000
2014	245,000	14,958	167,063	228,867	94,101	----	21,405	177,100	178,080	586,000	283,150	54,956	2,350,000
2015	222,000	16,789	160,000	234,936	92,900	----	19,610	129,000	186,065	554,000	269,310	56,689	2,280,000
2016	204,000		160,000	236,000	98,000			199,000	207,000	347,000	222,000	49,000	2,090,000
2017[1]	179,000			78,600	214,000	103,000		345,000	215,000	366,000	214,000	48,400	2,160,000
2018[2]	170,000			80,000	160,000	110,000		560,000	210,000	340,000	210,000	44,000	2,300,000

[1] Preliminary. [2] Estimate. [3] Content of nickel sulfate and concentrates. *Source: U.S. Geological Survey (USGS)*

Salient Statistics of Nickel in the United States — In Metric Tons (Contained Nickel)

Year	Net Import Reliance As a % of Apparent Consumption	Production Plant[4]	Production Secondary[5]	Alloy Sheets	Cast Iron	Copper Base Alloys	Electro-plating Anodes	Nickel Alloys	Stainless & Heat Resisting Steels	Super Alloys	Chemicals	Apparent Consumption	Stocks, Dec. 31 At Consumer Plants	Stocks, Dec. 31 At Producer Plants	Primary & Secondary Exports	Primary & Secondary Imports	Avg. Price LME $/Lb.
2012	49	----	89,710	5,080	2,130	5,530	9,330	22,600	126,000	26,600	1,670	215,000	16,800	6,380	68,730	155,300	7.95
2013	47	----	88,620	5,500	258	2,100	8,080	16,400	129,000	26,700	2,020	199,000	18,400	10,020	71,700	152,300	6.81
2014	58	----	90,910	3,330	273	2,300	8,280	15,000	133,000	26,200	2,130	264,000	23,300	9,030	66,700	195,000	7.65
2015	52	----	90,050	4,960	272	2,300	8,100	15,000	133,000	25,700	2,120	226,000	19,200	10,300	61,510	157,100	5.37
2016	46	----										224,000	15,100	10,500	74,000	143,300	4.35
2017[1]	53	----										262,000	14,700		62,500	188,100	4.72
2018[2]	52	----										270,000	15,000		90,000	200,000	6.20

[1] Exclusive of scrap. [2] Preliminary. [3] Estimate. [4] Smelter & refinery. [5] From purchased scrap (ferrous & nonferrous). W = Withheld proprietary data. NA = Not available. *Source: U.S. Geological Survey (USGS)*

Average Price of Nickel[1] in the United States — In Cents Per Pound

Year	Jan.	Feb.	Mar.	Apr.	May	June	July	Aug.	Sept.	Oct.	Nov.	Dec.	Average
2014	703.14	708.28	774.92	855.13	943.44	906.85	927.94	907.24	883.35	778.75	773.39	784.30	828.89
2015	731.81	722.45	690.11	647.56	676.12	641.79	574.56	572.69	572.69	572.69	461.43	446.04	609.16
2016	436.45	428.81	445.47	452.40	446.34	454.59	514.86	518.41	512.33	515.34	553.42	548.30	485.56
2017	502.04	530.43	513.62	488.28	465.54	454.74	480.54	543.29	557.15	563.12	594.41	568.56	521.81
2018	633.85	665.30	667.55	672.22	672.22	----	----	----	----	----	----	----	662.23

[1] Plating material, briquettes. *Source: American Metal Market (AMM)*

Oats

Oats are seeds or grains of a genus of plants that thrive in cool, moist climates. There are about 25 species of oats that grow worldwide in the cooler temperate regions. The oldest known cultivated oats were found inside caves in Switzerland and are believed to be from the Bronze Age. Oats are usually sown in early spring and harvested in mid to late summer, but in southern regions of the northern hemisphere, they may be sown in the fall. Oats are used in many processed foods such as flour, livestock feed, and furfural, a chemical used as a solvent in various refining industries. The oat crop year begins in June and ends in May. Oat futures and options are traded at the CME Group.

Prices – CME oat futures prices (Barchart.com electronic symbol ZO) on the nearest-futures chart moved lower early in 2018 but then rallied to finally close the year up about +3.6% at $2.75 per bushel. Regarding cash prices, the average monthly price received by farmers for oats in the U.S. in the first six months of the 2018/19 marketing year (June/May) fell -1.9% yr/yr to $2.69 per bushel.

Supply – World oat production in 2018/19 is expected to fall -3.0 % yr/yr to 22.705 million metric tons, moderately above the record low of 19.625 million metric tons posted in 2010-11. World annual oat production in the past three decades has dropped very sharply from levels above 50 million metric tons in the early 1970s. The world's largest oat producers in 2018/19 are expected to be the European Union with 35.5% of world production, Russia with 21.1%,

Canada with 15.2%, and Australia with 4.0%.

U.S. oat production in the 2017/18 marketing year is expected to rise 13.6% yr/yr to 56.130 million bushels, which is up from last year's record low of 49.391. U.S. oat production has fallen sharply from levels mostly above 1 billion bushels seen from the early 1900s into the early 1960s. U.S. farmers are expected to harvest 865,000 acres of oats in 2018/19, up 8.0% yr/yr. However, that is far below the almost 40 million acres harvested back in the 1950s. The oat yield in 2018/19 is expected to rise +5.2% to 64.9 bushels per acre. Oat stocks in the U.S. as of September 2018 were up +4.0% yr/yr to 74.862 million bushels. The largest U.S. oat-producing states in 2018 were the states of South Dakota with 15.3% of U.S. production, Minnesota and North Dakota with 14.8%, and Wisconsin with 11.6%.

Demand – U.S. usage of oats in 2018/19 is expected to rise +5.7% yr/yr to 154.000 million bushels, above the 2011-12 record low of 106.360 million bushels. U.S. usage of oats in 2018/19 is expected to be 48.7% for feed and residual, 47.1% for food, alcohol and industrial, 4.2% for seed, and the rest for export.

Trade – U.S. exports of oats in 2018/19 are expected to fall -17.1% yr/yr to 2.000 million bushels. U.S. imports of oats in 2018/19 are expected to rise +6.3% yr/yr to 95.000 million bushels, but still below the 2007 record high of 123.29 million bushels.

World Production of Oats   In Thousands of Metric Tons

Crop Year	Argen-tina	Australia	Belarus	Brazil	Canada	Chile	China	European Union	Kazak-stan	Russia	Ukraine	United States	World Total
2009-10	182	1,162	552	253	2,912	381	215	8,641	204	5,401	731	1,321	22,970
2010-11	660	1,128	442	379	2,451	564	220	7,500	134	3,218	458	1,188	19,340
2011-12	345	1,262	448	354	3,158	451	295	7,927	258	5,332	506	728	21,953
2012-13	496	1,121	422	361	2,830	680	250	7,909	200	4,027	630	892	20,766
2013-14	445	1,255	352	380	3,928	610	235	8,380	305	4,932	467	938	23,175
2014-15	525	1,198	522	307	2,977	421	255	7,821	226	5,267	610	1,019	22,104
2015-16	553	1,300	492	351	3,425	533	265	7,524	244	4,527	498	1,300	22,046
2016-17[1]	785	2,266	390	828	3,231	713	290	8,044	335	4,750	510	940	24,174
2017-18[2]	492	1,120	500	634	3,733	571	300	8,072	285	5,441	481	717	23,406
2018-19[3]	600	900	460	770	3,450	675	305	8,050	340	4,800	475	815	22,705

[1] Preliminary.   [2] Estimate.   [3] Forecast.   Source: Foreign Agricultural Service, U.S. Department of Agriculture (FAS-USDA)

Official Oats Crop Production Reports in the United States   In Thousands of Bushels

Year	July 1	Aug. 1	Sept. 1	Oct. 1	Dec. 1	Final	Year	July 1	Aug. 1	Sept. 1	Oct. 1	Dec. 1	Final
2007	100,921	98,341	----	----	----	90,430	2013	74,459	75,210	----	----	----	64,642
2008	92,872	89,897	----	----	----	89,135	2014	75,507	77,267	----	----	----	70,232
2009	91,277	91,960	----	----	----	93,081	2015	83,640	85,456	----	----	----	89,535
2010	87,726	87,239	----	----	----	81,190	2016	76,609	76,854	----	----	----	64,770
2011	56,551	57,489	----	----	----	53,649	2017	53,674	53,719	----	----	----	49,585
2012	65,276	66,519	----	----	----	61,486	2018[1]	66,384	65,668	----	----	----	56,130

[1] Preliminary.   Source: National Agricultural Statistics Service, U.S. Department of Agriculture (NASS-USDA)

Oat Stocks in the United States   In Thousands of Bushels

	On Farms				Off Farms				Total Stocks			
Year	Mar. 1	June 1	Sept. 1	Dec. 1	Mar. 1	June 1	Sept. 1	Dec. 1	Mar. 1	June 1	Sept. 1	Dec. 1
2009	30,200	17,480	54,500	43,000	65,250	66,619	73,875	67,629	95,450	84,099	128,375	110,629
2010	30,900	17,600	46,250	34,100	67,091	62,716	70,722	66,911	97,991	80,316	116,972	101,011
2011	26,950	14,580	31,000	24,900	59,361	53,049	47,391	54,235	86,311	67,629	78,391	79,135
2012	19,750	11,120	34,100	26,100	55,044	43,869	50,872	47,051	74,794	54,989	84,972	73,151
2013	18,900	11,380	37,150	25,650	33,726	24,957	26,339	22,394	52,626	36,337	63,489	48,044
2014	19,800	9,710	41,400	31,300	15,323	15,029	32,910	35,670	35,123	24,739	74,310	66,970
2015	20,810	15,120	47,800	36,750	38,609	38,625	46,066	45,981	59,419	53,745	93,866	82,731
2016	26,800	18,350	37,400	30,430	48,429	38,452	41,190	45,003	75,229	56,802	78,590	75,433
2017	22,320	13,540	33,950	23,300	40,885	36,790	38,039	43,166	63,205	50,330	71,989	66,466
2018[1]	17,240	11,410	39,200	25,410	37,699	29,606	35,573	41,824	54,939	41,016	74,773	67,234

[1] Preliminary.   Source: National Agricultural Statistics Service, U.S. Department of Agriculture (NASS-USDA)

Supply and Utilization of Oats in the United States   In Millions of Bushels

| Crop Year Beginning June 1 | Acreage | | | | | | | Food, | | | | | Findley | | |
| | Planted | Harvested | Yield Per Acre | Production | Imports | Total Supply | Feed & Residual | Alcohol & Industrial | Seed | Exports | Total Use | Ending Stocks | Farm Price | Loan Rate | Target Price |
	--- 1,000 Acres ---		(Bushels)	In Millions of Bushels									---- Dollars Per Bushel ----		
2009-10	3,404	1,379	67.5	93.1	94.9	272.1	115.2	66.2	8.2	191.8	2.2	80.3	2.02	1.33	1.44
2010-11	3,138	1,263	64.3	81.2	85.1	247.3	102.9	67.2	6.8	179.7	2.9	67.6	2.52	1.39	1.79
2011-12	2,496	939	57.1	53.6	94.1	211.8	78.5	68.8	7.2	156.9	2.4	54.9	3.49	1.39	1.79
2012-13	2,700	1,005	61.2	61.5	92.9	209.3	95.7	68.1	7.8	172.9	1.4	36.3	3.89	1.39	1.79
2013-14	2,980	1,009	64.1	64.6	97.1	198.1	98.4	66.2	7.2	173.4	1.6	24.7	3.75	1.39	1.79
2014-15	2,753	1,035	67.9	70.2	108.9	203.8	71.2	69.0	8.0	148.2	1.8	53.7	3.21	1.39	1.79
2015-16	3,088	1,276	70.2	89.5	85.6	228.8	93.5	69.4	7.1	170.1	2.0	56.8	2.12	1.39	1.79
2016-17	2,829	981	66.0	64.8	90.2	211.8	81.8	69.9	6.4	158.1	3.4	50.3	2.06	1.39	1.79
2017-18[1]	2,588	801	61.7	49.6	89.3	189.1	68.1	70.7	6.8	145.6	2.4	41.0	2.59		
2018-19[2]	2,746	865	64.9	56.1	95.0	192.1	75.0	72.5	6.5	154.0	2.0	36.1	2.55-2.75		

[1] Preliminary.   [2] Forecast.   [3] Less than 500,000 bushels.   NA = Not available.
Source: Economic Research Service, U.S. Department of Agiculture (ERS-USDA)

Production of Oats in the United States, by States   In Thousands of Bushels

Year	Illinois	Iowa	Michigan	Minnesota	Nebraska	New York	North Dakota	Ohio	Pennsylvania	South Dakota	Texas	Wisconsin	Total
2009	1,625	6,175	3,465	12,070	2,070	4,620	11,220	3,375	4,880	6,570	2,820	13,260	93,081
2010	1,950	4,340	4,080	11,385	1,700	3,886	6,405	3,500	4,720	7,560	4,160	9,860	81,190
2011	1,360	3,250	1,920	5,940	1,300	1,700	4,420	2,052	2,760	4,130	2,100	7,130	53,649
2012	1,140	3,770	2,100	8,370	1,026	3,250	6,510	2,576	3,965	3,060	3,185	7,800	61,486
2013	1,725	3,960	1,860	5,985	1,625	3,082	8,370	1,575	3,100	9,240	1,840	6,825	64,642
2014	2,000	3,520	2,760	7,875	2,400	2,520	7,665	2,205	3,480	9,300	1,710	8,680	70,232
2015	1,925	4,161	3,350	12,480	2,680	2,320	10,360	2,520	3,575	12,615	2,640	14,040	89,535
2016	1,620	3,268	1,740	8,160	1,500	3,300	7,260	1,850	3,350	9,020	3,000	6,600	64,770
2017	1,580	3,234	2,160	7,125	1,715	1,925	4,640	1,400	2,320	4,200	2,700	5,015	49,585
2018[1]	2,075	2,079	3,150	6,195	1,518	2,322	8,610	1,950	1,610	7,790	2,500	5,490	56,130

[1] Preliminary.   Source: National Agricultural Statistics Service, U.S. Department of Agriculture (NASS-USDA)

Average Cash Price of No. 2 Heavy White Oats in Toledo   In U.S. Dollars Per Bushel

Year	Jan.	Feb.	Mar.	Apr.	May	June	July	Aug.	Sept.	Oct.	Nov.	Dec.	Average
1996-97	NQ	2.45	2.34	2.19	2.02	1.96	1.96	1.99	2.16	2.26	2.12	2.08	2.14
1997-98	2.12	1.79	1.84	1.80	1.77	NQ	NQ	NQ	NQ	NQ	NQ	NQ	1.86
1998-99	NQ	NQ	NQ	NQ	NQ	NQ	NQ	NQ	NQ	NQ	NQ	NQ	NQ
1999-00	NQ	NQ	NQ	NQ	NQ	NQ	NQ	NQ	NQ	NQ	NQ	NQ	NQ
2000-01	NQ	NQ	NQ	NQ	NQ	NQ	NQ	NQ	NQ	NQ	NQ	NQ	NQ
2001-02	NQ	NQ	NQ	NQ	NQ	NQ	NQ	NQ	NQ	NQ	NQ	NQ	NQ
2002-03	NQ	NQ	NQ	NQ	NQ	NQ	NQ	NQ	NQ	NQ	NQ	NQ	NQ
2003-04	NQ	NQ	NQ	NQ	NQ	NQ	NQ	NQ	NQ	NQ	NQ	NQ	NQ
2004-05	NQ	NQ	NQ	NQ	NQ	NQ	NQ	NQ	NQ	NQ	NQ	NQ	NQ
2005-06[1]	NQ	NQ	NQ										

[1] Preliminary.   NQ = No quotes.   Source: Economic Research Service, U.S. Department of Agriculture (ERS-USDA)

OATS

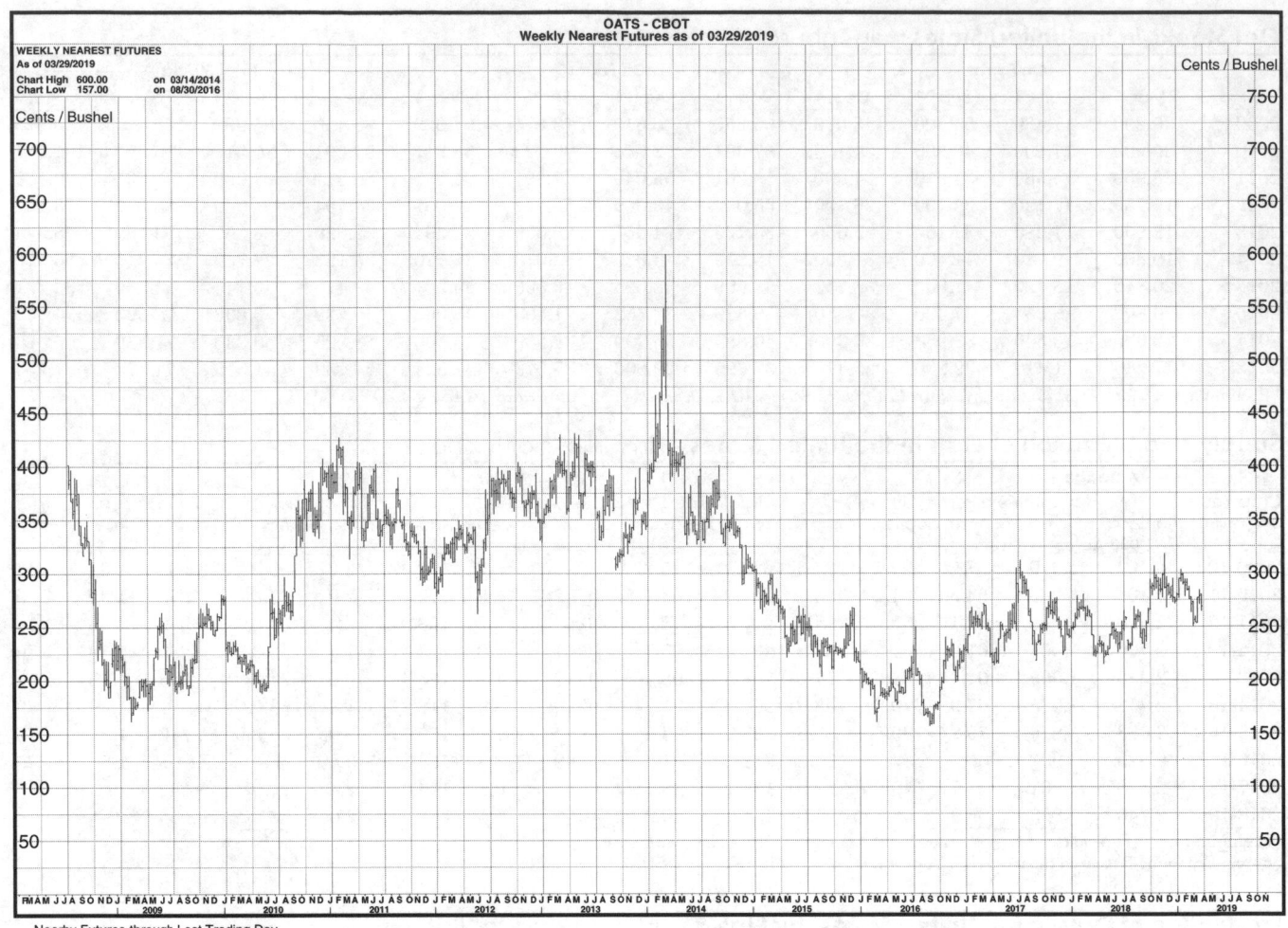

Nearby Futures through Last Trading Day.

Volume of Trading in Oats Futures in Chicago   In Contracts

Year	Jan.	Feb.	Mar.	Apr.	May	June	July	Aug.	Sept.	Oct.	Nov.	Dec.	Total
2009	17,494	34,259	19,035	34,277	25,365	41,961	19,370	24,801	20,076	29,720	29,328	18,619	314,305
2010	31,060	32,283	23,890	37,409	21,363	54,174	26,097	23,735	22,430	25,743	30,649	15,754	344,587
2011	28,513	41,210	32,798	35,451	25,962	42,810	17,687	26,037	24,613	23,352	41,624	9,259	349,316
2012	19,267	27,361	29,511	22,787	28,013	31,967	16,898	20,154	15,311	22,011	28,859	17,431	279,570
2013	21,246	34,411	16,949	31,035	16,891	28,267	18,156	16,459	17,388	21,863	22,977	9,316	254,958
2014	18,860	30,902	18,786	18,113	11,938	19,491	11,446	13,556	11,300	16,754	21,903	7,482	200,531
2015	14,618	19,923	12,461	25,243	15,152	21,734	11,399	13,953	9,614	13,216	24,979	12,283	194,575
2016	15,634	25,543	14,663	26,235	14,762	34,447	11,971	19,094	9,399	21,957	21,435	10,090	225,230
2017	15,129	16,691	13,180	17,122	10,845	24,381	10,292	11,920	8,370	11,522	19,561	10,239	169,252
2018	15,633	14,913	14,719	21,901	10,995	16,616	7,060	16,254	9,029	17,965	20,659	7,195	172,939

Contract size = 5,000 bu.   *Source: CME Group; Chicago Board of Trade (CBT)*

Average Open Interest of Oats in Chicago   In Contracts

Year	Jan.	Feb.	Mar.	Apr.	May	June	July	Aug.	Sept.	Oct.	Nov.	Dec.
2009	16,519	16,927	14,367	15,142	13,304	14,380	13,805	13,649	13,684	13,526	13,593	11,976
2010	12,601	13,869	15,662	17,612	17,244	16,838	10,329	10,956	11,664	13,477	13,452	11,707
2011	13,104	14,297	13,191	13,677	12,577	12,457	12,287	13,127	14,082	15,902	16,557	12,802
2012	13,363	11,924	10,849	10,879	11,516	11,021	9,959	10,708	11,328	11,802	11,567	10,439
2013	10,568	11,022	10,619	9,356	8,634	10,207	8,659	9,000	9,941	10,805	9,767	8,937
2014	10,414	11,168	9,529	8,350	7,356	7,793	7,292	8,382	8,987	9,787	9,813	8,151
2015	7,684	8,794	8,965	8,729	8,375	8,570	7,926	8,408	8,902	10,129	10,793	8,789
2016	9,457	10,452	10,883	10,418	9,947	10,282	9,969	10,511	10,755	9,261	8,304	6,946
2017	7,314	7,952	6,597	6,656	6,104	6,764	6,687	6,369	5,902	6,674	7,795	6,561
2018	6,491	5,995	5,740	6,470	5,468	5,232	4,898	4,723	3,990	6,113	6,608	5,712

Contract size = 5,000 bu.   *Source: CME Group; Chicago Board of Trade (CBT)*

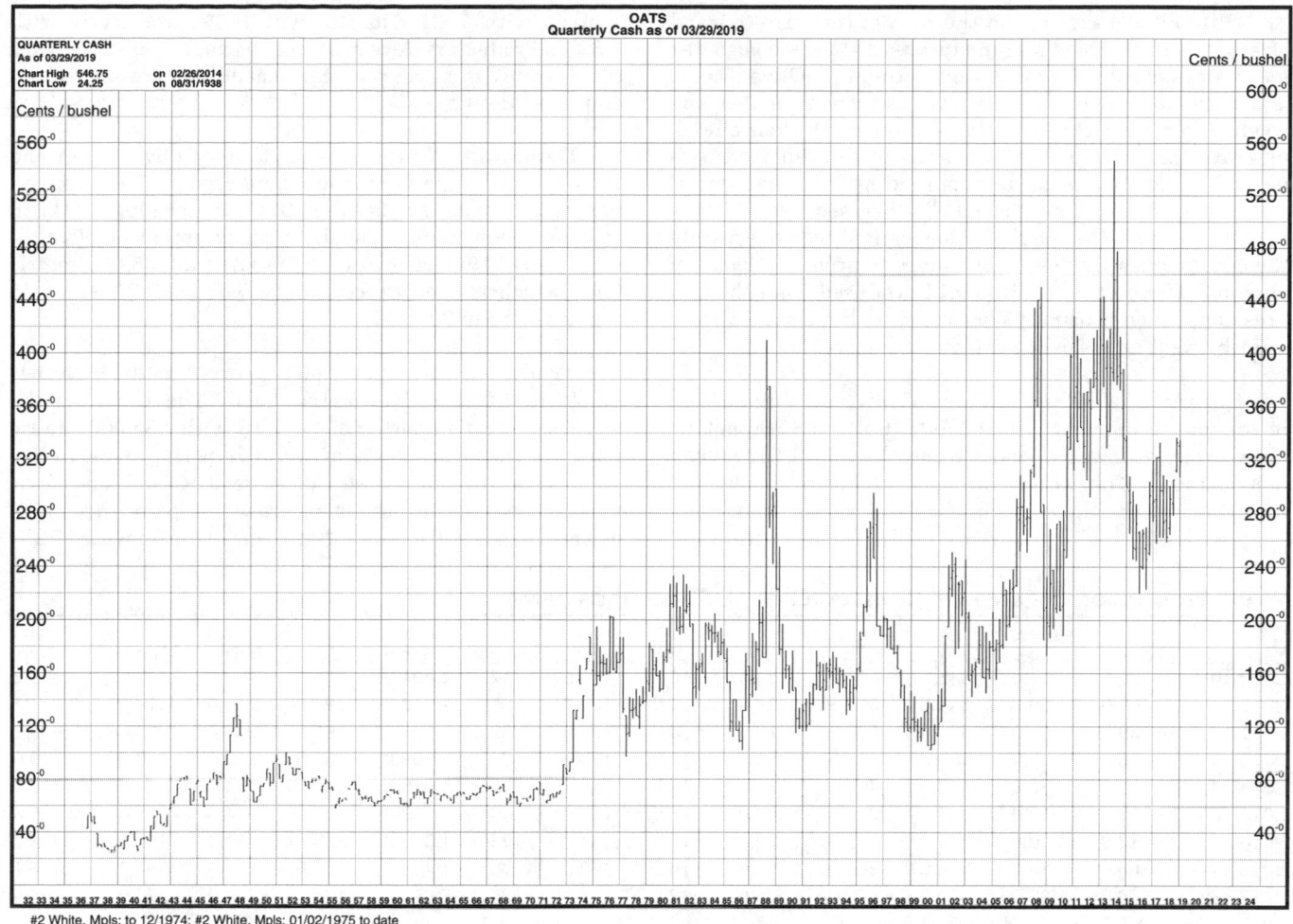

#2 White, Mpls: to 12/1974; #2 White, Mpls: 01/02/1975 to date

Average Cash Price of No. 2 Heavy White Oats in Minneapolis   In U.S. Dollars Per Bushel

Year	June	July	Aug.	Sept.	Oct.	Nov.	Dec.	Jan.	Feb.	Mar.	Apr.	May	Average
2009-10	2.33	2.15	2.12	2.03	2.34	2.56	2.56	2.44	2.30	2.19	2.10	1.98	2.26
2010-11	2.39	2.58	2.69	3.14	3.56	3.54	3.88	3.93	4.08	3.55	3.83	3.55	3.39
2011-12	3.68	3.68	3.69	3.72	3.51	3.36	3.30	3.16	3.46	3.48	3.55	3.48	3.50
2012-13	3.37	3.95	3.99	3.89	3.98	3.85	3.94	3.79	4.07	4.26	4.13	3.99	3.93
2013-14	4.21	3.84	3.78	3.40	3.57	3.79	3.80	4.30	4.64	4.66	4.58	4.03	4.05
2014-15	3.88	3.85	3.83	3.86	3.68	3.53	3.49	3.26	3.11	3.14	2.94	2.75	3.44
2015-16	2.89	2.82	2.63	2.70	2.58	2.67	2.60	2.64	2.60	2.43	2.49	2.49	2.63
2016-17	2.58	2.61	2.34	2.29	2.67	2.84	2.97	2.92	3.07	2.90	2.86	2.88	2.74
2017-18	2.95	3.17	2.98	2.87	2.97	2.94	2.90	2.73	2.96	2.79	2.72	2.89	2.90
2018-19[1]	2.88	2.84	2.91	2.91	3.18	3.22	3.28	3.31	3.23				3.08

[1] Preliminary.   *Source: Economic Research Service, U.S. Department of Agriculture (ERS-USDA)*

Average Price Received by Farmers for Oats in the United States   In U.S. Dollars Per Bushel

Year	June	July	Aug.	Sept.	Oct.	Nov.	Dec.	Jan.	Feb.	Mar.	Apr.	May	Average
2009-10	2.37	2.03	1.86	1.82	2.03	2.02	2.22	2.19	2.30	2.29	2.25	2.20	2.13
2010-11	2.11	2.11	2.09	2.30	2.55	3.07	2.94	3.13	3.27	3.28	3.54	3.55	2.83
2011-12	3.43	3.35	3.20	3.67	3.69	3.38	3.57	3.56	3.47	3.77	3.84	4.12	3.59
2012-13	3.80	3.70	3.82	3.76	3.93	3.88	3.90	4.06	4.14	4.20	4.43	4.45	4.01
2013-14	3.93	3.88	3.67	3.57	3.49	3.63	3.59	3.70	3.75	4.13	3.96	3.98	3.77
2014-15	3.73	3.49	3.24	3.20	3.16	2.95	3.21	3.02	3.08	2.96	2.82	2.90	3.15
2015-16	2.83	2.33	2.07	2.04	2.20	2.11	2.12	1.93	2.21	2.20	1.97	2.26	2.19
2016-17	1.98	1.89	1.84	1.97	2.03	2.23	2.35	2.31	2.39	2.39	2.32	2.63	2.19
2017-18	2.74	2.33	2.32	2.56	2.55	2.68	2.94	3.29	2.64	2.80	2.93	3.14	2.74
2018-19[1]	3.04	2.61	2.47	2.62	2.68	2.72	2.77	2.70					2.70

[1] Preliminary.   *Source: National Agricultural Statistics Service, U.S. Department of Agriculture (NASS-USDA)*

Olive Oil

Olive oil is derived from the fruit of the olive tree and originated in the Mediterranean area. Olives designated for oil are picked before ripening in the fall. Olive picking is usually done by hand. The olives are then weighed and washed in cold water. The olives, along with their oil-rich pits, are then crushed and kneaded until a homogeneous paste is formed. The paste is spread by hand onto metal plates, which are then stacked and pressed hydraulically to yield a liquid. The liquid is then centrifuged to separate the oil. It takes 1,300 to 2,000 olives to produce 1 quart of olive oil. The best olive oil is still produced from the first pressing, which is usually performed within 24 to 72 hours after harvest and is called *extra virgin* olive oil.

Supply – World production of olive oil (pressed oil) in the marketing year 2017/18 fell -10.2% to 3.396 million metric tons, below last year's record high of 3.782 million metric tons. The world's largest producers of olive oil in 2017/18 were Spain with 39.8% of world production, Italy with 11.8%, Greece with 10.3%, Turkey with 8.1%,

Tunisia with 7.8%, Morocco with 4.5%, and Syria with 3.8%. Production levels in the various countries vary considerably from year-to-year depending on weather and crop conditions.

Demand – World consumption of olive oil in the 2017/18 marketing year rose +2.0% yr/yr to 3.152 million metric tons, not far below the 2011/12 record high of 3.356 million metric tons. The U.S. consumption of olive oil in the 2017/18 period rose +3.7% yr/yr to 335,000 metric tons, which is a new record high. That is 9.7% of world consumption in 2016-17.

Trade – World olive oil imports in 2017/18 rose +8.5% to 1.004 million metric tons. The U.S. was the world's largest importer in 2017/18 with 335,000 metric tons, representing 33.4% of world imports. World olive oil exports in 2017/18 rose +12.1% to 1,044 million metric tons. The world's largest exporters were Spain with 30.7% of world exports, Italy with 20.6%, and Tunisia with 17.2%.

World Production of Olive Oil (Pressed Oil)   In Thousands of Metric Tons

Crop Year	Algeria	Argen-tina	Greece	Italy	Jordan	Libya	Morocco	Portugal	Spain	Syria	Tunisia	Turkey	World Total
2009-10	26.5	17.0	346.0	557.7	29.5	15.0	151.5	57.5	1,494.5	163.0	170.0	157.0	3,298.2
2010-11	67.0	20.0	334.0	551.8	28.0	15.0	137.0	67.9	1,512.9	196.0	140.0	174.0	3,384.4
2011-12	39.5	32.0	322.6	576.0	19.5	15.0	126.5	82.3	1,701.9	165.0	202.0	205.0	3,629.1
2012-13	66.0	17.0	393.9	440.5	21.5	15.0	107.0	64.6	709.6	155.0	240.0	209.0	2,573.0
2013-14	44.0	30.0	146.6	491.5	19.0	18.0	140.0	102.9	1,913.0	147.0	84.0	149.0	3,440.3
2014-15	69.5	15.0	333.0	235.3	23.0	15.5	132.0	69.0	959.3	113.0	374.0	174.0	2,685.6
2015-16[1]	82.0	20.0	354.0	498.3	29.5	18.0	142.0	123.0	1,518.0	127.0	154.0	164.0	3,422.2
2016-17[2]	63.0	35.0	216.0	200.0	20.0	16.0	120.0	78.0	1,408.0	127.0	124.0	191.0	3,782.1
2017-18[3]	80.0	30.0	350.0	400.0	25.0	18.0	152.0	135.0	1,350.0	130.0	265.0	276.0	3,395.5

[1] Preliminary.   [2] Estimate.   [3] Forecast.   *Source: The Oil World*

World Imports and Exports of Olive Oil (Pressed Oil)   In Thousands of Metric Tons

Crop Year	Australia	Brazil	Italy	Japan	Spain	United States	World Total	Greece	Italy	Spain	Tunisia	Turkey	World Total
			--- Imports ---							--- Exports ---			
2009-10	35.6	51.3	56.8	42.6	17.9	272.0	740.7	13.7	213.8	208.0	115.3	27.2	731.5
2010-11	32.0	65.0	57.5	37.7	16.5	292.0	802.0	14.4	243.3	229.2	109.0	12.9	808.1
2011-12	31.9	71.0	73.9	45.6	21.4	317.4	895.4	18.1	254.9	285.8	149.5	19.4	902.8
2012-13	28.8	74.9	79.8	54.0	61.5	298.2	950.0	20.1	235.3	223.5	178.3	80.7	940.1
2013-14	28.9	73.6	29.1	56.2	20.4	312.4	894.7	17.9	255.6	333.8	84.0	34.9	919.6
2014-15	22.8	67.8	98.2	61.9	119.8	312.1	1,046.8	18.8	220.5	282.5	313.1	16.9	1,056.1
2015-16[1]	26.9	50.6	42.6	56.7	57.5	331.5	933.6	21.4	232.0	348.2	114.3	12.8	919.1
2016-17[2]	29.6	58.5	37.1	56.9	60.3	316.6	925.2	20.3	219.2	340.5	99.3	34.7	931.0
2017-18[3]	31.0	65.0	45.0	59.0	85.0	335.0	1,004.2	22.0	215.0	320.0	180.0	90.0	1,043.5

[1] Preliminary.   [2] Estimate.   [3] Forecast.   *Source: The Oil World*

World Consumption and Ending Stocks of Olive Oil (Pressed Oil)   In Thousands of Metric Tons

Crop Year	Brazil	Morocco	Syria	Tunisia	Turkey	United States	World Total	European Union	Morocco	Syria	Tunisia	Turkey	World Total
			--- Consumption ---						--- Ending Stocks ---			
2009-10	51.3	89.4	133.0	32.0	116.8	272.0	3,184.2	577.0	85.0	20.4	33.0	28.0	822.8
2010-11	65.0	96.7	138.1	34.5	129.2	284.8	3,294.2	775.0	90.0	45.0	30.0	60.0	1,105.9
2011-12	71.0	113.3	136.6	37.8	155.7	298.7	3,356.0	959.9	95.0	50.0	45.0	90.0	1,371.6
2012-13	74.9	116.3	139.5	40.0	153.3	304.1	3,125.9	459.7	75.0	40.0	67.0	65.0	824.6
2013-14	73.6	120.1	144.7	43.5	149.2	309.3	3,237.0	692.7	90.0	20.0	26.0	30.0	1,002.9
2014-15	67.8	130.7	119.8	45.5	149.7	310.0	3,068.4	339.0	60.0	10.0	43.0	40.0	610.8
2015-16[1]	50.6	132.5	111.2	46.0	157.7	321.0	3,169.7	586.1	55.0	15.0	42.0	35.0	877.9
2016-17[2]	58.5	129.9	108.9	46.2	161.3	322.9	3,089.6	350.2	29.0	----	24.0	30.0	564.6
2017-18[3]	65.0	132.0	110.0	47.0	166.0	335.0	3,152.0	493.5	29.0	----	65.0	50.0	768.8

[1] Preliminary.   [2] Estimate.   [3] Forecast.   *Source: The Oil World*

Onions

Onions are the bulbs of plants in the lily family. Onions can be eaten raw, cooked, pickled, used as a flavoring or seasoning, or dehydrated. Onions rank in the top 10 vegetables produced in the U.S. in terms of dollar value. Since 1629, onions have been cultivated in the U.S., but are believed to be indigenous to Asia.

The two main types of onions produced in the U.S. are yellow and white onions. Yellow varieties comprise approximately 75% of all onions grown for bulb production in the U.S. Onions that are planted as a winter crop in warm areas are milder in taste and odor than onions planted during the summer in cooler regions.

Prices – Onion prices in 2018 averaged $14.56 per hundred pounds, down -2.9% yr/yr.

Supply – U.S. production in 2015 fell -17.9% to 6.503 billion pounds, far below the 2004 record high of 12.031 billion pounds. The farm value of the U.S. production crop in 2017 fell -6.6% to $851,358, well below the 2006 record high of $1.084 billion. In 2017 U.S. farmers harvested only 130,000 acres, down -0.2% yr/yr to a new 2-decade low. The yield in 2017 was down -6.9% at 525 pounds per acre, down from the 2016 record high of 542 pounds per acre.

Demand – U.S. per capita consumption of onions in 2012 rose +3.4% yr/yr to 21.3 pounds.

Trade – U.S. exports of fresh onions in 2012 totaled 648 million pounds, and imports totaled 849 million pounds.

Salient Statistics of Onions in the United States

Crop Year	Harvested Acres	Yield Per Acre	Pro- duction 1,000 Cwt.	Price Per Cwt.	Farm Value $1,000	Jan. 1 Pack Frozen	Anual Pack Frozen	Imports Canned	Exports (Fresh)	Imports (Fresh)	Per Capita[3] Utilization -- Lbs., Farm Weight -- All	Fresh
							In Millions of Pounds					
2012	146,870	487	71,495	14.20	942,340	73.7	----	21.1	651.6	876.8	20.8	19.5
2013	143,340	486	69,654	15.00	969,183	58.0	----		702.4	994.4	19.4	18.5
2014	139,150	523	72,806	13.60	933,630	49.8	----		657.1	1,134.7	19.8	18.3
2015	132,900	507	67,380	17.60	993,360	45.0	----		605.5	1,109.7	20.3	18.9
2016	132,600	542	71,866	16.80	925,833	45.0	----		671.6	1,190.6	20.8	19.0
2017[1]	138,000	532	73,460	13.50	971,236	62.1	----		679.1	1,153.6	22.4	21.9
2018[2]	138,400	506	69,998	13.00	891,413	69.8	----					

[1] Preliminary. [2] Forecast. [3] Includes fresh and processing. *Source: Economic Research Service, U.S. Department of Agriculture (ERS-USDA)*

Production of Onions in the United States   In Thousands of Hundredweight (Cwt.)

Crop Year	Arizona	Cali- fornia	Texas	Total (All)	Cali- fornia	Colo- rado	Idaho	Mich- igan	Minne- sota	Mexico	New York	Oregon, Malheur	Texas	Total (All)	Grand Total
		---- Spring ----							Summer						
2009	576	2,460	3,003	8,523	14,287	2,739	6,512	1,330	----	----	4,275	7,840	----	67,076	75,599
2010	----	2,542	2,666	7,484	13,050	2,880	6,840	880	----	----	3,087	8,588	----	66,115	73,599
2011	----	2,520	3,360	8,845	12,980	2,864	7,176	816	----	----	1,891	8,249	----	65,252	74,097
2012	----	2,480	3,090	8,008	12,354	2,604	6,205	644	----	----	2,480	7,950	----	63,487	71,495
2013	----	2,720	3,492	9,209	11,700	1,700	7,380	810	----	----	2,015	7,848	----	60,445	69,654
2014	----	2,992	2,340	7,917	16,120	1,800	5,658	925	----	----	2,360	7,440	----	64,889	72,806
2015[1]	----	3,015	800	6,503	14,450	1,476	6,048	816	----	----	2,312	6,480	----	62,616	69,119

[1] Preliminary. *Source: Agricultural Statistics Board, U.S. Department of Agiculture (ASB-USDA)*

Cold Storage Stocks of Frozen Onions in the United States, on First of Month   In Thousands of Pounds

Year	Jan.	Feb.	Mar.	Apr.	May	June	July	Aug.	Sept.	Oct.	Nov.	Dec.
2013	58,030	53,882	55,947	52,566	52,835	51,059	50,557	53,048	50,048	50,252	49,506	52,770
2014	49,806	50,425	47,054	46,423	46,175	50,046	55,773	64,252	60,862	52,736	50,282	45,791
2015	45,001	43,865	48,055	48,960	52,702	56,379	56,673	53,467	53,428	48,106	48,935	46,921
2016	45,024	46,533	48,136	50,950	58,093	57,549	57,806	54,588	61,991	58,574	59,158	59,871
2017	62,106	61,514	63,908	66,174	72,770	76,063	71,368	68,219	73,667	70,900	64,044	67,319
2018[1]	69,847	68,858	73,548	79,789	84,899	85,349	84,870	81,347	76,309	72,265	64,388	65,213

[1] Preliminary. *Source: National Agricultural Statistics Service, U.S. Department of Agiculture (NASS-USDA)*

Average Price Received by Growers for Onions in the United States   In Dollars Per Hundred Pounds (Cwt.)

Year	Jan.	Feb.	Mar.	Apr.	May	June	July	Aug.	Sept.	Oct.	Nov.	Dec.	Season Average
2013	32.30	28.80	21.10	NQ	NQ	NQ	NQ	NQ	NQ	NQ	NQ	NQ	15.00
2014	NQ	NQ	NQ	25.10	27.20	17.30	23.50	14.50	11.90	10.30	9.12	9.56	13.60
2015	8.39	7.67	7.89	18.90	19.30	30.20	31.90	15.60	11.80	12.50	12.00	12.20	17.60
2016	14.40	15.30	14.90	21.10	25.80	27.70	26.70	12.70	9.78	7.58	6.76	6.43	16.80
2017	11.10	8.82	7.77	14.00	14.00	20.90	22.30	13.60	16.40	16.30	15.60	17.00	15.00
2018[1]	15.00	13.20	11.60	14.80	17.10	18.20	21.40	15.20	11.20	11.20	11.30	10.90	

[1] Preliminary.   NQ = Not quoted.   *Source: Economic Research Service, U.S. Department of Agiculture (ERS-USDA)*

Oranges and Orange Juice

The orange tree is a semi-tropical, non-deciduous tree, and the fruit is technically a hesperidium, a kind of berry. The three major varieties of oranges include the sweet orange, the sour orange, and the mandarin orange (or tangerine). In the U.S., only sweet oranges are grown commercially. Those include Hamlin, Jaffa, navel, Pineapple, blood orange, and Valencia. Sour oranges are mainly used in marmalade and in liqueurs such as triple sec and curacao.

Frozen Concentrated Orange Juice (FCOJ) was developed in 1945, which led to oranges becoming the main fruit crop in the U.S. The world's largest producer of orange juice is Brazil, followed by Florida. Two to four medium-sized oranges will produce about 1 cup of juice, and modern mechanical extractors can remove the juice from 400 to 700 oranges per minute. Before juice extraction, orange oil is recovered from the peel. Approximately 50% of the orange weight is juice, the remainder is peel, pulp, and seeds, which are dried to produce nutritious cattle feed.

The U.S. marketing year for oranges begins December 1 of the first year shown (e.g., the 2005-06 marketing year extends from December 1, 2005 to November 30, 2006). Orange juice futures prices are subject to upward spikes during the U.S. hurricane season (officially June 1 to November 30), and the Florida freeze season (late-November through March).

Frozen concentrate orange juice futures and options are traded at the Intercontinental Exchange (ICE). The ICE orange juice futures contract calls for the delivery of 15,000 pounds of orange solids and is priced in terms of cents per pound.

Prices – ICE frozen concentrate orange juice (FCOJ) futures prices (Barchart.com symbol OJ) traded sideways to higher the first half of 2018 and posted a 1-3/4 year high in May of 172.45 cents. Global orange production concerns boosted prices after 2018/19 orange production in Brazil, the world's largest orange producer, fell to 275.75 million boxes, down -31% yr/yr and -12% below the 10-year average due to drought. Also, U.S. weather concerns spurred fund buying after Colorado State University forecast that the 2018 Atlantic hurricane season would be above average. U.S. 2017/18 orange production was already decimated by Hurricane Irma with the 2017/18 Florida orange crop plunging to a 73-year low of 45 million boxes, down -35% yr/yr. However, FCOJ prices ratcheted lower the rest of the year as the Atlantic hurricane season remained quiet and U.S. orange crop estimates were raised. The USDA in December estimated that the 2018/19 Florida orange crop would jump +71% yr/yr to 78 million boxes on ideal weather conditions. FCOJ prices finished 2018 down -8.0% yr/yr at 125.15 cents.

Supply – World production of oranges in the 2017/18 marketing year are forecasted to fall -7.6% yr/yr to 49,282 million metric tons. The world's largest producers of oranges in 2017/18 marketing year are forecasted to be Brazil with 35.2% of world production, followed by the China with 14.8%, European Union with 12.7%, Mexico with 9.3%, and the U.S. with 7.3%.

U.S. production of oranges in 2016/17 fell -15.1% yr/yr to 120.420 million boxes (1 box equals 90 lbs). Florida's production in 2016/17 fell -14.0% yr/yr to 68.750 million boxes and California's production fell -15.9% yr/yr to 50.300 million boxes.

World Production of Oranges   In Thousands of Metric Tons

Year	Argentina	Australia	Brazil	China	Egypt	European Union	Mexico	Morocco	South Africa	Turkey	United States	Vietnam	World Total
2008-09	900	430	17,014	6,000	2,372	6,530	4,193	790	1,445	1,430	8,281	679	50,833
2009-10	770	380	15,830	6,500	2,401	6,244	4,051	823	1,459	1,690	7,478	694	49,181
2010-11	850	300	22,603	5,900	2,430	6,198	4,080	904	1,428	1,710	8,078	729	55,990
2011-12	565	390	20,482	6,900	2,350	6,023	3,666	850	1,466	1,650	8,166	531	53,841
2012-13	550	435	16,361	7,000	2,450	5,890	4,400	784	1,659	1,600	7,501	521	49,862
2013-14	800	430	17,870	7,600	2,570	6,550	4,533	1,001	1,723	1,700	6,140	590	52,236
2014-15	800	430	16,714	6,600	2,635	5,954	4,515	868	1,645	1,650	5,763	566	48,752
2015-16[1]	800	455	14,414	6,900	2,930	6,038	4,603	925	1,275	1,800	5,523	637	47,057
2016-17[2]	620	480	20,400	7,000	3,000	6,779	4,640	1,037	1,400	1,850	4,685	635	53,265
2017-18[3]	850	480	17,340	7,300	3,180	6,258	4,600	935	1,430	1,905	3,618	635	49,282

[1] Preliminary.   [2] Estimate.   [3] Forecast.   NA = Not available.   *Source: Foreign Agricultural Service, U.S. Department of Agriculture (FAS-USDA)*

Salient Statistics of Oranges & Orange Juice in the United States

	Production[4]					Florida Crop Processed				Frozen Concentrated Orange Juice - Florida			
Year	California	Florida	Total U.S.	Farm Price $ Per Box	Farm Value Million $	Frozen Concentrates	Chilled Products	Total Processed	Yield Per Box Gallons[5]	Carry-in	Pack	Total Supply	Total Season Movement
	Million Boxes					Million Boxes				In Millions of Gallons (42 Deg. Brix)			
2007-08	62.0	170.2	234.4	9.36	2,198.8	80.8	84.7	165.5	1.7	52.1	135.6	187.7	137.7
2008-09	46.5	162.5	210.7	9.22	1,970.1	72.5	82.6	156.2	1.7	108.0	153.9	261.9	143.9
2009-10	57.5	133.7	192.8	10.24	1,997.2	52.7	74.9	128.2	1.6	118.0	82.3	200.3	130.2
2010-11	62.5	140.5	204.9	10.90	2,230.4	51.8	82.6	135.2	1.6	95.0	82.1	177.1	148.5
2011-12	58.0	146.7	206.1	12.70	2,621.6	65.4	75.5	141.3	1.6	51.6	175.4	227.0	124.3
2012-13	54.5	133.6	189.9	10.85	2,073.6	48.0	79.2	127.6	1.6	61.1	127.9	189.0	108.4
2013-14	49.5	104.7	156.0	14.29	2,254.3	22.7	76.0	99.2	1.6	76.9	85.4	162.3	97.3
2014-15[1]	48.2	97.0	146.6	13.29	1,963.4	19.2	71.9	92.0	1.5	66.0	72.6	138.5	86.2
2015-16[2]	58.5	81.7	141.9	13.55	1,927.3	15.8	61.8	77.8	1.4	70.8	63.7	134.5	88.2
2016-17[3]	50.3	68.8	120.4	15.16	1,844.5	12.6	53.2	65.9	1.4	52.7	55.9	108.6	87.4

[1] Preliminary.   [2] Estimate.   [3] Forecast.   4/ Fruit ripened on trees, but destroyed prior to picking not included.   [5] 42 deg. Brix equivalent.
Source: Economic Research Service, U.S. Department of Agriculture (ERS-USDA); Florida Department of Citrus

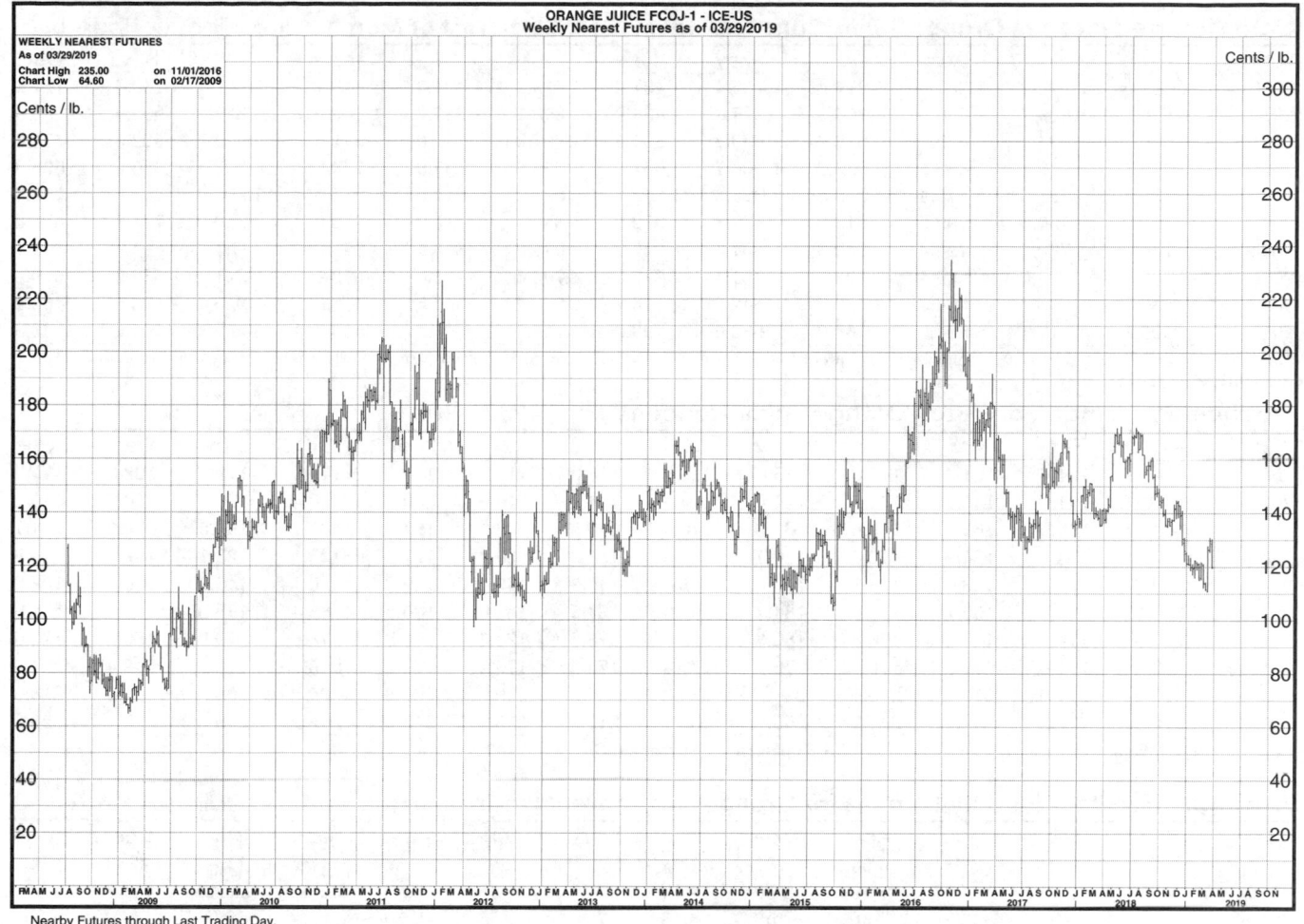

ORANGE JUICE FCOJ-1 - ICE-US
Weekly Nearest Futures as of 03/29/2019

WEEKLY NEAREST FUTURES
As of 03/29/2019
Chart High 235.00 on 11/01/2016
Chart Low 64.60 on 02/17/2009

Nearby Futures through Last Trading Day.

Volume of Trading of Frozen Concentrated Orange Juice Futures in New York   In Contracts

Year	Jan.	Feb.	Mar.	Apr.	May	June	July	Aug.	Sept.	Oct.	Nov.	Dec.	Total
2009	28,514	63,757	31,766	67,156	30,396	81,964	56,197	65,286	40,276	86,071	28,426	77,186	656,995
2010	55,002	62,671	42,726	73,654	36,599	63,734	37,098	64,224	50,953	72,996	34,959	96,967	691,583
2011	39,184	63,134	43,077	63,680	41,142	89,150	28,260	80,733	32,920	59,502	24,493	62,335	627,610
2012	59,578	68,746	29,672	58,405	42,001	56,218	28,654	57,465	31,796	51,993	36,729	65,518	586,775
2013	46,432	54,711	37,532	67,361	31,399	63,622	26,724	43,047	29,937	40,275	24,295	39,684	505,019
2014	27,095	39,560	29,605	51,337	24,033	51,811	21,141	36,438	18,068	35,974	27,182	35,685	398,529
2015	21,377	37,435	34,855	39,065	23,789	42,032	18,914	42,607	24,694	48,774	28,965	36,060	398,567
2016	28,008	34,218	25,553	40,101	20,743	50,207	24,414	47,704	24,848	49,991	22,202	45,915	413,904
2017	30,883	37,187	35,311	33,218	25,193	34,836	18,627	36,316	34,697	25,936	16,504	34,791	363,499
2018	23,671	29,581	16,795	36,685	27,571	36,726	16,771	40,982	18,075	46,573	25,131	38,293	356,854

Contract size = 15,000 lbs.   Source: ICE Futures U.S. (ICE)

Average Open Interest of Frozen Concentrated Orange Juice Futures in New York   In Contracts

Year	Jan.	Feb.	Mar.	Apr.	May	June	July	Aug.	Sept.	Oct.	Nov.	Dec.
2009	27,889	28,234	26,905	27,982	29,370	31,608	30,602	31,281	28,806	30,805	29,677	34,210
2010	35,442	34,435	35,991	31,854	29,524	29,143	26,424	27,037	27,400	29,340	28,707	29,996
2011	31,885	31,086	27,618	27,153	31,594	36,039	35,046	28,253	23,967	25,308	27,118	27,105
2012	26,892	23,743	21,892	20,278	22,652	25,461	21,779	23,214	23,078	23,687	22,412	24,458
2013	20,672	20,900	18,819	20,972	20,719	22,432	19,760	19,241	16,646	15,809	14,609	14,636
2014	15,542	15,905	16,793	18,372	18,487	17,605	13,552	13,068	12,175	13,385	13,798	12,089
2015	10,973	12,605	15,506	15,799	14,630	14,192	12,421	13,196	13,358	15,172	14,651	14,759
2016	12,887	12,224	12,408	13,452	13,239	17,154	18,182	16,433	16,312	15,940	16,285	14,857
2017	12,528	11,357	10,887	11,104	11,212	11,929	11,277	11,441	8,972	8,741	9,378	9,882
2018	10,670	10,703	12,349	13,460	14,934	15,644	15,041	14,133	13,370	16,227	17,994	16,807

Contract size = 15,000 lbs.   Source: ICE Futures U.S. (ICE)

ORANGES AND ORANGE JUICE

Cold Storage Stocks of Orange Juice Concentrate[2] in the U.S., on First of Month   In Millions of Pounds

Year	Jan.	Feb.	Mar.	Apr.	May	June	July	Aug.	Sept.	Oct.	Nov.	Dec.
2009	1,088.0	1,193.2	1,261.2	1,291.4	1,415.4	1,497.2	1,519.7	1,404.3	1,316.7	1,252.2	1,150.3	1,127.2
2010	1,185.2	1,289.7	1,300.4	1,305.1	1,377.6	1,434.2	1,353.1	1,235.7	1,133.9	1,036.8	903.6	795.3
2011	809.7	834.7	869.2	842.0	835.2	864.5	797.3	732.0	641.5	588.9	522.3	479.6
2012	632.1	710.1	788.8	889.0	1,006.7	1,057.6	956.6	857.9	773.6	675.6	606.4	598.0
2013	695.4	781.6	875.4	946.8	1,021.3	1,042.3	996.2	915.0	864.6	795.8	785.9	732.6
2014	739.5	750.5	799.3	813.0	877.8	872.9	853.7	815.9	773.0	712.0	721.9	676.8
2015	734.8	720.7	728.4	832.3	857.5	947.9	943.8	868.1	807.8	757.1	695.9	641.7
2016	639.3	623.0	633.4	702.0	751.4	772.5	766.5	711.0	653.1	603.1	579.9	519.6
2017	516.6	503.4	506.3	517.1	542.2	575.4	544.4	505.5	471.5	495.6	493.5	468.1
2018[1]	505.1	517.1	501.0	564.0	632.6	730.9	733.7	691.1	633.4	609.0	566.4	528.8

[1] Preliminary.   [2] Adjusted to 42.0 degrees Brix equivalent (9.896 pounds per gallon).   Source: Agricultural Statistics Board, U.S. Department of Agriculture (ASB-USDA)

Producer Price Index of Frozen Orange Juice Concentrate   1982 = 100

Year	Jan.	Feb.	Mar.	Apr.	May	June	July	Aug.	Sept.	Oct.	Nov.	Dec.	Average
2009	124.6	124.4	124.4	117.6	125.0	118.0	118.0	119.8	119.1	119.0	119.0	128.8	121.5
2010	141.3	141.1	141.5	144.5	144.5	144.5	144.7	145.0	150.0	150.4	150.4	150.6	145.7
2011	164.1	163.9	163.9	169.6	169.8	170.4	170.8	188.8	187.6	181.7	190.5	175.7	174.7
2012	177.5	188.7	184.9	173.4	170.7	133.5	131.6	130.0	127.0	125.5	123.1	132.0	149.8
2013	130.8	122.6	123.0	124.1	145.6	148.6	145.5	149.2	149.2	136.7	140.1	140.9	138.0
2014	138.3	139.0	135.1	184.0	184.4	184.6	184.5	184.0	190.2	183.4	178.3	178.1	172.0
2015	177.8	178.2	178.2	176.5	180.3	178.3	178.8	178.6	178.3	178.6	179.0	180.4	178.6
2016	169.5	171.6	171.8	176.8	176.6	177.4	178.0	170.8	170.4	215.1	215.6	216.4	184.2
2017	218.0	217.9	219.8	218.5	220.7	220.8	229.5	229.9	209.8	209.8	209.8	211.0	218.0
2018[1]	210.2	210.2	243.5	247.7	255.5	255.1	215.2	215.2	215.6	215.2	215.6	216.1	226.3

[1] Preliminary.   Source: Bureau of Labor Statistics, U.S. Department of Labor (BLS)

Average Price Received by Farmers for Oranges (Equivalent On-Tree) in the U.S.   In Dollars Per Box

Year	Jan.	Feb.	Mar.	Apr.	May	June	July	Aug.	Sept.	Oct.	Nov.	Dec.	Average
2009	5.74	6.04	7.08	6.54	6.61	7.04	7.38	8.58	W	W	11.61	6.13	7.28
2010	6.41	6.78	7.97	7.49	8.00	8.85	7.10	7.49	6.88	6.96	11.47	6.66	7.67
2011	6.58	6.50	6.77	7.00	7.53	8.46	7.74	7.53	7.60	8.47	8.86	7.29	7.53
2012	7.65	8.25	8.52	9.53	10.35	12.49	9.60	7.81	9.08	9.57	8.92	6.64	9.03
2013	6.85	7.05	7.84	8.46	9.27	12.85	10.64	10.00	12.24	12.94	13.07	6.93	9.85
2014	8.24	10.71	10.90	9.68	10.27	11.12	14.60	14.78	15.84	13.82	16.26	9.43	12.14
2015	9.35	9.85	11.32	10.78	10.74	10.53	10.79	12.01	15.25	17.73	17.35	9.59	12.11
2016	8.96	9.78	9.30	9.08	9.47	8.21	8.19	8.62	8.66	10.11	16.57	9.64	9.72
2017	9.63	11.62	12.35	11.81	12.46	18.53	20.33	18.18	20.52	25.61	16.47	12.55	15.84
2018[1]	15.06	20.57	14.96	14.20	16.41	23.05	18.90	17.78	21.18	19.02	15.71	10.68	17.29

[1] Preliminary.   Source: Economic Research Service, U.S. Department of Agriculture (ERS-USDA)

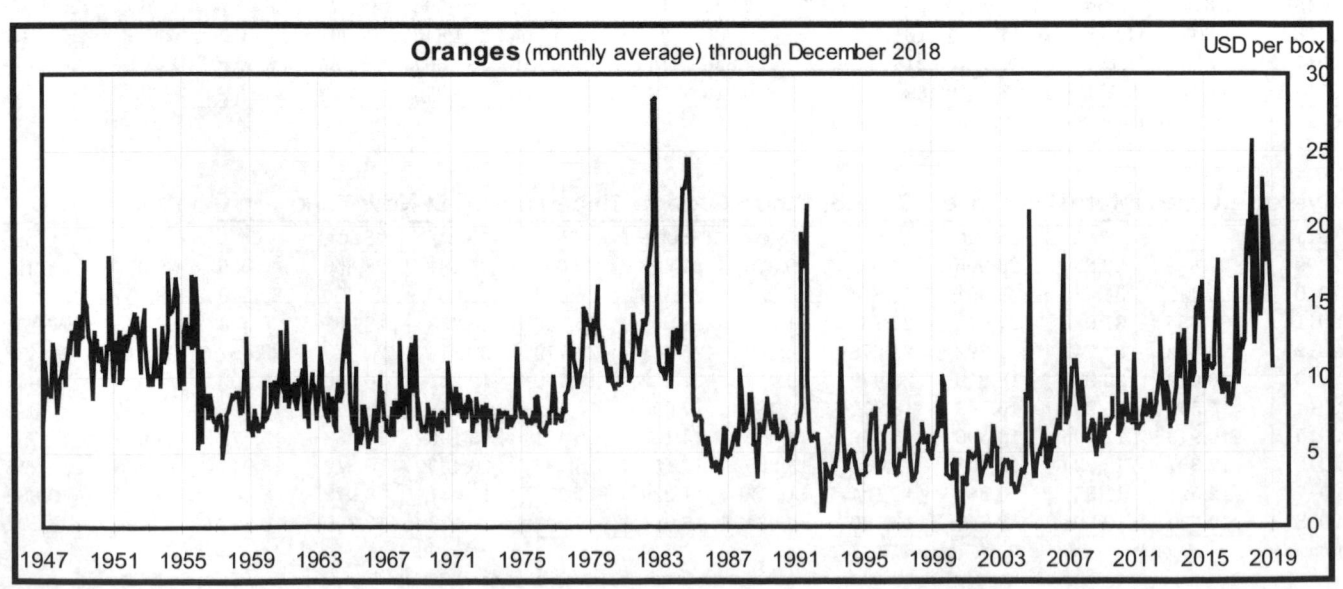

Oranges (monthly average) through December 2018   USD per box

Palm Oil

Palm oil is an edible vegetable oil produced from the flesh of the fruit of the oil palm tree. The oil palm tree is a tropical palm tree that is a native of the west coast of Africa and is different from the coconut palm tree. The fruit of the oil palm tree is reddish, about the size of a large plum, and grows in large bunches. A single seed, the palm kernel, is contained in each fruit. Oil is extracted from both the pulp of the fruit (becoming palm oil) and the kernel (palm kernel oil). About 1 metric ton of palm kernel oil is obtained for every 10 metric tons of palm oil.

Palm oil is commercially used in soap, ointments, cosmetics, detergents, and machinery lubricants. It is also used worldwide as cooking oil, shortening, and margarine. Palm kernel oil is a lighter oil and is used exclusively for food use. Crude palm oil and crude palm kernel oil are traded on the Kuala Lumpur Commodity Exchange.

Prices – The monthly average wholesale price of palm oil (CIF, bulk, U.S. ports) in 2017 rose by +14.6% yr/yr to 39.42 cents per pound, but still below the 2011 record high of 55.98 cents per pound.

Supply – World production of palm oil in the 2017/18 marketing year rose by +7.6% to 69.774 million metric tons. World palm oil production has grown by more than thirty times the production level of 1.922 million metric tons seen back in 1970. Indonesia and Malaysia are the world's two major global producers of palm oil. Indonesian production in 2017/18 rose +6.9% yr/yr to a record high of 38.500 million metric tons and Indonesian production will account for 55.2% of world production. Malaysian production in 2017/18 rose +8.7% to a record high of 20.500 million metric tons and Malaysian production will account for 31.0% of world production. Other smaller global producers include Thailand with 3.9% of world production, Columbia with 2.3%, and Nigeria with 1.4%.

Demand – U.S. total disappearance of palm oil in 2017/18 rose +4.7% yr/yr to 1.629 million metric tons which is a new record high.

Trade – World palm oil exports in 2017/18 rose +2.7% to 50.121 million metric tons, which is a new record high. The world's largest exporters were Indonesia with a 56.9% share of world exports and Malaysia with a share of 34.5%. World palm oil imports in 2017/18 rose +2.8% to 47.177 million metric tons. The world's largest importers were India with a 22.5% share of world imports and the European Union with a 13.8% share.

World Production of Palm Oil   In Thousands of Metric Tons

Crop Year	Brazil	Colombia	Costa Rica	Cote d'Ivoire	Ecuador	Guatemala	Honduras	Indonesia	Malaysia	Nigeria	Papua New Guinea	Thailand	World Total
2008-09	240	778	207	345	418	194	280	20,500	17,259	850	501	1,540	44,502
2009-10	250	805	227	330	429	177	275	22,000	17,763	850	510	1,287	46,401
2010-11	270	753	242	360	380	231	320	23,600	18,211	971	488	1,832	49,221
2011-12	310	945	260	371	473	291	395	26,200	18,202	970	580	1,892	52,565
2012-13	340	974	230	418	539	365	425	28,500	19,321	970	520	2,135	56,430
2013-14	370	1,041	210	415	499	434	460	30,500	20,161	970	500	2,000	59,362
2014-15	400	1,110	210	415	484	510	470	33,000	19,879	970	520	2,068	61,872
2015-16[1]	405	1,275	250	415	520	625	490	32,000	17,700	970	580	1,804	58,902
2016-17[2]	400	1,147	270	415	565	740	545	36,000	18,860	970	522	2,500	64,874
2017-18[3]	410	1,628	270	415	593	740	545	38,500	20,500	970	530	2,700	69,774

[1] Preliminary.   [2] Estimate.   [3] Forecast.   *Source: The Oil World*

World Trade of Palm Oil   In Thousands of Metric Tons

	------------------------------ Imports ------------------------------						------------------------------ Exports ------------------------------						
Crop Year	China	European Union	India	Pakistan	Other	World Total	Benin	European Union	Indonesia	Malaysia	Papua/ New Guinea	United Arab Emirates	World Total
2007-08	5,223	4,967	4,329	1,958	13,932	30,409	358	134	13,969	15,040	451	336	32,775
2008-09	6,118	5,509	6,090	1,957	13,711	33,385	352	131	15,964	15,990	496	232	35,276
2009-10	5,760	5,442	5,674	1,987	15,739	34,602	466	144	16,573	16,610	520	344	36,444
2010-11	5,711	4,944	5,584	2,062	17,296	35,597	255	200	16,423	17,151	578	400	37,272
2011-12	5,841	5,707	7,201	2,217	17,617	38,583	253	169	18,453	17,586	585	385	39,836
2012-13	6,589	6,812	8,364	2,245	18,123	42,133	430	135	20,373	18,524	564	217	43,157
2013-14	5,573	6,969	7,820	2,725	18,905	41,992	600	162	21,719	17,344	537	250	43,215
2014-15[1]	5,696	6,936	9,139	2,826	20,127	44,724	500	116	25,964	17,378	602	250	47,467
2015-16[2]	4,689	6,700	8,860	2,800	20,186	43,235	550	130	23,000	16,621	615	240	43,868
2016-17[3]	5,100	6,650	10,000	3,100	21,349	46,199	580	80	25,700	17,500	560	250	47,485

[1] Preliminary.   [2] Estimate.   [3] Forecast.   *Source: The Oil World*

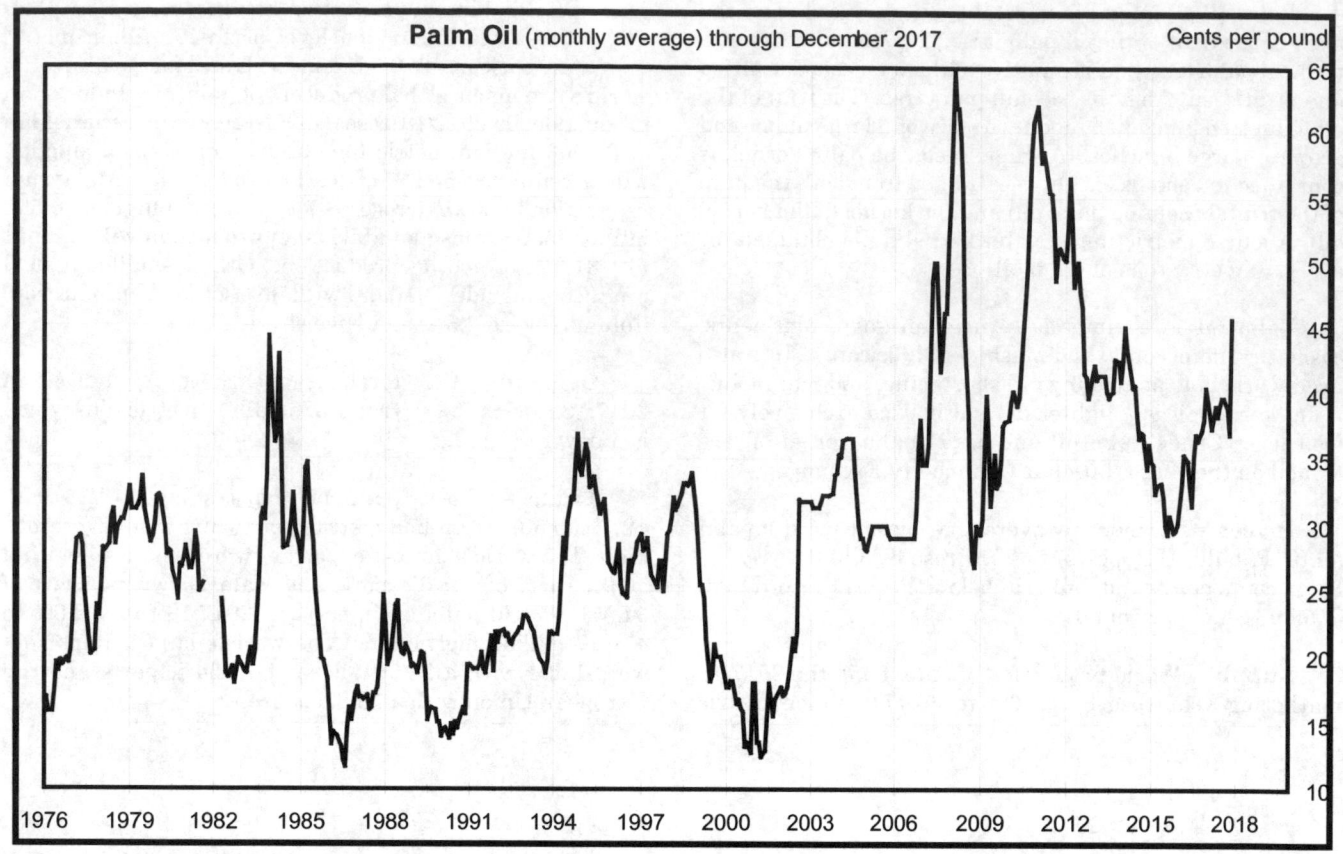

Palm Oil (monthly average) through December 2017 — Cents per pound

Supply and Distribution of Palm Oil in the United States   In Thousands of Metric Tons

Crop Year Beginning Oct. 1	Stocks Oct. 1	Imports	Total Supply	Consumption Edible Products	Consumption Inedible Products	Consumption Total End Products	Total Disappearance	Exports	U.S. Import Value[4]	Malaysia, F.O.B., RBD	Palm Kernel Oil, Malaysia, C.I.F Rotterdam
				------ In Millions of Pounds ------					--------- U.S. $ Per Metric Ton ---------		
2008-09	73.0	1,036.0	1,109.0	973.6	W	973.6	1,109.0	20.0	----	628	662
2009-10	130.0	994.0	1,124.0	1,140.8	W	1,140.8	1,124.0	16.0	----	807	972
2010-11	151.0	980.0	1,131.0	1,049.7	W	1,049.7	1,131.0	27.0	----	1146	1741
2011-12	147.0	1,032.0	1,179.0	NA	NA	NA	1,179.0	18.0	----	1053	1220
2012-13	118.0	1,293.0	1,411.0	----	----	----	1,411.0	37.0	----	835	836
2013-14	136.0	1,220.0	1,356.0	----	----	----	1,356.0	13.0	----	867	1146
2014-15	136.0	1,143.0	1,279.0	----	----	----	1,279.0	22.0	----	659	941
2015-16[1]	165.0	1,307.0	1,472.0	----	----	----	1,472.0	14.0	----	655	1126
2016-17[2]	189.0	1,367.0	1,556.0	----	----	----	1,556.0	17.0	----	751	1436
2017-18[3]	184.0	1,445.0	1,629.0	----	----	----	1,629.0	21.0	----		

[1] Preliminary.   [2] Estimate.   [3] Forecast.   [4] Market value in the foreign country, excluding import duties, ocean freight and marine insurance.
W = Withheld.   *Sources: The Oil World; Economic Research Service, U.S. Department of Agriculture (ERS-USDA)*

Average Wholesale Palm Oil Prices, CIF, Bulk, U.S. Ports   In Cents Per Pound

Year	Jan.	Feb.	Mar.	Apr.	May	June	July	Aug.	Sept.	Oct.	Nov.	Dec.	Average
2008	51.48	54.66	64.63	61.96	61.90	59.70	55.41	44.43	38.52	30.11	27.41	26.91	48.09
2009	29.98	29.32	30.32	35.46	39.86	36.45	31.40	35.39	32.90	33.24	34.66	37.53	33.88
2010	37.83	37.91	39.35	40.11	39.60	38.97	39.64	44.57	47.00	49.55	54.00	58.60	43.93
2011	60.88	62.06	60.44	57.80	58.44	57.56	55.40	55.25	53.25	48.63	51.00	51.05	55.98
2012	50.25	50.19	52.60	56.56	52.94	48.20	50.06	47.75	46.63	41.44	41.25	39.69	48.13
2013	41.38	42.06	41.00	41.38	41.35	41.31	40.19	39.70	40.00	40.19	42.65	42.38	41.13
2014	40.90	42.50	45.00	43.44	42.40	40.38	40.63	38.35	36.56	37.00	36.94	34.19	39.86
2015	36.05	34.88	34.50	32.38	33.05	33.19	32.15	29.88	29.25	30.75	29.50	29.60	32.10
2016	30.06	31.44	32.80	35.35	34.94	33.00	31.45	35.25	36.85	36.44	37.13	37.95	34.39
2017	40.38	39.56	38.50	37.38	39.06	38.30	39.00	39.63	39.69	38.94	36.88	45.75	39.42

Source: Economic Research Service, U.S. Department of Agriculture (ERS-USDA)

Paper

The earliest known paper that is still in existence was made from cotton rags around 150 AD. Around 800 AD, paper made its appearance in Egypt but was not manufactured there until 900 AD. The Moors introduced the use of paper to Europe, and around 1150, the first papermaking mill was established in Spain, followed by England in 1495, and the U.S. in 1690.

During the 17th and 18th centuries, the increased usage of paper created a shortage of cotton rags, which were the only source for papermaking. The solution to this problem lead to the introduction of the ground-wood process of pulp-making in 1840 and the first chemical pulp process 10 years later.

Today, the paper and paperboard industries, including newsprint, are sensitive to the economic cycle. As the economy strengthens, paper use increases, and vice versa.

Prices – The average monthly index price (1982 = 100) for paperboard in 2018 rose +6.2% yr/yr to 273.6, a new record high. The average monthly producer price index of standard newsprint paper in 2018 rose by +16.9% to 138.5, well below the 11-year high of 151.8 posted in 2006.

Supply – U.S. production of paper and paperboard in 2017 rose +0.2% yr/yr to 72.045 million metric tons.

The U.S. is the world's largest producer of paper and paperboard by far with 17.6% of the world's supply, followed by Germany at 5.6%. Canada with 2.4%, Finland and Sweden both with 2.5%.

Production of Paper and Paperboard by Selected Countries   In Thousands of Metric Tons

Year	Austria	Canada	Finland	France	Germany	Italy	Nether-lands	Norway	Russia/3	Spain	Sweden	United Kingdom	United States
2012	5,004	10,756	10,847	8,354	22,603	8,588	2,761	1,209	7,670	6,177	11,417	4,292	74,492
2013	4,837	11,174	10,592	8,043	22,401	8,652	2,792	1,079	7,747	6,685	10,792	4,561	71,732
2014	4,865	10,775	10,408	8,096	22,540	8,648	2,767	1,023	8,023	6,036	10,419	4,397	73,093
2015	4,965	10,300	10,320	7,984	22,601	8,840	2,643	979	8,068	6,195	10,255	3,970	72,397
2016	4,995	9,911	10,140	7,984	22,629	8,888	2,671	1,099	8,547	6,219	10,102	3,677	71,902
2017[1]	4,860	9,867	10,280	8,022	22,931	8,888	2,983	1,097	8,569	6,218	10,261	3,855	72,045

[1] Preliminary.   *Source: Food and Agriculture Organization of the United Nations (FAO)*

Production of Newsprint by Selected Countires (Monthly Average)   In Thousands of Metric Tons

Year	Australia	Brazil	Canada	China	Finland	France	Germany	India	Japan	Korea, South	Russia	Sweden	United States
2013	----	----	----	305.4	----	----	176.4	----	268.2	124.1	132.1	127.4	----
2014	----	----	----	282.5	----	----	NA	----	261.1	118.1	136.3	104.0	----
2015	----	----	----	278.9	----	----	----	----	248.7	113.7	124.1	99.7	----
2016	----	----	----	244.5	----	----	----	----	242.1	117.9	122.5	84.7	----
2017[1]	----	----	----	212.9	----	----	----	----	231.6	100.0	119.9	84.2	----
2018[2]	----	----	----	158.0	----	----	----	----	224.5		124.4	80.4	----

[1] Preliminary.   [2] Estimate.   *Source: Food and Agriculture Organization of the United Nations (FAO)*

Index Price of Paperboard   (1982 = 100)

Year	Jan.	Feb.	Mar.	Apr.	May	June	July	Aug.	Sept.	Oct.	Nov.	Dec.	Average
2012	226.4	226.3	225.9	226.1	226.0	225.9	224.9	226.1	226.6	230.3	235.5	235.7	228.0
2013	235.7	235.8	236.8	236.8	241.1	246.4	247.7	249.3	249.0	249.0	248.8	248.3	243.7
2014	249.0	249.6	249.7	249.2	249.3	249.3	249.2	248.8	247.7	247.3	247.0	246.9	248.6
2015	246.9	245.2	244.5	242.6	243.6	242.6	241.9	241.4	242.2	242.1	242.2	242.0	243.1
2016	241.2	236.0	232.2	230.6	230.9	230.5	230.6	230.0	230.0	232.3	236.2	240.7	233.4
2017	244.7	244.1	244.2	249.3	252.5	262.7	264.0	264.5	265.5	266.3	266.1	266.6	257.5
2018[1]	265.5	265.9	264.8	266.6	275.6	276.8	278.3	278.1	277.9	278.2	277.5	277.9	273.6

[1] Preliminary.   *Source: Bureau of Labor Statistics, U.S. Department of Commerce (BLS) (0914)*

Producer Price Index of Standard Newsprint   (1982 = 100)

Year	Jan.	Feb.	Mar.	Apr.	May	June	July	Aug.	Sept.	Oct.	Nov.	Dec.	Average
2012	138.9	138.6	143.9	144.1	144.1	138.7	138.4	138.2	138.3	138.1	137.9	138.1	139.8
2013	136.3	132.6	130.1	129.7	129.1	127.8	130.8	129.6	129.4	129.9	131.3	130.3	130.6
2014	130.7	130.5	130.2	129.2	128.3	129.2	129.1	129.0	128.7	128.4	128.1	127.2	129.1
2015	126.3	123.3	121.4	119.1	116.1	114.4	112.9	106.5	106.3	105.6	105.4	105.4	113.6
2016	106.7	109.6	111.9	112.3	113.3	114.9	116.4	117.8	118.3	118.4	118.1	118.3	114.7
2017	118.8	118.3	117.4	117.0	117.3	118.1	118.0	117.5	118.0	118.1	120.8	122.9	118.5
2018[1]	124.8	127.0	128.1	130.4	136.0	141.2	143.5	146.0	146.3	146.2	146.1	146.3	138.5

[1] Preliminary.   *Source: Bureau of Labor Statistics, U.S. Department of Commerce (BLS) (0913-02)*

Peanuts and Peanut Oil

Peanuts are the edible seeds of a plant from the pea family. Although called a nut, the peanut is actually a legume. Ancient South American Inca Indians were the first to grind peanuts to make peanut butter. Peanuts originated in Brazil and were later brought to the U.S. via Africa. The first major use of peanuts was as feed for pigs. It wasn't until the Civil War that peanuts were used as human food when both Northern and Southern troops used the peanut as a food source during hard times. In 1903, Dr. George Washington Carver, a talented botanist who is considered the "father of commercial peanuts," introduced peanuts as a rotation crop in cotton-growing areas. Carver discovered over 300 uses for the peanut including shaving cream, leather dye, coffee, ink, cheese, and shampoo.

Peanuts come in many varieties, but there are four basic types grown in the U.S.: Runner, Spanish, Valencia, and Virginia. Over half of Runner peanuts are used to make peanut butter. Spanish peanuts are primarily used to make candies and peanut oil. Valencia peanuts are the sweetest of the four types. Virginia peanuts are mainly roasted and sold in and out of the shell.

Peanut oil is extracted from shelled and crushed peanuts through hydraulic pressing, expelled pressing, or solvent extraction. Crude peanut oil is used as a flavoring agent, salad oil, and cooking oil. Refined, bleached and deodorized peanut oil is used for cooking and in margarines and shortenings. The by-product called press cake is used for cattle feed along with the tops of the plants after the pods are removed. The dry shells can be burned as fuel.

Prices – The average monthly price received by farmers for peanuts (in the shell) in the first four months of the 2018/19 marketing year (Aug/July) fell -4.6% to 21.9 cents per pound. The record high is 34.7 cents posted in 1990/91. The average monthly price of peanut oil in the 2018/19 marketing year (through December 2019) fell – 1.4% yr/yr to 65.72 cents per pound, below the 2007/08 record high of 100.91 cents per pound.

Supply – World peanut production in 2018/19 is forecasted to fall -2.1% to 44.508 million metric tons, down from last year's record high of 45.561. The world's largest peanut producers are expected to be China with 39.1% of world production, India with 14.3%, U. S. with 7.2%, and Nigeria with 7.0%.

U.S. peanut production in the 2018/19 marketing year is expected to fall by -23.1% yr/yr to 5.472 billion pounds, down from last year's record high of 7.115. U.S. farmers are expected to harvest 1.345 million acres of peanuts in 2018/19, down -24.2% yr/yr. That will be below the 30-year high harvest of 2.015 million acres in 1992-93. U.S. peanut yield in 2018/19 is expected to rise +1.5% yr/yr to 4,066 pounds per acre, still below the 2012/13 record high of 4,211 pounds per acre. The largest peanut producing states in the U.S. in 2018 were Georgia with 51.5% of U.S. production, Alabama with 11.6%, Florida with 9.3%, Texas with 8.2%, North Carolina with 7.1%, and South Carolina with 5.2%. U.S. crude peanut oil production in 2017/18 fell -20.1% to 358.282 million pounds.

Demand – U.S. disposition of peanuts in 2018/19 is expected to fall -2.2% yr/yr to 5.996 billion pounds. Of that disposition, 53.9% of the peanuts will go for food, 20.0% for exports, 13.4% for crushing into peanut oil, and 12.6% for seed, loss and residual. The most popular type of peanut grown in the U.S. is the Runner peanut with 88.0% of U.S. production in 2017/18. This was followed by the Virginia peanut with 11.2% of production and the Spanish peanut far behind with only 1.25% of production. Peanut butter is a primary use for Runner and Virginia peanuts. It accounts for 58.2% of Runner peanut usage and 49.8% of Virginia peanut usage. In lagging third place, only about 5% of Spanish peanuts was used for peanut butter. Snack peanuts is also a key usage category and accounts for 32.4% of Virginia peanut usage, 21.4% of Runner peanut usage, and 20.7% of Spanish peanut usage. Candy accounts for 80.9% of Spanish peanut usage, 17.1% of Runner peanut usage, and 5.8% of Virginia peanut usage.

Trade – U.S. exports of peanuts in 2018/19 are expected to fall -5.7% yr/yr to 1.200 billion pounds. U.S. imports of peanuts are expected to fall by -50.1% yr/yr in 2018/19 to 75 million pounds.

World Production of Peanuts (in the Shell)   In Thousands of Metric Tons

Crop Year	Argen-tina	Burma	Came-roon	China	India	Indo-nesia	Nigeria	Senegal	Sudan	Tanzania	United States	Vietnam	World Total
2009-10	836	1,305	503	14,708	5,120	1,250	2,978	1,033	942	348	1,675	525	36,369
2010-11	1,033	1,362	536	15,644	5,840	1,250	3,799	1,287	763	465	1,886	441	39,922
2011-12	1,020	1,399	564	16,046	6,015	1,165	2,963	528	1,185	651	1,660	471	39,364
2012-13	1,016	1,372	634	16,692	4,334	1,145	3,314	693	1,032	810	3,064	468	41,157
2013-14	997	1,375	636	16,972	6,482	1,160	2,475	677	1,767	1,425	1,893	455	42,583
2014-15	1,188	1,375	579	16,482	4,855	1,150	3,399	669	1,871	1,635	2,354	452	42,128
2015-16	930	1,375	609	16,440	4,470	1,130	3,467	1,050	1,042	1,836	2,722	441	41,711
2016-17	1,288	1,375	748	17,290	6,700	1,120	3,029	945	1,826	1,100	2,532	462	44,858
2017-18[1]	880	1,375	600	17,800	6,500	1,075	3,200	1,412	1,400	1,100	3,281	450	45,561
2018-19[2]	1,070	1,375	600	18,100	6,000	1,060	3,200	1,000	1,400	1,100	2,776	450	44,598

[1] Preliminary.   [2] Estimate.   *Source: Foreign Agricultural Service, U.S. Department of Agriculture (FAS-USDA)*

Salient Statistics of Peanuts in the United States

Crop Year Beginning Aug. 1	Acreage Planted (1,000 Acres)	Acreage Harvested for Nuts (1,000 Acres)	Average Yield Per Acre In Lbs.	Pro-duction (1,000 Lbs)	Season Farm Price (Cents Lb.)	Farm Value (Million Dollars)	In Thousands of Pounds			
							Exports		Imports	
							Unshelled	Shelled	Unshelled	Shelled
2009-10	1,116.0	1,079.0	3,421	3,691,650	21.7	793.1	592,000	402,732	71,972	49,454
2010-11	1,288.0	1,255.0	3,312	4,156,840	22.5	938.6	606,000	395,554	64,592	46,031
2011-12	1,140.6	1,080.6	3,386	3,658,590	31.8	1,168.6	546,000	352,994	253,897	163,852
2012-13	1,638.0	1,604.0	4,211	6,753,880	30.1	2,026.3	1,190,000	741,103	118,743	72,871
2013-14	1,067.0	1,043.0	4,001	4,173,170	24.9	1,055.1	1,096,000	708,141	88,000	60,738
2014-15	1,353.5	1,322.5	3,923	5,188,665	22.0	1,158.3	1,080,000	676,509	90,000	64,345
2015-16	1,625.0	1,560.9	3,845	6,001,357	19.3	1,160.6	1,544,000		94,000	
2016-17	1,671.0	1,536.0	3,634	5,581,570	19.7	1,088.2	1,328,000		162,000	
2017-18[1]	1,871.6	1,775.6	4,007	7,115,410	22.9	1,638.1	1,273,000		171,000	
2018-19[2]	1,425.5	1,368.5	3,991	5,461,600	19.25-23.25		1,250,000		75,000	

[1] Preliminary. [2] Estimate. Source: Economic Research Service, U.S. Department of Agriculture (ERS-USDA)

Supply and Disposition of Peanuts (Farmer's Stock Basis) in the United States

Crop Year Beginning Aug. 1	Supply				Disposition				
	Pro-duction	Imports	Stocks Aug. 1	Total	Exports	Crushed for Oil	Seed, Loss & Residual	Food	Total Disap-pearance
	In Millions of Pounds								
2010-11	1,829	4,157	65	6,050	2,840	587	350	606	4,382
2011-12	1,516	3,659	254	5,428	2,805	604	470	546	4,425
2012-13	1,003	6,754	119	7,876	2,735	656	524	1,190	5,105
2013-14	2,771	4,173	88	7,032	2,886	663	530	1,096	5,174
2014-15	1,858	5,189	90	7,136	2,982	675	298	1,080	5,035
2015-16	2,101	6,001	94	8,197	3,053	709	1,100	1,544	6,406
2016-17	1,791	5,582	162	7,534	3,086	880	799	1,328	6,093
2017-18[1]	1,442	7,115	171	8,728	3,149	705	885	1,273	6,011
2018-19[2]	2,717	5,462	75	8,254	3,108	690	824	1,250	5,872

[1] Preliminary. [2] Estimate. Source: Economic Research Service, U.S. Department of Agriculture (ERS-USDA)

Production of Peanuts (Harvested for Nuts) in the United States, by States   In Thousands of Pounds

Crop Year	Alabama	Florida	Georgia	Mississippi	New Mexico	North Carolina	Oklahoma	South Carolina	Texas	Virginia	Total
2009	495,000	336,000	1,797,800	54,000	21,700	244,200	42,900	148,800	506,850	44,400	3,691,650
2010	481,000	472,500	1,959,150	63,000	34,000	232,200	70,350	224,000	586,800	33,840	4,156,840
2011	489,700	549,500	1,645,750	56,000	19,800	291,600	54,600	240,900	249,240	61,500	3,658,590
2012	876,000	760,500	3,343,400	215,600	26,000	427,180	80,300	417,300	525,600	82,000	6,753,880
2013	489,900	517,450	1,887,180	122,100	21,700	315,900	59,200	273,000	423,540	63,200	4,173,170
2014	544,950	668,000	2,435,515	124,000	15,750	401,760	44,000	410,400	459,740	84,550	5,188,665
2015	637,000	648,000	3,364,410	143,500	15,337	302,760	30,600	262,400	528,000	69,350	6,001,357
2016	619,200	554,800	2,753,400	152,000	22,400	349,470	44,400	339,200	559,650	76,650	5,581,570
2017	704,450	638,250	3,572,250	172,000	26,600	479,700	79,380	472,000	697,200	119,880	7,115,410
2018[1]	550,800	504,000	2,892,500	96,000	16,500	382,200	46,500	278,800	478,500	100,800	5,461,600

[1] Preliminary. Source: Agricultural Statistics Board, U.S. Department of Agriculture (ASB-USDA)

Supply and Reported Uses of Shelled Peanuts and Products in the United States   In Thousands of Pounds

Crop Year Beginning Aug. 1	Shelled Peanuts -- Stocks, Aug. 1 --		Shelled Peanuts ----- Production -----		Reported Used (Shelled Peanuts - Raw Basis)					Shelled Peanuts Crushed[6]	Crude Oil Pro-duction	Cake & Meal Production
					Edible Grades Used In							
	Edible	Oil Stock[2]	Edible	Oil Stock[2]	Candy[3]	Snack[4]	Butter[5]	Other Products	Total			
2009-10	554,295	35,498	2,457,434	280,888	315,595	352,963	1,191,821	15,840	1,876,219	326,779	139,903	185,452
2010-11	473,878	43,380	2,450,639	357,130	395,452	395,177	1,213,229	16,890	2,020,748	441,017	190,110	250,043
2011-12	466,310	52,883	2,399,094	345,565	394,678	390,068	1,197,748	19,661	2,002,155	453,835	188,479	250,037
2012-13	547,965	33,883	3,125,786	351,284	381,914	400,429	1,227,859	20,664	2,030,866	493,205	210,702	270,328
2013-14	519,824	25,364	3,098,392	373,008	395,726	429,796	1,218,170	29,103	2,072,795	497,272	209,808	268,554
2014-15	431,674	31,012	2,997,078	391,728	375,856	428,477	1,303,755	53,179	2,161,267	506,677	214,041	278,380
2015-16	467,139	65,350	3,141,099	442,650	377,505	505,692	1,299,634	61,388	2,244,219	531,770	226,219	291,193
2016-17	482,010	26,372	2,944,760	448,377	407,701	470,292	1,338,195	56,769	2,272,957	659,966	283,689	357,751
2017-18[1]	535,730	24,232	2,853,147	358,282	379,504	524,845	1,314,567	95,943	2,314,859	528,750	231,748	282,346

[1] Preliminary. [2] Includes straight run oil stock peanuts. [3] Includes peanut butter made by manufacturers for own use in candy. [4] Formerly titled "Salted Peanuts." [5] Includes peanut butter made by manufacturers for own use in cookies and sandwiches, but excludes peanut butter used in candy.
[6] All crushings regardless of grade. Source: National Agricultural Statistics Service, U.S. Department of Agriculture (NASS-USDA)

PEANUTS AND PEANUT OIL

Shelled Peanuts (Raw Basis) Used in Primary Products, by Type   In Thousands of Pounds

Crop Year Beginning Aug. 1	Virginia				Runner				Spanish			
	Candy[2]	Peanuts	Butter[3]	Total	Candy[2]	Peanuts	Butter[3]	Total	Candy[2]	Peanuts	Butter[3]	Total
2008-09	26,342	52,925	110,737	191,770	276,212	303,730	981,546	1,569,531	13,721	10,823	W	34,990
2009-10	17,361	50,812	W	198,497	286,277	290,358	1,056,699	1,646,454	11,957	11,793	W	31,269
2010-11	16,070	62,708	W	211,194	365,260	319,529	1,076,521	1,774,346	14,122	12,940	W	35,207
2011-12	17,856	78,333	W	203,958	360,797	303,631	1,091,541	1,770,809	16,025	8,104	W	27,390
2012-13	17,731	83,722	82,981	192,888	347,428	309,860	1,143,108	1,812,591	16,755	6,847	W	25,389
2013-14	17,109	85,298	86,759	202,536	W	337,934	1,128,206	1,844,490	15,996	6,564	W	W
2014-15	12,079	91,909	102,340	232,768	348,367	329,930	1,196,277	1,901,311	15,410	6,638	W	27,188
2015-16	14,319	89,766	108,156	238,494	346,831	408,726	1,186,810	1,977,495	16,355	7,200	W	28,225
2016-17	13,427	92,331	118,109	247,473	379,549	370,766	1,215,212	1,998,683	14,725	7,195	W	26,801
2017-18[1]	15,455	84,479	129,823	258,754	346,985	434,139	1,179,186	2,027,253	17,064	6,227	W	28,851

[1] Preliminary.   [2] Includes peanut butter made by manufacturers for own use in candy.   [3] Includes peanut butter made by manufacturers for own use in cookies and sandwiches, but excludes peanut butter used in candy.
Source: National Agricultural Statistics Service, U.S. Department of Agriculture (NASS-USDA)

Production, Consumption, Stocks and Foreign Trade of Peanut Oil in the United States   In Millions of Pounds

Crop Year Beginning Aug. 1	Production		Consumption		Stocks, Dec. 31		Imports for Con-sumption	Exports
	Crude	Refined	In Refining	In End Products	Crude	Refined		
2002-03	267.7	166.3	W	277.6	52.9	3.5	----	----
2003-04	180.7	115.8	W	203.8	23.0	1.8	----	----
2004-05	135.7	91.0	W	181.9	40.3	2.4	----	----
2005-06	188.0	119.9	W	152.1	15.4	3.7	----	----
2006-07	173.8	115.1	W	W	35.5	5.6	----	----
2007-08	168.7	111.2	W	W	14.1	1.8	----	----
2008-09	150.8	99.9	W	W	17.6	3.0	----	----
2009-10[1]	146.3	96.6	W	W	18.1	2.1	----	----
2010-11[2]	196.9	132.0	W	W	----	----	----	----
2011-12[2]	NA	NA	NA	NA	NA	NA	----	----

[1] Preliminary.   [2] Forecast.   W = Withheld.   Source: Bureau of the Census, U.S. Department of Commerce

Farmer Stock Equivalent Total[2/3] Stocks of Peanuts in the United States at End of Month   In Million Pounds

Crop Year	Aug.	Sept.	Oct.	Nov.	Dec.	Jan.	Feb.	Mar.	Apr.	May.	June	July
2009-10	1,837.6	1,657.4	2,922.1	3,973.0	3,862.4	3,602.9	3,541.8	3,153.2	2,785.9	2,451.9	2,158.8	1,828.7
2010-11	1,502.4	1,778.9	3,651.7	4,150.9	3,887.3	3,565.5	3,258.3	2,867.1	2,443.1	2,148.3	1,820.9	1,515.9
2011-12	1,171.5	1,252.4	2,888.2	3,389.3	3,237.9	2,938.7	2,652.9	2,333.0	1,966.5	1,553.1	1,261.8	1,003.3
2012-13	669.6	1,623.1	5,050.1	5,758.2	5,570.7	5,184.7	4,792.2	4,382.6	3,953.0	3,559.0	3,202.7	2,770.7
2013-14	2,427.0	2,172.4	3,776.3	4,641.5	4,710.1	4,299.6	3,919.4	3,505.5	3,092.3	2,741.2	2,304.4	1,857.8
2014-15	1,426.7	1,330.5	4,246.1	4,717.3	4,573.2	4,297.1	3,893.3	3,487.2	3,105.8	2,717.9	2,401.4	2,101.0
2015-16	1,455.3	1,846.4	4,496.2	5,317.9	5,360.6	4,863.2	4,347.8	3,798.7	3,279.7	2,656.4	2,108.6	1,790.9
2016-17	1,239.1	1,509.3	4,156.1	4,701.6	4,389.9	3,992.8	3,550.0	3,087.8	2,668.3	2,241.0	1,806.7	1,441.6
2017-18	1,013.5	1,806.4	4,739.2	5,587.7	5,379.1	5,032.3	4,585.7	4,225.5	3,787.6	3,357.5	2,982.1	2,717.1
2018-19[1]	2,309.8	2,594.7	4,195.3	5,002.8	58,056.8	4,793.9						

[1] Preliminary.   [2] Excludes stocks on farms. Includes stocks owned by or held for account of peanut producers and CCC in commercial storage facilities. Farmer stock on net weight basis.   [3] Actual farmer stock, plus roasting stock, plus shelled peanuts.   W = Withheld.   Source: Agricultural Marketing Service, U.S. Department of Agriculture (AMS-USDA)

Farmer Stock Peanuts[2], Total All Types, in the United States at End of Month   In Millions of Pounds

Crop Year	Aug.	Sept.	Oct.	Nov.	Dec.	Jan.	Feb.	Mar.	Apr.	May.	June	July
2009-10	1,037.5	859.2	2,113.7	3,143.5	3,035.0	2,783.8	2,656.9	2,258.7	1,903.9	1,595.4	1,286.0	991.4
2010-11	711.4	1,064.9	2,900.3	3,394.2	3,178.3	2,852.9	2,501.4	2,066.1	1,657.1	1,343.8	1,027.3	769.0
2011-12	472.0	613.8	2,300.1	2,780.8	2,581.2	2,239.4	1,888.5	1,514.2	1,145.2	772.3	507.9	272.8
2012-13	98.2	1,164.8	4,442.1	5,098.6	4,865.5	4,447.0	4,032.1	3,548.0	3,073.4	2,629.0	2,266.4	1,925.0
2013-14	1,527.6	1,296.5	2,909.0	3,790.8	3,876.1	3,472.0	3,045.7	2,615.1	2,195.8	1,819.1	1,423.3	1,059.5
2014-15	661.8	573.0	3,517.7	4,046.4	3,947.9	3,622.6	3,224.0	2,789.6	2,394.6	2,056.4	1,697.5	1,445.3
2015-16	874.6	1,305.6	3,883.8	4,690.3	4,733.5	4,207.8	3,621.4	3,058.7	2,584.2	1,948.7	1,413.6	1,051.1
2016-17	648.2	960.2	3,594.2	4,093.3	3,747.5	3,317.9	2,828.0	2,342.8	1,919.8	1,465.8	1,050.4	733.0
2017-18	393.9	1,252.0	4,131.7	4,977.2	4,679.2	4,283.4	3,831.6	3,351.3	2,906.0	2,508.7	2,192.0	1,916.8
2018-19[1]	1,568.9	1,811.5	3,426.7	4,286.5	4,301.9	3,980.0						

[1] Preliminary.   [2] Excludes stocks on farms. Includes stocks owned by or held for account of peanut producers and CCC in commercial storage facilities. Farmer stock on net weight basis.   Source: Agricultural Marketing Service, U.S. Department of Agriculture (AMS-USDA)

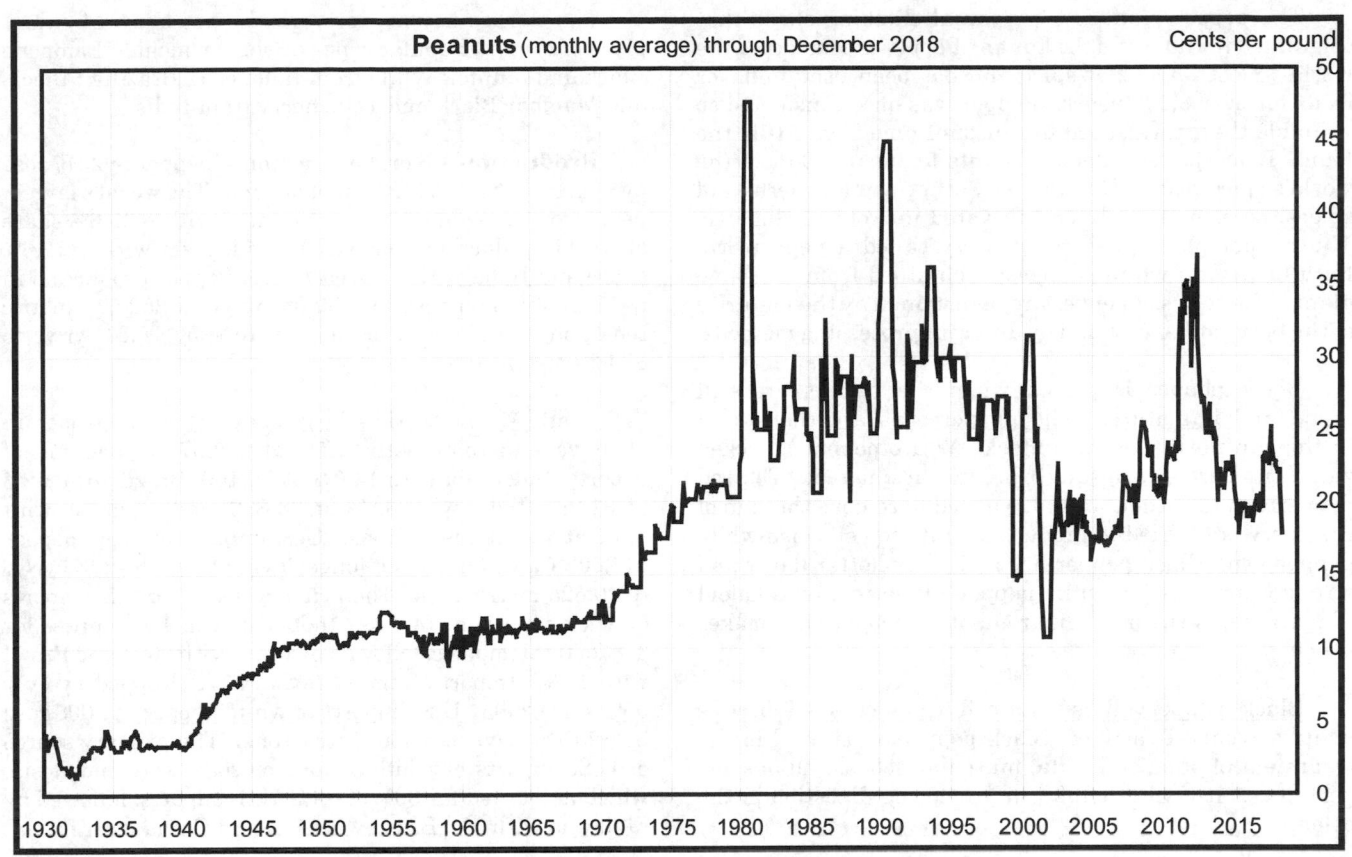

Peanuts (monthly average) through December 2018 — Cents per pound

Average Price[2] Received by Farmers for Peanuts (in the Shell) in the United States — In Cents Per Pound

Year	Aug.	Sept.	Oct.	Nov.	Dec.	Jan.	Feb.	Mar.	Apr.	May.	June	July	Average[1]
2009-10	23.1	23.3	23.7	21.7	21.7	20.7	21.0	20.6	20.4	20.5	21.6	21.5	21.7
2010-11	20.7	19.9	21.4	22.3	24.0	23.0	23.5	23.4	23.1	22.8	23.3	23.9	22.6
2011-12	23.4	23.5	28.9	33.2	30.8	33.7	32.9	34.8	35.1	33.8	34.4	34.5	31.6
2012-13	29.3	35.2	33.7	32.6	36.9	31.2	28.2	27.8	26.8	27.1	27.0	24.7	30.0
2013-14	25.1	25.3	26.0	26.6	24.6	25.4	24.3	25.0	24.2	23.7	20.0	21.7	24.3
2014-15	22.1	21.5	21.0	21.4	20.9	22.5	22.2	22.5	22.1	22.5	21.8	23.0	22.0
2015-16	20.7	19.6	18.8	18.5	17.8	19.3	19.8	19.5	19.8	19.6	19.5	19.0	19.3
2016-17	19.0	19.1	19.5	19.0	18.6	19.8	20.1	20.6	19.8	19.4	19.7	20.5	19.6
2017-18	19.7	23.0	23.2	22.7	23.0	22.9	22.6	25.1	23.9	22.8	22.7	22.4	22.8
2018-19[1]	22.0	22.2	22.1	21.2	17.8	22.2							21.3

[1] Preliminarly.   [2] Weighted average by sales.   Source: National Agricultural Statistics Service, U.S. Department of Agriculture (NASS-USDA)

Average Price of Domestic Crude Peanut Oil (in Tanks) F.O.B. Southeast Mills — In Cents Per Pound

Year	Oct.	Nov.	Dec.	Jan.	Feb.	Mar.	Apr.	May	June	July	Aug.	Sept.	Average
2009-10	51.20	52.00	52.20	59.00	59.50	58.75	63.60	67.63	67.75	67.80	68.38	68.81	61.39
2010-11	71.40	75.13	77.90	80.06	79.63	77.50	78.70	82.81	78.50	88.05	95.56	97.50	81.90
2011-12	97.00	98.75	96.10	95.81	95.00	96.60	102.38	106.13	111.00	110.00	110.00	104.50	101.94
2012-13	103.00	99.90	98.56	96.75	86.00	79.05	77.50	80.00	82.75	84.00	83.00	82.00	87.71
2013-14	81.00	78.70	75.38	65.70	62.06	59.06	57.75	57.20	58.25	58.63	62.80	61.75	64.86
2014-15	59.95	60.63	60.13	56.15	55.56	54.69	54.81	54.65	56.31	58.15	58.63	58.69	57.36
2015-16	57.70	58.06	58.50	56.19	55.00	55.55	56.20	61.38	61.10	62.10	61.00	61.60	58.70
2016-17	64.88	66.00	63.10	62.88	63.13	65.80	69.69	70.75	76.20	75.75	69.63	66.60	67.87
2017-18	65.44	65.00	65.20	66.13	66.63	67.00	66.88	66.50	67.70	68.00	68.00	67.63	66.68
2018-19[1]	66.63	64.80	62.25	61.88	61.13								63.34

[1] Preliminary.   Source: Agricultural Marketing Service, U.S. Department of Agriculture (AMS-USDA)

Pepper

The pepper plant is a perennial climbing shrub that originated in India and Sri Lanka. Pepper is considered the world's most important spice and has been used to flavor foods for over 3,000 years. Pepper was once considered so valuable that it was used to ransom Rome from Attila the Hun. Black pepper alone accounts for nearly 35% of the world's spice trade. Unlike many other popular herbs and spices, pepper can only be cultivated in tropical climates. The pepper plant produces a berry called a peppercorn. Both black and white pepper are obtained from the same plant. The colors of pepper are determined by the maturity of the berry at harvest and by different processing methods.

Black pepper is picked when the berries are still green and immature. The peppercorns are then dried in the sun until they turn black. White pepper is picked when the berries are fully ripe and bright red. The red peppercorns are then soaked, washed to remove the skin of the berry, and dried to produce a white to yellowish-white peppercorn. Black pepper has a slightly hotter flavor and stronger aroma than white pepper. Piperine, an alkaloid of pyridine, is the active ingredient in pepper that makes it hot.

Black pepper oil is obtained from crushed berries using solvent extraction. Black pepper oil is used in the treatment of pain, chills, flu, muscular aches, and in some perfumes. It is also helpful in promoting digestion in the colon.

The world's key pepper varieties are known by their place of origin. Popular types of pepper include Lampong Black and Muntok White from Indonesia, Brazilian Black, and Malabar Black and Tellicherry from India.

Production – World production of pepper in 2017 rose by +11.1% yr/yr to 690,467 metric tons. The world's largest pepper producer in 2017 was Vietnam with a 36.6% share of world production, followed by Indonesia with a 12.6% share and India with a 10.4% share. Pepper production in 2017 in Vietnam rose by +39.6% yr/yr to 252,576 metric tons and in Indonesia production rose by +0.8% yr/yr to 87,029 metric tons.

Trade – The world's largest exporters of pepper in 2016 were Vietnam with 37.5% at 142,375 metric tons of exports, Indonesia with 14.0% at 50,100, Brazil with 8.2% at 31,085, India with 6.3% at 23,863, and Malaysia with 3.3% at 12,549 metric tons. U.S. imports of black pepper in 2008 (later data is no longer available) fell -2.6% yr/yr to 49,625 metric tons. The primary source of U.S. imports of black pepper in 2008 was Indonesia which accounted for 41% of total imports, followed by India with 20%, and Brazil with 17%. Imports from Malaysia have dropped by over 95% since 2003. U.S. imports of white pepper in 2008 rose by +25.1% yr/yr to 6,960 metric tons. The primary source of U.S. imports of white pepper in 2008 were Indonesia, which accounted for 69% of total U.S. imports, followed by Malaysia with 5%, Brazil with 1%, and China with 1%.

World Production of Pepper   In Metric Tons

Year	Brazil	Cambodia	China	India	Indonesia	Madagascar	Malaysia	Mexico	Philippines	Sri Lanka	Thailand	Vietnam	World Total
2010	52,137	2,447	30,210	51,020	83,700	5,012	24,227	3,640	3,348	26,620	6,391	105,400	482,568
2011	44,610	2,439	29,206	52,000	87,100	4,838	25,600	3,453	3,369	25,770	4,395	111,964	483,714
2012	43,345	2,400	31,200	41,000	87,841	4,824	26,000	3,025	3,248	24,950	2,241	120,276	478,643
2013	42,312	2,468	31,410	53,000	91,000	4,894	26,500	3,199	2,716	26,730	1,332	125,023	500,399
2014	42,339	2,513	32,862	51,000	87,400	4,465	27,500	3,309	2,563	27,847	1,174	151,761	527,989
2015	51,739	2,509	34,113	65,000	81,501	6,881	28,300	3,567	1,847	28,833	1,405	176,789	576,708
2016[1]	54,425	2,521	34,459	55,000	86,334	6,979	29,245	5,206	1,436	28,995	1,533	216,432	621,595
2017[2]	79,371	2,534	35,389	72,000	87,029	6,425	30,433	7,951	1,369	29,289	1,400	252,576	690,467

[1] Preliminary.   [2] Estimate.   *Source: Food and Agricultural Organization of the United Nations (FAO-UN)*

World Imports of Pepper   In Metric Tons

Year	European Union	France	Germany	India	Japan	Netherlands	Pakistan	Russia	Singapore	United Arab Em.	United Kingdom	United States	World Total
2009	88,822	8,357	26,219	17,444	8,785	15,765	6,564	9,358	12,437	1,643	7,761	65,855	301,739
2010	100,359	9,719	28,948	11,913	8,908	19,856	7,267	10,244	10,130	4,000	10,269	70,470	308,003
2011	96,875	8,827	25,480	13,548	8,855	18,331	8,893	8,603	11,923	2,572	10,799	68,489	314,361
2012	95,998	7,882	27,653	16,009	8,130	16,950	5,691	9,705	11,936	6,013	11,944	62,458	325,951
2013	----	8,690	30,706	15,919	8,514	15,077	6,602	9,797	20,254	18,467	12,946	71,741	364,291
2014	----	9,564	25,978	23,068	8,833	15,863	8,105	7,996	27,005	19,967	10,936	68,987	380,933
2015[1]	----	10,203	29,239	21,460	9,068	13,630	7,119	6,922	20,177	18,363	12,038	80,357	400,871
2016[2]	----	11,505	29,452	23,484	8,741	12,450	10,160	7,699	6,452	14,969	14,270	75,178	376,220

[1] Preliminary.   [2] Estimate.   *Source: Food and Agricultural Organization of the United Nations (FAO-UN)*

World Exports of Pepper   In Metric Tons

Year	Brazil	European Union	Germany	India	Indonesia	Malaysia	Mexico	Netherlands	Singapore	Sri Lanka	United States	Vietnam	World Total
2009	35,770	31,812	10,850	26,281	50,642	13,153	6,175	9,974	9,570	6,576	5,472	134,300	337,418
2010	30,761	32,982	11,128	25,847	62,599	14,107	6,590	9,153	9,777	12,236	5,605	116,859	343,021
2011	32,696	36,163	11,031	37,419	36,487	14,237	5,998	10,848	9,119	5,057	7,110	123,800	330,494
2012	29,129	40,977	10,915	29,263	62,608	10,613	6,122	13,903	12,504	10,488	9,213	116,842	350,450
2013	30,605	----	13,310	38,576	47,908	12,099	7,434	10,526	18,603	21,330	9,730	132,763	384,632
2014	34,269	----	11,709	27,415	34,733	13,634	7,176	12,858	25,405	7,930	11,790	159,433	408,418
2015[1]	38,034	----	14,067	34,801	58,075	13,910	8,216	10,115	19,088	16,657	15,933	132,791	421,328
2016[2]	31,085	----	14,841	23,863	53,100	12,549	8,556	9,283	5,485	7,876	14,129	142,375	379,242

[1] Preliminary.   [2] Estimate.   *Source: Food and Agricultural Organization of the United Nations (FAO-UN)*

Petroleum

Crude oil is petroleum that is acquired directly from the ground. Crude oil was formed millions of years ago from the remains of tiny aquatic plants and animals that lived in ancient seas. Ancient societies such as the Persians, 10th century Sumatrans, and pre-Columbian Indians believed that crude oil had medicinal benefits. Around 4,000 BC in Mesopotamia, bitumen, a tarry crude, was used as caulking for ships, as a setting for jewels and mosaics, and as an adhesive to secure weapon handles. The walls of Babylon and the famed pyramids were held together with bitumen, and Egyptians used it for embalming. During the 19th century in America, an oil find was often met with dismay. Pioneers who dug wells to find water or brine, were disappointed when they struck oil. It wasn't until 1854, with the invention of the kerosene lamp, that the first large-scale demand for petroleum emerged. Crude oil is a relatively abundant commodity. The world has produced approximately 650 billion barrels of oil, but another trillion barrels of proved reserves have yet to be extracted. Crude oil was the world's first trillion-dollar industry and accounts for the single largest product in world trade.

Crude Oil futures and options are traded at the CME Group, the ICE Futures Europe, and the JSE Securities Exchange. Futures are also traded at the Dubai Mercantile Exchange (DME), the Multi Commodity Exchange of India (MCX), the Thailand Futures Exchange, and the Tokyo Commodity Exchange (TOCOM). The CME trades two main types of crude oil: light sweet crude oil and Brent crude oil. The light sweet futures contract calls for the delivery of 1,000 barrels of crude oil in Cushing, Oklahoma. Light sweet crude is preferred by refiners because of its low sulfur content and relatively high yield of high-value products such as gasoline, diesel fuel, heating oil, and jet fuel. The Brent blend crude is based on a light, sweet North Sea crude oil. Brent blend crude production is approximately 500,000 barrels per day, and is shipped from Sullom Voe in the Shetland Islands.

Prices – CME West-Texas Intermediate (WTI) crude oil prices (Barchart.com symbol CL) traded sideways to higher into Q4-2018 on a weak dollar and the prospects for diminished global crude supplies. The dollar index sank to a 4-year low in February, which lifted the prices of most commodities priced in dollars. Meanwhile, global oil inventories continued to decline after OPEC+ in late-Nov 2017 extended their 2017 production cut agreement through 2018. Geopolitical concerns in the Middle East kept crude prices firm and the U.S. revived its sanctions against Iranian crude oil as of November. Also, the U.S. added additional sanctions on Venezuela, which further reduced global crude supplies. U.S. crude supplies at Cushing, Oklahoma, the delivery point for WTI futures, declined steadily into August to a 4-year low, which also underpinned crude prices. In October, crude prices jumped to a 4-year high of $76.90 a barrel on ramped up tensions between the U.S. and Saudi Arabia after Saudi Arabia implicitly threatened to use oil as a weapon if it incurred U.S. sanctions over the apparent murder of journalist Khashoggi. Crude prices then plunged into December to a 1-1/2 year low of $42.36 a barrel on increased supplies and global economic concerns. U.S. crude output rose steadily through 2018 and climbed to a record 11.7 million bpd the week ended November 9 and OPEC Nov crude production rose for a sixth month to a 2-year high of 33.15 million bpd. Weaker economic activity in China, the world's second-largest crude oil consumer, also weighed on crude oil prices after the China's Dec manufacturing PMI fell to a 3-year low of 49.4. Crude oil finished the year down -24.8% yr/yr at $45.41 a barrel.

Supply – World crude oil production in 2017 rose +0.3% yr/yr to 81.068 million barrels per day, which was a new record high. The world's largest oil producers in 2017 were Russia with 13.1% of the world production, Saudi Arabia with 12.5%, the United States with 11.5%, Iran & Iraq each with 5.5%, and Canada with 4.9%. U.S. crude oil production in 2017 rose by +5.0% yr/yr to 9.301 million barrels per day. Alaskan production in 2017 rose by +1.0% yr/yr to 494,656 barrels per day and was far below the peak level of 2.017 million barrels per day seen in 1988.

Demand – U.S. demand for crude oil in 2017 rose +2.5% yr/yr to 16.593 million barrels per day, which is a record high. Most of that demand went for U.S. refinery production of products such as gasoline fuel, diesel fuel, aviation fuel, heating oil, kerosene, asphalt, and lubricants.

Trade – The U.S. is still highly dependent on imports of crude oil to meet its energy needs and imports in 2017 rose +0.8% yr/yr to 7.911 million barrels per day, although that is well below the 2005 record high of 10.126 million barrels. U.S. exports of crude oil in 2017 rose sharply by +87% yr/yr to 1.105 million barrels per day.

World Production of Crude Petroleum   In Thousands of Barrels Per Day

Year	Canada	China	Iran	Iraq	Kuwait	Mexico	Nigeria	Russia	Saudi Arabia	United Arab Em	United States	Venezuela	World Total
2008	2,579	3,790	4,050	2,375	2,586	2,839	2,165	9,357	9,261	2,821	5,000	2,510	74,301
2009	2,579	3,796	4,037	2,391	2,350	2,646	2,208	9,495	8,250	2,560	5,349	2,520	73,121
2010	2,741	4,078	4,080	2,399	2,300	2,621	2,408	9,694	8,900	2,570	5,478	2,410	74,887
2011	2,901	4,052	4,054	2,626	2,530	2,600	2,474	9,774	9,458	2,849	5,654	2,500	74,908
2012	3,138	4,074	3,387	2,983	2,635	2,593	2,457	9,922	9,832	2,994	6,502	2,500	76,382
2013	3,325	4,164	3,113	3,054	2,650	2,562	2,307	10,054	9,693	2,938	7,467	2,500	76,449
2014	3,613	4,208	3,239	3,368	2,642	2,469	2,347	10,107	9,735	3,010	8,759	2,500	78,348
2015	3,677	4,278	3,293	4,045	2,784	2,302	2,171	10,253	10,168	3,149	9,431	2,500	80,716
2016[1]	3,679	3,981	4,151	4,444	2,905	2,187	1,871	10,551	10,461	3,243	8,831	2,277	80,801
2017[2]	3,977	3,838	4,469	4,454	2,753	1,981	1,946	10,580	10,134	3,174	9,352	2,007	81,068

Includes lease condensate.   [1] Preliminary.   [2] Estimate.   *Source: Energy Information Administration, U.S. Department of Energy (EIA-DOE)*

PETROLEUM

World Imports of Crude Petroleum In Thousands of Barrels Per Day

Year	China	France	Germany	India	Italy	Japan	Korea, South	Nether-lands	Singa-pore	Spain	United Kingdom	United States	World Total
2007	3,277	1,636	2,157	2,480	1,790	4,036	2,390	977	1,164	1,161	1,007	10,031	44,313
2008	3,583	1,666	2,122	2,516	1,662	3,841	2,342	998	1,165	1,178	1,036	9,783	43,831
2009	4,076	1,442	1,979	2,812	1,532	3,416	2,324	975	884	1,056	951	9,013	41,912
2010	4,773	1,294	1,883	3,040	1,540	3,467	2,401	1,033	953	1,059	959	9,213	42,852
2011	5,096	1,296	1,828	3,366	1,449	3,398	2,528	996	980	1,053	1,003	8,935	42,840
2012	5,428	1,139	1,881	3,746	1,377	3,429	2,583	1,008	974	1,184	1,083	8,527	43,498
2013	5,658	1,120	1,829	3,857	1,154	3,393	2,475	953	948	1,169	1,016	7,730	42,276
2014	6,193	1,082	1,805	3,785	1,059	3,205	2,525	959	954	1,192	940	7,344	42,019
2015[1]	6,737	1,146	1,843	3,927	1,230	3,203	2,802	1,055	993	1,305	862	7,363	43,879
2016[2]	7,621	1,092	1,837	4,255	1,217	3,147	2,946	1,090	1,057	1,292	798	7,850	45,166

Includes lease condensate. [1] Preliminary. [2] Estimate. *Source: Energy Information Administration, U.S. Department of Energy (EIA-DOE)*

World Exports of Crude Petroleum In Thousands of Barrels Per Day

Year	Angola	Canada	Iran	Iraq	Kuwait	Mexico	Nigeria	Norway	Russia	Saudi Arabia	United Arab Em	Vene-zuela	World Total
2007	1,591	1,486	2,492	1,637	1,613	1,808	2,152	1,989	5,179	6,909	2,358	1,835	42,990
2008	1,635	1,553	2,412	1,835	1,739	1,505	1,961	1,838	4,843	7,105	2,405	1,841	42,424
2009	1,770	1,515	2,235	1,902	1,348	1,312	2,071	1,776	4,997	5,977	2,051	1,697	40,638
2010	1,711	1,590	2,269	1,890	1,491	1,446	2,322	1,600	4,991	5,979	2,108	1,730	41,184
2011	1,585	1,808	2,328	2,163	1,816	1,421	2,222	1,455	4,943	7,077	2,487	1,785	41,858
2012	1,663	1,933	1,455	2,414	2,070	1,333	2,288	1,314	4,759	7,397	2,571	1,741	41,954
2013	1,677	2,218	1,086	2,363	2,058	1,270	2,028	1,226	4,700	7,553	2,654	1,857	41,186
2014	1,632	2,382	1,084	2,518	1,995	1,208	2,120	1,294	4,500	7,120	2,651	1,729	40,656
2015[1]	1,746	2,661	1,113	2,990	1,964	1,210	2,114	1,312	4,937	7,242	2,593	1,872	42,486
2016[2]	1,681	2,750	1,897	3,577	2,128	1,236	1,655	1,395	5,114	7,334	2,488	1,725	43,607

Includes lease condensate. [1] Preliminary. [2] Estimate. *Source: Energy Information Administration, U.S. Department of Energy (EIA-DOE)*

World Production of Petroleum Products In Thousands of Barrels Per Day

Year	Brazil	Canada	China	Germany	India	Italy	Japan	Korea, South	Russia	Saudi Arabia	United Kingdom	United States	World Total
2005	2,180	2,102	6,354	2,617	2,745	2,116	4,360	2,502	4,361	2,088	1,823	17,800	82,535
2006	2,167	2,069	6,495	2,580	2,896	2,050	4,262	2,559	4,548	2,289	1,757	17,975	82,611
2007	2,184	2,117	7,018	2,539	3,122	2,112	4,215	2,552	4,568	2,146	1,719	17,994	81,606
2008	2,007	2,029	7,069	2,484	3,226	1,971	4,136	2,535	4,803	2,103	1,678	18,146	81,772
2009	2,237	1,962	8,209	2,333	3,836	1,823	3,863	2,476	4,935	1,935	1,570	17,882	82,410
2010	2,467	2,015	8,737	2,197	4,220	1,886	3,857	2,537	5,299	1,935	1,532	18,453	84,163
2011	2,472	1,905	9,298	2,183	4,356	1,791	3,658	2,686	5,390	1,901	1,578	18,673	84,687
2012	2,555	1,926	9,880	2,207	4,506	1,693	3,645	2,789	5,516	1,971	1,436	18,564	85,182
2013[1]	2,810	1,893	10,345	2,151	4,776	1,506	3,689	2,697	5,770	1,884	1,380	19,106	86,426
2014[2]	2,899	1,877	10,852	2,126	4,793	1,418	3,536	2,772	6,174	2,221	1,301	19,654	87,766

Includes lease condensate. [1] Preliminary. [2] Estimate. *Source: Energy Information Administration, U.S. Department of Energy (EIA-DOE)*

Supply and Disposition of Crude Oil in the United States In Thousands of Barrels Per Day

	Supply						Stock Withdrawal[3]		Disposition		Ending Stocks		
	-- Field Production --		------- Imports -------			Unaccounted for Crude							Other
	Total Domestic	Alaskan	Total	SPR[2]	Other	Oil	SPR[2]	Other	Refinery Inputs	Exports	Total	SPR[2]	Primary
Year	In Thousands of Barrels Per Day										In Millions of Barrels		
2010	5,475	600	9,213	----	----	----	----	----	14,724	42	1,039	727	312
2011	5,643	561	8,935	----	----	----	----	----	14,806	47	1,004	696	308
2012	6,497	526	8,527	----	----	----	----	----	14,999	67	1,033	695	338
2013	7,466	515	7,730	----	----	----	----	----	15,312	134	1,023	696	327
2014	8,753	496	7,344	----	----	----	----	----	15,848	351	1,052	691	361
2015	9,408	483	7,363	----	----	----	----	----	16,188	465	1,144	695	449
2016	8,857	490	7,850	----	----	----	----	----	16,187	591	1,180	695	485
2017[1]	9,301	495	7,911	----	----	----	----	----	16,592	1,105	1,086	664	422

[1] Preliminary. [2] Strategic Petroleum Reserve. [3] A negative number indicates a decrease in stocks and a positive number indicates an increase.
Source: Energy Information Administration, U.S. Department of Energy (EIA-DOE)

Crude Petroleum Refinery Operations Ratio[2] in the United States   In Percent of Capacity

Year	Jan.	Feb.	Mar.	Apr.	May	June	July	Aug.	Sept.	Oct.	Nov.	Dec.	Average
2009	82.3	81.5	81.5	82.7	84.0	86.0	84.2	84.1	84.9	81.5	81.1	81.3	82.9
2010	79.9	81.1	83.2	88.7	88.2	90.7	91.2	89.1	86.5	82.5	86.5	88.4	86.3
2011	84.8	80.0	84.4	82.9	85.3	89.0	90.2	90.3	88.7	84.9	87.0	86.5	86.2
2012	85.6	86.5	85.6	86.6	90.6	92.5	92.5	91.1	87.6	87.1	88.6	90.4	88.7
2013	83.8	81.7	84.0	85.8	88.2	91.7	92.6	91.5	90.7	86.9	90.6	92.0	88.3
2014	87.2	86.6	85.8	90.7	90.2	90.3	94.6	93.7	91.8	87.7	92.0	94.2	90.4
2015	88.4	87.6	88.7	92.0	92.5	94.0	95.1	93.9	90.5	86.6	91.8	92.6	91.1
2016	89.4	88.3	88.8	88.6	89.9	91.1	92.2	92.1	90.4	85.4	89.6	91.3	89.8
2017	88.4	85.0	88.0	92.7	94.3	94.3	95.0	92.8	85.3	88.3	92.5	94.7	90.9
2018[1]	91.1	88.1	91.3	92.0	93.3	97.0	95.1	96.6	93.5	90.0	94.1	95.4	93.1

[1] Preliminary.   [2] Based on the ration of the daily average crude runs to stills to the rated capacity of refineries per day.   *Source: Energy Information Administration, U.S. Department of Energy (EIA-DOE)*

Crude Oil Refinery Inputs in the United States   In Thousands of Barrels Per Day

Year	Jan.	Feb.	Mar.	Apr.	May	June	July	Aug.	Sept.	Oct.	Nov.	Dec.	Average
2009	14,146	14,134	14,118	14,382	14,483	14,850	14,636	14,593	14,710	14,095	13,898	13,983	14,336
2010	13,666	13,950	14,314	15,131	15,215	15,382	15,519	15,110	14,740	14,000	14,637	14,976	14,724
2011	14,423	13,676	14,451	14,231	14,718	15,294	15,589	15,556	15,275	14,570	14,960	14,842	14,799
2012	14,374	14,615	14,476	14,609	15,097	15,637	15,665	15,325	14,910	14,843	15,085	15,330	14,997
2013	14,567	14,230	14,703	14,864	15,305	15,833	16,042	15,793	15,636	14,991	15,633	16,069	15,306
2014	15,311	15,128	15,116	15,864	15,946	15,817	16,534	16,460	16,074	15,361	16,043	16,469	15,844
2015	15,456	15,342	15,640	16,273	16,402	16,701	16,879	16,700	16,168	15,440	16,458	16,742	16,183
2016	15,951	15,843	16,082	15,920	16,237	16,433	16,621	16,593	16,340	15,454	16,235	16,516	16,186
2017	16,118	15,493	16,048	16,954	17,222	17,204	17,317	16,981	15,460	16,061	16,840	17,274	16,581
2018[1]	16,599	15,932	16,665	16,766	16,989	17,666	17,355	17,612	16,986	16,409	17,152	17,409	16,962

[1] Preliminary.   *Source: Energy Information Administration, U.S. Department of Energy (EIA-DOE)*

Production of Major Refined Petroleum Products in Continental United States   In Millions of Barrels

Year	Asphalt	Aviation Gasoline	Fuel Oil Distillate	Fuel Oil Residual	Gasoline	Jet Fuel	Kero- sene	Natural Gas Plant Liquids	Lubri- cants	Liquified Gasses Total	Liquified Gasses at L.P.G.[2]	Liquified Gasses AT L.P.G.[3]
2008	150.9	5.5	1,569.6	227.1	3,072	539.5	12.0	651.9	63.2	786.1	556.2	229.9
2009	131.0	5.0	1,476.7	218.6	3,199	510.2	6.9	688.5	55.4	821.1	591.3	229.8
2010	132.1	5.4	1,384.7	200.8	3,298	519.7	7.2	730.4	47.6	869.3	631.7	237.6
2011	129.6	5.4	1,405.1	175.3	3,189	520.2	4.4	825.0	45.3	915.5	689.1	226.4
2012	124.5	5.0	1,369.8	126.2	3,185	512.2	1.4	830.7	41.4	992.0	762.6	229.4
2013	117.0	4.2	1,727.0	170.4	3,347	547.8	4.0	809.0	59.8	1,162.2	933.1	229.1
2014	118.7	4.3	1,463.7	93.9	3,257	536.6	3.2	940.7	45.2	1,322.3	1,081.9	240.3
2015	125.4	4.2	1,451.1	94.7	3,344	561.6	2.4	1,038.1	49.4	1,418.1	1,194.6	223.4
2016	128.8	4.1	1,419.1	130.6	3,414	587.9	2.6	1,114.4	47.4	1,501.5	1,272.9	228.6
2017[1]	128.7	4.1	1,437.3	130.9	3,401	613.8	1.6	1,363.7	39.7	1,593.1	1,363.7	229.4

[1] Preliminary.   [2] Gas processing plants.   [3] Refineries.   *Source: Energy Information Administration, U.S. Department of Energy (EIA-DOE)*

Stocks of Petroleum and Products in the United States on January 1   In Millions of Barrels

Year	Crude Petroleum	Strategic Reserve	Refined Products Total	Asphalt	Aviation Gasoline	Fuel Oil Distillate	Fuel Oil Residual	Finished Gasoline	Jet Fuel	Kero- sene	Gases[2]	Lubri- cants	Motor Gasoline Total	Motor Gasoline Finished[3]
2009	1,026.1	701.8	367.8	20.3	1.2	145.9	36.2	98.2	38.2	2.2	126.9	10.7	----	98
2010	1,051.8	726.6	375.1	17.9	1.0	164.7	37.8	85.9	43.4	2.5	113.2	8.9	----	86
2011	1,058.5	726.5	357.4	19.9	1.1	164.5	41.3	63.4	43.2	2.4	121.3	8.2	----	63
2012	1,026.8	696.0	332.7	19.6	1.1	149.7	34.1	61.4	41.7	2.4	111.1	9.9	----	61
2013	1,060.3	695.3	313.6	22.1	1.0	134.7	33.9	56.8	39.5	1.7	140.9	9.6	----	57
2014	1,053.6	696.0	291.3	21.4	0.9	127.3	37.7	39.7	37.2	1.9	112.7	10.1	----	40
2015	1,084.7	691.0	286.9	21.2	1.1	136.1	33.7	30.6	37.5	2.1	154.8	11.2	----	31
2016	1,176.5	695.1	325.1	24.6	0.9	160.7	42.2	28.5	40.3	2.6	176.7	13.5	----	28
2017	1,179.4	695.1	329.7	22.9	1.0	165.5	41.5	28.6	42.8	2.3	178.4	12.4	----	29
2018[1]	1,084.0	663.7	291.6	21.5	1.0	145.6	29.4	24.6	41.2	2.1	184.8	12.0	----	25

[1] Preliminary.   [2] Includes ethane & ethylene at plants and refineries.   [3] Includes oxygenated.
Source: Energy Information Administration, U.S. Department of Energy (EIA-DOE)

PETROLEUM

Stocks of Crude Petroleum in the United States, on First of Month   In Millions of Barrels

Year	Jan.	Feb.	Mar.	Apr.	May	June	July	Aug.	Sept.	Oct.	Nov.	Dec.
2009	1,055.1	1,063.1	1,079.7	1,089.7	1,081.2	1,071.2	1,069.5	1,059.7	1,060.1	1,057.6	1,063.0	1,051.8
2010	1,063.4	1,069.8	1,085.8	1,089.9	1,088.5	1,092.1	1,084.2	1,085.9	1,089.3	1,094.1	1,079.0	1,060.0
2011	1,071.6	1,075.0	1,086.8	1,093.1	1,094.9	1,082.3	1,064.6	1,043.2	1,026.1	1,032.9	1,032.8	1,026.6
2012	1,039.4	1,044.4	1,069.1	1,078.8	1,083.9	1,083.9	1,068.6	1,058.4	1,064.9	1,071.3	1,074.4	1,060.8
2013	1,073.5	1,080.9	1,088.1	1,091.8	1,088.2	1,071.7	1,062.5	1,059.5	1,067.1	1,079.8	1,072.5	1,053.6
2014	1,059.7	1,069.3	1,079.7	1,086.5	1,085.0	1,074.9	1,059.7	1,051.6	1,051.9	1,073.0	1,078.5	1,084.7
2015	1,112.4	1,139.0	1,165.8	1,174.3	1,171.7	1,163.4	1,150.6	1,152.9	1,155.9	1,181.8	1,182.5	1,176.5
2016	1,166.9	1,187.3	1,199.9	1,204.4	1,207.0	1,196.0	1,188.6	1,181.8	1,166.6	1,186.3	1,185.8	1,179.7
2017	1,201.9	1,220.2	1,230.1	1,213.1	1,201.3	1,180.7	1,162.3	1,138.8	1,143.2	1,128.7	1,114.3	1,084.5
2018[1]	1,084.1	1,089.0	1,088.9	1,099.0	1,093.4	1,074.9	1,069.3	1,066.9	1,076.2	1,087.3	1,098.2	1,090.9

[1] Preliminary.   Source: Energy Information Administration; U.S. Department of Energy

Production of Crude Petroleum in the United States   In Thousands of Barrels Per Day

Year	Jan.	Feb.	Mar.	Apr.	May	June	July	Aug.	Sept.	Oct.	Nov.	Dec.	Average
2009	5,138	5,236	5,210	5,278	5,374	5,263	5,389	5,406	5,555	5,515	5,378	5,438	5,348
2010	5,390	5,548	5,506	5,383	5,391	5,381	5,299	5,442	5,611	5,621	5,567	5,602	5,478
2011	5,492	5,399	5,612	5,552	5,613	5,578	5,430	5,651	5,583	5,886	6,001	6,032	5,652
2012	6,161	6,245	6,301	6,296	6,351	6,269	6,421	6,329	6,563	6,946	7,037	7,088	6,501
2013	7,025	7,144	7,208	7,355	7,316	7,268	7,483	7,531	7,784	7,699	7,873	7,899	7,465
2014	8,051	8,136	8,274	8,573	8,612	8,718	8,782	8,886	9,041	9,221	9,303	9,467	8,755
2015	9,385	9,511	9,578	9,650	9,464	9,344	9,430	9,400	9,460	9,388	9,318	9,251	9,431
2016	9,197	9,055	9,081	8,866	8,824	8,670	8,635	8,670	8,519	8,787	8,888	8,778	8,831
2017	8,840	9,083	9,140	9,085	9,168	9,074	9,230	9,244	9,495	9,703	10,103	10,040	9,350
2018[1]	9,995	10,248	10,461	10,475	10,464	10,672	10,936	11,325	11,470	11,559	11,905	11,849	10,947

[1] Preliminary.   Source: Energy Information Administration, U.S. Department of Energy (EIA-DOE)

U.S. Foreign Trade of Petroleum and Products   In Thousands of Barrels Per Day

	---- Exports ----		---- Imports ----				
Year	Total[2]	Petroleum Products	Crude	Petroleum Products	Distillate Fuel Oil	Residual Fuel Oil	Net Imports[3]
2008	1,802	1,773	9,783	2,570	213	349	11,114
2009	2,024	1,980	9,013	2,121	225	331	9,667
2010	2,353	2,311	9,213	1,985	228	366	9,441
2011	2,986	2,939	8,935	1,994	179	328	8,450
2012	3,205	3,137	8,527	1,689	126	256	7,393
2013	3,621	3,487	7,730	1,749	155	225	6,237
2014	4,176	3,824	7,344	1,529	195	173	5,065
2015	4,738	4,273	7,363	1,694	200	192	4,711
2016	5,261	4,670	7,850	1,854	147	205	4,795
2017[1]	6,271	5,166	7,911	1,832	143	190	3,805

[1] Preliminary.   [2] Includes crude oil.   [3] Equals imports minus exports.
Source: Energy Information Administration, U.S. Department of Energy (EIA-DOE)

Domestic First Purchase Price of Crude Petroleum at Wells[2]   In U.S. Dollars Per Barrel

Year	Jan.	Feb.	Mar.	Apr.	May	June	July	Aug.	Sept.	Oct.	Nov.	Dec.	Average
2009	35.00	34.14	42.46	45.22	52.69	63.08	60.43	65.28	65.27	69.82	71.99	70.42	56.32
2010	72.87	72.74	75.77	78.80	70.91	70.77	71.37	72.07	71.23	76.02	79.20	83.98	74.64
2011	85.66	86.69	99.19	108.80	102.46	97.30	97.82	89.00	90.22	92.28	100.18	98.71	95.69
2012	98.99	102.04	105.42	103.62	95.57	83.59	86.10	92.53	95.98	92.24	89.64	89.81	94.63
2013	95.00	95.01	95.54	94.41	94.75	93.82	101.41	102.96	102.32	96.18	88.70	91.85	96.00
2014	89.57	96.86	96.17	96.49	95.74	98.68	96.70	90.72	86.87	78.84	71.07	54.86	87.71
2015	43.06	44.35	42.66	49.30	54.38	55.88	47.70	39.98	41.60	42.33	38.19	32.26	44.31
2016	27.02	25.51	31.87	35.59	41.02	43.96	40.70	40.46	40.54	45.00	41.65	47.12	38.37
2017	48.19	49.41	46.39	47.23	45.19	42.19	43.42	44.96	47.17	49.13	55.19	56.98	47.95
2018[2]	62.25	61.20	60.68	63.50	66.16	62.80	67.00	62.64	63.55	65.18	55.65	47.72	61.53

[1] Preliminary.   [2] Buyers posted prices.   Source: Energy Information Administration, U.S. Department of Energy (EIA-DOE)

Refiner Sales Prices of Residual Fuel Oil In U.S. Dollars Per Gallon

Year	Jan.	Feb.	Mar.	Apr.	May	June	July	Aug.	Sept.	Oct.	Nov.	Dec.	Average
2011	NA	2.100	2.344	2.555	2.463	2.467	2.547	2.394	2.368	2.512	2.566	2.473	2.389
2012	2.591	2.739	2.921	2.805	2.589	2.275	2.271	2.586	2.558	2.464	2.385	2.341	2.548
2013	2.530	2.571	2.479	2.354	2.316	2.285	2.282	2.331	2.359	2.338	2.296	2.315	2.371
2014	2.337	2.459	2.470	2.401	2.350	2.358	2.287	2.148	2.100	1.893	1.639	1.237	2.140
2015	0.936	1.150	1.093	1.124	1.198	1.175	1.080	0.797	0.819	0.812	0.766	0.552	0.959
2016	0.477	0.475	0.582	0.633	0.729	0.850	0.876	0.842	0.846	0.961	0.920	1.024	0.768
2017	1.099	1.174	1.103	1.038	0.986	0.937	1.026	1.042	1.150	1.153	1.302	1.254	1.105
2018[1]	1.301	1.221	1.227	1.311	1.462	1.487	1.543	1.499	1.520	1.620	1.360	1.252	1.400

Sulfur 1% or less, excluding taxes. [1] Preliminary. Source: Energy Information Administration, U.S. Department of Energy (EIA-DOE)

Refiner Sales Prices of No. 2 Fuel Oil In U.S. Dollars Per Gallon

Year	Jan.	Feb.	Mar.	Apr.	May	June	July	Aug.	Sept.	Oct.	Nov.	Dec.	Average
2011	2.585	2.737	2.996	3.167	3.039	2.956	3.024	2.927	2.927	2.915	3.050	2.928	2.907
2012	3.027	3.166	3.211	3.153	2.976	2.635	2.774	2.988	3.128	3.155	3.049	3.003	3.031
2013	3.069	3.168	2.977	2.793	2.708	2.741	2.894	2.954	2.973	2.955	2.910	3.011	2.966
2014	3.059	3.051	2.979	2.911	2.883	2.878	2.825	2.784	2.701	2.476	2.371	2.050	2.747
2015	1.669	1.850	1.847	1.740	1.852	1.813	1.654	1.461	1.438	1.411	1.356	1.126	1.601
2016	0.976	0.948	1.070	1.113	1.291	1.404	1.305	1.307	1.341	1.443	1.386	1.507	1.258
2017	1.560	1.553	1.495	1.499	1.447	1.375	1.392	1.522	1.668	1.695	1.781	1.841	1.569
2018[1]	1.990	1.889	1.848	1.982	2.143	2.089	2.079	2.114	2.214	2.281	2.098	1.796	2.044

Excluding taxes. [1] Preliminary. Source: Energy Information Administration, U.S. Department of Energy (EIA-DOE)

Refiner Sales Prices of No. 2 Diesel Fuel In U.S. Dollars Per Gallon

Year	Jan.	Feb.	Mar.	Apr.	May	June	July	Aug.	Sept.	Oct.	Nov.	Dec.	Average
2011	2.621	2.820	3.134	3.296	3.116	3.079	3.135	3.032	3.035	3.035	3.157	2.927	3.034
2012	3.018	3.163	3.308	3.252	3.039	2.741	2.907	3.206	3.278	3.265	3.117	3.022	3.109
2013	3.046	3.259	3.082	2.969	2.958	2.923	3.015	3.084	3.095	3.006	2.949	2.998	3.028
2014	2.981	3.091	3.031	3.027	2.987	2.973	2.921	2.900	2.806	2.639	2.558	1.980	2.825
2015	1.616	1.861	1.815	1.805	1.973	1.881	1.729	1.562	1.551	1.572	1.456	1.176	1.666
2016	1.015	1.043	1.189	1.251	1.432	1.531	1.426	1.440	1.471	1.592	1.469	1.606	1.372
2017	1.636	1.641	1.581	1.627	1.552	1.465	1.533	1.681	1.847	1.852	1.936	1.918	1.689
2018[1]	2.042	1.972	1.952	2.099	2.258	2.203	2.192	2.203	2.282	2.379	2.130	1.794	2.126

Excluding taxes. [1] Preliminary. Source: Energy Information Administration, U.S. Department of Energy (EIA-DOE)

Refiner Sales Prices of Kerosine-Type Jet Fuel In U.S. Dollars Per Gallon

Year	Jan.	Feb.	Mar.	Apr.	May	June	July	Aug.	Sept.	Oct.	Nov.	Dec.	Average
2011	2.585	2.783	3.095	3.259	3.188	3.101	3.090	3.040	3.025	2.962	3.089	2.951	3.014
2012	3.059	3.186	3.296	3.255	3.076	2.747	2.850	3.129	3.245	3.182	3.015	2.982	3.080
2013	3.093	3.250	3.036	2.884	2.763	2.784	2.899	2.995	3.017	2.928	2.868	2.978	2.953
2014	2.964	2.981	2.939	2.911	2.932	2.917	2.882	2.882	2.823	2.547	2.410	1.998	2.766
2015	1.612	1.722	1.731	1.709	1.933	1.813	1.655	1.479	1.443	1.451	1.400	1.207	1.596
2016	1.022	1.017	1.100	1.155	1.311	1.428	1.354	1.313	1.366	1.471	1.406	1.511	1.288
2017	1.561	1.592	1.520	1.545	1.459	1.378	1.436	1.587	1.771	1.704	1.795	1.846	1.600
2018[1]	1.969	1.911	1.893	2.032	2.175	2.152	2.140	2.148	2.214	2.296	2.100	1.812	2.070

Excluding taxes. [1] Preliminary. Source: Energy Information Administration, U.S. Department of Energy (EIA-DOE)

Refiner Sales Prices of Propane[2] In U.S. Dollars Per Gallon

Year	Jan.	Feb.	Mar.	Apr.	May	June	July	Aug.	Sept.	Oct.	Nov.	Dec.	Average
2011	1.380	1.401	1.403	1.433	1.515	1.503	1.513	1.522	1.557	1.511	1.498	1.444	1.467
2012	1.341	1.282	1.293	1.163	0.950	0.762	0.809	0.875	0.910	0.979	0.955	0.894	1.033
2013	0.928	0.953	0.952	0.949	0.932	0.861	0.903	1.059	1.114	1.154	1.219	1.342	1.048
2014	1.641	1.654	1.198	1.121	1.057	1.054	1.075	1.055	1.097	1.044	0.966	0.819	1.148
2015	0.713	0.748	0.689	0.566	0.475	0.404	0.405	0.402	0.469	0.524	0.505	0.499	0.533
2016	0.460	0.470	0.497	0.458	0.511	0.497	0.476	0.453	0.494	0.608	0.588	0.703	0.518
2017	0.788	0.792	0.671	0.641	0.631	0.585	0.634	0.742	0.864	0.942	0.997	0.991	0.773
2018[1]	0.990	0.889	0.827	0.792	0.867	0.807	0.854	0.907	0.951	0.948	0.826	0.799	0.871

[1] Preliminary. [2] Consumer Grade, Excluding taxes. Source: Energy Information Administration, U.S. Department of Energy (EIA-DOE)

CRUDE OIL, LIGHT - NYMEX
Weekly Nearest Futures as of 03/29/2019

WEEKLY NEAREST FUTURES
As of 03/29/2019
Chart High 114.83 on 05/02/2011
Chart Low 26.05 on 02/11/2016

Nearby Futures through Last Trading Day.

Volume of Trading of Crude Oil Futures in New York   In Thousands of Contracts

Year	Jan.	Feb.	Mar.	Apr.	May	June	July	Aug.	Sept.	Oct.	Nov.	Dec.	Total
2009	11,369	11,411	11,340	10,106	9,939	11,367	11,924	11,823	11,462	13,179	11,600	11,906	137,428
2010	10,894	12,772	13,298	17,433	17,591	14,458	11,427	14,494	16,018	14,423	13,429	12,416	168,652
2011	17,948	17,757	15,675	12,089	15,126	15,815	11,571	17,178	13,488	14,785	13,609	9,994	175,036
2012	12,557	14,693	13,290	10,627	12,402	12,593	10,870	11,687	10,572	11,660	11,055	8,524	140,532
2013	12,028	11,540	10,515	13,354	13,825	13,111	15,384	12,849	11,139	13,792	10,569	9,586	147,691
2014	11,162	9,862	11,700	11,467	10,283	11,398	13,174	11,016	12,824	15,939	12,204	14,119	145,147
2015	16,514	20,263	17,884	17,638	13,553	13,995	14,863	19,197	16,605	17,484	16,145	18,064	202,202
2016	21,710	25,607	22,954	23,614	21,494	20,790	18,841	23,051	24,332	23,019	27,375	23,981	276,768
2017	22,430	20,528	26,417	21,225	27,527	29,141	27,618	34,725	27,571	25,031	27,636	20,205	310,053
2018	28,504	26,784	25,003	27,977	30,951	28,578	23,056	19,661	21,113	24,507	27,571	22,909	306,613

Contract size = 1,000 bbl.   *Source: CME Group; New York Mercantile Exchange (NYMEX)*

Average Open Interest of Crude Oil Futures in New York   In Thousands of Contracts

Year	Jan.	Feb.	Mar.	Apr.	May	June	July	Aug.	Sept.	Oct.	Nov.	Dec.
2009	1,232.4	1,223.3	1,190.2	1,163.0	1,159.6	1,180.5	1,170.7	1,176.0	1,174.2	1,231.2	1,207.8	1,200.4
2010	1,303.5	1,304.8	1,324.1	1,375.8	1,416.3	1,307.3	1,252.7	1,262.3	1,338.2	1,419.1	1,414.1	1,380.0
2011	1,494.0	1,540.7	1,551.4	1,565.5	1,591.3	1,531.0	1,517.1	1,521.8	1,433.7	1,406.6	1,332.6	1,321.5
2012	1,374.6	1,475.5	1,565.8	1,561.7	1,520.9	1,446.8	1,408.6	1,473.6	1,575.5	1,574.3	1,548.8	1,514.8
2013	1,504.5	1,636.4	1,690.3	1,751.8	1,753.7	1,813.5	1,835.7	1,872.0	1,896.1	1,821.8	1,682.1	1,631.0
2014	1,607.4	1,628.5	1,653.4	1,654.8	1,633.4	1,703.8	1,687.6	1,572.7	1,518.4	1,495.4	1,464.1	1,450.3
2015	1,699.2	1,713.6	1,725.0	1,734.5	1,683.7	1,648.2	1,693.9	1,702.7	1,661.4	1,652.0	1,666.0	1,674.5
2016	1,741.4	1,821.0	1,774.8	1,751.3	1,708.3	1,737.3	1,727.7	1,810.2	1,842.7	1,851.9	1,982.7	2,063.4
2017	2,143.1	2,148.1	2,181.9	2,190.6	2,241.2	2,168.4	2,158.7	2,259.7	2,379.9	2,446.4	2,550.6	2,513.1
2018	2,589.4	2,509.2	2,444.7	2,567.8	2,662.5	2,501.2	2,425.1	2,292.2	2,246.9	2,182.7	2,044.7	2,065.2

Contract size = 1,000 bbl.   *Source: CME Group; New York Mercantile Exchange (NYMEX)*

Plastics

Plastics are moldable, chemically fabricated materials produced mostly from fossil fuels, such as oil, coal, or natural gas. The word plastic is derived from the Greek *plastikos*, meaning "to mold," and the Latin *plasticus*, meaning "capable of molding." Leo Baekeland created the first commercially successful thermosetting synthetic resin in 1909. More than 50 families of plastics have since been produced.

All plastics can be divided into either thermoplastics or thermosetting plastics. The difference is the way in which they respond to heat. Thermoplastics can be repeatedly softened by heat and hardened by cooling. Thermosetting plastics harden permanently after being heated once.

Prices – The average monthly producer price index (1982=100) of plastic resins and materials in the U.S. in 2018 rose +4.7% yr/yr to 243.7, remaining below the 2014 record high of 257.0. The average monthly producer price index of thermoplastic resins in the U.S. in 2018 rose +4.8% yr/yr to 247.0, remaining below the 2014 record high of 262.1. The average monthly producer price index of thermosetting resins in the U.S. in 2018 rose +4.7% to 240.8, but still below the 2014 record high of 244.4.

Supply – Total U.S. plastics production in 2016 rose +1.6% yr/yr to 112.227 billion pounds, which was still below the 2007 record high of 115.793 billion pounds. U.S. plastics production has more than doubled in the past two decades. By sector, the thermoplastics sector is by far the largest, with 2016 production up +1.5 yr/yr to 95.721 billion pounds and accounting for 85.3% of total U.S. plastic production. Production in the thermosetting plastic sector (polyester unsaturated, phenolic, and epoxy) rose +2.0% yr/yr in 2016 to 16.506 billion pounds and accounted for 14.7% of total U.S. plastics production. The category of "other plastics" back in 2008 was 11.952 billion pounds and accounted for about 12% of total U.S. plastics production in that year.

Demand – Total usage of plastic resins by important markets in 2017 in the U.S. fell -0.2% to 78.963 billion pounds. The breakdown by market shows that the largest single consumption category is "Packaging" with 26.847 billion pounds of usage in 2017, accounting for 34.0% of total U.S. consumption. After packaging, the largest categories are "Consumer and Industrial" (20.0% of U.S. consumption), and "Building and Construction" (17.0% of U.S. consumption).

Trade – U.S. exports of plastics in 2017 fell -14.4% yr/yr to 14.213 billion pounds, down from last year's record high. U.S. exports accounted for 18.0% of U.S. supply disappearance in 2017.

Plastics Production by Resin in the United States   In Millions of Pounds

| | ------------ Thermosets ------------ | | | | ---------------------------------- Thermoplastics ---------------------------------- | | | | | | | | | | |
Year	Polyester Unsaturated	Phenolic	Epoxy	Total Thermosets	Thermoplastic Polyester	Polyvinyl Chloride	Polystyrene	Polypropylene	Nylon	Low Density Polyethylene[1]	High Density Polyethylene	Total Thermoplastics	Total Selected Plastics	Other Plastics	Total Plastics
2007	3,471	4,838	642	8,951	8,745	14,606	6,015	19,445	1,295	21,511	18,222	92,835	101,786	14,007	115,793
2008	2,798	4,233	583	15,091	8,159	12,789	5,220	16,768	1,148	19,061	10,247	86,455	89,594	11,952	101,546
2009	NA	NA	535	12,713	NA	12,754	4,865	16,623	943	19,793	16,956	85,983	98,696	NA	98,696
2010	NA	NA	610	13,214	NA	14,017	5,055	17,254	1,027	20,530	16,887	89,592	102,806	NA	102,806
2011	----	----	613	13,800	----	14,434	5,472	16,418	1,106	20,130	17,116	89,408	103,208	----	103,208
2012	----	----	545	14,519	----	15,310	5,452	16,326	1,193	20,328	17,738	91,426	105,945	----	105,945
2013	----	----	499	14,975	----	15,373	5,405	16,427	1,238	20,772	17,899	92,547	107,522	----	107,522
2014	----	----	561	15,814	----	15,038	5,408	16,446	1,299	20,969	18,585	92,369	108,183	----	108,183
2015	----	----	544	16,188	----	14,704	5,375	17,153	----	21,622	18,870	94,290	110,478	----	110,478
2016	----	----	537	16,506	----	15,455	5,411	17,152	----	21,764	19,250	95,721	112,227	----	112,227

[1] Includes LDPE and LLDPE.   *Source: American Plastics Council (APC)*

Total Resin Sales and Captive Use by Important Markets   In Millions of Pounds (Dry Weight Basis)

Year	Adhesive, Inks & Coatings	Building & Construction	Consumer & Industrial	Electrical & Electronics	Exports	Furniture & Furnishings	Industrial & Machinary	Packaging	Transportation	Other	Total
2008	937	12,313	15,461	1,755	11,962	2,671	834	24,097	2,751	1,375	74,156
2009	798	11,102	14,717	1,519	14,691	1,877	678	23,702	1,971	972	72,025
2010	846	10,914	14,782	1,561	14,488	1,894	774	25,041	2,558	1,200	74,057
2011	801	11,036	14,743	1,618	14,858	1,818	781	25,302	2,649	1,206	74,811
2012	334	11,704	14,613	1,643	14,588	1,471	845	25,828	2,725	1,259	75,010
2013	322	12,287	14,739	1,731	14,232	1,470	852	25,998	2,791	1,293	75,714
2014	327	12,626	14,968	1,770	12,666	1,372	861	26,081	3,005	1,352	75,028
2015	----	12,474	15,592	1,559	14,813	1,559	780	26,507	3,118	1,559	77,962
2016	----	11,864	15,028	1,582	16,610	1,582	791	26,893	3,164	1,582	79,096
2017	----	13,424	15,793	1,579	14,213	1,579	790	26,847	3,159	1,579	78,963

[1] Included in other.   *Source: American Plastics Council (APC)*

PLASTICS

Average Producer Price Index of Plastic Resins and Materials (066) in the United States   (1982 = 100)

Year	Jan.	Feb.	Mar.	Apr.	May	June	July	Aug.	Sept.	Oct.	Nov.	Dec.	Average
2009	184.6	190.1	188.6	183.5	185.9	185.9	194.4	194.5	196.4	194.5	194.5	196.8	190.8
2010	195.0	206.4	208.2	222.4	213.1	208.1	212.7	211.1	210.7	215.0	210.3	208.4	210.1
2011	213.2	218.8	223.2	229.1	239.5	238.4	236.7	233.8	235.3	229.2	231.5	227.2	229.7
2012	232.0	234.9	238.0	239.6	238.7	236.3	233.8	234.8	231.8	234.4	234.2	233.9	235.2
2013	239.7	244.1	247.1	245.9	244.6	245.4	244.4	245.1	245.5	245.8	247.9	247.7	245.3
2014	250.6	253.8	256.6	257.5	257.3	255.2	257.1	259.4	261.7	263.0	259.7	252.4	257.0
2015	243.2	237.3	230.2	229.4	230.3	231.5	230.5	227.7	221.3	218.9	217.7	218.1	228.0
2016	215.0	216.3	213.5	213.7	216.7	219.5	219.3	220.1	221.0	225.6	223.1	218.4	218.5
2017	220.5	225.2	232.3	235.8	234.3	232.8	230.4	230.3	232.9	237.7	239.7	240.2	232.7
2018[1]	235.1	236.4	240.3	238.3	241.9	243.8	248.5	252.3	250.2	245.6	246.4	245.2	243.7

[1] Preliminary.   *Source: Bureau of Labor Statistics, U.S. Department of Commerce (BLS)*

Average Producer Price Index of Thermoplastic Resins (0662) in the United States   (1982 = 100)

Year	Jan.	Feb.	Mar.	Apr.	May	June	July	Aug.	Sept.	Oct.	Nov.	Dec.	Average
2009	179.3	187.1	185.9	180.3	183.1	183.2	193.2	192.9	194.5	192.2	192.8	194.9	188.3
2010	193.2	206.8	208.8	225.7	214.9	208.8	214.3	212.6	212.1	217.2	211.7	209.3	211.3
2011	214.7	221.1	226.0	232.6	244.6	242.1	239.9	236.3	238.1	230.9	233.6	228.6	232.4
2012	234.3	237.6	241.1	242.9	241.7	238.8	235.6	236.8	233.2	236.2	236.1	235.4	237.5
2013	242.8	247.4	250.7	249.4	247.7	248.7	246.7	247.7	249.2	249.6	251.8	251.7	248.6
2014	254.9	258.5	261.7	262.8	262.1	260.0	262.3	265.0	267.2	269.0	265.3	255.9	262.1
2015	245.6	239.2	231.3	230.5	233.0	234.3	233.2	229.8	222.1	219.8	218.4	218.9	229.7
2016	215.7	217.1	214.0	214.7	218.1	221.2	221.2	222.0	223.0	227.7	224.6	219.0	219.9
2017	221.4	226.8	235.7	239.2	237.4	235.8	233.0	233.0	236.1	241.5	243.9	244.5	235.7
2018[1]	238.5	238.5	243.2	240.4	244.7	246.9	252.3	257.5	254.9	248.9	249.7	247.9	247.0

[1] Preliminary.   *Source: Bureau of Labor Statistics, U.S. Department of Commerce (BLS)*

Average Producer Price Index of Thermosetting Resins (0663) in the United States   (1982 = 100)

Year	Jan.	Feb.	Mar.	Apr.	May	June	July	Aug.	Sept.	Oct.	Nov.	Dec.	Average
2009	226.7	219.3	216.2	213.5	213.9	213.7	213.5	215.5	219.7	220.0	216.2	220.0	217.4
2010	218.0	216.8	217.1	216.7	216.1	217.2	216.3	215.2	215.3	215.4	215.3	216.1	216.3
2011	218.0	219.4	220.6	223.0	224.8	231.9	233.0	233.7	234.0	233.9	233.8	233.4	228.3
2012	233.2	234.0	235.1	235.9	236.4	236.6	238.1	237.6	238.6	238.6	238.1	239.3	236.8
2013	236.4	240.1	241.8	241.4	241.8	241.8	246.2	245.6	239.7	239.9	240.7	240.2	241.3
2014	241.5	242.6	243.4	243.7	245.9	244.3	243.5	244.2	246.3	245.7	244.6	247.6	244.4
2015	244.6	241.0	237.9	237.2	229.2	230.1	229.5	229.6	230.5	227.7	226.9	226.7	232.6
2016	224.4	224.9	223.4	221.6	222.4	222.9	221.8	222.7	223.3	228.0	228.4	228.0	224.3
2017	228.6	230.1	227.6	231.3	230.9	230.2	230.1	229.4	229.3	230.5	230.6	230.8	230.0
2018[1]	230.9	240.1	239.9	242.3	242.1	242.0	242.8	238.3	238.6	242.6	243.6	246.3	240.8

[1] Preliminary.   *Source: Bureau of Labor Statistics, U.S. Department of Commerce (BLS)*

Average Producer Price Index of Styrene Plastics Materials (0662-06) in the United States   (1982 = 100)

Year	Jan.	Feb.	Mar.	Apr.	May	June	July	Aug.	Sept.	Oct.	Nov.	Dec.	Average
1995	129.0	127.0	132.5	134.7	135.9	137.5	135.1	133.2	132.1	130.1	127.9	126.1	131.8
1996	125.7	123.5	125.0	118.3	120.1	122.7	123.4	123.3	123.6	122.8	122.0	120.9	122.6
1997	120.6	123.1	123.0	121.6	121.6	121.6	122.7	117.7	118.0	116.5	113.5	113.7	119.5
1998	113.3	113.9	115.5	114.9	114.1	112.8	111.3	111.2	107.6	107.9	107.1	106.3	111.3
1999	103.5	102.4	103.5	104.7	103.0	102.3	103.1	101.5	101.4	99.8	99.4	100.5	102.1
2000	103.0	104.3	110.5	113.0	116.2	116.9	118.5	116.5	115.0	114.1	112.1	110.4	112.5
2001	110.5	109.2	107.9	108.0	101.8	99.9	97.6	95.7	87.3	89.4	90.0	85.4	98.6
2002	85.7	85.8	87.9	88.5	90.4	91.7	93.7	100.6	100.5	108.9	108.1	103.9	95.5
2003[1]	102.9	110.2	119.5	127.2	126.7	119.1	118.0	113.3	112.8	113.6	113.7	111.6	115.7
2004[1]	Data no longer available												

[1] Preliminary.   *Source: Bureau of Labor Statistics, U.S. Department of Commerce (BLS)*

Platinum-Group Metals

Platinum (atomic symbol Pt) is a relatively rare, chemically inert metallic element that is more valuable than gold. Platinum is a grayish-white metal that has a high fusing point, is malleable and ductile, and has a high electrical resistance. Chemically, platinum is relatively inert and resists attack by air, water, single acids, and ordinary reagents. Platinum is the most important of the six-metal group, which also includes ruthenium, rhodium, palladium, osmium, and iridium. The word "platinum" is derived from the Spanish word *platina* meaning silver.

Platinum is one of the world's rarest metals with new mine production totaling only about 5 million troy ounces a year. All the platinum mined to date would fit in the average-size living room. Platinum is mined all over the world with supplies concentrated in South Africa. South Africa accounts for nearly 80% of world supply, followed by Russia, and North America.

Because platinum will never tarnish, lose its rich white luster, or even wear down after many years, it is prized by the jewelry industry. The international jewelry industry is the largest consumer sector for platinum, accounting for 51% of total platinum demand. In Europe and the U.S., the normal purity of platinum is 95%. Ten tons of ore must be mined and a five-month process is needed to produce one ounce of pure platinum.

The second major consumer sector for platinum is for auto catalysts, with 21% of total platinum demand. Catalysts in autos are used to convert most of vehicle emissions into less harmful carbon dioxide, nitrogen, and water vapor. Platinum is also used in the production of hard disk drive coatings, fiber optic cables, infra-red detectors, fertilizers, explosives, petrol additives, platinum-tipped spark plugs, glassmaking equipment, biodegradable elements for household detergents, dental restorations, and in anti-cancer drugs.

Palladium (atomic symbol Pd) is very similar to platinum and is part of the same general metals group. Palladium is mined with platinum, but it is somewhat more common because it is also a by-product of nickel mining. The primary use for palladium is in the use of automotive catalysts, with that sector accounting for about 63% of total palladium demand. Other uses for palladium include electronic equipment (21%), dental alloys (12%), and jewelry (4%).

Rhodium (atomic symbol Rh), another member of the platinum group, is also used in the automotive industry in pollution control devices. To some extent palladium has replaced rhodium. Iridium (atomic symbol Ir) is used to process catalysts and it has also found use in some auto catalysts. Iridium and ruthenium (atomic symbol Ru) are used in the production of polyvinyl chloride. As the prices of these metals change, there is some substitution. Therefore, strength of platinum prices relative to palladium should lead to the substitution of palladium for platinum in catalytic converters.

Platinum futures and options and palladium futures

are traded at the CME Group. Platinum and palladium futures are traded on the Tokyo Commodity Exchange (TOCOM). The CME platinum futures contract calls for the delivery of 50 troy ounces of platinum (0.9995 fineness) and the contract trades in terms of dollars and cents per troy ounce. The CME palladium futures contract calls for the delivery of 50 troy ounces of palladium (0.9995 fineness) and the contract is priced in terms of dollars and cents per troy ounce.

Prices – CME platinum futures prices (Barchart.com symbol PL) on the nearest-futures chart in 2018 started the year at $934.20 per troy ounce, moved higher in January and February but then moved lower the rest of the year to finally settle down -14.8% at $795.30 per troy ounce. CME palladium futures prices (Barchart.com symbol PA) on the nearest-futures chart in 2018 moved lower until mid-year but then turned higher the rest of the year to close up +12.8% at $1,097.20 per troy ounce.

Supply – World mine production of platinum in 2018 fell -19.6% yr/yr to 100,000 kilograms and remained below the 2006 record high of 218,000 kilograms. South Africa is the world's largest producer of platinum by far with 68.8% of world production in 2018, followed by Russia with 13.1%, Zimbabwe with 8.8%, Canada with 5.9% and the U.S. with 2.6%. World mine production of palladium in 2018 was down -6.7% at 210,000 kilograms, which was below the record high production level of 224,000 kg in 2007. The world's largest palladium producers are Russia with 40.5% of world production in 2018, South Africa with 32.4%, Canada with 8.1%, and the U.S. with 6.7%. World production of platinum group metals other than platinum and palladium in 2016 rose by 18.0% yr/yr to 70,300 kilograms, but still below the 2005 record high of 77,700 kilograms.

U.S. mine production of platinum in 2018 rose +3.0% yr/yr to 4,100 kilograms, but still below the record high of 4,390 kilograms posted in 2002. U.S. mine production of palladium in 2018 rose +2.9% yr/yr to 14,000 kilograms, but still below the record high of 14,800 kilograms posted in 2002. U.S. refinery secondary production of scrap platinum and palladium in 2016 rose +3.8% yr/yr to 40,500 kilograms, down slightly from 2013's 20-year record high of 43,000 kilograms.

Demand – This data is no longer available but in 2004 the total of platinum-group metals sold to consuming industries in the U.S. was 91,434 kilograms. At that time the two main U.S. industries that used platinum were the auto industry, which accounted for about 74% of U.S. platinum usage in 2004, and the jewelry industry, which accounted for about 26% of U.S. platinum usage.

Trade – U.S. imports of refined platinum and palladium in 2018 for consumption fell -58.0% yr/yr to 222,978 kilograms. U.S. exports of refined platinum and palladium in 2017 fell -13.3% yr/yr to 265,344 kilograms and still well below the record high of 403,640 kilograms in 2013. The U.S. relied on imports for 73% of its platinum and palladium consumption in 2018.

PLATINUM-GROUP METALS

World Mine Production of Platinum   In Kilograms

Year	Australia	Canada	Colombia[3]	Finland	Japan	Russia	Serbia/Montenegro	Africa	United States	Zimbabwe	World Total
2009	230	4,000	929	265	1,417	24,500	12	140,819	3,830	6,849	185,000
2010	130	3,500	997	718	1,331	25,000	----	147,790	3,450	8,800	193,000
2011	95	8,000	1,231	836	1,765	27,300	6	148,008	3,700	10,826	202,000
2012	160	7,870	1,460	429	1,735	26,500	3	128,590	3,670	10,500	181,000
2013	170	8,900	1,836	946	1,963	25,200	2	137,024	3,720	13,100	193,000
2014	170	11,000	1,135	1,060	1,724	24,300	3	93,991	3,660	12,500	150,000
2015	170	11,600	861	1,030	1,864	23,800	4	139,125	3,670	12,600	195,000
2016	90	12,600	700	700	2,033	23,000	4	133,241	3,890	14,900	191,000
2017[1]		9,500				21,800		143,000	3,980	14,000	199,000
2018[2]		9,500				21,000		110,000	4,100	14,000	160,000

[1] Preliminary.   [2] Estimate.   [3] Placer platinum.   W = Withheld.   *Source: U.S. Geological Survey (USGS)*

World Mine Production of Palladium and Other Group Metals   In Kilograms

	Palladium										Other Group Metals		
Year	Australia	Canada	Finland	Japan	Russia	Serbia/Montenegro	South Africa	United States	Zimbabwe	Total	Russia	South Africa	World Total
2009	800	7,000	560	6,675	83,200	38	75,117	12,700	5,680	195,000	11,900	55,456	69,500
2010	650	11,000	1,493	6,107	84,700	22	82,222	11,600	7,000	208,000	12,000	57,292	71,500
2011	350	17,400	1,058	7,534	84,100	4	82,731	12,407	8,241	216,000	12,000	58,111	72,700
2012	550	13,800	1,100	8,052	81,700	22	74,738	12,300	8,140	203,000	8,200	51,010	62,100
2013	600	15,700	1,100	6,239	80,200	25	76,008	12,600	10,200	204,000	8,300	51,156	63,000
2014	600	19,300	902	6,969	82,700	23	58,410	12,400	10,100	193,000	8,200	36,043	48,000
2015	600	20,400	2,400	7,073	81,000	31	82,691	12,500	10,100	218,000	7,600	53,699	65,100
2016	590	21,000	2,000	7,172	79,400		76,273	13,100	12,000	212,000	11,500	54,139	70,300
2017[1]		17,000			85,200		86,800	13,600	12,000	225,000			
2018[2]		17,000			85,000		68,000	14,000	12,000	210,000			

[1] Preliminary.   [2] Estimate.   *Source: U.S. Geological Survey (USGS)*

Salient Statistics of Platinum and Allied Metals[3] in the United States   In Kilograms

Year	Net Import Reliance as a % of Apparent Consump	Mine Production Platinum	Mine Production Palladium	Refinery Production (Secondary)	Total Refined	Refiner, Importer & Dealer Stocks as of Dec. 31 Platinum	Palladium	Other[4]	Total	Imports Refined	Imports Total	Exports Refined	Exports Total	Apparent Consumptio
2009	95	3,830	12,700	15,030	15,030	261	----	18	279	286,688	----	51,140	----	----
2010	91	3,450	11,600	12,230	12,230	261	----	18	279	253,206	----	61,040	----	----
2011	89	3,700	12,400	33,000	33,000	261	----	18	279	257,138	----	45,820	----	----
2012	73	3,670	12,300	37,600	37,600	261	----	18	279	276,160	----	128,310	----	----
2013	67	3,720	12,600	43,000	43,000	261	----	18	279	227,217	----	403,540	----	----
2014	69	3,660	12,400	42,600	42,600	261	----	15	276	274,682	----	292,234	----	----
2015	66	3,670	12,500	39,000	39,000	261	----	15	276	270,848	----	284,940	----	----
2016	66	3,890	13,100	40,500	40,500	261	----	15	276	302,137	----	306,030	----	----
2017[1]	71	3,980	13,600				----			530,576	----	265,344	----	----
2018[2]	73	4,100	14,000				----			222,978	----		----	----

[1] Preliminary.   [2] Estimate.   [3] Includes platinum, palladium, iridium, osmium, rhodium, and ruthenium.   [4] Includes iridium, osmium, rhodium, and ruthenium.   W = Withheld.   *Source: U.S. Geological Survey (USGS)*

Average Producer Price of Rhodium in the United States   In Dollars Per Troy Ounce

Year	Jan.	Feb.	Mar.	Apr.	May	June	July	Aug.	Sept.	Oct.	Nov.	Dec.	Average
2009	1,147.62	1,178.95	1,169.32	1,346.90	1,417.50	1,463.64	1,490.91	1,671.43	1,650.00	1,782.95	2,332.89	2,410.71	1,588.57
2010	2,668.75	2,483.75	2,514.57	2,846.43	2,768.75	2,484.09	2,341.67	2,148.86	2,203.57	2,279.76	2,341.25	2,361.98	2,453.62
2011	2,436.90	2,475.00	2,396.74	2,340.00	2,120.24	2,067.05	1,982.50	1,876.09	1,817.86	1,625.00	1,660.00	1,475.00	2,022.70
2012	1,390.00	1,513.75	1,484.09	1,383.25	1,345.91	1,250.00	1,224.52	1,123.26	1,175.00	1,184.78	1,137.50	1,091.50	1,275.30
2013	1,123.64	1,226.00	1,254.00	1,184.32	1,127.95	1,037.00	988.64	1,000.23	1,000.00	987.83	958.50	916.43	1,067.05
2014	1,047.73	1,068.00	1,092.14	1,134.52	1,071.67	1,118.81	1,187.27	1,375.24	1,310.48	1,228.70	1,224.44	1,206.36	1,172.11
2015	1,195.95	1,184.50	1,166.59	1,146.90	1,105.75	976.14	857.05	847.86	772.38	767.95	741.90	678.70	953.47
2016	650.00	654.29	711.52	740.00	690.91	657.27	647.38	640.22	675.00	692.14	786.14	782.95	693.99
2017	833.41	874.05	959.57	1,023.50	955.65	982.05	1,023.81	1,052.83	1,160.24	1,401.14	1,443.86	1,607.62	1,109.81
2018	1,709.57	1,848.75	1,932.27	2,070.71	2,137.17	2,255.24	2,296.36	2,360.22	2,468.25	2,511.52	2,515.68	2,533.33	2,219.92

Source: American Metal Market (AMM)

PLATINUM
Quarterly Cash as of 03/29/2019

QUARTERLY CASH
As of 03/29/2019

| Chart High | 2275.00 | on 03/04/2008 |
| Chart Low | 29.50 | on 06/28/1935 |

USD / troy oz.

Producer: to 03/2006; Ind Engelhard: 04/2006 to 06/2009; Composite; 07/2009 to date.

Average Merchant's Price of Platinum in the United States   In Dollars Per Troy Ounce

Year	Jan.	Feb.	Mar.	Apr.	May	June	July	Aug.	Sept.	Oct.	Nov.	Dec.	Average
2009	949.76	1,037.26	1,084.59	1,169.57	1,134.45	1,220.41	1,163.82	1,248.24	1,294.71	1,335.86	1,401.26	1,447.20	1,207.26
2010	1,567.15	1,525.63	1,602.65	1,718.33	1,633.45	1,556.77	1,530.57	1,543.82	1,598.57	1,692.29	1,702.35	1,715.05	1,615.55
2011	1,790.62	1,828.68	1,773.26	1,804.00	1,792.24	1,771.45	1,766.65	1,810.52	1,745.43	1,539.81	1,607.65	1,461.81	1,724.34
2012	1,510.85	1,664.50	1,660.05	1,590.85	1,474.45	1,450.05	1,425.86	1,455.70	1,629.89	1,639.26	1,578.85	1,583.00	1,555.28
2013	1,646.43	1,676.95	1,586.30	1,497.23	1,478.95	1,431.20	1,405.14	1,496.50	1,454.05	1,415.52	1,423.85	1,355.25	1,488.95
2014	1,423.73	1,411.30	1,457.52	1,435.38	1,461.07	1,457.81	1,497.05	1,449.90	1,362.10	1,263.61	1,213.00	1,222.48	1,387.91
2015	1,247.38	1,200.79	1,140.00	1,154.33	1,143.25	1,091.77	1,011.23	985.86	966.38	978.95	885.10	863.30	1,055.70
2016	857.19	924.14	971.78	997.19	1,036.73	986.50	1,087.29	1,123.91	1,047.36	961.10	955.91	919.27	989.03
2017	970.55	1,009.75	965.22	963.35	934.35	933.64	921.52	975.65	968.76	924.00	937.73	912.52	951.42
2018	991.85	991.20	956.82	927.05	907.78	887.90	835.27	807.91	807.20	833.57	849.45	793.62	882.43

Source: American Metal Market (AMM)

Average Dealer Price[1] of Palladium in the United States   In Dollars Per Troy Ounce

Year	Jan.	Feb.	Mar.	Apr.	May	June	July	Aug.	Sept.	Oct.	Nov.	Dec.	Average
2009	189.81	207.63	203.73	228.29	230.45	247.18	250.64	278.38	295.86	324.45	354.84	376.60	265.66
2010	437.15	429.16	464.48	535.33	495.05	465.18	459.86	493.45	543.24	596.33	687.75	760.05	530.59
2011	797.48	823.47	766.48	777.30	743.38	774.55	794.80	766.57	710.14	620.45	637.70	650.57	738.57
2012	664.28	708.05	689.86	660.65	624.68	617.95	582.95	607.04	664.00	637.78	639.20	694.95	649.28
2013	716.62	755.68	761.20	710.27	723.91	716.70	725.18	746.23	711.75	727.61	737.20	721.45	729.48
2014	738.59	733.90	783.19	804.62	829.67	841.19	880.95	884.10	844.57	784.30	783.78	810.71	809.96
2015	788.29	789.95	789.55	771.86	787.00	729.77	643.64	598.24	612.76	693.82	575.57	555.96	694.70
2016	505.67	510.48	572.78	578.81	582.64	557.27	649.19	703.57	686.32	652.62	700.68	706.20	617.19
2017	749.09	780.35	780.65	803.90	797.04	867.68	859.29	917.26	937.52	963.91	1,005.45	1,028.48	874.22
2018	1,097.74	1,027.60	990.91	974.81	984.70	990.00	936.41	924.17	1,017.90	1,089.52	1,147.50	1,254.14	1,036.28

[1] Based on wholesale quantities, prompt delivery.   Source: American Metal Market (AMM)

PLATINUM-GROUP METALS

Nearby Futures through Last Trading Day.

Volume of Trading of Platinum Futures in Chicago   In Contracts

Year	Jan.	Feb.	Mar.	Apr.	May	June	July	Aug.	Sept.	Oct.	Nov.	Dec.	Total
2009	31,090	35,199	82,949	30,849	34,962	104,413	46,045	48,650	134,462	55,865	63,896	134,504	802,884
2010	85,446	83,630	176,594	91,365	133,781	144,344	71,314	74,099	188,874	99,204	151,998	185,858	1,486,507
2011	123,012	97,150	235,375	105,524	113,655	216,647	95,589	188,066	293,142	156,172	136,109	232,822	1,993,263
2012	150,111	172,872	252,464	136,954	181,216	283,780	138,326	217,759	371,411	211,656	183,154	322,051	2,621,754
2013	280,979	275,013	335,276	277,634	243,442	388,436	188,942	216,194	341,340	222,190	185,380	307,949	3,262,775
2014	217,465	194,296	389,315	182,628	239,397	379,860	210,163	179,938	399,265	271,921	211,151	360,542	3,235,941
2015	243,017	200,204	408,528	217,744	211,710	434,374	262,007	268,391	443,850	281,094	261,514	408,711	3,641,144
2016	284,203	262,873	413,082	248,758	249,861	435,018	279,689	278,246	456,092	302,621	360,457	423,172	3,994,072
2017	345,619	286,893	515,593	280,575	354,263	529,562	321,062	394,884	528,953	344,217	381,004	569,535	4,852,160
2018	444,074	346,507	562,720	423,705	392,326	652,863	393,517	412,710	580,643	383,720	372,849	498,165	5,463,799

Contract size = 50 oz.   *Source: CME Group; New York Mercantile Exchange (NYMEX)*

Average Open Interest of Platinum Futures in Chicago   In Contracts

Year	Jan.	Feb.	Mar.	Apr.	May	June	July	Aug.	Sept.	Oct.	Nov.	Dec.
2009	18,300	20,041	20,388	20,506	21,045	23,755	21,952	25,303	28,571	31,236	33,730	33,542
2010	34,160	34,637	36,720	37,368	33,840	30,242	28,369	31,026	35,528	38,402	36,959	37,115
2011	40,572	41,823	35,986	35,925	36,214	35,150	32,278	37,063	39,229	37,910	38,779	42,652
2012	43,893	44,519	43,028	40,337	45,372	50,530	50,160	53,902	57,555	63,289	60,641	62,626
2013	64,184	70,544	64,608	63,193	63,406	62,590	61,937	65,515	61,739	59,391	59,092	63,028
2014	59,980	63,324	69,278	65,308	68,150	68,004	71,271	64,416	64,103	59,701	61,768	65,647
2015	66,436	66,642	70,775	69,165	71,645	79,378	79,326	76,953	73,817	72,160	72,938	73,105
2016	68,301	65,306	62,884	59,152	64,862	63,825	72,441	80,327	74,296	70,022	66,480	65,869
2017	62,849	66,421	66,618	65,191	72,742	73,137	72,273	72,013	76,162	75,280	78,273	85,097
2018	86,391	87,064	78,963	76,759	80,900	86,235	81,652	83,049	86,436	74,712	72,385	81,227

Contract size = 50 oz.   *Source: CME Group; New York Mercantile Exchange (NYMEX)*

PALLADIUM - NYMEX
Weekly Selected Futures as of 03/29/2019

WEEKLY SELECTED FUTURES
As of 03/29/2019
Chart High 1599.10   on 03/22/2019
Chart Low 176.10   on 01/15/2009

USD / troy oz.

Nearby Futures through Last Trading Day.

Volume of Trading of Palladium Futures in Chicago   In Contracts

Year	Jan.	Feb.	Mar.	Apr.	May	June	July	Aug.	Sept.	Oct.	Nov.	Dec.	Total
2009	14,284	41,726	14,509	17,332	51,635	23,403	25,689	57,502	25,393	29,401	71,228	28,719	400,821
2010	48,438	90,368	48,314	58,104	134,435	45,840	45,847	87,366	55,399	69,623	156,495	61,355	901,584
2011	72,121	121,271	94,402	85,897	132,608	80,665	66,290	139,208	80,932	72,895	119,732	73,508	1,139,529
2012	74,977	125,721	75,910	61,833	136,033	67,710	59,308	123,731	85,209	84,730	145,835	77,483	1,118,480
2013	126,987	198,821	87,681	122,520	181,016	93,497	77,175	163,892	82,470	99,944	182,133	69,880	1,486,016
2014	87,502	158,760	136,126	111,648	195,880	101,610	97,809	208,474	126,132	115,708	161,947	72,376	1,573,972
2015	99,787	146,928	100,748	78,232	131,105	91,044	102,665	185,094	87,201	92,284	162,382	66,956	1,344,426
2016	90,129	151,159	96,917	93,887	142,585	94,937	104,219	169,852	88,440	113,977	198,537	91,224	1,435,863
2017	111,959	141,648	98,308	97,861	191,603	120,488	82,725	164,153	80,618	87,270	153,217	72,890	1,402,740
2018	98,800	164,476	101,277	145,138	127,272	93,661	98,611	176,108	89,368	116,003	148,110	74,888	1,433,712

Contract size = 100 oz.   Source: CME Group; New York Mercantile Exchange (NYMEX)

Average Open Interest of Palladium Futures in Chicago   In Contracts

Year	Jan.	Feb.	Mar.	Apr.	May	June	July	Aug.	Sept.	Oct.	Nov.	Dec.
2009	12,442	12,596	12,230	14,237	15,594	16,288	17,150	20,669	21,877	21,881	22,650	22,692
2010	23,356	22,566	22,944	23,905	23,152	21,271	19,732	19,808	23,036	24,706	24,747	23,089
2011	22,340	22,939	21,584	21,325	20,376	20,615	21,809	21,576	19,590	19,074	19,368	18,558
2012	18,051	21,035	20,978	21,174	22,931	21,951	22,676	23,304	19,987	20,172	22,005	25,798
2013	31,036	37,519	37,181	37,118	36,554	36,219	35,682	38,564	34,971	37,152	39,264	36,781
2014	39,059	40,226	41,494	42,071	43,466	39,964	43,791	44,286	38,776	33,587	34,170	32,060
2015	33,813	33,807	31,897	32,138	31,396	33,426	36,629	34,717	27,329	25,978	27,440	25,030
2016	26,200	27,339	22,964	23,573	23,912	23,048	24,043	28,475	25,272	23,968	24,431	26,124
2017	27,919	29,500	29,601	34,312	35,204	35,544	33,508	35,549	32,465	32,910	35,411	35,320
2018	38,468	29,987	24,894	23,645	23,008	23,045	21,676	22,511	19,056	26,129	27,046	26,158

Contract size = 100 oz.   Source: CME Group; New York Mercantile Exchange (NYMEX)

Potatoes

The potato is a member of the nightshade family. The leaves of the potato plant are poisonous, and a potato will begin to turn green if left too long in the light. This green skin contains solanine, a substance that can cause the potato to taste bitter and even cause illness in humans.

In Peru, the Inca Indians were the first to cultivate potatoes around 200 BC. The Indians developed potato crops because their staple diet of corn would not grow above an altitude of 3,350 meters. In 1536, after conquering the Incas, the Spanish Conquistadors brought potatoes back to Europe. At first, Europeans did not accept the potato because it was not mentioned in the Bible and was therefore considered an "evil" food. But after Marie Antoinette wore a crown of potato flowers, it finally became a popular food. In 1897, during the Alaskan Klondike gold rush, potatoes were so valued for their vitamin C content that miners traded gold for potatoes. The potato became the first vegetable to be grown in outer space in October 1995.

The potato is a highly nutritious, fat-free, cholesterol-free and sodium-free food, and is an important dietary staple in over 130 countries. A medium-sized potato contains only 100 calories. Potatoes are an excellent source of vitamin C and provide B vitamins as well as potassium, copper, magnesium, and iron. According to the U.S. Department of Agriculture, "a diet of whole milk and potatoes would supply almost all of the food elements necessary for the maintenance of the human body."

Potatoes are one of the largest vegetable crops grown in the U.S. and are grown in all fifty states. The U.S. ranks about 4th in world potato production. The top three types of potatoes grown extensively in the U.S. are white, red, and Russets (Russets account for about two-thirds the U.S. crop). Potatoes in the U.S. are harvested in all four seasons, but the vast majority of the crop is harvested in fall. Potatoes harvested in the winter, spring and summer are used mainly to supplement fresh supplies of fall-harvested potatoes and are also important to the processing industries. The four principal categories for

U.S. potato exports are frozen, potato chips, fresh, and dehydrated. Fries account for approximately 95% of U.S. frozen potato exports.

Prices – The average monthly price received for potatoes by U.S. farmers in 2018 rose +17.9% to $10.73 per hundred pounds, a new record high.

Supply – The total U.S. potato crop in 2017 fell -0.1% to 43.897 billion pounds, well below the record high of 50.936 billion pounds posted in 2000. The fall crop in 2017 fell by -1.9% to 39.893 billion pounds and it accounted for 90.9% of the total crop. Stocks of the fall crop (as of Dec 1, 2017), were 26.675 billion pounds. In 2018, the spring crop fell -11.3% to 1.755 billion pounds, the summer crop fell -8.9% to 1.975 billion pounds.

The largest producing states for the 2017 crop were Idaho with 32.8% of the crop, Washington with 24.8%, Wisconsin with 7.3%, North Dakota with 6.39%, and Colorado with 5.4%. For the spring crop, the largest producing states were California with 64.7% of the crop and Florida with 35.3% of the crop. Farmers harvested 1.025 million acres in 2017, up +0.6% yr/yr. The yield per harvested acre in 2017 was down -0.5% to 431 pounds per acre, falling below last year's record high of 433.

Demand – Total utilization of potatoes in 2017 was up +0.2% yr/yr at 44.203 billion pounds, and still above the 2010 record low of 40.427 billion pounds. The breakdown shows that the largest consumption category for potatoes is frozen French fries with 35.2% of total consumption, followed closely by table stock with 24.2%, chips, shoestrings with 13.3%, and dehydration with 10.4%. U.S. per capita consumption of potatoes in 2014 fell -1.1% to 112.1 pounds, below the record high of 145.0 pounds per capita seen in 1996.

Trade – U.S. exports of potatoes in 2016 rose +18.7% to 1.074 billion pounds, a new record high. U.S. imports in 2011 rose +19.2% to 910 million pounds, down from the 2008 record high of 1.071 million pounds.

Salient Statistics of Potatoes in the United States

Crop Year	Acreage Planted	Acreage Harvested	Yield Per Harvested Acre Cwt.	Total Production	Seed & Feed	Shrinkage & Loss	Sold[2]	Farm Price ($ Cwt.)	Value of Production[3]	Value of Sales	Stocks Jan. 1 (1,000 Cwt)	Exports (Fresh)	Imports	Consumption[4] Fresh	Consumption[4] Total
	--- 1,000 Acres ---			--------- In Thousands of Cwt. ---------					---- Million $ ----			-- Millions of Lbs. --		-- In Pounds --	
2009	1,071	1,044	414	432,601	4,535	29,135	398,931	8.25	3,558	3,292	234,300	728,800	794,611	36.7	113.4
2010	1,026	1,008	401	404,273	4,220	24,990	375,063	9.20	3,722	3,449	209,400	855,597	762,876	36.8	113.8
2011	1,099	1,077	399	429,647	4,142	27,755	397,750	9.37	4,041	3,743	NA	989,979	909,645	34.0	110.3
2012	1,155	1,139	408	464,970	4,869	28,356	429,541	8.63	4,017	3,728	NA	986,497		34.5	114.7
2013	1,064	1,051	414	434,652	4,323	26,211	404,118	9.75	4,237	3,943	NA	1,055,601		34.5	113.3
2014	1,063	1,051	421	442,170	4,192	26,762	411,216	8.88	3,928	3,658		922,366		33.5	112.1
2015	1,066	1,054	418	441,205	4,631	26,509	410,065	8.76	3,866	3,597		904,958		34.1	113.7
2016	1,057	1,038	434	450,324	4,284	26,460	410,667	9.08	4,009	3,736		1,073,734		33.2	
2017	1,053	1,045	432	450,921	4,380	24,737	412,917	9.10	4,021	3,768					
2018[1]	1,033	1,023	444	454,314											

[1] Preliminary. [2] For all purposes, including food, seed processing & livestock feed. [3] Farm weight basis, excluding canned and frozen potatoes.
[4] Calendar year. Source: Economic Research Service, U.S. Department of Agriculture (ERS-USDA)

Potato Crop Production Estimates, Stocks and Disappearance in the United States   In Millions of Cwt.

Year	Crop Production Estimates — Total Crop — Oct. 1	Nov. 1	Dec. 1	Fall Crop — Oct. 1	Nov. 1	Dec. 1	Total Storage Stocks[2] — Following Year — Jan. 1	Feb. 1	Mar. 1	Apr. 1	May 1	Fall Crop — 1,000 Cwt. — Production	Disappearance (Sold)	Stocks Dec. 1	Average Price ($/Cwt.)	Value of Sales ($1,000)
2009	----	429.7	----	----	391.5	265.8	234.3	203.5	169.7	128.7	89.6	383,962	361,316	265,800	7.62	2,751,550
2010	----	399.2	----	----	361.4	240.2	209.4	180.3	148.5	111.0	72.0	357,467	339,051	240,200	8.79	2,981,528
2011	----	429.6	----	----	391.2	253.0	NA	187.5	NA	115.7	NA	382,318	360,620	253,000	8.87	3,197,096
2012	----	467.2	----	----	422.0	271.5	NA	204.6	NA	NA	NA	410,367	385,767	271,500	8.05	3,111,362
2013	----	439.7	----	----	401.5	NA	NA	NA	NA	119.1	NA	396,655	404,118	NA	9.05	3,320,712
2014	----	442.8	----	----	406.2	265.7	NA	200.8	NA	128.7	NA	406,080	411,216	265,700	8.35	3,113,990
2015	----	441.2	----	----	404.7	262.7	NA	198.1	NA	125.7	NA	409,281	410,667	262,700	8.27	3,094,832
2016	----	439.6	----	----	405.2	272.9	NA	203.1	NA	131.4	NA	412,688	412,917	272,900	8.45	3,180,605
2017	----	439.0	----	----	398.9	274.9	NA	208.6	NA	137.5	NA	406,800		274,900		
2018[1]	----	452.6	----	----	417.5	283.6	NA	213.9	NA		NA	420,281		283,600		

[1] Preliminary.   [2] Held by growers and local dealers in the fall producing areas.
Source: Agricultural Statistics Board, U.S. Department of Agriculture (ASB-USDA)

Production of Fall Potatoes in the United States   In Thousands of Cwt.

Year	California	Colorado	Idaho	Maine	Michigan	Minnesota	Nebraska	New York	North Dakota	Oregon	Washington	Wisconsin	U.S. Total
2009	3,960	22,080	132,500	15,263	15,660	20,700	8,756	4,950	19,125	21,460	87,230	28,980	383,962
2010	2,828	21,528	112,970	15,892	15,660	17,010	7,719	5,120	22,000	20,058	88,440	24,293	357,467
2011	4,312	21,291	128,760	14,310	15,180	16,685	7,800	4,050	18,865	23,342	97,600	25,938	382,318
2012	3,901	19,980	141,820	16,088	16,100	18,800	10,369	5,130	25,200	22,935	95,940	30,360	410,367
2013	3,504	20,304	131,131	15,660	15,840	17,325	8,418	4,959	22,620	21,582	96,000	26,040	396,655
2014	3,901	23,196	132,880	14,645	15,725	16,400	7,943	4,345	23,870	22,562	101,475	26,240	406,080
2015	3,528	22,575	130,400	16,160	17,550	16,200	6,885	4,144	27,600	21,784	100,300	27,813	409,281
2016	3,516	22,236	139,320	15,113	17,390	17,200	7,380	3,552	21,600	22,951	105,625	27,840	412,688
2017	3,321	21,220	134,850	15,200	18,315	18,428	9,025	4,032	24,420	25,245	99,220	29,750	406,800
2018[1]	3,225	21,722	140,175	15,345	18,240	18,705	9,361	4,118	23,360	28,060	105,600	28,400	420,281

[1] Preliminary.   *Source: Agricultural Statistics Board, U.S. Department of Agriculture (ASB-USDA)*

Utilization of Potatoes in the United States   In Thousands of Cwt.

Crop Year	Table Stock	For Processing — Chips, Shoe-strings	Dehydration	Frozen French Fries	Other Frozen Products	Canned Potatoes	Other Canned Products[2]	Starch & Flour	Other Sales — Livestock Feed	Seed	Total Sales	Non-Sales — Used on Farms Where Grown	Shrinkage & Loss	Total Non-Sales	Total
2008	109,351	50,988	40,646	134,123	19,519	2,070	790	5,288	803	20,900	384,478	3,315	26,438	30,576	415,055
2009	116,326	42,548	44,477	138,589	21,004	1,983	748	6,504	6,533	20,219	398,931	3,346	29,135	33,670	432,601
2010	107,407	54,508	34,164	135,703	13,374	1,659	700	6,334	593	20,621	375,063	3,002	24,990	29,210	404,273
2011	102,655	58,703	45,511	144,626	15,188	1,650	716	6,013	825	21,863	397,750	3,012	27,755	31,897	429,647
2012	118,535	59,304	49,894	142,993	20,635	1,741	734	7,919	4,080	23,706	429,541	3,286	28,356	33,225	462,766
2013	106,930	60,485	47,411	134,966	18,451	188	1,089	8,579	1,251	22,431	404,118	3,215	26,211	30,534	434,652
2014	107,344	73,960	48,707	152,832	9,208	435	886	6,907	768	22,774	411,216	3,343	26,762	30,954	442,170
2015	110,960	56,807	48,016	152,329	13,573	985	730	6,420	919	25,648	410,065	3,765	26,509	31,140	441,205
2016	113,634	60,266	48,015	156,985	12,695	1,234	698	6,000	1,083	26,310	410,667	3,605	26,460	30,744	441,411
2017[1]	107,235	58,751	45,761	155,798	13,803	1,152	703	6,160	1,815	24,747	412,917	3,526	24,737	29,117	442,034

[1] Preliminary.   [2] Hash, stews and soups.   *Source: Agricultural Statistics Board, U.S. Department of Agriculture (ASB-USDA)*

Cold Storage Stocks of All Frozen Potatoes in the United States, on First of Month   In Millions of Pounds

Year	Jan.	Feb.	Mar.	Apr.	May	June	July	Aug.	Sept.	Oct.	Nov.	Dec.
2009	1,098.6	1,171.0	1,192.1	1,226.8	1,221.4	1,203.2	1,245.1	1,187.5	1,094.8	1,130.2	1,162.9	1,108.1
2010	1,043.8	1,091.3	1,113.6	1,100.5	1,093.7	1,077.3	1,141.9	1,063.9	1,036.3	1,070.1	1,122.9	1,127.5
2011	1,018.9	1,095.0	1,102.9	1,086.1	1,070.3	1,073.8	1,073.8	1,073.8	1,073.8	1,073.8	1,073.8	1,073.8
2012	999.9	1,072.0	1,111.7	1,129.0	1,138.7	1,091.6	1,161.5	1,065.7	1,019.8	1,123.4	1,184.7	1,144.2
2013	1,110.4	1,175.1	1,232.7	1,226.8	1,222.4	1,181.3	1,270.3	1,138.4	1,091.3	1,137.6	1,175.3	1,150.8
2014	1,095.3	1,104.8	1,124.1	1,044.3	1,009.2	983.4	1,012.8	924.2	936.6	1,039.7	1,099.5	1,105.6
2015	1,030.4	1,091.7	1,132.9	1,146.4	1,127.2	1,135.6	1,151.7	1,065.4	1,047.0	1,058.0	1,093.0	1,055.6
2016	1,006.9	1,021.7	1,046.0	1,072.2	1,095.0	1,122.2	1,175.8	1,149.0	1,160.5	1,217.2	1,253.5	1,180.5
2017	1,124.6	1,195.7	1,210.6	1,212.3	1,219.7	1,209.3	1,230.6	1,201.7	1,190.2	1,237.0	1,273.5	1,274.1
2018[1]	1,183.0	1,258.3	1,265.2	1,225.8	1,192.8	1,156.7	1,216.6	1,101.0	1,140.7	1,185.0	1,250.2	1,198.6

[1] Preliminary.   *Source: Agricultural Statistics Board, U.S. Department of Agriculture (ASB-USDA)*

POTATOES

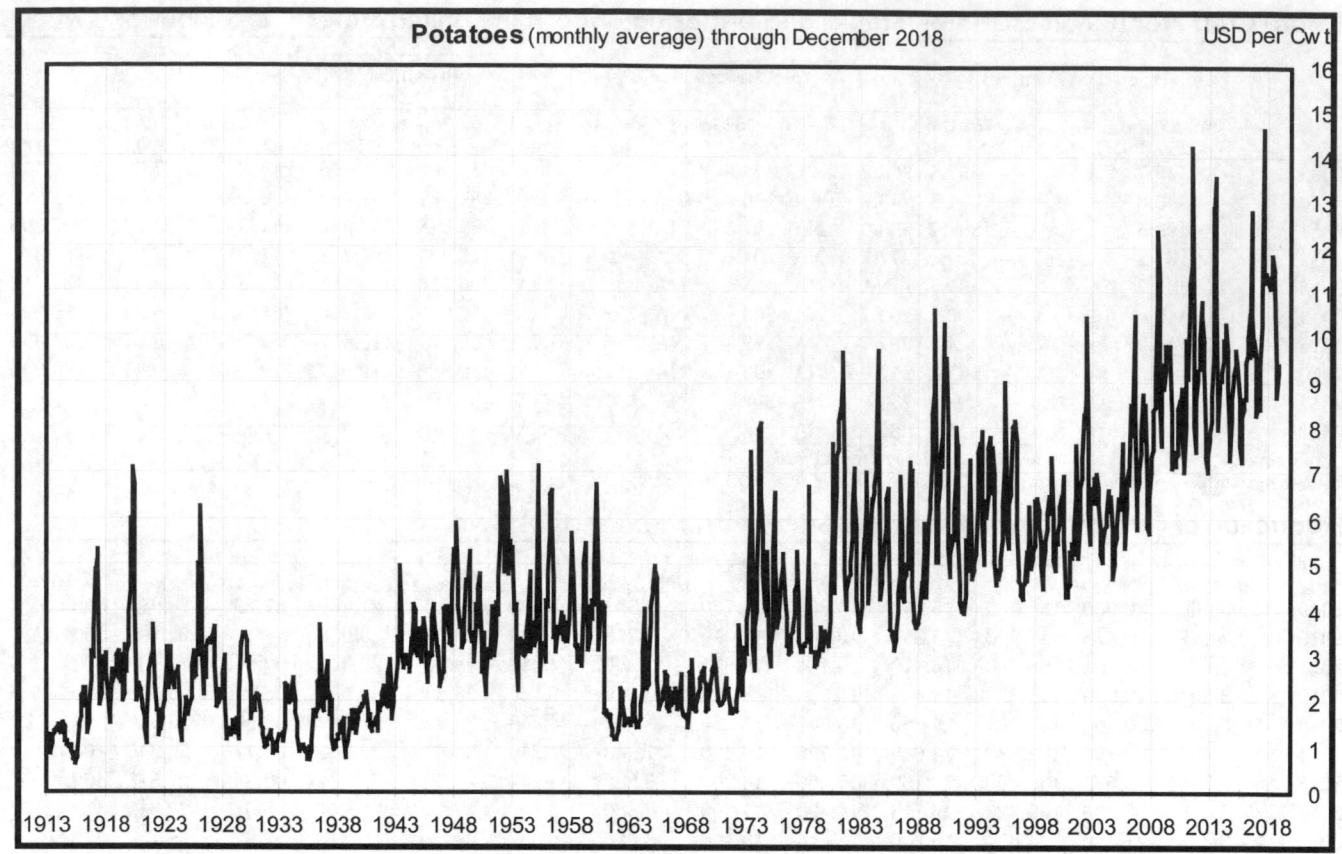

Potatoes (monthly average) through December 2018   USD per Cwt

Average Price Received by Farmers for Potatoes in the U.S.   In Dollars Per Hundred Pounds (Cwt.)

Year	Jan.	Feb.	Mar.	Apr.	May	June	July	Aug.	Sept.	Oct.	Nov.	Dec.	Season Average
2009	9.40	8.87	9.27	9.81	9.62	9.48	9.81	9.61	8.27	7.11	7.22	7.47	8.25
2010	7.17	7.34	7.42	8.42	8.57	8.25	8.83	7.78	7.22	7.03	8.01	9.94	9.20
2011	9.08	9.26	10.74	11.17	11.17	11.59	14.19	10.47	8.05	7.46	8.58	9.06	9.37
2012	9.23	9.31	9.98	10.75	10.44	9.93	9.29	7.80	7.31	7.02	7.39	7.74	8.63
2013	7.87	8.12	8.72	9.63	12.89	12.57	13.56	11.15	8.48	7.96	8.87	9.02	9.75
2014	9.02	9.22	9.47	9.92	9.53	10.28	9.72	8.88	7.76	7.30	8.19	8.63	8.88
2015	9.12	9.14	9.38	9.69	9.26	9.27	8.62	8.45	7.58	7.24	8.23	8.38	8.76
2016	8.63	8.64	9.41	9.61	9.98	10.52	9.58	12.80	10.48	9.59	9.91	9.59	9.08
2017	8.27	8.42	8.65	8.40	9.40	10.25	10.79	14.61	13.86	11.33	11.22	11.39	9.10
2018[1]	11.30	11.20	11.10	11.20	11.40	11.80	11.50	11.20	9.44	8.65	9.22	9.37	

[1] Preliminary.   *Source: Agricultural Statistics Board, U.S. Department of Agriculture (ASB-USDA)*

Per Capita Utilization of Potatoes in the United States   In Pounds (Farm Weight)

Year	Total	Fresh	Freezing	Chips & Shoestring	Dehydrating	Canning	Total Processing
2005	125.4	41.3	54.3	16.1	12.8	0.9	84.1
2006	123.7	38.6	53.2	18.6	12.4	0.8	85.0
2007	124.3	38.7	53.2	18.6	13.0	0.9	85.6
2008	118.3	37.8	51.5	15.7	12.4	0.9	80.5
2009	113.3	36.7	50.4	13.7	11.8	0.8	76.8
2010	113.8	36.8	50.2	15.0	11.2	0.7	77.2
2011	110.3	34.1	48.2	16.8	10.6	0.7	76.3
2012	114.7	34.4	48.4	17.0	13.9	0.8	80.4
2013[1]	113.3	34.8	49.3	16.7	12.9	0.8	80.6
2014[2]	112.1	----	----	----	----	----	----

[1] Preliminary.   [2] Forecast.   *Source: Agricultural Statistics Board, U.S. Department of Agriculture (ASB-USDA)*

Potatoes Processed[1] in the United States, Eight States   In Thousands of Cwt.

States	Storage Season	to Dec. 1	to Jan. 1	to Feb. 1	to Mar. 1	to Apr. 1	to May 1	to June 1	Entire Season
Idaho and Oregon-Malheur Co.	2010-11	21,040	26,840	32,700	39,240	46,180	52,830	59,440	70,050
	2011-12	28,060	34,800	41,800	49,460	56,680	63,800	71,510	84,780
	2012-13	27,900	34,740	41,890	49,980	57,750	65,430	73,430	89,780
	2013-14	25,770	32,060	39,090	46,320	53,755	61,780	70,425	85,280
	2014-15	27,685	33,995	40,850	47,985	54,665	63,025	70,600	86,870
	2015-16	26,850	33,115	39,655	46,455	53,710	61,050	68,435	86,250
	2016-17	25,720	32,650	39,475	46,880	54,625	61,950	70,110	92,760
	2017-18	24,840	31,920	38,950	46,610	54,060	61,285	69,840	87,379
	2018-19	25,170	31,985	39,535					
Maine[2]	2010-11	1,860	2,390	3,000	3,620	4,320	4,980	5,645	7,490
	2011-12	1,860	2,380	3,095	3,695	4,360	4,940	5,345	6,790
	2012-13	1,890	2,380	3,005	3,600	4,290	5,075	5,740	7,720
	2013-14	1,570	1,990	2,510	3,060	3,680	4,240	4,800	6,315
	2014-15	1,410	1,845	2,415	2,930	3,475	3,980	4,445	5,622
	2015-16	1,170	1,590	2,050	2,490	2,980	3,495	4,065	5,724
	2016-17	1,260	1,665	2,175	2,660	3,080	3,470	3,825	5,059
	2017-18	1,510	1,880	2,370	2,880	3,460	4,010	4,560	4,829
	2018-19	1,470	1,890	2,400					
Washington & Oregon-Other	2010-11	27,670	33,570	38,815	46,700	53,660	60,145	67,655	77,940
	2011-12	31,750	38,165	44,475	51,630	58,515	65,320	73,040	84,105
	2012-13	31,295	37,730	43,820	51,765	57,915	64,500	70,470	80,400
	2013-14	31,575	37,990	45,420	52,690	59,025	64,905	72,325	80,655
	2014-15	31,870	37,190	42,715	50,380	57,340	64,525	72,365	88,615
	2015-16	33,955	39,970	46,320	54,455	60,985	67,560	74,285	91,720
	2016-17	36,700	42,180	47,835	55,365	62,125	68,705	76,635	90,785
	2017-18	32,885	39,925	46,515	54,355	61,780	68,555	76,495	91,160
	2018-19	36,395	43,385	50,300					
Other States[3]	2010-11	11,820	14,785	17,435	20,370	23,215	25,775	28,690	35,430
	2011-12	14,205	16,770	19,525	21,930	24,910	27,230	29,960	36,200
	2012-13	14,270	16,765	19,785	22,520	25,170	28,320	31,100	40,395
	2013-14	11,365	14,280	17,470	20,475	23,695	26,990	30,195	37,425
	2014-15	13,705	17,295	20,865	24,685	28,550	32,080	35,415	40,456
	2015-16	8,995	12,515	16,380	20,720	24,550	28,665	33,020	38,742
	2016-17	10,035	13,570	17,140	21,005	25,085	28,505	32,385	38,631
	2017-18	10,030	14,181	18,075	22,740	26,535	30,425	34,740	42,856
	2018-19	10,738	14,578	18,381					
Total	2010-11	62,390	77,585	91,950	109,930	127,375	143,730	161,430	190,910
	2011-12	75,875	92,115	108,895	126,715	144,465	161,290	179,855	211,875
	2012-13	75,355	91,615	108,500	127,865	145,125	163,325	180,740	218,295
	2013-14	70,280	86,320	104,490	122,545	140,155	157,915	177,745	209,675
	2014-15	74,670	90,325	106,845	125,980	144,030	163,610	182,825	221,563
	2015-16	70,970	87,190	104,405	124,120	142,225	160,770	179,805	222,436
	2016-17	73,715	90,065	106,625	125,910	144,915	162,630	182,955	227,235
	2017-18	69,265	87,906	105,910	126,585	145,835	164,275	185,635	226,224
	2018-19	73,773	91,838	110,616					
Dehydrated[4]	2010-11	7,960	10,795	13,645	16,485	19,415	22,740	25,855	32,700
	2011-12	13,375	16,845	20,875	24,410	28,070	31,533	35,310	42,585
	2012-13	13,965	17,640	22,000	26,105	30,135	34,610	38,945	47,305
	2013-14	12,065	15,875	19,835	23,380	27,140	31,095	34,895	44,385
	2014-15	13,045	16,325	19,965	23,645	26,345	31,515	35,490	46,340
	2015-16	12,155	15,885	19,620	23,560	27,605	31,585	35,645	45,735
	2016-17	11,560	15,305	19,085	22,675	26,565	30,545	34,890	46,317
	2017-18	10,595	14,304	18,085	21,680	25,775	29,800	34,410	44,263
	2018-19	13,655	17,030	20,820					

[1] Total quantity received and used for processing regardless of the State in which the potatoes were produced. Amount excludes quantities used for potato chips in Maine, Michigan and Wisconsin.   [2] Includes Maine grown potatoes only.   [3] Colorado, Minnesota, , Nevada, North Dakota and Wisconsin.
[4] Dehydrated products except starch and flour. Included in above totals. Includes CO, ID, NV, ND, OR, WA, and WI.
Source: National Agricultural Statistics Service, U.S. Department of Agriculture (NASS-USDA)

Rice

Rice is a grain that is cultivated on every continent except Antarctica and is the primary food for half the people in the world. Rice cultivation probably originated as early as 10,000 BC in Asia. Rice is grown at varying altitudes (sea level to about 3,000 meters), in varying climates (tropical to temperate), and on dry to flooded land. The growth duration of rice plants is 3-6 months, depending on variety and growing conditions. Rice is harvested by hand in developing countries or by combines in industrialized countries. Asian countries produce about 90% of rice grown worldwide. Rough rice futures and options are traded at the CME Group.

Prices – CME rough rice prices (Barchart.com electronic symbol ZR) on the nearest-futures chart rose early in the year to a high of $13.215 in April and then fell the rest of the year to close the year 2018 at $10.885 per hundred pounds, down -10.9% Regarding cash prices, the average monthly price of rice received by farmers in the U.S. in the first four months of the 2018/19 marketing year (i.e., August 2018 through July 2019) fell -0.5% yr/yr to $12.55 per hundred pounds (cwt).

Supply – World rice production in the 2018/19 marketing year is expected to fall -0.7% to 733.771 million metric tons, down from the 2017/18 record high of 739.081. The world's largest rice producers are expected to be China with 28.0% of world production in 2018/19, India with 22.7%, Indonesia with 8.0%, Bangladesh with 7.1%, Vietnam with 6.3%, and Thailand with 4.3%. U.S. production of rice in 2018/19 is expected to rise +22.5 % yr/yr to 218.290 million cwt (hundred pounds).

Demand – World consumption of rice in 2018/19 is expected to rise +0.8% to a record high of 486.715 million metric tons. U.S. rice consumption in 2018/19 is expected to fall -1.3% yr/yr to 133.000 million cwt (hundred pounds), below the 2010/11 record high of 136.921 million cwt (hundred pounds).

Trade – World exports of rice in 2018/19 is expected to rise +1.6% yr/yr to 48.105 million metric tons, which is a record high. The world's largest rice exporters will be India with 26.0% of world exports, Thailand with 21.4%, Vietnam with 14.6%, Pakistan with 8.8%, the U.S. with 6.5%, and Burma with 6.2%. U.S. rice imports in 2018/19 are expected to rise +0.4% yr/yr to 27.000 million cwt (hundred pounds), which is a record high. U.S. rice exports in 2018/19 are expected to rise +12.6% yr/yr to 98.000 million cwt.

World Production of Rough Rice   In Thousands of Metric Tons

Year	Bangla-desh	Brazil	Burma	China	India	Indo-nesia	Japan	Pakistan	Philip-pines	Thailand	United States	Vietnam	World Total
2012-13	50,735	11,819	18,305	206,531	157,877	57,559	11,080	8,305	18,140	30,606	9,069	44,059	709,678
2013-14	51,590	12,206	18,683	206,286	159,985	57,165	11,154	10,198	18,822	31,000	8,615	45,058	717,649
2014-15	51,755	12,449	19,688	209,609	158,239	56,000	11,098	10,506	18,911	28,409	10,079	45,066	719,203
2015-16	51,755	10,603	19,000	212,141	156,628	57,008	10,819	10,204	17,473	23,939	8,761	44,134	710,237
2016-17[1]	51,872	12,328	19,766	211,094	164,563	58,505	10,891	10,275	18,549	29,091	10,167	43,840	732,783
2017-18[2]	48,980	12,071	20,625	212,676	169,382	58,268	10,696	11,176	19,421	30,864	8,084	45,554	739,081
2018-19[3]	51,755	12,000	20,500	205,117	166,517	58,740	10,577	11,101	19,286	31,364	9,901	46,510	733,771

[1] Preliminary.   [2] Estimate.   [3] Forecast.   *Source: Foreign Agricultural Service, U.S. Department of Agriculture (FAS-USDA)*

World Imports of Rice (Milled Basis)   In Thousands of Metric Tons

Year	China	Cote d'Ivoire	European Union	Indo-nesia	Iran	Iraq	Malaysia	Nigeria	Philip-pines	Saudi Arabia	Senegal	South Africa	World Total
2012-13	3,150	1,150	1,395	650	2,100	1,411	885	2,800	1,400	1,326	1,000	908	36,744
2013-14	4,000	800	1,530	1,225	1,500	950	989	2,800	1,200	1,459	1,100	975	38,708
2014-15	4,700	1,300	1,706	1,350	1,350	1,170	1,051	2,600	1,800	1,601	1,200	980	41,528
2015-16	4,800	1,250	1,804	1,050	1,100	850	823	2,100	1,600	1,260	1,020	943	38,321
2016-17[1]	5,300	1,300	1,841	350	1,600	1,070	900	2,500	1,100	1,195	1,100	1,005	41,286
2017-18[2]	5,500	1,400	1,997	2,150	1,300	1,150	900	2,000	1,300	1,250	1,150	1,000	47,380
2018-19[3]	5,000	1,450	2,000	800	1,400	1,300	1,000	2,400	1,800	1,300	1,250	1,000	45,260

[1] Preliminary.   [2] Estimate.   [3] Forecast.   *Source: Foreign Agricultural Service, U.S. Department of Agriculture (FAS-USDA)*

World Exports of Rice (Milled Basis)   In Thousands of Metric Tons

Year	Argen-tina	Brazil	Burma	Cam-bodia	Guyana	India	Pakistan	Para-guay	Thailand	United States	Uruguay	Vietnam	World Total
2012-13	533	840	1,163	1,075	265	10,869	3,578	365	6,722	3,385	1,012	6,700	39,407
2013-14	467	819	1,688	1,000	346	10,619	3,950	380	10,969	3,004	890	6,325	43,057
2014-15	312	931	1,735	1,150	446	12,238	3,800	371	9,779	3,078	766	6,606	43,634
2015-16	526	547	1,300	1,050	486	10,240	4,200	557	9,867	3,396	972	5,088	40,351
2016-17[1]	343	830	3,350	1,150	431	11,772	3,516	500	11,615	3,645	950	6,488	47,250
2017-18[2]	380	950	2,800	1,250	455	12,200	4,300	625	10,700	2,763	900	6,700	47,334
2018-19[3]	360	850	3,000	1,300	480	12,500	4,250	650	10,300	3,143	800	7,000	48,105

[1] Preliminary.   [2] Estimate.   [3] Forecast.   *Source: Foreign Agricultural Service, U.S. Department of Agriculture (FAS-USDA)*

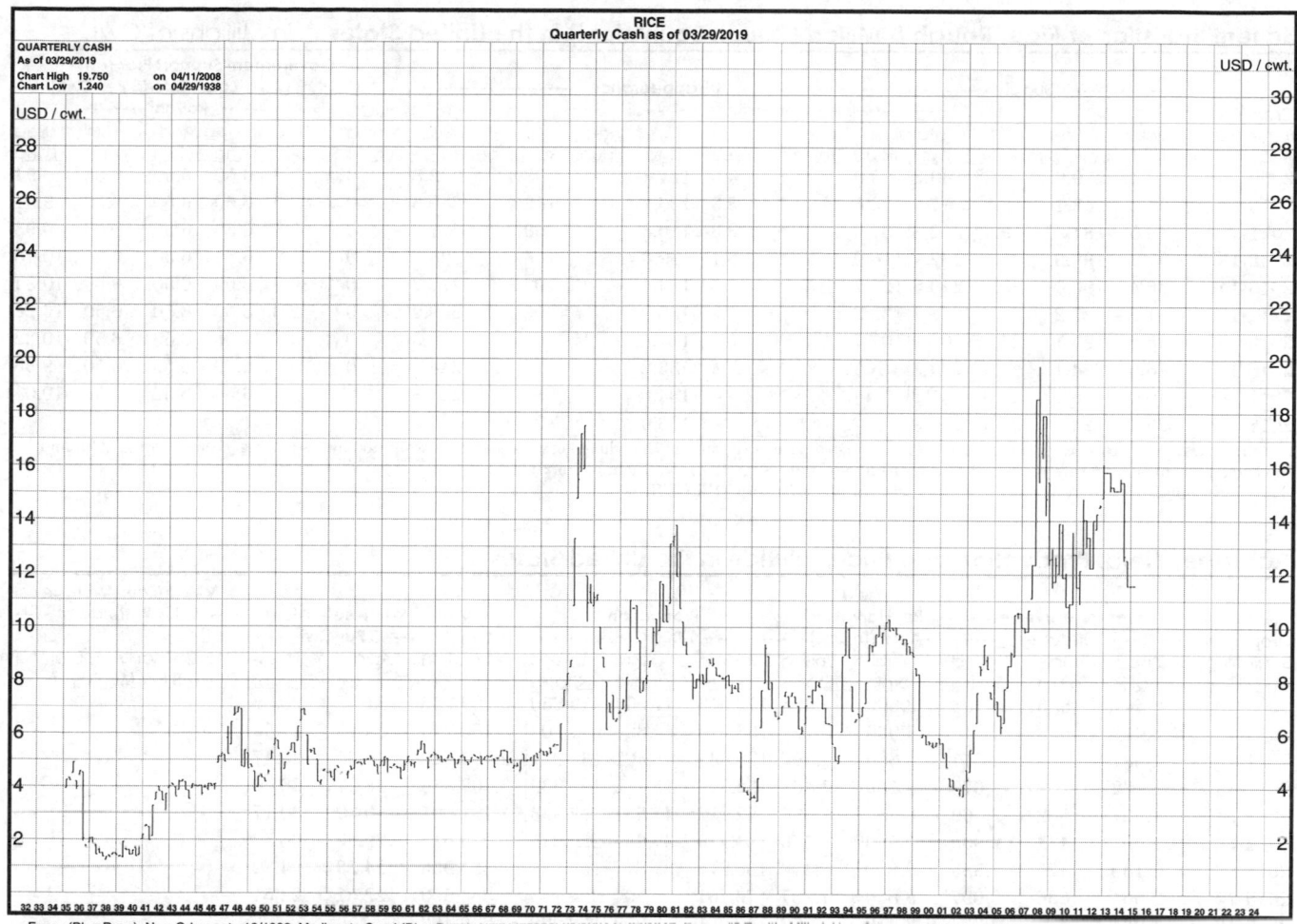

Faney (Blue Rose), New Orleans to 12/1833, Medium to Good (Blue Rose), New Orleans: 01/1934 to 07/1947; Fancy, #2 Zenith, Milled, New Orleans: 08/1947 to 04/1972; #2 Medium, SW Louisiana: 05/1972 to 12/2004; Milled, #2 Long grain, Louisiana: 01/2005 to date.

Average Wholesale Price of Rice No. 2 (Medium)[2] Southwest Louisiana   In Dollars Per Cwt. Bagged

Year	Jan.	Feb.	Mar.	Apr.	May	June	July	Aug.	Sept.	Oct.	Nov.	Dec.	Average
2008-09	40.63	43.10	43.25	43.06	42.88	43.25	43.25	42.15	42.25	42.25	42.25	42.25	42.55
2009-10	41.05	35.75	33.25	33.05	32.75	32.75	32.63	32.15	31.56	30.35	29.25	28.88	32.79
2010-11	28.35	28.16	29.69	32.70	33.75	34.15	34.75	34.75	34.00	33.75	33.75	33.75	32.63
2011-12	33.75	33.75	32.55	32.06	31.50	30.70	30.31	29.75	29.75	29.75	29.75	29.75	31.11
2012-13	29.75	29.75	29.75	29.75	29.75	29.75	30.19	30.38	30.38	30.38	30.38	30.38	30.05
2013-14	30.44	30.50	32.00	32.00	32.00	32.00	32.00	32.00	32.00	30.25	32.00	32.00	31.60
2014-15	30.50	29.00	29.00	29.00	29.00	28.75	28.00	28.00	28.00	28.00	28.00	28.00	28.60
2015-16	28.00	28.00	28.00	28.00	28.00	28.00	28.00	28.00	28.00	28.00	28.00	28.00	28.00
2016-17	28.00	28.00	28.00	26.00	22.00	22.00	22.00	22.00	22.00	22.00	22.00	22.20	23.85
2017-18[1]	23.00	23.60	24.50	24.50	24.50	25.63	28.00						24.82

[1] Preliminary.   [2] U.S. No. 2 -- broken not to exceed 4%.   Source: Economic Research Service, U.S. Department of Agriculture (ERS-USDA)

Average Price Received by Farmers for Rice (Rough) in the United States   In Dollars Per Hundred Pounds (Cwt.)

Year	Jan.	Feb.	Mar.	Apr.	May	June	July	Aug.	Sept.	Oct.	Nov.	Dec.	Average[2]
2009-10	14.70	14.60	14.30	14.00	14.40	15.00	14.80	14.30	14.30	13.80	13.20	12.60	14.17
2010-11	11.60	11.10	11.50	12.50	13.80	14.00	13.40	13.00	13.10	12.70	12.10	12.90	12.64
2011-12	13.60	14.40	14.70	15.00	14.70	15.20	14.10	14.10	14.40	14.10	14.20	14.40	14.41
2012-13	14.60	14.30	14.40	14.60	14.80	15.30	15.00	15.20	15.40	15.50	15.50	15.60	15.02
2013-14	15.80	15.60	15.80	16.20	16.50	17.10	16.70	16.40	16.20	16.20	16.30	16.10	16.24
2014-15	15.60	14.40	14.00	14.30	13.60	15.10	12.80	12.60	12.60	12.50	12.00	11.60	13.43
2015-16	12.00	11.90	12.20	12.50	12.80	13.30	12.10	11.80	11.50	11.70	11.70	12.10	12.13
2016-17	11.80	10.60	10.30	10.40	10.50	10.90	10.10	10.10	10.10	10.20	10.20	10.70	10.49
2017-18	11.30	11.50	12.20	13.30	12.90	13.70	12.60	12.70	12.90	12.90	13.30	13.70	12.75
2018-19[1]	13.90	12.20	11.90	12.20	11.90	12.40							12.42

[1] Preliminary.   [2] Weighted average by sales.   Source: Economic Research Service, U.S. Department of Agriculture (ERS-USDA)

RICE

Salient Statistics of Rice, Rough & Milled (Rough Equivalent) in the United States   In Millions of Cwt.

Crop Year Beginning Aug. 1	Supply				Disappearance							Government Support Program					
					Domestic								Put Under	Loan Rate ($ Per Cwt.)			
	Stocks Aug. 1	Pro-duction	Imports	Total Supply	Food	Brewers	Seed	Total	Resi-dual	Exports	Total Disap-pearance	CCC Stocks July 31	Price Support	Rough[3]			Milled Long
														Long	Med-ium	All Classes	
2009-10	30.4	219.9	19.0	269.3	120.0	4	4.5	124.4	4	108.4	232.8	0	67.6	6.50	6.50	6.50	9.94
2010-11	36.5	243.1	18.3	297.9	133.6	4	3.3	136.9	4	112.6	249.5	0	86.5	6.50	6.50	6.50	9.91
2011-12	48.5	184.9	19.4	252.8	107.5	4	3.3	110.8	4	100.9	211.7	0	65.8	6.50	6.50	6.50	9.93
2012-13	41.1	199.9	21.1	262.1	116.0	4	3.1	119.0	4	106.6	225.7	0	65.9	6.50	6.50	6.50	10.13
2013-14	36.4	190.0	23.1	249.5	120.7	4	3.6	124.4	4	93.3	217.7	0	36.0	6.50	6.50	6.50	10.34
2014-15	31.8	222.2	24.7	278.7	131.2	4	3.2	133.9	4	96.3	230.2	0	42.3	6.50	6.50	6.50	10.25
2015-16	48.5	193.1	24.1	264.9	107.7	4	3.9	112.4	4	107.0	219.3	0		6.50	6.50	6.50	10.22
2016-17	46.5	224.1	23.5	294.1	NA	4	NA	133.2	4	114.8	248.0	0		6.50	6.50	6.50	9.98
2017-18[1]	46.0	178.2	26.9	251.2	----	4	----	134.8	4	87.0	221.8			6.50	6.50	6.50	10.01
2018-19[2]	29.4	224.2	27.0	275.9	----	4	----	133.0	4	98.0	231.0						

[1] Preliminary.   [2] Forecast.   [3] Loan rate for each class of rice is the sum of the whole kernels' loan rate weighted by its milling yield (average 56%) and the broken kernels' loan rate weighted by its milling yield (average 12%).   [4] Included in Food.
Source: Economic Research Service, U.S. Department of Agriculture (ERS-USDA)

Acreage, Yield, Production and Prices of Rice in the United States

Crop Year Beginning Aug. 1	Acreage Harvested 1,000 Acres			Yield Per Harvested Acre (In Lbs.)		Production 1,000 Cwt.			Value of Pro-duction ($1,000)	Wholesale Prices $ Per Cwt.		Milled Rice, Average C.I.F. Rotterdam		
	Southern States	Cali-fornia	United States	Cali-fornia	United States	Southern States	Cali-fornia	United States		Arkan-sas[2]	Hous-ton[2]	U.S. No. 2[4]	Thai "A"[5]	Thai "B"[5]
												$ Per Metric Ton		
2009-10	2,547	556	3,103	8,600	7,085	172,046	47,804	219,850	3,209,236	31.47	26.52	----	----	----
2010-11	3,062	553	3,615	8,020	6,725	198,778	44,326	243,104	3,183,213	33.21	27.52	----	----	----
2011-12	2,037	580	2,617	8,350	7,067	136,539	48,402	184,941	2,737,423	30.64	28.47	----	----	----
2012-13	2,122	557	2,679	8,150	7,463	154,526	45,413	199,939	3,067,365	28.27	28.46	----	----	----
2013-14	1,907	562	2,469	8,480	7,694	142,312	47,641	189,953	3,181,993	30.39	30.17	----	----	----
2014-15	2,491	442	2,933	8,580	7,576	184,279	37,936	222,215	3,075,618	29.87	26.52	----	----	----
2015-16	2,159	426	2,585	8,890	7,472	155,271	37,877	193,148	2,421,955	24.23	24.72	----	----	----
2016-17	2,561	536	3,097	8,840	7,237	176,751	47,394	224,145	2,384,690	22.51	22.51	----	----	----
2017-18	1,931	443	2,374	8,410	7,507	140,951	37,277	178,228	2,246,483			----	----	----
2018-19[1]	2,411	504	2,915	8,620	7,692	180,786	43,425	224,211				----	----	----

[1] Preliminary.   [2] F.O.B. mills, Arkansas, medium.   [3] Houston, Texas (long grain).   [4] Milled, 4%, container, FAS.
[5] SWR, 100%, bulk.   NA = Not available.   *Source: Economic Research Service, U.S. Department of Agriculture (ERS-USDA)*

U.S. Exports of Milled Rice, by Country of Destination   In Thousands of Metric Tons

Trade Year Beginning October	Canada	Haiti	Iran	Ivory Coast	Jamaica	Mexico	Nether-lands	Peru	Saudi Arabia	South Africa	Switzer-land	United Kingdom	Total
2008-09	207.8	239.7	31.7	15.3	26.4	790.9	6.9	.3	129.8	.7	1.3	57.1	3,388
2009-10	220.0	327.5	.0	.4	28.3	827.0	4.4	3.2	116.1	1.2	.3	65.5	4,260
2010-11	229.1	324.1		1.9	23.3	942.0	5.1	1.5	120.3	1.7	.6	47.4	3,920
2011-12	219.9	287.3	3.1	.3	9.1	804.2	5.6	.7	133.4	2.1	.3	36.2	3,578
2012-13	231.6	365.0	125.7	14.9	2.7	885.8	4.6	.3	126.2	2.6	.6	21.4	3,848
2013-14	242.6	346.0	.2	13.5	2.3	741.2	5.4	6.8	106.1	2.3	.6	23.6	3,355
2014-15	219.2	392.1		.1	2.6	837.4	5.3	9.0	111.9	1.6	.6	30.6	3,971
2015-16	207.1	413.5	61.4	16.0	2.5	769.6	6.7	6.6	115.7	.9	.7	28.0	3,806
2016-17	212.6	478.0		17.2	3.1	962.0	6.0	8.7	130.1	.8	.6	34.0	3,986
2017-18[1]	213.2	450.0		19.0	3.8	714.7	7.4	.2	89.6	.3	.5	22.3	3,048

[1] Preliminary.   *Source: Economic Research Service, U.S. Department of Agriculture (ERS-USDA)*

Production of Rice (Rough) in the United States, by Type and Variety   In Thousands of Cwt.

Year	Long Grain	Medium Grain	Short Grain	Total	Year	Long Grain	Medium Grain	Short Grain	Total
2009	152,725	63,291	3,834	219,850	2014	162,665	57,222	2,328	222,215
2010	183,296	57,144	2,664	243,104	2015	133,401	57,041	2,706	193,148
2011	116,352	65,562	3,027	184,941	2016	166,465	54,533	3,147	224,145
2012	144,280	51,819	3,840	199,939	2017	127,850	47,867	2,511	178,228
2013	131,896	54,915	3,142	189,953	2018[1]	163,956	57,339	2,916	224,211

[1] Preliminary.   *Source: National Agricultural Statistics Service, U.S. Department of Agriculture (NASS-USDA)*

Rubber

Rubber is a natural or synthetic substance characterized by elasticity, water repellence, and electrical resistance. Pre-Columbian Native South Americans discovered many uses for rubber such as containers, balls, shoes, and waterproofing for fabrics such as coats and capes. The Spaniards tried to duplicate these products for many years but were unsuccessful. The first commercial application of rubber began in 1791 when Samuel Peal patented a method of waterproofing cloth by treating it with a solution of rubber and turpentine. In 1839, Charles Goodyear revolutionized the rubber industry with his discovery of a process called vulcanization, which involves combining rubber and sulfur and heating the mixture.

Natural rubber is obtained from latex, a milky white fluid, from the Hevea Brasiliensis tree. The latex is gathered by cutting a chevron shape through the bark of the rubber tree. The latex is collected in a small cup, with approximately 1 fluid ounce per cutting. The cuttings are usually done every other day until the cuttings reach the ground. The tree is then allowed to renew itself before a new tapping is started. The collected latex is strained, diluted with water, and treated with acid to bind the rubber particles together. The rubber is then pressed between rollers to consolidate the rubber into slabs or thin sheets and is air-dried or smoke-dried for shipment.

During World War II, natural rubber supplies from the Far East were cut off, and the rubber shortage accelerated the development of synthetic rubber in the U.S. Synthetic rubber is produced by chemical reactions, condensation or polymerization, of certain unsaturated hydrocarbons. Synthetic rubber is made of raw material derived from petroleum, coal, oil, natural gas, and acetylene and is almost identical to natural rubber in chemical and physical properties.

Natural rubber and Rubber Index futures are traded on the Osaka Mercantile Exchange (OME). The OME's natural rubber contract is based on the RSS3 ribbed smoked sheet No. 3. The OME's Rubber Index Futures Contract is based on a composite of 8 component grades from 6 rubber markets in the world. Rubber futures are also traded on the Shanghai Futures Exchange (SHFE), the Singapore Exchange (SGX), and the Tokyo Commodity Exchange (TOCOM).

Prices – Singapore SGX Rubber futures prices (Barchart.com symbol U6K) on the nearest-futures chart in 2018 rose briefly for 4 months and then fell the rest of the year to close the year down -13.1% at $148.50 per metric ton.

Supply – World production of natural rubber in 2016 fell -0.4% to 13.151 million metric tons, down from the 2014 record high of 13.258. The world's largest producers of natural rubber in 2016 were Thailand with 34.0% of world production, Indonesia with 24.0%, Vietnam with 7.9%, India with 7.2%, China with 6.2%, and Malaysia with 5.1%.

Trade – World exports of natural rubber in 2013 rose +8.8% yr/yr to 1.253 million metric tons. The world's largest exporter of natural rubber in 2013 was Thailand with 82.9% of world exports. U.S. imports of natural dry rubber in 2013 fell by -4.6% yr/yr to 881,396 metric tons.

World Production of Natural Rubber   In Thousands of Metric Tons

Year	Brazil	China	Côte d'Ivoire	India	Indonesia	Liberia	Malaysia	Nigeria	Philip-pines	Sri Lanka	Thailand	Vietnam	Total
2007	111.4	588.4	188.5	825.3	2,755.2	120.8	1,199.6	143.0	404.1	117.6	3,024.2	605.8	10,603.2
2008	120.9	547.9	203.0	864.5	2,751.3	84.8	1,072.4	136.0	411.0	129.2	3,166.9	660.0	10,749.5
2009	127.0	618.9	209.5	831.4	2,440.3	59.5	857.3	145.0	391.0	136.0	3,090.3	711.3	10,269.9
2010	134.0	690.8	235.0	862.0	2,734.9	62.1	939.2	144.7	395.2	153.0	3,051.8	751.7	10,838.8
2011	164.5	750.9	238.7	800.0	2,990.2	62.5	996.3	144.4	425.7	158.2	3,348.9	789.6	11,593.3
2012	177.1	802.3	256.6	900.0	3,012.3	78.1	923.0	147.6	443.0	150.6	4,139.4	877.1	12,663.0
2013	185.7	864.8	289.6	900.0	3,107.5	74.4	826.4	149.7	444.8	130.4	4,305.1	946.9	13,005.4
2014	192.4	840.2	307.0	940.0	3,153.2	75.0	668.6	151.8	453.1	113.4	4,566.3	961.1	13,257.9
2015[1]	191.5	816.1	305.6	950.7	3,145.4	76.2	722.1	154.1	398.1	133.5	4,466.1	1,012.8	13,205.4
2016[2]	189.4	811.3	310.7	952.8	3,157.8	73.7	673.5	156.3	362.6	130.9	4,476.6	1,035.3	13,151.6

[1] Preliminary.   [2] Estimate.   Source: Food and Agricultural Organization of the United Nations (FAO-UN)

World Imports of Natural Rubber   In Metric Tons

Year	Brazil	Canada	China	European Union	Germany	Italy	Korea, South	Malaysia	Mexico	Pakistan	United Kingdom	United States	Total
2007	13,024	20,366	256,643	294,455	114,432	38,012	23,399	361,713	22,527	22,497	22,635	89,160	1,204,584
2008	13,649	20,552	257,702	249,299	75,878	34,597	21,342	341,173	22,928	22,293	22,772	93,714	1,145,247
2009	14,003	14,233	312,771	194,890	67,388	24,955	21,036	357,254	18,918	16,634	15,620	69,930	1,104,422
2010	17,180	22,241	262,089	152,269	40,107	24,604	21,316	348,487	20,323	17,218	19,031	53,222	1,027,962
2011	17,752	23,058	280,663	138,609	31,817	24,123	19,252	306,561	19,433	14,819	20,376	49,264	975,316
2012	17,397	23,315	327,683	133,535	29,621	20,253	19,306	330,910	19,963	14,021	20,337	44,887	1,032,232
2013	17,849	22,309	345,330	160,483	32,169	20,894	20,130	344,581	19,318	14,023	28,656	45,939	1,094,304
2014	29,611	18,870	375,538	213,039	26,123	21,480	33,718	315,711	21,531	20,086	45,644	49,914	1,219,492
2015[1]	28,053	18,802	386,157	140,216	18,092	21,065	34,398	318,300	21,795	14,223	38,546	50,278	1,156,963
2016[2]	27,825	3,088	432,273	123,104	21,089	22,518	34,302	318,419	22,967	6,722	19,313	48,619	1,148,804

[1] Preliminary.   [2] Estimate.   Source: Food and Agricultural Organization of the United Nations (FAO-UN)

RUBBER

World Exports of Natural Rubber   In Metric Tons

Year	Belgium	Came-roon	Hong Kong	Germany	Guate-mala	India	Indonesia	Malaysia	Myanmar	Nether-lands	Thailand	United States	Total
2007	42,653	9,173	8,487	10,563	22,800	13,069	7,610	56,704	947	16,650	887,544	5,365	1,118,072
2008	31,402	6,396	5,723	6,732	20,355	13,141	8,547	44,599	1,388	22,650	836,404	5,888	1,031,926
2009	13,266	6,614	3,813	5,076	19,821	7,690	9,147	38,752	1,170	5,857	1,007,957	3,386	1,149,035
2010	14,255	8,160	3,224	6,039	20,603	7,407	12,929	47,773	1,886	694	898,454	5,369	1,056,340
2011	26,934	6,627	2,031	6,273	22,742	9,943	9,502	41,586	1,378	3,127	876,382	7,279	1,037,161
2012	37,031	4,826	1,675	7,332	23,301	4,499	7,620	31,748	50	2,288	949,103	7,909	1,151,861
2013	54,754	9,866	1,414	8,209	24,068	4,635	5,907	33,538	80	3,328	1,038,421	5,398	1,253,098
2014	80,932	7,169	1,802	5,980	42,899	815	5,410	32,370	----	12,967	1,057,520	6,470	1,348,497
2015[1]	19,980	5,596	2,346	5,136	41,910	653	6,410	31,904	889	17,834	1,072,710	7,119	1,302,309
2016[2]	37,911	6,300	1,692	6,070	36,287	2,148	6,067	30,375	1,840	20,240	1,240,189	6,045	1,499,360

[1] Preliminary.   [2] Estimate.   *Source: Food and Agricultural Organization of the United Nations (FAO-UN)*

World Imports of Natural Dry Rubber   In Metric Tons

Year	Brazil	Canada	China	European Union	France	Germany	Italy	Japan	Korea, South	Malaysia	Spain	United States	Total
2007	208,453	123,287	1,490,358	1,379,825	233,711	261,495	136,895	842,246	354,553	245,317	199,911	939,367	6,359,097
2008	220,959	121,907	1,506,462	1,211,480	208,921	234,608	123,850	839,170	337,790	219,637	181,472	958,558	6,180,191
2009	138,010	91,646	1,500,896	882,331	131,546	189,322	80,071	584,577	311,067	381,483	126,787	634,888	5,314,528
2010	232,161	128,087	1,724,502	1,304,121	171,252	367,791	103,302	731,498	366,255	329,683	177,182	891,688	6,512,249
2011	205,351	124,911	1,935,738	1,560,294	192,644	392,475	117,765	770,804	382,908	360,872	171,838	999,373	7,179,882
2012	163,742	120,209	1,962,901	1,341,258	162,806	338,306	93,204	685,966	378,016	541,519	141,411	923,981	7,126,938
2013	205,903	109,375	2,241,937	1,314,459	159,935	342,548	97,455	711,490	376,217	660,136	143,491	881,396	7,494,686
2014	211,843	110,737	2,352,994	1,411,036	154,532	361,112	107,043	678,929	383,051	589,328	164,149	897,012	7,829,740
2015[1]	191,039	113,698	2,460,397	1,458,367	161,966	353,750	115,196	677,828	367,806	639,001	169,108	899,721	8,107,058
2016[2]	206,383	118,204	2,178,576	1,469,796	160,774	315,651	116,682	655,319	361,975	611,916	162,042	897,493	7,830,607

[1] Preliminary.   [2] Estimate.   *Source: Food and Agricultural Organization of the United Nations (FAO-UN)*

World Exports of Natural Dry Rubber   In Metric Tons

Year	Côte d'Ivoire	Germany	Guate-mala	India	Indonesia	Liberia	Malaysia	Nigeria	Philip-pines	Sri Lanka	Thailand	Vietnam	Total
2007	182,397	40,572	45,474	39,294	2,399,146	120,800	960,241	33,792	30,417	46,083	2,077,771	247,331	6,425,892
2008	199,721	28,113	53,008	26,031	2,286,910	84,800	870,997	25,900	36,323	42,476	1,995,524	212,850	6,077,168
2009	218,555	56,089	57,770	12,787	1,982,116	59,500	664,306	31,700	24,899	50,246	1,731,787	239,580	5,378,189
2010	238,701	96,979	55,695	8,601	2,338,986	70,620	853,108	42,435	36,355	46,924	1,834,828	782,213	6,824,352
2011	259,459	130,568	65,351	28,154	2,546,237	70,339	904,494	58,088	42,209	41,052	2,120,597	817,502	7,499,757
2012	267,368	112,745	64,267	8,893	2,436,819	70,606	739,426	56,847	38,614	35,313	2,049,683	799,489	7,055,019
2013	259,860	110,488	64,182	22,134	2,696,087	58,946	813,714	51,332	66,930	23,007	2,398,556	674,342	7,648,372
2014	352,543	148,976	65,355	2,171	2,618,061	67,688	689,352	38,760	87,162	15,415	2,351,793	697,068	7,737,321
2015[1]	409,815	142,222	60,862	4,685	2,623,903	55,819	674,589	37,115	78,604	12,050	2,579,309	660,669	8,038,537
2016[2]	497,174	98,908	52,842	5,882	2,572,097	66,276	611,588	33,216	68,788	15,529	2,356,971	617,135	7,698,756

[1] Preliminary.   [2] Estimate.   *Source: Food and Agricultural Organization of the United Nations (FAO-UN)*

U.S. Imports of Natural Rubber (Includes Latex & Guayule)   In Metric Tons

Year	Jan.	Feb.	Mar.	Apr.	May	June	July	Aug.	Sept.	Oct.	Nov.	Dec.	Total
2009	84,464	52,281	73,285	48,921	51,743	31,137	60,976	48,537	52,110	64,798	64,970	71,598	704,819
2010	78,014	76,988	94,797	87,496	69,664	71,136	79,947	76,970	77,572	73,544	69,665	89,177	944,969
2011	82,559	83,695	100,449	94,540	104,094	82,569	92,187	95,040	68,872	90,280	79,167	75,984	1,049,435
2012	80,134	87,794	93,327	95,541	75,109	62,804	68,098	83,118	88,059	75,963	80,187	78,828	968,960
2013	75,848	66,517	84,667	80,380	72,054	82,234	77,067	72,617	76,176	76,111	88,195	76,234	928,100
2014	80,647	75,094	87,363	95,293	70,447	72,062	79,663	82,402	71,885	77,073	74,484	80,532	946,946
2015	84,504	57,323	86,017	81,059	102,381	78,643	83,734	79,336	83,083	77,489	73,360	65,115	952,042
2016	77,751	72,275	77,523	85,225	88,091	79,224	86,991	80,035	70,754	83,342	72,110	72,826	946,147
2017	78,217	71,901	88,085	85,883	64,955	97,920	82,746	79,584	82,898	80,086	71,825	88,396	972,495
2018[1]	82,600	75,326	96,446	75,441	101,791	86,553	65,733	84,977	87,418	97,657	73,051	70,410	997,403

[1] Preliminary.   *Source: Economic Research Service, U.S. Department of Agriculture (ERS-USDA)*

Rye

Rye is a cereal grain and a member of the grass family. Hardy varieties of rye have been developed for winter planting. Rye is most widely grown in northern Europe and Asia. In the U.S., rye is used as an animal feed and as an ingredient in bread and some whiskeys. Bread using rye was developed in northern Europe in the Middle Ages where bakers developed dark, hearty bread consisting of rye, oat and barley flours. Those were crops that grew more readily in the wet and damp climate of northern Europe, as opposed to wheat which fares better in the warmer and drier climates in central Europe. Modern rye bread is made with a mixture of white and rye flours. Coarsely ground rye flour is also used in pumpernickel bread and helps provide the dark color and course texture, along with molasses. The major producing states are North and South Dakota, Oklahoma, and Georgia. The crop year runs from June to May.

Supply – World rye production in 2017/18 marketing year is forecasted to rise by +0.1% yr/yr to 12.420 million metric tons. The world's largest producers of rye are the European Union with 60.5% of world production in 2017/18, followed by Russia with 20.1%, Belarus with 6.4%, and the Ukraine with 3.6%. U.S. production of rye accounted for only 2.0% of world production.

U.S. production of rye in 2016 (latest data) rose +15.8% to 13.451 million bushels, far below the production levels of over 20 million bushels seen from the late 1800s through the 1960s. U.S. production of rye fell off in the 1970's and fell to a record low of 6.311 million bushels in 2007.

U.S. acreage harvested with rye in 2017/18 is expected to fall -30.9% yr/yr to 286,000 acres. U.S. farmers in the late 1800s through the 1960s typically harvested more than 1 million acres of rye, showing how domestic planting of rye has dropped off sharply in the past several decades. Rye yield in 2017/18 is expected to rise +4.3% to 33.9 bushels per acre which is a new record high.

Demand – Total U.S. domestic usage of rye in 2016-27 rose +2.1% yr/yr to 20.625 million bushels. The breakdown of domestic usage shows that 52.9% of rye in 2016/17 was used for feed and residual, 17.7% for food, 14.8% for seed, and 14.5% for industry.

Trade – World exports of rye in the 2017/18 marketing year are expected to rise +36.6% yr/yr to 336,000 metric tons, above the record low of 225,000 metric tons in 2008-09. The largest exporters will be Canada with 150,000 metric tons of exports .and the European Union with 125,000 metric tons. World imports of rye are expected to rise +4.8% to 350,000 metric tons. U.S. imports of rye in 2016/17 ae expected to rise +3.6% yr/yr to 230,000 metric tons.

World Production of Rye   In Thousands of Metric Tons

Crop Year	Argen-tina	Australia	Belarus	Canada	Chile	European Union	Kazak-hstan	Norway	Russia	Turkey	Ukraine	United States	World Total
2009-10	55	34	1,227	281	5	9,955	75	27	4,333	343	954	172	17,522
2010-11	40	33	735	237	1	7,576	42	34	1,642	365	464	190	11,407
2011-12	45	40	801	241	1	6,900	28	16	2,967	366	579	154	12,191
2012-13	40	40	1,082	337	4	8,763	50	5	2,132	370	676	166	13,713
2013-14	52	20	648	223	4	10,151	43	13	3,360	365	638	194	15,761
2014-15	97	20	867	218	5	8,864	61	38	3,279	300	475	183	14,459
2015-16	61	22	753	226	5	7,833	37	66	2,084	330	394	295	12,154
2016-17[1]	79	26	661	436	5	7,440	41	20	2,598	300	394	342	12,328
2017-18[2]	86	26	670	342	5	7,411	39	42	2,544	320	510	246	12,293
2018-19[3]	95	26	650	235	5	6,600	25	42	1,850	320	400	214	10,514

[1] Preliminary.   [2] Estimate.   [3] Forecast.   Source: Foreign Agricultural Service, U.S. Department of Agriculture (FAS-USDA)

World Imports and Exports of Rye   In Thousands of Metric Tons

Year	Imports European Union	Japan	Korea, South	Norway	Russia	United States	World Total	Exports Belarus	Canada	European Union	Russia	United States	World Total
2009-10	----	103	7	13	----	108	246	2	124	97	12	2	293
2010-11	21	101	11	11	150	141	458	20	189	108	----	4	362
2011-12	291	46	11	16	----	152	538	11	166	57	238	4	490
2012-13	98	27	12	19	25	228	454	----	189	113	133	8	462
2013-14	77	37	8	22	5	234	425	----	118	169	74	7	420
2014-15	102	22	4	8	5	237	408	----	86	184	114	6	413
2015-16	51	16	5	1	8	222	335	20	98	161	48	5	353
2016-17[1]	16	24	4	3	4	167	228	11	142	76	9	4	254
2017-18[2]	60	21	3	4	5	225	352	----	193	80	85	4	400
2018-19[3]	50	20	5	10	25	254	384	20	150	100	70	5	415

[1] Preliminary.   [2] Estimate.   [3] Forecast.   Source: Foreign Agricultural Service, U.S. Department of Agriculture (FAS-USDA)

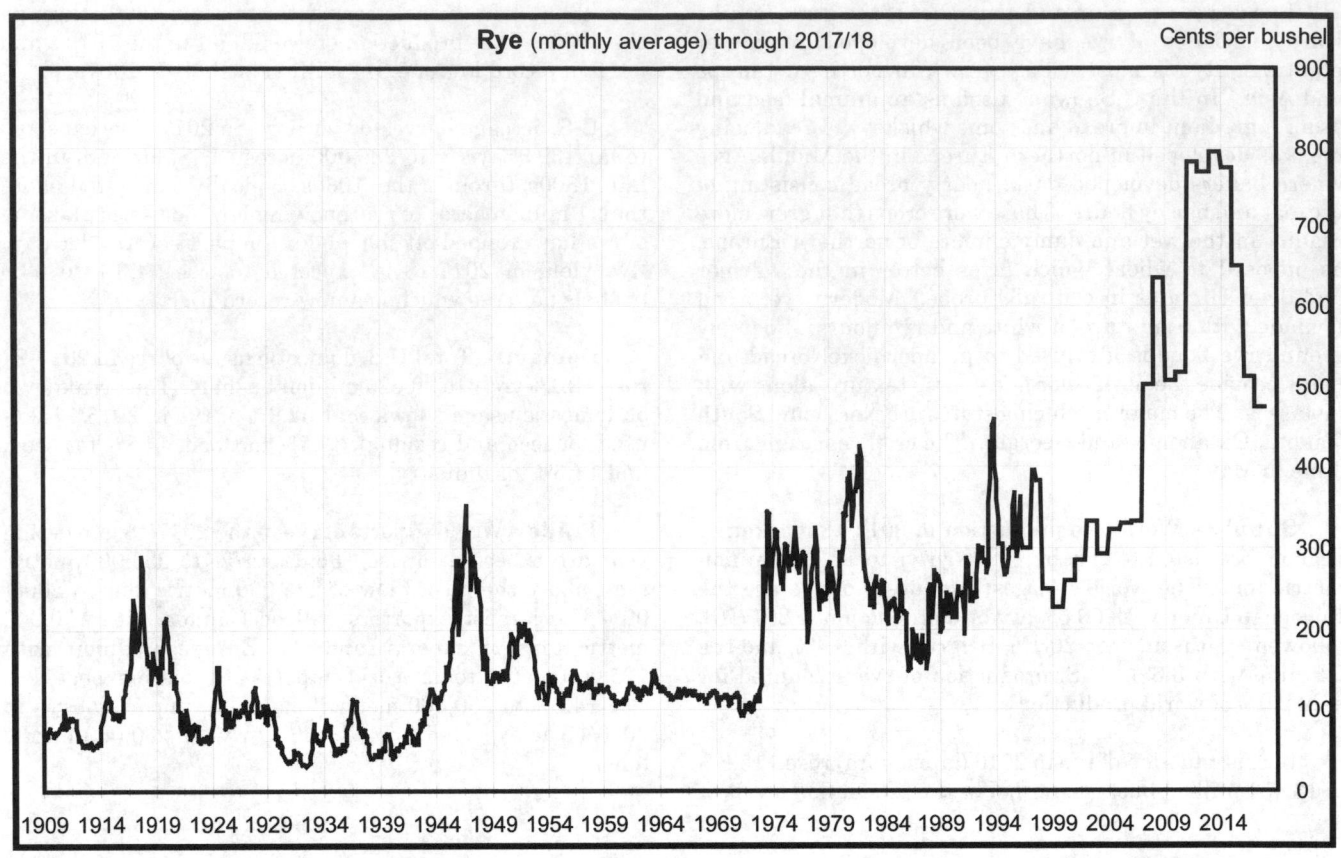

Rye (monthly average) through 2017/18 — Cents per bushel

Production of Rye in the United States   In Thousands of Bushels

Year	Georgia	North Dakota	Oklahoma	South Dakota	Other States[2]	Total
2009	525	----	560	----	5,908	6,791
2010	960	----	1,500	----	4,971	7,480
2011	945	----	825	----	4,556	6,051
2012	575	----	1,680	----	4,287	6,542
2013	1,080	----	1,600	----	4,946	7,626
2014	540	----	495	----	6,154	7,189
2015	420	----	2,040	----	9,156	11,616
2016	630	----	1,875	----	10,832	13,337
2017	475	----	1,080	----	8,697	10,252
2018[1]	390	----	1,100	----	6,942	8,432

[1] Preliminary.   [2] Includes IL, KS, ME, MD, MI, MN, NE, NJ, NY, NC, ND, PA, SC, SD, TX, VA, and WI.   *Source: Agricultural Statistics Board, U.S. Department of Agriculture (ASB-USDA)*

Salient Statistics of Rye in the United States   In Thousands of Bushels

Crop Year Beginning June 1	Supply — Stocks June 1	Supply — Production	Supply — Imports	Supply — Total Supply	Domestic Use — Food	Domestic Use — Industry	Domestic Use — Seed	Domestic Use — Feed & Residual	Domestic Use — Total	Exports	Total Disappearance	Acreage — Planted 1,000 Acres	Acreage — Harvested for Grain 1,000 Acres	Yield Per Harvested Acre (Bushels)
2009-10	509	6,791	4,251	11,551	3,330	2,161	2,560	2,495	10,546	73	10,619	1,241	252	27.8
2010-11	932	7,480	5,552	13,964	3,350	2,176	2,520	4,968	13,014	149	13,163	1,211	265	28.0
2011-12	801	6,051	5,994	12,846	3,380	2,531	2,610	3,716	12,237	157	12,394	1,266	242	26.1
2012-13	452	6,542	8,966	15,960	3,400	2,786	2,990	6,073	15,249	310	15,559	1,300	248	28.0
2013-14	401	7,626	9,213	17,240	3,430	3,399	2,970	6,888	16,687	268	16,955	1,451	278	27.4
2014-15	285	7,189	9,319	16,793	3,450	3,173	3,200	6,141	15,964	240	16,204	1,434	258	27.9
2015-16	589	11,616	8,757	20,962	3,480	5,321	3,840	7,685	20,326	181	20,507	1,584	365	31.8
2016-17[1]	455	13,337	6,586	20,378	3,500	5,727	4,130	6,262	19,619	175	19,794	1,891	411	32.5
2017-18[2]	698	10,252	8,842	19,792	3,530	5,800	4,250	4,906	18,486	157	18,643	1,961	300	34.2
2018-19[3]	593	8,432	10,000	19,025	3,550	6,000	4,140	4,565	18,255	200	18,455	2,011	273	30.9

[1] Preliminary.   [2] Estimate.   [3] Forecast   *Source: Economic Research Service, U.S. Department of Agriculture (ERS-USDA)*

Salt

Salt, also known as sodium chloride, is a chemical compound that is an essential element in the diet of humans, animals, and even many plants. Since prehistoric times, salt has been used to preserve foods and was commonly used in the religious rites of the Greeks, Romans, Hebrews, and Christians. Salt, in the form of salt cakes, served as money in ancient Ethiopia and Tibet. As long ago as 1450 BC, Egyptian art shows records of salt production.

The simplest method of obtaining salt is through the evaporation of salt water from areas near oceans or seas. In most regions, rock salt is obtained from underground mining or by wells sunk into deposits. Salt is soluble in water, is slightly soluble in alcohol, but is insoluble in concentrated hydrochloric acid. In its crystalline form, salt is transparent and colorless, shining with an ice-like luster.

Prices – The price of salt in 2018 (FOB mine, vacuum and open pan) was unchanged from 2017 at $200.00 per metric ton, which is a new record high.

Supply – World production of salt in 2018 rose +4.2% yr/yr to 300.000 million metric tons. The world's largest salt producers were China with 22.7% and the U.S. with 14.0% of world production. U.S. salt production in 2018 rose +5.0% yr/yr to 42.000 million metric tons.

Demand – U.S. consumption of salt in 2018 rose +16.3% to 57.000 million metric tons, but still down from the 2014 record high of 65.300 million.

Trade – U.S. imports of salt for consumption in 2017 rose +7.4% yr/yr to 13.000 million metric tons, down from the 2015 record high of 21.600. The U.S. relied on imports for 30% of its salt consumption in 2018. U.S. exports of salt in 2018 fell by -15.2% to 950,000 metric tons, with the bulk of those exports going to Canada.

World Production of All Salt   In Thousands of Metric Tons

Year	Australia	Canada	China	France	Germany	India	Italy	Mexico	Poland	Spain	United Kingdom	United States	World Total
2011	12,250	12,625	67,420	5,430	17,443	16,002	2,912	8,812	4,282	4,503	6,060	45,055	273,000
2012	12,500	12,820	69,120	5,460	14,656	17,002	3,098	8,730	4,183	4,109	6,460	37,245	261,000
2013	12,900	12,244	73,676	5,890	17,396	26,888	2,879	9,461	4,743	4,278	6,930	39,955	280,000
2014	13,000	14,473	70,497	5,810	13,338	23,017	1,501	10,251	4,127	4,300	4,690	45,385	275,000
2015	11,000	14,343	66,655	6,000	12,480	24,241	1,600	9,088	4,119	4,300	5,000	45,125	277,000
2016	12,000	14,000	67,000	6,000	12,890	25,000	1,700	9,000	4,170	4,300	5,100	41,795	274,000
2011[1]	11,000	12,000	67,000	4,500	13,000	28,000		9,000	4,450	4,500	5,100	40,000	288,000
2018[2]	12,000	13,000	68,000	4,500	13,000	29,000		9,000	4,500	4,500	5,100	42,000	300,000

[1] Preliminary.   [2] Estimate.   Source: U.S. Geological Survey (USGS)

Salient Statistics of the Salt Industry in the United States   In Thousands of Metric Tons

Year	Net Import Reliance As a % of Apparent Consumption	Average Value FOB Mine Vacuum & Open Pan ($ Per Ton)	Production Total	Open & Vacuum Pan	Solar	Rock	Brine	Sold or Used, Producers Open & Vacuum Pan	Rock	Brine	Total Salt	Imports for Consumption Value[3] Million $	Imports for Consumption	Exports Total	Exports To Canada	Apparent Consumption
2011	24	174.00	45,000	4,080	3,230	18,500	19,200	4,000	18,500	19,200	45,500	1,770.0	13,800	846	754	58,500
2012	22	169.93	37,200	4,240	2,760	13,300	16,900	4,200	11,300	16,900	34,900	1,460.0	9,880	809	728	44,000
2013	22	172.09	39,900	4,130	3,580	14,800	17,400	4,090	18,300	17,400	43,100	1,980.0	11,900	525	434	54,500
2014	29	180.61	45,300	4,140	3,900	20,000	17,300	4,080	20,800	17,500	46,000	2,180.0	20,200	935	809	65,300
2015	33	188.87	45,100	4,190	3,590	20,400	16,900	4,220	18,200	17,000	42,800	2,360.0	21,600	830	699	63,600
2016	22	197.78	41,700	4,050	2,900	17,900	16,900	4,040	16,100	16,700	40,200	2,190.0	12,100	716	581	51,600
2017[1]	23	200.00	40,000								38,000		12,600	1,120		49,000
2018[2]	28	200.00	42,000								41,000		17,000	950		57,000

[1] Preliminary.   [2] Estimate.   [3] Values are f.o.b. mine or refinery & do not include cost of cooperage or containers.   Source: U.S. Geological Survey (USGS)

Salt Sold or Used by Producers in the U.S. by Classes & Consumers or Uses   In Thousands of Metric Tons

Year	Chemical[2]	Tanning Leather	Textile & Dyeing	Meat Packers[3]	Canning	Baking	Agricultural Distribution	Feed Dealers	Feed Manufacturers	Rubber	Oil	Paper & Pulp	Metal Processing	Water Treatment	Grocery Stores	Water Conditioning Distrib.	Ice Control and/or Stabilization
2009	17,940	32	48	271	215	324	357	1,310	377	5	314	58	24	1,011	812	469	16,850
2010	20,190	39	59	275	258	364	359	1,330	425	5	325	59	26	913	761	461	18,640
2011	18,530	42	49	260	195	162	375	1,170	438	5	322	67	44	312	706	493	19,560
2012	16,824	36	41	248	182	160	253	1,010	392	7	441	61	53	446	591	472	11,100
2013	17,990	38	39	258	179	162	351	913	516	5	409	66	42	472	665	627	20,340
2014	20,360	39	38	240	171	158	389	939	514	6	400	71	56	603	708	504	24,490
2015	19,430	38	39	275	175	181	306	849	336	3	302	69	46	723	707	440	22,760
2016[1]	19,050	36	64	283	181	171	428	660	377	4	316	63	41	469	669	437	20,300

[1] Preliminary.   [2] Chloralkali producers and other chemical.   Source: U.S. Geological Survey (USGS)

Sheep and Lambs

Sheep and lambs are raised for both their wool and meat. In countries that have high wool production, there is also demand for sheep and lamb meat due to the easy availability. Production levels have declined in New Zealand and Australia, but that has been counteracted by a substantial increase in China.

Prices – The average monthly wholesale price of slaughter lambs (choice) at San Angelo, Texas in 2018 was virtually unchanged yr/yr at 143.56 cents per pound, which was still well below the record high of 160.75 cents per pound posted in 2011.

Supply – World sheep and goat numbers in 2016 rose by +1.7% to 2.176 billion head, a new record high. The world's largest producers of sheep and goats are China with 14.3% of world production in 2016, India with 9.0%, Turkey with 1.9%, and the United Kingdom with 1.6%.

The number of sheep and lambs on U.S. farms in 2018 (Jan 1) was down -0.4% yr/yr to 5.230 million head. The U.S. states with the most sheep and lambs are Texas with 14.3% of the U.S. total, California with 10.9%, Colorado with 8.5%, Wyoming with 6.6%, and Utah with 5.9%.

World Sheep and Goat Numbers in Specified Countries on January 1   In Thousands of Head

Year	Argentina	Australia	China	India	Kazakhstan	New Zealand	Romania	Russia	South Africa	Spain	Turkey	United Kingdom	World Total
2008	20,238	79,638	285,877	209,732	16,080	34,184	9,334	21,503	31,623	22,912	31,749	33,223	1,982,774
2009	19,528	76,140	281,056	207,387	16,770	32,466	9,780	21,770	31,347	22,652	29,568	31,533	1,978,316
2010	19,062	71,585	284,729	205,065	17,370	32,658	10,059	21,986	30,776	21,455	26,923	31,177	1,987,186
2011	19,011	76,599	281,085	202,766	17,988	31,218	9,658	21,820	30,468	19,696	29,383	31,728	2,014,889
2012	19,047	78,272	282,549	200,242	18,092	31,353	9,770	22,858	30,533	18,977	32,310	32,313	2,050,100
2013	18,950	79,098	285,209	197,800	17,633	30,867	10,100	24,180	30,556	18,729	35,783	32,954	2,087,741
2014	18,934	76,182	290,524	196,000	17,561	29,901	10,449	24,337	30,094	18,136	38,510	33,843	2,095,178
2015	19,580	74,510	303,308	194,250	18,016	29,196	10,935	24,683	29,810	19,533	41,485	33,438	2,177,398
2016[1]	19,576	71,193	311,154	198,431	18,184	27,696	11,250	24,881	28,906	19,051	41,924	34,047	2,214,106
2017[2]	19,563	75,725	301,267	196,417	18,329	27,625	11,359	24,844	28,164	19,023	41,329	34,936	2,236,837

[1] Preliminary.   [2] Forecast.   *Source: Food and Agricultural Organization of the United Nations (FAO-UN)*

Salient Statistics of Sheep & Lambs in the United States (Average Live Weight)   In Thousands of Head

	Inventory, Jan. 1				Marketings[3]		Slaughter					Production (Live Weight)	Farm Value Jan. 1
Year	Without New Crop Lambs	With New Crop Lambs	Lamb Crop	Total Supply	Sheep	Lambs	Farm	Commercial	Total[4]	Net Exports	Total Disappearance	(Mil. Lbs.)	Total
2009	5,747	5,855	3,690	9,545	625	3,532	95	2,516	2,611	----	----	421.6	765.2	133.0
2010	5,620	5,727	3,570	9,297	645	3,429	95	2,458	2,553	----	----	405.3	761.1	135.0
2011	5,470	5,579	3,490	9,069	----	----	93	2,164	2,258	----	----	----	938.4	170.0
2012	5,375	5,484	3,445	8,929	----	----	93	2,183	2,275	----	----	----	----	----
2013	5,360	5,467	3,370	8,837	----	----	94	2,319	2,412	----	----	----	----	----
2014	5,245	5,356	3,440	8,796	----	----	95	2,310	2,404	----	----	----	----	----
2015	5,280	5,385	3,275	8,660	----	----	95	2,224	2,319	----	----	----	----	----
2016	5,300	5,405	3,250	8,655	----	----	95	2,238	2,333	----	----	----	----	----
2017[1]	5,250	5,356	3,230	8,586	----	----	96	2,178	2,274	----	----	----	----	----
2018[2]	5,265	5,372	3,235	8,607	----	----	92	2,250	2,343	----	----	----	----	----

[1] Preliminary.   [2] Estimate.   [3] Excludes interfarm sales.   [4] Includes all commercial and farm.
Source: Economic Research Service, U.S. Department of Agriculture (ERS-USDA)

Sheep and Lambs[3] on Farms in the United States on January 1   In Thousands of Head

Year	California	Colorado	Idaho	Iowa	Minnesota	Montana	New Mexico	Ohio	Dakota	Texas	Utah	Wyoming	Total
2011	600	370	235	200	130	230	110	129	265	850	280	365	5,470
2012	570	460	240	195	150	225	100	126	285	650	305	370	5,375
2013	570	435	235	175	135	235	100	121	275	700	295	375	5,360
2014	590	365	250	155	135	220	81	117	270	730	280	355	5,245
2015	600	420	260	175	130	215	90	121	255	720	290	345	5,280
2016	575	435	255	175	125	230	90	120	265	725	285	355	5,300
2017	600	420	250	175	130	230	97	117	250	710	275	360	5,250
2018	570	445	235	165	130	225	96	119	250	750	275	345	5,265
2019[1]	550	420	220	153	125	215	100	121	255	750	290	350	5,230

[1] Preliminary.   [2] Includes sheep & lambs on feed for market and stock sheep & lambs.   *Source: Economic Research Service, U.S. Department of Agriculture (ERS-USDA)*

Average Wholesale Price of Slaughter Lambs (Choice[2]) at San Angelo Texas In Dollars Per Hundred Pounds (Cwt.)

Year	Jan.	Feb.	Mar.	Apr.	May	June	July	Aug.	Sept.	Oct.	Nov.	Dec.	Average
2010	95.04	106.63	109.95	112.00	104.47	102.05	109.17	112.15	125.38	129.69	138.50	156.67	116.81
2011	164.19	182.63	177.15	152.88	160.20	160.88	169.47	162.13	152.80	154.00	156.80	135.83	160.75
2012	147.40	148.13	141.94	136.75	128.50	116.00	103.64	83.32	80.88	96.20	84.67	88.67	113.01
2013	114.25	109.57	98.76	88.90	92.50	93.76	91.90	86.50	104.38	146.50	143.09	163.33	111.12
2014	165.00	168.38	154.88	150.97	135.17	160.83	150.23	152.94	164.90	159.25	162.00	166.83	157.62
2015	155.25	148.75	137.75	137.38	147.25	147.88	140.50	148.00	150.20	139.00	148.67	139.88	145.04
2016	139.00	134.07	127.45	136.56	136.40	135.50	130.66	139.90	142.00	130.50	126.13	139.00	134.76
2017	138.10	139.25	139.38	140.50	159.00	160.88	146.00	147.00	138.88	127.50	130.17	136.00	141.89
2018[1]	130.88	133.75	135.50	149.05	155.63	159.91	157.29	145.58	140.98	136.58	134.35	131.98	142.62

[1] Preliminary.   Source: Economic Research Service, U.S. Department of Agriculture (ERS-USDA)

Federally Inspected Slaughter of Sheep & Lambs in the United States   In Thousands of Head

Year	Jan.	Feb.	Mar.	Apr.	May	June	July	Aug.	Sept.	Oct.	Nov.	Dec.	Total
2010	173.2	167.4	249.4	174.9	167.3	194.2	178.3	184.8	186.0	184.6	201.1	200.0	2,261.1
2011	150.5	145.5	183.5	191.8	165.8	168.2	149.6	182.6	162.8	160.8	171.9	167.2	2,000.2
2012	153.8	154.6	180.0	165.8	164.4	154.8	164.5	185.5	160.6	189.5	165.5	173.3	2,012.1
2013	164.7	150.3	184.0	174.9	188.4	167.7	192.9	189.5	167.2	186.5	169.5	184.6	2,120.1
2014	166.9	155.4	176.5	204.0	176.5	175.3	188.9	161.4	172.7	186.8	157.1	182.8	2,104.6
2015	153.0	149.9	190.0	179.1	152.7	172.8	166.8	155.5	167.4	166.3	162.6	182.3	1,998.4
2016	144.4	159.9	187.5	169.7	166.7	174.0	152.4	173.3	170.1	163.0	169.6	178.9	2,009.5
2017	161.6	144.8	177.3	156.1	157.1	165.5	146.3	171.9	153.9	165.1	167.3	170.1	1,937.0
2018[1]	161.9	146.0	185.2	163.3	177.8	158.8	158.0	174.1	148.1	176.1	174.1	176.2	1,999.6

[1] Preliminary.   Source: Economic Research Service, U.S. Department of Agriculture (ERS-USDA)

Average Live Weight of Sheep & Lambs Slaughtered in the United States   In Pounds per Head

Year	Jan.	Feb.	Mar.	Apr.	May	June	July	Aug.	Sept.	Oct.	Nov.	Dec.	Average
2010	141	143	137	141	142	138	134	129	130	134	134	140	137
2011	142	144	148	142	148	141	136	135	137	138	138	142	141
2012	151	153	152	147	157	152	144	145	148	140	140	138	147
2013	143	145	142	143	142	142	136	134	128	127	130	133	137
2014	140	140	142	140	147	141	135	131	130	132	135	137	138
2015	144	144	142	142	145	142	141	137	132	131	134	135	139
2016	142	145	141	138	144	138	138	132	128	130	133	135	137
2017	141	144	143	133	134	136	135	134	131	131	136	138	136
2018[1]	144	148	142	141	140	141	138	136	137	134	136	134	139

[1] Preliminary.   Source: Economic Research Service, U.S. Department of Agriculture (ERS-USDA)

Federally Inspected Slaughter of Goats in the United States   In Thousands of Head

Year	Jan.	Feb.	Mar.	Apr.	May	June	July	Aug.	Sept.	Oct.	Nov.	Dec.	Total
2010	42.9	39.3	58.3	46.8	45.7	52.8	50.2	58.5	56.5	50.7	57.7	52.5	612.1
2011	40.8	37.7	42.6	47.4	44.5	49.5	50.3	60.3	50.8	51.6	58.6	55.2	589.1
2012	43.3	38.4	44.1	45.9	45.5	44.6	52.0	54.3	44.4	52.5	44.6	48.3	557.9
2013	39.8	34.0	44.8	42.0	44.7	40.7	53.3	48.6	43.7	49.5	41.6	45.3	528.0
2014	35.4	31.5	36.4	41.6	39.8	44.3	45.3	40.9	42.7	43.9	37.2	47.4	486.5
2015	34.9	28.3	38.2	35.5	33.8	40.1	38.5	37.2	40.4	36.5	36.2	41.7	441.3
2016	31.1	32.5	38.1	32.0	35.5	39.9	35.4	41.8	40.8	38.1	38.8	44.9	448.9
2017	36.9	32.2	36.8	38.1	45.1	42.9	38.9	43.9	41.7	43.2	42.4	46.7	488.8
2018[1]	39.4	35.3	42.4	38.6	45.8	42.6	43.0	47.7	36.8	46.0	46.4	50.1	514.1

[1] Preliminary.   Source: Economic Research Service, U.S. Department of Agriculture (ERS-USDA)

Cold Storage Holdings of Lamb and Mutton in the United States, on First of Month   In Thousands of Pounds

Year	Jan.	Feb.	Mar.	Apr.	May	June	July	Aug.	Sept.	Oct.	Nov.	Dec.
2010	14,519	11,759	12,922	16,313	16,453	20,448	22,972	22,059	19,859	18,046	16,189	16,500
2011	15,206	13,278	12,582	12,874	13,279	15,062	18,097	21,034	21,209	22,218	20,021	19,014
2012	16,857	19,275	20,851	21,846	19,711	19,680	22,460	24,291	24,233	23,453	23,210	18,978
2013	21,379	18,768	19,833	17,624	21,463	19,793	19,307	23,324	21,988	23,444	23,967	21,697
2014	24,508	25,658	26,191	28,076	26,536	25,208	31,119	33,968	40,157	39,693	38,686	31,366
2015	33,942	35,206	36,771	34,250	37,004	38,360	35,470	39,064	41,883	41,921	40,742	44,693
2016	41,452	47,111	40,051	40,648	39,787	44,816	39,518	40,979	36,563	32,736	29,439	21,876
2017	26,140	20,361	25,694	25,792	28,603	29,859	26,177	26,770	32,383	31,415	31,594	28,977
2018[1]	26,714	26,790	28,280	28,615	33,992	35,591	38,678	42,129	39,386	40,466	39,320	37,860

[1] Preliminary.   Source: Economic Research Service, U.S. Department of Agriculture (ERS-USDA)

Silk

Silk is a fine, tough, elastic fiber produced by caterpillars, commonly called silkworms. Silk is one of the oldest known textile fibers. Chinese tradition credits Lady Hsi-Ling-Shih, wife of the Emperor Huang Ti, with the discovery of the silkworm and the invention of the first silk reel. Dating to around 3000 BC, a group of ribbons, threads, and woven fragments was found in China. Also found, along the lower Yangzi River, were 7,000-year-old spinning tools, silk thread, and fabric fragments.

Silk filament was first woven into cloth in Ancient China. The Chinese successfully guarded this secret until 300AD, when Japan, and later India, learned the secret. In 550 AD, two Nestorian monks were sent to China to steal mulberry seeds and silkworm eggs, which they hid in their walking staffs, and then brought them back to Rome. By the 17th century, France was the silk center of the West. Unfortunately, the silkworm did not flourish in the English climate, nor has it ever flourished in the U.S.

Sericulture is the term for the raising of silkworms. The blind, flightless moth, Bombyx mori, lays more than 500 tiny eggs. After hatching, the tiny worms eat chopped mulberry leaves continuously until they are ready to spin their cocoons. After gathering the complete cocoons, the first step in silk manufacturing is to kill the insects inside the cocoons with heat. The cocoons are then placed in boiling water to loosen the gummy substance, sericin,

holding the filament together. The filament is unwound, and then rewound in a process called reeling. Each cocoon's silk filament is between 600 and 900 meters long. Four different types of silk thread may be produced: organzine, crepe, tram, and thrown singles. During the last 30 years, despite the use of man-made fibers, world silk production has doubled.

Raw silk is traded on the Kansai Agricultural Commodities Exchange (KANEX) in Japan. Dried cocoons are traded on the Chuba Commodity Exchange (CCE). Raw silk and dried cocoons are traded on the Yokohama Commodity Exchange.

Supply – World production of silk in 2014 (latest data), rose + 0.2% yr/yr to 168.333 metric tons, just below the 2012 record high of 168,470 metric tons. China is the world's largest producer of silk by far with a 74.9% share of world production in 2014. Other key producers include India with 14.1% of world production, Vietnam (4.0%), and Thailand (1.0%).

Trade – In 2013 (latest data), the world's largest exporters of silk were China with 82.7 % of world exports, North Korea with 0.7%, and Japan with 0.4%. In 2013, the world's largest importers of silk were India with 14.5% of world imports, Italy with 2.7%, and Japan with 4.9%.

World Production of Raw Silk   In Metric Tons

Year	Brazil	China	India	Iran	Japan	Korea, North	Korea, South	Kyrgy-zstan	Thailand	Turkmen-istan	Uzbek-istan	Vietnam	World Total
2005	1,200	111,950	16,500	900	150	350	3	50	1,600	4,500	1,200	11,475	152,448
2006	1,250	123,491	17,305	900	117	350	3	50	1,600	4,500	1,200	10,413	163,765
2007	1,300	125,001	18,475	900	105	350	3	50	1,600	4,500	1,200	10,110	166,180
2008	1,000	126,001	18,320	900	120	350	3	50	1,600	4,500	1,200	7,746	164,377
2009	800	126,001	18,370	900	150	400	3	50	1,600	4,500	1,200	7,367	163,933
2010	600	126,001	19,690	900	130	400	3	50	1,600	4,500	1,200	7,107	164,767
2011	500	126,001	20,410	900	280	400	3	50	1,600	4,500	1,200	7,057	165,488
2012	400	126,001	23,060	900	250	400	3	50	1,600	4,500	1,200	7,517	168,470
2013[1]	400	126,001	23,679	900	250	400	3	50	1,600	4,500	1,200	6,360	167,932
2014[2]	400	126,001	23,679	900	250		3	50	1,600	4,500	1,200	6,761	168,333

[1] Preliminary.   [2] Estimate.   NA = Not avaliable.   *Source: Food and Agricultural Organization of the United Nations (FAO-UN)*

World Trade of Silk by Selected Countries   In Metric Tons

	Imports							Exports					
Year	France	Hong Kong	India	Italy	Japan	Korea, South	World Total	Brazil	China	Hong Kong	Japan	Korea, South	World Total
2007	150	2	7,922	1,463	791	989	15,931	18	13,758	2	10	277	15,696
2008	191	----	8,392	1,040	932	724	16,371	13	13,431	----	16	137	14,903
2009	111	17	7,338	501	733	656	12,552	8	9,243	16	8	100	10,860
2010	109	34	4,525	698	737	645	9,992	6	8,543	34	36	57	10,406
2011	110	9	5,597	711	563	533	16,803	----	7,122	----	35	59	8,608
2012	135	----	5,235	692	607	503	21,161	----	7,676	2	25	245	9,158
2013	248	----	3,609	676	570	410	24,917	----	6,690	----	18	118	8,454
2014	230	----	3,403	785	497	346	8,741	----	6,359	----	1	73	8,341
2015	185	----	3,454	733	391	313	8,270	----	6,695	----	----	17	8,948
2016[1]	156	----	3,757	710	395	310	9,167	----	6,927	----	----	97	8,962

[1] Preliminary.   *Source: Food and Agricultural Organization of the United Nations (FAO-UN)*

Silver

Silver is a white, lustrous metallic element that conducts heat and electricity better than any other metal. In ancient times, many silver deposits were on or near the earth's surface. Before 2,500 BC, silver mines were worked in Asia Minor. Around 700 BC, ancient Greeks stamped a turtle on their first silver coins. Silver assumed a key role in the U.S. monetary system in 1792 when Congress based the currency on the silver dollar. However, the U.S. discontinued the use of silver in coinage in 1965. Today Mexico is the only country that uses silver in its circulating coinage.

Silver is the most malleable and ductile of all metals, apart from gold. Silver melts at about 962 degrees Celsius and boils at about 2212 degrees Celsius. Silver is not very chemically active, although tarnishing occurs when sulfur and sulfides attack silver, forming silver sulfide on the surface of the metal. Because silver is too soft in its pure form, a hardening agent, usually copper, is mixed into the silver. Copper is usually used as the hardening agent because it does not discolor the silver. The term "sterling silver" refers to silver that contains at least 925 parts of silver per thousand (92.5%) to 75 parts of copper (7.5%).

Silver is usually found combined with other elements in minerals and ores. In the U.S., silver is mined in conjunction with lead, copper, and zinc. In the U.S., Nevada, Idaho, Alaska, and Arizona are the leading silver-producing states. For industrial purposes, silver is used for photography, electrical appliances, glass, and as an antibacterial agent for the health industry.

Silver futures and options are traded at the CME Group and the London Metal Exchange (LME). Silver futures are traded on the Tokyo Commodity Exchange (TOCOM). The CME silver futures contract calls for the delivery of 5,000 troy ounces of silver (0.999 fineness) and is priced in terms of dollars and cents per troy ounce.

Prices – CME silver futures prices (Barchart.com symbol SI) posted the high for 2018 in January at $17.705 an ounce. Dollar weakness early in 2018 pushed silver prices higher as the dollar index tumbled to a 4-year low in January. Silver prices traded sideways into Q3 and then trended lower into November, posting a 3-year low of $13.86 an ounce. Expectations for tighter Fed policy undercut precious metals prices the second half of 2018 as the Fed continued to raise interest rates. Also, U.S. tariffs on Chinese goods took a negative toll on China's economy as Chinese industrial output trended lower throughout 2018 and slowed to a 2-year low of +6.2% yr/yr pace in December. China's Q4 2018 GDP eased to a 9-year low of 6.4%. Silver prices bounced higher from their worst levels into year-end after a sell-off on global equity markets in December spurred safe-haven buying of precious metals. Silver prices finished 2018 down -9.4% yr/yr at $15.54 an ounce.

Supply – World mine production of silver in 2018 rose 0.7% yr/yr to 27,000 metric tons, to match the record high posted in both 2014 and 2915. The world's largest silver producers in 2018 were Mexico with 22.6% of world production, Peru with 15.9%, China with 13.3%, and both Poland & Chili with 4.8%. U.S. production of refined silver in 2018 (annualized through October) fell by -0.5% yr/yr yr/yr to 4,654 metric tons, down from the 2011 record high of 6,375 metric tons.

Trade – U.S. exports of refined silver in 2015 rose +125.7% yr/yr to 781,000 kilograms. The major destinations for U.S. silver exports are Canada with 55.1% of the total exports and India with 36.4%. U.S. imports of silver mullion in 2015 rose +19.5% yr/yr to 4.660 million kilograms. The bulk of those imports came from Mexico with 42.5% and Canada with 41.2% of the total.

World Mine Production of Silver — In Thousands of Kilograms (Metric Ton)

Year	Australia	Bolivia	Canada[3]	Chile	China	Kazak-hstan	Mexico	Peru	Poland	Russia	Sweden	United States	World Total[2]
2009	1,635	1,326	617	1,301	2,900	618	3,554	3,923	1,207	1,590	289	1,250	22,600
2010	1,879	1,259	591	1,287	3,500	552	3,499	3,640	1,181	1,545	302	1,280	23,300
2011	1,725	1,214	582	1,291	3,192	547	4,778	3,473	1,270	1,198	283	1,120	23,600
2012	1,727	1,206	685	1,195	3,401	545	5,358	3,547	1,284	1,384	306	1,060	24,600
2013	1,840	1,281	640	1,174	3,529	611	5,513	3,754	1,170	1,428	337	1,050	25,600
2014	1,675	1,345	493	1,574	3,499	590	5,795	3,821	1,264	1,434	396	1,180	27,000
2015	1,570	1,310	380	1,510	3,390	538	5,900	4,230	1,290	1,570	494	1,090	27,600
2016	1,420	1,350		1,500	2,380	1,180	5,360	4,370	1,270	1,570		1,150	25,700
2017[1]	1,200	1,240		1,260	3,500	1,200	6,110	4,300	1,290	1,120		1,030	26,800
2018[2]	1,200	1,200		1,300	3,600		6,100	4,300	1,300	1,200		900	27,000

[1] Preliminary.   [2] Estimate.   [3] Shipments.   *Source: U.S. Geological Survey (USGS)*

SILVER

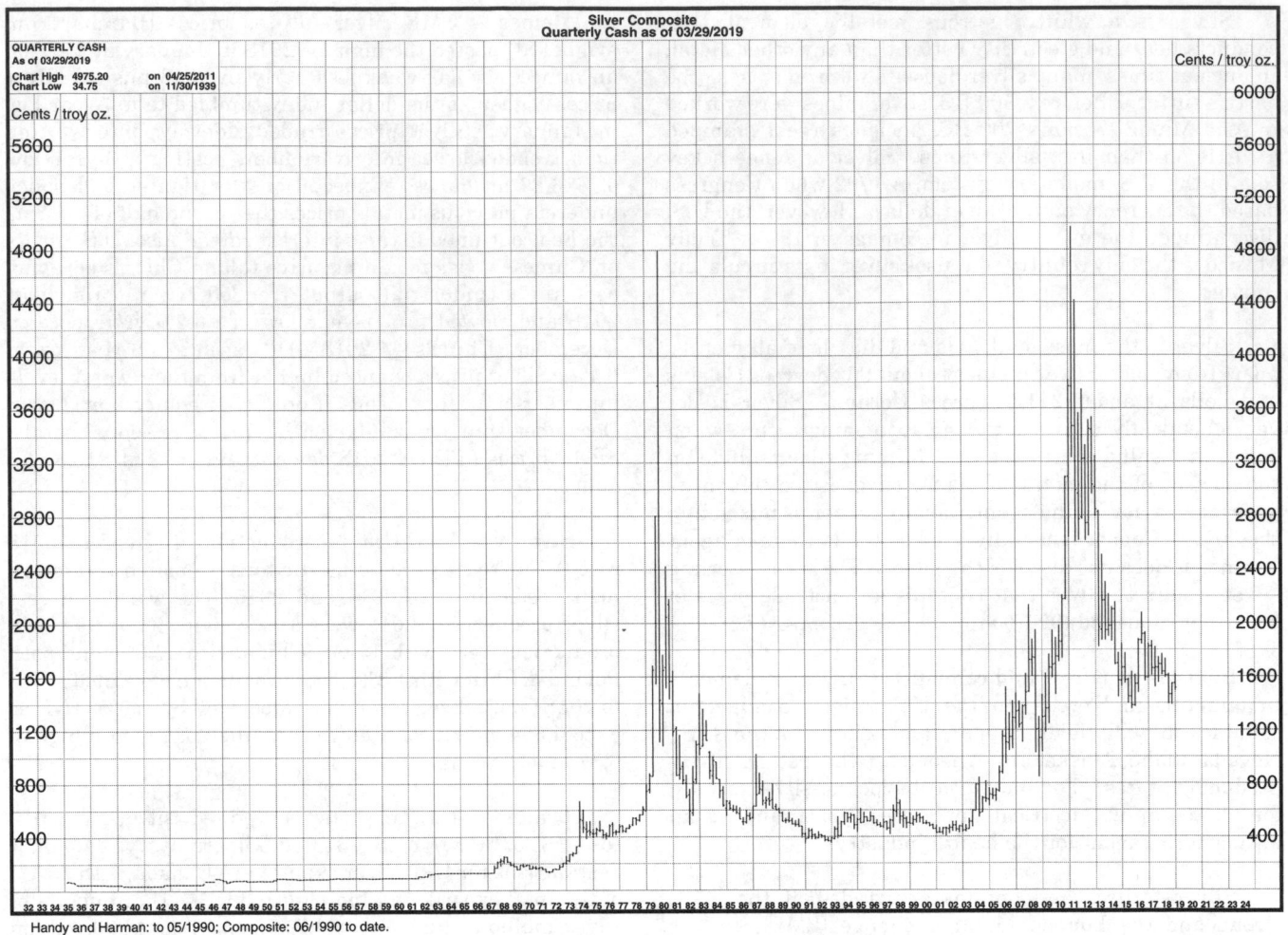

Handy and Harman: to 05/1990; Composite: 06/1990 to date.

Average Price of Silver in New York (Handy & Harman)   In Cents Per Troy Ounce (.999 Fine)

Year	Jan.	Feb.	Mar.	Apr.	May	June	July	Aug.	Sept.	Oct.	Nov.	Dec.	Average
2009	1,139.90	1,343.68	1,311.50	1,252.02	1,411.30	1,465.93	1,338.64	1,443.05	1,648.74	1,726.34	1,787.68	1,765.68	1,469.54
2010	1,775.05	1,587.21	1,717.11	1,816.83	1,841.90	1,853.43	1,793.98	1,849.25	2,061.12	2,346.86	2,657.20	2,933.00	2,019.41
2011	2,855.15	3,085.61	3,594.61	4,264.45	3,702.67	3,584.09	3,832.95	4,035.17	3,802.10	3,206.33	3,336.08	3,028.07	3,527.27
2012	3,095.25	3,421.95	3,296.32	3,154.65	2,882.00	2,810.29	2,739.74	2,891.35	3,379.18	3,328.57	3,271.00	3,177.13	3,120.62
2013	3,112.05	3,027.53	2,878.90	2,525.25	2,301.95	2,111.53	1,968.66	2,208.02	2,249.40	2,201.43	2,072.35	1,962.29	2,384.95
2014	1,987.52	2,086.53	2,071.60	1,973.64	1,934.19	1,989.24	2,092.25	1,973.56	1,837.10	1,716.33	1,596.61	1,629.48	1,907.34
2015	1,723.55	1,678.71	1,624.00	1,634.00	1,683.28	1,607.45	1,505.32	1,494.12	1,475.02	1,581.25	1,445.22	1,408.55	1,571.71
2016	1,411.18	1,516.72	1,546.45	1,636.02	1,694.71	1,728.61	1,999.18	1,958.74	1,932.98	1,764.07	1,740.74	1,644.62	1,714.50
2017	1,690.20	1,793.32	1,761.96	1,803.34	1,674.48	1,693.11	1,615.20	1,695.17	1,743.15	1,694.14	1,697.71	1,616.50	1,706.52
2018	1,712.71	1,658.24	1,647.30	1,664.84	1,648.99	1,654.14	1,572.30	1,498.70	1,427.17	1,459.67	1,435.34	1,477.24	1,571.39

Source: American Metal Market (AMM)

Average Price of Silver in London (Spot Fix)   In Pence Per Troy Ounce (.999 Fine)

Year	Jan.	Feb.	Mar.	Apr.	May	June	July	Aug.	Sept.	Oct.	Nov.	Dec.	Average
2009	787.02	931.98	923.81	850.16	912.88	894.99	816.90	872.89	1,010.76	1,065.91	1,076.27	1,087.91	935.96
2010	1,098.45	1,016.07	1,140.22	1,184.58	1,256.63	1,255.90	1,172.41	1,181.47	1,323.37	1,479.95	1,665.70	1,880.21	1,304.58
2011	1,808.34	1,912.09	2,224.65	2,602.69	2,266.24	2,209.81	2,373.37	2,466.59	2,410.10	2,032.85	2,111.63	1,942.66	2,196.75
2012	1,994.05	2,164.96	2,082.42	1,970.51	1,811.54	1,806.56	1,756.42	1,839.55	2,097.22	2,070.91	2,049.00	1,967.97	1,967.59
2013	1,949.80	1,957.31	1,908.68	1,649.50	1,505.82	1,362.47	1,296.54	1,424.04	1,416.94	1,368.26	1,286.22	1,197.73	1,526.94
2014	1,206.90	1,259.53	1,246.67	1,178.50	1,148.47	1,175.94	1,225.31	1,181.77	1,126.82	1,067.60	1,012.22	1,042.49	1,156.02
2015	1,138.45	1,094.75	1,084.93	1,092.25	1,089.22	1,031.34	967.53	958.94	961.93	1,031.14	951.23	940.07	1,028.48
2016	980.88	1,060.00	1,084.79	1,142.90	1,166.93	1,216.44	1,520.83	1,494.89	1,470.13	1,430.05	1,399.15	1,318.71	1,273.81
2017	1,368.47	1,436.17	1,426.87	1,426.35	1,295.78	1,321.55	1,242.52	1,308.41	1,309.00	1,283.21	1,283.06	1,205.93	1,325.61
2018	1,238.59	1,187.71	1,178.66	1,183.28	1,224.89	1,245.10	1,193.92	1,163.69	1,093.05	1,121.87	1,113.01	1,166.61	1,175.87

Source: American Metal Market (AMM)

Nearby Futures through Last Trading Day.

Volume of Trading of Silver Futures in Chicago   In Thousands of Contracts

Year	Jan.	Feb.	Mar.	Apr.	May	June	July	Aug.	Sept.	Oct.	Nov.	Dec.	Total
2009	415.6	652.2	433.8	575.7	418.4	869.1	476.6	842.9	657.0	809.6	1,159.3	680.3	7,990.5
2010	755.9	1,065.2	750.2	994.8	936.9	1,079.3	642.8	978.6	757.1	1,314.2	2,282.2	1,269.6	12,826.7
2011	1,429.7	1,674.7	1,685.7	3,014.6	2,461.1	1,768.9	1,325.0	1,982.8	1,220.4	952.6	1,327.4	765.6	19,608.6
2012	826.9	1,478.7	1,120.1	1,224.1	1,028.2	1,416.8	804.5	1,231.9	1,068.8	874.2	1,437.3	804.2	13,315.7
2013	1,021.7	1,346.4	780.3	1,980.5	1,172.0	1,555.4	932.3	1,652.5	958.1	948.4	1,270.3	857.7	14,475.6
2014	915.0	1,498.8	973.7	1,388.9	883.1	1,459.4	957.2	1,216.7	990.8	1,013.7	1,435.1	964.7	13,697.2
2015	979.5	1,196.0	875.8	1,431.4	886.3	1,499.6	988.4	1,511.0	822.3	1,107.5	1,291.7	864.9	13,454.4
2016	960.5	1,694.2	1,212.5	1,974.1	1,183.6	1,828.3	1,458.7	1,939.3	1,290.1	1,327.6	2,214.4	1,135.5	18,218.7
2017	1,414.0	1,809.3	1,495.9	2,120.9	1,904.5	2,371.5	1,829.7	2,604.7	1,730.4	1,826.4	2,539.5	1,388.1	23,035.0
2018	2,186.6	2,155.7	1,842.3	2,625.8	1,702.2	2,486.3	1,582.4	2,364.1	1,648.3	1,793.5	2,299.1	1,300.6	23,987.1

Contract size = 5,000 oz.   *Source: CME Group; Commodity Exchange (COMEX)*

Average Open Interest of Silver Futures in Chicago   In Contracts

Year	Jan.	Feb.	Mar.	Apr.	May	June	July	Aug.	Sept.	Oct.	Nov.	Dec.
2009	87,525	96,902	92,756	93,855	95,420	106,283	99,018	103,076	122,052	133,409	137,261	124,797
2010	126,921	118,619	112,234	123,849	122,547	129,561	118,619	126,117	145,022	153,013	148,547	133,596
2011	133,030	138,901	135,793	143,245	124,278	118,740	115,246	117,217	109,908	103,939	107,600	100,220
2012	103,766	108,478	110,777	117,254	113,514	122,240	122,555	124,907	125,957	140,254	145,146	141,906
2013	143,032	141,751	149,900	156,813	145,964	147,042	133,417	130,278	113,116	116,266	130,050	133,668
2014	137,682	145,743	141,847	157,064	152,154	161,079	161,447	161,613	168,883	172,012	169,706	148,854
2015	158,200	167,554	171,411	177,026	176,403	190,678	190,121	173,457	155,598	164,457	167,660	164,215
2016	161,725	167,337	170,875	190,935	203,017	203,311	217,206	207,634	197,360	192,183	177,922	161,707
2017	172,215	198,811	194,560	220,791	202,476	203,230	207,098	192,201	187,569	190,554	198,941	199,229
2018	197,597	198,883	207,295	218,714	199,496	220,429	212,471	233,201	206,398	201,730	211,615	175,572

Contract size = 5,000 oz.   *Source: CME Group; Commodity Exchange (COMEX)*

SILVER

Mine Production of Recoverable Silver in the United States   In Metric Tons

Year	Arizona	Idaho	Montana	Nevada	New Mexico	Other States	U.S. Total
2009	W	W	W	203	W	1,040	1,250
2010	W	W	W	224	W	1,050	1,280
2011	W	W	W	209	W	913	1,120
2012	W	W	W	250	W	805	1,060
2013	W	W	W	255	W	791	1,050
2014	W	W	W	326	W	858	1,180
2015	W	W	W	296	W	777	1,070
2016	W	W	W	276	W	871	1,150
2017	W	W	W	265	W	766	1,030
2018[1]	W	W	W	238	W	686	923

[1] Preliminary.   W = Withheld proprietary data; included in "Other States".   *Source: U.S. Geological Survey (USGS)*

Production[2] of Refined Silver in the United States, from All Sources   In Metric Tons

Year	Jan.	Feb.	Mar.	Apr.	May	June	July	Aug.	Sept.	Oct.	Nov.	Dec.	U.S. Total
2009	456	182	270	326	337	394	363	495	535	676	530	778	5,342
2010	553	504	794	503	510	356	383	534	439	460	547	441	6,024
2011	626	512	748	477	485	462	493	491	499	522	426	634	6,375
2012	559	443	443	419	457	426	423	375	344	385	407	393	5,073
2013	505	438	421	486	376	337	415	365	364	450	292	431	4,880
2014	431	334	348	399	450	418	458	386	506	456	430	474	5,080
2015	515	507	473	505	434	479	467	498	453	480	390	547	5,750
2016	496	476	581	507	496	429	455	575	545	503	475	481	6,020
2017	507	497	398	461	390	426	485	348	326	374	425	345	4,980
2018[1]	480	379	316	357	458	304	394	423	382	392	382	411	4,676

[1] Preliminary.   [2] Includes U.S. mine production of recoverable silver plus imports of refined silver.   *Source: U.S. Geological Survey (USGS)*

Mine Production of Recoverable Silver in the United States   In Metric Tons

Year	Jan.	Feb.	Mar.	Apr.	May	June	July	Aug.	Sept.	Oct.	Nov.	Dec.	U.S. Total
2009	103.0	94.0	108.0	105.0	107.0	107.0	97.3	106.0	100.0	104.0	103.0	104.0	1,238.3
2010	113.0	92.0	116.0	114.0	109.0	105.0	107.0	105.0	103.0	117.0	91.0	101.0	1,273.0
2011	98.1	85.2	103.0	95.2	99.3	92.6	91.5	91.0	88.4	84.7	90.2	103.0	1,122.2
2012	83.0	78.7	85.5	80.9	84.0	88.5	85.4	91.0	84.5	85.0	94.3	101.0	1,041.8
2013	88.8	84.2	88.5	90.2	89.6	91.5	90.3	86.2	83.9	86.4	79.0	88.3	1,046.9
2014	95.5	86.2	95.5	94.2	102.0	90.8	106.0	101.0	103.0	103.0	105.0	110.0	1,180.0
2015	94.2	90.1	99.5	89.8	90.6	87.5	88.0	90.8	83.6	93.9	89.2	94.2	1,090.0
2016	94.0	95.4	98.0	92.2	93.8	90.6	91.0	104.0	98.5	100.0	94.6	96.1	1,150.0
2017	98.4	84.1	94.3	87.5	82.9	85.4	84.7	83.6	74.5	82.4	87.6	82.4	1,030.0
2018[1]	74.6	67.2	69.3	73.7	76.5	78.6	72.8	79.3	77.9	86.5	79.5	87.4	923.3

[1] Preliminary.   *Source: U.S. Geological Survey (USGS)*

Mine Production of Recoverable Silver in Nevada   In Metric Tons

Year	Jan.	Feb.	Mar.	Apr.	May	June	July	Aug.	Sept.	Oct.	Nov.	Dec.	U.S. Total
2009	NA	NA	17.4	18.1	15.0	18.3	14.8	15.8	14.1	18.0	17.2	16.6	194.0
2010	16.6	13.3	20.2	17.8	17.2	18.0	14.8	16.7	15.7	20.0	17.7	16.2	204.2
2011	18.8	16.8	19.9	18.0	17.9	19.6	16.8	17.2	14.0	14.8	17.6	17.6	209.0
2012	15.8	16.5	19.3	21.0	23.6	20.8	19.1	23.5	19.9	22.1	24.3	24.1	250.0
2013	21.1	18.4	20.6	23.6	21.0	22.0	17.7	23.1	20.9	23.0	19.5	24.2	255.1
2014	25.0	23.9	26.5	24.9	29.2	28.3	29.1	29.1	28.3	29.9	29.6	31.1	326.0
2015	25.1	23.7	25.6	26.0	26.2	25.3	24.8	24.2	22.5	22.8	21.5	22.9	290.0
2016	22.1	20.7	21.6	22.6	22.9	22.0	23.5	24.3	23.6	23.9	24.5	25.8	276.0
2017	23.1	22.1	22.1	22.2	22.8	23.1	20.7	19.4	19.2	21.5	22.6	23.2	265.0
2018[1]	18.8	18.4	19.6	19.4	18.9	18.4	19.0	19.4	19.6	22.2	21.1	22.8	237.6

[1] Preliminary.   *Source: U.S. Geological Survey (USGS)*

U.S. Imports of Silver Bullion   In Metric Tons

Year	Jan.	Feb.	Mar.	Apr.	May	June	July	Aug.	Sept.	Oct.	Nov.	Dec.	U.S. Total
2009	353.0	87.8	162.0	221.0	230.0	287.0	266.0	389.0	435.0	572.0	427.0	674.0	4,103.8
2010	440.0	412.0	678.0	389.0	401.0	251.0	276.0	429.0	336.0	343.0	456.0	340.0	4,751.0
2011	528.0	427.0	645.0	382.0	386.0	369.0	401.0	400.0	411.0	437.0	336.0	531.0	5,253.0
2012	476.0	364.0	357.0	338.0	373.0	337.0	338.0	284.0	259.0	300.0	313.0	292.0	4,031.0
2013	416.0	354.0	332.0	396.0	286.0	245.0	325.0	279.0	280.0	364.0	213.0	343.0	3,833.0
2014	335.0	248.0	252.0	305.0	348.0	327.0	352.0	285.0	403.0	353.0	325.0	364.0	3,900.0
2015	421.0	417.0	373.0	415.0	343.0	391.0	379.0	407.0	369.0	386.0	301.0	453.0	4,660.0
2016	402.0	381.0	483.0	415.0	402.0	338.0	364.0	471.0	446.0	403.0	380.0	385.0	4,870.0
2017	409.0	413.0	304.0	373.0	307.0	341.0	400.0	264.0	251.0	292.0	337.0	263.0	3,950.0
2018[1]	405.0	312.0	247.0	283.0	381.0	225.0	321.0	344.0	304.0	305.0	302.0	324.0	3,753.0

[1] Preliminary.   Source: U.S. Geological Survey (USGS)

Commodity Exchange Warehouse of Stocks of Silver, on First of Month   In Thousands of Troy Ounces

Year	Jan. 1	Feb. 1	Mar. 1	Apr. 1	May 1	June 1	July 1	Aug. 1	Sept. 1	Oct. 1	Nov. 1	Dec. 1
2009	125,536	123,902	124,121	123,615	119,910	120,879	118,519	117,818	117,796	116,159	116,159	112,494
2010	110,588	110,588	110,588	115,786	116,178	119,452	114,015	110,244	110,765	111,075	107,785	107,393
2011	104,548	103,594	102,549	105,495	102,014	100,968	101,720	104,176	104,085	106,012	107,096	110,415
2012	126,218	129,403	130,318	137,073	142,125	143,150	145,933	139,218	140,678	142,047	142,362	145,284
2013	148,205	154,577	162,830	164,163	166,050	165,749	166,746	164,711	163,771	165,329	169,012	169,985
2014	173,927	179,297	182,831	179,791	174,483	175,267	175,517	175,317	179,292	182,194	181,185	177,008
2015	174,359	178,053	177,163	176,650	176,310	179,287	182,384	175,671	170,562	165,009	162,813	158,954
2016	160,671	158,266	154,261	154,999	151,780	153,898	151,481	154,090	162,921	173,354	173,583	178,616
2017	183,006	180,805	186,606	190,223	196,524	201,367	208,937	215,512	217,741	218,121	225,904	235,906
2018	244,724	246,977	251,320	260,510	262,948	270,519	275,911	286,599	295,357	289,725	290,258	295,015

Source: CME Group; Commodity Exchange (COMEX)

U.S. Exports of Refined Silver   In Kilograms

Year	Australia	Canada	Germany	Hong Kong	India	Italy	Japan	Mexico	Singapore	Switzerland	United Arab Emirates	United Kingdom	Total
2006	104,000	169,000	27,200	----	----	301	17,000	1,790	----	----	----	1,170,000	1,500,000
2007	472	117,000	35,200	55,900	385,000	793	24,900	584	----	62	----	22,600	660,000
2008	37,300	123,000	38,500	----	106,000	328	65,800	1,360	----	750	----	25,100	413,000
2009	76,100	12,100	35,900	4,580	----	19	51	29,900	1,360	3,720	----	164	167,000
2010	97,300	104,000	33,000	4,320	----	43	38,600	218,000	8,590	2,070	----	12,100	523,000
2011	20,700	98,400	6,030	8,830	----	237	148,000	288,000	9,700	823	1,100	19,500	625,000
2012	27,800	79,200	16,900	5,670	19,100	115	86,200	250,000	4,010	12,100	270	320,000	837,000
2013	124,000	77,300	8,760	4,030	36,300	302	----	76,300	11,800	64	28	73	347,000
2014	55,300	200,000	1,190	1,330	1,180	3,410	----	62,400	9,820	1,090	198	1,550	346,000
2015[1]	24,000	430,000	8,720	2,720	284,000	5,880	----	8,650	6,560	1,700	----	2,690	781,000

[1] Preliminary.   Source: U.S. Geological Survey (USGS)

U.S. Imports of Silver From Selected Countries   In Kilograms

	Ores and Concentrates				Refined Bullion						
Year	Canada	Mexico	Other Countries	Total	Canada	Chile	Mexico	Peru	Uruguay	United Kingdom	Total
2006	----	----	----	----	1,470,000	34,400	2,300,000	411,000	----	171	4,280,000
2007	----	----	----	381	1,080,000	37,500	2,430,000	571,000	----	5	4,210,000
2008	----	----	----	32	781,000	69,500	2,370,000	500,000	----	274	3,860,000
2009	----	----	----	87	747,000	125,000	1,630,000	204,000	----	534	2,800,000
2010	3,230	----	----	3,230	1,580,000	80,000	2,040,000	38,200	----	454,000	4,630,000
2011	84,200	----	----	84,200	1,260,000	97,100	2,100,000	29,600	----	20,500	5,250,000
2012	73,800	7,770	----	82,700	1,330,000	73,100	2,390,000	44,100	----	330	4,030,000
2013	26	10,700	----	10,700	1,600,000	8,350	2,010,000	38,300	----	20,700	3,830,000
2014	----	----	59	59	1,120,000	119	2,140,000	77,800	----	41,000	3,900,000
2015[1]	----	----	253	253	1,920,000	----	1,980,000	90,300	----	3,000	4,660,000

[1] Preliminary.   Source: U.S. Geological Survey (USGS)

Soybean Meal

Soybean meal is produced through processing and separating soybeans into oil and meal components. If the soybeans are of particularly good quality, then the processor can get more meal weight by including more hulls in the meal while still meeting a 48% protein minimum. Soybean meal can be further processed into soy flour and isolated soy protein, but the bulk of soybean meal is used as animal feed for poultry, hogs and cattle. Soybean meal accounts for about two-thirds of the world's high-protein animal feed, followed by cottonseed and rapeseed meal, which together account for less than 20%. Soybean meal consumption has been moving to record highs in recent years. The soybean meal marketing year begins in October and ends in September. Soybean meal futures and options are traded at the CME Group. The CME soybean meal futures contract calls for the delivery of 100 tons of soybean meal produced by conditioning ground soybeans and reducing the oil content of the conditioned product and having a minimum of 48.0% protein, minimum of 0.5% fat, maximum of 3.5% fiber, and maximum of 12.0% moisture.

Soybean crush – The term soybean "crush" refers to both the physical processing of soybeans and also to the dollar-value premium received for processing soybeans into their component products of meal and oil. The conventional model says that processing 60 pounds (one bushel) of soybeans produces 11 pounds of soybean oil, 44 pounds of 48% protein soybean meal, 3 pounds of hulls, and 1 pound of waste. The Gross Processing Margin (GPM) or crush equals (0.22 times Soybean Meal Prices in dollars per ton) + (11 times Soybean Oil prices in cents/pound) – Soybean prices in $/bushel. A higher crush value will occur when the price of the meal and oil products are strong relative to soybeans, e.g., because of supply disruptions or because of an increase in demand for the products. When the crush value is high, companies will have a strong incentive to buy raw soybeans and boost the output of the products. That supply increase should eventually bring the crush value back into line with the long-term equilibrium.

Prices – CME soybean meal futures prices (Barchart.com electronic symbol ZM) opened the year 2018 at about $124.02 per short ton, moved down in mid-year, but then moved up to finally close the year down -1.6% at $122.01 per short ton.

Supply – World soybean meal production in 2018/19 is expected to rise +4.3% yr/yr to a new record high of 242.343 million metric tons. The world's largest soybean meal producers are expected to be China with 30.2% of world production in 2018/19, the U.S. with 18.4%, Argentina with 13.7%, and Brazil with 13.6%.

U.S. production of soybean meal in 2018/19 is expected to fall -0.1% yr/yr to 49.147 million short tons, just below last year's new record high. U.S. soybean meal ending stocks in 2018/19 are expected to fall -18.6% yr/yr to 450,000 short tons.

Demand – World consumption of soybean meal in 2018/19 is expected to rise +4.3% yr/yr to 238.893 million metric tons, a new record high. China is expected to account for 30.3% of that consumption, the U.S. for 13.6% and the European Union for 13.1%. U.S. consumption of soybean meal in 2018/19 is expected to rise +3.2% yr/yr to 32.524 million metric tons, a new record high.

Trade – World exports of soybean meal in 2018/19 is expected to rise +2.8% to 66.259 million metric tons. Argentina is expected to account for 45.0% of world total exports and the U.S. for 18.8%. World imports of soybean meal in 2018/19 is expected to rise +3.5% yr/yr to 62.530 million metric tons, a record high. U.S. exports of soybean meal in 2018/19 are expected to fall -7.3% yr/yr to 13.750 million short tons. U.S. imports of soybean meal in 2018/19 are expected to fall -29.3% yr/yr to 350,000 short tons.

Supply and Distribution of Soybean Meal in the United States — In Thousands of Short Tons

Crop Year Beginning Oct. 1	For Stocks Oct. 1	Pro-duction	Total Supply	Domestic	Exports	Total	Decatur 48% Protein Solvent	Decatur 44% Protein Solvent	Brazil FOB 45-46% Protein	Rotter-dam CIF
2009-10	235	41,707	39,484	30,640	11,159	41,800	311.27	343	327	391
2010-11	302	39,251	42,101	30,278	9,104	39,381	345.52	381	383	418
2011-12	350	41,025	39,731	31,548	9,743	41,291	393.53	434	442	461
2012-13	300	39,875	41,591	29,031	11,114	40,145	468.11	516	489	538
2013-14	275	40,685	40,420	29,547	11,546	41,093	489.94	540	500	533
2014-15	250	45,062	41,343	32,277	13,108	45,384	368.49	406	376	403
2015-16	260	44,672	45,645	33,118	11,954	45,072	324.56	358	335	351
2016-17[1]	264	44,787	45,336	33,420	11,580	45,000	316.88	349	322	336
2017-18[2]	401	49,216	45,347	34,733	14,826	49,559	345.02	380	368	382
2018-19[3]	553	49,147	46,800	35,950	13,750	49,700	295-335	345	339	341

[1] Preliminary. [2] Estimate. [3] Forecast. *Source: Economic Research Service, U.S. Department of Agriculture (ERS-USDA)*

World Production of Soybean Meal   In Thousands of Metric Tons

Crop Year	Argentina	Bolivia	Brazil	China	European Union	India	Japan	Mexico	Para-guay	Russia	Taiwan	United States	World Total
2009-10	26,624	1,200	26,120	38,808	9,950	6,240	1,908	2,850	1,300	1,497	1,581	37,836	165,784
2010-11	29,312	1,420	28,160	43,560	9,741	7,480	1,647	2,870	1,310	1,615	1,620	35,608	175,025
2011-12	27,945	1,580	29,510	48,312	9,164	8,240	1,483	2,910	706	1,655	1,588	37,217	180,888
2012-13	26,089	1,700	27,310	51,480	10,033	8,640	1,447	2,890	2,315	1,734	1,510	36,174	182,247
2013-14	27,892	1,760	28,540	54,569	10,349	6,960	1,487	3,185	2,787	2,600	1,513	36,909	190,447
2014-15	30,928	1,915	31,300	59,004	11,416	6,160	1,627	3,300	2,905	2,837	1,555	40,880	208,482
2015-16	33,211	1,995	30,750	64,548	11,811	4,400	1,723	3,480	2,983	3,152	1,555	40,525	215,926
2016-17	33,280	1,605	31,280	69,696	11,376	7,200	1,805	3,635	2,945	3,467	1,606	40,630	225,556
2017-18[1]	28,010	1,840	34,500	71,280	11,811	6,160	1,773	4,152	2,985	3,625	1,688	44,648	232,394
2018-19[2]	33,050	1,760	33,100	73,260	13,114	7,520	1,773	4,192	3,065	3,940	1,767	44,586	242,343

Crop year beginning October 1.   [1] Preliminary.   [2] Forecast.   Source: Foreign Agricultural Service, U.S. Department of Agriculture (FAS-USDA)

World Exports of Soybean Meal   In Thousands of Metric Tons

Crop Year	Argen-tina	Bolivia	Brazil	Canada	China	European Union	India	Korea, South	Norway	Para-guay	Russia	United States	World Total
2009-10	24,914	1,114	12,985	126	1,181	471	3,527	75	165	1,040	3	10,125	55,935
2010-11	27,615	1,097	13,987	210	472	609	5,169	72	152	1,018	28	8,238	58,887
2011-12	26,043	1,208	14,678	173	966	884	4,877	38	165	505	10	8,845	58,705
2012-13	23,667	1,562	13,242	245	1,365	536	4,943	115	148	2,020	92	10,111	58,394
2013-14	24,972	1,608	13,948	241	2,017	296	3,252	179	153	2,428	507	10,504	60,648
2014-15	28,575	1,674	14,290	212	1,595	362	1,521	112	175	2,569	505	11,891	64,405
2015-16	30,333	1,726	15,407	335	1,909	304	409	76	201	2,552	479	10,844	65,517
2016-17	31,323	1,289	13,762	291	1,111	334	2,008	100	181	2,407	323	10,505	64,574
2017-18[1]	25,350	1,550	16,065	357	1,175	393	1,844	41	180	2,600	384	13,450	64,458
2018-19[2]	29,800	1,450	15,225	350	900	300	1,500	40	180	2,580	250	12,474	66,259

Crop year beginning October 1.   [1] Preliminary.   [2] Forecast.   Source: Foreign Agricultural Service, U.S. Department of Agriculture (FAS-USDA)

World Imports of Soybean Meal   In Thousands of Metric Tons

Crop Year	Algeria	European Union	Indo-nesia	Iran	Japan	Korea, South	Malaysia	Mexico	Peru	Philip-pines	Thailand	Vietnam	World Total
2009-10	934	20,879	2,508	1,524	2,106	1,737	1,076	1,209	1,072	1,720	2,513	2,879	53,538
2010-11	1,078	21,877	3,069	1,742	2,208	1,658	1,028	1,500	1,059	1,975	2,318	2,719	56,871
2011-12	861	20,872	3,278	2,192	2,282	1,571	1,078	1,548	1,113	1,879	2,936	2,276	57,018
2012-13	1,333	16,941	3,600	2,099	1,765	1,654	1,276	1,295	1,099	1,968	2,874	2,981	54,067
2013-14	1,441	18,140	3,806	2,683	1,976	1,825	1,397	1,410	1,173	2,335	2,665	3,344	57,770
2014-15	1,101	19,623	3,902	1,948	1,699	1,751	1,465	1,795	1,145	2,204	3,068	4,311	60,685
2015-16	1,438	19,213	4,203	1,420	1,721	2,118	1,291	2,367	1,277	2,618	2,433	5,094	61,874
2016-17	1,276	18,794	4,255	1,507	1,621	1,764	1,427	1,991	1,327	2,662	2,782	4,945	60,412
2017-18[1]	1,375	18,372	4,650	1,113	1,728	1,846	1,525	1,818	1,400	2,750	3,191	4,800	60,393
2018-19[2]	1,400	18,500	4,800	1,250	1,770	1,870	1,500	2,000	1,450	2,850	2,900	5,000	62,530

Crop year beginning October 1.   [1] Preliminary.   [2] Forecast.   Source: Foreign Agricultural Service, U.S. Department of Agriculture (FAS-USDA)

U.S. Exports of Soybean Cake & Meal by Country of Destination   In Thousands of Metric Tons

Year	Algeria	Australia	Canada	Dominican Republic	Italy	Japan	Mexico	Nether-lands	Philip-pines	Russia	Spain	Vene-zuela	Total
2009	----	121.9	1,154.3	362.4	48.5	366.3	1,323.0	0.2	803.4	20.0	90.0	487.1	8,791
2010	----	208.0	1,069.3	384.4	28.1	389.2	1,382.3	0.8	860.3	22.0	50.6	571.0	9,318
2011	17.4	0.5	1,048.5	358.4	33.7	338.6	1,423.7	0.4	869.5	22.6	0.2	636.1	7,821
2012	16.5	41.8	1,073.0	393.9	63.2	211.6	1,343.0	0.2	1,305.9	25.1	50.5	705.8	9,691
2013	17.3	69.0	895.1	331.6	229.6	180.2	1,269.5	0.9	1,120.1	0.1	198.4	755.1	10,133
2014	3.0	0.1	971.6	374.4	253.0	211.0	1,593.3	1.6	1,104.3	15.0	267.0	842.6	10,281
2015	30.6	0.2	805.4	472.8	75.2	174.4	2,001.4	10.3	1,509.2	----	315.5	540.9	11,394
2016	27.3	0.5	755.9	506.2	0.4	158.4	2,130.3	1.1	1,848.0	----	0.0	311.9	10,540
2017	15.1	0.7	894.6	489.4	2.0	250.0	1,599.8	2.5	2,042.5	----	114.3	301.8	10,594
2018[1]		0.6	978.1	494.4	125.1	330.6	1,766.0	4.5	2,164.1	----	354.7	182.8	12,936

[1] Preliminary.   Source: Foreign Agricultural Service, U.S. Department of Agriculture (FAS-USDA)

SOYBEAN MEAL

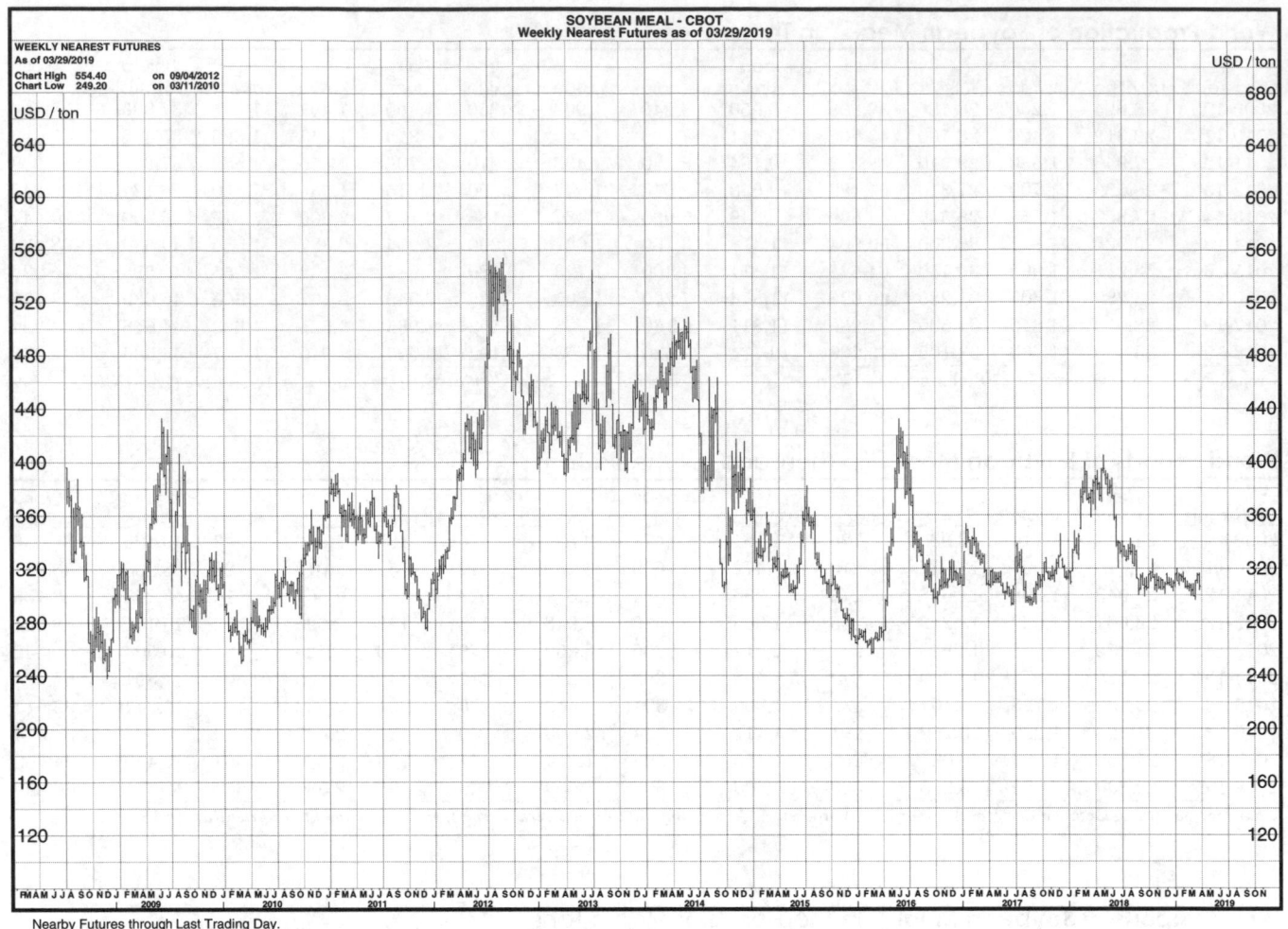

Nearby Futures through Last Trading Day.

Volume of Trading of Soybean Meal Futures in Chicago   In Thousands of Contracts

Year	Jan.	Feb.	Mar.	Apr.	May	June	July	Aug.	Sept.	Oct.	Nov.	Dec.	Total
2009	909.2	988.7	841.7	1,195.1	1,071.4	1,390.1	1,146.6	1,071.8	974.6	1,012.1	1,222.7	1,056.6	12,881
2010	994.1	1,134.5	1,330.1	1,264.3	850.7	1,349.0	1,134.2	1,057.8	1,136.4	1,054.7	1,590.7	1,156.3	14,053
2011	1,115.7	1,437.9	1,475.1	1,546.9	1,141.0	1,642.3	1,211.5	1,485.3	1,726.2	1,329.8	1,511.7	1,296.8	16,920
2012	1,182.2	1,484.7	1,545.3	1,914.5	1,481.2	1,812.1	1,848.1	1,594.8	1,389.8	1,263.9	1,436.3	1,234.5	18,187
2013	1,520.3	1,758.3	1,277.9	1,985.6	1,558.3	1,839.5	1,919.1	1,797.3	1,433.2	1,632.4	1,881.6	1,633.7	20,237
2014	1,519.1	1,918.1	1,409.7	1,711.2	1,138.3	1,811.9	1,703.3	1,664.5	1,613.9	2,456.8	2,070.8	1,619.9	20,637
2015	1,558.6	1,863.0	1,627.7	2,118.1	1,655.7	2,861.9	2,181.3	2,145.4	1,942.1	2,106.6	2,147.4	2,107.4	24,315
2016	1,547.6	2,055.5	1,696.5	3,289.2	2,564.1	2,971.6	2,027.7	1,880.0	1,738.5	1,967.8	2,156.9	2,058.7	25,954
2017	1,858.5	2,157.2	1,854.4	2,379.1	1,812.1	2,591.4	2,356.1	2,184.0	1,940.2	1,781.8	2,591.0	2,490.8	25,996
2018	2,482.4	3,466.9	2,294.9	3,361.6	2,275.4	3,268.2	2,417.4	2,725.2	2,329.5	2,641.3	2,470.2	2,105.7	31,839

Contract size = 100 tons.   Source: CME Group; Chicago Board of Trade (CBT)

Average Open Interest of Soybean Meal Futures in Chicago   In Contracts

Year	Jan.	Feb.	Mar.	Apr.	May	June	July	Aug.	Sept.	Oct.	Nov.	Dec.
2009	118,930	121,722	110,580	123,445	160,515	190,481	174,733	167,301	155,388	150,639	159,393	165,141
2010	170,924	198,651	200,438	196,464	177,726	187,838	197,981	200,131	208,773	195,256	201,589	194,033
2011	203,340	215,886	213,717	226,365	228,210	223,375	180,790	176,598	187,326	186,973	204,468	206,053
2012	193,344	187,100	226,979	261,896	251,386	253,037	263,064	255,541	235,650	211,525	217,752	222,206
2013	248,644	287,037	281,914	262,103	264,520	305,549	285,970	266,192	267,963	272,131	279,717	274,139
2014	272,424	307,186	312,283	321,497	310,358	320,237	309,536	319,263	340,910	362,209	382,227	353,605
2015	347,095	363,919	341,479	342,428	352,507	402,421	400,309	385,239	379,936	401,497	422,294	415,217
2016	411,932	416,103	376,318	369,967	367,597	389,845	373,020	359,333	362,886	375,331	373,239	350,214
2017	356,312	382,823	366,137	377,335	379,196	399,940	353,194	370,584	381,819	380,034	403,480	409,863
2018	401,624	465,945	454,202	506,093	522,647	510,772	518,013	507,407	524,092	525,893	503,197	448,462

Contract size = 100 tons.   Source: CME Group; Chicago Board of Trade (CBT)

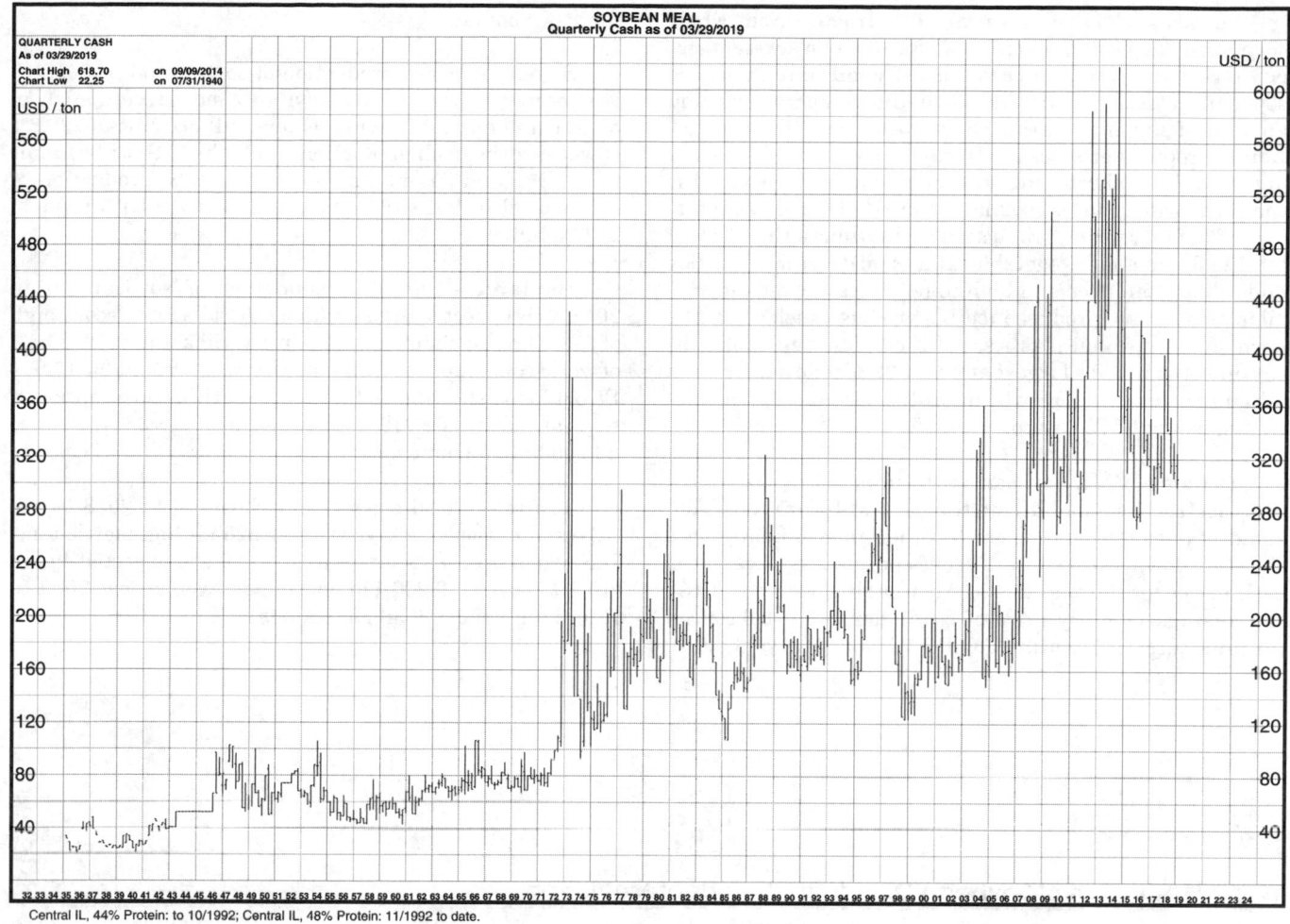

SOYBEAN MEAL
Quarterly Cash as of 03/29/2019

QUARTERLY CASH
As of 03/29/2019
Chart High 618.70 on 09/09/2014
Chart Low 22.25 on 07/31/1940

Central IL, 44% Protein: to 10/1992; Central IL, 48% Protein: 11/1992 to date.

Average Price of Soybean Meal (48% Solvent) in Decatur Illinois   In Dollars Per Short Ton -- Bulk

Year	Oct.	Nov.	Dec.	Jan.	Feb.	Mar.	Apr.	May.	June	July	Aug.	Sept.	Average
2009-10	325.69	328.18	333.93	314.23	295.79	277.61	291.21	287.85	305.78	325.56	331.76	317.65	311.27
2010-11	321.92	341.78	351.93	368.54	358.59	345.43	335.87	342.30	347.45	346.52	349.60	336.32	345.52
2011-12	301.45	290.37	281.65	310.65	330.37	365.95	394.29	415.17	422.59	515.82	564.69	529.37	393.53
2012-13	488.46	465.64	459.40	431.39	440.66	437.33	422.07	465.72	496.78	544.59	464.90	500.39	468.11
2013-14	443.63	451.13	498.10	479.54	509.25	495.71	514.01	519.38	501.72	450.79	490.32	526.72	489.94
2014-15	381.50	441.39	431.73	380.03	370.38	357.83	336.61	320.23	335.03	375.71	357.85	333.62	368.49
2015-16	327.97	308.60	289.78	279.56	273.61	276.22	303.81	376.35	408.57	371.49	340.80	337.95	324.56
2016-17	323.37	322.41	321.02	332.34	334.42	320.34	305.67	307.63	300.72	326.04	301.05	307.70	316.89
2017-18	315.23	313.52	319.22	322.60	362.85	379.85	385.84	393.55	355.71	341.08	332.50	318.32	345.02
2018-19	319.15	310.62	311.70	314.92	306.83								312.64

Source: Economic Research Service, U.S. Department of Agriculture (ERS-USDA)

Average Price of Soybean Meal (44% Solvent) in Decatur Illinois   In Dollars Per Short Ton -- Bulk

Year	Oct.	Nov.	Dec.	Jan.	Feb.	Mar.	Apr.	May.	June	July	Aug.	Sept.	Average
1992-93	168.6	170.9	176.4	175.6	167.5	172.4	175.6	181.7	181.3	217.6	206.9	186.5	181.8
1993-94	180.6	195.7	192.5	185.9	184.4	182.0	176.4	191.1	183.0	168.1	165.6	162.5	180.7
1994-95	156.4	150.9	145.4	145.1	149.4	145.7	151.0	148.1	149.1	160.1	157.5	171.8	152.5
1995-96	183.4	194.1	213.6	220.5	216.7	215.7	237.9	232.3	227.9	242.3	251.1	265.5	225.1
1996-97	238.0	242.7	240.9	240.7	253.6	270.4	277.7	296.0	275.9	261.5	261.6	265.7	260.4
1997-98	216.0	231.6	214.9	193.1	182.1	165.3	152.8	150.3	157.8	173.3	135.7	126.9	175.0
1998-99	129.4	139.3	139.6	131.0	124.4	127.2	128.6	127.0	131.7	125.7	135.9	144.1	132.0
1999-00	147.2	148.1	145.4	155.0	163.6	166.6	168.1	180.1	170.2	156.8	151.4	166.9	160.0
2000-01	166.0	173.7	187.9	175.6	158.3	149.1	149.7	155.6	163.1	183.9	170.6	163.5	166.4
2001-02	157.7	157.2	146.6	Discontinued									153.8

Source: Economic Research Service, U.S. Department of Agriculture (ERS-USDA)

Soybean Oil

Soybean oil is the natural oil extracted from whole soybeans. Typically, about 19% of a soybean's weight can be extracted as crude soybean oil. The oil content of U.S. soybeans correlates directly with the temperatures and amount of sunshine during the soybean pod-filling stages. Edible products produced with soybean oil include cooking and salad oils, shortening, and margarine. Soybean oil is the most widely used cooking oil in the U.S. It accounts for 80% of margarine production and for more than 75% of total U.S. consumer vegetable fat and oil consumption. Soy oil is cholesterol-free and high in polyunsaturated fat. Soy oil is also used to produce inedible products such as paints, varnish, resins, and plastics. Of the edible vegetable oils, soy oil is the world's largest at about 32%, followed by palm oil and rapeseed oil. Soybean oil futures and options are traded at the CME Group.

Prices – CME soybean oil futures prices (Barchart.com electronic symbol ZL) on the nearest-futures chart fell steadily until late in the year but then rose to finally close the year down -8.8% at 30.17 cents per pound. Regarding cash prices for the year 2018/19 (through November 2018), the average monthly price of crude domestic soybean oil (in tank cars) in Decatur (F.O.B.) fell -6.2% yr/yr to 28.19 cents per pound.

Supply – World production of soybean oil in 2018/19 is expected to rise +4.2% yr/yr to a new record high of 57.541 million metric tons. China will account for 28.8% of world soybean oil production, while the U.S. will account for 18.9%, and Argentina for 14.6%. U.S. production of soybean oil in 2018/19 is expected to rise +1.1% yr/yr to 24.025 billion pounds.

Demand – World consumption of soybean oil in 2018/19 is expected to rise +4.5% yr/yr to a new record high of 57.054 million metric tons. China will account for 30.5% of world consumption, while the U.S. will account for 17.6%, Brazil for 12.2%, and India for 6.7%. U.S. consumption of soybean oil in 2018/19 is expected to rise +3.9% yr/yr to 22.200 billion pounds.

Trade – World exports of soybean oil in 2018/19 are expected to rise +7.9% yr/yr to 11.226 million metric tons. U.S. exports of soybean oil in 2018/19 are expected to fall -10.1% yr/yr to 2.200 billion pounds, well below 2009/10 record high of 3.359 billion pounds.

World Production of Soybean Oil   In Thousands of Metric Tons

Crop Year	Argentina	Bolivia	Brazil	China	European Union	India	Japan	Mexico	Paraguay	Russia	Taiwan	United States	World Total
2009-10	6,476	277	6,470	8,781	2,290	1,404	480	643	307	340	358	8,897	38,971
2010-11	7,181	320	6,970	9,856	2,343	1,683	417	648	310	367	367	8,568	41,478
2011-12	6,839	355	7,310	10,931	2,204	1,854	380	657	167	376	360	8,954	42,816
2012-13	6,364	405	6,760	11,648	2,413	1,944	379	653	545	394	345	8,990	43,348
2013-14	6,785	415	7,074	12,347	2,489	1,566	389	720	665	591	343	9,131	45,239
2014-15	7,687	455	7,759	13,350	2,746	1,386	414	745	700	645	352	9,706	49,288
2015-16	8,433	475	7,627	14,605	2,841	990	445	785	720	717	352	9,956	51,549
2016-17[1]	8,395	380	7,755	15,770	2,736	1,620	466	820	711	788	364	10,035	53,719
2017-18[2]	7,310	435	8,535	16,128	2,841	1,386	458	937	720	824	383	10,781	55,227
2018-19[3]	8,390	417	8,195	16,576	3,154	1,692	458	946	740	896	401	10,898	57,541

Crop year beginning October 1.   [1] Preliminary.   [2] Forecast.   *Source: Foreign Agricultural Service, U.S. Department of Agriculture (FAS-USDA)*

World Consumption of Soybean Oil   In Thousands of Metric Tons

Crop Year	Algeria	Argentina	Bangladesh	Brazil	China	Egypt	European Union	India	Iran	Korea, South	Mexico	United States	World Total
2009-10	395	1,915	369	4,980	10,050	560	2,760	2,750	560	445	875	7,173	38,161
2010-11	475	2,520	404	5,205	11,400	669	2,400	2,550	620	443	840	7,506	40,477
2011-12	490	3,020	483	5,390	12,050	432	2,050	2,900	600	445	845	8,396	42,462
2012-13	540	2,245	493	5,534	12,550	562	1,850	3,000	600	445	860	8,522	42,590
2013-14	590	2,844	551	5,705	13,650	442	1,990	3,350	600	440	905	8,576	45,312
2014-15	640	2,401	668	6,215	14,200	752	2,040	4,100	660	435	961	8,600	47,733
2015-16	700	2,840	785	6,290	15,350	960	2,285	5,250	680	440	1,020	9,145	52,127
2016-17[1]	710	2,985	1,005	6,570	16,350	610	2,205	5,200	700	450	1,070	9,010	53,415
2017-18[2]	710	3,155	990	6,915	16,550	760	2,225	4,620	720	470	1,060	9,696	54,588
2018-19[3]	750	3,275	1,000	6,985	17,400	810	2,255	4,950	740	490	1,150	10,070	57,054

Crop year beginning October 1.   [1] Preliminary.   [2] Forecast.   *Source: Foreign Agricultural Service, U.S. Department of Agriculture (FAS-USDA)*

World Exports of Soybean Oil   In Thousands of Metric Tons

Crop Year	Argentina	Bolivia	Brazil	Canada	European Union	Malaysia	Para- guay	Russia	South Africa	Ukraine	United States	Vietnam	World Total
2009-10	4,453	230	1,449	47	386	126	253	170	30	44	1,524	----	9,186
2010-11	4,561	232	1,668	66	463	134	232	136	62	43	1,466	28	9,619
2011-12	3,794	224	1,885	72	742	146	123	142	68	49	664	73	8,525
2012-13	4,244	285	1,251	102	1,011	127	519	129	76	70	981	44	9,329
2013-14	4,087	371	1,378	92	766	157	630	332	94	118	852	91	9,422
2014-15	5,094	392	1,510	118	1,010	170	699	423	71	136	914	104	11,118
2015-16	5,698	444	1,550	151	915	148	709	431	64	152	1,017	17	11,769
2016-17[1]	5,387	249	1,241	175	819	137	680	529	55	177	1,159	35	11,245
2017-18[2]	4,133	350	1,511	157	902	135	697	568	50	192	1,110	40	10,407
2018-19[3]	5,100	320	1,350	150	1,000	137	710	585	50	155	998	40	11,226

Crop year beginning October 1.   [1] Preliminary.   [2] Forecast.   *Source: Foreign Agricultural Service, U.S. Department of Agriculture (FAS-USDA)*

World Imports of Soybean Oil   In Thousands of Metric Tons

Crop Year	Algeria	Bangla- desh	China	Colom- bia	Egypt	European Union	India	Iran	Korea, South	Peru	Morocco	Vene- zuela	World Total
2009-10	402	354	1,514	184	243	547	1,354	275	318	379	352	302	8,483
2010-11	516	377	1,319	238	644	906	817	704	300	397	315	366	9,380
2011-12	438	439	1,502	257	----	386	1,190	411	343	367	344	415	7,997
2012-13	575	400	1,409	216	324	322	1,081	543	300	364	363	374	8,508
2013-14	629	442	1,353	288	230	329	1,804	551	278	444	355	403	9,268
2014-15	631	508	773	304	480	253	2,815	421	257	432	395	365	10,035
2015-16	732	639	586	372	674	325	4,269	299	250	465	382	157	11,639
2016-17[1]	667	830	711	352	246	285	3,534	257	306	497	449	157	10,837
2017-18[2]	720	780	546	355	227	284	2,984	213	276	492	500	170	9,835
2018-19[3]	760	780	800	375	250	200	3,400	250	300	515	500	175	10,738

Crop year beginning October 1.   [1] Preliminary.   [2] Forecast.   *Source: Foreign Agricultural Service, U.S. Department of Agriculture (FAS-USDA)*

Supply and Distribution of Soybean Oil in the United States   In Millions of Pounds

| | | | | | Domestic Disappearance | | | | | | | | | |
| | | | | | Food | | | | | | Non-Food | | | |
Crop Year	Pro- duction	Imports	Stocks Oct. 1	Exports	Total Domestic	Short- ening	Mar- garine	Cooking & Salad Oils	Other Edible	Total Food	Paint & Varnish	Resins & Plastics	Total Non- Food	Total Disap- pearance
2009-10	19,615	103	2,861	3,359	15,814	3,895	W	9,595	NA	13,490	W	W	3,166	19,173
2010-11	18,888	159	3,406	3,233	16,544	3,670	W	9,541	NA	13,211	NA	NA	NA	20,027
2011-12	19,740	149	2,425	1,464	18,510	NA	NA	NA	NA	NA	NA	NA	NA	19,775
2012-13	19,820	196	2,540	2,164	18,787	----	----	----	----	----	----	----	----	20,851
2013-14	20,130	165	1,655	1,877	18,908	----	----	----	----	----	----	----	----	20,785
2014-15	21,399	264	1,165	2,014	18,959	----	----	----	----	----	----	----	----	20,973
2015-16	21,950	288	1,855	2,243	20,163	----	----	----	----	----	----	----	----	22,406
2016-17	22,123	319	1,687	2,556	19,862	----	----	----	----	----	----	----	----	22,418
2017-18[1]	23,767	335	1,711	2,447	21,376	----	----	----	----	----	----	----	----	23,824
2018-19[2]	24,570	300	1,990	2,250	22,600	----	----	----	----	----	----	----	----	24,850

Crop year beginning October 1.   [1] Preliminary .   [2] Forecast.   *Source: Economic Research Service, U.S. Department of Agriculture (ERS-USDA)*

U.S. Exports of Soybean Oil[2], by Country of Destination   In Metric Tons

Crop Year	Canada	Ecuador	Ethiopia	Haiti	India	Mexico	Morocco	Pakistan	Panama	Peru	Turkey	Vene- zuela	Total
2008-09	41,500	----	840	19,127	146,086	173,041	110,249	----	1,715	37,061	2,598	54,438	994,927
2009-10	41,390	----	720	24,616	162,342	211,456	231,996	6,795	5,151	92,004	54	52,702	1,523,384
2010-11	35,001	8,722	700	13,314	49	167,760	291,890	20,900	6,123	44,999	1,120	57,707	1,466,468
2011-12	25,417	15	890	3,156	12	151,224	159,917	----	2,307	7	1,092	22,942	664,111
2012-13	30,867	28	----	2,230	113,104	187,117	23,248	0	6,374	193	76	51,377	981,345
2013-14	31,755	13	390	1,576	22	189,759	29,702	0	4,139	42,121	----	18,988	852,074
2014-15	28,755	11	450	649	39	245,163	64,658	9,190	5,434	104,743	----	61,920	913,704
2015-16	15,647	6	----	2,687	51	235,554	50,521	11,165	6,054	75,355	----	50,055	1,017,200
2016-17	22,658	8	----	1,307	139	265,028	30,432	7,137	7,055	2	75	32,437	1,159,229
2017-18[1]	21,213	9	----	----	105	167,513	11,798	----	7,723	93,051	17	48,345	1,109,990

Crop year beginning October 1.   [1] Preliminary.   [2] Crude & Refined oil combined as such.   *Source: Foreign Agricultural Service, U.S. Department of Agriculture (FAS-USDA)*

SOYBEAN OIL

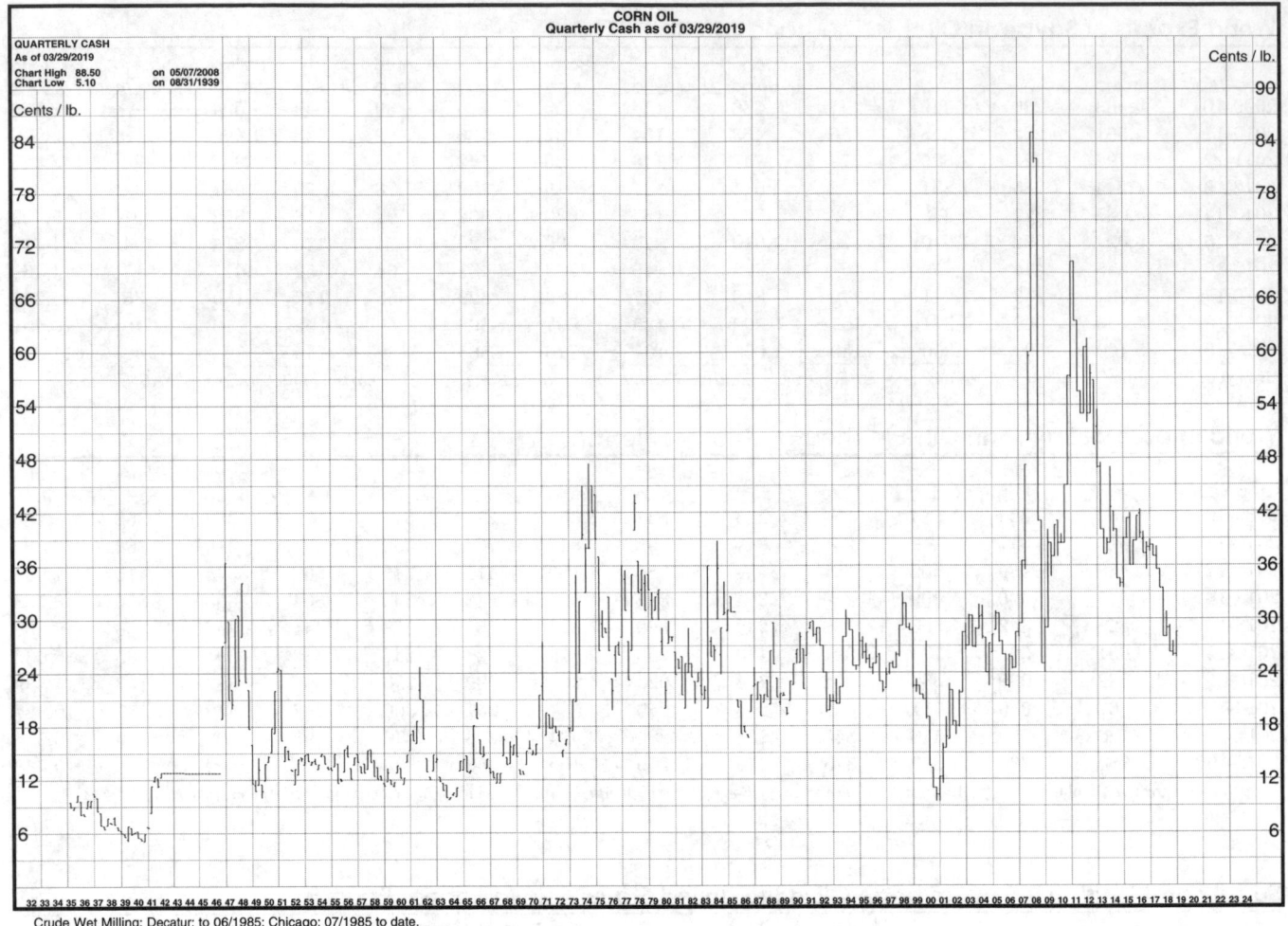

CORN OIL
Quarterly Cash as of 03/29/2019

QUARTERLY CASH
As of 03/29/2019

Chart High 88.50 on 05/07/2008
Chart Low 5.10 on 08/31/1939

Cents / lb.

Crude Wet Milling: Decatur: to 06/1985; Chicago: 07/1985 to date.

Production of Soybean Oil in the United States   In Millions of Pounds

Year	Oct.	Nov.	Dec.	Jan.	Feb.	Mar.	Apr.	May	June	July	Aug.	Sept.	Total
2009-10	1,825.2	1,854.0	1,898.3	1,844.9	1,690.1	1,727.7	1,518.1	1,481.6	1,442.2	1,440.5	1,418.4	1,474.4	19,615.0
2010-11	1,790.5	1,771.2	1,731.5	1,722.9	1,500.0	1,623.8	1,504.6	1,491.2	1,438.0	1,504.7	1,458.8	1,350.4	18,888.0
2011-12	----	----	----	----	----	----	----	----	----	----	----	----	19,740.0
2012-13	----	----	----	----	----	----	----	----	----	----	----	----	19,820.0
2013-14	----	----	----	----	----	----	----	----	----	----	----	----	20,130.0
2014-15	----	----	----	----	----	----	----	----	----	----	----	----	21,399.0
2015-16	1,962.9	1,901.9	1,929.0	1,864.9	1,795.9	1,943.5	1,840.3	1,876.2	1,787.2	1,789.4	1,642.5	1,616.6	21,950.0
2016-17	2,028.5	1,961.3	1,950.2	1,977.2	1,752.5	1,857.1	1,731.7	1,839.3	1,735.6	1,801.4	1,762.2	1,701.8	22,098.8
2017-18	2,016.9	1,977.0	2,015.3	1,995.6	1,889.8	2,079.1	1,964.9	1,966.5	1,936.9	2,043.3	1,945.0	1,936.9	23,767.2
2018-19[1]	2,134.6	2,060.6	2,135.4	2,114.0									25,333.8

[1] Preliminary.   Source: Economic Research Service, U.S. Department of Agriculture (ERS-USDA)

U.S. Exports of Soybean Oil (Crude and Refined)   In Millions of Pounds

Year	Jan.	Feb.	Mar.	Apr.	May	June	July	Aug.	Sept.	Oct.	Nov.	Dec.	Total
2009	96.4	145.9	161.3	350.3	277.9	86.5	247.6	302.9	164.2	332.1	241.1	390.3	2,797
2010	513.9	399.5	408.0	148.0	77.2	129.1	179.1	365.7	174.5	440.3	432.5	394.5	3,662
2011	466.3	301.2	330.1	188.6	91.7	129.7	120.0	114.6	223.6	78.0	107.8	59.6	2,211
2012	91.4	142.5	69.8	121.2	193.6	123.8	198.1	206.7	71.6	253.1	274.6	358.6	2,105
2013	258.9	339.7	136.7	135.9	79.3	75.1	70.7	92.8	87.9	71.4	135.9	320.2	1,805
2014	267.2	277.5	195.5	92.6	45.8	79.7	198.0	119.0	75.6	159.2	231.4	236.2	1,978
2015	256.7	220.5	233.5	125.7	72.5	157.4	64.6	154.6	101.9	179.6	233.0	320.7	2,121
2016	168.0	114.6	233.1	126.2	103.8	158.4	281.8	93.1	227.2	241.0	236.7	235.5	2,219
2017	259.4	238.7	294.5	258.3	161.2	138.2	199.4	163.1	130.2	212.8	132.0	173.0	2,361
2018[1]	180.7	181.1	201.5	212.3	431.4	228.3	174.7	197.6	121.7	146.1	215.8	170.5	2,462

[1] Preliminary.   Source: Bureau of the Census, U.S. Department of Commerce

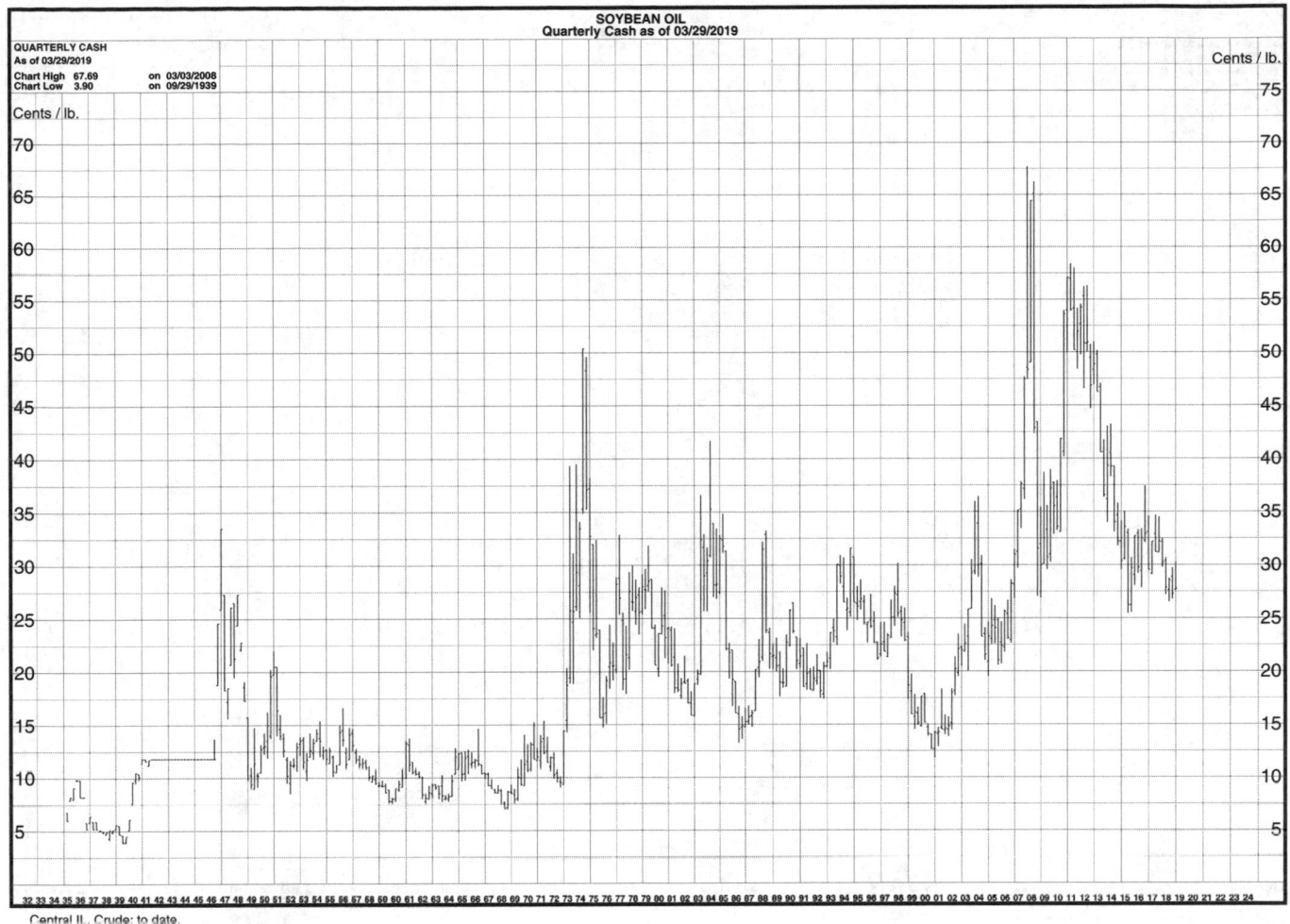

SOYBEAN OIL
Quarterly Cash as of 03/29/2019

QUARTERLY CASH
As of 03/29/2019

Chart High 67.69 on 03/03/2008
Chart Low 3.90 on 09/29/1939

Cents / lb.

Central IL, Crude: to date.

Stocks of Soybean Oil (Crude and Refined) at Factories and Warehouses in the U.S.   In Millions of Pounds

Year	Oct. 1	Nov. 1	Dec. 1	Jan. 1	Feb. 1	Mar. 1	Apr. 1	May 1	June 1	July 1	Aug. 1	Sept. 1
2009-10	2,861.0	2,809.4	2,990.5	3,150.5	3,221.7	3,295.7	3,317.6	3,414.8	3,521.9	3,597.5	3,594.1	3,337.8
2010-11	3,406.0	3,285.0	3,349.5	3,531.9	3,415.4	3,375.5	3,409.8	3,342.1	3,177.3	3,153.1	3,128.9	2,868.1
2011-12	2,425.0	----	----	----	----	----	----	----	----	----	----	----
2012-13	2,540.0	----	----	----	----	----	----	----	----	----	----	----
2013-14	1,655.0	----	----	----	----	----	----	----	****	****	----	----
2014-15	1,165.0	----	----	----	----	----	----	----	----	----	----	----
2015-16	1,854.8	1,940.4	1,965.9	1,972.5	2,110.8	2,280.2	2,324.9	2,420.0	2,466.1	2,424.1	2,214.3	1,985.7
2016-17	1,686.8	1,795.3	1,780.7	1,872.3	2,112.6	2,205.9	2,353.4	2,233.8	2,269.3	2,142.9	2,000.6	1,810.3
2017-18	1,711.0	1,626.2	1,690.6	1,950.7	2,239.8	2,425.4	2,444.5	2,688.8	2,374.1	2,304.8	2,383.6	2,214.8
2018-19[1]	1,990.0	2,047.6	1,900.3	1,945.8								

On First of Month.   [1] Preliminary.   *Source: Economic Research Service, U.S. Department of Agriculture (ERS-USDA)*

Average Price of Crude Domestic Soybean Oil (in Tank Cars) F.O.B. Decatur   In Cents Per Pound

Year	Oct.	Nov.	Dec.	Jan.	Feb.	Mar.	Apr.	May	June	July	Aug.	Sept.	Average
2009-10	33.15	36.59	36.81	34.88	34.69	36.39	37.11	35.41	34.47	35.07	37.57	39.21	35.95
2010-11	44.02	47.62	51.51	53.84	54.21	54.07	56.65	56.09	55.68	55.16	54.39	55.13	53.20
2011-12	51.73	51.44	50.17	50.99	52.36	53.43	54.96	50.69	48.65	51.96	52.65	53.81	51.90
2012-13	49.31	46.27	47.16	48.85	49.33	48.62	49.28	49.31	47.84	45.19	42.33	42.12	47.13
2013-14	39.66	39.58	37.63	34.95	37.11	40.82	41.87	40.68	39.84	37.60	35.04	33.99	38.23
2014-15	34.10	33.45	32.56	32.33	31.57	30.89	31.13	32.65	33.73	31.54	28.87	26.43	31.60
2015-16	27.14	26.42	29.72	28.89	29.79	30.86	32.45	30.76	30.35	28.75	31.21	31.99	29.86
2016-17	33.86	34.52	35.57	33.58	32.00	30.86	29.57	30.60	30.74	32.82	33.17	33.28	32.55
2017-18	32.35	33.43	32.27	31.61	30.63	30.28	29.70	29.40	28.30	27.21	27.60	27.73	30.04
2018-19[1]	28.89	27.49	28.14	28.44	29.58								28.51

[1] Preliminary.   *Source: Economic Research Service, U.S. Department of Agriculture (ERS-USDA)*

SOYBEAN OIL

WEEKLY NEAREST FUTURES
As of 03/29/2019
Chart High 60.40 on 04/11/2011
Chart Low   25.38 on 08/24/2015

Cents / lb.

Nearby Futures through Last Trading Day.

Volume of Trading of Soybean Oil Futures in Chicago   In Thousands of Contracts

Year	Jan.	Feb.	Mar.	Apr.	May	June	July	Aug.	Sept.	Oct.	Nov.	Dec.	Total
2009	1,211.9	1,518.5	1,189.8	1,429.7	1,202.9	1,993.4	1,543.9	1,400.4	1,217.9	1,342.1	1,527.1	1,554.4	17,132
2010	1,184.3	1,787.0	1,414.2	1,924.2	1,224.4	2,198.2	1,721.4	1,646.8	1,561.7	1,588.9	2,297.3	2,242.9	20,791
2011	1,660.1	2,427.9	2,153.7	2,276.7	1,613.1	2,427.4	1,616.1	1,924.0	2,027.5	1,866.4	2,296.1	1,867.6	24,157
2012	1,649.0	2,155.3	2,107.2	2,732.0	2,333.5	2,846.1	2,394.5	2,206.0	1,958.3	2,392.5	2,683.3	2,169.7	27,628
2013	2,043.6	2,403.6	1,465.9	2,453.7	1,831.6	2,213.7	1,918.7	1,850.1	1,560.5	1,908.5	2,263.2	1,892.7	23,806
2014	1,752.1	2,531.9	1,657.5	2,058.5	1,450.2	2,199.9	1,869.4	1,775.4	1,768.9	2,199.9	2,386.3	2,119.2	23,769
2015	1,985.3	2,348.9	1,683.5	2,527.2	2,042.6	3,236.5	2,358.9	2,412.7	2,190.7	2,519.5	2,667.4	2,924.0	28,897
2016	1,713.2	2,310.9	1,866.0	3,407.3	2,476.6	2,822.7	2,165.3	2,385.6	2,143.2	2,393.9	3,144.7	2,599.8	29,429
2017	2,001.6	2,737.6	2,421.6	2,639.6	1,882.5	2,952.5	2,467.6	2,721.7	2,451.3	2,125.4	3,128.1	2,702.9	30,232
2018	2,127.2	3,503.1	2,185.3	3,210.2	2,097.3	3,481.7	2,175.5	2,203.0	2,375.4	2,312.2	3,139.3	2,455.6	31,266

Contract size = 60,000 lbs.   Source: CME Group; Chicago Board of Trade (CBT)

Average Open Interest of Soybean Oil Futures in Chicago   In Contracts

Year	Jan.	Feb.	Mar.	Apr.	May	June	July	Aug.	Sept.	Oct.	Nov.	Dec.
2009	204,502	211,632	206,299	208,101	217,198	246,451	245,978	239,386	217,068	229,387	248,176	229,970
2010	219,042	283,115	282,973	290,577	299,379	319,098	284,484	292,426	290,685	325,697	358,850	347,185
2011	375,563	391,930	358,625	357,657	313,673	322,642	287,408	278,784	287,250	297,663	305,955	305,279
2012	296,889	314,752	340,827	380,916	386,924	377,817	329,673	332,182	314,359	322,262	347,898	310,982
2013	313,467	327,562	329,956	353,044	351,425	357,052	340,600	308,032	291,005	314,235	333,607	344,607
2014	364,056	339,211	302,398	326,545	313,757	333,690	325,337	347,395	373,086	391,486	395,330	365,382
2015	370,576	385,819	367,203	383,502	394,773	410,233	372,932	390,494	413,151	420,227	448,872	412,621
2016	404,388	411,898	415,026	457,557	404,143	389,896	361,443	378,813	399,625	443,699	446,001	407,110
2017	391,377	386,979	385,217	423,805	412,142	414,657	398,719	416,321	438,439	440,831	469,775	467,647
2018	480,781	499,421	496,026	519,883	514,763	505,702	512,638	534,033	575,527	539,882	556,831	497,905

Contract size = 60,000 lbs.   Source: CME Group; Chicago Board of Trade (CBT)

Soybeans

Soybean is the common name for the annual leguminous plant and its seed. The soybean is a member of the oilseed family and is not considered a grain. The soybean seeds are contained in pods and are nearly spherical in shape. The seeds are usually light yellow in color. The seeds contain 20% oil and 40% protein. Soybeans were an ancient food crop in China, Japan, and Korea and were only introduced to the U.S. in the early 1800s. Today, soybeans are the second largest crop produced in the U.S. behind corn. Soybean production in the U.S. is concentrated in the Midwest and the lower Mississippi Valley. Soybean crops in the U.S. are planted in May or June and are harvested in autumn. Soybean plants usually reach maturity 100-150 days after planting depending on growing conditions.

Soybeans are used to produce a wide variety of food products. The key value of soybeans lies in the relatively high protein content, which makes it an excellent source of protein without many of the negative factors of animal meat. Popular soy-based food products include whole soybeans (roasted for snacks or used in sauces, stews and soups), soy oil for cooking and baking, soy flour, protein concentrates, isolated soy protein (which contains up to 92% protein), soy milk and baby formula (as an alternative to dairy products), soy yogurt, soy cheese, soy nut butter, soy sprouts, tofu and tofu products (soybean curd), soy sauce (which is produced by a fermentation process), and meat alternatives (hamburgers, breakfast sausage, etc.).

The primary market for soybean futures is at the CME Group. The CME's soybean contract calls for the delivery of 5,000 bushels of No. 2 yellow soybeans (at contract par), No. 1 yellow soybeans (at 6 cents per bushel above the contract price), or No. 3 yellow soybeans (at 6 cents under the contract price). Soybean futures are also traded at exchanges in Brazil, Argentina, China, and Tokyo.

Prices – CME soybean futures prices (Barchart.com electronic symbol ZS) pushed higher in Q1-2018 and posted a 2-year high in March of $10.71 a bushel. Stellar Chinese demand for U.S. soybeans along with drought concerns in Argentina lifted soybean prices in Q1. China 2017 soybean imports rose +13.9% yr/yr to a record 95.54 MMT, while a La Nina weather system in the eastern Pacific Ocean curbed precipitation in Argentina, the world's third-biggest soybean producer. Also, the USDA's Prospective Plantings report in March gave soybean prices a lift after the USDA forecast that U.S. 2018 soybean acreage would decline by -1.2 million acres yr/yr to 88.982 million acres. Soybean prices then fell sharply in the spring on increased trade tensions between China and the U.S. that prompted China to boost its soybean purchases from Brazil at the expense of U.S. supplies. China May soybean imports from Brazil, now China's number one soybean supplier, jumped +17% yr/yr to 12.4 MMT, the most ever for the month of May. Another bearish factor for soybeans was the outlook for a record global crop and robust supplies as the USDA in July projected a record 2018/19 soybean crop of 359.49 MMT and that global 2018/19 soybean ending stocks would climb by +2.3% yr/yr to a record 98.27 MMT. This confluence of bearish factors caused soybean prices to sink to a 10-year low of $8.105 a bushel in July. Soybean prices recovered slightly in Q4 after the U.S. announced a new

trade deal with Mexico and Canada, which sparked some short covering. However, the slump in Chinese demand for U.S. soybeans undercut by soybean prices as China's 2018 soybean imports from the U.S. plunged by -49% yr/yr to 16.64 MMT. China boosted its 2018 soybean imports from Brazil by 30% yr/yr to 66.1 MMT as shipments from Brazil accounted for 75% of China's total soybean imports in 2018. Soybean prices finished 2018 down -7.3% yr/yr at $8.825 a bushel.

Supply – World soybean production during the 2018/19 marketing year (Sep-Aug) is forecasted to rise +8.8% yr/yr to 369.203 million metric tons. World soybean production has risen sharply from the 80 million metric ton level seen back in the 1980's. The world's largest soybean producers in 2018/19 are expected to be the U.S. with 33.9% of world production, Brazil with 33.0%, Argentina with 15.0%, China with 4.3%, and India with 3.0%. China's soybean production has roughly doubled since 1980. Brazil's production has risen by almost eight times since 1980.

U.S. soybean production in 2018/19 is forecasted to rise by 4.3% yr/yr to 4.599 billion bushels, a new record high. U.S. farmers are expected to harvest 88.343 million acres of soybeans in 2018/19, falling by -1.3% yr/yr, down from last year's record high. The average yield in 2018/19 is forecasted to be up +5.7% yr/yr to 52.1, which is a new record high. U.S. ending stocks for the 2018/19 marketing year is expected to rise by +45.3% yr/yr to 438.1 million bushels.

Demand – Total U.S. distribution in 2018/19 fell -4.4% yr/yr to 4.108 billion bushels. the distribution tables for U.S. soybeans for the 2018/19 marketing year are expected to show that 50.6% of U.S. soybean usage went for crush, exports, 46.3% went for exports, and 3.1% for seed, feed, and residual. The quantity of U.S. soybeans that will go for crushing is expected to rise +1.2% yr/yr in 2018/19 to 2.080 billion bushels. The world soybean crush in 2018/19 is expected to rise +4.4% yr/yr to a new record high of 308.189 million metric tons, a new record high and which is about triple the level seen in 1993-94.

Trade – World exports of soybeans in 2018/19 are forecasted to rise +1.9% yr/yr to a new record high of 156.094 million metric tons. The world's largest soybean exporters in 2018/19 are expected to be Brazil with 51.9% of world exports, the U.S. with 33.1%. and Paraguay with 3.7%, Canada with 3.4%, and Argentina with 3.2%. Brazil's soybean exports have more than doubled in the past decade and Canada's exports have almost tripled. U.S. soybean exports in 2018/19 are forecasted to fall by -8.8% yr/yr to 1.945 billion bushels.

World imports in 2018/19 are expected to fall -0.7% yr/yr to 152.460 million metric tons. The world's largest importers of soybeans in 2018/19 are expected to be China with 59.0% of world imports, the European Union with 10.4%, Mexico with 3.3%, and Japan with 2.2%. China's imports in 2018/19 are expected to fall -4.4% yr/yr to 90.000 million metric tons, which is down from last year's record level.

SOYBEANS

World Production of Soybeans In Thousands of Metric Tons

Crop Year[4]	Argen-tina	Bolivia	Brazil	Canada	China	European Union	India	Para-guay	Russia	Ukraine	United States	Uruguay	World Total
2009-10	54,500	1,934	69,000	3,581	14,982	951	9,700	6,462	873	1,044	91,470	1,987	260,733
2010-11	49,000	2,320	75,300	4,445	15,357	1,198	10,130	7,128	1,133	1,680	90,663	1,855	264,684
2011-12	40,100	2,429	66,500	4,467	15,020	1,220	11,940	4,043	1,641	2,264	84,291	2,726	240,955
2012-13	49,300	2,646	82,000	5,086	13,553	948	12,186	8,202	1,683	2,410	82,791	3,650	269,076
2013-14	53,400	2,814	86,700	5,356	12,513	1,211	9,477	8,190	1,517	2,774	91,389	3,163	283,335
2014-15	61,450	3,106	97,200	6,045	12,690	1,832	8,711	8,154	2,362	3,900	106,878	3,109	320,691
2015-16	58,800	3,205	96,500	6,456	12,360	2,320	6,929	9,217	2,707	3,932	106,857	2,208	316,553
2016-17[1]	55,000	2,107	114,600	6,597	13,644	2,410	10,992	10,336	3,134	4,286	116,920	3,212	349,298
2017-18[2]	37,800	2,600	120,300	7,717	15,200	2,667	8,350	9,810	3,621	3,890	120,039	1,334	339,467
2018-19[3]	55,500	2,700	122,000	7,300	16,000	2,700	11,000	9,800	3,900	4,400	125,179	2,500	369,203

[1] Preliminary. [2] Estimate. [3] Forecast. [4] Spilt year includes Northern Hemisphere crops harvested in the late months of the first year shown combined with Southern Hemisphere crops harvested in the early months of the following year. *Sources: Foreign Agricultural Service, U.S. Department of Agriculture (FAS-USDA)*

World Crushings of Soybeans In Thousands of Metric Tons

Crop Year	Argen-tina	Bolivia	Brazil	China	European Union	India	Japan	Mexico	Para-guay	Russia	Taiwan	United States	World Total
2009-10	34,127	1,520	33,700	49,000	12,595	7,800	2,535	3,600	1,658	1,900	2,010	47,673	210,481
2010-11	37,614	1,800	36,330	55,000	12,330	9,350	2,149	3,625	1,670	2,050	2,060	44,851	222,217
2011-12	35,886	2,000	38,083	61,000	11,600	10,300	1,960	3,675	900	2,100	2,020	46,348	229,126
2012-13	33,611	2,175	35,235	65,000	12,700	10,800	1,915	3,650	2,950	2,200	1,920	45,967	231,813
2013-14	36,173	2,250	36,861	68,900	13,100	8,700	1,969	4,030	3,550	3,300	1,925	47,192	242,857
2014-15	40,235	2,450	40,435	74,500	14,450	7,700	2,150	4,175	3,700	3,600	1,980	50,975	264,756
2015-16	43,267	2,550	39,747	81,500	14,950	5,500	2,283	4,400	3,800	4,000	1,980	51,335	275,130
2016-17[1]	43,309	2,050	40,411	88,000	14,400	9,000	2,392	4,600	3,750	4,400	2,045	51,742	287,424
2017-18[2]	36,984	2,350	44,500	90,000	14,950	7,700	2,350	5,250	3,800	4,600	2,150	55,926	295,239
2018-19[3]	43,000	2,250	42,700	92,500	16,600	9,400	2,350	5,300	3,900	5,000	2,250	56,608	308,189

[1] Preliminary. [2] Estimate. [3] Forecast. *Sources: Foreign Agricultural Service, U.S. Department of Agriculture (FAS-USDA)*

World Exports of Soybeans In Thousands of Metric Tons

Crop Year	Argen-tina	Bolivia	Brazil	Canada	China	India	Para-guay	Russia	Serbia	Ukraine	United States	Uruguay	World Total
2009-10	13,088	50	28,578	2,247	184	15	4,659	----	5	263	40,798	1,974	92,063
2010-11	9,206	24	29,951	2,943	190	18	5,094	1	82	989	40,959	1,820	91,575
2011-12	7,368	322	36,257	2,933	275	39	3,162	90	17	1,338	37,186	2,607	91,774
2012-13	7,738	523	41,904	3,470	266	115	5,082	102	6	1,323	36,129	3,527	100,378
2013-14	7,842	141	46,829	3,469	215	183	4,844	24	23	1,261	44,594	3,150	112,737
2014-15	10,575	8	50,612	3,763	143	234	4,576	312	136	2,422	50,136	3,114	126,226
2015-16	9,922	91	54,383	4,236	114	134	5,400	456	68	2,369	52,870	2,124	132,572
2016-17[1]	7,026	13	63,137	4,592	114	269	6,129	375	186	2,904	58,960	3,224	147,503
2017-18[2]	2,112	10	76,195	4,925	150	217	6,200	892	28	2,757	57,945	1,250	153,163
2018-19[3]	5,000	15	81,000	5,300	100	250	5,800	800	150	3,100	51,710	2,370	156,094

[1] Preliminary. [2] Estimate. [3] Forecast. *Sources: Foreign Agricultural Service, U.S. Department of Agriculture (FAS-USDA)*

World Imports of Soybeans In Thousands of Metric Tons

Crop Year	China	Egypt	European Union	Indo-nesia	Japan	Korea, South	Mexico	Russia	Taiwan	Thailand	Turkey	Vietnam	World Total
2009-10	50,338	1,638	12,683	1,620	3,401	1,197	3,523	1,037	2,469	1,660	1,648	231	87,510
2010-11	52,339	1,644	12,472	1,898	2,917	1,239	3,498	1,000	2,454	2,139	1,351	932	89,787
2011-12	59,231	1,661	12,070	1,922	2,758	1,139	3,606	741	2,285	1,907	1,057	1,290	94,552
2012-13	59,865	1,730	12,538	1,795	2,830	1,115	3,409	717	2,286	1,867	1,249	1,291	97,195
2013-14	70,364	1,694	13,293	2,241	2,894	1,271	3,842	2,048	2,335	1,798	1,608	1,564	113,068
2014-15	78,350	1,947	13,914	2,006	3,004	1,246	3,819	1,986	2,520	2,411	2,197	1,707	124,362
2015-16	83,230	1,300	15,120	2,274	3,186	1,249	4,126	2,336	2,476	2,798	2,283	1,602	133,340
2016-17[1]	93,495	2,115	13,441	2,649	3,175	1,286	4,126	2,221	2,566	3,078	2,271	1,646	144,372
2017-18[2]	94,125	3,255	14,584	2,500	3,256	1,256	4,873	2,237	2,666	2,482	2,777	1,850	153,538
2018-19[3]	90,000	3,350	15,800	2,725	3,300	1,365	5,030	2,450	2,730	3,150	2,600	2,200	152,460

[1] Preliminary. [2] Estimate. [3] Forecast. *Sources: Foreign Agricultural Service, U.S. Department of Agriculture (FAS-USDA)*

World Ending Stocks of Soybeans   In Thousands of Metric Tons

Crop Year	Argentina	Bolivia	Brazil	Canada	China	European Union	India	Japan	Paraguay	Turkey	Ukraine	United States	World Total
2009-10	20,729	285	17,480	305	13,169	541	1,251	227	158	701	150	4,106	60,063
2010-11	20,623	414	23,636	297	14,675	826	833	168	463	644	103	5,852	70,054
2011-12	14,719	326	13,024	231	16,351	1,482	1,235	154	383	338	----	4,610	54,212
2012-13	19,472	24	15,355	158	12,803	1,076	1,210	221	500	206	99	3,825	56,403
2013-14	25,271	139	15,870	246	14,465	1,253	600	256	243	287	265	2,504	63,145
2014-15	31,750	433	19,178	466	17,562	843	200	212	68	359	166	5,188	78,717
2015-16	33,650	635	18,758	301	17,138	1,559	338	259	31	274	113	5,354	81,046
2016-17[1]	35,464	414	26,812	277	20,663	1,150	890	217	436	313	151	8,208	97,529
2017-18[2]	34,524	279	25,150	632	23,538	1,526	219	217	180	460	26	11,923	101,295
2018-19[3]	41,304	359	21,350	587	19,838	1,501	479	261	210	335	100	25,995	115,334

[1] Preliminary.   [2] Estimate.   [3] Forecast.   Sources: Foreign Agricultural Service, U.S. Department of Agriculture (FAS-USDA)

Supply and Distribution of Soybeans in the United States   In Millions of Bushels

Crop Year Beginning Sept. 1	Stocks, Sept. 1 — Farms	Stocks, Sept. 1 — Mills, Elevators[3]	Total Stocks	Production	Imports	Total Supply	Crushings	Seed, Feed & Residual Use	Exports	Total Distribution	Ending Stocks
2009-10	35.1	103.1	138.2	3,359	15	3,514	1,752	112	1,499	3,363	151
2010-11	35.4	115.5	150.9	3,329	14	3,497	1,648	129	1,505	3,282	215
2011-12	48.5	166.5	215.0	3,094	16	3,328	1,703	91	1,365	3,159	169
2012-13	38.3	131.1	169.4	3,042	41	3,252	1,689	95	1,328	3,111	141
2013-14	39.6	101.0	140.6	3,358	72	3,570	1,734	107	1,638	3,478	92
2014-15	21.3	70.7	92.0	3,927	33	4,052	1,873	146	1,842	3,862	191
2015-16	49.7	140.9	190.6	3,926	24	4,140	1,886	115	1,942	3,944	197
2016-17	41.6	155.2	196.7	4,296	22	4,515	1,901	146	2,166	4,214	302
2017-18[1]	87.9	213.7	301.6	4,412	22	4,735	2,055	113	2,129	4,297	438
2018-19[2]	101.0	337.1	438.1	4,544	20	5,002	2,100	127	1,875	4,102	900

[1] Preliminary.   [2] Estimate.   [3] Also warehouses.   Source: Economic Research Service, U.S. Department of Agriculture (ERS-USDA)

Salient Statistics & Official Crop Production Reports of Soybeans in the United States   In Millions of Bushels

Year	Acreage Planted (1,000 Acres)	Acreage Harvested (1,000 Acres)	Yield Per Acre (Bu.)	Farm Price ($/Bu.)	Farm Value (Million Dollars)	Yield of Oil (Lbs. Per Bushel Crushed)	Yield of Meal (Lbs. Per Bushel Crushed)	Crop Production Reports In Thousands of Bushels — Aug. 1	Sept. 1	Oct. 1	Nov. 1	Dec. 1	Final
2009-10	77,451	76,372	44.0	9.61	32,145	11.10	43.82	3,199,172	3,245,292	3,250,113	3,319,270	----	3,359,011
2010-11	77,404	76,610	43.5	12.17	37,547	11.54	44.39	3,433,370	3,482,899	3,408,211	3,375,067	----	3,329,181
2011-12	75,046	73,776	41.9	13.13	38,498	----	----	3,055,882	3,085,340	3,059,987	3,045,558	----	3,093,524
2012-13	77,198	76,144	40.0	14.53	43,723	----	----	2,692,014	2,634,310	2,860,290	2,971,022	----	3,042,044
2013-14	76,840	76,253	44.0	13.32	43,683	----	----	3,255,444	3,149,166	NA	3,257,746	----	3,357,984
2014-15	83,276	82,591	47.5	10.00	39,475	----	----	3,815,679	3,913,079	3,926,812	3,958,272	----	3,927,090
2015-16	82,650	81,732	48.0	9.18	35,192	----	----	3,916,448	3,935,277	3,887,721	3,981,337		3,926,339
2016-17	83,453	82,706	51.9	9.46	40,691	----	----	4,060,188	4,200,985	4,268,884	4,361,023	----	4,296,496
2017-18[1]	90,162	89,542	49.3	9.38	41,007	----	----	4,381,053	4,431,043	4,430,621	4,425,279	----	4,411,633
2018-19[2]	89,196	88,110	51.6	8.58		----	----	4,585,916	4,693,135	4,689,628	4,599,530	----	4,543,883

[1] Preliminary.   [2] Forecast.   NA = Not available.   Source: National Agricultural Statistics Service, U.S. Department of Agriculture (NASS-USDA)

Stocks of Soybeans in the United States   In Thousands of Bushels

Year	On Farms Mar. 1	On Farms June 1	On Farms Sept. 1	On Farms Dec. 1	Off Farms Mar. 1	Off Farms June 1	Off Farms Sept. 1	Off Farms Dec. 1	Total Stocks Mar. 1	Total Stocks June 1	Total Stocks Sept. 1	Total Stocks Dec. 1
2009	656,500	226,300	35,100	1,229,500	645,289	369,859	103,098	1,109,050	1,301,789	596,159	138,198	2,338,550
2010	609,200	232,600	35,400	1,091,000	660,868	338,523	115,485	1,187,084	1,270,068	571,123	150,885	2,278,084
2011	505,000	217,700	48,500	1,139,000	743,800	401,583	166,513	1,230,885	1,248,800	619,283	215,013	2,369,885
2012	555,000	179,000	38,250	910,000	819,488	488,465	131,120	1,056,161	1,374,488	667,465	169,370	1,966,161
2013	456,700	171,100	39,550	955,000	541,320	263,564	101,007	1,198,621	998,020	434,664	140,557	2,153,621
2014	381,900	109,100	21,325	1,218,000	611,928	295,945	70,666	1,309,744	993,828	405,045	91,991	2,527,744
2015	609,200	246,300	49,700	1,308,500	717,399	380,768	140,910	1,405,577	1,326,599	627,068	190,610	2,714,077
2016	727,500	281,300	41,560	1,335,000	803,406	590,481	155,169	1,563,379	1,530,906	871,781	196,729	2,898,379
2017	668,500	332,500	87,900	1,485,000	1,070,433	633,356	213,695	1,675,679	1,738,933	965,856	301,595	3,160,679
2018[1]	855,000	377,000	101,000	1,935,000	1,254,303	842,329	337,105	1,801,212	2,109,303	1,219,329	438,105	3,736,212

[1] Preliminary.   Source: National Agricultural Statistics Service, U.S. Department of Agriculture (NASS-USDA)

SOYBEANS

Commercial Stocks of Soybeans in the United States, on First of Month   In Millions of Bushels

Year	Jan.	Feb.	Mar.	Apr.	May	June	July	Aug.	Sept.	Oct.	Nov.	Dec.
2005	26.5	21.5	19.5	16.0	14.8	12.1	11.5	8.8	5.4	17.0	36.7	36.1
2006	36.8	30.2	26.1	25.7	17.6	20.5	14.6	14.5	14.5	19.0	40.1	43.7
2007	42.0	36.5	37.3	34.3	29.7	27.4	26.6	24.6	25.5	32.0	54.0	61.3
2008	51.1	45.5	41.8	36.3	28.2	25.6	19.2	14.8	11.4	19.6	40.5	46.1
2009	44.6	36.8	27.0	15.6	13.9	11.8	10.0	5.8	5.9	24.7	40.5	44.3
2010	30.0	28.5	20.1	22.3	10.8	8.0	8.2	4.5	3.3	19.2	45.0	32.0
2011	32.6	23.2	16.0	11.3	10.2	5.9	6.2	5.7	4.6	9.8	49.4	50.7
2012	42.7	34.8	29.9	28.5	27.1	23.8	16.6	10.4	5.2	18.8	41.6	33.8
2013	25.2	20.3	16.1	10.0	6.4	6.6	4.1	2.9	2.1	27.2	36.9	35.5
2014	30.7	20.4	15.5	12.2	7.0	5.1	5.2	2.3	----	----	----	----

This report was discontinued as of August 26, 2014.   Source: Livestock Division, U.S. Department of Agriculture (LD-USDA)

Production of Soybeans for Beans in the United States, by State   In Millions of Bushels

Year	Arkansas	Illinois	Indiana	Iowa	Kentucky	Michigan	Minnesota	Mississippi	Missouri	Nebraska	Ohio	Tennessee	Total
2009-10	122.6	430.1	266.6	486.0	68.2	79.6	284.8	77.1	230.6	259.4	222.0	68.9	3,359.0
2010-11	110.3	466.1	258.5	496.2	47.3	88.7	329.0	76.2	210.4	267.8	220.3	43.7	3,329.2
2011-12	126.3	423.2	240.7	475.3	57.7	85.4	274.6	70.2	190.2	261.4	217.9	40.3	3,093.5
2012-13	137.0	384.0	225.3	419.0	58.8	85.6	304.5	87.8	158.1	207.1	206.6	46.7	3,042.0
2013-14	140.9	474.0	267.3	420.9	83.0	85.4	278.0	91.5	202.0	255.2	222.3	72.1	3,358.0
2014-15	158.4	547.1	301.9	498.3	83.1	86.7	301.7	113.9	259.9	287.8	246.2	74.1	3,927.1
2015-16	155.3	544.3	275.0	553.7	88.7	99.0	377.5	104.4	181.0	305.7	237.0	79.1	3,926.3
2016-17	145.2	593.0	323.7	566.4	89.0	104.0	389.5	97.0	271.5	314.2	263.8	73.4	4,296.5
2017-18	178.5	611.9	320.8	566.6	102.8	96.5	384.3	115.0	292.5	326.0	252.0	83.0	4,411.6
2018-19[1]	165.2	698.8	346.3	564.9	103.5	109.4	389.4	119.4	261.0	333.4	288.8	76.8	4,543.9

[1] Preliminary.   Source: Agricultural Statistics Board, U.S. Department of Agriculture (ASB-USDA)

U. S. Exports of Soybeans   In Millions of Bushels

Year	Sept.	Oct.	Nov.	Dec.	Jan.	Feb.	Mar.	Apr.	May	June	July	Aug.	Total
2009-10	39.1	198.1	299.0	226.1	226.5	170.0	131.6	55.5	32.0	28.2	37.4	56.3	1,499.9
2010-11	68.2	296.4	257.8	195.9	185.5	169.5	125.9	66.4	34.7	31.6	30.4	43.6	1,505.8
2011-12	47.6	193.3	184.2	151.2	175.0	153.5	116.0	74.8	67.5	53.9	73.8	76.5	1,367.1
2012-13	96.8	274.3	255.4	186.4	194.5	141.6	72.1	34.6	22.1	19.5	13.7	17.4	1,328.3
2013-14	55.3	290.1	331.5	255.0	259.0	198.7	117.0	42.9	32.2	22.2	19.2	16.4	1,639.5
2014-15	77.9	329.9	405.3	301.7	257.5	166.6	94.1	49.7	44.0	34.4	39.7	42.6	1,843.5
2015-16	86.4	369.0	336.3	250.1	218.1	207.5	95.8	52.3	33.8	36.8	98.5	152.6	1,937.1
2016-17	138.5	415.9	378.6	291.2	272.9	162.4	114.7	89.4	53.3	66.0	83.2	113.1	2,179.3
2017-18	170.6	347.1	332.1	237.2	211.9	154.9	119.1	79.7	110.0	119.7	126.0	123.8	2,131.9
2018-19[1]	119.0	205.2	186.3	150.9									1,984.2

[1] Preliminary.   Source: Economic Research Service, U.S. Department of Agriculture (ERS-USDA)

Soybean Crushed (Factory Consumption) in the United States   In Millions of Bushels

Year	Sept.	Oct.	Nov.	Dec.	Jan.	Feb.	Mar.	Apr.	May	June	July	Aug.	Total
2009-10	113.3	163.5	168.7	173.1	167.2	153.9	156.1	136.5	133.0	129.2	129.4	128.1	1,751.7
2010-11	130.4	157.2	155.1	153.0	149.2	129.4	140.3	128.0	128.0	123.6	129.6	125.0	1,648.0
2011-12	----	516.6	----	----	524.0	----	----	453.9	----	----	299.0	----	1,703.0
2012-13	----	631.2	----	----	453.5	----	----	442.3	----	----	267.3	----	1,688.9
2013-14	----	675.8	----	----	457.0	----	----	422.0	----	----	285.6	----	1,733.9
2014-15	----	687.3	----	----	480.2	----	----	522.7	----	151.6	155.8	144.6	1,873.5
2015-16	134.6	170.1	165.8	167.0	160.5	154.6	166.4	158.2	160.9	154.1	153.5	140.6	1,886.3
2016-17	138.3	175.9	170.7	169.0	170.4	151.0	160.0	149.8	158.0	148.2	155.6	151.6	1,898.5
2017-18	145.4	175.9	173.3	176.3	174.7	165.0	182.2	171.6	172.5	169.6	178.9	169.9	2,055.3
2018-19[1]	169.3	183.6	178.1	183.8	182.9								2,154.5

[1] Preliminary.   Source: Economic Research Service, U.S. Department of Agriculture (ERS-USDA)

Nearby Futures through Last Trading Day.

Volume of Trading of Soybean Futures in Chicago   In Thousands of Contracts

Year	Jan.	Feb.	Mar.	Apr.	May	June	July	Aug.	Sept.	Oct.	Nov.	Dec.	Total
2009	2,773.7	2,892.5	2,576.2	3,638.9	2,635.5	3,439.7	2,845.7	2,417.6	2,348.2	3,996.4	2,820.8	3,373.7	35,759
2010	2,659.0	3,392.5	2,932.8	3,414.4	2,078.2	2,946.5	2,546.1	2,266.1	2,553.0	4,660.2	3,455.9	4,029.3	36,934
2011	3,572.5	4,577.6	3,906.0	4,143.1	2,790.6	3,822.9	2,708.7	3,332.7	4,053.1	5,309.5	3,004.7	3,922.4	45,144
2012	3,342.4	4,370.8	4,388.0	5,314.9	4,556.2	4,887.6	5,195.8	3,879.3	3,925.5	5,272.1	3,027.3	3,881.7	52,042
2013	3,628.0	4,568.4	3,193.0	4,516.5	3,522.9	3,644.1	3,328.3	4,132.9	3,442.2	5,288.6	3,401.3	4,054.9	46,721
2014	3,692.7	5,090.5	3,613.9	4,191.9	2,914.6	3,929.4	3,765.7	2,967.5	3,672.1	7,261.6	3,661.2	4,408.2	49,169
2015	3,570.3	4,867.3	4,011.2	5,029.8	3,422.5	6,284.1	4,425.8	4,256.8	3,693.6	6,251.6	3,314.6	4,967.4	54,095
2016	3,846.1	5,203.8	4,455.3	8,380.0	6,211.8	7,135.0	4,779.8	3,432.5	3,373.1	5,936.7	4,085.1	4,891.6	61,731
2017	3,760.7	5,197.1	3,837.0	4,612.5	3,781.0	5,251.6	5,287.5	4,132.3	3,629.0	6,075.2	3,726.4	5,213.9	54,504
2018	4,066.9	6,799.5	5,116.2	6,789.1	4,592.8	6,603.2	3,794.3	4,088.9	3,151.9	5,831.5	3,439.6	4,264.6	58,539

Contract size = 5,000 bu.   Source: CME Group; Chicago Board of Trade (CBT)

Average Open Interest of Soybean Futures in Chicago   In Contracts

Year	Jan.	Feb.	Mar.	Apr.	May	June	July	Aug.	Sept.	Oct.	Nov.	Dec.
2009	297,316	313,704	292,160	358,857	415,599	454,846	410,718	401,752	428,320	461,463	438,531	464,281
2010	446,212	465,666	434,272	477,138	459,342	462,796	470,087	514,703	553,196	633,086	624,213	643,091
2011	643,422	673,796	618,157	624,350	559,493	582,529	529,949	524,547	590,297	567,081	521,277	525,510
2012	474,050	532,738	623,973	793,781	787,884	769,806	805,353	748,382	732,388	704,191	609,007	588,185
2013	549,767	615,897	589,572	565,212	565,761	596,479	517,022	535,645	615,389	626,484	582,859	625,222
2014	589,906	675,981	649,898	645,604	601,103	616,406	622,020	642,043	724,924	766,218	664,485	668,492
2015	644,320	698,627	708,314	746,322	698,151	722,449	663,522	653,707	675,762	701,419	673,127	681,902
2016	674,273	721,934	723,375	824,649	840,893	859,598	747,309	668,100	636,957	657,062	642,826	709,587
2017	681,161	736,942	691,919	729,828	654,509	695,963	648,861	645,305	666,063	723,614	712,476	747,181
2018	762,139	781,574	846,901	923,139	879,489	893,661	838,433	797,279	846,361	839,514	743,667	723,335

Contract size = 5,000 bu.   Source: CME Group; Chicago Board of Trade (CBT)

SOYBEANS

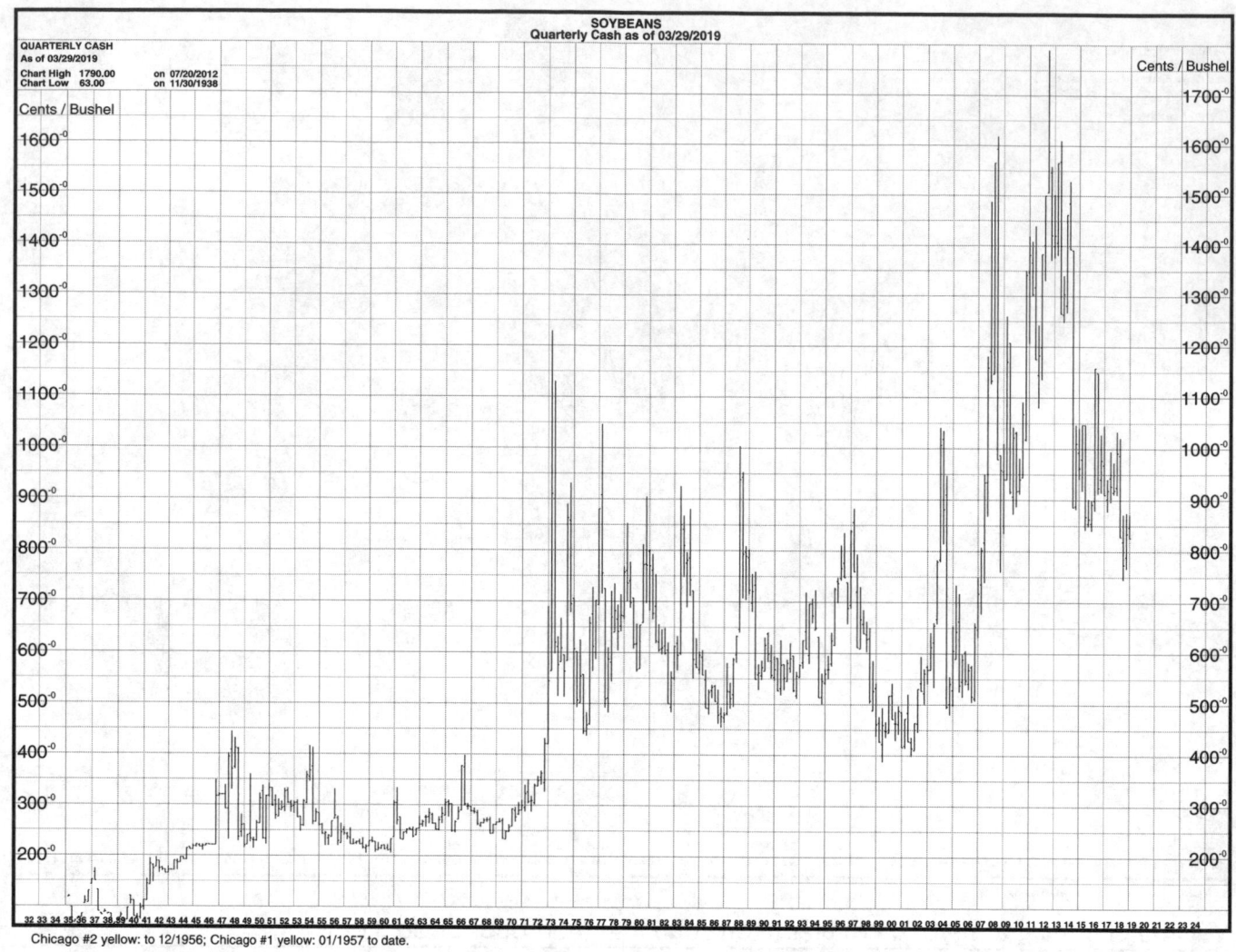

Chicago #2 yellow: to 12/1956; Chicago #1 yellow: 01/1957 to date.

Average Price Received by Farmers for Soybeans in the United States   In Dollars Per Bushel

Year	Sept.	Oct.	Nov.	Dec.	Jan.	Feb.	Mar.	Apr.	May	June	July	Aug.	Average
2009-10	9.75	9.43	9.53	9.80	9.79	9.41	9.39	9.47	9.41	9.45	9.79	10.10	9.61
2010-11	9.98	10.20	11.10	11.60	11.60	12.70	12.70	13.10	13.20	13.20	13.20	13.40	12.17
2011-12	12.20	11.80	11.70	11.50	11.90	12.20	13.00	13.80	14.00	13.90	15.40	16.20	13.13
2012-13	14.30	14.20	14.30	14.30	14.30	14.60	14.60	14.40	14.90	15.10	15.30	14.10	14.53
2013-14	13.30	12.50	12.70	13.00	12.90	13.20	13.70	14.30	14.40	14.30	13.10	12.40	13.32
2014-15	10.90	9.97	10.20	10.30	10.30	9.91	9.85	9.69	9.58	9.58	9.95	9.71	10.00
2015-16	9.05	8.81	8.68	8.76	8.71	8.51	8.56	9.01	9.76	10.20	10.20	9.93	9.18
2016-17	9.41	9.30	9.47	9.64	9.71	9.86	9.69	9.33	9.29	9.10	9.42	9.24	9.46
2017-18	9.35	9.18	9.22	9.30	9.30	9.49	9.81	9.83	9.84	9.55	9.08	8.59	9.38
2018-19[1]	8.77	8.58	8.37	8.57	8.63								8.58

[1] Preliminary.   *Source: Economic Research Service, U.S. Department of Agriculture (ERS-USDA)*

Average Cash Price of No. 1 Yellow Soybeans at Illinois Processor   In Cents Per Bushel

Year	Sept.	Oct.	Nov.	Dec.	Jan.	Feb.	Mar.	Apr.	May	June	July	Aug.	Average
2001-02	469	430	441	438	437	440	464	471	492	519	575	567	479
2002-03	579	541	575	566	570	590	580	611	640	635	601	589	590
2003-04	639	729	763	772	823	872	975	992	958	890	809	641	822
2004-05	562	519	534	545	539	544	628	622	644	701	703	639	598
2005-06	565	553	574	592	576	575	569	562	581	576	577	542	570
2006-07	535	580	661	657	683	735	730	718	749	792	801	804	704
2007-08	907	944	1,032	1,123	1,216	1,335	1,312	1,292	1,324	1,499	1,516	1,288	1,232
2008-09	1,140	903	893	868	991	938	917	1,025	1,166	1,237	1,096	1,136	1,026
2009-10	1,012	978	1,009	1,033	984	944	949	975	955	955	1,030	1,066	991
2010-11[1]	1,065	1,148	1,252	1,311	1,378	1,386	1,350	1,364	1,368	1,382	1,384	1,381	1,314

[1] Preliminary.   *Source: Economic Research Service, U.S. Department of Agriculture (ERS-USDA)*

Stock Index Futures - U.S.

A stock index simply represents a basket of underlying stocks. Indexes can be either price-weighted or capitalization-weighted. In a price-weighted index, such as the Dow Jones Industrial Average, the individual stock prices are simply added up and then divided by a divisor, meaning that stocks with higher prices have a higher weighting in the index value. In a capitalization-weighted index, such as the Standard and Poor's 500 index, the weighting of each stock corresponds to the size of the company as determined by its capitalization (i.e., the total dollar value of its stock). Stock indexes cover a variety of different sectors. For example, the Dow Jones Industrial Average contains 30 blue-chip stocks that represent the industrial sector. The S&P 500 index includes 500 of the largest blue-chip U.S. companies. The NYSE index includes all the stocks that are traded at the New York Stock Exchange. The Nasdaq 100 includes the largest 100 companies that are traded on the Nasdaq Exchange. The most popular U.S. stock index futures contract is the E-mini S&P 500 futures contract, which is traded at the CME Group.

Prices – The S&P 500 index (Barchart.com symbol $SPX) struggled in 2018, finally closing the year down -6.2%. The S&P 500 index in early 2018 extended the rally that began in 2016 to post a new record high but then fell sharply in early 2018 when President Trump imposed tariffs on imported solar panels and washing machines and then later on steel and aluminum as well. Mr. Trump also imposed tariffs on $250 billion of imported Chinese products, leading China to impose retaliatory tariffs on $110 billion of U.S. goods exported to China. However, the stock market weakness from tariffs was short-lived and the S&P 500 index resumed its rise to reach a new record high in September 2018.

The stock market then fell sharply late in 2018 and closed the year lower because of (1) slowing global economic growth, (2) the cumulative effect of the Fed's four interest rate hikes during 2018, (3) the plunge in oil prices in late 2018 that hurt energy stocks, and (4) concern about the ongoing U.S.-Chinese trade war. However, the stock market hit its low in late December and then started to rebound higher as the market anticipated that the Fed would have to halt its rate-hike regime and after President Trump and Chinese President Xi on December 1, 2018 agreed to formal trade talks with a 90-day moratorium on any new tariff hikes.

Stocks were supported during 2018 by very strong earnings growth for the S&P 500 companies of about +24% yr/yr. Earnings growth was boosted mainly by the big tax cut implemented on January 1, 2018. Congress slashed the top U.S. corporate tax rate to 21% from 35%. In addition, Congress forced the repatriation of some of the $2.6 trillion of U.S. corporate cash parked overseas, which was used in part to finance larger stock buyback program and higher dividends.

The U.S. stock market during 2018 was able to largely shake off the negative effects of the Federal Reserve's four interest rate hikes that totaled one percentage point during the year. However, by the end of 2018, stock market investors started to get concerned about the Fed's guidance for three more interest rate hikes in 2019 and a continuation of its balance sheet drawdown program indefinitely, thus leading to the sharp sell-off seen in stocks in late 2018. The stock market was able to recover sharply in early 2019, however, after the Fed shifted to a neutral policy and retracted its guidance for higher interest rates in 2019.

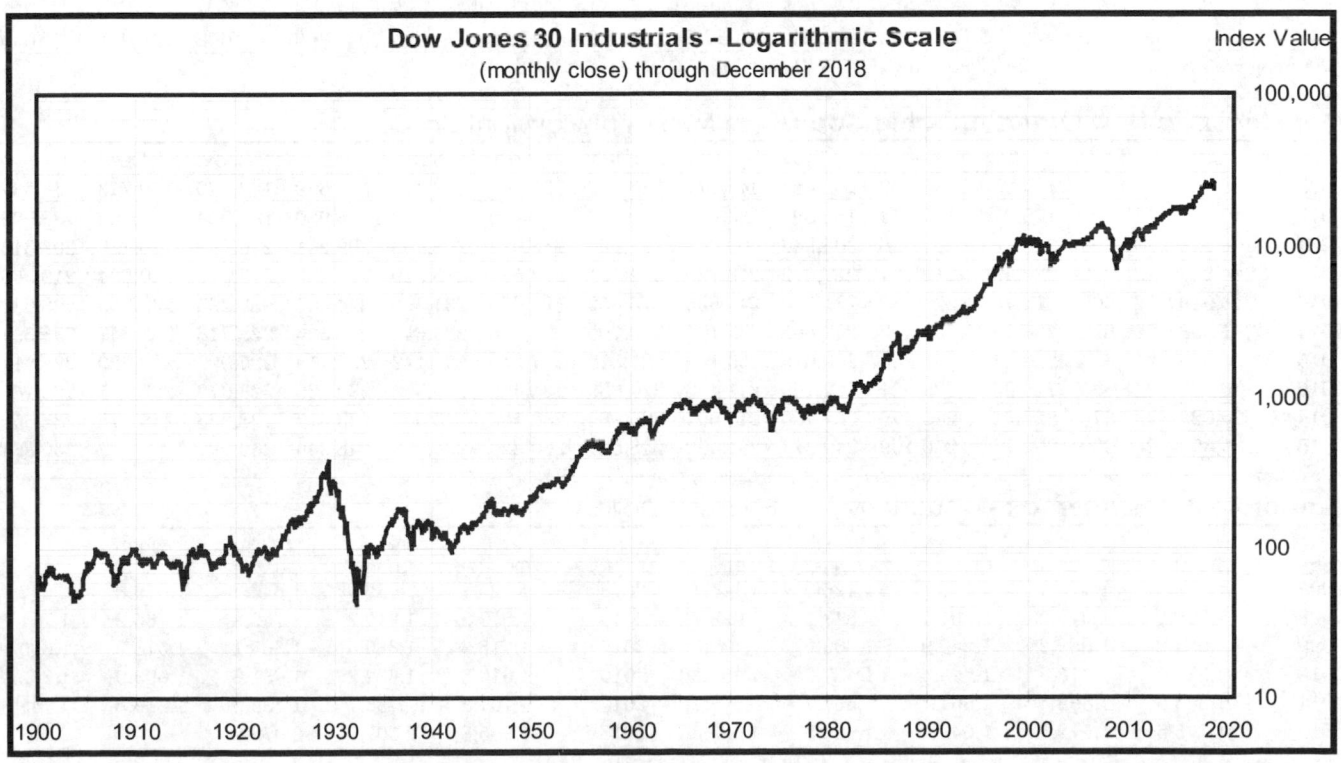

Dow Jones 30 Industrials - Logarithmic Scale
(monthly close) through December 2018

STOCK INDEX FUTURES - U.S.

Composite Index of Leading Indicators   (1992 = 100)

Year	Jan.	Feb.	Mar.	Apr.	May	June	July	Aug.	Sept.	Oct.	Nov.	Dec.	Average
2006	104.7	104.4	104.6	104.4	103.7	103.9	103.7	103.3	103.7	103.9	103.8	104.4	104.0
2007	104.0	103.7	104.1	103.9	104.0	103.9	104.6	103.6	103.7	103.2	102.8	102.6	103.7
2008	102.1	101.9	101.9	102.0	101.9	101.9	101.2	100.3	100.3	99.4	99.0	98.8	100.9
2009	98.8	98.3	98.1	99.2	100.6	101.3	102.5	103.1	104.2	104.7	105.8	106.2	101.9
2010	106.7	107.2	108.6	108.6	109.0	108.8	109.0	109.1	109.9	110.1	111.4	112.3	109.2
2011	91.8	92.7	93.7	93.7	94.2	94.2	94.4	93.7	93.2	93.8	94.1	92.2	93.5
2012	92.2	92.9	93.1	92.9	93.3	92.7	93.1	92.7	93.2	93.4	93.4	94.3	93.1
2013	94.8	95.3	95.1	95.8	96.0	96.1	96.5	97.2	98.2	98.5	99.4	113.8	98.1
2014	113.7	114.3	115.4	115.8	116.5	117.2	118.4	118.5	119.2	119.9	120.5	121.0	117.5
2015[1]	121.2	120.9	121.2	121.9	122.9	123.6	Discontinued						122.0

[1] Preliminary.   Source: The Conference Board

Consumer Confidence, The Conference Board   (2004 = 100)

Year	Jan.	Feb.	Mar.	Apr.	May	June	July	Aug.	Sept.	Oct.	Nov.	Dec.	Average
2006	106.8	102.7	107.5	109.8	104.7	105.4	107.0	100.2	105.9	105.1	105.3	110.0	105.9
2007	110.2	111.2	108.2	106.3	108.5	105.3	111.9	105.6	99.5	95.2	87.8	90.6	103.4
2008	87.3	76.4	65.9	62.8	58.1	51.0	51.9	58.5	61.4	38.8	44.7	38.6	58.0
2009	37.4	25.3	26.9	40.8	54.8	49.3	47.4	54.5	53.4	48.7	50.6	53.6	45.2
2010	56.5	46.4	52.3	57.7	62.7	54.3	51.0	53.2	48.6	49.9	57.8	63.4	54.5
2011	64.8	72.0	63.8	66.0	61.7	57.6	59.2	45.2	46.4	40.9	55.2	64.8	58.1
2012	61.5	71.6	69.5	68.7	64.4	62.7	65.4	61.3	68.4	73.1	71.5	66.7	67.1
2013	58.4	68.0	61.9	69.0	74.3	82.1	81.0	81.8	80.2	72.4	72.0	77.5	73.2
2014	79.4	78.3	83.9	81.7	82.2	86.4	90.3	93.4	89.0	94.1	91.0	93.1	86.9
2015[1]	103.8	98.8	101.4	94.3	94.6	101.4	Discontinued						99.1

[1] Preliminary.   Source: The Conference Board (TCB) Copyrighted.

Capacity Utilization Rates (Total Industry)   In Percent

Year	Jan.	Feb.	Mar.	Apr.	May	June	July	Aug.	Sept.	Oct.	Nov.	Dec.	Average
2009	70.0	69.4	68.3	67.7	67.0	66.7	67.5	68.3	68.9	69.2	69.6	69.9	68.5
2010	70.9	71.3	71.9	72.3	73.5	73.8	74.2	74.6	74.9	74.8	74.9	75.6	73.6
2011	75.6	75.3	76.0	75.7	75.8	76.0	76.3	76.6	76.5	76.9	76.7	77.0	76.2
2012	77.4	77.4	76.9	77.4	77.4	77.2	77.3	76.9	76.8	76.8	77.1	77.2	77.2
2013	77.1	77.4	77.6	77.5	77.4	77.5	77.1	77.6	77.9	77.7	77.9	78.1	77.6
2014	77.6	78.2	78.9	78.9	79.1	79.2	79.2	79.1	79.2	79.1	79.6	79.4	79.0
2015	78.8	78.4	78.1	77.7	77.3	76.9	77.3	77.2	76.9	76.6	76.1	75.7	77.3
2016	76.3	75.7	75.1	75.2	75.0	75.3	75.4	75.3	75.1	75.2	75.0	75.7	75.3
2017	75.4	75.1	75.5	76.2	76.2	76.2	76.1	75.7	75.7	76.8	77.1	77.3	76.1
2018[1]	77.0	77.2	77.5	78.2	77.5	77.8	78.0	78.5	78.5	78.6	78.9	78.8	78.0

[1] Preliminary.   Source: Bureau of Economic Analysis, U.S. Department of Commerce (BEA)

Manufacturers New Orders, Durable Goods   In Millions of Constant Dollars

Year	Jan.	Feb.	Mar.	Apr.	May	June	July	Aug.	Sept.	Oct.	Nov.	Dec.	Average
2009	153,567	146,163	144,350	143,769	150,684	145,217	156,453	158,160	157,770	162,629	162,170	159,713	153,387
2010	182,987	176,497	179,211	187,274	186,393	186,484	190,077	192,410	200,338	194,980	195,734	194,759	188,929
2011	204,128	194,899	210,464	201,736	205,946	200,008	208,990	215,074	208,403	209,201	216,898	226,410	208,513
2012	224,677	224,092	220,496	218,897	217,012	218,729	224,611	202,598	216,919	218,153	218,345	230,294	219,569
2013	216,919	229,202	211,757	220,286	231,193	240,895	215,452	221,749	231,395	224,605	238,295	230,735	226,040
2014	221,898	229,822	233,750	236,290	232,665	238,124	290,709	238,736	235,647	230,525	228,416	223,741	236,694
2015	226,806	219,304	230,337	226,960	220,679	233,102	231,512	227,210	221,142	227,110	225,927	220,920	225,917
2016	226,580	215,886	218,633	229,021	222,159	211,453	220,039	221,425	220,333	233,739	223,079	223,681	222,169
2017	223,020	220,970	227,324	230,479	227,750	244,004	225,984	232,140	243,008	233,017	238,226	245,875	232,650
2018[1]	235,508	246,039	252,760	250,109	249,374	251,499	248,571	260,223	260,178	248,945	250,794		250,364

[1] Preliminary.   Source: Bureau of Economic Analysis, U.S. Department of Commerce (BEA)

Corporate Profits After Tax -- Quarterly   In Billions of Dollars

Year	First Quarter	Second Quarter	Third Quarter	Fourth Quarter	Total	Year	First Quarter	Second Quarter	Third Quarter	Fourth Quarter	Total
2007	1,109.9	1,179.4	1,149.1	1,126.0	1,141.1	2013	1,622.7	1,642.9	1,646.2	1,679.8	1,647.9
2008	1,090.2	1,079.2	1,101.7	847.8	1,029.7	2014	1,577.2	1,710.2	1,792.2	1,766.2	1,711.5
2009	1,082.8	1,088.2	1,249.9	1,309.6	1,182.6	2015	1,716.3	1,680.6	1,665.1	1,578.2	1,660.1
2010	1,386.0	1,378.3	1,523.4	1,537.2	1,456.2	2016	1,610.8	1,632.2	1,631.6	1,693.9	1,642.1
2011	1,384.9	1,506.4	1,561.7	1,661.7	1,528.7	2017	1,707.8	1,733.7	1,735.9	1,816.8	1,748.6
2012	1,705.5	1,672.4	1,643.4	1,628.9	1,662.5	2018[1]	1,965.3	2,007.5	2,076.8		2,016.5

[1] Preliminary.   Source: Bureau of Economic Analysis, U.S. Department of Commerce (BEA)

Change in Manufacturing and Trade Inventories — In Billions of Dollars

Year	Jan.	Feb.	Mar.	Apr.	May	June	July	Aug.	Sept.	Oct.	Nov.	Dec.	Average
2006	85.9	-49.7	129.5	82.7	169.3	169.3	92.2	93.2	65.9	22.9	28.3	4.2	85.2
2007	37.8	43.6	-17.0	59.5	68.1	55.0	75.6	62.7	87.7	23.8	53.3	96.3	53.4
2008	169.4	78.5	35.6	81.4	66.2	133.3	202.6	34.8	-64.9	-99.6		-250.0	35.2
2009	-170.2	-188.5	-232.1	-197.4	-196.7	-218.1	-159.1	-232.5	-46.8	59.8	75.6	-14.9	-126.7
2010	27.9	104.4	95.5	95.3	54.9	136.3	173.2	139.3	179.6	190.5	63.3	173.4	119.5
2011	167.1	129.1	226.8	154.7	184.1	50.0	75.1	114.0	-26.5	158.7	69.4	79.7	115.2
2012	139.9	118.4	47.8	46.5	56.8	27.0	128.1	85.0	118.2	60.8	37.4	33.6	75.0
2013	205.4	30.2	-18.8	66.4	-1.8	17.5	62.3	71.5	117.8	137.2	95.7	82.0	72.1
2014	65.6	74.8	82.9	124.5	104.5	64.6	70.8	32.9	54.1	52.7	20.9	15.3	63.6
2015[1]	-29.5	57.0	25.4	83.8	59.8	Discontinued							39.3

[1] Preliminary. *Source: Bureau of Economic Analysis, U.S. Department of Commerce (BEA)*

Productivity: Index of Output per Hour, All Persons, Nonfarm Business -- Quarterly (1992 = 100)

Year	First Quarter	Second Quarter	Third Quarter	Fourth Quarter	Total	Year	First Quarter	Second Quarter	Third Quarter	Fourth Quarter	Total
2007	90.7	91.1	92.0	92.7	91.7	2013	100.3	100.0	100.5	101.3	100.5
2008	92.0	92.9	93.1	92.5	92.6	2014	100.4	101.2	102.1	101.6	101.3
2009	93.4	95.3	96.8	98.1	95.9	2015	102.3	102.9	103.0	102.3	102.6
2010	98.6	98.9	99.5	99.7	99.2	2016	102.3	102.6	102.9	103.2	102.8
2011	99.0	99.3	98.8	99.5	99.1	2017	103.4	103.8	104.3	104.3	103.9
2012	99.8	100.3	100.1	99.8	100.0	2018[1]	104.3	105.1	105.7		105.0

[1] Preliminary. *Source: Bureau of Economic Analysis, U.S. Department of Commerce (BEA)*

Civilian Unemployment Rate - U3

Year	Jan.	Feb.	Mar.	Apr.	May	June	July	Aug.	Sept.	Oct.	Nov.	Dec.	Average
2009	7.7	8.2	8.6	8.9	9.4	9.5	9.4	9.7	9.8	10.1	10.0	10.0	9.3
2010	9.7	9.8	9.9	9.9	9.6	9.4	9.5	9.5	9.5	9.5	9.8	9.4	9.6
2011	9.1	9.0	9.0	9.1	9.0	9.1	9.0	9.0	9.0	8.8	8.6	8.5	8.9
2012	8.2	8.3	8.2	8.2	8.2	8.2	8.2	8.1	7.8	7.8	7.8	7.9	8.1
2013	7.9	7.7	7.5	7.5	7.5	7.5	7.3	7.2	7.2	7.2	7.0	6.7	7.4
2014	6.6	6.7	6.6	6.2	6.3	6.1	6.2	6.1	5.9	5.7	5.8	5.6	6.2
2015	5.7	5.5	5.4	5.4	5.5	5.3	5.2	5.1	5.0	5.0	5.0	5.0	5.3
2016	4.9	4.9	5.0	5.0	4.7	4.9	4.9	4.9	4.9	4.8	4.6	4.7	4.9
2017	4.8	4.7	4.5	4.4	4.3	4.4	4.3	4.4	4.2	4.1	4.1	4.1	4.4
2018[1]	4.1	4.1	4.1	3.9	3.8	4.0	3.9	3.8	3.7	3.8	3.7	3.9	3.9

[1] Preliminary. *Source: Bureau of Economic Analysis, U.S. Department of Commerce (BEA)*

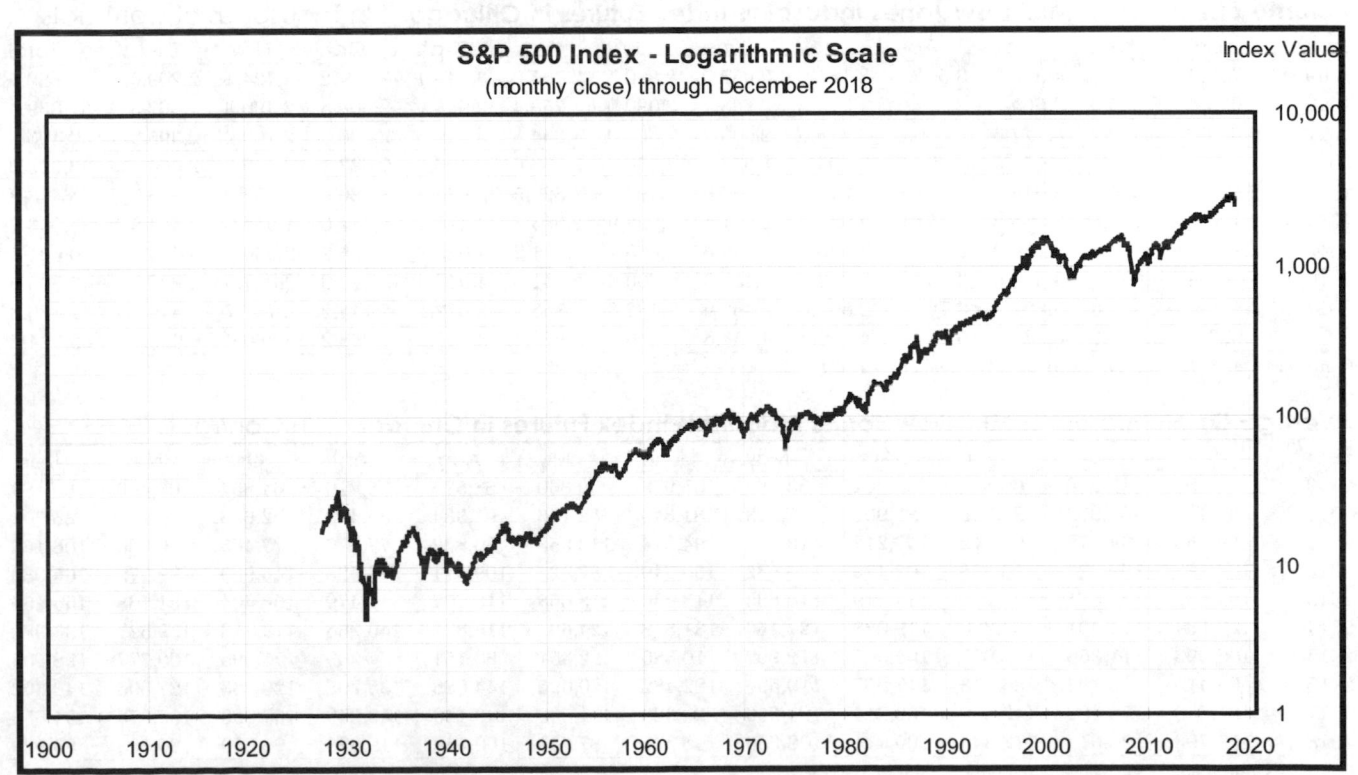

S&P 500 Index - Logarithmic Scale
(monthly close) through December 2018

STOCK INDEX FUTURES - U.S.

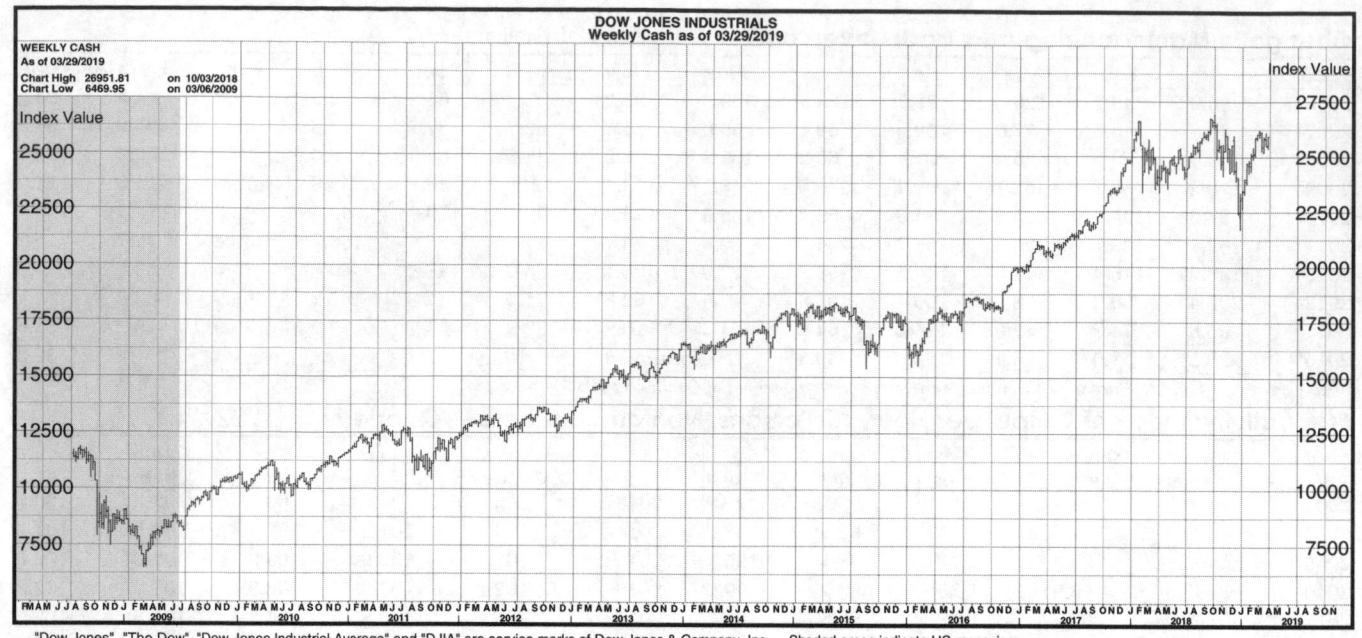

"Dow Jones", "The Dow", "Dow Jones Industrial Average" and "DJIA" are service marks of Dow Jones & Company, Inc.   Shaded areas indicate US recessions.

Average Value of Dow Jones Industrials Index (30 Stocks)

Year	Jan.	Feb.	Mar.	Apr.	May	June	July	Aug.	Sept.	Oct.	Nov.	Dec.	Average
2009	8,396.2	7,690.5	7,235.5	7,992.1	8,398.4	8,593.0	8,679.8	9,375.1	9,635.0	9,857.3	10,227.6	10,433.4	8,876.1
2010	10,471.2	1,021.5	10,677.5	11,052.2	10,500.2	10,159.3	10,222.2	10,350.4	10,598.1	11,044.5	11,198.6	11,465.3	9,896.7
2011	11,802.4	12,190.0	12,081.5	12,434.9	12,580.0	12,097.3	12,512.3	11,326.6	11,175.5	11,515.9	11,804.2	12,075.7	11,966.4
2012	12,550.9	12,889.1	13,079.5	13,030.8	12,721.1	12,544.9	12,814.1	13,134.9	13,418.5	13,380.7	12,896.4	13,144.2	12,967.1
2013	13,615.3	13,967.3	14,418.3	14,675.9	15,172.2	15,035.8	15,390.2	15,195.3	15,269.8	15,289.8	15,870.8	16,095.8	14,999.7
2014	16,243.6	15,958.4	16,308.6	16,399.5	16,567.3	16,843.8	16,988.3	16,775.2	17,098.1	16,701.9	17,649.0	17,754.2	16,774.0
2015	17,542.3	17,945.4	17,931.7	17,970.5	18,124.7	17,927.2	17,795.0	17,061.6	16,340.0	17,182.3	17,723.8	17,542.9	17,590.6
2016	16,305.3	16,299.9	17,302.1	17,844.4	17,692.3	17,754.9	18,341.2	18,495.2	18,267.4	18,184.6	18,697.3	19,712.4	17,908.1
2017	19,908.2	20,424.1	20,823.1	20,684.7	20,936.8	21,317.8	21,581.3	21,914.1	22,173.4	23,036.2	23,557.9	24,545.4	21,741.9
2018	25,804.0	24,981.5	24,582.2	24,304.2	24,572.5	24,790.1	24,978.2	25,630.0	26,232.7	25,609.3	25,258.7	23,805.5	25,045.8

Source: New York Stock Exchange (NYSE)

Volume of Trading of Mini Dow Jones Industrials Index Futures in Chicago   In Thousands of Contracts

Year	Jan.	Feb.	Mar.	Apr.	May	June	July	Aug.	Sept.	Oct.	Nov.	Dec.	Total
2009	3,707.9	4,164.2	4,915.8	3,595.5	3,161.6	3,052.0	2,830.5	2,795.0	3,249.1	3,434.2	2,724.1	2,260.0	39,889.8
2010	2,610.4	2,565.0	2,664.0	2,684.3	4,019.8	3,688.7	3,090.0	2,758.4	2,958.0	2,668.3	2,490.3	1,862.3	34,059.5
2011	2,086.5	2,020.2	3,177.6	1,830.8	2,475.5	2,990.4	2,367.0	4,344.6	3,249.6	2,790.5	2,769.2	2,395.0	32,496.9
2012	1,873.4	2,057.1	2,582.9	2,398.8	3,488.5	3,359.7	2,570.8	2,236.0	2,406.3	2,623.1	2,745.3	2,560.3	30,902.0
2013	2,143.3	2,525.2	3,044.9	3,417.8	3,212.1	4,386.6	2,492.1	2,820.5	2,934.8	3,480.8	2,494.0	2,496.7	35,448.8
2014	3,180.8	3,115.6	3,965.0	3,351.6	2,637.7	2,641.1	3,028.9	2,683.7	3,476.0	5,444.0	1,954.8	3,574.5	39,053.7
2015	4,146.7	2,343.8	3,126.0	2,988.1	2,558.3	3,546.6	3,063.7	4,651.2	4,649.7	3,226.2	2,566.1	3,734.5	40,601.1
2016	5,169.8	4,307.1	3,300.6	3,164.9	3,083.4	4,152.0	2,600.0	2,641.6	4,047.4	3,274.0	3,887.6	2,927.5	42,555.9
2017	2,515.6	2,343.6	3,891.9	2,722.0	2,564.0	3,465.6	2,132.3	2,858.2	2,672.1	2,144.2	2,707.7	2,849.1	32,866.3
2018	3,623.3	6,592.1	6,939.8	5,479.4	4,405.7	4,558.5	3,310.8	2,989.4	3,521.3	7,088.2	4,886.0	6,929.7	60,324.2

Contract value = $5.   *Source: Chicago Board of Trade (CBT)*

Average Open Interest of Mini Dow Jones Industrials Index Futures in Chicago   In Contracts

Year	Jan.	Feb.	Mar.	Apr.	May	June	July	Aug.	Sept.	Oct.	Nov.	Dec.
2009	65,403	75,276	65,501	52,362	53,660	55,979	59,860	68,575	75,719	64,854	66,490	69,164
2010	66,488	66,853	85,812	85,906	77,273	81,840	82,146	91,334	88,463	92,636	100,170	86,604
2011	89,055	94,278	97,112	117,217	113,517	94,274	113,353	86,802	77,776	77,465	86,666	106,153
2012	102,192	109,321	116,358	102,473	103,582	100,349	87,422	109,011	128,525	115,960	99,172	105,089
2013	104,630	122,311	131,290	114,419	118,633	113,230	113,658	115,707	119,479	106,434	131,168	134,255
2014	127,534	114,491	134,383	119,028	127,150	131,818	124,601	115,822	140,265	119,716	139,521	135,980
2015	106,993	111,350	109,677	104,565	112,992	110,880	92,351	93,151	77,209	75,595	100,777	98,535
2016	65,416	62,194	83,643	117,857	119,596	122,482	120,095	144,885	135,208	120,288	127,896	140,802
2017	131,853	130,492	145,630	130,214	121,956	129,328	131,569	149,149	159,249	157,990	155,973	154,854
2018	153,793	126,347	118,343	100,414	102,356	96,326	87,601	100,558	112,896	95,850	80,908	80,929

Contract value = $5.   *Source: Chicago Board of Trade (CBT)*

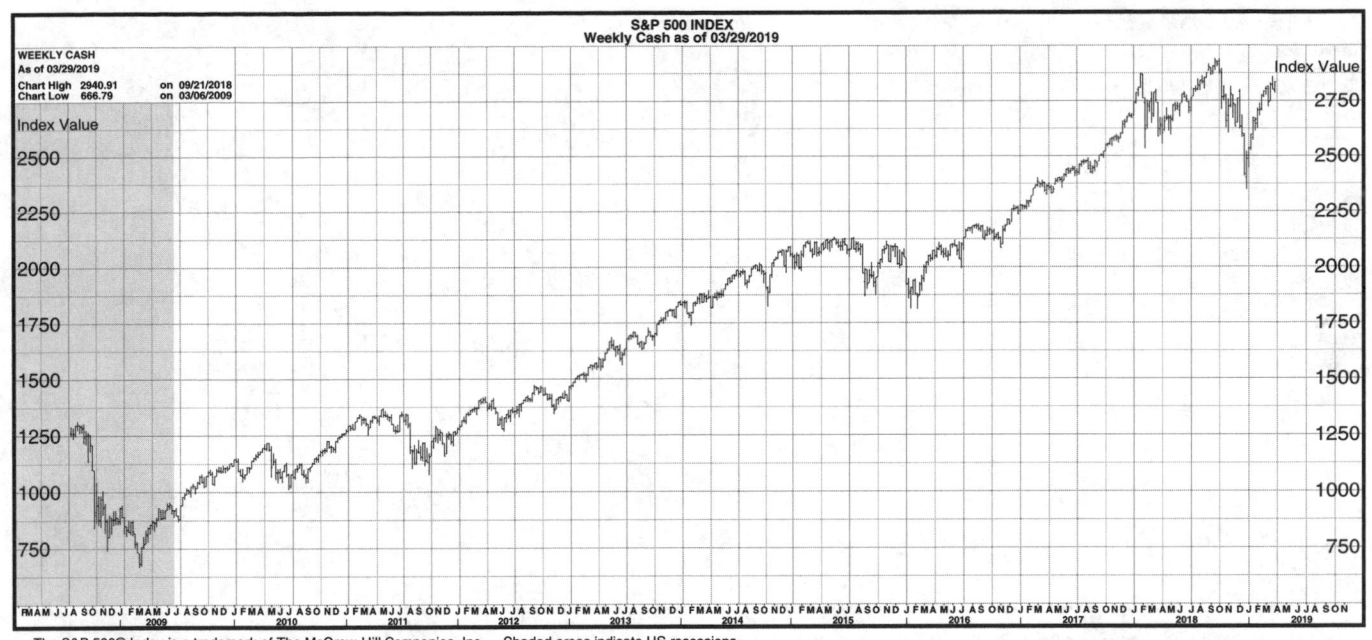

The S&P 500® Index is a trademark of The McGraw-Hill Companies, Inc.   Shaded areas indicate US recessions.

Average Value of Standard & Poor's 500 Index

Year	Jan.	Feb.	Mar.	Apr.	May	June	July	Aug.	Sept.	Oct.	Nov.	Dec.	Average
2009	865.6	805.2	757.1	848.2	902.4	926.1	935.8	1,009.7	1,044.6	1,067.7	1,088.1	1,110.4	946.7
2010	1,123.6	1,089.2	1,152.1	1,197.3	1,125.1	1,083.4	1,079.8	1,087.3	1,122.1	1,171.6	1,198.9	1,241.5	1,139.3
2011	1,282.6	1,321.1	1,304.5	1,331.5	1,338.3	1,287.3	1,325.2	1,185.3	1,173.9	1,207.2	1,226.4	1,243.3	1,268.9
2012	1,300.6	1,352.5	1,389.2	1,386.4	1,341.3	1,323.5	1,359.8	1,403.5	1,443.4	1,437.8	1,394.5	1,422.3	1,379.6
2013	1,480.4	1,512.3	1,550.8	1,570.7	1,639.8	1,618.8	1,668.7	1,670.1	1,687.2	1,720.1	1,783.5	1,807.8	1,642.5
2014	1,822.4	1,817.0	1,863.5	1,864.3	1,889.8	1,947.1	1,973.1	1,961.5	1,993.2	1,937.3	2,044.6	2,054.3	1,930.7
2015	2,028.2	2,082.2	2,080.0	2,094.9	2,111.9	2,099.3	2,094.1	2,039.9	1,944.4	2,024.8	2,080.6	2,054.1	2,061.2
2016	1,918.6	1,904.4	2,022.0	2,075.5	2,065.6	2,083.9	2,148.9	2,177.5	2,157.7	2,143.0	2,165.0	2,246.6	2,092.4
2017	2,275.1	2,329.9	2,366.8	2,359.3	2,395.4	2,434.0	2,454.1	2,456.2	2,492.8	2,557.0	2,593.6	2,664.3	2,448.2
2018	2,789.8	2,705.2	2,702.8	2,653.6	2,701.5	2,754.4	2,793.6	2,857.8	2,901.5	2,785.5	2,723.2	2,567.3	2,744.7

Source: Index and Option Market (IOM), division of the Chicago Mercantile Exchange (CME)

Volume of Trading of E-mini S&P 500 Stock Index Futures in Chicago   In Thousands of Contracts

Year	Jan.	Feb.	Mar.	Apr.	May	June	July	Aug.	Sept.	Oct.	Nov.	Dec.	Total
2009	45,814	49,498	69,321	49,293	46,060	48,779	42,273	38,448	46,864	46,352	36,951	36,662	556,314
2010	40,765	42,986	46,644	43,563	64,388	61,258	44,454	42,196	46,366	41,921	45,468	35,320	555,329
2011	38,684	36,320	60,440	32,705	43,114	59,180	43,083	82,693	71,646	55,044	51,593	45,850	620,369
2012	34,720	32,505	44,161	35,956	47,447	54,942	38,614	33,377	38,685	36,912	39,528	37,433	474,279
2013	30,743	35,953	43,787	41,242	41,901	52,896	29,323	34,906	39,752	39,069	28,689	34,028	452,291
2014	33,770	33,265	43,038	34,460	27,653	33,330	33,263	28,020	40,843	54,465	22,223	40,690	425,020
2015	38,362	25,643	38,949	26,801	24,516	39,037	32,990	46,325	48,962	36,264	28,643	43,312	429,803
2016	47,987	42,532	44,628	34,639	33,049	48,583	31,172	33,429	49,729	32,532	38,250	36,148	472,679
2017	28,663	26,871	43,248	27,397	28,105	40,315	22,213	32,605	33,473	24,444	27,662	30,604	365,602
2018	29,153	42,946	47,450	35,694	28,915	35,955	23,295	25,086	33,325	53,156	37,153	53,071	445,199

Contract value = $50.   Source: Index and Option Market (IOM), division of the Chicago Mercantile Exchange (CME)

Average Open Interest of E-mini S&P 500 Stock Index Futures in Chicago   In Thousands of Contracts

Year	Jan.	Feb.	Mar.	Apr.	May	June	July	Aug.	Sept.	Oct.	Nov.	Dec.
2009	2,512.9	2,896.4	3,123.3	2,489.2	2,680.4	2,690.2	2,429.6	2,622.9	2,582.3	2,397.1	2,593.6	2,688.5
2010	2,510.1	2,808.4	2,866.0	2,468.7	2,680.5	2,937.2	2,797.2	2,839.5	2,872.0	2,668.2	2,810.5	2,826.7
2011	2,581.7	2,829.5	2,960.3	2,704.1	2,762.3	2,887.0	2,578.6	3,318.6	3,424.6	3,008.7	2,955.1	2,903.6
2012	2,651.8	2,769.8	2,904.4	2,797.2	2,949.5	2,964.8	2,799.8	2,945.7	3,182.3	2,951.7	3,088.0	3,116.6
2013	2,872.7	3,117.0	3,199.6	3,038.9	3,279.6	3,245.5	2,778.0	2,910.8	2,954.2	2,717.7	2,848.0	2,973.0
2014	2,865.8	3,123.2	3,283.5	2,800.4	2,949.6	3,160.0	2,946.3	2,985.7	3,153.2	2,821.8	2,990.2	3,025.6
2015	2,724.4	2,820.5	3,000.4	2,707.2	2,776.2	2,863.5	2,672.8	2,893.6	3,179.8	2,921.9	2,889.2	2,801.6
2016	2,792.2	3,072.3	3,109.5	2,863.7	2,884.5	3,056.9	2,971.7	2,971.2	3,115.3	2,960.2	2,985.0	2,989.9
2017	2,833.2	2,991.5	3,112.3	2,905.0	3,049.8	3,062.1	2,924.0	3,192.3	3,279.6	3,104.8	3,293.9	3,348.8
2018	3,310.8	3,366.2	3,200.3	3,017.3	3,081.8	2,985.4	2,745.8	2,833.8	2,950.5	2,887.7	2,993.6	3,024.4

Contract value = $50.   Source: Index and Option Market (IOM), division of the Chicago Mercantile Exchange (CME)

STOCK INDEX FUTURES - U.S.

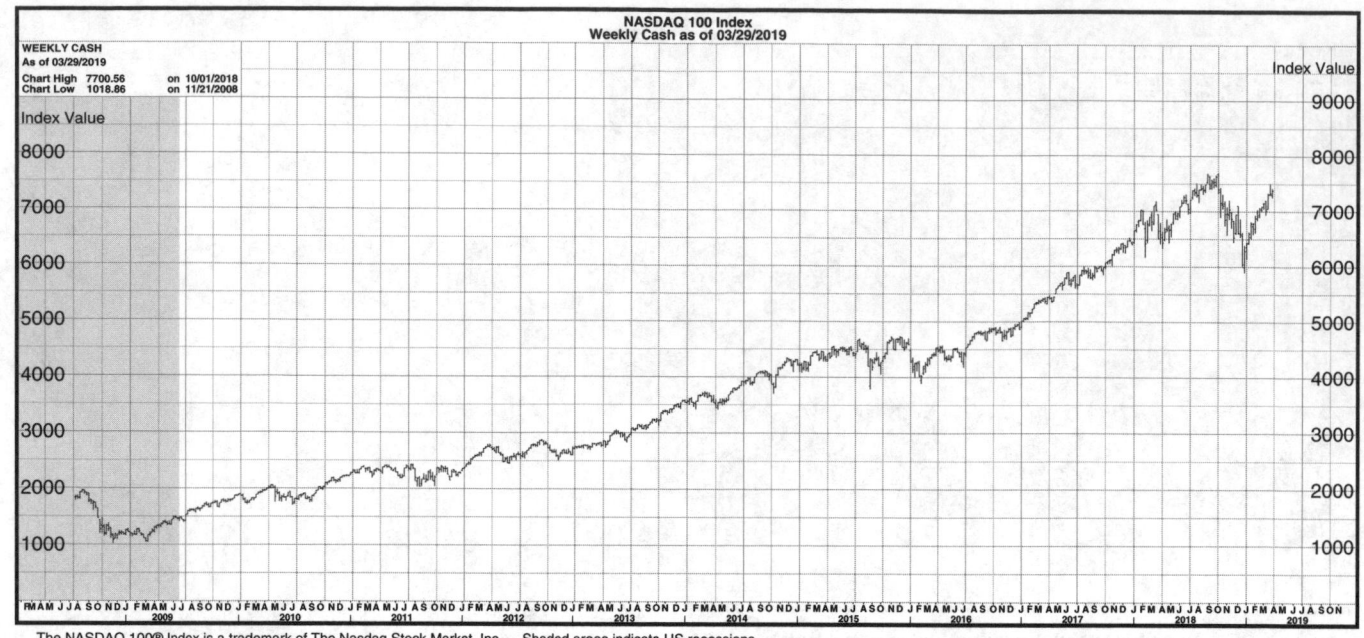

NASDAQ 100 Index
Weekly Cash as of 03/29/2019

WEEKLY CASH
As of 03/29/2019
Chart High 7700.56 on 10/01/2018
Chart Low 1018.86 on 11/21/2008

The NASDAQ 100® Index is a trademark of The Nasdaq Stock Market, Inc.   Shaded areas indicate US recessions.

Average Value of NASDAQ 100 Index

Year	Jan.	Feb.	Mar.	Apr.	May	June	July	Aug.	Sept.	Oct.	Nov.	Dec.	Average
2009	1,206.5	1,199.4	1,167.3	1,332.2	1,393.5	1,472.2	1,515.8	1,618.0	1,688.0	1,722.1	1,761.8	1,816.5	1,491.1
2010	1,850.2	1,784.7	1,920.6	2,011.0	1,892.7	1,847.2	1,827.2	1,839.1	1,939.9	2,066.0	2,148.4	2,211.4	1,944.9
2011	2,291.2	2,353.4	2,298.7	2,344.1	2,364.6	2,255.1	2,379.5	2,173.8	2,224.5	2,298.7	2,291.8	2,279.2	2,296.2
2012	2,404.3	2,567.0	2,699.0	2,716.1	2,589.0	2,549.9	2,605.7	2,739.1	2,820.9	2,735.9	2,616.6	2,658.8	2,641.9
2013	2,736.9	2,748.2	2,795.3	2,818.6	2,981.2	2,937.3	3,033.0	3,105.5	3,187.5	3,292.0	3,399.5	3,513.8	3,045.7
2014	3,557.9	3,615.0	3,661.1	3,554.5	3,621.1	3,792.1	3,926.7	3,979.4	4,070.3	3,964.6	4,221.1	4,260.8	3,852.0
2015	4,182.6	4,343.5	4,389.2	4,418.9	4,476.4	4,481.7	4,528.3	4,422.3	4,261.6	4,445.5	4,653.2	4,628.0	4,435.9
2016	4,259.3	4,129.6	4,377.1	4,491.9	4,379.4	4,427.0	4,592.6	4,785.7	4,813.3	4,845.3	4,791.8	4,886.3	4,564.9
2017	5,056.8	5,261.2	5,386.2	5,447.9	5,687.4	5,767.0	5,816.1	5,874.4	5,954.9	6,088.5	6,328.2	6,398.0	5,755.5
2018	6,790.5	6,704.4	6,844.9	6,606.9	6,875.9	7,159.6	7,296.6	7,453.1	7,528.0	7,171.6	6,855.0	6,498.0	6,982.0

Source: Index and Option Market (IOM), division of the Chicago Mercantile Exchange (CME)

Volume of Trading of E-mini NASDAQ 100 Index Futures in Chicago   In Thousands of Contracts

Year	Jan.	Feb.	Mar.	Apr.	May	June	July	Aug.	Sept.	Oct.	Nov.	Dec.	Total
2009	5,713.2	6,789.4	8,800.1	6,383.4	6,240.6	6,721.8	6,243.3	5,958.8	6,808.0	7,048.1	5,686.2	5,579.4	77,972.1
2010	6,711.7	6,179.6	6,447.8	5,937.9	8,666.0	8,054.5	6,905.1	6,619.3	7,365.6	6,249.0	5,996.6	4,504.7	79,637.7
2011	4,986.1	4,764.0	8,138.5	4,912.7	5,944.0	6,778.1	5,276.4	8,884.3	8,034.8	6,813.7	5,807.2	4,825.6	75,165.3
2012	3,623.4	4,274.5	6,068.6	5,655.0	6,428.6	6,100.5	4,852.6	4,448.9	5,148.7	5,578.6	5,845.3	5,506.0	63,530.8
2013	4,420.0	4,365.7	4,911.6	5,226.0	4,549.5	6,411.2	4,222.9	4,686.9	5,210.9	6,077.2	4,280.9	5,030.3	59,393.1
2014	5,641.0	5,236.1	7,514.0	7,765.8	5,541.1	5,252.7	5,305.9	4,774.4	7,103.7	10,105.5	4,013.9	7,229.6	75,483.7
2015	6,833.3	3,985.2	6,094.0	4,617.1	3,880.7	5,542.4	5,100.7	7,432.1	7,310.1	5,782.1	4,431.2	6,301.3	67,310.3
2016	8,223.6	6,818.4	5,768.6	5,007.9	4,813.8	6,045.0	3,857.8	4,059.2	6,567.4	4,716.0	5,396.7	4,476.2	65,750.5
2017	3,626.6	3,403.0	5,698.7	4,376.9	5,129.1	9,012.5	5,528.7	7,491.5	6,785.4	5,498.9	6,481.7	6,526.1	69,559.1
2018	7,000.4	10,100.0	12,243.8	10,030.7	7,692.8	8,400.0	7,283.8	7,592.7	9,416.3	16,684.0	13,094.0	14,657.0	124,195.5

Contract value = $20.   *Source: Index and Option Market (IOM), division of the Chicago Mercantile Exchange (CME)*

Average Open Interest of E-mini NASDAQ 100 Index Futures in Chicago   In Contracts

Year	Jan.	Feb.	Mar.	Apr.	May	June	July	Aug.	Sept.	Oct.	Nov.	Dec.
2009	245,830	281,273	302,750	256,064	286,754	284,962	272,424	332,576	341,802	321,653	329,991	338,692
2010	338,217	402,622	362,520	329,709	353,999	353,720	316,651	349,380	397,910	441,782	442,146	401,214
2011	367,204	361,772	350,534	351,601	370,994	321,623	346,518	350,282	369,902	321,427	325,938	308,063
2012	335,164	435,422	484,224	435,734	402,222	376,770	354,698	422,296	480,174	390,199	382,542	380,507
2013	313,000	337,571	376,894	365,878	419,450	381,375	361,111	391,874	393,462	380,763	406,143	439,961
2014	427,403	428,404	452,936	352,802	355,239	383,300	365,320	359,978	399,636	349,013	357,410	376,694
2015	314,070	325,766	352,413	335,425	322,640	342,629	327,815	337,292	287,155	285,539	348,170	334,859
2016	287,540	269,926	244,045	227,743	227,844	237,463	242,541	295,495	301,601	303,400	269,558	247,601
2017	224,988	233,695	249,237	256,682	273,541	324,978	286,106	295,726	292,471	278,159	286,310	306,756
2018	264,915	239,065	250,925	242,489	243,195	251,523	243,189	244,958	268,030	250,113	245,902	240,458

Contract value = $20.   *Source: Index and Option Market (IOM), division of the Chicago Mercantile Exchange (CME)*

Average Value of Dow Jones Transportation Index (20 Stocks)

Year	Jan.	Feb.	Mar.	Apr.	May	June	July	Aug.	Sept.	Oct.	Nov.	Dec.	Average
2009	3,238.3	2,857.3	2,499.9	2,986.8	3,163.7	3,266.6	3,321.5	3,697.2	3,863.1	3,844.4	3,915.2	4,117.2	3,397.6
2010	4,119.6	3,971.7	4,308.5	4,597.7	4,427.6	4,259.5	4,217.9	4,280.6	4,439.9	4,670.6	4,846.8	5,067.4	4,434.0
2011	5,135.4	5,130.2	5,110.7	5,319.1	5,431.5	5,212.9	5,395.0	4,569.8	4,420.8	4,628.8	4,820.8	4,943.3	5,009.8
2012	5,206.5	5,245.1	5,225.4	5,239.7	5,121.6	5,050.9	5,117.2	5,088.7	5,038.1	5,041.0	5,056.3	5,218.7	5,137.4
2013	5,665.7	5,908.1	6,167.2	6,073.4	6,370.3	6,225.1	6,420.2	6,438.7	6,555.1	6,767.9	7,131.0	7,220.9	6,412.0
2014	7,361.9	7,235.3	7,512.0	7,587.8	7,854.6	8,135.4	8,308.7	8,272.8	8,534.2	8,308.9	9,033.8	9,025.7	8,097.6
2015	8,853.6	9,005.2	8,942.9	8,725.1	8,592.8	8,361.0	8,214.8	8,134.2	7,929.8	8,117.2	8,174.0	7,658.2	8,392.4
2016	6,871.7	7,133.1	7,771.2	7,919.7	7,700.9	7,615.7	7,817.1	7,845.3	7,913.3	8,054.3	8,622.5	9,207.6	7,872.7
2017	9,192.9	9,368.9	9,184.5	9,096.5	9,058.9	9,382.3	9,542.7	9,208.8	9,573.3	9,901.8	9,665.7	10,463.4	9,470.0
2018	11,106.0	10,471.7	10,477.7	10,427.8	10,631.9	10,795.0	10,663.5	11,220.3	11,443.3	10,604.3	10,507.1	9,544.1	10,657.7

Source: New York Stock Exchange (NYSE)

Average Value of Dow Jones Utilities Index (15 Stocks)

Year	Jan.	Feb.	Mar.	Apr.	May	June	July	Aug.	Sept.	Oct.	Nov.	Dec.	Average
2009	371.3	356.3	315.8	331.6	339.3	350.6	361.4	373.3	376.0	375.6	373.4	398.9	360.3
2010	393.8	371.9	378.1	384.3	372.7	366.9	379.8	389.8	396.6	404.8	400.5	400.8	386.7
2011	410.1	411.9	409.9	416.5	434.8	427.0	435.3	419.9	431.7	439.9	443.0	451.5	427.6
2012	451.0	451.3	454.8	459.4	467.9	475.6	485.0	479.3	471.5	479.2	449.7	453.9	464.9
2013	463.6	474.7	493.1	522.2	511.0	481.1	496.7	490.3	480.7	492.3	499.5	485.4	490.9
2014	491.9	513.0	519.8	540.7	540.0	556.0	557.5	547.2	555.3	569.2	596.5	609.7	549.7
2015	634.5	610.4	582.6	589.7	584.5	564.1	570.8	587.1	558.1	588.0	566.9	567.7	583.7
2016	585.1	621.9	649.2	655.4	657.7	682.6	712.9	686.2	676.4	654.6	642.6	650.1	656.2
2017	658.2	674.0	696.8	703.8	705.4	726.4	712.0	738.2	736.9	740.9	760.2	742.3	716.3
2018	694.2	671.0	679.0	693.4	687.0	683.9	719.6	729.3	729.1	734.2	730.9	734.5	707.2

Source: New York Stock Exchange (NYSE)

Average Value of Standard & Poor's MidCap 400 Index

Year	Jan.	Feb.	Mar.	Apr.	May	June	July	Aug.	Sept.	Oct.	Nov.	Dec.	Average
2009	519.6	488.7	457.9	532.0	565.8	582.8	588.6	649.3	680.6	692.7	690.4	715.4	597.0
2010	737.0	720.5	781.4	823.8	779.1	749.4	741.9	745.8	778.1	817.3	849.5	898.5	785.2
2011	921.6	959.0	959.6	991.0	990.7	950.8	980.4	843.9	829.1	841.9	867.8	872.2	917.3
2012	917.3	975.0	988.8	978.7	949.4	915.3	939.9	962.7	1,001.1	986.0	979.7	1,010.8	967.1
2013	1,070.4	1,104.0	1,132.3	1,133.9	1,188.1	1,163.1	1,214.3	1,221.6	1,230.2	1,270.6	1,297.6	1,311.4	1,194.8
2014	1,333.5	1,333.4	1,373.9	1,355.0	1,361.6	1,410.5	1,413.6	1,402.5	1,415.2	1,351.5	1,435.2	1,438.2	1,385.3
2015	1,440.1	1,493.5	1,509.4	1,527.7	1,525.0	1,528.8	1,499.9	1,463.3	1,399.8	1,427.8	1,449.2	1,413.6	1,473.2
2016	1,299.3	1,296.5	1,408.0	1,456.5	1,458.3	1,489.2	1,534.0	1,559.7	1,546.7	1,526.0	1,571.6	1,668.8	1,484.5
2017	1,684.1	1,720.7	1,715.5	1,715.7	1,724.7	1,749.1	1,763.1	1,722.3	1,754.8	1,822.3	1,845.6	1,892.9	1,759.2
2018	1,959.7	1,876.7	1,902.7	1,886.0	1,930.2	1,981.1	1,988.5	2,016.0	2,032.4	1,892.6	1,859.1	1,715.6	1,920.0

Source: Index and Option Market (IOM), division of the Chicago Mercantile Exchange (CME)

Civilian Unemployment Rate - U6

Year	Jan.	Feb.	Mar.	Apr.	May	June	July	Aug.	Sept.	Oct.	Nov.	Dec.	Average
2009	14.0	15.0	15.6	15.8	16.4	16.5	16.4	16.8	17.0	17.4	17.2	17.3	16.3
2010	16.5	16.8	16.9	17.1	16.6	16.5	16.5	16.7	17.1	17.0	17.0	16.7	16.8
2011	16.1	15.9	15.7	15.9	15.8	16.2	16.1	16.2	16.5	16.2	15.6	15.2	16.0
2012	15.1	15.0	14.5	14.5	14.8	14.8	14.9	14.7	14.7	14.5	14.4	14.4	14.7
2013	14.4	14.3	13.8	13.9	13.8	14.3	14.0	13.6	13.6	13.7	13.1	13.1	13.8
2014	12.7	12.6	12.7	12.3	12.2	12.1	12.2	12.0	11.7	11.5	11.4	11.2	12.1
2015	11.3	11.0	10.9	10.8	10.8	10.5	10.4	10.3	10.0	9.8	9.9	9.9	10.5
2016	9.9	9.7	9.8	9.7	9.7	9.6	9.7	9.7	9.7	9.5	9.3	9.2	9.6
2017	9.4	9.2	8.9	8.6	8.4	8.6	8.6	8.6	8.3	7.9	8.0	8.1	8.6
2018[1]	8.2	8.2	8.0	7.8	7.6	7.8	7.5	7.4	7.5	7.4	7.6	7.6	7.7

The U6 unemployment rate counts not only people without work seeking full-time employment (the more familiar U-3 rate), but also counts "marginally attached workers and those working part-time for economic reasons." Note that some of these part-time workers counted as employed by U-3 could be working as little as an hour a week. And the "marginally attached workers" include those who have gotten discouraged and stopped looking, but still want to work. The age considered for this calculation is 16 years and over.

[1] Preliminary.   Source: Bureau of Economic Analysis, U.S. Department of Commerce (BEA)

STOCK INDEX FUTURES - U.S.

Volume of Trading of S&P 500 Index Futures in Chicago   In Contracts

Year	Jan.	Feb.	Mar.	Apr.	May	June	July	Aug.	Sept.	Oct.	Nov.	Dec.	Total
2009	674,413	744,280	2,026,304	555,285	534,711	1,637,512	453,521	427,329	1,338,260	473,281	384,606	1,186,410	10,435,912
2010	403,627	432,016	1,084,473	363,465	650,746	1,195,283	412,661	433,120	1,027,932	296,761	415,770	974,107	7,689,961
2011	321,230	330,793	1,161,950	306,622	309,799	1,027,261	283,409	713,632	1,124,309	389,089	394,757	857,769	7,220,620
2012	228,210	222,899	812,486	232,960	301,759	818,852	243,463	247,857	729,728	192,426	257,122	744,888	5,032,650
2013	263,398	248,841	699,646	203,842	232,649	693,771	151,373	190,394	584,401	186,798	136,416	564,970	4,156,499
2014	200,461	192,965	525,447	137,151	145,735	500,052	135,986	118,435	518,784	229,310	152,715	530,699	3,387,740
2015	200,265	109,971	521,653	132,407	134,537	455,419	131,114	218,785	465,263	145,559	134,391	382,196	3,031,560
2016	177,856	168,307	332,830	116,852	98,936	336,958	100,807	94,459	311,370	101,081	111,981	286,440	2,237,877
2017	110,481	99,344	255,028	77,484	97,315	207,957	52,266	80,197	190,828	65,559	78,261	194,543	1,509,263
2018	93,762	173,394	235,765	136,742	108,631	157,986	98,813	62,472	217,043	127,769	98,505	143,941	1,654,823

Contract value = $250.   Source: Index and Option Market (IOM), division of the Chicago Mercantile Exchange (CME)

Average Open Interest of S&P 500 Index Futures in Chicago   In Contracts

Year	Jan.	Feb.	Mar.	Apr.	May	June	July	Aug.	Sept.	Oct.	Nov.	Dec.
2009	518,589	583,132	566,284	439,705	467,060	456,209	391,596	393,499	400,489	386,593	398,242	379,761
2010	334,063	379,277	384,532	320,130	323,367	354,304	308,220	320,409	327,551	314,245	352,215	341,358
2011	295,221	328,406	351,308	312,007	326,135	314,542	277,586	351,944	367,322	292,018	295,609	285,435
2012	247,547	249,536	248,980	234,595	260,383	266,290	236,315	235,725	225,849	199,981	217,709	215,589
2013	193,514	217,014	202,882	169,581	189,144	203,898	162,175	170,134	196,824	159,233	167,647	168,253
2014	150,125	197,844	198,079	126,277	142,806	163,129	144,257	161,528	165,415	142,572	149,630	146,618
2015	130,204	146,778	154,302	112,920	126,006	132,006	106,046	127,294	149,564	104,817	103,028	97,764
2016	104,123	134,488	109,898	73,227	77,419	84,363	93,313	95,738	84,687	77,392	87,557	76,983
2017	63,927	74,879	72,959	58,118	74,418	59,727	49,623	63,689	57,097	54,499	70,733	68,740
2018	62,941	79,712	64,362	75,398	101,975	84,641	60,976	66,560	57,264	47,401	57,130	56,018

Contract value = $250.   Source: Index and Option Market (IOM), division of the Chicago Mercantile Exchange (CME)

Volume of Trading of E-mini S&P 400 Index Futures in Chicago   In Contracts

Year	Jan.	Feb.	Mar.	Apr.	May	June	July	Aug.	Sept.	Oct.	Nov.	Dec.	Total
2009	638,571	639,126	1,040,605	715,017	672,835	855,038	609,479	654,219	963,292	921,161	691,942	731,938	9,133,223
2010	575,430	529,499	749,214	556,649	771,715	870,496	612,694	575,424	829,573	526,247	476,898	583,533	7,657,372
2011	421,293	362,478	797,744	427,817	519,082	768,346	407,619	937,031	976,312	687,489	628,695	755,400	7,689,306
2012	408,514	411,301	751,336	513,459	613,049	820,825	494,705	410,688	615,845	453,404	431,072	612,709	6,536,907
2013	309,335	334,867	582,358	434,406	403,614	726,068	369,807	400,705	622,836	478,458	338,633	600,460	5,601,547
2014	369,537	360,548	604,474	385,135	334,222	500,963	343,309	283,606	618,774	648,830	242,848	593,469	5,285,715
2015	414,909	332,866	599,168	325,498	293,658	554,697	369,498	498,662	649,465	402,087	332,728	607,797	5,381,033
2016	529,519	442,219	633,841	325,445	347,829	654,024	305,479	313,218	626,528	336,632	352,772	538,251	5,405,757
2017	356,153	255,217	592,956	327,303	308,302	537,053	246,470	308,005	431,674	229,221	282,517	457,169	4,332,040
2018	316,880	430,453	590,759	332,663	294,698	498,591	268,791	227,276	481,588	531,815	363,033	614,553	4,951,100

Contract value = $20.   Source: Index and Option Market (IOM), division of the Chicago Mercantile Exchange (CME)

Stock Index Futures - WorldWide

World stocks – World stock markets in 2018 closed mostly lower. The MSCI World Index, a benchmark for large companies based in 23 developed countries, closed moderately lower by -10.4%, partially reversing the sharp +20.1% gain seen in 2017. World stocks fell sharply in late 2018 due to trade tensions and the Federal Reserve's hawkish monetary policy that produced the fourth interest rate hike of the year in December.

Small-Capitalization Stocks – The MSCI World Small-Cap Index, which tracks companies with market caps between $200 million and $1.5 billion, fell by -15.2% in 2018, reversing part of the +20.9% gain seen in 2017. The -15.2% decline in the MSCI World Small-Cap Index in 2018 was 4.7 percentage points worse than the -10.4% decline in the large-cap MSCI World Index. Small caps in 2018 under-performed large caps, breaking the string of three consecutive years of out-performance.

World Industry Groups – Nine of the ten MSCI industry groups showed declines in 2018 as the world stock markets were generally weak. The Health Care sector rose +1.0% and was the only sector with a gain. The Utilities (-1.0%) and Information Technology (-3.5%) sectors showed small declines. Consumer Discretionary showed a decline of -6.8%. The other five sectors showed double-digit declines: Consumer Staples (-12.1%), Telecom (-13.3%), Industrials (-16.0%), Energy (-18.2%), and Materials (-18.8%).

Emerging markets – The MSCI Emerging Markets Free Index, which tracks companies based in 26 emerging countries, fell by -16.6% in 2018, reversing about one-half of 2017's gain of +34.3%. The emerging markets fell in 2018 on the overall downward correction seen in global stocks in Q4-2018 and fell by more than the -10.4% decline seen in the MSCI World Index.

G7 – The G7 stock markets in 2018 were weak and all showed declines. The U.S. S&P 500 index showed the smallest decline but still fell by -6.2% due to trade tensions and the Federal Reserve's hawkish monetary policy during 2018. The European stock markets were weak due to slower Eurozone economic growth and Brexit concerns with the French CAC-40 index falling by -11.0%, the UK FTSE 100 falling by -12.5%, the German Dax index falling by -18.3%, and the Italian MIB index falling by -16.1%. Canada's Toronto Composite Index fell by -11.6% on carry-over weakness from the U.S. stock market and the sharp drop in crude oil prices seen in late 2018. Japan's Nikkei index fell -12.1% in 2018 due to trade tensions and carry-over weakness from China.

North America – In North America, the U.S. S&P 500 index in 2018 showed the smallest decline of -6.2% due to trade tensions and the Fed's four interest rate hikes in 2018. Canada's Toronto Composite index fell by -11.6% in 2018 due to NAFTA trade tensions early in the year and a sharp drop in oil prices later in the year. Mexico's Bolsa index fell by -15.6% on trade tensions and political uncertainty as a new Mexican president took power.

Latin America – The Latin American stock markets in 2018 closed mixed with downward pressure from the sharp sell-off seen in global stocks in late 2018. The ranked returns are as follows: Jamaica's Stock Exchange Index +31.7%, Venezuela's Stock Market Index +27.1%, Brazil's Bovespa Index +15.0%, Ecuador's Guayaqui Bolsa Index +9.2%, Argentina's Merval Index +0.8%, Columbia's General Index -2.9%, Peru's Lima General Index -3.1%, Chile's Stock Market Select Index -8.3%.

Europe – European stocks in 2018 performed poorly due to the weak Eurozone economy, the conclusion of the European Central Bank's bond-buying program at the end of 2018, and concerns about Brexit. The Euro Stoxx 50 index in 2018 fell by -13.1%, more than reversing the +5.6% gain seen in 2017. The ranked returns in 2018 were as follows: French CAC 40 index -11.0%, UK FTSE 100 index -12.5%, Spanish IBEX 35 index -15.0%, Italian MIB index -16.1%, and German DAX index -18.3%.

Asia – The Asian stock markets in 2018 closed mostly lower. The MSCI Far East Index in 2018 fell by -11.8%, breaking the string of three consecutive annual gains. The ranked returns for the Asian stock markets in 2018 were as follows: India's Mumbai Sensex 30 index +5.9%, New Zealand's Exchange 50 Index +4.9%, Indonesia's Jakarta Composite Index -2.5%, Malaysia's Kuala Lumpur Composite index -5.9%, Australia's All-Ordinaries Index -7.4%, Pakistan's 100 Index -8.4%, Taiwan's TAIEX Index -8.6%, Vietnam's Stock Index -9.3%, Singapore's Straights Times Index -9.8%, Thailand's Stock Exchange index -10.8%, Japan's Nikkei 225 Index -12.1%, Philippines' Composite index -12.8%, Hong Kong's Hang Seng -13.6%, South Korea's Composite Index -17.3%, China's Shanghai Composite Index -24.6%.

STOCK INDEX FUTURES - WORLDWIDE

Comparison of International Indices (2010=100)

Year	Jan.	Feb.	Mar.	Apr.	May	June	July	Aug.	Sept.	Oct.	Nov.	Dec.	Average
United States													
2012	126.8	130.2	132.2	131.7	128.5	126.8	129.5	132.7	135.6	135.2	130.3	132.8	131.0
2013	137.6	141.1	145.7	148.3	153.3	151.9	155.5	153.5	154.3	154.5	160.4	162.6	151.6
2014	164.1	161.2	164.8	165.7	167.4	170.2	171.7	169.5	172.8	168.8	178.3	179.4	169.5
2015	177.3	181.3	181.2	181.6	183.1	181.1	179.8	172.4	165.1	173.6	179.1	177.3	177.7
2016	164.8	164.7	174.8	180.3	178.8	179.4	185.3	186.9	184.6	183.7	188.9	199.2	180.9
2017	201.2	206.4	210.4	209.0	211.6	215.4	218.1	221.4	224.0	232.8	238.0	248.0	219.7
2018	260.7	252.4	248.4	245.6	248.3	250.5	252.4	259.0	265.1	258.8	255.2	240.5	253.1
Canada													
2012	102.2	104.0	103.2	100.5	96.5	95.2	96.3	98.7	101.8	102.2	100.8	101.8	100.3
2013	104.9	105.5	105.8	101.9	104.3	101.2	103.4	104.6	106.2	108.2	111.0	110.5	105.6
2014	113.7	115.7	118.3	119.6	121.2	123.9	126.5	127.5	127.2	119.8	122.8	118.7	121.2
2015	119.8	125.5	123.6	126.7	125.3	122.9	119.6	116.1	111.6	113.9	111.2	108.6	118.7
2016	102.4	104.6	110.9	113.1	114.7	116.3	119.7	121.6	121.2	121.9	122.8	126.4	116.3
2017	128.3	129.6	128.5	129.6	128.3	126.8	125.5	125.2	126.6	131.1	132.8	133.3	128.8
2018	134.8	127.8	128.3	127.4	132.2	134.6	136.1	135.3	133.6	127.9	125.4	120.5	130.3
France													
2012	86.7	91.3	93.1	86.7	82.3	81.5	85.4	91.5	93.1	91.7	92.4	96.9	89.4
2013	99.6	98.2	101.0	99.7	105.9	101.2	103.4	108.0	109.9	112.8	114.2	111.0	105.4
2014	113.4	114.8	115.8	118.4	119.7	120.7	116.4	113.4	118.1	110.2	113.7	113.7	115.7
2015	117.0	127.2	133.4	138.0	135.0	131.5	132.2	130.4	120.8	125.8	131.0	124.5	128.9
2016	115.8	111.7	118.1	118.6	116.7	114.6	115.2	118.1	118.7	120.0	120.2	127.1	117.9
2017	129.8	129.3	133.6	137.0	142.8	140.5	138.1	136.7	139.0	143.8	144.0	143.4	138.2
2018	146.3	140.3	138.8	142.6	147.8	144.3	144.3	145.1	143.6	138.0	134.3	128.0	141.1
Germany													
2012	101.5	109.7	112.6	108.8	103.8	99.9	105.9	112.3	117.6	117.8	117.0	122.4	110.8
2013	125.2	123.9	127.9	124.8	134.4	130.7	131.9	134.7	137.3	142.2	148.2	149.3	134.2
2014	153.8	153.7	151.0	153.4	156.9	160.5	157.6	149.9	155.8	145.0	153.4	158.6	154.1
2015	163.8	177.4	190.5	193.2	187.5	181.6	182.4	174.8	160.9	165.2	177.6	172.5	177.3
2016	158.8	150.2	159.4	162.0	161.8	159.3	161.0	170.2	169.8	171.7	171.2	181.3	164.7
2017	187.8	189.8	194.7	197.7	204.6	205.4	200.4	196.4	201.7	210.3	212.7	211.4	201.1
2018	214.5	201.4	196.6	200.6	208.7	204.7	203.3	201.4	196.9	188.4	183.6	175.1	197.9
Italy													
2012	73.0	78.1	78.9	69.8	63.9	63.0	64.6	69.8	75.3	74.3	73.2	75.8	71.6
2013	82.6	77.9	75.1	75.3	81.8	76.1	75.5	80.8	83.1	89.4	89.9	86.9	81.2
2014	92.8	95.1	98.9	102.8	100.4	103.9	99.4	94.4	99.1	91.7	92.1	91.2	96.8
2015	92.0	101.1	107.9	111.5	110.8	109.1	109.2	108.3	102.2	105.3	105.6	10.2	97.8
2016	91.9	81.1	87.3	85.9	84.8	80.4	78.0	79.0	79.0	79.8	78.7	88.2	82.8
2017	92.0	89.7	94.3	95.9	101.0	99.1	101.1	103.1	105.4	106.8	106.7	105.8	100.1
2018	110.5	107.4	106.6	111.2	111.0	103.7	103.6	99.6	99.7	92.5	90.5	89.1	102.1
Japan													
2012	86.1	92.3	99.5	96.2	88.3	86.3	87.5	89.4	89.4	88.2	90.5	98.0	91.0
2013	107.4	113.2	122.4	132.1	144.8	130.9	143.0	137.1	143.6	143.2	149.2	156.4	135.3
2014	155.6	146.0	146.8	144.6	143.3	151.2	153.6	153.4	159.3	153.8	171.6	175.2	154.6
2015	172.6	180.4	191.8	197.5	199.5	203.8	203.5	199.0	179.3	183.6	195.6	191.8	191.5
2016	172.9	163.3	168.8	165.3	166.0	160.5	161.5	165.7	167.2	170.3	176.7	190.5	169.1
2017	191.8	191.7	193.2	187.2	197.1	200.3	200.3	196.5	199.1	212.5	225.0	227.5	201.8
2018	236.9	219.7	213.7	218.5	225.7	225.4	222.9	224.7	231.4	226.7	219.5	210.1	222.9
United Kingdom													
2012	104.2	107.8	107.5	104.7	99.9	100.2	103.1	106.0	106.2	106.7	105.9	108.3	105.0
2013	112.7	115.5	117.7	116.3	121.6	115.2	119.2	119.3	119.8	120.2	122.4	120.2	118.4
2014	122.8	122.4	121.3	121.7	125.0	124.4	123.9	122.8	124.0	117.2	121.5	119.7	122.2
2015	120.9	125.8	125.9	128.3	127.7	124.1	121.6	118.1	111.3	116.0	115.4	112.7	120.6
2016	108.3	107.6	112.6	114.7	112.8	112.9	121.7	124.8	124.6	128.2	124.4	127.3	118.3
2017	131.9	132.4	134.6	132.8	135.8	136.5	135.3	135.5	134.1	137.3	136.1	136.8	134.9
2018	140.8	132.7	129.7	133.3	140.7	140.0	Discontinued		----	----	----	----	136.2

Not Seasonally Adjusted.   Source: *Economic and Statistics Administration, U.S. Department of Commerce (ESA)*

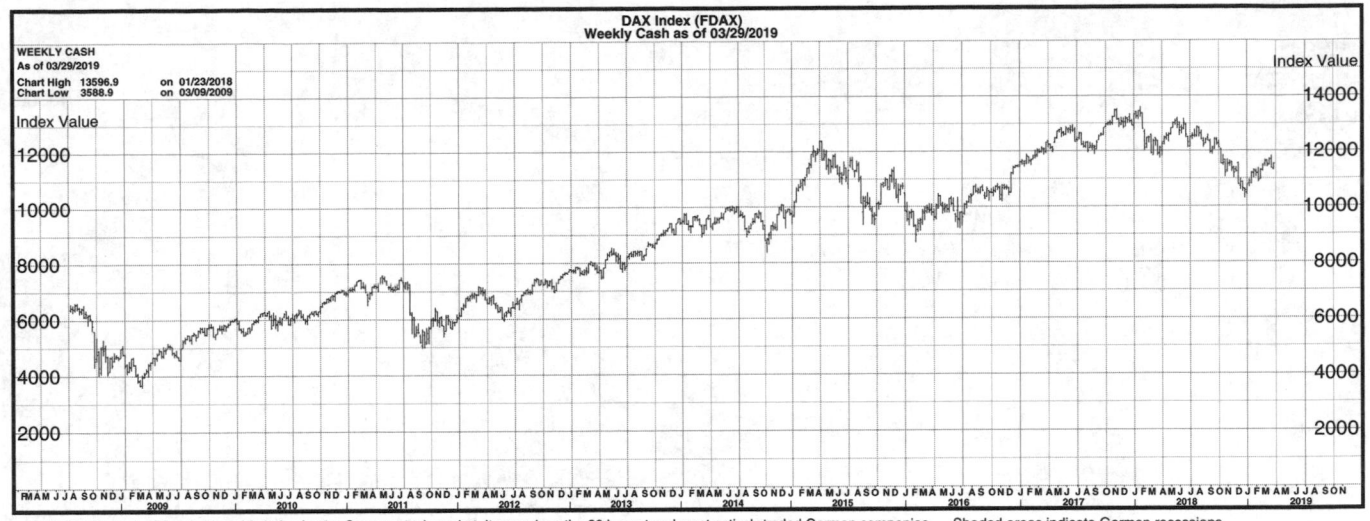

DAX® is Deutsche Börse's blue chip index for the German stock market. It comprises the 30 largest and most actively traded German companies.   Shaded areas indicate German recessions.

Average Value of Deutscher Aktienindex (DAX)

Year	Jan.	Feb.	Mar.	Apr.	May	June	July	Aug.	Sept.	Oct.	Nov.	Dec.	Average
2009	4,534.2	4,265.0	3,969.2	4,519.1	4,886.4	4,930.8	4,949.6	5,395.2	5,584.0	5,680.0	5,642.2	5,836.6	5,016.0
2010	5,863.2	5,584.7	5,965.1	6,215.3	5,966.6	6,080.8	6,061.3	6,122.4	6,214.9	6,436.3	6,744.4	6,991.9	6,187.2
2011	7,039.7	7,294.2	6,952.0	7,227.1	7,330.6	7,158.7	7,292.8	5,923.8	5,402.3	5,871.8	5,826.5	5,867.8	6,598.9
2012	6,278.3	6,789.6	6,966.5	6,731.9	6,424.8	6,184.0	6,549.6	6,949.8	7,274.4	7,288.2	7,238.6	7,576.2	6,854.3
2013	7,747.6	7,666.7	7,913.9	7,723.1	8,317.4	8,089.2	8,161.8	8,332.5	8,497.8	8,800.5	9,170.6	9,235.0	8,304.7
2014	9,516.8	9,509.5	9,339.9	9,490.0	9,709.5	9,927.4	9,751.8	9,273.1	9,638.7	8,971.9	9,490.3	9,812.3	9,535.9
2015	10,133.6	10,977.1	11,784.9	11,956.3	11,599.1	11,236.3	11,288.1	10,818.0	9,953.3	10,222.3	10,986.3	10,673.0	10,969.0
2016	9,827.1	9,291.4	9,859.9	10,023.2	10,010.6	9,859.2	9,960.5	10,530.3	10,504.5	10,624.2	10,595.5	11,214.9	10,191.8
2017	11,620.1	11,745.4	12,047.6	12,232.6	12,661.1	12,710.6	12,397.5	12,153.8	12,479.5	13,012.1	13,159.4	13,079.9	12,441.6
2018	13,270.7	12,459.4	12,165.9	12,411.6	12,911.2	12,667.6	12,581.7	12,458.9	12,185.2	11,659.1	11,359.6	10,834.5	12,247.1

Source: EUREX

The FTSE 100 Index covers 100 of the largest companies traded on the LSE.   Shaded areas indicate United Kingdom recessions.

Average Value of FTSE 100 Stock Index

Year	Jan.	Feb.	Mar.	Apr.	May	June	July	Aug.	Sept.	Oct.	Nov.	Dec.	Average
2009	4,281.85	4,074.38	3,760.23	4,046.33	4,393.78	4,349.25	4,374.50	4,755.63	5,033.13	5,161.18	5,242.29	5,309.54	4,565.17
2010	5,411.65	5,231.92	5,621.03	5,720.73	5,238.81	5,139.26	5,158.39	5,276.00	5,514.67	5,687.17	5,735.84	5,874.87	5,467.53
2011	5,971.31	6,021.12	5,858.24	6,007.85	5,937.95	5,792.18	5,909.81	5,271.31	5,228.50	5,408.62	5,402.52	5,480.08	5,690.79
2012	5,694.45	5,893.35	5,875.40	5,725.58	5,461.45	5,480.44	5,636.47	5,796.96	5,805.45	5,831.81	5,787.52	5,922.72	5,742.63
2013	6,161.87	6,316.35	6,435.58	6,361.01	6,647.35	6,299.43	6,517.86	6,521.48	6,552.36	6,571.95	6,694.32	6,572.98	6,471.05
2014	6,714.51	6,690.79	6,631.69	6,651.96	6,834.80	6,804.31	6,772.02	6,712.21	6,777.75	6,408.63	6,644.12	6,542.62	6,682.12
2015	6,612.63	6,878.54	6,884.51	7,012.39	6,981.68	6,783.17	6,646.60	6,455.96	6,087.34	6,340.81	6,306.91	6,162.31	6,596.07
2016	5,922.67	5,881.74	6,155.24	6,271.90	6,164.88	6,175.30	6,655.88	6,821.69	6,813.75	7,011.20	6,803.33	6,961.04	6,469.89
2017	7,211.36	7,240.42	7,359.53	7,263.60	7,422.66	7,463.97	7,395.85	7,409.18	7,334.65	7,508.18	7,441.23	7,481.74	7,377.70
2018	7,695.65	7,255.90	7,090.09	7,288.22	7,690.22	7,656.93	Discontinued		----	----	----	----	7,446.17

Source: Euronext LIFFE

STOCK INDEX FUTURES - WORLDWIDE

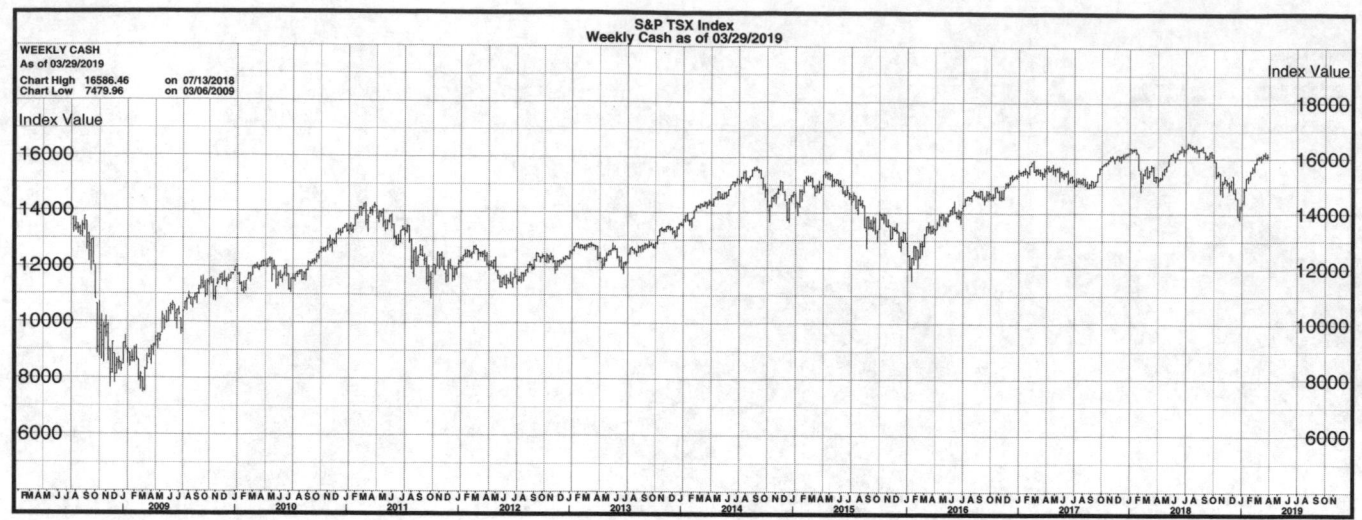

Average Value of S&P TSX Index

Year	Jan.	Feb.	Mar.	Apr.	May	June	July	Aug.	Sept.	Oct.	Nov.	Dec.	Average
2009	8,886.5	8,437.6	8,314.1	9,224.7	10,031.3	10,372.3	10,292.8	10,816.4	11,255.1	11,291.5	11,413.6	11,580.1	10,159.7
2010	11,654.3	11,453.7	11,966.8	12,154.2	11,816.5	11,680.2	11,558.6	11,728.5	12,163.8	12,569.5	12,843.2	13,275.4	12,072.1
2011	13,392.8	13,908.2	13,932.9	13,962.4	13,621.2	13,126.1	13,294.7	12,380.7	12,130.8	11,922.8	12,038.1	11,860.7	12,964.3
2012	12,331.8	12,552.7	12,464.0	12,135.4	11,644.1	11,495.7	11,626.9	11,921.0	12,285.6	12,337.7	12,163.2	12,290.3	12,104.0
2013	12,668.8	12,737.0	12,777.3	12,299.2	12,585.1	12,221.4	12,479.7	12,622.7	12,818.9	13,057.7	13,396.1	13,339.2	12,750.3
2014	13,728.1	13,964.5	14,281.4	14,440.5	14,635.7	14,960.5	15,268.3	15,389.4	15,353.5	14,460.8	14,824.8	14,330.5	14,636.5
2015	14,460.9	15,155.0	14,921.6	15,299.3	15,127.2	14,835.9	14,436.4	14,010.4	13,477.6	13,751.9	13,424.2	13,115.1	14,334.6
2016	12,361.0	12,632.4	13,382.1	13,650.4	13,851.9	14,042.4	14,445.8	14,680.8	14,634.0	14,718.2	14,821.9	15,254.5	14,039.6
2017	15,486.6	15,639.7	15,515.3	15,642.3	15,486.8	15,308.8	15,153.5	15,108.9	15,284.5	15,826.0	16,032.6	16,092.8	15,548.2
2018	16,272.5	15,430.6	15,490.4	15,380.4	15,964.4	16,253.3	16,432.6	16,332.4	16,125.6	15,441.2	15,144.0	14,546.8	15,734.5

Source: Toronto Stock Exchange

The CAC 40® is a free float market capitalization weighted index that reflects the performance of the 40 largest and most actively traded shares listed on Euronext Paris, and is the most widely used indicator of the Paris stock market. Shaded areas indicate French recessions.

Average Value of CAC 40 Index

Year	Jan.	Feb.	Mar.	Apr.	May	June	July	Aug.	Sept.	Oct.	Nov.	Dec.	Average
2009	3,099.7	2,911.5	2,725.3	3,007.2	3,244.0	3,242.9	3,212.0	3,539.9	3,732.7	3,780.0	3,752.7	3,851.9	3,341.6
2010	3,925.2	3,687.1	3,922.2	3,973.7	3,561.5	3,558.0	3,539.3	3,616.9	3,723.6	3,799.4	3,818.4	3,848.5	3,747.8
2011	3,960.7	4,086.4	3,941.7	4,020.3	3,998.6	3,853.3	3,818.0	3,201.9	2,983.1	3,148.4	3,033.0	3,091.9	3,594.8
2012	3,250.6	3,420.4	3,490.0	3,248.8	3,084.4	3,055.9	3,199.6	3,427.4	3,490.9	3,435.7	3,461.5	3,631.8	3,349.7
2013	3,734.0	3,679.4	3,786.4	3,735.1	3,968.7	3,792.5	3,876.6	4,046.3	4,117.7	4,228.0	4,279.9	4,161.4	3,950.5
2014	4,248.4	4,301.1	4,338.1	4,437.3	4,484.8	4,522.0	4,362.0	4,249.6	4,425.3	4,129.8	4,261.0	4,262.2	4,335.1
2015	4,384.2	4,768.5	5,000.7	5,173.4	5,058.2	4,927.9	4,956.2	4,887.1	4,526.6	4,715.6	4,910.3	4,665.7	4,831.2
2016	4,340.1	4,184.8	4,427.5	4,445.2	4,373.5	4,293.9	4,317.6	4,425.4	4,448.6	4,497.6	4,504.3	4,764.5	4,418.6
2017	4,863.6	4,846.7	5,008.4	5,134.6	5,352.0	5,263.8	5,175.0	5,122.7	5,208.8	5,389.8	5,398.0	5,373.0	5,178.0
2018	5,483.0	5,257.8	5,200.6	5,345.3	5,537.6	5,408.3	5,409.4	5,438.3	5,381.7	5,170.1	5,035.1	4,798.2	5,288.8

Source: Euronext Paris

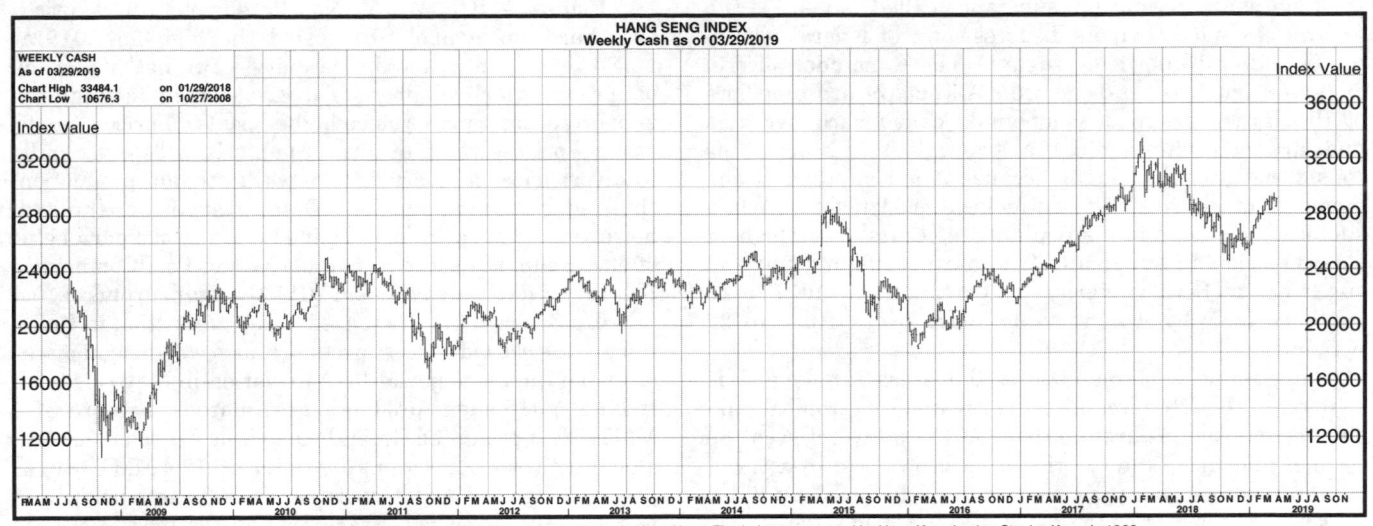

The Hang Seng Index is a freefloat-adjusted market capitalization-weighted stock market index in Hong Kong. The Index was created by Hong Kong banker Stanley Kwan in 1969.

Average Value of Hang Seng Index

Year	Jan.	Feb.	Mar.	Apr.	May	June	July	Aug.	Sept.	Oct.	Nov.	Dec.	Average
2009	13,794.0	13,166.7	12,795.0	15,029.3	17,124.3	18,342.5	18,903.7	20,475.5	20,920.5	21,654.3	22,219.4	21,747.9	18,014.4
2010	21,408.8	20,244.1	21,089.4	21,623.8	19,945.4	20,104.0	20,445.7	21,108.7	21,657.7	23,301.0	23,804.9	23,057.3	21,482.6
2011	23,864.8	23,196.7	23,110.2	24,009.1	23,133.3	22,342.4	22,280.3	20,333.7	19,007.3	18,352.1	18,865.3	18,585.7	21,423.4
2012	19,455.8	21,128.5	21,013.0	20,665.8	19,615.2	18,940.3	19,372.3	19,946.2	20,226.8	21,293.3	21,650.2	22,406.2	20,476.1
2013	23,470.7	23,148.3	22,518.0	22,054.3	22,933.1	21,063.9	21,298.5	22,009.5	22,932.7	23,102.2	23,304.5	23,370.8	22,600.5
2014	22,725.2	22,188.3	21,980.8	22,598.5	22,584.9	23,144.9	23,760.0	24,812.1	24,341.8	23,301.2	23,779.1	23,386.2	23,216.9
2015	24,209.9	24,670.4	24,306.8	27,451.5	27,656.2	27,009.0	25,032.2	23,223.2	21,365.1	22,649.3	22,509.5	21,910.2	24,332.8
2016	19,733.6	19,134.5	20,299.8	20,986.5	20,174.0	20,646.4	21,497.8	22,663.9	23,543.0	23,406.1	22,618.9	22,229.6	21,411.2
2017	22,814.5	23,725.3	24,029.6	24,262.7	25,189.4	25,828.2	26,326.0	27,532.4	27,790.9	28,394.4	29,213.7	29,109.6	26,184.7
2018	31,831.9	30,969.3	30,898.1	30,376.0	30,698.7	30,070.3	28,466.1	27,925.8	27,275.6	25,705.4	26,081.0	26,075.6	28,864.5

Source: Hong Kong Futures Exchange

The Nikkei Stock Average is owned by and proprietary to Nihon Keisai Shimbun.   Shaded areas indicate Japan recessions.

Average Value of Nikkei 225 Index

Year	Jan.	Feb.	Mar.	Apr.	May	June	July	Aug.	Sept.	Oct.	Nov.	Dec.	Average
2009	8,331.5	7,694.8	7,764.6	8,768.0	9,304.4	9,810.3	9,691.1	10,430.4	10,302.9	10,066.2	9,641.0	10,169.0	9,331.2
2010	10,661.6	10,175.1	10,671.5	11,139.8	10,104.0	9,786.1	9,456.8	9,268.2	9,346.7	9,455.1	9,797.2	10,254.5	10,009.7
2011	10,449.5	10,622.3	9,852.5	9,644.6	9,650.8	9,541.5	9,996.7	9,072.9	8,695.4	8,733.6	8,506.1	8,506.0	9,439.3
2012	8,616.7	9,242.3	9,962.4	9,627.4	8,842.5	8,638.1	8,760.7	8,949.9	8,948.6	8,827.4	9,059.9	9,814.4	9,107.5
2013	10,750.9	11,327.3	12,254.7	13,224.1	14,494.3	13,106.6	14,317.5	13,726.7	14,372.1	14,329.0	14,931.7	15,655.2	13,540.8
2014	15,578.3	14,617.6	14,694.8	14,475.3	14,343.2	15,131.8	15,379.3	15,358.7	15,948.5	15,394.1	17,179.0	17,541.7	15,470.2
2015	17,274.4	18,053.2	19,197.6	19,767.9	19,974.2	20,403.8	20,372.6	19,919.1	17,944.2	18,374.1	19,581.8	19,202.6	19,172.1
2016	17,302.3	16,347.0	16,897.3	16,543.5	16,612.7	16,068.8	16,168.3	16,586.1	16,737.0	17,044.5	17,689.5	19,066.0	16,921.9
2017	19,194.1	19,188.7	19,340.2	18,736.4	19,726.8	20,045.6	20,044.9	19,670.2	19,924.4	21,267.5	22,525.2	22,769.9	20,202.8
2018	23,712.2	21,991.7	21,395.5	21,868.8	22,590.1	22,562.9	22,309.1	22,494.1	23,159.3	22,690.8	21,967.9	21,032.4	22,314.6

Source: Singapore Exchange

Sugar

The white crystalline substance called "sugar" is the organic chemical compound sucrose, one of several related compounds all known as sugars. These include glucose, dextrose, fructose, and lactose. All sugars are members of the larger group of compounds called carbohydrates and are characterized by a sweet taste. Sucrose is considered a double sugar because it is composed of one molecule of glucose and one molecule of fructose. While sucrose is common in many plants, it occurs in the highest concentration in sugarcane (Saccharum officinarum) and sugar beets (Beta vulgaris). Sugarcane is about 7 to 18 percent sugar by weight while sugar beets are 8 to 22 percent.

Sugarcane is a member of the grass family and is a perennial. Sugarcane is cultivated in tropical and subtropical regions around the world roughly between the Tropics of Cancer and Capricorn. It grows best in hot, wet climates where there is heavy rainfall followed by a dry season. The largest cane producers are Florida, Louisiana, Texas, and Hawaii. On a commercial basis, sugarcane is not grown from seeds but from cuttings or pieces of the stalk.

Sugar beets, which are produced in temperate or colder climates, are annuals grown from seeds. Sugar beets do best with moderate temperatures and evenly distributed rainfall. The beets are planted in the spring and harvested in the fall. The sugar is contained in the root of the beet, but the sugars from beets and cane are identical. Sugar beet production takes place mostly in Europe, the U.S., China, and Japan. The largest sugar beet producing states are Minnesota, Idaho, North Dakota, and Michigan. Sugar beets are refined to yield white sugar and very little raw sugar is produced.

Sugar beets and sugarcane are produced in over 100 countries around the world. Of all the sugar produced, about 25% is processed from sugar beets and the remaining 75% is from sugar cane. The trend has been that production of sugar from cane is increasing relative to that produced from beets. The significance of this in that sugarcane is a perennial plant while the sugar beet is an annual, and due to the longer production cycle, sugarcane production and the sugar processed from that cane, may not be quite as responsive to changes in price.

Sugar futures are traded at the Intercontinental Exchange (ICE), the Bolsa de Mercadorias & Futuros (BM&F), Kansai Commodities Exchange (KANEX), the Tokyo Grain Exchange (TGE), and the London International Financial Futures and Options Exchange (LIFFE).

Raw sugar is traded on the ICE exchange while white sugar is traded on the London International Financial Futures Exchange (LIFFE). The most actively traded contract is the No. 11 (World) sugar contract at the ICE exchange. The No. 11 contract calls for the delivery of 112,000 pounds (50 long tons) of raw cane centrifugal sugar from any of 28 foreign countries of origin and the United States. The ICE exchange also trades the No. 14 sugar contract (Domestic), which calls for the delivery of raw centrifugal cane sugar in the United States. Futures on white sugar are traded on the London International Financial Futures Exchange and call for the delivery of 50 metric tons of white beet sugar, cane crystal sugar, or refined sugar of any origin from the crop current at the time of delivery.

Prices – ICE World No. 11 sugar futures prices (Barchart.com symbol SB) posted the high for 2018 at 15.37 cents per pound in January. Strength in crude oil prices, which climbed to a 4-year high in January, supported sugar prices since higher crude oil prices benefit ethanol prices, which in turn prompts Brazil's sugar mills to divert more cane crushing toward ethanol production, thus reducing sugar supplies. Gains in sugar were limited, however, and sugar prices declined into Q3 on a global glut of sugar supplies after researcher Green Pool Commodity Specialists forecasted a global 2017/18 sugar surplus of 10.4 MMT, a 5-year high. Increased sugar production in India, the world's second-largest producer, also weighed on prices after the Indian Sugar Mills Association in May raised its India 2017/18 sugar production estimate to a record 31.5 MMT. That prompted Green Pool to hike its global 2017/18 global sugar surplus estimate to a record 18.4 MMT. Sugar prices plunged to an 11-year low of 9.83 cents per pound in September after the Brazilian real tumbled to a 3-1/4 year low against the dollar. The weaker real encouraged Brazil's sugar producers to boost sugar exports, which are priced in dollars. Sugar prices recovered into October on signs of lower output from Brazil, the world's biggest producer, after Unica predicted that Brazil's Center South 2018/19 sugar production would fall -28% yr/yr to 26 MMT. The upside for sugar prices was limited after the USDA's FAS in November projected a record 2017/18 global sugar surplus of 10.73 MMT and record global 2017/18 sugar production of 184.95 MMT. Sugar prices finished 2018 down -20.6% yr/yr at 12.03 cents per pound.

Supply – World production of centrifugal (raw) sugar in the 2018/19 marketing year (Oct 1 to Sep 30) is forecasted to fall -4.5% yr/yr to 185.886 million metric tons, down from last year's record high. The world's largest sugar producers in 2018/19 are expected to be India with 9.3% of world production, Brazil with 16.5%, and the European Union with 10.%. U.S. sugar production in 2018/19 is expected to fall 3.0% yr/yr to 8.178 million metric tons, down from last year's record high. World ending stocks in 2017/18 rose +22.0% yr/yr to 51.529 million metric ton, a record high. The stocks/consumption ratio in 2017/18 was 30.0%. U.S. production of cane sugar in 2017/18 is expected to rise +1.8% to 3.912 million short tons and beet sugar production is expected to rise +0.4% yr/yr to 5.017 million short tons.

Demand – World domestic consumption of centrifugal (raw) sugar in 2017/18 fell by -0.2% yr/yr to 171.559, down slightly from the 2016/17 record high of 171.867 million metric tons. U.S. domestic disappearance (consumption) of sugar in 2017/18 rose +1.8% yr/yr to 12.703 million short tons. U.S. per capita sugar consumption in 2014/15 rose +0.6% yr/yr to 68.39 pounds per year, which was only about two-thirds of the levels seen in the early 1970s.

Trade – World exports of centrifugal sugar in 2018/19 are expected to fall -9.4% yr/yr to 57.880 million metric tons, down from last year's record high of 63.876. The world's largest sugar exporter in 2018/19 will continue to be Brazil, with 33.9% of world exports, even though its exports are expected to fall -30.5% yr/yr to 19,600 million metric tons. The next largest exporters are expected to be Thailand with 19.9% of world exports, India with 6.9% and Australia with 6.7%. U.S. sugar exports in 2017/18 fell -80.0% yr/yr to 25,000 short tons, which is down from the 3-decade high of 422,000 seen in 2006-07. U.S. sugar imports in 2018/19 are expected to fall -14.5% yr/yr to 2.541 million metric tons.

World Production, Supply & Stocks/Consumption Ratio of Sugar   In 1000's of Metric Tons (Raw Value)

Marketing Year	Beginning Stocks	Production	Imports	Total Supply	Exports	Domestic Consumption	Ending Stocks	Stocks As a % of Consumption
2009-10	29,836	153,184	48,261	231,281	48,327	154,926	28,028	18.1
2010-11	28,028	162,221	49,119	239,368	53,939	155,938	29,491	18.9
2011-12	29,491	172,349	48,563	250,403	54,996	160,217	35,190	22.0
2012-13	35,190	177,833	51,444	264,467	55,742	166,437	42,288	25.4
2013-14	42,288	175,971	51,450	269,709	57,931	166,960	44,818	26.8
2014-15	44,818	177,582	50,248	272,648	55,013	168,864	48,771	28.9
2015-16	48,771	164,868	54,671	268,310	53,959	170,256	44,095	25.9
2016-17[1]	44,095	174,030	54,518	272,643	58,625	171,784	42,234	24.6
2017-18[2]	42,234	194,574	53,547	290,355	63,876	171,784	51,529	30.0
2018-19z[3]	51,529	185,886	50,978	288,393	57,880	174,950		

[1] Preliminary.   [2] Estimate.   [3] Forecast.   *Source: Foreign Agricultural Service, U.S. Department of Agriculture (FAS-USDA)*

World Production of Sugar (Centrifugal Sugar-Raw Value)   In Thousands of Metric Tons

Year	Australia	Brazil	China	Cuba	European Union	India	Indonesia	Mexico	Pakistan	Thailand	United States	Ukraine	World Total
2009-10	4,700	36,400	11,429	1,250	16,897	20,637	1,910	5,115	3,420	6,930	1,382	7,224	153,184
2010-11	3,700	38,350	11,199	1,150	15,939	26,574	1,770	5,495	3,920	9,663	1,540	7,104	162,221
2011-12	3,683	36,150	12,341	1,400	18,320	28,620	1,830	5,351	4,520	10,235	2,300	7,700	172,349
2012-13	4,250	38,600	14,001	1,600	16,655	27,337	2,300	7,393	5,000	10,024	2,400	8,148	177,833
2013-14	4,380	37,800	14,263	1,650	16,020	26,605	2,300	6,382	5,630	11,333	1,196	7,676	175,971
2014-15	4,700	35,950	11,000	1,850	18,449	30,460	2,100	6,344	5,164	10,793	1,728	7,853	177,582
2015-16	4,900	34,650	9,050	1,625	14,283	27,385	2,025	6,484	5,265	9,743	1,638	8,155	164,868
2016-17[1]	5,100	39,150	9,300	1,800	18,314	22,200	2,050	6,314	6,825	10,033	2,156	8,137	174,030
2017-18[2]	4,800	38,870	10,300	1,100	20,896	34,110	2,100	6,371	7,425	14,710	2,326	8,430	194,574
2018-19[3]	5,000	30,600	10,800	1,600	19,525	35,870	2,200	6,386	6,525	13,800	2,315	8,178	185,886

[1] Preliminary.   [2] Estimate.   [3] Forecast.   *Source: Foreign Agricultural Service, U.S. Department of Agriculture (FAS-USDA)*

World Stocks of Centrifugal Sugar at Beginning of Marketing Year   In Thousands of Metric Tons (Raw Value)

Year	Australia	Brazil	China	Cuba	European Union	India	Indonesia	Iran	Mexico	Philippines	Russia	United States	World Total
2009-10	487	-1,135	3,784	102	2,232	5,880	340	475	623	581	481	1,392	29,836
2010-11	413	-835	2,355	114	1,433	6,223	750	475	973	730	399	1,359	28,028
2011-12	193	260	1,621	59	1,974	6,299	602	650	806	934	350	1,250	29,491
2012-13	64	260	4,140	109	3,303	7,163	409	640	1,024	932	390	1,795	35,190
2013-14	83	10	6,793	170	3,836	9,373	879	700	1,548	942	395	1,958	42,288
2014-15	111	350	9,977	160	3,066	8,227	1,299	700	881	1,032	370	1,642	44,818
2015-16	140	960	10,890	195	4,161	10,607	949	400	860	997	100	1,647	48,771
2016-17[1]	230	750	9,591	130	1,241	9,294	1,098	450	1,099	1,054	150	1,863	44,095
2017-18[2]	220	850	7,811	135	2,238	6,570	1,743	535	1,062	1,054	360	1,702	42,234
2018-19[3]	110	920	6,511	110	2,234	13,729	1,763	490	1,479	954	460	1,808	51,529

[1] Preliminary.   [2] Estimate.   [3] Forecast.   *Source: Foreign Agricultural Service, U.S. Department of Agriculture (FAS-USDA)*

Centrifugal Sugar (Raw Value) Imported into Selected Countries   In Thousands of Metric Tons

Year	Algeria	Canada	China	European Union	Indonesia	Iran	Japan	Korea, South	Malaysia	Nigeria	Russia	United States	World Total
2009-10	1,260	1,114	1,535	2,561	3,200	1,643	1,199	1,617	1,537	1,431	2,223	3,010	48,261
2010-11	1,193	1,135	2,143	3,755	3,082	1,292	1,199	1,688	1,813	1,495	2,510	3,391	49,119
2011-12	1,594	1,103	4,430	3,552	3,027	1,079	1,301	1,668	1,721	1,399	510	3,294	48,563
2012-13	2,014	1,156	3,802	3,790	3,570	1,553	1,244	1,806	1,966	1,450	735	2,925	51,444
2013-14	1,854	1,007	4,275	3,262	3,570	1,629	1,360	1,909	1,897	1,470	1,020	3,395	51,450
2014-15	1,844	1,184	5,058	2,918	2,950	266	1,360	1,882	2,063	1,465	1,100	3,223	50,248
2015-16	1,834	1,229	6,116	3,055	3,724	822	1,275	1,900	2,009	1,470	750	3,031	54,671
2016-17[1]	2,061	1,139	4,600	2,942	4,918	962	1,232	1,757	1,893	1,820	379	2,943	54,518
2017-18[2]	2,349	1,241	4,200	1,500	4,298	271	1,240	1,864	2,002	1,870	280	2,972	53,547
2018-19[3]	2,265	1,340	4,000	1,500	4,250	281	1,326	1,965	2,090	1,870	300	2,541	50,978

[1] Preliminary.   [2] Estimate.   [3] Forecast.   *Source: Foreign Agricultural Service, U.S. Department of Agriculture (FAS-USDA)*

SUGAR

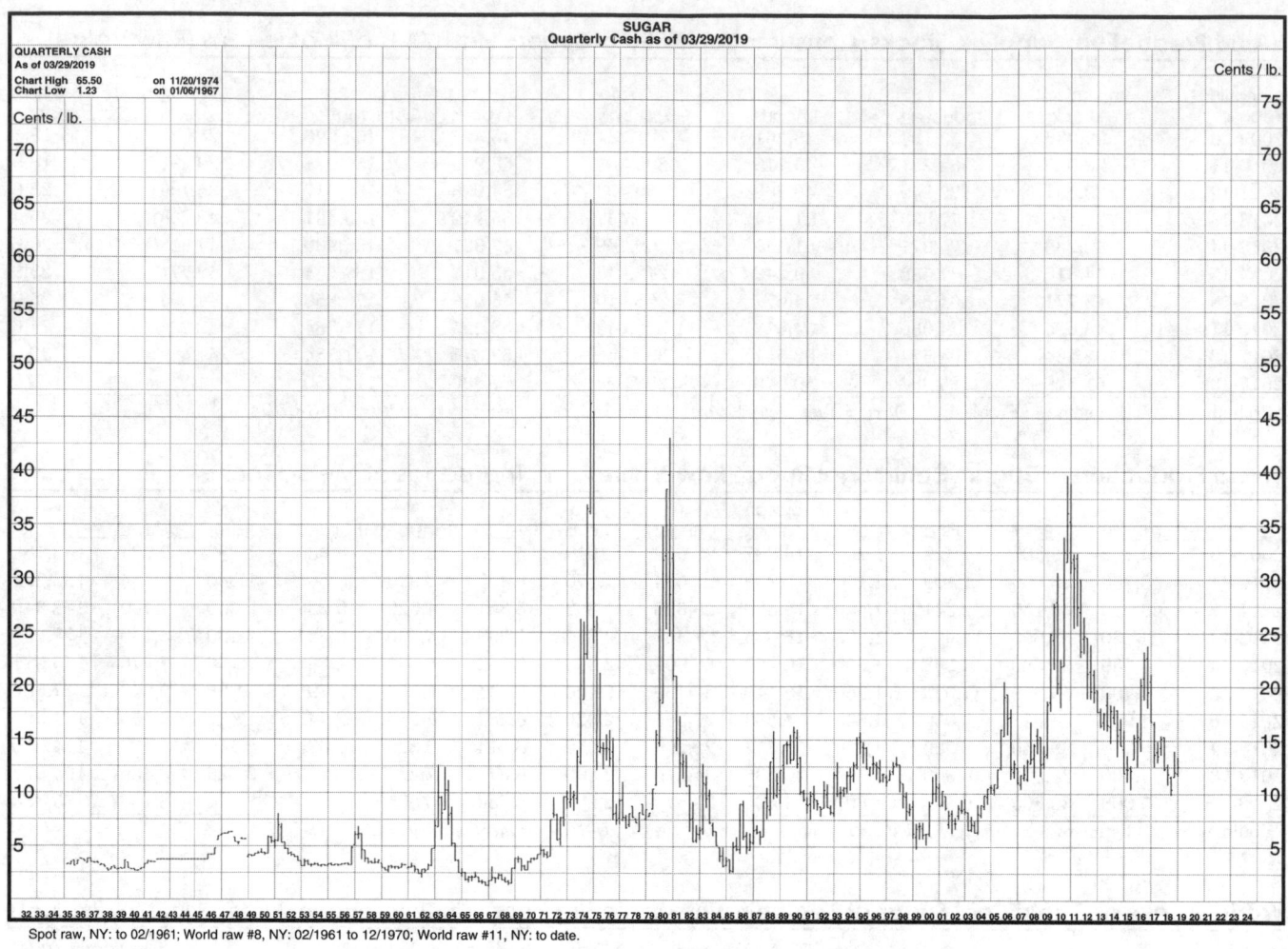

QUARTERLY CASH
As of 03/29/2019
Chart High 65.50 on 11/20/1974
Chart Low 1.23 on 01/06/1967

Cents / lb.

Spot raw, NY: to 02/1961; World raw #8, NY: 02/1961 to 12/1970; World raw #11, NY: to date.

Centrifugal Sugar (Raw Value) Exported From Selected Countries   In Thousands of Metric Tons

Year	Australia	Brazil	Colom-bia	Cuba	Dominican Republic	European Union	Guate-mala	India	Mauritius	South Africa	Swazi-land	Thailand	World Total
2009-10	3,600	24,300	870	538	261	350	2,647	1,815	225	271	754	4,930	48,327
2010-11	2,750	25,800	830	577	204	320	1,113	1,544	3,903	338	400	6,642	53,939
2011-12	2,800	24,650	876	830	211	315	2,343	1,619	3,764	370	271	7,898	54,996
2012-13	3,100	27,650	542	775	165	353	1,662	1,911	1,261	384	356	6,693	55,742
2013-14	3,242	26,200	900	937	208	412	1,552	2,100	2,806	416	868	7,200	57,931
2014-15	3,561	23,950	835	895	186	641	1,582	2,340	2,580	457	772	8,252	55,013
2015-16	3,700	24,350	584	1,031	186	665	1,548	2,029	3,800	463	305	7,055	53,959
2016-17[1]	4,000	28,500	695	1,094	185	587	1,509	1,978	2,125	474	218	7,016	58,625
2017-18[2]	3,800	28,200	700	570	185	525	3,600	1,894	1,800	390	770	10,500	63,876
2018-19[3]	3,900	19,600	700	580	200	710	3,000	1,888	4,000	350	1,190	11,500	57,880

[1] Preliminary.   [2] Estimate.   [3] Forecast.   Source: Foreign Agricultural Service, U.S. Department of Agriculture (FAS-USDA)

Average Wholesale Price of Refined Beet Sugar[2]--Midwest Market   In Cents Per Pound

Year	Jan.	Feb.	Mar.	Apr.	May	June	July	Aug.	Sept.	Oct.	Nov.	Dec.	Average
2009	35.00	35.00	35.00	34.25	34.40	35.50	35.40	38.00	42.00	42.60	45.00	45.00	38.10
2010	50.50	53.00	52.25	48.20	45.00	50.00	53.40	59.50	59.00	54.40	56.50	57.00	53.23
2011	54.50	54.00	56.50	56.80	54.00	55.00	55.40	57.00	58.60	59.00	58.75	55.10	56.22
2012	51.75	51.00	51.00	50.25	47.81	45.00	42.00	41.20	38.25	36.00	34.60	31.75	43.38
2013	30.50	28.50	27.60	26.63	26.30	26.50	26.00	25.50	26.25	27.38	28.00	27.50	47.22
2014	26.50	26.25	26.50	29.75	31.60	35.00	36.00	36.60	37.50	36.60	36.00	36.00	32.86
2015	36.00	35.25	35.13	35.50	34.30	34.00	33.80	33.13	33.00	32.40	32.00	32.00	33.88
2016	32.00	31.00	31.00	30.50	30.00	29.75	29.00	28.50	28.50	28.50	28.50	28.50	29.65
2017	28.50	28.63	29.10	29.50	29.50	30.70	31.88	32.13	32.90	33.50	34.63	35.00	31.33
2018[1]	35.25	36.00	36.00	36.00	36.00	36.00	36.00	36.00	36.00	33.38	34.90	35.00	35.54

[1] Preliminary.   [2] These are f.o.b. basis prices in bulk, not delivered prices.   Source: Economic Research Service, U.S. Department of Agriculture (ERS-)

Average Price of World Raw Sugar[1]   In Cents Per Pound

Year	Jan.	Feb.	Mar.	Apr.	May	June	July	Aug.	Sept.	Oct.	Nov.	Dec.	Average
2009	13.09	13.90	13.83	14.43	16.89	16.94	18.57	22.37	23.11	23.22	22.96	25.28	18.72
2010	28.94	27.29	21.36	19.87	19.59	21.24	23.42	25.09	31.19	34.80	35.44	36.10	27.03
2011	36.11	35.01	33.22	29.35	26.64	29.75	30.51	28.87	27.71	26.30	24.52	23.42	29.28
2012	24.05	25.81	24.73	22.98	20.25	20.44	22.76	20.53	19.47	20.39	19.31	19.50	21.69
2013	18.37	18.28	18.33	17.71	17.08	16.79	16.38	16.44	17.33	18.81	17.58	16.41	17.46
2014	15.42	16.28	17.58	17.01	17.50	17.22	17.18	15.89	14.60	16.48	15.89	14.99	16.34
2015	15.06	14.52	12.84	12.93	12.70	11.75	11.88	10.67	11.32	14.14	14.89	15.00	13.14
2016	14.29	13.31	15.43	15.00	16.68	19.34	19.69	20.01	21.30	22.92	20.81	18.83	18.13
2017	20.54	20.40	18.06	16.32	15.66	13.53	14.11	13.80	13.92	14.23	14.66	14.43	15.81
2018[1]	13.99	13.56	12.83	11.82	11.85	12.06	11.17	10.46	10.78	13.18	12.78	12.55	12.25

[1] Contract No. 11, f.o.b. stowed Caribbean port, including Brazil, bulk spot price. [2] Preliminary. *Source: Economic Research Service, U.S. Department of Agriculture (ERS-USDA)*

Average Price of Raw Sugar in New York (C.I.F., Duty/Free Paid, Contract #12 & #14)   In Cents Per Pound

Year	Jan.	Feb.	Mar.	Apr.	May	June	July	Aug.	Sept.	Oct.	Nov.	Dec.	Average
2009	20.15	19.83	19.75	21.58	21.64	22.47	23.02	26.18	28.91	30.48	31.86	33.30	24.93
2010	39.36	40.13	35.11	30.86	30.89	32.73	33.66	34.24	38.17	39.30	38.84	38.35	35.97
2011	38.46	39.69	39.65	38.32	35.04	35.65	37.93	40.16	40.15	38.19	37.92	36.32	38.12
2012	34.69	33.57	34.94	31.87	30.20	28.89	28.68	28.84	26.27	23.89	22.52	22.41	28.90
2013	21.20	20.72	20.82	20.38	19.51	19.31	19.22	20.97	21.05	21.82	20.61	19.95	20.46
2014	20.27	21.65	22.03	24.33	24.66	25.65	24.78	25.64	25.36	26.41	24.26	24.81	24.15
2015	25.24	24.62	24.07	24.39	24.61	24.76	24.67	24.50	24.21	25.04	26.63	25.83	24.88
2016	25.76	25.50	26.32	27.90	27.26	27.68	28.15	28.54	28.16	28.57	28.76	29.24	27.65
2017	29.44	30.59	29.95	28.72	28.41	27.83	26.77	25.11	26.90	27.09	27.28	26.93	27.92
2018[1]	26.60	25.83	24.73	24.92	24.59	25.72	25.56	25.60	25.40	25.21	25.04	25.23	25.37

[1] Preliminary. *Source: Economic Research Service, U.S. Department of Agriculture (ERS-USDA)*

Supply and Utilization of Sugar (Cane and Beet) in the United States   In Thousands of Short Tons (Raw Value)

Year	Cane	Beet	Total	Foreign	Terri-tories	Total	Beginning Stocks	Total Supply	Total Use	Exports	Net Changes in Invisible Stocks	Refining Loss Ad-justment	In Poly-hydric Alcohol[4]	Total	Per Capita Pounds
2009-10	3,387	4,575	7,963	3,320	0	3,320	1,534	12,817	11,319	211	-45	0	35	11,152	63.4
2010-11	3,172	4,659	7,831	3,738	0	3,738	1,498	13,067	11,689	248	19	0	33	11,193	66.0
2011-12	3,588	4,900	8,488	3,632	0	3,632	1,378	13,498	11,519	269	-64	0	33	11,141	65.9
2012-13	3,905	5,076	8,981	3,224	0	3,224	1,979	14,185	12,027	274	-23	0	185	11,511	66.7
2013-14	3,667	4,794	8,462	3,742	0	3,742	2,158	14,362	12,552	306	0	0	346	11,819	68.0
2014 15	3,763	4,893	8,656	3,553	0	3,553	1,810	14,019	12,204	185	0	0	28	11,888	68.4
2015-16	3,870	5,119	8,989	3,341	0	3,341	1,815	14,145	12,091	74	-33	0	22	11,881	69.2
2016-17[1]	3,867	5,103	8,970	3,244	0	3,244	2,054	14,267	12,391	95	38	0	29	12,102	69.7
2017-18[2]	4,014	5,279	9,293	3,277	0	3,277	1,876	14,445	12,438	170	82	0	28	12,048	69.2
2018-19[3]	4,099	5,004	9,103	2,862	0	2,862	2,008	13,973	12,305	35	0	0	25	12,125	

[1] Preliminary. [2] Estimate. [3] Forecast. [4] Includes feed use. *Source: Economic Research Service, U.S. Department of Agriculture (ERS-USDA)*

Sugarcane for Sugar & Seed and Production of Cane Sugar and Molasses in the United States

Year	Acreage Harvested (1,000 Acres)	Yield of Cane Per Havested Acre Net Tons	for Sugar	for Seed	Total	Sugar Yield Per Acre (Short Tons)	Farm Price ($ Per Ton)	of Cane Used for Sugar	of Cane Used for Sugar & Seed	Total (1,000 Tons)	Per Ton of Cane (In Lbs.)	Refined Basis (1,000 Tons)	Edible	Total[3]
2009	873.9	34.8	28,484	1,938	30,432	4.16	34.8	991,424	1,056,613	3,395	----	----	----	----
2010	877.5	31.2	25,663	1,697	27,360	3.83	41.7	1,069,537	1,140,636	3,161	----	----	----	----
2011	872.6	33.5	27,738	1,486	29,224	4.35	47.2	1,308,951	1,379,498	3,599	----	----	----	----
2012	902.4	35.7	30,500	1,727	32,227	4.57	41.9	1,276,631	1,348,361	3,905	----	----	----	----
2013	910.8	33.8	29,023	1,738	30,761	4.27	31.4	910,377	962,807	3,667	----	----	----	----
2014	868.5	35.0	28,895	1,529	30,424	4.57	34.7	1,054,657	1,083,180	3,763	----	----	----	----
2015	874.7	36.7	30,555	1,567	32,122	4.66	31.2	1,000,620		3,870	----	----	----	----
2016	903.1	35.6	30,371	1,747	32,118	4.53	32.6	1,043,953		3,869	----	----	----	----
2017[1]	904.1	36.8	31,182	2,056	33,238						----	----	----	----
2018[2]	908.2	38.3	32,825	1,929	34,754						----	----	----	----

[1] Preliminary. [2] Estimate. [3] Excludes edible molasses. *Source: Economic Research Service, U.S. Department of Agriculture (ERS-USDA)*

SUGAR

U.S. Sugar Beets, Beet Sugar, Pulp & Molasses Produced from Sugar Beets and Raw Sugar Spot Prices

Year of Harvest	Planted ---- 1,000	Harvested Acres ----	Yield Per Harvested Acre (Sh. Tons)	Pro- duction (1,000 Tons)	Sugar Yield Per Acre (Sh. Tons)	Price[3] (Dollars)	Farm Value (1,000 $)	Equiv- alent Raw Value[4] - 1,000	Refined Basis Short Tons -	World[5] Refined #5 ------ In	#11 World Cents Per	N.Y. Duty Paid Pound	Wholesale List Price HFCS (42%) Midwest
2009	1,186	1,149	25.9	29,783	3.98	51.50	1,532,634	4,575	----	22.13	18.72	24.93	31.51
2010	1,172	1,156	27.7	32,024	4.03	66.90	2,142,162	4,659	----	27.78	27.03	35.97	26.56
2011	1,233	1,213	23.8	28,896	4.04	69.40	2,004,116	4,900	----	31.68	29.28	38.12	30.11
2012	1,230	1,204	29.3	35,224	4.22	66.40	2,338,789	5,076	----	26.50	21.69	28.90	32.92
2013	1,198	1,154	28.4	32,789	4.15	46.90	1,536,422	4,794	----	22.17	17.46	20.46	35.86
2014	1,163	1,146	27.3	31,285	4.27	46.00	1,440,068	4,893	----	20.05	16.34	24.15	29.96
2015	1,160	1,145	30.9	35,359	4.47	47.20	1,669,310	5,119	----	16.94	13.14	24.88	32.75
2016	1,163	1,126	32.8	36,920	4.53	35.50	1,311,851	5,106	----	22.63	18.13	27.65	37.68
2017[1]	1,132	1,114	31.7	35,317					----	19.62	15.81	27.92	39.79
2018[2]	1,113	1,095	30.3	33,145					----	15.56	12.25	25.37	----

[1] Preliminary. [2] Estimate. [3] Includes support payments, but excludes Gov't. sugar beet payments. [4] Refined sugar multiplied by factor of 1.07.
[5] F.O.B. Europe. Source: Economic Research Service, U.S. Department of Agriculture (ERS-USDA)

Sugar Deliveries and Stocks in the United States   In Thousands of Short Tons (Raw Value)

Year	Quota Allocation	Actual Imports	Cane Sugar Refineries Deliveries	Beet Sugar Factories Deliveries	Importers of Direct Con- sumption Sugar	Mainland Cane Sugar Mills[3]	Total Deliveries	Total Domestic Con- sumption	Cane Sugar Re- fineries	Beet Sugar Factories	CCC	Refiners' Raw	Mainland Cane Mills	Total
2009	----	----	5,493	4,324	667	----	10,485	10,657	440	1,464	0	468	1,612	3,984
2010	----	----	5,635	4,514	843	----	10,992	11,231	484	1,456	0	346	1,274	3,559
2011	----	----	5,572	4,552	995	----	11,118	11,370	466	1,691	0	257	1,455	3,869
2012	----	----	5,648	4,633	977	----	11,257	11,405	315	1,597	0	498	1,370	3,780
2013	----	----	5,849	4,777	949	----	11,575	12,124	388	2,013	0	574	1,646	4,621
2014	----	----	6,069	4,875	760	----	11,704	11,831	572	1,603	0	592	1,714	4,481
2015	----	----	6,285	4,614	1,034	----	11,933	12,067	351	1,589	0	556	1,634	4,130
2016	----	----	6,386	4,809	921	----	12,115	12,287	413	1,889	0	322	1,336	3,960
2017[1]	----	----	5,976	5,425	682	----	12,083	12,232	325	2,041	0	362	1,623	4,351
2018[2]	----	----	6,230	5,130	704	----	12,065	12,203	316	1,716	0	538	1,529	4,099

[1] Preliminary. [2] Estimate. [3] Sugar for direct consumption only. [4] Refined. Source: Economic Research Service,
U.S. Department of Agriculture (ERS-USDA)

Sugar, Refined--Deliveries to End User in the United States   In Thousands of Short Tons

Year	Bakery & Cereal Products	Bev- erages	Confec- tionery[2]	Hotels, Restar. & Insti- tutions	Ice Cream & Dairy Products	Canned, Bottled & Frozen Foods	All Other Food Uses	Retail Grocers[3]	Wholesale Grocers[4]	Non-food Uses	Non- Industrial Uses	Industrial Uses	Total Deliveries
2009	2,286	351	1,085	127	587	427	573	1,241	2,360	84	3,907	5,393	9,300
2010	2,400	422	1,070	124	583	391	609	1,270	2,471	111	4,079	5,587	9,666
2011	2,324	404	1,048	120	622	411	625	1,239	2,511	128	4,104	5,562	9,665
2012	2,330	486	1,044	130	674	412	687	1,172	2,374	123	3,959	5,755	9,715
2013	2,296	547	1,149	112	678	399	760	1,109	2,427	117	4,040	5,947	9,987
2014	2,435	598	1,142	118	756	434	853	1,193	2,151	118	3,965	6,336	10,300
2015	2,391	755	1,172	103	764	473	791	1,230	2,086	162	3,832	6,509	10,341
2016	2,517	695	1,156	92	764	433	880	1,303	2,248	179	4,094	6,625	10,719
2017	2,519	680	1,171	105	753	420	1,048	1,250	2,206	137	4,055	6,729	10,784
2018[1]	2,468	725	1,222	91	812	375	1,147	1,224	2,175	138	3,836	6,877	10,713

[1] Preliminary. [2] And related products. [3] Chain stores, supermarkets. [4] Jobbers, sugar dealers.
Source: Economic Research Service, U.S. Department of Agriculture (ERS-USDA)

Deliveries[1] of All Sugar by Primary Distributors in the United States, by Quarters   In Thousands of Short Tons

Year	First Quarter	Second Quarter	Third Quarter	Fourth Quarter	Total	Year	First Quarter	Second Quarter	Third Quarter	Fourth Quarter	Total
2007	2,364	2,604	2,735	2,471	10,173	2012	2,663	2,915	2,954	2,873	11,405
2008	2,532	2,728	2,865	2,775	10,900	2013	2,720	2,954	3,222	3,229	12,124
2009	2,431	2,649	2,823	2,754	10,657	2014	2,742	3,053	3,189	2,847	11,831
2010	2,565	2,759	3,074	2,833	11,231	2015	2,861	3,070	3,274	2,862	12,067
2011	2,649	2,809	3,131	2,781	11,370	2016	2,992	2,946	3,250	3,098	12,287
2012	2,663	2,915	2,954	2,873	11,405	2017[2]	2,869	3,130	3,161	3,090	12,250

[1] Includes for domestic consumption and for export. [2] Preliminary. Source: Economic Research Service, U.S. Department of Agriculture (ERS-USDA)

SUGAR #11 - ICE-US
Weekly Selected Futures as of 03/29/2019

WEEKLY SELECTED FUTURES
As of 03/29/2019

Chart High 36.08 on 02/02/2011
Chart Low 9.83 on 09/27/2018

Nearby Futures through Last Trading Day using selected contract months: March, May, July and October.

Volume of Trading of World Sugar #11 Futures in New York   In Thousands of Contracts

Year	Jan.	Feb.	Mar.	Apr.	May	June	July	Aug.	Sept.	Oct.	Nov.	Dec.	Total
2009	1,624.6	2,040.3	1,867.0	2,995.5	2,229.3	3,359.1	1,741.5	2,833.2	3,219.5	1,824.3	1,576.4	1,989.5	27,300
2010	2,348.9	2,986.5	2,772.9	2,754.5	1,730.0	2,936.0	1,840.3	2,184.6	3,366.7	1,978.1	2,629.3	1,524.7	29,053
2011	2,180.8	3,341.9	1,774.8	2,338.8	1,832.4	3,266.1	1,702.0	1,986.6	2,555.9	1,258.7	1,286.7	1,104.7	24,629
2012	1,999.3	2,765.1	2,316.0	2,765.4	1,941.5	3,460.7	2,251.7	2,049.8	2,736.2	1,781.4	1,633.1	1,426.4	27,127
2013	2,368.0	3,038.0	2,039.9	3,086.2	1,908.9	3,974.1	2,037.0	2,117.1	3,791.9	2,279.9	1,559.9	1,612.7	29,814
2014	2,461.6	4,157.3	2,477.4	2,857.3	1,906.5	3,370.3	1,981.4	1,853.3	3,657.9	1,651.3	1,574.3	1,448.0	29,397
2015	2,547.7	3,635.6	2,790.0	3,850.9	2,274.2	3,789.2	2,260.8	2,315.0	4,329.7	2,600.5	2,303.8	1,697.0	34,394
2016	3,182.7	3,772.8	2,652.9	3,517.9	2,596.7	4,210.0	1,738.1	2,008.6	3,963.5	1,721.8	1,964.4	1,786.0	33,115
2017	2,494.1	3,269.3	2,773.6	3,294.8	2,484.6	3,515.7	1,859.0	2,291.5	3,359.1	1,665.9	2,055.1	1,898.4	30,961
2018	3,212.7	3,692.3	2,839.4	4,157.9	3,195.2	3,984.1	2,003.6	2,836.6	4,144.2	3,216.5	2,129.3	1,599.2	37,011

Contract size = 112,000 lbs.   Source: ICE Futures U.S. (ICE)

Average Open Interest of World Sugar #11 Futures in New York   In Contracts

Year	Jan.	Feb.	Mar.	Apr.	May	June	July	Aug.	Sept.	Oct.	Nov.	Dec.
2009	664,303	656,033	644,829	681,177	703,355	764,799	735,556	838,638	821,646	770,085	772,808	813,238
2010	842,463	830,888	745,170	667,291	656,182	635,744	587,509	627,022	651,093	585,353	584,909	592,044
2011	619,904	648,027	597,384	613,301	583,047	627,566	630,027	598,737	544,893	489,135	495,699	533,588
2012	612,932	699,780	729,307	728,645	728,515	744,254	669,730	688,099	705,221	697,064	726,541	756,324
2013	796,708	824,203	804,682	852,113	846,873	901,021	848,276	878,813	870,124	818,823	803,346	810,753
2014	834,655	838,471	787,473	792,420	809,219	870,191	842,551	885,193	851,724	766,320	811,959	828,791
2015	824,778	848,192	862,965	876,247	853,458	885,602	805,457	837,922	790,609	766,704	838,992	861,944
2016	870,944	830,246	795,043	820,305	841,639	894,893	837,385	880,629	885,571	841,889	837,131	818,873
2017	828,436	824,169	778,676	791,551	790,116	833,483	768,669	812,524	773,437	700,720	709,575	752,794
2018	844,185	891,797	915,120	1,003,293	1,012,957	977,622	973,446	1,041,981	871,673	774,976	791,152	840,548

Contract size = 112,000 lbs.   Source: ICE Futures U.S. (ICE)

Sulfur

Sulfur (atomic symbol S) is an odorless, tasteless, light yellow, nonmetallic element. As early as 2000 BC, Egyptians used sulfur compounds to bleach fabric. The Chinese used sulfur as an essential component when they developed gunpowder in the 13th century.

Sulfur is widely found in both its free and combined states. Free sulfur is found mixed with gypsum and pumice stone in volcanic regions. Sulfur dioxide is an air pollutant released from the combustion of fossil fuels. The most important use of sulfur is the production of sulfur compounds. Sulfur is used in skin ointments, matches, dyes, gunpowder, and phosphoric acid.

Supply – World production of all forms of sulfur in 2018 was down -0.2% yr/yr at 80.000 million metric tons, which is down from the 2017 record high. The world's largest producers of sulfur are China with 21.3% of the world's production, the U.S. with 12.1%, Russia with 8.9%, and Canada with 6.9%. U.S. production of sulfur in 2018 rose +0.6% yr/yr to 9.700 million metric tons, still above the 2009 record low of 8.940 million metric tons.

Demand – U.S. consumption of all forms of sulfur in 2018 was unchanged at 10.000 million metric tons, but still above the 4-decade low of 9.460 million metric tons seen in 2009. U.S. consumption of elemental sulfur in 2015 fell -1.5% yr/yr to 9.310 million metric tons. U.S. consumption of sulfuric acid in 2015 fell by -1.4% yr/yr to 6.320 million metric tons.

Trade – U.S. exports of recovered sulfur in 2016 rose +10.3% yr/yr to 2.040 million metric tons, but still above the 25-year low of 635,000 metric tons in 2006. U.S. imports of recovered sulfur in 2016 fell by -12.5% yr/yr to 1.960 million metric tons, down from the 2011 record high of 3.270 million metric tons.

World Production of Sulfur (All Forms) In Thousands of Metric Tons

Year	Canada	China	France	Germany	Kazakh-stan	Japan	Mexico	Poland	Russia	Saudi Arabia	Spain	United States	World Total
2011	6,523	9,700	650	3,908	3,205	2,700	1,440	1,166	7,557	4,579	675	8,950	69,900
2012	6,260	9,900	728	3,820	3,503	2,740	1,012	1,230	7,690	4,092	257	9,000	71,400
2013	6,300	8,110	478	3,800	3,465	3,050	1,030	1,080	7,300	3,900	270	9,210	69,800
2014	5,840	8,840	478	3,800	3,503	3,070	993	1,160	6,860	4,400	270	9,630	71,300
2015	5,750	8,800	478	3,800	3,421	3,120	859	1,200	6,960	4,900	----	9,540	73,800
2016	5,320	8,800	478	3,800	3,420	3,120	673	1,210	6,960	4,900	----	9,740	73,500
2017[1]	5,460	17,400	----	888	3,490	3,520	551	1,240	7,080	6,000	----	9,640	80,200
2018[2]	5,500	17,000	----	890	3,500	3,500	550	1,200	7,100	6,000	----	9,700	80,000

[1] Preliminary.   [2] Estimate.   *Source: U.S. Geological Survey (USGS)*

Salient Statistics of Sulfur in the United States In Thousands of Metric Tons (Sulfur Content)

	Production of										Sales Value of Shipments		
	Elemental Sulfur					By-product Sulfuric Acid[4]	Other Sulf. Acid Compounds	Imports Sulfuric Acid[4]	Exports Sulfuric Acid[4]	Producer Stocks, Dec. 31[5]	Apparent Consumption (All Forms)	F.O.B. Mine/Plant	
	Native - Sulfur[3] -	---- Recovered -----			Total Elemental Sulfur							Frasch	Recovered Average
Year	Frasch	Petroleum & Cole	Natural Gas	Total									Total
2011	----	7,080	1,130	8,230	720	----	8,950	2,670	332	175	11,700	----	----	159.88
2012	----	7,370	1,040	8,410	586	----	9,000	2,850	161	132	11,000	----	----	123.54
2013	----	7,580	1,020	8,590	616	----	9,210	2,980	165	160	11,300	----	----	68.71
2014	----	8,040	1,000	9,040	587	----	9,630	3,070	160	141	11,000	----	----	80.07
2015	----	7,910	984	8,890	646	----	9,540	3,540	172	138	11,000	----	----	87.62
2016	----	8,290	781	9,070	673	----	9,740			144	10,500	----	----	37.88
2017[1]	----	8,410	662	9,070	575	----	9,640			124	10,000	----	----	46.40
2018[2]	----	8,338	625	8,965	670	----	9,700			110	10,000	----	----	70.00

[1] Preliminary.   [2] Estimate.   [3] Or sulfur ore; Withheld included in natural gas.   [4] Basis 100% H2SO4, sulfur equivalent.   [5] Frasch & recovered.
W = Withheld proprietary data.   Source: U.S. Geological Survey (USGS)

Sulfur Consumption & Foreign Trade of the United States In Thousands of Metric Tons (Sulfur Content)

	Consumption			Sulfuric Acid Sold or Used, by End Use[2]						Foreign Trade				
	Native Sulfur (Frasch)	Recovered Sulfur	Total Elemental Form	Pulpmills & Paper Products	Inorganic Chemicals[3]	Synthetic Rubber & Plastic	Phosphatic Fertilizers	Petroleum Refining[4]	Frasch	Exports		Imports		
Year										Frasch covered	Re-covered	Value $1,000	Frasch covered	Re-covered	Value $1,000
2009	----	----	8,380	7,740	188	286	64	5,430	283	----	1,430	82,200	----	1,700	54,100
2010	----	----	9,870	6,980	79	31	6	5,700	368	----	1,450	171,000	----	2,950	214,000
2011	----	----	10,200	7,650	168	118	70	5,740	422	----	1,310	266,000	----	3,270	301,000
2012	----	----	9,520	7,410	168	107	70	5,420	423	----	1,860	366,000	----	2,930	238,000
2013	----	----	9,810	7,780	168	101	70	5,270	1,270	----	1,770	235,000	----	2,990	202,000
2014	----	----	9,450	6,410	129	74	6	4,810	410	----	2,010	315,000	----	2,370	134,000
2015	----	----	9,310	6,320	124	128	6	4,610	428	----	1,850	284,000	----	2,240	136,000
2016[1]	----	----	8,850	7,550	119	79	6	5,820	387	----	2,040	213,000	----	1,960	79,800

[1] Preliminary.   [2] Sulfur equivalent.   [3] Including inorganic pigments, paints & allied products, and other inorganic chemicals & products.
[4] Including other petroleum and coal products.   W = Withheld proprietary data.   NA = Not available.   *Source: U.S. Geological Survey (USGS)*

Sunflowerseed, Meal and Oil

Sunflowers are native to South and North America but are now grown almost worldwide. Sunflower-seed oil accounts for approximately 14% of the world production of seed oils. Sunflower varieties that are commercially grown contain from 39% to 49% oil in the seed. Sunflower crops produce about 50 bushels of seed per acre on average, which yields approximately 50 gallons of oil.

Sunflower-seed oil accounts for around 80% of the value of the sunflower crop. Refined sunflower-seed oil is edible and used primarily as a salad and cooking oil and in margarine. Crude sunflower-seed oil is used industrially for making soaps, candles, varnishes, and detergents. Sunflower-seed oil contains 93% of the energy of U.S. No. 2 diesel fuel and is being explored as a potential alternate fuel source in diesel engines. Sunflower meal is used in livestock feed and when fed to poultry, increases the yield of eggs. Sunflower seeds are also used for birdfeed and as a snack for humans.

Prices – The average monthly price received by U.S. farmers for sunflower seeds in the first three months of the 2018/19 marketing year (Sep/Aug) fell -3.2% to $16.80 per hundred pounds, well below the 2011-12 record high of $28.96 per hundred pounds.

Supply – World sunflower-seed production in the 2018/19 is expected to rise +6.5% yr/yr to 50.469 million metric tons. The world's largest sunflower-seed producers

will be the Ukraine with 29.7% of the world production, Russia with 22.8%, European Union with 19.6%, Argentina with 8.7%, China with 6.4%, Turkey with 3.6%, and the U.S. with 1.7%.

U.S. production of sunflower seeds in 2018/19 is expected to fall by -10.2% yr/yr to 878,000 metric tons, far below the record production level of 3.309 million metric tons posted in 1979-80. U.S. farmers are expected to harvest 1.240 million acres of sunflowers in 2018/19, down -7.0% yr/yr, well below the 10-year high of 2.610 million acres posted in 2005-06. U.S sunflower yield in 2018/19 is expected to be 15.60 hundred pounds per acre, down -3.5% yr/yr, below the 2016/17 record high of 17.31.

Demand – Total U.S. disappearance of sunflower seeds in 2018/19 is expected to fall -15.3% yr/yr to 1.137 million metric tons, of which 43.4% went to non-oil and seed use, 39.3% went to crushing for oil and meal, and 5.2% went to exports.

Trade – World sunflower seed exports in 2018/19 are expected to fall -7.6% yr/yr to 2.299 million metric tons. The world's largest exporters will be Moldova which accounted for 28.3% of world exports, China with 16.5%, and both the European Union and Kazakhstan with 15.2%. World sunflower seed imports in 2018/19 are expected to fall -6.2% yr/yr to 2.022 million metric tons. The world's largest importers will be the European Union with 27.2% of world imports and Turkey with 24.7% of world imports.

World Production of Sunflowerseed   In Thousands of Metric Tons

Crop Year	Argen-tina	China	European Union	India	Kazakh-stan	Pakistan	Russia	Serbia	South Africa	Turkey	Ukraine	United States	World Total
2011-12	3,341	2,313	8,455	620	409	283	9,002	415	522	925	9,800	925	38,618
2012-13	3,100	2,323	7,088	615	400	243	7,495	350	557	1,125	9,000	1,241	34,993
2013-14	2,065	2,424	9,054	580	573	200	9,842	425	832	1,400	11,600	917	41,511
2014-15	3,160	2,492	8,974	383	513	200	8,374	525	661	1,200	10,200	1,007	39,189
2015-16	3,000	2,698	7,721	323	534	90	9,173	450	755	1,100	11,900	1,326	40,540
2016-17	3,547	2,990	8,598	318	755	75	10,858	650	874	1,320	15,200	1,203	48,008
2017-18[1]	3,538	3,120	9,679	230	903	90	10,362	540	859	1,550	13,700	978	47,406
2018-19[2]	3,400	3,250	9,900	324	1,000	75	11,500	680	760	1,800	15,000	878	50,469

[1] Preliminary. [2] Forecast. Source: Economic Research Service, U.S. Department of Agriculture (ERS-USDA)

World Exports of Sunflowerseed   In Thousands of Metric Tons

Crop Year	Argen-tina	Canada	China	European Union	Israel	Kazakh-stan	Moldova	Russia	Serbia	Turkey	Ukraine	United States	World Total
2011-12	80	33	186	596	4	36	194	332	15	38	282	106	1,927
2012-13	84	44	158	521	4	31	196	39	50	38	127	136	1,453
2013-14	74	49	173	712	3	145	322	135	106	33	70	120	1,957
2014-15	63	34	244	518		116	342	61	77	28	45	116	1,657
2015-16	308	29	286	424	2	163	316	107	134	42	83	99	2,008
2016-17	75	18	365	353	1	269	522	368	127	47	191	90	2,440
2017-18[1]	50	17	415	629	1	350	630	94	112	56	39	79	2,489
2018-19[2]	70	20	380	350	1	350	650	100	150	50	100	59	2,299

[1] Preliminary. [2] Forecast. Source: Economic Research Service, U.S. Department of Agriculture (ERS-USDA)

World Imports of Sunflowerseed   In Thousands of Metric Tons

Crop Year	Belarus	Canada	Egypt	European Union	Iran	Mexico	Moldova	Morocco	Pakistan	Russia	Turkey	United States	World Total
2011-12	35	33	77	280	27	15	1	18	159	28	834	44	1,702
2012-13	12	27	52	214	30	14	1	37	2	29	628	54	1,362
2013-14	13	25	56	319	42	18	2	1	197	35	581	65	1,624
2014-15	19	30	57	266	69	18	3	38	178	88	470	75	1,559
2015-16	25	22	63	622	82	20	6	15	94	121	396	72	1,866
2016-17	53	30	62	694	144	27	5	8	40	107	591	80	2,171
2017-18[1]	27	22	74	512	150	27	3	19	50	46	720	97	2,156
2018-19[2]	55	23	65	550	150	28	3	10	50	50	500	84	2,022

[1] Preliminary. [2] Forecast. Source: Economic Research Service, U.S. Department of Agriculture (ERS-USDA)

SUNFLOWERSEED, MEAL AND OIL

World Production of Sunflowerseed Oil In Thousands of Metric Tons

Crop Year	Argen-tina	Burma	China	European Union	India	Pakistan	Russia	Serbia	South Africa	Turkey	Ukraine	United States	World Total
2011-12	1,565	143	348	2,824	195	153	3,304	170	272	688	3,976	146	14,347
2012-13	980	112	476	2,581	193	97	2,891	130	289	731	3,638	194	12,860
2013-14	934	112	481	3,196	179	148	3,785	123	347	774	4,759	195	15,631
2014-15	1,153	131	466	3,232	121	144	3,428	161	298	696	4,429	146	14,967
2015-16	1,142	131	502	3,042	105	68	3,552	153	335	587	5,010	205	15,376
2016-17	1,288	131	609	3,338	105	38	4,171	191	348	761	6,351	211	18,181
2017-18[1]	1,300	131	663	3,634	75	44	4,130	212	352	912	5,891	200	18,232
2018-19[2]	1,400	131	717	3,718	112	40	4,460	225	352	935	6,235	188	19,251

[1] Preliminary. [2] Forecast. *Source: Economic Research Service, U.S. Department of Agriculture (ERS-USDA)*

World Production of Sunflowerseed Meal In Thousands of Metric Tons

Crop Year	Argen-tina	Burma	China	European Union	India	Kazakh-stan	Pakistan	Russia	South Africa	Turkey	Ukraine	United States	World Total
2011-12	1,621	140	532	3,629	260	129	160	3,284	275	853	3,930	181	15,602
2012-13	1,021	110	726	3,318	258	127	101	2,874	293	935	3,595	238	14,149
2013-14	963	110	732	4,108	238	144	155	3,571	356	990	4,646	240	16,833
2014-15	1,147	128	709	4,131	156	135	150	3,407	302	880	4,254	179	16,165
2015-16	1,141	128	763	3,888	135	129	71	3,530	340	743	4,811	252	16,495
2016-17	1,270	128	927	4,266	135	176	40	4,146	353	963	6,030	259	19,349
2017-18[1]	1,285	128	1,008	4,644	97	201	46	4,105	357	1,128	5,658	245	19,607
2018-19[2]	1,380	128	1,090	4,752	146	242	42	4,433	357	1,155	5,989	227	20,663

[1] Preliminary. [2] Forecast. *Source: Economic Research Service, U.S. Department of Agriculture (ERS-USDA)*

Sunflowerseed Statistics in the United States In Thousands of Metric Tons

Crop Year Beginning Sept. 1	Acres Harvested (1,000)	Harvested Yield Per CWT	Farm Price ($/Metric Ton)	Value of Pro-duction (Million $)	Stocks, Sept. 1	Pro-duction	Imports	Total Supply	Crush	Exports	Non-Oil Use & Seed	Total Disap-pearance
2011-12	1,458	13.98	642	589.3	117	925	44	1,086	349	106	544	1,086
2012-13	1,840	14.87	560	700.0	87	1,241	54	1,382	451	136	641	1,382
2013-14	1,465	13.80	472	443.3	154	917	65	1,136	463	120	462	1,136
2014-15	1,510	14.69	478	497.8	91	1,007	75	1,173	366	116	583	1,173
2015-16	1,799	16.25	432	574.2	108	1,326	72	1,506	495	99	725	1,506
2016-17	1,532	17.31	384	464.0	187	1,203	80	1,470	508	90	605	1,470
2017-18[1]	1,334	16.03	388	389.2	267	978	97	1,342	481	79	607	1,342
2018-19[2]	1,223	17.31			175	878	84	1,137	447	59	494	1,137

[1] Preliminary. [2] Forecast. *Source: Economic Research Service, U.S. Department of Agriculture (ERS-USDA)*

Sunflower Oil Statistics in the United States In Thousands of Metric Tons

Crop Year Beginning Sept. 1	Stocks, Oct. 1	Production	Imports	Total Supply	Exports	Domestic Use	Total Disap-pearance	Price $ Per Metric Ton (Crude Mpls.)
2011-12	27	146	74	247	19	205	224	1,871
2012-13	23	194	32	249	28	198	226	1,473
2013-14	23	195	35	253	37	193	230	1,305
2014-15	23	146	80	249	29	197	226	1,449
2015-16	23	205	42	270	39	197	236	1,309
2016-17	34	211	54	299	32	226	258	1,182
2017-18[1]	41	200	73	314	40	241	281	1,205
2018-19[2]	33	188	68	289	36	217	253	1,181

[1] Preliminary. [2] Forecast. *Source: Economic Research Service, U.S. Department of Agriculture (ERS-USDA)*

Sunflower Meal Statistics in the United States In Thousands of Metric Tons

Crop Year Beginning Sept. 1	Stocks, Oct. 1	Production	Imports	Total Supply	Exports	Domestic Use	Total Disap-pearance	Price USD Per Metric Ton 28% Protein
2011-12	5	181	----	186	3	178	186	264
2012-13	5	238	----	243	19	219	243	279
2013-14	5	240	11	256	8	243	256	270
2014-15	5	179	20	204	7	192	204	224
2015-16	5	252	21	278	12	261	278	175
2016-17	5	259	11	275	5	265	275	161
2017-18[1]	5	245	1	251	6	240	251	190
2018-19[2]	5	227	9	241	9	227	241	190

[1] Preliminary. [2] Forecast. *Source: Economic Research Service, U.S. Department of Agriculture (ERS-USDA)*

Average Price Received by Farmers for Sunflower[2] in the United States   In Dollars Per Hundred Pounds (Cwt.)

Year	Sept.	Oct.	Nov.	Dec.	Jan.	Feb.	Mar.	Apr.	May	June	July	Aug.	Average
2011-12	32.90	29.60	29.00	29.60	28.90	29.50	28.80	28.40	27.80	27.20	27.00	28.80	28.96
2012-13	28.80	25.90	26.70	24.80	26.00	26.10	24.60	24.80	24.00	24.40	23.70	23.70	25.29
2013-14	22.60	23.00	20.70	18.80	19.60	22.80	21.60	22.30	24.10	22.80	22.10	22.40	21.90
2014-15	20.20	21.70	20.30	19.70	19.10	21.50	22.50	23.20	26.40	25.40	26.40	24.20	22.55
2015-16	25.20	18.40	18.30	19.30	20.10	20.40	21.10	20.90	19.50	20.10	19.00	19.60	20.16
2016-17	17.90	17.00	16.40	17.20	17.20	17.60	17.40	17.90	17.30	17.60	17.90	19.10	17.54
2017-18	17.40	16.80	16.60	17.00	17.60	17.70	17.30	18.00	17.90	17.70	17.40	16.90	17.36
2018-19[1]	16.70	16.70	17.00	16.40	17.40								16.84

[1] Preliminary.   [2] KS, MN, ND and SD average.   Source: Economic Research Service, U.S. Department of Agriculture (ERS-USDA)

Average Price of Crude Sunflower Oil at Minneapolis   In Cents Per Pound

Year	Sept.	Oct.	Nov.	Dec.	Jan.	Feb.	Mar.	Apr.	May	June	July	Aug.	Average
2011-12	94.80	92.50	91.00	91.00	88.75	86.00	82.00	79.00	80.00	80.20	78.00	75.00	84.85
2012-13	75.00	74.00	70.30	67.50	65.25	65.00	64.60	64.00	64.00	64.00	64.00	64.00	66.80
2013-14	63.75	60.50	57.40	57.00	57.00	57.00	58.00	59.00	59.00	57.50	61.00	63.00	59.18
2014-15	63.00	63.00	61.75	58.00	63.00	65.63	65.56	65.50	65.00	69.75	73.40	75.00	65.72
2015-16	75.00	72.00	64.50	62.00	58.00	54.25	53.80	53.80	54.00	54.20	55.20	56.00	59.40
2016-17	56.00	56.00	56.00	56.00	56.00	55.00	52.00	51.00	50.50	50.80	51.25	52.75	53.61
2017-18	55.20	56.00	55.50	54.80	55.50	55.00	54.00	54.00	54.00	54.00	54.00	54.00	54.67
2018-19[1]	54.00	54.00	52.80	53.50	53.50								53.56

[1] Preliminary.   Source: Economic Research Service, U.S. Department of Agriculture (ERS-USDA)

Average Price of Sunflower Meal (26% protein) in the United States   In Cents Per Pound

Year	Sept.	Oct.	Nov.	Dec.	Jan.	Feb.	Mar.	Apr.	May	June	July	Aug.	Average
2011-12	263.75	232.50	224.00	225.63	223.50	191.88	191.88	211.25	230.50	226.88	300.50	348.13	239.20
2012-13	354.38	287.00	269.38	266.67	252.00	237.50	231.25	222.00	215.00	233.13	245.50	221.25	252.92
2013-14	218.13	236.25	246.88	277.50	283.75	285.00	271.25	267.50	265.00	250.00	192.50	151.25	245.42
2014-15	139.50	162.50	208.13	245.00	247.50	225.63	202.50	202.50	192.50	180.50	214.38	222.50	203.60
2015-16	216.00	212.50	187.50	163.13	156.88	131.88	120.00	109.38	149.50	165.63	151.88	141.00	158.77
2016-17	148.75	148.75	140.50	145.00	159.00	161.88	155.00	147.50	144.00	140.00	130.63	134.50	146.29
2017-18	134.38	153.00	165.00	185.00	178.00	185.63	187.50	191.88	201.50	175.63	155.50	153.13	172.18
2018-19[1]	150.63	164.00	171.25	187.50	190.50								172.78

[1] Preliminary.   Source: Economic Research Service, U.S. Department of Agriculture (ERS-USDA)

Production of Sunflower in the United States   In Thousands of Pounds

Crop Year	California	Colorado	Kansas	Minnesota	Nebraska	North Dakota	Oklahoma	South Dakota	Texas	Total
2011	44,300	124,200	149,400	46,100	75,900	766,250	5,275	776,950	49,900	2,038,275
2012	68,575	52,720	97,950	93,925	26,460	1,430,460	4,720	859,250	102,000	2,736,060
2013	75,150	45,600	82,000	69,250	32,975	600,560	5,180	996,800	114,250	2,021,765
2014	61,925	95,700	91,540	87,870	47,375	847,420	3,200	876,620	137,400	2,219,050
2015	44,720	85,200	135,560	166,050	79,410	1,068,800	6,600	1,230,040	107,350	2,923,730
2016	61,875	90,500	82,660	113,550	58,150	1,137,450	----	1,057,050	50,400	2,651,635
2017	51,305	86,200	84,520	68,475	61,800	704,250	----	1,020,000	61,200	2,137,750
2018[1]	76,500	61,950	74,250	114,050	47,380	739,400	----	975,300	27,580	2,116,410

[1] Preliminary.   Source: Economic Research Service, U.S. Department of Agriculture (ERS-USDA)

Production of Sunflower Oil in the United States   In Thousands of Pounds

Crop Year	California	Colorado	Kansas	Minnesota	Nebraska	North Dakota	Oklahoma	South Dakota	Texas	Total
2011	39,500	97,000	123,900	35,100	45,500	690,000	4,875	664,950	21,850	1,722,675
2012	65,075	40,120	74,750	70,300	20,650	1,283,500	4,180	761,600	39,600	2,359,775
2013	72,150	29,600	58,000	51,200	19,975	504,000	3,480	820,800	78,000	1,637,205
2014	57,200	44,800	57,540	65,250	29,000	683,400	2,100	668,000	56,800	1,664,090
2015	42,900	68,400	80,560	123,750	42,660	889,350	4,800	1,048,000	82,650	2,383,870
2016	60,075	68,400	57,540	96,000	37,800	1,055,300	----	960,300	33,600	2,369,015
2017	49,875	73,000	65,000	64,350	37,050	628,650	----	848,000	45,600	1,847,525
2018[1]	74,100	53,900	61,500	99,000	34,080	665,000	----	887,550	21,280	1,896,410

[1] Preliminary.   Source: Economic Research Service, U.S. Department of Agriculture (ERS-USDA)

Tallow and Greases

Tallow and grease are derived from processing (rendering) the fat of cattle. Tallow is used to produce both edible and inedible products. Edible tallow products include margarine, cooking oil, and baking products. Inedible tallow products include soap, candles, and lubricants. Production of tallow and greases is directly related to the number of cattle produced. Those countries that are the leading cattle producers are also the largest producers of tallow. The American Fats and Oils Association provides specifications for a variety of different types of tallow and grease, including edible tallow, lard (edible), top white tallow, all beef packer tallow, extra fancy tallow, fancy tallow, bleachable fancy tallow, prime tallow, choice white grease, and yellow grease. The specifications include such characteristics as the melting point, color, density, moisture content, insoluble impurities, and others.

Prices – The monthly average wholesale price of tallow (inedible, No. 1 Packers-Prime, delivered Chicago) in 2015 fell -27.0% yr/yr to 28.42 cents per pound. The wholesale price of inedible tallow in 2015 fell -26.7% yr/yr to 26.87 cents per pound.

Supply – World production of tallow and greases (edible and inedible) in 2017 (latest data), rose + 1.4% yr/yr to 9.511million metric tons, which is a new record high.

The world's largest producer of tallow and greases by far is the U.S. with 47.0% of world production, followed by Brazil far behind with 6.5%, Australia with 5.5%, and Canada with 2.7%. U.S. production of edible tallow in 2017 fell -4.2% yr/yr to 2.053 billion pounds, close to the 2012 record high of 2.055 billion pounds. U.S. production of inedible tallow and greases in 2011 fell -37.9% yr/yr to 3.654 billion pounds, well below the record high of 7.156 billion pounds posted in 2002.

Demand – U.S. consumption of inedible tallow and greases in 2011 fell 0.9% yr/yr to 1.560 billion pounds, of which virtually all went for animal feed. U.S. consumption of edible tallow in 2017 rose +0.8% yr/yr to 1.945 billion pounds, but still below the 2011 record high of 1.954 billion pounds. U.S. per capita consumption of edible tallow in 2010 rose from 0.7 pounds per person to 3.4 pounds per person yr/yr, down from the 2000 and 2004 record high of 4.0 pounds.

Trade – U.S. exports of inedible tallow and grease in 2011 fell -3.2% yr/yr to 752.990 million pounds and accounted for 48.3% of total U.S. supply. U.S. exports of edible tallow in 2017 fell by -31.8% yr/yr to 181 million pounds and accounted for 8.5% of U.S. supply.

World Production of Tallow and Greases (Edible and Inedible)   In Thousands of Metric Tons

Year	Argentina	Australia	Brazil	Canada	France	Germany	Korea, South	Nether-lands	New Zealand	Russia	United Kingdom	United States	World Total
2008	189	499	564	261	196	131	16	122	189	189	138	3,695	8,389
2009	204	483	547	252	188	131	16	123	168	195	134	3,655	8,304
2010	160	488	566	262	200	134	16	131	169	200	141	3,575	8,331
2011	153	493	551	255	209	134	15	121	167	198	144	4,529	9,186
2012	160	494	587	242	198	131	18	106	166	199	139	4,488	9,190
2013	175	548	654	241	191	130	21	103	169	207	138	4,457	9,319
2014	167	601	635	248	192	131	20	101	167	213	142	4,225	9,189
2015	171	605	600	238	196	132	20	105	176	218	145	4,205	9,191
2016[1]	167	507	621	248	198	132	19	108	165	224	147	4,432	9,377
2017[2]	180	525	619	260	201	130	19	111	171	228	146	4,469	9,511

[1] Preliminary.   [2] Forecast.   Source: Foreign Agricultural Service, U.S. Department of Agriculture (FAS-USDA)

Salient Statistics of Tallow and Greases (Inedible) in the United States   In Millions of Pounds

	-------------------- Supply ---------------------			---------------- Consumption -----------------				Wholesale ------ Prices, Cents Per Lb. ------	
Year	Production	Stocks, Jan. 1	Total	Exports	Soap	Feed	Total	Edible, (Loose) Chicago	Inedible, Chicago No. 1
2006	6,460	309	6,769	730	W	2,585	2,585	18.6	16.9
2007	6,369	291	6,661	795	W	2,385	2,385	30.7	27.8
2008	6,224	350	6,573	703	W	2,095	2,095	38.0	34.2
2009	5,878	315	6,193	727	W	1,770	1,770	27.5	25.2
2010	5,887	286	6,174	778	W	1,574	1,574	35.1	33.3
2011	3,654	281	3,934	753	W	1,560	1,560	53.2	49.6
2012[1]	NA	NA	NA	NA	NA	NA	NA	47.8	43.8
2013[2]	NA	NA	NA	NA	NA	NA	NA	42.6	40.4
2014[2]	----	----	----	----	----	----	----	38.7	36.7
2015[2]	----	----	----	----	----	----	----	28.4	26.9

[1] Preliminary.   [2] Forecast.   Source: Foreign Agricultural Service, U.S. Department of Agriculture (FAS-USDA)

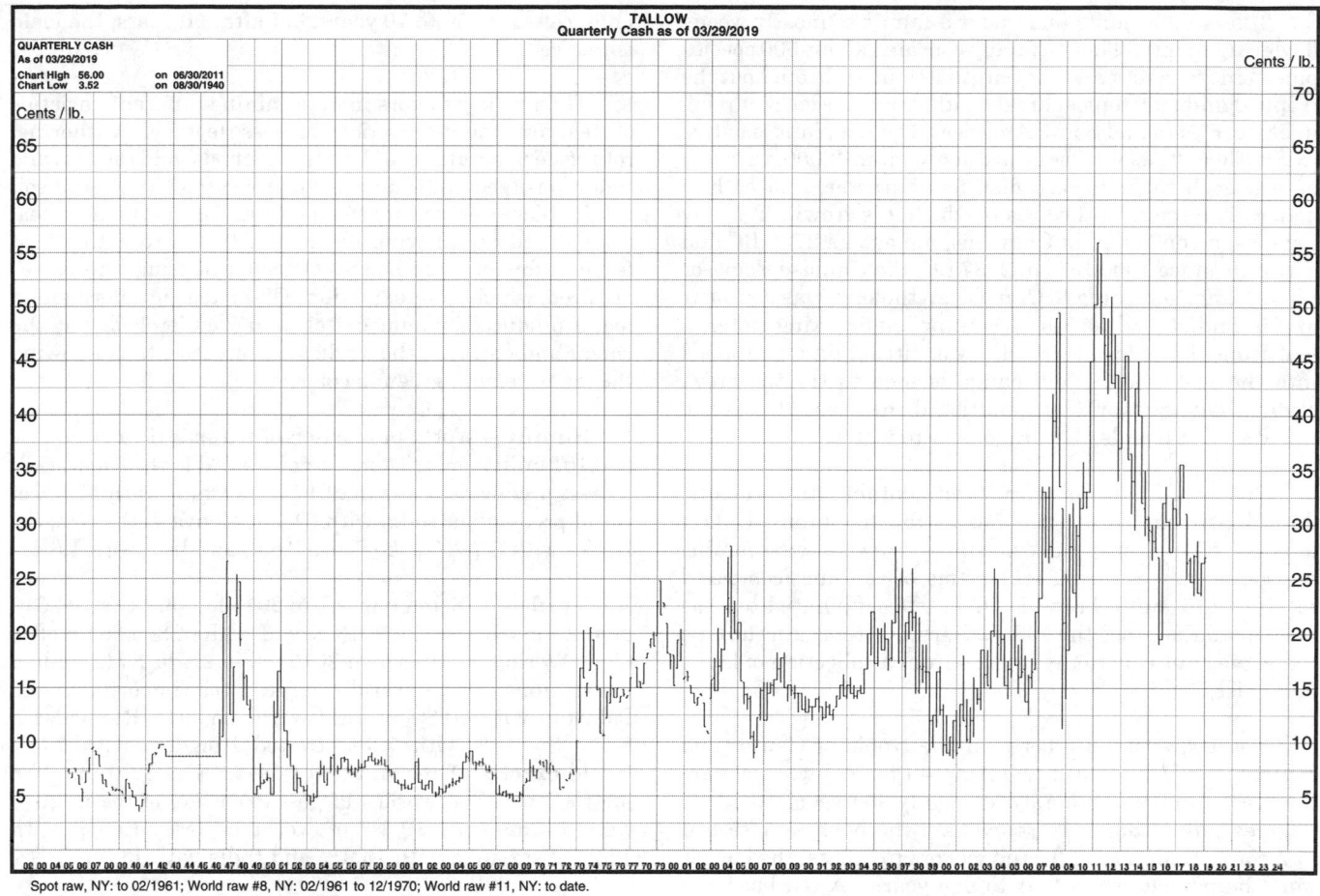

TALLOW
Quarterly Cash as of 03/29/2019

QUARTERLY CASH
As of 03/29/2019
Chart High 56.00 on 06/30/2011
Chart Low 3.52 on 08/30/1940

Cents / lb.

Spot raw, NY: to 02/1961; World raw #8, NY: 02/1961 to 12/1970; World raw #11, NY: to date.

Supply and Disappearance of Edible Tallow in the United States   In Millions of Pounds, Rendered Basis

	---------- Supply ----------			---------------------------------- Disappearance ----------------------------------					
Year	Stocks, Jan. 1	Production	Total Supply	Domestic Disap- pearance	Exports	Total Disap- pearance	Direct Use	Baking or Frying Fats	Per Capita (Lbs.)
2008	39	1,794	1,863	1,648	185	1,833	896	W	2.9
2009	30	1,837	1,903	1,711	162	1,873	212	W	0.7
2010	31	1,859	1,913	1,693	183	1,876	1,050	W	3.4
2011	38	2,050	2,116	1,954	132	2,086	NA	NA	NA
2012	30	2,055	2,137	1,940	166	2,107	NA	NA	NA
2013	30	2,043	2,122	1,935	157	2,092	----	----	----
2014	30	1,922	2,004	1,884	90	1,974	----	----	----
2015	30	1,928	2,003	1,830	143	1,973	----	----	----
2016[1]	30	2,143	2,235	1,929	265	2,194	----	----	----
2017[2]	41	2,053	2,159	1,945	181	2,126	----	----	----

[1] Preliminary.   [2] Forecast.   W = Withheld.   *Sources: Economic Research Service, U.S. Department of Agriculture (ERS-USDA); Bureau of the Census, U.S. Department of Commerce*

Average Wholesale Price of Tallow, Inedible, No. 1 Packers (Prime), Delivered, Chicago   In Cents Per Pound

Year	Jan.	Feb.	Mar.	Apr.	May	June	July	Aug.	Sept.	Oct.	Nov.	Dec.	Average
2009	22.86	19.57	16.72	21.83	25.80	29.53	26.17	31.75	30.44	22.27	25.89	29.09	25.16
2010	28.37	27.42	31.57	32.74	33.08	32.73	32.15	32.28	32.93	33.88	40.52	42.50	33.35
2011	47.83	47.61	49.49	51.59	52.33	54.52	53.69	49.36	50.02	47.36	44.35	47.21	49.61
2012	44.17	45.67	48.16	47.33	48.98	45.39	45.38	44.59	45.72	40.07	34.05	36.20	43.81
2013	40.00	40.00	42.42	43.06	41.67	45.00	45.39	42.74	40.53	33.37	35.14	35.14	40.37
2014	31.95	31.61	38.52	42.60	44.57	42.04	39.96	39.85	34.90	29.51	32.47	32.09	36.67
2015	28.77	28.84	30.42	28.22	28.64	29.72	28.50	29.21	28.71	22.41	19.48	19.50	26.87
2016	23.14	26.50	29.64	32.93	32.67	31.34	29.04	27.50	27.50	27.90	31.49	31.64	29.27
2017	31.35	31.11	30.11	30.33	33.49	35.40	35.50	35.37	33.96	27.83	26.36	26.50	31.44
2018[1]	26.38	25.00	25.59	24.61	24.20	26.35	28.05	27.88	25.20	23.76	25.85	26.50	25.78

[1] Preliminary.   *Sources: Economic Research Service, U.S. Department of Agriculture (ERS-USDA)*

Tea

Tea is the common name for a family of mostly woody flowering plants. The tea family contains about 600 species placed in 28 genera and they are distributed throughout the tropical and subtropical areas, with most species occurring in eastern Asia and South America. The tea plant is native to Southeast Asia. There are more than 3,000 varieties of tea, each with its own distinct character, and each is generally named for the area in which it is grown. Tea may have been consumed in China as long ago as 2700 BC and certainly since 1000 BC. In 2737 BC, the Chinese Emperor Shen Nung, according to Chinese mythology, was a scholar and herbalist. While his servant boiled drinking water, a leaf from the wild tea tree he was sitting under dropped into the water and Shen Nung decided to try the brew. Today, half the world's population drinks tea. Tea is the world's most popular beverage next to water.

Tea is a healthful drink and contains antioxidants, fluoride, niacin, folic acid, and as much vitamin C as a lemon. The average 5 oz. cup of brewed tea contains approximately 40 to 60 milligrams of caffeine (compared to 80 to 115 mg in brewed coffee). Decaffeinated tea has been available since the 1980s. Herbal tea contains no true tea leaves but is actually brewed from a collection of herbs and spices.

Tea grows mainly between the tropic of Cancer and the tropic of Capricorn, requiring 40 to 50 inches of rain per year and a temperature ideally between 50 to 86 degrees Fahrenheit. To rejuvenate the bush and keep it at a convenient height for the pickers to access, the bushes must be pruned every four to five years. A tea bush can produce tea for 50 to 70 years, but after 50 years, the yield is reduced.

The two key factors in determining different varieties of tea are the production process (sorting, withering, rolling, fermentation, and drying methods) and the growing conditions (geographical region, growing altitude, and soil type). Black tea, often referred to as fully fermented tea, is produced by allowing picked tea leaves to wither and ferment for up to 24 hours. After fermenting, the leaves are fired, which stops oxidation. Green tea, or unfermented tea, is produced by immediately and completely drying the leaves and omitting the oxidization process, thus allowing the tea to remain green in color.

Supply – World production of tea in 2017 rose +3.2% to 6.101 million metric tons, a new record high. The world's largest producers of tea in 2017 were China with 40.5% of world production, India with 21.7%, Kenya with 7.2%, Sri Lanka with 5.7%, Turkey with 3.8%, and Iran with 1.6%.

Trade – U.S. tea imports in 2018 fell -3.9% to 194,313 metric tons, below the 2013 record high of 216,864 metric tons. World tea imports in 2016 fell -6.2% to 1.741 million metric tons. The world's largest tea importers were Pakistan with 10.8% of total world imports, Russia with 9.4%, the U.S with 7.5%, United Kingdom with 7.3%. World exports of tea in 2016 fell -2.8% to 1.701 million metric tons. The world's largest exporters of tea in 2016 were China with 19.8% of world exports, Kenya with 17.2%, Sri Lanka with 16.9%, and India with 13.5%.

World Tea Production, in Major Producing Countries   In Metric Tons

Year	Argentina	Bang-ladesh	China	India	Indo-nesia	Iran	Japan	Kenya	Malawi	Sri Lanka	Turkey	Ex-USSR[2]	World Total
2011	92,892	60,500	1,640,310	1,095,460	146,603	112,084	82,100	377,912	47,006	327,500	221,600	3,701	4,839,700
2012	82,813	62,524	1,804,655	1,135,070	143,413	103,890	85,900	369,400	42,490	330,000	225,000	3,258	5,042,470
2013	80,423	66,259	1,939,175	1,208,780	145,855	97,475	84,800	432,400	46,460	340,230	212,400	3,958	5,328,737
2014	82,887	63,780	2,110,770	1,207,310	154,369	72,277	83,600	445,105	45,480	338,032	226,800	2,496	5,510,386
2015	82,492	66,101	2,291,405	1,233,140	132,615	196,957	79,500	399,100	47,552	341,678	239,028	2,925	5,810,097
2016	85,015	64,500	2,326,018	1,250,490	144,015	132,492	80,200	473,000	48,277	349,580	243,000	4,465	5,913,955
2017[1]	80,608	81,850	2,473,443	1,325,050	139,362	100,580	81,119	439,857	48,412	349,699	234,000	3,629	6,101,062

[1] Preliminary.   [2] Mostly Georgia and Azerbaijan.   Sources: Foreign Agricultural Service, U.S. Department of Agriculture (FAS-USDA); Food and Agriculture Organization of the United Nations (FAO-UN)

World Exports of Tea from Producing Countries   In Metric Tons

Year	Argentina	Bang-ladesh	Brazil	China	India	Indonesia	Kenya	Malawi	Papua New Guinea	Sri Lanka	Vietnam	Zim-babwe	Total
2010	85,695	1,981	2,542	307,777	234,560	87,101	417,661	49,999	4,581	312,908	136,515	10,023	2,022,762
2011	86,650	945	1,965	327,650	322,548	75,450	306,678	46,007	4,224	321,074	133,900	11,221	1,983,292
2012	78,056	838	1,643	319,357	225,082	70,071	234,181	34,679	3,737	318,396	146,898	11,540	1,805,977
2013	77,291	665	623	332,172	254,841	70,842	448,809	43,245	2,943	317,710	90,296	11,863	2,051,373
2014	76,892	2,475	447	307,480	212,606	66,399	271,244	47,510	1,933	325,141	84,125	12,790	1,839,040
2015[1]	76,029	574	399	331,751	235,132	61,915	259,524	38,785	1,303	304,835	71,836	13,959	1,749,454
2016[2]	78,177	646	367	336,618	230,456	51,317	293,231	40,915	896	286,760	73,571	11,083	1,701,061

[1] Preliminary.   [2] Estimate.   Source: Food and Agriculture Organization of the United Nations (FAO-UN)

Imports of Tea in the United States   In Metric Tons

Year	Jan.	Feb.	Mar.	Apr.	May	June	July	Aug.	Sept.	Oct.	Nov.	Dec.	Total
2013	14,553	13,598	15,806	22,615	22,506	20,012	21,375	21,577	22,286	14,247	15,366	12,923	216,865
2014	13,547	13,957	16,120	20,541	19,683	18,582	17,249	18,959	21,658	18,299	17,616	15,148	211,359
2015	13,344	13,018	19,870	18,794	19,750	20,863	19,625	20,091	23,682	15,621	15,734	13,692	214,084
2016	14,278	14,512	20,720	20,168	21,535	22,102	19,136	20,903	18,424	13,513	13,264	13,260	211,815
2017	14,923	12,784	16,132	18,980	21,458	19,263	20,082	19,684	18,930	12,874	13,657	13,349	202,116
2018[1]	15,231	11,716	11,611	17,712	20,164	18,202	17,370	18,866	17,850	13,205	13,993	12,314	188,234

[1] Preliminary.   Source: Foreign Agricultural Service, U.S. Department of Agriculture (FAS-USDA)

Tin

Tin (atomic symbol Sn) is a silvery-white, lustrous gray metallic element. Tin is soft, pliable and has a highly crystalline structure. When a tin bar is bent or broken, a crackling sound called a "tin cry" is produced due to the breaking of the tin crystals. People have been using tin for at least 5,500 years. Tin has been found in the tombs of ancient Egyptians. In ancient times, tin and lead were considered different forms of the same metal. Tin was exported to Europe in large quantities from Cornwall, England, during the Roman period, from approximately 2100 BC to 1500 BC. Cornwall was one of the world's leading sources of tin for much of its known history and into the late 1800s.

The principal ore of tin is the mineral cassiterite, which is found in Malaya, Bolivia, Indonesia, Thailand, and Nigeria. About 80% of the world's tin deposits occur in unconsolidated placer deposits in riverbeds and valleys, or on the sea floor, with only about 20% occurring as primary hard-rock lodes. Tin deposits are generally small and are almost always found closely allied to the granite from which it originates. Tin is also recovered as a by-product of mining tungsten, tantalum, and lead. After extraction, tin ore is ground and washed to remove impurities, roasted to oxidize the sulfides of iron and copper, washed a second time, and then reduced by carbon in a reverberatory furnace. Electrolysis may also be used to purify tin.

Pure tin, rarely used by itself, was used as currency in the form of tin blocks and was considered legal tender for taxes in Phuket, Thailand, until 1932. Tin is used in the manufacture of coatings for steel containers used to preserve food and beverages. Tin is also used in solder alloys, electroplating, ceramics, and in plastic. The world's major tin research and development laboratory, ITRI Ltd, is funded by companies that produce and consume tin. The focus of the research efforts have been on possible new uses for tin that would take advantage of tin's relative non-toxicity to replace other metals in various products. Some of the replacements could be lead-free solders, antimony-free flame-retardant chemicals, and lead-free shotgun pellets. No tin is currently mined in the U.S.

Tin futures and options trade on the London Metal Exchange (LME). Tin has traded on the LME since 1877 and the standard tin contract began in 1912. The futures contract calls for the delivery of 5 metric tons of tin ingots of at least 99.85% purity. The contract trades in terms of U.S. dollars per metric ton.

Prices – The average monthly price of tin (straights) in New York in 2018 rose by +0.5% yr/yr to $12.49 per pound, but still below the 2011 record high of $15.87 per pound. The price was far above the 3-decade low of $2.83 per pound seen in 2002. The average monthly price of ex-dock tin in New York in 2018 rose +0.3% yr/yr to $9.40 per pound.

Supply – World mine production of tin in 2018 fell -1.0% yr/yr to 310,000 metric tons, remaining below the 2011 record high of 315,000 metric tons. The world's largest mine producers of tin are China with 29.0% of world production in 2018, Indonesia with 26.8%, Burma with 14.5%, and Brazil, Bolivia & Peru with 5.8% each. World smelter production of tin in 2016 fell -3.7% yr/yr to 341,000 metric tons, which is a new record high. The world's largest producers of smelted tin are China with 46.7% of world production in 2016 (latest data), Indonesia with 13.2%, and Malaysia with 7.9%. The U.S. does not mine tin, and therefore its supply consists only of scrap and imports. U.S. tin recovery in 2018 fell -30.4% yr/yr to 3,450 metric tons for a new record low.

Demand – U.S. consumption of tin (pig) in 2018 fell -13.1% yr/yr to 22,173 metric tons (annualized through September) for a new record low. The breakdown of U.S. consumption of tin by finished products in 2016 shows that the largest consuming industry of tin is chemicals with 20.9% of consumption, followed by tinplate with 18.3%, solder with 16.6%, and bronze and brass with 6.7%.

Trade – The U.S. relied on imports for 78% of its tin consumption in 2018. U.S. imports of unwrought tin metal in 2017 rose +0.6% yr/yr to 32,400 metric tons, up slightly from 2016's 25-year low of 32,200 metric tons. The largest sources of U.S. imports in 2016 were Indonesia with 26.6%, Malaysia with 23.5%, and Bolivia with 18.6%. U.S. exports of tin in 2016 fell -43.3% yr/yr to 1,900 metric tons.

World Mine Production of Tin   In Metric Tons (Contained Tin)

Year	Australia	Bolivia	Brazil	Burma	China	Congo	Indonesia	Malaysia	Nigeria	Peru	Rwanda	Vietnam	World Total
2009	13,268	19,575	9,500	1,000	97,200	9,900	46,078	2,412	400	37,503	2,400	5,400	246,000
2010	18,263	20,190	10,400	4,000	115,000	8,000	43,258	2,668	160	33,848	3,300	5,400	266,000
2011	14,014	20,373	10,725	11,000	120,000	5,600	89,600	3,340	270	28,882	4,400	5,400	315,000
2012	6,158	19,702	13,667	10,600	110,000	4,800	44,202	3,725	340	26,105	2,900	5,400	249,000
2013	6,472	19,282	16,830	17,000	97,000	4,500	59,412	3,697	2,600	23,668	3,100	5,400	260,000
2014	6,900	19,802	25,534	30,000	104,000	6,500	51,801	3,777	2,800	23,105	4,200	5,400	285,000
2015	7,000	20,000	25,000	34,271	110,156	6,400	52,000	3,800	2,500	19,511	2,000	5,400	289,000
2016	6,640	17,000	25,000	54,000	92,000	5,500	52,000	4,000	2,290	18,800	2,200	5,500	288,000
2017[1]	7,200	18,500	18,000	47,000	93,000	9,500	83,000	3,810	5,960	17,800	2,860	4,560	313,000
2018[2]	7,000	18,000	18,000	45,000	90,000	9,000	83,000	4,000	6,000	18,000	2,900	5,000	310,000

[1] Preliminary.   [2] Estimate.   Source: U.S. Geological Survey (USGS)

TIN

World Smelter Production of Primary Tin   In Metric Tons

Year	Australia	Belgium	Bolivia	Brazil	China	Indo-nesia	Japan	Malaysia	Peru	Russia	Thailand	United States	World Total
2007	518	5,000	12,251	9,634	149,000	64,127	879	25,263	36,004	4,200	23,104	12,200	346,000
2008	570	5,000	12,667	11,300	140,000	53,417	956	31,691	38,865	1,730	21,860	11,700	334,000
2009	400	8,700	14,995	8,561	140,000	51,418	757	36,407	34,388	1,430	19,423	11,100	331,000
2010	400	9,900	15,003	9,348	150,000	51,418	841	38,771	36,451	1,381	20,000	11,100	348,000
2011	400	10,000	14,295	9,632	156,000	43,832	947	40,281	32,290	726	20,000	11,000	344,000
2012	400	11,400	14,626	12,205	148,000	51,400	1,133	37,823	24,811	700	19,996	11,200	342,000
2013	400	12,000	14,862	14,971	159,000	48,800	1,786	32,633	24,181	550	19,088	10,600	346,000
2014	400	9,810	15,439	25,784	187,000	58,233	1,746	35,018	24,462	550	16,929	10,100	394,000
2015	400	8,860	15,700	26,250	166,900	48,000	1,700	30,260	20,396	550	16,500	10,100	354,000
2016[1]	400	8,540	16,800	26,000	166,000	45,000	1,620	26,849	19,390	----	11,088	10,100	341,000

[1] Preliminary.   Source: U.S. Geological Survey (USGS)

United States Foreign Trade of Tin   In Metric Tons

		Concentrates[2] (Ore)			Imports for Consumption — Unwrought Tin Metal								
Year	Exports (Metal)	Total All Ore	Bolivia	Peru	Total All Metal	Bolivia	Brazil	China	Indo-nesia	Malaysia	Singa-pore	Thailand	United Kingdom
2007	6,410	----	----	----	34,600	4,340	2,600	4,230	1,680	14	1,730	15	881
2008	9,800	----	----	----	36,300	4,980	1,570	2,380	2,000	1,740	706	1,670	225
2009	3,170	----	----	----	33,000	6,300	1,050	1,210	3,220	169	451	15	4
2010	5,630	----	----	----	35,300	6,060	75	887	3,970	4,500	996	1,310	4
2011	5,450	----	----	----	34,200	5,680	676	1,490	4,930	3,980	645	2,310	18
2012	5,560	----	----	----	36,900	5,100	2,930	174	6,180	4,590	424	1,750	1
2013	5,870	----	----	----	34,900	6,510	3,100	1,610	5,560	4,190	101	2,380	----
2014	5,700	----	----	----	35,600	4,570	3,030	3,470	8,140	6,050	375	291	----
2015	3,350	----	----	----	33,600	6,260	2,950	1,230	5,210	9,990	225	20	
2016[1]	1,900	----	----	----	32,200								

[1] Preliminary.   [2] Tin content.   [4] Less than 1/2 unit.   Source: U.S. Geological Survey (USGS)

Consumption (Total) of Tin (Pig) in the United States   In Metric Tons

Year	Jan.	Feb.	Mar.	Apr.	May	June	July	Aug.	Sept.	Oct.	Nov.	Dec.	Total
2009	2,642	2,546	2,610	2,573	2,525	2,521	2,630	2,552	2,626	2,646	2,675	2,564	31,110
2010	2,678	2,673	2,689	2,698	2,666	2,655	2,706	2,740	2,724	2,730	2,599	2,951	32,509
2011	2,782	2,769	2,833	2,831	2,862	2,983	2,961	2,823	3,064	3,061	2,973	2,750	34,692
2012	2,718	2,748	2,868	2,829	2,908	2,775	2,735	2,745	2,696	2,724	2,684	2,725	33,155
2013	2,959	2,970	3,009	2,989	2,970	2,949	2,099	2,140	2,079	2,069	2,026	2,047	30,306
2014	1,819	1,818	1,878	1,938	2,164	2,212	2,202	2,202	2,212	2,182	2,193	2,143	24,963
2015	2,183	2,181	2,211	2,241	2,211	2,271	2,251	2,261	2,261	2,231	2,161	2,191	26,590
2016	2,239	2,239	2,179	2,179	2,189	2,209	2,189	2,239	2,209	2,197	2,165	2,127	26,360
2017	2,137	2,127	2,155	2,165	2,194	2,176	2,166	2,195	2,158	2,187	2,061	1,804	25,525
2018[1]	1,870	1,832	1,835	1,874	1,856	1,843	1,823	1,859	1,838				22,173

[1] Preliminary.   Source: U.S. Geological Survey (USGS)

Tin Stocks (Pig-Industrial) in the United States, on First of Month   In Metric Tons

Year	Jan.	Feb.	Mar.	Apr.	May	June	July	Aug.	Sept.	Oct.	Nov.	Dec.
2009	7,970	7,890	7,660	7,640	7,620	7,640	7,570	7,630	7,590	7,540	7,520	7,470
2010	7,450	7,030	7,080	7,060	7,080	7,180	7,270	7,220	7,130	7,060	7,090	7,090
2011	6,920	6,660	6,710	6,740	6,750	6,820	6,860	6,880	6,860	6,860	6,800	6,700
2012	5,230	6,810	6,860	6,780	6,710	6,750	6,790	7,290	7,280	7,340	7,310	6,360
2013	6,470	6,670	6,640	6,590	6,640	7,110	6,660	6,670	6,680	6,580	6,570	6,480
2014	6,520	6,540	6,560	6,570	6,490	6,800	6,800	6,770	6,740	7,360	7,060	6,970
2015	7,010	6,860	6,910	6,960	6,910	6,910	7,360	6,970	6,900	7,510	6,930	6,940
2016	6,420	6,420	6,400	6,350	6,380	6,310	6,220	6,220	6,210	6,320	6,480	6,510
2017	6,490	6,550	6,570	6,580	6,480	6,540	6,520	6,580	6,590	6,560	6,550	6,570
2018[1]	6,300	6,330	6,300	6,430	6,280	6,360	6,400	6,310	6,400			

[1] Preliminary.   Source: U.S. Geological Survey (USGS)

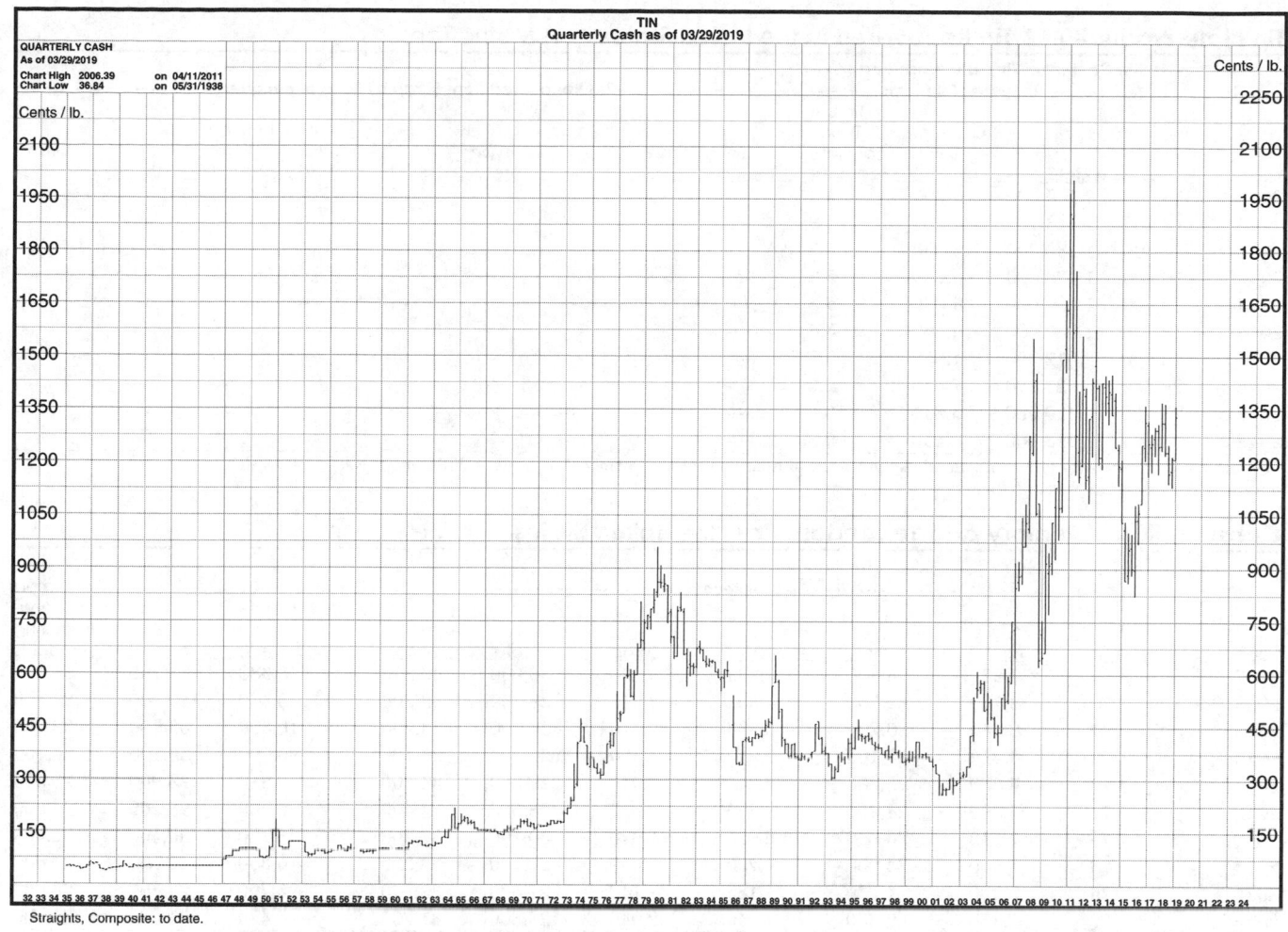

TIN
Quarterly Cash as of 03/29/2019

QUARTERLY CASH
As of 03/29/2019
Chart High 2006.39 on 04/11/2011
Chart Low 36.84 on 05/31/1938

Straights, Composite: to date.

Average Price of Ex-Dock Tin in New York[1]   In Cents Per Pound

Year	Jan.	Feb.	Mar.	Apr.	May	June	July	Aug.	Sept.	Oct.	Nov.	Dec.	Average
2009	539.32	523.68	508.12	554.44	646.09	702.56	657.47	694.15	695.88	701.13	698.44	721.79	636.92
2010	823.31	764.25	818.62	870.50	821.34	809.88	851.80	967.17	1,057.81	1,223.59	1,191.80	1,211.71	950.98
2011	1,274.29	1,456.60	1,422.69	1,501.64	1,339.50	1,188.91	1,271.42	1,137.37	1,055.80	1,019.31	998.78	913.27	1,214.96
2012	1,005.52	1,136.74	1,074.53	1,034.47	958.73	905.04	874.07	879.88	972.20	998.11	969.71	1,065.21	989.52
2013	1,147.61	1,132.62	1,088.32	1,016.82	968.64	946.60	914.64	1,008.60	1,062.18	1,076.08	1,064.68	1,061.89	1,040.71
2014	1,026.81	1,061.00	1,074.64	1,088.65	1,083.18	1,059.89	1,041.12	1,037.98	983.57	929.95	931.02	925.65	1,020.29
2015	910.45	857.51	818.81	754.37	745.34	721.70	NQ	NQ	NQ	733.84	694.41	693.59	770.00
2016	653.01	737.23	797.61	798.88	786.39	796.12	834.14	861.60	913.95	940.57	987.73	990.44	841.47
2017	965.02	907.96	925.11	931.47	943.03	920.97	946.70	959.93	971.40	953.69	913.47	907.11	937.15
2018	965.23	1,009.51	987.72	993.12	974.52	962.92	918.93	900.01	887.62	891.53	893.21	898.89	940.27

Source: American Metal Market (AMM)

Average Price of Tin (Straights) in New York   In Cents Per Pound

Year	Jan.	Feb.	Mar.	Apr.	May	June	July	Aug.	Sept.	Oct.	Nov.	Dec.	Average
2009	711.20	686.02	664.21	724.55	841.83	920.39	862.04	902.14	899.35	911.42	922.75	964.64	834.21
2010	1,090.89	1,011.26	1,082.71	1,149.23	1,084.11	1,067.12	1,117.84	1,268.74	1,386.44	1,597.89	1,552.75	1,588.29	1,249.77
2011	1,661.33	1,906.31	1,857.97	1,958.08	1,750.23	1,555.57	1,663.54	1,486.24	1,378.26	1,330.78	1,298.42	1,191.48	1,586.52
2012	1,312.08	1,481.62	1,404.14	1,351.56	1,251.34	1,180.70	1,142.08	1,148.33	1,269.91	1,300.73	1,264.64	1,393.41	1,291.71
2013	1,502.64	1,480.17	1,422.82	1,328.61	1,265.73	1,252.58	1,200.86	1,321.68	1,391.23	1,413.19	1,392.13	1,391.85	1,363.62
2014	1,345.40	1,388.75	1,406.24	1,423.40	1,416.15	1,388.17	1,365.31	1,362.21	1,289.78	1,219.57	1,223.03	1,211.06	1,336.59
2015	1,193.00	1,125.26	1,076.19	989.76	978.73	930.77	924.68	933.28	945.21	973.65	908.21	909.01	990.65
2016	854.30	965.15	1,050.78	1,056.03	1,037.46	1,051.94	1,105.23	1,143.75	1,208.97	1,246.19	1,309.82	1,314.74	1,112.03
2017	1,282.89	1,205.68	1,232.26	1,233.41	1,251.83	1,218.85	1,253.86	1,272.12	1,289.49	1,263.32	1,212.57	1,207.57	1,243.65
2018	1,282.77	1,342.47	1,316.42	1,321.32	1,294.62	1,280.95	1,223.25	1,191.67	1,175.96	1,185.53	1,182.02	1,194.59	1,249.30

Source: U.S. Geological Survey (USGS)

Tin Plate Production & Tin Recovered in the United States   In Metric Tons

| | Tin Content of Tinplate Produced | | | | Tin Recovered from Scrap by Form of Recovery | | | | | | | | |
| | Tinplate (All Forms) | | | | | | | | | | | | |
Year	Tinplate Waste ----- Gross Weight -----		Tin Content (Met. Ton)	Tin per Tonne of Plate (Kilograms)	Tin Metal	Bronze & Brass	Solder	Type Metal	Babbitt	Anti-monial Lead	Chemical Com-pounds	Misc.[2]	Grand Total
2009	14,500	1,150,000	6,200	5.4	----	----	----	----	----	----	----	----	----
2010	18,163	1,416,758	6,920	4.9	----	----	----	----	----	----	----	----	----
2011	21,500	1,230,000	6,330	5.2	----	----	----	----	----	----	----	----	----
2012	16,300	1,160,000	6,090	5.2	----	----	----	----	----	----	----	----	----
2013	20,800	1,090,000	6,030	5.5	----	----	----	----	----	----	----	----	----
2014	32,900	1,030,000	5,680	5.5	----	----	----	----	----	----	----	----	----
2015	43,800	812,000	4,650	5.7	----	----	----	----	----	----	----	----	----
2016	29,800	623,000	7,840	12.6	----	----	----	----	----	----	----	----	----
2017	27,700	496,000	5,340	10.8	----	----	----	----	----	----	----	----	----
2018[1]		373,000	3,450	9.3	----	----	----	----	----	----	----	----	----

[1] Preliminary.   [2] Includes foil, terne metal, cable lead, and items indicated by symbol "W".   W = Withheld.   NA = Not available.
Source: U.S. Geological Survey (USGS)

Consumption of Primary and Secondary Tin in the United States   In Metric Tons

| Year | Net Import Reliance as a % of Apparent Consump | Stocks, Jan. 1[2] | Net Receipts | | | | Available Supply | Stocks, Dec. 31 (Total Available Less Total Processed) | Total Pro-cessed | Consumed in Manu-facturing Products |
			Primary	Secondary	Scrap	Total				
2007	72	7,230	25,600	4,950	3,030	33,600	40,800	8,980	31,700	31,100
2008	70	8,760	22,700	4,300	2,410	29,400	38,200	8,460	29,800	29,400
2009	74	8,940	26,200	5,930	2,170	34,300	43,200	10,300	32,900	32,600
2010	73	6,210	25,100	2,910	1,920	29,900	36,100	6,000	30,100	30,100
2011	73	5,830	25,200	2,840	916	29,000	34,800	5,880	28,900	28,500
2012	72	5,800	24,900	2,810	892	28,600	34,400	6,200	28,200	27,800
2013	75	7,110	25,600	2,620	1,970	30,100	37,300	6,820	30,400	30,400
2014	76	5,530	24,000	1,250	2,450	27,700	33,200	5,350	27,800	27,500
2015	76	5,330	24,200	1,180	2,140	27,500	32,800	5,700	27,100	26,800
2016[1]	76	5,430	22,600	1,140	2,040	25,800	31,200	5,470	25,700	25,400

[1] Preliminary.   [2] Includes tin in transit in the U.S.   NA = Not available.   *Source: U.S. Geological Survey (USGS)*

Consumption of Tin in the United States, by Finished Products   In Metric Tons (Contained Tin)

Year	Tin-plate[2]	Solder	Babbitt	Bronze & Brass	Tinning	Chem-icals[3]	Tin Powder	Bar Tin & Anodes	White Metal	Other	Total
2007	7,010	10,400	604	2,800	451	6,070	W	788	W	1,120	31,100
2008	6,840	5,110	604	2,460	395	5,440	227	767	W	5,370	29,200
2009	6,130	5,110	322	2,200	340	9,290	193	245	W	7,000	32,600
2010	6,920	7,340	288	2,460	387	9,470	192	W	W	811	30,100
2011	6,230	4,100	315	3,810	552	9,990	W	W	W	757	28,500
2012	6,090	4,930	281	2,460	467	9,860	W	W	W	726	27,800
2013	6,030	5,940	820	2,380	511	6,790	W	W	W	807	30,400
2014	5,940	4,860	282	1,720	514	5,420	W	W	W	4,780	27,500
2015	5,880	4,400	312	1,750	463	5,410	W	W	W	6,090	26,800
2016[1]	4,660	4,220	289	1,710	405	5,320	W	W	W	6,190	25,400

[1] Preliminary.   [2] Includes small quantity of secondary pig tin and tin acquired in chemicals.   [3] Including tin oxide.
W = Withheld proprietary data.   *Source: U.S. Geological Survey (USGS)*

Salient Statistics of Recycling Tin in the United States

| Year | New Scrap[1] | Old Scrap[2] | Recycled Metal[3] | Apparent Supply | Percent Recycled | New Scrap[1] | Old Scrap[2] | Recycled Metal[3] | Apparent Supply |
	In Metric Tons					Value in Thousands of Dollars			
2009	2,310	11,100	13,400	44,700	30.0	42,500	204,000	247,000	825,000
2010	2,680	11,100	13,800	44,100	31.0	73,400	303,000	376,000	1,200,000
2011	2,530	11,000	13,600	42,800	32.0	87,900	383,000	470,000	1,490,000
2012	2,380	11,200	13,500	46,900	31.0	67,300	316,000	383,000	1,220,000
2013	2,150	10,600	12,700	45,100	28.0	49,300	243,000	292,000	1,050,000
2014	2,060	10,600	12,600	44,900	27.0	46,400	238,000	285,000	1,040,000
2015	1,120	10,100	11,200	43,800	26.0	18,700	168,000	186,000	722,000
2016	1,050	10,300	11,300	43,100	27.0	19,400	190,000	209,000	788,000

[1] Scrap that results from the manufacturing process.   [2] Scrap that results from consumer products.   [3] Metal recovered from new plus old scrap.
Source: U.S. Geological Survey (USGS)

Titanium

Titanium (atomic symbol Ti) is a silver-white, metallic element used primarily to make light, strong alloys. It ranks ninth in abundance among the elements in the crust of the earth but is never found in the pure state. It occurs as an oxide in various minerals. It was first discovered in 1791 by Rev. William Gregor and was first isolated as a basic element in 1910. Titanium was named after the mythological Greek god Titan for its strength.

Titanium is extremely brittle when cold but is malleable and ductile at a low red heat, and thus easily fabricated. Due to its strength, low weight, and resistance to corrosion, titanium is used in metallic alloys and as a substitute for aluminum. It is used extensively in the aerospace industry, in desalinization plants, construction, medical implants, paints, pigments, and lacquers.

Supply – World production of titanium ilmenite concentrates in 2018 fell -2.5% yr/yr to 5.400 million metric tons, still down from the 2013 record high of 8.270 million metric tons. The world's largest producers of titanium ilmenite concentrates are China with 15.7% of world production in 2018, Australia with 13.0%, India with 5.6%, Ukraine with 4.3%, and Vietnam and Norway with 3.7% each. World production of titanium rutile concentrates in 2018 fell -2.6% yr/yr to 750,000 metric tons. The world's largest producers are Australia with 33.3% of world production in 2018 followed by Sierra Leone with 22.7%, and the Ukraine and South Africa with 13.3% each.

Demand – U.S. consumption of titanium dioxide pigment in 2018 rose +5.7% yr/yr to 920,000 metric tons, remaining below 2004's record high of 1.170 million metric tons. U.S. consumption of ilmenite in 2005 fell –12.8% yr/yr to 1.290 million metric tons, down from 2004's 8-year high of 1.480 million metric tons. U.S. consumption of rutile in 2005 fell 4.7% yr/yr to a 7-year low of 424,000 metric tons.

Trade – U.S. imports of titanium dioxide pigment in 2018 rose +5.7% yr/yr to 270,000 metric tons, still below the 2005 record high of 341,000 metric tons. U.S. imports of ilmenite in 2017 rose +28.4% yr/yr to 760,000 metric tons.

World Produciton of Titanium Ilmenite Concentrates   In Thousands of Metric Tons

Year	Australia[2]	Brazil	China	Egypt	India	Malaysia	Norway	Ukraine	United States	Vietnam	World Total	-- Titaniferous Slag[4] --- Canada	Africa
2009	1,611	53	112	----	700	16	671	500	311	699	5,480	765	1,084
2010	1,651	166	1,400	----	729	19	864	500	400	912	7,760	1,090	1,210
2011	1,501	115	1,420	----	550	29	869	261	400	841	7,330	878	1,367
2012	1,570	115	1,330	----	340	22	831	247	300	978	7,250	900	1,300
2013	1,560	130	1,700	20	436	16	826	670	300	1,030	8,270	900	1,170
2014	1,250	135	1,860	----	320	8	864	450	200	558	7,640	900	1,030
2015	1,160	133	1,780	----	300	6	430	350	300	282	6,980	700	950
2016	1,300	130	1,400	----	300	30	439	350	100	400	7,000	900	830
2017	730	50	840	----	300		220	230	100	200	5,540	880	550
2018[1]	700	50	850	----	300		200	230	100	200	5,400	850	500

[1] Preliminary. [2] Includes leucoxene. [3] Approximately 10% of total production is ilmenite. Beginning in 1988, 25% of Norway's ilmenite production was used to produce slag containing 75% TiO2. NA = Not available. *Source: U.S. Geological Survey (USGS)*

Salient Statistics of Titanium in the United States   In Metric Tons

Year	--- Titanium Dioxide Pigment --- Production	Imports[3]	Apparent Consumption	------ Ilmenite ------ Imports[3]	Consumption	-- Titanium Slag --- Imports[3]	Consumption	------- Rutile[4] -------- Imports[3]	Consumption	Ores & Concentrates	Scrap	Dioxide & Pigments	Ingots, Billets, Etc.
2009	1,230,000	175,000	757,000	250,000	----	414,000	----	279,600	----	14,800	4,200	617,000	7,240
2010	1,320,000	204,000	767,000	377,000	----	475,000	----	351,000	----	18,900	3,480	717,000	8,450
2011	1,290,000	200,000	706,000	377,000	----	513,000	----	381,000	----	26,600	5,150	741,000	15,600
2012	1,140,000	203,000	722,000	374,000	----	618,000	----	389,000	----	43,000	8,760	587,000	13,800
2013	1,280,000	213,000	826,000	389,000	----	681,000	----	406,000	----	11,500	4,700	624,000	12,500
2014	1,260,000	224,000	802,000	355,000	----	678,000	----	342,500	----	2,240	4,610	685,000	11,500
2015	1,220,000	221,000	792,000	649,000	----	399,000	----	394,000	----	2,040	6,860	649,000	10,400
2016	1,240,000	247,000	840,000	592,000	----	402,000	----	349,700	----	7,330	9,720	651,000	10,100
2017[1]	1,260,000	239,000	870,000	760,000	----	479,000	----	334,200	----	8,940	9,480	634,000	10,900
2018[2]	1,200,000	270,000	920,000		----		----		----			550,000	

[1] Preliminary. [2] Estimate. [3] For consumption. [4] Natural and synthetic. W = Withheld. *Source: U.S. Geological Survey (USGS)*

World Production of Titanium Rutile Concentrates   In Metric Tons

Year	Australia	Brazil	India	Mada-gascar	Malaysia	Mozam-bique	Sierra Leone	South Africa	Sri Lanka	Ukraine	United States	World Total
2011	474,000	2,474	18,800	9,000	10,810	6,455	67,916	149,000	1,970	60,000	W	800,000
2012	439,000	2,090	24,000	12,000	20,000	4,000	94,500	150,000	1,970	58,000	W	811,000
2013	232,000	2,250	26,000	11,000	5,980	4,000	120,000	70,000	1,590	162,000	W	640,000
2014	212,000	2,040	19,100	6,900	3,070	6,100	114,000	120,000	1,750	110,000	W	660,000
2015	320,000	2,220	20,000	4,800	198	5,980	126,000	100,000	1,810	90,000	W	760,000
2016	400,000	2,000	20,000	4,800	200	7,780	148,000	110,000	2,000	100,000	W	889,000
2017	290,000		10,000	9,000			160,000	95,000		95,000	W	770,000
2018[1]	250,000		10,000	8,000			170,000	100,000		100,000	W	750,000

[1] Preliminary.   Source: U.S. Geological Survey (USGS)

World Production of Titanium Sponge Metal & U.S. Consumption of Titanium Concentrates

	Production of Titanium (In Metric Tons) Sponge Metal[2]						U.S. Consumption of Titanium Concentrates, by Products (In Metric Tons) Ilmenite (TiO$_2$ Content)			Rutile (TiO$_2$ Content)			
Year	China	Japan	Russia	United Kingdom	United States	Total	Pigments	Misc.	Total	Welding Rod Coatings	Pigments	Misc.	Total
2011	60,000	40,000	25,800	----	W	156,000	NA	NA	1,500,000	----	----	----	----
2012	80,000	40,000	44,000	----	W	200,000	NA	NA	1,590,000	----	----	----	----
2013	105,000	42,000	44,000	----	W	209,000	NA	NA	1,460,000	----	----	----	----
2014	110,000	25,000	42,000	----	W	194,000	NA	NA	1,430,000	----	----	----	----
2015	62,000	42,000	40,000	----	W	160,000	NA	NA	1,390,000	----	----	----	----
2016	60,000	54,000	38,000	----	W	170,000	NA	NA	1,390,000	----	----	----	----
2017	72,000	51,000	40,000	----	W	181,000				----	----	----	----
2018[1]	70,000	52,000	40,000	----	W	180,000				----	----	----	----

[1] Preliminary.   [2] Unconsolidated metal in various forms.   [4] Included in Pigments.   NA = Not available.   W = Withheld.
Source: U.S. Geological Survey (USGS)

Average Prices of Titanium in the United States

Year	Ilmenite FOB Australian Ports[2]	Slag, 85% TiO2 FOB Richards Bay, South Africa	Rutile Large Lots Bulk, FOB U.S. East Coast[3]	Rutile Bagged FOB Australian Ports	Avg. Price of Grade A Titanium Sponge, FOB Shipping Point	Titanium Metal Sponge	Titanium Dioxide Pigments FOB US Plants Anatase	Titanium Dioxide Pigments FOB US Plants Rutile
	Dollars Per Metric Ton				Dollars Per Pound			
2009	$60 - $85	$401 - $439	$525 - $540	$700 - $800	----	$4.50 - $7.07	----	----
2010	$65 - $85	$367 - $433	$530 - $550	$760 - $805	----	$3.50 - $6.24	----	----
2011	$140 - $250	$468 - $494	$1,300-$1,400	$1,348-$1,600	----	$3.27 - $6.74	----	----
2012	$250 - $350	$512 - $763	$2,050-$2,400	$2,500-$2,800	----	$3.53 - $6.95	----	----
2013	$230 - $300	$405 - $455	$1,100-$1,400	$1,200-$1,500	----	$3.20 - $6.23	----	----
2014	$150 - $165	$690 - $835	$820 - $950	$840 - $1,000	----	$4.07 - $5.96	----	----
2015	$100 - $120	$630 - $751	$790 - $890	$800 - $840	----	$3.32 - $5.36	----	----
2016[1]	$100 - $110	$674 - $676	$710 - $770	$770 - $850	----	$5.03 - $5.42	----	----

[1] Preliminary.   NA = Not available.   Source: U.S. Geological Survey (USGS)

Average Price of Titanium[1] in United States   In Dollars Per Pound

Year	Jan.	Feb.	Mar.	Apr.	May	June	July	Aug.	Sept.	Oct.	Nov.	Dec.	Average
2013	10.40	10.25	10.25	10.25	10.25	10.25	10.25	9.80	9.55	9.09	8.76	8.59	9.81
2014	8.26	8.07	8.13	8.13	8.26	8.38	8.38	8.66	8.75	8.75	8.63	8.50	8.41
2015	8.50	8.50	8.50	8.38	8.38	8.38	8.56	8.62	8.62	8.62	8.62	8.62	8.53
2016	8.62	8.62	8.62	8.62	8.48	8.38	8.38	8.38	8.38	8.38	8.12	8.12	8.43
2017	8.16	8.25	8.25	8.25	8.25	8.25	8.25	8.25	8.25	8.09	8.02	8.02	8.19
2018	8.02	8.02	8.02	8.10	8.12	8.12	8.12	8.12	8.12	8.30	8.38	8.38	8.15

[1] Ingot, 6Al - 4V.   Source: American Metal Market (AMM)

Average Price of Titanium[1] in United States   In Dollars Per Pound

Year	Jan.	Feb.	Mar.	Apr.	May	June	July	Aug.	Sept.	Oct.	Nov.	Dec.	Average
2013	29.07	27.50	27.50	27.50	27.50	27.50	27.50	26.77	25.90	25.50	25.50	25.50	26.94
2014	25.50	25.50	25.50	25.50	25.76	26.00	26.00	26.00	26.00	26.00	25.75	25.50	25.75
2015	25.50	25.50	25.50	25.50	25.50	25.50	25.50	25.50	25.50	25.50	25.50	25.50	25.50
2016	25.50	25.50	25.50	25.50	25.50	25.50	25.50	25.50	25.50	25.50	25.50	25.50	25.50
2017	26.40	28.50	28.50	28.02	28.00	28.00	28.80	29.00	29.00	29.00	29.00	29.00	28.44
2018	29.00	29.00	29.00	30.43	31.00	31.00	29.48	29.00	29.00	29.70	30.00	30.00	29.72

[1] Plate, Alloy.   Source: American Metal Market (AMM)

Tobacco

Tobacco is a member of the nightshade family. It is commercially grown for its leaves and stems, which are rolled into cigars, shredded for use in cigarettes and pipes, processed for chewing, or ground into snuff. Christopher Columbus introduced tobacco cultivation and use to Spain after observing natives from the Americas smoking loosely rolled tobacco-stuffed tobacco leaves.

Tobacco is cured, or dried, after harvesting and then aged to improve its flavor. The four common methods of curing are: air cured, fire cured, sun cured, and flue cured. Flue curing is the fastest method of curing and requires only about a week compared with up to 10 weeks for other methods. Cured tobacco is tied into small bundles of about 20 leaves and aged one to three years.

Virginia tobacco is by far the most popular type used in pipe tobacco since it is the mildest of all blending tobaccos. Approximately 60% of the U.S. tobacco crop is Virginia-type tobacco. Burley tobacco is the next most popular tobacco. It is air-cured, burns slowly and provides a relatively cool smoke. Other tobacco varieties include Perique, Kentucky, Oriental, and Latakia.

Prices – U.S. tobacco farm prices in 2017 rose +3.1% to 206.9 cents per pound, below the 2013 record high of 217.7 cents per pound.

Supply – World production of leaf tobacco in 2016 fell -4.6% yr/yr to 6.654 million metric tons, down from the 2013 record high of 7.615 million metric tons. The world's largest producers of tobacco are China with 42.1% of world production, followed at a distance by India with 11.4%, Brazil with 10.1%, and the U.S. with 4.3%.

U.S. production in 2016 fell -12.6% yr/yr at 265.181 metric tons, where it was down by about two-thirds from the 2-decade high of 810,750 metric tons posted in 1997. Tobacco in the U.S. is grown primarily in the mid-Atlantic States and they account for the vast majority of U.S. production. Specifically, the largest tobacco producing states in the U.S. are North Carolina with 46.4% of U.S. production in 2018, Kentucky with 26.4%, Virginia with 8.8%, Tennessee with 7.2%, Georgia with 4.1%, and South Carolina with 3.7%.

U.S. production of flue-cured tobacco (type 11-14), the most popular tobacco type grown in the U.S., fell by -20.8% yr/yr to 341.900 million pounds in 2018. The second most popular type is burley tobacco (type 31-32), which saw U.S. production in 2018 fall -29.8% yr/yr to 116.180 million pounds. Total U.S. production of tobacco in 2018 fell -22.9% yr/yr to 547.812 million pounds, which is less than one-third of the 2-decade high of 1.787 billion pounds posted in 1997. U.S. farmers have sharply reduced the planting acreage for tobacco. In 2018, harvested tobacco acreage fell -6.1% yr/yr to 301.980 acres, which was just mildly above the 2005 record low of 297,080 but still far below the 25-year high of 836,230 posted in 1997. Yield in 2018 fell -17.9% to 1,184 pounds per acre, well below the 15-year high of 2,323 pounds per acre posted in 2009. The farm value of the U.S. tobacco crop in 2017 rose +16.4% yr/yr to $1.469 billion.

Trade – U.S. tobacco exports in 2017 fell -12.4% yr/yr to 317.1 million pounds which is a new record low.

World Production of Leaf Tobacco   In Metric Tons

Year	Brazil	Canada	China	Greece	India	Indo-nesia	Italy	Japan	Pakistan	Turkey	United States	Zim-babwe	World Total
2008	851,058	39,234	2,839,947	27,062	490,000	168,037	92,560	38,500	107,765	93,403	363,101	109,376	6,647,544
2009	863,079	37,303	3,067,928	26,776	622,830	176,510	97,860	36,600	108,100	81,053	373,115	126,107	7,142,371
2010	787,817	34,904	3,005,928	29,948	690,000	135,700	89,112	29,300	119,323	53,018	325,764	109,737	6,944,875
2011	951,933	32,780	3,158,737	32,043	830,000	214,600	70,130	23,600	102,834	45,435	271,361	125,056	7,481,169
2012	810,550	30,723	3,408,142	34,250	820,000	260,800	50,620	19,700	97,878	73,285	345,957	139,179	7,593,955
2013	850,673	28,620	3,375,400	40,613	765,154	260,200	49,770	19,800	108,307	93,158	328,208	147,068	7,606,741
2014	862,396	26,549	2,997,050	40,940	735,742	196,300	53,925	20,000	129,878	74,696	397,533	184,003	7,305,312
2015	867,355	24,456	2,678,604	37,031	765,523	193,790	51,406	18,700	120,022	75,000	326,210	171,083	6,838,675
2016[1]	677,472	22,453	2,575,371	29,890	782,582	126,728	48,470	17,900	115,851	70,000	285,180	170,762	6,399,092
2017[2]	880,881	22,100	2,392,090	28,200	799,960	152,319	46,060	19,000	117,750	80,000	322,120	181,643	6,501,646

[1] Preliminary.   [2] Estimate.   *Source: Food and Agriculture Organization of the United Nations (FAO-UN)*

TOBACCO

Production and Consumption of Tobacco Products in the United States

	Cigar-ettes	Cigars[3]	Chewing Tobacco — Plug	Twist	Loose-leaf	Smoking Total Tobacco	Snuff[4]	Cigar-ettes	Cigars[3]	Cigar-ettes	Cigars[3]	Smoking Tobacco	Chewing Tobacco	Total Products
Year	- Billions -	- Millions -	--- In Millions of Pounds ---					----- Number -----		----------------- In Pounds -----------------				
2000	593.2	2,825	2.6	0.8	46.0	49.4	13.6	69.5	2,049	38.0	3.40	.62	.13	.48	4.10
2001	562.8	3,741	2.4	0.8	43.9	47.1	12.8	70.9	2,051	41.2	3.50	.68	.15	.47	4.30
2002	484.3	3,816	2.2	0.8	41.5	44.5	15.5	72.7	1,982	41.8	3.40	.68	.16	.43	4.16
2003	499.4	4,017	1.7	0.7	39.2	41.6	17.8	73.8	1,890	44.5	3.20	.73	.16	.40	3.97
2004	492.7	4,342	1.7	0.7	37.0	39.3	16.1	79.3	1,814	47.9	3.10	.79	.15	.37	3.87
2005	498.7	3,674	1.4	0.6	37.2	39.2	17.4	86.7	1,716	46.9	2.90	.77	.16	.36	3.69
2006	483.7	4,256	1.3	0.6	36.4	38.3	16.5	81.8	1,691	47.8	2.90	.78	.15	.37	3.69
2007	449.7	4,797	1.2	0.5	35.1	36.8	NA	NA	NA	NA	NA	NA	NA	NA	NA
2008[1]	396.1	4,984	1.1	0.5	30.9	32.5	----	----	----	----	----	----	----	----	----
2009[2]	338.1	8,232	0.9	0.5	28.0	29.3	----	----	----	----	----	----	----	----	----

[1] Preliminary. [2] Estimate. [3] Large cigars and cigarillos. [4] Includes loose-leaf. [5] Consumption of tax-paid tobacco products. Unstemmed rocessing weight. [6] 18 years and older. NA = Not available. *Source: Economic Research Service, U.S. Department of Agriculture (ERS-USDA)*

Production of Tobacco in the United States, by States   In Thousands of Pounds

Year	Georgia	Kentucky	North Carolina	Ohio	Pennsyl-vania	South Carolina	Tennessee	Virginia	Total
2009	28,014	206,900	423,856	6,800	18,660	38,850	49,960	46,530	822,581
2010	26,790	181,760	352,625	5,125	19,965	36,000	45,740	44,299	718,190
2011	26,775	172,140	251,565	3,360	20,655	26,350	45,363	48,125	598,252
2012	22,500	195,800	381,190	3,990	22,985	25,200	53,000	53,599	762,709
2013	22,400	187,240	362,660	4,620	21,260	24,650	44,570	52,613	723,579
2014	34,500	214,280	453,860	4,300	22,250	33,180	52,155	57,651	876,415
2015	32,400	149,830	380,250	3,610	18,090	26,000	48,770	55,655	719,171
2016	28,350	136,280	331,800	----	20,460	24,700	35,690	51,440	628,720
2017	26,250	183,300	360,040	----	18,990	25,200	43,000	53,381	710,161
2018[1]	23,750	134,370	251,925	----	17,400	22,140	39,610	44,046	533,241

[1] Preliminary. *Source: Agricultural Statistics Board, U.S. Department of Agriculture (ASB-USDA)*

Salient Statistics of Tobacco in the United States

Year	Acres Harvested 1,000 Acres	Yield Per Acre Pounds	Pro-duction Million Pounds	Farm Price cents Lb.	Farm Value Million $	Tobacco (June - July) Exports[2]	Imports[3]	U.S. Exports of — Cigar-ettes	Cigars & Cheroots	All Tobacco	Smoking Tobacco[4]	Stocks of Tobacco[5] Various Types — All Tobacco	Fire Cured[6]	Cigar Filler[7]	Mary-land
						- Million Pounds -		---- In Millions -----				--------------- In Millions of Pounds ---------------			
2009	354.0	2,323	823	183.7	1,511	----	----	----	----	----	----	----	----	----	----
2010	337.5	2,128	718	178.2	1,280	----	----	----	----	----	----	----	----	----	----
2011	325.0	1,841	598	184.7	1,105	----	----	----	----	----	----	----	----	----	----
2012	336.2	2,268	763	207.2	1,580	----	----	----	----	----	----	----	----	----	----
2013	355.7	2,034	724	217.7	1,575	----	----	----	----	----	----	----	----	----	----
2014	378.4	2,316	876	209.4	1,835	----	----	----	----	----	----	----	----	----	----
2015	328.7	2,188	719	200.3	1,441	----	----	----	----	----	----	----	----	----	----
2016	319.7	1,967	629	200.7	1,262	----	----	----	----	----	----	----	----	----	----
2017	321.5	2,209	710	206.9	1,469	----	----	----	----	----	----	----	----	----	----
2018[1]	291.4	1,830	533			----	----	----	----	----	----	----	----	----	----

[1] Preliminary. [2] Domestic. [3] For consumption. [4] In bulk. [5] Flue-cured and cigar wrapper, year beginning July 1; for all other types, October 1. [6] Kentucky-Tennessee types 22-23. [7] Types 41-46. *Source: Economic Research Service, U.S. Department of Agriculture (ERS-USDA)*

Tobacco Production in the United States, by Types   In Thousands of Pounds (Farm-Sale Weight)

Year	Class 1, Flue-cured (11-14)	Class 2, Fire-cured (21-23)	Class 3A, Light air-cured (31-32)	Class 3B, Dark air-cured (35-37)	Total Cigar types (41-61)	US Total
2009	525,414	52,990	219,726	17,040	7,411	822,581
2010	451,290	48,379	192,520	15,180	10,821	718,190
2011	344,610	51,721	178,265	16,082	7,574	598,252
2012	472,900	53,764	211,550	15,250	9,245	762,709
2013	454,350	50,388	197,165	13,790	7,886	723,579
2014	572,880	59,146	217,860	17,490	9,039	876,415
2015	489,475	56,125	148,195	17,050	8,326	719,171
2016	431,450	39,520	143,890	10,020	3,840	628,720
2017	460,650	59,531	165,460	20,200	4,320	710,161
2018[1]	338,690	58,926	103,515	26,590	5,520	533,241

[1] Preliminary. *Source: Agricultural Statistics Board, U.S. Department of Agriculture (ASB-USDA)*

U.S. Exports of Unmanufactured Tobacco   In Millions of Pounds (Declared Weight)

Year	Australia	Belgium-Luxem.	Denmark	France	Germany	Italy	Japan	Nether-lands	Sweden	Switzer-land	Thailand	United Kingdom	Total U.S. Exports
2009	6.4	3.6	6.4	7.7	23.9	.4	.0	37.7	.3	59.1	2.8	.1	380.3
2010	5.2	44.6	4.5	8.3	20.8	.6	.0	44.7	.4	34.7	3.0	1.1	394.0
2011	.8	10.0	.7	8.9	25.9	.8	.0	27.2	.5	65.6	3.7	6.0	406.5
2012	.7	10.3	.8	11.8	20.2	.5	.2	29.6	.2	46.2	3.6	2.9	353.4
2013	.3	3.8	.7	6.5	20.1	1.5	.0	25.0	.5	62.2	2.7	1.4	349.9
2014	.1	9.8	1.2	9.8	14.4	.5	.0	14.3	.4	63.5	3.2	3.2	330.2
2015	.1	10.9	1.1	5.2	15.2	.6	.0	7.9	.4	89.7	1.8	1.0	343.0
2016	.0	20.5	.9	2.0	11.9	6.3	.2	8.5	.3	79.5	.6	1.1	362.2
2017		14.6	.9	1.2	6.6	7.2	.3	7.5	.4	76.6		1.0	317.8
2018[1]		13.8	.9	2.9	5.5	8.6	.2	9.4	.1	70.4		1.2	329.7

[1] Preliminary.   Source: Economic Research Service, U.S. Department of Agriculture (ERS-USDA)

U.S. Salient Statistics for Flue-Cured Tobacco (Types 11-14) in the United States   In Millions of Pounds

Year	Acres Harvested 1,000	Yield Per Acre Pounds	Mar-ketings	Stocks Oct. 1	Total Supply	Exports	Domestic Disap-pearance	Total Disap-pearance	Farm Price cents/Lb.	Placed Under Gov't Loan (Mil. Lb.)	Price Support Level (cents/) Lb.	Loan Stocks Nov. 30	Uncom-mitted
2009-10	223.8	2,348	----	----	----	----	----	----	----	175.4	----	----	----
2010-11	210.9	2,140	----	----	----	----	----	----	----	----	----	----	----
2011-12	206.9	1,666	----	----	----	----	----	----	----	----	----	----	----
2012-13	206.0	2,296	----	----	----	----	----	----	----	----	----	----	----
2013-14	228.8	1,986	----	----	----	----	----	----	----	----	----	----	----
2014-15	245.3	2,335	----	----	----	----	----	----	----	----	----	----	----
2015-16	220.0	2,225	----	----	----	----	----	----	----	----	----	----	----
2016-17	213.5	2,021	----	----	----	----	----	----	----	----	----	----	----
2017-18[1]	209.5	2,199	----	----	----	----	----	----	----	----	----	----	----
2018-19[2]	197.8	1,712	----	----	----	----	----	----	----	----	----	----	----

[1] Preliminary.   [2] Estimate.   NA = Not available.   Source: Economic Research Service, U.S. Department of Agriculture (ERS-USDA)

Salient Statistics for Burley Tobacco (Type 31) in the United States   In Millions of Pounds

Year	Acres Harvested 1,000	Yield Per Acre Pounds	Mar-ketings	Stocks Oct. 1	Total Supply	Exports	Domestic Disap-pearance	Total Disap-pearance	Farm Price cents/Lb.	Gross Sales[3]	Price Support Level cents/Lb.	Loan Stocks Nov. 30	Uncom-mitted
2009-10	101.9	2,109	----	----	----	----	----	----	----	170.9	----	----	----
2010-11	97.6	1,922	----	----	----	----	----	----	----	----	----	----	----
2011-12	88.9	1,938	----	----	----	----	----	----	----	----	----	----	----
2012-13	101.4	2,021	----	----	----	----	----	----	----	----	----	----	----
2013-14	99.0	1,944	----	----	----	----	----	----	----	----	----	----	----
2014-15	101.5	2,100	----	----	----	----	----	----	----	----	----	----	----
2015-16	78.9	1,834	----	----	----	----	----	----	----	----	----	----	----
2016-17	80.0	1,747	----	----	----	----	----	----	----	----	----	----	----
2017-18[1]	81.5	1,977	----	----	----	----	----	----	----	----	----	----	----
2018-19[2]	61.1	1,645	----	----	----	----	----	----	----	----	----	----	----

[1] Preliminary.   [2] Estimate.   [3] Before Christmas holidays.   NA = Not available.
Source: Economic Research Service, U.S. Department of Agriculture (ERS-USDA)

Exports of Tobacco from the United States (Quantity and Value)   In Metric Tons

Year	Flue-Cured	Value 1,000 USD	Burley	Value 1,000 USD	Total	Value 1,000 USD	Manu-factured	Value 1,000 USD
2009	86,429	659,772	37,395	300,744	172,504	1,158,970	4,654	489,480
2010	85,789	662,648	32,687	265,927	178,726	1,167,644	4,981	454,459
2011	88,876	643,946	33,385	256,006	184,369	1,148,991	7,472	489,454
2012	77,073	607,725	32,051	243,411	160,308	1,101,214	18,405	482,614
2013	78,079	650,887	32,124	265,809	158,728	1,137,947	21,930	485,412
2014	76,239	645,462	25,441	217,329	149,758	1,085,958	18,111	426,981
2015	77,942	657,188	26,100	226,807	155,578	1,108,756	21,880	423,179
2016	88,283	707,889	20,202	166,246	164,278	1,085,439	18,620	408,341
2017[1]	77,830	643,791	16,335	139,327	144,136	1,010,325	16,321	197,428
2018[2]	82,281	674,237	19,967	165,723	149,551	1,053,664	14,528	184,628

[1] Preliminary.   [2] Forecast.   Source: Foreign Agricultural Service, U.S. Department of Agriculture (FAS-USDA)

Tungsten

Tungsten (atomic symbol W) is a grayish-white, lustrous, metallic element. The atomic symbol for tungsten is W because of its former name of Wolfram. Tungsten has the highest melting point of any metal at about 3410 degrees Celsius and boils at about 5660 degrees Celsius. In 1781, the Swedish chemist Carl Wilhelm Scheele discovered tungsten.

Tungsten is never found in nature but is instead found in the minerals wolframite, scheelite, huebnertite, and ferberite. Tungsten has excellent corrosion resistance qualities and is resistant to most mineral acids. Tungsten is used as filaments in incandescent lamps, electron and television tubes, alloys of steel, spark plugs, electrical contact points, cutting tools, and in the chemical and tanning industries.

Prices – The average monthly price of tungsten at U.S. ports in 2018 rose +29.3% yr/yr to $313.15 per short ton, but still below the 2012 record high of $375.16.

Supply – World concentrate production of tungsten in 2018 fell -0.1% yr/yr to 82,000 metric tons. The world's largest producer of tungsten by far is China with 67,000 metric tons of production in 2018, which was 81.7% of total world production. Russia is the next largest producer at 2.6% with miniscule production of only 2,100 metric tons.

Trade – The U.S. in 2017 relied on imports for somewhat over 50% of its tungsten consumption., which is down from 95% in 1994. U.S. imports for consumption in 2018 rose +1.8% yr/yr to 4,000 metric tons. U.S. exports in 2018 fell -30.5% yr/yr to 370 metric tons.

World Concentrate Production of Tungsten   In Metric Tons (Contained Tungsten[3])

Year	Austria	Bolivia	Brazil	Burma	Canada	China	Korea, North	Mongolia	Portugal	Russia	Rwanda	Thailand	Total
2011	861	1,124	244	140	1,966	61,800	110	13	819	3,314	480	160	73,900
2012	706	1,247	381	131	2,194	64,400	100	66	763	4,281	830	80	77,700
2013	850	1,253	494	140	2,128	71,100	65	274	692	4,191	1,100	140	85,400
2014	819	1,252	510	111	2,344	71,000	70	557	671	3,775	1,000	100	88,500
2015	861	1,460	510	90	1,600	73,000	70	351	474	3,262	850	30	89,700
2016	954	1,110	510	90	----	72,000	50	753	549	3,100	820	30	88,100
2017[1]	975	994				67,000		150	724	2,090	720		82,100
2018[2]	980	1,000				67,000			770	2,100	830		82,000

[1] Preliminary.   [2] Estimate.   [3] Conversion Factors: WO_3 to W, multiply by 0.7931; 60% WO_3 to W, multiply by 0.4758.
Source: U.S. Geological Survey (USGS)

Salient Statistics of Tungsten in the United States   In Metric Tons (Contained Tungsten)

Year	Net Import Reliance as a % Apparent Consump sumption	Total Con- sumption	Steel Tool	Stainless & Heat Assisting	Alloy Steel[3]	Super- alloys	Cutting & Wear Resistant Materials	Products Made From Metal Powder	Miscel- laneous	Chemical and Ceramic	Exports	Imports for Con- sumption	Stocks, Dec. 31 -- Concentrates -- Con- sumers	Pro- ducers
2011	40	W	W	96	W	W	6,760	W	----	88	169	3,640	W	W
2012	39	W	W	123	W	W	6,800	W	----	90	186	3,610	W	W
2013	41	W	W	86	W	W	6,260	W	----	88	1,050	3,690	W	W
2014	>25	W	W	82	W	W	6,880	W	----	88	1,230	4,080	W	W
2015	>25	W	W	205	W	W	6,310	W	----	88	398	3,970	W	W
2016	>25	W	W	94	W	W	5,760	W	----	88	183	3,580	W	W
2017[1]	>50	W	W	W	W	W	W	W	----		532	3,930	W	W
2018[2]	>50	W	W	W	W	W	W	W	----		370	4,000	W	W

[1] Preliminary.   [2] Estimate.   [3] Other than tool.   [4] Included with stainless & heat assisting.   W = Withheld.
Source: U.S. Geological Survey (USGS)

Average Price of Tungsten at U.S. Ports (Including Duty)   In Dollars Per Short Ton

Year	Jan.	Feb.	Mar.	Apr.	May	June	July	Aug.	Sept.	Oct.	Nov.	Dec.	Average
2011	263.45	307.00	307.00	307.00	307.00	307.00	307.00	307.00	307.00	385.67	425.00	425.00	329.59
2012	420.50	395.00	393.64	389.64	382.84	402.50	402.50	390.00	360.00	346.96	320.50	297.78	375.16
2013	297.74	329.45	351.29	351.50	356.73	382.55	406.86	417.28	407.13	392.50	387.29	378.50	371.57
2014	374.39	368.18	367.12	363.64	368.81	376.00	369.60	363.57	353.81	345.00	329.31	309.19	357.39
2015	293.18	281.80	272.64	254.20	243.45	228.50	222.95	207.90	188.81	184.77	173.33	176.28	227.32
2016	171.79	167.74	175.43	189.52	217.82	212.75	188.69	191.74	190.00	192.45	198.89	191.39	190.68
2017	194.33	200.30	211.83	211.18	217.80	221.68	222.76	252.28	310.60	286.02	280.68	296.79	242.19
2018	311.96	321.62	327.93	327.55	338.02	349.36	341.50	307.52	282.50	283.48	285.00	281.31	313.15

U.S. Spot Quotations, 65% WO_3, Basis C.I.F.   *Source: U.S. Geological Survey (USGS)*

Turkeys

During the past three decades, the turkey industry has experienced tremendous growth in the U.S. Turkey production has more than tripled since 1970, with a current value of over $7 billion. Turkey was not a popular dish in Europe until aDuring the past three decades, the turkey industry has experienced tremendous growth in the U.S. Turkey production has more than tripled since 1970, with a current value of over $7 billion. Turkey was not a popular dish in Europe until a roast turkey was eaten on June 27, 1570, at the wedding feast of Charles XI of France and Elizabeth of Austria. The King was so impressed with the birds that the turkey subsequently became a popular dish at banquets held by French nobility.

The most popular turkey product continues to be the whole bird, with heavy demand at Thanksgiving and Christmas. The primary breeders maintain and develop the quality stock, concentrating on growth and conformation in males and fecundity in females, as well as characteristics important to general health and welfare. Turkey producers include large companies that produce turkeys all year round, and relatively small companies and farmers who produce turkeys primarily for the seasonal Thanksgiving market.

Prices – The average monthly price received by farmers for turkeys in the U.S. in 2018 fell -20.7% yr/yr to 51.2 cents per pound, well below the 2016 record high of 82.5 cents per pound. The monthly average retail price of turkeys (whole frozen) in the U.S. in 2018 fell -5.1% yr/yr to 150.1 cents per pound, below the 2013 record high of 164.9 cents per pound.

Supply – World production of turkeys in 2014 fell -1.4% yr/yr to 5.288 million metric tons. World production of turkeys has grown by more than two and one-half times since 1980 when production was 2.090 million metric tons.

The U.S. was the largest producer of turkeys by far with 2.600 million metric tons of production in 2014, which is 49.2% of world production. The value of U.S. turkey production in the U.S. in 2017 was $4.842 billion.

Demand – World consumption of turkeys in 2014 fell -2.5% yr/yr to 4.937 million metric tons. U.S. turkey consumption was 2.253 million metric tons in 2014, which accounts for 45.6% of world consumption. U.S. per-capita consumption of turkeys in 2019 is expected to fall -7.8% yr/yr to 14.9 pounds per person per year. U.S. per-capita consumption of turkeys has been in the range of 16-18 pounds since 1990, but the USDA is projecting that per-capita consumption will drop somewhat, which appears to be happening.

Production of Turkey Meat, by Selected Countries   In Thousands of Metric Tons (RTC)

	Production							Consumption						
Year	Brazil	Canada	European Union	Mexico	Russia	United States	World Total	Brazil	Canada	European Union	Mexico	Russia	United States	World Total
2005	360	155	1,919	14	11	2,464	4,936	199	143	1,888	194	118	2,247	4,857
2006	353	163	1,858	14	16	2,543	4,960	197	144	1,841	197	107	2,297	4,866
2007	458	170	1,790	15	30	2,664	5,143	281	150	1,770	211	105	2,404	5,026
2008	465	180	1,830	15	39	2,796	5,337	261	163	1,836	212	107	2,434	5,101
2009	466	167	1,795	11	31	2,535	5,018	302	151	1,802	155	72	2,363	4,911
2010	485	159	1,946	11	70	2,527	5,212	327	143	1,913	163	105	2,306	5,023
2011	489	160	1,950	13	90	2,592	5,308	348	150	1,886	164	117	2,273	5,010
2012	510	161	2,010	14	100	2,671	5,480	340	142	1,953	173	120	2,282	5,105
2013[1]	520	168	1,950	10	100	2,599	5,361	359	150	1,893	166	112	2,291	5,063
2014[2]	470	170	1,920	9	105	2,600	5,288	350	152	1,848	158	115	2,253	4,937

[1] Preliminary. [2] Forecast. Source: Foreign Agricultural Service, U.S. Department of Agriculture (FAS-USDA)

Salient Statistics of Turkeys in the United States

			Liveweight		Value of Production	Ready-to-Cook Basis			Consumption			Production Costs		Wholesale Ready-to-Cook	
Year	Poults Placed[3] --- In Thousands ----	Number Raised[4]	Pro-duced Mil Lbs	Price cents Per Lb.	of Pro-duction Million $	Pro-duction	Be-ginning Stocks	Exports	Total	Per Capita Lbs.	Feed	Total	Pro-duction Costs	3-Region Weighted Avg Price[5]
						In Millions of Pounds					Liveweight Basis -			
2009	273,992	247,359	7,149.3	49.9	3,573.3	5,588	396,144	535	5,201	16.9	----	----	----	----
2010	275,384	244,188	7,108.2	61.2	4,372.4	5,644	261,838	583	5,084	16.4	----	----	----	----
2011	277,931	248,500	7,313.2	68.0	4,987.6	5,791	191,560	703	5,013	16.1	----	----	----	----
2012	283,550	253,500	7,561.9	71.9	5,452.1	5,967	210,787	797	5,028	16.0	----	----	----	----
2013	260,571	240,000	7,277.5	66.4	4,839.6	5,806	296,479	741	5,068	16.0	----	----	----	----
2014	267,142	237,500	7,217.0	73.2	5,304.5	5,756	237,407	775	5,052	15.8	----	----	----	----
2015	260,184	233,100	7,038.1	81.1	5,707.9	5,627	193,429	529	5,136	16.0	----	----	----	----
2016	255,978	241,418	7,487.0	82.5	6,184.2	5,981	201,011	569	5,386	16.6	----	----	----	----
2017[1]	267,840	242,500	7,494.6	64.5	4,841.5	5,979	278,741	621		16.4	----	----	----	----
2018[2]	257,910	240,000		51.0		5,970	309,625	645		16.1	----	----	----	----

[1] Preliminary. [2] Estimate. [3] Poults placed for slaughter by hatcheries. [4] Turkeys place August 1-July 31. [5] Regions include central, eastern and western. Central region receives twice the weight of the other regions in calculating the average.
Source: Economic Research Service, U.S. Department of Agriculture (ERS-USDA)

TURKEYS

Turkey-Feed Price Ratio in the United States   In Pounds[2]

Year	Jan.	Feb.	Mar.	Apr.	May	June	July	Aug.	Sept.	Oct.	Nov.	Dec.	Average
2009	4.1	4.6	4.8	4.7	4.7	4.8	5.1	5.2	5.3	5.6	5.7	5.6	5.0
2010	4.8	5.3	5.6	5.9	6.2	6.9	6.9	6.7	6.6	6.8	6.4	5.6	6.1
2011	4.6	4.2	4.4	4.5	4.6	4.8	4.7	4.7	5.2	5.8	5.9	5.4	4.9
2012	4.8	4.7	4.8	5.0	5.0	5.1	4.4	4.3	4.8	4.9	4.7	4.3	4.7
2013	4.0	3.9	4.1	4.2	4.1	4.1	4.3	4.6	5.0	5.8	5.3	5.5	4.6
2014	5.2	5.4	5.3	5.1	5.4	5.6	6.2	6.8	7.6	8.3	8.1	7.1	6.3
2015	6.3	6.6	6.8	7.1	7.9	8.4	8.5	9.4	10.0	10.6	10.2	9.8	8.5
2016	8.7	9.0	9.0	9.2	8.8	8.9	9.3	9.5	10.3	9.9	9.3	8.4	9.2
2017	7.6	7.3	7.5	7.5	7.7	7.4	7.3	7.2	6.9	7.1	6.5	6.0	7.2
2018[1]	5.7	5.5	5.2	5.2	5.1	5.3	5.7	5.8	5.9	5.7	6.0	5.5	5.6

[1] Preliminary.   [2] Pounds of feed equal in value to one pound of turkey, liveweight.   Source: Economic Research Service, U.S. Department of Agriculture (ERS-USDA)

Average Price Received by Farmers for Turkeys in the United States (Liveweight)   In Cents Per Pound

Year	Jan.	Feb.	Mar.	Apr.	May	June	July	Aug.	Sept.	Oct.	Nov.	Dec.	Average
2009	43.8	46.5	47.1	47.6	50.1	52.5	52.0	51.1	48.5	52.1	54.1	53.7	49.9
2010	46.5	49.1	52.2	53.7	56.1	61.7	64.7	66.8	69.0	73.4	73.6	67.7	61.2
2011	56.4	57.8	59.9	65.7	67.9	69.5	67.5	70.7	73.1	77.3	78.1	71.5	68.0
2012	65.7	65.0	69.0	73.7	72.7	73.9	72.9	74.4	76.2	76.9	75.1	67.4	71.9
2013	62.9	62.7	65.0	66.2	64.9	65.7	67.7	67.4	67.9	72.4	65.6	68.7	66.4
2014	64.5	66.4	68.3	68.7	72.6	72.8	74.0	75.6	77.5	82.2	82.1	73.4	73.2
2015	66.2	66.9	68.3	70.2	75.9	81.2	84.8	89.7	92.5	97.2	92.2	88.6	81.1
2016	78.9	79.4	78.9	83.2	83.1	86.5	86.6	84.3	87.8	85.2	81.5	74.4	82.5
2017	68.9	67.2	69.0	66.6	68.6	65.8	67.8	64.7	62.3	62.7	57.7	52.9	64.5
2018[1]	50.8	50.6	49.9	50.0	49.8	50.8	51.9	51.7	53.1	51.1	53.0	49.8	51.0

[1] Preliminary.   Source: Economic Research Service, U.S. Department of Agriculture (ERS-USDA)

Average Wholesale Price of Turkeys[1] (Hens, 8-16 Lbs.) in New York   In Cents Per Pound

Year	Jan.	Feb.	Mar.	Apr.	May	June	July	Aug.	Sept.	Oct.	Nov.	Dec.	Average
2009	71.73	74.32	75.22	76.59	78.71	82.00	82.68	81.33	80.26	82.52	84.96	83.95	79.52
2010	72.71	75.25	78.90	80.43	82.46	90.28	94.67	97.15	102.02	107.22	106.05	97.90	90.42
2011	88.14	89.97	92.38	96.68	99.75	103.14	104.00	105.39	109.79	114.83	113.57	106.54	102.02
2012	98.35	100.15	103.70	106.89	107.77	106.00	106.43	108.53	110.54	110.27	108.86	99.08	105.55
2013	96.27	95.00	96.58	97.30	97.59	98.18	99.09	99.28	101.22	106.75	105.64	103.83	99.73
2014	99.78	99.88	102.34	103.52	106.15	107.18	108.56	109.15	112.79	116.20	118.78	106.79	107.59
2015	99.12	99.12	100.57	104.06	108.82	112.53	120.86	126.62	131.65	135.68	130.63	123.96	116.14
2016	114.71	114.77	114.73	116.17	116.00	117.21	119.45	118.95	123.57	121.84	122.54	105.33	117.11
2017	99.81	100.56	100.90	99.25	99.44	98.54	97.61	96.38	96.59	94.97	88.76	80.16	96.08
2018[1]	79.10	79.64	79.31	79.50	79.31	79.98	79.11	80.03	82.09	82.00	82.24	79.85	80.18

[1] Ready-to-cook.   [2] Preliminary.   Source: Economic Research Service, U.S. Department of Agriculture (ERS-USDA)

Certified Federally Inspected Turkey Slaughter in the U.S. (Ready-to-Cook Weights)   In Thousands of Pounds

Year	Jan.	Feb.	Mar.	Apr.	May	June	July	Aug.	Sept.	Oct.	Nov.	Dec.	Total
2009	465,481	441,630	467,717	472,243	448,772	490,672	482,278	460,690	463,836	504,415	475,287	453,227	5,626,248
2010	421,098	423,251	487,985	452,759	437,480	486,999	463,890	478,199	464,079	521,672	517,999	458,594	5,614,005
2011	460,910	432,774	500,414	453,806	494,571	516,341	445,675	499,115	470,843	521,508	509,314	456,916	5,762,187
2012	474,530	464,839	499,864	475,184	516,910	504,083	494,852	526,318	450,670	576,265	512,931	438,521	5,934,967
2013	522,128	458,794	470,052	502,276	505,780	471,529	512,059	482,373	438,111	514,181	477,015	420,380	5,774,678
2014	451,344	419,636	454,990	468,525	469,331	484,245	497,961	480,569	490,385	558,196	478,421	472,065	5,725,668
2015	489,634	431,503	498,992	493,905	432,442	455,913	446,207	447,301	450,088	522,359	466,917	458,298	5,593,559
2016	472,415	451,760	500,407	482,346	496,204	532,226	476,204	535,290	492,914	514,928	511,897	475,553	5,942,144
2017	495,763	454,965	526,631	433,274	520,061	519,205	581,127	673,714	581,261	686,143	642,370	573,273	6,687,787
2018[1]	633,654	571,596	598,038	597,493	633,247	603,743	604,483	644,881	531,593	710,416	619,092	558,969	7,307,205

[1] Preliminary.   Source: Economic Research Service, U.S. Department of Agriculture (ERS-USDA)

Per Capita Consumption of Turkeys in the United States   In Pounds

Year	First Quarter	Second Quarter	Third Quarter	Fourth Quarter	Total	Year	First Quarter	Second Quarter	Third Quarter	Fourth Quarter	Total
2008	4.0	4.1	4.3	5.3	17.6	2014	3.4	3.5	3.9	5.0	15.8
2009	3.7	3.9	4.0	5.3	16.9	2015	3.5	3.6	3.9	4.9	16.0
2010	3.5	3.6	4.1	5.2	16.4	2016	3.6	3.9	4.2	4.9	16.6
2011	3.5	3.5	4.0	5.0	16.1	2017	3.7	3.7	4.0	5.0	16.4
2012	3.5	3.6	4.1	4.9	16.0	2018[1]	3.5	3.8	3.9	4.9	16.1
2013	3.7	3.6	4.0	4.8	16.0	2019[2]	3.5	3.6	3.9	4.9	15.9

[1] Preliminary.   [2] Estimate.   Source: Economic Research Service, U.S. Department of Agriculture (ERS-USDA)

Storage Stocks of Turkeys (Frozen) in the United States on First of Month   In Thousands of Pounds

Year	Jan.	Feb.	Mar.	Apr.	May	June	July	Aug.	Sept.	Oct.	Nov.	Dec.
2009	396,144	446,197	462,395	513,384	571,708	585,745	594,742	641,060	653,546	613,891	517,463	244,480
2010	261,838	302,058	342,418	379,720	422,064	461,805	507,174	501,511	502,175	473,745	410,161	174,110
2011	191,560	253,527	288,976	325,688	364,503	447,895	508,657	524,846	528,396	509,650	406,864	194,227
2012	210,787	297,736	349,577	375,268	438,384	498,419	547,091	547,465	547,766	521,810	453,378	255,191
2013	296,479	360,018	394,755	401,246	457,575	521,556	566,475	581,357	580,069	541,183	434,493	221,221
2014	237,407	275,787	310,756	336,383	375,013	422,502	462,586	489,758	494,786	484,547	390,654	187,563
2015	193,429	280,400	321,337	345,578	394,415	441,388	462,020	494,037	477,579	449,622	351,828	190,268
2016	201,011	289,746	341,094	368,073	398,719	454,147	504,385	530,278	532,579	511,199	400,355	236,862
2017	278,741	339,493	378,370	428,752	471,484	529,904	565,123	595,623	600,013	569,963	460,856	288,536
2018[1]	309,625	375,188	427,618	462,899	493,833	536,026	561,858	590,247	606,320	564,745	445,016	274,123

[1] Preliminary.   Source: Economic Research Service, U.S. Department of Agriculture (ERS-USDA)

Average Retail Price of Turkeys (Whole frozen) in the United States   In U.S. Dollars Per Pound

Year	Jan.	Feb.	Mar.	Apr.	May	June	July	Aug.	Sept.	Oct.	Nov.	Dec.	Average
2009	1.365	1.369	1.347	1.354	1.366	1.410	1.445	1.461	1.454	1.480	1.336	1.365	1.396
2010	1.398	1.375	1.425	1.479	1.464	1.474	1.554	1.521	1.566	1.677	1.407	1.380	1.477
2011	1.459	1.526	1.572	1.562	1.596	1.581	1.603	1.641	1.676	1.673	1.541	1.574	1.584
2012	1.671	1.671	1.812	1.791	1.608	1.557	1.561	1.586	1.621	1.661	1.488	1.433	1.622
2013	1.579	1.591	1.593	1.649	1.654	1.595	1.624	1.663	1.819	NA	1.721	1.650	1.649
2014	1.713	1.699	1.733	1.610	1.602	1.606	1.641	1.604	1.584	1.667	1.425	1.331	1.601
2015	1.445	1.480	1.503	1.487	1.527	1.541	1.568	1.546	1.538	1.558	1.424	1.448	1.505
2016	1.528	1.494	1.509	1.488	1.527	1.515	1.586	1.622	1.649	1.692	1.527	1.495	1.553
2017	1.581	1.570	1.585	1.567	1.532	1.576	1.622	1.615	1.623	1.656	1.556	1.502	1.582
2018[1]	1.399	1.435	1.512	1.483	1.526	1.529	1.585	1.567	1.578	1.582	1.400	1.413	1.501

[1] Preliminary.   Source: Economic Research Service, U.S. Department of Agriculture (ERS-USDA)

Average Retail-to-Consumer Price Spread of Turkeys (Whole) in the United States   In Cents Per Pound

Year	Jan.	Feb.	Mar.	Apr.	May	June	July	Aug.	Sept.	Oct.	Nov.	Dec.	Average
2008	38.0	37.5	23.7	21.6	27.3	23.4	25.1	23.0	23.4	18.0	33.9	48.8	28.6
2009	NA	NA	NA	NA	NA	51.0	53.9	56.0	56.2	56.3	39.4	43.7	50.9
2010	55.6	50.6	51.9	55.5	52.2	NA	NA	42.8	42.9	49.3	22.7	28.8	45.2
2011	48.8	NA	NA	NA	NA	NA	NA	49.7	48.8	43.5	31.5	41.9	44.0
2012	59.8	58.0	68.5	63.2	44.0	40.7	40.7	41.1	42.6	46.8	30.9	35.2	47.6
2013	52.6	55.1	53.7	58.6	58.8	52.3	54.3	58.0	71.7	NA	57.5	52.2	56.8
2014	62.5	61.0	62.0	48.5	45.1	44.4	46.5	42.3	36.6	41.5	14.7	17.3	43.5
2015	36.4	39.9	40.7	35.6	34.9	32.6	26.9	19.0	NA	NA	2.8	11.8	28.1
2016	29.1	25.6	27.2	23.6	27.7	25.3	30.2	34.3	32.3	38.4	21.2	35.2	29.2
2017[1]	49.3	47.4	48.6	48.5	44.8	Discontinued	----	----	----	----	----	----	47.7

[1] Preliminary.   Source: Economic Research Service, U.S. Department of Agriculture (ERS-USDA)

Uranium

Uranium (atomic symbol U) is a chemically reactive, radioactive, steel-gray, metallic element and is the main fuel used in nuclear reactors. Uranium is the heaviest of all the natural elements. Traces of uranium have been found in archeological artifacts dating back to 79 AD. Uranium was discovered in pitchblende by German chemist Martin Heinrich Klaproth in 1789. Klaproth named it uranium after the recently discovered planet Uranus. French physicist Antoine Henri Becquerel discovered the radioactive properties of uranium in 1896 when he produced an image on a photographic plate covered with a light-absorbing substance. Following Becquerel's experiments, investigations of radioactivity led to the discovery of radium (atomic symbol Ra) and to new concepts of atomic organization.

The principal use for uranium is fuel in nuclear power plants. Demand for uranium concentrates is directly linked to the level of electricity generated by nuclear power plants. Uranium ores are widely distributed throughout the world and are primarily found in Canada, DRC (formerly Zaire), and the U.S. Uranium is obtained from primary mine production and secondary sources. Two Canadian companies, Cameco and Cogema Resources, are the primary producers of uranium from deposits in the Athabasca Basin of northern Saskatchewan. Secondary sources of uranium include excess inventories from utilities and other fuel cycle participants, used reactor fuel, and dismantled Russian nuclear weapons.

Prices – CME uranium swap futures prices (Barchart. com symbol UX) during 2018 started the year at $23.90 per pound, moved lower into April and then moved higher the rest of the year to finally end the year up +17.0% at $28.80 per pound. Uranium prices have fallen sharply from levels above $100 per pound seen around 2007.

Supply – World production of uranium oxide (U308) concentrate in 2016 rose + 6.1% yr/yr to 59,875 metric tons, a new record high. The world's largest uranium producers in 2014 were Kazakhstan with 41.0% of world production, Canada with 23.4%, Australia with 10.5%, Namibia with 6.1%, and Niger with 5.8%.

Trade – U.S. imports of uranium in 2017 fell -17.0% yr/yr to 42.100 million pounds. The record high of 66.100 million pounds was posted in 2004. The U.S. has generally been forced to import more uranium as domestic production steadily declined. U.S. exports of uranium in 2017 fell -18.6% yr/yr to 14.000 million pounds, which is below the record high of 23.500 million pounds posted in 2009.

Uranium Industry Statistics in the United States   In Millions of Pounds U_3O_8

	----- Production -----		Concent-rate	-------------- Employment - Person Years ----------						Avg Price		Avg Price Delivered	
Year	Mine	Concent-rate	Ship-ments	Explor-ation	Mining	Milling	Pro-cessing	Total[1]	Deliveries to U.S. Utilities[2]	Avg Price Delivered Uranium $/lb U_3O_8	Imports	Uranium Imports $/lb U_3O_8	Exports
2008	3.9	3.902	4.130	457	558	W	W	1,563	53.4	45.88	57.1	41.30	17.2
2009	4.1	3.708	3.620	175	441	W	W	1,096	49.8	45.86	58.9	41.23	23.5
2010	4.2	4.228	5.137	211	400	W	W	1,073	46.6	49.29	55.3	47.01	23.1
2011	4.1	3.991	4.000	208	462	W	W	1,191	54.8	55.64	54.4	54.00	16.7
2012	4.3	4.146	3.911	161	462	W	W	1,196	57.5	54.99	56.2	51.44	18.0
2013	4.6	4.659	4.655	149	392	W	W	1,156	57.4	51.99	57.3	48.24	18.9
2014	4.9	4.891	4.593	86	246	W	W	787	53.3	46.16	58.6	44.11	20.0
2015	3.7	3.343	4.023	58	251	W	W	625	56.5	44.13	64.1	42.96	25.7
2016	2.5	2.917	3.018	38	255	W	W	560	50.6	42.43	50.7	40.45	17.2
2017	1.2	2.443	2.277	50	136	W	W	424	43.0	38.80	42.1	37.09	14.0

[1] From suppliers under domestic purchases.   Source: Energy Information Administration, U.S. Department of Energy (EIA-DOE)

Commercial and U.S. Government Stocks of Uranium, End of Year   In Millions of Pounds U_3O_8 Equivalent

	------------------ Utility ------------------		----------- Domestic Supplier -------------		Total	DOE Owned ----------- & USEC Held ---------------	
Year	Natural Uranium	Enriched Uranium[1]	Natural Uranium	Enriched Uranium[1]	Commercial Stocks	Natural Uranium	Enriched Uranium[1]
2008	58.8	24.2	(/2)	27.0	110.0	W	W
2009	53.6	31.2	(/2)	26.8	111.5	W	W
2010	48.8	37.7	W	24.7	111.3	W	W
2011	50.6	39.2	W	22.3	112.1	W	W
2012	45.0	52.6	W	23.3	120.9	W	W
2013	56.5	56.6	W	21.3	134.4	W	W
2014	59.9	54.2	W	18.7	132.7	W	W
2015	68.8	52.4	W	14.3	135.5	W	W
2016	74.4	53.6	W	16.7	144.6	W	W
2017	74.0	49.7	W	19.0	142.7	W	W

[1] Includes amount reported as UF_6 at enrichment suppliers.   DOE = Department of Energy   USEC = U.S. Energy Commission
Source: Energy Information Administration, U.S. Department of Energy (EIA-DOE)

World Production of Uranium Oxide (U3O8) Concentrate   In Metric Tons (Uranium Content)

Year	Australia	Canada	China	Czech Republic	Kazakh-stan	Namibia	Niger	Russia	South Africa	United States	Ukraine	Uzbeki-stan	World Total
2010	5,900	9,775	1,350	254	17,803	4,503	4,199	3,562	582	837	1,630	2,874	51,806
2011	5,967	9,145	1,400	229	19,450	3,954	4,264	2,993	556	873	1,582	2,500	52,266
2012	7,009	8,998	1,450	228	21,240	5,026	4,773	2,862	467	1,012	1,667	2,400	56,816
2013	6,350	9,000	1,450	215	22,500	5,627	4,277	3,133	540	1,075	1,792	2,400	58,103
2014	5,001	9,134	1,500	193	23,127	3,255	4,156	2,990	393	926	1,919	2,400	54,282
2015	5,654	11,709	1,616	155	23,800	2,993	4,116	3,055	322	1,200	1,256	2,385	56,452
2016[1]	6,315	14,039	1,616	138	24,575	3,654	3,479	3,004	490	1,005	1,125	2,404	59,887
2017[2]	5,882	13,116	1,885		23,391	4,224	3,449	2,917	308	550	940	2,404	57,083

[1] Preliminary.   [2] Estimate.   *Source: Food and Agriculture Organization of the United Nations (FAO-UN)*

Total Production of Uranium Concentrate in the United States, by Quarters   In Pounds U3O8

Year	First Quarter	Second Quarter	Third Quarter	Fourth Quarter	Total	Year	First Quarter	Second Quarter	Third Quarter	Fourth Quarter	Total
2007	1,162,737	1,119,536	1,075,460	1,175,845	4,533,578	2013	1,147,031	1,394,232	1,171,278	946,301	4,658,842
2008	810,189	1,073,315	980,933	1,037,946	3,902,383	2014	1,242,179	1,095,011	1,468,608	1,085,534	4,891,332
2009	880,036	982,760	956,657	888,905	3,708,358	2015	1,154,408	789,980	774,541	624,278	3,343,207
2010	876,084	1,055,102	1,150,725	1,153,104	4,235,015	2016	626,522	745,306	818,783	725,947	2,916,558
2011	1,063,047	1,189,083	846,624	892,013	3,990,767	2017[1]	450,215	726,375	643,212	622,987	2,442,789
2012	1,078,404	1,061,289	1,048,018	957,936	4,145,647	2018[2]	226,780	365,421	528,870	345,425	1,466,496

[1] Preliminary.   [2] Estimate.   *Source: Energy Information Administration, U.S. Department of Energy (EIA-DOE)*

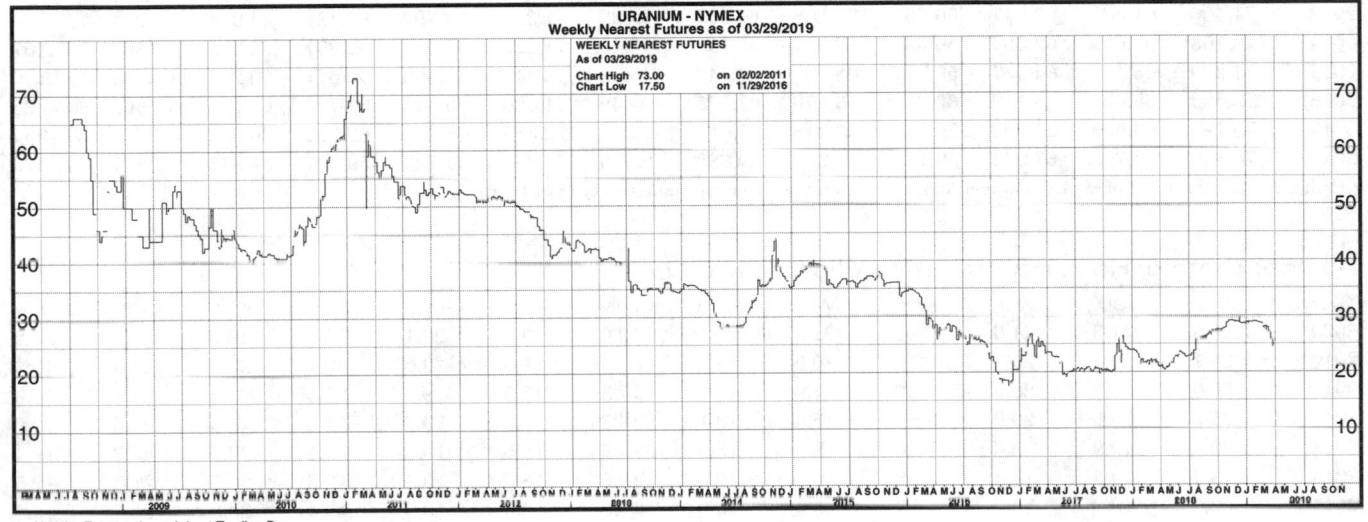

URANIUM - NYMEX
Weekly Nearest Futures as of 03/29/2019
WEEKLY NEAREST FUTURES
As of 03/29/2019
Chart High 73.00   on 02/02/2011
Chart Low 17.50   on 11/29/2016

Nearby Futures through Last Trading Day.

Volume of Trading of Uranium Futures   In Contracts

Year	Jan.	Feb.	Mar.	Apr.	May	June	July	Aug.	Sept.	Oct.	Nov.	Dec.	Total
2012	421	1,109	400	817	306	12	1,000	202	965	976	400	1,505	8,113
2013	1,203	201	155	268	432	58	1,751	1,207	34	201	----	1,005	6,515
2014	564	7	181	77	----	200	825	----	224	821	186	368	3,453
2015	186	706	300	----	1	1,154	----	1	600	402	----	1,198	4,548
2016	400	400	3,119	1,120	1,054	400	----	----	200	600	2	288	7,583
2017	370	1,180	744	200	915	530	286	232	17	----	978	941	6,393
2018	650	35	200	27	100	431	521	190	1,298	827	2,169	714	7,162

Contract size = 250 pounds of U3O8.   *Source: CME Group; New York Mercantile Exchange (NYMEX)*

Average Open Interest of Uranium Futures   In Contracts

Year	Jan.	Feb.	Mar.	Apr.	May	June	July	Aug.	Sept.	Oct.	Nov.	Dec.
2012	5,159	5,045	4,567	4,407	3,676	3,278	3,604	3,938	4,484	5,019	5,223	5,028
2013	5,171	5,615	5,456	5,705	5,368	5,300	5,973	7,186	7,714	7,789	7,310	7,177
2014	6,733	6,477	6,456	6,540	6,215	6,237	5,973	6,452	6,233	5,994	5,318	4,870
2015	4,202	4,368	4,614	4,529	4,439	4,816	4,605	4,549	4,492	4,537	4,242	4,193
2016	4,238	17,036	5,899	7,102	6,882	6,195	5,376	4,851	4,837	4,980	4,708	4,323
2017	4,100	4,447	4,768	4,348	4,565	4,808	4,447	4,288	4,236	4,191	3,785	3,810
2018	3,707	2,952	2,926	2,764	2,719	2,628	2,499	3,026	3,420	4,636	4,619	4,097

Contract size = 250 pounds of U3O8.   *Source: CME Group; New York Mercantile Exchange (NYMEX)*

URANIUM

Uranium Industry Statistics in the United States   In Millions of Pounds U₃O₈

Year	Total Operable Units[2/3] Number	Net Summer Capacity of Operable Units[3/4] Million Kilowatts	Nuclear Electricity Net Generation Million Kilowatthours	Nuclear Share of Electricity Net Gen. Percent	Capacity Factor Percent	Year	Total Operable Units[2/3] Number	Net Summer Capacity of Operable Units[3/4] Million Kilowatts	Nuclear Electricity Net Generation Million Kilowatthours	Nuclear Share of Electricity Net Gen. Percent	Capacity Factor Percent
2005	104.0	100.0	781,986	19.3	89.3	2012	104.0	101.9	769,331	19.0	86.1
2006	104.0	100.3	787,219	19.4	89.6	2013	100.0	99.2	789,016	19.4	89.9
2007	104.0	100.3	806,425	19.4	91.8	2014	99.0	99.1	797,167	19.5	91.7
2008	104.0	100.8	806,208	19.6	91.1	2015	99.0	98.6	797,177	19.6	92.3
2009	104.0	101.0	798,855	20.2	90.3	2016	99.0	99.5	805,325	19.9	92.3
2010	104.0	101.2	806,968	19.6	91.1	2017	99.0	99.6	804,950	20.1	92.2
2011	104.0	101.4	790,204	19.3	89.1	2018[1]		99.5	802,277	19.2	92.2

[1] Preliminary.   [2] Total of nuclear generating units holding full-power licenses, or equivalent permission to operate, at end of period.
[3] At end of period.   [4] Beginning in 2011, monthly capacity values are estimated in two steps: 1) uprates and derates reported on Form EIA-860M are added to specific months; and 2) the difference between the resulting year-end capacity and final capacity is allocated to the month of January. purchases.   Source: Energy Information Administration, U.S. Department of Energy (EIA-DOE)

Nuclear Electricity Net Generation   In Million Kilowatthours

Year	Jan.	Feb.	Mar.	Apr.	May	June	July	Aug.	Sept.	Oct.	Nov.	Dec.	Total
2009	74,102	64,227	67,241	59,408	65,395	69,735	72,949	72,245	65,752	58,021	59,069	70,710	798,855
2010	72,569	65,245	64,635	57,611	66,658	68,301	71,913	71,574	69,371	62,751	62,655	73,683	806,968
2011	72,743	64,789	65,662	54,547	57,013	65,270	72,345	71,339	66,849	63,337	64,474	71,837	790,204
2012	72,381	63,847	61,729	55,871	62,081	65,140	69,129	69,602	64,511	59,743	56,713	68,584	769,331
2013	71,406	61,483	62,947	56,767	62,848	66,430	70,539	71,344	65,799	63,184	64,975	71,294	789,016
2014	73,163	62,639	62,397	56,385	62,947	68,138	71,940	71,129	67,535	62,391	65,140	73,363	797,167
2015	74,270	63,462	64,547	59,757	65,833	68,546	71,412	72,415	66,466	60,571	60,264	69,634	797,177
2016	72,525	65,638	66,149	62,365	66,576	67,175	70,349	71,526	65,448	60,733	65,179	71,662	805,325
2017	73,121	63,560	65,093	56,743	61,313	67,011	71,314	72,384	68,098	65,995	66,618	73,700	804,950
2018[1]	74,649	64,790	67,033	59,133	67,320	69,688	72,456	72,282	64,725	59,397	63,948	71,657	807,078

[1] Preliminary.   Source: Energy Information Administration, U.S. Department of Energy (EIA-DOE)

Nuclear Share of Electricity Net Generation   In Percent

Year	Jan.	Feb.	Mar.	Apr.	May	June	July	Aug.	Sept.	Oct.	Nov.	Dec.	Average
2009	20.9	21.3	21.6	20.5	21.0	20.1	19.6	19.0	20.1	18.9	19.9	20.2	20.2
2010	20.1	20.4	20.7	20.0	20.3	18.2	17.6	17.5	20.0	20.4	20.5	20.3	19.6
2011	20.0	20.7	20.6	18.0	17.6	17.7	17.3	17.5	19.8	20.5	21.2	21.4	19.3
2012	21.3	20.6	20.0	18.9	18.4	18.1	16.7	17.6	19.3	19.2	18.5	20.5	19.0
2013	20.5	19.9	19.3	19.0	19.5	18.6	17.9	18.5	19.3	20.1	20.7	20.2	19.4
2014	19.4	19.3	18.8	18.9	19.4	19.0	18.6	18.5	19.9	19.8	20.5	21.7	19.5
2015	20.6	19.0	19.9	20.3	20.4	18.9	17.8	18.5	19.0	19.4	20.0	21.5	19.6
2016	20.6	20.9	21.7	21.3	21.0	18.2	17.1	17.4	18.6	19.4	21.9	20.8	19.9
2017	21.3	21.9	20.5	19.3	19.0	18.7	17.6	18.8	20.3	20.6	21.5	20.9	20.0
2018[1]	19.9	21.2	20.9	19.6	19.8	18.7	17.6	17.7	18.1	18.2	19.8	21.2	19.4

[1] Preliminary.   Source: Energy Information Administration, U.S. Department of Energy (EIA-DOE)

Capacity Factor   In Percent

Year	Jan.	Feb.	Mar.	Apr.	May	June	July	Aug.	Sept.	Oct.	Nov.	Dec.	Average
2009	98.6	94.6	89.5	81.7	87.0	95.9	97.1	96.1	90.4	77.2	81.2	94.1	90.3
2010	96.4	96.0	85.9	79.1	88.6	93.8	95.5	95.1	95.2	83.4	86.0	97.9	91.1
2011	96.6	95.3	87.2	74.9	75.7	89.5	96.0	94.6	91.6	84.0	88.4	95.2	89.1
2012	95.8	90.3	81.7	76.4	82.1	89.0	91.3	91.8	88.0	78.8	77.3	90.5	86.1
2013	93.9	90.3	83.4	77.6	83.3	93.1	95.6	96.7	92.2	85.7	91.0	96.6	89.9
2014	99.1	94.0	84.5	78.8	85.2	95.4	97.5	96.4	94.6	84.5	91.3	99.6	91.7
2015	101.3	95.8	88.0	84.3	89.8	96.4	97.3	98.6	93.6	82.5	84.8	94.9	92.3
2016	98.5	95.3	89.9	88.1	90.5	94.2	94.5	96.1	90.9	81.7	90.9	96.7	92.3
2017	98.7	94.9	87.8	79.1	82.7	93.4	96.2	97.6	94.9	89.0	92.9	99.4	92.2
2018[1]	100.7	96.7	90.4	82.4	90.8	97.1	97.7	97.5	90.4	80.5	89.4	96.9	92.5

[1] Preliminary.   [2] Beginning in 2008, capacity factor data are calculated using a new methodology.   Source: Energy Information Administration, U.S. Department of Energy (EIA-DOE)

Vanadium

Vanadium (atomic symbol V) is a silvery-white, soft, ductile, metallic element. Discovered in 1801, but mistaken for chromium, vanadium was rediscovered in 1830 by Swedish chemist Nils Sefstrom, who named the element in honor of the Scandinavian goddess Vanadis.

Never found in the pure state, vanadium is found in about 65 different minerals such as carnotite, roscoelite, vanadinite, and patronite, as well as in phosphate rock, certain iron ores, some crude oils, and meteorites. Vanadium is one of the hardest of all metals. It melts at about 1890 degrees Celsius and boils at about 3380 degrees Celsius.

Vanadium has good structural strength and is used as an alloying agent with iron, steel, and titanium. It is used in aerospace applications, transmission gears, photography as a reducing agent, and as a drying agent in various paints.

Prices – The price of vanadium in 2018 rose sharply by +84.0% yr/yr to $14.00 per pound but remaining well below the record high of $16.28 per pound in 2005.

Supply – Virtually all (99%) of vanadium is produced from ores, concentrates, and slag, with the remainder coming from petroleum residues, ash, and spent catalysts.

World production in 2018 from ore, concentrates, and slag rose +2.5% yr/yr to 73,000 metric tons. World production of all vanadium in 2015 fell -4.0% yr/yr to 79,400 metric tons. The world's largest producer of vanadium from ores, concentrates, and slag is China with 40,000 metric tons of production in 2018 which was 54.8% of total world production. The two other major producers are Russia with 18,000 metric tons of production which was 24.7% of world production in 2018, and South Africa with 13,000 metric tons of production which was 12.5% of world production.

Production in Russia and South Africa has been relatively stable in recent years, while China's production grew sharply in the late 1990s. China's production level of 48,000 metric tons in 2014 was a new record high and more than four times the levels seen in the early 1990s.

Trade – U.S. exports of vanadium in 2018 were in the forms of vanadium pent-oxide & anhydride at 400 metric tons (up +270.4% yr/yr), ferro-vanadium at 280 metric tons (up +22.3% yr/yr) and oxides & hydroxides at 50 metric tons (down -49.0% yr/yr). U.S. imports of vanadium in 2018 were in the forms of ferro-vanadium at 3,000 metric tons (up +6.8% yr/yr), vanadium pent-oxide at 4,700 metric tons (up +38.2% yr/yr); ore, slag, and residues at 4,800 metric tons (unchanged yr/yr); and oxides & hydroxides at 160 metric tons (up +8.1% yr/yr).

World Production of Vanadium   In Metric Tons (Contained Vanadium)

	From Ores, Concentrates and Slag						From Petroleum Residues Ash, Spent Catalysts			
Year	Australia	China[3]	Kazak-hstan	Russia	South Africa	Total[4]	Japan[5]	United States[6]	Total	World Total
2013	----	45,000	14,400	21,397	591	81,400	580	----	580	81,000
2014	1,030	48,000	15,100	21,600	----	85,700	580	----	580	82,700
2015	5,800	45,000	16,000	17,788	----	84,600	600	----	600	79,400
2016	8,000	45,000	16,000	10,000	----	79,000	----	----	----	----
2017[1]	5,210	40,000	18,000	7,960	----	71,200	----	----	----	----
2018[2]	6,300	40,000	18,000	9,100	----	73,000	----	----	----	----

[1] Preliminary.   [2] Estimate.   [3] In vanadiferous slag product.   [4] Excludes U.S. production.   [5] In vanadium pentoxide product.   [6] In vanadium pentoxide and ferrovanadium products.   Source: U.S. Geological Survey (USGS)

Salient Statistics of Vanadium in the United States   In Metric Tons (Contained Vanadium)

	Con-sumer & Producer Stocks,	Vanadium Consumption by Uses in the U.S.									Average $ Per Lb.	Exports			Imports			
Year	Dec. 31	Tool Steel	Cast Irons	High Strength, Low Alloy	Stainless & Heat Resisting	Super-alloys	Carbon	Full Alloy	Total		V_2O_5	Vanadium Pent-oxide Anhydride	Oxides & Hydr-oxides	Ferro-Vana-dium	Ores, Slag, Residues	Vanadium Pent-oxide Anhydride	Oxides & Hydr-oxides	Ferro-Vana-dium
2012	219	165	----	W	62	9	759	1,510	3,960		6.49	62	305	337	2,210	1,640	905	4,190
2013	220	161	W	W	61	9	671	1,510	3,980		6.04	90	407	299	4,190	2,040	205	3,710
2014	225	W	W	W	61	8	710	1,540	4,070		5.61	201	350	253	6,160	3,410	104	3,230
2015	W	W	W	W	59	2	532	1,470	3,930		4.16	356	100	122	8,210	2,870	94	1,980
2016[1]	W	W	W	W					3,830		3.38	5	81	400	5,030	2,460	660	1,590
2017[2]									3,000		5.20	77	120	270	4,800	2,700	150	3,000

[1] Preliminary.   [2] Estimate.   W = Withheld.   *Source: U.S. Geological Survey (USGS)*

Average Price of Vanadium Pentoxide   In Dollars Per Pound

Year	Jan.	Feb.	Mar.	Apr.	May	June	July	Aug.	Sept.	Oct.	Nov.	Dec.	Average
2013	6.37	6.64	6.75	6.35	5.78	5.68	5.68	5.46	5.78	5.80	5.80	5.82	5.99
2014	5.83	5.82	5.80	5.79	5.39	5.54	5.31	5.30	5.27	5.25	5.24	5.10	5.47
2015	4.97	4.55	3.94	3.80	3.97	4.25	3.83	3.44	3.09	2.72	2.51	2.38	3.62
2016	2.73	3.10	2.88	3.20	3.62	3.49	3.09	3.50	3.85	3.87	4.71	4.97	3.58
2017	5.13	5.16	5.10	5.76	5.98	5.54	5.98	9.28	10.67	7.76	7.30	9.26	6.91
2018	11.42	13.46	14.89	15.59	14.63	15.86	18.85	18.85	20.36	24.19	28.26	21.95	18.19

Source: American Metal Market (AMM)

Vegetables

Vegetables are the edible products of herbaceous plants, which are plants with soft stems. Vegetables are grouped according to the edible part of each plant including leaves (e.g., lettuce), stalks (celery), roots (carrot), tubers (potato), bulbs (onion), fruits (tomato), seeds (pea), and flowers (broccoli). Each of these groups contributes to the human diet in its own way. Fleshy roots are high in energy value and good sources of the vitamin B group, seeds are relatively high in carbohydrates and proteins, while leaves, stalks, and fruits are excellent sources of minerals, vitamins, water, and roughage. Vegetables are an important food for the maintenance of health and prevention of disease. Higher intakes of vegetables have been shown to lower the risks of cancer and coronary heart disease.

Vegetables are best consumed fresh in their raw state to derive the maximum benefits from their nutrients. While canned and frozen vegetables are often thought to be inferior to fresh vegetables, they are sometimes nutritionally superior to fresh produce because they are usually processed immediately after harvest when nutrient content is at its peak. When cooking vegetables, aluminum utensils should not be used, because aluminum is a soft metal that is affected by food acids and alkalis. Scientific evidence shows that tiny particles of aluminum from foods cooked in aluminum utensils enter the stomach and can injure the sensitive lining of the stomach.

Prices – The monthly average index of fresh vegetable prices received by growers in the U.S. in 2018 fell -2.0% yr/yr to 233.4, a new record high.

Demand – The leading vegetable in terms of U.S. per capita consumption in 2016 was the potato with 111.2 pounds of consumption, tomatoes with 82.5 pounds, lettuce with 27.2 pounds, onions with 20.3 pound, and sweet corn with 19.9 pounds. Total U.S. per capita vegetable consumption in 2016 was 384.9 pounds.

Index of Prices Received by Growers for Fresh Vegetables in the United States   (1990-92=100)

Year	Jan.	Feb.	Mar.	Apr.	May	June	July	Aug.	Sept.	Oct.	Nov.	Dec.	Average
2009	179.8	163.6	167.4	182.3	134.1	182.5	149.8	144.3	140.4	180.6	197.8	210.4	169.4
2010	178.6	190.6	310.4	274.1	215.4	158.6	177.1	157.3	171.2	153.7	156.0	186.7	194.1
2011	211.2	341.1	267.7	184.7	156.9	174.2	148.7	146.6	174.1	171.4	199.1	169.7	195.5
2012	146.9	129.5	150.2	133.7	144.2	156.2	147.1	159.4	163.7	143.2	164.7	154.0	149.4
2013	240.8	182.0	236.8	201.0	211.6	195.8	175.1	229.1	188.8	222.2	218.5	177.0	206.6
2014	197.0	193.3	197.1	200.2	195.9	214.6	197.3	184.7	191.0	219.6	249.1	229.0	205.7
2015	253.2	197.1	200.5	211.0	230.2	213.5	209.9	206.2	235.1	229.4	228.3	284.0	224.9
2016	343.7	266.3	222.6	209.1	240.2	226.3	225.4	184.8	217.0	205.8	179.7	182.3	225.3
2017	185.1	223.6	244.6	332.3	266.8	228.1	211.8	185.4	209.9	262.3	268.3	239.8	238.2
2018[1]	252.3	160.8	247.0	183.7	235.5	189.5	173.9	197.7	190.2	221.6	317.3	431.8	233.4

[1] Preliminary.   Not seasonally adjusted.   *Source: National Agricultural Statistics Service, U.S. Department of Agriculture (NASS-USDA)*

Producer Price Index of Canned[2] Processed Vegetables in the United States   (1982 = 100)

Year	Jan.	Feb.	Mar.	Apr.	May	June	July	Aug.	Sept.	Oct.	Nov.	Dec.	Average
2009	168.9	169.0	170.5	170.7	171.0	171.1	171.3	170.9	170.6	170.7	169.9	169.2	170.3
2010	169.8	167.3	167.2	167.0	166.7	166.0	164.1	164.6	161.6	161.1	162.0	161.7	164.9
2011	162.2	162.0	162.7	164.4	164.4	164.9	166.9	168.1	169.8	169.7	170.3	170.3	166.3
2012	171.3	171.1	171.7	171.5	170.7	172.9	172.4	175.6	175.0	175.3	174.2	174.3	173.0
2013	173.9	174.1	173.9	174.6	174.0	173.7	173.9	174.1	174.0	173.9	173.6	173.6	173.9
2014	173.2	173.4	173.0	172.4	172.3	172.9	173.0	173.7	174.2	174.6	174.7	174.8	173.5
2015	175.7	176.3	179.4	175.0	174.9	177.0	176.2	172.6	172.1	172.3	172.6	168.8	174.4
2016	166.7	168.4	165.4	166.6	167.3	166.0	165.9	166.2	165.9	165.4	165.4	165.5	166.2
2017	164.2	164.6	163.6	165.4	166.4	165.7	165.6	166.4	165.5	165.8	167.6	167.4	165.7
2018[1]	167.4	170.2	168.8	169.1	168.6	169.5	168.5	170.8	171.5	171.9	175.2	175.3	170.6

[1] Preliminary.   [2] Includes canned vegetables and juices, including hominy and mushrooms.   Not seasonally adjusted.   *Source: Bureau of Labor Statistics, U.S. Department of Labor (BLS)*

Producer Price Index of Frozen Processed Vegetables in the United States   (1982 = 100)

Year	Jan.	Feb.	Mar.	Apr.	May	June	July	Aug.	Sept.	Oct.	Nov.	Dec.	Average
2009	176.5	178.1	178.5	178.1	178.1	178.5	178.1	177.4	179.3	180.3	180.4	180.1	178.6
2010	179.9	180.3	180.8	180.2	180.5	180.3	179.6	179.8	179.0	174.9	175.5	175.9	178.9
2011	174.8	175.2	175.3	176.0	176.1	177.7	183.9	185.1	186.0	186.5	191.4	193.3	181.8
2012	193.8	193.7	193.7	194.1	194.1	194.5	194.5	194.1	193.6	193.6	193.9	193.9	194.0
2013	194.0	194.5	194.4	194.4	194.6	194.6	194.6	192.4	192.5	192.3	192.4	192.3	193.6
2014	192.2	192.3	192.3	192.4	192.4	192.3	192.3	192.9	193.2	193.5	193.5	193.5	192.7
2015	193.8	193.1	193.2	193.3	193.5	193.3	193.3	193.1	195.9	195.8	195.3	195.3	194.1
2016	195.2	195.2	195.2	195.2	195.3	195.4	195.5	195.3	195.3	195.6	196.0	196.0	195.4
2017	198.6	199.5	199.6	199.5	199.6	199.6	202.7	202.7	204.3	205.7	205.7	206.8	202.0
2018[1]	208.0	208.1	209.3	209.5	209.6	210.3	211.5	211.5	213.6	213.9	213.5	211.3	210.8

[1] Preliminary.   Not seasonally adjusted.   *Source: Bureau of Labor Statistics, U.S. Department of Labor (BLS)*

Per Capita Use of Selected Commercially Produced Fresh and Processing Vegetables and Melons in the United States   In Pounds, farm weight basis

Crop	2008	2009	2010	2011	2012	2013	2014	2015	2016[10]	2017[11]
Asparagus, All	1.5	1.5	1.6	1.6	1.7	1.6	1.8	1.6	1.8	1.8
Fresh	1.2	1.3	1.4	1.4	1.4	1.4	1.6	1.5	1.5	1.6
Canning	0.2	0.2	0.1	0.1	0.1	0.1	0.1	0.1	0.1	0.1
Freezing	0.1	0.1	0.1	0.1	0.1	0.1	0.1	0.1	0.2	0.1
Snap beans, All	7.4	7.2	7.5	6.4	6.5	6.6	6.0	6.4	6.9	6.5
Fresh	2.0	1.8	1.9	1.7	1.6	1.6	1.5	1.6	1.7	1.5
Canning	3.3	3.6	3.7	3.2	2.9	2.9	2.8	2.9	3.2	3.1
Freezing	2.1	1.9	2.0	1.5	1.9	2.1	1.8	1.9	2.0	1.9
Broccoli, All [1]	8.7	8.7	8.4	8.6	8.9	9.4	9.2	10.0	10.1	9.5
Fresh	6.0	6.2	6.0	5.9	6.3	6.9	6.6	7.4	7.4	7.1
Freezing	2.7	2.5	2.5	2.7	2.6	2.5	2.6	2.6	2.6	2.4
Cabbage, All	9.0	8.1	8.5	7.6	7.4	8.0	7.8	7.5	7.3	7.4
Fresh	8.1	7.3	7.5	6.6	6.3	6.9	6.7	6.3	5.9	6.0
Canning (kraut)	0.9	0.9	1.0	1.0	1.2	1.1	1.1	1.2	1.4	1.4
Carrots, All [2]	10.6	9.7	10.0	9.9	9.9	10.5	10.4	10.8	10.7	10.7
Fresh	8.1	7.4	7.8	7.5	7.9	8.0	8.5	8.8	7.8	7.3
Canning	1.0	0.9	0.7	0.8	0.8	0.8	0.7	0.7	1.0	1.1
Freezing	1.5	1.5	1.5	1.6	1.2	1.7	1.2	1.4	1.9	2.3
Cauliflower, All [1]	2.0	2.1	1.7	1.7	1.5	1.7	1.6	1.9	2.0	2.7
Fresh	1.6	1.7	1.3	1.2	1.2	1.3	1.3	1.6	1.6	2.2
Freezing	0.4	0.4	0.4	0.4	0.3	0.3	0.4	0.3	0.4	0.5
Celery	6.2	6.2	6.1	6.0	6.0	5.5	5.5	5.4	5.0	4.6
Sweet Corn, All [3]	25.1	25.8	24.6	23.7	24.3	21.6	21.1	22.0	20.3	21.4
Fresh	9.1	9.2	9.2	8.2	8.7	8.9	7.6	8.6	7.2	7.5
Canning	6.7	7.6	6.9	5.8	5.9	5.8	5.8	5.3	5.2	5.4
Freezing	9.3	9.1	8.5	9.8	9.8	7.0	7.7	8.0	7.9	8.5
Cucumbers, All	9.9	11.9	10.5	9.2	10.1	10.5	11.3	11.0	11.3	11.4
Fresh	6.4	6.8	6.7	6.4	7.1	7.3	7.4	7.6	8.2	7.5
Pickling	3.5	5.1	3.7	2.8	3.0	3.2	3.9	3.4	3.1	3.8
Melons	26.7	26.2	26.4	25.5	----	----	----	----	----	----
Watermelon	15.6	14.9	15.7	14.8	----	----	----	----	----	----
Cantaloupe	8.9	9.1	8.6	8.7	----	----	----	----	----	----
Honeydew	1.7	1.6	1.5	1.5	----	----	----	----	----	----
Other	0.5	0.6	0.6	0.5	----	----	----	----	----	----
Lettuce, All	27.3	26.1	27.9	27.5	27.9	25.5	25.2	24.6	27.0	25.8
Head lettuce	16.9	16.1	15.9	15.8	15.9	14.1	14.5	13.6	14.3	13.3
Romaine & Leaf	10.4	10.0	12.0	11.7	11.9	11.4	10.8	11.0	12.7	12.5
Onions, All	21.7	21.5	20.9	20.4	20.8	19.4	19.8	20.3	20.8	22.4
Fresh	20.2	19.6	19.6	19.1	19.5	18.5	18.3	18.9	19.0	21.9
Dehydrating	1.5	1.9	1.3	1.3	1.3	1.0	1.5	1.4	1.8	0.5
Green Peas, All [4]	2.9	3.0	2.6	2.4	2.7	2.4	2.3	2.3	1.8	1.8
Canning	1.1	1.3	1.1	0.8	0.8	0.9	0.7	0.8	0.8	0.6
Freezing	1.8	1.7	1.5	1.6	1.9	1.5	1.6	1.5	1.0	1.2
Peppers, All	15.8	16.4	11.2	11.4	11.6	10.9	11.6	11.6	12.0	12.4
Bell Peppers, All	9.6	9.8	10.3	10.6	10.7	10.0	10.7	10.7	11.0	11.4
Chile Peppers, All	6.2	6.6	0.8	0.8	0.9	0.9	0.9	0.9	1.0	1.0
Tomatoes, All	85.6	89.9	91.3	86.7	87.3	86.1	87.8	76.8	81.8	93.5
Fresh	18.5	19.6	20.6	21.0	20.8	20.2	20.6	20.5	20.4	20.3
Canning	67.1	70.3	70.8	65.7	66.5	65.9	67.2	56.3	61.5	73.3
Other, Fresh [5]	19.1	18.5	18.3	18.8	19.3	18.8	20.4	18.2	20.8	20.2
Other, Canning [6]	2.5	2.3	2.5	2.6	2.7	2.6	2.5	2.9	3.0	2.9
Other, Freezing [7]	4.0	4.3	4.5	4.3	4.5	4.3	4.6	4.7	4.6	4.2
Subtotal, All [8]	286.0	263.3	262.7	253.3	258.0	250.6	254.0	242.9	252.2	261.3
Fresh	170.0	141.4	144.7	141.9	144.7	140.9	142.2	141.7	144.4	145.0
Canning	92.6	98.7	97.1	89.4	91.0	90.2	92.0	80.8	87.1	95.2
Freezing	21.9	21.4	20.9	21.9	22.3	19.5	19.8	20.4	20.6	21.1
Potatoes, All	118.3	113.5	113.8	110.3	114.7	113.3	112.8	115.3	110.0	115.8
Fresh	37.8	36.7	36.8	34.0	34.5	34.5	33.6	34.1	33.6	33.4
Processing	80.5	76.8	77.0	76.3	80.2	78.8	79.3	81.2	76.4	82.4
Sweet Potatoes	5.1	5.3	6.3	7.1	6.9	6.3	7.5	7.6	7.2	8.0
Mushrooms	3.6	3.6	3.7	3.8	3.8	3.8	3.8	3.9	4.0	3.9
Dry Peas & Lentils [9]	0.4	0.9	1.6	1.0	0.8	1.0	0.8	1.2	2.3	3.5
Dry Edible Beans	6.5	6.1	6.7	5.4	5.9	5.8	5.6	7.2	6.9	8.2
Total, All Items	419.9	392.7	394.9	381.0	390.1	380.8	384.5	378.1	382.5	400.7

[1] All production for processing broccoli and cauliflower is for freezing.   [2] Industry allocation suggests that 27 percent of processing carrot production is for canning and 73 percent is for freezing.   [3] On-cob basis.   [4] In-shell basis.   [5] Includes artichokes, brussels sprouts, eggplant, endive/escarole, garlic, radishes, green limas, squash, and spinach. In 2000, okra, pumpkins, kale, collards, turnip greens and mustard greens added.   [6] Includes beets, green limas (1992-2003), spinach, and miscellaneous imports (1990-2001).   [7] Includes green limas, spinach, and miscellaneous freezing vegetables.   [8] Fresh, canning, and freezing data do not sum to the total because onions for dehydrating are included in the total.   [9] Production from new areas in upper midwest added in 1998. A portion of this is likely for feed use.   [10] Preliminary.   [11] Forecast.   NA = Not available.   *Source: Economic Research Service, U.S. Department of Agriculture (ERS-USDA)*

VEGETABLES

Average Price Received by Growers for Broccoli in the United States   In Dollars Per Cwt

Year	Jan.	Feb.	Mar.	Apr.	May	June	July	Aug.	Sept.	Oct.	Nov.	Dec.	Season Average
2011	57.10	45.40	40.80	33.90	40.20	55.70	28.70	35.60	33.60	33.10	42.90	51.60	35.40
2012	28.80	23.70	33.70	24.10	31.40	49.20	30.00	30.20	40.40	30.30	35.40	28.20	33.80
2013	80.40	38.10	30.60	NA	NA	NA	NA	NA	NA	NA	NA	NA	43.20
2014	NA	NA	NA	40.10	48.00	49.60	31.80	47.10	53.40	34.60	45.00	33.10	40.70
2015	67.30	29.90	47.80	50.60	54.50	34.70	38.20	49.90	57.10	58.10	65.10	84.70	49.10
2016	50.80	26.80	30.90	39.30	48.10	49.30	41.60	28.00	36.60	37.70	35.90	34.80	38.20
2017	55.70	54.10	70.90	95.60	82.60	50.50	51.00	62.10	82.10	66.60	54.80	40.30	46.00
2018[1]	45.00	28.50	46.80	39.70	56.90	46.80	37.60	53.90	51.40	56.50	70.70	85.50	51.61

[1]Preliminary.   NA = Not available.   *Source: National Agricultural Statistics Service, U.S. Department of Agriculture (NASS-USDA)*

Average Price Received by Growers for Carrots in the United States   In Dollars Per Cwt

Year	Jan.	Feb.	Mar.	Apr.	May	June	July	Aug.	Sept.	Oct.	Nov.	Dec.	Season Average
2011	38.00	40.70	44.60	46.20	44.80	35.10	28.40	20.40	17.30	14.80	14.10	25.50	32.50
2012	26.30	26.30	26.80	27.60	27.40	27.50	28.10	24.20	21.70	26.00	26.70	27.40	26.60
2013	28.20	28.50	30.80	NA	NA	NA	NA	NA	NA	NA	NA	NA	28.60
2014	NA	NA	NA	28.20	27.20	25.50	25.10	23.00	21.50	26.90	28.00	33.40	27.10
2015	33.80	33.00	32.20	31.80	31.40	30.60	29.90	30.20	30.40	31.30	31.00	32.90	30.50
2016	34.40	35.80	34.90	38.60	39.30	31.80	29.90	29.30	28.90	28.90	28.90	27.90	32.20
2017	28.60	28.40	28.00	27.80	27.80	25.70	25.90	28.90	30.80	24.20	31.30	31.30	30.10
2018[1]	31.40	31.00	27.90	27.30	27.70	26.70	27.10	25.80	26.30	26.60	26.50	26.40	27.56

[1]Preliminary.   NA = Not available.   *Source: National Agricultural Statistics Service, U.S. Department of Agriculture (NASS-USDA)*

Average Price Received by Growers for Cauliflower in the United States   In Dollars Per Cwt

Year	Jan.	Feb.	Mar.	Apr.	May	June	July	Aug.	Sept.	Oct.	Nov.	Dec.	Season Average
2011	41.10	55.90	51.30	43.10	56.80	52.80	38.40	30.90	29.70	30.30	67.30	66.20	46.80
2012	31.90	32.10	39.00	28.50	35.40	38.90	27.90	29.60	39.20	29.40	47.70	40.00	35.90
2013	69.90	43.30	46.00	NA	NA	NA	NA	NA	NA	NA	NA	NA	44.50
2014	NA	NA	NA	65.80	79.10	66.30	43.10	31.80	64.70	43.20	67.60	84.80	50.10
2015	58.40	40.10	85.10	87.80	108.00	49.60	31.10	42.80	55.50	68.60	121.00	184.00	61.50
2016	59.10	45.30	39.80	53.70	82.00	62.20	41.00	39.10	42.70	42.80	42.40	81.10	55.60
2017	56.70	65.00	134.00	136.00	70.60	55.60	44.90	35.60	49.90	56.00	73.20	90.10	47.00
2018[1]	47.80	42.90	87.60	60.80	78.60	35.50	38.40	39.80	45.30	46.40	95.50	74.80	57.78

[1]Preliminary.   NA = Not available.   *Source: National Agricultural Statistics Service, U.S. Department of Agriculture (NASS-USDA)*

Average Price Received by Growers for Celery in the United States   In Dollars Per Cwt

Year	Jan.	Feb.	Mar.	Apr.	May	June	July	Aug.	Sept.	Oct.	Nov.	Dec.	Season Average
2011	25.10	46.50	29.50	19.30	33.10	17.10	20.00	16.70	16.30	16.30	15.00	14.90	19.70
2012	20.10	12.60	12.50	12.70	15.80	13.50	23.60	22.10	24.80	19.10	20.30	21.20	18.20
2013	39.70	47.00	29.20	NA	NA	NA	NA	NA	NA	NA	NA	NA	25.40
2014	NA	NA	NA	15.50	15.80	14.50	20.60	18.70	17.90	16.90	26.60	28.70	17.10
2015	19.40	14.60	14.00	18.60	26.80	17.60	17.10	23.50	22.70	28.00	40.60	59.80	24.80
2016	67.20	29.90	18.80	20.00	26.20	18.80	17.70	16.40	15.80	18.60	26.60	17.30	18.50
2017	17.50	15.60	24.50	39.30	79.90	42.40	27.70	17.70	17.30	19.20	29.60	23.60	20.60
2018[1]	20.80	19.20	25.20	30.70	27.10	24.70	21.10	16.80	18.60	20.20	30.50	46.60	25.13

[1]Preliminary.   NA = Not available.   *Source: National Agricultural Statistics Service, U.S. Department of Agriculture (NASS-USDA)*

Average Price Received by Growers for Sweet Corn in the United States   In Dollars Per Cwt

Year	Jan.	Feb.	Mar.	Apr.	May	June	July	Aug.	Sept.	Oct.	Nov.	Dec.	Season Average
2011	62.20	51.80	42.40	21.50	19.90	24.30	32.90	20.70	24.40	26.40	26.60	14.90	26.70
2012	37.30	31.00	33.70	22.90	21.10	22.80	25.60	16.60	22.70	25.60	26.60	27.80	17.40
2013	30.40	36.70	33.30	NA	NA	NA	NA	NA	NA	NA	NA	NA	24.10
2014	NA	NA	NA	26.00	25.40	32.00	37.70	29.00	23.10	42.20	40.70	41.40	23.90
2015	39.80	40.00	31.70	29.60	26.80	27.70	33.70	29.50	32.30	47.90	24.40	26.00	21.80
2016	43.80	58.70	67.50	34.30	26.20	25.40	29.50	23.60	28.20	33.60	37.40	37.50	20.70
2017	30.90	35.70	26.20	30.80	29.80	34.30	30.70	26.80	21.30	32.50	54.70	34.10	29.10
2018[1]	35.40	24.70	26.90	32.60	28.30	27.10	26.20	24.40	30.50	30.50	45.80	31.70	30.34

[1]Preliminary.   NA = Not available.   *Source: National Agricultural Statistics Service, U.S. Department of Agriculture (NASS-USDA)*

Average Price Received by Growers for Head Lettuce in the United States   In Dollars Per Cwt

Year	Jan.	Feb.	Mar.	Apr.	May	June	July	Aug.	Sept.	Oct.	Nov.	Dec.	Season Average
2009	28.50	17.80	19.40	27.70	18.20	18.90	16.90	16.70	16.60	27.20	49.60	38.70	22.40
2010	17.30	14.10	20.80	19.00	24.30	25.70	26.00	23.30	17.20	20.20	35.40	17.50	21.10
2011	27.20	54.40	35.20	17.80	26.40	17.10	19.40	14.70	14.80	17.00	30.50	17.40	23.00
2012	13.40	12.60	12.00	17.90	19.00	19.00	19.10	19.20	20.50	17.70	20.10	12.80	17.70
2013	44.80	31.70	46.90	NA	NA	NA	NA	NA	NA	NA	NA	NA	26.70
2014	NA	NA	NA	18.20	26.10	35.30	29.00	29.60	32.90	33.40	49.10	15.90	24.40
2015	38.20	15.20	19.10	23.10	25.10	30.30	18.80	35.70	48.90	34.40	60.10	51.90	29.10
2016	42.00	20.90	15.40	20.80	32.50	25.90	26.00	20.70	20.80	20.60	26.60	30.20	27.30
2017	29.10	51.40	49.60	82.50	26.10	22.80	25.60	24.70	31.70	42.20	23.00	30.50	36.40
2018[1]	26.00	27.00	46.70	25.50	28.90	25.90	20.90	27.80	25.90	28.60	76.70	74.80	36.23

[1]Preliminary.   NA = Not available.   *Source: National Agricultural Statistics Service, U.S. Department of Agriculture (NASS-USDA)*

Average Price Received by Growers for Tomatoes in the United States   In Dollars Per Cwt

Year	Jan.	Feb.	Mar.	Apr.	May	June	July	Aug.	Sept.	Oct.	Nov.	Dec.	Season Average
2009	29.30	32.70	41.50	45.40	33.20	67.20	31.70	35.90	34.40	40.20	73.70	65.00	40.40
2010	58.90	84.60	109.00	103.00	65.20	37.30	33.60	35.50	38.40	32.00	38.10	37.30	48.20
2011	51.90	108.00	98.70	67.60	49.10	44.60	33.10	30.30	35.50	26.60	42.40	26.50	36.10
2012	28.90	30.60	36.60	26.70	34.10	45.10	24.70	23.70	26.20	20.90	45.30	49.40	30.50
2013	34.10	37.70	53.50	NA	NA	NA	NA	NA	NA	NA	NA	NA	44.60
2014	NA	NA	NA	45.20	39.10	57.60	27.00	33.20	34.70	54.60	71.80	66.70	41.50
2015	34.80	49.40	44.20	45.20	24.00	33.50	41.30	36.30	35.80	41.80	39.30	42.50	46.30
2016	108.00	88.30	70.90	38.60	30.40	32.00	30.40	28.10	34.50	37.50	42.80	29.40	42.50
2017	28.40	28.50	30.20	32.90	62.80	43.90	28.20	30.10	37.20	42.40	62.40	80.20	37.30
2018[1]	47.90	34.40	40.00	25.70	35.40	28.30	15.30	29.90	29.00	39.60	55.50	57.20	36.52

[1]Preliminary.   NA = Not available.   *Source: National Agricultural Statistics Service, U.S. Department of Agriculture (NASS-USDA)*

Frozen Vegetables: January 1 and July 1 Cold Storage Holdings in the United States   In Thousands of Pounds

Crop	2014 July 1	2015 Jan. 1	July 1	2016 Jan. 1	July 1	2017 Jan. 1	July 1	2018 Jan. 1	July 1	2019[1] Jan. 1
Asparagus	15,185	13,603	14,457	11,926	14,490	11,395	11,137	10,188	11,137	8,106
Limas, Fordhook	----	----	----	----	----	----	----	----	----	----
Limas, Baby	34,333	54,530	41,133	57,841	40,193	55,895	36,817	54,024	36,817	38,647
Green Beans, Reg. Cut	96,376	182,136	113,449	199,994	121,414	209,496	115,498	191,291	115,498	152,495
Green Beans, Fr. Style	8,194	14,754	8,025	15,279	9,912	14,482	8,923	15,187	8,923	13,747
Broccoli, Spears	34,093	27,108	27,821	25,023	27,650	21,870	30,877	23,877	30,877	26,691
Broccoli, Chopped & Cut	33,394	36,143	42,211	39,398	37,574	42,915	31,521	32,738	31,521	37,761
Brussels sprouts	12,480	15,960	14,691	19,843	13,061	22,021	16,253	21,878	16,253	15,680
Carrots, Diced	97,279	168,289	99,334	161,755	99,573	161,641	97,296	142,941	97,296	125,994
Carrots, Other	102,942	180,493	88,645	166,317	119,697	191,102	112,691	164,466	112,691	110,822
Cauliflower	16,497	20,567	18,203	26,448	22,634	27,325	28,013	34,083	28,013	29,760
Corn, Cut	250,726	529,586	262,028	520,804	287,223	522,396	220,012	479,654	220,012	475,712
Corn, Cob	101,087	223,053	88,817	220,295	91,313	207,064	73,922	257,185	73,922	269,689
Mixed vegetables	49,422	53,082	58,099	55,067	60,593	62,424	69,734	57,762	69,734	53,845
Okra	14,800	39,375	16,337	56,080	27,167	33,964	24,246	27,190	24,246	44,156
Onion Rings	11,141	9,057	13,135	12,004	16,005	13,769	12,810	12,375	12,810	17,160
Onions, Other	44,632	35,944	43,538	33,020	41,801	48,337	58,558	57,472	58,558	51,663
Blackeye Peas	1,655	1,565	2,869	2,434	1,377	1,600	1,804	1,484	1,804	1,479
Green Peas	284,293	243,251	314,155	274,778	360,749	323,820	322,460	277,206	322,460	207,808
Peas and Carrots Mixed	7,274	7,671	7,580	7,052	8,348	6,884	8,989	7,914	8,998	7,262
Spinach	52,579	38,024	60,413	42,629	57,913	54,850	68,427	50,731	68,427	30,994
Squash, Summer/Zucchini	42,958	62,828	39,517	65,550	42,122	64,176	48,617	66,948	48,617	60,482
Southern greens	14,873	11,253	19,717	18,405	19,105	18,899	18,600	12,803	18,600	12,174
Other Vegetables	281,639	381,070	302,891	391,886	327,268	453,978	397,044	626,616	397,044	582,039
Total	1,607,852	2,359,342	1,697,065	2,423,828	1,847,182	2,570,303	1,814,249	2,626,013	1,814,249	2,374,166
Potatoes, French Fries	807,376	842,464	916,294	809,569	889,492	893,453	954,888	940,958	954,888	944,230
Potatoes, Other Frozen	205,458	187,967	235,411	197,327	287,996	231,118	275,721	242,085	275,721	230,329
Potatoes, Total	1,012,834	1,030,431	1,151,705	1,006,896	1,177,488	1,124,571	1,230,609	1,183,043	1,230,609	1,174,559
Grand Total	2,620,686	3,389,773	2,848,770	3,430,724	3,024,670	3,694,874	3,044,858	3,809,056	3,044,858	3,548,725

VEGETABLES

Cold Storage Stocks of Frozen Green Beans[2] in the United States, on First of Month   In Thousands of Pounds

Year	Jan.	Feb.	Mar.	Apr.	May	June	July	Aug.	Sept.	Oct.	Nov.	Dec.
2013	252,309	203,122	201,608	179,446	164,526	152,338	143,931	166,636	237,400	252,315	224,385	200,790
2014	181,073	162,305	149,444	139,195	125,882	109,855	96,376	147,470	225,135	253,066	235,830	205,861
2015	182,136	161,510	153,916	135,211	123,221	119,151	113,449	155,410	226,850	255,661	243,986	225,001
2016	199,994	180,082	158,534	142,228	136,727	131,014	122,127	169,238	242,529	265,200	263,320	233,980
2017	209,496	190,073	174,009	159,278	144,992	132,483	115,498	138,593	196,016	238,830	230,850	216,052
2018[1]	191,291	172,673	155,853	132,434	109,337	93,324	81,164	115,005	173,836	202,123	190,920	173,655

[1] Preliminary.   [2] Regular cut.   *Source: Economic Research Service, U.S. Department of Agriculture (ERS-USDA)*

Cold Storage Stocks of Frozen Sweet Corn[2] in the United States, on First of Month   In Thousands of Pounds

Year	Jan.	Feb.	Mar.	Apr.	May	June	July	Aug.	Sept.	Oct.	Nov.	Dec.
2013	465,827	450,464	410,588	369,771	330,335	282,126	249,147	226,862	397,483	585,455	630,849	581,072
2014	550,708	492,643	460,752	397,092	345,504	296,765	250,726	273,738	462,352	596,616	631,669	576,419
2015	529,586	464,026	431,593	395,330	348,564	313,388	262,028	287,729	446,215	621,237	640,668	582,672
2016	520,804	488,940	479,571	412,766	381,312	339,900	289,897	301,633	464,716	587,865	600,062	552,697
2017	522,396	463,549	414,754	371,774	316,608	275,307	220,012	216,938	377,400	519,847	568,117	521,589
2018[1]	479,654	446,194	403,945	356,223	312,153	276,599	240,908	257,798	443,887	558,378	592,617	530,664

[1] Preliminary.   [2] Cut.   *Source: Economic Research Service, U.S. Department of Agriculture (ERS-USDA)*

Cold Storage Stocks of Frozen Sweet Corn[2] in the United States, on First of Month   In Thousands of Pounds

Year	Jan.	Feb.	Mar.	Apr.	May	June	July	Aug.	Sept.	Oct.	Nov.	Dec.
2013	235,766	219,301	202,672	173,684	150,267	123,501	100,019	83,647	151,447	244,077	271,819	251,382
2014	238,575	225,426	200,562	174,569	156,311	121,262	101,087	108,477	175,199	258,604	268,087	240,784
2015	223,053	206,000	175,910	156,425	132,387	110,912	88,817	112,873	165,657	239,922	244,687	229,113
2016	220,295	216,834	198,513	164,351	135,956	112,977	91,597	97,354	177,551	223,337	250,261	227,305
2017	207,064	197,123	177,461	150,107	128,032	101,904	73,922	74,754	181,921	278,137	297,466	286,139
2018[1]	257,185	231,840	207,582	176,477	142,642	107,713	79,134	105,145	208,223	276,776	307,074	288,031

[1] Preliminary .   [2] Cob.   *Source: Economic Research Service, U.S. Department of Agriculture (ERS-USDA)*

Cold Storage Stocks of Frozen Green Peas in the United States, on First of Month   In Thousands of Pounds

Year	Jan.	Feb.	Mar.	Apr.	May	June	July	Aug.	Sept.	Oct.	Nov.	Dec.
2013	219,559	195,388	165,683	138,449	112,263	99,542	240,208	392,588	349,572	305,131	285,313	256,457
2014	228,586	192,134	168,608	136,081	111,179	95,529	284,293	427,634	395,401	354,716	314,577	285,406
2015	243,251	205,887	189,997	154,385	127,621	127,985	314,155	414,632	397,020	372,987	335,536	308,934
2016	274,778	251,096	225,590	195,128	166,005	173,146	360,749	455,262	437,827	401,126	361,786	343,397
2017	323,820	294,248	267,497	238,263	205,494	191,203	322,460	428,002	410,645	381,666	342,202	305,457
2018[1]	277,206	247,040	223,679	198,966	190,125	177,152	284,008	341,192	319,549	303,905	268,893	244,255

[1] Preliminary.   *Source: Economic Research Service, U.S. Department of Agriculture (ERS-USDA)*

Cold Storage Stocks of Other Frozen Vegetables in the United States, on First of Month   In Thousands of lbs

Year	Jan.	Feb.	Mar.	Apr.	May	June	July	Aug.	Sept.	Oct.	Nov.	Dec.
2013	387,366	363,899	352,909	350,651	349,274	301,871	298,588	310,171	369,266	436,882	455,362	433,678
2014	425,010	371,053	366,772	359,294	311,776	285,450	281,639	310,021	348,093	402,271	415,446	392,454
2015	381,070	357,718	335,823	327,915	319,475	307,475	302,891	321,753	364,047	397,496	407,400	391,876
2016	391,886	368,774	346,407	326,102	322,249	328,465	331,768	340,474	405,041	441,482	476,689	463,852
2017	453,978	447,244	447,065	451,698	416,977	385,932	397,044	418,221	518,807	618,682	660,094	646,967
2018[1]	626,616	563,016	504,878	463,011	406,019	383,227	383,963	429,509	502,853	569,778	623,597	603,237

[1] Preliminary.   *Source: Economic Research Service, U.S. Department of Agriculture (ERS-USDA)*

Cold Storage Stocks of Total Frozen Vegetables in the United States, on First of Month   In Millions of Pounds

Year	Jan.	Feb.	Mar.	Apr.	May	June	July	Aug.	Sept.	Oct.	Nov.	Dec.
2013	2,366.0	2,203.9	2,046.3	1,874.4	1,760.8	1,581.4	1,646.3	1,763.7	2,090.0	2,431.0	2,578.5	2,480.2
2014	2,360.4	2,157.4	2,025.0	1,842.1	1,660.2	1,519.9	1,607.9	1,863.8	2,232.8	2,530.6	2,663.6	2,546.8
2015	2,359.3	2,144.9	1,995.5	1,850.1	1,714.1	1,620.7	1,697.1	1,889.1	2,222.9	2,570.1	2,688.7	2,580.2
2016	2,423.8	2,302.3	2,169.7	1,973.7	1,861.4	1,769.2	1,855.6	2,028.6	2,413.9	2,626.6	2,757.7	2,695.1
2017	2,570.3	2,407.5	2,256.6	2,125.7	1,954.2	1,803.6	1,814.2	1,938.1	2,366.1	2,731.8	2,866.1	2,788.6
2018[1]	2,626.0	2,413.1	2,221.9	2,025.8	1,842.0	1,695.3	1,719.7	1,881.8	2,276.0	2,544.6	2,670.4	2,548.5

[1] Preliminary.   *Source: Economic Research Service, U.S. Department of Agriculture (ERS-USDA)*

Wheat

Wheat is a cereal grass, but before it was cultivated it was just a wild grass. It has been grown in temperate regions and cultivated for food since prehistoric times. Wheat is believed to have originated in southwestern Asia. Archeological research indicates that wheat was grown as a crop in the Nile Valley about 5,000 BC. Wheat is not native to the U.S. and was first grown here in 1602 near the Massachusetts coast. The common types of wheat grown in the U.S. are spring and winter wheat. Wheat planted in the spring for summer or autumn harvest is mostly red wheat. Wheat planted in the fall or winter for spring harvest is mostly white wheat. Winter wheat accounts for nearly three-fourths of total U.S. production. Wheat is used mainly as a human food and supplies about 20% of the food calories for the world's population. The primary use for wheat is flour, but it is also used for brewing and distilling, and for making oil, gluten, straw for livestock bedding, livestock feed, hay or silage, newsprint, and other products.

Wheat futures and options are traded at the CME Group, the Mercado a Termino de Buenos Aires (MAT), Sydney Futures Exchange (SFE), London International Financial Futures and Options Exchange (LIFFE), Marche a Terme International de France (MATIF), Budapest Commodity Exchange (BCE), the Kansas City Board of Trade (KCBT), the Minneapolis Grain Exchange (MGE), and the Winnipeg Commodity Exchange (WCE). The CME's wheat futures contract calls for the delivery of soft red wheat (No. 1 and 2), hard red winter wheat (No. 1 and 2), dark northern spring wheat (No. 1 and 2), No.1 northern spring at 3 cents/bushel premium, or No. 2 northern spring at par.

Prices – CME wheat futures prices (Barchart.com electronic symbol ZW) posted the low for the year in January of $4.1325 a bushel. The outlook for record global output and abundant supplies was bearish for wheat prices as the USDA projected global 2017/18 wheat production at a record 755.21 MMT and global 2017/18 wheat ending stocks at a record 268.42 MMT. Prices moved sideways to higher the first half of 2018 on concern about U.S wheat output as the USDA projected U.S. 2017/18 wheat production would fall to a 15-year low of 1.741 billion bushels due to a drop in 2017/18 U.S. wheat acreage to 46 million acres, the fewest wheat acres since 1919. Wheat prices then soared to a 3-1/2 year high of $5.93 a bushel in July on drought concerns in Russia, the world's third-largest wheat producer, that prompted the USDA to cut its Russia 2018/19 wheat crop estimate to 67 MMT, the first decline in 6 years. Wheat prices then fell back as beneficial rains improved Russia's wheat crop and prompted Russia's Agriculture Ministry to raise its Russia 2018/19 wheat harvest estimate to 69 MMT from a prior estimate of 64.4 MMT. Reduced crop concerns allowed Russia to maintain its record export pace as Russia 2017/18 wheat exports rose to a record 40 MMT and the Russian government extended its zero export tax on wheat until July 2019, which reduced demand for more-expensive U.S. wheat. Wheat prices then stabilized and moved sideways into year-end on the outlook for smaller global output after the USDA in its October WASDE report cut its global 2018/19 wheat production estimate to a 4-year low of 730.92 MMT and cut its forecast of U.S. 2018/19 wheat production to only 1.884 billion bushels, the second lowest production level of the past 12 years. Wheat prices finished 2018 up +17.9% yr/yr at $5.0325 a bushel.

Supply – World wheat production in the 2018/19 marketing year is forecasted to fall -3.9% yr/yr to 733.414 million metric tons, down from last year's record high of 763.060. The world's largest wheat producers in 2018/19 are expected to be the European Union with 18.8% of world production, China with 18.1%, India with 13.6%, Russia with 9.5%), and the U.S. with 7.0%. China's wheat production in 2018/19 is expected to fall -1.4% yr/yr to 132.502 million metric tons, down from last year's record high of 134.334. India's wheat production in 2018/19 is expected to rise by +13.6% yr/yr to a record high of 99.700 million metric tons. The world land area harvested with wheat in 2018/19 is expected to fall -1.0% yr/yr to 217.3 million hectares (1 hectare equals 10,000 square meters or 2.471 acres). World wheat yield in 2018/19 is expected to fall -2.7% yr/yr to 3.36 metric tons per acre, down from last year's record high of 3.45.

U.S. wheat production in 2018/19 is forecasted to rise by +6.3% yr/yr to 1.884 billion bushels, which will be below the record crop of 2.785 billion bushels seen in 1981-82. Ending stocks for U.S. wheat for 2017.18 fell by -6.8% yr/yr to 1.100 billion bushels. The U.S. winter wheat crop in 2018 fell by -6.7% yr/yr to 1.184 billion bushels, which was well below the record winter wheat crop of 2.097 billion bushels seen in 1981. U.S. production of durum wheat in 2018 rose by 41.1% yr/yr to 77.287 million bushels. U.S. production of other spring wheat in 2018 rose +50.0% yr/yr to 623.232 million bushels. The largest U.S. producing states of winter wheat in 2018 were Kansas with 23.4% of U.S. production, Washington with 10.7%, Colorado and Montana with 6.4% each, and Texas with 7%%. U.S. farmers planted 46.012 million acres of wheat in 2017 (latest data), which was down 8.2% yr/yr. U.S. wheat yield in 2018/19 is expected to be up by +2.8% yr/yr to 47.6 bushels per acre, down from the 2016/17 record high of 52.7.

Demand – World wheat utilization in 2018/19 is forecasted to rise +0.2% yr/yr to 743.7 million metric tons. U.S. consumption of wheat in 2018/19 is expected to rise +6.0% yr/yr to 1.152 billion bushels, but still below the 2012/13 record high of 1.389 billion bushels. The wheat consumption breakdown in 2018/19 is expected to be 84.2% for food, 10.4% for feed and residuals, and 5.4% for seed.

Trade – World trade in wheat in 2018/19 is expected to rise by +0.7% yr/yr to 183.9 million metric tons, a new record high. U.S. exports of wheat in 2018/19 are expected to rise by +13.8% yr/yr to 1.025 billion bushels but remain below the record high of 1.771 billion bushels of exports seen in 1981/82. U.S. imports of wheat in 2018/19 are expected to fall -14.2% yr/yr to 135.0 million bushels, and remain below the 2013/14 record high of 172.5 million bushels.

WHEAT

World Production of Wheat   In Thousands of Metric Tons

Crop Year	Australia	Canada	China	European Union	India	Iran	Kazakh-stan	Pakistan	Russia	Turkey	Ukraine	United States	World Total
2009-10	21,834	26,950	115,834	139,720	80,679	13,485	17,051	24,033	61,770	18,450	20,866	60,117	688,180
2010-11	27,410	23,300	116,141	136,667	80,804	13,500	9,638	23,311	41,508	17,000	16,844	58,868	650,662
2011-12	29,905	25,288	118,625	138,182	86,874	12,400	22,732	25,214	56,240	18,800	22,324	54,244	698,682
2012-13	22,856	27,246	122,540	133,949	94,882	13,800	9,841	23,473	37,720	16,000	15,761	61,298	660,373
2013-14	25,303	37,589	123,710	144,583	93,506	14,000	13,941	24,211	52,091	18,750	22,278	58,105	716,518
2014-15	23,743	29,442	128,321	156,912	95,850	13,000	12,996	25,979	59,080	15,250	24,750	55,147	730,375
2015-16	22,275	27,647	132,639	160,480	86,530	14,500	13,748	25,086	61,044	19,500	27,274	56,117	738,415
2016-17[1]	31,819	32,140	133,271	145,369	87,000	14,500	14,985	25,633	72,529	17,250	26,791	62,833	756,509
2017-18[2]	21,300	29,984	134,334	151,264	98,510	14,000	14,802	26,674	84,992	21,000	26,981	47,345	763,060
2018-19[3]	17,000	31,800	132,502	137,600	99,700	14,500	15,000	25,500	70,000	19,000	25,000	51,287	733,414

[1] Preliminary.   [2] Estimate.   [3] Forecast.   Source: Foreign Agricultural Service, U.S. Department of Agriculture (FAS-USDA)

World Supply and Demand of Wheat   In Millions of Metric Tons/Hectares

Year	Area Harvested	Yield	Production	World Trade	Utilization Total	Ending Stocks	Stocks as a % of Utilization
2009-10	225.8	3.05	687.3	136.8	649.9	203.7	31.3
2010-11	217.1	3.00	649.6	133.0	653.4	198.9	30.4
2011-12	221.3	3.16	697.3	157.6	690.1	198.9	28.8
2012-13	216.2	3.05	660.4	138.1	680.8	179.0	26.3
2013-14	220.0	3.26	716.5	165.9	698.5	197.0	28.2
2014-15	222.1	3.29	730.4	164.2	705.1	222.3	31.5
2015-16	224.0	3.30	738.4	172.8	716.3	244.4	34.1
2016-17[1]	222.7	3.40	756.5	183.3	739.8	261.0	35.3
2017-18[2]	220.1	3.47	763.2	181.2	744.2	280.0	37.6
2018-19[3]	216.8	3.39	734.7	178.7	747.2	267.5	35.8

[1] Preliminary.   [2] Estimate.   [3] Forecast.   Source: Foreign Agricultural Service, U.S. Department of Agriculture (FAS-USDA)

Salient Statistics of Wheat in the United States

Year	Planting Intentions	Acreage Harvested Winter	Spring	All	Average All Yield Per Acre in Bushels	Value of Production $1,000	Foreign Trade[5] Domestic Exports[2]	Imports[3]	Per Capita[4] Consumption Flour	Cereal
		1,000 Acres					In Millions of Bushels		In Pounds	
2009-10	59,168	34,510	15,383	49,893	44.5	10,654,115	879.3	118.6	134.7	----
2010-11	53,593	31,741	15,878	47,619	46.3	12,827,254	1,291.4	96.9	135.0	----
2011-12	54,409	32,314	13,391	45,705	43.7	14,322,909	1,051.1	113.1	133.0	----
2012-13	55,294	34,609	14,149	48,758	46.2	17,383,149	1,012.1	124.3	134.0	----
2013-14	56,236	32,650	12,672	45,332	47.1	14,604,442	1,176.2	172.5	135.0	----
2014-15	56,841	32,299	14,086	46,385	43.7	11,914,954	864.3	151.2	----	----
2015-16	54,999	32,346	14,972	47,318	43.6	10,018,323	777.8	112.8	----	----
2016-17	50,116	20,235	13,613	43,848	52.7	9,179,424	1,050.9	118.0	----	----
2017-18	46,052	25,301	12,254	37,555	46.3	8,142,065	901.1	157.4	----	----
2018-19[1]	47,800	24,742	14,863	39,605	47.6		1,000.0	140.0	----	----

[1] Preliminary.   [2] Includes flour milled from imported wheat.   [3] Total wheat, flour & other products.   [4] Civilian only.   [5] Year beginning June.
Source: Economic Research Service, U.S. Department of Agriculture (ERS-USDA)

Supply and Distribution of Wheat in the United States   In Millions of Bushels

Crop Year Beginning June 1	Stocks, June 1 On Farms	Mills, Elevators[3]	Total Stocks	Pro-duction	Imports[4]	Total Supply	Food	Seed	Feed & Residual[5]	Total	Exports[4]	Total Disap-pearance
2009-10	140.7	515.8	656.5	2,218.1	118.6	2,993.2	918.9	68.0	142.2	1,129.1	879.3	2,008.4
2010-11	209.9	765.7	975.6	2,206.9	96.9	3,235.6	925.6	70.7	84.8	1,081.1	1,291.4	2,372.6
2011-12	130.9	731.3	862.2	1,999.3	113.1	2,969.2	941.4	75.6	158.5	1,175.5	1,051.1	2,226.6
2012-13	112.0	630.6	742.6	2,252.3	124.3	3,119.2	950.8	73.1	365.3	1,389.3	1,012.1	2,401.4
2013-14	120.2	597.7	717.9	2,135.0	172.5	3,025.3	955.1	75.6	228.2	1,258.8	1,176.2	2,435.1
2014-15	97.0	493.3	590.3	2,026.3	151.2	2,767.8	958.3	79.4	113.4	1,151.1	864.3	2,015.4
2015-16	155.2	597.3	752.4	2,061.9	112.8	2,927.1	957.1	67.2	149.5	1,173.8	777.8	1,951.5
2016-17	197.2	778.4	975.6	2,308.7	118.0	3,402.3	949.0	61.3	160.5	1,170.8	1,050.9	2,221.7
2017-18[1]	191.8	988.8	1,180.6	1,739.6	157.4	3,078.9	964.4	63.4	51.2	1,079.0	901.1	1,980.1
2018-19[2]	130.5	968.4	1,098.9	1,884.5	140.0	3,123.3	970.0	63.0	80.0	1,113.0	1,000.0	2,113.0

[1] Preliminary.   [2] Estimate.   [3] Also warehouses and all off-farm storage not otherwise designated, including flour mills.   [4] Imports & exports are for wheat, including flour & other products in terms of wheat.   [5] Mostly feed use.
Source: Economic Research Service, U.S. Department of Agriculture (ERS-USDA)

Stocks, Production and Exports of Wheat in the United States, by Class   In Millions of Bushels

Year	Hard Spring Stocks June 1	Hard Spring Pro-duction	Hard Spring Exports[3]	Durum[2] Stocks June 1	Durum[2] Pro-duction	Durum[2] Exports[3]	Hard Winter Stocks June 1	Hard Winter Pro-duction	Hard Winter Exports[3]	Soft Red Winter Stocks June 1	Soft Red Winter Pro-duction	Soft Red Winter Exports[3]	White Stocks June 1	White Pro-duction	White Exports[3]
2009-10	142	548	214	25	109	44	254	920	370	171	404	109	64	237	143
2010-11	234	564	340	35	101	44	385	1,006	617	242	219	109	80	272	182
2011-12	185	396	243	35	47	27	387	783	397	171	453	165	85	314	219
2012-13	151	503	233	25	82	29	317	998	382	185	413	194	64	257	175
2013-14	165	491	246	23	58	32	343	747	446	124	568	283	63	271	170
2014-15	169	556	274	22	54	37	237	739	272	113	455	134	50	224	147
2015-16	212	568	254	26	84	29	294	830	227	154	359	120	67	221	147
2016-17	272	491	319	28	104	25	446	1,082	453	157	345	91	74	286	163
2017-18	235	384	228	36	55	18	589	750	371	215	293	91	105	259	193
2018-19[1]	191	587	300	35	77	30	581	662	320	205	286	130	87	272	220

[1] Preliminary.   [2] Includes "Red Durum."   [3] Includes four made from U.S. wheat & shipments to territories.
Source: Economic Research Service, U.S. Department of Agriculture (ERS-USDA)

Seeded Acreage, Yield and Production of all Wheat in the United States

Year	Seed Acreage - 1,000 Acres Winter	Seed Acreage - 1,000 Acres Other Spring	Seed Acreage - 1,000 Acres Durum	Seed Acreage - 1,000 Acres All	Yield Per Harvested Acre (Bushels) Winter	Yield Per Harvested Acre (Bushels) Other Spring	Yield Per Harvested Acre (Bushels) Durum	Yield Per Harvested Acre (Bushels) All	Production (Million Bushels) Winter	Production (Million Bushels) Other Spring	Production (Million Bushels) Durum	Production (Million Bushels) All
2009	43,346	13,268	2,554	59,168	44.2	45.1	44.9	44.5	1,524.6	584.4	109.0	2,218.1
2010	37,335	13,698	2,560	53,593	46.8	46.1	42.1	46.3	1,484.9	616.0	106.1	2,206.9
2011	40,646	12,394	1,369	54,409	46.2	37.7	38.5	43.7	1,493.7	455.2	50.5	1,999.3
2012	40,897	12,259	2,138	55,294	47.1	44.9	38.4	46.2	1,630.4	540.4	81.5	2,252.3
2013	43,230	11,606	1,400	56,236	47.3	47.1	43.3	47.1	1,542.9	534.1	58.0	2,135.0
2014	42,409	13,025	1,407	56,841	42.6	46.7	40.2	43.7	1,377.2	595.0	54.1	2,026.3
2015	39,681	13,367	1,951	54,999	42.5	46.3	43.5	43.6	1,374.7	603.2	84.0	2,061.9
2016	36,149	11,555	2,412	50,116	55.3	47.3	44.0	52.7	1,672.6	532.2	103.9	2,308.7
2017	32,726	11,019	2,307	46,052	50.2	41.0	26.0	46.3	1,270.3	415.9	54.8	1,739.6
2018[1]	32,535	13,200	2,065	47,800	47.9	48.3	39.3	47.6	1,183.9	623.2	77.3	1,884.5

[1] Preliminary.   *Source: Economic Research Service, U.S. Department of Agriculture (ERS-USDA)*

Production of Winter Wheat in the United States, by State   In Thousands of Bushels

Year	Colorado	Idaho	Illinois	Kansas	Missouri	Montana	Nebraska	Ohio	Okla-homa	Oregon	Texas	Wash-ington	US Total
2009	98,000	56,700	45,920	369,600	34,310	89,540	76,800	70,560	77,000	42,000	61,250	96,760	1,524,608
2010	105,750	58,220	16,520	360,000	12,600	93,600	64,070	45,750	120,900	54,270	127,500	117,990	1,484,861
2011	78,000	63,140	46,665	276,500	34,000	89,790	65,250	49,300	70,400	63,525	49,400	129,750	1,493,677
2012	68,200	59,200	40,960	382,200	39,440	84,630	53,300	30,600	154,800	51,810	95,700	116,900	1,630,387
2013	40,750	63,640	56,280	321,100	56,145	81,700	39,900	44,800	105,400	48,360	68,150	115,230	1,542,902
2014	89,300	58,400	44,890	246,400	42,920	91,840	71,050	40,330	47,600	40,700	67,500	85,280	1,377,216
2015	81,030	58,220	33,800	321,900	32,330	91,020	45,980	32,160	98,800	34,545	106,500	89,040	1,374,690
2016	105,120	66,740	34,780	467,400	39,900	105,350	70,740	44,800	136,500	35,500	89,600	130,260	1,672,582
2017	86,860	53,600	35,720	333,600	36,720	66,780	46,920	34,040	98,600	43,470	68,150	120,450	1,270,282
2018[1]	70,200	61,200	36,960	277,400	30,680	78,500	49,490	33,750	70,000	46,565	56,000	125,400	1,183,939

[1] Preliminary.   *Source: Crop Reporting Board, U.S. Department of Agriculture (CRB-USDA)*

Official Winter Wheat Crop Production Reports in the United States   In Thousands of Bushels

Crop Year	May 1	June 1	July 1	August 1	September 1	Current December	Final
2009-10	1,502,074	1,491,769	1,524,771	1,537,348	----	----	1,524,608
2010-11	1,458,350	1,482,364	1,505,493	1,522,902	----	----	1,484,861
2011-12	1,424,357	1,450,115	1,491,739	1,497,429	----	----	1,493,677
2012-13	1,693,710	1,683,667	1,670,346	1,682,726	----	----	1,630,387
2013-14	1,485,757	1,509,142	1,543,095	1,542,605	----	----	1,542,902
2014-15	1,402,505	1,381,060	1,367,432	1,396,742	----	----	1,377,216
2015-16	1,471,802	1,505,072	1,455,516	1,438,278	----	----	1,374,690
2016-17	1,427,084	1,506,626	1,627,664	1,657,440	----	----	1,672,582
2017-18	1,246,392	1,250,192	1,279,363	1,287,133	----	----	1,270,282
2018-19[1]	1,191,542	1,197,716	1,192,585	1,189,199	----	----	1,183,939

[1] Preliminary.   *Source: Crop Reporting Board, U.S. Department of Agriculture (CRB-USDA)*

WHEAT

Production of All Spring Wheat in the United States, by State — In Thousands of Bushels

			Durum Wheat							Other Spring Wheat				
Year	Arizona	Cali-fornia	Montana	North Dakota	South Dakota	Total	Idaho	Minne-sota	Montana	North Dakota	Oregon	South Dakota	Wash-ington	Total
2009	12,400	17,000	16,585	61,230	207	109,042	40,810	82,150	70,500	289,800	6,858	64,680	26,325	584,411
2010	9,085	10,450	18,020	66,750	555	106,080	47,970	85,250	103,740	277,200	9,316	59,220	29,900	615,975
2011	7,979	12,535	10,780	18,233	196	50,482	52,080	69,000	74,400	167,750	10,990	37,820	38,130	455,188
2012	9,880	12,720	15,260	42,720	115	81,501	37,240	74,670	95,700	256,500	5,766	41,410	27,775	540,419
2013	7,548	4,900	15,225	29,453	168	57,976	39,270	66,120	104,710	235,290	5,544	51,260	30,300	534,101
2014	8,436	3,150	13,330	28,223	180	54,056	34,580	64,900	104,300	291,650	3,744	71,680	23,180	595,038
2015	15,150	6,695	18,755	42,463	246	84,009	30,450	85,800	78,740	319,200	4,650	60,480	22,860	603,240
2016	9,408	4,042	31,365	58,118	231	103,914	34,365	74,340	75,960	269,100	4,437	47,250	27,030	532,227
2017	8,989	2,484	12,560	28,920	108	54,777	35,275	75,710	48,090	270,050	4,599	20,770	22,050	415,851
2018[1]	7,420	3,135	23,250	42,463	84	77,287	42,275	92,630	95,880	318,010	5,025	40,530	27,810	623,232

[1] Preliminary. Source: Crop Reporting Board, U.S. Department of Agriculture (CRB-USDA)

Stocks of All Wheat in the United States — In Thousands of Bushels

	On Farms				Off Farms				Total Stocks			
Year	Mar. 1	June 1	Sept. 1	Dec. 1	Mar. 1	June 1	Sept. 1	Dec. 1	Mar. 1	June 1	Sept. 1	Dec. 1
2009	280,400	140,745	836,000	558,800	759,664	515,760	1,373,338	1,222,891	1,040,064	656,505	2,209,338	1,781,691
2010	348,250	209,900	812,100	550,000	1,008,107	765,737	1,637,517	1,382,946	1,356,357	975,637	2,449,617	1,932,946
2011	288,010	130,915	633,000	405,400	1,137,292	731,331	1,513,669	1,257,318	1,425,302	862,246	2,146,669	1,662,718
2012	217,100	112,030	572,900	399,500	982,245	630,590	1,531,837	1,271,079	1,199,345	742,620	2,104,737	1,670,579
2013	236,970	120,150	555,000	398,400	997,860	597,739	1,314,637	1,076,451	1,234,830	717,889	1,869,637	1,474,851
2014	237,530	96,995	713,450	472,800	819,435	493,288	1,193,770	1,056,830	1,056,965	590,283	1,907,220	1,529,630
2015	278,710	155,170	650,200	503,450	861,697	597,224	1,446,889	1,242,457	1,140,407	752,394	2,097,089	1,745,907
2016	319,800	197,210	728,200	571,280	1,051,862	778,393	1,816,830	1,506,042	1,371,662	975,603	2,545,030	2,077,322
2017	349,500	191,755	491,800	394,080	1,309,175	988,847	1,774,275	1,479,335	1,658,675	1,180,602	2,266,075	1,873,415
2018[1]	259,310	130,475	632,700	503,980	1,236,131	968,414	1,757,071	1,495,304	1,495,441	1,098,889	2,389,771	1,999,284

[1] Preliminary. Source: National Agricultural Statistics Service, U.S. Department of Agriculture (NASS-USDA)

Stocks of Durum Wheat in the United States — In Thousands of Bushels

	On Farms				Off Farms				Total Stocks			
Year	Mar. 1	June 1	Sept. 1	Dec. 1	Mar. 1	June 1	Sept. 1	Dec. 1	Mar. 1	June 1	Sept. 1	Dec. 1
2009	18,700	13,300	74,100	50,600	13,571	11,774	27,686	25,181	32,271	25,074	101,786	75,781
2010	34,300	23,900	71,200	46,600	21,216	10,749	28,931	21,742	55,516	34,649	100,131	68,342
2011	35,700	22,100	34,900	24,500	20,720	13,366	28,828	24,006	56,420	35,466	63,728	48,506
2012	17,900	15,200	43,600	36,700	17,899	10,270	24,842	24,306	35,799	25,470	68,442	61,006
2013	21,400	13,600	42,900	32,800	21,088	9,450	23,465	21,175	42,488	23,050	66,365	53,975
2014	20,700	12,800	38,700	23,900	17,430	8,724	19,121	20,147	38,130	21,524	57,821	44,047
2015	16,200	10,250	44,900	35,700	21,454	15,406	29,146	24,787	37,654	25,656	74,046	60,487
2016	17,700	12,190	65,500	49,200	24,785	15,609	26,386	23,696	42,485	27,799	91,886	72,896
2017	32,400	18,350	33,400	30,700	20,584	17,953	32,756	25,351	52,984	36,303	66,156	56,051
2018[1]	25,800	14,950	51,800	46,700	23,740	19,996	38,260	36,913	49,540	34,946	90,060	83,613

[1] Preliminary. Source: National Agricultural Statistics Service, U.S. Department of Agriculture (NASS-USDA)

Wheat Supply and Distribution in Canada, Australia and Argentina — In Millions of Metric Tons

	Canada (Year Beginning Aug. 1)					Australia (Year Beginning Oct. 1)					Argentina (Year Beginning Dec. 1)				
	Supply			Disappearance		Supply			Disappearance		Supply			Disappearance	
Crop Year	Stocks Aug. 1	New Crop	Total Supply	Domestic	Exports[3]	Stocks Oct. 1	New Crop	Total Supply	Domestic	Exports[3]	Stocks Dec. 1	New Crop	Total Supply	Domestic	Exports[3]
2009-10	6.6	27.0	33.6	7.2	19.0	3.1	21.8	24.9	5.2	14.8	1.3	12.0	13.3	5.8	5.1
2010-11	7.7	23.3	31.0	7.5	16.6	5.1	27.4	32.5	5.8	18.6	2.3	17.2	19.5	6.0	9.5
2011-12	7.4	25.3	32.6	9.8	17.4	8.2	29.9	38.1	6.5	24.7	4.1	15.5	19.6	6.0	12.9
2012-13	5.9	27.2	33.2	9.6	19.0	7.1	22.9	29.9	6.7	18.6	0.7	9.3	10.0	6.2	3.6
2013-14	5.1	37.6	42.7	9.5	23.3	4.7	25.3	30.0	7.0	18.6	0.3	10.5	10.8	6.1	2.3
2014-15	10.4	29.4	39.8	9.1	24.2	4.6	23.7	28.3	7.2	16.6	2.5	13.9	16.4	6.4	5.3
2015-16	7.1	27.6	34.7	8.0	22.1	4.7	22.3	26.9	7.1	16.1	4.8	11.3	16.1	5.7	9.6
2016-17	5.2	32.1	37.3	10.8	20.2	3.9	31.8	35.7	7.5	22.6	0.8	18.4	19.2	5.2	13.8
2017-18[1]	6.9	30.0	36.8	9.4	22.0	5.7	21.3	27.0	7.5	13.8	0.2	18.5	18.7	5.7	12.2
2018-19[2]	5.9	31.8	37.7	9.3	24.0	5.9	17.3	23.2	9.2	10.0	0.9	19.5	20.4	5.7	14.2

[1] Preliminary. [2] Forecast. [3] Including flour. Source: Foreign Agricultural Service, U.S. Department of Agriculture (FAS-USDA)

Quarterly Supply and Disappearance of Wheat in the United States   In Millions of Bushels

Crop Year Beginning June 1	Supply				Disappearance					Total Disappearance	Ending Stocks		
					Domestic Use								
	Beginning Stocks	Pro-duction	Imports[3]	Total Supply	Food	Seed	Feed & Residual	Total	Exports[3]	pearance	Gov't Owned[4]	Privately Owned[5]	Total Stocks
2008-09	306.0	2,499.0	127.0	2,932.0	924.0	75.0	256.0	1,255.0	1,016.0	2,271.0	----	----	657.0
June-Aug.	306.0	2,499.0	28.0	2,833.0	236.0	2.0	393.0	631.0	345.0	976.0	----	----	1,858.0
Sept.-Nov.	1,858.0	----	28.0	1,886.0	238.0	54.0	-124.0	168.0	295.0	463.0	----	----	1,422.0
Dec.-Feb.	1,422.0	----	36.0	1,459.0	219.0	1.0	28.0	248.0	170.0	418.0	----	----	1,040.0
Mar.-May	1,040.0	----	35.0	1,075.0	231.0	18.0	-41.0	208.0	206.0	414.0	----	----	657.0
2009-10	657.0	2,218.0	119.0	2,994.0	917.0	69.0	150.0	1,136.0	881.0	2,017.0	----	----	976.0
June-Aug.	657.0	2,218.0	28.0	2,902.0	231.0	1.0	261.0	493.0	200.0	693.0	----	----	2,209.0
Sept.-Nov.	2,209.0	----	24.0	2,234.0	237.0	46.0	-83.0	200.0	252.0	452.0	----	----	1,782.0
Dec.-Feb.	1,782.0	----	30.0	1,812.0	221.0	1.0	31.0	253.0	202.0	455.0	----	----	1,356.0
Mar.-May	1,356.0	----	37.0	1,393.0	228.0	21.0	-59.0	190.0	227.0	417.0	----	----	976.0
2010-11	976.0	2,207.0	96.0	3,279.0	930.0	80.0	170.0	1,180.0	1,288.0	2,468.0	----	----	862.0
June-Aug.	976.0	2,207.0	27.0	3,212.0	235.0	2.0	262.0	499.0	266.0	765.0	----	----	2,450.0
Sept.-Nov.	2,450.0	----	24.0	2,473.0	242.0	52.0	-63.0	231.0	310.0	541.0	----	----	1,933.0
Dec.-Feb.	1,933.0	----	23.0	1,956.0	221.0	1.0	-2.0	220.0	311.0	531.0	----	----	1,425.0
Mar.-May	1,425.0	----	22.0	1,448.0	233.0	73.0	-65.0	241.0	401.0	642.0	----	----	862.0
2011-12	862.0	1,993.1	112.1	2,968.2	941.4	75.6	157.4	1,174.4	1,051.2	2,225.6	----	----	742.6
June-Aug.	862.0	1,993.1	20.8	2,876.9	230.0	4.7	200.8	435.5	294.8	730.3	----	----	2,146.7
Sept.-Nov.	2,146.7	----	32.3	2,178.9	244.0	51.0	-16.4	278.5	237.9	516.4	----	----	1,662.5
Dec.-Feb.	1,662.5	----	30.1	1,692.6	230.9	1.4	43.5	275.9	217.4	493.3	----	----	1,199.3
Mar.-May	1,199.3	----	28.9	1,228.2	236.5	18.5	-70.5	184.5	301.1	485.6	----	----	742.6
2012-13	742.6	2,252.3	124.3	3,119.2	950.8	73.1	365.3	1,389.3	1,012.1	2,401.4	----	----	717.9
June-Aug.	742.6	2,252.3	25.5	3,020.4	237.6	1.4	402.7	641.7	263.7	905.3	----	----	2,115.1
Sept.-Nov.	2,115.1	----	32.9	2,148.0	246.6	55.4	-22.4	279.6	197.9	477.5	----	----	1,670.6
Dec.-Feb.	1,670.6	----	34.7	1,705.3	229.0	1.4	4.9	235.3	235.2	470.4	----	----	1,234.8
Mar.-May	1,234.8	----	31.2	1,266.0	237.6	15.0	-19.9	232.8	315.4	548.1	----	----	717.9
2013-14	717.9	2,135.0	172.5	3,025.3	955.1	75.6	228.2	1,258.8	1,176.2	2,435.1	----	----	590.3
June-Aug.	717.9	2,135.0	35.7	2,888.5	234.8	4.1	422.4	661.4	357.5	1,018.9	----	----	1,869.6
Sept.-Nov.	1,869.6	----	48.0	1,917.7	249.3	52.7	-168.0	134.0	308.8	442.8	----	----	1,474.9
Dec.-Feb.	1,474.9	----	42.0	1,516.9	231.1	1.9	-0.8	232.2	227.7	459.9	----	----	1,057.0
Mar.-May	1,057.0	----	46.7	1,103.7	239.9	16.8	-25.4	231.3	282.1	513.4	----	----	590.3
2014-15	590.3	2,026.3	151.2	2,767.8	958.3	79.4	113.4	1,151.1	864.3	2,015.4	----	----	752.4
June-Aug.	590.3	2,026.3	44.2	2,660.8	238.9	6.4	255.7	501.0	252.5	753.5	----	----	1,907.2
Sept.-Nov.	1,907.2	----	34.6	1,941.8	248.2	48.8	-92.6	204.4	207.7	412.1	----	----	1,529.6
Dec.-Feb.	1,529.6	----	36.7	1,566.4	230.8	2.1	7.9	240.9	185.1	426.0	----	----	1,140.4
Mar.-May	1,140.4	----	35.8	1,176.2	240.3	22.1	-57.6	204.8	219.0	423.8	----	----	752.4
2015-16	752.4	2,061.9	112.8	2,927.1	957.1	67.2	149.5	1,173.8	777.8	1,951.5	----	----	975.6
June-Aug.	752.4	2,061.9	26.5	2,840.9	240.2	1.0	297.8	539.0	204.8	743.8	----	----	2,097.1
Sept.-Nov.	2,097.1	----	27.0	2,124.1	248.7	44.2	-107.2	185.8	192.4	378.2	----	----	1,745.9
Dec.-Feb.	1,745.9	----	34.4	1,780.3	229.5	1.7	2.2	233.5	175.2	408.6	----	----	1,371.7
Mar.-May	1,371.7	----	24.9	1,396.5	238.6	20.3	-43.4	215.5	205.5	420.9	----	----	975.6
2016-17	975.6	2,308.7	118.0	3,402.3	949.0	61.3	160.5	1,170.8	1,050.9	2,221.7	----	----	1,180.6
June-Aug.	975.6	2,308.7	32.6	3,316.9	237.6	0.6	265.8	504.0	267.8	771.9	----	----	2,545.0
Sept.-Nov.	2,545.0	----	29.5	2,574.5	245.5	40.6	-30.3	255.8	239.4	495.2	----	----	2,079.4
Dec.-Feb.	2,079.4	----	24.6	2,104.0	227.9	1.3	-13.0	216.2	229.1	445.3	----	----	1,658.7
Mar.-May	1,658.7	----	31.3	1,689.9	238.0	18.7	-61.9	194.8	314.5	509.3	----	----	1,180.6
2017-18[1]	1,180.6	1,740.9	157.4	3,078.9	964.4	63.4	51.2	1,079.0	901.1	1,980.1	----	----	1,098.9
June-Aug.	1,180.6	1,740.9	42.1	2,963.6	238.8	0.9	165.1	404.7	292.0	696.8	----	----	2,266.8
Sept.-Nov.	2,266.8	----	36.0	2,302.8	250.6	40.1	-54.9	235.7	193.5	429.2	----	----	1,873.5
Dec.-Feb.	1,873.5	----	37.3	1,910.9	233.0	1.7	-14.3	220.4	195.0	415.4	----	----	1,495.4
Mar.-May	1,495.4	----	42.0	1,537.5	242.1	20.6	-44.6	218.1	220.5	438.6	----	----	1,098.9
2018-19[2]	1,098.9	1,884.5	140.0	3,123.3	970.0	63.0	80.0	1,113.0	1,000.0	2,113.0	----	----	1,010.3
June-Aug.	1,098.9	1,884.5	41.6	3,024.9	239.3	2.4	190.3	432.1	203.1	635.1	----	----	2,389.8
Sept.-Nov.	2,389.8	----	30.7	2,420.4	251.5	37.0	-73.3	215.3	205.9	421.2	----	----	1,999.3

[1] Preliminary.   [2] Forecast.   [3] Imports & exports include flour and other products expressed in wheat equivalent.   [4] Uncommitted, Government only.
[5] Includes total loans.   [6] Includes alcoholic beverages.   *Source: Economic Research Service, U.S. Department of Agriculture (ERS-USDA)*

WHEAT

Exports of Wheat (Only)[2] from the United States   In Thousands of Bushels

Year	June	July	Aug.	Sept.	Oct.	Nov.	Dec.	Jan.	Feb.	Mar.	Apr.	May	Total
2009-10	63,786	58,627	69,238	99,164	77,991	67,671	54,517	62,600	78,109	73,880	76,978	67,517	850,079
2010-11	71,980	81,324	106,435	126,086	89,925	89,324	91,113	109,785	101,352	123,860	147,691	129,159	1,268,035
2011-12	105,733	83,453	100,102	99,523	72,101	61,287	71,503	72,751	69,020	86,759	103,778	104,449	1,030,459
2012-13	88,538	70,378	97,627	92,901	52,669	46,420	61,495	77,006	91,861	103,441	111,234	95,236	988,805
2013-14	94,904	114,879	142,197	151,935	87,681	64,108	73,735	80,725	68,543	77,859	102,988	95,876	1,155,431
2014-15	77,912	73,314	95,989	97,967	58,258	45,692	59,967	51,471	68,363	74,564	74,102	64,539	842,136
2015-16	59,531	60,229	79,422	90,351	44,850	50,968	62,994	51,899	54,281	70,087	65,495	63,676	753,784
2016-17	83,009	75,485	103,565	103,742	63,389	65,525	80,095	60,537	82,555	98,116	98,570	112,397	1,026,986
2017-18	109,661	87,501	89,071	86,753	48,308	54,467	73,059	65,821	51,423	78,069	71,212	66,391	881,738
2018-19[1]	56,270	65,187	76,846	67,192	70,050	63,452	82,208						824,924

[1] Preliminary.   [2] Grains.   Source: Economic Research Service, U.S. Department of Agriculture (ERS-USDA)

Wheat Government Loan Program Data in the United States   Loan Rates--Cents Per Bushel

| | | | ---------- Farm Loan Prices ----------- | | | | | | | ------------------ Stocks, May 31 ------------------ | | | | |
| | | | | Central & Southern | Northern | | | | Acquired | | Total --- Outstanding --- | | | |
Crop Year Beginning June 1	National Average[3]	Target Rate[4]	Corn Belt (Soft Red Winter)	Plains (Hard Winter)	Plains (Spring & Durum)	Pacific Northwest (White)	Placed Under Loan	% of Pro-duction	by CCC Under Program	Total Stocks May 31	CCC Stocks May 31	CCC Loans	Farmer-Owned Reserve	"Free"
							---------------------------- In Millions of Bushels ----------------------------							
2007-08	275	392	----	----	----	----	36	1.8	0	306	0	NA	NA	NA
2008-09	275	392	----	----	----	----	84	3.4	0	657	0	----	----	----
2009-10	275	392	----	----	----	----	103	4.6	0	976	0	----	----	----
2010-11	294	417	----	----	----	----	67	3.0	0	862	0	----	----	----
2011-12	294	417	----	----	----	----	36	1.8	0	743	0	----	----	----
2012-13	294	417	----	----	----	----	28	1.2	0	718	0	----	----	----
2013-14	294	417	----	----	----	----	25	1.2	0	590	0	----	----	----
2014-15	294	550	----	----	----	----	43	2.1	0	752	0	----	----	----
2015-16[1]	294	550	----	----	----	----	81	3.9	0	976	0	----	----	----
2016-17[2]	294	550	----	----	----	----	151	6.5	0.21	1,181	0	----	----	----

[1] Preliminary.   [2] Estimate.   [3] The national average loan rate at the farm as a percentage of the parity-priced wheat at the beginning of the marketing year.   [4] 1996-97 through 2001-02 marketing year, target prices not applicable.   NA = Not avaliable.
Source: Agricultural Marketing Service, U.S. Department of Agriculture (AMS-USDA)

United States Wheat and Wheat Flour Imports and Exports   In Thousands of Bushels

| | ------------------------- Imports ------------------------- | | | | | --- Exports --- | | | | | | |
| | ------- Wheat -------- | | | | | | | | | | | |
Crop Year Beginning June 1	Suitable for Milling	Wheat Unfit for Human Consump.	Grain	Flour & Products[2]	Total	P.L. 480	Foreign Donations Sec. 416	Aid[3]	Total con-cessional	CCC Export Credit	Export Enhance-ment Program	Total U.S. Wheat
			-- Wheat Equivalent --			---------------------------- In Thousands of Metric Tons ----------------------------						
2010-11	69,053	----	69,053	27,866	96,918	521	0	----	673	2,785	0	34,583
2011-12	83,336	----	83,336	28,733	112,069	595	13	----	661	2,388	0	----
2012-13	96,103	----	96,103	28,214	124,317	----	----	----	----	----	----	----
2013-14	141,665	----	141,665	30,802	172,467	----	----	----	----	----	----	----
2014-15	116,973	----	116,973	34,276	151,249	----	----	----	----	----	----	----
2015-16	76,433	----	76,433	36,292	112,725	----	----	----	----	----	----	----
2016-17[1]	83,849	----	83,849	34,291	118,140							

[1] Preliminary.   [2] Includes macaroni, semolina & similar products.   [3] Shipment mostly under the Commodity Import Program, financed with foreign aid funds.   NA = Not available.   Source: Economic Research Service, U.S. Department of Agriculture (ERS-USDA)

Comparative Average Cash Wheat Prices   In Dollars Per Bushel

| | | | | | -- Minneapolis -- | | | | | ------- Export Prices2 (U.S. $ Per Metric Ton) ------- | | | |
| | | | No 1 Hard Red | | No 1 Dark | | No 1 Soft | No 2 Western | | | Canada | | | Rotterdam C.I.F. |
Crop Year June to May	Received by U.S. Farmers	No. 2 Soft Red Winter, Chicago	Ordinary Protein, Kansas City	No 2 Soft Red Winter, St. Louis	Northern Spring 14%	No 1 Hard Amber Durum	White , Portland, Oregon	White Pacific Northwest	No 2 Soft White, Toledo	Aust-ralian Standard White	Vancouver No 1 CWRS 13 1/2%	Argen-tina F.O.B. B.A.	U.S. Gulf No. 2 Hard Winter	U.S. No 2 Hard Winter
2011-12	7.24	6.36	7.81	6.59	10.13	----	6.69	----	6.50	249	416	271	290	----
2012-13	7.77	7.82	8.95	7.91	9.61	----	8.34	----	7.71	324	359	330	332	----
2013-14	6.87	6.52	8.34	6.71	8.82	----	7.26	----	6.38	281	331	327	309	----
2014-15	5.99	5.31	7.04	5.32	8.08	----	6.65	----	5.13	253	285	270	252	----
2015-16	4.89	4.90	5.58	4.60	6.34	----	5.38	----	4.99	218	232	209	187	----
2016-17	3.89	4.06	4.60	4.14	6.28	----	4.79	----	4.09	195	216	191	157	----
2017-18	4.72	4.46	5.58	4.58	7.62	----	5.35	----	4.49	227	260	198	188	----
2018-19[1]	5.05-5.25	5.04	6.24	5.21	6.86	----	6.13	----	5.12	289	258	239	214	----

[1] Preliminary.   [2] Calendar year.   NA = Not available.   Source: Economic Research Service, U.S. Department of Agriculture (ERS-USDA)

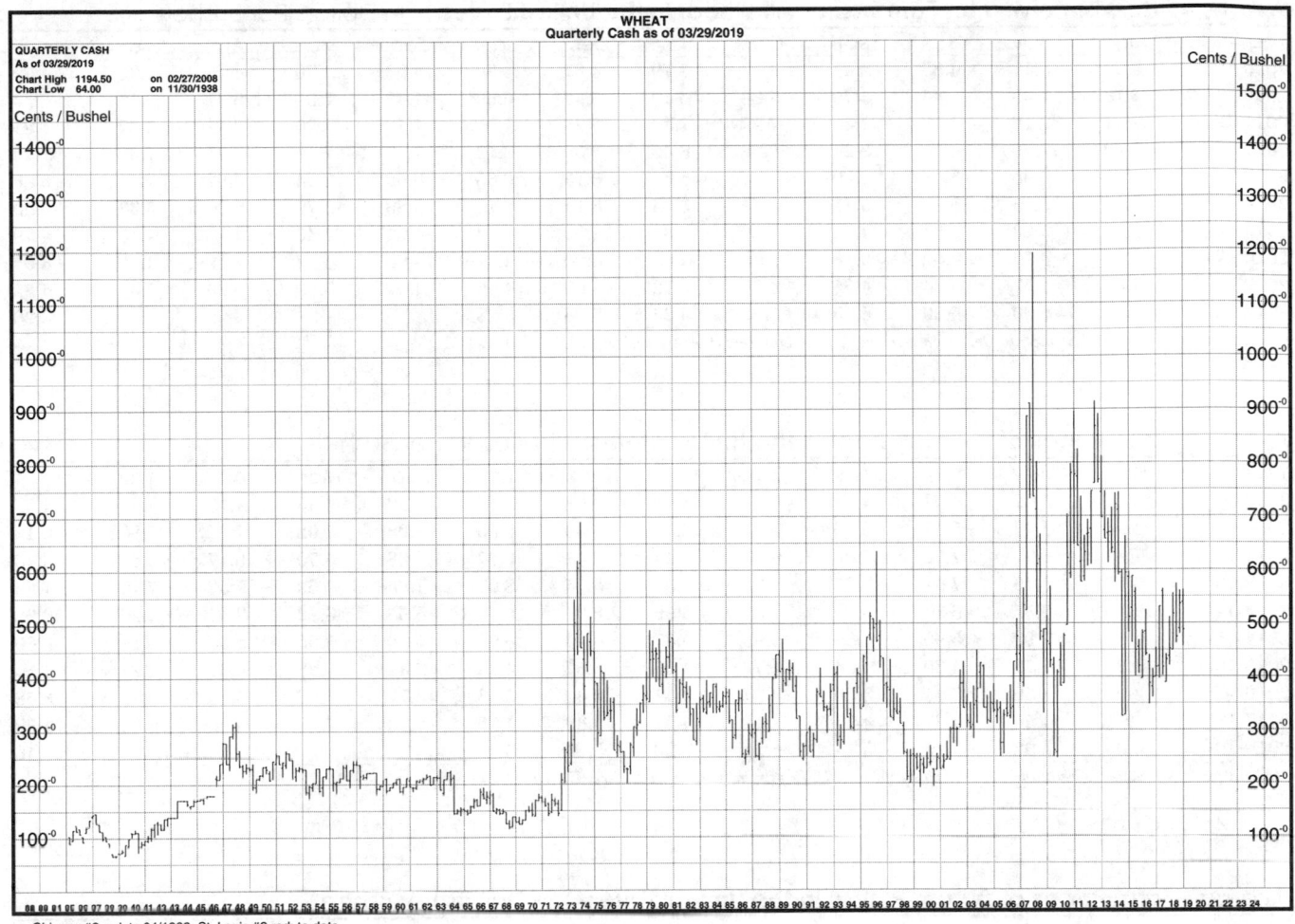

Chicago #2 red: to 04/1982; St. Louis #2 red: to date.

Average Price of No. 2 Soft Red Winter (30 Days) Wheat in Chicago   In Dollars Per Bushel

Year	June	July	Aug.	Sept.	Oct.	Nov.	Dec.	Jan.	Feb.	Mar.	Apr.	May	Average
2009-10	4.96	4.45	4.18	3.70	4.01	4.53	4.67	4.55	4.37	4.38	4.43	4.49	4.39
2010-11	4.26	5.38	6.29	6.43	5.97	6.20	7.20	7.55	7.99	6.95	7.56	7.44	6.60
2011-12	6.71	6.54	7.03	6.40	5.96	6.09	5.94	6.23	6.44	6.44	6.24	6.29	6.36
2012-13	6.56	8.57	8.70	8.62	8.49	8.58	8.03	7.69	7.40	7.18	6.97	7.01	7.82
2013-14	6.94	6.60	6.26	6.41	6.77	6.46	6.23	5.86	6.08	6.01	6.91	6.86	6.52
2014-15	5.87	5.30	5.34	4.82	5.04	5.43	6.21	5.56	5.19	5.07	5.02	4.87	5.31
2015-16	5.17	5.40	5.00	4.86	5.02	4.98	4.83	4.75	4.69	4.70	4.71	4.65	4.90
2016-17	4.70	4.12	3.99	3.76	3.82	3.88	3.94	4.16	4.26	4.06	3.93	4.08	4.06
2017-18	4.41	4.96	4.12	4.23	4.22	4.13	4.12	4.27	4.55	4.69	4.74	5.08	4.46
2018-19[1]	4.92	4.98	5.32	4.81	4.88	5.01	5.24	5.20	4.97				5.04

[1] Preliminary.   Source: Economic Research Service, U.S. Department of Agriculture (ERS-USDA)

Average Price of No. 1 Hard Red Winter (Ordinary Protein) Wheat in Kansas City   In Dollars Per Bushel

Year	June	July	Aug.	Sept.	Oct.	Nov.	Dec.	Jan.	Feb.	Mar.	Apr.	May	Average
2009-10	6.63	5.58	5.15	4.56	5.06	5.58	5.37	5.24	5.10	4.99	4.86	4.78	5.24
2010-11	4.50	5.26	6.76	7.01	7.04	7.13	8.04	8.54	9.23	8.44	9.28	9.38	7.55
2011-12	8.61	8.03	8.63	8.30	7.77	7.74	7.46	7.69	7.59	7.52	7.11	7.24	7.81
2012-13	7.61	9.13	9.43	9.56	9.62	9.73	9.36	9.09	8.70	8.35	8.30	8.53	8.95
2013-14	8.32	8.14	8.12	8.00	8.70	8.44	8.03	7.56	8.04	8.87	8.81	9.01	8.34
2014-15	8.23	7.61	7.33	7.11	7.35	7.20	7.54	6.75	6.44	6.46	6.22	6.18	7.04
2015-16	6.40	6.27	5.70	5.44	5.62	5.55	5.60	5.46	5.28	5.34	5.22	5.08	5.58
2016-17	5.04	4.24	4.15	4.24	4.40	4.64	4.56	4.91	5.04	4.80	4.37	4.80	4.60
2017-18	5.24	5.65	4.80	5.07	5.11	5.30	5.38	5.73	5.93	6.05	6.09	6.56	5.58
2018-19[1]	6.35	6.20	6.61	6.03	6.11	6.18	6.36	6.26	6.02				6.24

[1] Preliminary.   Source: Economic Research Service, U.S. Department of Agriculture (ERS-USDA)

WHEAT

Average Price Received by Farmers for All Wheat in the United States   In Dollars Per Bushel

Year	June	July	Aug.	Sept.	Oct.	Nov.	Dec.	Jan.	Feb.	Mar.	Apr.	May	Average
2009-10	5.72	5.17	4.85	4.48	4.47	4.79	4.87	4.90	4.73	4.70	4.41	4.33	4.79
2010-11	4.16	4.49	5.44	5.79	5.88	6.10	6.44	6.69	7.42	7.55	8.01	8.16	6.34
2011-12	7.41	7.10	7.59	7.54	7.27	7.30	7.20	7.05	7.10	7.20	7.11	6.67	7.21
2012-13	6.70	7.89	8.04	8.27	8.38	8.47	8.30	8.12	7.97	7.79	7.71	7.68	7.94
2013-14	7.37	6.95	6.88	6.80	6.94	6.85	6.73	6.65	6.50	6.74	6.82	7.08	6.86
2014-15	6.49	6.15	5.97	5.71	5.71	6.04	6.14	6.15	5.89	5.70	5.56	5.33	5.90
2015-16	5.42	5.23	4.84	4.72	4.86	4.86	4.75	4.82	4.61	4.40	4.46	4.45	4.79
2016-17	4.20	3.75	3.68	3.48	3.68	3.88	3.90	4.01	4.16	4.37	4.16	4.05	3.94
2017-18	4.37	4.77	4.84	4.65	4.64	4.72	4.50	4.65	4.92	5.10	5.29	5.39	4.82
2018-19[1]	5.17	5.00	5.30	5.15	5.22	5.23	5.28	5.28					5.20

[1] Preliminary.   *Source: Economic Research Service, U.S. Department of Agriculture (ERS-USDA)*

Average Farm Prices of Winter Wheat in the United States   In Dollars Per Bushel

Year	June	July	Aug.	Sept.	Oct.	Nov.	Dec.	Jan.	Feb.	Mar.	Apr.	May	Average
2009-10	5.47	5.02	4.67	4.20	4.27	4.60	4.68	4.57	4.53	4.45	4.19	4.21	4.57
2010-11	4.05	4.47	5.47	5.76	5.83	6.02	6.40	6.35	7.03	7.02	7.37	7.80	6.13
2011-12	7.13	6.77	7.27	7.00	6.53	6.44	6.41	6.57	6.68	6.70	6.47	6.42	6.70
2012-13	6.55	7.76	7.92	8.25	8.33	8.38	8.15	8.01	7.85	7.63	7.52	7.49	7.82
2013-14	7.18	6.85	6.81	6.80	7.07	6.96	6.84	6.72	6.58	6.92	7.07	7.26	6.92
2014-15	6.34	5.99	5.90	5.69	5.65	5.87	6.14	6.02	5.70	5.55	5.50	5.19	5.80
2015-16	5.20	5.15	4.80	4.64	4.76	4.66	4.57	4.63	4.47	4.28	4.31	4.28	4.65
2016-17	3.97	3.56	3.41	3.25	3.37	3.41	3.40	3.53	3.77	3.82	3.70	3.77	3.58
2017-18	4.11	4.56	4.27	4.11	4.17	4.07	3.89	4.15	4.63	4.73	4.90	5.05	4.39
2018-19[1]	5.05	4.92	5.23	5.14	5.21	5.20	5.24	5.25					5.16

[1] Preliminary.   *Source: Economic Research Service, U.S. Department of Agriculture (ERS-USDA)*

Average Farm Prices of Durum Wheat in the United States   In Dollars Per Bushel

Year	June	July	Aug.	Sept.	Oct.	Nov.	Dec.	Jan.	Feb.	Mar.	Apr.	May	Average
2009-10	6.83	7.57	4.95	4.86	4.59	4.91	4.94	4.94	4.61	4.57	4.17	4.28	5.10
2010-11	4.58	4.44	4.45	4.89	5.07	5.55	5.71	7.09	8.45	8.09	8.60	7.86	6.23
2011-12	9.18	10.20	10.20	10.80	9.60	10.30	10.30	8.84	8.98	8.39	9.22	8.95	9.58
2012-13	8.31	8.67	7.76	7.77	7.61	8.11	8.31	8.24	8.19	8.12	8.01	8.06	8.10
2013-14	8.51	8.32	7.73	7.84	7.03	6.72	6.90	7.01	6.43	6.69	6.80	7.21	7.27
2014-15	7.96	8.13	8.03	8.25	8.48	11.00	10.70	9.89	10.10	9.50	7.79	8.02	8.99
2015-16	9.16	8.74	7.28	6.36	6.57	6.97	6.93	6.60	6.08	6.03	6.24	6.57	6.96
2016-17	6.50	6.47	5.66	5.61	5.51	6.00	6.07	5.90	5.71	5.72	5.90	5.82	5.91
2017-18	6.69	6.30	6.89	6.31	6.41	6.55	6.25	6.05	6.20	5.67	5.66	6.02	6.25
2018-19[1]	6.33	5.79	5.05	5.00	4.91	4.72	4.77	4.86					5.18

[1] Preliminary.   *Source: Economic Research Service, U.S. Department of Agriculture (ERS-USDA)*

Average Farm Prices of Other Spring Wheat in the United States   In Dollars Per Bushel

Year	June	July	Aug.	Sept.	Oct.	Nov.	Dec.	Jan.	Feb.	Mar.	Apr.	May	Average
2009-10	6.66	5.96	5.54	4.85	5.00	5.19	5.18	5.30	5.04	5.04	4.89	4.61	5.27
2010-11	4.58	4.71	5.47	5.97	6.14	6.35	6.60	7.14	7.68	8.07	8.67	8.85	6.69
2011-12	9.26	8.45	8.28	8.09	8.19	8.43	8.25	8.09	8.01	8.04	7.96	7.93	8.25
2012-13	7.78	8.39	8.27	8.38	8.56	8.65	8.48	8.34	8.11	7.95	7.90	7.84	8.22
2013-14	7.72	7.30	6.97	6.71	6.66	6.70	6.55	6.48	6.40	6.56	6.61	6.85	6.79
2014-15	6.60	6.23	5.93	5.51	5.57	5.73	5.80	5.84	5.55	5.53	5.51	5.29	5.76
2015-16	5.20	5.15	4.71	4.68	4.78	4.91	4.80	4.81	4.56	4.47	4.55	4.64	4.77
2016-17	4.61	4.48	4.26	4.22	4.38	4.48	4.66	4.74	4.83	4.86	4.83	4.81	4.60
2017-18	5.35	6.09	5.86	5.62	5.56	5.78	5.62	5.72	5.65	5.74	5.78	5.84	5.72
2018-19[1]	5.66	5.41	5.40	5.16	5.26	5.33	5.38	5.37					5.37

[1] Preliminary.   *Source: Economic Research Service, U.S. Department of Agriculture (ERS-USDA)*

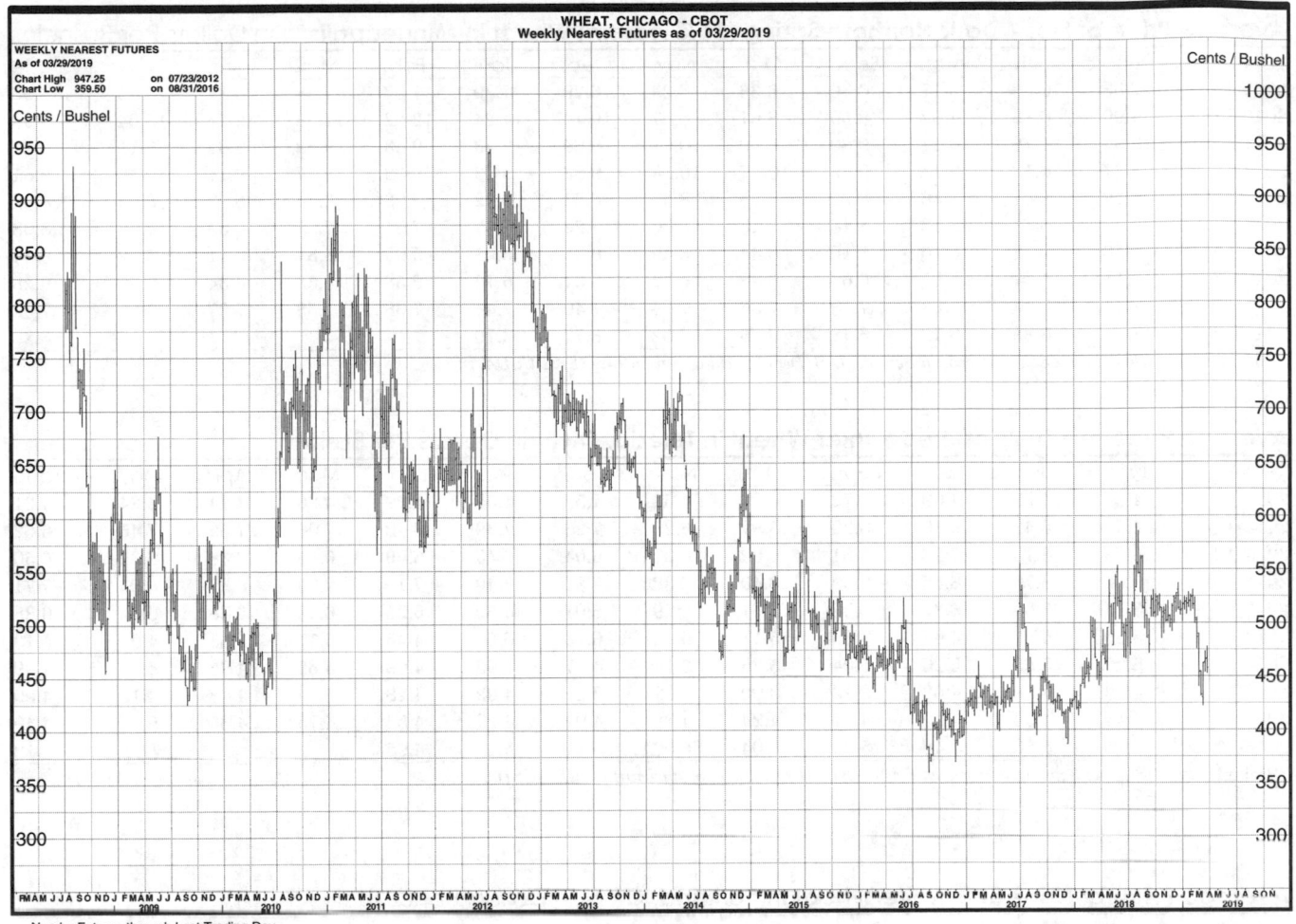

WHEAT, CHICAGO - CBOT
Weekly Nearest Futures as of 03/29/2019

WEEKLY NEAREST FUTURES
As of 03/29/2019

Chart High 947.25   on 07/23/2012
Chart Low   359.50   on 08/31/2016

Cents / Bushel

Cents / Bushel

Nearby Futures through Last Trading Day.

Volume of Trading of Wheat Futures in Chicago   In Thousands of Contracts

Year	Jan.	Feb.	Mar.	Apr.	May	June	July	Aug.	Sept.	Oct.	Nov.	Dec.	Total
2009	986.9	1,505.7	1,213.8	1,747.8	1,300.1	2,350.9	1,298.1	1,926.4	1,040.0	1,451.2	1,952.5	904.2	17,677.5
2010	1,297.9	1,936.2	1,289.8	2,029.8	1,392.3	2,547.3	2,394.8	3,386.6	1,501.6	1,527.8	2,383.2	1,402.9	23,090.3
2011	1,651.7	2,601.4	2,131.8	2,475.9	2,095.9	2,857.2	1,699.9	2,301.0	1,470.5	1,504.1	2,217.0	1,186.8	24,283.3
2012	2,014.0	2,433.7	2,088.5	2,563.3	2,670.7	3,244.9	2,404.1	2,433.4	1,541.6	1,776.4	2,769.4	1,439.5	27,379.4
2013	2,006.5	2,679.0	1,937.3	2,888.9	1,872.7	2,488.8	1,872.6	2,487.0	1,329.5	1,741.4	2,312.0	1,235.7	24,845.5
2014	1,888.8	2,681.9	2,375.1	2,605.2	2,389.1	3,028.9	2,210.8	3,064.6	1,804.6	1,793.2	2,387.5	1,962.5	28,192.3
2015	1,787.2	2,612.3	2,394.8	3,074.8	2,433.3	4,087.8	2,753.5	2,961.6	1,919.4	2,322.0	3,144.4	1,611.0	31,102.0
2016	1,820.7	3,224.7	2,084.5	3,611.5	2,355.1	3,693.2	2,353.2	3,410.3	1,457.6	2,200.7	3,270.0	1,578.1	31,059.7
2017	2,384.5	3,190.9	2,293.9	3,293.2	2,515.3	4,132.5	3,121.2	3,381.6	1,891.5	2,200.8	3,692.9	1,619.4	33,717.8
2018	2,699.7	3,731.2	3,045.3	3,473.5	3,416.5	4,219.7	2,990.5	4,177.6	2,082.6	2,407.8	3,073.7	1,486.9	36,805.2

Contract size = 5,000 bu.   *Source: CME Group; Chicago Board of Trade (CBT)*

Average Open Interest of Wheat Futures in Chicago   In Contracts

Year	Jan.	Feb.	Mar.	Apr.	May	June	July	Aug.	Sept.	Oct.	Nov.	Dec.
2009	268,513	297,116	291,831	309,503	302,088	335,407	317,024	327,977	320,607	331,678	355,414	353,774
2010	388,660	431,434	427,821	457,548	469,103	490,351	477,461	504,547	487,184	516,982	507,512	480,059
2011	515,137	538,874	482,060	482,702	457,289	451,965	428,043	427,516	411,468	426,188	411,485	376,671
2012	435,379	458,289	446,242	462,078	431,133	425,379	450,423	456,537	450,653	462,690	478,767	444,929
2013	463,359	470,154	457,785	436,052	410,871	414,728	404,821	399,943	358,054	366,743	394,264	396,016
2014	429,507	413,808	350,290	371,767	371,689	389,610	407,989	417,932	400,815	419,886	403,348	372,284
2015	382,618	415,559	426,147	453,404	444,906	432,352	402,961	406,381	372,538	377,775	381,822	351,546
2016	396,301	436,358	430,193	437,750	404,026	411,893	457,192	456,866	460,023	483,899	494,269	445,295
2017	473,794	458,494	463,099	508,045	445,294	441,396	430,971	452,301	433,612	486,843	551,386	521,674
2018	546,304	499,112	481,428	477,365	489,652	514,394	472,514	483,532	460,995	500,521	493,664	435,278

Contract size = 5,000 bu.   *Source: CME Group; Chicago Board of Trade (CBT)*

WHEAT

Average Price of No. 1 Dark Northern Spring (14% Protein) Wheat in Minneapolis   In Dollars Per Bushel

Year	June	July	Aug.	Sept.	Oct.	Nov.	Dec.	Jan.	Feb.	Mar.	Apr.	May	Average
2009-10	7.96	6.82	6.17	6.30	6.36	7.29	6.79	7.39	7.57	7.48	6.88	6.55	6.96
2010-11	6.90	6.89	7.92	8.35	8.61	8.67	10.14	11.24	12.22	12.36	12.76	13.04	9.93
2011-12	12.97	11.16	10.21	9.80	9.80	10.61	9.69	9.43	9.53	9.62	9.63	9.11	10.13
2012-13	9.31	10.12	9.71	9.82	10.17	10.15	9.83	9.43	9.33	9.17	9.11	9.15	9.61
2013-14	9.18	8.57	8.36	8.22	8.78	8.40	8.64	9.32	9.03	9.64	8.72	8.95	8.82
2014-15	9.00	8.66	8.18	8.48	8.12	8.50	8.22	7.37	7.51	7.91	7.39	7.62	8.08
2015-16	7.56	7.12	6.16	6.15	6.44	6.49	6.25	6.05	5.93	5.84	6.11	6.02	6.34
2016-17	6.11	5.74	5.87	5.62	6.48	6.32	6.64	6.75	6.58	6.33	6.34	6.60	6.28
2017-18	7.66	8.64	7.64	7.18	7.36	7.66	7.40	7.41	7.68	7.58	7.57	7.66	7.62
2018-19[1]	7.14	6.86	6.72	6.48	6.76	7.02	6.77	6.79	7.17				6.86

[1] Preliminary.   Source: Economic Research Service, U.S. Department of Agriculture (ERS-USDA)

Average Price of No. 2 Soft Red Winter Wheat in Toledo, OH   In Dollars Per Bushel

Year	June	July	Aug.	Sept.	Oct.	Nov.	Dec.	Jan.	Feb.	Mar.	Apr.	May	Average
2009-10	4.85	4.21	4.09	3.72	4.09	4.54	4.56	4.57	4.29	4.26	4.24	4.24	4.31
2010-11	4.34	5.42	6.10	6.20	5.97	6.20	7.26	7.69	8.12	7.06	7.59	7.46	6.62
2011-12	6.75	6.73	7.28	6.61	6.09	6.07	6.04	6.45	6.69	6.58	6.38	6.30	6.50
2012-13	6.62	8.70	8.69	8.59	8.40	8.38	7.91	7.40	7.10	7.00	6.87	6.91	7.71
2013-14	6.75	6.50	6.32	6.32	6.61	6.29	6.01	5.60	5.91	6.73	6.78	6.74	6.38
2014-15	5.89	5.41	4.65	3.65	5.13	5.44	6.19	5.54	4.45	5.17	5.08	4.92	5.13
2015-16	5.22	5.58	5.20	5.04	5.25	5.16	4.97	4.93	4.69	4.61	4.63	4.61	4.99
2016-17	4.69	4.22	4.03	3.72	3.90	3.92	3.80	4.09	4.28	4.14	4.08	4.19	4.09
2017-18	4.44	4.94	4.20	4.27	4.24	4.18	4.04	4.22	4.54	4.75	4.85	5.24	4.49
2018-19[1]	5.15	5.20	5.48	5.04	5.04	5.00	5.14	5.12	4.95				5.12

[1] Preliminary.   Source: Economic Research Service, U.S. Department of Agriculture (ERS-USDA)

Average Price of No. 1 Soft White Wheat in Portland, OR   In Dollars Per Bushel

Year	June	July	Aug.	Sept.	Oct.	Nov.	Dec.	Jan.	Feb.	Mar.	Apr.	May	Average
2009-10	5.91	5.32	4.90	4.53	4.67	4.89	4.96	4.83	4.76	4.64	4.76	4.76	4.91
2010-11	4.57	4.88	6.30	6.46	6.00	6.29	7.34	7.83	8.31	7.44	7.92	7.84	6.77
2011-12	7.45	6.75	6.92	6.75	6.25	6.05	5.93	6.27	6.98	7.07	7.03	6.87	6.69
2012-13	6.97	8.53	8.69	8.77	8.75	8.87	8.56	8.53	8.59	8.16	7.93	7.71	8.34
2013-14	----	7.23	7.32	7.17	7.27	7.04	6.97	6.78	7.20	7.55	7.65	7.65	7.26
2014-15	6.99	6.69	6.88	6.75	6.79	7.00	7.19	6.52	6.49	6.36	6.23	5.94	6.65
2015-16	----	----	5.55	5.38	5.49	5.37	----	5.31	5.30	----	5.33	5.34	5.38
2016-17	5.46	5.07	4.89	4.77	4.65	4.64	4.57	4.63	4.74	4.70	4.61	4.77	4.79
2017-18	4.91	5.40	5.13	5.19	5.30	5.26	5.22	5.30	5.39	5.64	5.63	5.79	5.35
2018-19[1]	5.92	5.88	6.18	5.98	6.11	6.25	6.23	6.29	6.36				6.13

[1] Preliminary.   Source: Economic Research Service, U.S. Department of Agriculture (ERS-USDA)

Average Producer Price Index of Wheat Flour (Spring[2])   June 1983 = 100

Year	Jan.	Feb.	Mar.	Apr.	May	June	July	Aug.	Sept.	Oct.	Nov.	Dec.	Average
2009	187.4	185.3	186.5	183.4	185.0	196.2	176.4	171.1	165.2	168.0	169.2	168.5	178.5
2010	167.2	168.1	163.7	162.5	167.1	161.7	169.7	190.5	190.6	190.1	200.5	204.9	178.1
2011	212.0	228.4	211.8	226.5	225.2	219.5	217.0	224.1	224.8	216.1	216.5	207.8	219.1
2012	206.8	216.4	219.2	219.7	214.3	214.4	231.2	226.5	232.0	232.4	236.4	233.8	223.6
2013	231.0	223.5	219.6	220.6	229.1	230.2	226.0	219.8	218.4	225.5	220.1	218.4	223.5
2014	223.3	224.9	235.6	229.5	234.8	225.5	225.7	218.8	231.5	225.3	225.6	230.5	227.6
2015	213.4	214.5	214.5	210.5	212.2	216.1	214.3	193.5	189.1	192.6	191.2	196.3	204.9
2016	194.3	192.1	193.5	193.4	195.2	195.1	186.3	183.8	183.8	187.9	186.4	186.2	189.8
2017	188.9	189.2	184.5	181.1	187.4	194.5	215.4	197.9	194.0	193.1	197.1	193.1	193.0
2018[1]	194.8	193.0	196.0	196.4	197.0	197.9	193.3	196.5	191.8	193.1	194.0	193.3	194.8

[1] Preliminary.   [2] Standard patent.   Source: Bureau of Labor Statistics, U.S. Department of Commerce (BLS) (0212-0301)

World Wheat Flour Production (Monthly Average)   In Thousands of Metric Tons

Year	Australia	France	Germany	Hungary	India	Japan	Kazak-hstan	Korea, South	Mexico	Poland	Russia	Turkey	United Kingdom
2009	----	449.5	429.1	59.2	195.1	379.9	255.0	150.7	249.3	143.2	774.1	349.7	----
2010	----	461.9	458.0	NA	212.5	401.0	NA	160.5	257.5	122.6	746.7	371.4	----
2011	----	443.8	446.7	----	215.0	408.9	----	159.9	266.8	118.3	753.5	399.1	----
2012	----	NA	453.5	----	NA	404.8	----	161.9	266.5	124.5	735.1	374.6	----
2013	----	----	465.3	----	----	403.1	----	156.9	277.2	125.4	759.4	407.5	----
2014	----	----	487.3	----	----	403.0	290.6	163.6	277.6	125.4	738.0	455.6	----
2015	----	----	498.1	----	----	404.7	287.8	167.0	260.6	129.7	758.1	552.2	----
2016	----	----	510.4	----	----	403.0	308.3	170.3	254.7	134.3	745.4	544.2	----
2017[1]	----	----	508.7	----	----	406.1	309.1	171.0	270.2	147.2	704.0	596.2	----
2018[2]	----	----	503.7	----	----	399.3	339.1		283.6	146.3	684.8	429.8	----

[1] Preliminary.   [2] Estimate.   NA = Not available.   *Source: United Nations (UN)*

United States Wheat Flour Exports (Grain Equivalent[2])   In Thousands of Bushels

Year	June	July	Aug.	Sept.	Oct.	Nov.	Dec.	Jan.	Feb.	Mar.	Apr.	May	Total
2009-10	887	1,490	1,704	1,496	2,255	1,609	1,195	1,231	1,722	2,401	1,774	1,992	19,755
2010-11	1,158	912	897	1,005	1,727	914	1,130	1,638	1,644	1,227	1,973	1,116	15,343
2011-12	1,099	863	1,771	1,104	1,021	1,182	736	766	727	1,115	817	1,529	12,731
2012-13	1,264	1,885	1,619	1,790	1,241	1,027	987	1,080	1,147	928	781	1,505	15,252
2013-14	1,626	975	836	1,005	1,218	986	1,173	955	807	954	1,141	1,140	12,816
2014-15	955	1,214	1,067	1,301	1,182	1,430	1,096	1,057	1,283	1,524	1,062	1,315	14,486
2015-16	1,222	1,225	1,208	1,431	1,466	1,491	1,521	1,457	1,085	1,685	1,303	1,467	16,562
2016-17	1,711	1,338	1,399	1,672	1,872	1,774	1,469	1,624	1,430	1,288	1,191	1,574	18,344
2017-18	1,463	1,437	1,663	905	712	870	1,073	964	1,094	1,157	1,088	1,360	13,786
2018-19[1]	1,365	940	1,097	1,269	1,373	1,188	1,249						14,539

[1] Preliminary.   [2] Includes meal, groats and durum.   *Source: Economic Research Service, U.S. Department of Agriculture (ERS-USDA)*

Supply and Distribution of Wheat Flour In the United States

Year	Wheat Ground -- 1,000 Bu. --	Milfeed Production - 1,000 Tons -	Flour Production[9]	Flour & Product Imports[2]	Total Supply In 1,000 Cwt.	Exports — Flour	Exports — Products	Domestic Disap-pearance	Total Population July 1 -- Millions --	Per Capita Disap-pearance -- Pounds --
2008	907,979	6,753	416,283	10,822	427,105	4,925	6,179	416,001	304.5	136.6
2009	896,060	6,460	414,658	10,313	424,971	5,911	5,338	413,722	307.2	134.7
2010	901,843	6,480	417,396	11,206	428,602	7,004	3,930	417,667	309.8	134.8
2011	895,255	6,402	411,745	11,698	423,443	6,309	3,615	413,519	312.2	132.5
2012	921,853	6,637	420,365	11,991	432,356	5,997	3,894	422,465	314.5	134.3
2013	919,830	6,367	424,550	12,281	436,831	5,274	3,755	427,803	316.8	135.0
2014	921,264	6,423	424,949	13,859	438,808	5,303	3,664	429,841	319.2	134.7
2015	923,641	6,641	424,910	14,753	439,663	6,376	3,567	429,720	323.0	133.0
2016	914,635	6,559	423,846	15,059	438,905	7,368	2,973	428,565	325.5	131.7
2017[1]	917,816	6,447	426,399	14,863	441,262	6,204	2,773	432,284	328.0	131.8

[1] Preliminary.   [2] Commercial production of wheat flour, whole wheat, industrial and durum flour and farina reported by Bureau of Census.
Source: Economic Research Service, U.S. Department of Agriculture (ERS-USDA)

Wheat and Flour Price Relationships at Milling Centers in the United States   In Dollars

	At Kansas City					At Minneapolis				
	Cost of Wheat to Produce 100 lb. Flour[1]	Wholesale Price of — Bakery Flour 100 lb. Flour[2]	By-Products Obtained 100 lb. Flour[3]	Total Products — Actual	Over Cost of Wheat	Cost of Wheat to Produce 100 lb. Flour[1]	Wholesale Price of — Bakery Flour 100 lb. Flour[2]	By-Products Obtained 100 lb. Flour[3]	Total Products — Actual	Over Cost of Wheat
Year										
2011-12	19.21	18.76	2.96	21.71	2.51	23.10	21.87	3.11	24.98	1.88
2012-13	21.29	19.92	3.62	23.53	2.25	21.91	19.46	4.06	23.52	1.61
2013-14	19.20	19.23	2.70	21.93	2.73	20.17	19.17	2.79	21.96	1.78
2014-15	16.16	17.24	1.91	19.15	2.99	19.35	18.75	1.86	20.61	1.37
2015-16	13.16	14.00	1.61	15.61	2.45	14.00	14.34	1.28	15.62	1.17
2016-17	12.74	13.14	1.35	14.49	1.75	14.32	14.51	.65	15.16	.84
2017-18	15.33	15.51	1.79	17.31	1.97	17.38	17.24	.73	17.96	.59
2018-19	14.87	15.79	1.85	17.64	2.77	15.57	15.28	.79	16.06	.48
June-Aug.	15.44	16.43	1.67	18.11	2.67	15.75	15.65	.76	16.41	.65
Sept.-Nov.	14.30	15.15	2.02	17.17	2.87	15.39	14.90	.81	15.71	.31

[1] Based on 73% extraction rate, cost of 2.28 bushels: At Kansas City, No. 1 hard winter 13% protein; and at Minneapolis, No. 1 dark northern spring, 14% protein.   [2] quoted as mid-month bakers' standard patent at Kansas City and spring standard patent at Minneapolis, bulk basis.   [3] Assumed 50-50 millfeed distribution between bran and shorts or middlings, bulk basis.   *Source: Agricultural Marketing Service, U.S. Department of Agriculture*

Wool

Wool is light, warm, absorbs moisture, and is resistant to fire. Wool is also used for insulation in houses, for carpets and furnishing, and for bedding. Sheep are sheared once a year and produce about 4.3 kg of "greasy" wool per year.

Greasy wool is wool that has not been washed or cleaned. Wool fineness is determined by fiber diameter, which is measured in microns (one millionth of a meter). Fine wool is softer, lightweight, and produces fine clothing. Merino sheep produce the finest wool.

Prices – Average monthly wool prices at U.S. mills in 2018 (through September) rose by +38.5% yr/yr to $6.04 per pound, a new record high. The value of U.S. wool production in 2017 fell -3.4% yr/yr to $36.424 million,

below the 2011 record high of $48.925 million.

Supply – World production of wool has been falling in the past decade due to the increased use of polyester fabrics. Greasy wool world production in 2013 rose +1.6% yr/yr to 2.176 million metric tons. The world's largest producers of greasy wool in 2013 were China with 22.2% of world production, followed by Australia with 17.0%, and New Zealand with 7.8%. U.S. wool production of 14,000 metric tons in 2013 accounted for only 0.7% of world production.

Trade – U.S. exports of domestic wool in 2016 fell -0.3% yr/yr to 7.826 million pounds. U.S. imports in 2016 fell -1.8% to 3.909 million pounds.

World Production of Wool, Greasy   In Metric Tons

Year	Argentina	Australia	China	Kazakhstan	New Zealand	Pakistan	Romania	Russia	South Africa	United Kingdom	United States	Uruguay	World Total
2004	60,000	467,580	373,902	28,499	217,700	39,900	17,505	47,111	44,000	60,000	17,046	37,271	2,158,877
2005	63,696	465,700	393,172	30,444	215,500	40,000	17,600	48,033	44,000	60,000	16,865	42,009	2,209,767
2006	67,794	472,530	388,777	32,389	224,700	40,100	19,378	50,276	44,000	57,552	16,284	46,709	2,213,761
2007	68,743	450,220	363,470	34,200	217,900	40,600	21,025	52,022	42,000	62,000	15,750	46,709	2,192,715
2008	65,000	407,880	367,687	35,200	157,500	41,000	22,051	53,491	41,583	63,290	14,952	45,085	2,091,810
2009	65,000	370,600	364,002	36,400	185,800	41,540	22,352	54,658	43,320	65,393	13,770	41,057	2,065,570
2010	54,000	352,740	386,768	37,600	176,300	42,000	20,457	53,521	41,091	67,000	13,776	34,700	2,020,030
2011	48,000	368,330	443,981	38,500	163,700	42,500	19,026	52,575	41,197	67,500	13,286	34,700	2,089,520
2012[1]	45,000	362,100	437,119	38,437	165,000	43,000	18,600	55,253	39,904	68,000	14,000	36,000	2,093,600
2013[2]	45,000	360,520	471,111	37,638	165,000	43,600	18,600	54,651	39,904	68,000	14,000	36,000	2,126,900

[1] Preliminary.   [2] Estimate.   NA = Not avaliable.   *Source: Food and Agriculture Organization of the United Nations (FAO-UN)*

Average Wool Prices[1] of Australian 64's, Type 62, Duty Paid at U.S. Mills   In Dollars Per Pound

Year	Jan.	Feb.	Mar.	Apr.	May	June	July	Aug.	Sept.	Oct.	Nov.	Dec.	Average
2009	2.29	2.23	2.30	2.50	2.87	2.95	2.95	3.18	3.39	3.79	3.86	3.92	3.02
2010	4.23	4.04	4.12	4.04	3.81	3.79	3.81	3.81	3.90	4.19	4.50	4.79	4.09
2011	5.17	5.44	5.86	6.37	6.43	7.42	7.13	6.49	6.10	5.62	4.50	6.24	6.06
2012	6.35	6.67	6.68	6.35	6.07	5.76	5.78	5.36	5.17	5.33	5.42	5.89	5.90
2013	5.87	5.95	5.84	5.38	5.17	5.09	4.71	4.67	4.79	5.45	5.37	4.89	5.27
2014	5.18	5.06	4.86	4.92	5.04	4.98	5.02	4.86	4.79	4.71	4.68	4.56	4.89
2015	4.34	4.27	4.21	4.34	4.90	5.17	4.64	4.62	4.30	4.28	4.43	4.55	4.50
2016	4.53	4.65	4.72	4.89	4.80	4.86	5.17	5.23	5.06	4.99	4.90	4.94	4.90
2017	5.14	5.16	5.28	5.10	5.23	5.40	5.48	5.97	5.77	5.70	5.81	5.96	5.50
2018	6.60	6.86	6.85	6.92	7.26	7.95	7.67	7.70	7.47	7.23	7.08	7.17	7.23

[1] Raw, clean basis.   *Source: Economic Research Service, U.S. Department of Agriculture (ERS-USDA)*

United States Imports[2] of Unmanufactured Wool (Clean Yield)   In Thousands of Pounds

Year	Jan.	Feb.	Mar.	Apr.	May	June	July	Aug.	Sept.	Oct.	Nov.	Dec.	Total
2009	1,061.7	982.9	1,043.0	803.5	536.2	745.1	833.8	847.4	447.4	798.8	626.0	627.0	9,352.8
2010	705.5	340.8	663.7	757.1	424.3	576.4	1,183.0	702.2	652.4	607.1	594.8	385.4	7,592.7
2011	857.1	451.2	564.5	681.2	698.5	503.3	1,046.5	1,306.0	1,590.9	1,168.2	635.5	404.2	9,907.1
2012	711.7	968.1	1,018.9	880.7	919.9	944.7	715.9	536.0	779.2	693.8	610.2	416.4	9,195.5
2013	457.3	251.4	358.7	819.7	909.1	891.0	796.5	889.8	437.1	919.6	458.2	430.8	7,619.2
2014	597.6	379.1	348.3	583.8	868.5	553.2	707.7	718.8	544.0	967.5	403.5	420.5	7,092.5
2015	504.8	800.1	420.0	657.0	765.2	585.8	681.5	619.8	404.9	664.2	527.1	655.5	7,285.9
2016	564.6	321.8	600.5	942.4	514.6	746.8	419.2	229.9	330.1	300.3	488.1	568.8	6,027.1
2017	488.1	490.8	747.9	706.3	427.9	552.7	341.0	627.6	486.6	357.7	283.0	171.7	5,681.3
2018[1]	279.8	281.0	485.3	624.8	416.8	383.4	629.0	591.4	550.5	443.1	449.3	328.9	5,463.3

[1] Preliminary.   [2] Data are imports for consumption.   *Source: Economic Research Service, U.S. Department of Agriculture (ERS-USDA)*

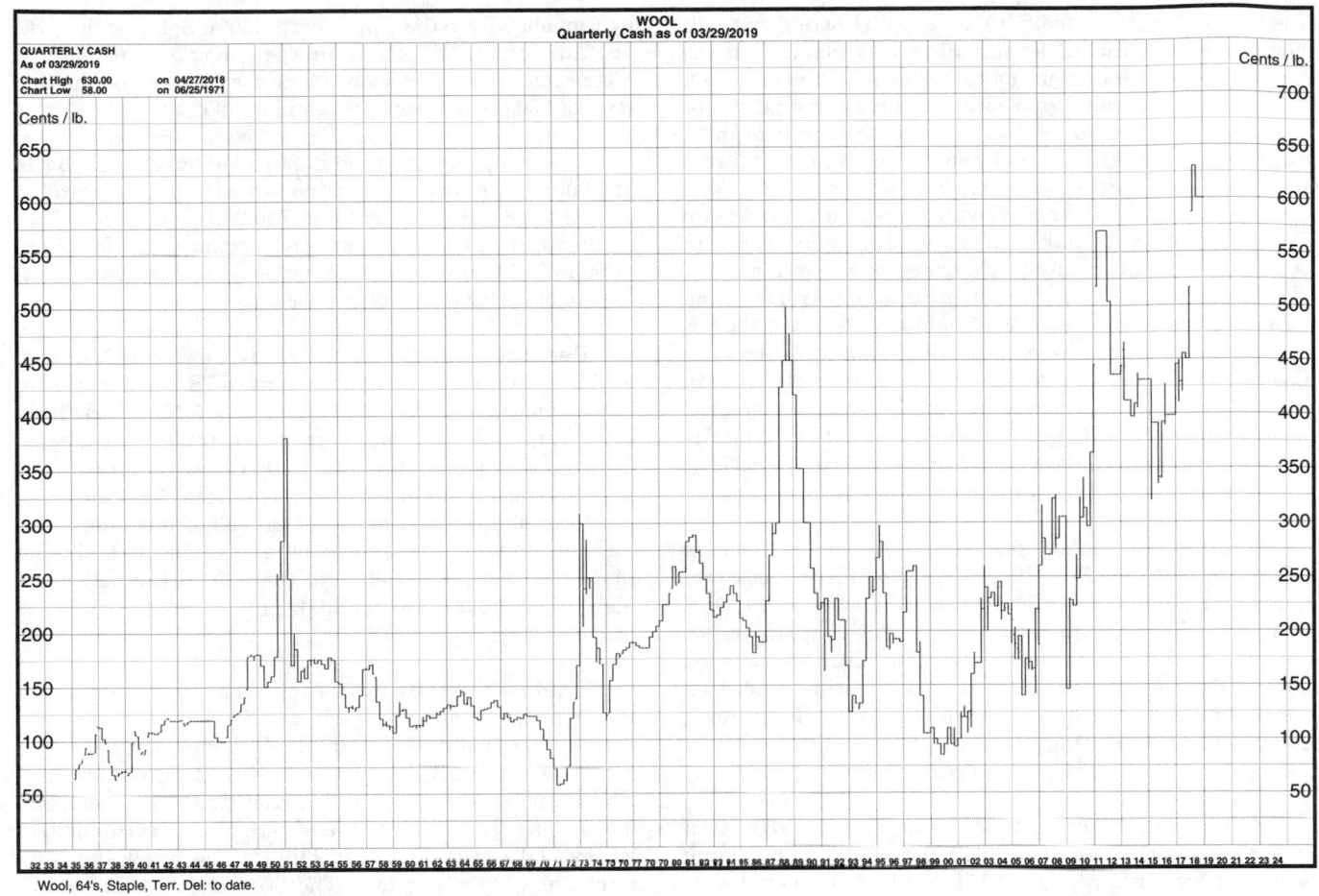

WOOL
Quarterly Cash as of 03/29/2019

QUARTERLY CASH
As of 03/29/2019
Chart High 630.00 on 04/27/2018
Chart Low 58.00 on 06/25/1971

Wool, 64's, Staple, Terr. Del: to date.

Salient Statistics of Wool in the United States

			Shorn					Total			Dutiable Imports for Consump-	Total	Duty Free Raw Imports	Mill - Consumption -	
	Sheep & Lambs Shorn[4]	Weight per Fleece	Wool Pro- duction	Price per	Value of Pro- duction	Shorn Wool Support	Shorn Wool Payment	Wool Pro- duction	Domestic Pro- duction	Domestic Wool Exports	tion[3] (48's & Finer)	New Supply[2]	(Not Finer than 46's)	Apparel	Carpet
Year	-1,000's-	-In Lbs.-	1,000 Lbs.	Lb.	-$1,000-	\-- Cents Per Lb. --	Rate	\---------------------- In Thousands of Pounds ----------------------							
2011	4,030	7.30	29,290	167.0	48,925	115	40.0	29,280	15,465	9,586	3,791	14,364	4,694	----	----
2012	3,750	7.30	27,400	152.0	41,595	115	40.0	27,630	14,467	7,741	4,564	15,841	4,551	----	----
2013	3,700	7.30	26,990	145.0	39,209	115	40.0	26,990	14,256	9,998	3,858	11,857	3,746	----	----
2014	3,680	7.30	26,680	146.0	38,909	115	40.0	26,680	14,200	7,918	3,917	13,247	3,363	----	----
2015	3,675	7.40	27,015	145.0	39,205	115	40.0	27,015	14,300	7,847	3,980	13,718	3,321	----	----
2016	3,585	7.30	26,050	145.0	37,721	115	40.0	26,050	13,800	7,826	3,909	12,015	2,178	----	----
2017	3,435	7.20	24,810	148.0	36,774				13,100	11,000	3,396		2,285		
2018[1]	3,372	7.20	24,400	175.0	42,772				13,000	12,000				----	----

[1] Preliminary. [2] Production minus exports plus imports; stocks not taken into consideration. [3] Apparel wool includes all dutiable wool; carpet wool includes all duty-free wool. [4] Includes sheep shorn at commercial feeding yards.
Source: Economic Research Service, U.S. Department of Agriculture (ERS-USDA)

Shorn Wool Prices   In Dollars Per Pound

	US Farm	Australian Offering Price, Clean[2]						Graded Territory Shorn Wool, Clean Basis[4]				
	Price Shorn Wool Greasy Basis[1]	Grade 70's type 61	Grade 64's type 63	Grade 62's type 64	Grade 60/62's type 64A	Grade 58's-56's 433-34	Market Indicator[3]	62's Staple 3"& up	60's Staple 3"& up	58's Staple 3 1/4"& up	56's Staple 3 1/4"& up	54's Staple 3 1/2"& up
Year	-- cents/Lb --	\------------------ In Dollars Per Pound ------------------					- Cents/Kg. -	\------------------ In Dollars Per Pound ------------------				
2010	115.0	5.34	4.10	4.24	3.78	2.78	NA	3.27	2.54	2.15	1.89	1.48
2011	167.0	7.61	6.30	6.55	6.02	5.62	NA	2.81	4.36	4.07	3.40	NA
2012	152.0	5.77	5.90	5.98	5.78	5.66	NA	4.23	1.65	3.46	2.17	NA
2013	145.0	5.59	5.34	5.39	5.24	3.69	1,073	4.23	3.36	3.01	2.47	2.21
2014	146.0	5.03	4.89	4.91	4.80	3.39	1,046	4.17	3.44	3.00	2.47	2.21
2015	145.0	4.71	4.50	4.54	4.38	3.58	1,198	3.58	3.15	3.04	2.63	2.39
2016	145.0	5.19	4.89	4.98	4.79	3.69	1,293	3.94	3.22	3.21	2.43	2.36
2017	148.0	6.67	5.50	5.84	5.13	3.80	1,540	4.36	3.57	3.24	2.36	NA

[1] Annual weighted average. [2] F.O.B. Australian Wool Corporation South Carolina warehouse in bond. [3] Index of prices of all wool sold in Australia for the crop year July-June. [4] Wool principally produced in Texas and the Rocky Mountain States.
Source: Economic Research Service, U.S. Department of Agriculture (ERS-USDA)

Zinc

Zinc (atomic symbol Zn) is a bluish-while metallic element that is the 24th most abundant element in the earth's crust. Zinc is never found in its pure state but rather in zinc oxide, zinc silicate, zinc carbonate, zinc sulfide, and in minerals such as zincite, hemimorphite, smithsonite, franklinite, and sphalerite. Zinc is utilized as a protective coating for other metals, such as iron and steel, in a process known as galvanizing. Zinc is used as an alloy with copper to make brass and also as an alloy with aluminum and magnesium. There are, however, a number of substitutes for zinc in chemicals, electronics, and pigments. For example, with aluminum, steel and plastics can substitute for galvanized sheets. Aluminum alloys can also replace brass. Zinc is used as the negative electrode in dry cell (flashlight) batteries and also in the zinc-mercuric-oxide battery cell, which is the round, flat battery typically used in watches, cameras, and other electronic devices. Zinc is also used in medicine as an antiseptic ointment.

Zinc futures and options are traded on the London Metals Exchange (LME). The LME zinc futures contract calls for the delivery of 25 metric tons of at least 99.995% purity zinc ingots (slabs and plates). The contract trades in terms of U.S. dollars per metric ton. Zinc first started trading on the LME in 1915. Zinc futures are traded on the Commodity Exchange (COMEX), the Hong Kong Exchanges and Clearing, the Multi Commodity Exchange of India, and the Shanghai Futures Exchange.

Prices – Zinc prices in 2018 rose +1.3% yr/yr to a monthly average of 141.36 cents per pound but remaining below the 2006 record high of 158.44 cents per pound.

Supply – World smelter production of zinc in 2016 fell -0.9% yr/yr to 13.800 million metric tons, down from last year's record high. The world's largest producer of zinc is China with 45.7% of world smelter production, followed by Canada with 5.0%, Japan with 3.9%, Spain with 3.6%, and Australia with 3.4%. China's production of 6.3 million metric tons in 2016 was more than ten times its production level of 550,000 metric tons seen in 1990.

U.S. smelter production in 2018 fell by -26.7% yr/yr to 126,000 metric tons. U.S. mine production of recoverable zinc in 2018 fell -2.4% yr/yr to 730,200 metric tons U.S. production in 2016 of slab zinc on a primary basis fell -6.9% yr/yr to 135,000 metric tons, while secondary production fell -44.5% yr/yr to 29,300 metric tons.

Demand – U.S. consumption of slab zinc in 2018 rose by 6.2% yr/yr to 880,000 metric tons. U.S. consumption of refined zinc in 2018 fell -2,8% yr/yr to 806,100 metric tons, down from the 2014 record high of 965,000. The breakdown of consumption by industries for 2016 showed that 85.9% of slab zinc consumption was for galvanizers, 5.8% for brass products, and the rest for other miscellaneous industries. The consumption breakdown by grades for 2016 showed that 49.2% was for re-melt and other, 29.4% was for special high grade, 16.9% was for high grade, and 4.6% was for prime western.

Trade – The U.S. in 2017 relied on imports for 85% of its consumption of zinc, up sharply from the 35% average seen in the 1990s. U.S. imports for consumption of slab zinc rose by +6.2% yr/yr to 770,000 metric tons in 2018 while imports of zinc ore in 2013 fell -58.5% yr/yr to 2,550 metric tons. The dollar value of U.S. zinc imports in 2015 fell by -8.0% yr/yr to $2.072 billion, well below the 2007 record high $3.091 billion. The breakdown of imports in 2018 shows that most zinc is imported as blocks; pigs and slabs (715.400 metric tons); ores (31,000 metric tons), dust, powder and flakes (27,229 metric tons); waste and scrap (13,551 metric tons); dross, ashes and fume (4,412 metric tons); and sheets, plates, other (5,606 metric tons).

Salient Statistics of Zinc in the United States   In Metric Tons

| | Slab Zinc Production | | Mine Production | Imports for Consumption | | Exports | | Consumption | | | Net Import Reliance As a % of Apparent | High-Grade, Price |
Year	Primary	Secondary	Recovered	Slab Zinc	Ore (Zinc Content)	Slab Zinc	Ore (Zinc Content)	Slab Zinc	Consumed as Ore	All Classes[3]	Consump	-Cents/Lb.-
2009	94,000	109,000	736,000	686,000	74,200	2,960	785,000	893,000	----	----	77	77.91
2010	120,000	129,000	748,000	671,000	32,200	4,200	752,000	907,000	----	----	73	101.98
2011	110,000	138,000	769,000	716,000	26,700	18,400	653,000	939,000	----	----	74	106.24
2012	114,000	147,000	738,000	655,000	6,140	14,200	591,000	902,000	----	----	71	95.80
2013	106,000	127,000	784,000	713,000	2,550	11,500	669,000	935,000	----	----	75	95.60
2014	110,000	70,000	831,000	805,000	2	19,800	644,000	965,000	----	----	81	107.10
2015	145,000	52,800	825,000	771,000	----	13,000	708,000	931,000	----	----	81	95.50
2016	135,000	29,300	805,000	713,000	----	47,000	597,000	792,000	----	----	84	101.40
2017[1]			774,000	729,000	----	32,000	682,000	829,000	----	----	84	139.30
2018[2]			790,000	770,000	----	22,000	870,000	880,000	----	----	85	145.00

[1] Preliminary.   [2] Estimate.   [3] Based on apparent consumption of slab zinc plus zinc content of ores and concentrates and secondary materials used to make zinc dust and chemicals.   Source: U.S. Geological Survey (USGS)

World Smelter Production of Zinc[3]   In Thousands of Metric Tons

Year	Australia	Belgium	Canada	China	France	Germany	Italy	Japan	Kazak-hstan	Mexico	Spain	United States	World Total
2007	508.0	241.3	802.1	3,740.0	129.1	294.7	109.0	638.7	358.2	321.9	494.1	278.0	11,400
2008	505.0	239.0	764.3	4,000.0	117.9	292.3	100.0	615.5	365.6	305.4	456.1	286.0	11,700
2009	531.0	14.0	685.5	4,290.0	161.0	153.0	100.0	540.6	327.9	385.4	515.0	203.0	11,400
2010	499.0	260.0	691.2	5,210.0	163.0	165.0	105.0	574.0	318.9	327.7	480.1	249.0	12,900
2011	507.3	282.0	662.2	5,212.2	164.0	170.0	100.0	544.7	319.8	322.1	489.1	248.0	13,100
2012	498.3	250.0	648.6	4,890.0	161.0	169.4	100.0	571.0	319.8	323.6	489.5	261.0	12,600
2013	498.3	252.0	651.6	5,310.0	152.0	162.0	111.0	587.0	320.2	322.8	490.5	233.0	13,000
2014	481.6	262.0	649.2	5,780.0	171.0	168.0	138.1	583.0	324.9	320.9	491.3	180.0	13,400
2015[1]	489.0	260.0	683.1	6,090.0	169.0	169.0	139.2	567.0	323.8	326.6	493.8	172.0	13,900
2016[2]	464.2	236.0	691.4	6,300.0	149.0	170.0	140.0	534.0	325.0	321.2	500.0	126.0	13,800

[1] Preliminary.   [2] Estimate.   [3] Secondary metal included.   *Source: U.S. Geological Survey (USGS)*

Consumption (Reported) of Slab Zinc in the United States, by Industries and Grades   In Metric Tons

		------------------------------ By Industries ------------------------------					----------------------- By Grades -----------------------			
Year	Total	Galvanizers	Brass Products	Zinc-Base Alloy[3]	Zinc Oxide	Other	Special High Grade	High Grade	Remelt and Other	Prime Western
2007	484,000	304,000	39,700	W	[4]	141,000	242,000	80,700	92,700	69,000
2008	433,000	262,000	107,000	23,200	[4]	40,600	195,000	60,400	75,800	102,000
2009	306,000	226,000	45,500	17,900	[4]	17,200	170,000	46,600	55,000	34,600
2010	475,000	369,000	45,800	35,000	----	25,100	205,000	91,900	121,684	56,500
2011	604,000	496,000	40,400	40,400	----	27,600	177,000	111,000	237,233	78,000
2012	806,000	685,000	49,700	44,700	----	26,500	255,000	138,000	357,455	55,300
2013	428,000	369,000	24,900	24,200	----	9,660	105,000	85,200	208,038	30,300
2014	403,000	340,000	25,600	33,000	----	4,460	101,000	97,900	182,185	21,200
2015[1]	433,000	367,000	27,400	34,300	----	4,710	126,000	78,200	210,260	18,800
2016[2]	462,000	397,000	26,900	34,000	----	4,190	136,000	78,200	227,337	21,100

[1] Preliminary.   [2] Estimated.   [3] Die casters.   [4] Included in other.   W = Withheld.   NA = Not applicable.   *Source: U.S. Geological Survey (USGS)*

United States Foreign Trade of Zinc   In Metric Tons

	----------------- Imports for Consumption -----------------							------------------ Zinc Ore & Manufactures Exported ------------------					
								Blocks, Pigs, Anodes, etc. ---	------- Wrought & Alloys -------					Zinc Ore & Con-centrates
Year	Ores[3]	Blocks, Pigs, Slabs	Sheets, Plates, Other	Waste & Scrap	Dross, Ashes, Fume	Dust, Powder & Flakes	Total Value $1,000	Un-wrought	Un-wrought Alloys	Sheets, Plates & Strips	Angles, Bars, Rods, etc.	Waste & Scrap	Dust (Blue Powder)	
2009	74,200	686,000	3,010	9,100	8,610	20,400	1,336,134	2,960	6,280	6,160	16,600	47,100	12,100	785,000
2010	32,200	671,000	3,440	15,600	17,900	31,600	1,846,320	4,200	11,400	7,380	27,800	77,900	14,900	752,000
2011	26,600	716,000	3,650	18,500	14,400	30,100	2,023,910	19,000	13,500	8,730	25,700	85,600	15,600	660,000
2012	6,140	655,000	2,920	20,000	23,200	28,200	1,684,190	14,100	17,900	6,040	17,700	90,500	14,200	592,000
2013	2,550	713,000	3,570	21,000	13,000	24,500	1,787,320	11,500	23,200	6,500	8,580	87,500	10,700	670,000
2014	2	805,000	4,090	24,900	8,590	31,700	2,252,374	19,800	27,100	6,710	10,000	71,400	10,400	644,000
2015	22	771,000	3,680	18,000	5,610	29,100	2,072,026	12,700	19,700	8,010	15,400	55,200	12,300	708,000
2016	60	713,000	3,650	11,300	3,770	27,800		49,792	16,194	6,960	8,101	30,091	12,753	604,000
2017[1]	6,780	730,000	3,690	11,100	6,350	27,100		32,700	14,500	7,670	9,110	33,600	12,800	688,000
2018[2]	31,000	715,400	5,606	13,351	4,412	27,229		21,361	21,775	7,358	10,596	40,625	13,215	753,390

[1] Preliminary.   [2] Estimate.   [3] Zinc content.   *Source: U.S. Geological Survey (USGS)*

Mine Production of Recoverable Zinc in the United States   In Thousands of Metric Tons

Year	Jan.	Feb.	Mar.	Apr.	May	June	July	Aug.	Sept.	Oct.	Nov.	Dec.	Total
2009	69.3	54.0	55.2	58.4	56.1	58.6	57.0	62.1	60.5	65.2	49.9	62.1	710.0
2010	59.4	56.5	63.5	61.6	62.6	57.4	64.8	60.3	60.0	66.0	50.0	63.2	723.0
2011	69.5	54.9	62.1	59.3	66.2	57.9	70.0	63.6	60.0	55.4	58.5	67.8	743.0
2012	58.0	57.5	58.4	60.4	60.2	54.7	58.4	56.8	60.2	55.8	65.1	68.2	713.0
2013	64.1	54.5	56.0	63.2	65.8	61.3	61.7	67.2	66.7	68.0	68.8	68.7	761.0
2014	67.9	67.8	70.6	69.5	63.3	61.2	64.6	65.6	66.4	63.2	71.3	75.0	803.0
2015	67.3	63.6	72.4	68.5	74.5	70.4	62.5	65.9	58.4	58.9	59.6	56.9	781.0
2016	54.3	55.9	68.6	66.8	67.1	68.9	59.0	67.1	66.0	68.6	54.2	52.6	777.0
2017	58.2	50.5	60.0	62.3	53.7	53.4	64.9	71.3	62.9	73.7	72.2	62.5	748.0
2018[1]	63.9	55.5	51.9	65.7	69.5	74.9	74.7	68.3	70.5	79.1	56.5	77.0	807.5

[1] Preliminary.   *Source: U.S. Geological Survey (USGS)*

ZINC

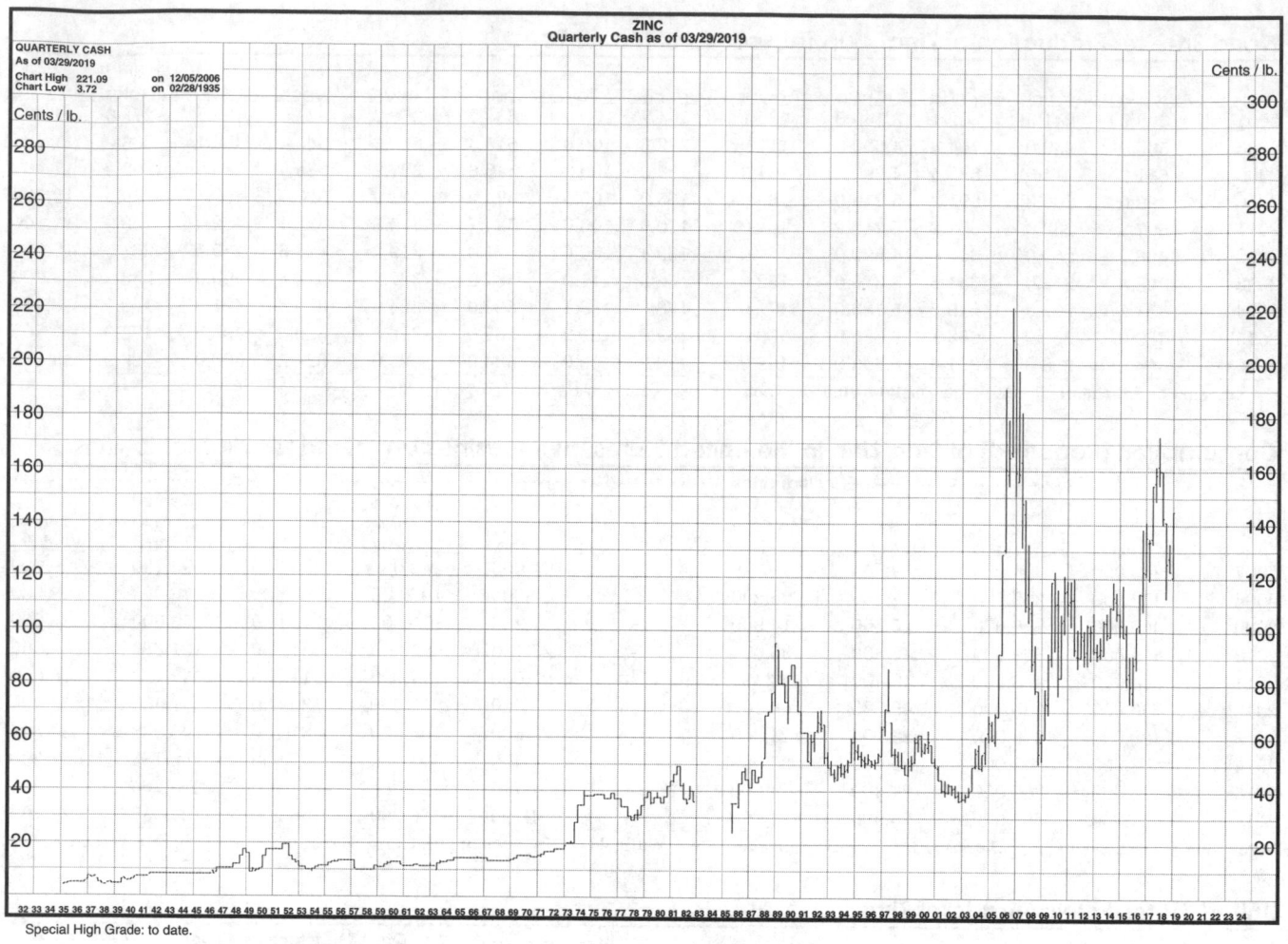

ZINC
Quarterly Cash as of 03/29/2019

QUARTERLY CASH
As of 03/29/2019
Chart High 221.09 on 12/05/2006
Chart Low 3.72 on 02/28/1935

Special High Grade: to date.

Average Price of Zinc, Prime Western Slab (Delivered U.S. Basis)   In Cents Per Pound

Year	Jan.	Feb.	Mar.	Apr.	May	June	July	Aug.	Sept.	Oct.	Nov.	Dec.	Average
2009	57.28	53.96	57.96	65.19	69.91	73.34	74.38	85.30	88.25	97.11	102.32	109.97	77.91
2010	113.30	100.72	106.15	110.33	93.02	83.34	88.25	97.11	102.16	112.55	109.67	108.04	102.05
2011	112.47	116.61	111.76	112.83	104.86	108.12	115.41	107.26	101.03	91.28	94.18	94.73	105.88
2012	97.62	101.31	99.99	98.01	95.19	91.62	91.32	89.77	98.67	94.43	94.32	100.33	96.05
2013	100.21	104.53	95.62	92.04	91.25	91.88	92.18	95.47	93.11	93.86	93.40	98.17	95.14
2014	101.35	101.41	100.58	101.54	102.75	105.78	113.91	114.56	112.82	112.02	111.17	107.09	107.08
2015	104.08	103.48	100.33	108.09	112.42	102.59	98.49	89.77	85.54	86.07	79.26	76.02	95.51
2016	75.65	84.61	88.64	90.59	91.48	98.21	105.64	110.08	110.30	111.42	122.23	127.26	101.34
2017	129.14	135.58	134.68	128.04	126.96	125.45	135.06	144.21	150.02	157.19	155.18	153.34	139.57
2018	164.74	169.02	157.64	153.85	147.33	149.04	129.11	122.68	119.08	129.99	126.18	127.68	141.36

Source: American Metal Market (AMM)

Consumption of Refined Zinc in the United States   In Thousands of Metric Tons

Year	Jan.	Feb.	Mar.	Apr.	May	June	July	Aug.	Sept.	Oct.	Nov.	Dec.	Total
2009	78.9	69.6	85.5	67.2	78.6	70.8	80.0	72.6	76.9	68.7	75.5	80.0	891.0
2010	79.1	72.7	84.3	76.1	76.5	71.9	66.9	98.5	66.7	73.2	75.8	76.0	919.0
2011	76.3	67.1	83.2	72.1	67.4	87.2	61.8	74.2	73.4	95.0	69.0	87.2	939.0
2012	73.1	71.4	72.9	77.0	77.4	85.2	71.7	74.6	71.7	77.1	69.0	78.6	904.0
2013	77.6	77.1	77.3	98.4	78.9	76.7	75.2	138.0	85.1	78.9	68.5	80.7	934.0
2014	106.0	62.4	69.2	86.7	116.0	69.3	70.6	92.3	72.2	62.4	79.3	79.2	965.0
2015	73.2	60.9	73.8	73.9	116.0	92.5	66.2	98.2	69.5	66.3	70.4	68.5	931.0
2016	----	41.2	63.2	56.7	95.5	60.3	69.8	67.4	72.7	68.9	73.5	64.8	789.0
2017	106.0	57.8	96.1	76.7	64.3	65.3	52.1	56.7	57.6	66.5	50.5	74.8	829.0
2018[1]	66.9	62.9	78.0	90.5	71.8	68.9	68.3	76.1	71.6	86.0	65.1	65.6	871.7

[1] Preliminary.   *Source: U.S. Geological Survey (USGS)*